Contemporary Authors®
NEW REVISION SERIES

Explore your options!
Gale databases offered in a variety of formats

DISKETTE/MAGNETIC TAPE

Many Gale databases are available on diskette or magnetic tape, allowing systemwide access to your most-used information sources through existing computer systems. Data can be delivered on a variety of mediums (DOS-formatted diskette, 9-track tape, 8mm data tape) and in industry-standard formats (comma-delimited, tagged, fixed-field).

CD-ROM

A variety of Gale titles are available on CD-ROM, offering maximum flexibility and powerful search software.

The information in this Gale publication is also available in some or all of the formats described here. Your Gale Representative will be happy to fill you in.

ONLINE

For your convenience, many Gale databases are available through popular online services, including DIALOG, NEXIS, DataStar, ORBIT, OCLC, Thomson Financial Network's I/Plus Direct, HRIN, Prodigy, Sandpoint's HOOVER, The Library Corporation's NLightN, and Telebase Systems.

A number of Gale databases are available on an annual subscription basis through GaleNet, a new online information resource that features an easy-to-use end-user interface, the powerful search capabilities of BRS/SEARCH retrieval software and ease of access through the World-Wide Web.

For information, call

GALE

1-800-877-GALE

ISSN 0275-7176

Contemporary Authors®

A Bio-Bibliographical Guide to
Current Writers in Fiction, General Nonfiction,
Poetry, Journalism, Drama, Motion Pictures,
Television, and Other Fields

JEFF CHAPMAN
PAMELA S. DEAR
Editors

NEW REVISION SERIES
volume **52**

GALE

DETROIT · NEW YORK · TORONTO · LONDON

STAFF

Jeff Chapman and Pamela S. Dear, *Editors, New Revision Series*

John D. Jorgenson, *Pre-Manuscript Coordinator*
Thomas Wiloch, *Sketchwriting Coordinator*

Deborah A. Stanley, Aarti Dhawan Stephens,
Kathleen Wilson, and Janet Witalec, *Contributing Editors*

George H. Blair, Daniel Jones, and Polly A. Vedder, *Associate Editors*

Bruce Boston, Frank DeSanto, Joan Goldsworthy, Anne Janette Johnson, Jane Kosek,
Jim McWilliams, Robert Miltner, Julie Monahan, John Mort, Trudy Ring, Bryan Ryan,
Kenneth R. Shepherd, Pamela L. Shelton, Andrea Votava, Denise Wiloch,
Michaela Swart Wilson, and Tim Winter-Damon, *Sketchwriters*

Tracy Arnold-Chapman, Jane Kosek, Doris Maxfield,
Emily J. McMurray, and Trudy Ring, *Copyeditors*

James P. Draper, *Managing Editor*

Victoria B. Cariappa, *Research Manager*

Barbara McNeil, *Research Specialist*

Alicia Noel Biggers, Julia C. Daniel, Michelle Lee, Tamara C. Nott,
Tracie A. Richardson, Norma Sawaya, and Cheryl L. Warnock, *Research Associates*

Laura C. Bissey, *Research Assistant*

∞™ This book is printed on acid-free paper that meets the minimum requirements
of American National Standard for Information Sciences-
Permanence Paper for Printed Library Materials, ANSI Z39.48-1984.

Library of Congress Catalog Card Number 81-640179

ISBN 0-7876-0123-3
ISSN 0275-7176

Printed in the United States of America.

10 9 8 7 6 5 4 3 2 1

Contents

Indexing note: All *Contemporary Authors New Revision Series* entries are indexed in the *Contemporary Authors* cumulative index, which is published separately and distributed with even-numbered *Contemporary Authors* original volumes and odd-numbered *Contemporary Authors New Revision Series* volumes.

As always, the most recent *Contemporary Authors* cumulative index continues to be the user's guide to the location of an individual author's listing.

Contemporary Authors
was named an
*"Outstanding
Reference Source" by
the American Library
Association Reference
and Adult Services
Division after its 1962
inception.
In 1985 it was listed by
the same organization
as one of the
twenty-five most
distinguished reference
titles published in the
past twenty-five years.*

Preface

The *Contemporary Authors New Revision Series* (*CANR*) provides completely updated information on authors listed in earlier volumes of *Contemporary Authors* (*CA*). Entries for individual authors from *any* volume of *CA* may be included in a volume of the *New Revision Series*. *CANR* updates only those sketches requiring significant change.

Authors are included on the basis of specific criteria that indicate the need for significant revision. These criteria include bibliographical additions, changes in addresses or career, major awards, and personal information such as name changes or death dates. All listings in this volume have been revised or augmented in various ways. Some sketches have been extensively rewritten, and many include informative new sidelights. As always, a *CANR* listing entails no charge or obligation.

How to Get the Most out of *CA*: Use the Index

The key to locating an author's most recent entry is the *CA* cumulative index, which is published separately and distributed with even-numbered original volumes and odd-numbered revision volumes. It provides access to *all* entries in *CA* and *CANR*. Always consult the latest index to find an author's most recent entry.

For the convenience of users, the *CA* cumulative index also includes references to all entries in these Gale literary series: *Authors and Artists for Young Adults, Authors in the News, Bestsellers, Black Literature Criticism, Black Writers, Children's Literature Review, Concise Dictionary of American Literary Biography, Concise Dictionary of British Literary Biography, Contemporary Authors Autobiography Series, Contemporary Authors Bibliographical Series, Contemporary Literary Criticism, Dictionary of Literary Biography, Dictionary of Literary Biography Documentary Series, Dictionary of Literary Biography Yearbook, DISCovering Authors, DISCovering Authors: British, DISCovering Authors: Canadian, DISCovering Authors: Modules, Drama Criticism, Hispanic Literature Criticism, Hispanic Writers, Junior DISCovering Authors, Major Authors and Illustrators for Children and Young Adults, Major 20th-Century Writers, Native North American Literature, Poetry Criticism, Short Story Criticism, Something about the Author, Something about the Author Autobiography Series, Twentieth-Century Literary Criticism, World Literature Criticism,* and *Yesterday's Authors of Books for Children.*

A Sample Index Entry:

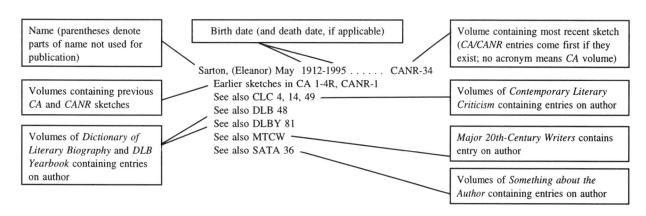

For the most recent *CA* information on Sarton, users should refer to Volume 34 of the *New Revision Series,* as designated by "CANR-34"; if that volume is unavailable, refer to CANR-1. And if CANR-1 is unavailable, refer to CA 1-4R, published in 1967, for Sarton's First Revision entry.

How Are Entries Compiled?

The editors make every effort to secure new information directly from the authors. Copies of all sketches in selected *CA* and *CANR* volumes previously published are routinely sent to listees at their last-known addresses, and returns from these authors are then assessed. For deceased writers, or those who fail to reply to requests for data, we consult other reliable biographical sources, such as those indexed in Gale's *Biography and Genealogy Master Index,* and bibliographical sources, such as *National Union Catalog, LC MARC,* and *British National Bibliography.* Further details come from published interviews, feature stories, and book reviews, and often the authors' publishers supply material.

* Indicates that a listing has been compiled from secondary sources believed to be reliable but has not been personally verified for this edition by the author sketched.

What Kinds of Information Does an Entry Provide?

Sketches in *CANR* contain the following biographical and bibliographical information:

- **Entry heading:** the most complete form of author's name, plus any pseudonyms or name variations used for writing

- **Personal information:** author's date and place of birth, family data, educational background, political and religious affiliations, and hobbies and leisure interests

- **Addresses:** author's home, office, or agent's addresses as available

- **Career summary:** name of employer, position, and dates held for each career post; resume of other vocational achievements; military service

- **Membership information:** professional, civic, and other association memberships and any official posts held

- **Awards and honors:** military and civic citations, major prizes and nominations, fellowships, grants, and honorary degrees

- **Writings:** a comprehensive, chronological list of titles, publishers, dates of original publication and revised editions, and production information for plays, television scripts, and screenplays

- **Adaptations:** a list of films, plays, and other media which have been adapted from the author's work

- **Work in progress:** current or planned projects, with dates of completion and/or publication, and expected publisher, when known

- **Sidelights:** a biographical portrait of the author's development; information about the critical reception of the author's works; revealing comments, often by the author, on personal interests, aspirations, motivations, and thoughts on writing

- **Biographical and critical sources:** a list of books and periodicals in which additional information on an author's life and/or writings appears

Related Titles in the *CA* Series

Contemporary Authors Autobiography Series complements *CA* original and revised volumes with specially commissioned autobiographical essays by important current authors, illustrated with personal photographs they provide. Common topics include their motivations for writing, the people and experiences that shaped their careers, the rewards they derive from their work, and their impressions of the current literary scene.

Contemporary Authors Bibliographical Series surveys writings by and about important American authors since World War II. Each volume concentrates on a specific genre and features approximately ten writers; entries list works written by and about the author and contain a bibliographical essay discussing the merits and deficiencies of major critical and scholarly studies in detail.

Available in Electronic Formats

CD-ROM. Full-text bio-bibliographic entries from the entire *CA* series, covering approximately 100,000 writers, are available on CD-ROM through lease and purchase plans. The disc combines entries from the *CA, CANR,* and *Contemporary Authors Permanent Series* (*CAP*) print series to provide the most recent author listing. It can be searched by name, title, subject/genre, and personal data, and by using boolean logic. The disc will be updated every six months. For more information, call 1-800-877-GALE.

Magnetic Tape. *CA* is available for licensing on magnetic tape in a fielded format. Either the complete database or a custom selection of entries may be ordered. The database is available for internal data processing and nonpublishing purposes only. For more information, call 1-800-877-GALE.

Online. The *Contemporary Authors* database is made available online to libraries and their patrons through online public access catalog (OPAC) vendors. Currently, *CA* is offered through Ameritech Library Services' Vista Online (formerly Dynix), and is expected to become available through CARL Systems. More OPAC vendor offerings will follow soon.

GaleNet. *CA* is available on a subscription basis through GaleNet, a new online information resource that features an easy-to-use end-user interface, the powerful search capabilities of the BRS/Search retrieval software, and ease of access through the World-Wide Web. For more information, call Melissa Kolehmainen at 1-800-877-GALE, ext. 1598.

Suggestions Are Welcome

The editors welcome comments and suggestions from users on any aspects of the *CA* series. If readers would like to recommend authors whose entries should appear in future volumes of the series, they are cordially invited to write: The Editors, *Contemporary Authors,* 835 Penobscot Bldg., Detroit, MI 48226-4094; call toll-free at 1-800-347-GALE; fax to 1-313-961-6599; or e-mail at conauth@gale.com.

CA Numbering System and Volume Update Chart

Occasionally questions arise about the *CA* numbering system and which volumes, if any, can be discarded. Despite numbers like "29-32R," "97-100" and "150," the entire *CA* series consists of only 130 physical volumes with the publication of *CA New Revision Series* Volume 52. The following charts note changes in the numbering system and cover design, and indicate which volumes are essential for the most complete, up-to-date coverage.

CA First Revision	• 1-4R through 41-44R (11 books) *Cover:* Brown with black and gold trim. There will be no further First Revision volumes because revised entries are now being handled exclusively through the more efficient *New Revision Series* mentioned below.
CA Original Volumes	• 45-48 through 97-100 (14 books) *Cover:* Brown with black and gold trim. • 101 through 151 (51 books) *Cover:* Blue and black with orange bands. The same as previous *CA* original volumes but with a new, simplified numbering system and new cover design.
CA Permanent Series	• *CAP*-1 and *CAP*-2 (2 books) *Cover:* Brown with red and gold trim. There will be no further *Permanent Series* volumes because revised entries are now being handled exclusively through the more efficient *New Revision Series* mentioned below.
CA New Revision Series	• *CANR*-1 through *CANR*-52 (52 books) *Cover:* Blue and black with green bands. Includes only sketches requiring extensive changes; **sketches are taken from any previously published *CA*, *CAP*, or *CANR* volume.**

If You Have:	You May Discard:
CA First Revision Volumes 1-4R through 41-44R **and** *CA Permanent Series* Volumes 1 and 2	*CA* Original Volumes 1, 2, 3, 4 and Volumes 5-6 through 41-44
CA Original Volumes 45-48 through 97-100 **and** 101 through 151	**NONE:** These volumes will not be superseded by corresponding revised volumes. Individual entries from these and all other volumes appearing in the left column of this chart may be revised and included in the various volumes of the *New Revision Series*.
CA New Revision Series Volumes *CANR*-1 through *CANR*-52	**NONE:** The *New Revision Series* does not replace any single volume of *CA*. Instead, volumes of *CANR* include entries from many previous *CA* series volumes. All *New Revision Series* volumes must be retained for full coverage.

A Sampling of Authors and Media People
Featured in This Volume

Renata Adler

Adler is an Italian-born American journalist and fiction writer whose novel *Speedboat* won the Ernest Hemingway Prize for best first novel in 1976. Known for her provocative views represented in such nonfiction collections as *Toward a Radical Middle* and *Politics and Media: Essays,* Adler's work consistently creates controversy.

Jeffrey Archer

A former member of the British House of Commons, Archer is primarily a novelist but also writes plays, short stories, and children's fiction. Much of his more controversial and popular fiction examines political themes. These works include *Not a Penny More, Not a Penny Less, Shall We Tell the President?, A Matter of Honor,* and *The Prodigal Daughter.*

Paul Auster

After spending many years as a relatively unknown poet, essayist, and translator, Auster attracted extensive critical attention as a novelist with his Edgar Award nominated *City of Glass,* the first book of his "New York Trilogy," which also includes *Ghosts* and *The Locked Room.* While experimenting with elements of the mystery genre, the novels address the relationship between past and present and the elusive nature of language and identity. Auster also directed the film *Blue in the Face,* the companion piece to his screenplay *Smoke.*

Gwendolyn Brooks

A critically acclaimed and highly respected writer, Brooks is an American poet whose works center on the experiences of the urban poor. With her 1949 collection *Annie Allen,* Brooks became the first African-American author to win the Pulitzer Prize in poetry. Brooks has received numerous other awards and honors, including an appointment as Poetry Consultant to the Library of Congress.

Edna Buchanan

A Pulitzer Prize winning journalist with the *Miami Herald,* Buchanan has written of her experiences with violent crime cases in books such as *The Corpse Had a Familiar Face: Covering Miami, America's Hottest Beat* and *Never Let Them See You Cry: More from Miami, America's Hottest Beat.* These experiences also inform her novels, including the Edgar Award nominated *Nobody Lives Forever.*

William S. Burroughs

A former drug addict, Burroughs is one of the most influential of the Beat generation writers. His literary reputation is based primarily on his controversial novel *Naked Lunch.* The first American edition, published in 1962, was the focus of a landmark obscenity trial featuring the testimony of Norman Mailer and Allen Ginsberg among others.

Joan Didion

Known for the elegance and precision of her prose, Didion is an acclaimed American novelist and journalist. Her works typically explore social disintegration and include the National Book Award nominated best-seller *Play It as It Lays,* and the Morton Dauwen Zabel award winning *The White Album.*

Bruce Jay Friedman

Friedman established himself as a popular American novelist, short fiction writer, and playwright in the mid-1960s with works such as *Stern, A Mother's Kisses, Black Angels* and *23 Pat O'Brien Movies.* Known primarily as a black humorist, Friedman has also written screenplays, including *Stir Crazy* and *Splash!.*

William Gibson

Labeled "cyberpunk," Gibson's *Neuromancer* was the first novel to win the Hugo, Nebula, and Philip K. Dick awards. Written with a hip cynicism and an acclaimed, economical prose, Gibson's science fiction novels depict a future in which multinational corporations use technology to manipulate society.

L. Ron Hubbard

A prolific writer, Hubbard published nearly six hundred books, stories, and articles during his lifetime. Despite his stature as one of the science fiction field's most influential authors, Hubbard is primarily known for his involvement with the controversial Church of Scientology, which he founded after the success of his *Dianetics: The Modern Science of Mental Health.*

Tama Janowitz

Known as much for her flamboyant personality and association with the late Andy Warhol as for her fiction, Janowitz is an American novelist whose works center on the inner life of New York City. Janowitz's works include *American Dad, A Cannibal in Manhattan,* and the popular short story collection, *Slaves of New York.*

Erica Jong

Jong is known primarily for her best-selling first novel *Fear of Flying,* credited with revolutionizing the perception of female sexuality. In addition to writing fiction, Jong has also been acclaimed as a poet and critic, for such works as *Fruits and Vegetables, Here Comes, and Other Poems,* and *The Devil at Large: Erica Jong on Henry Miller.*

Stephen King

Perhaps the most popular and prolific horror writer of all time, King is an American novelist, short story writer, and screenwriter. Combining elements of horror, fantasy, science fiction, and humor, King's novels, including *The Shining, Cujo, Misery,* and *Rose Madder,* are consistent best-sellers. Credited with reviving the horror genre in both fiction and film, King also revived the serial novel in 1996 with *The Green Mile.*

Dean R. Koontz

Koontz is a best-selling American novelist whose works are known for rich characterization and tightly constructed plots. After achieving initial success in the science fiction genre with such works as *Beastchild,* Koontz moved into mainstream suspense and horror with such novels as *Strangers, Watchers,* and *Intensity.*

Milan Kundera

A Czech-born French novelist, short story writer, playwright, and poet, Kundera is considered one of Europe's outstanding contemporary novelists. His works, which include *The Book of Laughter and Forgetting, The Unbearable Lightness of Being,* and *Immortality,* are known for their structural innovation and thematic complexity. In 1996, Kundera published *Slowness,* his first novel written originally in French.

Ursula K. Le Guin

A highly respected and influential science fiction and fantasy writer, Le Guin has received numerous awards and award nominations for her short stories, novelettes, novellas, and novels. In addition to her science fiction novels, which include the Hugo, Nebula, and Jupiter award winning *The Dispossessed: An Ambiguous Utopia,* Le Guin is also the author of numerous children's books.

Philip Levine

Winner of the 1995 Pulitzer Prize for Poetry for his collection *The Simple Truth: Poems,* Levine is an acclaimed American poet whose works focus on working class life. In his essay collection *The Bread of Time: Toward an Autobiography,* Levine explored the subjects and events that have shaped his life and poetry.

Bill Moyers

A well-known broadcast journalist, Moyers has garnered numerous prestigious awards including multiple Emmy, George Peabody, and George Polk awards for his television series, essays, and commentaries. His television series include "Creativity," "A Walk through the Twentieth Century," and "Facing Evil."

Paul Muldoon

Muldoon achieved prominence during the 1960s and 1970s as the youngest member of a group of Northern Ireland poets which included Seamus Heaney. His works, which include *Why Brownlee Left, Quoof,* and *The Annals of Chile,* are known for their terse language and multiplicity of meaning. He received the T. S. Eliot Prize in 1994.

Ruth Rendell

A mystery writer, Rendell has been praised for her ingenious and surprising plots and for the depth of her characterization. She has received numerous awards including Edgar Awards for *The Fallen Curtain and Other Stories* and *A Dark-Adapted Eye,* and Gold Dagger Awards for *A Demon in My View, Live Flesh,* and *A Fatal Inversion.*

Charles Simic

Simic is a Yugoslavian-born poet, essayist, and translator whose works include the Pulitzer Prize winning collection *The World Doesn't End.* Considered by many critics to be among the finest of America's postmodern poets, Simic has received numerous other prestigious awards, including the PEN Translation award and the MacArthur Foundation "Genius Grant."

Frank Yerby

After winning the O. Henry Memorial Award for best first short story in 1944, Yerby became a prolific and best-selling novelist despite being virtually dismissed by critics. His works included *The Foxes of Harrow, The Vixens,* and the acclaimed *The Dahomean: An Historical Novel.*

Contemporary Authors®

NEW REVISION SERIES

*Indicates that a listing has been compiled from secondary sources believed to be reliable but has not been personally verified for this edition by the author sketched.

ADLER, Irene
    See STORR, Catherine (Cole)

*   *   *

ADLER, Renata   1938-
    (Brett Daniels)

PERSONAL: Born October 19, 1938, in Milan, Italy; daughter of Frederick L. and Erna (Strauss) Adler. *Education:* Bryn Mawr College, A.B., 1959; Sorbonne, University of Paris, D.d'E.S., 1961; Harvard University, M.A., 1962; Yale University, law degree.

ADDRESSES: Home—Hattertown Rd., Newton, CT 06470. *Agent*—Lynn Nesbit, International Creative Management, 40 West 57th St., New York, NY 10019.

CAREER: Novelist, journalist, film critic. *New Yorker,* New York City, writer-reporter, 1962-68 and 1970-82; *New York Times,* New York City, film critic, 1968-69. Fellow of Trumbull College, Yale University, 1969-72; associate professor of theater and cinema, Hunter College of City University of New York, 1972-73. Judge in arts and letters for National Book Awards, 1969.

MEMBER: PEN (member of executive board, 1964-70).

AWARDS, HONORS: Guggenheim fellow, 1973-74; first prize in O. Henry Short Story Awards, Doubleday, 1974; American Academy and Institute of Arts and Letters Award, 1976; Ernest Hemingway Prize, 1976, for best first novel; elected to American Academy and Institute of Arts and Letters, 1987.

WRITINGS:

Toward a Radical Middle: Fourteen Pieces of Reporting and Criticism, Random House (New York City), 1969.
A Year in the Dark: Journal of a Film Critic, 1968-69, Random House, 1970.
Reckless Disregard: Westmoreland v. CBS et al.; Sharon v. Time, Knopf (New York City), 1986.
Politics and Media: Essays, St. Martin's (New York City), 1988.

NOVELS

Speedboat, Random House, 1976.
Pitch Dark, Knopf, 1983.

OTHER

Contributor of articles and short stories, sometimes under pseudonym Brett Daniels, to *National Review, Vanity Fair, New Yorker, Harper's Bazaar, Commentary, Atlantic,* and other periodicals. Member of editorial board, *American Scholar,* 1969-75; consulting editor, *Vanity Fair,* 1983.

SIDELIGHTS: Renata Adler is known for her work as a journalist, novelist, and controversial film critic. Trained as a journalist, Adler worked for twenty years at the *New Yorker,* and her first two books were collections of essays and reviews written on assignment for that magazine and for the *New York*

Times, where she worked one year as a film critic. In 1969, having had "about enough" of film reviewing and convinced, as she told *New York* contributor Jesse Kornbluth, "that if you're going to write, after a certain point some of it better be fiction," Adler turned to short stories. Her early work surfaced in the *New Yorker,* and she eventually collected and reshaped much of this short fiction into her award-winning first novel, *Speedboat.* Seven years later her second novel, *Pitch Dark,* appeared. Well before its 1983 publication, however, Adler had decided that "you can't really be a journalist and not know the law," as she told Kornbluth, so she enrolled at the Yale Law School. The influence of her legal training is apparent in her 1986 book, an exhaustive investigation into shoddy news reporting practices entitled *Reckless Disregard: Westmoreland v. CBS et al.; Sharon v. Time.*

Despite the scope of her interests, Adler brings a constancy of outlook to all her writing. Adler grew up during the postwar Eisenhower years, "part of an age group," she once told *CA,* "that through being skipped, through never having had a generational voice, was forced into the broadest possible America. . . . We have no journals we publish, no exile we share, no brawls, no anecdotes, no way, no solidarity, no mark. In a way . . . we are the last custodians of language . . . because history, in our time, has rung so many changes on the meaning of terms, and we, having never generationally perpetuated anything, have no commitment to any distortion of them." Adler's use of language, her insistence on factual accuracy, and her original way of thinking have established her as a cultural critic whose work often contains what Kornbluth calls "bombshells."

The "bombshells" to which Kornbluth refers include many of her film reviews. Adler's generally negative film reviews so angered the movie making industry that in 1968 United Artists took out a full-page *New York Times* ad denouncing her. She further outraged the film community in 1979 by publishing a *New York Review of Books* critique of colleague Pauline Kale's work. Her negative assessment of Kale's *When the Lights Go Down* pronounced the collection of film reviews "jarringly, piece by piece, line by line, and without interruption, worthless," and created a minor scandal within the film community. But even when she is dealing in the realm of imagination rather than analysis, Adler's work can provoke literary controversy, as evidenced by critical reaction to her first book of fiction, *Speedboat.*

Labeled a novel by its publisher, *Speedboat* defies many novelistic conventions. *Atlantic* reviewer Richard Todd believes "calling it a novel perhaps stretches a point. It is a gathering of stories. . . . And the stories themselves are assemblages of small moments that lack the coherence of plot but nevertheless overlap and iridesce like the scales of a fish." The episodes vary in length from a few lines to several pages and seem to be organized in random fashion. In one incident (from which the novel takes its name), a young woman takes a joy ride in a new speedboat and exaggerates each bounce of the boat against the waves until she breaks her back. In another, a different woman imagines that she is being followed by rats.

By juxtaposing episodes like these with personal observations, Adler creates a disturbing portrait of contemporary urban life. But, unlike a traditional novel that builds to a climax, *Speedboat* offers neither "engrossing narrative" nor "sustained psychological rendering of character," *New York Times Book Review* contributor Robert Towers believes. What holds the book together is the sensibility of Jen Fain, its fictional narrator. Patterned, critics believe, after Adler herself, Fain is a career woman about thirty-five years old, living in New York and working at a newspaper while teaching college part-time. Adler grew up in the fifties and her narrator represents that age group in *Speedboat.* "Associate Professor Fain (to use her part-time academic title) epitomizes a whole generation of educationally privileged Americans who came of age at the end of the Eisenhower era. She often writes as a historian of this generation, as a survivor," writes Towers. Like her reticent creator, "Fain does not declare herself; she has to be pieced together by the reader from what she chooses to report and generalize about," John Leonard observes in *Harper's* magazine.

Though written in the first-person, *Speedboat,* according to critics, is cool, dispassionate, and always carefully controlled. "For all its attention to modern woes, *Speedboat* is free of stock response," notes Todd. "No lamentations of vulgarity. No intimations of systematic evil. No love of madness, no chic despair. It is the work of someone who simply won't relinquish the right to say . . . 'how strange.'" Other reviewers also note Adler's unique way of recording events. Her voice, "although in the familiar tradition of wise, witty, perceptive, resigned New York cool, is original in its avoidance . . . of the mawkishly tough or languidly hysterical, in the exact grace of its prose and its vigilant self-scrutiny," notes *Times*

Literary Supplement contributor Eric Korn. Describing the book as "wonderfully fresh and thoughtful," *New Republic* contributor Anne Tyler surmises that *Speedboat* was "written as if the author neither knew nor cared how other people wrote; she would proceed in her own remarkable way."

Because it is composed of unrelated incidents, *Speedboat* presents some structural challenges that not all reviewers believe Adler has overcome. For instance, in one of the few negative reviews of the book, *New York Times* critic Anatole Broyard dismisses *Speedboat* as "little more than a series of witty jottings, a collection of small, contemporary curiosities set down one after another in the conviction that they would all eventually work in apposition. . . . It is all extremely clever, but, in my opinion, it is not what I mean—and I decline the semantic challenge—by a novel. I do not believe that *Speedboat* is important either." More representative of critical opinion is *Saturday Review* contributor Jane Larkin Crain's assertion that "as a series of sketches, vignettes, tableaus, the novel has already more force and stature than is ordinarily found in contemporary fiction, even in those offerings that attend faithfully, as Adler's work does not, to narrative conventions." Towers recommends reading the book in parts, "one section at a sitting, with frequent pauses for rereading," to relieve any "clogging effect."

The literary controversy that attended publication of Adler's first novel resumed in earnest when her second book of fiction, *Pitch Dark,* appeared in 1983. Variously described as an "antinovel" in the *New York Times,* a "meditation on writing a novel" in *Harper's,* and a "genre unto itself" in the *New York Times Book Review, Pitch Dark* emerged as one of the most widely discussed books of the year. Similar in style and structure to her first novel, *Pitch Dark* is also related by a first-person narrator who resembles Adler. Furthermore, according to Tyler, "it conveys the same sense of freshness, or originality practiced not for its own sake but because the author is absolutely desperate to tell us how . . . her heroine feels." In this book Adler narrows her focus from the general malaise of city life to the private pain accompanying the end of a love affair.

The plot, which is skeletal, revolves around narrator Kate Ennis's attempts to break off an extended affair with a married man. "Though the situation is essentially banal, Kate's methods of coping with emotional crises are so extraordinary that the book becomes a series of excursions into history, literature, philoso-

phy, human relations, memory and fantasy," writes Elaine Kendall in the *Los Angeles Times Book Review.* "Some of these are hilarious; others ominous; several so remote from the matter at hand they seem imported from another book entirely."

To convey her story, Adler creates three loosely connected sections, the first and third of which are comprised of diverse episodes, reflections, and observations arranged non-chronologically, almost like journal entries reflecting her state of mind. The longest episode in the first part is a five-page parable about an ailing raccoon that seems to overcome its wildness and takes up residence on Kate's stove. "I thought he was growing to trust me, when in fact he was dying," Kate writes. Developing this incident into a metaphor for her relationship to Jake, she continues: "So are we all, of course. But we do not normally mistake progressions of weakness, the loss of the simple capacity to escape, for the onset of love." *Village Voice* contributor Eliot Fremont-Smith describes the narrator's agonizing over the raccoon's fate as "a typical rumination in the book" and points out that "there are as many of these as there are half-mind's of Kate." In fact, the novel is studded with incidents that "at the time seemed only peripherally connected or connected not at all to the love affair," but in memory become "inextricably and painfully bound up with it," writes Steven Simmons in *Harper's.*

In the second section, Adler shifts to a more traditional narrative, chronicling a visit Kate makes to an Irish castle to get her mind off Jake. Adopting the tone of a thriller, this segment "is sensationally effective," according to Simmons. "The Irish passages, by turns scary and funny, brilliantly evoke a very modern sense of paranoia, and they also reveal Adler's real and rather old-fashioned gift for sketching characters vividly and economically." It is here, as Kate plots a surreptitious departure from Ireland, that her identity and Adler's temporarily merge. At the airport, while trying to convince herself that adopting a false name would provide good cover, Kate writes: "I should make the name as like my own as possible to account for the mistake. Alder, I thought." After experimenting with variations, the name she eventually chooses is Hadley, but as *New York Times Book Review* contributor Muriel Spark notes: "Her own name is Ennis, and Alder, Haddock, Hadley do not resemble Ennis, could not possibly pose as either a visual or aural mistake. . . . Does Miss Adler mean to suggest that she herself is

Kate Ennis? Illogical characters are fine, but this has the effect of professional illogic. It breaks the fiction and, for a brief moment, we have autobiography."

One strategy for deciphering the story, suggests Toronto *Globe and Mail* contributor Gale Garnett, is to read it as "a long letter from one lover to another, filled with all of the accumulated grievances, angers and desires that pile up over the course of a long alliance with a very busy married man. . . . Instead she gives him what she believes he does not know: her feelings, her thoughts, her frustrations at his perpetually unfulfilled promise to take her to New Orleans. Toward the end, she even becomes bored with sustaining the existence of 'Kate Ennis and tells a story of selecting' Hadley as a pseudonym. . . . Perhaps Adler intended that the reader do some inductive and deductive sleuthing through her printed words."

By forcing the reader to piece her story together from fragments, Adler is affirming what Roger Shattuck calls "the 'innarratability principle.' You cannot tell your essential story straight out; Adler-Ennis quotes Emily Dickinson on telling it 'slant.' As the symbolist poets hesitated to name anything for fear of destroying the fragile essence of the object so rudely named, Adler fears to narrate. She proceeds by indirection, giving us only glancing views of the breakup with Jake," he writes in the *New York Review of Books*.

Critics typically associate this kind of minimalist approach with modernist fiction. But Adler, in an interview with *New York Times* reporter Samuel G. Freedman, expresses a wariness about aligning herself with that school: "I think *Pitch Dark* either works emotionally or it doesn't work at all. . . . If it is modernist in form, then I hope that form can accommodate a certain amount of feeling, because the relationship of modernism to feeling has been, at best, skittish. Modernism might be comic. It might be rueful. But it's all astringent. Someone said my writing was ironic. I don't think there's any irony, because in irony, there's a certain safety and reserve."

Arguing that Adler does indeed take risks in the novel, *New York Times* critic Michiko Kakutani concludes that "in the end, Kate's personality and voice—which, one suspects, closely echoes Miss Adler's own—help *Pitch Dark* transcend the limits of its structure; they make the book not only engaging intellectually, but also emotionally compelling."

Between the publication of her first and second novels, Adler enrolled at Yale University and by the time *Pitch Dark* was published, she had earned her law degree. Her fifth book reflects that legal training. In *Reckless Disregard: Westmoreland v. CBS et al.; Sharon v. Time,* Adler abandons the imaginary drama of fiction to portray the real-life theatrics of courtroom law. Her most controversial book to date, *Reckless Disregard* has been criticized less for how it is written than for what it implies. The book took shape when, through a coincidence, two military leaders filed separate, but remarkably similar, libel suits charging that their reputations had been wrongfully damaged by major news organizations. Both suits were filed in the U.S. District Court of Manhattan between October of 1984 and February of 1985 and both defendants were represented by what Adler calls "the large and powerful New York law firm, Cravath, Swaine & Moore."

In the Sharon case, former Defense Minister of Israel General Ariel Sharon filed suit against Time, Inc., to protest a news story in *Time* magazine's February 21, 1983, issue suggesting that Sharon had abetted the massacre of civilian Palestinians by Lebanese Christian Phalangists. That story, which claimed that Sharon had "reportedly discussed . . . the need for the Phalangists to take revenge" was judged "false and defamatory" by the jury. But because Sharon had not, in the court's eyes, "proved by clear and convincing evidence" that *Time* knew the story was false before publishing it, "actual malice" could not be proved. Despite being cleared of libel charges, *Time* correspondent David Halevy, who filed the story, was singled out by the jury in an amplifying statement for having "acted negligently and carelessly."

In the Westmoreland case, former commander of American forces in South Vietnam General William Westmoreland filed charges against the Columbia Broadcasting System, Inc. (CBS) news reporter Mike Wallace and others because of a documentary aired January 23, 1982. Entitled "The Uncounted Enemy: A Vietnam Deception," the program suggested that "a conspiracy at the highest levels of American military intelligence" had resulted in underestimating the number of North Vietnamese forces in 1967-68 so it would look like the war was being won. Unlike *Time,* which had simply neglected to verify information provided by its correspondent, CBS was guilty of deliberate misrepresentation, Adler believes. "They took a thesis; found witnesses more or less to support it; interviewed those witnesses, and cut those parts of the interviews which did not support the thesis," she argues at length, concluding that "in short, they were acting not as press but as producers and directors casting for a piece of theatre." Despite the apparent merit of his case, Westmoreland dropped the charges before they reached a jury.

As she investigated both cases, Adler became convinced that the defendants had refused to acknowledge even the possibility of error, that their lawyers had behaved with what she called "almost mindless aggressiveness," and that together they displayed "a concerted disregard for the fundamental . . . goals of truth and accuracy," writes *New York Times Book Review* contributor Marvin E. Frankel. Her conclusions so angered CBS management that the network had Cravath file a fifty-plus page document charging that *Reckless Disregard* represented "plainly false, gross misrepresentations and distortions of the record" and should be withdrawn. Though delayed for several months, the manuscript was published without a single factual change.

Adler's clash with Cravath was closely followed by the press, and syndicated columnist Edwin M. Yoder, Jr., dubbed it "the publishing scandal of the fall." When *Reckless Disregard* finally appeared in November, 1986, there were some scattered objections to specific minor issues, such as whether or not *Time* and CBS could even be considered legitimate news sources and whether or not Adler was truly as impartial as she appeared to be. Several critics also noted her affinity for complex sentences, studded with dependent clauses and parenthetical asides. *Washington Post Book World* critic William V. Shannon asks: "Is there no editor at *The New Yorker* or Knopf who dares cry, 'Block that parenthesis!'?" In general, however, most critics applauded Adler's courage and firmly endorsed her book.

"*Reckless Disregard* is the best book about American journalism of our time . . . yet another parable of how law, in our overly litigious society, can overcome and even devour professional and ethical scruples," Yoder writes in the *Washington Post.* Shannon describes it as "brilliant in its analysis, relentlessly argued, and unsparing in its moral and professional journalistic judgments. Adler leaves in shreds and tatters the professional reputations of both *Time* and CBS and their respective employees involved in these two cases. She proves that both organizations were wrong in their original news pre-

sentations, refused when challenged to admit error, and deployed their huge financial and legal resources to obscure the truth and defeat justice." Concludes *Chicago Tribune Books* reviewer Edward P. Bassett, "Given the apparent breakdown in ethics in a number of fields today, the journalist (and lawyer?) and citizen interested in encouraging those in our society to discourse should read this book and take pains to understand the author's messages."

Adler's 1988 publication *Politics and Media: Essays* is a collection of a dozen pieces, eleven of which were previously published in magazines. The book's scope is broader than its title indicates. Seven of the essays take on political subjects, including the National Guard, the Watergate affair, and Robert Bork's nomination to the Supreme Court. The rest serve up Adler's special brand of cultural criticism, including her thoughts on soap operas, game shows, and movies. Her critique of Pauline Kael also appears in the collection and is singled out as one of its best offerings by *Publishers Weekly* reviewer Genevieve Stuttaford, who calls it "hilarious, a masterpiece of invective." Stuttaford names the Bork piece as another standout essay, one that "reflects [Adler's] polemical skill and fierce intelligence." Although she says the interest and impact of some of the political writing from the 1970s has faded with time, Stuttaford concludes that the book's "best passages give full play to her dangerous wit and trenchant observations."

Kimberly G. Allen, a reviewer for *Library Journal,* offers another opinion of *Politics,* however. She states that while readers familiar with Adler's work might expect the book to be fascinating, "alas, it is tedious. . . . Wading through these excessively long and lackluster essays is a painful bore. Very disappointing." A *Kirkus Reviews* contributor differs strongly, however. Like Stuttaford, this reviewer points out that some of the pieces are too dated to be compelling; however, he finds that "in her cultural criticism, Adler shines" and concludes that overall, the book provides a healthy portion of "bold and bristly commentary from a porcupine essayist with acid-dipped quills."

BIOGRAPHICAL/CRITICAL SOURCES:

BOOKS

Contemporary Literary Criticism, Gale (Detroit), Volume 8, 1978, Volume 31, 1985.

PERIODICALS

Atlantic, October, 1976.

Booklist, September 1, 1988, p. 9.

Chicago Tribune, October 28, 1986.

Commentary, June, 1984.

Detroit News, January 29, 1984.

Kirkus Reviews, September 15, 1988, p. 1369.

Globe and Mail (Toronto), January 28, 1984.

Harper's, November, 1976; February, 1984.

Library Journal, October 15, 1988, p. 82.

Los Angeles Times, November 18, 1986.

Los Angeles Times Book Review, December 18, 1983; December 7, 1986.

Ms., November, 1976.

Nation, November 6, 1976; February 18, 1984.

New Republic, December 5, 1983.

Newsweek, October 11, 1976; December 19, 1983; November 10, 1986.

New York, December 12, 1983.

New York Review of Books, August 14, 1980; March 15, 1984.

New York Times, January 28, 1970; September 23, 1976; December 5, 1983; December 27, 1983; August 28, 1986; October 25, 1986; November 6, 1986.

New York Times Book Review, March 29, 1970; September 26, 1976; December 18, 1983; November 9, 1986.

Publishers Weekly, August 26, 1988, p. 71.

Saturday Review, April 4, 1970; October 2, 1976.

Spectator, September 10, 1977.

Time, October 11, 1976; December 5, 1983.

Times (London), July 19, 1984.

Times Literary Supplement, August 26, 1977; July 20, 1984.

Tribune Books (Chicago), December 14, 1986.

Village Voice, October 11, 1976.

Voice Literary Supplement, December, 1983.

Washington Post, August 18, 1984; November 4, 1986; November 14, 1986; November 23, 1986.

Washington Post Book World, October 24, 1976; December 25, 1983; November 9, 1986.*

*   *   *

ALCOCK, John   1942-

PERSONAL: Born November 13, 1942, in Charlottesville, VA; son of John Powell (a chemical engineer) and Mariana (Collins) Alcock; married Susanne Eleanor Coates, October 26, 1968; children:

John, Nicholas. *Education:* Amherst College, B.A., 1965; Harvard University, Ph.D., 1969. *Politics:* Democrat. *Religion:* Society of Friends (Quakers).

ADDRESSES: Home—705 East Loyola Dr., Tempe, AZ 85282. *Office*—Department of Zoology, Arizona State University, Tempe, AZ 85287-1501.

CAREER: University of Washington, Seattle, assistant professor, 1969-72; Arizona State University, Tempe, assistant professor, 1972-74, associate professor, 1974-80, professor of zoology, 1980—.

WRITINGS:

Animal Behavior: An Evolutionary Approach, Sinauer Associates (Sunderland, MA), 1975, 5th edition, 1993.

The Evolution of Insect Mating System, Harvard University Press (Cambridge, MA), 1983.

Sonoran Desert Spring, University of Chicago Press (Chicago), 1985.

The Kookaburra's Song, University of Arizona Press (Tucson), 1988.

Sonoran Desert Summer, University of Arizona Press, 1990.

The Masked Bobwhite Rides Again, University of Arizona Press, 1993.

*   *   *

ALPERN, Andrew   1938-

PERSONAL: Born November 1, 1938, in New York, NY; son of Dwight K. (a college professor, chemist, engineer, metallurgist, mineralogist, and writer) and Grace (in fashion industry and public relations; maiden name, Michelman) Alpern. *Education:* Columbia University, B.Arch., 1964; Benjamin N. Cardoza School of Law, J.D. (magna cum laude), 1992.

ADDRESSES: Office—Hughes Hubbard & Reed, 24 Whitehall St., New York, NY 10004.

CAREER: Haines Lundberg Waehler, New York City, student trainee, 1959-63, architect, 1964-67; W. T. Grant (department store), New York City, consulting architect, 1967-68; Saphier, Lerner, Schindler, Environetics, project manager, 1968-72; Environmental Research and Development, Inc., New York City, vice-president and director of architecture, 1972-75; independent consulting architect, 1975-77, 1988-92; Hellmuth, Obata & Kassabaum, P.C., New York City, project manager, 1977-78; Coopers & Lybrand, New York City, manager of real estate and planning, 1978-88; Coopers & Lybrand, consulting lawyer, 1992-94; Hughes Hubbard & Reed, New York City, special counsel, 1994—. Certified by National Council of Architectural Registration Boards, 1967; registered architect in New York, California, and Washington, DC; admitted to the bar in New York and in Federal District Court (eastern and southern districts of New York). National arbitrator for American Arbitration Association, 1971-86. Lecturer at the City College of the City University of New York and Institute for Architecture and Urban Studies. Member of advisory board, Institute of Applied Psychotherapy, 1969-72.

MEMBER: American Bar Association, American Institute of Architects, Friends of Cast Iron Architecture, Society of Architectural Historians, Architectural League of New York, New York Historical Society, New York State Association of Architects, New York State Bar Association, Real Estate Board of New York (member, Landmark Buildings Committee, hall of fame selection jury), Association of the Bar of the City of New York (member, construction law committee), Brooklyn Historical Society, Municipal Art Society, Fifth Avenue Association of New York (member of design awards jury), Coffee House Club.

AWARDS, HONORS: Sc.D. from London College of Applied Science, 1971; named as jury member to Hall of Fame of the Real Estate Board of the State of New York, 1988; presidential citation from the New York State Association of Architects, 1991, for "Statutes of Repose and the Construction Industry: A Proposal for New York"; West Publishing Award for academic excellence, 1992.

WRITINGS:

Apartments for the Affluent: A Historical Survey of Buildings in New York, McGraw-Hill (New York City), 1975.

Alpern's Architectural Aphorisms, McGraw-Hill, 1979.

(Editor-in-chief) *Handbook of Specialty Elements in Architecture,* McGraw-Hill, 1981.

(With Seymour Durst) *Holdouts!,* McGraw-Hill, 1984.

New York's Fabulous Luxury Apartments, Dover (New York City), 1987.

(Managing editor and contributor with Jon Heller) *Civil Practice and Litigation in Federal and State Courts,* 5th edition, ALI-ABA, 1992.

Luxury Apartment Houses of Manhattan: An Illustrated History, Dover, 1993.

Historic Manhattan Apartment Houses, Dover, 1995.

Regular contributor of articles to *N.Y. Habitat;* also contributor to other periodicals, including *Cardoza Law Forum, Cardoza Law Review, Chelsea Clinton News, Environetics Today,* and *Metropolis.* Editorial advisor and consultant to McGraw-Hill periodicals for architects. Editor of twice-monthly periodical *Legal Briefs for the Construction Industry,* 1978-92. Member of *Cardoza Law Review,* 1990-92.

SIDELIGHTS: Andrew Alpern told *CA:* "The practice of architecture encompasses science, technology, business, and art, and it is a wonderfully challenging and stimulating profession, but writing about architecture and buildings can reach a larger audience than mere construction. And through the written word (and copious illustrative material) the crucial, intimate, and often tempestuous interrelationships between architects, developers, and the world-at-large can be described. Buildings are stone and glass and steel, of course, but far more important, they represent physical manifestations of human needs. Perhaps the most important basic need after food and water, is enough of a shelter to call home."

Concerning the future outlook for architecture and architects, Alpern remarked: "The relentless pressure of economic realities is forcing architects, and indeed our entire society, to reevaluate how we deal with our built environment within the context of our ever-changing needs as human beings and as a society. The days of bulldozing the old to make way for the new every twenty years or so are over. The philosophy that progress means a total rejection of what went before has proven disastrously wrong, both in social terms and in economic ones. At long last America has come around to a recognition of its significant architectural heritage and resource that does not necessarily have to be destroyed when it no longer meets its functional or economic imperatives.

"Architectural preservation has come out of the closet with a vengeance. But has it gone too far? Any city that relentlessly destroys its past destroys its soul and its humanity. But one that is loath to raze any structure that retains a bit of classical molding or a graceful cornice will rapidly doom itself to economic and social obsolescence. What is sorely needed is a rational balance that preserves the best of the old, recognizes the need for continual change and rejuvenation, and that fosters the wisdom of knowing when and how to compromise in a reasonable and realistic way. Extreme positions and blind zealotry may make good newspaper copy, but they cannot yield a truly livable yet economically viable place in which humans can function. It is only through cooperation, careful analysis, and a ready willingness to compromise that the architecture produced by our entire society (guided and aided by our architects) will be the responsive resource it has the capability of being."

*   *   *

ANDREW, Prudence (Hastings) 1924-

PERSONAL: Born May 23, 1924, in London, England; daughter of Percy and Margaret (Bridge) Petch; married G. H. L. Andrew, 1946; children: Jane, Sarah. *Education:* St. Anne's College, Oxford, B.A. (with honors), 1946. *Avocational interests:* Music (jazz and classical), ballet, history, cats and dogs.

ADDRESSES: Office—c/o Heinemann Ltd., 81 Fulham Road, London SW3 6RB, England.

CAREER: Joseph Lucas, Ltd., Birmingham, England, personnel department, 1944-45; Nuffield Institute of Colonial Affairs, Oxford, England, staff member, 1945-47; St. Michael's Convent School, Monmouthshire, England, history teacher, 1956-60; writer, 1960—.

WRITINGS:

ADULT FICTION

The Hooded Falcon, Hutchinson (London), 1960, Putnam (New York City), 1961.
Ordeal by Silence: A Story of Medieval Times, Hutchinson, 1961, Putnam, 1961.
A Question of Choice, Hutchinson, 1962, Putnam, 1962.
The Earthworms, Hutchinson, 1963, also published as *The Constant Star,* Putnam, 1968.
A Sparkle from the Coal, Hutchinson, 1964.
A New Creature, Hutchinson, 1968, Putnam, 1968.
A Man with Your Advantages, Hutchinson, 1970.

CHILDREN'S FICTION

The Christmas Card, illustrated by Mary Russon, Hamish Hamilton (London), 1966.
Mr. Morgan's Marrow, illustrated by Janet Duchesne, Hamish Hamilton, 1967.
Dog!, illustrated by Trevor Stubley, Hamish Hamilton, 1968, Nelson (Nashville), 1973.
Mister O'Brien, Heinemann (London), 1972, Nelson, 1973.
Una and Grubstreet, Heinemann, 1972, also published as *Una and the Heaven Baby,* Nelson, 1975.
Rodge, Silvie, and Munch, illustrated by Jael Jordan, Heinemann, 1973.
Goodbye to the Rat, Heinemann, 1974.
The Heroic Deeds of Jason Jones, illustrated by Jordan, Heinemann, 1975.
Where Are You Going To, My Pretty Maid?, Heinemann, 1977.
Robinson Daniel Crusoe, Heinemann, 1978, also published as *Close within My Own Circle,* Elsevier Nelson, 1980.
The Other Side of the Park, Heinemann, 1984.

"GINGER" SERIES

Ginger over the Wall, illustrated by Charles Mozley, Lutterworth Press (London), 1962.
Ginger and Batty Billy, illustrated by Mozley, Lutterworth Press, 1963.
Ginger and Number Ten, illustrated by Mozley, Lutterworth Press, 1964.
Ginger among the Pigeons, illustrated by Mozley, Lutterworth Press, 1966.

SIDELIGHTS: British author Prudence Andrew has written a number of popular books for children, reluctant readers, and young adults. "Andrew writes well-constructed, entertaining stories about both boys and girls; although she tackles unusual themes and gives the reader an insight into the characters, there is plenty of action and humor to keep the story moving at a steady pace," Sheila G. Ray writes in *Twentieth-Century Children's Writers.* "Through their experiences, Andrew's heroes and heroines develop and grow and, in doing so, provide a rewarding and enriching reading experience."

Andrew's first series of books for children follows the adventures of a boy named Ginger and his friends—all working-class kids from a variety of ethnic backgrounds who live in the city. Ray notes in *Twentieth-Century Children's Writers* that, when the

"Ginger" series was first published in the 1960s, it was among the earliest "to include black characters as an integral part of the story." In *Ginger among the Pigeons,* the fourth book in the series, Ginger and his friends help old Mr. Bean protect his champion homing pigeon from a competitor who will do anything to win. "The climax . . . is built up, and exploded, superbly," declares a reviewer in the *Times Literary Supplement.*

Mister O'Brien, published in 1972, tells the inspirational story of Christopher Porter, who wears a brace on one leg but learns to overcome his handicap. Mister O'Brien is a colorful, one-legged man who appears in Christopher's imagination whenever he needs to make an important decision. With the encouragement of Mister O'Brien and his friend Penny—who manages to maintain a positive outlook despite the fact that her family lives in a dirty and depressing slum apartment—Christopher decides to enter a ten-mile walk for charity. Although "every aching yard of that terrible ten-mile walk can be felt in the reader's own limbs," a critic for the *Times Literary Supplement* says "the book is full of unsentimental warmth, humour and common sense."

Andrew's next book for children, *Una and Grubstreet* (also published as *Una and the Heaven Baby*), also features a child with an active imagination. Una is a motherless eleven-year-old who spends a lot of time alone while her father is at work. She fills her lonely hours by creating a fantasy life in which she receives advice from her toy bear, Grubstreet, and makes up scenarios to explain the behavior of a neighbor family, the Heavens. When her father announces that he is going on vacation with a new lady friend, Una feels neglected and decides to take action. Since she identifies strongly with the Heavens' neglected baby, Una kidnaps him and takes him to an abandoned building in order to keep him safe. Una's father discovers her desperate act, and his sensitive reaction allows Una to accept her own situation. Writing in *Books and Bookmen,* Gladys Williams calls it "an exciting, convincing story that many girls will find fascinating."

Andrew profiles another lonely teenager in *Robinson Daniel Crusoe* (also published as *Close within My Own Circle*). The story is told by thirteen-year-old Jimmy, whose older brother, Daniel, has trouble coping with the pressure their bullying father places on him to succeed. Jimmy is popular and a good soccer player, while Daniel is serious and a gifted student. As their father becomes increasingly ob-

sessed with Daniel's future, Daniel rebels and refuses to go to school during exam week. As Daniel retreats into his own world—which Andrew reveals through excerpts from Daniel's diary—tension builds and the family slowly disintegrates. The book ends as Daniel builds a raft, like that of his hero Robinson Crusoe, and sails down a river to almost certain death. A *Junior Bookshelf* reviewer calls the book "beautiful in its truth, its contemporary freshness," while *Growing Point* critic Margery Fisher praises it as a "striking study of early adolescence."

In her 1984 book, *The Other Side of the Park,* Andrew presents a teenager who is struggling to understand and accept her family. Fifteen-year-old Judy suffers the loss of her beloved great-grandmother, who had become somewhat senile but was very supportive of Judy's talents in ventriloquism. Her great-grandmother died when she fell down a flight of stairs, but as Judy notices how materialistic her father and sister have become, she begins to suspect them of playing a role in her death. She works through her questions and doubts about her family with the help of her ventriloquist's dummy, Tatty 'Ead, and her sensible, working-class boyfriend. In the process, Judy grows up and becomes more independent. In a review for the *Times Educational Supplement,* Neil Philip states that "teenage girls may well identify with her, though they may also resent the too easy ending." A *Junior Bookshelf* reviewer declares that Andrew's "characterization is first rate," adding that *The Other Side of the Park* contains "much to be recommended."

BIOGRAPHICAL/CRITICAL SOURCES:

BOOKS

Twentieth-Century Children's Writers, 4th edition, St. James Press (Detroit, MI), 1995, pp. 26-27.

PERIODICALS

Booklist, May 15, 1973, p. 903.

Books and Bookmen, May, 1973, p. 13.

Bulletin of the Center for Children's Books, May, 1976; July-August, 1980.

Growing Point, October, 1975, pp. 2721-22; September, 1977, p. 3176; March, 1979, p. 3483; September, 1987, p. 4873.

Horn Book, August, 1980, pp. 412-13.

Junior Bookshelf, June, 1979, p. 164; October, 1984, p. 213.

Kirkus Reviews, July 1, 1973, p. 684.
Library Journal, April 15, 1973, p. 1384.
School Library Journal, March, 1976, p. 109; February, 1980, p. 63.
Times Educational Supplement, January 4, 1985, p. 20.
Times Literary Supplement, November 24, 1966, p. 1085; April 28, 1972, p. 5660; July 11, 1975, p. 770.

* * *

ANSON, Robert Sam   1945-

PERSONAL: Born March 12, 1945, in Cleveland, OH; son of Sam B. and Virginia Anson; married Amanda Kay Kyser (an artist), August 17, 1986; children: Christian Kennedy, Sam Gideon, Georgia Grace. *Education:* University of Notre Dame, B.A. (cum laude), 1967. *Religion:* Catholic.

*ADDRESSES: Home and office—*1047 25th St, Santa Monica, CA 90403.

CAREER: Writer. *Time,* New York City, correspondent in Chicago, Los Angeles, New York City, and Indochina, 1966-72; WNET-TV, New York City, producer and anchor, 1972-78; *New Times,* New York City, senior writer, 1975-78; *Esquire,* New York City, contributing editor, 1978-81, and 1991-95; *Manhattan, Inc.,* New York City, contributing editor, 1985-87; *Los Angeles,* Los Angeles, CA, editor-in-chief, 1995.

WRITINGS:

McGovern, Holt (New York City), 1972.
"They've Killed the President!": The Search for the Murderers of John F. Kennedy, Bantam (New York City), 1975.
Gone Crazy and Back Again: The Rise and Fall of the Rolling Stone Generation, Doubleday (New York City), 1981.
Exile: The Unquiet Oblivion of Richard M. Nixon, Simon & Schuster (New York City), 1984.
Best Intentions: The Education and Killing of Edmund Perry, Random House (New York City), 1987.
War News: A Young Reporter in Indochina, Simon & Schuster, 1989.
The Rules of the Magic, Pantheon (New York City), 1996.

Contributor to periodicals, including *Esquire* and *Life.*

ADAPTATIONS: Best Intentions: The Education and Killing of Edmund Perry was made into a television movie.

SIDELIGHTS: Robert Sam Anson is a prominent figure in American journalism. He entered the field as a correspondent for *Time* while he was still a student at the University of Notre Dame in the mid-1960s, and upon graduation he worked for the magazine's Chicago and Los Angeles bureaus. Anson eventually covered the Vietnam War, and in 1970 he was captured by the North Vietnamese soldiers fighting with Cambodia's Communist forces, the Khmer Rouge. He initially feared for his life, particularly since other American journalists had already been killed by the Communists. But Anson succeeded in befriending his captors, and after three weeks he was freed in a ceremony led by ranking Cambodian and Vietnamese officers. Prior to the ceremony he supplied comments on his captivity to North Vietnamese radio for later broadcast—the comments, however, were never used. Once released, Anson was also interviewed by the Western press, to whom he conveyed his impressions of his captors as dedicated and compassionate. "They treated me like a brother," he declared in announcing that he would no longer cover the war. "I have friends on both sides now. I don't want to see my friends dead."

In 1972 Anson left *Time* and began working as an anchor and producer for WNET-TV, New York City's public television station. That same year he published *McGovern,* a biography of Democratic presidential candidate and U.S. Senator George S. McGovern. Anson's book appeared prior to the 1972 election—which McGovern lost, overwhelmingly, to incumbent Richard M. Nixon—and was commended as a reasoned, unflinching account of McGovern's career. A critic for the *Times Literary Supplement* reported that *McGovern* afforded readers a frank appraisal of the senator's career, and L. W. Koenig, writing in the *Saturday Review,* praised Anson's book as a "shrewd and informing study."

While working at WNET-TV Anson also began writing for the investigative magazine *New Times.* He became one of the periodical's leading political writers, and in his years with the magazine—from 1975 to 1978, when it ceased publication—he produced pieces on prominent political figures such as Hubert

H. Humphrey, Ronald Reagan, and Jimmy Carter. His best-known articles, however, are probably those exploring the 1963 assassination of President John F. Kennedy. As author of an article entitled "The Greatest Cover-up of All," Anson cited flagrant distortions in the official investigation, which concluded that Lee Harvey Oswald was the sole assassin of the president, and he presented evidence that Kennedy was the victim of a conspiracy most probably involving right-wing Cubans and members of organized crime. Anson's piece gained notoriety for its accompanying cover illustration featuring a shaken Kennedy with blood spraying from a head wound, but the article was nonetheless important for delineating various aspects of the assassination, including Oswald's ties to right-wing extremists and to both Soviet and American espionage organizations.

In 1975, the same year of the *New Times* report, Anson presented a more detailed investigation of the Kennedy assassination and its related controversies in *"They've Killed the President!": The Search for the Murderers of John F. Kennedy.* The book, like the aforementioned article, explores the possibility that Kennedy's death resulted from conspiracy and presents evidence that at least one individual—and possibly more—posed as Oswald. In addition, Anson argues that a 1966 investigation conducted by Jim Garrison, who was then district attorney of New Orleans, had the effect of besmirching the integrity of sincere conspiracy theorists. In a field rife with preposterous speculation and misinformation, Anson's *"They've Killed the President!"* is viewed as among the more plausible and keenly researched reports. D. C. Anderson, writing in the *New York Times Book Review,* called Anson's book "a powerful piece of journalistic scholarship" and praised Anson's "exhaustive documentation." In addition, Anderson commended Anson's "thoroughness" and cited his "capacity for backbreaking research."

By 1978 *New Times* had ceased publication and Anson had resigned his position at WNET-TV. His next work as a writer was *Gone Crazy and Back Again: The Rise and Fall of the Rolling Stone Generation,* an entertaining analysis of the 1960s counterculture as it was reflected in the development of *Rolling Stone* magazine. The book was dismissed as trivial by some reviewers and considered highly readable, if not particularly profound, by others.

Anson followed *Gone Crazy and Back Again* with *Exile: The Unquiet Oblivion of Richard M. Nixon,*

which detailed Nixon's life in the decade following his resignation from the American presidency. Anson was unable to secure Nixon's cooperation on *Exile* and thus relied heavily on research and interviews. Despite this seeming drawback, the book elicited positive responses from critics such as J. Anthony Lukas, who wrote in the *New York Times Book Review* that Anson's inclusion of voluminous notes constituted "a model of journalist attribution," and the *Los Angeles Times*'s reviewer, who called *Exile* a "fascinating account" and a "fastpaced, colorful, highly readable narrative."

Anson's next book was *Best Intentions: The Education and Killing of Edmund Perry,* in which he explored the circumstances behind the 1985 death of a Harlem youth killed while attempting to rob a plainclothes policeman. The seeming contradiction of Perry's action—a criminal act perpetrated by an admired Exeter Academy student—led Harlem residents to accuse New York City's police of racist violence. But Anson traced Perry's life in Harlem and at the exclusive Exeter preparatory school and discovered that Perry was a confused, angry youth capable of both earning an academic scholarship and committing a violent crime. Anson reported that Perry was perceived in Harlem as a model citizen and an inspiration to others hoping to avoid a life of poverty and crime. But Anson also disclosed that at Exeter the usually soft-spoken Perry portrayed himself as a streetwise militant who used and sold drugs. *Best Intentions* ultimately portrayed Perry as a confused young man whose inability to sustain conflicting lifestyles led to self-destruction. *Best Intentions* earned Anson further recognition as a keen reporter of provocative subjects. *Newsweek*'s David Gates found the book "engrossing," and a *People* reviewer described it as "profoundly moving."

Anson told *CA:* "Following *Best Intentions,* which was made into a network television movie, I wrote *War News: A Young Reporter in Indochina,* a memoir of my days as a combat correspondent for *Time.* The book was widely well-reviewed. In 1990, I moved to Los Angeles to begin work on *The Rules of the Magic,* a history of Michael Eisner's management of the Walt Disney Company. In May, 1995, I was named editor of *Los Angeles* magazine, a Cap Cities/ABC publication. Shortly after my appointment, Cap Cities/ABC was purchased by Disney. In October, 1995, I—who have written several articles critical of Disney chairman and chief executive officer Michael Eisner—was discharged as editor."

BIOGRAPHICAL/CRITICAL SOURCES:

PERIODICALS

Booklist, September 15, 1989, p. 118.
Chicago Tribune Book World, August 26, 1984.
JQ: Journalism Quarterly, spring, 1990, p. 226.
Kirkus Reviews, July 1, 1989, p. 961.
Library Journal, September 15, 1989, p, 119.
Los Angeles Times, February 26, 1981; July 1, 1984.
Newsweek, September 7, 1970; June 1, 1987.
New Times, April 18, 1975; March 19, 1976.
New York Times, February 10, 1981; June 28, 1984.
New York Times Book Review, June 4, 1972; January
    4, 1976; July 1, 1984; August 27, 1989, p. 9.
People, August 3, 1987.
Publishers Weekly, July 21, 1989, p. 45.
Saturday Review, June 3, 1972.
Time, September 7, 1970; August 17, 1987.
Times Literary Supplement, June 30, 1972.
Virginia Quarterly Review, winter, 1991, p. 34.
Washington Post, March 14, 1981.
WJR: Washington Journalism Review, October, 1989,
    p. 58.

*   *   *

ANTHONY, Geraldine (Cecilia) 1919-

PERSONAL: Born October 5, 1919, in Brooklyn, NY; daughter of William (a pharmacist) and Agnes (Murphy) Anthony. *Education:* Attended Boston College, 1945-47; Mount St. Vincent University, B.A., 1951; St. John's University, Jamaica, NY, M.A., 1956, Ph.D., 1963; post-doctoral study at Exeter College, Oxford, University of Minnesota, and Columbia University.

ADDRESSES: Home—51 Marlwood Dr., Wedgewood Park, Halifax, Nova Scotia, Canada B3M 3H4. *Office*—Mount St. Vincent Motherhouse, 150 Bedford Highway, Halifax, Nova Scotia, Canada B3M 3J5.

CAREER: Member of Roman Catholic women's congregation, the Sisters of Charity, 1939—; junior high school teacher at Roman Catholic schools in Dorchester, MA, 1942-48, Lowell, MA, 1948-51, and Bellmore, NY, 1951-62; high school teacher of English in Halifax, Nova Scotia, 1963-65; Mount St. Vincent University, Halifax, assistant professor, 1965-71, associate professor, 1971-77, professor of English, 1977-87, professor emeritus, 1987—, direc-

tor of summer school, 1966-68, chair of department, 1983-86. Visiting professor at Hofstra University, summers, 1970-74. Coordinator of annual Mount St. Vincent University/Oxford University summer school, 1984-90. Historian and biographer for the congregation of Sisters of Charity, Halifax, Nova Scotia.

MEMBER: Modern Language Association of America, Association for Canadian Theatre History (founding member, president, and member of executive board), Association of Canadian and Quebecois Literature, Association of Canadian University Teachers of English, Delta Kappa Gamma (founding member of Nova Scotia chapter).

AWARDS, HONORS: Wall Street Journal fellow at University of Minnesota, 1965; MSVU grants, 1975, 1976, 1978, and Canada Council grant, 1977, for research to complete books on Canadian dramatists; British High Council grant, 1983; Social Science and Humanities Research Council of Canada grant, 1991; received the Commemorative Medal of Canada, 1992, for community service.

WRITINGS:

John Coulter, G. K. Hall (Boston), 1976.
(Editor) *Profiles in Canadian Drama,* three volumes,
    Gage, 1977.
Stage Voices, Doubleday (New York City), 1978.
Gwen Pharis Ringwood, G. K. Hall, 1981.
(Contributor) *Canadian Biographical Dictionary,*
    University of British Columbia Press (Vancouver,
    Canada), 1982.
Nunc et Semper: A Call to Radical Sisterhood (mul-
    timedia documentary play), first produced in
    Halifax, Nova Scotia, July 3, 1988.
*Rebel, Reformer, Religious Extraordinaire: The Life
    of Sister Irene Farmer,* University of Calgary
    Press (Calgary, Canada), 1996.

Also coauthor of *This Is Barbara's Life,* 1956. Contributor to various periodicals, including *Canadian Book Review Annual, Atlantis, Canadian Drama, Canadian Theatre Review, Canadian Library Journal, Cithara, World Literature, Canadian Children's Literature, Canadian Review of American Studies, Prairie Forum, Theatre History in Canada, Great Plains Quarterly, Nashwaak Review, Books in Canada, Ottawa Journal,* and *Canadian Literature.* Member of editorial board of *Canadian Drama/L'Art Dramatique Canadien, Catholic Literary World, Oxford Companion to Canadian Theatre,* and *World Encyclopedia of Contemporary Theatre.*

WORK IN PROGRESS: The History of the Federation of Sisters of Charity, 1947-1997.

SIDELIGHTS: Geraldine Anthony told *CA* her interest in theater "stemmed from my childhood in New York and my father's keen interest in the Broadway plays. He stimulated me to a love of theatre that has become a passion, transferred from American to Canadian drama when I moved to Canada in 1963 and discovered that very little had been done in the way of Canadian dramatic literary criticism. Today many Canadian scholars are devoting more and more time to research in this field. I am happy to have been one of the first."

Anthony continued: "Thirty years ago, I had the temerity to write a few children's plays and had them produced in St. Barnabas School in New York in the 1950s. Until recently, the only other creative theatre venture was a slide projection show with voice-over on the life of the Sisters of Charity, plus a book on the same topic: *This Is Barbara's Life.* In 1988, at the request of the Congregation, I wrote a multimedia documentary on the three hundred year history of the Sisters of Charity from its foundation in France in the seventeenth century by St. Vincent de Paul, to its American foundation by St. Elizabeth Ann Seton in the early nineteenth century, to its Halifax branch in 1849, and finally to the extraordinary changes in today's religious life after Vatican II in 1968. The present status of Roman Catholic religious congregations of women is highlighted in this play, *Nunc et Semper: A Call to Radical Sisterhood.*

"Present day supporters of the feminist movement might see in this play all the desirable elements of the feminist cause, such as independence, a flexible life style, financial support for higher education in professional fields, colleague support in the strength and dedicated love of fellow religious, concentrated work for the poor and destitute in North America and in Third World countries. Again, theatre provides the means for a graphic portrayal of contemporary life— this time in the lives of nuns moving rapidly into the twenty-first century, dedicated to solidarity with the economically poor. I am glad that my academic life centered on theatre. It has made all the difference in my own life in my contacts with the Canadian theatre people whom I am proud to call my friends.

"When I retired from my academic career in 1987, my religious community asked me to become one of their historians and biographer. This was a new venture for me as I left the world of theatre for that of religious women, their lives and works. To date I have given four academic papers at university conferences in the United States and Canada on the careers of religious women. I have completed a biography on the life of Sister Irene Farmer, soon (1996) to be published by the University of Calgary Press. I am presently commissioned to write the history of fourteen congregations of religious women in the Federation of Sisters of Charity. Now in my 77th year, I am as actively engaged as ever and thoroughly fulfilled in this new research on religious women into the twenty-first century."

*   *   *

AOKI, Haruo   1930-

PERSONAL: Born April 1, 1930, in Kunsan, Korea; son of Akira and Yae Aoki; married Mary Ann Schroeder, August 30, 1958 (divorced, 1977); children: Kanna, Akemi, Mieko. *Education:* Hiroshima University, B.A., 1953; University of California, Los Angeles, M.A., 1958, University of California, Berkeley, Ph.D., 1965.

ADDRESSES: Office—Department of East Asian Languages, University of California, Berkeley, CA 94720.

CAREER: University of California, Berkeley, assistant professor, 1965-69, associate professor, 1969-72, professor of East Asian languages, 1972-91, professor emeritus, 1991—.

MEMBER: Cercle Linguistique de Copenhagne, Keiryoo Kokugo Gakkai, Kokugogakkai, Kokugo Kenkyuukai, Linguistic Association of Great Britain, Linguistic Society of Japan, Nihon Gengogakkai, American Oriental Society, Linguistic Society of America.

AWARDS, HONORS: Fulbright fellow, 1953-54.

WRITINGS:

Nez Perce Grammar, University of California Press (Santa Cruz), 1970.
Horobiyuku-kotoba o Otte (title means "In Pursuit of a Vanishing Language"), Sanseido Press (Tokyo), 1972.
Nez Perce Texts, University of California Press, 1979.
(With others) *Basic Structure in Japanese,* Asian Humanities Press, 1984.

(With Shigeko Okamoto) *Rules for Conversational Rituals in Japanese,* Taishu-kan, 1988.

(With Deward E. Walker, Jr.) *Nez Perce Oral Narratives,* University of California Press, 1989.

Nez Perce Dictionary, University of California Press, 1994.

Associate editor of *Northwestern Anthropological Research Notes,* 1967—, and *Papers in Japanese Linguistics,* 1973—.

* * *

ARCHER, Jeffrey (Howard) 1940-

PERSONAL: Born April 15, 1940, in Mark, near Weston-super-Mare, Somerset, England; son of William (a professional soldier) and Lola (a journalist; maiden name, Cook) Archer; married Mary Weeden (a chemist), 1966; children: two sons. *Education:* Attended Brasenose College, Oxford, 1963-66; received diploma in sports education from Oxford Institute. *Politics:* Conservative. *Avocational interests:* Theater, squash, watching Somerset play cricket.

ADDRESSES: Home—93 Albert Embankment, London S.E.1, England; and The Old Vicarage, Grantchester, England.

CAREER: Writer. Arrow Enterprises Ltd., London, chair of the board, beginning 1968; Conservative member of the British Parliament, 1969-74; deputy chair, British Conservative Party, 1985-86. Chair, Nigeria Consultants, Inc. Member, Greater London Council for Havering, 1966-70; executive, British Theatre Museum.

MEMBER: Royal Society of the Arts (fellow), Oxford University Athletics Club (president, 1965), Somerset Amateur Athletics Association (president), Carlton Cricket Club, Marylebone Cricket Club.

AWARDS, HONORS: Created Life Peer in the Queen's Birthday Honors, 1992.

WRITINGS:

NOVELS

Not a Penny More, Not a Penny Less, Doubleday (New York City), 1976.

Shall We Tell the President?, Viking (New York City), 1977.

Kane & Abel (Literary Guild alternate selection), Simon & Schuster (New York City), 1980.

The Prodigal Daughter, Linden Press (New York City), 1982.

First among Equals, Linden Press, 1984.

A Matter of Honor, Linden Press, 1986.

As the Crow Flies, HarperCollins (New York City), 1991.

Honor among Thieves, HarperCollins, 1993.

STORIES

A Quiver Full of Arrows, Linden Press, 1982.

A Twist in the Tale, HarperCollins, 1989.

Twelve Red Herrings, HarperCollins, 1994.

FOR CHILDREN

By Royal Appointment, Octopus (London), 1980.

Willy Visits the Square World, Octopus, 1980.

Willy and the Killer Kipper, Hodder & Stoughton (London), 1981.

The First Miracle, HarperCollins, 1994.

PLAYS

Beyond Reasonable Doubt (produced on West End, London, 1987), Samuel French (London), 1989.

Exclusive, first produced on West End, London, 1989.

OTHER

(With others) *Gemma Levine's Faces of the 80s,* Collins, 1987.

(Editor with Simon Bainbridge) *Fools, Knaves, and Heroes: Great Political Short Stories,* Norton (New York City), 1991.

ADAPTATIONS: Not a Penny More, Not a Penny Less was adapted for British television and serialized on British radio; *Kane & Abel* was made into a miniseries for Columbia Broadcasting System (CBS-TV), fall, 1985. Steven Spielberg has purchased the film rights to *A Matter of Honor.*

SIDELIGHTS: It has often been said that Jeffrey Archer's career is reflected in his fiction—or, in some cases, that his fiction is reflected in his career. Both have attracted much public attention and have become the center of much controversy. A man of boundless energy, Archer has walked the corridors of power with England's politicians and has earned a reputation as one of the most popular authors in both England and America. A writer for *Books* magazine declares Archer to be "Britain's top-selling novelist." "The great contradiction of Jeffrey Archer's life," declares Bill Bryson in the *New York Times Magazine,* "is that the one thing he has tried hardest to do—become a successful politician—is the one thing he has most signally failed to accomplish."

Archer founded his own company, Arrow Enterprises, after leaving school. Drawing on his experiences in fundraising and public relations for the university as well as his own tremendous energy, he quickly earned a fortune. "I think energy is a God-given gift," he tells *CA,* "in the way the ability to play a violin, the ability to sing, the ability to paint is a gift. People underestimate energy. If you have one gift plus energy, you'll go to the very top. I've always said the formula is: one gift plus energy, you'll be a king; energy and no gift, you're a prince; a gift and no energy, you're a pauper. I think energy is much underestimated. You will see it in the truly successful. It's the one thing Maria Callas, Pablo Picasso, and Margaret Thatcher have in common."

In 1969, Archer put his money to work by running for, and winning by a landslide, a seat in Parliament. Only 29 years old, he took his place in the House of Commons as its youngest member. For five years he served as a Conservative politician, enjoying political power and personal wealth—including a house in a posh London district, expensive sports cars, and a heavy investment in a famous art gallery. In 1974, however, Archer's dream of a political career exploded in his face. He had borrowed over £250,000 and invested it in a Canadian industrial cleaning company called Aquablast. The directors of the company embezzled the funds and Aquablast collapsed with over $8 million in debts. "I lost every penny," Archer tells Bryson. "The shares were £3.20 on one day and 7 pence the next day. I never had a chance." Although Archer was a victim of the fraud, he felt obliged to not seek reelection and to devote himself to repaying his debts of $620,000. He left Parliament, borrowed a room in Oxford, and went to work writing a book loosely based on his own experiences.

Not a Penny More, Not a Penny Less tells about four men—a doctor, a college professor, an art dealer, and a member of the aristocracy—who invest 1 million dollars in a company to exploit oil in the North Sea. The businessperson who runs the company proves to be dishonest, however, and the quartet determine to get their money back by cheating him in return. *Not a Penny More, Not a Penny Less* went on to become an instant best-seller in the United States (where it was first published) after having been turned down by a dozen British publishers. Its success surprised Archer, among others, who revealed to Ross that he had "absolutely" no previous experience as a writer, and no previous ambitions to become an author. "I'd been to university and was certainly educated, but I'd never done any writing at all, which makes me think that probably there are a lot of storytellers out there, or, more important, people who could do a second career and haven't thought about it. . . . I am by nature a person who enjoys other people's company. But I didn't mind being on my own during that time, because I needed to readjust, and I needed to put some work in to make up for my own stupidity."

Although *Not a Penny More, Not a Penny Less* did not earn enough to pay all of Archer's debts, its great success encouraged him to write more. *Shall We Tell the President?,* Archer's second novel, did not make the best-seller lists in the United States, but it did generate a great deal of controversy. Set in the early 1980s, it tells of a plan to assassinate President Edward Kennedy. American reviewers were outraged by what they perceived as Archer's callousness. Jacqueline Kennedy Onassis, President John F. Kennedy's widow, resigned her position as an editor with Viking, although she had no direct connection with the book. "The new editions in the bookshops," Archer reveals to Ross, "have Florentyna Kane"— the heroine of his novel *The Prodigal Daughter*—"as the president, not Edward Kennedy." Skillful marketing of the book and its paperback and movie rights netted Archer around $750,000—enough to pay off all his debts.

Archer's next novel, *Kane & Abel,* is also partially based on real people. It tells the story of William Kane, a Boston banker, and Abel Rosnovski, a Polish immigrant and hotelier, and their ferocious hatred for each other. Kane earns Rosnovski's hostility when his bank withholds crucial help from the Pole's American benefactor after the stock market crash of 1929. The benefactor then commits suicide, and Rosnovski launches a vendetta against Kane that lasts for decades. "I met two such men in New York," Archer explains to Ross. "They were very close friends, unlike Kane and Abel, who were enemies. But they came from totally different backgrounds.

One was a Polish aristocrat, and the other was one of America's most successful multimillionaires. They both told me their [stories]. I was quite interested in that, but I thought it would be much more interesting if they were deadly enemies. So I wrote the book with them as background material, but my own story." *Kane and Abel* sold more than a quarter million copies in hardcover and eight times that in paperback.

The Prodigal Daughter, a sequel about Rosnovski's daughter, followed *Kane and Abel* in 1982. It tells how Florentyna Rosnovski—now married to Kane's son Richard—becomes the first female president of the United States. "I wanted to write the story of the first woman president of the United States," Archer confides to Ross. "I wanted an Englishman to write it, so that the Americans would realize that we're still awake over here. And you must remember that it was written some time before Geraldine Ferraro was chosen to be a vice-presidential candidate [in the 1984 election]. People laughed at me to begin with. They said it could never happen." Like *Kane and Abel, The Prodigal Daughter* topped best-seller lists in Great Britain and the United States.

Archer established a precedent in *The Prodigal Daughter* by creating two versions of the story: one for his British audience and another for his American fans. For instance, he made changes in the novel to simplify the American political system. "The British, of course," Archer explains to Ross, "find reading *The Prodigal Daughter* a fairly simple way of learning about the American system." More sweeping changes are apparent in the two versions of Archer's *First among Equals,* which tells about the competition between four British candidates for the office of Prime Minister. One of the main characters in the British version of the book is almost totally absent in the American counterpart, and each version of the book has a different prologue and a different ending. "The Americans do seem interested," Archer confides to Ross. "They have a desire to learn about other countries. *First among Equals* is a very simple way of understanding our strange parliamentary system."

Shall We Tell the President? received some harsh criticism for its lack of sensitivity toward the Kennedy family—*Times Literary Supplement* contributor Charles Wheeler calls it "a sick idea"—but Betty Lukas, writing in the *Los Angeles Times Book Review,* labels *The Prodigal Daughter* "pure ro-

mance," and adds, "Don't knock it. . . . Archer creates so much suspense in the dialogue that the usual chase scene seems like a turtle race." "Settle into the blankets" and enjoy it, she advises. "It's that kind of novel."

Critical opinion has been similarly divided over Archer's more recent novels. *As the Crow Flies* tells the story of Charlie Trumper, a man of working-class origins who serves in World War I and then rises to become the founder and head of a chain of department stores. Ken Gross, reviewing the book for *People,* praises Archer's choice of theme and his execution of it. The author "doesn't possess the prose skills of a Fitzgerald or the thundering moral outrage of Dostoevsky. But he tells a nice story." The reviewer concludes that the novel "is like a long, languid, comforting soak in a warm tub." Maggie Scarf, writing in the *New York Times Book Review* about the same book, makes a similar comment: "If [Archer's] writing does appear somewhat naive at times . . . it nevertheless conveys the message that what is right will be rewarded and what is evil will inevitably be punished." "Jeffrey Archer may not be portraying the world as it is," she concludes, "but he is giving us an uncomplicated view of life that was deeply comfortable and gratifying. Archer's simpler world is, in many ways, far preferable to the one we inhabit."

In *Honor among Thieves* Archer tried his hand at the international spy-novel genre. The book has a long, complicated plot about Iraqi president Saddam Hussein's plan to steal the original Declaration of Independence and burn it live on television. Sent to foil Hussein's plot are a Yale University law professor named Scott Bradley and a model-turned-Mossad-agent named Hannah Kopec. Simon Louvish, in a review for *New Statesman and Society,* asserts that the book "appears to have been written by a committee of ten year olds as an assignment," and accuses Archer of maintaining some pulp magazine prejudices. "But who needs the muse," he concludes, "if the cash tills sing so well unaided?" On the other hand, Gene Lyons states in *Entertainment Weekly* that Archer "has an undeniable flair for . . . ingeniously plotted, grandiose tales of derring-do." However, he also complains that the story is too formulaic. Archer himself has few pretensions about his fiction. "I'm a storyteller," the author tells Ross. "I never know what's going to be in the next line, the next paragraph, or the next page. And if I did, you would. If I don't know what's on the next page, how can you know?"

Archer's success in writing helped bring him back into politics. In 1985, Margaret Thatcher, Prime Minister of Great Britain and a reputed Archer fan (as well as a main character in *First among Equals*), appointed the author to the post of deputy chair of the Conservative party. A purely honorary job, the position nonetheless recognized Archer's devotion to the Conservatives and exploited his huge popularity and his fundraising prowess.

Late in 1986, however, a scandal resembling an episode from one of his novels made international headlines. A prostitute, backed by two English tabloid newspapers—the *Star* and the *News of the World*—claimed that she had sex with Archer and that he paid her to leave the country. Archer denied any personal contact with the woman, but admitted that he had given her money in order to avoid bad publicity. He resigned his position and sued both papers. In 1987 he was awarded $800,000 in damages from the *Star,* plus legal costs and a public apology. Most of the money, Archer reveals to Bryson, "went into the new roof of Ely Cathedral." "Politically, it was terrible," he confesses. "Things were just beginning to turn for me. We were near a general election. I was actually doing some good. So, of course, it was a tremendous disappointment to have to step down."

Archer currently divides his time between his writing and the Playhouse, a West End theater he owns. Archer remains a firm supporter of Conservative politicians; after Margaret Thatcher left the Prime Minister's office, another of his friends, John Major, took her place. Most analysts believed that Archer had no future in politics, but in 1993, he was elevated to the House of Lords. "The things that have happened to him," newspaper editor John Bryant tells Bryson, "would have buried the political career of anyone else. But you can never count Jeffrey Archer out."

BIOGRAPHICAL/CRITICAL SOURCES:

BOOKS

Contemporary Literary Criticism, Volume 28, Gale (Detroit), 1986.

PERIODICALS

Booklist, November 15, 1988.
Books, July-August, 1993, pp. 8-9.
Chicago Tribune, August 8, 1982; September 10, 1985; January 3, 1989; August 26, 1994, Sec. 3, pp. 1, 4.
Chicago Tribune Book World, April 27, 1980.
Detroit Free Press, September 5, 1985.
Entertainment Weekly, July 30, 1993, p. 51.
Globe and Mail (Toronto), September 13, 1986.
Guardian, July 11, 1993, p. 28.
Kirkus Reviews, June 15, 1994, pp. 786-787.
Los Angeles Times, August 19, 1982; October 24, 1982; March 11, 1983; July 21, 1984; January 22, 1989.
Los Angeles Times Book Review, April 27, 1980.
New Statesman and Society, July 2, 1993, p. 38.
New York Times, August 30, 1984; November 10, 1984; October 10, 1985; July 30, 1993.
New York Times Book Review, October 23, 1977; May 4, 1980; July 6, 1980; July 11, 1982; November 28, 1982; June 19, 1983; February 19, 1989, p. 23; June 9, 1991, p. 52; August 15, 1993, p. 18.
New York Times Magazine, November 25, 1990, pp. 35, 75-78.
Observer, September 18, 1988, p. 43; June 9, 1991, p. 59; July 17, 1994, p. 18.
People, August 5, 1991, pp. 25-26.
Publishers Weekly, November 4, 1988, p. 72; April 26, 1991, pp. 42-43; June 21, 1993, pp. 86-87; June 20, 1994, p. 96.
Quill and Quire, May, 1991, p. 29.
Spectator, July 10, 1993, p. 31; July 16, 1994, p. 28.
Time, July 28, 1986; November 10, 1986; July 26, 1993.
Times (London), October 27, 1986.
Times Literary Supplement, September 10, 1976; October 28, 1977; November 21, 1980; December 5, 1986; June 28, 1991, p. 18.
Washington Post, March 7, 1980; April 16, 1986; July 27, 1986; January 26, 1989.
Washington Post Book World, July 23, 1982; August 5, 1984.

*   *   *

ARNOLD, Eve   1913-

PERSONAL: Born in 1913; married. *Education:* Studied medicine; attended New School for Social Research, 1947-48 (studied photography with Alexey Brodovitch).

ADDRESSES: Home—26 Mount St., Flat 3, London W1Y 5RB, England. *Agent*—Magnum Photos, 151 West 25th St., New York, NY 10001; Magnum Photos Ltd., 5 Old Street, London EC1V 9HL, England.

CAREER: Photojournalist. Magnum Photos (cooperative photography agency), New York and Paris, freelance photographer for advertising agencies and periodicals, including *Life, Stern, Match, Vogue,* London *Sunday Times,* and London *Times,* 1951—. Filmmaker; films include *Behind the Veil,* 1973. Exhibitions of photographs include "In China," Brooklyn Museum, 1980, United States tour, 1980-82; a showing of her photographs of Marilyn Monroe at the Knoedler Gallery, London, 1987; "In Retrospect," International Center of Photography, 1996, Menil Museum, 1996, HRHRC at the University of Texas, 1996, the Barbican, 1996; and "Women around the World," Tokyo, 1996.

AWARDS, HONORS: American Library Association selected *In China* as a notable book of 1980; Lifetime Achievement Award, American Society of Magazine Photographers, 1980; Royal Photographic Society fellow, 1995; Master Photographer citation, New York's International Center of Photography, 1995.

WRITINGS:

SELF-ILLUSTRATED

The Unretouched Woman, Knopf/Random House (New York City), 1976.
Flashback!: The 50s, Knopf, 1978, published as *The Fifties,* 1985.
In China, Knopf, 1980.
In America, Knopf, 1983.
Marilyn Monroe: An Appreciation, Borzoi/Knopf, 1987.
All in a Day's Work, Bantam (New York City), 1989.
The Great British, Knopf, 1991, published in England as *In Britain,* Sinclair-Stevenson, 1991.
In Retrospect, Knopf, 1995.

PHOTOGRAPHER

(With others) *For God's Sake, Care,* introduction by David Frost, foreword by General Frederick Coutts, Constable (London), 1967.

The Opening Ceremony of Cullinan Hall, October 10, 1958, Houston, Texas (photographic essay), text by Hugo V. Neuhaus, Jr., [Houston], 1972.
(With others) *The 1974 Marilyn Monroe Datebook,* commentary by Norman Mailer, Alskog/Simon & Schuster (New York City), 1973.
Private View: Inside Baryshnikov's American Ballet Theatre, text by John Fraser, Bantam, 1988.

OTHER

Contributor of articles to *Le Nouveau Photocinema* and *Camera 35.* Some of Arnold's books have been published in France, Spain, Italy, Japan, Germany, Canada, and England.

SIDELIGHTS: While Eve Arnold was studying to become a doctor in the 1940s, her boyfriend presented her with a Rolleicord camera. She soon enrolled in Alexey Brodovitch's photography class at the New School for Social Research in New York City and with one of her first assignments—a fashion show—determined the tenor of her future photographic works. Instead of snapping glossy, high-fashion pictures, Arnold sought to convey the vitality of local shows in Harlem. Brodovitch liked the project so much that he encouraged his student to pursue it for a year and a half; the study eventually culminated in a major article for London's *Picture Post.*

Arnold gave up medicine and joined the prestigious Magnum photography agency in 1951, becoming its first American woman member. During the 1950s she often photographed stories that dealt with women, the aged, the poor, and blacks for popular magazines. She treated her subjects kindly and candidly, attempting to capture honestly the common flow of life. In the 1960s and 1970s Arnold's photographs concentrated on the more political subjects of the civil-rights struggle and the women's movement, yet her photos still retained an emphasis on individuals.

In *Flashback!: The 50s,* Arnold presents a portfolio of her photographs, with personal commentary, from the 1950s—a decade that Douglas Davis describes in *Newsweek* as "the golden age of American postwar photojournalism" in "its last and sweetest phase." Picture magazines like *Life* and *Look* were popular and photographers were encouraged to use extreme measures to capture powerful, memorable images. The life of the photojournalist in that era, Arnold recalls in her book, was "free and adventurous."

Because of her affiliation with the Magnum agency, Arnold photographed numerous celebrities and prominent figures—including Dwight D. Eisenhower, Joseph McCarthy, Marilyn Monroe, and Joan Crawford—in addition to her studies of minority and political subjects. She also covered current events, religious gatherings, fads, and fashions. According to Davis, the 1950s was the last decade to be defined by photojournalism before television assumed the role, and *Flashback!* is "a superb collection of some of the decade's most sharp-eyed pictures." He also maintains that "Eve Arnold's prints are so bound up with the 50s, so faithful to the pace and rhythm of the decade, that they exert an irresistible nostalgic attraction." A critic in the *New Republic* expresses a similar sentiment: "[This] is sharp-eyed, unpretentious photojournalism at its best. Arnold's pictures of the decade of Ike, falsies, McCarthy, Marilyn and Little Rock (touchstone words she cites in her graceful account of her work) literally tell the stories. . . . The impact of such pictures is not easy or ephemeral: they stick." *Village Voice* reviewer Eliot Fremont-Smith deems all the photos in the book "revealing" and some "deeply affecting." He concludes: "This is one of the more rewarding photo books of the year."

In 1973 Arnold made a film, *Behind the Veil,* about harems in Arabia and the position of women in Muslim society. In 1976 she expanded on that theme for her second collection, *The Unretouched Woman.* In this collection she examined the humor, incongruities, and pathos of the lives of women around the world. "I am a woman and I wanted to know about women," Arnold states. "I realize now that through my work . . . I have been searching for myself, my time, and the world I live in." Taken over a span of nearly twenty-five years, the pictures range from peasants performing backbreaking daily tasks with great dignity to Joan Crawford putting on makeup. In *Ms.,* Annie Gottlieb deems *The Unretouched Woman* an "eloquent, poignant feast of images." The reviewer adds, "Arnold's photographs are formally and technically superb. In the manner of the best art, they move the heart through the balance of the eye. . . . Reality is enhanced by light but never censored or romanticized." *Newsweek* book critic Walter Clemons finds the collection to be "expert photojournalism."

In 1979 Arnold made two trips to China—the first to the more familiar places; the second to remote regions not usually visited by foreigners. The trip resulted in the book *In China,* a collection of 179 photographs with text under the four headings

"Landscape," "People," "Work," and "Living." Fremont-Smith acknowledges that the volume was one of "the year's best book 'portraits' of faraway lands" but wondered if the photos were truly representative. "The celebrative factor . . . seems generically to preclude ugliness, poverty, boring routine, anger and landscapes and artifacts that are less than quaintly or arrestingly photogenic," he observes. Beverly Beyette of the *Los Angeles Times Book Review* disagrees, however, noting that Arnold "does not take picture post-cards. She photographs laundry drying on the balconies of a modern apartment house, a dormitory for women oil-field workers, a demonstration by people out of work in Shanghai." A *New York Times Book Review* critic calls *In China* "surely one of the handsomest picture books of the year," showing "the most appealing faces since Steichen's Family of Man exhibit."

Arnold followed *In China* with *In America,* a photographic look at her native country. *Newsweek*'s Mark Stevens judges it "an enjoyable melting pot of the many styles and races and characters that make up modern America." Her highest achievement in the collection, he claims, is "not a single image, but the composite portrait carried away of a vigorous and varied nation." In the collection *The Great British,* published in England as *In Britain,* Arnold gathers together a wide selection of photographs she has taken of her adopted country. Ranging from portraits of the queen to candid behind-the-scenes looks at film stars, and from nuns to office workers, the photographs reveal an England of many social and economic strata. "This book," writes Ardys Kozbial in the *Boston Review,* "presents a varied, candid look at the British by a practiced, imaginative eye." According to Quentin Crisp, reviewing the book in the *New York Times Book Review,* "Arnold's camera . . . bestows a keen interest and a kindness on whatever it sees. . . . This is a beautifully produced record, full of sly humor and deep compassion."

Arnold's work spans a wide range of subjects. She has traveled the world and photographed people and scenes in more than thirty countries, including Jamaica, Cuba, Haiti, Malta, Tunisia, Austria, the former U.S.S.R., Egypt, South Africa, and Portugal. As Crisp notes, "Arnold has enjoyed a full life." *All in a Day's Work,* an all-color volume, collects photos from Arnold's many travels, with sample photos from many of the countries she has visited. The collection *In Retrospect* gathers together photographs from all aspects of Arnold's varied career, including photojournalism assignments for magazines, personality profiles, publicity stills for films, advertising spreads, and the books she has published.

BIOGRAPHICAL/CRITICAL SOURCES:

BOOKS

Harbutt, Charles, and Lee Jones, editors, *America in Crisis: Photographs for Magnum,* Holt, 1969.

PERIODICALS

Boston Review, February, 1992, pp. 29-30.
British Journal of Photography, November 21, 1991, pp. 28-29.
Chicago Tribune Book World, December 7, 1980.
Esquire, August, 1987, p. 120.
Library Journal, September 15, 1991, p. 53.
Los Angeles Times Book Review, November 30, 1980.
Ms., June, 1977.
New Republic, December 16, 1978.
New Statesman & Society, November 29, 1991, p. 34.
Newsweek, December 13, 1976; September 25, 1978; December 12, 1983.
New York Times Book Review, November 23, 1980; December 4, 1983; July 21, 1985, p. 22; December 27, 1987, p. 19; December 1, 1991, p. 51.
Publishers Weekly, September 19, 1980; October 9, 1995, p. 71.
Times (London), September 4, 1987.
Times Educational Supplement, December 6, 1991, p. 27.
Times Literary Supplement, November 14, 1980.
Tribune Books (Chicago), December 3, 1989, p. 7.
Village Voice, December 13, 1976; September 18, 1978; December 10, 1980.
Wall Street Journal, December 3, 1991, p. A12.
Washington Post Book World, November 30, 1980.
You and Your Camera, May 10, 1979.

*   *   *

ASARE, Meshack (Yaw)   1945-

PERSONAL: Surname pronounced "*Ah*-suh-ree"; born September 18, 1945, in Nyankumasi, Ghana; son of Joseph Kwaku (an accountant) and Adjoa (a trader; maiden name, Adoma) Asare; married Rose Tachie Menson (a bank clerk), 1969; children: Akosua (daughter), Kwajo (son), Kofi, Kwaku. *Education:* Attended University of Science and Technology (Kumasi, Ghana); University of Wisconsin—Madison; School of Journalism and Television (Berkshire, England). *Politics:* "Universalism." *Religion:* Christian.

ADDRESSES: Office—c/o Educational Press and Manufacturers, P.O. Box 9184, Airport, Accra, Ghana.

CAREER: Teacher in elementary school in Tema, Ghana, 1966-68; Lincoln Community School, Accra, Ghana, teacher, 1969-79; Educational Press and Manufacturers, Accra, art director and illustrator, 1979—. Artist, illustrator, and designer; has made sculptures for the government and for public buildings.

MEMBER: Ghana Association of Artists.

AWARDS, HONORS: National Book Award (Ghana), 1980, for *Tawia Goes to Sea;* Noma Award for publishing in Africa, 1982, for *The Brassman's Secret.*

WRITINGS:

SELF-ILLUSTRATED CHILDREN'S FICTION

Tawia Goes to Sea, Ghana Publishing (Accra, Ghana), 1970, Panther House, 1972.
I Am Kofi, Ghana Publishing, 1972.
Mansa Helps at Home, Ghana Publishing, 1972.
The Brassman's Secret, Educational Press (Accra, Ghana), 1981.
The Canoe's Story, Three Brothers and Cousins (Accra, Ghana), 1982.
Chipo and the Bird on the Hill: A Tale of Ancient Zimbabwe, Zimbabwe Publishing House (Harare, Zimbabwe), 1984.
Die Katze sucht sich einen Freund, Verlag Jungbrunen (Vienna, Austria), 1984, translation published as *Cat in Search of a Friend,* Kane/Miller (Brooklyn, NY), 1986.
Halima, Macmillan (London), 1992.
The Frightened Thief, Heinemann (London), 1993.

OTHER

(With others) *Ghana Welcomes You,* Valco, 1968.
(Illustrator) Alero and Cecile McHardy, *Akousa in Brazil,* 1970.
Seeing the World, Ghana Publishing, 1975.

(Illustrator) Tony Fairman, reteller, *Bury My Bones But Keep My Words: African Tales for Retelling,* HarperCollins (London), 1991, Puffin Books (New York City), 1994.

Also author of playlets *Ananse and Wisdom* and *The Outdooring,* and the play *The Hunter.* Contributor of articles on Ghanian culture to magazines.

SIDELIGHTS: A native of the west African country of Ghana, Meshack Asare "is an imaginative story-teller and talented artist who skillfully weaves cultural traditions and daily realities of life into picture stories for African children," Nancy J. Schmidt comments in *Twentieth-Century Children's Writers.* His picture books portray both everyday activities of children and folk tales from the oral tradition.

In his award-winning book *The Brassman's Secret,* Asare combines the two types of tales when a boy, after helping his father craft some goldweights, falls asleep and learns of the goldweight's history in a dream. Other stories tell of the fisherfolk of southern Ghana (*Tawia Goes to Sea* and *The Canoe's Story*), the Great Bird of Zimbabwean legend (*Chipo and the Bird on the Hill: A Tale of Ancient Zimbabwe*), and the everyday lives of young Africans (*I Am Kofi* and *Mansa Helps at Home*). Children in America may be familiar with Asare's *Cat in Search of a Friend,* a folktale in which a cat seeking protection discovers her own strength, or his illustrations for Tony Fairman's folktale collection *Bury My Bones But Keep My Words: African Tales for Retelling.* Whatever their subjects, according to Schmidt, "Asare's picture stories skillfully incorporate the cultural content of specific African settings in a manner that makes them widespread in their appeal to African children regardless of their cultural background."

Asare once commented: "Sometimes it is hard to tell what I am, but I like to think that I am an Artist. I feel that is a better way to think of myself, because then everything I am doing is art. . . . I sculpt and draw and design beautiful things. That is creativity. I enjoy doing those.

"But writing is different. My work in writing is very important to me. I consider writing to be a kind of construction; precisely, a kind of construction that bridges the gaps to reality—for even dreams and imagination are, in fact, reality. There are no dreams without images. Neither is there imagination without images. And, for that matter, no thought. Writing creates images. That is why it is so important. It creates images of time and life. Writing enables one to perceive the depth and roundness of civilization. It does not simply record it and enrich it.

"Who needs help in perceiving reality more than young people? The world is too complex to be perceived in its wholeness. . . . But there is a part of the world that is unchanging, unaffected and perhaps [permanent] in value. It is the warmth of knowing that there is something about you that the other person appreciates, something that everyone has a feeling for. It is a very exclusively human 'something' that universally communicates—and appeals. It is this 'something' that I try to write about."

BIOGRAPHICAL/CRITICAL SOURCES:

BOOKS

Twentieth-Century Children's Writers, 4th edition, St. James Press (Detroit, MI), 1995.

PERIODICALS

Emergency Librarian, January, 1992, p. 61.
Publishers Weekly, December 14, 1992, p. 57.
School Library Journal, March, 1987, p. 140.

* * *

AUSTER, Paul 1947-

PERSONAL: Born February 3, 1947, in Newark, NJ; son of Samuel and Queenie (Bogat) Auster; married Lydia Davis (a writer), October 6, 1974 (divorced, 1979); married Siri Hustuedt, June 16, 1981; children: (first marriage) Daniel; (second marriage) Sophie. *Education:* Columbia University, B.A., 1969, M.A., 1970.

ADDRESSES: c/o Paul Slovak, Viking Press Inc., 375 Hudson St., New York, NY 10014.

CAREER: Employed in a variety of jobs, including a merchant seaman, a census taker, a tutor, a telephone operator for the Paris bureau of the *New York Times,* and as the caretaker of a farmhouse in Provence, France; translator, critic, poet, novelist. Teacher in creative writing program, Princeton University, 1986-90. Director of the short film *Blue in the Face,* 1994.

AWARDS, HONORS: Poetry grant from Ingram Merrill Foundation, 1975 and 1982; PEN Translation Center grant, 1977; National Endowment for the Arts fellowship for poetry, 1979, and for creative writing, 1985; *City of Glass* was nominated for an Edgar Award for best mystery novel, 1986; *The Locked Room* was nominated for a *Boston Globe* Literary Press Award for fiction; Morton Dauwen Zabel Award, American Academy and Institute of Arts and Letters, 1990; PEN/Faulkner Award nomination, 1991, for *The Music of Chance;* Chevalier de l'Ordre des Arts et des Lettres, 1993; Prix Medicis for foreign literature, 1993, for *Leviathan.*

WRITINGS:

NOVELS

City of Glass (first novel in *The New York Trilogy;* also see below), Sun & Moon Press (Los Angeles), 1985.

Ghosts (second novel in *The New York Trilogy;* also see below), Sun & Moon Press, 1986.

The Locked Room (third novel in *The New York Trilogy;* also see below), Sun & Moon Press, 1987.

In the Country of Last Things, Viking (New York City), 1987.

Moon Palace, Viking, 1989.

The Music of Chance, Viking, 1990.

The New York Trilogy (contains *City of Glass, Ghosts,* and *The Locked Room*), Penguin Books (New York City), 1990.

Leviathan, Viking, 1992.

Mr. Vertigo, Viking, 1994.

EDITOR

The Random House Book of Twentieth-Century French Poetry, Random House (New York City), 1982.

(And translator) Joseph Joubert, *The Notebooks of Joseph Joubert: A Selection,* North Point Press (Berkeley, CA), 1983.

TRANSLATOR

A Little Anthology of Surrealist Poems, Siamese Banana Press, 1972.

Jacques Dupin, *Fits and Starts: Selected Poems of Jacques Dupin,* Living Hand (Stanfordville, NY), 1974.

(With Lydia Davis) Saul Friedlander and Mahmoud Hussein, *Arabs and Israelis: A Dialogue,* Holmes & Meier (New York City), 1975.

The Uninhabited: Selected Poems of Andre de Bouchet, Living Hand, 1976.

(With L. Davis) Jean-Paul Sartre, *Life Situations,* Pantheon (New York City), 1978.

(With L. Davis) Jean Chesneaux, *China: The People's Republic,* Pantheon, 1979.

(With L. Davis) Chesneaux and others, *China from the 1911 Revolution to Liberation,* Pantheon, 1979.

Stephane Mallarme, *A Tomb for Anatole,* North Point Press, 1983.

Maurice Blanchot, *Vicious Circles,* Station Hill (Barrytown, NY), 1985.

Philippe Petit, *On the High Wire,* Random House, 1985.

(With Margit Rowell) Joan Miro, *Selected Writings,* G. K. Hall (Boston), 1986.

(With Stephen Romer and David Shapiro) Jacques Dupin, *Jacques Dupin: Selected Poems,* Bloodaxe Books (Newcastle-upon-Tyne, England), 1992.

OTHER

Unearth: Poems, 1970-1972, Living Hand, 1974.

Wall Writing: Poems, 1971-1975, Figures (Berkeley, CA), 1976.

Eclipse (play), first produced in New York City by Artists' Theatre, March, 1977.

Facing the Music, Station Hill, 1980.

White Spaces (nonfiction), Station Hill, 1980.

The Invention of Solitude (memoir), SUN (New York City), 1982.

Disappearances: Selected Poems, Overlook Press (Woodstock, NY), 1988.

The Art of Hunger: Essays, Prefaces, Interviews, Sun & Moon Press, 1992.

Smoke and Blue in the Face: Two Screenplays, Hyperion/Miramax Books (New York City), 1995.

Also author of *Fragments from Cold,* 1977. Contributor of articles and translations of poetry to magazines, including *New York Times Book Review, Art News, Poetry, New York Review of Books, Harper's* and *Saturday Review.*

ADAPTATIONS: The Music of Chance was adapted into the 1993 film of the same title, directed by Philip Haas and starring James Spader and Mandy Patinkin; the film rights to *Mr. Vertigo* were purchased by Miramax, 1994; *City of Glass* was adapted into a comic book by Paul Karasik and David Mazzucchelli, 1994; *Smoke,* starring Harvey Keitel and William Hurt, directed by Wayne Wang, and

Blue in the Face, directed by Auster, starring Keitel, Michael J. Fox, and Roseanne Barr, were both filmed in 1994.

SIDELIGHTS: Paul Auster "is one of our most intellectually stimulating fiction writers but [his] reputation outside a small cult is based on a fuzzy perception that he is some sort of genre writer (mysteries? science fiction?) with cryptic pretensions," observes Joseph Coates in the *Chicago Tribune.* The perception of Auster as a genre writer has been due in part to the manner in which he entered the publishing world. For years, he labored in relative obscurity as a poet, essayist, and translator of French literature; many of those years he lived in France. Then, in the mid-1980s, he began to attract serious critical attention with his "New York Trilogy," a trio of post-modern detective novels. Appreciation for Auster's mysteries built slowly at first. A grim and intellectually puzzling mystery, *The City of Glass,* the first book in the trilogy, was rejected by seventeen different publishers. Nevertheless, when Sun & Moon Press finally issued the novel in 1985, it attracted far more notice than Auster's earlier work and generated considerable interest in the remaining two projected volumes. Completed in 1987, the trilogy has raised Auster's visibility and marked him as a talent to watch. From critics such as Toronto *Globe and Mail* contributor Margaret Cannon, he began to evoke the highest praise: "As a novelist, Paul Auster has gone beyond excellence and given the phrase 'experimental fiction' a good name. . . . Auster has created bona fide literary works, with all the rigor and intellect demanded of contemporary literature."

Each of the three novels tells a different story, but all share common properties. In addition to their New York setting, the books are linked by style and theme. In one of the books, Auster appears as a character in his own novel, and in all three he intentionally blurs the distinction between author and text. This post-modern device, as Jack Fuller notes in the Chicago *Tribune Books,* raises questions of identity that resonate throughout the series: "Who exactly is the client? Who is the villain? Who is the author? There are doppelgangers and chilling coincidences. And in the less literal sense, there is the identification of the hunter with his quarry."

While instances of confused or mistaken identity are common in the mystery genre, some critics say that Auster takes this convention and develops it into a metaphor for contemporary urban life. "In his detec-

tives who degenerate beyond the standard seediness into self-jailing voyeurs and bagpersons in the cramped streets of New York City, he has provided a striking vision of contemporary American stasis," writes *Washington Post Book World* contributor Dennis Drabelle. He labels the novels "*post-existentialist private eye.*"

Auster's dark vision emerges in the trilogy's first novel, *City of Glass.* On the surface, it appears to be a mystery novel that exploits the conventions of the detective genre. "The real mystery, however, is one of confused character identity," suggests *New York Times Book Review* contributor Toby Olson, "the descent of a writer into a labyrinth in which fact and fiction become increasingly difficult to separate." The novel opens when Quinn, a pseudonymous detective novelist, receives a phone call intended for a real detective (whose name we will later learn is Paul Auster). Lonely and bored, Quinn takes on Auster's identity and accepts the case. His job is to trail a madman named Stillman, recently released from a mental institution to which he had been committed for isolating his son in a locked room for nine years. Stillman, once a brilliant linguist, had segregated his son in hopes of recapturing the primordial human language spoken by Adam and Eve. Now that Stillman has been released, his son's life is in danger. Thus a detective is hired.

Critical reception to *City of Glass* has been highly enthusiastic. At the same time that he satisfies mystery readers' appetites for a good story, Auster moves into the realm of serious literature, his supporters say. "*City of Glass* is about the degeneration of language, the shiftings of identity, the struggle to remain human in a great metropolis, when the city itself is cranking on its own falling-apart mechanical life that completely overrides any and every individual," notes *Los Angeles Times Book Review* critic Carolyn See. She deems the book "an experimental novel that wanders and digresses and loses its own narrative thread, but with all that . . . thoughtfully and cleverly draws our attention to these questions of self." The way the novel subtly shifts from a standard mystery story to an existential quest for identity also captures *New York Times Book Review* reviewer Toby Olson's attention: "Each detail, each small revelation must be attended to as significant. And such attention brings ambiguity, confusion, and paranoia. Is it important that Quinn's dead son has the same name as Stillman? What can it mean that 'Quinn' rhymes with 'twin' and 'sin'?" As Canon puts it, "This is a novel that's full of intellectual puzzles, not all of them resolved." Despite its challenges, Olson believes that "the book is a pleasure to read, full of suspense and action."

In *Ghosts,* the second volume of the trilogy, Auster continues his investigation of lost identity on a more abstract plane. "A client named White hires a detective named Blue to follow a man named Black," Drabelle explains. "Gradually Blue realizes he's been ruined. All he can do is stare at Black, eternally writing a book in the rented room across the street, and draw a weekly paycheck. Black and White are probably the same person, and Blue is 'trapped . . . into doing nothing, into being so inactive as to reduce his life to almost no life at all.'" Auster's choice of names for his protagonists coupled with his coy and knowing tone throughout the book suggest that he is playing mind games with the reader. The real mystery, he implies, is not within the story but "on some higher level," as Rebecca Goldstein observes. "We are not being asked to submerge ourselves in this story, to believe in its reality," Goldstein continues in the *New York Times Book Review.* "We are to stay above it, to read it as, well, metaphor; and our fanatical attention to details and frenetic attempts at deduction (both necessary for reading a mystery novel correctly) are to be directed upward toward the question, what does it all mean?" Goldstein acknowledges that *Ghosts,* which solves the internal mystery but leaves the larger questions unanswered, does not fit the mold of the traditional detective novel. Nonetheless, she judges the work "nearly perfect." Others are less impressed. Margaret Cannon, citing problems with continuity, concludes that *Ghosts* has "as much weight as any middle-of-three work can have. It provides the history and heft for the next book, but it cannot really stand alone as a mystery with a beginning, a middle, and an end."

The trilogy's concluding volume, *The Locked Room,* is widely judged to be the richest and by far the most compelling book of the trilogy. Less abstract and more accessible, this story features flesh and blood characters with whom readers can easily identify. Several reviewers suggest that Auster's use of a first-person narrator enhances the book. "When Auster finally allows himself the luxury of character, what a delicious treat he serves up for the reader!" Carolyn See writes in the *Los Angeles Times.* Though *The Locked Room* is a mystery like the first two installments, this "story is told in the first person by a genuine character who feels love and pain and envy." Because of the first-person narration "Mr.

Auster's philosophical asides now sound heartfelt instead of stentorian and his descents into semiological *Angst* feel genuinely anguished and near," Steven Schiff suggests in the *New York Times Book Review.* He and other critics hypothesize that the nameless narrator represents Auster himself.

The story begins when the narrator is summoned by the wife of an old friend from childhood with whom he has lost touch. Fanshawe, as the friend is called, has disappeared and is presumed dead. A fantastically gifted writer, Fanshawe has left behind some unpublished writings as well as instructions for his friend to see them into print. As time passes, the narrator easily moves into Fanshawe's existence, marrying his wife, publishing his work, and eventually engendering rumors that he is actually Fanshawe or, at least, the man who created the works. When he receives a communication from the real Fanshawe, the narrator is plunged into danger. "What happens next cannot be revealed," See insists in her book review, "because . . . Auster has created characters so fragile and believable that their privacy should only be broken by a respectful reader who cares enough to buy their book."

Without revealing the ending, Schiff concludes that "the novel's most vivid passages conjure up a true dark night of the soul. . . . Mr. Auster puts his finger on the pulsing locus of language and identity. He understands that the detective of the self is trapped, forced to use that clumsiest of tools, language, to ferret out what mere language can never discover. Putting a name on something makes it at once available and all the more elusive. . . . In *The Locked Room,* Mr. Auster proclaims the urgency of that dilemma, not just for writers but for all those who seek the truth behind the fictions they read and the fictions they live."

In the same year that *The Locked Room* appeared, Auster published another novel, *In the Country of Last Things.* At first glance, this novel seems a science fiction tale about a future apocalypse. Anna Blume travels from one continent to a large metropolis on another, where she hopes to find her missing brother. She finds instead a city in chaos filled with ruined buildings, ruined lives, criminals ruling and exploiting the desperate and homeless, "Runners" running themselves to death, and "Leapers" jumping to their deaths from the city's crumbling skyscrapers. Anna relates her search through this hellish environment in a letter to someone left behind on the other continent.

Even though Auster seems to have shifted from mystery to science fiction in *In the Country of Last Things,* the novel shares stylistic and thematic concerns with "The New York Trilogy." "Once more, as in the three volumes of *The New York Trilogy,* it's all done with mirrors," comments Katharine Washburn in the *Review of Contemporary Fiction.* "This time, the game is played with, if anything, greater cunning and obliqueness behind the same screen of lucid and uncompromising prose." Washburn also challenges the initial impression that this novel is a typical science fiction piece. "*In the Country of Last Things* is occupied not with a future dystopia but with a hellish present," she contends. "Its citizens are no more inhabitants of the future than Swift's Houyhnhnms are native to some unmapped mid-Atlantic island. They belong to the here and now, to its ethical, spiritual, and cultural chaos." And, she concludes that "Auster has succeeded with Swiftian guile and ferocity in constructing a world of demolished things which we are forced, immediately and painfully to recognize as our own."

The perception of Auster as a genre writer has begun to change in recent years with his publication of novels which cannot be easily categorized. A *Kirkus Reviews* contributor, noting Auster's high standing as an author of serious intent, calls him "a postmodern fabulator who grounds his odd and challenging fictions in conventional and accessible narrative structures." *Moon Palace,* a novel of lost family, represents the first of these. Marco Stanley Fogg is raised by his mother in New York City, never knowing his father. She dies when Marco is eleven and he goes to live with his mother's older brother, Victor. After Victor's death, Marco (now a young man) goes to work for an old rich man who turns out to be his paternal grandfather. The remainder of the novel follows Marco on his journey of discovery and then loss of this unknown side of his family.

Joyce Reiser Kornblatt notes in a *New York Times Book Review* article on *Moon Palace* that Auster seems unconcerned with creating something realistic or novel: "The plot of the novel is so unbelievable, its narrator often has trouble being convinced by it himself. And the motifs are extremely familiar: the beleaguered orphan, the missing father, the doomed romance, the squandered fortune, the totemic power of the West, the journey as initiation." She adds, however, that "the story is, finally, so good-hearted and hopeful, so verbally exuberant, that its obvious architecture, its shameless borrowings, may be forgivable." *Review of Contemporary Fiction* contribu-

tor Steven Weisenburger finds that Auster violates "realistic conventions" to achieve an artistic end. "Clearly," suggests the reviewer, "one aim of Auster's technique is to push those conventions over the top, into a kind of metafictional counterpractice." Paul Hoover offers a similar conclusion in his Chicago *Tribune Books* review. "Story and characterization are secondary to how the work is wrought, its overall structure and patterns," he writes. "Credibility is therefore not the issue; from the beginning events are clearly improbable. The work investigates the act of reading, the tangled waltz of reader and author."

"*The Music of Chance* is an accessible, readable story that can be enjoyed by readers of all levels," Digby Diehl comments in the *Los Angeles Times Book Review.* "It is an exceptional novel about the interplay of freedom and chance which takes you on an engrossing tour of a man's inner life." On its surface, this novel begins as an "odyssey of self-invention," as *New York Times* critic Michiko Kakutani puts it, bringing to mind such fictional characters as Mark Twain's Huck Finn, John Updike's Rabbit Angstrom, and Jack Kerouac's Dean Moriarty. Jim Nashe hits the road in search of himself after his wife leaves him and he receives an inheritance from his deceased father. His tour of the country winds down at about the same time as his money runs out. He then meets a young gambler, Pozzi, who entices him into a poker game with two eccentric lottery winners from Pennsylvania. The two lose what they have and fall further into debt. In order to pay off the debt, Nashe and Pozzi are forced to build a stone wall for the eccentrics.

"Writing in brisk, precise prose," comments Kakutani in the *New York Times,* "Mr. Auster lends these events all the suspense and pace of a best-selling thriller." Yet, as the reviewer adds, the novel is more than a thriller. Auster "gives Nashe's adventures a brooding philosophical subtext that enables him to explore some of his favorite preoccupations: the roles of randomness and causality, the consequences of solitude, and the limitations of freedom, language and free will in an indifferent world." "The result," finds Kakutani, "[is] a chilling little story that's entertaining and provocative, resonant without being overly derivative."

Madison Smartt Bell, writing in the *New York Times Book Review,* faults Auster's characterization in *The Music of Chance.* "Nashe's sometime girlfriend Fiona, a hooker called Tiffany and especially Pozzi are not rendered well enough to convince," he comments. "Pozzi's monologues are shakily, inconsistently written and, unfortunately, too much hangs on his role as a credible and engaging picaro." Paul Bray suggests that Auster may have other literary aims. In the *Review of Contemporary Fiction,* he writes that "as a piece of fiction [*The Music of Chance*] is shaped in ways that subvert just about every expectation a reader could have with respect to conflict, rising action, resolution, and so forth. Its pacing is all its own. . . . Auster has a unique sense of fictional structure which allows him to impart a lyrical and at times sinister significance to narrated events solely on the strength of their being on the page in the first place." Bray concludes, "With *The Music of Chance* Auster, perhaps the most significant American author to emerge during the eighties, has quite simply invented a whole new kind of fiction."

In *Leviathan,* Auster continues to pursue the thematic and stylistic concerns of his previous novels, which *Times Literary Supplement* reviewer Julia O'Faolain calls "'meta-mysteries', whose latent puzzles can be as intriguing as the ones they solve." In these novels, she adds, "Auster has been perfecting his tropes, redeploying a stereotyped cast, burrowing into obsessions, dazzling critics with the ingenuity of his related plots, and keeping the balls of picaresque parable in play." The title of Auster's seventh novel brings to mind the legendary ocean beast, Thomas Hobbes's idea of the polemical political state which he likened to an "artificial man," and, according to Mark Osteen, writing in the *Review of Contemporary Fiction,* the Hebrew word meaning "joined." Osteen finds that the novel's title fits well the themes of the book: secrets, multiple selves, and connections.

"Only a courageous and confident novelist takes the kind of chance Paul Auster takes in *Leviathan,* his seventh novel," contends Mark Childress in the *Los Angeles Times Book Review.* "On the very first page, he unveils the climax of his story. The rest of the book is spent explaining how we got to that shattering beginning." The opening event of *Leviathan* is the death, by explosion, of a New York writer, Benjamin Sachs. Peter Aaron, another New York writer, learns of Sachs's bizarre death and becomes obsessed with writing the story of his friend "because he is afraid lest the authorities—police of some sort, probably the FBI (who shortly make an appearance)—will misrepresent the career of Benjamin Sachs," explains Robert M. Adams in the *New York Review of Books.* Aaron's investigation uncovers a world of secrets, multiple and exchanged identities, and previously unknown connections between characters. The result, believes Childress, "is rather like falling through a succession of trapdoors, each deceptive moment of stillness opening up to another precipitous tumble."

Both O'Faolain and Childress find weaknesses in this Auster novel. O'Faolain writes that "this time, although he re-deploys his clutch of themes as captivatingly as ever, their significance has shrunk." Childress notes that "at crucial moments, the author reminds us that we are reading a novel. Characters open their mouths and Authorspeak comes out." Even so, the reviewer concludes that "the intelligence and agility of the author's voice shines through, largely redeeming these missteps." The book's lesson seems clearer to Osteen, who suggests that the meaning of the book's title may be found in how "Aaron nevertheless comes to understand that every life is a leviathan, that connections stop nowhere, and that a person's public self is merely the tip of a colossal iceberg shaped by chance, destiny, and secrecy." Osteen adds, "The novel thus reaffirms Auster's idea that every single life contains a multitude; moreover, it suggests that the liberty of absolute solitude is a phantom and that true liberty emerges only through the covenants and bonds of social life."

Auster's 1994 novel, *Mr. Vertigo,* tells the story of Walter Rawley, also known as "Walt the Wonder Boy," and "Mr. Vertigo." In the Midwest of the 1920s, Walt is an orphaned street urchin who is offered a new life by a mystical showman named Master Yehudi. On a Kansas farm, Master Yehudi teaches Walt to levitate. The two, along with a Sioux Indian woman and an Ethiopian boy, barnstorm the country, growing more and more famous, on their way toward Broadway. But on the verge of stardom, Walt loses his gift for levitating. He begins to wander and eventually ends up in Chicago in the world of mobsters. Jonathan Yardley, writing in the *Washington Post Book World,* calls *Mr. Vertigo* "nothing less than the story of America itself: a parable that moves from rough beginnings through transcendent triumph before settling into middle age, a story of 'black magic and adventure' that evokes in miniature the glory and frustration of the American dream."

Critical response to *Mr. Vertigo* has varied. According to *New Statesman* contributor Phil Edwards, "The young Walt's dialogue is a constant outpouring of bad puns and smart answers, just the kind of linguistic jangle Auster has previously banished from his writing." He adds, "Shorn of the intense self-consciousness of the typical Auster narrator, the book's symbolism seems laboured and arbitrary." Joanna Scott offers a different view in the *Los Angeles Times Book Review.* She comments that "*Mr. Vertigo* is surely one of Auster's most absorbing tales, written in a prose that is precise, confident in its use of vernacular and sometimes smoothly lyrical." And Yardley states, "Like its predecessors, it is as much a fable as novel, but unlike them it has an antic air that comes as both a delight and a surprise." He summarizes that "the end result is a winning, accessible book that establishes its author not merely as a gifted literary stylist but also as a completely ingratiating entertainer."

BIOGRAPHICAL/CRITICAL SOURCES:

BOOKS

Contemporary Literary Criticism, Volume 47, Gale (Detroit), 1988.

PERIODICALS

Atlanta Journal and Constitution, May 24, 1987, p. J6; September 13, 1992, p. N9; October 2, 1994, p. N11.
Boston Globe, December 13, 1985, p. 79; March 30, 1989, p. 78; October 8, 1990, p. 67; September 13, 1992, p. 106; December 13, 1992, p. B40; July 31, 1994, p. B25.
Chicago Tribune, January 28, 1993, sec. 5, p. 3.
Contemporary Literature, Volume 33, 1992, pp. 1-23.
Esquire, August, 1994, p. 123.
Globe and Mail (Toronto), March 14, 1987.
Interview, April, 1989, p. 18.
Kirkus Reviews, September 15, 1985, p. 957; June 1, 1986, p. 822; December 15, 1986, p. 1812; January 1, 1987, p. 3; December 15, 1988, p. 1755; August 1, 1990, p. 1020; June 15, 1992, p. 732.
Los Angeles Times, September 1, 1986; March 2, 1987, p. V4; June 18, 1987, p. V10; March 30, 1989, p. V21.
Los Angeles Times Book Review, November 17, 1985; October 21, 1990, p. 2, 8; October 4, 1992, p. 2; July 31, 1994, p. 2.
Nation, November 20, 1982.
New Republic, March 27, 1989, p. 36.

New Statesman and Society, January 22, 1988, p. 33; March 22, 1991, p. 45; April 8, 1994, p. 37.
Newsweek, September 5, 1994.
New Yorker, December 30, 1985; July 18, 1994, p. 25.
New York Review of Books, August 17, 1989, p. 52; January 17, 1991, p. 31; December 3, 1992, pp. 14, 16.
New York Times, March 7, 1989, p. C19; October 2, 1990, p. C15; September 8, 1992, p. C14.
New York Times Book Review, January 23, 1983; February 27, 1983; January 15, 1984; November 3, 1985; May 25, 1986; June 29, 1986; January 4, 1987, p. 14; May 17, 1987, p. 11; March 19, 1989, p. 8-9; November 4, 1990, p. 15; September 20, 1992, p. 9; August 28, 1994, p. 12; October 2, 1994, p. 32.
New York Times Magazine, August 30, 1992, p. 41.
Review of Contemporary Fiction, spring, 1994, pp. 30-87.
Time, September 5, 1994, p. 76.
Times Literary Supplement, August 30, 1985; October 23, 1992, p. 20.
Tribune Books (Chicago), March 29, 1987, p. 3; March 19, 1989, p. 4; November 4, 1990, p. 5; November 1, 1992, p. 5; September 4, 1994, p. 4.
USA Today, March 17, 1989, p. D4; October 14, 1992, p. D7.
Vogue, August, 1994, p. 158.
Wall Street Journal, September 21, 1990, p. A12; September 15, 1992, p. A14.
Washington Post, October 10, 1990, p. D2.
Washington Post Book World, December 5, 1982; June 15, 1986; March 29, 1987; March 26, 1989, p. 3; September 6, 1992, p. 5; August 28, 1994, p. 3.
World Literature Today, spring, 1995.*

*   *   *

AUSTIN, Carrie
See SEULING, Barbara

*   *   *

AXTON, David
See KOONTZ, Dean R(ay)

B

BACHMAN, Richard
See KING, Stephen (Edwin)

* * *

BANKS, Russell (Earl) 1940-

PERSONAL: Born March 28, 1940, in Newton, MA; son of Earl and Florence Banks; married Darlene Bennett, June, 1960 (divorced, February 1962); married Mary Gunst (a poet), October 29, 1962 (marriage ended, 1977); married Kathy Banks (an editor), 1982 (divorced, 1988); married Chase Twichell (a poet), 1988; children: Leona Stamm, Caerthan, Maia, Danis (all daughters). *Education:* Attended Colgate University, 1958; University of North Carolina, A.B., 1967.

ADDRESSES: Agent—Ellen Levine Literary Agency, Suite 1801, 15 East 26th St., New York, NY 10010.

CAREER: Writer, 1975—. Plumber in New Hampshire, 1959-64; Lillabulero Press, Inc., Chapel Hill, NC, and later Northwood Narrows, NH, publisher and editor, 1966-75; instructor at Emerson College, Boston, 1968-71, University of New Hampshire, Durham, 1968-75, New England College, Henniker, NH, 1975, 1977-81, Princeton University, Princeton, NJ, 1981—, and Sarah Lawrence University.

MEMBER: International PEN, Coordinating Council of Literary Magazines (member of board of directors, 1967-73), Phi Beta Kappa.

AWARDS, HONORS: Woodrow Wilson fellowship, 1968; Guggenheim fellowship, 1976; St. Lawrence Award for Fiction from St. Lawrence University and *Fiction International,* 1976; American Academy and Institute of Arts and Letters Award for work of distinction, 1986; recipient of Fels Award, O. Henry Memorial Award, and other short story awards.

WRITINGS:

(With William Matthews and Newton Smith) *15 Poems,* Lillabulero Press (Chapel Hill, NC), 1967.
Waiting to Freeze, Lillabulero Press (Northwood Narrows, NH), 1967.
30/6 (poems), Quest (New York City), 1969.
Snow: Meditations of a Cautious Man in Winter, Granite Press (Hanover, NH), 1975.
Searching for Survivors, Fiction Collective (New York City), 1975.
Family Life, Avon (New York City), 1975, revised edition, Sun & Moon (Los Angeles), 1988.
The New World (stories), University of Illinois Press (Urbana, IL), 1978.
Hamilton Stark (novel), Houghton (Boston), 1978.
The Book of Jamaica (novel), Houghton, 1980.
Trailerpark (stories), Houghton, 1981.
(With others) *Antaeus, No. 45-56: The Autobiographical Eye,* Ecco (New York City), 1982.
The Relation of My Imprisonment (novel), Sun & Moon (College Park, MD), 1984.
Continental Drift (novel), Harper (New York City), 1985.
Success Stories, Harper, 1986.
Affliction, Harper, 1989.
Brushes with Greatness, Coach House (Toronto), 1989.
The Sweet Hereafter, HarperCollins (New York City), 1991.

Rule of the Bone, HarperCollins, 1995.

Coeditor of *Lillabulero.*

SIDELIGHTS: Russell Banks is a native New Englander who has drawn on his experience in the region's small towns hard hit by economic decline to create fiction that captures the lives of Northeastern people. As Banks has continued to add to the body of his novels, "he has ever more clearly emerged as a writer from the white working class," notes Fred Pfeil in the *Voice Literary Supplement,* "writing directly about the rage and damage, the capitulations, self-corruptions, and small resistances of subordinated lives." Banks offered his own view of the character of his fiction in an interview in the *New York Times Book Review.* "I grew up in a working-class family," he explained. For this reason, he added, "I have a less obstructed path as a writer to get to the center of their lives. Part of the challenge of what I write is uncovering the resiliency of that kind of life, and part is in demonstrating that even the quietest lives can be as complex and rich, as joyous, conflicted and anguished, as other, seemingly more dramatic lives." These characteristics support Pfeil's belief that "Banks has now become . . . the most important living white male American on the official literary map, a writer we, as readers *and* writers, can actually learn from, whose books help and urge us to change."

Trailerpark and *Hamilton Stark* both take place in New Hampshire. Both works feature desperate, not always admirable, lead characters. In *Trailerpark,* for instance, the inhabitants of the trailers gathered in the poor part of town include a demented woman who raises dozens of guinea pigs, a drug pusher, and other outcasts. *New York Times Book Review* writer Ivan Gold finds fault with Bank's omnipresent narrator in this collection—the "imprecise crackerbarrel tone and the equally arbitrary departure from it are accompanied by sometimes illuminating, more often disorienting, leaps in time," he remarks. However, in his *Washington Post Book World* review, Jonathan Yardley sees the collection as individual pieces of art: "Each [is] uncommonly good, and the whole of *Trailerpark* is greater than the sum of its parts; it is an odd, quirky book that offers satisfactions different from those provided by the conventional, or even unconventional, novel." Yardley further states that he sees in *Trailerpark* "brief stories of hope and disappointment, of infidelity and murder, of betrayal and alienation. They are bleak stories set in a bleak place, yet there is a wicked comic edge to them.

Banks has a terrific eye, mordant yet affectionate, for the bric-a-brac and the pathos of the American dream."

With *Hamilton Stark,* the author presents a title character with very few redeeming qualities. *Newsweek* critic Margo Jefferson describes him as "a misanthropic New Hampshire pipefitter [who is] frequently drunk and abusive. He hurls furniture into the fields surrounding his house, then fires his rifle at it for sport. . . . He rejects love of any sort, finding hate the more interesting emotion. . . . To his neighbors he is possibly a madman." Nevertheless, at least two people find Stark fascinating: Stark's grown daughter and the book's narrator, each of whom is trying to write a novel about this quirky character. While the narrator's novel is about Hamilton Stark, Banks's novel is about the narrator, "the way *The Great Gatsby* is more about Nick Carroway than Jay Gatsby," as Terence Winch points out in a *Washington Post Book World* review. Winch also speculates that Banks is portraying Hamilton Stark himself as the narrator, "or a version of the narrator. . . . But ultimately these issues—Who is Hamilton Stark? Or who is the narrator? And are they the same person?—are academic." What is important, says the critic, is that "Banks has skillfully used his repertoire of contemporary techniques to write a novel that is classically American—a dark, but sometimes funny, romance with echoes of Poe and Melville."

The Book of Jamaica and *Continental Drift* both concern themselves with travel and self-discovery. In the former, a thirty-five-year-old New Hampshire college professor travels to the Caribbean to finish a novel and finds himself so drawn to the exotic island of Jamaica that he decides to live there among its natives. In the beginning, the unnamed narrator "finds daunting mysteries and complexities at every turn," according to *New York Times Book Review* critic Darryl Pinckney. But "what he lacks in intuition and skepticism he makes up for with a self-lacerating sensitivity of which he is quite proud." *Washington Post* reviewer James W. Marks believes that "the most distinctive feature of the novel is Banks' rigorous exploitation of point of view. A melange of voices results from the novel's medium-is-the-message: 'You will see what you want to see.' Shifts in point of view define the structure and specify the stages in the hero's progress." Marks concludes that despite some "self-conscious sermonizing" in the book, the author "deserves praise for the novel's weight of thought; he has read much and pondered long."

Much critical attention greeted the publication of *Continental Drift,* often acknowledged as one of Banks's most ambitious novels. The story covers the lives of two characters who are worlds apart culturally and geographically, but who share the same dreams of bettering their lives by moving to a new home. For thirty-year-old Bob Dubois, a New Hampshire oil-burner repairman with a wife, two daughters, and a girlfriend, the solution to his aimless life lies in moving the family to Florida, where he hopes to gain a partnership in his brother's liquor store. At the same time, Vanise Dorsinville, a Haitian woman who looks after her infant son and her nephew, longs to emigrate to America to start a new life. Within these parameters, Banks has constructed tragic, interlocking stories in a novel "that will surely imprint [the author's] name on the roster of important contemporary novelists. The physical world with its natural beauties and blights is played off against what Banks sees as an abandonment of enduring social values by modern man for the seductive promises of material success," as Ralph B. Sipper comments in the *Los Angeles Times Book Review.* "It is clear that the electronic age has freed man's mind," continues Sipper. "What has happened to his heart is a question that [*Continental Drift*] explores."

In his *New York Review of Books* article, Robert Towers describes *Continental Drift* as Banks's most potentially "commercial" novel and notes that "admirers of [the author's] early fiction, which resisted conventional narrative, may find this objectionable, but his new book strikes me as the most interesting he has yet produced. [The novel] is an absorbing and powerful book that ambitiously attempts to 'speak' to the times." *Nation* critic James Marcus also finds Banks's move away from experimental fiction a successful one, declaring that, in *Continental Drift,* the author has "developed a vigorous, unornamented style which moves easily between narrative and authorial aside. This facility allows a double-edged view of Bob, as an eloquently fleshed-out character and as a type, a subject for speculation. Banks steps onstage repeatedly to discuss Bob's character, intelligence and sexuality, but these lectures don't seem condescending; nor does Banks outfit Bob with the usual bloodless accouterments of the common man—sentimental honesty or sentimental ingenuity. Average, yes, but also solid, painful and real."

An "excellent, disturbing book" is how Garrett Epps describes *Continental Drift* in the *New Republic.* Epps points out that "the novel is not without its flaws. For one thing, it is unremittingly, grindingly grim, unleavened by hope, humor, or wit." The critic also says he found himself wondering "whether Banks had not diminished his characters by showing them as victims and pawns of a malign structure so much larger than they." But James Atlas sees a difference between the way Banks handles the tragedies and emptiness of his characters' lives. "By witnessing his characters' doom he rescues their lives from oblivion, invests them with significance," writes Atlas in *Atlantic.* "Every life, he reminds us, is sanctified by the same exhaustive intensity, the same will to matter." Atlas sums up that Banks's "ability to evoke the texture of American life . . . rivals [John] Updike's. *Continental Drift* is the most convincing portrait I know of contemporary America: its greed, its uprootedness, its indifference to the past. This is a novel about the way we live now." *Continental Drift* "constantly assumes the stance of a major novel, and perhaps it is," concludes Stephen Dobyns in a *Chicago Tribune* article. "There is hardly any piece of contemporary fiction in which one finds a story so well told, in which the characters are so fully developed and completely believable, in which the issues confronted are the major issues of our time."

Banks's novel *Affliction* is a "gripping, most beautiful, grim and wide-sweeping novel," writes Carol Ascher in the *Women's Review of Books.* "The book is a requiem for a working-class manhood, no longer viable if it ever had been, that careens between decency, even sweetness, and brutal violence." The novel is Rolfe Whitehouse's attempt to reconstruct the recent events of his older brother Wade's life in order to understand his disappearance. Wade is in his forties and works as a jack-of-all-trades in his hometown, a small town in New Hampshire. He takes after his father in his tendencies to excessive drinking and abusive behavior. These have cost him his first marriage and the affection of his daughter. Wade becomes obsessed by the death of a visiting union official in a hunting accident.

As Robert F. Gish suggests in the *Bloomsbury Review,* "What Banks tries to do—and succeeds in doing with empathy but not sentimentality—is understand why an ordinary guy, like Wade Whitehouse . . . goes berserk one cold November day and . . . does something terrible, something so cruel and violent and criminal that all he has worked for, all that he himself represents and thinks he 'is,' disappears into the thin-air statistics of fugitives, a man on the lam ironically 'wanted' for reasons never anticipated." *New York Times Book Review* contributor Elizabeth

Tallent is also drawn to Banks's portrayal of Wade's obsession. "A novel of obsession is moving—is successful—in direct proportion to its ability to implicate the reader in its own warped and passionate view of the world," Tallent writes. She concludes that "this wintry novel, breathing cold from every page, brimming with that violence, is magnificently convincing."

Eric Larsen is not convinced. He comments in the *Los Angeles Times Book Review,* "The book has at its heart a firm, lean, real, observed, honest story; but all around that heart, as if it's felt just not to be sufficient in itself, are built-up thicknesses and protections of the derivative, inflated and excessive, of the posturing and often just plain false-toned." Fred Pfeil views the same characteristics among *Affliction*'s strengths. He believes that "Banks avoids the twin dangers of a mere 'sociological' accuracy on the one hand and a voyeuristic sensationalism on the other, through a wise combination of elevation and distancing techniques."

With *Affliction,* observes Sven Birkerts in the *New Republic,* Banks returns to fiction that is both geographically and spiritually closer to home. "Where [*Continental Drift*] charted a grand scheme of cultural migration, seeking to isolate the larger as well as the human-sized circulations of malaise," writes Birkerts, "*Affliction* stays rooted in place, hews to a single scale. Its study is the deeper ramifications of blood and kinship; it roots in to find the wellsprings of the will to violence." Birkerts concludes, "Bank's idiom is now vigorous and gritty, perfectly suited to the life of his characters and place. With his last few books, but with *Affliction* especially, he joins that group of small-town realists—writers like William Kennedy, Andre Dubus, and Larry Woiwode—who have worked to sustain what may in time be seen as our dominant tradition. Like them, Banks unfolds the sufferings of the ordinary life, of those who must worry, who can't be happy."

In *The Sweet Hereafter,* "Russell Banks has used a small town's response to tragedy to write a novel of compelling moral suspense," Richard Eder points out in the *Los Angeles Times Book Review.* The town is Sam Dent, a small burg in the Adirondack Mountains of upstate New York. The tragedy is an accident; a school bus swerves off a snowy road and falls into a quarry pond. Fourteen of the town's children die, and several other people are injured. Banks tells the story of the tragedy and its aftermath through four narrators in sequence. The narrators are Dolores Driscoll, the bus driver, Billy Ansel, a garage owner who has lost his two daughters, Mitchell Stevens, a New York lawyer who comes to capitalize on the town's misfortune, and Nicole Burnell, a promising teenager left paralyzed by the accident. The four accounts follow the town through its process of dealing with this tragedy.

Eder calls *The Sweet Hereafter* "a remarkable book, a sardonic and compassionate account of a community and its people, and of a catastrophe that vividly characterizes them even as it brutally acts upon them. His portrait of the small northern town is complex and spare at the same time; every detail stands out." Donna Rifkind also commends Banks's careful treatment of the theme of this book. She notes "the hard truth is that this catastrophe was villainless: it was a cruelly whimsical event, beyond control. This fact, and Banks's subtle handling of it, are what lift the novel up out of ordinary gritty realism toward something approaching the sublime." Eder admits that "there are one or two rough passages, but Banks, one of our strongest writers, has touched his unglamorous small-town Americans with light, and written, I think, his best book."

Rule of the Bone is Russell Banks's nod to Mark Twain, J. D. Salinger, and other chroniclers of wayward youth. Bone, a Huck Finn for the 1990s, is a mall rat from a working-class family in upstate New York. He runs away from his dysfunctional family and sets off in search of a new role models. He first tries a gang of bikers and eventually finds a Rastafarian who lives in a bus. This Jamaican, I-Man, becomes to Bone what Jim became to Huck Finn, and the two set off on a journey to Jamaica. In Bone's travels, the reader learns of what his world has and lacks. "Banks gives the entire story over to a child," observes Ann Hulbert in the *New Republic,* "and the result is brutally, often fantastically, picaresque." *Atlanta Journal-Constitution* contributor Hal Crowther says Bone's story is "a tour de force of a monologue, it's a guidebook to an underworld we never visit, and it answers our first question—what's lurking in the brain beneath that ghastly mohawk?"

Like other novels that draw their inspiration from the classics of teenage passage, *Rule of the Bone* is held up to the originals for serious scrutiny. Walter Kirn makes a favorable comparison in *New York* magazine. "Unlike the hundreds of other novelists who've given us teenage boys on the lam,. . . Banks doesn't borrow from Twain as much as steal outright, and he does it so well that Twain would approve, I suspect." He concludes that "*Rule of the Bone* is Twain, but darker, with wackier contrasts and sicker cameo players. It's an inspired rip-off. A great book." *New York Times* reviewer Michiko Kakutani offers a dimmer view, stating, "most of the allusions to *The Catcher in the Rye* and *The Adventures of Huckleberry Finn* turn out to be completely gratuitous: in the end, they're self-conscious literary references that serve no real purpose, except to try to make 'Rule of the Bone' seem like a larger and better book than it is."

For some reviewers, *Rule of the Bone* succeeds not because it pays homage to previous coming-of-age novels, but because it gives voice to a new generation of Huck Finns and Holden Caufields. As Crowther puts it, "Russell Banks has a singular gift for articulating the feelings of characters who would pass for inarticulate in the world. He trades in stunted lives and undernourished spirits; he gives them voices. And he knows there's beauty in a spirit almost crushed that somehow finds the soil and light to grow in." Gail Caldwell offers a similar view in a *Boston Globe* article. "Banks has the voice just right: Bone alternately manages to irritate, endear and outrage, just like thousands of other misbegotten kids through the ages. The end of the novel, after a few ludicrously unmoving events, is lovely in its simplicity. What Russell Banks has given us in his fiction is the truth—sometimes creepily intimate—about what's going on in the underpasses of America's highways." Caldwell adds that Banks "also writes better about race, from a white man's perspective, than most of his peers."

BIOGRAPHICAL/CRITICAL SOURCES:

BOOKS

Contemporary Literary Criticism, Gale (Detroit), Volume 37, 1986, Volume 72, 1992.
Dictionary of Literary Biography, Volume 130: *American Short-Story Writers since World War II,* Gale, 1993.

PERIODICALS

America, May 2, 1992, p. 391.
Atlantic, February, 1985.
Bloomsbury Review, November-December, 1989, p. 7; March, 1992, p. 3.

Boston Globe, September 10, 1989, p. 100; October 4, 1989, p. 69; August 25, 1991, p. M15; January 19, 1992, p. A14; May 14, 1995, p. 33; May 28, 1995, p. B30.
Chicago Tribune, March 17, 1985.
Chicago Tribune Book World, July 6, 1980.
Christian Science Monitor, September 20, 1989, p. 13; September 24, 1991, p. 14.
Commonweal, October 24, 1986, p. 570.
Journal-Constitution (Atlanta), September 17, 1989, p. L10; May 14, 1995, p. M11.
Listener, October 10, 1985, p. 29; September 13, 1990, p. 34.
Los Angeles Times, August 20, 1989, p. B10; September 30, 1991, p. E1.
Los Angeles Times Book Review, February 17, 1985, p. 5; June 22, 1986, p. 3; August 20, 1989, p. 10; September 1, 1991, p. 3; May 21, 1995, p. 3.
Maclean's, September 18, 1989, p. 68.
Nation, February 10, 1972; April 27, 1985, p. 505; September 13, 1986, p. 226; December 16, 1991, p. 786; June 12, 1995, p. 826.
New Republic, April 1, 1985, p. 38; September 11, 1989, p. 38; May 29, 1995, p. 40.
New Statesman, September 5, 1986, p. 28; September 21, 1990, p. 41.
Newsweek, June 26, 1978; February 25, 1985, p. 86; June 2, 1986, p. 72; September 18, 1989, p. 76; September 16, 1991, p. 62.
New York, May 8, 1995, p. 70.
New Yorker, April 15, 1985, p. 126; October 28, 1991, p. 119.
New York Review of Books, April 11, 1985, p. 36; December 7, 1989, p. 46.
New York Times, February 27, 1985, p. 18; May 31, 1986, p. 13; September 8, 1989, p. C26; September 6, 1991, p. C21; May 19, 1995, p. B8.
New York Times Book Review, April 20, 1975; May 18, 1975; July 2, 1978; February 25, 1979; June 1, 1980; November 22, 1981; April 1, 1984; March 24, 1985, p. 11; September 17, 1989, p. 7; December 7, 1989, p. 46; September 15, 1991, p. 1; May 7, 1995, p. 13; June 18, 1995, p. 3.
New York Times Magazine, September 10, 1989, p. 53.
Publishers Weekly, March 15, 1985.
Quill and Quire, October, 1989, p. 27.
Saturday Review, May, 1980; October, 1981.
Time, September 4, 1989, p. 66; June 5, 1995, p. 65.
Times Literary Supplement, October 25, 1985, p. 1203; October 26, 1990, p. 1146; April 17, 1992, p. 20.

Tribune Books (Chicago), September 3, 1989, p. 1; September 15, 1991, p. 1.
Voice Literary Supplement, September, 1989, p. 25.
Washington Post, April 18, 1980.
Washington Post Book World, July 2, 1978; October 4, 1981; April 29, 1984; March 3, 1985, p. 3; September 24, 1989, p. 7; September 8, 1991, p. 3; October 13, 1991, p. 15; August 16, 1992, p. 12.
Women's Review of Books, April, 1990, p. 21.

—*Sketch by Bryan Ryan*

* * *

BANNING, Lance (Gilbert)   1942-

PERSONAL: Born January 24, 1942, in Kansas City, MO; son of E. Willis (a painter) and Marie (Gilbert) Banning; married Lana June Sampson, July 11, 1964; children: Clinton Edward. *Education:* University of Missouri, Kansas City, B.A., 1964; Washington University, St. Louis, MO, Ph.D., 1971.

ADDRESSES:Home—604 Cromwell Way, Lexington, KY 40503. *Office*—Department of History, University of Kentucky, 1737 Patterson Office Tower 27, Lexington, KY 40506.

CAREER: Brown University, Providence, RI, lecturer in American civilization, 1971-73; University of Kentucky, Lexington, assistant professor, 1973-78, associate professor, 1978-86, professor of history, 1986—.

MEMBER: Organization of American Historians, Southern Historical Association, Society for Historians of the Early American Republic.

AWARDS, HONORS: National Endowment for the Humanities younger humanist fellowship, 1974-75; Guggenheim fellowship, 1979-80; National Humanities Center fellow, 1986-87; Center for the History of Freedom fellow, 1991; Pulitzer Prize finalist, 1996.

WRITINGS:

The Jeffersonian Persuasion: Evolution of a Party Ideology, Cornell University Press (Ithaca, NY), 1978.

(Editor) *After the Constitution: Party Conflict in the New Republic,* Wadsworth (Belmont, CA), 1989.
Jefferson and Madison: Three Conversations from the Founding, Madison House (Madison, WI), 1995.
The Sacred Fire of Liberty: James Madison and the Founding of the Federal Republic, Cornell University Press, 1995.

Also coeditor of University Press of Kansas series, "American Political Thought." Contributor of articles and reviews to history journals and collections.

SIDELIGHTS: Lance Banning is an American historian whose work focuses on the era of the founding fathers. In *Jefferson and Madison: Three Conversations from the Founding,* Banning discusses the different views of Thomas Jefferson and James Madison concerning such topics as individual rights and the national debt. He bases his research primarily on a few primary sources, including the Declaration of Independence and the correspondence between the two men. In *The Sacred Fire of Liberty: James Madison and the Founding of the Federal Republic,* Banning discusses the view that Madison was "one of the leading champions of strong national government," comments Evan Cornog in the *New York Times Book Review.* Cornog calls the book "brilliant and original," and concludes: "At times the Madison presented here may seem unreal to the modern mind—so rigorous in his thinking, so nice in his distinctions, so principled. That he should seem so strange a figure is an indictment not of Mr. Banning, but of our age."

BIOGRAPHICAL/CRITICAL SOURCES:

PERIODICALS

Library Journal, February 1, 1995, p. 87.
New Republic, February 26, 1996, pp. 37-39.
New York Times Book Review, October 29, 1995, p. 39.

* * *

BARKER, Wendy B.   1942-

PERSONAL: Born September 22, 1942, in Summit, NJ; daughter of G. Clarke (a banker) and Pamela (a homemaker; maiden name, Dodwell) Bean; married Laurence Barker (a choral music conductor and university professor), August 11, 1962; children: Clarke

David. *Education:* Arizona State University, B.A. (with honors), 1966, M.A., 1974; University of California, Davis, Ph.D., 1981.

ADDRESSES: Home—26502 Fox Briar Lane, Boerne, TX 78006. *Office*—Division of English, Classics, and Philosophy, University of Texas at San Antonio, San Antonio, TX 78249-0643.

CAREER: High school English teacher in Scottsdale, AZ, and Berkeley, CA, 1966-72; University of California at Davis, lecturer, master teacher, associate, teaching assistant, 1974-82; University of Texas at San Antonio, assistant professor, 1982-88, associate professor, 1988-92, professor of English, 1992—. Co-founder of alternative school for gifted students in Berkeley, 1972. Gives poetry readings, workshops, and lectures in many venues including universities and academic conferences .

MEMBER: Emily Dickinson International Society, Modern Language Association, Associated Writing Programs, Society for the Study of the Multi-Ethnic Literature of the United States, Texas Institute of Letters, Texas Association of Creative Writing Teachers.

AWARDS, HONORS: Poetry award from Southwest Women Artists and Writers, 1982, for "Winter Chickens"; fellow of National Endowment for the Arts, 1986; poetry series award, Ithaca House, 1990; distinguished citizen award, city of San Antonio, TX, 1991; Mary Elinore Smith Poetry Prize, *American Scholar,* 1991; residency fellowship, Rockefeller Foundation, 1994.

WRITINGS:

Lunacy of Light: Emily Dickinson and the Experience of Metaphor, Southern Illinois University Press (Carbondale), 1987.
Winter Chickens and Other Poems, Corona (San Antonio, TX), 1990.
Let the Ice Speak, Ithaca House Books, Greenfield Review Press (Greenfield Center, NY), 1991.
Poems from Paradise, Aark Arts Publishers (London), 1996.
(Editor with Sandra M. Gilbert) *The House Is Made of Poetry: The Art of Ruth Stone,* Southern Illinois University Press, in press.

Work represented in many anthologies, including *Green Rain: A Collection for Young People of All Ages,* edited by Cyra Sweet Dumitru, San Antonio

Independent School District, 1983; *Women Poets of the World,* edited by Joanna Bankier and Deidre Lashgari, Macmillan, 1987; *Anthology of Magazine Verse and Yearbook of American Poetry, 1986/88,* edited by Alan F. Pater, Monitor Book (Beverly Hills, CA), 1988; *Mother Songs: Poems for, by, and about Mothers,* edited by Sandra M. Gilbert and Diana O Hehir, W. W. Norton (New York City), 1995; and *I Feel a Little Jumpy around You,* edited by Naomi Shihab Nye and Paul Janeczko, Simon and Schuster (New York City), 1996. Contributor of more than 100 articles, poems, translations, and reviews to magazines, including *Poetry, Southern Poetry Review, Nimrod, Viaztlan, American Scholar, North American Review,* and *Cedar Rock.* Member of poetry editorial board of *California Quarterly,* 1979.

Lunacy of Light: Emily Dickinson and the Experience of Metaphor was translated into Japanese in 1991.

WORK IN PROGRESS: Way of Whiteness, collection of poems; *The Berkeley Years,* collection of prose poems; *Generation,* collection of lyric and narrative poems; *Rabindranath Tagore, The Last Poems,* book of translations with Saranindra N. Tagore.

BIOGRAPHICAL/CRITICAL SOURCES:

PERIODICALS

San Antonio Light, August 2, 1987.
Women's Review of Books, December, 1987.

* * *

BAUMGARTNER, Frederic J(oseph) 1945-

PERSONAL: Born September 26, 1945, in Medford, WI; son of Michael and Theresa (Stauner) Baumgartner, married Lois Ann Hoffman, January 31, 1970; children: two. *Education:* Mount St. Paul College, B.A., 1967; University of Wisconsin—Madison, M.A., 1969, Ph.D., 1972.

ADDRESSES: Home—1109 Lora Lane, Blacksburg, VA 24060. *Office*—Department of History, Virginia Polytechnic Institute and State University, Blacksburg, VA 24061-0117.

CAREER: Georgia College, Milledgeville, assistant professor of history, 1972-76; Virginia Polytechnic Institute and State University, Blacksburg, assistant professor, 1976-80, associate professor, 1980-87, professor of history, 1987—. Member of council, Sixteenth-Century Studies Conference, 1982-85. President, Southern Historical Association, European section, 1991-92.

MEMBER: American Catholic Historical Association, American Society for Reformation Research, Society for French Historical Studies, Southern Historical Association.

WRITINGS:

Radical Reactionaries: The Political Thought of the French Catholic League, Librairie Droz, 1976.
Change and Continuity in the French Episcopate: The Bishops and the Wars of Religion, Duke University Press (Durham, NC), 1986.
Henry II: King of France, Duke University Press, 1988.
From Spear to Flintlock, Praeger (New York City), 1991.
Louis XII, St. Martin's Press (New York City), 1994.
France in the Sixteenth Century, St. Martin's (New York City), 1995.

Contributor of over sixty articles and reviews to history journals.

WORK IN PROGRESS: Astrology and the Scientific Revolution.

BIOGRAPHICAL/CRITICAL SOURCES:

PERIODICALS

American Historical Review, December, 1977.
Renaissance Quarterly, winter, 1987.
Sixteenth Century Journal, fall, 1988; spring, 1995.

*   *   *

BAXTER, Craig   1929-
     (David Dunbar)

PERSONAL: Born February 16, 1929, in Elizabeth, NJ; son of William James (an engineer) and Grace (Craig) Baxter; married Carol Alice Smart, September 17, 1955 (divorced, 1984); married Barbara Townsend Stevens (an attorney), May 28, 1984; children: (first marriage) Craig, Louise Stuart. *Edu-*

cation: University of Pennsylvania, B.S., 1951, M.A., 1954, Ph.D., 1967; studied Hindi and Urdu at Foreign Service Institute, 1960-61.

ADDRESSES: Office—Department of Political Science, Juniata College, Huntingdon, PA 16652.

CAREER: U.S. Department of State, Foreign Service officer, 1956-80, program officer for International Educational Exchange Service, 1956-58, vice consul in Bombay, India, 1958-60, political officer in New Delhi, India, 1961-64, deputy principal officer and political officer in Lahore, Pakistan, 1965-68, analyst for India, 1968-69, senior political officer for Pakistan and Afghanistan, 1969-71, political counselor in Accra, Ghana, 1974-76, and Dhaka, Bangladesh, 1976-78, officer in charge of international scientific relations for the Near East, South Asia, and Africa, 1978-80. United States Military Academy, West Point, NY, visiting professor, 1971-74; Mount Vernon College, Washington, DC, lecturer in South Asian studies, 1981; Juniata College, Huntingdon, PA, visiting professor of political science and diplomat in residence, 1981-82, professor of politics and history, 1982—, chair of department of political science, 1991-94. Adjunct lecturer in history and international relations, Northern Virginia Center, University of Virginia, 1969-71; lecturer at a number of other universities, including Harvard University, Columbia University, the United States Military Academy, College of William and Mary, and University of Pennsylvania.

Member of National Seminar on Pakistan and Bangladesh, Columbia University, 1969-74, Pakistan Studies Development Committee, 1969-75, 1979—, and Bengal Studies Conference, 1982—; cochair of South Asia panel, National Council on Foreign Languages and International Studies, 1980-81; chair of founding committee, American Institute of Bangladesh Studies, 1983-88, president, 1988—. Director, Juniata Summer Seminar in India, 1986; American Institute of Pakistan Studies, trustee, 1988—, member of executive committee, 1991-93, president, 1993—; Middle Atlantic Region, Association of Asian Studies, member of advisory council, 1986-88, member of executive committee, 1988-89, 1994—, treasurer, 1989-92, vice president, 1992-93, president, 1993-94. Consultant to National Foreign Estimate Center, U.S. Department of State, United States Information Agency, American Institute of Indian Studies, Asia Foundation, and Asia Society, Georgetown University Center for Strategic and International Studies, Middle East Institute, National

Defense University, and Frost and Sullivan. Expert witness, House Committee of Foreign Affairs, and subcommittees on Asia and the Pacific and Human Rights and International Organizations. *Military service:* United States Army, 1952-54.

MEMBER: American Foreign Service Association, Association for Asian Studies, Middle East Institute, Bengal Studies Conference, Research Committee on the Punjab (member, executive committee, 1986-89).

WRITINGS:

The Jana Sangh: A Biography of an Indian Political Party, University of Pennsylvania Press (Philadelphia), 1969, Oxford University Press (Bombay), 1971.
District Voting Trends in India: A Research Tool, Columbia University Press (New York City), 1969.
Bangladesh: A New Nation in an Old Setting, Westview (Boulder, CO), 1984, second edition, 1996.
(Editor and translator) Syed Nur Ahmad, *From Martial Law to Martial Law: Politics in Punjab, 1919-1958,* Westview, 1985, Vanguard Press (Lahore, Pakistan), 1985.
(Editor and contributor) *Zia's Pakistan: Politics and Stability in a Frontline State,* Westview, 1985, Vanguard Press, 1986.
(With Yogendra K. Malik, Charles H. Kennedy, and Robert C. Oberst) *Government and Politics in South Asia,* Westview, 1987, Vanguard Press, 1988, third edition, 1993.
(With Syedur Rahman) *Historical Dictionary of Bangladesh,* Scarecrow (Metuchen, NJ), 1989, second edition, 1996.

Contributor to books, including *South Asian Politics and Religion,* edited by Donald E. Smith, Princeton University Press (Princeton, NJ), 1966; *Pakistan and Bangladesh: Bibliographic Essays in the Social Sciences,* edited by W. Eric Gustafson, University of Islamabad Press (Pakistan), 1976; *Gulf Security in the Iran-Iraq War,* edited by Thomas Naff, National Defense University Press (Washington, DC), 1985; *Friendly Tyrants,* edited by Adam Garfinkle, St. Martin's Press (New York City), 1991; and *Pakistan under Military Rule: A Decade of Zia ul-Haq,* Westview, 1991. Also contributor to *Yearbook on International Communist Affairs,* 1973 and 1974, *Encyclopedia of Asian History, World Encyclopedia of Political Systems and Parties,* and *Handbook for Asia and the Pacific.* Also contributor of articles,

sometimes under pseudonym David Dunbar, to professional journals and newspapers, including *Asian Survey, Journal of Asian Studies, World Today, Journal of Asian and African Studies, Current History, Washington Quarterly,* and *Journal of International Affairs.*

WORK IN PROGRESS: Works on South Asian history and politics; editor, with Syed Razi Wasti, and contributor, *Pakistan: Emerging Democracy.*

*　*　*

BLAKE, Jennifer
See MAXWELL, Patricia

*　*　*

BLAYLOCK, James P(aul) 1950-

PERSONAL: Born September 20, 1950, in Long Beach, CA; son of Loren Calvin (an orthotist) and Daisy (a nurse; maiden name, Teeslink) Blaylock; married Viki Lynn Martin (a secretary), August 12, 1972; children: John Andrew, Daniel Robert. *Education:* California State University, Fullerton, B.A., 1972, M.A., 1974. *Politics:* "Unidentifiable." *Religion:* Protestant.

ADDRESSES: Home—Orange, CA. *Agent*—Writers House, Inc., 21 West 26th St., New York, NY 10010.

CAREER: Clerk at pet food store in Garden Grove, CA, 1967-72; construction worker in Placentia, CA, 1972-80; California State University, Fullerton, part-time instructor of English, 1980—. Part-time instructor at Fullerton Community College, 1976—.

MEMBER: Blake Society (vice president, 1979—).

AWARDS, HONORS: World Fantasy Award, 1986, for the short story "Paper Dragons."

WRITINGS:

SCIENCE FICTION/FANTASY

The Elfin Ship, Ballantine (New York City), 1982.
The Disappearing Dwarf, Ballantine, 1983.

The Digging Leviathan, Ace Books (New York City), 1984.

Homunculus, Ace Books, 1986.

Land of Dreams, Ace Books, 1987.

The Last Coin, Ace Books, 1988.

The Stone Giant, Ace Books, 1989.

The Magic Spectacles (young adult), Morrigan Books, 1991.

The Paper Grail, Ace Books, 1991.

Lord Kelvin's Machine, Arkham House (Sauk City, WI), 1992.

Night Relics, Ace Books, 1994.

All the Bells on Earth, Ace Books, 1995.

SIDELIGHTS: Science fiction novelist James P. Blaylock is known for his fantasy "steampunk" novels, a subgenre akin to "cyberpunk" but set in the 19th-century. His 1992 novel, *Lord Kelvin's Machine,* is a "tale of obsessive grief, time travel, mad scientists and gentlemanly adventure," summarizes a *Publishers Weekly* reviewer. Dan Chow, reviewing the novel in *Locus,* comments: "Blaylock has created a story which ranges from the blatantly sentimental . . . to the richly complex." Gerald Jonas in the *New York Times Book Review* calls the novel "regressive in more ways than one," but Chow concludes that *Lord Kelvin's Machine* "faithfully reflects both its antecedents and a more contemporary Weltschmertz."

The protagonist of Blaylock's 1994 novel *Night Relics,* Pete Travers, "can't get over his failed marriage—though he has a growing relationship with another woman; when his ex-wife and son disappear, he faces a crisis," summarizes a *Washington Post Book World* reviewer. Pete begins seeing a woman and boy walking in the hills near his home, and realizes that they are not his missing wife and son, but rather ghosts connected to his cabin in a story of long-forgotten murder. The reviewer for the *Washington Post Book World* concludes: "*Night Relics* is a powerful story full of creepy moments, made meaningful by a cast of well-drawn characters, living and dead." A reviewer for the *Library Journal* calls the book "gracefully written and splendidly told."

BIOGRAPHICAL/CRITICAL SOURCES:

PERIODICALS

Booklist, May 15, 1989, p. 1613.

Library Journal, April 15, 1991, p. 129; February 15, 1994, p. 188.

Locus, March, 1992, p. 31.

New York Times Book Review, March 15, 1992.

Publishers Weekly, March 22, 1991, p. 74; January 6, 1992, p. 52.

Village Voice Literary Supplement, October, 1984.

Washington Post Book World, November 29, 1987; July 26, 1992; February 27, 1994, p. 11.

*   *   *

BOND, Ruskin   1934-

PERSONAL: Born May 19, 1934, in Kasauli, Himachal, India; son of Aubrey Alexander (in the Royal Air Force) and Edith (Clerke) Bond. *Education:* Attended Bishop Cotton School, Simla, India, 1943-50. *Avocational interests:* Folk songs, American operetta (favorite singers include Nelson Eddy and Jeannette MacDonald), and ghost stories.

ADDRESSES: Home—Ivy Cottage, Landour Cantt, Mussoorie, Uttar Pradesh 2481279, India.

CAREER: Freelance writer, 1956—. Managing editor, *Imprint* magazine, 1975-79; worked for Cooperative for American Relief Everywhere (CARE).

AWARDS, HONORS: John Llewellyn Rhys Memorial Prize, 1957, for *The Room on the Roof;* Sahitya Academy award for English writing in India, 1992.

WRITINGS:

JUVENILE NOVELS

The Hidden Pool, illustrated by Arup Das, Children's Book Trust (New Delhi), 1966.

Grandfather's Private Zoo, illustrated by Mario Miranda, India Book House (Bombay), 1967.

Panther's Moon, illustrated by Tom Feelings, Random House (New York City), 1969.

The Last Tiger, Government of Indian Publications (New Delhi), 1971.

Angry River, illustrated by Trevor Stubley, Hamish Hamilton (London), 1972.

The Blue Umbrella, illustrated by Stubley, Hamish Hamilton, 1974.

Night of the Leopard, illustrated by Eileen Green, Hamish Hamilton, 1979.

Big Business, illustrated by Valerie Littlewood, Hamish Hamilton, 1979.

The Cherry Tree, illustrated by Littlewood, Hamish Hamilton, 1980, published with illustrations by Allan Eitzen, Boyds Mills Press, 1991.

Flames in the Forest, illustrated by Littlewood, MacRae (New York City), 1981.

The Adventures of Rusty, illustrated by Imtiaz Dharker, Thompson (New Delhi), 1981.

Tigers Forever, illustrated by Littlewood, MacRae, 1983.

Earthquake, illustrated by Littlewood, MacRae, 1984.

Getting Granny's Glasses, illustrated by Barbara Walker, MacRae, 1985.

Cricket for the Crocodile, illustrated by Walker, MacRae, 1986.

The Adventures of Rama and Sita, illustrated by Littlewood, MacRae, 1987.

The Eyes of the Eagle, illustrated by Littlewood, MacRae, 1987.

Ghost Trouble, MacRae, 1989.

Dust on the Mountain, MacRae, 1990.

Snake Trouble, illustrated by Mickey Patel, MacRae, 1990.

Tiger Roars, Eagle Soars, Walker, 1994.

Binya's Blue Umbrella, illustrated by Vera Rosenberry, Boyds Mills Press, 1995.

JUVENILE STORY COLLECTIONS

The Road to the Bazaar, illustrated by Littlewood, MacRae, 1980.

Panther's Moon, and Other Stories, illustrated by Suddhasattwa Basu, Puffin (New Delhi), 1990.

Ruskin Bond Children's Omnibus, Rupa (New Delhi), 1994.

Quakes and Flames, illustrated by Subir Roy, National Book Trust, 1994.

JUVENILE POETRY

The Wonderful World of Insects, Trees, and Wild Flowers, illustrated by Kamal Kishore, India Book House, 1968.

Tales Told at Twilight (folktales), illustrated by Madhu Powle, India Book House, 1970.

World of Trees, illustrated by Siddhartha Banerjee, National Book Trust, 1974.

Who's Who at the Zoo, photographs by Raghu Rai, National Book Trust, 1974.

Once upon a Monsoon Time (autobiography), Orient Longman, 1974.

Man of Destiny: A Biography of Jawaharlal Nehru, Orient Longman, 1976.

A Garland of Memories (essays), Mukul Prakashan (New Delhi), 1982.

Tales and Legend of India, illustrated by Sally Scott, MacRae and F. Watts, 1982.

To Live in Magic, Thompson, 1983.

An Island of Trees: Nature Stories and Poems, illustrated by Basu, Ratna Sagar (Delhi), 1992.

(Editor) *The Green Book,* Roli (New Delhi), 1995.

ADULT NOVELS

The Room on the Roof, Deutsch (London), 1956, Coward McCann, 1957.

An Axe for the Rani, Hind (Delhi), 1972.

Love Is a Sad Song, Orient Longman, 1975.

A Flight of Pigeons, India Book House, 1980.

The Young Vagrants, India Book House, 1981.

ADULT STORY COLLECTIONS

The Neighbour's Wife, and Other Stories, Higginbothams (Madras), 1967.

My First Love, and Other Stories, Pearl (Bombay), 1968.

The Man-Eater of Manjari, Sterling (New Delhi), 1974.

A Girl from Copenhagen, India Paperbacks, 1977.

Ghosts of a Hill Station, India Book House, 1983.

The Night Train at Deoli, and Other Stories, Penguin India (New Delhi), 1988.

Time Stops at Shamli, and Other Stories, Penguin (London), 1990.

Our Trees Still Grow in Dehra, Penguin India, 1991.

Delhi Is Not Far: The Best of Bond, Penguin India, 1995.

ADULT POETRY

It Isn't Time That's Passing: Poems, 1970-1971, Writers Workshop (Calcutta), 1972.

Lone Fox Dancing: Lyric Poems, Writers Workshop, 1975.

OTHER

Strange Men, Strange Places, Pearl, 1969.

Beautiful Garhwal, English Book Depot (Dehra Dun), 1988.

Ganga Descends, English Book Depot, 1992.

Mussoorie and Landour: Days of Wine and Roses, illustrated by Ganesh Saili, Lustre Press (New Delhi), 1992.

Rain in the Mountains: Notes from the Himalayas, Viking (New Delhi), 1993.

(Editor) *Penguin Book of Indian Ghost Stories*, Penguin India, 1993.

(Editor) *Penguin Book of Indian Railway Stories*, Penguin India, 1994.

Also contributor of short stories to numerous anthologies and periodicals, including *Blackwood's, Christian Science Monitor, Cricket, Highlights for Children, New Renaissance, Reader's Digest, School,* and *Short Story International.*

Several of Bond's books have been translated into French, German, Danish, Dutch, and Spanish.

The author's manuscripts are housed at the Mugar Memorial Library, Boston University.

ADAPTATIONS: A Flight of Pigeons was adapted as the Hindi film *Junoon.*

SIDELIGHTS: Born in India to British parents, author Ruskin Bond paints sensitive, colorful portraits of life in his native country to capture the imagination of his young readers. One of India's most noted children's authors, he depicts the many facets of India's natural and social landscape through his simple stories—from a temple near a quiet, rural village or a bazaar in a small provincial town to a narrow city street brimming with buses, bicycles, and the clamor of people. As Bond notes in his *Rain in the Mountains: Notes from the Himalayas,* "I have been writing in order to sustain the sort of life I like to lead—unhurried, even-paced, sensual, in step with the natural world, most at home with humble people."

A natural storyteller, Bond found that his talent enabled him to make a living away from the more highly industrialized, congested areas of India. Following the philosophy he outlined in "What's Your Dream?," an autobiographical essay from 1982's *A Garland of Memories,* Bond has found "a room of his own" at Ivy Cottage, a house in the foothills of the Himalayan Mountains, and has pursued his single dream by dedicating his life to being a storyteller.

Bond had his first success as a writer very early in his career. In fact, he was not even twenty when he published *The Room on the Roof,* a novel that dealt with growing up in a changing India. When Rusty, the tale's orphaned protagonist, discovers that he is of mixed Indian-English heritage, he decides to strike out on his own and work as a tutor in the town of Dehra Dun. His naive romantic relationship with the mother of his young charge leads to discovery by her alcoholic husband. Rusty is forced to leave the life he has made for himself and move to another city to find a new place in society. Although Helen W. Coonley senses the author's youth—Bond was seventeen when he wrote the novel—and notes in *Kliatt* that *The Room on the Roof* incorporates a somewhat immature outlook, she concludes that "though awkward in parts, the book is still fresh and likable." *The Room on the Roof* was the winner of the John Llewellyn Rhys Memorial Prize in 1957, an annual award given to a quality work of fiction written by a resident of the British Commonwealth (which then included India) under the age of thirty.

The Room on the Roof made its author something of a celebrity in India, not only because of his young age but because he was able to capture the spirit of the land and its people so sensitively through his fiction. Throughout his twenties Bond continued to write adult novels about his childhood, not turning to writing for children until he had reached his thirties. Since then, he has written numerous stories and poems that capture his nostalgia for the days of his boyhood: the natural beauty and tranquility of his grandparent's home and the close, secure, loving relationships that he experienced with friends and family.

"Bond illustrates his vision of childhood as a carefree age of mischief and joy where the only worries are associated with cricket matches, beetle races, and parental anger at bad report cards," explains Meena Khorana in *Twentieth-Century Children's Writers.* "In this comfortable and familiar world, there is a sense of security in friendship and the love and guidance of adults." In books such as *The Cherry Tree, The Adventures of Rusty,* and *Getting Granny's Glasses,* relationships among friends and family are warmly illustrated through incidents in the lives of each of Bond's youthful characters. *The Cherry Tree,* for example, is Bond's heartwarming story of six-year-old Rakhi's attempt to grow a cherry tree from a seed. A *Publishers Weekly* reviewer praises the book as "abound[ing] with quiet wisdom and love of life."

Drama and suspense are often found in Bond's fiction for children. In *Flames in the Forest,* young Romi finds himself caught in a forest fire. He and another boy must help each other race to the river—along with frightened birds and animals and even an elephant herd—to escape the smoke and flames. The determined Romi and his partner manage to survive the tragedy in a story that Ellen D. Warwick describes in *School Library Journal* as full of "action, suspense, local color, even a bit of humor."

Angry River is another of Bond's dramatic adventures. The novel features a young girl who has been left alone on her island home while her grandfather takes his dying wife to the hospital. As the river surrounding her island rises, Sita climbs a tree to safety; after the tree is washed downriver by the raging water, she is rescued by the providential appearance of a boy in a boat. "The power and size of the river, the fear and the danger are all present," states a *Times Literary Supplement* reviewer, "as is the sense of smallness in a vast world. . . . This really is India you feel."

"At the heart of [Bond's] writings is the value placed on simplicity and a selfless attitude toward life," explains Khorana. "Although the stories deal with the pleasures of humble people, their lives are enriched by meaningful experiences and a profound insight into life." Bond himself gains much of his inspiration from his surroundings and develops many of his ideas for children's books on the long walks he takes on the mountains near his home. "My interests (mountains, animals, trees, wild flowers) are embodied in these and other writings," Bond once explained. "I live in the foothills of the Himalayas and my window opens out on the forest and the distant snow-peaks—the highest mountains in the world. . . . I sit here and, inspired by the life of the hill people and the presence of birds and trees, write my stories and poems." Of his preoccupation with the landscape that features so prominently in his work, Bond once explained, "Once you have lived in the mountains, you belong to them and must come back again and again. There is no escape."

BIOGRAPHICAL/CRITICAL SOURCES:

BOOKS

Bond, Ruskin, *Rain in the Mountains: Notes from the Himalayas,* Viking, 1993.
Twentieth-Century Children's Writers, St. James Press (Detroit), 1995, pp. 123-26.

PERIODICALS

Booklist, March 15, 1995, p. 1327.

Growing Point, July, 1982, p. 3923; November, 1987, p. 4876; September, 1990, p. 5408.
Junior Bookshelf, June, 1980, p. 125; June, 1985, p. 125; February, 1991, p. 29.
Kliatt, September, 1989, p. 4.
Publishers Weekly, November 15, 1991, p. 71.
School Librarian, September, 1980, p. 262; December, 1985, p. 234; February, 1991, p. 21; November, 1992, p. 149.
School Library Journal, May, 1969, p. 83; August, 1981, p. 63; March, 1992, p. 208.
Times Literary Supplement, July 14, 1972, p. 804; July 5, 1974, p. 722.*

*   *   *

BRAMS, Steven J(ohn) 1940-

PERSONAL: Born November 28, 1940, in Concord, NH; son of Nathan (a shoe clerk) and Isabelle (Tryman) Brams (a teacher); married Eva Floderer (a ballet dancer and social worker), November 12, 1971; children: Julie, Michael. *Education:* Massachusetts Institute of Technology, S.B., 1962; Northwestern University, Ph.D., 1966.

ADDRESSES: Home—4 Washington Square Village, Apt. 17I, New York, NY 10012. *Office*—Department of Politics, New York University, 715 Broadway, 4th Fl., New York, NY 10003.

CAREER: National Institutes of Health, Office of the Director, Bethesda, MD, program analyst, summer, 1962; Office of the Secretary of Defense, Washington, DC, executive trainee, summer, 1963; Institute for Defense Analyses, Arlington, VA, research associate, 1965-67; Syracuse University, Syracuse, NY, assistant professor of political science, 1967-69; New York University, New York City, assistant professor, 1969-73, associate professor, 1973-76, professor of politics, 1976—. Visiting lecturer at University of Michigan, 1969-70, and University of Pennsylvania, spring, 1972, fall, 1977, fall, 1978; visiting professor at University of Rochester, spring, 1967, 1968-69, fall, 1971, 1972-73, Yale University, spring, 1977, fall, 1981, spring, 1991, Institute for Advanced Studies, Vienna, 1978, University of California, Irvine, 1979, and University of Haifa, 1984. Modules and Monographs in Undergraduate Mathematics and Its Applications Project (UMAP), national steering committee member, 1976-80, consortium council member, 1980-83.

MEMBER: American Association for the Advancement of Science, American Political Science Association (delegate, 1983-86), International Studies Association, Public Choice Society, Policy Studies Organization, Peace Science Society (International) (president, 1990-91), Society for Judgment and Decision Making.

AWARDS, HONORS: National Science Foundation grants, 1968-70, 1970-71, 1974-75, 1980-83, 1984-85, 1986-87, 1988-91; Ford Foundation grant, 1984-85; Sloan Foundation grant, 1986-95; United States-Israel Binational Science Foundation grant, 1985-88; Guggenheim fellowship, 1986-87; U.S. Institute of Peace grant, 1988-89; American Association for the Advancement of Science fellowship, 1992.

WRITINGS:

Game Theory and Politics, Free Press (New York City), 1975.

Paradoxes in Politics: An Introduction to the Nonobvious in Political Science, Free Press, 1976.

The Presidential Election Game, Yale University Press (New Haven, CT), 1978.

(Editor with A. Schotter and G. Schwodiaver and contributor) *Applied Game Theory: Proceedings of a Conference, Vienna, 1978,* Physica-Verlag (Wurzburg, Germany), 1979.

Biblical Games: A Strategic Analysis of Stories in the Old Testament, MIT Press (Cambridge, MA), 1980.

(Editor and contributor with William F. Lucas and Philip D. Straffin Jr.) *Modules in Applied Mathematics: Political and Related Models,* Volume 2, Springer-Verlag (New York City), 1983.

(With Peter C. Fishburn) *Approval Voting,* Birkhaeuser Boston (Cambridge, MA), 1983.

Superior Beings: If They Exist, How Would We Know? Game-Theoretic Implications of Omniscience, Omnipotence, Immortality, and Incomprehensibility, Springer-Verlag, 1983.

Superpower Games: Applying Game Theory to Superpower Conflict, Yale University Press, 1985.

Rational Politics: Decision, Games, and Strategy, CQ Press (Washington, DC), 1985.

(With D. Marc Kilgour) *Game Theory and National Security,* Basil Blackwell (New York City), 1988.

Negotiation Games: Applying Game Theory to Bargaining and Arbitration, Routledge (New York City), 1990.

Theory of Moves, Cambridge University Press (Cambridge, England), 1994.

(With Alan D. Taylor) *Fair Division: From Cake-Cutting to Dispute Resolution,* Cambridge University Press, 1995.

OTHER

Contributor to numerous books, including *The Presidency in American Politics,* edited by Paul Brace, Christine Harrington, and Gary King, New York University Press, 1989; *Systematic Analysis in Dispute Resolution,* edited by Stuart S. Nagel and Miriam K. Mills, Quorum (New York City), 1991; *Frontiers of Game Theory,* edited by Ken Binmore, Alan Kirman, and Piero Tani, MIT Press, 1993; and *Cooperative Models in International Relations Research,* edited by Michael D. Intrilgator and Urs Luterbacher, Kluwer (Norwell, MA), 1994. Contributor to journals and member of editorial boards of *Journal of Politics,* 1968-73, 1978-82, 1991—, *Behavioral Science,* 1972—, *Theory and Decision,* 1982—, *Public Choice,* 1973-90, *American Political Science Review,* 1978-82, *Mathematical Social Sciences,* 1980—, *Journal of Behavioral Decisionmaking,* 1987-90, *Journal of Theoretical Politics,* 1988—, *Group Decision and Negotiation,* 1991—, and *Control and Cybernetics,* 1993—.

SIDELIGHTS: In a *Science '81* review of Steven J. Brams's *Biblical Games: A Strategic Analysis of Stories in the Old Testament,* Jake Page remarks, "This curiously compelling book is likely to irritate humanists, enrage theologians, and dissatisfy certain mathematicians—wherein, of course, lies its charm and perhaps its ultimate effectiveness. The author is a political scientist who has taken it into his head to apply modern game theory to the enduringly fascinating and therefore unquestionably important stories of the Old Testament." Leonard Silk states in the *New York Times,* "Marvel of marvels, the mathematical theory of games appears to predict correctly the strategic choices of God and the human characters in the Bible, as well as the outcome of the conflicts between them." *Biblical Games,* Silk continues, "is neither religious nor sacrilegious; it is logical and deeply rooted in its sources." And a reviewer for the *Los Angeles Times* suggests that the reader of this book does not "have to agree with the author's rationale to be stimulated by his unusual approach."

Group Decision and Negotiation contributor D. Marc Kilgour comments on Brams's 1994 book *Theory of*

Moves: "Systems like the Theory of Moves will undoubtedly be the vehicles that deliver strategic support to the policy makers and the negotiators of the future. The amazing collection of examples that Steven Brams uses to illustrate *Theory of Moves* is not only a delight on its own, it is also a compelling demonstration of how many new and significant problems game-theory-based methods can insightfully address."

BIOGRAPHICAL/CRITICAL SOURCES:

PERIODICALS

Choice, January, 1979.
Discover, March, 1995, pp. 49-57.
Group Decision and Negotiation, May, 1995, pp. 287-88.
Los Angeles Times, July 24, 1980.
New Scientist, June 17, 1995, pp. 42-48.
New York Times, September 7, 1981.
Science '81, January/February, 1981.
Times Literary Supplement, November 30, 1979.

*   *   *

BROCK, Delia
    See EPHRON, Delia

*   *   *

BROME, (Herbert) Vincent   1910-

PERSONAL: Born July 14, 1910, in London, England; son of Nathaniel Gregory and Emily Maud Brome. *Education:* Attended schools in Streatham, England; also privately educated. *Religion:* None.

ADDRESSES: Home and office—45 Great Ormond St., London WC1, England.

CAREER: Daily Chronicle, London, feature writer, 1930-35; editor of *Menu* (magazine), 1935-39; Ministry of Information, London, journalist, 1942-44; *Medical World,* London, assistant editor, 1944-46; writer, 1946—. Member of British Library Advisory Committee.

WRITINGS:

(Editor) *My Favorite Quotations: An Anthology,* Methuen (London), 1934.
Europe's Free Press: The Underground Newspapers of Occupied Lands Described as Far as the Censor Permits, Feature Books (London), 1943.
Clement Attlee, Lincolns-Prager (London), 1949.
H. G. Wells, Longmans, Green (London), 1951, reprinted, R. West, 1979.
The Way Back: The Story of Lieutenant Commander Pat O'Leary, Cassell (London), 1953, 2nd edition, 1957, Norton (New York City), 1958.
Aneurin Bevan: A Biography, Longmans, Green, 1953.
Acquaintance with Grief (novel), Cassell, 1954.
The Last Surrender (novel), A. Dakers (London), 1954.
Six Studies in Quarrelling, Cresset Press (London), 1958, reprinted, Greenwood Press (Westport, CT), 1973.
Sometimes at Night, Cassell, 1959.
Frank Harris, Cassell, 1959, published as *Frank Harris: The Life and Loves of a Scoundrel,* T. Yoseloff, 1960.
We Have Come a Long Way (nonfiction), Cassell, 1962.
The Problem of Progress, Cassell, 1963.
Love in Our Time, Cassell, 1964.
Four Realist Novelists: Arthur Morrison, Edwin Pugh, Richard Whiting, and William Pett Ridge, Longmans, Green, 1965.
The International Brigades: Spain, 1936-39 (nonfiction), Heinemann (London), 1965, Morrow (London), 1966.
The World of Luke Simpson, Heinemann, 1966.
The Embassy (novel), Cassell, 1967, published as *The Ambassador and the Spy,* Crown (New York City), 1973.
Freud and His Early Circle: The Struggle of Psychoanalysis, Heinemann, 1967, Morrow, 1968, published as *Freud and His Disciples,* Caliban Press (Dover, NH), 1984.
The Surgeon (novel), Cassell, 1967, published as *The Operating Theatre,* Simon & Schuster (New York City), 1968.
Man at Large (three-act play), first produced in Edinburgh, Scotland, at Princess Theatre, 1967.
The Revolution (novel), Cassell, 1969.
Confessions of a Writer, Hutchinson (London), 1970.
The Brain Operators, Cassell, 1971.
Reverse Your Verdict: A Collection of Private Prosecutions, Hamish Hamilton (London), 1971.
The Day of Destruction, Cassell, 1974.
The Happy Hostage, Cassell, 1976.

Jung: Man and Myth, Atheneum (New York City), 1978.

Havelock Ellis: Philosopher of Sex, Routledge & Kegan Paul (London), 1979.

Ernest Jones: Freud's Alter Ego, Caliban Books, 1982, published as *Ernest Jones: A Biography,* Norton, 1983.

The Day of the Fifth Moon (novel), Gollancz (London), 1984.

J. B. Priestley, Hamish Hamilton, 1988.

The Other Pepys, Weidenfeld & Nicolson (London), 1992.

Also author of *The Imaginary Crime,* 1969, *London Consequences,* 1972, and *Diary of a Revolution,* 1978. Author of seven television and radio plays. Contributor to periodicals, including *New Society, Observer, Times, New Statesman, Encounter, Spectator, Washington Post, New York Times,* and *Nation.*

SIDELIGHTS: Vincent Brome, according to Robert Calder in the *Dictionary of Literary Biography,* is "one of the last of a vanishing breed—the man of letters earning his living by his pen." In a career spanning some fifty years, Brome has produced novels, biographies, magazine and newspaper articles, radio and television scripts, and a variety of other kinds of writing. Perhaps Brome's most widely appreciated works have been his biographies of such prominent writers as H. G. Wells, Frank Harris and J. B. Priestley. Brome has, Calder believes, "illuminated the lives of important literary figures of our time for a great many general readers."

Brome's first successful biography, *H. G. Wells,* appeared in 1951. The biography of the popular British novelist "is an eminently readable, careful, and thoughtful analysis of Wells as artist, scientist, and social agitator," according to Calder. Partly based on Brome's own conversations with the author, the biography is nonetheless more reticent about Wells's personal life than are more recent accounts. One reason for this was that in 1951, many people who figured prominently in Wells's life—several mistresses who bore him illegitimate children, for example—were still alive and able to legally prevent any biography that was unflattering to them. Despite such restrictions, Brome's record of Wells's career is written with "an admirable sense of balance, a steady common sense and with evident liking and sympathy," according to H. F. West in the *New York Times.* Although judging the book to have "little to do with serious scholarship, research, or literary

criticism," the reviewer for the *Manchester Guardian* nonetheless calls it "a lively impressionistic sketch."

Following a handful of other publications, Brome returned to literary biography with *Frank Harris: The Life and Loves of a Scoundrel.* Harris, a writer and editor at the turn of the century, was known for his extravagant claims about his accomplishments, his megalomania and his often disreputable behavior, including blackmail. His own autobiography, in which he claimed to have been a murderer and thief as a young man, was banned in several countries because of its explicit pornographic passages. Brome presents the story of Harris's life in what John Randolph in the *Chicago Sunday Tribune* finds is "a fair and clean and balanced book." Less enthusiastic about the biography, Evelyn Waugh, in a review for the *Spectator,* calls Harris "a most insignificant person" and suggests that Brome may have "found his subject more odious than he hoped, and lost zest for the investigation." But Robert Conquest, writing in the *Manchester Guardian,* calls *Frank Harris: The Life and Loves of a Scoundrel* a "lively and judicious book."

In *Jung: Man and Myth* Brome explores the life and career of one of the most controversial figures in the field of twentieth-century psychiatry. *Los Angeles Times* critic Robert Kirsch writes: "One bonus of Brome's biographical method is that [the author] accepts change as part of the process of evoking the whole man. This would seem to be a truism about biography, yet apart from the obvious differences between infancy, youth and old age, many biographers . . . often see character as static and consistent, rather than functioning along a chronological line." *Spectator* reviewer Hans Keller also offers praise, calling the biography "simply unprecedented—not only as the first full-length biography of one of the most complicated major talents of our time, but as an insistently factual report on a tumultuous and confusing life, produced by the rarest of all biographical gifts—the sympathetic fancy of the fact-lover."

In 1988 Brome published a biography of J. B. Priestley, a prolific British novelist who died in 1984. The author of some one hundred books, Priestley was often compared to Charles Dickens for writing large, entertaining novels for the general public. Brome's goal in this biography, Calder argues, "is to deconstruct the public persona of Priestley—that of the bluff, down-to-earth, pipe-smoking Yorkshireman—that he had built around himself. As he had done with Wells and Harris, Brome presents his subject as a man of many roles." According to Bernard Crick in a *Listener* review, Brome, "himself an old-fashioned man of letters, . . . is someone suited to tackle this difficult life. The result is everything a good biography should be." Although J. L. Carr in the *Spectator* finds that Brome's account of Priestley's early years is "more illuminating and livelier reading than the remaining five-sixths" of the book, Anthony Burgess, writing in the *Times Literary Supplement,* sees *J. B. Priestley* as displaying "a total candour of portraiture, as well as the kind of affection that admits occasional exasperation." Crick concludes that Brome "tells [the story of Priestley's life] as if to a friend, informally but carefully, weighing the evidence." Calder concludes that *J. B. Priestley* is "not only the best of Brome's work but the best example of his strengths as a biographer: intelligence, common sense, and lively, readable prose."

BIOGRAPHICAL/CRITICAL SOURCES:

BOOKS

Dictionary of Literary Biography, Volume 155: *Twentieth-Century British Literary Biographers,* Gale (Detroit), 1995.

PERIODICALS

British Book News, November, 1984, p. 687; December, 1984, p. 718.
Chicago Sunday Tribune, June 17, 1951, p. 6; April 10, 1960, p. 11.
Economist, November 5, 1988, p. 105.
Listener, November 10, 1988, p. 28.
London Review of Books, January 5, 1989, p. 26.
Los Angeles Times, November 21, 1978.
Manchester Guardian, March 6, 1951, p. 3; February 20, 1959, p. 4.
Nation, May 26, 1951, p. 496.
New Statesman & Nation, February 24, 1951, p. 220.
New Yorker, May 26, 1951, p. 27; April 23, 1960, p. 179.
New York Herald Tribune Book Review, July 1, 1951, p. 8.
New York Times, May 27, 1951, p. 19.
New York Times Book Review, May 8, 1960, p. 7; December 24, 1978.
Observer, October 16, 1988, p. 43.
San Francisco Chronicle, May 29, 1960, p. 21.

Saturday Review of Literature, August 18, 1951, p. 10.
Spectator, February 23, 1951, p. 252; February 20, 1959, p. 268; November 11, 1978, p. 19; January 7, 1989, p. 24; November 14, 1992, p. 40.
Stand, winter, 1989, p. 64.
Time, March 21, 1960, p. 102.
Times Literary Supplement, February 23, 1951, p. 116; February 20, 1959, p. 91; May 6, 1983; December 7, 1984, p. 1420; October 21, 1988, p. 1163; July 30, 1993, p. 23.
Washington Post Book World, January 6, 1985, p. 13.

*   *   *

BROOKHOUSE, (John) Christopher 1938-

PERSONAL: Born January 6, 1938, in Cincinnati, OH; married Diane Banks, June 14, 1959 (divorced, October, 1972); married Anne Ponder, March 3, 1973; children: (first marriage) Stephen, Nathaniel. *Education:*Stanford University, A.B., 1959; Harvard University, M.A., 1960, Ph.D., 1964. *Politics:* Independent.

ADDRESSES: Home—Sunbear Woods, Pittsboro, NC. *Office*—Department of English, University of North Carolina, Chapel Hill, NC 27515. *Agent*—John Hawkins, Paul R. Reynolds, Inc., 12 East 41st St., New York, NY 10017.

CAREER: Harvard University, Cambridge, MA, instructor in English, 1964-66; University of North Carolina at Chapel Hill, 1966—, began as assistant professor, currently associate professor of English.

MEMBER: Authors League of America, Phi Beta Kappa.

WRITINGS:

(Editor) *Sir Amadace and the Avowing of Arthur,* Rosenkilde & Bagger, 1968.
Scattered Light (poems), University of North Carolina Press (Chapel Hill), 1969.
Running Out, Little, Brown (Boston), 1970.
Genesis House, Loom Press, 1974.
If Lost, Return, Loom Press, 1974.
Wintermute, Dutton (New York City), 1978.
Dear Otto, Permanent Press (Sag Harbor, NY), 1995.

SIDELIGHTS: Christopher Brookhouse has published work both as a poet and a novelist. He is also a professor of English, and in his first novel, *Running Out,* some of the action takes place in a setting very familiar to him—a North Carolina college campus. The central characters are two men and a woman, recent graduates, who are all struggling with emotional pain and preoccupation with death. Evaluating *Running Out* in the *New York Times Book Review,* Millicent Bell compared it to earlier classics such as Virginia Woolf's *Mrs. Dalloway.* Both novels employ a stream-of-consciousness narrative, a solipsistic viewpoint and a poetic style. Bell concluded that *Running Out* was "rather exquisite." A *Library Journal* contributor also reacted positively to the book, calling it "a work of some distinction."

Brookhouse's novel *Wintermute* is set in a remote Vermont mansion owned by eccentric millionaire Sy Brinton. Brinton invites several of his college classmates to his isolated retreat for a twenty-fifth reunion and then proceeds to take his revenge on them. A *Kirkus Reviews* writer described *Wintermute* as "a short book that, though sometimes nicely voiced, seems unconsciously long." A *Booklist* reviewer found Brinton's motivations unconvincing, but allowed that *Wintermute* provided a spooky, enjoyable read. A *Publishers Weekly* contributor gave an even more enthusiastic appraisal, stating that the book could appeal to almost any reader, and that its plot twists were never gimmicky. "The ending is quite surprising and has much of the bizarre quality of some of [John] Fowles's storytelling," concluded the reviewer.

Brookhouse used another isolated setting for his novel *Dear Otto.* In this story, three aspiring novelists attend a writing workshop held near an isolated Amish village. As with *Wintermute,* the plot is full of surprising twists. A *Publishers Weekly* reviewer praised *Dear Otto* as "a set of finely drawn portraits" that "bring to life the complex nature of modern relationships."

BIOGRAPHICAL/CRITICAL SOURCES:

PERIODICALS

Booklist, March 15, 1978.
Kirkus Reviews, January 15, 1978, p. 56.
Library Journal, February 15, 1970.
New Yorker, October 24, 1970, p. 170.
New York Times, May 12, 1970, p. 37.
New York Times Book Review, May 3, 1970, p. 5.

Publishers Weekly, January 16, 1978, p. 92; October 2, 1995, p. 54.
Saturday Review, July 11, 1970, p. 29.*

*   *   *

BROOKS, Gwendolyn 1917-

PERSONAL: Born June 7, 1917, in Topeka, KS; daughter of David Anderson and Keziah Corinne (Wims) Brooks; married Henry Lowington Blakely II, September 17, 1939; children: Henry Lowington III, Nora. *Education:* Graduate of Wilson Junior College, 1936.

ADDRESSES: Home—5530 South Shore Drive, Chicago, IL 60637.

CAREER: Poet and novelist. Publicity director, National Association for the Advancement of Colored People (NAACP) Youth Council, Chicago, IL, 1937-38. Taught poetry at numerous colleges and universities, including Columbia College, Elmhurst College, Northeastern Illinois State College (now Northwestern Illinois University), and University of Wisconsin-Madison, 1969; Distinguished Professor of the Arts, City College of the City University of New York, 1971; currently professor at Chicago State University. Member, Illinois Arts Council.

MEMBER: National Institute of Arts and Letters, American Academy of Arts and Letters, Society of Midland Authors (Chicago), Cliff Dwellers Club, Tavern Club (honorary memeber), Caxton Club (honorary member).

AWARDS, HONORS: Named one of ten women of the year, *Mademoiselle* magazine, 1945; National Institute of Arts and Letters grant in literature, 1946; American Academy of Arts and Letters Award for creative writing, 1946; Guggenheim fellowships, 1946 and 1947; Eunice Tietjens Memorial Prize, *Poetry* magazine, 1949; Pulitzer Prize in poetry, 1950, for *Annie Allen;* Robert F. Ferguson Memorial Award, Friends of Literature, 1964, for *Selected Poems;* Thormod Monsen Literature Award, 1964; Anisfield-Wolf Award, 1968, for *In the Mecca;* named Poet Laureate of Illinois, 1968; National Book Award nomination, for *In the Mecca;* Black Academy of Arts and Letters Award, 1971, for outstanding achievement in letters; Shelley Memorial Award, 1976; Poetry Consultant to the Library of

Congress, 1985-86; inducted into National Women's Hall of Fame, 1988; Lifetime Achievement Award, National Endowment for the Arts, 1989; Society for Literature Award, University of Thessoloniki (Athens, Greece), 1990; Kuumba Liberation Award; Frost Medal, Poetry Society of America; approximately fifty honorary degrees from universities and colleges, including Columbia College, 1964, Lake Forest College, 1965, and Brown University, 1974.

WRITINGS:

POETRY

A Street in Bronzeville (also see below), Harper (New York City), 1945.

Annie Allen (also see below), Harper, 1949, reprinted, Greenwood Press, 1972 (Westport, CT).

The Bean Eaters (also see below), Harper, 1960.

In the Time of Detachment, In the Time of Cold, Civil War Centennial Commission of Illinois, 1965.

In the Mecca (also see below), Harper, 1968.

For Illinois 1968: A Sesquicentennial Poem, Harper, 1968.

Riot (also see below), Broadside Press (Highland Park, MI), 1969.

Family Pictures (also see below), Broadside Press, 1970.

Aloneness, Broadside Press, 1971.

Aurora, Broadside Press, 1972.

Beckonings, Broadside Press, 1975.

Primer for Blacks, Black Position Press, 1980.

To Disembark, Third World Press (Chicago, IL), 1981.

Black Love, Brooks Press, 1982.

Mayor Harold Washington [and] *Chicago, The I Will City,* Brooks Press, 1983.

The Near-Johannesburg Boy, and Other Poems, David Co., 1987.

Gottschalk and the Grande Tarantelle, David Co., 1988.

Winnie, Third World Press, 1988.

Children Coming Home, David Co., 1991.

Also author of *A Catch of Shy Fish* (also see below), 1963.

JUVENILE

Bronzeville Boys and Girls (poems), Harper, 1956.

The Tiger Who Wore White Gloves: Or You Are What You Are, Third World Press, 1974, reissued, 1987.

FICTION

Maud Martha (novel; also see below), Harper, 1953.

Stories included in books, including *Soon One Morning: New Writing by American Negroes, 1940-1962* (includes "The Life of Lincoln West"), edited by Herbert Hill, Knopf (New York City), 1963, published in England as *Black Voices,* Elek, 1964; and *The Best Short Stories by Negro Writers: An Anthology from 1899 to the Present,* edited by Langston Hughes, Little, Brown (Boston), 1967.

COLLECTED WORKS

Selected Poems, Harper, 1963.

The World of Gwendolyn Brooks (contains *A Street in Bronzeville, Annie Allen, Maud Martha, The Bean Eaters,* and *In the Mecca;* also see below), Harper, 1971.

Blacks (includes *A Street in Bronzeville, Annie Allen, The Bean Eaters, Maud Martha, A Catch of Shy Fish, Riot, In the Mecca,* and most of *Family Pictures*), David Co., 1987.

The Gwendolyn Brooks Library, Moonbeam Publications, 1991.

OTHER

(With others) *A Portion of That Field: The Centennial of the Burial of Lincoln,* University of Illinois Press (Champaign), 1967.

(Editor) *A Broadside Treasury* (poems), Broadside Press, 1971.

(Editor) *Jump Bad: A New Chicago Anthology,* Broadside Press, 1971.

Report from Part One: An Autobiography, Broadside Press, 1972.

(With Keorapetse Kgositsile, Haki R. Madhubuti, and Dudley Randall) *A Capsule Course in Black Poetry Writing,* Broadside Press, 1975.

Young Poet's Primer (writing manual), Brooks Press, 1981.

Very Young Poets (writing manual), Brooks Press, 1983.

The Day of the Gwendolyn: A Lecture (sound recording), Library of Congress (Washington, DC), 1986.

Also author of broadsides *The Wall* and *We Real Cool,* for Broadside Press, and *I See Chicago,* 1964. Contributor to books, including *New Negro Poets USA,* edited by Langston Hughes, Indiana University Press, 1964; *The Poetry of Black America: Anthology of the Twentieth Century,* edited by Arnold Adoff, Harper, 1973; and *Celebrate the Midwest! Poems and Stories for David D. Anderson,* edited by Marcia Noe, Lake Shore, 1991. Contributor of poems and articles to *Ebony, McCall's, Nation, Poetry,* and other periodicals. Contributor of reviews to Chicago *Sun-Times, Chicago Daily News, New York Herald Tribune,* and *New York Times Book Review.*

WORK IN PROGRESS: A sequel to *Maud Martha.*

SIDELIGHTS: In 1950 Gwendolyn Brooks, a highly regarded poet, became the first black author to win the Pulitzer Prize. Her poems from this period, specifically *A Street in Bronzeville* and *Annie Allen,* were "devoted to small, carefully cerebrated, terse portraits of the Black urban poor," Richard K. Barksdale comments in *Modern Black Poets: A Collection of Critical Essays.* Jeanne-Marie A. Miller calls this "city-folk poetry" and describes Brooks's characters as "unheroic black people who fled the land for the city only to discover that there is little difference between the world of the North and the world of the South."

"One learns from them," Miller continues in the *Journal of Negro Education,* "their dismal joys and their human griefs and pain." Audiences in Chicago, inmates in prisons around the country, and students of all ages have found her poems accessible and relevant. Haki Madhubuti, cited in Jacqueline Trescott's *Washington Post* article on Brooks, points out that Brooks "has, more than any other nationally acclaimed writer, remained in touch with the community she writes about. She lives in the core of Chicago's black community. . . . She is her work." In addition, notes Toni Cade Bambara in the *New York Times Book Review,* Brooks "is known for her technical artistry, having worked her word sorcery in forms as disparate as Italian terza rima and the blues. She has been applauded for revelations of the African experience in America, particularly her sensitive portraits of black women."

Though best known for her poetry, in the 1950s Brooks published her first novel. *Maud Martha* presents vignettes from a ghetto woman's life in short chapters, says Harry B. Shaw in *Gwendolyn Brooks.* It is "a story of a woman with doubts about herself and where and how she fits into the world. Maud's concern is not so much that she is inferior but that she is perceived as being ugly." Eventually, she takes a stand for her own dignity by turning her back

on a patronizing, racist store clerk. "The book is . . . about the triumph of the lowly," comments Shaw.

"[Brooks] shows what they go through and exposes the shallowness of the popular, beautiful white people with 'good' hair. One way of looking at the book, then, is as a war with . . . people's concepts of beauty." Its other themes include "the importance of spiritual and physical death," disillusionment with a marriage that amounts to "a step down" in living conditions, and the discovery "that even through disillusionment and spiritual death life will prevail," Shaw maintains.

Other reviewers feel that Brooks is more effective when treating the same themes in her poetry, but David Littlejohn, writing in *Black on White: A Critical Survey of Writing by American Negroes,* feels the novel "is a striking human experiment, as exquisitely written . . . as any of Gwendolyn Brook's poetry in verse. . . . It is a powerful, beautiful dagger of a book, as generous as it can possibly be. It teaches more, more quickly, more lastingly, than a thousand pages of protest." In a *Black World* review, Annette Oliver Shands appreciates the way in which *Maud Martha* differs from the works of other early black writers: "Miss Brooks does not specify traits, niceties or assets for members of the Black community to acquire in order to attain their just rights. . . . So, this is not a novel to inspire social advancement on the part of fellow Blacks. Nor does it say *be poor, Black and happy.* The message is to accept the challenge of being human and to assert humanness with urgency."

Although, as Martha Liebrum notes in the *Houston Post,* Brooks "wrote about being black before being black was beautiful," in retrospect her poems have been described as sophisticated, intellectual, and European, or "conditioned" by the established literary tradition. Like her early favorites Emily Dickinson, John Keats, and Percy Bysshe Shelley, Brooks expresses in poetry her love of "the wonders language can achieve," as she told Claudia Tate in an interview for *Black Women Writers at Work.* Barksdale states that by not directly emphasizing any "rhetorical involvement with causes, racial or otherwise," Brooks was merely reflecting "the literary mood of the late 1940's." He suggests that there was little reason for Brooks to confront the problems of racism on a large scale since, in her work, "each character, so neatly and precisely presented, is a racial protest in itself and a symbol of some sharply etched human dilemma."

However, Brooks's later poems show a marked change in tone and content. Just as her first poems reflected the mood of their era, her later works mirror their age by displaying what *National Observer* contributor Bruce Cook calls "an intense awareness of the problems of color and justice." Bambara comments that at the age of fifty "something happened [to Brooks], a something most certainly in evidence in 'In the Mecca' (1968) and subsequent works—a new movement and energy, intensity, richness, power of statement and a new stripped lean, compressed style. A change of style prompted by a change of mind."

"Though some of her work in the early 1960s had a terse abbreviated style, her conversion to direct political expression happened rapidly after a gathering of black writers at Fisk University in 1967," Trescott reports. Brooks told Tate, "They seemed proud and so committed to their own people. . . . The poets among them felt that black poets should write as blacks, about blacks, and address themselves *to* blacks." If many of her earlier poems had fulfilled this aim, it was not due to conscious intent, she said; but from this time forward, Brooks has thought of herself as an African who has determined not to compromise social comment for the sake of technical proficiency.

Although *In the Mecca* and later works are characterized as tougher and possess what a reviewer for the *Virginia Quarterly Review* describes as "raw power and roughness," critics are quick to indicate that these poems are neither bitter nor vengeful. Instead, according to Cook, they are more "about bitterness" than bitter in themselves. *Dictionary of Literary Biography* essayist Charles Israel suggests that *In the Mecca*'s title poem, for example, shows "a deepening of Brooks's concern with social problems." A mother has lost a small daughter in the block-long ghetto tenement, the Mecca; the long poem traces her steps through the building, revealing her neighbors to be indifferent or insulated by their own personal obsessions. The mother finds her little girl, who "never learned that black is not beloved," who "was royalty when poised, / sly, at the A and P's fly-open door," under a Jamaican resident's cot, murdered. A *Virginia Quarterly Review* contributor compares the poem's impact to that of Richard Wright's fiction. R. Baxter Miller, writing in *Black American Poets between Worlds, 1940-1960,* comments, "*In the Mecca* is a most complex and intriguing book; it seeks to balance the sordid realities of urban life with an imaginative process of reconcilia-

tion and redemption." Other poems in the book, occasioned by the death of Malcolm X or the dedication of a mural of black heroes painted on a Chicago slum building, express the poet's commitment to her people's awareness of themselves as a political as well as a cultural entity.

Her interest in encouraging young blacks to assist and appreciate fledgling black publishing companies led her to leave Harper & Row. In the seventies, she chose Dudley Randall's Broadside Press to publish her poetry (*Riot, Family Pictures, Aloneness, Aurora,* and *Beckonings*) and *Report from Part One,* the first volume of her autobiography. She edited two collections of poetry—*A Broadside Treasury* and *Jump Bad: A New Chicago Anthology*—for the Detroit-based press. The Chicago-based Third World Press, run by Haki R. Madhubuti (formerly Don L. Lee, one of the young poets she had met during the sixties), has also brought two Brooks titles into print. She does not regret having given her support to small publishers who dedicated themselves to the needs of the black community. Brooks was the first writer to read in Broadside's Poet's Theatre Series when it began and was also the first poet to read in the second opening of the series when the press revived under new ownership in 1988.

Riot, Family Pictures, Beckonings, and other books brought out by black publishers were given brief notice by critics of the literary establishment who "did not wish to encourage Black publishers," said Brooks. Some were disturbed by the political content of these poems. *Riot,* in particular, in which Brooks is the spokesman for the "HEALTHY REBELLION" going on then, as she calls it, was accused of "celebrating violence" by L. L. Shapiro in a *School Library Journal* review. Key poems from these books, later collected in *To Disembark,* call blacks to "work together toward their own REAL emancipation," Brooks indicated. Even so, "the strength here is not in declamation but in [the poet's] genius for psychological insight," claims J. A. Lipari in the *Library Journal.* Addison Gayle points out that the softer poems of this period—the ones asking for stronger interpersonal bonds among black Americans—are no less political: "To espouse and exult in a Black identity, outside the psychic boundaries of white Americans, was to threaten. . . . To advocate and demand love between one Black and another was to begin a new chapter in American history. Taken together, the acknowledgment of a common racial identity among Blacks throughout the world and the suggestion of a love based upon the brotherhood and sisterhood of the oppressed were meant to transform Blacks in America from a minority to a majority, from world victims to, to use Madhubuti's phrase, 'world makers'."

In the same essay, printed in *Black Women Writers (1950-1980): A Critical Evaluation,* Gayle defends *Riot* and the later books, naming them an important source of inspiration to a rising generation: "It may well be . . . that the function of poetry is not so much to save us from oppression nor from Auschwitz, but to give us the strength to face them, to help us stare down the lynch mob, walk boldly in front of the firing squad. It is just such awareness that the poetry of Gwendolyn Brooks has given us, this that she and those whom she taught/learned from have accomplished for us all. They have told us that for Black Americans there are no havens, that in the eyes of other Americans we are, each and every one of us, rioters. . . . These are dangerous times for Black people. The sensitive Black poet realizes that fact, but far from despairing, picks up his pen, . . . and echoes Gwendolyn Brooks: 'My aim . . . is to write poems that will somehow successfully "call" . . . all black people . . . in gutters, in schools, offices, factories, prisons, the consulate; I wish to teach black people in pulpits, black people in mines, on farms, on thrones.'" Brooks pointed out "a serious error" in this quote; she wants to "reach" people, not "teach" them. She added, "The times for Black people—when*ever* in the clutches of white *manipulation,* have ALWAYS been dangerous." She also advised young poets, "Walking in front of a firing squad is *crazy.* Your effort should be in preventing the *formation* of a firing squad."

"The poet's search "for an *expression* relevant to all manner of blacks," as she described her change in focus to Tate, did not alter her mastery of her craft. "While quoting approvingly Ron Karenga's observation that 'the fact that we are black is our ultimate reality,' blackness did not, to her, require simplification of language, symbol, or moral perception," notes C. W. E. Bigsby in *The Second Black Renaissance: Essays in Black Literature.* It did include "the possibility of communicating directly to those in the black community." In the bars and on the street corners were an audience not likely to "go into a bookstore" to buy poetry by anyone, she told George Stavros in a *Contemporary Literature* interview reprinted in *Report from Part One: An Autobiography.* And in the late sixties, Brooks reported, "some of those folks DID" enter bookstores to buy poetry and read it "standing up." To better reach the street

audience, Brooks's later poems use more open, less traditional poetic forms and techniques. Penelope Moffet, writing in the *Los Angeles Times,* records the poet's statement that since 1967, she has been "successfully escaping from close rhyme, because it just isn't natural. . . . I've written hundreds . . . of sonnets, and I'll probably never write another one, because I don't feel that this is a sonnet time. It seems to me it's a wild, raw, ragged free verse time." She told Stavros, "I want to write poems that will be non-compromising. I don't want to stop a concern with words doing good jobs, which has always been a concern of mine, but I want to write poems that will be meaningful to those people I described a while ago, things that will touch them." Speaking of later works aimed for that audience, Robert F. Kiernan offers in *American Writing since 1945: A Critical Survey,* "She remains, however, a virtuoso of the lyric and an extraordinary portraitist—probably the finest black poet of the post-Harlem generation."

When *Report from Part One* came out in 1972, some reviewers complained that it did not provide the level of personal detail or the insight into black literature that they had expected. "They wanted a list of domestic spats," remarked Brooks. Bambara notes that it "is not a sustained dramatic narrative for the nosey, being neither the confessions of a private woman poet or the usual sort of mahogany-desk memoir public personages inflict upon the populace at the first sign of a cardiac. . . . It documents the growth of Gwen Brooks." Other reviewers value it for explaining the poet's new orientation toward her racial heritage and her role as a poet. In a passage she has presented again in later books as a definitive statement, she writes: "I—who have 'gone the gamut' from an almost angry rejection of my dark skin by some of my brainwashed brothers and sisters to a surprised queenhood in the new Black sun—am qualified to enter at least the kindergarten of new consciousness now. New consciousness and trudge-toward-progress. I have hopes for myself. . . . I know now that I am essentially an essential African, in occupancy here because of an indeed 'peculiar' institution. . . . I know that Black fellow-feeling must be the Black man's encyclopedic Primer. I know that the Black-and-white integration concept, which in the mind of some beaming early saint was a dainty spinning dream, has wound down to farce. . . . I know that the Black emphasis must be not *against white* but *FOR Black.* . . . In the Conference-That-Counts, whose date may be 1980 or 2080 (woe betide the Fabric of Man if it is 2080), there will be no looking up nor looking down." In the future, she envisions "the profound and frequent shaking of hands, which in Africa is so important. The shaking of hands in warmth and strength and union."

Brooks put some of the finishing touches on the second volume of her autobiography while serving as Poetry Consultant to the Library of Congress. Brooks was sixty-eight when she became the first black woman to be appointed to the post. Of her many duties there, the most important, in her view, were visits to local schools. Similar visits to colleges, universities, prisons, hospitals, and drug rehabilitation centers characterize her tenure as Poet Laureate of Illinois. In that role, she has sponsored and hosted annual literary awards ceremonies at which she presents prizes paid for "out of [her] own pocket, which, despite her modest means, is of legendary depth," Reginald Gibbons relates in Chicago *Tribune Books*. She has honored and encouraged many poets in her state through the Illinois Poets Laureate Awards and Significant Illinois Poets Awards programs. At one ceremony, says Gibbons, "poetry was, for a time, the vital center of people's lives."

Brook's objectivity is considered by some reviewers as one of the most widely acclaimed features of her poetry. Janet Overmeyer notes in the *Christian Science Monitor* that Brooks's "particular, outstanding, genius is her unsentimental regard and respect for all human beings. . . . She neither foolishly pities nor condemns—she creates." Overmeyer continues, "From her poet's craft bursts a whole gallery of wholly alive persons, preening, squabbling, loving, weeping; many a novelist cannot do so well in ten times the space." Brooks achieves this effect through a high "degree of artistic control," claims Littlejohn. "The words, lines, and arrangements," he states, "have been worked and worked and worked again into poised exactness: the unexpected apt metaphor, the mock-colloquial asides amid jewelled phrases, the half-ironic repetitions—she knows it all." More importantly, Brooks's objective treatment of issues such as poverty and racism "produces genuine emotional tension," he writes.

This quality also provides her poems with universal appeal. Blyden Jackson states in *Black Poetry in America: Two Essays in Historical Interpretation* that Brooks "is one of those artists of whom it can truthfully be said that things like sex and race, important as they are, . . . appear in her work to be sublimated into insights and revelations of universal application." Although Brooks's characters are primarily

black and poor and live in Northern urban cities, she provides, according to Jackson, through "the close inspection of a limited domain, . . . a view of life in which one may see a microscopic portion of the universe intensely and yet, through that microscopic portion see all truth for the human condition wherever it is." And although the goals and adjustments of black nationalism have been her frequent topics, Houston A. Baker, Jr., says of Brooks in the *CLA Journal*: "The critic (whether black or white) who comes to her work seeking only support for his ideology will be disappointed for, as Etheridge Knight pointed out, she has ever spoken the truth. And truth, one likes to feel, always lies beyond the boundaries of any one ideology. Perhaps Miss Brooks' most significant achievement is her endorsement of this point of view. From her hand and fertile imagination have come volumes that transcend the dogma on either side of the American veil." Baker feels that Brooks "represents a singular achievement. Beset by a double consciousness, she has kept herself from being torn asunder by crafting poems that equal the best in the black and white American literary traditions."

Proving the breadth of Brooks's appeal, poets representing a wide variety of "races and . . . poetic camps" gathered at the University of Chicago to celebrate the poet's seventieth birthday in 1987, reports Gibbons. Brooks brought them together, he says, "in . . . a moment of good will and cheer." In recognition of her service and achievements, a junior high school in Harvey, Illinois, has been named for her. She is also honored at Western Illinois University's Gwendolyn Brooks Center for African-American Literature.

Summing up the poet's accomplishments, Gibbons writes that beginning with *A Street in Bronzeville*, Brooks has brought national attention to "a part of life that had been grossly neglected by the literary establishment. . . . And because Brooks has been a deeply serious artist . . ., she has created works of special encouragement to black writers and of enduring importance to all readers."

BIOGRAPHICAL/CRITICAL SOURCES:

BOOKS

Authors in the News, Volume 1, Gale, 1976.
Baker, Houston A., Jr., *Singers of Daybreak: Studies in Black American Literature,* Howard University Press, 1974.

Berry, S. L., *Gwendolyn Brooks,* Creative Education, 1993.

Bigsby, C. W. E., editor, *The Black American Writer, Volume 2: Poetry and Drama,* Deland, 1969.

Bigsby, C. W. E., *The Second Black Renaissance: Essays in Black Literature,* Greenwood Press, 1980.

Black Literature Criticism, Gale, 1992.

Brooks, Gwendolyn, *In the Mecca,* Harper, 1968.

Brooks, Gwendolyn, *Report from Part One: An Anthology,* Broadside Press, 1972.

Brown, Patricia L., Don L. Lee, and Francis Ward, editors, *To Gwen with Love: An Anthology Dedicated to Gwendolyn Brooks,* Johnson Publishing, 1971.

Children's Literature Review, Volume 27, Gale, 1992.

Concise Dictionary of American Literary Biography: The New Consciousness, 1941-1968, Gale, 1985.

Contemporary Literary Criticism, Gale, Detroit, Volume 1, 1973, Volume 2, 1974, Volume 4, 1975, Volume 5, 1976, Volume 15, 1980, Volume 49, 1988.

Dembo, L. S., and C. N. Pondrom, editors, *The Contemporary Writer: Interviews with Sixteen Novelists and Poets,* University of Wisconsin Press, 1972.

Dictionary of Literary Biography, Gale, Volume 5: *American Poets since World War II,* 1980, Volume 75: *Afro-American Writers, 1940-1955,* 1988.

Drotning, Philip T., and Wesley W. Smith, editors, *Up from the Ghetto,* Cowles, 1970.

Emanuel and Gross, editors, *Dark Symphony: Negro Literature in America,* Free Press, 1968.

Evans, Mari, editor, *Black Women Writers (1950-1980): A Critical Evaluation,* Anchor/Doubleday, 1984.

Gates, Henry Louis, Jr., editor, *Black Literature and Literary Theory,* Methuen, 1984.

Gayle, Addison, editor, *Black Expression,* Weybright & Talley, 1969.

Gibson, Donald B., editor, *Modern Black Poets: A Collection of Critical Essays,* Prentice-Hall, 1973.

Gould, Jean, *Modern American Women Poets,* Dodd, Mead, 1985.

Jackson, Blyden, and Louis D. Rubin, Jr., *Black Poetry in America: Two Essays in Historical Interpretation,* Louisiana State University Press, 1974.

Kent, George, *Gwendolyn Brooks: A Life,* University Press of Kentucky, 1988.

Kiernan, Robert F. *American Writing since 1945: A Critical Survey,* Continuum (New York City), 1983.

Kufrin, Joan, *Uncommon Women,* New Century Publications, 1981.

Littlejohn, David, *Black on White: A Critical Survey of Writing by American Negroes,* Viking, 1966.

Madhubuti, Haki R., *Say that the River Turns: The Impact of Gwendolyn Brooks,* Third World Press, 1987.

Melhem, D. H., *Gwendolyn Brooks: Poetry and the Heroic Voice,* University Press of Kentucky, 1987.

Miller, R. Baxter, *Langston Hughes and Gwendolyn Brooks: A Reference Guide,* Hall, 1978.

Miller, R. Baxter, *Black American Poets between Worlds, 1940-1960,* University of Tennessee Press, 1986.

Mootry, Maria K., and Gary Smith, editors, *A Life Distilled: Gwendolyn Brooks, Her Poetry and Fiction,* University of Illinois Press, 1987.

Newquist, Roy, *Conversations,* Rand McNally, 1967.

Poetry Criticism, Gale, Detroit, Volume 7, 1994.

Redmond, Eugene B., *Drumvoices: The Mission of Afro-American Poetry,* Doubleday, 1976.

Shaw, Harry F., *Gwendolyn Brooks,* Twayne, 1980.

Tate, Claudia, *Black Women Writers at Work,* Continuum, 1983.

World Literature Criticism, Gale, 1992.

PERIODICALS

African American Review, summer, 1992, p. 197-211.

American Literature, December, 1990, pp. 606-16.

Atlantic Monthly, September, 1960.

Best Sellers, April 1, 1973.

Black American Literature Forum, spring, 1977; winter, 1984; fall, 1990, p. 567.

Black Enterprise, June, 1985.

Black Scholar, March, 1981; November, 1984.

Black World, August, 1970; January, 1971; July, 1971; September, 1971; October, 1971; January, 1972; March, 1973; June, 1973; December, 1975.

Book Week, October 27, 1963.

Book World, November 3, 1968.

Chicago Tribune, January 14, 1986; June 7, 1987; June 12, 1989.

Christian Science Monitor, September 19, 1968.

CLA Journal, December, 1962; December, 1963; December, 1969; September, 1972; September, 1973; September, 1977; December, 1982.

Contemporary Literature, March 28, 1969; winter, 1970.

Critique, summer, 1984.

Discourse, spring, 1967.
Ebony, July, 1968; June, 1987, p. 154.
English Journal, November, 1990, p. 84-8.
Essence, April, 1971; September, 1984.
Explicator, April, 1976; Volume 36, number 4, 1978.
Houston Post, February 11, 1974.
Jet, May 30, 1994, p. 37.
Kenyon Review, winter, 1995, p. 136.
Journal of Negro Education, winter, 1970.
Library Journal, September 15, 1970.
Los Angeles Times, November 6, 1987; September 14, 1993, p. F3.
Los Angeles Times Book Review, September 2, 1984.
Modern Fiction Studies, winter, 1985.
Nation, September, 1962; July 7, 1969; September 26, 1987, p. 308.
National Observer, November 9, 1968.
Negro American Literature Forum, fall, 1967; summer, 1974.
Negro Digest, December, 1961; January, 1962; August, 1962; July, 1963; June, 1964; January, 1968.
New Statesman, May 3, 1985.
New Yorker, September 22, 1945; December 17, 1949; October 10, 1953; December 3, 1979.
New York Times, November 4, 1945; October 5, 1953; December 9, 1956; October 6, 1963; March 2, 1969; April 30, 1990, p. C11.
New York Times Book Review, October 23, 1960; October 6, 1963; March 2, 1969; January 2, 1972; June 4, 1972; December 3, 1972; January 7, 1973; June 10, 1973; December 2, 1973; September 23, 1984; July 5, 1987; March 18, 1990, p. 21.
Phylon, summer, 1961; March, 1976.
Poetry, December, 1945; Volume 126, 1950; March, 1964.
Publishers Weekly, June 6, 1970.
Ramparts, December, 1968.
Saturday Review, February 1, 1964.
Saturday Review of Literature, January 19, 1946; September 17, 1949; May 20, 1950.
Southern Review, spring, 1965.
Southwest Review, winter, 1989, pp. 25-35.
Studies in Black Literature, autumn, 1973; spring, 1974; summer, 1974; spring, 1977.
Tribune Books (Chicago), July 12, 1987.
Virginia Quarterly Review, winter, 1969; winter, 1971.
Washington Post, May 19, 1971; April 19, 1973; March 31, 1987.
Washington Post Book World, November 11, 1973; May 4, 1994, p. C1.
Women's Review of Books, December, 1984.
World Literature Today, winter, 1985.

BUCHANAN, Edna (Rydzik) 1939(?)-

PERSONAL: Born c. 1939 (one source says c. 1946), near Paterson, NJ; daughter of a factory worker/tavern operator and a respiratory therapist; married Jim Buchanan (a reporter) (divorced, 1965); married Emmett Miller (a police officer) (divorced). *Education:* Attended creative writing classes at Montclair State Teachers College.

ADDRESSES: Home—Miami, FL. *Office—Miami Herald,* One Herald Plaza, P.O. Box 615, Miami, FL 33152. *Agent*—Michael Congdon, Don Congdon Associates, Suite 625, 156 Fifth Ave., New York, NY 10010.

CAREER: Western Electric Co., Paterson, NJ, switchboard wirer; affiliated with *Daily Sun,* Miami, FL; *Miami Herald,* Miami, general assignment and criminal court reporter, 1970-73, police beat reporter, 1973—.

MEMBER: Miami Sherlock Holmes Club.

AWARDS, HONORS: Awards from American Bar Association, National Newspaper Association, and Florida Society of Newspapers, all during 1970s; Green Eye Shade Award from Society of Professional Journalists, 1982, for deadline reporting; Pulitzer Prize, 1986, for general reporting; Edgar Award nominee for Best Novel, 1990, for *Nobody Lives Forever,* and 1994, for *Miami, It's Murder.*

WRITINGS:

FICTION

Nobody Lives Forever, Random House (New York City), 1990.
Contents Under Pressure, Hyperion (New York City), 1992.
Miami, It's Murder, Hyperion, 1994.
Suitable for Framing, Hyperion, 1995.

NONFICTION

Carr: Five Years of Rape and Murder; From the Personal Account of Robert Frederick Carr III, Dutton (New York City), 1979.
The Corpse Had a Familiar Face: Covering Miami, America's Hottest Beat, Random House, 1987.
Never Let Them See You Cry: More from Miami, America's Hottest Beat, Random House, 1992.

Contributor of articles to magazines, including *Fame, Family Circle, Cosmopolitan,* and *Rolling Stone.*

ADAPTATIONS: Walt Disney Productions purchased the film rights to *The Corpse Had a Familiar Face: Covering Miami, America's Hottest Beat.*

SIDELIGHTS: Since 1973 Edna Buchanan has covered more than five thousand violent crime cases— most of them murders—as the police beat reporter for the *Miami Herald.* "In Miami," asserted Calvin Trillin in the *New Yorker,* "a few figures are regularly discussed by first name among people they have never actually met. One of them . . . is Edna." Working a beat many journalists dread, Buchanan gained recognition by being a tough but sympathetic reporter—strong enough to coolly sort out factual details in the midst of grisly murder scenes, yet empathetic enough to comfort survivors before asking them questions. "Clearly a feminist heroine," as Anne Rice described her in the *New York Times Book Review,* "[Buchanan] is also an old-fashioned American in many ways. A self-made woman with unabashed ideals and a healthy suspicion of anyone who tries to hide the truth, she is an individual to the core."

As one of the first female crime reporters in Miami, Buchanan initially experienced difficulty with male police officers, who treated her as "some empty-headed blond," Buchanan told Cheryl Lavin in the *Chicago Tribune.* Buchanan soon convinced the officers that she was serious about her work, gradually earning the respect, if not the admiration, of many of the forty-five hundred police officers in the Miami area. "I think now that being a woman can sometimes be an advantage," Buchanan told Lavin. "Some of the macho-type cops prefer whispering secrets into the ear of a woman than of some cigar-smoking male reporter." Buchanan's journalistic work, which garnered her a Pulitzer Prize in 1986, is highlighted by what Trillin called the "classic Edna lead," which generally consists of a simple, factual statement intended to jolt the reader. She related to Trillin that a good lead should cause a typical morning reader to "spit out his coffee, clutch his chest, and say, 'My God, Martha! Did you read this!'" One example often cited comes from a story in which a man was killed in a fast-food chicken restaurant. Buchanan began her article: "Gary Robinson died hungry."

In 1979 Buchanan published her first book, *Carr: Five Years of Rape and Murder; From the Personal Account of Robert Frederick Carr III,* an account of a serial rapist. Robert Carr, an automobile salesman who scored well on intelligence quotient (IQ) tests, left his family in 1971 because he had an uncontrollable desire to rape. He embarked on a five-year journey around the country in search of victims and, through his charismatic personality, often succeeded in gaining the confidence of women he subsequently assaulted. Once arrested, Carr made a full confession to police and later to Buchanan, who then wrote *Carr,* a book some have described as a rare examination of the criminal psyche. About Carr's willingness to talk, Buchanan told *CA:* "In the cases of criminals, their willingness to talk is often because they like to have their stories told. It's sort of an ego trip with them; many of them want to talk about it, and they're really glad somebody's interested. The police just want to know the details of the crime. A reporter is more interested in what made them become what they are and will ask them questions about where they're from and what they think and what they were like when they were children. People in jail get very bored. They love to have somebody to talk to."

In 1987 Buchanan published her memoirs as *The Corpse Had a Familiar Face: Covering Miami, America's Hottest Beat.* The book recounts the stories surrounding several of the thousands of cases Buchanan covered for the *Miami Herald.* Among the many disturbing tales are those of a young, rookie policeman startled by a naked man throwing a severed head at him, and of Arthur McDuffie, a black insurance executive who was killed on his motorcycle in 1980. Buchanan's investigation of McDuffie's death turned up evidence that led to the indictment of five white police officers. The eventual release of the five officers set off race riots that killed eighteen people. Rice asserted that "Buchanan's prose is clean, precise and ultimately irresistible. As a sordid yet exciting world unfolds, we are always aware of Ms. Buchanan's wholesome presence, reassured by her unobtrusive moral overview of the shocking scenes she brings to life." Michele Landsberg wrote in the Toronto *Globe and Mail* that Buchanan "writes about these gory years [of reporting for the *Miami Herald*] in classic detective-story prose, only better: punchy, pared-down, darkly funny, nearly every paragraph ending with a terse zinger that hot-wires your brain."

"The cases that haunt me the most are not necessarily the most gory or gruesome," Buchanan told *CA.* "They're the missing people who are never found, the murder that goes forever unsolved, the unidentified bodies that we never name or return to their families. But, of course, there have been some cases that are unforgettable because they're so bizarre. There was the case of the naked man who threw the severed head at the young police officer. There was the case of Carl Brown, a paranoid high school teacher who suspected that a welding shop had overcharged him for repairs to his bicycle. He went back the next day heavily armed and killed eight people in the welding shop—the owner, the owner's mother, the secretary, the workers—and wounded three others. As he was making his getaway, a passing motorist, who realized what he had done and happened to have a gun in the car, killed him. When the police arrived there were nine dead people and three seriously wounded. That was a pretty terrible case."

Buchanan's first novel, entitled *Nobody Lives Forever,* was published in 1990 and garnered her an Edgar Award nomination. Set in Miami, the novel features characters similar to those described in *The Corpse Had a Familiar Face:* Rick, an alluring police sergeant, Dusty, a sensuous female detective, Jim, an aged and exhausted policeman, and a variety of criminals and victims. Although Margaret Cannon claimed in the Toronto *Globe and Mail* that Buchanan was much better at writing nonfiction than fiction, Eugene Izzi disagreed. In the *Washington Post,* Izzi maintained that "Buchanan states her case flawlessly, sensibly allowing her characters to make the points she wishes to get across, never getting in the way as they make their choices and live with them. There are enough twists and turns here to satisfy the most discriminating readers and enough dark humor to have them laughing aloud, lulled into a false sense of security until Buchanan assaults them with the next barrage of suspense and high excitement."

Contents Under Pressure, Buchanan's 1992 novel, is again set in Miami. The story revolves around the death of a black football star at the hands of the Miami police, allegedly for resisting arrest. This leads eventually to race riots, which Charles Champlin in the *Los Angeles Times Book Review* called "a sensational stretch of narrative writing, with an awful immediacy and power." As Michelle J. Bearden noted in a *Publishers Weekly* interview with Buchanan, *Contents Under Pressure* is "the first in a planned series of thrillers featuring Miami reporter Britt Montero," the Cuban-American heroine of *Contents.* Champlin finds Britt Montero "right in the mode of the new crime heroines," and sees her as the perfect conduit for Buchanan's portrait of Miami "in all its complexities and contrasts of race, wealth and worries." Richard Martins in *Tribune Books* argued that although Buchanan has "a reporter's eye for detail . . . [she] lacks the novelist's ear to create characters who sound like more than sources." Josh Rubins in the *New York Times Book Review* commented that Buchanan "has problems with pacing, with sustaining tone and tension over the course of a novel," but concluded that "the Britt Montero stories are bound to improve with time. Britt herself, and the feverish Miami she inhabits, are already in perfect shape."

Miami, It's Murder, the second Britt Montero novel, revolves around a 22-year-old murder and rape. Britt's prime suspect is gubernatorial candidate Eric Fielding, a young man at the time of the crime. *Booklist* reviewer Wes Lukowsky argued that despite the ending, where Britt encounters the murderer, being "a little hokey," Buchanan has "no trouble translating her experiences on the crime beat into first-rate mystery fiction." Britt Montero returned again in Buchanan's 1995 novel *Suitable for Framing,* for which she received a second Edgar Award nomination. In this novel, after helping young Trish Tierney get work as a reporter, Montero finds herself the suspect in a brutal murder. Wes Lukowsky in *Booklist* called *Suitable for Framing* "a quick and entertaining read," despite the book's "busy, busy plot." A *Publishers Weekly* reviewer argued that *Suitable for Framing* "offers atmosphere and entertainment" but has "neither the polish nor the punch" of *Miami, It's Murder.* A *Kirkus Reviews* reviewer concluded that "even on deadline, Buchanan couldn't write a boring page."

Into her third decade of writing about Miami homicides, Buchanan claimed that, far from becoming emotionally numb or exhausted, she continued to enjoy her job, telling *People:* "I still love it because the police beat is the only one on the paper where you can learn about people. Sex, greed, violence, lust, passion, it's all there. You try to learn what brings out the best in people—and what makes them go berserk."

Buchanan told *CA:* "When I applied for my first newspaper job, the editor asked if I'd ever worked on a newspaper before, if I had studied journalism in school. My heart sank. I thought I had lost my chance. I said, 'No,' and he said, 'Good. Then we won't have to unteach you anything.' I think I learned it the hard way, as I did everything. I worked at a small newspaper for five years, doing a little bit of everything. That was my real education, on-the-job training. And of course I had to be getting paid at the time; I needed a job. I have often felt that maybe I could have done better had I had a college degree or studied journalism. But I guess I've done OK. I was lucky. I just fell into the newspaper career—and fell into Miami, which was the best thing that ever happened to me, because I really love it here. It's the most enduring love affair I've ever had. . . . It's a very captivating place. It feeds creativity; there are a lot of good writers down here, and it's a wonderful place to be a writer. I've lived here now for more than twenty-five years, and yet it still excites me to see banana trees growing in my backyard and palm trees outlined against the sky and the water."

BIOGRAPHICAL/CRITICAL SOURCES:

PERIODICALS

Belles Lettres, winter, 1992, p. 58.
Booklist, December 1, 1993, p. 659; January 15, 1995, p. 868.
Chicago Tribune, October 16, 1987; December 27, 1987.
Globe and Mail (Toronto), October 31, 1987; December 5, 1987; March 3, 1990.
Kirkus Reviews, December 1, 1994, p. 1574.
Library Journal, March 1, 1994, p. 123.
Los Angeles Times, December 4, 1987.
Los Angeles Times Book Review, February 17, 1987; September 20, 1992, p. 8; February 12, 1995, p. 4.
New Yorker, February 17, 1986.
New York Times Book Review, December 13, 1987; October 18, 1992, p. 38; February 19, 1995.
Observer (London), August 29, 1993, p. 51.
People, January 18, 1988.
Publishers Weekly, November 13, 1987; September 28, 1992, p. 54; December 19, 1994; January 16, 1995. p. 440.
Time, September 28, 1987.
Times Literary Supplement, March 18, 1988.
Tribune Books (Chicago), September 20, 1992, p. 4; February 5, 1995, section 14, p. 7.
Washington Post, November 8, 1987; December 10, 1987; February 15, 1990; March 3, 1992, p. B2.

*   *   *

BUCKERIDGE, Anthony (Malcolm) 1912-

PERSONAL: Born June 20, 1912, in London, England; son of Ernest George (a bank official) and Gertrud (Smith) Buckeridge; married Sylvia Brown (marriage ended); married Eileen Selby, October, 1962; children: Sally, Timothy, Corin. *Education:* Attended Seaford College, Sussex; University College, London, 1933-35. *Politics:* Liberal. *Religion:* Church of England.

ADDRESSES: Home—East Crink, Barcome Mills, Lewes, Sussex, England.

CAREER: Schoolmaster at boys' preparatory schools in England, with last teaching post at St. Lawrence College, Ramsgate, Kent, 1945-50; writer of series of radio plays, *Jennings at School,* produced by British Broadcasting Corp., 1948-74. *Wartime service:* National Fire Service, 1939-45.

MEMBER: Society of Authors, Writers Guild of Great Britain, British Actors' Equity Association.

AWARDS, HONORS: Jennings at School was once voted the most popular program of the year by radio listeners in England.

WRITINGS:

"JENNINGS" SERIES

Jennings Goes to School, Collins (London), 1950.
Jennings Follows a Clue, Collins, 1951.
Jennings' Little Hut, Collins, 1951.
Jennings and Darbishire, Collins, 1952.
Jennings' Diary, Collins, 1953.
According to Jennings, Collins, 1954.
Our Friend Jennings, Collins, 1955, Penguin (New York City), 1967.
Thanks to Jennings, Collins, 1957.
Take Jennings, for Instance, Collins, 1958.
Jennings as Usual, Collins, 1959.
The Trouble with Jennings, Collins, 1960.
Just Like Jennings, Collins, 1961.
Leave It to Jennings, Collins, 1963.
Jennings, of Course!, Collins, 1964.
Especially Jennings!, Collins, 1965.
A Bookful of Jennings, Collins, 1966, revised edition published as *The Best of Jennings,* 1972.
Jennings Abounding, Collins, 1966, published as *Jennings Unlimited,* Macmillan (London), 1993.
Jennings in Particular, Collins, 1968.
Trust Jennings!, Collins, 1969.
The Jennings Report, Collins, 1970.
Typically Jennings, Collins, 1971.
Speaking of Jennings, Collins, 1973.
Jennings at Large, Armada (London), 1977.

Jennings Again!, illustrated by Rodney Sutton, Macmillan, 1991.
That's Jennings!, Macmillan, 1994.

The "Jennings" books have been translated into twelve languages, including German, French, Norwegian, Dutch, Danish, Swedish, and Hebrew.

"REX MILLIGAN" SERIES

Rex Milligan's Busy Term, Lutterworth (London), 1953.
Rex Milligan Raises the Roof, Lutterworth, 1955.
Rex Milligan Holds Forth, Lutterworth, 1955.
Rex Milligan Reporting, Lutterworth, 1961.

PLAYS

Jennings at School (radio series), BBC Children's Hour, 1948-74.
Draw the Line Somewhere, first produced in Ramsgate, Kent, England, 1948.
Happy Christmas, Jennings, first produced in Lewes, Sussex, England, 1969.
Jennings Abounding! (music by Hector Cortes and William Gomez, first produced in Lewes, 1978), Samuel French (New York City), 1980.
It Happened in Hamelin, music by Corin Buckeridge, first produced in Lewes, 1980.
The Cardboard Conspiracy, music by Corin Buckeridge, first produced in Edinburgh, Scotland, 1985.
Scaling the Cock, first produced in Chichester, England, 1986.

Also author of radio plays *A Funny Thing Happened!*, 1953, and *Liz*, 1974. Author of radio serial scripts for the BBC program *Fourth Dimension*.

OTHER

A Funny Thing Happened, Lutterworth, 1953.
Rex Milligan (television series), BBC-TV, 1954-55.
(Editor) *Stories for Boys*, Faber (London), 1956.
(Editor) *In and Out of School*, British Book Service, 1958.
(Editor) *Stories for Boys 2*, Faber, 1965.
Jennings (television series), BBC-TV, 1958, 1966.

Contributor to *Stirring Stories for Boys*, edited by Eric Duthie, Odhams, 1966.

SIDELIGHTS: Anthony Buckeridge has gained a worldwide following as the creator of the popular schoolboy hero J. C. T. Jennings, a character who has appeared in books, plays, on radio, and on television in England and other countries for more than four decades. Jennings, an eleven-year-old British boarding school student, is based on Buckeridge's experiences as a teacher and schoolmaster in England. To entertain his young pupils, he would make up comical stories about Jennings and his friends' misadventures at Linbury Court Preparatory School. It wasn't until some time later that Jennings was first introduced to the world on the BBC *Children's Hour*. Two years later, in 1950, the first Jennings book was published, and Buckeridge has been writing stories about him ever since.

"The trouble with Jennings," Buckeridge once explained, "is the way he ticks—not out loud of course, except when he is being a space rocket in orbit. It is rather that he has his own peculiar way of doing things. Simple matters become complicated to the point of chaos whenever he takes command. The humor of the Jennings stories is based upon the logical absurdities of all small boys. As an ex-schoolmaster, I enjoy writing humor set against a background with which I am familiar. If I had been an undertaker instead of a teacher, I would write funny stories about funerals!"

In a 1986 article covering several of the Jennings titles, *Times Literary Supplement* reviewer Alan Jenkins describes Buckeridge's famous character as "a natural leader, honest, truthful, loyal, respectful towards his elders; his preoccupations, with sport and tuck, and his lack of academic zeal, are presented benignly and shared by all his pre-pubescent tribe. The trouble he attracts is consequent on well-meaning misreadings of the world and irrepressible high spirits." With such an appealing character as Jennings, plot becomes secondary in Buckeridge's books. Each book is more a collection of episodes in which Jennings and his friend Darbishire get into various sorts of trouble—often with their stuffy headmaster, Mr. Pemberton-Oakes—than a fully-plotted story.

What has surprised some literary experts is not that the Jennings stories were popular three or four decades ago, but that they are still enormously popular today, not only in England but throughout Europe. The type of prep school that Jennings attends, in which students must adhere to a strict code of rules, is a thing of the past in England today. Such a school was never a cultural institution in continental Europe and Scandinavia, where the books are also popular, yet children have discovered hilarity in both the old and newer publications. Even when, after publishing

Jennings at Large, Buckeridge put aside his lovable schoolboy for fourteen years, the next Jennings adventure—1991's *Jennings Again!*—proved just as popular as ever. In a review of the new book, a *Junior Bookshelf* contributor remarks, "Nothing lasts forever, yet some characters seem to defy the truism. One such is Jennings. . . . The hilarity of old still pervades this full-length novel."

Speaking of his character's popularity throughout the world, Buckeridge once stated: "Jennings is essentially an English-sounding name and for this reason some European translators have adopted instead a name that comes more readily to the lips of their readers. In Germany, Jennings is known as Fredy, in Norway, where he is also the hero of several films, he is called Stompa. In France, they call him Bennett. Thus it seems that, as well as being popular in their own country, Jennings and his friends at Linbury Court have completely won the affection of boys and girls in countries where boarding schools are unknown and school uniforms are unheard of!"

BIOGRAPHICAL/CRITICAL SOURCES:

BOOKS

Fisher, Margery, *Intent upon Reading,* Brockhampton Press, 1961.
Townsend, John Rowe, *Written for Children,* Garnet Miller, 1965.
Trease, Geoffrey, *Tales Out of School,* Oxford University Press (New York City), 1948.
Twentieth-Century Children's Writers, 4th edition, St. James Press (Detroit), 1995.

PERIODICALS

Junior Bookshelf, December, 1991, p. 258.
Publishers Weekly, May 29, 1967, p. 66.
Times Educational Supplement, February 22, 1980, p. 29.
Times Literary Supplement, May 25, 1967, p. 443; December 3, 1971, p. 1512; April 11, 1986, p. 385.

*   *   *

BULLOUGH, Vern (LeRoy) 1928-

PERSONAL: Born July 24, 1928, in Salt Lake City, UT; son of David Vernon (a tool and die maker) and Augusta (Rueckert) Bullough; married Bonnie Uckerman (a nurse and teacher), August 2, 1947; children: David (deceased), James, Steven, Susan, Robert, Michael. *Education:* University of Utah, B.A., 1951; University of Chicago, M.A., 1951, Ph.D., 1954; California State University, Long Beach, R.N., 1980.

ADDRESSES: Home and office—17434 Mayall St., Northridge, CA 91325.

CAREER: Salt Lake Tribune-Telegram, Salt Lake City, UT, summer employee, 1945; employed with *Desert News,* Salt Lake City, 1948-51; Youngstown University, Youngstown, OH, associate professor of history, 1954-59; California State University, Northridge, 1959-80, began as assistant professor, became professor of history; State University of New York College at Buffalo, dean of natural and social sciences, 1980-90, distinguished professor, 1987-93; distinguished professor emeritus, 1993—. Morris Fishbein Lecturer, University of Chicago, 1970; Beaumont Lecturer, University of Vermont, 1975; guest lecturer at numerous universities, 1979—, including California College of Medicine, Los Angeles; School of Public Health, University of California, Los Angeles; and University of Southern California; adjunct professor of nursing and history, State University of New York at Buffalo; invited lecturer to China, Netherlands, Germany, Norway, Egypt, Greece, Italy, Spain, France, England, Canada, and most of the United States. Member of southern California board, American Civil Liberties Union, 1965-80; boardmember of Los Angeles Building Commission, 1975-78; member of Housing Opportunities Made Equal, 1981-87; president of International Humanist and Ethical Union, 1995—. *Military service:* U.S. Army, Army Security Agency, 1946-48.

MEMBER: International Society for Comparative Study of Civilizations, American Historical Association, American Association for Advancement of Science, American Association for History of Medicine, American Association for History of Nursing, American Nurses Association, Mediaeval Academy, Renaissance Society, History of Technology Society, Society for Study of Social Problems, History of Science Society, Society for the Scientific Study of Sex (fellow, 1981; president, 1981-83).

AWARDS, HONORS: Named outstanding professor, California State Universities and Colleges, 1969;

President's Award, California State University, 1978; Distinguished Humanist Award, 1979; Founders Award, Center for Sex Research, 1980; laureate, Humanist Academy, 1984; Garrison Lecturer, American Association for History of Medicine, 1988; Distinguished Scientific Award, Society for Scientific Study of Sex, 1990; Distinguished Humanist Award, International Humanist and Ethical Union, 1993; Kinsey Award, 1995; Newberry fellowship; Huntington Library fellowship; Fulbright exchange scholar; recipient of grants from American Philosophical Society, National Science Foundation, Rockefeller Foundation, American Council of Learned Societies, U.S. Department of Education, and Erickson Educational Foundation.

WRITINGS:

The History of Prostitution, University Books (Secaucus, NJ), 1964.

The Development of Medicine as a Profession: The Contribution of the Medieval University to Modern Medicine, S. Karger (New York City), 1966.

Man in Western Civilization, Holt (New York City), 1970.

The Scientific Revolution, Holt, 1970.

(With Raoul Naroll and Frada Naroll) *Military Deterrence in History: A Statistical Survey,* State University of New York Press (Albany), 1971.

Sex, Society, and History, Neale Watson (New York City), 1976.

Sexual Variance in Society and History, Wiley (New York City), 1976.

(With others) *Annotated Bibliography of Homosexuality,* Garland (New York City), 1977.

(With Barett Elcano) *Bibliography of Prostitution,* Garland, 1978.

Homosexuality: A History, New American Library (New York City), 1979.

(Editor) *The Frontiers of Sex Research,* Prometheus (Buffalo, NY), 1979.

(With James Brundage) *Sexual Practice and the Medieval Church,* Prometheus, 1982.

(With Olga Church and Alice Stein) *American Nursing: A Biographical Dictionary,* Garland, 1988.

(With Brenda Shelton and Sarah Slavin) *Subordinated Sex,* University of Georgia Press (Athens), 1988.

The Society for the Scientific Study of Sex: A Brief History, FSS Sexuality, 1989.

(With Lilli Sentz and Alice Stein) *American Nursing, A Biographical Dictionary,* Volume 2, Garland, 1992.

(With Sentz) *Prostitution: A Guide to Sources,* Garland, 1992.

(With Sarah Freeman) *A Guide to Fertility,* Prometheus, 1993.

(With Tim Madigan) *Toward a New Enlightenment: The Philosophy of Paul Kurtz,* Transaction (New Brunswick, NJ), 1993.

Science in the Bedroom, Basic (New York City), 1994.

(With James Brundage) *Handbook of Medieval Sexuality,* Garland, 1995.

WITH WIFE, BONNIE BULLOUGH

What Color Are Your Germs? (pamphlet), Committee to End Discrimination in Chicago Medical Institutions, 1954.

The Emergence of Modern Nursing, Macmillan (New York City), 1964, 2nd edition, 1969.

(Editors) *Issues in Nursing,* Springer (New York City), 1966.

(Editors) *New Directions for Nurses,* Springer, 1971.

Poverty, Ethnic Identity, and Health Care, Appleton-Century-Crofts (East Norwalk, CT), 1972.

The Subordinate Sex: A History of Attitudes toward Women, University of Illinois Press (Champaign), 1973.

Sin, Sickness, and Sanity: A History of Sexual Attitudes, New American Library, 1977.

(Editors) *Expanding Horizons in Nursing,* Springer, 1977.

Prostitution: An Illustrated Social History, Crown (New York City), 1978.

The Care of the Sick, Neale Watson, 1978.

Nursing: An Historical Bibliography, Garland, 1981.

Health Care for the Other Americans, Appleton-Century-Crofts, 1982.

(Editors with Mary Claire Soukup) *Nursing Issues and Strategies for the Eighties,* Springer, 1983.

History and Politics of Nursing, Appleton-Century-Crofts, 1984.

(Coeditors with Jane Garvey and Karen Miller Allen) *Issues Nursing,* Garland, 1985.

Prostitution and Society, Prometheus, 1987.

Nursing in the Community, Mosby (St. Louis, MO), 1990.

Contraception: A Guide to Modern Methods of Birth Control, Prometheus, 1990.

(With Marietta Stanton) *Nightengale and Her Era,* Garland, 1990.

Cross-Dressing, Sex, and Gender, University of Pennsylvania Press (Philadelphia), 1993.

American Sexuality: An Encyclopedia, Garland, 1994.

Nursing Issues and Nursing Strategies for the 90's, Springer, 1995.

Sexual Attitudes: Myths and Realities, Prometheus, 1995.

Gender and Transgender: Issues and Challenges to Traditional Concepts, Prometheus, in press.

OTHER

Editor of approximately twenty volumes in "Human Sexuality" series for Prometheus. Contributor of chapters to over sixty books. Also contributor of over three hundred articles to a variety of journals and magazines. Associate editor of *American Journal of Professional Nursing,* 1993-95; senior editor of *Free Inquiry.*

Some of Bullough's works have been translated into Italian, Japanese, Chinese, and Russian.

WORK IN PROGRESS: How I Got Into Sex, with William Hartman and Marilyn Fithian; *Intellectual and Creative Achievement: The Myth of IQ.*

SIDELIGHTS: Vern Bullough told *CA:* "I was always interested in writing but my first published experience came in high school, first on the school newspaper and then as a stringer for a local newspaper in Salt Lake City. Based on my work as a high-school correspondent, I was hired by the *Salt Lake Tribune-Telegram* as a summer employee in 1945 (World War II was still on and I was too young for the draft). After returning from the army, I went to work for the *Desert News* in Salt Lake City, holding various part-time jobs as I finished my degree at the University of Utah. After moving to Chicago for graduate school, I did freelance work and helped ghost-write some books for professors and for a Chicago publisher. Once I received my Ph.D, I continued to write, both in professional journals and in more popular ones, with increasing success. My first book was published in 1964 . . . and since that time I have always had a book or books under way or under contract, sometimes as sole author, but mostly with my wife, Bonnie, as coauthor or coeditor. Occasionally I have collaborated with others. All the time I continued to do freelance and published in a variety of journals. I also began doing book reviews in large numbers and continue to do so. I regard this last as a way to continually keep broadening my knowledge base since I review in a variety of fields."

BURFORD, E(phraim) J(ohn)   1905-

PERSONAL: Born July 15, 1905, in London, England; married Anne de Bruss. *Education:* Attended schools in London, England. *Politics:* Liberal. *Religion:* Agnostic.

ADDRESSES: Home—111 Addison House, Grove End Rd., London NW8 9EJ, England.

CAREER: Democrat/Die Demokraat, Johannesburg, South Africa, joint editor, c. 1946-49; commerce director of a London, England, export house, 1949-70; historical writer, 1970—.

WRITINGS:

The Queen of the Bawds: The Story of Donna Britannica Hollandia (biography), Neville Spearman (Essex, England), 1973.

The Orrible Synne: A Look at London Lechery, Calder & Boyars (London), 1973.

A History of the Clink: England's Oldest Prison, New England Library (London), 1975.

Bawds and Lodgings: The Bishop's Bankside Brothels, Peter Owen (London), 1976, expanded edition published as *The Bishop's Brothels,* Robert Hale (London), 1993.

(Editor) *A Pleasant Collection of Bawdy Ballads,* Penguin (Middlesex, England), 1982, reprinted as *Bawdy Verse: A Pleasant Collection,* 1982.

Wits, Wenchers, and Wantons: London's Low Life; Covent Garden in the Eighteenth Century, Robert Hale, 1986.

Royal St. James: Kings Clubmen and Courtezans, Robert Hale, 1990.

London: The Synfulle Citie, Robert Hale, 1990.

(With Sandra Shulman) *From Bridles to Burnings: A Social History of Female Punishments,* Robert Hale, 1992.

(With Joy Wotton) *Private Vices, Public Virtues,* Robert Hale, 1995.

Also author of unpublished books "A History of London Bridge," "A Book of Bawdy Ballads (from Middle Ages to 1800)," and "A Bibliography of Georgian Rakes and Courtezans."

WORK IN PROGRESS: An unbiased study of homosexuality.

SIDELIGHTS: E. J. Burford once told *CA:* "My particular interests are ancient history and archaeology, and the history of social and sexual mores in

London. I have traveled extensively all over Europe, including the eastern bloc. Because of my interest in philology and languages I speak French, German, Afrikaans, and Spanish, as well as some Russian. I have also traveled throughout eastern and central Africa, having lived in South Africa for almost twenty years.

"I write of those aspects of London's history that most other historians tend to ignore. They believe that politics, economics, and, above all, the successions of kings and queens are more important than chronicling the lives and sufferings of the poor, indigent, and especially that mass of womenfolk compelled to sell their bodies for bread. By writing about prostitutes I try to expose the villainies of the groups who make profit from the degradation of these women and show that such activities have existed from ancient times. My books should serve as weapons in the hands of all who seek true emancipation of womankind."

BIOGRAPHICAL/CRITICAL SOURCES:

PERIODICALS

Spectator, October 27, 1973.

* * *

BURNS, Robert I(gnatius)   1921-

PERSONAL: Born August 16, 1921, in San Francisco, CA; son of Harry (a railroad engineer) and Viola (Whearty) Burns. *Education:* Attended University of San Francisco, 1939-40, and University of Santa Clara; Gonzaga University, B.A. (with honors), 1945, M.A. (philosophy) and Phil.Lic., 1947; Fordham University, M.A. (history), 1949; Jesuit Faculty of Theology, S.Th.B. and S.Th.Lic., 1953; graduate study at Villa Machiavelli, Florence, Italy, 1953-54, Gregorian University, Rome, Italy, 1954-55, and Campion Hall, Oxford, 1955-56; Johns Hopkins University, Ph.D. (with honors), 1958; University of Fribourg, Doc. es Sc. Hist. (double summa cum laude), 1961.

ADDRESSES: Home—Xavier Hall, 7101 West 80th St., Los Angeles, CA 90045. *Office*—Department of History, Graduate School, University of California, Los Angeles, CA 90024.

CAREER: Entered Society of Jesus (Jesuits), 1940, ordained Roman Catholic priest, 1952. Jesuit Historical Archives, Spokane, WA, assistant archivist, 1946-47; University of San Francisco, San Francisco, CA, instructor, 1947-48, assistant professor, 1958-63, associate professor, 1963-66, professor of history, 1967-76; University of California, Los Angeles, senior professor of history, 1976—, member of staff of Near Eastern Center and of Center for Medieval and Renaissance Studies, 1977—. Visiting professor of history at College of Notre Dame, Belmont, CA, 1963—; visiting James Chair Professor, Brown University, 1970; member of faculty, Institute for Advanced Study, Princeton University, 1972; visiting lecturer at universities in United States, Italy, Spain, Germany, Israel, and Canada. Director, Institute of Medieval Mediterranean Spain, 1976—; member of executive committee, Hill Monastic Library, 1977-81; member of committee, California State Legislature's "Joint Quinquennial Committee" for Columbus Quinquennial, 1990-93. Member of international advisory board of American Bibliographical Center, 1982-90, University of California Press, 1985—, and Patronato Nacional del "Misteri de Elche" [government of Spain], 1986—. Served briefly as civilian relief chaplain to U.S. Air Force near Casablanca and in pastoral work during study periods in England and Italy. Has conducted research in Europe, Near East, and North Africa.

MEMBER: North American Catalan Society (member of board of directors, 1978—), Medieval Academy of America (elected fellow, 1978; Scribe, 1987-89), American Historical Association (Pacific Coast branch vice president, 1978; president, 1979-80), American Society of Church History (Pacific Coast branch vice president, 1962), American Catholic Historical Association (life member; vice president, 1974; president, 1975), Society for Spanish and Portuguese Historical Studies, Academy of Research Historians on Medieval Spain (president, 1976-78), Conference on Peace Research in History, Medieval Association of the Pacific.

AWARDS, HONORS: Guggenheim fellowship to Spain, 1963-64; Pierre Charles Award of Mission Institute, 1966; John Gilmary Shea Prize from American Catholic Historical Society, 1966, for *The Jesuits and the Indian Wars of the Northwest,* and 1968, for *The Crusader Kingdom of Valencia: Reconstruction on a Thirteenth-Century Frontier;* American Association for State and Local History award, 1967; Pacific Coast Branch of American Historical Association award, 1968, for *The Crusader*

Kingdom of Valencia: Reconstruction on a Thirteenth-Century Frontier; National Endowment for the Humanities fellowships, 1971, 1973-82; American Council of Learned Societies fellowship, 1972; Catholic Press Association of the United States and Canada book award, 1975, for *Islam under the Crusaders: Colonial Survival in the Thirteenth-Century Kingdom of Valencia;* Phi Alpha Theta book award, 1976, for *Medieval Colonialism: Postcrusade Exploitation of Islamic Valencia;* Haskins Gold Medal from Medieval Academy of America, 1976; Medieval Academy of America elected fellow, 1978; Accio Cultural del Pais Valencia, 1979; Premi de la Critica "Serra d'Or," 1982; Premi Catalonia from Institut d'Estudis Catalans, 1982; Hispanic Society of America elected fellow, 1985; Celtic Foundation award, 1985; Creu de Sant Jordi (Cross of St. George), 1989; grants from the Ford Foundation, Guggenheim Foundation, and Robb Foundation; D.Litt. from Gonzaga University, 1968, Marquette University, 1977, Loyola University of Chicago, 1978, Boston College, 1982, Georgetown University, 1982, University of San Francisco, 1983, Fordham University, 1984, and Universidad de Valencia, Spain, 1985.

WRITINGS:

The Jesuits and the Indian Wars of the Northwest, Yale University Press (New Haven, CT), 1966.

The Crusader Kingdom of Valencia: Reconstruction on a Thirteenth-Century Frontier, two volumes, Harvard University Press (Cambridge, MA), 1967.

Islam under the Crusaders: Colonial Survival in the Thirteenth-Century Kingdom of Valencia, Princeton University Press (Princeton, NJ), 1974.

Medieval Colonialism: Postcrusade Exploitation of Islamic Valencia, Princeton University Press, 1975.

(Coauthor) *Islam and Cultural Change in the Middle Ages,* University of California Press (Berkeley), 1975.

(Coauthor) *Contributions to Mediterranean Studies,* Royal University of Malta Press, 1977.

Moors and Crusaders in Mediterranean Spain, Variorum Reprints (London), 1978.

(Coauthor) *Islamic Middle Ages, 700-1900,* Darwin Press (Princeton, NJ), 1981.

Jaume I i els Valencians del segle XIII, [Valencia], 1981.

Muslims, Christians, and Jews in the Crusader Kingdom of Valencia: Societies in Symbiosis (essays), Cambridge University Press (New York City), 1984, 2nd edition, 1986.

Diplomatarium Regni Valentiae, Princeton University Press, Volume 1: *Society and Documentation in Crusader Valencia,* 1985; Volume 2: *Foundations of Crusader Valencia,* 1991.

(Editor) *The Worlds of Alfonso the Learned and James the Conqueror: Intellect and Force in the Middle Ages,* Princeton University Press, 1985.

(Editor) *Alfonso X the Learned: Emperor of Culture,* Fordham University Press (Bronx, NY), 1985.

Jewish Communities in the Notarial Culture: Latinate Jewish Wills in the Realms of Arago-Catalonia 1250-1350, University of California Press, 1996.

Contributor to books, including *I Lift My Lamp,* Newman Press, 1955. Also associate editor of *Encyclopedia of Iberia in the Middle Ages,* Garland Publishing. Contributor of more than one hundred articles on Spain to encyclopedias; also contributor to proceedings of international historical congresses. Contributor of about seventy articles to periodicals and history journals, including *Speculum, Mid-America, Anuario de estudios medievales,* and *American Historical Review.* Regular abstracter for *Historical Abstracts* and *America: History and Life.* Coeditor, *Viator,* 1980-90; member of board of editors, *Trends in History,* 1978—, *Anuario de Estudios Medievales* (Spain), 1985—, and *Bulletin of the Society of Cantigueiros,* 1986—.

Many of Burns' works have been translated into Spanish and Catalan. The library of the University of California, Los Angeles, maintains a permanent deposit for Burns' manuscript drafts and correspondence in its special collection.

WORK IN PROGRESS: Four additional volumes of *Diplomatarium Regni Valentiae* and six volumes of *Regnante Jacobo I Ejus Conquistatoris,* both for Princeton University Press; *Siete partidas,* University of Pennsylvania Press; *Bilingual Treatises in Muslim-Crusader Spain under James the Conqueror.*

SIDELIGHTS: Historian Robert I. Burns reads Italian, French, German, Spanish, Catalan, Latin, and Greek.

BIOGRAPHICAL/CRITICAL SOURCES:

BOOKS

Simon, Larry, et al., editor, *Iberia and the Mediterranean World of the Middle Ages: Studies in Honor of Robert I. Burns,* E. J. Brill (New York City), Volume 1, 1995, Volume 2, 1996.

PERIODICALS

Catholic Historical Review, October, 1990, p. 828.
English Historical Review, February, 1994, p. 143.
Hispanic American Historical Review, May, 1991, p. 385.
Times Literary Supplement, December 1, 1966; January 17, 1975; April 4, 1986; July 18, 1986.

*   *   *

BURROUGHS, William S(eward) 1914-
(William Lee, Willy Lee)

PERSONAL: Born February 5, 1914, in St. Louis, MO; son of Mortimer P. (a businessperson) and Laura (Lee) Burroughs; married Ilse Herzfeld Klapper, 1937 (divorced, 1946); married Joan Vollmer, January 17, 1946 (died September 7, 1951, of an accidental gunshot wound); children: (second marriage) William Seward, Jr. (died March 3, 1981). *Education:* Harvard University, A.B., 1936, graduate study, 1938; attended University of Vienna, 1937, and Mexico City College, 1949-50.

ADDRESSES: Office—William S. Burroughs Communications, P.O. Box 147, Lawrence, KS 66044.

CAREER: Writer. Advertising copywriter in New York City, early 1940s; has also worked as bartender, exterminator, and private detective. Has given lectures and readings across the United States. Appeared in film *Drugstore Cowboy,* Avenue Pictures, 1989. *Military service:* U.S. Army, 1942.

AWARDS, HONORS: National Institute of Arts and Letters and American Academy, award in literature, 1975, named member, 1983; the Nova Convention, a four-day arts festival held in New York City in 1978, and the Final Academy, held in London in 1982, were organized as tributes to Burroughs.

WRITINGS:

NOVELS

(Under pseudonym William Lee) *Junkie: Confessions of an Unredeemed Drug Addict* (bound with *Narcotic Agent* by Maurice Helbrant), Ace Books (New York City), 1953, published separately under name William S. Burroughs, 1964, unexpurgated edition published as *Junky,* Penguin (New York City), 1977.
The Naked Lunch (also see below), Olympia Press (Paris), 1959, published as *Naked Lunch,* Grove (New York City), 1962.
The Soft Machine (also see below), Olympia Press, 1961, revised edition, Grove, 1966.
The Ticket That Exploded (also see below), Olympia Press, 1962, revised edition, Grove, 1967.
Dead Fingers Talk (contains excerpts from *Naked Lunch, The Soft Machine,* and *The Ticket That Exploded*), Calder/Olympia Press, 1963.
Nova Express (also see below), Grove, 1964.
The Wild Boys: A Book of the Dead (also see below), Grove, 1971, revised edition, Calder, 1979.
Exterminator!, Viking/Seaver (New York City), 1973.
Port of Saints, Convent Garden Press (London), 1975, Blue Wind Press, 1979.
Short Novels, Calder, 1978.
Blade Runner: A Movie, Blue Wind Press, 1979.
The Soft Machine, Nova Express [and] *The Wild Boys,* Grove, 1980.
Cities of the Red Night, Holt (New York City), 1981.
The Place of Dead Roads, Holt, 1984.
Queer, Viking (New York City), 1986.
The Western Lands, Viking, 1987.
Interzone, edited by James Grauerholz, Viking, 1989.

Also author, with Jack Kerouac, of unpublished novel *And the Hippos Were Boiled in Their Tanks.*

OTHER

(With Brion Gysin) *The Exterminator,* Auerhaun Press (San Francisco), 1960.
(With Gysin, Sinclair Beiles, and Gregory Corso) *Minutes to Go* (poems), Two Cities Editions (Paris), 1960, Beach Books, 1968.
(With Allen Ginsberg) *The Yage Letters,* City Lights (San Francisco), 1963.
Takis (exhibition catalog), [New York], 1963.
(Under pseudonym Willy Lee) *Roosevelt after Inauguration,* F——— You Press, 1964, published as *Roosevelt after Inauguration and Other Atrocities,* City Lights, 1979.
Valentine's Day Reading, American Theatre for Poets, 1965.
The White Subway (also see below), Aloes Books, 1965.
Health Bulletin: APO:33: A Metabolic Regulator, F——— You Press, 1965, published as *APO:33: A Report on the Synthesis of the Apomorphine Formula,* Beach Books, 1966.

(With Lee Harwood) *Darayt,* Lovebooks, 1965.

Time (poems), "C" Press, 1965.

(With Claude Pelieu and Carl Weissner) *So Who Owns Death TV?,* Beach Book Texts and Documents, 1967.

They Do Not Always Remember, Delacorte, 1968.

(Author of preface) Jeff Nuttall, *Pig,* Fulcrum Press, 1969.

Ali's Smile, Unicorn Books, 1969.

The Dead Star, Nova Broadcast Press, 1969.

Entretiens avec William Burroughs, Editions Pierre Belfond (Paris), 1969, translation published as *The Job: Interviews with William S. Burroughs,* Grove, 1970, new edition, 1974.

(With Weissner) *The Braille Film,* Nova Broadcast Press, 1970.

(With Gysin) *Third Mind,* Grove, 1970.

The Last Words of Dutch Schultz: A Fiction in the Form of a Film Script, Cape Goliard Press, 1970, Viking/Seaver, 1975.

(With Pelieu) *Jack Kerouac* (in French), L'Herne (Paris), 1971.

Electronic Revolution (also see below), Blackmoor Head Press, 1971.

(With Gysin and Ian Somerville) *Brion Gysin Let the Mice In,* Something Else Press, 1973.

Mayfair Academy Series More or Less, Urgency Press Rip-Off, 1973.

The Book of Breathing (also see below), OU Press (Ingatestone, England), 1974, Blue Wind Press, 1975, 2nd edition, 1980.

(With Charles Gatewood) *Sidetripping,* Strawberry Hill, 1975.

(With Eric Mottram) *Snack: Two Tape Transcripts,* Aloes Books, 1975.

Cobblestone Gardens (also see below), Cherry Valley, 1976.

The Retreat Diaries (also see below), City Moon, 1976.

(Author of text) *23 Skidoo,* first produced in New York City at the Washington Square Methodist Church, April, 1978.

Naked Scientology, Expanded Media Editions (Bonn), 1978.

Doctor Benway: A Variant Passage from "The Naked Lunch," Bradford Morrow, 1979.

Ah Pook Is Here and Other Texts: The Book of Breathing, Electronic Revolution, Calder, 1979.

Early Routines, Cadmus Editions, 1981.

Letters to Allen Ginsberg, 1953-1957, Full Court Press, 1981.

A William Burroughs Reader, Pan Books, 1982.

The Burroughs File (includes *The White Subway, Cobblestone Gardens,* and *The Retreat Diaries*), City Lights, 1984.

The Adding Machine: Collected Essays, Calder, 1985.

(With Keith Haring) *Apocalypse* (catalogue), George Mulder Fine Arts (New York City), 1988.

Tornado Alley, Cherry Valley Editions (Cherry Valley, NY), 1988.

William S. Burroughs: Paintings, Galerie Carzaniga + Ueker (Basel), 1989.

William S. Burroughs: Exposition, 23 mars/21 avril 1990, Galerie K. Paris, Le Galerie (Paris), 1990.

Ghost of Chance, illustrated by George Condo, Library Fellows of the Whitney Museum of American Art (New York City), 1991.

The Cat Inside, Viking, 1992.

Everything Is Permitted: The Making of "Naked Lunch," edited by Ira Silverberg, Grove Weidenfeld (New York City), 1992.

The Letters of William S. Burroughs, 1945-1959, edited and with an introduction by Oliver Harris, Viking, 1993.

My Education: A Book of Dreams, Viking, 1995.

Also author, with Pelieu and Weissner, of *Fernseh-Tuberkulose,* 1969, and of films, with Gysin, *Towers Open Fire,* 1963, with Antony Balch, *Bill and Tony,* 1966, and of *The Cut-Ups.* Contributor to books, including *A Casebook on the Beat,* edited by Thomas Parkinson, Crowell, 1961, and *The Final Academy: Statements of a Kind,* edited by Robert Fly, Final Academy, 1982.

RECORDINGS

Call Me Burroughs, English Bookshop, 1965.

William S. Burroughs/John Giorno, Giorno Poetry Systems, 1975.

You're the Man I Want to Share My Money With, Giorno Poetry Systems, 1981.

Nothing Here Now but the Recordings, Industrial Records, 1981.

Dead City Radio, Island, 1990.

(Narrator) *A Thanksgiving Prayer,* Island Records, 1990.

Spare Ass Annie and Other Tales, Island Red Label, 1993.

Also composer of song "Old Lady Sloan," recorded by Mortal Micronotz on the album *The Mortal Micronotz,* Fresh Sounds, 1982. Also contributor to *Revolutions per Minute (The Art Record),* Ronald Feldmann Fine Arts, 1982, and *Life Is a Killer,* Giorno Poetry Systems.

ADAPTATIONS: Burroughs' novel *Naked Lunch* was adapted for a film directed by David Cronenberg, produced by Jeremy Thomas, and released by Twentieth Century-Fox, in 1991.

SIDELIGHTS: A drug addict turned experimental novelist, William S. Burroughs embodies for many observers the artist as outsider and rebel. He has had a tremendous influence as one of the Beat generation of writers, as an avant-garde theorist, and as a counter-culture forerunner. His novel *Junkie: Confessions of an Unredeemed Drug Addict* outlines his life as a morphine addict; *Naked Lunch* successfully overturned America's obscenity laws; his innovative "cut-up" writing technique, his attacks on the control systems enslaving mankind, and his outspoken homosexuality have made him "one of the most controversial and influential writers of the past decades," says Bob Halliday in the *Washington Post Book World.* Henry Allen, writing in the same publication, calls Burroughs "the model of modern man as pariah: eminence grise of the Beat generation, black sheep of the Burroughs adding machine family, junkie, intellectual crank . . . , esoteric novelist . . . , punk saint and grand old man of the seamy underbelly." Robert E. Burkholder admits in the *Dictionary of Literary Biography Yearbook 1981* that Burroughs occupies "a strange cultural position as a major figure of contemporary avant-garde fiction and the so-called Godfather of Punk."

Burroughs comes from a distinguished family. His mother is descended from Civil War leader Robert E. Lee, while his paternal grandfather, for whom Burroughs is named, invented the adding machine and founded the Burroughs Corporation which today manufactures computer equipment. Burroughs has made clear on several occasions that his grandfather sold his share of the company upon retirement and that his family, although of prominent social standing, was not wealthy. He lives entirely on the royalties from his books.

Raised in St. Louis and educated in private schools, Burroughs, Jennie Skerl writes in the *Dictionary of Literary Biography,* was "alienated from a suburban social environment perceived as both boring and hostile. He felt his homosexuality was only part of the reason for his alienation. . . . Timid and solitary, he turned to extensive reading for solace and dreamed of becoming a writer. . . . He early formed a view of the artist as an outlaw and adventurer." In 1936 Burroughs graduated from Harvard University, where he studied English literature. After graduation

he tried his hand at several careers. He attended medical school in Vienna with the hope of becoming a doctor; he studied anthropology at Harvard's graduate school; he served in the U.S. Army for several months before being discharged for psychological reasons (he had deliberately cut off the first joint of a finger to impress a friend); and he worked as an advertising copywriter, exterminator, bartender, and private detective. "Burroughs's own description of his life during the years 1936 to 1944," Skerl recounts, "is one of aimless drifting and boredom."

This aimlessness ended in the mid-1940s when Burroughs was living in New York City. At that time he met several people who were to fundamentally alter the course of his later life. He met and married Joan Vollmer, a widow, in 1946. (Burroughs had previously married a German woman to allow her to legally enter the United States from Nazi Germany. They were divorced in 1946.) Joan introduced him to her friend Jack Kerouac, then a student at Columbia University, who in turn introduced Burroughs to Allen Ginsberg, an aspiring poet.

Ginsberg relates in *Jack's Book: An Oral Biography of Jack Kerouac* that he and Kerouac found Burroughs "so interesting and intelligent and worldly wise that he seemed like some sort of intellectual spiritual man of distinction to us." In the same book, Burroughs recalls their initial meeting: "Joan and I were older, and we had done some more reading than they had at the time. I didn't think anything special about it. I recommended a number of books." Burroughs's apartment soon became a gathering place where the three men, later to form the core of the Beat literary movement, shared and discussed their ideas. In 1944 Burroughs also met Herbert Huncke, a drug addict, thief, and male prostitute who introduced him to morphine. Burroughs soon became an addict himself and was to remain one, despite several attempts at a cure, until 1957.

Kerouac and Ginsberg's efforts to become writers inspired the older Burroughs to turn to fiction writing. He had made an earlier attempt in the 1930s to write detective stories, but that had ended in failure and Burroughs had not written anything since. He began to write seriously only in the 1940s. As Burroughs tells Charles Platt in *Dream Makers, Volume II: The Uncommon Men and Women Who Write Science Fiction,* "I didn't write anything till I was thirty-five." He explains in *Jack's Book* that Kerouac "had suggested that I write and I wasn't too interested for a long time." He and Kerouac collaborated on a novel in the 1940s entitled "And the Hippos Were Boiled in Their Tanks," a title inspired by a radio broadcast about a fire in the St. Louis zoo.

But Burroughs's writing efforts were soon superseded by his troubles with the law. Because of police pressure in New York, brought on by his morphine addiction and resultant association with the underworld, Burroughs was obliged to move to Texas. When police pressure increased there because he was raising marijuana on his farm, Burroughs moved to Louisiana. After a police raid on his home in Louisiana in early 1949, Burroughs and Joan fled to Mexico to avoid drug and illegal weapons charges. The couple found Mexico to their liking. Morphine could be easily obtained by prescription; and benzedrine, which Joan used, was sold over the counter. For a time Burroughs attended Mexico City College, where he studied architecture, Aztec history, and the Mayan codices.

The Burroughs's stay in Mexico was ended in 1951 with the shooting death of Joan Burroughs. For many years after, stories circulated that Burroughs had killed her in cold blood. In 1984, Burroughs finally explained the incident in "Burroughs," a documentary film made about his life. While living in Mexico, he relates, he and his wife had been arguing frequently. Burroughs had been neglecting her for his homosexual companions. At a drinking party with two visiting Army friends, Joan balanced a glass on her head and dared Burroughs to shoot it off in William Tell style. Burroughs's bullet struck her in the forehead and she died instantly. As Dennis McNally writes in *Desolate Angel: Jack Kerouac, the Beat Generation, and America,* Burroughs "was obsessed with handguns, and Joan's death wish was legendary. The month before, Allen [Ginsberg] and Lucien [Carr] had visited . . . , and Allen had been terrified at Lucien's and Joan's suicidal drunken driving. In any case, there was a gun, a .38 revolver. Bill fired it, and it killed Joan." The authorities ruled Joan's death an accident and Burroughs was released without charges. In *Queer,* a novel written shortly after the accident but not published until 1986, Burroughs dealt indirectly with his wife's death. He states in the book's preface that when he reread the manuscript for publication, it had made him feel threatened. It was "painful to an extent I feel it difficult to read, let alone write about. Every word and gesture sets the teeth on edge. The reason for this reluctance becomes clearer as I force myself to look: the book is motivated and formed by an event which is never mentioned, in fact is carefully avoided: the accidental shooting death of my wife."

Some of Burroughs' evolution as a writer can be traced through his letters to Allen Ginsberg and others, published in *Letters to Allen Ginsberg, 1953-1957,* and *The Letters of William S. Burroughs, 1945-1959.* "After the death of Joan by his hand in 1951," explains Scott Vickers in the *Bloomsbury Review,* "Burroughs became convinced that he was, in a most medieval sense, possessed by a demonic entity whom he later named 'the Ugly Spirit.' Henceforth, his life became a battle against invasion, and the only power he could summon against possession became his writing; letter writing in particular seemed to bring up all the unconscious data and supraconscious creativity that were to form the hallucinogenic 'routines' of his novels." "Many letters are first drafts of episodes that would later appear in *Naked Lunch* and the cut-up trilogy that followed," *Washington Post Book World* contributor Steven Moore declares, ". . . and many of the incomprehensible episodes in those works are clarified by the biographical contexts of these letters."

For several years after his wife's death Burroughs travelled, visiting South America, Morocco, and New York City. He finished his first novel, *Junkie: Confessions of an Unredeemed Drug Addict,* in 1951 while living in Morocco. Ginsberg served as his literary agent, placing the manuscript with the New York paperback publisher Ace Books. The book's subject matter caused Ace to publish an edited version, filled with disclaimers, in a double-book format with Maurice Helbrant's novel *Narcotic Agent* in 1953. Burroughs used the pseudonym William Lee, taken from his mother's maiden name, on the book. The complete, unedited manuscript was finally published under his real name and with the original title, *Junky,* by Penguin in 1977.

Junkie is a "luridly hyperbolic, quasi-autobiographical first-person account of the horrors of drug addiction," as Donald Palumbo writes in the *Dictionary of Literary Biography.* Nelson Algren, writing in the *Chicago Tribune Book World* in 1981, finds that *Junkie* was "the first American report on the drug experience and remains the most authentic." In his introduction to the complete edition, Ginsberg cites as *Junkie's* virtues its "intelligent fact, the clear perception, precise bare language, direct syntax & mind pictures—as well as the enormous sociological grasp, culture-revolutionary attitude toward bureaucracy & law, and the stoic cold-humor'd eye on crime."

Junkie tells the story of William Lee, an "unredeemed" drug addict who becomes involved with the underworld and is forced to travel to avoid the law. Essentially plotless, the novel recounts Lee's withdrawals and cures from four drug addictions and ends with him leaving for the jungles of South America in search of the native drug yage, rumored to give its user telepathic powers. Much of *Junkie* is Burroughs's own life fictionalized in a pulp confessional style. Burroughs's journey to South America was in search of yage; he, too, travelled widely to escape the law; and his own drug experiences parallel those of Lee. As McNally relates, *Junkie* "was a generally straightforward description of [Burroughs's] drug life."

Although this first novel is written in a realistic style not found in Burroughs's subsequent books, it introduces many of the concerns later developed in the more experimental works. *"Junkie,"* Skerl explains, "introduces many of Burroughs's continuing themes, characters, images, and settings." Burkholder believes that *Junkie* "is important to an understanding of [Burroughs's] later work. . . . Burroughs's literal description of scenes . . . would eventually be inflated to abstract images, ultimately becoming part of the allegorical war of control in later novels. . . . Later narratives . . . attempt to make the drug experience an archetype for modern man."

Because *Junkie* was a first novel published by a small paperback publisher, it did not receive much critical attention. *Queer,* another book written at this time—concerning a homosexual romance in Mexico City—would not find a publisher until 1986. Burroughs's writing career seemed at a standstill. In 1953 he moved to Tangier, Morocco, where he lived until 1958, writing in seclusion. During this time, Burroughs filled over one thousand pages with fragmentary notes about his travels and drug use and with social satire attacking contemporary society. From these notes came his next four novels: *Naked Lunch, The Soft Machine, The Ticket That Exploded,* and *Nova Express.*

By 1957 Burroughs's drug addiction was severely restricting his ability to function normally. He recalls in an article for *Evergreen Review:* "I lived in one room in the Native Quarter of Tangier. I had not taken a bath in a year nor changed my clothes or

removed them except to stick a needle every hour in the fibrous grey wooden flesh of terminal addiction. . . . I did absolutely nothing. I could look at the end of my shoe for eight hours." When his habit became too expensive, jumping from thirty grains to sixty grains a day and still not enough, Burroughs realized he had to quit. He travelled to London to undergo a new drug rehabilitation treatment developed by Dr. John Yerby Dent. This method involved using apomorphine, a substance produced by boiling morphine in hydrochloric acid. The apomorphine serves as a kind of metabolic regulator to satisfy the addict's craving for drugs without damaging his health. After undergoing Dent's apomorphine treatments, Burroughs was permanently cured of his addiction.

The Naked Lunch, first published in Paris in 1959 and retitled *Naked Lunch* in its American edition of 1962, was assembled from the many notes Burroughs wrote while living in Tangier. Several friends—including Ginsberg, Brion Gysin, Sinclair Beiles, and Alan Ansen—helped Burroughs choose the material to use in the book. Kerouac typed most of the manuscript and provided the book's title, which Burroughs explains in the novel's "Atrophied Preface" as the "frozen moment when everyone sees what is on the end of every fork." Paul Bowles, a novelist who also lives in Tangier, describes in *Big Table* the process by which Burroughs composed the novel. Speaking of a visit to Burroughs's apartment, Bowles writes: "The litter on his desk and under it, on the floor, was chaotic, but it consisted only of pages of *Naked Lunch,* at which he was constantly working. When he read aloud from it, at random (any sheet of paper he happened to grab would do) he laughed a good deal, as well he might, since it is very funny."

Naked Lunch is a series of sketches arranged in a random order. Because of the unstructured nature of the book—further enhanced by the random stacking of manuscript pages on a table at his publisher's office which Burroughs held to be as good an ordering of the contents as any—*Naked Lunch* has, Tony Tanner writes in his *City of Words: American Fiction, 1950-1970,* "no narrative continuity, and no sustained point of view; the separate episodes are not interrelated, they coexist in a particular field of force brought together by the mind of Burroughs which then abandons them." Alvin J. Seltzer, in his study *Chaos in the Novel: The Novel in Chaos,* finds that in *Naked Lunch* "all structure is discarded: one can pick up the novel and start his reading anywhere, then go forward, backward or jump around at will. . . . The novel is set up to break down any rational approach to it, any logical system which attempts to reduce a multilevel experience directed toward our central nervous system."

While Burroughs deals only with drug addiction in *Junkie,* in *Naked Lunch* he explores many forms of addiction in human society. As Jerry Bryant writes in *The Open Decision,* "drug addiction is both a literal example of human imprisonment and thought control and a figurative representation of similar forces at work in human society at large." Burroughs argues that mankind is addicted to such things as image, sex, power, language, and government. As he explains in the novel, "there are many forms of addiction, and I think they all obey basic laws."

These addictions are used by those in control to subdue the population. William Lee, the protagonist and Burroughs-surrogate of *Junkie,* reappears in *Naked Lunch* as an addict who cures himself only to find that "all of humanity is victimized by some form of addiction. He realizes that the body is a biological trap and that society is run by 'control addicts' who use the needs of the body to satisfy their obsession with power. Thus the terms *addiction* and *junk* . . . are also metaphors for the human condition," Skerl writes. McNally explains that the "manipulative addict-dealer structure . . . was a harsh and simplified replica of modern society's web of electronic and political controls. Junk was a virus of addiction, but the deceitful words of government agencies, advertisements and the mass media were a virus as well. *Naked Lunch* and Burrough's succeeding volumes were designed to innoculate the reader against the virus with a silence of perfect awareness that canceled out the insidious desire to be controlled, the mainstay of the liberal technocratic ideology Burroughs despised."

The style of *Naked Lunch* deliberately subverts the language "addiction" of the average reader. Robin Lydenberg of the *Review of Contemporary Fiction* describes the purpose of the book as the curing of "the 'image addiction' and 'morality addiction' of Western thought by producing a text which will defy and destroy these systems." Burroughs uses no metaphors, believing them to be one of the "kicks" the language addiction provides, and writes instead in a literal style. Lydenberg writes that Burroughs has a "distrust of allegory and metaphor. . . . Allegory or symbol screens out the literal, the fact, the signifier, to illuminate the idea; nothing happens, life fades and is replaced by abstraction." The purpose of

Burroughs's literal style, Lydenberg argues, is "to reveal a more naked truth." The language addiction—and the purposes of the control systems using language—are further subverted by the novel's random structure. Burroughs, writes Burkholder, "fights the artificial reality of the subject-verb-object order by freeing language from its dependence upon that order. . . . Burroughs views [*Naked Lunch's*] incoherence as the liberator of his reader's mind."

Because *Naked Lunch* contains graphic sex and violence, no American or English publisher would at first accept it. The book was first published in Paris in 1959. Though there was no American edition of the book until 1962, and the post office would not allow copies of the Paris edition to be mailed to the United States, milder excerpts from the book appeared in American magazines.

The first American edition of *Naked Lunch* appeared in 1962 from Grove Press and was met by a lawsuit in Boston on grounds of obscenity. The subsequent trial brought out Ginsberg, Mailer, and other literary figures to speak on behalf of the novel's redeeming social value, the criteria at the time for acceptable literature. Ginsberg described Burroughs's intentions as "moral . . . defending the good," while Mailer called him a "religious writer" and *Naked Lunch* "a vision of how mankind would act if man was totally divorced from eternity." Burroughs did not appear at the trial, but in an article for *Evergreen Review* he defends "certain passages in the book that have been called pornographic" as being "a tract against Capital Punishment in the manner of Jonathan Swift's Modest Proposal. These sections are intended to reveal capital punishment as the obscene, barbaric and disgusting anachronism that it is." In a landmark decision, a federal court ruled *Naked Lunch* not obscene. As Skerl relates, "*Naked Lunch* was a ground-breaking book in helping to eliminate censorship of the printed word in the United States."

The novel also met with opposition from many members of the literary community. John Wain, in a review for *New Republic,* for example, believes *Naked Lunch* "is of very small significance. It consists of a prolonged scream of hatred and disgust. . . . A book like *Naked Lunch* requires far less talent in the writer, and for that matter less intelligence in the reader than the humblest magazine story or circulating-library novel. From the literary point of view, it is the merest trash, not worth a second glance."

Despite the negative comments and controversy, *Naked Lunch* has received critical praise from most quarters. It was a national best-seller, made Burroughs's literary reputation, and remains his most widely known book. Robert Peters, writing in the *Los Angeles Times Book Review,* calls it "the best American novel of its decade." Jack Kerouac "thought it was wonderful, superseding Genet, De Sade, and Aleister Crowley," according to McNally. Paul Ableman of *Spectator* judges it to be "the most brilliant satire in English since *Gulliver's Travels.*" And Skerl finds *Naked Lunch* "a brilliant work. . . . It significantly contributes to the craft of fiction in subject matter and technique, thus gaining it a permanent place in the history of the novel and the history of the avant-garde."

In his next three novels Burroughs consciously expanded the random structuring used in *Naked Lunch* by introducing the "cut-up" method of composition. The cut-up is derived from the collage of the visual arts, a technique of combining unrelated elements into a new work. Burroughs learned of the cut-up from the experiments of his friend Brion Gysin. Gysin had been cutting newspaper articles into sections and then rearranging the sections at random, while looking away. The resulting juxtapositions of words intrigued Burroughs. He took the method further, cutting texts down the center and placing unrelated halves together to form new sentences. He cut up the works of other writers, his own writings, newspapers, poems, and magazine articles. From the resulting texts he chose fragments and phrases of the most interest and included them in the completed work. Burroughs also developed the fold-in method in which sections of text are folded in half and juxtapositioned to create new works. Throughout the 1960s he experimented with cut-ups in fiction, film, and tape recordings.

Burroughs explains to Platt the importance of the cut-up: "It's closer to the actual facts of perception. . . . I'm talking about how things are actually perceived by the brain." By coming closer to the way the brain perceives information, the cut-up method also frees the author and reader from the traditional constraints of fiction. Cut-ups, according to Burkholder, realize Burroughs's "notion that we need to escape the constructs of Aristotelian logic and the declarative sentence to free ourselves from the false reality and authorial control that traditional fiction has always presented." Similarly, Tanner finds that the cut-up method manages "to cut the Word Lines which predetermine your response to reality."

The Soft Machine, The Ticket That Exploded, and *Nova Express* are all written in the cut-up method, utilizing the notes Burroughs took in Tangier. Because of this, the novels are not in "straight-forward linear form. The reader must piece [the story] together from flashes, obsessive phrases, and incomplete scenes, struggling through disjointed chronology and abrupt changes of narrators, or cryptic cut-ups," Gerard Cordesse writes in *Caliban XII.* The three novels continue the story begun in *Naked Lunch,* forming a tetralogy. The addictions to word, image, power, sex and drugs uncovered by William Lee in *Naked Lunch* are found in the subsequent novels to be the work of the Nova Mob, a group of aliens who control the earth. The Nova Mob takes on the form of viruses to infect mankind with addictions. Through these addictions they have manipulated Earthlings for three thousand years. "Drugs, sex, and power control the body," Skerl explains, "but 'word and image locks' control the mind, that is, conventional patterns of perceiving, thinking, and speaking which determine our interactions with environment and society." Countering the Mob are the Nova Police, who work to regulate man's addictions and use silence and cut-ups to destroy the perception habits enslaving mankind. "The cut-up," Skerl writes, "is a way of exposing word and image controls and thus freeing oneself from them." Bryant sees the Nova Mob as "the symbol of a tyrannical society that flourishes on the destruction of its citizens' independence and integrity. . . . Only those free of the destructive force of the totalitarian state—be it fascist or welfare—can operate as individuals."

The Soft Machine (the title refers to the human brain) outlines the use of control systems throughout human history, tracing the Nova Mob's influence and focusing in particular on the Mayan civilization. The Mayan priesthood maintained social control through the manipulation of their calendar, which was a word and image system forming the basis of the agricultural, social, and religious life of the people. When Lee, an agent of the Nova Police, travels through time to the Mayan civilization, he restructures the calendar and causes the breakdown of the priests' totalitarian system. Vernon finds *The Soft Machine* to be Burroughs's "best use of cut-ups" because he establishes "a dynamic rhythm of cohesion and fragmentation which becomes the experience of the novel."

In *The Ticket That Exploded* the use of cut-ups to destroy language systems and thereby liberate the mind is explicitly presented. The novel even "includes its own book of exercises for the reader to help himself break out of the control system which lives his life for him," Seltzer writes. Using a host of concepts borrowed from science fiction, the novel takes place in several imaginary settings on other worlds. One of these is the Garden of Delights, where the Nova Police exhibit all the control systems used by the Mob. The city of Minraud, ruled by insect creatures who use "mind tapes" to control individuals and a "reality film" to control the actions of their society, is a Burroughs totalitarian fantasy. The book's cut-up sequences are a means of liberation from such totalitarianism. They are "images of apocalyptic destruction of linguistic social systems and of the liberated consciousness that results," Skerl writes.

The final novel of the tetralogy, *Nova Express,* summarizes and condenses the concerns of the previous books while introducing the idea that writing is a powerful tool in resisting control, an idea Burroughs develops in later novels. The science fiction aspect of the tetralogy becomes dominant in *Nova Express* as giant space battles take place between aliens and Earthlings. The novel ends in a deadlock between the forces of the Nova Mob and Nova Police.

Speaking of the tetralogy as a whole, Seltzer sees a fundamental difference in Burroughs's approach to the writing of the novel. "Whereas the novel traditionally has tried to universalize experience," Seltzer writes, "Burroughs seems intent on personalizing it. That is, in fact, his message for the reader: resist all control systems and storm the reality studio where your life is being programmed by the parasitic exploiters . . . who, by sending images through the soft machine inside your head, are controlling your mental associative patterns, and ultimately your body, your soul, your life." Writing of Burroughs's intentions, Marshall McLuhan finds in the *Nation* that he "is not asking merit marks as a writer, he is trying to point to the shut-on button of an active and lethal environmental process."

With *The Wild Boys: A Book of the Dead,* published in 1971, and his following books, Burroughs abandoned the extensive cut-ups of his tetralogy in favor of a more conventionally organized narrative. He writes in a popular style and borrows heavily from established commercial genres, suggesting that the elements of popular culture can be used by the writer as tools of liberation. Set in an apocalyptic near-

future, *The Wild Boys* tells of a group of homosexual hashish smokers who can travel through time and space and who, through their indifference to the images of society, are beyond social control. The story of their ongoing rebellion is told in a series of eighteen related scenes written in the "simple narrative style of popular fiction, especially the pulp fiction [Burroughs] read in his youth," Skerl explains in the *Review of Contemporary Fiction.*

Although there is a change in Burroughs's style in *The Wild Boys,* he is still concerned with personal freedom, the control systems of society, and the efforts to free oneself from social restrictions. These concerns are given a new perspective, however. In *The Wild Boys* "the tide," Cordesse explains, "has turned: language that was the instrument of nova oppression has become a weapon of liberation." As Skerl writes, *The Wild Boys* and the novels that follow it express "more hope for the individual and for change through 'utopian dreams.'" The novel ends with the narrator attempting to break through the time barrier to join the wild boys in the future.

The characters in *The Wild Boys* reappear in *Cities of the Red Night,* a novel interweaving three plot lines set in different times and places. One story follows private detective Clem Snide as he tries to solve a case of ritual murder in the present. Another is set one hundred thousand years in the past where the red virus has broken out in the ancient cities of the Gobi Desert. The primary story is set in the eighteenth century and concerns a group of homosexual pirates who establish a series of libertarian republics in South America and battle the Spanish conquistadors. Each of these narratives is told in the style and language of popular fiction and borrows heavily from the detective, science fiction, and boys' adventure genres.

Burroughs explains in his introduction to the novel that his pirate tale is inspired by the life of Captain Mission, a pirate who founded the visionary republic of Libertatia in Madagascar a hundred years before the French Revolution. In this community all wealth was shared equally, government officials were elected by popular vote, and the death penalty was abolished. Because Mission's community was overrun and destroyed by natives, Burroughs argues that "Your right to live where you want, with companions of your choosing, under laws to which you agree, died in the eighteenth century with Captain Mission. Only a miracle or a disaster could restore it."

This lost utopia is contrasted with the dictatorship of the ancient Cities of the Red Night and with the violence of the present day. All three plot lines end in confusion as their characters, settings, and actions are joined and tangled into one giant, unresolved battle at novel's end. This battle includes pirates, aliens, marines, assassins, western gunslingers, gladiators, thugees, the CIA, the KGB, and many others. "All of time is merged in this absurd and frightening battle," Burkholder states. "Then," John Richy writes in the *Los Angeles Times Book Review,* "Burroughs smashes his own anarchy. Like a crazy movie, the book 'unwinds.'" Skerl maintains that "Burroughs merges his three narratives in order to emphasize their fictionality."

The novel ends with the narrator explaining that, through his fictional fantasizing, he has "blown a hole in time. . . . Let others step through." "Perhaps Burroughs's point," writes Burkholder, "is that whether artifice or not, the escape from time he offers is 'real' in the truest sense, since he suggests that entering the 'gate in time' he has created in *Cities of the Red Night* and his other work is the only way to escape from the inevitability of the 'great mushroom-shaped cloud' that was his childhood nightmare and is the final dark image of this . . . novel." Skerl also sees the novel's ending as positive. Burroughs, she writes, "wants to stimulate readers to create their own stories, rather than passively consume his creations. . . . *Cities of the Red Night* shows the reader how to create alternative realities with the basic human ability to dream and tell stories."

Critical reaction to *Cities of the Red Night* was divided. Thomas M. Disch, referring to the novel's graphic violence, comments in the *New York Times Book Review* that "opium addicts who are sexually aroused by witnessing and/or enacting garrotings and hangings will find 'Cities' a veritable gallows of delight." Similarly, Peter S. Prescott of *Newsweek* finds that "the inspiration behind [*Cities of the Red Night*] seems retarded: the masturbatory fantasies of a 12-year-old boy who dreams, as boys will, of plague and violent death, of hiding out with his chums in a secret jungle fort and beating up on the adults around him. For a book that seemed to promise some kind of allegory or at least an apocalyptic vision of the world's end, it is a poor dream to come down to." Algren found himself "so moved by all this cardboard surrealism that, when I came to, the galley proofs were on the floor and the reading lamp was still burning."

But other observers were kinder in their assessments of the novel. Perry Meisel, writing in the *New York Times Book Review,* calls *Cities of the Red Night* Burroughs's "best novel," while Steven Shaviro of the *Review of Contemporary Fiction* defines it as a "homoerotic quest romance, in the great American tradition of *Moby Dick.*" John Tytell, in an article for the *American Book Review,* finds that "though not as formally explosive as *Naked Lunch, Cities of the Red Night* is a powerful book and a hauntingly macabre entertainment." Rechy describes the novel as "Burroughs' masterpiece. In it, the world ends with a bang—and a barely perceived whimper, disguised by the wicked smile of one of the most dazzling magicians of our time."

Speaking of *Cities of the Red Night* in an article for the *New York Times Book Review,* Burroughs explains his intentions: "In 'Cities of the Red Night' I parachute my characters behind enemy lines in time. Their mission is to correct retroactively certain fatal errors at crucial turning points in human history. I am speaking of biological errors that tend to block man's path to his biological and spiritual destiny in space. I postulate a social structure offering maximum variation of small communes, as opposed to the uniformity imposed by industrialization and over-population."

Burroughs's next novel, *The Place of Dead Roads,* is set in the 1890s and features a protagonist named William Seward Hall, an author of Westerns under the pen name of Kim Carsons. "Born in St. Louis, largely self-taught (teachers hate him), openly homosexual, fascinated by disease, violence, and extreme, often drug-induced, states of mind, the Kim who gradually takes shape in this novel is, we soon realize, very much a fictional version of Burroughs himself," Jay Tolson writes in the *Washington Post Book World.* This fictionalized Burroughs is, Gerald Nicosia claims in the *Chicago Tribune Book World,* "a classic grotesque and a quintessential American youth. He is a morbid homosexual who performs elaborate rituals of black magic to curse the prigs who condemn him. But he is also sensitive, honest according to his own code, and highly inventive. He wants most of all to be left alone by those who feel the urge to control his life."

To achieve this freedom, Kim forms an outlaw gang called the Wild Fruits and establishes a string of secret bases across the western frontier. The gang wages a guerrilla war against "straight" society in order to create a utopian society where they can live in peace as homosexuals. Nicosia points out that "Burroughs equates the writer with the warrior in that both must outmaneuver mortality—the warrior with his weapons and military expertise, the writer with his ability to 'unwrite' the existing world and replace it with another more congenial to his own nature." To create a new world the writer can only use the memories of his own past—"the place of dead roads"—but he does this "at the peril of becoming trapped by them and repeating his errors, instead of breaking free," Nicosia writes.

As in *The Wild Boys* and *Cities of the Red Night* Burroughs uses a popular narrative style in *The Place of Dead Roads*. Luc Sante of the *New York Review of Books* finds that in *Cities of the Red Night* and *The Place of Dead Roads* Burroughs "has somehow been inspired to emulate the language and themes of such pulp masters as Sax Rohmer, H. P. Lovecraft, Max Brand, and . . . Nick Carter." But Meisel makes clear that "despite a largely naturalistic style and an often conventional mode of storytelling, 'The Place of Dead Roads' slips and slides in time and place—almost unaccountably until one is again reminded that a transpersonal web links everything together."

Like the earlier Wild Boys, the Wild Fruits travel through time and space, and like the pirates of *Cities of the Red Night,* they battle against alien invaders. The story "loops back and forth," writes David Donnell in the Toronto *Globe & Mail,* "between gay cowboys and social satire, between tech futurism and Mayan altars." The book is structured around a gunfight between Kim Carsons and Mike Chase. The opening scene depicts one version of this gunfight in which both men are shot dead. The novel ends with the same gunfight, but this time only Carsons is killed.

"The first serious gay western," as Donnell describes *The Place of Dead Roads,* is thought by most reviewers to be a highly personal fiction, although there is disagreement as to its ultimate merit. Anatole Broyard of the *New York Times* sees little to praise: "For a celebrated author to publish a novel as poor as 'The Place of Dead Roads' requires a degree of collusion or encouragement on our part. He must have a certain confidence in our credulity, must assume that bad taste is a good bet, that age cannot wither, nor customs stale the appeal of an established reputation." But Nicosia deems the novel "a moving personal saga as well as a record of revolutionary vision," and Tolson believes the book "would be pretty

dull fare were it not for the force of Burroughs' genius, his almost terrifying independence, and his refusal to accept any values but his own."

Burroughs capped the two volumes of *Cities of the Red Night* and *The Place of Dead Roads* with *The Western Lands,* which, according to some critics, completes a trilogy with the two earlier volumes. "The latest work, whose title refers to the Egyptian goal of immortality," declares *New Statesman* contributor Oliver Harris, "brings one of the most remarkable of 20th-century literary oeuvres to a close." In *The Western Lands,* the writer William Seward Hall becomes disgusted with his work and begins a journey to find and win immortality. "The journey to the Western Lands," writes Danny Karlan in the *London Review of Books,* "is punctuated by violent purgative encounters with 'fraudulent human stock' and its predators, enemies of the free self." "And so, exploring new words," states novelist John Rechy in the *Los Angeles Times Book Review,* "'William Seward Hall sets out to write his way out of death . . . to reach the western lands . . . to achieve freedom from fear'—and not by 'cowering' in his 'physical body for eternity.'" By the end of the book, however, Hall has exhausted himself in the pursuit of an unrealizable goal. "Death can only be paid in person," Karlan explains, "in the gold coin of identity."

To some critics, *The Western Lands* reads like Burroughs' farewell to his life's work. "Reviewers," explains Karlan, "have interpreted it as a valediction to that phase of the Post-Modernist enterprise of which *The Naked Lunch* was the first resounding blast." "Other modern writers have converted the form," Rechy states. "But Burroughs seems to have taken aim at all conventional storytelling—and fired." The results, the critic determines, mix diverse genres, including autobiography, adventure, Western, and science fiction, and bits and pieces from the Bible and modern literature. "*The Western Lands* concludes with echoes of two texts repeatedly incorporated into his writing," Harris concludes, "Eliot's 'Waste Land' and Joyce's story 'The Dead,' as the snow flakes fall softly on the dying writer and the last call is heard for the last time; 'Hurry up, please. It's time.' His pilgrimage through the place of dead roads to the western lands, picking up the last bric-a-brac pieces for his mythology, aspires to the immortality of the writer, his after-life dependent on his readers."

Burroughs' consistent individualism has won him a loyal readership despite some critical hostility to his style and themes. Two festivals, the Nova Convention in New York in 1978 and the Final Academy in London in 1982, were organized by admirers as tributes to him. These festivals included films, readings, and panels about his work and attracted devotees from the fields of music, literature, and film. As Tolson acknowledges, "I have met a few [of Burroughs's fans] and know that their regard for the man borders on devotion."

Burroughs has been influential in several areas. In literature, he had a tremendous impact on the Beat writers of the 1950s, particularly his friends Ginsberg and Kerouac. George Dordess explains in the *Dictionary of Literary Biography* that both Ginsberg and Kerouac "saw in their older friend . . . a fearless, sardonic experimenter with drugs, sex, and crime, as well as a coolly precise student of those analysts of society's ills, Korzybski, Spengler, and Freud. A good teacher, also, Burroughs willingly passed on his information to his younger friends. He even undertook an informal psychoanalysis of both young men and also served as literary critic." Ginsberg's *Reality Sandwiches,* a book of poems, is directly inspired by *Naked Lunch;* Burroughs appears as a character in several of Kerouac's novels: as Will Dennison in *The Town and the City,* as Old Bull Lee in *On the Road,* as Frank Carmody in *The Subterraneans,* as Bull Hubbard in *Book of Dreams* and *Desolation Angels,* and as Wilson Holmes Hubbard in *Vanity of Duluoz: An Adventurous Education, 1935-46.* Among today's younger experimental writers, too, Burroughs has had a considerable influence. "In their various ways, writers Hunter Thompson, Tom Wolfe and Ken Kesey all are Burroughs' disciples," Larry Kart writes in the *Chicago Tribune Book World.*

But it is possibly outside of literature that Burroughs has enjoyed his greatest following. As a prominent member of the Beat writers, Burroughs helped to inspire the hippie and punk movements of the 1960s and 1970s. His *Junkie* foreshadowed the drug use of the 1960s, and his tetralogy reflected the decade's chaotic rebellion. *Naked Lunch,* Meisel explains, "not only exemplified the Beat subculture out of which Mr. Burroughs emerged; it also prophesied the wider fate of the American sensibility well into the next two decades. By the time the counterculture of the 1960's succeeded the Beats, license had become the law, and Mr. Burroughs had become a principal avatar of the liberationist esthetic he helped create." The publication of *Naked Lunch* effectively ended America's last obscenity laws, opening the way for greater freedom in all the arts and allowing explicit sexual material to be legally published in this country. Burroughs "has had considerably greater cultural impact than the extent of his present readership might indicate," Bruce Cook writes in the *Detroit News.* "It would not be an overstatement to say that he is one of the secret shapers of American culture—such as it is today."

"The master's influence," Kart writes, "also has been felt in the world of rock." The term "heavy metal," a name for a type of rock and roll, comes from *Naked Lunch.* The group Steely Dan borrowed their name from Burroughs's writings. Such groups as the Rolling Stones have written songs about his characters, while David Bowie and Patti Smith admit to using the cut-up method to compose their songs. The book *With William Burroughs: A Report from the Bunker* contains transcripts of conversations between Burroughs and such rock figures as Mick Jagger, Patti Smith, Lou Reed, and Richard Hell. Burroughs even hit the British record charts with his "Nothing Here but the Recordings," an album containing readings from his work and some cut-up tape recorder experiments. As a *New York Times* writer sums up, "There can be no doubt that Mr. Burroughs has been one of the principal literary influences on rock music." Sante believes that "youth culture since the Sixties has abounded in allusions to his work the way earlier generations drew on Shakespeare or the Bible."

Though his influence in literature and popular culture has been substantial, Burroughs has not yet achieved full academic acceptance. His controversial cut-up method and his graphic writing about drug use and homosexuality have made Burroughs difficult for some observers to evaluate objectively. Seymour Krim of the *Washington Post Book World* points out that one problem with Burroughs's writing is its refusal to fulfill a reader's preconceptions. "Many a decent-minded reader," Krim writes, "is going to give up out of a feeling of bewilderment and impotence because he expects to be spoonfed in the grand American custom. But Burroughs doesn't make these concessions." As Norman Snider writes in the Toronto *Globe & Mail,* "Burroughs is not the sort of writer whose reputation will ever settle into general and genial acceptance. His work will always have its passionate detractors and ferocious admirers."

Among the detractors is David Lodge, who argues in his *The Novelist at the Crossroads and Other Essays on Fiction and Criticism* that Burroughs "has, principally, two claims on the attention of serious readers: as a moralist, and as an innovator. On both counts, it seems to me, he cannot be considered as more than a minor, eccentric figure. Undoubtedly he has a certain literary talent, particularly for comedy and the grotesque, but in both precept and practice he is deeply confused and ultimately unsatisfying." Broyard wonders why Burroughs has been long described as "irreverent." "Who are all these reverent people ostensibly being mocked here," Broyard writes, "and what is it that they are alleged to revere, as opposed to Mr. Burroughs? Is it heterosexuality? Staying alive? Pleasant odors? It seems to me that the man in the street has a more sophisticated—or irreverent—sense of humor than this Peck's Bad Boy of literature."

Even a more sympathetic critic, Alfred Kazin of the *New York Times Book Review,* while allowing that Burroughs "is indeed a serious man and a considerable writer," nevertheless feels that "his books are not really books, they are compositions that astonish, then pall. They are subjective experiences brought into the world for the hell of it and by the excitement of whatever happens to be present to Burroughs's consciousness when he writes." Sante, too, is of a mixed opinion as to Burroughs's stature. He calls *Naked Lunch* "still his best. . . . It remains a milestone of a kind, going further than any book in plumbing the untouchable aspects of American life." But Sante also believes that Burroughs "shot his wad with this volume."

Part of the resistance to Burroughs's work is perhaps explained by Bruce Cook in his *The Beat Generation.* Cook gives his opinion that Burroughs "is a very considerable prose artist—intellectually accomplished, technically innovative," and then allows that, if "given different subject matter, [Burroughs] would have enormous appeal to academic critics." Krim sees the subjective nature of Burroughs's work as another possible drawback to its wide acceptance. Burroughs, Krim writes, "gives the very definite impression that he is including us in a private ceremonial obsession over which he has little control. . . . We feel that Burroughs is composing in a trance that removes his work from what we ordinarily think of as 'fiction' or even 'art.'It's as if we had gotten hold of a black ticket to his unconscious, and anyone who makes the trip will see sights and feel feelings that are unique and mind-bending. . . . Totting it all up is of course another, highly subjective story."

But a number of critics praise Burroughs's innovative prose and his exploration of new literary terrain. Harry Marten, for example, writes in the *New York Times Book Review* that Burroughs "has been mixing the satirist's impulse toward invective with the cartoonist's relish for exaggerated gesture, the collage artist's penchant for radical juxtapositions with the slam-bang pace of the carnival barker. In the process, he has mapped a grotesque modern landscape of disintegration whose violence and vulgarity is laced with manic humor." Anthony Burgess, speaking of the tetralogy in his *The Novel Now: A Guide to Contemporary Fiction,* finds Burroughs's style innovative and leading to a "new medium . . . a medium totally fantastic, spaceless, timeless, in which the normal sentence is fractured, the cosmic tries to push its way through bawdry, and the author shakes the reader as a dog shakes a rat." Theodore Solotaroff, in his *The Red Hot Vacuum and Other Pieces on the Writing of the Sixties,* calls Burroughs "one of the small group of American novelists today who are both vital and complex," while Hugo Williams of *New Statesman* believes that "if there is anyone truly creative in novel-writing today, as distinct from merely interpretive, it must be him." Speaking to the Edinburgh International Writer's Conference, Mailer proclaimed Burroughs as "the only American novelist living today who may conceivably be possessed by genius."

After living abroad for many years Burroughs returned to the United States in 1973, living for a time in New York City and then moving to rural Kansas. In the 1970s he began to give public readings from his work, and has since given over one hundred and fifty readings in the United States, Canada, and in several European countries. He has also read his work on the "Saturday Night Live" television program. "These readings," Burroughs tells *CA,* "are *performances* carefully rehearsed. I am, despite previous disclaimers, an entertainer, in fact a stand-up comic." Through his readings Burroughs's distinctive persona—a gaunt figure dressed impeccably in a dark suit—has become familiar to many of his readers. He possesses a "sad, nasty drawl, a voice that goes well with his face, which has the odd quality of being soft and haggard at the same time, a face that can writhe with tics, then gaze with reptilian stillness," Allen writes. Platt recalls that Burroughs's "complexion is ghostly pale; he peers out into daylight like the caretaker for a mausoleum." Sante likens Burroughs to "the dangerous figure in a worn business outfit who haunts schoolyards and mutters vague fragments about planetary conspiracy."

Speaking of his writing, Burroughs tells *CA* he has been deeply influenced by the authors Denton Welch, Joseph Conrad, Graham Greene, Louis-Ferdinand Celine, Samuel Beckett, Jean Genet, Arthur Rimbaud, and Saint-John Perse. As to his literary intentions, Burroughs explains: "My purpose in writing any book is to do the best job of writing I can do. And that's it."

BIOGRAPHICAL/CRITICAL SOURCES:

BOOKS

Authors in the News, Volume II, Gale, 1976.
Bartlett, Lee, editor, *The Beats: Essays in Criticism,* Mc-Farland, 1981.
Bockris, Victor, *With William Burroughs: A Report from the Bunker,* Seaver, 1981.
Bowles, Paul, *Without Stopping,* Putnam, 1972.
Bryant, Jerry H., *The Open Decision: The Contemporary American Novel and Its Intellectual Background,* Free Press, 1970.
Burgess, Anthony, *The Novel Now: A Guide to Contemporary Fiction,* Norton, 1967.
Burroughs, William, Jr., *Kentucky Ham,* Dutton, 1973.
Burroughs, William S., *Junky,* Penguin, 1977.
Burroughs, William S., *Cities of the Red Night,* Holt, 1981.
Charters, Ann, *Kerouac: A Biography,* Straight Arrow Books, 1973.
Contemporary Fiction in America and England, 1950-1970, Gale, 1976.
Contemporary Literary Criticism, Gale, Volume 1, 1973, Volume 2, 1974, Volume 5, 1976, Volume 15, 1980, Volume 22, 1982, Volume 42, 1987, Volume 75, 1993.
Cook, Bruce, *The Beat Generation,* Scribner, 1971.
Dictionary of Literary Biography, Gale, Volume II: *American Novelists since World War II,* 1978, Volume VIII: *Twentieth Century American Science Fiction Writers,* 1981, Volume XVI: *The Beats: Literary Bohemians in Postwar America,* 1983.
Dictionary of Literary Biography Yearbook: 1981, Gale, 1982.
Gifford, Barry and Lawrence Lee, *Jack's Book: An Oral Biography of Jack Kerouac,* St. Martin, 1978.
Goodman, Michael Barry, *William S. Burroughs: An Annotated Bibliography of His Works and Criticism,* Garland Publishing, 1975.
Goodman, Michael Barry, *Contemporary Literary Censorship: The Case History of Burroughs' Naked Lunch,* Scarecrow, 1981.
Goodman, Michael Barry, and Lemuel B. Coley, *William S. Burroughs; A Reference Guide,* Garland Publishing, 1990.
Harrison, Gilbert A., editor, *The Critic as Artist: Essays on Books, 1920-1970,* Liveright, 1972.
Hassan, Ihab, *The Dismemberment of Orpheus,* Oxford University Press, 1971.
Itinerary 3: Criticism, Bowling Green University, 1977.
Kazin, Alfred, editor, *Writers at Work: The Paris Review Interviews,* Viking, 1967.
Kazin, Alfred, *Bright Book of Life: American Novelists and Storytellers from Hemingway to Mailer,* Atlantic/Little, Brown, 1973, pp. 243-282.
Kirsch, Hans-Christian, *Dies Land ist unser: Die Beat-Poeten William S. Burroughs, Allen Ginsburg, Jack Kerouac,* List (Munich), 1993.
Lemaire, Gerard-Georges, *Colloque de Tanger,* Christian Bourgois Editeur, 1976.
Lodge, David, *The Novelist at the Crossroads and Other Essays on Fiction and Criticism,* Cornell University Press, 1971.
Lodge, David, *Modes of Modern Writing,* Cornell University Press, 1977.
Lydenberg, Robin, *Word Culture: Radical Theory and Practice in William S. Burroughs' Fiction,* University of Illinois Press (Urbana, IL), 1987.
Mattram, Eric, *William Burroughs: The Algebra of Need,* Marion Boyars, 1977.
Maynard, Philippe, *William S. Burroughs,* Seghers, 1975.
McCaffery, Larry and Jim McMenamin, *William Burroughs: An Interview,* Northouse & Northouse (Dallas, TX), 1988.
McCarthy, Mary, *The Writing on the Wall and Other Literary Essays,* Harcourt, 1970.
McNally, Dennis, *Desolate Angel: Jack Kerouac, the Beat Generation, and America,* Random House, 1979.
Miles Associates, compilers, *A Descriptive Catalogue of the William S. Burroughs Archive,* Covent Garden Press, 1973.
Miles, Barry, *William Burroughs: El hombre invisible, a Portrait,* Hyperion, 1993.
Morgan, Ted, *Literary Outlaw: The Life and Times of William S. Burroughs,* Holt, 1988.
Nelson, Cary, *The Incarnate Word: Literature and Verbal Space,* University of Illinois Press, 1973.
Odier, Daniel, *The Job: Interviews with William S. Burroughs,* Grove, 1970.
Parkinson, Thomas, editor, *A Casebook on the Beat,* Crowell, 1961.
Pastor Garcia, Daniel, *El individualismo anarquico y radical de William S. Burroughs,* Universidad de Salamanca (Salamance), 1988.
Pearce, Richard, *Stages of the Clown: Perspectives on Modern Fiction from Dostoevsky to Beckett,* Southern Illinois University Press, 1970.

Platt, Charles, *Dream Makers,* Volume 2: *The Uncommon Men and Women Who Write Science Fiction,* Berkley Publishing, 1983.

Seltzer, Alvin J., *Chaos in the Novel: The Novel in Chaos,* Schocken, 1974.

Skerl, Jennie, *William S. Burroughs,* Twayne, 1985.

Skerl, Jennie, and Robin Lydenberg, *William S. Burroughs at the Front: Critical Reception, 1959-1989,* Southern Illinois University Press (Carbondale, IL), 1991.

Solotaroff, Theodore, *The Red Hot Vacuum and Other Pieces on the Writing of the Sixties,* Atheneum, 1970.

Tanner, Tony, *City of Words: American Fiction, 1950-1970,* Harper, 1971.

Tytell, John, *Naked Angels: The Lives and Literature of the Beat Generation,* McGraw-Hill, 1976.

Vernon, John, *The Garden and the Map: Schizophrenia in Twentieth Century Literature and Culture,* University of Illinois Press, 1973.

Wilson, Terry and others, *Here to Go: Planet R-101,* Re-Search Publications (San Francisco), 1982.

PERIODICALS

Advocate, July 16, 1991, p. 38.
Ambit, Number 27, 1966.
American Book Review, May-June, 1981.
American Scholar, spring, 1965.
Atlantic, December, 1968; April, 1981.
Big Table, summer, 1959.
Bloomsbury Review, May/June, 1994, p. 7.
Calaban XII, Volume XI, number 1, 1975.
Chicago Tribune, June 15, 1984.
Chicago Tribune Book World, March 1, 1981; February 9, 1984; June 17, 1984.
Comparative Literature Studies, December, 1978.
Critical Quarterly, autumn, 1966.
Criticism, Number 22, 1980.
Critique, spring, 1963.
Denver Post, June 15, 1975.
Detroit News, March 22, 1981.
Encounter, April, 1963; January, 1967.
Esquire, September, 1971; February, 1992, p. 112.
Evergreen Review, January-February, 1962; April-May, 1964.
Extrapolation, winter, 1979.
Film Quarterly, spring, 1992, p. 2.
Forum, Number 14, 1976.
Globe & Mail (Toronto), March 10, 1984; February 22, 1986.
Guardian, October 1, 1982.
Harper's, February, 1974.
Harper's Bazaar, November, 1992, p. 62.

High Performance, Number 4, winter, 1982.
High Times, March, 1979.
Hollins Critic, April, 1977.
Hudson Review, autumn, 1967.
Il Verri, December, 1968.
Interview, April, 1991, p. 118.
Intrepid, fall/winter, 1969-70.
Iowa Review, spring, 1972.
Journal for the Protection of All Beings, Number 1, 1961.
Journal of Aesthetics and Art Criticism, summer, 1967.
Kulchur, autumn, 1962.
Library Journal, September 1, 1978; November 15, 1980.
Life, November 30, 1959; February 15, 1967.
London Review of Books, April 16-May 6, 1981; June 2, 1988, pp. 9-10; September 23, 1993, pp. 18-19.
Los Angeles Times, February 10, 1986.
Los Angeles Times Book Review, March 15, 1981; September 19, 1982; July 6, 1986; December 13, 1987, pp. 2, 8.
Massachusetts Review, Number 8, 1967.
Modern Occasions, winter, 1972.
My Own Mag, August, 1965.
Nation, December 28, 1964; January 25, 1965.
New Republic, August 5, 1967; April 18, 1981.
New Statesman, March 29, 1974; March 27, 1981; March 11, 1988, p. 30.
New Statesman & Society, September 3, 1993, p. 38.
Newsweek, March 9, 1981; September 6, 1993, p. 50.
New Worlds, Number 142, 1964.
New Yorker, August 11, 1980; January 16, 1995, pp. 83-84.
New York Review of Books, May 10, 1984.
New York Times, December 1, 1978; February 25, 1981; July 22, 1981; February 15, 1984; January 17, 1995, p. C18.
New York Times Book Review, September 16, 1962; December 12, 1971; June 22, 1975; March 15, 1981; February 19, 1984; November 3, 1985; August 17, 1986; January 15, 1995, pp. 9, 11.
Observer, August 22, 1993, p. 48.
Paris Review, fall, 1965.
Partisan Review, spring, 1963; spring, 1974.
Penthouse, March, 1972.
Premiere, January, 1992, p. 35.
Quill & Quire, March, 1988, p. 82.
Re/Search, Number 4/5, 1982.
Review of Contemporary Fiction, Volume 4, number 1, 1984.
Revue des Langues Vivants, Number 42, 1976.

Rolling Stone, May 11, 1972.

Saturday Review, June 27, 1959; January 6, 1979.

Search & Destroy, Number 10, 1978.

Semiotext(e), Volume 4, number 2, 1982.

Serif, summer, 1974.

SF Horizons, Number 2, 1975.

Spectator, July 29, 1960; March 16, 1974; April 4, 1981.

Sphinx, Number 11, 1980.

Style, Number 10, 1976.

Telos, fall, 1972.

Time, November 30, 1962.

Time Out, September 24-30, 1982.

Times (London), April 26, 1984.

Times Literary Supplement, December 21, 1979; March 27, 1981; January 24, 1986; March 18-24, 1988; October 15, 1993, p. 22.

Transatlantic Review, winter, 1969-70.

Tribune Books (Chicago), September 5, 1993, pp. 1, 9; February 5, 1995, pp. 7, 11.

Tri-Quarterly, spring, 1968.

Twentieth Century Literature, October, 1965; summer, 1978.

Twentieth Century Studies, November, 1969.

Unspeakable visions of the individual, Number 4, 1974; Number 5, 1977.

Variety, May 16, 1990, p. 98.

Village Voice Literary Supplement, September, 1982; March, 1984; July 20, 1993, p. 60.

Washington Post, February 3, 1984; January 19, 1992, p. G1.

Washington Post Book World, March 1, 1981; February 19, 1984; December 29, 1985; August 15, 1993, pp. 1, 14.

West Coast Review, fall, 1969.

World Literature Today, spring, 1981.

*   *   *

BURTCHAELL, James Tunstead 1934-

PERSONAL: Born March 31, 1934, in Portland, OR; son of James Tunstead, Jr (an executive) and Marion Margaret (Murphy) Burtchaell. *Education:* University of Notre Dame, A.B. (magna cum laude), 1956; Pontifical Gregorian University, Rome, Italy, S.T.B., 1958; Catholic University of America, S.T.L., 1960; Ecole Biblique et Archeologique Francaise de Jerusalem, graduate study, 1961-63; Pontifical Biblical Commission, Rome, S.S.B., 1961, S.S.L., 1964; Gonville and Caius College, Cambridge University, Ph.D., 1966.

ADDRESSES: Office—Our Lady of Princeton, Great Road at Drakes Corner, Princeton, NJ 08540-1298.

CAREER: Ordained Catholic priest of Congregation of Holy Cross (C.S.C.), 1960; University of Notre Dame, Notre Dame, IN, assistant professor, 1966-69, associate professor, 1969-75, professor of theology, 1975-92, chairperson of department, 1968-70, provost, fellow, and trustee, 1970-77. Cambridge University, Gonville and Caius College, S.A. Cook Bye Fellow, 1965-66, St. Edmund's House, visiting fellow, 1965-66, senior Fulbright scholar, 1985-86; visiting fellow, Princeton University, 1980-81, 1990-93.

Member of board of governors, Ave Maria Press, 1968-70; Danforth Foundation, associate, 1968-86, member of advisory council, 1970-74; chairperson of constituting committee, Council on the Study of Religion, 1969-70; member of advisory screening committee in religion, Committee on International Exchange of Persons, 1970-73; member of commission of higher education, North Central Accrediting Association, 1972-75; National Endowment for the Humanities, panelist, 1975, member of national board of consultants, 1975-82; chairperson of advisory board, Center for Constitutional Studies, 1977-79; member of advisory board, Our Sunday Visitor Institute, 1978-80; member of board of directors, East Asia History of Science, Inc., 1980—; delegate, U.S. Roman Catholic-Presbyterian/Reformed Consultation, 1982-85; Council for the Retarded, member of protective services board, 1982-90, vice chairperson, 1987-90; JustLife education fund, member of advisory board, 1988-89, member of board of directors, 1989-92; project director, Madison Center Research Project, 1992-96.

MEMBER: American Academy of Religion (member of executive committee, 1969-74; vice president, 1969; president, 1970), Institute Council of Religion and Public Life, Society for Religion/Values in Higher Education, Society for the Study of Egyptian Antiquities (honorary trustee), Associates for Religion and Intellectual Life, Catholic Commission on Intellectual and Cultural Affairs, Phi Beta Kappa, Phi Kappa Delta.

AWARDS, HONORS: D.H.L. from St. Mary's College of California, 1974, Rose-Hulman Institute of Technology, 1976, and College of Mount St. Joseph, 1987; Christopher Book Award, 1982, for *Rachel Weeping, and Other Essays on Abortion.*

WRITINGS:

Catholic Theories of Biblical Inspiration since 1810, Cambridge University Press (Cambridge, England), 1969.

Philemon's Problem: The Daily Dilemma of the Christian, Life in Christ, 1973.

(Editor) *Marriage among Christians: A Curious Tradition,* Ave Maria Press (Notre Dame, IN), 1977.

(Editor) *Abortion Parley,* Andrews & McMeel (Kansas City, MO), 1980.

Rachel Weeping, and Other Essays on Abortion, Andrews & McMeel, 1982.

For Better, for Worse: Sober Thoughts on Passionate Promises, Paulist Press (Mahwah, NJ), 1985.

Major Decisions: How to Pick Your Major in College, privately printed, 1986.

(Editor) *A Just War No Longer Exists: The Teaching and Trial of Don Lorenzo Milani,* University of Notre Dame Press (Notre Dame, IN), 1988.

The Giving and Taking of Life: Essays Ethical, University of Notre Dame Press, 1989.

From Synagogue to Church: Public Services and Offices in the Earliest Christian Communities, Cambridge University Press, 1992.

CONTRIBUTOR

Cambridge Sermons on Christian Unity, Oldbourne, 1966.

Andrew Bauer, editor, *The Debate on Birth Control,* Hawthorne, 1969.

Peter Foote, John Hill, Laurence Kelly, John McCudden, and Theodore Stone, editors, *Church: Vatican II's Dogmatic Constitution on the Church,* Holt (New York City), 1969.

Willis W. Bartlett, editor, *Evolving Religious Careers,* Center for Applied Research in the Apostolate, 1970.

Paul T. Jersild and Dale A. Johnson, editors, *Moral Issues and Christian Response,* Holt, 1971.

Claude Welch, editor, *Religion in the Undergraduate Curriculum: An Analysis and Interpretation,* Association of American Colleges (Washington, DC), 1972.

Ninian Smart, John Clayton, Steven Katz, and Patrick Sherry, editors, *Religious Thought in the Nineteenth Century,* Cambridge University Press, 1981.

The 1988 Catholic College and University Handbook, SMS Publications, 1987.

OTHER

Also author of tape cassettes, including "Bread and Salt: A Cassette Catechism," 1978. Contributor to *Ann Landers Encyclopedia A to Z,* 1978, and *Report of the Human Fetal Tissue Transplantation Research Panel,* 1988. Also contributor of book reviews and articles to *Commonweal, America, Christian Century,* and numerous other journals; member of editorial advisory board, *First Things,* 1989—.

WORK IN PROGRESS: "A study of the secularization process in church-affiliated colleges in the United States and a study on analogy as the most persuasive ethical argument."

SIDELIGHTS: Discussing his beliefs about the difference between sound and bad theology, James Tunstead Burtchaell says this in a *Commonweal* article: "We Christians . . . hold ourselves answerable to the more durable insights our ancestors in faith left us from their graced experience. But we think that we too have the Spirit, and that we never learn what the tradition has to teach us until we can see and say it sensibly shown in our own experience. Bad theology comes when we say in ancient words what ancients told, but cannot say it as something we relearned ourselves (at their cue)." Burtchaell concludes later in the article: "Sound theology must close the synapse between what ancients said to us and what we have seen for ourselves."

BIOGRAPHICAL/CRITICAL SOURCES:

PERIODICALS

Commonweal, January 30, 1981.
Los Angeles Times Book Review, September 19, 1982.

C

CARPELAN, Bo (Gustaf Bertelsson) 1926-

PERSONAL: Surname is pronounced "*Car*-pel-an"; born October 25, 1926, in Helsinki, Finland; son of Bertel Gustaf (an engineer) and Ebba (Lindahl) Carpelan; married Barbro Eriksson (a reservations clerk for Finnair), April 13, 1954; children: Anders, Johanna. *Education:* University of Helsinki, Ph.D., 1960.

ADDRESSES: Home—Nyckelpigvaagen 2B, Tapiola, Finland.

CAREER: Writer. City Library, Helsinki, Finland, assistant chief librarian, 1963-80, professor of arts, 1980—.

MEMBER: PEN, Finnish-Swedish Authors Society.

AWARDS, HONORS: Finnish State Prize and Nils Holgersson Prize, 1969, for *Baagen: Beraettelsen om en sommar som var annorlunda;* Nordic Councils Prize, 1977, for *I de moerka rummen, i de ljusa;* Pro Finlandia Medal, 1980; Finlandia Prize, 1993, for *Urwind;* Samfundet De Nios Prize and Aniara Prize, both 1995.

WRITINGS:

POETRY

Som en dunkel vaerme, Holger Schildt (Helsinki, Finland), 1946.
Du moerka oeverlevande, Bonnnier (Stockholm, Sweden), 1948.

Variationer, Holger Schildt, 1950.
Minus sju, Bonnier, 1952.
Objekt foer ord, Bonnier, 1954.
Landskapets foervandlingar, Holger Schildt, 1957.
(Translator into Swedish with others) Eino S. Repo and Nils B. Stormbom, compilers, *Ny finsk lyrik* (anthology), Holger Schildt, 1960.
Den svala dagen, Holger Schildt, 1961.
Sjuttiotre dikter, Bonnier, 1966.
(Compiler) *Findlandssvenska lyrikboken* (anthology), Forum (Stockholm), 1967.
Gaarden, Holger Schildt, 1969.
Kaellan, Holger Schildt, 1973.
I de moerka rummen, i de ljusa, Holger Schildt, 1976.
Dihter fraen trettio aer (selected poems), Holger Schildt, 1980.
Dagen vaender, Holger Schildt, 1983.
(Compiler) *Modern finsk lyrik* (anthology), Holger Schildt, 1984.
Marginalia, Holger Schildt, 1984.
Room without Walls (selected poems), translated by Anne Born, Forest Books, 1987.
Ar som loev, Schildt/Bonnier, 1989.
Homecoming, translated by David McDuff, Carcanet, 1993.
J det seddan, Schildt/Bonnier, 1995.

OTHER

Anders paa oen (juvenile), Bonnier, 1959.
(Contributor) *Jag lever i republiken Finland* (essays), Soederstroem (Helsinki), 1961.
Anders i stan (juvenile), Bonnier, 1962.
(With others) *Aaret i norden* (nonfiction), Bonnier, 1962.

Baagen: Beraettelsen om en sommar som var annorlunda (young adult), Bonnier, 1968, translation by Sheila La Farge published as *Bow Island: The Story of a Summer That Was Different,* Delacorte, 1972 (published in England as *The Wide Wings of Summer,* Heinemann, 1972).

Roesterna i den sena timmen (novel), Holger Schildt, 1971, translation published as *Voices at a Late Hour* (also see below), University of Georgia Press, 1988.

Paluu nuoruuteen (play), first produced in Helsinki at Kansallisteatteri, 1971.

Paradiset: Beraettelsen om Marvins och Johans vaenskap (young adult), Bonnier, 1973, translation by La Farge published as *Dolphins in the City,* Delacorte, 1976.

Din gestalt bakom doerren: En beraettelse (novel), Holger Schildt, 1975.

Vandrande skugga: En smaestadsberaettelse (novel), Holger Schildt, 1977.

Jag minns att jag droemde (short stories), Holger Schildt, 1979.

Julius Blom (juvenile), Bonnier, 1982.

Axel (novel; also see below), Holger Schildt, 1986.

Urwind (novel), Schildt/Bonnier, 1993.

Also author of works for television, theater, and radio, including radio play, *Voices at a Late Hour,* produced by Canadian Broadcasting Corp. (CBC-Radio). A translation of *Axel* was published by Carcanet Press in 1989.

BIOGRAPHICAL/CRITICAL SOURCES:

PERIODICALS

Swedish Book Review, May, 1984.

*   *   *

CARTER, Dan T.   1940-

PERSONAL: Born June 17, 1940, in Florence, SC; son of Dewey L. and Lalla (Lawhon) Carter; married Jane Winkler, August 29, 1964; children: Alicia Lee, David Charles. *Education:* University of South Carolina, B.A., 1962; University of Wisconsin, M.A., 1964; University of North Carolina, Ph.D., 1967. *Religion:* Presbyterian.

ADDRESSES: Home—1121 Springdale Road, NE, Atlanta, GA 30306. *Office*—Department of History, Emory University, Atlanta, GA 30322.

CAREER: University of Maryland, College Park, assistant professor, 1967-69, associate professor, 1970-71, professor of history, 1971-75; Emory University, Atlanta, GA, Andrew W. Mellon Professor of History, 1976-93, William Rand Kenan, Jr. Professor, 1994—. Visiting professor at University of Wisconsin, 1969-70; Fulbright lecturer, Central Polytechnic, London, 1979-80; Pitt professor, Cambridge University, Cambridge, England, 1995-96.

MEMBER: Society of American Historians, Organization of American Historians, Southern Historical Association (president, 1994-95).

AWARDS, HONORS: Woodrow Wilson Fellow, 1962-63; Anisfield-Wolfe Award, 1969; Lillian Smith Award, 1969; Bancroft Prize, 1970, for *Scottsboro: A Tragedy of the American South;* Jules Landry Prize, 1970, 1985; Lh.D., Francis Marion College, 1983; Avery Craven Prize, 1986; Georgia Governor's Award in the Humanities, 1991; Robert F. Kennedy Book Prize, 1996, for *The Politics of Rage: George Wallace, the Origins of the New Conservatism, and the Transformation of American Politics.*

WRITINGS:

Scottsboro: A Tragedy of the American South, Louisiana State University Press (Baton Rouge), 1969, revised edition, 1979.

(Editor with Amy Friedlander) Mayo, A. D., *Southern Women in the Recent Educational Movement of the South,* Louisiana State University Press, 1979.

When the War Was Over: The Failure of Self-Reconstruction in the South, 1865-1867, Louisiana State University Press, 1985.

George Wallace, Richard Nixon, and the Transformation of American Politics, (lectures) Markham Press Fund (Waco, TX), 1992.

The Politics of Rage: George Wallace, the Origins of the New Conservatism, and the Transformation of American Politics, Simon & Schuster (New York City), 1995.

Co-editor, with Elizabeth Jacoway, of *The Adaptable South,* 1991. Contributor of autobiographical essay to *Historians and Race: Autobiography and the Writing of History,* edited by Paul A. Cimbala and Robert F. Himmelburg, Indiana University Press, 1996. Also contributor to *American Heritage* and *Journal of Southern History.*

SIDELIGHTS: Dan T. Carter attracted national attention in 1991 with his assertion that a bestselling memoir of a Native American was in fact a hoax penned by a white supremacist. *The Education of Little Tree,* by Forrest Carter, was for a time the top-selling paperback in the United States. This lyrical reminiscence of a Cherokee boy's childhood during the Depression proved especially popular with environmentalists and New Age enthusiasts. Yet Dan Carter stepped forward at the height of the book's popularity to say that Forrest Carter was in fact Asa Earl Carter, an Alabama native who was a member of the Ku Klux Klan and the author of George Wallace's "segregation forever" speech. *Little Tree*'s alleged author died in 1979; his book continued to rise in popularity until it hit the top of the bestseller lists in 1991. It was then that Dan Carter, a distant relative of Asa Carter, publicly announced that despite thorough investigation, he had been unable to locate anyone who had ever known Little Tree in the region where the young Native American had supposedly grown up. He further said that he had been unable to trace anyone in the family tree published in the alleged autobiography. Doubts about Forrest Carter's identity had been raised years before and denied, but Dan Carter had discovered new evidence that Forrest and Asa Carter were one and the same while he was researching a book on George Wallace.

New York Times Book Review contributor Richard Brookhiser called Carter's 1995 book, *The Politics of Rage: George Wallace, the Origins of the New Conservatism, and the Transformation of American Politics,* "a useful, if ultimately unsatisfactory, look at the career of the Alabama Governor [Wallace]." Fred Hobson, in the *Los Angeles Times Book Review,* called *The Politics of Rage* "the finest of those written about the Alabamian-who-would-be-president; indeed, it is one of the finest political biographies of this or any other year." Commenting that "Carter's conclusion is irresistible: Wallace was the most important loser in 20th Century American history," *Chicago Tribune* reviewer Stanley Kutler found the book "sure-footed in its understanding of the local [Alabama] psyche," and concluded: "Carter certainly has it right: Wallace was a major influence on the politics of the past quarter-century—and probably beyond."

Carter's interest and expertise in Southern history reaches far beyond the Wallace era. In 1986, he published *When the War Was Over: The Failure of Self-Reconstruction in the South 1865-1867,* described by *Journal of American Studies* reviewer W.

T. M. Riches as a "well-written, closely argued defence of the role of southern conservatives during Presidential Reconstruction." William C. Harris, writing in the *Journal of American History,* also praised the book as "well-researched and well-written . . . a valuable addition to the growing literature on the post-Civil War South."

BIOGRAPHICAL/CRITICAL SOURCES:

PERIODICALS

Chicago Tribune, October 6, 1991, section 1, p. 6; December 24, 1995.
Choice, October, 1985, p. 351.
Journal of American History, March, 1986, pp. 963-64.
Journal of American Studies, August, 1986, pp. 319-20.
Los Angeles Times Book Review, January 28, 1996.
New York Times, October 4, 1991, p. A11.
New York Times Book Review, October 29, 1995.
Times Literary Supplement, May 17, 1996, p. 10.
Washington Post, October 5, 1991, pp. D1, D4.

*　　*　　*

CHAMPLIN, John Michael 1937-(Tim Champlin)

PERSONAL: Born October 11, 1937, in Fargo, ND; son of John B. (a veterinarian) and Elizabeth I. (a teacher; maiden name, Hushaw) Champlin; married Ellen Hosey (an artist), October 26, 1967; children: Christopher, Kenneth, Liz. *Education:* Middle Tennessee State College (now University), B.S., 1960; George Peabody College for Teachers, M.A., 1964. *Politics:* "Independent, but mostly Democrat." *Religion:* Roman Catholic. *Avocational interests:* Travel, sailing, tennis, coin collecting.

ADDRESSES: Home—2926 Leatherwood, Nashville, TN 37214.

CAREER: U.S. Department of the Interior, recreation resource specialist in Ann Arbor, MI, 1967-68; Stewart Air Force Base, Smyrna, TN, civilian youth director, 1968-70; Veterans Administration, Nashville, TN, veterans' benefits counselor, 1970-77, supervisor, 1977-94. *Military service:* U.S. Naval Reserve, radar operator, 1955-63.

MEMBER: Western Writers of America.

AWARDS, HONORS: Citation from Catholic Press Association, 1978, for article "The Irish Travelers: Always on the Go, but Seldom Changing."

WRITINGS:

WESTERN NOVELS; UNDER NAME TIM CHAMPLIN

Summer of the Sioux, Ballantine (New York City), 1982.
Dakota Gold, Ballantine, 1982.
Staghorn, Ballantine, 1984.
Shadow Catcher, Ballantine, 1985.
Great Timber Race, Ballantine, 1986.
Iron Horse, Ballantine, 1987.
Colt Lightning, Ballantine, 1989.
King of the Highbinders, Ballantine, 1989.
Flying Eagle, M. Evans (New York City), 1990.
The Last Campaign, Thorndike Press (Thorndike, ME), 1996.
The Survivor, Thorndike Press, 1996.

Contributor of stories and articles to magazines, including *Bay and Delta Yachtsman, All Outdoors, Encounter, American Way, Louis L'Amour Western Magazine, Seek, Great West,* and *Gracious Living.*

WORK IN PROGRESS: Deadly Season and *The Tombstone Conspiracy,* both for Thorndike Press, publication expected in 1997; a novel about the Pony Express.

SIDELIGHTS: John Michael Champlin, better known as Tim Champlin, told *CA:* "I have wanted to write ever since I was a little boy. At the age of twelve, I attempted to write a mystery similar to the 'Hardy Boys' books. I quit about two hundred handwritten pages into it, when I got my heroes into such a jam that I couldn't get them out.

"I started writing for publication in 1970, and had some success. I grew up in North Dakota, Nebraska, Missouri, and Arizona, and loved western history. In 1977 I decided to attempt a western historical novel. *Summer of the Sioux* was the result.

"The western novels and short stories I have written are all set in the period between 1876 and 1890. From Indian campaigns to gold mining to riverboat trade to lumbering, I am attempting to portray aspects of frontier America as they really existed. In researching these things, I try to make my books

more adventurous than violent. Certainly there was violence on the frontier, but it wasn't always the six-gun violence we have come to expect in western novels. There was the violence of the blizzard, of the plagues of grasshoppers, of prairie fires, and of epidemics of cholera. There were stampedes and mine cave-ins, accidental drownings, and broken bones from breaking horses.

"I see the American frontier west primarily as a huge, ever-changing block of space and time in which an individual had more freedom than the average person has today. True, it was a freedom to fail as well as to succeed, but the opportunities were there. A person then was not crushed by the burdens of personal income tax, a thirty-year mortgage, and the worry of trespassing on someone else's property if he stepped off his own. For the most part, the population was widely spaced and transient. It was an era of building, of boom and bust and boom again. The resources and the future seemed unlimited. For those brave, and sometimes desperate, souls who ventured west looking for a better life, it must have been an exciting time to be alive. If I can capture even a little of this on paper for current readers I will be satisfied."

*   *   *

CHAMPLIN, Tim
   See CHAMPLIN, John Michael

*   *   *

CHANDLER, David (Geoffrey)   1934-

PERSONAL: Born January 15, 1934, in England; son of Geoffrey Edmund (a clergyperson) and Joyce Mary (Ridsdale) Chandler; married Gillian Dixon (an indexer), February 18, 1961; children: Paul Geoffrey, John Roger, Mark David. *Education:* Keble College, Oxford, B.A. (with second class honors), 1955, Diploma of Education, 1956, M.A., 1960. *Politics:* Conservative. *Religion:* Church of England. *Avocational interests:* Sailing, war games, model ship construction, gardening, camping.

ADDRESSES: Home—Hindford, Monteagle Lane, Yateley, near Camberley, Surrey, GU17 7LT, England.

CAREER: Royal Military Academy Sandhurst, Camberley, Surrey, England, lecturer in politics and modern history, 1960-64, senior lecturer in military history, 1964-70, deputy head of department, 1970-80, head of department of war studies and international affairs, 1980-94. Visiting lecturer, Naval War College, 1974 and 1983; visiting professor, Ohio State University, 1970, Virginia Military Institute, 1988, USMC University, 1991. *Military service:* British Army, 1957-60; seconded to Nigerian Military Forces; became captain.

MEMBER: International Commission of Military History (international vice president, 1975-95), Royal Historical Society (fellow), Society for Army Historical Research (council member), Army Records Society (council member), European Union Re-enactment Society (international president, 1990-95).

AWARDS, HONORS: D.Litt., Keble College, Oxford, 1991.

WRITINGS:

(Editor) *A Traveller's Guide to the Battlefields of Europe,* two volumes, Hugh Evelyn, 1965, Chilton, 1966.

The Campaigns of Napoleon, Macmillan (New York City), 1966.

Robert Parker and Comte de Merode-Westerloo: The Marlborough Wars, Shoe String, 1968.

Marlborough as Military Commander, Scribner, 1973, new edition, 1979.

Napoleon, Saturday Review Press, 1974.

Art of Warfare on Land, Hamlyn (London), 1974.

Art of War in the Age of Marlborough, Batsford (London), 1976.

A Dictionary of the Napoleonic Wars, Macmillan, 1979.

An Atlas of Military Strategy, 1618-1878, Free Press (New York City), 1980.

Waterloo: The Hundred Days, Macmillan, 1980.

The Journal of John Marshall Deane, Society for Army Historical Research (London), 1984.

Sedgemoor 1685: An Account and an Anthology, St. Martin's, 1985.

(Editor) *Napoleon's Marshalls,* Macmillan, 1987.

(Editor) *The Dictionary of Battles,* Holt (New York City), 1987.

(Editor) *The Military Maxims of Napoleon,* Macmillan, 1987.

Battles and Battle-scenes of World War II, Macmillan, 1989.

(Editor) *Land Battles of the Second World War,* Colour Library Books (Surrey), 1990.

Austerlitz 1805, Osprey (London), 1990.

World War II on Land, Mallard, 1990.

The Illustrated Napoleon, Holt, 1990.

(Editor) *Great Battles of the British Army as Commemorated in the Sandhurst Companies,* University of South Carolina Press (Columbia), 1991.

Sandhurst: The Royal Military Academy—250 Years, Harmony House, 1991.

Jena 1806, Osprey, 1993.

(Editor with Brigadier General J. L. Collins) *D-Day Encyclopedia,* Simon & Schuster (New York City), 1993.

On the Napoleonic Wars, Greenhill (London), 1994.

(Editor with Ian Beckett) *The Oxford Illustrated History of the British Army,* Oxford University Press (Oxford, England), 1994.

Contributor to books, including *Great Military Battles,* edited by C. Falls, Weidenfeld & Nicolson (London), 1965; *Victorian Military Campaigns,* edited by Brian Bond, Hutchinson (London), 1967; *History of the Second World War,* Purnell & Sons, 1967; and *New Cambridge Modern History,* Cambridge University Press, 1971. Also contributor to military and historical journals.

WORK IN PROGRESS: On the Marlburian Wars.

SIDELIGHTS: David Chandler has made lecture tours to British bases in the Mediterranean, Far East, Germany, Russia, Czechoslovakia, and to universities and other institutions in the United States. He has also led battlefield tours to Flanders, northern Italy, Belgium, Germany, the United States, and France. He has been involved in several television productions on military history for British television, including *War and Peace, Campaigns in History,* and *Military Leaders.*

BIOGRAPHICAL/CRITICAL SOURCES:

PERIODICALS

Guardian (London), December 21, 1981.
St. Louis Post-Dispatch, December 17, 1967.

* * *

CHANEY, Jill 1932-

PERSONAL: Born June 5, 1932, in Hertfordshire, England; daughter of Walter Sidney (a barrister) and Barbara (Webb) Chaney; married Walter Francis

Leeming (a chartered civil engineer), August 26, 1960; children: Catherine Frances, Matthew John. *Education:* Attended private schools in England; attended Waterperry Horticultural School, 1949-51; Royal Horticultural Society diploma, 1950.

ADDRESSES: Home—Glen Rosa, Colleyland, Chorleywood, Hertfordshire, England.

CAREER: Author. Worked as a gardener in London, England, 1951-61, primarily at a retirement home operated by the Jewish Board of Guardians. Director of Chorleywood Bookshop, 1971-88.

MEMBER: Royal Horticultural Society, Religious Society of Friends (Quakers), National Trust.

WRITINGS:

CHILDREN'S FICTION

On Primrose Hill, illustrated by Jane Paton, Methuen (London), 1962.
Half a Candle, illustrated by Carolyn Dinan, Dobson (London), 1968, Crown (New York City), 1969.
A Penny for the Guy, illustrated by John Dyke, Dobson, 1970.
Mottram Park, illustrated by Dinan, Dobson, 1971.
Christopher's Dig, illustrated by Dyke, Dobson, 1972.
Return to Mottram Park, illustrated by Dinan, Dobson, 1974.
Taking the Woffle to Pebblecombe-on-Sea, illustrated by Elizabeth Ogan, Dobson, 1974.
Christopher's Find, illustrated by Dyke, Dobson, 1975.
The Buttercup Field, illustrated by Ogan, Dobson, 1976.
Woffle, R.A., illustrated by daughter, Catherine Leeming, Dobson, 1976.
Canary Yellow, illustrated by Dinan, Dobson, 1977.
Angel Face, illustrated by Dinan, Dobson, 1979.
Vectis Diary, illustrated by Leeming, Dobson, 1979.
Leaving Mottram Park, illustrated by Dinan, Book Guild (Lewes, England), 1989.
Three Weeks in August, Cross, 1995.

SIDELIGHTS: British author Jill Chaney "writes equally successfully for the eight-year-old level and the older adolescent reader," according to Ann G. Hay in *Twentieth-Century Children's Writers.* Chaney has written several popular series of books for each audience. She explains to Hay that her books "seem to be about people trying to get on well

with each other, not wanting to quarrel. The books for older children are also about bridging the gap between childish expectations and adult reality."

Chaney shows a "real understanding of young love" in her popular "Mottram Park" series for young adults, according to Ann Thwaite in the *New Statesman.* The series follows the developing romance between Sheila and Gary. In *Mottram Park,* the first book in the series, Sheila runs away from home, with the reluctant help of Gary, when she cannot get along with her domineering grandmother. When their decision to make love leads to a traumatic experience, however, the couple go their separate ways. In the anxiously awaited sequel, *Return to Mottram Park,* Sheila's grandmother dies, which allows her family life to return to normal. When she meets Gary, whom she has not seen in a year, they realize that they still love each other, though they both feel it is best for their relationship to proceed very slowly. Gary travels abroad for several weeks and returns to find that his parents have separated. In his shock, he asks Sheila to marry him. As a *Junior Bookshelf* reviewer notes, "I am sure that many young girls and some boys, perhaps secretly, will read this novel with real enjoyment and understanding." The story of Sheila and Gary continues in *Leaving Mottram Park,* published in 1989.

Chaney is also the author of three successful books for younger readers about Christopher, who wants nothing more than to dig up the bones of a dinosaur. After reading about Mary Anning, a nineteenth-century girl from Dorset who dug up a plesiosaurus, Christopher decides to find a dinosaur himself. In *Christopher's Dig,* he has a hard time finding a place to excavate in London, and he gets into trouble for digging in the city parks. His parents and friends are skeptical about his ambitions. While digging on the banks of the Thames, however, Christopher finds a box of buried treasure that provides enough money to fund a real search for dinosaur bones on the Dorset coast. In the sequel, *Christopher's Find,* Christopher goes on holiday with his sister Margie and their friend Roy and again sets out to find his dinosaur skeleton, while Margie and Roy pursue their own interests. In a review for *Growing Point,* Margery Fisher remarks that Chaney "has an eye for youthful behaviour and a brisk, easy way of describing it."

Another of Chaney's popular series for younger readers features a big, hairy, invisible creature known as the Woffle. In *Taking the Woffle to*

Pebblecombe-on-Sea, Joseph and Annabel notice a pair of boots walking by themselves in the woods. They come to learn that the boots are actually being worn by the invisible Woffle, and they make friends with him. When the Woffle wants to go to Pebblecombe to visit his aunt, the children take him on the train with hilarious results. A *Junior Bookshelf* reviewer calls it "a splendid imaginative book." The sequel, *Woffle, R.A.,* describes what happens when the children bring the Woffle home to live in their shed. In order to keep him out of trouble, Joseph and Annabel give the Woffle a set of paints. But his paintings turn out to be so popular that they appear in an exhibition, and the children are hard pressed by the people of the village to produce the artist. In *Growing Point,* Fisher considers the story to be "entertaining enough," but noted that "the humour cannot help but be interrupted by the intrusive improbabilities of the plot."

Chaney returned to writing for a young adult audience with the 1977 publication of *Canary Yellow.* In this novel, sixteen-year-old Julia has a fight with her parents and runs away from home. She meets an old man who shortly afterward has an accident, and while he is in the hospital she lives on his houseboat and takes care of his canary. Julia also baby-sits for a troubled neighbor family. When the kids are placed in foster care and the mother is institutionalized, however, Julia realizes that she has fallen in love with the father, Dave. Dave takes advantage of the situation, and their relationship turns out badly. In a review for the *Times Literary Supplement,* David Rees praises Chaney for not glamorizing the life of a runaway, stating that she "is exceptionally good at conveying to the reader the feelings of boredom, loneliness and guilt which the young runaway usually experiences, also how the attraction and excitement of new experience can rapidly turn to fear and pain." Assessing Chaney's writing, Hay finds that her stories tend to be "sensitively handled," so that "the teenager will not feel 'talked-down-to' as she reads them."

BIOGRAPHICAL/CRITICAL SOURCES:

BOOKS

Twentieth-Century Children's Writers, St. James Press (Detroit), 1995, pp. 196-97.

PERIODICALS

Growing Point, October, 1975, pp. 2721-23; April, 1976, pp. 2849-52; January, 1977, pp. 3040-43; March, 1979, p. 3484.

Junior Bookshelf, February, 1975, pp. 33, 57; August, 1976, pp. 195-96; April, 1977, p. 107; December, 1978, p. 326; April, 1979, p. 112; April, 1980, p. 92.
Kirkus Reviews, April 15, 1969, p. 450.
New Statesman, November 12, 1971, p. 661.
Times Literary Supplement, October 3, 1968, p. 1107; October 30, 1970, p. 1262; October 22, 1971, p. 1318; April 6, 1973, p. 383; September 29, 1978, p. 1083.

*   *   *

CHAPPLE, Christopher Key 1954-

PERSONAL: Born September 4, 1954, in Medina, NY; son of H. Edward (a horseman) and Julia (a librarian; maiden name, Peton) Chapple; married Maureen Shannon (a first grade teacher), August 10, 1974; children: Dylan Edward, Emma Catherine. *Education:* State University of New York at Stony Brook, B.A., 1976; Fordham University, M.A., 1978, Ph.D., 1980.

ADDRESSES: Home—5839 W. 78th Pl., Los Angeles, CA 90045. *Office*—Department of Theology, Loyola Marymount University, Los Angeles, CA 90045.

CAREER: State University of New York at Stony Brook, lecturer in religious studies, 1980-85; Loyola Marymount University, Los Angeles, assistant professor, 1985-89, associate professor, 1989-94, professor of theological studies, 1994—, cofounder and acting director of Asian and Pacific studies, 1989-90, Charles S. Casassa Chair of Social Values, 1989-91, chairperson of Department of Theology, 1990-94, director of Casassa Conferences, 1990 and 1991. Margaret Demerest Lecturer, Casper College, Casper, WY, 1989. Coordinator of Moksha Community Education Center, 1979-85; assistant director of Institute for Advanced Studies of World Religions, 1980-85; coordinator of Southern California Seminar on South Asia, 1986—.

MEMBER: American Academy of Religion, College Theology Society, Society for Asian and Comparative Philosophy, Society for Buddhist-Christian Studies.

AWARDS, HONORS: Research and travel award, International Association Against Painful Experiments on Animals (London), 1984; summer research grants from Loyola Marymount University, 1987, 1988, 1993, 1994, and 1996; certificate of appreciation, California Women in Higher Education, 1989; National Endowment for the Humanities grant, 1992.

WRITINGS:

(Compiler) *Religious Experience and Scientific Paradigms: Proceedings of the IASWR Conference,* Institute for Advanced Studies of World Religions (Fort Lee, NJ), 1985.
Karma and Creativity, State University of New York Press (Albany, NY), 1986.
(Translator with Yogi Anand Viraj) *The Yoga Sutras of Patanjali: An Analysis of the Sanskrit with Accompanying English Translation,* Sri Satgura Publications (Delhi, India), 1990.
Nonviolence to Animals, Earth, and Self in Asian Traditions, State University of New York Press, 1993.

EDITOR

Samkhya-Yoga (proceedings of a conference), Institute for Advanced Studies of World Religions, 1982.
Bhagavad Gita, State University of New York Press, 1984.
The Jesuit Tradition in Education and Missions, University of Scranton Press (Scranton, PA), 1993.
Ecological Prospects: Scientific, Religious, and Aesthetic Perspectives, State University of New York Press, 1994.

OTHER

Contributor to periodicals. Editor of *Hindu Text Information,* 1980-85, and *Sikh Religious Studies Information,* 1981-85.

WORK IN PROGRESS: Research on the development of Yoga in medieval India, particularly as interpreted in the Sanskrit Yoga texts of Harilhadra, an Eighth Century Jaina scholar.

SIDELIGHTS: Christopher Key Chapple told *CA:* "*Karma and Creativity* explores the constructive side of Indian religious traditions, which too often are dismissed as fatalistic. Used properly, action can be seen as a means to bring one closer to liberation, rather than condemning one to continual rebirth. This book was written both for the scholar or student and

for those with a personal interest in the applications of Eastern thought in a contemporary context.

"Asian religion and philosophy offer great riches to the world. By exploring topics such as karma, nonviolence, and yoga, I have been able to find issues and interests that extend beyond the specific locale of India and speak to perennial human concerns."

*   *   *

CHEHAK, Susan Taylor   1951-

PERSONAL: Surname is pronounced "*Chee*-hock"; born February 16, 1951, in Cedar Rapids, IA; daughter of Robert Harmon (an actuary) and Mary Frances (a homemaker; maiden name, Zuercher) Taylor; married Thomas Archer Chehak (a television writer), May 18, 1974; children: Parker Thomas, Jesse Taylor. *Education:* Attended University of Chicago, 1969-70, and Mills College, 1971; University of Iowa, B.A. (with honors), 1973; University of Iowa Writer's Workshop, M.F.A., 1975. *Religion:* Protestant.

ADDRESSES: Home—Los Angeles, CA. *Agent*—Kim Witherspoon, Witherspoon Associates, Inc., 157 West 57th Street, New York, NY 10019.

CAREER: Writer. Teacher of fiction writing, Kirkwood Community College, Cedar Rapids, IA, 1975-76, and University of California, Los Angeles, Extension, 1992-95; University of Southern California, visiting lecturer, 1993-96. Member of guidance committee, UCLA Extension Writers' Program, 1995.

MEMBER: PEN, Mystery Writers of America, Authors Guild, Writers Guild of America.

AWARDS, HONORS: Edgar Award nominee for best first novel, Mystery Writers of America, 1990, for *The Story of Annie D.;* Hammett Award nomination, International Association of Crime Writers, 1996, for *Smithereens.*

WRITINGS:

NOVELS

The Story of Annie D., Houghton (Boston), 1989.
Harmony, Ticknor & Fields (New York City), 1990.

Dancing on Glass, Ticknor & Fields, 1993.
Smithereens, Doubleday (New York City), 1995.

OTHER

(With husband, Tom Chehak) *Last Chance Cafe* (two-act play), first produced in Los Angeles, CA, at Colony Theater, October, 1985.

Also author, with T. Chehak, of "One Fine Day," and "All the Young Dudes," both one hour dramatic series pilots for the Fox Broadcasting Company. Contributor to *Sisters in Crime,* Volume 5. Also contributor to the *Chariton Review.*

Chehak's papers are housed in the Twentieth-Century Archives, Munger Memorial Library, Boston University.

WORK IN PROGRESS: A novel, tentatively titled *Carried Away;* a screenplay adaptation of *Smithereens.*

SIDELIGHTS: Susan Taylor Chehak has established a reputation as a fine storyteller and an accomplished stylist through her mystery novels. In her first novel, *The Story of Annie D.,* she weaves a tale of a seemingly tranquil small town that is touched by violence. Marilyn Stasio, contributor to the *New York Times Book Review,* described *The Story of Annie D.* as "absolutely stunning" and found Chehak's voice "mesmerizing." The author's prose, according to Stasio, is "smooth and hard as a rock without being barren," and her narrative has "the force and generational sweep of some ancient rural myth." A *Publishers Weekly* writer was similarly impressed, referring to Chehak's "clear, dry voice, stripped of sentiment or passion," and concluding that "this authentically and distinctively cadenced first novel marks a promising debut."

Chehak sought to fulfill that promise in subsequent novels. Like *The Story of Annie D., Harmony* revealed the dark underside of small-town life. The narrator, Clodine Wheeler, tells readers of her violent marriage and her fascination with Lilly Duke, an amoral teenaged mother who drifts into the town of Harmony. A *Publishers Weekly* contributor described *Harmony* as "haunting . . . infused with a dark, edgy presence." Discussing the novel in the *New York Times Book Review,* Robert F. Moss asserted that Chehak's plot "is a highly sophisticated parquet of past and present events. Portents and harbingers— bloody, lacerated flesh, images of drowned bodies— brood over the story, opaquely foretelling some awful doom. . . . The town's name embodies the reassuring stability of Midwestern hamlets, while ironically accentuating the disharmony that lurks there as well." Moss cautioned that *Harmony* "is not a major work," yet he concluded that "it gives abundant evidence of a rapidly maturing talent" and asserted: "Susan Taylor Chehak's future as a novelist should be no mystery."

Dancing on Glass, Chehak's third novel, is a moody story of "family, place and sensibility, written in a prose of an almost hypnotic lyricism," in the opinion of *New York Times Book Review* contributor Daniel Woodrell. He praised the author's style, declaring Chehak's sentences to be "long and looping, occasionally breathless with detail. The frequent descriptions of the physical world are beautifully done, and the scenes of the human throng . . . are handled with a master's ease." He concluded that "though sometimes it seems that too many pages are given over to peripheral characters . . . Ms. Chehak's sentences are always rewarding."

In *Smithereens,* Chehak presents May Caldwell, a well-behaved teenager from a respectable Iowa family. May quickly unravels when she falls under the influence of Frankie Crane, a disadvantaged, manipulative girl from rural Kentucky. For years, May's mother has sponsored Frankie in a mail-order foster-child program. The girl's arrival on the Caldwells' doorstep sets off a chain of events that culminate in a tragic conflagration. Insecure May is irresistibly drawn to Frankie, and "her old personality and former innocence are slowly erased" under Frankie's tutelage, "supplanted by a rampant appetite for all kinds of transgressive pleasure," Judith Freeman reported in the *Los Angeles Times Book Review.* She went on to say that "Chehak is a very accomplished storyteller, always in control of her narrative, which moves ahead with grace and speed." *Smithereens* has "brooding, ominous atmosphere, sexual awakening, loss of innocence, murder," Diane White recounted in the *Boston Globe.* "Several murders, actually. It could be described as a gothic coming-of-age novel, but it's far too good to lend itself to any label. Susan Taylor Chehak is a meticulous writer, an evocative stylist whose mastery is evident on every page."

BIOGRAPHICAL/CRITICAL SOURCES:

PERIODICALS

Booklist, July, 1995, p. 1858.
Boston Globe, July 20, 1995, p. 53.

Library Journal, June 15, 1995, p. 93.
Los Angeles Times, August 18, 1989, p. V10.
Los Angeles Times Book Review, July 23, 1995, pp. 3, 8.
New York Times Book Review, July 9, 1989, p. 24; December 9, 1990, p. 29; January 16, 1994, p. 18; July 30, 1995, p. 15.
Publishers Weekly, March 31, 1989, p. 45; August 24, 1990, p. 54; May 8, 1995, p. 284.
Tribune Books (Chicago), May 28, 1989, p. 4.
Washington Post, October 4, 1993, p. B2.

*   *   *

CHETWIN, Grace

PERSONAL: Born in Nottingham, England; immigrated to the United States, 1964; daughter of Charles William and Ada (Fletcher) Chetwin; married Arthur G. Roberts (a professional tennis player); children: Claire, Briony (daughters). *Education:* University of Southampton, B.A. (with honors).

ADDRESSES: Home and office—37 Hitching Post Lane, Glen Cove, NY 11542. *Agent*—Jean V. Naggar, Jean V. Naggar Literary Agency, 336 East 73rd St., New York, NY 10021.

CAREER: High school English and French teacher in Auckland, New Zealand, in 1950s and 1960s; high school English teacher and department head in Devon, England, in 1960s; director of drama group in Auckland in 1970s; writer, 1983—; founder of Feral Press, 1995. Directed her own dance company in New Zealand for four years; producer of amateur plays and operas.

WRITINGS:

YOUNG ADULT NOVELS

On All Hallow's Eve, Lothrop (New York City), 1984.
Out of the Dark World, Lothrop, 1985.
Gom on Windy Mountain, Lothrop, 1986.
The Riddle and the Rune, Bradbury (Scarsdale, NY), 1987.
The Crystal Stair: From the Tales of Gom in the Legends of Ulm, Bradbury, 1988.
The Starstone, Bradbury, 1989.
Collidescope, Bradbury, 1990.
Child of the Air, Bradbury, 1991.

Friends in Time, Bradbury, 1992.
The Chimes of Alyafaleyn, Bradbury, 1993.
(Self-illustrated) *Jason's Seven Magical Night Rides,* Bradbury, 1994.

PICTURE BOOKS

Mr. Meredith and the Truly Remarkable Stone, illustrated by Catherine Stock, Bradbury, 1988.
Box and Cox, illustrated by David Small, Bradbury, 1990.
(Self-illustrated) *Rufus,* Feral Press (Glen Cove, NY), 1995.

OTHER

The Atheling: Volume I of the Last Legacy (adult), Tor Books (New York City), 1987.

Contributor to textbook, *Battling Dragons: Issues and Controversy in Children's Literature,* edited by Susan Lehr, Heinemann (London), 1995.

ADAPTATIONS: Rufus has been recorded on audio cassette.

SIDELIGHTS: Grace Chetwin is best known as the author of fantasy and science fiction books for young adults. Chetwin's first two books feature two sisters, Meg and Sue. *On All Hallow's Eve* tells the story of the sisters' recent immigration to the United States from England, Meg's dislike of her new home, and her struggle to deal with Kenny, a classmate who is a tease and a bully. Meg gets her revenge by humiliating Kenny at a Halloween party. When Meg and Sue run for home, they find themselves caught in a different world and time, and they must fight a battle that pits good against evil. Writing in *Booklist,* reviewer Barbara Elleman states: "The children's adventures . . . contain enough chilling effects to keep readers immersed in the struggle."

Sisters Meg and Sue appear again in Chetwin's second novel, *Out of the Dark World,* a book Karen P. Smith, writing in *School Library Journal,* calls "an unusual science fiction fantasy which combines Welsh lore with modern-day computer technology." In this complicated fantasy, Meg materializes the spirits of Peter Saltifer—an abrupt, outspoken Welshman—and the infamous enchantress Morgan le Fay to help her save her dying cousin from the forces of evil.

Chetwin's fantasies have been influenced by European folktales, especially the four books in her series about the wizard Gom. Gom is the tenth son of woodcutter Stig and his Wife, a mysterious woman who disappeared on the day of Gom's birth, leaving him only a rune, or magic stone. By his tenth birthday, Gom is small and dwarf-like, has three moles on his chin, and can communicate with animals. His strange powers lead him to a hidden cache of gold where he meets Dismas Skeller, whom Kathleen Brachmann in *School Library Journal* calls "as evil a gold-seeking malefactor as ever trod his way across the pages of a fantasy." When Stig dies, Gom sets off for Far Away to find his mother, his heritage, and his destiny.

During his quest for the gold, Gom discovers that his mother was really Harga the Brown, a great wizard. In the second book of the series, *The Riddle and the Rune,* Gom uses the stone, his only clue to his mother's existence, to reunite the pair. However, the reunion is short-lived. In *The Crystal Stair: From the Tales of Gom in the Legends of Ulm,* Harga is called off to do battle against the destruction of Ulm; Gom must become a wizard himself to be of any help, and his mother leaves him with the names of three wizards who might become his mentor. *Voice of Youth Advocates* contributor Barbara Evans finds that "the story is well-written and the action exciting."

The final book of the series, *The Starstone,* finds Gom on his own, having to use Harga's old notebooks to complete his education in order to thwart the evil Katak's plans to take over the world of Ulm. In the midst of this cosmic struggle between good and evil, the teenage Gom finds a love interest. Anne Raymer, writing in *Voice of Youth Advocates,* calls *The Starstone* a "pure fantasy adventure where a young boy comes of age through a fight with phantom and flesh enemies," and Ruth S. Vose in *School Library Journal* claims that "followers of Gom's adventures will devour this new addition to his story."

Chetwin returned to fantasy for young adults in a book Lesa M. Holstine, writing in *Voice of Youth Advocates,* describes as "a riveting story of time travel in which three civilizations collide." *Collidescope* tells the story of Hahn, a cyborg (a bionically-enhanced human being) from the future, Frankie, a present-day Long Island teenager, and Sky-fire-trail, a Delaware Indian of pre-Colonial America. When these three, traveling from different points in time, do meet, they manage to offer each other help, solace, and friendship in what Susan L. Rogers of *School Library Journal* calls "fast-paced,

action-packed pursuits through time and space." Chetwin once explained that *Collidescope* is "an examination of what humanity is, of what makes a human being."

The time travel theme reappears in *Friends in Time,* which tells of Emma Gibson, a lonely sixth grader who suddenly finds a friend in Abigail Bentley, a ten-year-old who has been mysteriously transported to the present from 1846. The action in *The Chimes of Alyafaleyn* takes place in a different world all together: a world where floating golden spheres, called "heynim," control the weather and have healing powers. Because of her ability to attract these spheres away from their rightful owners, young Caidrun is forced to suppress her talents. When she grows older and runs off to take her revenge, her only friend, Tamborel, sets out to find her. A contributor to *Kirkus Reviews* labels the book a "soft-edged romantic fantasy," and an "entertaining, if far-fetched, love story."

A different sort of relationship is the foundation for Chetwin's 1994 work, *Jason's Seven Magical Night Rides.* Eleven-year-old Jason is being raised by his mother, but he longs to know what it would be like to have a father in his life. One night, a mysterious stranger appears and offers him seven rides on famous mythical horses, including Pegasus, Chiron the centaur, and the Trojan Horse. As a *Kirkus Reviews* critic notes, "each episode teaches the fatherless boy a bit about maturity and responsibility."

In 1995, Chetwin produced her first book for Feral Press, a publishing company she founded. *Rufus,* Chetwin explained, "deals with loss and honesty." In the work, a child's beloved pet dies. "The child keeps her dignity by acknowledging the loss and deciding on her own if she wants to accept a new animal," Chetwin said.

BIOGRAPHICAL/CRITICAL SOURCES:

PERIODICALS

Booklist, October 15, 1984, p. 304.

Horn Book, November/December, 1986, pp. 743-744; May/June, 1990, p. 321.

Kirkus Reviews, February 1, 1988, p. 168; October 29, 1993; April 15, 1994.

New York Times Book Review, July 1, 1990.

Publishers Weekly, January 29, 1988, p. 418; March 10, 1989, p. 87.

School Library Journal, January, 1986, pp. 64-65; May, 1986, p. 89; June, 1989, p. 103; August, 1989, p. 116; May, 1990, p. 122; July, 1992, p. 72.

Voice of Youth Advocates, December, 1986, p. 234; June, 1988, p. 95; October, 1989, p. 220; April, 1990, p. 37; August, 1991, p. 178; October, 1992, p. 236.

Washington Post Book World, May 13, 1990, p. 18.

Wilson Library Bulletin, June, 1993, p. 112.

* * *

CHEUSE, Alan 1940-

PERSONAL: Born January 23, 1940, in Perth Amboy, NJ; son of Philip and Henrietta (Diamond) Cheuse; married Mary Agan, October 7, 1964 (divorced, 1974); married Marjorie Lee Pryse, June 22, 1975 (divorced, 1984); married Kristin M. O'Shee, August 17, 1991; children: (first marriage) Joshua Todd; (second marriage) Emma Cordelia, Sonya Ruth. *Education:* Attended Lafayette College, 1957-58; Rutgers University, B.A., 1961, Ph.D., 1974.

ADDRESSES: Home—3700 33rd Place NW, Washington, DC 20008. *Office*—Department of English, George Mason University, Fairfax, VA 22030.

CAREER: New Jersey Turnpike Authority, NJ, toll taker, 1961; Fairchild Publications, reporter, 1962-63; *Kirkus Reviews* Service, staff member, 1963-64; Butler Institute, Guadalajara, Jalisco, Mexico, teacher of history and English, 1965-66; New York City Department of Welfare, New York City, case worker, 1966-67; Bennington College, Bennington, VT, member of Division of Literature and Languages, 1970-78; University of the South, Sewanee, TN, writer in residence, 1984; University of Michigan, Ann Arbor, writer in residence, 1984-86; Bennington College, acting director of writing workshops, 1986-87; George Mason University, Fairfax, VA, member of writing faculty, 1987—. Visiting writer, University of Virginia, spring, 1987. Producer and host of radio magazine "The Sound of Writing," for National Public Radio (NPR), 1989—

MEMBER: National Book Critics Circle.

AWARDS, HONORS: National Endowment for the Arts writing fellowship, 1979-80.

WRITINGS:

(Editor with Richard M. Koffler) *The Rarer Action: Essays in Honor of Francis Fergusson,* Rutgers University Press (New Brunswick, NJ), 1971.

Candace and Other Stories, Applewood Press (Cambridge, MA), 1980.

The Bohemians: John Reed and His Friends Who Shook the World (novel), Applewood Books, 1982.

The Grandmothers' Club (novel), Peregrine Smith (Salt Lake City, UT), 1986, new edition with afterword by John W. Aldridge, Southern Methodist University Press (Dallas), 1994.

Fall Out of Heaven: An Autobiographical Journey (memoir), Peregrine Smith, 1987.

(Editor with Caroline Marshall) *The Sound of Writing,* Anchor Books (New York City), 1990.

The Tennessee Waltz and Other Stories, Peregrine Smith, 1990.

The Light Possessed (novel), Peregrine Smith, 1991.

(Editor with Marshall) *Listening to Ourselves,* Anchor Books, 1993.

(Editor with Nicholas Delbanco) *Talking Horse: Bernard Malamud on Life and Art,* Columbia University Press (New York City), 1996.

Contributor of short stories, articles, and reviews to periodicals, including the *New Yorker, Black Warrior Review, Nation, New York Times Book Review, Los Angeles Times Book Review, Saturday Review, Chicago Tribune, Ms., Dallas Morning News,* and *Antioch Review.* Member of editorial board, *Studies on the Left,* 1964-65. Book commentator for NPR evening news magazine "All Things Considered," 1982—.

WORK IN PROGRESS: Novels and stories.

SIDELIGHTS: Alan Cheuse's novel *The Grandmothers' Club* relates the experience of the Jewish immigrant in the United States. Specifically, it discloses the misfortunes of Rabbi Emmanuel (Manny) Bloch through the monologues of his mother, Minnie. As Jerome Charyn explains in the *New York Times Book Review,* "this is an unlikely novel concerning a group of grandmothers who meet to trade stories about sons, daughters-in-law and whatever else is on this side of the moon. Minnie Bloch does most of the talking. She's the 'leading lady in the grandmothers' club.'" In her own fashion, Minnie pieces together a record of her son's life; at age eight, we learn, Manny saw his father crushed to death beneath a milk wagon and that is why he has failed to move in rhythm with the rest of the world since. Readers also learn of Manny's more recent abandonment of his religious commitments for success on Wall Street, as well as his acceptance of a mistress when his wife experiences mental instability. Charyn believes *The Grandmothers' Club* "would be an ordinary Jewish family saga if Minnie were an ordinary woman. . . . It is this . . . grandmother's ability to thrust herself into her son's surroundings, to soak up his past and dream her way into his future, to hallucinate a life for him, that is both the virtue and the extraordinary sting of the book." Although in Charyn's opinion the novel is too long and at times overly melodramatic, he insists "we are all Jewish sons (and daughters) in Alan Cheuse's grip. His novel is a bitter, brilliant series of songs, heartless and tender, with a magical displacement of time and a language that rattles us and reminds us how close art and chaos really are."

Other critics value *The Grandmothers' Club* as well. In the *New York Times,* Christopher Lehmann-Haupt calls it a "haunting story. . . . A reader comes away from *The Grandmothers' Club* with the sense that he has read an epic of Jewish life in America and of the sometimes tragic conflict between blessedness and wealth." If the reader is able to overcome some of Minnie's longwindedness and forced humor, "*The Grandmothers' Club* is bound to work its powerful incantatory effects on you," maintains Lehmann-Haupt. As for *Chicago Tribune* reviewer Judy Bass, Minnie Bloch is "a character of stunning authenticity, one whose nuances render her both lifelike and endearing. . . . Above all, it is Minnie's humaneness that emerges with aching clarity, and her abundant sympathy for all those who stumble into crucibles from which there is no escape."

BIOGRAPHICAL/CRITICAL SOURCES:

BOOKS

Cheuse, Alan, *Fall Out of Heaven: An Autobiographical Journey* (memoir), Peregrine Smith, 1987.

PERIODICALS

Booklist, February 15, 1994, p. 1061.
Chicago Tribune, October 3, 1986.
College Literature, June, 1994, p. 183.
Kliatt Young Adult Paperback Book Guide, May, 1994, p. 21.
Library Journal, December, 1993, p. 179.
Los Angeles Times, October 1, 1987.

Los Angeles Times Book Review, December 7, 1986; January 16, 1994, p. 12; March 6, 1994, p. 6.
New York Times, November 20, 1986.
New York Times Book Review, November 9, 1980; March 28, 1982; October 26, 1986.
Publishers Weekly, December 6, 1993, p. 69.
Tribune Books (Chicago), September 20, 1987.
Washington Post Book World, March 14, 1982.

*   *   *

CLARK, Burton R(obert)   1921-

PERSONAL: Born September 6, 1921, in Pleasantville, NJ; son of Burton H. (in business) and Cornelia (Amole) Clark; married Adele Halitsky (an editor), August 31, 1949; children: Philip Neil (deceased), Adrienne. *Education:* University of California, Los Angeles, B.A., 1949, Ph.D., 1954.

ADDRESSES: Home—201 Ocean Ave., Apt. 1710B, Santa Monica, CA 90402. *Office*—Department of Education, University of California, Los Angeles, CA 90024.

CAREER: Stanford University, Stanford, CA, assistant professor of sociology, 1953-56; Harvard University, Cambridge, MA, research associate and assistant professor of education, 1956-58; University of California, Berkeley, associate professor, 1958-64, professor of education, 1964-66, associate research sociologist, 1958-64, research sociologist, 1964-66; Yale University, New Haven, CT, professor of sociology, 1966-80, chair of department, 1969-72, chair of Higher Education Research Group, 1973-80; University of California, Los Angeles, Allan M. Cartter Professor of Higher Education and Sociology, 1980-91, chair of Comparative Higher Education Research Group, 1982-91, professor emeritus, 1991—. *Military service:* U.S. Army, 1942-46.

MEMBER: International Sociological Association, American Sociological Association, National Academy of Education, American Educational Research Association, Association for the Study of Higher Education (president, 1979-80), American Association for Higher Education, Consortium of Higher Education Researchers, European Association for Institutional Research, British Society for the Study of Higher Education.

AWARDS, HONORS: Research award, American Educational Research Association and American College Testing Program, 1979; Research Achievement Award, Association for the Study of Higher Education, 1985; Distinguished Research Award, American Educational Research Association, Division J, 1988.

WRITINGS:

Adult Education in Transition, University of California Press (Berkeley), 1956.

The Open Door College, McGraw (New York City), 1960.

Educating the Expert Society, Chandler, 1962.

The Distinctive College: Antioch, Reed, and Swarthmore, Aldine, 1970.

(With Paul Heist, T. R. McConnell, Martin A. Trow, and George Yonge) *Students and Colleges,* Center for Research and Development in Higher Education, (Berkeley), 1972.

(With James S. Coleman and others) *Youth: Transition to Adulthood,* University of Chicago Press, 1973.

The Problems of American Education, F. Watts (New York City), 1975.

(With Ted I. K. Youn) *Academic Power in the United States,* American Association for Higher Education, 1976.

Academic Power in Italy, University of Chicago Press (Chicago), 1977.

(With John H. Van de Graaff and others) *Academic Power: Patterns of Authority in Seven National Systems of Higher Education,* Praeger (Westport, CT), 1978.

The Higher Education System: Academic Organization in Cross-National Perspective, University of California Press, 1983.

(Editor) *Perspectives on Higher Education,* University of California Press, 1984.

(Editor) *The School and the University,* University of California Press, 1985.

(Editor) *The Academic Profession,* University of California Press, 1987.

The Academic Life, Carnegie Foundation for the Advancement of Teaching and Princeton University Press (Princeton, NJ), 1987.

(Senior editor with Guy Neave), *Encyclopedia of Higher Education* (four volumes), Pergamm, 1992.

(Editor) *The Research Foundations of Higher Education: Germany, Britain, France, United States, Japan,* University of California Press, 1993.

Places of Inquiry: Research and Advanced Education in Modern Universities, University of California Press, 1995.

SIDELIGHTS: Burton R. Clark told *CA:* "My work centers on a sociological understanding of higher education. Since 1960, I have specialized in cross-national studies of how national systems of higher education are organized. This work has taken me, as researcher, lecturer, and consultant, to Japan, the United Kingdom, Sweden, Germany, France, Italy, Poland, Portugal, Canada, Mexico, Chile, Brazil, Australia, China, Norway, South Africa, Finland, and the Netherlands.

"I am impressed with the enormous diversity of American higher education, which makes our system open and flexible, but also leaves it with uneven standards and much confusion. I am convinced that international comparisons are the best way to grasp the special nature of our educational system."

*   *   *

CLEARY, Jon   1917-

PERSONAL: Born November 22, 1917, in Sydney, New South Wales, Australia; son of Matthew and Ida (Brown) Cleary; married Constantine Joy Lucas, September 6, 1946; children: Catherine, Jane (deceased). *Education:* Left school at end of second year of high school in Sydney, Australia. *Avocational interests:* Cricket, tennis.

ADDRESSES: Home—71 Upper Pitt St., Kirribilli, New South Wales, Australia. *Agent*—c/o Curtis Brown Ltd., 28-29 Haymarket, London SW1Y 4SP, England.

CAREER: Prior to World War II worked at "too many jobs to be listed," including commercial artist, salesperson, delivery man, laundry worker, bush worker, and sign painter; full-time writer, 1945—, except for a year in London, as journalist with Australian Government Bureau, and two years in New York City, with the Australian Bureau. *Military service:* Australian Army, 1940-45; served in Middle East, New Guinea, and New Britain campaigns; became lieutenant.

AWARDS, HONORS: Cowinner of first prize, National Play Award, Australian Broadcasting Commission, 1944; second prize, National Novel Contest, *Sydney Morning Herald,* 1946; Crouch gold medal for best Australian novel of 1950; Edgar Allan Poe award, Mystery Writers of America, 1974, for *Peter's Pence;* cowinner of Australian section, World Story Contest, *New York Herald Tribune.*

WRITINGS:

These Small Glories, Angus & Robertson (North Ryde, New South Wales), 1946.
You Can't See around Corners, Scribner (New York City), 1947, 4th edition, Horwitz, 1965.
The Long Shadow, Laurie (London), 1950, reprinted, Severn House (London), 1976.
Just Let Me Be, Laurie, 1951.
The Sundowners, Scribner, 1952, reprinted, 1984.
The Climate of Courage, Collins (New York City), 1954, reprinted, Magna Print Books (Skipton, N. Yorkshire, England), 1980.
Justin Bayard, Morrow (New York City), 1955.
The Green Helmet, Morrow, 1958, reprinted, Collins, 1983.
Back of Sunset, Morrow, 1959, reprinted, Ulverscroft Large Print Books (Anstey, Leicester, England), 1978.
North from Thursday, Morrow, 1961.
The Country of Marriage, Morrow, 1962.
Forests of the Night, Morrow, 1963.
A Flight of Chariots, Morrow, 1963.
The Fall of an Eagle, Morrow, 1964, reprinted, Collins, 1983.
The Pulse of Danger, Morrow, 1966.
The High Commissioner, Morrow, 1966.
The Long Pursuit, Morrow, 1967.
Season of Doubt, Morrow, 1968.
Remember Jack Hoxie, Morrow, 1969.
Helga's Web, Morrow, 1970.
The Liberators, Morrow, 1971, published in England as *Mask of the Andes,* Collins, 1971.
The Ninth Marquess, Morrow, 1972, published in England as *Man's Estate,* Collins, 1972.
Ransom, Morrow, 1973.
Peter's Pence, Morrow, 1974.
Sidecar Racers (screenplay), Universal, 1975.
The Safe House, Morrow, 1975.
A Sound of Lightning, Collins, 1975, Morrow, 1976.
High Road to China, Morrow, 1977.
Vortex, Collins, 1977, Morrow, 1978.
The Beaufort Sisters, Morrow, 1979.
A Very Private War, Morrow, 1980.
The Golden Sabre, Morrow, 1981.
The Faraway Drums, Collins, 1981, Morrow, 1982.
Spearfield's Daughter, Collins, 1982, Morrow, 1983.
The Phoenix Tree, Collins, 1984.

City of Fading Light, Collins, 1985, Morrow, 1986.
Dragons at the Party, Morrow, 1988.
Now and Then, Simon, Morrow, 1989.
Babylon South, Morrow, 1990.
Murder Song, Morrow, 1991.
Pride's Harvest, Morrow, 1992.
Dark Summer, Morrow, 1993.
Bleak Spring, Morrow, 1994.
Autumn Maze, Morrow, 1995.
Winter Chill, Morrow, 1996.
Endpeace, Morrow, 1996.

Also author of film scripts for Warner Brothers, Metro-Goldwyn-Mayer, Paramount Pictures, and Ealing Films. Author of television scripts for programs in the United States and England.

ADAPTATIONS: A screen adaptation of *Justin Bayard* was produced by Southern Pacific in 1958; the films *The Sundowners,* produced by Warner Bros. in 1960, *The Green Helmet,* produced by Metro-Goldwyn-Mayer in 1961, *The High Commissioner,* produced by Rank in 1968, and *High Road to China,* produced by Warner Bros. in 1984, were all based on Cleary's novels of the same titles; *You Can't See 'round Corners,* based on his novel *You Can't See around Corners,* was produced by Universal in 1969; *Scobie Malone,* based on his novel *Helga's Web,* was produced by Kingscroft in 1975; television adaptations were produced of *Ransom,* by Kokusai Hoei (Japan) in 1981, and of *Spearfield's Daughter,* by Metromedia (United States) in 1986.

BIOGRAPHICAL/CRITICAL SOURCES:

PERIODICALS

Armchair Detective, fall, 1993, p. 121.
Booklist, March 1, 1994, p. 1183, 1188.
Kirkus Reviews, December 1, 1989, p. 1707; February 1, 1994, p. 97.
Library Journal, February 1, 1994, p. 115.
Los Angeles Times, July 4, 1980.
Los Angeles Times Book Review, March 20, 1983.
New York Times Book Review, July 9, 1967; July 7, 1968; September 14, 1969; June 2, 1974; January 7, 1990, p. 29.
Publishers Weekly, October 27, 1989, p. 58; October 12, 1990, p. 48; January 10, 1994, p. 47.
Times Literary Supplement, July 17, 1969; March 16, 1973.
Tribune Books (Chicago), January 31, 1988; January 7, 1990, p. 6.

CLEVERLEY FORD, D(ouglas) W(illiam)   1914-

PERSONAL: Born March 4, 1914, in Sheringham, England; son of Arthur James (a clerk) and Mildred (Cleverley) Ford; married Olga Mary Gilbart-Smith, June 28, 1939 (died, 1993). *Education:* London College of Divinity, A.L.C.D. (with first class honors), 1936; University of London, B.D., 1937, M.Th., 1941. *Avocational interests:* Music, the arts, European travel, gardening and carpentry at his house in the country.

ADDRESSES: Home—Rostrevor, Lingfield, Surrey RH7 6BZ, England.

CAREER: Ordained priest of Church of England in St. Paul's Cathedral, London, 1937; London College of Divinity, London, tutor, 1937-39; Bridlington, Yorkshire, England, curate, 1939-42; Holy Trinity, Hampstead, London, vicar, 1942-55; Holy Trinity, South Kensington, London, vicar, 1955-74; senior chaplain to the Archbishop of Canterbury, Canterbury, England, 1975-80; Six Preacher of Canterbury Cathedral, Canterbury, 1982-91. Chaplain to Queen Elizabeth II, 1973-84. Honorary director, College of Preachers, 1960-73; rural dean of Westminster, 1965-74; prebendary of St. Paul's Cathedral, beginning 1968; provincial canon of York, 1969—. Chair of Queen Alexandra's House, Kensington Gore, 1966-74. Member of governing body, Westminster City School and United Westminster Schools, 1965-74.

MEMBER: British and Foreign Bible Society (life governor), Church's Ministry among the Jews, Athenaeum Club (London).

AWARDS, HONORS: Queen's Jubilee Medal, 1977.

WRITINGS:

Why Men Believe in Jesus Christ, Lutterworth (Cambridge, England), 1950.
A Key to Genesis, Society for Promoting Christian Knowledge (London), 1951.
An Expository Preacher's Notebook, Hodder & Stoughton (London), 1960, Harper (New York City), 1961.
A Theological Preacher's Notebook, Hodder & Stoughton, 1962.
(Coauthor) *The Churchman's Companion,* Hodder & Stoughton, 1964.
A Pastoral Preacher's Notebook, Hodder & Stoughton, 1965.

A Reading of St. Luke's Gospel, Lippincott, 1967.
Preaching at the Parish Communion, Mowbray (Oxford, England), Volume 1, 1967, Volume 2: *On the Epistles,* 1968, Volume 3: *On Saints' Days and Holy Days,* 1969, Volume 7, 1975.
Preaching Today, Society for Promoting Christian Knowledge, 1969.
Preaching through the Christian Year: Sermon Outlines for the Seasons of the Church's Year, Mowbray, 1971.
Praying through the Christian Year, Mowbray, 1973.
Have You Anything to Declare?, Mowbray, 1973.
Preaching on Special Occasions, Mowbray, Volume 1, 1975, Volume 2, 1982.
New Preaching from the Old Testament, Mowbray, 1976.
New Preaching from the New Testament, Mowbray, 1977.
The Ministry of the Word, Hodder & Stoughton, 1979, Eerdmans (Grand Rapids, MI), 1980.
Preaching through the Acts of the Apostles, Mowbray, 1980.
More Preaching from the New Testament, Mowbray, 1982.
More Preaching from the Old Testament, Mowbray, 1983.
Preaching through the Psalms, Mowbray, 1984.
Preaching through the Life of Christ, Mowbray, 1985, CBP Press, 1986.
Preaching on Devotional Occasions, Mowbray, 1986.
From Strength to Strength, Mowbray, 1987.
Preaching the Risen Christ, Mowbray, 1988.
Preaching the Great Themes, Mowbray, 1989.
God's Masterpieces, Bible Reading Fellowship (London), 1991.
Preaching the Incarnate Christ, Mowbray, 1992.
Preaching on the Crucifixion, Mowbray, 1993.
Preaching What We Believe, Mowbray, 1995.
Preaching on the Sayings of Jesus, Mowbray, 1996.
Day to Day with the Psalms, Bible Reading Fellowship, 1996.

Contributor to *Expository Times* and *Church Times.*

SIDELIGHTS: D. W. Cleverly Ford told *CA* that he began his writing career because people wanted to read what he had said in lectures in sermons. "Since my spoken word had always been carefully prepared, having been written and rewritten," he said, "this was not difficult. Writing for speaking is different from writing for reading, but it is good training in the art of clarity. I believe that a writer's work will be flat if it pays attention only to conveying information couched in a good literary style; it also needs to move the reader. This implies a sense of drama. I suppose a person either has or has not this sense. A rough and ready test of a good piece of writing is whether or not the reader is sorry when he has come to the end."

BIOGRAPHICAL/CRITICAL SOURCES:

PERIODICALS

Church Times, January 4, 1963.

*　　*　　*

CLEWES, Dorothy (Mary) 1907-

PERSONAL: Born July 6, 1907, in Nottingham, England; daughter of Frank and Annie Gertrude Parkin; married Winston David Armstrong Clewes (a writer), 1932 (died, 1957). *Education:* Attended private school in Nottingham, and University of Nottingham. *Religion:* Church of England. *Avocational interests:* Travel.

ADDRESSES: Home—Soleig, 1 Kings Ride, Alfriston, East Sussex BN26 5XP, England. *Agent*—Curtis Brown, 162-168 Regent St., London WIR 5TB, England.

CAREER: Secretary and dispenser to a physician in Nottingham, England, 1924-32; writer. Speaker at schools and libraries in England and the United States. *Wartime service:* Drove an ambulance during World War II.

MEMBER: PEN (member of executive committee), Society of Authors, National Book League.

AWARDS, HONORS: Junior Literary Guild award, 1957, for *The Runaway.*

WRITINGS:

YOUNG ADULT FICTION

The Rivals of Maidenhurst, Nelson (London), 1925.
The Cottage in the Wild Wood, illustrated by Irene Hawkins, Faber (London), 1945.
The Stream in the Wild Wood, illustrated by Hawkins, Faber, 1946.

The Treasure in the Wild Wood, illustrated by Hawkins, Faber, 1947.
The Wild Wood (contains *The Cottage in the Wild Wood* and *The Stream in the Wild Wood*), illustrated by Hawkins, Coward McCann (New York City), 1948.
The Fair in the Wild Wood, illustrated by Hawkins, Faber, 1949.
Henry Hare's Boxing Match, illustrated by Patricia W. Turner, Chatto & Windus (London), 1950, Coward McCann, 1950.
Henry Hare's Earthquake, illustrated by Turner, Chatto & Windus, 1950, Coward McCann, 1951.
Henry Hare, Painter and Decorator, illustrated by Turner, Chatto & Windus, 1951.
Henry Hare and the Kidnapping of Selina Squirrel, illustrated by Turner, Chatto & Windus, 1951.
The Adventure of the Scarlet Daffodil, illustrated by R. G. Campbell, Chatto & Windus, 1952, as *The Mystery of the Scarlet Daffodil,* Coward McCann, 1953.
The Mystery of the Blue Admiral, illustrated by J. Marianne Moll, Coward McCann, 1954, Collins (London), 1955.
The Secret, illustrated by Peggy Beetles, Hamish Hamilton (London), 1956, Coward McCann, 1956.
The Runaway, illustrated by Beetles, Hamish Hamilton, 1957, illustrated by Sofia, Coward McCann, 1957.
Adventure on Rainbow Island, illustrated by Shirley Hughes, Collins, 1957, as *Mystery on Rainbow Island,* Coward McCann, 1957.
The Jade Green Cadillac, illustrated by Shirley Hughes, Collins, 1958, as *The Mystery of the Jade Green Cadillac,* Coward McCann, 1958.
The Happiest Day, illustrated by Beetles, Hamish Hamilton, 1958, Coward McCann, 1959.
The Old Pony, illustrated by Beetles, Hamish Hamilton, 1959, Coward McCann, 1960.
Hide and Seek, illustrated by Beetles, Hamish Hamilton, 1959, Coward McCann, 1960.
The Lost Tower Treasure, illustrated by Shirley Hughes, Collins, 1960, as *The Mystery of the Lost Tower Treasure,* Coward McCann, 1960.
The Hidden Key, illustrated by Beetles, Hamish Hamilton, 1960, Coward McCann, 1961.
The Singing Strings, illustrated by Shirley Hughes, Collins, 1961, as *Mystery of the Singing Strings,* Coward McCann, 1961.
All the Fun of the Fair, illustrated by Juliette Palmer, Hamish Hamilton, 1961, Coward McCann, 1962.

Wilberforce and the Slaves, illustrated by Peter Edwards, Hutchinson (London), 1961.

Skyraker and the Iron Imp, illustrated by Edwards, Hutchinson, 1962.

The Purple Mountain, illustrated by Robert Broomfield, Collins, 1962, as *The Golden Eagle,* Coward McCann, 1962.

The Birthday, illustrated by Palmer, Hamish Hamilton, 1962, Coward McCann, 1963.

The Branch Line, illustrated by Palmer, Hamish Hamilton/Coward McCann, 1963.

Operation Smuggle, illustrated by Hughes, Collins, 1964, as *The Mystery of the Midnight Smugglers,* Coward McCann, 1964.

Boys and Girls Come out to Play, illustrated by Jane Paton, Hamish Hamilton, 1964.

The Holiday, illustrated by Janet Duchesne, Hamish Hamilton, 1964, Coward McCann, 1964.

Guide Dog, illustrated by Peter Burchard, Hamish Hamilton, 1965, Coward McCann, 1965, published as *Dog for the Dark,* White Lion (London), 1974.

Red Ranger and the Combine Harvester, illustrated by Edwards, Hutchinson, 1966.

Roller Skates, Scooter and Bike, illustrated by Constance Marshall, Hamish Hamilton, 1966, illustrated by Sofia, Coward McCann, 1966.

A Boy Like Walt, Collins, 1967, Coward McCann, 1967.

A Bit of Magic, illustrated by Robert Hales, Hamish Hamilton, 1967.

A Girl Like Cathy, Collins, 1968.

Adopted Daughter, Coward McCann, 1968.

Upside-Down Willie, illustrated by Edward Ardizzone, Hamish Hamilton, 1968.

Special Branch Willie, illustrated by Ardizzone, Hamish Hamilton, 1969.

Peter and the Jumbie, illustrated by Hales, Hamish Hamilton, 1969.

Fire-Brigade Willie, illustrated by Ardizzone, Hamish Hamilton, 1970.

Library Lady, illustrated by Hales, Chatto Boyd & Oliver (London), 1970, as *The Library,* illustrated by Reisie Lonette, Coward McCann, 1971.

Two Bad Boys, illustrated by Lynette Hemmant, Hamish Hamilton, 1971.

The End of Summer, Coward McCann, 1971.

Storm over Innish, Heinemann, 1972, Nelson (Nashville), 1973.

A Skein of Geese, illustrated by Duchesne, Chatto Boyd & Oliver, 1972.

Ginny's Boy, Heinemann, 1973.

Hooray for Me, illustrated by Michael Jackson, Heinemann, 1973.

Wanted—a Grand, illustrated by Robert Micklewright, Chatto & Windus, 1974.

Missing from Home, Heinemann, 1975, Harcourt, 1978.

Nothing to Declare, Heinemann, 1976.

The Testing Year, Heinemann, 1977.

The Adventures of Willie (includes *Upside-Down Willie, Special Branch Willie,* and *Fire-Brigade Willie*), illustrated by Caroline Crossland, MacRae (London), 1991.

CHILDREN'S NONFICTION

Guide Dogs for the Blind, photographs by Louis Klemantaski, Hamish Hamilton, 1966.

(Editor) *The Secret of the Sea: An Anthology of Underwater Exploration and Adventure,* illustrated by Jeroo Roy, Heinemann, 1973.

ADULT NOVELS

She Married a Doctor, Jenkins (London), 1943, as *Stormy Hearts,* Arcadia (New York City), 1944.

Shepherd's Hill, Sampson Low (London), 1945.

To Man Alone, Jenkins, 1945, Arcadia, 1945.

A Stranger in the Valley, Harrap (London), 1948.

The Blossom on the Bough, Harrap, 1949.

Summer Cloud, Harrap, 1951.

Merry-Go-Round, Hodder & Stoughton (London), 1954.

I Came to a Wood, Hale (London), 1956.

OTHER

Contributor to *The Eleanor Farjeon Giftbook.* Contributor to magazines and annuals for children.

ADAPTATIONS: The Adventure of the Scarlet Daffodil and *Operation Smuggle* were adapted for British television.

SIDELIGHTS: English author Dorothy Clewes has written many books for children of all ages—from pre-school to young adult—in a career that has spanned over three decades. From the popular "Willie" books to teen novels like *Storm over Innish,* her books have pleased both British and American readers with their interesting settings, intriguing subjects, and likeable, well-drawn characters.

"I have always written, as long as I can remember," Clewes once stated. "Fairy stories and animal stories for newspapers and magazines when I was in my earliest teens, a full length school novel when I was

15." Clewes began writing in her spare time while working for her family's doctor in Nottingham. Her first novel, *The Rivals of Maidenhurst,* a story about life at a girl's private school, was published in 1925. After marrying Winston Clewes, a prolific writer, in 1932, Dorothy was encouraged by her new husband to devote herself to writing on a full-time basis. Soon she was publishing a series of light romance novels and children's books. "I suppose this all began as a fascinating hobby," she once explained, "began to be a lucrative one, and then, when my husband died, I decided to use it as a serious career. I miss very much the discussions and criticisms he used to give, as he was a writer in a quite different field so that we could read each other's work quite objectively."

Several years after her husband's death, Clewes was working on a story about smuggling along the south of England near the English Channel coast. She fell in love with the area, left her home in London, and moved to the old smuggling village of Alfriston, Sussex—the same town where she had set her story. It would be in this new home that Clewes would write many of her popular books, including *The Library, Special Branch Willie,* and *Roller Skates, Scooter and Bike.*

Special Branch Willie is one of three books featuring Willie, a young boy whose overly-enthusiastic personality leads him to change his career plans constantly. In *Upside-Down Willie,* published in 1968, Willie decides to join the circus. Because the only acrobatic trick he knows is a handstand, he practices it constantly. In *Special Branch Willie,* he longs to be a policeman. But when he gets the chance to use the emergency number after he discovers a small fire, the attention and praise given him by the hardworking firemen cause Willie to yearn for a career as a fireman. Hoses and ladders and soaked parents come into play in *Fire-Brigade Willie,* as the boy's excessive enthusiasm leads him into more trouble. Clewes, a *Times Literary Supplement* reviewer believes, tells Willie's stories in a "direct, simple and entirely gripping" manner. The three books about Willie were reissued as *The Adventures of Willie* in 1991.

In *The Library,* Clewes tells the story of two older brothers who come under the sway of their little sister when Ginny gets a card at the town's brand new library. Ginny tries to get big brothers Dudley and Charlie interested in books instead of their gang of local toughs. "Family relationships are warm and realistic, particularly those between Ginny and her brothers," according to a *Bulletin of the Center for Children's Books* reviewer.

"I take most of my material from first-hand experience and information," Clewes once explained. "I like a real background in my stories and feel that coming fresh to the experience myself adds a freshness to my writing." The real background of *Guide Dog* is the result of the research she did in the breeding, training, and use of seeing-eye dogs. In the story, nineteen-year-old Roley Rolandson is blinded for life after a package explodes near his face during his part-time job delivering mail at the post office. With his dreams of becoming a doctor destroyed, Roley becomes bitter and depressed, but two friends encourage him to get a seeing-eye dog. Real-life use of seeing-eye dogs is detailed in Clewes' nonfiction book *Guide Dogs for the Blind,* in which she describes the work of the British Guide Dogs for the Blind Association.

Guide Dog is but one of many novels that Clewes has written for older teen readers. One of her most popular novels for this age group is 1972's *Storm over Innish,* which takes place on a remote island off the coast of Ireland where Letty Ward and her family have moved after her brother's death. Her parents' relationship begins to fall apart; they fight constantly while each tries vainly to cope with the loss, and fifteen-year-old Letty is left alone to deal with her own grief. When a young man is washed up on the beach during a storm suffering from amnesia, the family takes care of him, becoming revitalized in their own lives as a result. *Storm over Innish* tells, a *Publishers Weekly* critic notes, an "engrossing plot against a sharply realistic background of land and sea."

Throughout her writing career, Clewes has been praised by critics for creating realistic characters and vivid settings. "I do not find that English and American readers are so different," Clewes once explained, "and try and write an honest and unsentimental book, not pointing morals but leaving them there for children to find for themselves. I don't think I have ever written down, and don't really subscribe to the idea of children's books and adult books being in a strongly emphasized category—a good children's book I feel should be interesting to an adult, and vice versa."

BIOGRAPHICAL/CRITICAL SOURCES:

BOOKS

Twentieth-Century Children's Writers, 4th edition, St. James Press (Detroit), 1995.

PERIODICALS

Bulletin of the Center for Children's Books, November, 1967; April, 1971, p. 120; February, 1974; February, 1978.
Horn Book, August, 1965, pp. 394-95; August, 1967, p. 474; February, 1969, p. 58.
Junior Bookshelf, April, 1977, p. 107; June, 1978, p. 150.
Publishers Weekly, November 19, 1973, p. 61.
School Library Journal, June 15, 1966, pp. 3256-57; May 15, 1971, p. 1801; November, 1978, p. 58.
Times Literary Supplement, November 17, 1966, p. 1053; November 24, 1966, p. 1087; August 14, 1970, p. 909; December 11, 1970, p. 1459; July 14, 1972, p. 814; March 29, 1974, p. 326; July 5, 1974, p. 720.

*   *   *

COALE, Samuel Chase   1943-

PERSONAL: Born July 26, 1943, in Hartford, CT; son of Samuel Chase (a photographer) and Harriet (Kimberly) Coale; married Gray Emory, June 24, 1972; children: Samuel Chase. *Education:* Trinity College, Hartford, CT, B.A., 1965; Brown University, M.A. and Ph.D., both 1970.

ADDRESSES: Office—Department of English, Wheaton College, Norton, MA 02766.

CAREER: Wheaton College, Norton, MA, instructor, 1968-71, assistant professor, 1971-76, associate professor, 1976-81, professor of American literature, 1981—. Instructor, Poznan Summer Seminar, Poznan, Poland, 1977-79, 1984, and 1985; instructor, English Literature and Language Seminar in Czechoslovakia, 1983-86, 1988, and 1989; lecturer, speaker, consultant in Sweden, Pakistan, India, Egypt, Israel, Yugoslavia, and Brazil, 1981-95. Trinity Repertory Theatre, board of directors, 1974-84, humanities consultant and project coordinator, 1978-92; member of board of directors, Looking Glass Theatre, 1975-77, Rhode Island Dance Repertory Company, 1975-77, Rhode Island Bicentennial Commission, 1976, Foundation for Repertory Theatre, 1974-84, The Vestry of St. Martin's Church, 1988-92; Gordon School, East Providence, RI, board of governors, education committee, 1988-91, chair of committee on the arts, 1989-91.

MEMBER: National Book Critics Circle, Modern Language Association of America, College English Association, English-Speaking Union (president, 1975-78; program chair, 1978-83; scholarship chair, 1987-91), Hawthorne Society, Frost Society (chair, 1991), Poe Society, Phi Beta Kappa.

AWARDS, HONORS: Ford Foundation summer grants, 1970, 1971; grants for study in England, 1969, 1970, 1972; Fulbright fellowship in Greece, 1976-77, and Brazil, 1994; elected Knight of Mark Twain for book *John Cheever;* named outstanding young man, U.S. Jaycees, 1978; National Endowment for the Humanities fellowship, 1981; Fulbright Seminars Abroad Program in Pakistan, 1990.

WRITINGS:

John Cheever, Ungar (New York City), 1977.
Anthony Burgess, Ungar, 1981.
In Hawthorne's Shadow: American Romance from Melville to Mailer, University Press of Kentucky (Lexington, KY), 1985.
Paul Theroux, Twayne (Boston, MA), 1987.
Providence's Muse; or, It's Muse to Me (play), produced by Trinity Repertory Company, 1987.
William Styron Revisited, Twayne, 1991.

Contributor of articles and essays to anthologies on literature, including *Thor's Hammer: Essays on John Gardner,* edited by Jeff Henderson, University of Central Arkansas Press, 1985, and *Confronting AIDS Through Literature: The Responsibilities of Representations,* edited by Judith Laurence Pastore, University of Illinois Press, 1993. Contributor of articles and reviews to literature journals such as *American Literature, Modern Fiction Studies, American Transcendental Quarterly,* and *Essays in Literature.* Book reviewer, *Providence Journal;* theater and film reviewer, *East Side* (Providence, RI) and *Newport: This Week.* Contributing editor, *Critique: Studies in Modern Fiction,* 1982-89.

WORK IN PROGRESS: Mesmerism and Hawthorne: Mediums of American Romance, about American mysteries; *Blood Rites,* a novel of the Afghanistan War in Pakistan; *The Woods Are Lovely,* a gothic novel.

SIDELIGHTS: Samuel Chase Coale told *CA:* "Writing continues to occupy two or three hours a day, despite a heavy load of teaching American literature at Wheaton College. At the moment I'm working on writers and mysteries and how they both use and alter the standard mystery formula, looking at such writers as Walter Mosley, Amanda Cross, Tony Hillerman, and James Lee Burke. I continue to travel widely and lecture, as well as writing feature articles on various cultures and countries and theater reviews in Providence. My real hope is to break through into published fiction, an opportunity that consistently beckons and always seems about to happen."

BIOGRAPHICAL/CRITICAL SOURCES:

PERIODICALS

Los Angeles Times Book Review, January 10, 1982.
Times Literary Supplement, May 22, 1987.

*   *   *

COFFEY, Brian
  See KOONTZ, Dean R(ay)

*   *   *

COHN, Samuel Kline, Jr.   1949-

PERSONAL: Born April 13, 1949, in Birmingham, AL; son of Samuel Kline (a physician) and Mildred (an artist; maiden name, Hiller) Cohn. *Education:* Attended University of London, 1969-70; Union College, Schenectady, NY, B.A., 1971; University of Wisconsin—Madison, M.A., 1972; Harvard University, Ph.D., 1978. *Politics:* Socialist.

ADDRESSES: Home—13 Botanic Crescent, Glasgow, Scotland G20 8QQ. *Office*—Department of Medieval History, University of Glasgow, Scotland G12 8QQ.

CAREER: Wesleyan University, Middletown, CT, assistant professor of history, 1978-79; Brandeis University, Waltham, MA, assistant professor, 1979-85, associate professor, 1985-86, professor of history, 1986-95; University of Glasgow (Scotland), professor of medieval history, 1995—. Visiting professor, Brown University, 1991.

WRITINGS:

The Laboring Classes in Renaissance Florence, Academic Press (San Diego, CA), 1980.
Death and Property in Siena, 1205-1799: Strategies for the Afterlife, Johns Hopkins University Press (Baltimore, MD), 1988.
The Cult of Remembrance and the Black Death, Johns Hopkins University Press, 1992.
(With David Herlily) *The Black Death & the Transformation of the West,* Harvard University Press (Cambridge, MA), 1996.
Women in the Streets and Other Essays on the Renaissance, Johns Hopkins University Press, 1996.
(Editor with Steven Epstein) *Portraits of Medieval & Renaissance Life,* University of Michigan Press (Ann Arbor), 1996.

WORK IN PROGRESS: The Growth of the Florentine Territorial State as Seen from the Mountains.

BIOGRAPHICAL/CRITICAL SOURCES:

PERIODICALS

American Historical Review, June, 1990, p. 860; October, 1993, p. 1283.
Catholic Historical Review, January, 1990, p. 95; October, 1993, p. 740.
Historian, spring, 1994, p. 583.
History Today, January, 1994, p. 55.
Journal of Interdisciplinary History, spring, 1990, p. 672.
Renaissance Quarterly, winter, 1989, p. 833.
Times Literary Supplement, January 15, 1982.

*   *   *

COLT, Winchester Remington
  See HUBBARD, L(afayette) Ron(ald)

*   *   *

COREY, Stephen   1948-

PERSONAL: Born August 30, 1948, in Buffalo, NY; son of Dale B. (a certified public accountant) and Julienne (a homemaker and nurse; maiden name, Holmes) Corey; married Mary Gibson (a nurse),

January 28, 1970; children: Heather Lynn, Miranda Dawn, Rebecca Elizabeth Yeong Ae, Catherine Pamela Rose. *Education:* State University of New York at Binghamton, B.A., 1971, M.A., 1974; University of Florida, Ph.D., 1979.

ADDRESSES: Home—357 Parkway Dr., Athens, GA 30606-4951. *Office*—*The Georgia Review,* University of Georgia, Athens, GA 30602.

CAREER: University of Florida, Gainesville, instructor in English, 1979-80; University of South Carolina, Columbia, assistant professor of English, 1980-83; University of Georgia, Athens, assistant editor of *The Georgia Review,* 1983-86, associate editor, 1986—.

MEMBER: Poets and Writers, South Atlantic Modern Language Association.

AWARDS, HONORS: First Book Award from Water Mark Poets, and Excellence Award from Winthrop College, both 1981, both for *The Last Magician;* award from Swallow's Tale Press, 1984, for *Synchronized Swimming;* fellow of Florida Arts Council, 1979-80, South Carolina Arts Council, 1981-82, and Georgia Arts Council, 1985-86, 1988-89; Georgia Author of the Year in Poetry, 1992 and 1993.

WRITINGS:

POETRY

Twelve, Renaissance Press, 1978.
The Last Magician, Water Mark Press (Owings Mills, MD), 1981.
Fighting Death, State Street Press (Brockport, NY), 1983.
Gentle Iron Lace, Press of the Night Owl (Athens, GA), 1984.
Synchronized Swimming, Swallow's Tale Press, 1985.
Attacking the Pieta, State Street Press, 1988.
All These Lands You Call One Country, University of Missouri Press (Columbia), 1992.

OTHER

(Editor with Stanley W. Lindberg) *Necessary Fictions: Selected Stories From the Georgia Review,* University of Georgia Press (Athens), 1987.
(Editor with Lindberg) *Keener Sounds: Selected Poems from the Georgia Review,* University of Georgia Press, 1987.

Contributor of poetry and essays to anthologies, including *The Pushcart Press: Best of the Small Presses,* and *For a Living: The Poetry of Work.* Also contributor to periodicals, including *The American Poetry Review, Poetry, The New Republic, Poets and Writers,* and *Yellow Silk.* Editor of *Devil's Millhopper,* 1977-83.

WORK IN PROGRESS: Knotter (poems); *'She is startled at the big sound'* (essays).

BIOGRAPHICAL/CRITICAL SOURCES:

BOOKS

Swanson, Gayle and William B. Thesing, *Conversations With South Carolina Poets,* John F. Blair (Winston-Salem, NC), 1986.

PERIODICALS

Atlantic Journal and Constitution, March 1, 1987.
Southern Humanities Review, winter, 1994, p. 93.
Virginia Quarterly Review, spring, 1982.

*   *   *

COTTON, John   1925-

PERSONAL: Born March 7, 1925, in London, England; son of Arthur Edmund (a structural engineer) and Florence (Mandy) Cotton; married Peggy Midson (a secretary), December, 1948; children: Toby, Bevis. *Education:* University of London, B.A. (with honors), 1956.

ADDRESSES: Home—37 Lombardy Dr., Berkhamsted, Hertfordshire HP4 2LQ, England.

CAREER: Middlesex Education Authority, England, teacher of English, 1947-57; Southall Grammar Technical School, England, head of English department, 1957-63; Highfield Comprehensive School, Hemel Hempstead, England, headmaster, 1963-85. Tutor for the Arvon Foundation, Totleigh Barton, Devon and for Pearse House creative writing courses; member of literature panel, Eastern Arts. *Military service:* Royal Naval Commandos, 1942-46; served in the Far East.

MEMBER: National Poetry Society (member of council; chair of council, 1973-75, and 1977; treasurer, 1986-89).

AWARDS, HONORS: Publication award from Arts Council of Great Britain, 1971, for *Old Movies and Other Poems;* Page scholarship from English Speaking Union, 1975; appointed Deputy Lieutenant of the County of Hertfordshire, 1989.

WRITINGS:

POETRY

Fourteen Poems, Priapus (Berkhamsted, Herts, England), 1967.

Outside the Gates of Eden and Other Poems, Taurus Press, 1969.

Ampurias, Priapus, 1969.

Old Movies and Other Poems, Chatto & Windus (London), 1971.

The Wilderness, Priapus, 1971.

Columbus on St. Dominica, Sceptre Press (Peterborough), 1972.

Photographs, Sycamore Press (Oxford), 1973.

A Sycamore Press Broadsheet, Sycamore Press, 1973.

British Poetry since 1965: A Selected List, National Book League (London), 1973.

Kilroy Was Here (Poetry Book Society selection), Chatto & Windus, 1974.

Places, Priapus, 1981.

Day Books, Priapus, 1981.

Catullus at Sirmione, Priapus, 1982.

The Storyville Portraits, Headland Press (Hartlepool), 1984.

The Crystal Zoo, Oxford University Press (Oxford), 1985.

Dust, Starwheel Press, 1986.

Oh Those Happy Feet!, Poet and Printer, 1986.

The Poetry File, Macmillan (London and New York City), 1988.

(With Fred Sedgwick) *Two by Two,* Mary Glasgow (London), 1990.

The Tower, Bonnefant Press (Netherlands), 1991.

Here's Looking at You Kid, Headland, 1992.

First Things, Nelson (Surrey), 1993.

Oscar the Dog and Friends, Longmans (London), 1996.

(Editor) *I Am the Song* (poetry for young people), Nelson, 1996.

Contributor to anthologies, including *Poetry Introduction 1,* Faber & Faber (London), 1969; *Best Science Fiction, 1972,* edited by Harry Harrison and Brian Aldiss, Putnam (London), 1972; *New Poetry,* Hutchinson (London), Number 1, 1975, Number 2, 1976, Number 3, 1977, Number 7, 1981, Number 8, 1982, Number 9, 1983; and *Completing the Picture,* edited by William Oxley, Stride, 1995. Also contributor to PEN poetry annuals, 1965, 1967, 1974, and 1975; and *Poems for Shakespeare 1987,* Bishopsgate Press. Editor of *Priapus,* 1962-72, and *Private Library,* 1970-80; advisory editor for *Contemporary Poets of the English Language.*

BIOGRAPHICAL/CRITICAL SOURCES:

PERIODICALS

Hertfordshire Countryside, July, 1973.

Poetry Book Society Bulletin, number 69, summer, 1971; number 84, spring, 1975.

School Librarian, November, 1989, p. 171.

Stand, Volume 14, number 1, 1972.

Teacher, May, 1973.

Times Educational Supplement, April 5, 1991, p. 20.

Times Literary Supplement, September 6, 1985.

*   *   *

COULSON, Juanita (Ruth)   1933-
(John Jay Wells)

PERSONAL: Surname is pronounced "*Col*-son"; born February 12, 1933, in Anderson, IN; daughter of Grant Elmer (a tool and die maker) and Ruth Margaret (Oemler) Wellons; married Robert Stratton Coulson (a writer), August 21, 1954; children: Bruce Edward. *Education:* Ball State University, B.S., 1954, M.A., 1961. *Politics:* Independent. *Religion:* Unitarian Universalist.

ADDRESSES: Home—2677W-500N, Hartford City, IN 47348. *Agent*—James Allen, 538 East Harford St., Milford, PA 18337.

CAREER: Writer. Art editor and publisher of *Yandro* (science fiction magazine), 1953—. Elementary school teacher, 1954-55; collator, Heckman's Bookbindery, North Manchester, IN, 1955-57.

MEMBER: Science Fiction Writers of America.

AWARDS, HONORS: Joint nominee with husband, Robert S. Coulson, for Hugo Award, World Science Fiction Convention, 1960-64, 1966-67, for best amateur science fiction magazine, *Yandro,* and joint winner with R. S. Coulson, Hugo Award, 1965, for *Yandro;* Ralph Holland Memorial Award, Fan Art

Show, 20th World Science Fiction Convention, 1962; co-Fan Guest of Honor, with R. S. Coulson, 30th World Science Fiction Convention, 1972.

WRITINGS:

SCIENCE FICTION

Crisis on Cheiron, Ace Books (New York City), 1967.
The Singing Stones, Ace Books, 1968.
The Secret of Seven Oaks, Berkley Publishing (New York City), 1972.
Door into Terror, Berkley Publishing, 1972.
Stone of Blood, Ballantine (New York City), 1975.
Unto the Last Generation, Laser Books (New York City), 1975.
Space Trap, Laser Books, 1976.
Fear Stalks the Bayou, Ballantine, 1976.
Dark Priestess, Ballantine, 1977.
Web of Wizardry, Del Rey Books (New York City), 1978.
Fire of the Andes, Ballantine, 1979.
The Death God's Citadel, Del Rey Books, 1980.
Star Sister, Del Rey Books, 1990.

"CHILDREN OF THE STARS" SERIES; PUBLISHED BY DEL REY BOOKS

Tomorrow's Heritage, 1981.
Outward Bound, 1982.
Legacy of Earth, 1989.
The Past of Forever, 1989.

OTHER

Contributor to books, including *The Comic-Book Book,* edited by Richard A. Lupoff and Don Thompson, Arlington House (New York City), 1973; *Star Trek: The New Voyages,* edited by Sandra Marshak and Myrna Culbreath, Bantam (New York City), 1976; and *Goldmann Fantasy Foliant III,* edited by Peter Wilfert, Wilhelm Goldmann Verlag, 1985. Contributor to anthologies, including *Tales of Witch World IV,* edited by Andre Norton, and *Women at War,* Tor, 1996. Also contributor to periodicals, sometimes under pseudonym John Jay Wells, including *Fantasy and Science Fiction.* Art editor and publisher of Science Fiction Writers of America's *Forum* magazine, 1971-72.

Many of Coulson's books have been translated into German.

SIDELIGHTS: Juanita and Robert S. Coulson's publication, *Yandro,* is referred to by science fiction enthusiasts as a "fanzine"—an amateur science fiction magazine published by those interested in the genre—and is one of the longest-running large fanzines in the world.

Juanita Coulson adds: "In recent years, our amateur magazine *Yandro* has virtually ceased publication, due to increasing pressure of freelance writing. Originally, *Yandro* served as our forum, and that of our fellow science fiction and fantasy enthusiasts. Now we have acquired broader outlets—not to say considerably more profitable ones. My husband's interest in reviewing has been transferred to several professional periodicals, and I have been able to concentrate my creative focus on the writing of novels.

"Prior to the '80s, my work lay in the fields of women's genre, action/adventure-oriented SF and fantasy. When I was commissioned to write the 'Children of the Stars' series for Del Rey Books, I was forced into a very different mode. Following the dictum of 'stick to what you know—or can extrapolate from what you know,' I had never attempted even the fringes of so-called 'hard science' fiction. My degrees are in the 'soft sciences,' not astrophysics and computer technology, etc. However, I was able to pick the brains of a number of highly-trained friends employed in those fields. The results apparently are satisfactory; numerous readers, also qualified in high-tech industries, have complimented me not only on the characters and stories I have created but on the technological 'scenery' in the backgrounds of those books. It has certainly been the most challenging task of my writing career—to date.

"Now I would like to make the swing back to the quite different genre of fantasy adventure. Style and background requirements vary enormously in the science fiction and fantasy specialties, but the basics of solid characterizations and a narrative the reader can become involved in are constants. In *that* regard, I've found that storytelling in novel form really is the same; and I hope it continues to be indefinitely, for *my* enjoyment as well as the reader's."

BIOGRAPHICAL/CRITICAL SOURCES:

PERIODICALS

Locus, May, 1989, p. 46; November, 1989, p. 54; April, 1990, pp. 25, 35.

Science Fiction Chronicle, April, 1990, p. 34.
Science Fiction Review, November, 1981.

*   *   *

CUNLIFFE, John Arthur 1933-

PERSONAL: Born June 16, 1933, in Colne, Lancashire, England; married Sylvia May Thompson (a musician), 1960; children: Julian Edward. *Education:* Leeds School of Librarianship, A.L.A., 1955; Northwest London Polytechnic School of Librarianship, F.L.A., 1957; Charlotte Mason College of Education, Cert. ed., 1975.

ADDRESSES: Office—Andre Deutsch Ltd., 105-106 Great Russell St., London WC1B 3LJ, England.

CAREER: Branch librarian, Earby, Yorkshire, England, 1951-54; mobile librarian, Wooler, Northumberland, England, 1955-56; Decca Radar Research Laboratories, Tolworth, Surrey, England, deputy information officer, 1957-58; senior assistant librarian, Hendon, London, England, 1958; Foyle's (booksellers), London, manager of rare book department, 1958-59; regional children's librarian, Bletchley, Buckinghamshire, England, 1959-62; librarian in charge of work with young people, Reading, Berkshire, England, 1962-64, and Brighton, England, 1967-73; librarian, British Council, Belgrade, Yugoslavia, 1964-66; education librarian, Newcastle-upon-Tyne, England, 1966-67; Castle Park School, Kendal, Cumbria, England, teacher, 1975-79; Manchester Education Committee, Manchester, England, teacher-organizer, 1979-80; Crowcroft Park School, Manchester, deputy head teacher, 1981-85; freelance writer, 1985—.

MEMBER: Society of Authors, National Union of Teachers.

WRITINGS:

CHILDREN'S FICTION

The Adventures of Lord Pip, illustrated by Robert Hales, Deutsch (London), 1970.
The Giant Who Stole the World, illustrated by Faith Jacques, Deutsch, 1971.

Riddles and Rhymes and Rigamaroles, illustrated by Alexy Pendle, Deutsch, 1971.
The Giant Who Swallowed the Wind, illustrated by Jacques, Deutsch, 1972.
Giant Kippernose, and Other Stories, illustrated by Fritz Wegner, Deutsch, 1972.
The Great Dragon Competition, and Other Stories, illustrated by Pendle, Deutsch, 1973.
The King's Birthday Cake, illustrated by Jacques, Deutsch, 1973.
Small Monkey Tales, illustrated by Gerry Downes, Deutsch, 1974.
The Farmer, the Rooks, and the Cherry Tree, illustrated by Prudence Seward, Deutsch, 1975.
Giant Brog and the Motorway, illustrated by Pendle, Deutsch, 1975.
Sara's Giant and the Upside-down House, illustrated by Hillary Abrahams, Deutsch, 1980.
Our Sam: The Daftest Dog in the World, illustrated by Maurice Wilson, Deutsch, 1980.
Mr. Gosling and the Runaway Chair, illustrated by William Stobbs, Deutsch, 1981.
Standing on a Strawberry and Other Poems, illustrated by David Parkins, Deutsch, 1987.
Fog Lane School and the Great Racing Car Disaster, illustrated by Andrew Tiffen, Deutsch, 1988.
The Minister's Cat, illustrated by David Parkins, Deutsch, 1989.
(With Elizabeth Lindsay and Joan Stimson) *Readaloud Stories,* Hippo Books (London), 1990.
Ted Glen's New Year Promises, illustrated by Ray Mutimer, Hippo Books, 1990.
Granny Dryden's Runaway Pig, illustrated by Mutimer, Hippo Books, 1991.
Pat and the Puzzle Parcels, illustrated by Mutimer, Hippo Books, 1991.
Julian and the Vacuum Cleaner, Deutsch, 1991.
Miss Hubbard's New Hat, Hippo Books, 1992.
Jess and the Fish, illustrated by Joan Hickson, Deutsch, 1992.
Jess Goes Hunting, illustrated by Hickson, Scholastic (New York City), 1992.
Jess's New Bed, illustrated by Hickson, Deutsch, 1992.
A Song for Jess, illustrated by Hickson, Deutsch, 1992.
Dare You Go? (poetry), Deutsch, 1992.
Tots and the Brass Band, Hippo Books, 1995.

"FARMER BARNES" SERIES

Farmer Barnes Buys a Pig, illustrated by Carol Barker, Deutsch, 1964, Lion Press, 1968.

Farmer Barnes and Bluebell, illustrated by Barker, Deutsch, 1966.

Farmer Barnes at the County Show, illustrated by Jill McDonald, Deutsch, 1966, published as *Farmer Barnes at the County Fair,* Lion Press, 1969.

Farmer Barnes and the Goats, illustrated by McDonald, Deutsch, 1971.

Farmer Barnes Goes Fishing, illustrated by McDonald, Deutsch, 1972.

Farmer Barnes and the Snow Picnic, illustrated by Hickson, Deutsch, 1974.

Farmer Barnes Fells a Tree, illustrated by Hickson, Deutsch, 1977.

Farmer Barnes and the Harvest Doll, illustrated by Hickson, Deutsch, 1977.

Farmer Barnes' Guy Fawkes Day, illustrated by Hickson, Deutsch, 1978.

"POSTMAN PAT" SERIES

Postman Pat and the Mystery Thief, illustrated by Celia Berridge, Deutsch, 1981, Scholastic, 1993.

Postman Pat's Treasure Hunt, illustrated by Berridge, Deutsch, 1981.

Postman Pat's Secret, illustrated by Berridge, Deutsch, 1981.

Postman Pat's Rainy Day, illustrated by Berridge, Deutsch, 1982.

Postman Pat's Difficult Day, illustrated by Berridge, Deutsch, 1982.

Postman Pat's Foggy Day, illustrated by Berridge, Deutsch, 1982.

Postman Pat Takes a Message, illustrated by Berridge, Deutsch, 1982.

Postman Pat Goes Sledging, illustrated by Berridge, Deutsch, 1983.

Postman Pat's Tractor Express, illustrated by Berridge, Deutsch, 1983.

(With Ivor Wood) *Fun and Games with Postman Pat: An Activity Book,* illustrated by Hickson, Deutsch, 1983.

Postman Pat's Thirsty Day, illustrated by Berridge, Deutsch, 1983.

Postman Pat's Letters on Ice, illustrated by Berridge, Deutsch, 1984.

Postman Pat's Breezy Day, illustrated by Berridge, Deutsch, 1985.

Postman Pat to the Rescue, illustrated by Berridge, Deutsch, 1985, Scholastic, 1993.

Postman Pat Easy Readers, fourteen volumes, illustrated by Hickson, Deutsch, 1986-89.

Postman Pat Beginners, seven volumes, illustrated by Hickson, Deutsch, 1986-93.

Postman Pat's Summer Storybook, illustrated by Berridge, Deutsch, 1987.

Postman Pat's Winter Storybook, illustrated by Berridge, Deutsch, 1987.

The Postman Pat Fun Book, illustrated by Berridge, Deutsch, 1987.

Postman Pat's Parcel of Fun, illustrated by Stuart Trotter, Deutsch, 1987.

My Postman Pat Storytime Book, Treasure, 1987.

Postman Pat and the Letter Puzzle, illustrated by Hickson, Hippo Books, 1988.

Postman Pat Gets a Pet, Hippo Books, 1988.

Postman Pat Goes Sailing, Hippo Books, 1988, revised, 1993.

Postman Pat Goes to Town, Hippo Books, 1989.

Postman Pat's Cat-up-a-Tree Party, Hippo Books, 1989.

Postman Pat's Greendale Storybook, Hippo Books, 1989.

Postman Pat's Zodiac Storybook, illustrated by Berridge, Deutsch, 1989.

Postman Pat and the Toy Soldiers, Deutsch, 1991.

Postman Pat's Lost Hat, illustrated by Hickson and Emma Iliffe, Deutsch/National Deaf Children's Society, 1991.

(With Susannah Bradley) *Postman Pat and the Toy Soldiers Sticker Fun Book,* illustrated by Mutimer, Hippo Books, 1991.

Postman Pat Takes the Bus, Deutsch, 1992.

Postman Pat Wins a Prize, illustrated by Hickson, Hippo Books, 1992.

Postman Pat's Wild Cat Chase, illustrated by Mutimer, Deutsch, 1992.

My Favorite Postman Pat Stories, illustrated by Berridge, Dean, 1993.

Postman Pat and the Harvest Parcel, illustrated by Hickson, Hippo Books, 1993.

Postman Pat and the Greendale Bus, illustrated by Hickson, Hippo Books, 1993.

The Reverend Timms Gives a Film Show, illustrated by Mutimer, Deutsch, 1993.

Postman Pat's Market Day, illustrated by Hickson, Hippo Books, 1993.

Postman Pat and the Barometer, illustrated by Mutimer, Deutsch, 1994.

Postman Pat and the Tuba, illustrated by Mutimer, Scholastic, 1994.

Postman Pat and the Fly, illustrated by Mutimer, World, 1995.

Postman Pat and the Flood, illustrated by Mutimer, Hippo Books, 1995.

Also author of *Postman Pat and His Black and White Cat* (television series), British Broadcasting Corp.

(BBC), beginning 1981; also author of play *Postman Pat's Adventures,* produced in Wimbledon, England, 1987.

"ROSIE AND JIM" SERIES

Rosie and Jim and the Rainbow, Deutsch, 1991.

Rosie and Jim and the Water Wizard, Deutsch, 1991.

Rosie and Jim, illustrated by Hickson, Deutsch, 1992.

Rosie and Jim and the Man in the Wind, illustrated by Berridge, Deutsch, 1992.

Fun and Games with Rosie and Jim: An Activity Book, Deutsch, 1992.

(With Anita Ganeri) *Round the Year with Rosie and Jim,* illustrated by Hickson, 1992.

Rosie and Jim and the Drink of Milk, illustrated by Berridge, Hippo Books, 1993.

Rosie and Jim: A Family for Ducks, illustrated by Hickson, Scholastic, 1993.

Rosie and Jim: Jim Gets Lost, illustrated by Hickson, Scholastic, 1993.

Rosie and Jim and the Snowman, illustrated by Hickson, Scholastic, 1993.

Rosie and Jim's Apple, Banana, Carrot Alphabet Book, illustrated by Berridge, Deutsch, 1993.

Rosie and Jim at the Seaside, illustrated by Hickson, Scholastic, 1993.

Rosie and Jim and the Glass Blowers, illustrated by Berridge, Deutsch, 1993.

Rosie and Jim and the Magic Sausages, illustrated by Berridge, Deutsch, 1993.

OTHER

Play Logo, Deutsch, 1984.

Contributor to *Children's Book Review.* Several titles in the "Postman Pat" series have been translated into Welsh.

SIDELIGHTS: John Arthur Cunliffe "is a master of homely humour," Marcus Crouch states in *School Librarian.* A librarian and teacher, Cunliffe has used his sense of humor and his skills as a storyteller to compose numerous entertaining tales for children from a wide variety of age groups. As a *Junior Bookshelf* critic notes, "Cunliffe is a master of the art of telling a simple story which is closely related to the realities of contemporary life." Cunliffe has written numerous books based on the *Postman Pat* and *Rosie and Jim* television series, which are very popular with young children in England, as well as the Farmer Barnes series, set in rural England.

Cunliffe's ability to write stories drawing from ordinary life are especially evident in his books concerning the adventures of Farmer Barnes and Postman Pat. Busy, harried Farmer Barnes faces numerous domestic crises in a series of books that focus on everyday farm life in England. Cunliffe brings the farmer and his family—wife Emily, daughter Candy, and five-year-old son Little John—to life in simple stories that deal with the kinds of realistic problems young children can easily understand. In *Farmer Barnes and Bluebell,* for example, chaos reigns in a small village after Bluebell decides to escape her humdrum life as a dairy cow for some excitement beyond the barn. A stray goat rescued by a helicopter becomes the high-point in *Farmer Barnes and the Goats,* while a shopping trip to town in the Barnes family's Land Rover turns into a chilly overnight adventure in *Farmer Barnes and the Snow Picnic.*

One of Cunliffe's most popular characters is Postman Pat. The colorful series of picture books is based on a popular British children's television show and its characters designed by puppeteer Ivor Wood. The stories take place in the small village of Greendale, where Postman Pat and his cat Jess are drawn into the activities of the community during his daily rounds. Cunliffe's books "present an innocent, fanciful view of small-town life," Judith Elkin notes in *Twentieth-Century Children's Writers.*

Other of Cunliffe's children's stories focus on the many things surrounding us in the real world. For example, in his *Small Monkey Tales,* Cunliffe tells of a young monkey's first explorations into the world around him. The tales are "told in a delightfully animated way, [and] deserve to become classics," according to a *Times Literary Supplement* reviewer. And in *Our Sam: The Daftest Dog in the World,* Cunliffe recalls his own childhood in the north of England where he visited his grandmother who owned a cocker spaniel that went by the name of "Our Sam." "The background is authentic," states a reviewer in *Junior Bookshelf,* "and the human characters are colourful."

Far from the true-to-life worlds of Farmer Barnes or Postman Pat, giants and dragons roam the countryside in several of Cunliffe's other books for children. The great diversity among dragons is brought to light in *The Great Dragon Competition, and Other Stories,* a collection of ten stories that introduce young readers to the world of the fantastic in a humorous way. *Giant Kippernose, and Other Stories* is a collection of stories about giants that provides "most pleasant reading—especially aloud to others," according to George Shannon in *School Library Journal.*

BIOGRAPHICAL/CRITICAL SOURCES:

BOOKS

Twentieth-Century Children's Writers, 4th edition, St. James Press (Detroit), 1995.

PERIODICALS

British Book News, spring, 1982, p. 1.
Growing Point, March, 1979, p. 3476.
Junior Bookshelf, April, 1979, p. 93; October, 1980, p. 239; February, 1982, p. 14; August, 1987, p. 167; June, 1989, p. 118.
Library Journal, May 15, 1969, p. 2088.
School Librarian, December, 1982, p. 318; March, 1983, p. 25; August, 1991, p. 100; February, 1993, p. 26.
School Library Journal, September, 1979, p. 107; October, 1979, p. 148; November, 1980, p. 59; August, 1981, p. 63; October, 1981, p. 127.
Spectator, November 13, 1971, p. 700.
Times Literary Supplement, November 24, 1966, p. 1083; April 28, 1972, p. 483; November 3, 1972, p. 1333; July 5, 1974, p. 722; December 6, 1974, p. 1378.*

D

DALY, Cahal Brendan   1917-

PERSONAL: Born October 1, 1917, in Loughguile, County Antrim, Northern Ireland; son of Charles and Susan Daly. *Education:* Received B.A. (with honors) and M.A. from Queen's University, Belfast, Northern Ireland; received D.D. from St. Patrick's College, Maynooth, Ireland; received L.Ph. from Institut Catholique, France. *Religion:* Roman Catholic.

ADDRESSES: Home—Ara Coeli, Armagh, BT61 7ZY, Northern Ireland.

CAREER: Ordained Roman Catholic priest, 1941; classics master at secondary school in Belfast, Northern Ireland, 1945-46; Queen's University, Belfast, lecturer, 1946-63, reader in scholastic philosophy, 1963-67; St. Michael's, Longford, Ireland, bishop of Armagh and Clonmacnois, 1967-82; bishop of Down and Connor, 1982-90; Cardinal Archbishop of Armagh, 1990—. Member of British Broadcasting Corp. (BBC) Northern Ireland Religious Advisory Council, 1945-59; committee member, Northern Ireland Independent Television Authority, 1960-65; religious advisor to UTV.

MEMBER: Christus Rex Society (chair, 1941-66).

WRITINGS:

(Contributor) I. T. Ramsey, editor, *Prospect for Metaphysics,* G. Allen, 1961.
Morals, Law, and Life: An Examination of the Sanctity of Life and the Criminal Law by Granville Llewellyn Williams, Clonmore, 1962, Scepter, 1966.
Natural Law: Morality Today, Burns & Oates, 1965.

(Contributor) T. A. Langford and W. H. Poteat, editors, *Intellect and Hope,* Duke University Press (Durham, NC), 1968.
(Contributor) D. M. High, editor, *New Essays in Religious Language,* Oxford University Press, 1969.
Violence in Ireland and Christian Conscience, Veritas Publications (Dublin), 1973.
Theologians and the Magisterium, Veritas Publications, 1977.
Penance Renewed, Irish Messenger (Dublin), 1977.
(Editor with A. S. Worrall) *Ballymascanlon: An Irish Venture in Inter-Church Dialogue,* Veritas Publications, 1978.
Peace: The Work of Justice—Addresses on the Northern Tragedy, Veritas Publications, 1979.
Communities without Consensus: The Northern Irish Tragedy, Irish Messenger, 1984.
Renewed Heart for Peace, Irish Messenger, 1984.
Cry of the Poor, Irish Messenger, 1986.
The Price of Peace, Veritas Publications, 1991.
Morals and Law, Veritas Publications, 1993.
Tertullian the Puritan, Four Courts Press (Dublin), 1993.
Northern Ireland—Peace—Now Is the Time, Veritas Publications, 1994.
Love Begins at Home, Veritas Publications, 1995.

Also contributor to *Understanding the Eucharist,* 1969. Contributor to numerous theology and philosophy journals.

*   *   *

DANIELS, Brett
See ADLER, Renata

DAUNTON, M(artin) J(ames) 1949-

PERSONAL: Born February 7, 1949, in Cardiff, Wales; son of Ronald J. (a bank official) and Dorothy (a homemaker; maiden name, Bellett) Daunton; married Claire Gobbi (a university administrator), January 7, 1984. *Education:* University of Nottingham, B.A., 1970; University of Kent at Canterbury, Ph.D., 1973.

ADDRESSES: Home—14 Union Square, London N1 7DH, England. *Office*—University College London, Gower St., London WC1E 6BT, England.

CAREER: University of Durham, England, lecturer in economic history, 1973-79; University College London, England, lecturer, 1979-85, reader in history, 1985-89, professor, 1989—.

MEMBER: Royal Historical Society (treasurer, 1986-91), Economic History Society (member of council, 1985-88), Institute of Historical Research (chairperson, 1994—).

WRITINGS:

Coal Metropolis: Cardiff, 1870-1914, Leicester University Press (England), 1977.
House and Home in the Victorian City: Working Class Housing, 1850-1914, Edward Arnold (London), 1983.
Councillors and Tenants, Leicester University Press, 1985.
Royal Mail: The Post Office Since 1840, Athlone Press (London), 1986.
A Property Owning Democracy? Faber (London), 1987.
Housing the Workers, 1850-1914, Leicester University Press, 1990.
Progress and Poverty: An Economic and Social History of Britain, 1700-1850, Oxford University Press, 1995.
The Ransom of Riches: The Politics of Taxation in Britain since 1842, Longmans (London), 1996.

Contributor to economic and history journals. *Studies in History,* chairperson of editors, 1995—.

WORK IN PROGRESS: "A second volume of my economic and social history of Britain for Oxford University Press: *Wealth and Welfare: An Economic and Social History of Britain, 1850-1939,* which is scheduled for completion in 1997. I am also completing the editing of volume III of the Cambridge Urban History of Britain; and have recently edited a series of papers on *Charity, Self Interest and Welfare in the English Past* for publication by UCL Press."

SIDELIGHTS: M. J. Daunton's first book, *Coal Metropolis: Cardiff, 1870-1914,* was largely welcomed by critics as a much-needed and long overdue history of the Welsh city of Cardiff. The author considered the economic development of the city since 1870 and its social evolution as a city, extending his research into the areas of social culture and politics. Kenneth O. Morgan wrote in the *Times Literary Supplement:* "The result is impressive—a precise, fully documented, lucidly written and beautifully illustrated book which will be of great value and interest to historians . . . of the British urban experience."

House and Home in the Victorian City: Working Class Housing, 1850-1914, enjoyed a similar reception. In a *Times Literary Supplement* review, P. J. Waller commented that Daunton's second book "combines very different perspectives to illuminate a complex topic: those of physical form, class culture, distinctive local habit, and particular personal preference." The author analyzes various approaches to planning and housing, and studies the nineteenth-century trends which resulted in sweeping changes in the relationships between public and private space. Daunton surveys the types of housing that characterized various localities, examines housing from the perspective of rents and investment values, and considers the political issues involved in the relationships of landlords to tenants and public officials. According to Waller, "Daunton integrates the subject better than any historian before him," providing "a more complete picture than we have yet had."

Daunton wrote *CA:* "My work has now moved away from its earlier interest in the history of cities and architectural form to a concern for the nature of the modern British state, and the development of economic and social policy. The connection between the two sets of concerns is housing policy, which I analysed through international comparisons; my more recent publications have dealt with taxation and social policy. These themes have informed my general books on British economic and social history since 1700, as well as more specific studies. I hope in the future to move from Britain to a wider analysis of the British empire, considering issues such as taxation and land policy."

BIOGRAPHICAL/CRITICAL SOURCES:

PERIODICALS

Times Literary Supplement, March 4, 1977; January 20, 1984; November 29, 1985.

*   *   *

DAVIDSON, Paul   1930-

PERSONAL: Born October 23, 1930, in Brooklyn, NY; son of Charles and Lillian (Janow) Davidson; married Louise Tattenbaum, 1952; children: Robert Alan, Diane Carol, Greg Stuart. *Education:* Brooklyn College (now Brooklyn College of the City University of New York), B.S., 1950; City College (now City College of the City University of New York), M.B.A., 1955; University of Pennsylvania, Ph.D., 1959.

*ADDRESSES: Home—*2400 Craghead Lane, Knoxville, TN 37920. *Office—*Department of Economics, University of Tennessee, Knoxville, TN 37996.

CAREER: University of Pennsylvania, Philadelphia, instructor in physiological chemistry, 1951-52, instructor in economics, 1955-58; Rutgers University, New Brunswick, NJ, assistant professor of economics, 1958-60; Continental Oil Co., Houston, TX, assistant director of Economics Division, 1960-61; University of Pennsylvania, assistant professor, 1961-63, associate professor of economics, 1963-66; Rutgers University, professor of economics, 1966-87, associate director of Bureau of Economic Research, 1966-75, chairman of New Brunswick Department of Economics and Allied Sciences and director of Bureau of Economic Research, 1975-78; University of Tennessee, Knoxville, TN, distinguished professor of economics, 1987—. Visiting lecturer, University of Bristol, 1964-65; senior visiting lecturer, Cambridge University, 1970-71; George Miller Distinguished Lecturer, University of Illinois, 1972; Bernardin Distinguished Visiting Lecturer, University of Missouri, 1979; professor, International Summer School Centro di Studi Economici Avanzati, Trieste, Italy, 1980; visiting professor, Institute for Advanced Studies, Vienna, Austria, 1980, 1984. Member, Brookings Economic Panel, 1974; senior visitor, Bank of England, 1979. Participant in government conferences and witness before numerous Congressional committees. Consultant,

Resources for the Future, 1964-66, Ford Foundation energy policy project, 1973, International Communications Agency, U.S. Department of State, 1980, and to numerous public and private organizations, including Western Union, Federal Trade Commission, and the State of Alabama; member of national board of advisors, Public Interest Economics Center, 1972—. *Military service:* U.S. Army, 1953-55.

MEMBER: American Economic Association, Econometric Society, National Association of Business Economists, Royal Economic Society, Epsilon Phi Alpha.

AWARDS, HONORS: Ford Foundation fellow, 1956-57; Fulbright fellow, 1964-65; Rutgers faculty research fellow, 1970-71, 1980; Lindbeck Award for Research, 1975.

WRITINGS:

Theories of Aggregate Income Distribution, Rutgers University Press (New Brunswick, NJ), 1960.

(With Eugene Smolensky) *Aggregate Supply and Demand Analysis,* Harper (New York City), 1964.

(With C. J. Chiccetti and J. J. Seneca) *The Demand and Supply of Outdoor Recreation: An Econometric Study,* Bureau of Economic Research, Rutgers University, 1968.

Money and the Real World, Macmillan (New York City), 1972, 2nd edition, 1978.

(With Milton Friedman and others) *Milton Friedman's Monetary Theory: A Debate with His Critics,* University of Chicago Press (Chicago), 1974.

International Money and the Real World, Macmillan, 1981.

(With son, Greg S. Davidson) *Economics for a Civilized Society,* Norton (New York City), 1987, revised edition, Macmillan (London), 1996.

The Struggle over the Keynesian Heritage (audio tape narrated by Louis Rukeyser), Knowledge Products, 1989.

(Edited with J. A. Kregel) *Macroeconomic Problems and Policies of Income Distribution: Functional, Personal, International,* Edward Elgar (London), 1989.

(Edited by Louise Davidson) *Money and Employment, The Collected Writings of Paul Davidson,* Volume 1, Macmillan (London), 1990.

(Edited by Louise Davidson) *Inflations, Open Economies and Resources, The Collected Writings of Paul Davidson,* vol. 2, Macmillan, 1991, NYU Press (New York City), 1991.

Controversies in Post Keynesian Economics, Edward Elgar, 1991.

(With Kregel) *Economic Problems of the 1990s: Less Developed Countries, Europe and the United States,* Edward Elgar, 1991.

(Editor and author of introduction) *Can the Free Market Pick Winners?,* M. E. Sharpe (New York City), 1993.

Post Keynesian Macroeconomic Theory: A Foundation for Successful Economic Policy in the Twenty-first Century, Edward Elgar, 1994.

(With Kregel) *Employment, Growth and Finance; Economic Reality and Economic Growth,* Edward Elgar, 1994.

Also contributor to economic and public finance journals. Contributor to numerous books on economics, including *The Crisis in Economic Theory,* edited by D. Bell and I. Kristol, Basic Books, 1981; *Keynes, Money, and Monetarism,* edited by R. Hill, Macmillan, 1989; and *The Megacorp and Macrodynamics,* edited by W. Milberg, M. E. Sharpe, 1992. Editor, *Journal of Post Keynesian Economics,* 1978—; member of editorial board, *Energy Journal,* 1980-83.

* * *

DAVIS, Robert Murray   1934-

PERSONAL: Born September 4, 1934, in Lyons, KS; son of Mathew Cary (a dealer) and Elizabeth (Murray) Davis; married Barbara Hillyer, December 28, 1958 (divorced April 3, 1981); children: Megan, Jennifer, John. *Education:* Rockhurst College, B.S., 1955; University of Kansas, M.A., 1958; University of Wisconsin, Ph.D., 1964.

ADDRESSES: Office—Department of English, University of Oklahoma, 760 Van Vleet, Norman, OK 73019.

CAREER: Loyola University, Chicago, IL, assistant professor of English, 1962-65; University of California, Santa Barbara, assistant professor of English, 1965-67; University of Oklahoma, Norman, 1967—, currently professor of English. Visiting professor, University of New Brunswick, St. John, summer, 1981, and Dalhousie University, summers, 1984, 1986. Fulbright lecturer, Eotvos University, Budapest, 1981, and Kassuth University, Dabrecen, 1989; visiting lecturer, University of Paris, spring,

1983; United States Information Service lecturer in France, Yugoslavia, Hungary, and Germany, spring, 1983.

MEMBER: Western Literature Association.

AWARDS, HONORS: National Endowment for the Humanities summer stipend, 1969; DeGolyer Prize for American Studies, 1984.

WRITINGS:

(With others) *Evelyn Waugh: A Checklist of Primary and Secondary Material,* Whitston Publishing (Troy, NY), 1972.

(With others) *Donald Barthelme: A Bibliography,* Archon (Hamden, CT), 1977.

A Catalogue of the Evelyn Waugh Collection, Whitston Publishing, 1981.

Evelyn Waugh, Writer, Pilgrim, 1981.

A Bibliography of Evelyn Waugh, Whitston Publishing, 1986.

Evelyn Waugh and the Forms of His Time, Catholic University of America Press (Washington, DC), 1989.

Brideshead Revisited: The Past Redeemed, Twayne (Boston, MA), 1990.

Outside the Lines, Cow Hill, 1990.

Playing Cowboy: Low Culture and High Art in the Western, University of Oklahoma Press (Norman, OK), 1992.

Mid-Lands: A Family Album, University of Georgia Press (Atlanta), 1992.

A Lower-Middle-Class Education, University of Oklahoma Press, in press.

Postmarks, Rednecks Press, in press.

EDITOR

The Novel: Modern Essays in Criticism, Prentice-Hall (Englewood Cliffs, NJ), 1969.

Evelyn Waugh, B. Herder (England), 1969.

Steinbeck, Prentice-Hall, 1972.

Modern British Short Novels, Scott, Foresman (Glenview, IL), 1972.

Evelyn Waugh, Apprentice, Pilgrim, 1985.

Owen Wister's West, [New Mexico], 1987.

A Handful of Dust, Penguin (New York City), in press.

OTHER

Contributor to periodicals.

WORK IN PROGRESS: Volumes of poetry and reminiscences; *Rednecks,* a novel; collections of essays.

SIDELIGHTS: Robert Davis told *CA:* "After thirty years as a scholar and academic critic, I have, like many of my academic generations, become disenchanted with the political and philosophical biases of recent literary theory, especially with its fundamentally anhedonic bias. While it is true that words may be unreliable, they can, rightly used, give intense pleasure as well as convey information.

"As critical theory has become more abstract, my response to experience had become more concrete. Especially influential, in unexpected ways, was a Fulbright semester in Budapest in the fall of 1981. Professionally, I had just published two scholarly books on Evelyn Waugh and was looking for a new subject. Personally, I was alone for the first time in more than twenty years among people whose language and culture I did not understand. As a result, I began to think about what it meant to be not only an American but an American from a particular time and place. In this mood, learning to trust my feelings and explore my own life rather than someone else's work, I wrote my first poem and personal essay in more than twenty years.

"Back in the United States, I began to write and publish poems about the landscape of the American Southwest, about my family, and about my emotional life. In prose, I began to explore my past as a small-town Midwestern boy in the late 1940s. After a second trip to Hungary in 1989, during the collapse of communis rule, I finished *Mid-Lands,* a book I categorize as reminiscent social history. The sequel, *A Lower-Middle-Class Education,* deals with my college experience in the early and middle 1950s. A third volume, about the profession of English over the last forty years, is now in the planning stages.

"Although I have learned a good deal from my work as scholar and critic, I now see myself as a writer or man of letters. To be useful to the culture at large, to reflect as well as alter the sense of common experience, discourse must be more intelligible and more broadly humane than that current on either Left or Right. This sounds more solemn and conservative than my work is in tone and form. I can see the dangers of sentimentality and cynicism. But it's hard to be nostalgic if one has a good memory; it's hard to avoid the superiority of hindsight. And that's aside from all the other problems writers face."

BIOGRAPHICAL/CRITICAL SOURCES:

PERIODICALS

American Literature, March, 1993.
Journal of the West, January, 1994.
Kirkus Reviews, December 15, 1991.
Missourian, May 3, 1992.
Montana: The Magazine of Western History, autumn, 1993.
Times Literary Supplement, August 21, 1981; July 9, 1982.
Western American Literature, Volume 27, number 4; Volume 28, number 1.

*　　*　　*

DAWE, (Donald) Bruce 1930-

PERSONAL: Born February 15, 1930, in Geelong, Australia; son of Alfred (a laborer) and Mary Ann (Hamilton) Dawe; married Gloria Desley, January 1, 1964; children: Brian, Jamie, Katrina, Melissa. *Education:* University of Queensland, B.A., 1969, M.A., 1975, Ph.D., 1980; University of New England, Litt.B., 1973. *Religion:* Roman Catholic.

ADDRESSES: Home—30 Cumming St., Toowoomba, Queensland, Australia 4350.

CAREER: Worked as a laborer, postman, and gardener. Institute College of Advanced Education, Toowoomba, Australia, lecturer in literature, 1971-78, senior lecturer and teaching fellow, 1979-89, associate professor, 1990-93. *Military service:* Royal Australian Air Force, 1959-68; became sergeant.

AWARDS, HONORS: Myer Award for poetry, 1966, for *A Need of Similar Name,* and 1969, for *An Eye for a Tooth;* Ampol Arts Award for Creative Literature, 1967; Dame Mary Gilmore Medal, 1971, for *Condolences of the Season;* Grace Leven Poetry Prize, 1978, and Braille Book of the Year award, 1979, both for *Sometimes Gladness: Collected Poems, 1954-1978;* Patrick White Literary Award for contributions to Australian poetry, 1980; Christopher Bremmer Award, Order of Australia, 1984; honorary D. Litt., University of Southern Queensland, 1995.

WRITINGS:

No Fixed Address, Cheshire (Melbourne, Australia), 1962.

A Need of Similar Name, Cheshire, 1965.

An Eye for a Tooth, Cheshire, 1968.

Beyond the Subdivision, Cheshire, 1969.

Heat-Wave, Sweeny Reed (Melbourne), 1970.

Condolences of the Season, Cheshire, 1971.

Bruce Dawe Reads from His Own Work, University of Queensland Press (St. Lucia, Australia), 1971.

(Editor) *Dimensions,* McGraw (New York City), 1974.

Just a Dugong at Twilight, Cheshire, 1975.

Sometimes Gladness: Collected Poems, 1954-1978, Longman Cheshire, 1979, 4th edition published as *Sometimes Gladness: Collected Poems, 1954-1993,* 1993.

Over Here, Harv! and Other Stories, Penguin (Melbourne and Harmondsworth, Australia), 1983.

Towards Sunrise: Poems, 1979-1986, Longman Cheshire, 1986.

Speaking in Parables: A Reader, Longman Cheshire, 1987.

Bruce Dawe: Essays and Opinions, edited by Ken Goodman, Longman Cheshire, 1990.

This Side of Silence: Poems 1987-1990, Longman Cheshire, 1990.

Mortal Instruments: Poems 1990-1995, Longman, 1995.

SIDELIGHTS: Australian Bruce Dawe's "poetry sounds easy . . . but it represents a feat of strength," Clive James asserts in the *Times Literary Supplement.* James praises Dawe's ability to show his country's relationship to, and assimilation of, American culture. "Dawe was the first Australian poet to take measure of the junk media and find poetry in their pathos," James continues. "He wrote better about the Vietnam War than any other poet, including American poets; and he could do so because he wrote better about television."

Bruce Dawe told *CA:* "One of the reasons why the use of various verse forms may help me to capture something of the evanescence of the contemporary Australian idiom is that the use of various traditional rhyme-forms and some metrical regularity together with elements of the contemporary scene and idiom provide a 'mix' of past and present in an acceptable form overall.

"I never *consciously* chose the dramatic monologue form—it just occurred as a form frequently enough to confirm its possibilities. I am sure this is the general way things happen—forms choose us.

"Regional poetry is not (as in the United States) a very obvious and characteristic kind of poetry here, Australian society being culturally and linguistically far more homogeneous than American—urban and rural are the significant 'regions' rather than the Southwest, West, Midwest, East, etc. This is one of our greatest losses, I feel, artistically."

BIOGRAPHICAL/CRITICAL SOURCES:

BOOKS

Coldrey, B., *Bruce Dawe's Poetry: Notes,* Coles Australian Notes, Lothian Publishing (Melbourne, Australia), 1985.

Freeman, J., *Bruce Dawe: A Comprehensive Study Guide,* Australian Educational Materials (Highbury, South Australia), 1989.

Goodwin, K. L., *Adjacent Worlds: A Literary Life of Bruce Dawe,* Longman Cheshire, 1988.

Goodwin, *Selected Poems of Bruce Dawe,* Longman York Press, 1983.

Hansen, Ian Victor, editor, *Bruce Dawe: The Man Down the Street,* Victorian Association for the Teaching of English, 1972.

Kuch, P., *Bruce Dawe,* Oxford Australian Writers, (Melbourne, Australia), 1995.

Shaw, Basil, editor, *Times and Seasons: An Introduction to Bruce Dawe,* Cheshire, 1973.

PERIODICALS

Australian Book Review, February, 1991, p. 35.

Times Literary Supplement, November 27-December 3, 1987.

*　　*　　*

DEAK, Istvan 1926-

PERSONAL: Born May 11, 1926, in Szekesfehervar, Hungary; came to United States in 1956, naturalized in 1962; son of Istvan (an engineer) and Anna (Timar) Deak; married Gloria Alfano (a freelance editor and writer), July 4, 1959; children: Eva. *Education:* Attended University of Budapest, 1945-48, University of Paris, 1949-51, and University of Maryland, 1954-56; Ecole de Documentation, diploma, 1950; Columbia University, M.A., 1958, Ph.D., 1964.

ADDRESSES: *Home*—410 Riverside Dr., New York, NY 10025. *Office*—1229 International Affairs Building, Columbia University, New York, NY 10027.

CAREER: Freelance researcher and translator in New York City, 1956-59; Smith College, Northampton, MA, instructor, 1962-63; Columbia University, New York City, instructor, 1963-64, assistant professor, 1964-67, associate professor, 1967-71, professor of history, 1971-93, Seth Lon professor of history, 1993—, director of Institute on East Central Europe, 1967-78, acting director, 1979-80, 1983. Lecturer, University of Maryland Overseas Program, West Germany, 1961, and School of General Studies, Columbia University, 1961-62. Visiting lecturer, Yale University, spring, 1966; visiting professor, University of California, Los Angeles, 1975, and Universitaet Siegen, West Germany, 1981. German Academic Exchange fellow, 1960-61, Fulbright-Hays Travel fellow, 1973, 1984-85. Member, Joint Committee on Slavic Studies, 1967-69. International Research and Exchanges Board travel fellow, 1972, 1973, 1984-85, fellowship committee member, 1980-83, program committee member, 1983-1989. American Council of Learned Societies, committee member, 1972-74, fellow, 1981. Executive secretary, Committee to Promote Studies of the History of the Hapsburg Monarchy, 1974-77. Vice president, Conference Group for Slavic and East European History, 1975-77, president, 1985. Member, Institute for Advanced Study, Princeton, NJ, 1981. Woodrow Wilson International Center for Scholars, Smithsonian Institution, Washington, DC, fellow, 1985, advisory committee member, 1985-88.

MEMBER: World Association of Hungarian Historians (vice president, 1990—), American Association for the Advancement of Slavic Studies (president of Mid-Atlantic Association, 1977-78, member of board of directors, 1985-88), American Association for the Study of Hungarian History (awards committee chairman, 1974—, vice chairman, 1979-80, chairman, 1980-83), Hungarian Academy of Sciences.

AWARDS, HONORS: Scudder W. Johnston fellowship, Columbia University, 1959-60; Chamberlain fellow, Columbia University, 1966; study grant, School of International Affairs, Columbia University, 1969; Guggenheim fellowship, 1970-71; Lionel Trilling Book Award, Columbia University, 1977, for *The Lawful Revolution: Louis Kossuth and the Hungarians, 1848-1849,* and 1979; Wayne S. Vuchinich Book Prize, American Association for the Advancement of Slavic Studies, 1991, and outstanding academic book, *Choice,* both 1991, for *Beyond Nationalism: A Social and Political History of the Hapsburg Officer Corps, 1848-1918.*

WRITINGS:

Weimar Germany's Left-Wing Intellectuals: A Political History of the Weltbuehne and Its Circle, University of California Press (Berkeley), 1968.

(Editor with Sylvia Sinanian and Peter C. Ludz) *Eastern Europe in the 1970's* (conference papers), Praeger (New York City), 1972.

(Editor with Allan Mitchell) *Everyman in Europe: Essays in Social History,* two volumes, Prentice-Hall (Englewood Cliffs NJ), 1974, 3rd edition, 1989.

The Lawful Revolution: Louis Kossuth and the Hungarians, 1848-1849, Columbia University Press (New York City), 1979, translated as *Die rechtmassige Revolution,* Bohlau Verlag (Vienna-Cologne), Akademiai Kiado (Budhapest), 1989, *Kossuth Lajos es a magyarok,* Godalet (Budapest), 1983, 2nd edition, 1994.

Beyond Nationalism: A Social and Political History of the Hapsburg Officer Corps, 1848-1918, Oxford University Press (New York City), 1989, translated as *Der k.(u.)k. Offizier,* Bohlau Verlag (Vienna, Cologne, Weimar), 1991, *Volt egyszer egy tisztikar,* Gondolat (Budapest), 1993, *Gli ufficiali della monarchia asburgica. Oltre il nazionalismo,* Editrice Goriziana, 1994.

Also contributor to many books on history, particularly of Eastern Europe, including *The European Right: A Historical Profile,* edited by Hans Rogger and Eugen Weber, University of California Press, 1965; *The American and European Revolutions, 1776-1848,* edited by Jaroslaw Pelenski, University of Iowa Press (Iowa City), 1980; *The Holocaust in Hungary Forty Years Later,* edited by Randolph L. Braham and Bela Vago, Columbia University Press (New York City), 1985; and *Nationalism and Empire: The Hapsburg Empire and the Soviet Union,* edited by Richard L. Rudolph and David F. Good, St. Martin's (New York City), 1992. Contributor to *Encyclopedia Year Book 1973.* Contributor to *New York Review of Books, Slavonic and East European Review, Austrian History Yearbook, Oesterreichische Osthefte, East Central Europe, New Hungarian Quarterly, Romania Bulletin, American Historical Review, New Republic, Orbis,* and other journals. Author of book reviews for periodicals, including *New York Times, Slavic Review* and *American Historical Review.* Member of editorial advisory board, *Political Science Quarterly,* 1969-70, board of editors, *Austrian History Yearbook,* 1971-77, editorial board, *Slavic Review,* 1985-92.

DICKSON, Paul (Andrew) 1939-

PERSONAL: Born July 30, 1939, in Yonkers, NY; son of William A. and Isabelle (Cornell) Dickson, Jr.; married Nancy Hartman, April 13, 1968; children: Andrew Cary, Alexander Hartman. *Education:* Wesleyan University, B. A., 1961.

ADDRESSES: Home—Box 80, Garrett Park, MD 20896. *Agent*—Jonathan Dolger, The Jonathan Dolger Agency, 49 E. 96th St. #9B, New York, NY 10128.

CAREER: Writer. McGraw-Hill Book Co., New York City, regional editor, 1966-69. *Military service:* U. S. Navy, 1962-65.

MEMBER: National Press Club, Washington Independent Writers (president, board member and treasurer).

AWARDS, HONORS: American Political Science Association fellowship for reporters, 1969-70; Philip M. Stern Award, 1986; SABR-Macmillan Baseball Research Award, 1989.

WRITINGS:

Think Tanks, Atheneum (New York City), 1971.
The Great American Ice Cream Book, Atheneum, 1973.
The Future of the Workplace, Weybright, 1975.
The Electronic Battlefield, Indiana University Press (Bloomington, IN), 1976.
The Mature Person's Guide to Kites, Frisbees, Yo-Yos and Other Childlike Diversions, New American Library (New York City), 1977.
Out of This World: American Space Photography, foreword by R. Buckminster Fuller, Delacorte (New York City), 1977.
Future File: A Handbook for People with One Foot in the Twenty-first Century, Rawson (New York City), 1977.
Chow: A Cook's Tour of Military Food, New American Library, 1978.
The Official Rules, illustrated by Kenneth Tiews, Delacorte, 1978.
The Official Explanations, Delacorte, 1980.
Toasts: The Complete Book of the Best Toasts, Sentiments, Blessings, Curses, and Graces, Delacorte, 1981.
Words: A Connoisseur's Collection of Old and New, Weird and Wonderful, Useful and Outlandish Words, Delacorte, 1982.
(With Joseph C. Goulden) *There Are Alligators in Our Sewers, and Other American Credos,* Delacorte, 1983.

Jokes: Outrageous Bits, Atrocious Puns, and Ridiculous Routines for Those Who Love Jests, illustrated by Don Addis, Delacorte, 1984.
On Our Own: A Declaration of Independence for the Self-Employed, Facts on File (New York City), 1985.
Names: A Collector's Compendium of Rare and Unusual, Bold and Beautiful, Odd and Whimsical Names, Delacorte, 1986.
The Library in America: A Celebration in Words and Pictures, Facts on File, 1986.
Too Much Saxon Violence, Dell (New York City), 1986.
Waiter, There's a Fly in My Soup, Dell, 1986.
Family Words, Addison-Wesley (Reading, MA), 1988.
The Dickson Baseball Dictionary, Facts on File, 1989.
The New Official Rules: Maxims for Muddling through to the 21st Century, Addison-Wesley, 1989.
What Do You Call a Person from . . . ?: A Dictionary of Resident Names, Facts on File, 1990.
Slang!: The Topic-by-Topic Dictionary of Contemporary American Lingoes, Pocket Books (New York City), 1990.
Timelines: Day by Day and Trend by Trend from the Dawn of the Atomic Age to the Close of the Cold War, Addison-Wesley, 1990.
Baseball's Greatest Quotations, HarperCollins (New York City), 1991.
Dickson's Word Treasury, Wiley, (New York City), 1991.
Dickson's Joke Treasury, Wiley, 1992.
(With Douglas E. Evelyn) *On This Spot: Pinpointing the Past in Washington, D.C.,* Farragut Publishing Co., 1992.
(With William B. Mead) *Baseball: The President's Game,* Farragut Publishing Co., 1993.
(With Paul Clancy) *The Congress Dictionary,* Wiley, 1993.
(With Joseph C. Goulden) *Mythinformed,* Perigee Books (New York City), 1994.
War Slang!, Pocket Books, 1994.
The Worth Book of Softball, Facts on File, 1994.
(With Robert Skole) *The Volvo Guide to Halls of Fame,* Living Planet Press, 1995.
The Book of Thanksgiving, Perigee Books, 1995.
The Joy of Keeping Score, Walker & Co. (New York City), 1996.

Contributor to magazines, including *American Heritage, Esquire, Progressive, Town and Country,* and *Washington Monthly.* Editor, *The Washingtonian Magazine;* consulting editor, Merriam-Webster.

SIDELIGHTS: Paul Dickson's business card carries the motto: "Practice limited to subjects of interest," which covers a lot of ground. His books, both humorous and serious, have concentrated on such subjects as toys, think tanks, working conditions, congress, and ice cream. According to Dickson, two of his sports titles, *The Dickson Baseball Dictionary* and *Baseball's Greatest Quotations,* are considered major baseball reference works.

Dickson says his great passion is writing about the American language and he spends fully half his of his time working in this area. Dickson's book of words entitled *Words: A Connoisseur's Collection of Old and New, Weird and Wonderful, Useful and Outlandish Words* contains such rarities as "borborygmite," "wamble," "vomer," and "psithurism." Writes Charles Champlin for the *Los Angeles Times Book Review:* "it is unquestionably a word man's word book, a treasury for anyone whose love of words approaches (and indeed overtakes) the obsessive. . . . You realize afresh what an astonishing arsenal of invective English is." Additionally, *Time* reviewer Otto Friedrich believes the "novelty" of Dickson's word book lies in its organization. Dickson arranges his book into categories, including "Outdoors Words," "Alimentary (food-related) Words," and "Sexy Words." As for "new" words, Dickson presents words that have been deliberately developed to fill a void. A "nork," for instance, is, as Dickson defines it, "a product that looks especially appealing in its original context—an ad, a catalogue, a hotel gift shop—but then loses its appeal very shortly after you get it." In the end, Champlin concludes: "Once you've dipped . . . [into *Words*], only the steel-willed can stop."

BIOGRAPHICAL/CRITICAL SOURCES:

BOOKS

Dickson, Paul, *Words: A Connoisseur's Collection of Old and New, Weird and Wonderful, Useful and Outlandish Words,* Delacorte, 1982.

PERIODICALS

American Heritage, February, 1994, p. 105.
Booklist, June 1, 1990, p. 1926; December 1, 1993, p. 709.
Book World, October 31, 1971.
Chicago Tribune Book World, July 31, 1986.
Library Journal, April 1, 1990, p. 106; October 1, 1990, p. 80; September 15, 1993, p. 68.

Los Angeles Times, March 10, 1983.
Los Angeles Times Book Review, August 29, 1982.
New York Times, February 12, 1979; August 9, 1982; February 17, 1983; August 15, 1986.
New York Times Book Review, October 15, 1972.
Saturday Review, March 18, 1972.
Time, August 23, 1982.
Tribune Books (Chicago), September 9, 1990, p. 8.
Washington Post, December 8, 1989.
Washington Post Book World, October 15, 1972; June 17, 1990, p. 12; September 4, 1994, p. 13.

*   *   *

DIDION, Joan 1934-

PERSONAL: Born December 5, 1934, in Sacramento, CA; daughter of Frank Reese and Eduene (Jerrett) Didion; married John Gregory Dunne (a writer), January 30, 1964; children: Quintana Roo (daughter). *Education:* University of California, Berkeley, B.A., 1956.

ADDRESSES: Agent—Lynn Nesbit, Jauklow, and Nesbit, 598 Madison Ave., New York, NY 10022.

CAREER: Writer. *Vogue,* New York City, 1956-63, began as promotional copywriter, became associate feature editor. Visiting regents lecturer in English, University of California, Berkeley, 1976.

AWARDS, HONORS: First prize, *Vogue*'s Prix de Paris, 1956; Bread Loaf fellowship in fiction, 1963; National Book Award nomination in fiction, 1971, for *Play It as It Lays;* Morton Dauwen Zabel Award, National Institute of Arts and Letters, 1978; National Book Critics Circle Prize nomination in nonfiction, 1980, and American Book Award nomination in nonfiction, 1981, both for *The White Album; Los Angeles Times* Book Prize nomination in fiction, 1984, for *Democracy;* Edward MacDowell Medal, 1996.

WRITINGS:

NOVELS

Run River, Obolensky (New York City), 1963.
Play It as It Lays (also see below), Farrar, Straus (New York City), 1970.
A Book of Common Prayer, Simon & Schuster (New York City), 1977.

Democracy, Simon & Schuster, 1984.
The Last Thing He Wanted, Knopf (New York City), 1996.

SCREENPLAYS; WITH HUSBAND, JOHN GREGORY DUNNE

Panic in Needle Park (based on a James Mills book of the same title), Twentieth Century-Fox, 1971.
Play It as It Lays (based on Didion's book of the same title), Universal, 1972.
(With others) *A Star Is Born,* Warner Bros., 1976.
True Confessions (based on Dunne's novel of the same title), United Artists, 1981.
Hills Like White Elephants (based on Ernest Hemingway's short story), HBO, 1990.
Broken Trust (based on the novel *Court of Honor* by William Wood), TNT, 1995.
Up Close and Personal, Disney, 1996.

NONFICTION

Slouching towards Bethlehem, Farrar, Straus, 1968.
The White Album, Simon & Schuster, 1979.
Salvador, Simon & Schuster, 1983.
Miami, Simon & Schuster, 1987.
After Henry, Simon & Schuster, 1992, published in England as *Sentimental Journeys,* HarperCollins (London), 1993.

OTHER

Robert Graham: The Duke Ellington Memorial in Progress, Los Angeles County Museum of Art (Los Angeles), 1988.
(Author of introduction) Robert Mapplethorpe, *Some Women,* Bulfinch Press (Boston), 1992.

Author of column, with Dunne, "Points West," *Saturday Evening Post,* 1967-69, and "The Coast," *Esquire,* 1976-77; former columnist, *Life.* Contributor of short stories, articles, and reviews to periodicals, including *Vogue, Saturday Evening Post, Holiday, Harper's Bazaar,* and *New York Times Book Review, The New Yorker,* and *The New York Review of Books.* Former contributing editor, *National Review.*

SIDELIGHTS: An elegant prose stylist and celebrated journalist, Joan Didion possesses a distinct literary voice, widely praised for its precision and control. She began, by her own admission, as a nonintellectual writer, more concerned with images than ideas and renowned for her use of telling detail. In addition to being "a gifted reporter," according to *New York Times Magazine* contributor Michiko Kakutani, Didion "is also a prescient witness, finding in her own experiences parallels of the times. The voice is always precise, the tone unsentimental, the view unabashedly subjective. She takes things personally." For years, Didion's favorite subject was her native California, a state that seemed to supply ample evidence of the disorder in society. Though her theme has not changed, she has broadened her perspective in more recent years and turned to the troubled countries of Central America and Southeast Asia for new material.

Although she has been writing since 1963, Didion has produced a relatively small output, which may be the result of perfectionism. "I'm not much interested in spontaneity," the author explained to Digby Diehl of the *Los Angeles Times.* "What concerns me is total control." To this end, Didion revises her writing repeatedly, working and reworking the exact placement of important details. *Newsweek*'s Peter S. Prescott says she is "able to condense into a paragraph what others would take three pages to expound. Unerringly, she seizes the exact phrase that not only describes but comments on a scene." According to *New York Times* reviewer John Leonard, "nobody writes better English prose than Joan Didion. Try to rearrange one of her sentences, and you've realized that the sentence was inevitable, a hologram."

After graduating from the University of California at Berkley in 1956, Didion took a job at *Vogue* magazine's New York office, where she remained for eight years, rising from promotional copywriter to associate feature editor. During this period, she met John Gregory Dunne and, after several years of friendship, they married, becoming not just matrimonial partners but collaborators as well. While still at *Vogue,* Didion began writing her first novel, *Run River,* which was published in 1963. The following year she moved back to the West Coast with Dunne, determined to earn a living as a freelance reporter. Working on a series of magazine columns about California for the *Saturday Evening Post,* the couple earned a meager $7,000 in their first year. But their writing did attract widespread attention, and when Didion's columns were collected and published in 1968 as *Slouching towards Bethlehem,* her reputation as an essayist soared.

Slouching towards Bethlehem takes its theme from Yeats's poem "The Second Coming," which reads: "Things fall apart; the center cannot hold; / Mere anarchy is loosed upon the world." For Didion those words sum up the chaos of the sixties, a chaos so far-reaching that it affected her ability to perform. Convinced "that writing was an irrelevant act, that the world as I had understood it no longer existed," Didion, as she states in the book's preface, realized, "If I was to work again at all, it would be necessary for me to come to terms with disorder." She went to Haight Ashbury to explore the hippie movement and out of that experience came the title essay.

Most critics praise the book highly. Writing in the *Christian Science Monitor,* Melvin Maddocks suggests of Didion that "her melancholy voice is that of a last survivor dictating a superbly written wreckage report onto a tape she doubts will ever be played." And while *Best Sellers* reviewer T. O'Hara argues that "the devotion she gives to America-the-up-rooted-the-lunatic-and-the-alienated is sullied by an inability to modulate, to achieve a respectable distance," most critics applaud her subjectivity. "Nobody captured the slack-jawed Haight-Ashbury hippies any better," states *Saturday Review* contributor Martin Kasindorf.

In 1970, Didion published *Play It as It Lays,* a best-selling novel that received a National Book Award nomination and, at the same time, created enormous controversy with its apparently nihilistic theme. The portrait of a woman on what *New York Times Book Review* contributor Lore Segal calls a "downward path to wisdom," *Play It as It Lays* tells the story of Maria Wyeth's struggle to find meaning in a meaningless world. "The setting is the desert; the cast, the careless hedonists of Hollywood; the emotional climate, bleak as the surroundings," Kakutani reports in the *New York Times Magazine.* Composed of eighty-four brief chapters, some less than a page in length, the book possesses a cinematic quality and such technical precision that Richard Shickel remarks in *Harper's* that it is "a rather cold and calculated fiction—more a problem in human geometry . . . than a novel that truly lives."

New York Review of Books critic D. A. N. Jones finds himself unmoved by the novel: "Although [Maria] seems to be in hell, and although every event is charged with misery, *Play It as It Lays* cannot be honestly called depressing. The neat, cinematic construction, the harsh wit of the mean, soulless dialogue stimulate a certain exhilaration, as when we appreciate a harmonious and well-proportioned painting of some cruelly martyred saint in whom we do not believe." John Leonard in the *New York Times,*

on the other hand, expresses a far different view: "While the result is not exactly pleasant, it seems to me just about perfect according to its own austere terms. So long as novels are permitted to be about visions, to explore situations, to see truths beyond individual manipulation, then Miss Didion need not equip Maria with a Roto-Rooter or a dose of ideological uplift. The courage to say 'Why not?' to Nothingness is more than enough."

Didion originally got the idea for her third novel during a 1973 trip to Cartagena, Colombia, when her plane stopped over in the Panama airport for an hour. "My experience of that airport was very vivid, super-real," she told Diehl in the *Saturday Review.* "I could see the opening scene of a woman having a contretemps with a waitress in the coffee shop about boiling her water twenty minutes for a cup of tea. I started to think about what she was doing there and the novel began to unfold." *A Book of Common Prayer* continues the author's theme of social disintegration with the story of Charlotte Douglas, a Californian "immaculate of history, innocent of politics." Until her daughter Marin abandoned home and family to join a group of terrorists, Charlotte was one who "understood that something was always going on in the world but believed that it would turn out all right." When things fall apart, Charlotte takes refuge in Boca Grande, a fictitious Central American country embroiled in its own domestic conflicts. There she idles away her days at the airport coffee shop, futilely waiting for her daughter to surface and eventually losing her life in a military coup.

Because Charlotte's story is narrated by Grace, an American expatriate and long-time Boca Grande resident, the book presented several technical problems. "The narrator was not present during most of the events she's telling you about. And her only source is a woman incapable of seeing the truth," Didion explained to Diehl. In her *New York Times Book Review* article, Joyce Carol Oates speculates that Didion employs this technique because Grace permits Didion "a free play of her own speculative intelligence that would have been impossible had the story been told by Charlotte. The device of an uninvolved narrator is a tricky one, since a number of private details must be presented as if they were within the range of the narrator's experience. But it is a measure of Didion's skill as a novelist that one never questions [Grace's] near omniscience in recalling Charlotte's story." Christopher Lehmann-Haupt, on the other hand, maintains in the *New York Times* that Didion "simply asks too much of Charlotte, and overburdened as she is by the pitiless cruelty of the narrator's vision, she collapses under the strain."

After *A Book of Common Prayer,* Didion published *The White Album,* a second collection of magazine essays similar in tone to *Slouching towards Bethlehem.* "I don't have as many answers as I did when I wrote *Slouching,'* Didion explained to Kakutani. She called the book *The White Album* in consideration of a famous Beatles album that captured for her the disturbing ambience of the sixties. "I am talking here about a time when I began to doubt the premises of all the stories I had ever told myself," Didion writes in the title essay. "This period began around 1966 and continued until 1971." During this time, says Didion, "all I knew was what I saw: flash pictures in variable sequence, images with no 'meaning' beyond their temporary arrangement, not a movie but a cuttingroom experience."

Diagnosed at this time as "fundamentally pessimistic, fatalistic, and depressive," Didion includes not only such personal data as her psychiatric profile, but also public news about incidents as diverse as the Charles Manson murders and Robert Kennedy's death. "At times, it seems Didion's own fear and malaise run parallel like train tracks to those of the era," observes Hillary Johnson in the *Christian Science Monitor. New York Times Book Review* contributor Robert Towers calls her title essay, "the best short piece (37 pages) on the late 1960's that I have yet read," attributing its success in large part to "the use to which personal neurosis has been put. Joan Didion makes no bones about the seriousness of the neurosis, but she gives the impression of having refined it to the point where it vibrates in exquisite attunement to the larger craziness of the world. . . . It is her nerve-frayed awareness of the gap between the supposedly meaningful 'script' by which we try to live and the absurdities by which we are bombarded that has brought her vision to its preternaturally sharp focus and has helped make her the extraordinary reporter she is."

In her later work, Didion broadened her questioning approach while retaining her subjectivity. Under her scrutiny came the differences between North America and its southern neighbors. First surfacing in *A Book of Common Prayer* with its fictitious Central American setting, this subject is journalistically addressed in the nonfiction work *Salvador,* which chronicles two weeks that Didion and Dunne spent in the war-torn country of El Salvador in 1982. "Alternately detached and compassionate, this slim essay is many things at once," observes Carolyn Forche in the *Chicago Tribune Book World:* "a sidelong reflection on the limits of the now-old new journalism; a tourist guide manque; a surrealist docu-drama; a withering indictment of American foreign policy; and a poetic exploration in fear."

While highly acclaimed for its literary merits, *Salvador* has been criticized on other grounds. *Newsweek* reviewer Gene Lyon, for example, allows that "Didion gets exactly right both the ghastliness and the pointlessness of the current killing frenzy in El Salvador" but then suggests that "ghastliness and pointlessness are Didion's invariable themes wherever she goes. Most readers will not get very far in this very short book without wondering whether she visited that sad and tortured place less to report than to validate the Didion world view." Others question Didion's credentials as a historian. Leonel Gomez Videz, former deputy director of the Agrarian Reform Institute in El Salvador, faults the book for mystifying a subject that desperately needs to be understood. "What she provides is a horrific description of atrocity: 'The dead and pieces of the dead turn up in El Salvador everywhere, every day, as taken for granted as in a nightmare, or a horror movie,'" he writes, quoting *Salvador* in the *New Republic.* "What point is Didion making? Such lurid details make for compelling prose, but in the absence of any analysis of why such murders occur, they seem at best to bolster her thesis of mindless terror and at worst to suggest a penchant for gratuitous special effects."

Juan M. Vasquez, on the other hand, defends Didion's approach. "Didion's book is not for the seekers of solutions, those who would feed the contents of El Salvador into a computer and expect a tidy answer to emerge—pressed, neat, ready for consumption," he writes in the *Los Angeles Times Book Review.* "It is, rather, for those who can subscribe to the foolishness of such notions and who can appreciate that the way some people live—the way some countries live—is not always believable, but it is all too crushingly real." Moreover, Forche maintains that "Didion achieves in this slender volume what she seldom does in her fiction: a consummate political artwork. For the otherwise powerless artist, the tenacious pursuit of reality and the past, in countries where both are constantly thrown into doubt, constitutes the most meaningful act of defiance."

In 1984, one year after *Salvador* was published, Didion produced *Democracy.* The book was to have been the story of a family of American colonialists whose interests were firmly entrenched in the Pacific at a time when Hawaii was still a territory, but Didion abandoned this idea. The resulting novel features Inez Christian and her family. In the spring of 1975—at the time the United States completed its evacuation of Vietnam and Cambodia—Inez's father is arrested for a double murder with political and racial overtones. "The Christians and their in-laws are the emblems of a misplaced confidence," according to John Lownsbrough in Toronto's *Globe & Mail*, "the flotsam and jetsam of a Manifest Destiny no longer so manifest. Their disintegration as a family in the spring of 1975 . . . is paralleled by the fall of Saigon a bit later that year and the effective disintegration of the American expansionist dream in all its ethnocentric optimism." Somehow, her family's tragedy enables Inez to break free of her marriage to a self-serving politician and escape to Malaysia with Jack Lovett, a freelance CIA agent and the man she has always loved. Though he dies abruptly, Inez holds on to her freedom, choosing to remain in Kuala Lumpur where she works among the Vietnamese refugees.

New York Review of Books critic Thomas R. Edwards believes *Democracy* "finally earns its complexity of form. It is indeed 'a hard story to tell' and the presence in it of 'Joan Didion' trying to tell it is an essential part of its subject. Throughout one senses the author struggling with the moral difficulty that makes the story hard to tell—how to stop claiming what Inez finally relinquishes, 'the American exemption' from having to recognize that history records not the victory of personal wills over reality . . . but the 'undertow of having and not having, the convulsions of a world largely unaffected by the individual efforts of anyone in it.'" At the story's end, "when the retreat from Vietnam is finished and Inez is alone in Kuala Lumpur, a penitent working with the refugees democracy has created, we feel that along with the novelist and her characters, we too have learned something about the importance of memory," writes Peter Collier in the *Chicago Tribune Book World*. "We also note that Didion, who has earlier compared the writer to the aerialist, is still on the high wire, a little shaky perhaps, but in no real danger of falling."

Miami once again finds Didion on the literary high wire, in a work of nonfiction that focuses on the cultural, social, and political impact the influx of Cuban exiles has had upon Miami and, indeed, upon the entire United States. Culminating in an indict-

ment of American foreign policy from the presidential administrations of John F. Kennedy through Ronald Reagan, *Miami* "is a thoroughly researched and brilliantly written meditation on the consequences of power, especially on power's self-addictive delusions," according to *Voice Literary Supplement* reviewer Stacey D'Erasmo. The book explores the thirty-year history of the community of Cuban immigrants which now comprises over half the population of that city. Passionate in their desire to oust Fidel Castro since being driven from their homeland by his Communist revolution during the 1960s, these emigres have felt increasingly manipulated and betrayed by the government of the United States, beginning with the Bay of Pigs expedition and continuing through a series of betrayals by the CIA that followed in its wake.

Within a city that is now more Cuban than American, wealthy Cuban Americans have transformed a culture once American into one now distinctly Latin, and have formed characteristically Latin rivalries in plotting Castro's demise. Didion paints these emigres as existing within a country that threatens their political agenda, and a city full of enemies. "The shadowy missions, the secret fundings, the conspiracies beneath conspiracies, the deniable support by parts of the U.S. government and active discouragement by other parts," Richard Eder writes in the *Los Angeles Times Book Review*, paraphrasing Didion's argument, "all these things have fostered a tensely paranoid style in parts of our own political life. . . . Miami is us." While noting that Didion's intricate—if journalistic—style almost overwhelms her argument, Eder compares *Miami* to a luxury hunting expedition: "You may look out the window and see some casually outfitted huntsman trudging along. You may wonder whether his experience is more authentic than yours. Didion's tour is overarranged, but that is a genuine lion's carcass strapped to our fender."

Edward Said is critical of *Miami* in a review for *London Review of Books*. While praising the power of Didion's argument, Said comments: "It offers no politics beyond its sometimes admirably crafted turns of phrase, its arch conceits, its carefully designed but limited effects. We are never told what U.S. relations with Cuba or Nicaragua should be, beyond being made to realise that they shouldn't be like *this*. . . . Didion's way with all this [description of violence and brutality is]. . . to get her readers angry. But she goes no further." And D'Erasmo agrees, noting that while other writers on the topic of Miami "do not even approach her in sophistication, analytic precision, and stylistic grace. . . . A certain skepticism about Didion's persona as an investigative traveller—the Sphinx crossed with Alice in Wonderland—kept interfering with my desire to believe her. . . . She castigates the government for its paper promises and equally fragile empires, but her own methods are suspiciously similar."

After Henry, published in the United Kingdom as *Sentimental Journeys,* is a collection of twelve essays organized loosely around three geographical areas that Didion has focused on throughout her writing career: Washington, DC, California, and New York City. "For her they are our Chapels Perilous," declares Robert Dana in the *Georgia Review,* "where power and dreams fuse or collide." The title essay is a tribute to Didion's friend and mentor Henry Robbins, who served as her editor prior to his death in 1979.

Politics are discussed in the section titled "Washington." The essay "In the Realm of the Fisher King" is an analysis of the years of the Reagan presidency. Didion's analytic style received mixed reactions. "Her difficulty with politics is that she really doesn't know it as well as she imagines," states Jonathan Yardley in the *Washington Post Book World,* "and brings to it no especially useful insights." However, reviewer Hendrik Hertzberg lauds "Inside Baseball," Didion's essay on the 1988 presidential campaign, in the *New York Times Book Review:* "Her cool eye sees sharply when it surveys the rich texture of American public folly. . . . What she has to say about the manipulation of images and the creation of pseudo-events makes familiar territory new again." But, Hertzberg adds, Didion's "focus on the swirl of 'narratives' is useful as a way of exploring political image-mongering, but surprisingly limited as a way of describing the brute political and social realities against which candidates and ideas must in the end be measured."

Didion uses California as a topic in seven essays. Former kidnap victim-turned-terrorist and publishing heiress Patty Hearst is compared to a frontierswoman bent on survival in "Girl of the Golden West." Another essay, "Pacific Days," is a recollection of a trip taken to the University of California at Berkley, where Didion had been an undergraduate student. A resident of Los Angeles for many years, she examines the city and its politics in "Down at City Hall" and "Times Mirror Square." "Here we have Didion at her most pungent," comments Yardley. "Her unending search for 'subtext' has in this instance struck gold: a pungent insight into the civic character of Los Angeles."

Included among the remaining works in *After Henry* is "Sentimental Journey," a three-part "attack on New York City and the sentimentality that distorts and obscures much of what is said and done there, and which has brought the city to the edge of bankruptcy and collapse," according to Dana. One section explores the way in which the highly publicized 1990 rape of a white investment banker jogging in New York City's Central Park—and the trial that followed—was transformed by the media into what Didion terms a "false narrative." Combined with her illuminating discussion of the many rapes occurring in the city that are not given such intensive press coverage and the decreasing competitive edge possessed by the city when viewed in real terms, "Didion's portrait is one of a city drugged nearly to death on the crack of its own myths," according to Dana, "its own 'sentimental stories told in defense of its own lazy criminality.'"

While praising the essays in *After Henry* in a *National Review* article, David Klinghoffer identifies a change in Didion's characteristic approach. Remarking on Didion's early forays into a variety of situations to gather the material for such early works as *Slouching towards Bethlehem,* Klinghoffer maintains that she now uses major newspapers as her sources, with negative results. "She has begun to conflate the views of the press with the views of the population at large," he contends, adding that "readers of her earlier, and more exhilarating, work will regret that the reality of Joan Didion is now generally grey in color, and characterized by parallel columns running down either side of it." "In [*After Henry*] Didion works less with firsthand impressions, more with the texts that sift up from the culture," agrees Carol Anshaw in the *Village Voice.* "Which gives these essays an air of imposed distance, rather than self-imposed detachment from their subjects." Yardley, however, finds that much has remained similar in Didion's style: "Whether she is writing fiction or nonfiction, Didion's *self* is always at the center; it is," the critic finds, "for all the acuity of her perceptions, a presence that in time becomes obtrusive and annoying."

Didion's continuing emphasis on self-reflection, image, and detail mirrors her personal orientation. In a lecture she delivered at her alma mater, she explained the way her mind works: "During the years I was an undergraduate at Berkeley, I . . . kept trying to find that part of my mind that could deal in abstracts. But my mind kept veering inexorably back like some kind of boomerang I was stuck with—to the specific, to the tangible, to what was generally considered by everyone I knew, the peripheral. I would try to think about the Great Dialectic and I would find myself thinking instead about how the light was falling through the window in an apartment I had on the North Side. How it was hitting the floor."

Though she often builds a whole book around a single "picture," Didion's writing can seem fragmented, her chapters short and disjointed, her images unexplored. "Everything depends on the selection and placement of details," notes *Newsweek*'s Walter Clemons, who calls it "a perilous method. At her worse Didion sounds supercilious, an uncommitted connoisseur of fragments, a severe snob."

Didion knows her concerns are not the standard ones and in one of her better-known essays, "In the Islands," she describes herself as "a woman who for some time now has felt radically separated from most of the ideas that seem to interest other people." However, many critics and readers would hasten to disagree. "Her prose is a literary seismograph," describes Dana, "on which are clearly registered the tremors and tremblors that increasingly shake the bedrock of the American social dream."

BIOGRAPHICAL/CRITICAL SOURCES:

BOOKS

Authors in the News, Volume 1, Gale (Detroit), 1976.
Contemporary Literary Criticism, Gale, Volume 1, 1973, Volume 3, 1975, Volume 8, 1978, Volume 14, 1980.
Dictionary of Literary Biography, Volume 2: *American Novelists since World War II,* Gale, 1978.
Dictionary of Literary Biography Yearbook, Gale, 1981, 1986.
Didion, Joan, *Slouching towards Bethlehem,* Farrar, Straus, 1968.
Didion, *A Book of Common Prayer,* Simon & Schuster, 1977.
Didion, *The White Album,* Simon & Schuster, 1979.
Didion, *Democracy,* Simon & Schuster, 1984.
Didion, *After Henry,* Simon & Schuster, 1992.
Felton, Sharon, editor, *The Critical Response to Joan Didion,* Greenwood Press (Westport, CT), 1994.
Friedman, Ellen G., editor, *Joan Didion: Essays and Conversations,* Ontario Review Press, 1984.
Henderson, Katherine Usher, *Joan Didion,* Ungar (New York City), 1981.
Kazin, Alfred, *Bright Book of Life: American Novelists and Storytellers from Hemingway to Mailer,* Little, Brown (Boston), 1973.
Winchell, Mark Royden, *Joan Didion,* Twayne (Boston), 1980.

PERIODICALS

American Scholar, winter, 1970-71.
American Spectator, September, 1992.
Atlantic, April, 1977.
Belles Lettres, fall, 1992, p. 14.
Best Sellers, June 1, 1968; August 1, 1970.
Booklist, March 1, 1992.
Book World, July 28, 1968.
Boston Globe, May 17, 1992, p. 105.
Chicago Tribune, June 12, 1979.
Chicago Tribune Book World, July 1, 1979; April 3, 1983; April 15, 1984.
Chicago Tribune Magazine, May 2, 1982.
Christian Science Monitor, May 16, 1968; September 24, 1970; July 9, 1979; June 1, 1992, p. 13.
Commentary, June, 1984, pp. 62-67.
Commonweal, November 29, 1968; October 23, 1992.
Critique, spring, 1984, pp. 160-70.
Detroit News, August 12, 1979.
Dissent, summer, 1983.
Economist, August 22, 1992.
Georgia Review, winter, 1992, pp. 799-802.
Globe and Mail (Toronto), April 28, 1984.
Harper's, August, 1970; December, 1971.
Harvard Advocate, winter, 1973.
London Review of Books, December 10, 1987, pp. 3, 5-6; October 21, 1993, p. 12-13.
Los Angeles Times, May 9, 1971; July 4, 1976.
Los Angeles Times Book Review, March 20, 1983; September 27, 1987, pp. 3, 6.
Miami Herald, December 2, 1973.
Ms., February, 1977.
Nation, September 26, 1979.
National Review, June 4, 1968; August 25, 1970; October 12, 1979; November 23, 1987; June 22, 1992, pp. 53-54.
New Republic, June 6, 1983; April 9, 1984; November 23, 1987.
Newsweek, August 3, 1970; December 21, 1970; March 21, 1977; June 25, 1979; March 28, 1983; April 16, 1984.

New Yorker, June 20, 1977; April 18, 1983; January 25, 1988, p. 112.

New York Magazine, February 15, 1971; June 13, 1979.

New York Review of Books, October 22, 1970; May 10, 1984.

New York Times, July 21, 1970; October 30, 1972; March 21, 1977; June 5, 1979; March 11, 1983; April 6, 1984; September 14, 1984.

New York Times Book Review, July 21, 1968; August 9, 1970; April 3, 1977; June 17, 1979; March 13, 1983; April 22, 1984; October 25, 1987, p. 3; May 17, 1992, pp. 3, 39.

New York Times Magazine, June 10, 1979; February 8, 1987.

Observer (London), March 27, 1988, p. 43; January 24, 1993, p. 53.

Quill and Quire, December, 1987, p. 30.

San Francisco Review of Books, May, 1977.

Saturday Review, August 15, 1970; March 5, 1977; September 15, 1979; April 1982.

Sewanee Review, fall, 1977.

Time, August 10, 1970; March 28, 1977; August 20, 1979; April 4, 1983; May 7, 1984; June 29, 1992.

Times Literary Supplement, February 12, 1970; March 12, 1971; July 8, 1977; November 30, 1979; June 24, 1983; January 29, 1993, p. 10; November 5, 1993, p. 28.

Tribune Books (Chicago), May 10, 1992, pp. 3, 7.

Village Voice, February 28, 1977; June 25, 1979; May 26, 1992, pp. 74-76.

Voice Literary Supplement, October 1987, pp. 21-22.

Washington Post, April 8, 1983.

Washington Post Book World, June 17,179; March 13, 1983; April 15, 1984; May 10, 1992, p. 3.

*   *   *

DORF, Richard C.   1933-

PERSONAL: Born December 27, 1933, in New York, NY; son of William Carl (a sales representative) and Marion (a secretary; maiden name, Fraser) Dorf; married Joy McDonald (a Presbyterian minister), 1957; children: Christine, Renee. *Education:* Clarkson College of Technology (now Clarkson University), B.S.E.E., 1955; University of Colorado, M.S.E.E., 1957; U.S. Naval Postgraduate School, Ph.D., 1961. *Religion:* Presbyterian.

ADDRESSES: Home—705 Ave del oro, Sonoma, CA 95476. *Office*—Department of Electrical Engineering, Graduate School of Management, University of California, Davis, CA 95616.

CAREER: Clarkson College of Technology (now Clarkson University), Potsdam, NY, instructor in electrical engineering, 1956-58; U.S. Naval Postgraduate School, Monterey, CA, instructor, 1958-61, assistant professor of electrical engineering, 1961-63; University of Santa Clara, Santa Clara, CA, associate professor, 1963-65, professor of electrical engineering, 1965-69, chairperson of department, 1963-69, dean of College of Engineering and vice president of Educational Service, 1969-72; University of California, Davis, professor of electrical engineering, 1972—, dean of extended learning, 1972-81. Research associate at University of New Mexico, 1958-59; lecturer at University of Edinburgh, 1961-62; vice president of Ohio University, 1969-72; visiting fellow at Institute of Engineers, Australia, 1983. Member of board of directors of Boyd & Fraser Publishing Co., 1968-85, and KVIE-TV, 1979-81.

MEMBER: Institute of Electrical and Electronics Engineers (Fellow), American Society for Engineering Education.

WRITINGS:

Time-Domain Analysis and Design of Control Systems, Addison-Wesley (Reading, MA), 1965.

(With George Julius Thaler) *Algebraic Methods for Dynamic Systems,* National Aeronautics and Space Administration, 1966.

Modern Control Systems, Addison-Wesley, 1967, seventh edition, 1996.

Matrix Algebra: A Programmed Introduction, Wiley (New York City), 1969.

Introduction to Computers and Computer Science, Boyd & Fraser (San Francisco), 1972, abridged edition published as *Computers and Man,* 1974, third edition, 1982.

Technology, Society, and Man, Boyd & Fraser, 1974.

Technology and Society, Boyd & Fraser, 1974.

Energy, Resources, and Policy, Addison-Wesley, 1978.

Appropriate Visions, Boyd & Fraser, 1978.

The Energy Factbook, McGraw (New York City), 1981.

The Energy Answer, 1982-2000, Brick House (Andover, MA), 1982.

Robotics and Automated Manufacturing, Reston (Reston, VA), 1983.

A User's Guide to the IBM Personal Computer, Addison-Wesley, 1983.

International Encyclopedia of Robotics, Wiley, 1988.

Introduction to Electric Circuits, Wiley, 1989, third edition, 1996.

Electrical Engineering Handbook, CRC Press (Boca Raton, FL), 1993.

Field Programmable Gate Arrays, Wiley, 1994.

The Handbook of Manufacturing and Automation, Wiley, 1995.

Engineering Handbook, CRC Press, 1996.

*   *   *

DORRITT, Susan
   See SCHLEIN, Miriam

*   *   *

DOWNIE, Mary Alice (Dawe)   **1934-**
   (Dawe Hunter)

PERSONAL: Born February 12, 1934, in Alton, IL; brought to Canada, 1940; daughter of Robert Grant (a research scientist) and Doris Mary (Rogers) Hunter; married John Downie (a professor of chemical engineering), June 27, 1959; children: Christine, Jocelyn, Alexandra. *Education:* University of Toronto, B.A. (honors), 1955. *Religion:* Anglican.

ADDRESSES: Home—190 Union St., Kingston, Ontario, Canada, K7L 2P6. *E-mail*—downiej@post.queensu.ca.

CAREER: Writer, critic, and editor. Maclean-Hunter, Toronto, Ontario, stenographer, 1955; *Marketing Magazine,* Toronto, reporter, 1955-56; *Canadian Medical Association Journal,* Toronto, editorial assistant, 1956-57; Oxford University Press, Toronto, librarian and publicity manager, 1958-59; Kingston *Whig-Standard,* Kingston, Ontario, book review editor, 1973-78. Affiliated member, Senior Combination Room, Newnham College, Cambridge, 1988-89. Speaker at schools and workshops.

MEMBER: PEN, Writers Union of Canada (chair, membership committee, 1987-88).

AWARDS, HONORS: Ontario Arts Council Awards, 1970, 1975, 1978, 1981, 1987, 1989, 1990; Canada Council Arts Awards, 1972-73, 1981-82; Canada Council Short Term Award, 1979; (with John Downie) second prize, fourth Canadian Broadcasting Corp. Literary Competition, Children's Section, 1982, for "The Bright Paddles"; Exploration Grant (with E. Greene and M. A. Thompson), 1984; Ontario Heritage Foundation grant, 1988; Multicultural Directorate grant, 1990.

WRITINGS:

CHILDREN'S FICTION

(With husband, John Downie) *Honor Bound,* illustrated by Joan Huffman, Oxford University Press (New York City), 1971, revised edition illustrated by Wesley Bates, Quarry Press (Kingston, ON), 1991.

Scared Sarah, illustrated by Laszlo Gal, Thomas Nelson (Canada), 1974.

Dragon on Parade, illustrated by Mary Lynn Baker, PMA Books, 1974.

The King's Loon/Un Huart pour le Roi, illustrated by Ron Berg, Kids Can Press (Toronto), 1979.

The Last Ship, illustrated by Lissa Calvert, PMA Books, 1980.

(With George Rawlyk) *A Proper Acadian,* illustrated by Berg, Kids Can Press, 1981.

Jenny Greenteeth, illustrated by Anne Powell, Rhino Press (Victoria, BC), 1981, revised edition illustrated by Barbara Reid, Kids Can Press, 1984.

(With J. Downie) *Alison's Ghosts,* illustrated by Paul McCusker, Thomas Nelson, 1984.

The Cat Park, illustrated by Kathryn Naylor, Quarry Press, 1993.

Snow Paws, illustrated by Naylor, Stoddart, 1996.

FOLKTALES

The Magical Adventures of Pierre, illustrated by Yuksel Hassan, Thomas Nelson, 1974.

The Witch of the North: Folktales from French Canada, illustrated by Elizabeth Cleaver, Oberon Press (Ottawa), 1975.

The Wicked Fairy-Wife: A French-Canadian Folktale, illustrated by Kim Price, Kids Can Press, 1983.

How the Devil Got His Cat, illustrated by Jillian Gilliland, Quarry Press, 1988.

(With Mann Hwa Huang-Hsu) *The Buffalo Boy and the Weaver Girl,* illustrated by Gilliland, Quarry Press, 1989.

Cathal the Giant Killer and the Dun Shaggy Filly, illustrated by Gilliland, Quarry Press, 1991.

CHILDREN'S NONFICTION

(With Gilliland) *Seeds and Weeds: A Book of Country Crafts,* Four Winds Press (New York City), 1981.
(With Gilliland) *Stones and Cones: Country Crafts for Kids,* Scholastic (New York City), 1984.

EDITOR OR COMPILER

(With Barbara Robertson) *The Wind Has Wings: Poems from Canada,* illustrated by Cleaver, Oxford University Press, 1968, revised edition published as *The New Wind Has Wings: Poems from Canada,* 1984.
(With Mary Hamilton) *And Some Brought Flowers: Plants in a New World,* illustrated by John Revell, University of Toronto Press (Toronto), 1980.
(With Elizabeth Greene and M. A. Thompson) *The Window of Dreams: New Canadian Writing for Children,* Methuen (London), 1986.
(With Robertson) *The Well-Filled Cupboard: Everyday Pleasures of Home and Garden,* Lester & Orpen Dennys (Toronto), 1987.
(With Robertson) A. M. Klein, *Doctor Dwarf and Other Poems for Children,* illustrated by Gail Geltner, Quarry Press, 1990.
(With Thompson) *Written in Stone: A Kingston Reader,* Quarry Press, 1993.

OTHER

Contributor (sometimes with J. Downie) to anthologies. Founding editor, "Kids Canada" series, Kids Can Press, and "Northern Lights" series, Peter Martin Associates. Contributor of numerous stories, articles and reviews to *Horn Book, Pittsburgh Press, Ottawa Citizen, Globe and Mail, OWL, Chickadee, Montreal Gazette, Canadian Gardening,* and *Century Home.*

SIDELIGHTS: Mary Alice Downie is one of the best-known children's authors and editors in Canada. Besides rewriting traditional folk tales, Downie has drawn stories from actual events in Canada's past, resulting in fiction that "breathes life into distant periods of Canadian history," Joan McGrath writes in *Twentieth-Century Children's Writers.* McGrath says that Downi's "youthful Canadians of long ago are irresistible creations."

Downie's first book was a compilation of poems, entitled *The Wind Has Wings: Poems from Canada.* Works by forty-eight poets from a diverse variety of backgrounds—some translated from Yiddish, French, and Eskimo—cover such subjects as ice and cold, animal life, and Indians. Since then Downie has coedited several other anthologies that feature Canadian writing for children and adults, including an updated version of her first collection, *The New Wind Has Wings: Poems from Canada,* which Zena Sutherland of *Bulletin of the Center for Children's Books* calls "a fine anthology" with "variety and vitality."

Honor Bound was Downie's first historical fiction, written in collaboration with her husband, John Downie. The story draws upon Canada's early history when, after the American Revolution, loyalists to England left America to move to the wilderness of Canada; they became known as United Empire Loyalists. *Honor Bound* tells the story of one such family who leaves their "civilized" Philadelphia home to start a new life in the Canadian backwoods. Not only must the family leave behind their home and possessions, they must also move without their daughter, Honor, who was visiting relatives when Yankee vigilantes struck, and they do not know her fate. Terence Scully, writing for *Canadian Children's Literature,* comments on the double meaning of the title—the family's search for dignity in their new home as well as their effort to reunite the family—and notes that "the narrative has a rousing beginning, a convincing progression from episode to episode . . . and above all a satisfying distinct conclusion where 'Honor' has been reached."

Details of seventeenth-century life are vividly displayed in *The Last Ship,* a story told from the viewpoint of ten-year-old Madeleine. Every year, when the last supply ship leaves Quebec to return to France, the inhabitants feel cut off and exiled from their old lives. In this story, which *In Review* contributor Mary Anne Buchowski-Monnin calls "a pleasant introduction to Canadian history for young children," Madeleine fails in an attempt to sneak into the governor's ball, witnesses a fire, and comes to realize that it is Quebec, not France, that is now truly her home.

A Proper Acadian makes a complicated subject understandable for young readers. Twelve-year-old Timothy, living in Boston in the 1750s, is sent to live with his aunt when he is orphaned by his mother's death. His aunt and her family are Acadians, people of French descent living in Nova Scotia in an area that the French had ceded to England in the early 1700s. Timothy must make a choice between his native New England and his beloved adopted family when the deportation of Acadians is ordered and his aunt's family must go into exile. McGrath calls this story of conflicting family and national loyalties "vividly told."

Besides historical novels, Downie has also written books for younger readers. Among these is *Jenny Greenteeth,* a book that Cynthia Kittleson, in a review for *School Library Journal,* claims is a "silly story with a witch whose life goes beyond Halloween." In this story, everyone in the town of Denim is afraid of the once-popular water witch. When the mayor orders her captured, only young David is brave enough to confront her and offer a solution—a toothbrush and toothpaste. Praising the story's "lighthearted humor," Hope Bridgewater of *In Review* finds that the story's idea that fears should be confronted logically makes for "a worthwhile message."

Downie is also well-established as a reteller of folktales, many of them based on French-Canadian tales. *The Wicked Fairy-Wife: A French-Canadian Folktale* tells of a young farmgirl named Josette who marries a handsome prince. But an evil fairy usurps Josette's place as queen and orders her killed. The executioners, however, take pity on her—merely plucking out her eyes and leaving her alone in the forest. Josette not only survives, she bears the king's son, who grows up to avenge his mother and reunite his parents. Reviewer Mary Ainslie Smith comments in *Books in Canada* that "in spite of the violence of many of the incidents, Downie tells the story with cheerful humour."

How the Devil Got His Cat is a French-Canadian tale set at a convent in Quebec. When an old wooden bridge collapses, the only one who can repair it is a stranger who wants no money for the job—only the soul of the first creature to cross the bridge. The Mother Superior tricks the stranger, the devil in disguise, by sending her beloved black cat over the bridge. This traditional tale, combined with the striking silhouette illustrations of Jillian Gilliland, makes "a compelling and enjoyable story for young children," Eva Martin writes in *Canadian Children's Literature.*

The Buffalo Boy and the Weaver Girl, written with Mann Hwa Huang-Hsu, is based on an ancient Chinese legend about a young man who is driven from his home with only the family's buffalo. The animal has magical powers which help the young man find a new home and a beautiful wife. The work features more silhouette art by Gilliland, which "perfectly complements" Downie's "well-crafted, compelling text," according to Bernie Goedhart in *Quill & Quire.* Downie explores her Scottish roots for the tale of *Cathal the Giant Killer and the Dun Shaggy Filly,* about a man's search for his wife, who has been stolen by a local giant. Downie's narrative, writes *Canadian Children's Literature* contributor Gillian Harding-Russell, reads like written "dialect, with the lovely flowing rhythms of that language emphasized by . . . a periodic repetition." In *Cathal,* the critic adds, "we feel the magic touch of an artist storyteller."

"As a writer I spend a great deal of my time on the wrong track; for every book that has been published there is another manuscript in the attic," Downie once commented. "I get an idea (become obsessed by, is nearer the truth) or stumble across interesting material in the Queen's University stacks. With mounting enthusiasm I turn it into an un-publishable manuscript. After a certain amount of brooding about this, it occurs to me what I should really be doing and I set to work once more.

"*The Wind Has Wings* sprang from the ashes of an anthology for poetry for four-to-six-year olds (in that case the publisher saw what should be done); *Honor Bound* from an eighteenth-century diary owned by a landlady. *The Witch of the North,* a collection of French-Canadian witch and devil legends, resulted from reading done for an ill-fated sequel to *Honor Bound.*

"My husband, who acts as unpaid editor and occasionally as coauthor, describes me as a 'relentless follower of false trails.' There are undoubtedly more efficient ways of writing, but as the travel-articles say—the side roads are the most interesting. They still are."

BIOGRAPHICAL/CRITICAL SOURCES:

BOOKS

Twentieth-Century Children's Writers, 4th edition, St. James Press (Detroit), 1995.

PERIODICALS

Books for Young People, August, 1988, p. 4.
Books in Canada, January, 1984, p. 26; October, 1986, p. 38.

Bulletin of the Center for Children's Books, April, 1985, p. 145.

Canadian Children's Literature, Number 23/24, 1981, pp. 97-98; Number 29, 1983, pp. 77-80; Number 41, 1986, pp. 56-57; Number 57/58, 1990, pp. 116-17; Number 73, 1994, pp. 86-88.

In Review, February, 1981, pp. 35-36; April, 1982, p. 42.

Kirkus Reviews, January 1, 1972, p. 4.

Quill and Quire, June, 1982, p. 36; June, 1984, p. 35; September, 1989, p. 22.

School Library Journal, May, 1981, p. 54; May, 1985, p. 72; November, 1985, p. 83.

Times Literary Supplement, April 3, 1969, p. 353.

* * *

DRAGLAND, Stan L(ouis)   1942-

PERSONAL: Born December 2, 1942, in Calgary, Alberta, Canada; son of Kenneth Arthur (a gambler) and Mydra (a teacher; maiden name, Roberts) Dragland; married Truus Alberta Schalk, May 15, 1965 (divorced May, 1987); married Marion Margaret Parsons (a teacher), May 30, 1987; children: Michael Tobias, Simon Jesse, Rachel Emily. *Education:* University of Alberta, B.A., 1964, M.A., 1966; Queen's University, Kingston, Ontario, Ph.D., 1970.

ADDRESSES: Home—47 Briscoe St. W., London, Ontario, Canada N6J 1M4. *Office*—Department of English, University of Western Ontario, London, Ontario, Canada N6A 3K7.

CAREER: University of Alberta, Edmonton, lecturer in English, 1965-66; English teacher and department head at grammar school in Sudbury, England, 1966-67; University of Alberta, lecturer in English, 1967-68; University of Western Ontario, London, assistant professor, 1970-77, associate professor, 1977-92, professor, 1992—.

MEMBER: Association of Canadian and Quebec Literatures, Writers Union of Canada.

WRITINGS:

Wilson MacDonald's Western Tour, Coach House Press (Chicago, IL), 1975.

Peckertracks, Coach House Press, 1978.

Simon Jesse's Journey (juvenile), Groundwood, 1983.

Journeys Through Bookland, Coach House Press, 1984.

The Bees of the Invisible: Essays in Contemporary English Canadian Writing, Coach House Press, 1991.

Floating Voice: Duncan Campbell Scott and the Literature of Treaty 9, House of Anansi, 1994.

WORK IN PROGRESS: A novel set in Eastern Ontario, set in 1916; a book of outtakes—working title, *Apocrypha.*

SIDELIGHTS: Stan L. Dragland told *CA:* "[My] writing is done in a small hut looking out on 13 Island Lake, north of Kingston. I made the hut from materials left in or around the new cottage by Charley Tucker, man after my own heart, who built the place and never threw away so much as a bent nail. Mr. Tucker once owned a cedar strip canoe so narrow that no one but he could ply it without tipping. The canoe featured a built-in gramophone platform. Scrounge and build: that's how I write."

* * *

DRURY, Allen (Stuart)   1918-

PERSONAL: Born September 2, 1918, in Houston, TX; son of Alden Monteith and Flora (Allen) Drury. *Education:* Stanford University, B.A., 1939. *Avocational interests:* Theater, travel.

ADDRESSES: Office—c/o The Lantz Office, 888 Seventh Ave., Suite 2500, New York, NY 10106.

CAREER: Writer. *Tulare Bee,* Tulare, CA, editor, 1940-41; *Bakersfield Californian,* Bakersfield, CA, county editor, 1941-42; United Press International, Washington, DC, member of U.S. Senate staff, 1943-45; freelance correspondent, 1946; *Pathfinder* magazine, Washington, DC, national editor, 1947-53; *Washington Evening Star,* Washington, DC, member of national staff, 1953-54; *New York Times,* Washington, DC, member of U.S. Senate staff, 1954-59; *Reader's Digest,* Pleasantville, NY, political contributor, 1959-62. *Military service:* U.S. Army, 1942-43.

MEMBER: National Council on the Arts, National Press Club, Sigma Delta Chi, Alpha Kappa Lambda, Cosmos Club and University Club (Washington, DC), Bohemian Club (San Francisco).

AWARDS, HONORS: Sigma Delta Chi award for editorial writing, 1942; Pulitzer Prize in fiction, 1960, for *Advise and Consent;* Litt.D., Rollins College, 1961.

WRITINGS:

A Senate Journal, 1943-1945 (diary), McGraw (New York City), 1963.

Three Kids in a Cart: A Visit to Ike and Other Diversions (selected newspaper articles), Doubleday (New York City), 1965.

"A Very Strange Society": A Journey to the Heart of South Africa (nonfiction), Trident, 1967.

Courage and Hesitation: Notes and Photographs of the Nixon Administration (nonfiction), Doubleday, 1971.

Egypt, the Eternal Smile: Reflections on a Journey, with photographs by Alex Gotfryd (nonfiction), Doubleday, 1980.

NOVELS

Advise and Consent (Book-of-the-Month Club selection), Doubleday, 1959, limited edition reprint with illustrations by Franz Altschuler, Franklin Library, 1976.

A Shade of Difference, Doubleday, 1962.

That Summer, M. Joseph (London), 1965, Coward, 1966.

Capable of Honor, Doubleday, 1966.

Preserve and Protect, Doubleday, 1968.

The Throne of Saturn: A Novel of Space and Politics, Doubleday, 1971.

Come Nineveh, Come Tyre: The Presidency of Edward M. Jason, Doubleday, 1973.

The Promise of Joy: The Presidency of Orrin Knox, Doubleday, 1975.

A God against the Gods, Doubleday, 1976.

Return to Thebes, Doubleday, 1977.

Anna Hastings: The Story of a Washington Newspaperperson!, Morrow (New York City), 1977.

Mark Coffin, U.S.S.: A Novel of Capitol Hill, Doubleday, 1979.

The Hill of Summer: A Novel of the Soviet Conquest, Doubleday, 1981.

Decision, Doubleday, 1983.

The Roads of Earth, Doubleday, 1984.

Pentagon, Doubleday, 1986.

Toward What Bright Glory?, Morrow, 1990.

Into What Far Harbor?, Morrow, 1993.

A Thing of State, Scribner (New York City), 1995.

ADAPTATIONS: Advise and Consent was produced as a film.

SIDELIGHTS: Allen Drury had almost twenty years of experience covering politics in Washington, DC, as a newspaper correspondent before he published his first novel, the Pulitzer Prize-winning *Advise and Consent.* A tale of political and sexual scandal in the nation's capital, the book was an immediate sensation when it was released in 1959. Drury's later novels have continued to follow in the tradition of *Advise and Consent,* presenting the machinations of Washington insiders as they deal with crises that could be tomorrow's news. "Drury knows our imperial city as well as Livy knew Rome," Webster Schott writes in the *New York Times Book Review.* "His . . . Washington novels and his many years as a correspondent there have made him an expert." "Drury is very much a writer with a cause," M. Stanton Evans allows in the *National Review,* "and his cause is to expose the confusions of the liberal mind in American politics. To this endeavor he brings a remarkable instinct for issues and an intimate knowledge of the political and journalistic world of Washington."

Advise and Consent is set in a near-future Washington where the president has announced a controversial selection for Secretary of State, a man whose view of the Soviet Union alarms many senators. Their efforts to stop the appointment and the president's battle against them involve blackmail, a suicide and finally the untimely death of the president himself. Critics particularly noted the novel's realistic depiction of Washington political life. "What interests Mr. Drury most," Lewis Gannett notes in the *New York Herald Tribune Book Review,* "is not the ambivalent character of [the new secretary of state] but the interplay of force in the Senate battle over his confirmation." As Richard L. Neuberger remarks in the *New York Times Book Review,* Drury "knows Washington as Jim Bridger knew the mountain passes. He has spared no pages in giving his book color and substance in generous depth."

Because of Drury's intimate knowledge of the workings of the Senate, *Advise and Consent* spurred many readers to match Drury's characters with their supposed real-life counterparts. Such figures as Lyndon Johnson, Joseph McCarthy, and Franklin Roosevelt are obvious models, although each character possesses the attributes of more than one actual politician. "The moment a reader becomes convinced of the true identity of a given character," Ned Calmer explains in the *Saturday Review,* "the author drops in a twist that puts the whole surmise back in doubt."

Critical reaction to *Advise and Consent* was enthusiastic. Neuberger calls the novel "one of the finest and most gripping political novels of our era." Gannett claims that Drury "has written the most exciting, most discriminating and most intimate novel of Washington political life yet to appear." Critical reaction was matched by the novel's popularity with readers, who made the book a bestseller.

Drury told *CA* about his writing of the novel: "About seven years before it was published, I wrote the first couple of chapters, and then they just sat like many a newspaperman's American novel and nothing much happened. . . . Finally a friend of mine who had worked with me on the old *Pathfinder* magazine in Washington and was then acting as a scout for Doubleday called up and said that Ken McCormick, the editor, was going to be in town and was looking for manuscripts and would I like to have lunch with him. Well, practically simultaneously with that . . . I had finally made up my mind that I certainly wasn't getting any younger and that if I wanted ever to get this thing done I was going to have to get busy and do it. So everything sort of came together. I gave him the two chapters, which were virtually as they appear in the book today, and a very brief outline. . . . He took that back to New York and called me up two days later with the offer of a contract and advance." With contract in hand, Drury wrote *Advise and Consent* on weekends and his days off while working full-time as a journalist covering the U.S. Senate for the *New York Times.* "He set himself a weekly quota of 4,000-5,000 words," John Barkham writes in the *Saturday Review.* "During this period ·he virtually lived in and with the Senate—the real one by day, an imaginary one by night." With the overwhelming success of *Advise and Consent,* Drury left journalism to begin a new career as a novelist.

Drury's subsequent novels also concern themselves with near-future Washington scenarios in which high-level bureaucrats and politicians battle against diplomatic crises and insider scandals. In *A Shade of Difference,* for example, he focuses on the United Nations' role in the struggle of an African colony for independence from England. Writing in the *New York Times Book Review* of the novel, Sydney Hyman notes that "Drury reveals himself again to be a first-class reporter, if not a first-class novelist, skilled in weaving a fascinating narrative that branches and flares on a wide canvas." Geoffrey Godsell in the

Christian Science Monitor finds that "one must concede Mr. Drury's skill as a writer and admire his inventiveness."

Some reviewers do not agree with Drury's political opinions and color their criticism of his fiction accordingly. Gene Lyons, writing in the *New York Times Book Review,* believes that "the fictive land" Drury calls the United States in his novels is "a funhouse-mirror version of . . . the North American banana-eating republic of the same name." And Drury depicts leftists, Lyons claims, as a "pack of weak-willed hypocrites, sneering psychotics, liars, losers, time-servers and bullies." Drury once told *CA:* "I think there are some reviewers who are much more interested in defending what they conceive to be their political views against what they conceive to be mine." Speaking of what makes a novel controversial, Drury explained: "If a novel were written about abortion, it would arouse a very violent reaction on both sides. I think any subject that takes up anything that cuts close to general interest is bound to create controversy and is bound to get both strong good reactions and strong bad reactions."

Other reviewers criticize Drury's writing for what they see as its sometimes stilted qualities or occasional tendency to put politics before plot. Writing in *Time* magazine, John Skow claims that "it is no secret that Drury is not much of a novelist. . . . He advances his narrative by bringing his characters onstage alone to soliloquize about what has occurred and what bad results may be expected." Patrick Anderson, in a review of *The Hill of Summer: A Novel of the Soviet Conquest* for the *New York Times Book Review,* believes that in this novel "Drury has allowed his anger to overwhelm his artistry." Writing in the *National Observer,* Robert B. Semple, Jr., finds that "Drury's highly successful fiction . . . has always, in a sense, been at war with itself. On the one hand there is Mr. Drury's capacity for telling a first-rate story that is so compelling, so authentic in detail, that the reader simply cannot let go. On the other there is his tendency to proselytize, to grind political axes openly and unashamedly."

One point about Drury's fiction that reviewers often highlight is his ability to write a story that carries a reader along. Speaking of *Toward What Bright Glory?* in *Library Journal,* Beth Ann Mills finds that "the storytelling soon gathers momentum, engrossing the reader in the fate of the numerous characters." Similarly, the *Publishers Weekly* critic finds *A Thing of State* to contain "an overly expository beginning and prose that occasionally resembles a jungle thicket," but "the narrative quickly gathers pace and sweeps readers along toward a chilling conclusion."

Writing in the *Los Angeles Times Book Review,* Chris Wall describes Drury as "the political scientist's Robert Ludlum; the tension [in his stories] derives from crisp rhetoric, bold gambles and shrewd maneuvering. . . . The battles are fought with words, and most of the blood-spilling is done off-page. . . . It's skillfully written and quite engaging." Speaking of the novel *Pentagon,* in which Drury depicts an institution so stifled by bureaucracy and wracked by competing factions as to threaten national security, Schott finds that Drury makes the reader "feel his anger rise from a sense of despair."

BIOGRAPHICAL/CRITICAL SOURCES:

BOOKS

Contemporary Literary Criticism, Gale (Detroit), Volume 37, 1986.
Kemme, Tom, *Political Fiction, the Spirit of the Age, and Allen Drury,* Bowling Green State University Press (Bowling Green, OH), 1987.
Milne, Gordon, *The American Political Novel,* University of Oklahoma Press (Norman, OK), 1966.

PERIODICALS

Atlanta Journal & Constitution, July 15, 1990, p. N8.
Booklist, September 1, 1986, p. 2; May 1, 1990, p. 1666; February 15, 1993, p. 1011; September 1, 1995, p. 38.
Christian Science Monitor, September 20, 1962, p. 11.
Editor and Publisher, December 17, 1960, p. 32.
Kirkus Reviews, May 1, 1990, p. 600.
Library Journal, June 15, 1990, p. 134; July, 1995, p. 118.
Los Angeles Times Book Review, December 9, 1984, p. 6.
National Observer, September 26, 1966, p. 22.
National Review, December 3, 1968, pp. 1225-26.
New Republic, September 14, 1959.
Newsweek, January 16, 1960, p. 72.
New York Herald Tribune Book Review, August 16, 1959, p. 1.
New York Times Book Review, August 16, 1959, pp. 1, 20; September 23, 1962, p. 5; September 12, 1965; March 20, 1966; November 12, 1967;

September 28, 1968; March 16, 1975, pp. 24, 26; March 8, 1981, p. 10; September 30, 1984, p. 28; October 26, 1986, p. 18; July 8, 1990, p. 16.
Publishers Weekly, May 18, 1990, p. 134; June 19, 1995, p. 47.
Saturday Review, August 15, 1959, p. 17-18; September 29, 1962; November 5, 1966; February 3, 1968.
Time, November 23, 1959, p. 56; August 16, 1976, p. 72.
USA Today, January 7, 1987, p. A9.
Wall Street Journal, November 17, 1986, p. 32.
Washington Monthly, December, 1986, p. 55.
Washington Post Book World, November 2, 1986, p. 8.

* * *

DUNBAR, David
See BAXTER, Craig

* * *

DUNBAR, Leslie W(allace)   1921-

PERSONAL: Born January 27, 1921, in Lewisburg, WV; son of Marion Leslie and Minnie Lee (Crickenberger) Dunbar; married Peggy Rawls, July 5, 1942; children: Linda Dunbar Kravitz, Anthony Paul. *Education:* Cornell University, M.A., 1946, Ph.D., 1948.

ADDRESSES: Home and office—10 Whitburn Pl., Durham, NC 27705.

CAREER: Emory University, Atlanta, GA, assistant professor of political science, 1948-51; Atomic Energy Commission, Aiken, SC, chief of community affairs at Savannah River plant, 1951-54; Mount Holyoke College, South Hadley, MA, assistant professor of political science, 1955-58; Southern Regional Council, Atlanta, director of research, 1958-61, executive director, 1961-65; Field Foundation, New York City, executive director and secretary, 1965-80. Visiting professor at University of Arizona, 1981. Member of board of directors, Franklin and Eleanor Roosevelt Institute, 1976—, Winston Foundation for World Peace, 1984—, and Ruth Mott Fund, 1988—, chair, 1992-93; past president of

Nation Institute; past chair of advisory board of Center for National Security Studies; past member of board of directors of Amnesty International, U.S.A. and Field Foundation; past chair of Children's Foundation and Minority Rights Group of New York City; past member and chair of board of directors of Pelham Village library.

AWARDS, HONORS: Guggenheim fellow, 1954-55.

WRITINGS:

A Republic of Equals, University of Michigan Press (Ann Arbor, MI), 1966.
(Editor) *Minority Report: What Has Happened to Blacks, Hispanics, American Indians, and Other American Minorities in the Eighties,* Pantheon (New York City), 1984.
The Common Interest, Pantheon, 1988.
Reclaiming Liberalism, Norton (New York City), 1991.

Contributor to magazines.

*   *   *

DUNDES, Alan   1934-

PERSONAL: Surname is pronounced "*Dun*-deez"; born September 8, 1934, in New York, NY; son of Maurice (an attorney) and Helen (Rothschild) Dundes; married Carolyn Browne, September 8, 1958; children: Alison, Lauren, David. *Education:* Yale University, B.A., 1955, M.A.T., 1958; Indiana University, Ph.D., 1962.

ADDRESSES: Home—1590 La Vereda, Berkeley, CA 94708. *Office*—Department of Anthropology, University of California, Berkeley, CA 94720.

CAREER: University of Kansas, Lawrence, instructor in English, 1962-63; University of California, Berkeley, assistant professor of anthropology, 1963-65, associate professor, 1965-68, professor of anthropology and folklore, 1968—. *Military service:* U.S. Navy, 1955-57; became lieutenant.

MEMBER: American Folklore Society, American Anthropological Association, California Folklore Society.

AWARDS, HONORS: Second place in Chicago Folklore Prize competition, 1962, for *The Morphology of North American Indian Folktales;* Guggenheim fellowship, 1966-67; senior fellowship, National Endowment for the Humanities, 1972-73; first place in Chicago Folklore Prize competition, 1976, for *La Terra in Piazza: An Interpretation of the Palio of Siena;* Pitre Prize, Sigillo d'Oro (Seal of Gold), for lifetime achievement in folklore, 1993.

WRITINGS:

The Morphology of North American Indian Folktales, Academic Scientarium Fennica, 1964.
(With Alessandro Falassi) *La Terra in Piazza: An Interpretation of the Palio of Siena,* University of California Press (Berkeley), 1975.
(With Carl R. Pagter) *Urban Folklore from the Paperwork Empire,* American Folklore Society, 1975.
Analytic Essays in Folklore, Mouton, 1975.
(Compiler) *Folklore Theses and Dissertations in the United States,* University of Texas Press (Austin), 1976.
Interpreting Folklore, Indiana University Press (Bloomington), 1980.
(With Claudia A. Stibbe) *The Art of Mixing Metaphors: A Folkloristic Interpretation of the "Netherlands Proverbs," by Pieter Bruegel the Elder,* Academia Scientarium Fennica, 1981.
Life Is Like a Chicken Coop Ladder: A Portrait of German Culture through Folklore, Columbia University Press (New York City), 1984.
(With C. Banc) *First Prize: Fifteen Years! An Annotated Collection of Romanian Political Jokes,* Associated University Presses, 1986.
(With Pagter) *When You're Up to Your Ass in Alligators: More Urban Folklore from the Paperwork Empire,* Wayne State University Press (Detroit), 1987.
Cracking Jokes: Studies of Sick Humor Cycles and Stereotypes, Ten Speed Press, 1987.
Parsing through Customs: Essays by a Freudian Folklorist, University of Wisconsin Press (Madison), 1987.
Folklore Matters, University of Tennessee Press (Knoxville), 1989.
(With Pagter) *Never Try to Teach a Pig to Sing: Still More Urban Folklore from the Paperwork Empire,* Wayne State University Press, 1991.

EDITOR

The Study of Folklore, Prentice-Hall (Englewood Cliffs, NJ), 1965.

Every Man His Way: Readings in Cultural Anthropology, Prentice-Hall, 1968.

Mother Wit from the Laughing Barrel: Readings in the Interpretation of Afro-American Folklore, Prentice-Hall, 1973.

The Evil Eye: A Folklore Casebook, Garland Publishing (New York City), 1981.

(With Wolfgang Mieder) *The Wisdom of Many: Essays on the Proverb,* Garland Publishing, 1981.

Cinderella: A Folklore Casebook, Garland Publishing, 1982.

(With Lowell Edmunds) *Oedipus: A Folklore Casebook,* Garland Publishing, 1983.

Sacred Narrative: Readings in the Theory of Myth, University of California Press, 1984.

(With Galit Hasan-Rokem) *The Wandering Jew: Essays in the Interpretation of a Christian Legend,* Indiana University Press, 1986.

The Flood Myth, University of California Press, 1988.

Little Red Riding Hood: A Casebook, University of Wisconsin Press, 1989.

The Blood Libel Legend: A Casebook in Anti-Semitic Folklore, University of Wisconsin Press, 1991.

The Cockfight: A Casebook, University of Wisconsin Press, 1994.

(With Alison Dundes Rentein) *Folk Law: Essays in the Theory and Practice of Lex Non Scripta,* Garland Publishing, 1994.

Contributor to the *Book of Knowledge, Worldbook Encyclopedia,* and *Encyclopedia Britannica,* on subjects such as folklore, superstition, and primitive mythology. Also contributor of more than 150 articles to professional journals, including *Journal of American Folklore, Asian Folklore Studies, Western Folklore, International Folklore Review,* and *American Anthropologist.* Has served on editorial boards, including *Annals of Scholarship, Humor,* and *Journal of Latin American Folklore.*

SIDELIGHTS: Folklorist Alan Dundes writes about a wide range of sometimes unconventional material, from traditional fables to xeroxed office memos. *Cinderella: A Folklore Casebook* interprets the familiar story from several academic viewpoints. *Times Literary Supplement* contributor T. A. Shippey praises Dundes' even selection of essays by "structuralists, Jungians, anthroposophists *et al.*" He continues: "the main message of this collection is 'armchair critics should at least review the literature': and every facility is offered for that in future, with long bibliographies and masterly introductions by Dundes to each of the essays selected." *Cracking Jokes:*

Studies of Sick Humor Cycles and Stereotypes ties jokes with the often sexual or racial message they offhandedly convey. According to Dundes, jokes are "effective as socially sanctioned outlets for expressing taboo ideas and subjects." In Chicago *Tribune Books,* Clarence Petersen notes that Dundes "knows why jokes are funny, as well as to whom and under what circumstances. Because he knows, too, that brevity is the soul of wit, he does not analyze jokes to death." *When You're Up to Your Ass in Alligators: More Urban Folklore from the Paperwork Empire* also looks at common modern communication not always termed as folklore. "What others dismiss as dirty jokes, pranks and low-brow humor, Dundes defends as genuine American folklore," states Jeff Kunerth in the *Chicago Tribune.* He continues that Dundes' book "includes examples of phony correspondence, fake business cards, parodied poems, nonsensical instructions and satirical memos. Much of it reveals a cynical disgust with bureaucracy and incompetence." Most of the book's examples were initially transmitted through office photocopiers. "Not everyone can tell a joke," Dundes explains. "But anyone can operate a Xerox machine."

BIOGRAPHICAL/CRITICAL SOURCES:

BOOKS

The Psychoanalytic Study of Society, Volume 18: *Essays in Honor of Alan Dundes,* The Analytic Press (Hillsdale, NJ), 1993.

PERIODICALS

California Monthly, Volume 74, number 1, October, 1965.
Chicago Tribune, February 5, 1988.
Folklore, Volume 105, 1994, p. 114.
Journal of American Folklore, spring, 1991, p. 198.
Journal of Biblical Literature, winter, 1990, p. 737.
Los Angeles Times Book Review, July 7, 1985; July 28, 1991, p. 6.
New York Times Book Review, January 24, 1988.
Times Literary Supplement, July 22, 1983.
Tribune Books (Chicago), May 3, 1987.

* * *

DUPONT, Robert L(ouis) 1936-

PERSONAL: Born March 25, 1936, in Toledo, OH; son of Robert Louis (in sales) and Martha Ireton (a teacher; maiden name, Lancashire) DuPont; married Helen Gayden Spink (a manager), July 14, 1962; children: Elizabeth, Caroline. *Education:* Emory University, B.A., 1958; Harvard University, M.D., 1963.

ADDRESSES: Home—8708 Susanna Lane, Chevy Chase, MD 20815. *Office*—6191 Executive Blvd., Rockville, MD 20852.

CAREER: Western Reserve University (now Case Western Reserve University), Cleveland, Ohio, intern, 1963-64; Harvard Medical School, Boston, MA, resident in psychiatry, 1964-66; National Institutes of Health, Bethesda, MD, clinical associate, 1966-68; private practice of psychiatry, 1969—. President of Institute for Behavior and Health, Inc., 1978—, Center for Behavioral Medicine, 1978-89, and American Council for Drug Education, 1980-84; vice president of Bensinger, DuPont Associates, Inc., 1983—. Research psychiatrist and acting associate director for community services at District of Columbia Department of Corrections, 1968-70; administrator of Narcotics Treatment Administration, District of Columbia Department of Human Resources, 1970-73; U.S. Department of Health, Education and Welfare, director of National Institute on Drug Abuse, 1973-78, acting administrator of Alcohol, Drug Abuse, and Mental Health Administration, 1974; director of Special Action Office for Drug Abuse Prevention, Executive Office of the President, 1973-75; U.S. delegate to United Nations Commission on Narcotic Drugs, 1973-78. Member of advisory committee of Washington Junior League, 1972-76, and Coordinating Council on Juvenile Justice and Delinquency Prevention, U.S. Department of Justice, 1974-78. Associate clinical professor at George Washington University, 1972-80; visiting associate professor at Harvard University, 1978-82; clinical professor at Georgetown University, 1980—. Guest on television programs, including *Good Morning, America* and *Today Show. Military service:* U.S. Public Health Service, surgeon, 1966-68; became major.

MEMBER: World Psychiatric Association, Pan American Medical Association, American Psychiatric Association (fellow), Anxiety Disorders Association, Phobia Society of America (president, 1982-84), Washington Psychiatric Society, Washington Society for Performing Arts (member of board of directors, 1972-76).

WRITINGS:

Getting Tough on Gateway Drugs: A Guide for the Family, American Psychiatric Press, 1984.
(With John P. McGovern) *A Bridge to Recovery—An Introduction to 12-Step Programs,* American Psychiatric Press, 1994.
The Selfish Brain: Learning from Addiction, American Psychiatric Press, 1996.

Contributor to medical journals.

SIDELIGHTS: Robert L. DuPont, told *CA:* "As a practicing psychiatrist with experience ranging from research to public policy, I have focused on two areas: addiction and the anxiety disorders. Addiction is characterized by loss of control over the addictive behaviors and by denial. My fascination with addiction led me to write *The Selfish Brain: Learning from Addiction,* which is scheduled for publication in 1996. New brain research has shown that all addictive disorders are rooted in the brain's powerful pleasure mechanisms, managed by the neurotransmitter dopamine in the nucleus accumbens and the ventral tegmental area. Alcohol, nicotine, and other drugs literally turn on the brain's 'MORE, NOW' buttons for those who are addicted, producing a cascade of effects involving every aspect of the person as the selfish brain seeks repeated chemical rewards, virtually at any price. Learning to manage the vulnerability to addiction, which is hard-wired into the mammalian brain, is one of the major tasks of the next generation as we increasingly come to recognize the major role of addiction in many human problems from crime to loss of productivity, from AIDS to homelessness, from cancer to heart disease.

My father was a salesman. My mother was a teacher. My life in medicine has been an expression of the values I share with my family, including the importance of caring about others and of participating joyfully in the marketplace of ideas. Writing helps me to achieve these goals. Having discovered that the universal antidote to addiction is honesty, I have come to know and respect the tremendous power of the 12-step programs, Alcoholics Anonymous and the fellowships based on AA, as a uniquely American contribution to world culture."

*   *   *

DWYER, Deanna
See KOONTZ, Dean R(ay)

DWYER, K. R.
  See KOONTZ, Dean R(ay)

*   *   *

DYE, Thomas R(oy)   1935-

PERSONAL: Born December 16, 1935, in Pittsburgh, PA; son of James C. and Marguerite A. (Dewan) Dye; married Joan G. Wohleber, June, 1957; children: Roy Thomas, Cheryl Price. *Education:* Pennsylvania State University, B.A., 1957, M.A., 1959; University of Pennsylvania, Ph.D., 1961.

ADDRESSES: Home—1057 Del Haven Dr., Delray Beach, FL 33483. *Office*—Policy Sciences Center, Florida State University, Tallahassee, FL 32306; Suite 115, 1030 S. Federal Highway, Delray Beach, FL 33483.

CAREER: University of Wisconsin—Madison, assistant professor of political science, 1962-63; University of Georgia, Athens, assistant professor, 1963-65, associate professor of political science and chairperson of department, 1965-68; Florida State University, Tallahassee, professor of government, 1968-86, chairperson of department, 1969-72, director of Policy Sciences Center, 1978-91; McKenzie Professor of Government, 1986—. Visiting professor at Bar Ilan University, 1972, and University of Arizona, 1976; visiting scholar, Brookings Institution, 1984. *Military service:* U.S. Air Force Reserve, 1957-62; became first lieutenant.

MEMBER: American Political Science Association (secretary, 1969-72), National Association of Scholars (president of Florida chapter, 1994—), Policy Studies Organization (president, 1975-76), Southern Political Science Association (member of executive council; president, 1976-77), James Madison Institute (research associate), Lincoln Center for Public Service (research associate), Phi Beta Kappa, Omicron Delta Kappa, Phi Kappa Phi.

AWARDS, HONORS: U.S. Office of Education research grants, 1966-67, 1969-70; National Science Foundation grants, 1967, 1970-71; National Institutes of Health research grant, 1973-76; Lynde and Harry Bradley Foundation grant, 1986-88; Outstanding Teacher Award, Florida State University, 1987; Harold D. Lasswell Award, Policy Studies Organiza-

tion, 1988, for career contributions to the study of public policy; Donald C. Stone Award, American Society for Public Administration, 1992, for career contributions to the study of federalism.

WRITINGS:

(With Oliver P. Williams, S. Charles Liebman, and Harold Herman) *Suburban Differences and Metropolitan Policies,* University of Pennsylvania Press (Philadelphia), 1965.

Politics, Economics, and the Public, Rand McNally (Chicago), 1966.

(Editor with Brett W. Hawkins) *Politics in the Metropolis: A Reader in Conflict and Cooperation,* C. E. Merrill (Columbus, OH), 1967.

Politics in States and Communities, Prentice-Hall (Englewood Cliffs, NJ), 1969, ninth edition, 1997.

(With Lee Greene and George S. Parthemos) *American Government: Theory, Structure, and Process,* Wadsworth Publishing (Belmont, CA), 1969.

(Compiler) *American Public Policy,* C. E. Merrill, 1969.

(With Harmon Zeigler) *The Irony of Democracy,* Wadsworth, 1970, tenth edition, 1995.

The Politics of Equality, Bobbs-Merrill (New York City), 1971.

Understanding Public Policy, Prentice-Hall, 1972, eighth edition, 1995.

Power and Society, Brooks/Cole (Monterey, CA), 1975, sixth edition, 1993.

Who's Running America?: Institutional Leadership in the United States, Prentice-Hall, 1976, second edition published as *Who's Running America?: The Carter Years,* 1979, third edition published as *Who's Running America?: The Reagan Years,* 1983, fourth edition published as *Who's Running America?: The Conservative Years,* 1986, fifth edition published as *Who's Running America? The Bush Era,* 1990, sixth edition published as *Who's Running America? The Clinton Years,* 1994.

Policy Analysis: What Governments Do, Why They Do It, and What Difference It Makes, University of Alabama Press (University), 1976.

(Editor with Virginia Gray) *Determinants of Public Policy,* Heath (Lexington, MA), 1980.

(With Zeigler) *American Politics in the Media Age,* Brooks/Cole, 1983, fourth edition, 1992.

(Editor with G. William Domhoff) *Power Elites and Organizations,* Sage Publications (Beverly Hills, CA), 1987.

American Federalism: Competition among Governments, Lexington Press, 1990.

Politics in America, Prentice-Hall, 1994, second edition, 1997.

Editor of "Policy Analysis" series for Bobbs-Merrill; editor of *The Madison Review,* 1994—. Also contributor of numerous articles, essays, and reviews to social science journals.

WORK IN PROGRESS: "Writings on national and state politics, political leadership, and on public policy."

E

PERSONAL: Born March 14, 1912, in Lysvik, Sweden; married Astrid Persson, 1937; children: Joergen, Ranveig Jacobsson, Birgitta.

ADDRESSES: Home—Hagtornsgatan 3, 652 30 Karlstad, Sweden.

CAREER: Oskarshamns Nyheter, Oskarshamm, Sweden, chief editor, 1934-37; *Oestgoeten,* Linkoeping, Sweden, chief editor, 1938-44; *Ny Tid,* Gothenburg, Sweden, chief editor, 1945-56; Swedish ambassador to Norway, 1956-67; governor of Swedish province of Vaermland, 1967-77. Member of Swedish Parliament, 1940-44 and 1948-56. Delegate to Council of Europe, 1949-52, United Nations, 1952-55, 1957, 1960-61, Northern Council, 1953-56, and Disarmament Conference, 1961-65.

MEMBER: Swedish Press Club (president, 1951-53), Swedish Association of Writers, Pen Club, Swedish Association of Biologists, Swedish Royal Academy of Sciences, Swedish Society for Anthropology and Geography.

AWARDS, HONORS: Socrates Prize, 1972, from School of Adult Education; gold medal, 1974, from Royal Swedish Academy of Science; Doctor Honoris Causa, 1974, from University of Gothenburg; gold medal, 1976, from Geographical-Anthropological Society; Selma Lagerloef's Prize, 1976; Dag Hammarskjoeld Medal, 1978; King's Medal, 1981; gold medal from government of Sweden, 1984; Nordic Environmental Prize, 1984; Let Live! Award, 1985; Premio Mondiale delle Cultura, 1985; Natur och Kultur's Cultural Prize, 1987; the Edberg Foundation, an environmental organization, was founded in 1990.

WRITINGS:

Nansen, european: En studie i vilja och god-vilja (title means "Nansen, the European: A Study in Will and Good Will"), Tiden, 1961.

Spillran av ett moln, Norstedt, 1966, translation by Sven Aahman published as *On the Shred of a Cloud: Notes in a Travel Book,* University of Alabama Press, 1969, same translation published as *On the Shred of a Cloud: Reflections on Man and His Environment,* Harper, 1971.

Vid traedets fot, Norstedt, 1971, translation by David Mel Paul and Margareta Paul published as *At the Foot of the Tree: A Wanderer's Musings before the Fall,* University of Alabama Press, 1974.

Brev till Columbus (title means "Letters to Columbus"), Norstedt, 1973.

Ett hus i kosmos (title means "A House in the Cosmos"), Esselte Studium, 1974.

Dalens Ande, Norstedt, 1976, translation by Keith Bradfield published as *The Dream of Kilimanjaro,* Pantheon, 1979.

Skuggor oever Savannen (title means "Shadows across the Savannah"), Bra Boecker & Trevi, 1977.

De glittrande vattnens land (title means "The Land of Glittering Waters"), Bra Boecker & Norstedts, 1980.

(Editor) *Haer aer vi hemma* (title means "This Is Our Home"), Bra Boecker & Norstedts, 1982.

(Editor) *Vaart hotade hem* (title means "Our Threatened Home"), Bra Boecker & Norstedts, 1983.

Droppar av vatten, droppar av act (title means "Drops of Water, Drops of Years"), Bra Boecker & Norstedts, 1984.

... *Och de seglade staendigt* (title means ". . . and They Always Sailed"), Norstedts, 1986.
Aarsbarn med Plejaderna (title means "Born with the Pleiades"), Norstedts, 1987.
(With Alexey Yablokov) *Soendag aer foer sent* (title means "Sunday Is Too Late"), Norstedts, 1988.

Also author of *Ge dem en chans* (title means "Give Them a Chance"), 1939, *I morgon Norden* (title means "Tomorrow Nordic"), 1944, *Demokratisk linje* (title means "Democratic Line"), 1948, *Femte etappen* (title means "The Fifth Stage"), 1949, *Oeppna grindarna* (title means "Open the Gates"), 1952, and *Paa jordens villkor* (title means "On Earth's Terms"), 1974.

ADAPTATIONS: Dalens Ande was adapted as a symphony by the Finnish composer, Henrik Otto Donner.

SIDELIGHTS: Rolf Edberg writes to *CA:* "I grew up in a fresh and beautiful countryside and very early I got in contact with the science of evolution, which started a lifelong interest in natural sciences. The first book about man's condition was created in order to disentangle my own meditating threads and to put man's moment on earth in a bigger continuity. We have in our constantly greedy searching acquired an ever increasing richness in knowledge of details and have been forced into an even harder specialization.

"However, nature is interaction, not separation. What we have to do today is to place our varying knowledge under a unifying comprehensive view giving us a vision of our destiny. My ambition as a layman has been to arrive at such a comprehensive view.

"The scientific literature—especially in the environmental field—published in the United States has given me great inspiration in my work. Europe has a lot to learn from the American research which is the most advanced in the world. But I believe that America, highly urbanized, has some to learn from the Scandinavian people with their natural love of nature. And that is the way it ought to be: that we learn from each other's research, thinking, and experience."

BIOGRAPHICAL/CRITICAL SOURCES:

PERIODICALS

Chicago Tribune Book World, May 20, 1979.

EGAN, Gerard   1930-

PERSONAL: Born June 17, 1930, in Chicago, IL. *Education:* Loyola University, Chicago, A.B., 1953, M.A. (philosophy), 1959, M.A. (clinical psychology), 1963, Ph.D., 1969.

ADDRESSES: Office—Center for Organization Development, 820 N. Michigan Ave., Loyola University, Chicago, IL 60611.

CAREER: Loyola University of Chicago, Chicago, IL, 1969—, began as assistant professor, currently professor emeritus of Organization Development and Psychology in the Center for Organization Development. Consultant to various organizations and institutions.

MEMBER: American Psychological Association, American Association for Counseling and Development.

WRITINGS:

Encounter: Group Processes for Interpersonal Growth, Brooks/Cole (Monterey, CA), 1970.
(Editor) *Encounter Groups: Basic Readings,* Brooks/Cole, 1971.
Face to Face: The Small Group Experience and Interpersonal Growth, Brooks/Cole, 1973.
The Skilled Helper: A Model for Helping and Human Relations Training, Brooks/Cole, 1975, fifth edition published as *The Skilled Helper: A Problem-management Approach to Helping,* 1994.
Exercises in Helping Skills, Brooks/Cole, 1975, 2nd edition, 1981.
Interpersonal Living: A Skills/Contract Approach to Human Relations Training in Groups, Brooks/Cole, 1976.
You and Me: The Skills of Human Communication in Everyday Life, Brooks/Cole, 1977.
(With M. Cowan) *People in Systems: A Model Development for the Human Services Professions and Education,* Brooks/Cole, 1979.
(With Cowan) *Moving into Adulthood: Themes and Variations in Self-Directed Development,* Brooks/Cole, 1980.
Change Agent Skill for Helping and Human-Service Professionals, Brooks/Cole, 1985.
Change Agent Skills A: Assessing and Designing Excellence, University Associates (San Diego, CA), 1988.
Change Agent Skills B: Managing Innovation and Change, University Associates, 1988.

Adding Value: A Systematic Guide to Business-based Management and Leadership, Jossey-Bass (San Francisco, CA), 1993.

Working the Shadow Side: A Guide to Positive behind-the-scenes Management, Jossey-Bass, 1994.

Contributor to numerous books, including *Human Behavior and Its Encounter Groups,* Schenkman, 1971, *The Cutting Edge: Current Theory and Practice in Organization Development,* University Associates, 1978, and *Teaching Psychological Skills: Models for Giving Psychology Away,* Brooks/Cole, 1983. Also contributor of articles to various professional journals.

SIDELIGHTS: Gerald Egan wrote *CA:* "*The Skilled Helper* has been my most popular and enduring work. Since it is a problem-management and opportunity-development approach to helping, it is a triumph of common sense. It is currently in its fifth edition (1994) and I am working on the sixth. It has been translated into Chinese, Dutch, French, German, Italian, Japanese, and Spanish. It is rewarding to see how easily it crosses borders. I have been working with Chinese trainers to help them develop an indigenous training system.

"However, I currently spend most of my time consulting, literally around the world. As to my current writing, my aspiration is to help turn management, which is now a job, role, or position, into a profession. *Adding Value* and *Working the Shadow Side* are efforts in this direction."

*   *   *

EHRHART, W(illiam) D(aniel)   1948-

PERSONAL: Born September 30, 1948, in Roaring Spring, PA; son of John Harry (a minister) and Evelyn Marie (a teacher; maiden name, Conti) Ehrhart; married Anne Senter Gulick, June, 1981; children: Leela Gulick. *Education:* Swarthmore College, B.A., 1973; University of Illinois at Chicago Circle, M.A., 1978. *Politics:* "Somewhere to the left of the Democrats." *Religion:* "No formal affiliation; raised in United Church of Christ."

ADDRESSES: Home—6845 Anderson St., Philadelphia, PA 19119. *Office*—George School, Newton, PA 18940.

CAREER: Poet, writer, and lecturer. U.S. Merchant Marine, engineroom wiper, 1973-74; Panelrama, Inc., Havertown, PA, warehouse worker, 1974; Pennsylvania Department of Justice, Special Prosecutor's Office, Philadelphia, PA, evidence custodian, 1974-76; University of Illinois at Chicago Circle, part-time instructor in composition, 1977-78; Sandy Spring Friends School, Sandy Spring, MD, teacher of English and history, 1978-79; George School, Newton, PA, teacher of history, 1981-83. Coeditor, East River Anthology, 1975-78. Reporter, *The Daily Intelligencer,* Doylestown, PA, summers, 1967-78, 1980. *Military service:* U.S. Marine Corps, 1966-69; attained the rank of sergeant; served in Vietnam.

MEMBER: Poets & Writers, Inc., Poetry Society of America, Society of Professional Journalists.

AWARDS, HONORS: Collegiate award, Academy of American Poets, 1971, 1972, and 1973; Circle Center Poetry Prize, 1978; Mary Roberts Rinehart Foundation grant, 1980; Pennsylvania Council on the Arts fellowship in prose, 1981; Pennsylvania Council on the Arts fellowship in poetry, 1988; President's Medal, Veterans for Peace, Inc., 1988; Pew Fellowship in the Arts, for poetry, 1993.

WRITINGS:

POETRY:

A Generation of Peace, New Voices Publishing, 1975, revised edition, Samisdat (Richford, VT), 1977.

Rootless, Samisdat, 1977.

Empire, Samisdat, 1978.

The Samisdat Poems, Samisdat, 1980.

The Awkward Silence, Northwoods Press (Stafford, VA), 1980.

Matters of the Heart, Adastra Press (Easthampton, MA), 1981.

Channel Fever, Backstreet Editions, 1982.

To Those Who Have Gone Home Tired, Thunder's Mouth Press (New York City), 1984.

The Outer Banks & Other Poems, Adastra Press, 1984.

Winter Bells, Adastra Press, 1988.

Just for Laughs, Viet Nam Generation, Inc., & Burning Cities Press, 1990.

The Distance We Travel, Adastra Press, 1993.

Mostly Nothing Happens, Adastra Press, 1995.

MEMOIRS, ESSAYS

Vietnam-Perkasie: A Combat Marine Memoir, McFarland (Jefferson, NC), 1983.

Going Back: An Ex-Marine Returns to Vietnam, McFarland, 1987.

Passing Time: Memoir of a Vietnam Veteran against the War, McFarland, 1989.

In the shadows of Vietnam: Essays 1977-1991, McFarland & Co., Inc., 1991.

Busted: A Vietnam Veteran in Nixon's America, University of Massachusetts Press (Amherst, MA), 1995.

EDITOR

(With Jan Barry) *Demilitarized Zones: Veterans after Vietnam,* East River Anthology (Montclair, NJ), 1976.

Carrying the Darkness: the Poetry of the Vietnam War, Texas Tech Press (Lubbock, TX), 1989.

Unaccustomed Mercy: Soldier-Poets of the Vietnam War, Texas Tech Press, 1989.

OTHER

Contributor to anthologies, including *Winning Hearts and Minds: War Poems by Vietnam Veterans,* First Casualty Press, 1972; *Listen: The War,* U.S. Air Force Academy Association of Graduates, 1974; *Front Lines,* Indochina Curriculum Group, 1975; *Silent Voices,* Ally Press, 1978; *Anthology of Magazine Verse,* Monitor Books, 1981; *A Long-Term Underground Plan,* Raindance Press, 1981; *Peace Is Our Profession,* East River Anthology, 1981; *From A to Z,* Swallow Press, 1981; and *Leaving the Bough,* International Publishers, 1982. Contributor of poetry and prose to literary journals, including *American Poetry Review, Connecticut Poetry Review, Colorado Review, Friends Journal, The Greenfield Review, The Hollow Spring Review of Poetry, Nasi Razgledi* (Slovenia), *New Hampshire Gazette, New Letters, Poetry Australia, Poetry East, Poetry Wales, TriQuarterly, Van Nghe Quan Doi* (Vietnam), *Virginia Quarterly Review, Tulane Literary Magazine, Washington Post,* and *Win.* Also contributor of commentaries to newspapers, including Sacramento *Bee,* *Chicago Tribune, Cleveland Plain Dealer,* Los Angeles and San Francisco *Daily Journal,* Philadelphia *Daily News,* San Francisco *Examiner,* Philadelphia *Inquirer,* San Jose *Mercury News,* Houston *Post, Reader's Digest,* Baltimore *Sun,* San Diego *Union Tribune, USA Today,* and *Utne Reader.* Contributing

writer, *The Veteran,* Vietnam Veterans of America, Inc., Washington, DC, ongoing series, "Platoon 1005," 1994—.

SIDELIGHTS: W. D. Ehrhart told *CA:* "The greatest concern I have is the imminent prospect of nuclear extermination. All else that I do—my writing, my teaching, my lovemaking, my involvement in social issues from American imperialism to environmental preservation—is necessarily subordinated to that one vast negative which looms over us all. There was a time when writers could long for immortality; now it is all we can do to hope that our children will survive long enough to have children of their own. It is clear that governments are not capable of protecting us from mass suicide; the stockpiles of ever-more-destructive nuclear weapons only grow larger by the year. The question is: What are we willing to do to protect ourselves from governments?"

*   *   *

EISS, Harry Edwin   1950-

PERSONAL: Surname rhymes with "lease"; born May 17, 1950, in Minneapolis, MN; son of Harry Earl (a printer) and Helen (a nurse; maiden name, Holmgren) Eiss; married Betty Palm (a bookkeeper); children: Meghan, Israel, Angela, Jared, Ryan. *Education:* University of Minnesota, B.A. (English) and B.A. (humanities), both 1975; Mankato State University, M.S., 1976; University of North Dakota, Ph.D., 1982.

ADDRESSES: Office—Department of English, Eastern Michigan University, Ypsilanti, MI 48197.

CAREER: Walden's Tree and Lawn Service, owner, 1970-74; Border Bowl and Lounge, International Falls, MN, assistant manager, bowling alley and lounge manager, 1977-78; International Co-op, Grand Forks, ND, production manager, 1979; Olan Mills Studios, Grand Forks, ND, manager of telephone sales, 1982; Northern Montana College, Havre, instructor, 1982-83, assistant professor, 1983-87; Eastern Michigan University, Ypsilanti, assistant professor of English, 1987—. Member of Montana Committee for the Humanities, 1985-87, and Montana State Reading Council. Public speaker.

MEMBER: Canadian Book Council, International Research Society for Children's Literature, ALAN,

American Academy of Arts and Sciences, American Library Association, American Culture Association, Children's Literature Association, Modern Language Association of America, National Council of the Teachers of English, Poe Studies Association, Society of Children's Book Writers, Society for the Study of Myth and Tradition, Cousteau Society, Green Peace, People for the American Way, Popular Culture Association, Smithsonian Institution, Union of Concerned Scientists, Michigan College English Association, Eastern Michigan University chapter of American Association of University Professors, Chicago Museum of Modern Art, Sigma Tau Delta.

AWARDS, HONORS: Merit Award to Outstanding Faculty, Northern Montana College, 1983-84, and 1986-87; Jaycee Outstanding Young Men of America, 1984; Faculty Center for Instructional Effectiveness Grant for Teaching Innovations, Eastern Michigan University, 1988.

WRITINGS:

English 102: Composition 102 (correspondence course), University of North Dakota, 1981.
Dictionary of Language Games, Puzzles, Amusements, Greenwood Press (Westport, CT), 1986.
Dictionary of Mathematical Games, Puzzles, and Amusements, Greenwood Press, 1988.
Literature 100: The Reading of Literature (independent course), Eastern Michigan University (Ypsilanti, MI), 1988, revised, 1990.
Literature 207: Introduction to Children's Literature (correspondence course), Eastern Michigan University, 1988, revised, 1991.
Literature for Young People on War and Peace (bibliography), Greenwood Press, 1989.
ENG 225: Intermediate Composition, Distance Learning, Eastern Michigan University, 1993.
Images of the Child: Past, Present, and Future, Bowling Green State University Popular Press (Bowling Green, OH), 1994.

Contributor to books, including *Instructor,* Harcourt (New York City), 1982; *Rainbows, Dreams and Butterfly Wings,* Good Apple, Inc. (Carthage, IL), 1982; *Challenge,* Good Apple, Inc, 1984; *Guide to Biography,* St. James Press (Detroit), 1991; *Masterplots II: Juvenile and Young Adult Fiction,* Salem Press (Englewood Cliffs, NJ), 1991; *Masterplots II,* Salem Press, 1993; and *The Reader's Advisor,* 14th edition, R. R. Bowker (New York City). Work represented in anthologies, including *Society of American Poets, Inc., Anthology,* SAPL

(Tampa, FL), 1981; *World Treasury of Great Poems,* edited by Cole and Campbell, World of Poetry, 1981; *Our Twentieth Century's Greatest Poets,* edited by Cole and Campbell, World of Poetry, 1982; and *Today's Greatest Poems,* edited by Cole and Campbell, World of Poetry, 1983. Contributor to encyclopedias and dictionaries, including *Encyclopedia of U. S. Popular Culture,* Popular Press, Bowling Green State University; and *Dictionary of Literary Biography: British Children's Writers, 1914-1960,* Bruccoli Clark Layman (Columbia, SC), in press. Also contributor of poems and articles to magazines, including *Journal of Popular Culture Journal of Narrative Technique, Montana Range Reader,* and *Word Ways: The Journal of Recreational Linguistics.* Guest writer, *Mankato Reporter,* 1975-76.

WORK IN PROGRESS: Folklore: Development, Theories, and Future, Bowling Green State University Press; *Child of the Lake,* a novel.

SIDELIGHTS: Harry Edwin Eiss told *CA:* "I am interested in current peace movements, especially groups that are against nuclear weapons. My views on nuclear war and arms buildup are simply that, when looked at closely, they make no moral or military sense. They are being used by politicians and big businesses to further political and economic goals. Unfortunately, the United States is spending so much money on national defense that it is draining itself of all the economic, social, educational, and most every other kind of growth it could be making.

"I am also concerned about current U.S. policies in such places as Nicaragua. I have a strong attraction to all of the humanities and arts, and I find a need to explore philosophy. When I feel like letting my mind rest, I enjoy watching sports."

*   *   *

ELLIS, John H.   1931-

PERSONAL: Born September 29, 1931, in Memphis, TN; son of John H. and Esther (Sides) Ellis; married Wanda Roper, July 1, 1949; children: Elaine Ann Ellis Tucci, John L., Suzanne. *Education:* Memphis State University, B.S., 1955, M.A., 1957; Tulane University, Ph.D., 1962. *Religion:* Christian.

ADDRESSES: Home—1431 Dalehurst Dr., Bethlehem, PA 18018.

CAREER: Memphis State University, Memphis, TN, assistant professor of history, 1960-64; Georgia State University, Atlanta, assistant professor of history, 1964-65; U.S. Public Health Service, National Institute of General Medical Sciences, Bethesda, MD, postdoctoral research fellow, 1965-67; Georgetown College, Georgetown, KY, associate professor of history and director of institutional research, 1967-71; Lehigh University, Bethlehem, PA, associate professor, 1971-79, professor of history, 1979-93, professor emeritus, 1993—. *Military service:* U.S. Air Force, 1948-51; became sergeant.

MEMBER: Southern Historical Association.

WRITINGS:

Medicine in Kentucky, University Press of Kentucky (Lexington), 1977.
Yellow Fever and Public Health in the New South, University Press of Kentucky, 1992.

*   *   *

ELRON
    See HUBBARD, L(afayette) Ron(ald)

*   *   *

EMSHWILLER, Carol   1921-

PERSONAL: Born April 12, 1921, in Ann Arbor, MI; daughter of Charles Carpenter (a professor) and Agnes (Carswell) Fries; married Edmund Emshwiller (a filmmaker), August 30, 1949; children: Eve, Susan, Peter. *Education:* University of Michigan, B.A. (music), 1945, and B. Design, 1949; attended Ecole nationale superieure des Beaux-Arts, Paris, France.

ADDRESSES: Home—260 East 10th St., Apt. 10, New York, NY 10009.

CAREER: Teacher at Clarion Science Fiction Writing Workshop, East Lansing, MI, 1972-73; New York University, New York City, adjunct assistant professor in continuing education, 1974—. Guest member of faculty, Sarah Lawrence College, 1982.

MEMBER: Science Fiction Writers of America, Authors Guild of Authors League of America.

AWARDS, HONORS: MacDowell Colony fellowship, 1973; New York State Creative Artist Public Service grant, 1975; National Endowment for the Arts grant, 1980.

WRITINGS:

Joy in Our Cause (short stories), Harper (New York City), 1974.
Pilobolus and Joan (television script), WNET, New York City, 1974.
Verging on the Pertinent (short stories), Coffee House Press (Minneapolis), 1989.
Carmen Dog (novel), Mercury House (San Francisco), 1990.
The Start of the End of It All (short stories), Mercury House, 1991.
Venus Rising (novella), Edgewood Press (Cambridge, MA), 1992.
Ledoyt (novel), Mercury House, 1995.

Contributor of short stories to literary and science fiction magazines, including *TriQuarterly, Croton Review* and *Epoch.*

SIDELIGHTS: Carol Emshwiller's short stories are, according to a critic for *Publishers Weekly,* "like carnival mirrors that distort our perceptions, letting us see ourselves in new, wise ways." In her stories, which borrow elements from the science fiction and fantasy genres and are told from a feminist perspective, Emshwiller creates allegorical lessons about the condition of women in society. Writing in the *New York Times Book Review,* Deborah Stead explains that Emshwiller gets "at the truth of things by rendering them strange," while Kimberly G. Allen in *Library Journal* finds that "Emshwiller explores the feminine psyche in an otherworldly way."

Emshwiller's stories often make use of characters and situations found in science fiction and fantasy. In the story "The Start of the End of It All," for example, aliens bent on conquering Earth collaborate with divorced women against the ruling male establishment. Another story tells of a highly-evolved alien woman who, upon her arrival among contemporary Americans, becomes relegated to the inglorious role of housewife. In "Yukon," a woman leaves her husband in favor of living with a bear in the forest. Emshwiller's fiction, writes Peter Bricklebank in *Library Journal,* "is inventive, whimsical, outrageous, and wise." Critics also point to Emshwiller's prose style. According to a *Los Angeles Times Book Review* critic, Emshwiller's stories are told in "a nervous, edgy, witty style all her own." "It would not be misleading," claims Edward Bryant in *Locus,* "to think of Carol Emshwiller as a cleverer, frequently more subtle, John Irving."

In her two published novels, Emshwiller has taken two different approaches. Her first novel, *Carmen Dog,* takes the same fantastical approach found in her short stories, presenting a world in which human women have become animals, and animals have evolved into human women. Although the critic for *Publishers Weekly* believes Emshwiller "stretches a conceit past the breaking point in this uneven allegory," Charlotte Innes in the *New York Times Book Review* dubs *Carmen Dog* "a gentle exposition of human folly that nevertheless makes some tough points about the inequalities between the sexes." Katherine Dieckmann, writing in the *Voice Literary Supplement,* celebrates "Emshwiller's hilariously dead-on radical vision."

Emshwiller's second novel, *Ledoyt,* a realistic story set in the American west of the early twentieth century, concerns Oriana Cochran and Beal Ledoyt, two wildly different characters who nonetheless fall in love and marry. The story focuses on the couple's daughter Lotti who, stubborn and jealous, tries to destroy their marriage. Emshwiller tells the story in a "spare but lyrical prose and [with] a fine attention to detail," as Walter Satterthwait writes in the *New York Times Book Review.* Oriana and Beal "are endearing and admirable characters," Satterthwait concludes, and the novel contains moments "that are remarkably moving; there are scenes of great power."

BIOGRAPHICAL/CRITICAL SOURCES:

PERIODICALS

American Book Review, August, 1991, p. 12.
Booklist, November 15, 1989, p. 639; February 1, 1990, p. 1070; May 15, 1991, p. 1779.
Kirkus Reviews, October 1, 1989, pp. 1421-1422.
Library Journal, December, 1989, p. 168; April 15, 1990, p. 122; June 1, 1991, p. 188; November 15, 1991, p. 152.
Locus, May, 1992, p. 51.
Los Angeles Times Book Review, June 9, 1991, p. 6.
New York Time Book Review, March 18, 1990, p. 20; April 29, 1990, p. 38; October 29, 1995.
Publishers Weekly, November 17, 1989, p. 46; April 26, 1991, p. 54.
Review of Contemporary Fiction, fall, 1991, p. 284.

Science Fiction Chronicle, June, 1992, p. 35.
Small Press, June, 1990, p. 31; fall, 1991, p. 55.
Voice Literary Supplement, June, 1990, p. 19.

*   *   *

ENGELHARDT, Frederick
    See HUBBARD, L(afayette) Ron(ald)

*   *   *

EPHRON, Delia   1944-
    (Delia Brock)

PERSONAL: Born July 12, 1944, in Los Angeles, CA; daughter of Henry (a writer) and Phoebe (a writer; maiden name, Wolkind) Ephron; married Dan Brock (divorced, 1975); married Jerome Kass (a screenwriter), May 21, 1982; children: Julie, Adam (stepchildren). *Education:* Barnard College, B.A., 1966.

ADDRESSES: Agent—Lynn Nesbit, Janklow & Nesbit Associates, 598 Madison Ave., New York, NY 10022-1614.

CAREER: Writer. *New York* magazine, New York City, writer, 1975-78.

WRITINGS:

(With Lorraine Bodger, under name Delia Brock) *The Adventurous Crocheter,* Simon & Schuster (New York City), 1972.
(With Bodger, under name Delia Brock) *Gladrags: Redesigning, Remaking, Refitting All Your Old Clothes,* Simon & Schuster, 1975.
How to Eat Like a Child, and Other Lessons in Not Being a Grown-Up (also see below), Viking (New York City), 1978.
(With Bodger) *Crafts for All Seasons,* Universe Books (New York City), 1980.
Teenage Romance; or, How to Die of Embarrassment, Viking, 1981.
Santa and Alex, Little, Brown (Boston), 1983.
Funny Sauce: Us, the Ex, the Ex's New Mate, the New Mate's Ex, and the Kids, Viking, 1986.
(With John Forster and Judith Kahan) *How to Eat Like a Child and Other Lessons in Not Being a Grown-up* (musical based on book of same title), Samuel French (New York City), 1986.

"Do I Have to Say Hello?": Aunt Delia's Manners Quiz for Kids and Their Grownups, Viking, 1989.

(With sister, Nora Ephron) *This Is My Life* (screenplay; based on the novel by Meg Wolitzer), Twentieth Century-Fox, 1990.

The Girl Who Changed the World, Ticknor & Fields (New York City), 1993.

Hanging Up, Putnam (New York City), 1995.

Contributor to magazines, including *Vogue, Esquire, Glamour, Redbook, Cosmopolitan, House and Garden, Savvy, California, New York Times Magazine,* and *New York.*

ADAPTATIONS: *How to Eat Like a Child* was adapted for television by the National Broadcasting Corp. (NBC) in November, 1982.

SIDELIGHTS: Delia Ephron is known for her humorous books that appeal to both young people and adults. In *How to Eat Like a Child, and Other Lessons in Not Being a Grown-Up,* Ephron covers such topics as birthdays, Christmas, sibling torture, car rides, school, and pets. Her *Teenage Romance; Or, How to Die of Embarrassment* offers wry advice for the insecure teenager on dating, hiding pimples and other social embarrassments. *"Do I Have to Say Hello?": Aunt Delia's Manners Quiz for Kids and Their Grownups* is a humorous look at manners for children, listing obviously inappropriate behavior choices in quiz fashion, allowing the reader to choose which answer is best. With her first adult novel, *Hanging Up,* Ephron turned her humor to a more serious topic, a middle-aged woman's relationship with her dying father.

Ephron comes from a family of writers; her parents were successful screenwriters for Hollywood. Her first books, written in collaboration with Lorraine Bodger, focused on craft activities. But with *How to Eat Like a Child,* Ephron turned to humor. The book was inspired when she was eating chocolate pudding with a friend. She noticed that the two women had different ways of eating the same food. "I was sitting here, eating it my way," she tells Judy Klemesrud in the *New York Times,* "which means that I make a little hole in the pudding and scoop out all the best parts and save the skin until last. I thought, Gee, I want to write a piece about it." The resulting article appeared in the *New York Times Magazine.* When readers sent in letters explaining their own childish ways of eating food, Ephron decided to write a book on the idea. *How to Eat Like a Child,* aside from describing juvenile approaches to food, describes in a deadpan manner how to deal with parents, behave at school, and torture siblings. One chapter is taken up with a listing of ways Ephron bothered her sisters when they were young.

For her next collection of essays, *Teenage Romance; or, How to Die of Embarrassment,* Ephron interviewed about seventy-five teenagers in New York and California. She tells *People:* "They say teens today are more sophisticated, but I believe they're just as nervous and embarrassed as ever. The girls still worry about getting pregnant [from] kissing; the boys are as preoccupied as ever with 'getting it.'" As with *How to Eat Like a Child,* Ephron recalls many of her own tribulations as a teenager. She tells Jill Wolfson of the Jackson *News:* "One of my biggest activities then was driving past a particular guy's house to see if he was home."

A visit from one of Ephron's nephews prompted her to write *"Do I Have to Say Hello?": Aunt Delia's Manners Quiz for Kids and Their Grownups.* Written with good-natured sarcasm, the book presents a number of outlandish responses to how a child should behave in given situations. "The incorrect answers," notes Ann M. Martin in the *New York Times Book Review,* "are so amusing that readers won't skip a word." Each chapter offers a quiz on such topics as visiting manners, thank-you manners, and telephone manners. The critic for *Publishers Weekly* finds that "Ephron raises audible laughs as she makes painfully clear the difference between the ways we hope small fry will act and the ways they do."

Ephron focuses on a more adult audience with *Funny Sauce: Us, the Ex, the Ex's New Mate, the New Mate's Ex, and the Kids,* a humorous look at the often confused extended families of today. Displaying what a *Publishers Weekly* critic calls an "inimitable wit," Ephron covers the inevitable personal conflicts and awkward adjustments when parents have divorced and each remarries. Writing in the *New York Times Book Review,* Cyra McFadden claims that *Funny Sauce* "manages to be both funny and wise." The *Publishers Weekly* critic concludes that readers "will laugh loudly, but probably wince too as they recognize their households."

Ephron's gift for humor is evident in her first novel for adults, *Hanging Up.* Based in part on Ephron's own experiences, the novel tells the story of Eve, a woman in her forties who must come to terms with her father when his health begins to fail and he needs her help. An alcoholic and manic-depressive, the father has for years called her on the phone, either abusing her verbally or talking nonsense. Now that he is near death she is obliged to assist him. "The novel," writes Irene Lacher in the *Los Angeles Times,* "escapes grimness, trading on Ephron's peculiar ability to write about painful things in a funny way." Eric Kraft in the *New York Times Book Review* calls *Hanging Up* a "compassionate, funny and tremendously satisfying first novel." In the *Chicago Tribune,* Tananarive Due praises Ephron's "gift for the particulars and nuances of dialogue" which "keeps *Hanging Up* near its goal as a weighty work with a quirky sense of humor."

BIOGRAPHICAL/CRITICAL SOURCES:

PERIODICALS

Atlanta Journal & Constitution, December 21, 1986, p. F13.
Booklist, September 1, 1989, p. 27; November 15, 1993, p. 623; July, 1995, p. 1859.
Boston Globe, July 27, 1995, p. 50.
Chicago Tribune, November 23, 1986, p. 6; August 11, 1995, p. 3.
Kirkus Reviews, October 1, 1989, p. 1467; October 1, 1993, p. 1272.
Los Angeles Times, November 17, 1986, p. V1; August 24, 1995, p. E1.
Los Angeles Times Book Review, May 8, 1988, p. 14; August 6, 1995, p. 2.
Nation, November 21, 1981.
News (Jackson, MS), November 3, 1981.
Newsweek, December 4, 1989, p. 73.
New York Daily News, October 11, 1981, pp. 1, 4.
New York Times, November 17, 1978; November 17, 1986, p. B10; February 16, 1992, p. 22.
New York Times Book Review, September 5, 1982; October 12, 1986, p. 13; May 20, 1990, p. 46; January 30, 1994, p. 27; July 23, 1995, p. 8.
New York Times Magazine, September 14, 1986.
People, October 12, 1981.
Publishers Weekly, January 7, 1983; September 12, 1986, p. 75; March 11, 1988, p. 99; September 29, 1989, p. 53; September 27, 1993, p. 63.
Reader's Digest, March, 1979; August, 1979.
San Francisco Chronicle, October 15, 1986.
Saturday Evening Post, May, 1979.
School Library Journal, November, 1993, p. 106.
Utne Reader, January, 1990, p. 96.
Washington Post Book World, August 22, 1982.

ESTERBROOK, Tom
    See HUBBARD, L(afayette) Ron(ald)

*   *   *

ETTINGER, Elzbieta   1925-

PERSONAL: Born September 19, 1925, in Poland; immigrated to the United States, 1960s. *Education:* University of Warsaw, M.A., Ph.D.; Academy of Political Science, Warsaw, additional study.

ADDRESSES: Home—83 Brattle St., Cambridge, MA 02138. *Agent*—Mary Yost Associates, 141 East 55th St., New York, NY 10022. *Office*—Massachusetts Institute of Technology, 14N-328, Cambridge, MA 02139.

CAREER: Affiliated with Radcliffe Seminars, Harvard Extension, beginning 1970, senior fellow at Radcliffe Institute, 1972-74; Massachusetts Institute of Technology, Cambridge, 1973—, began as assistant professor, became professor of humanities and Thomas Meloy Professor of Rhetoric.

WRITINGS:

NOVELS

Kindergarten, Houghton (Boston), 1970.

NONFICTION

Rosa Luxemburg: A Life, Beacon Press (Boston), 1986.
Hannah Arendt/Martin Heidegger, Yale University Press (New Haven, CT), 1995.

OTHER

(Editor and translator) *Comrade and Lover: Rosa Luxemburg's Letters to Leo Jogisches,* MIT Press (Cambridge, MA), 1979.

Also author of critical articles and essays published in Polish. Translator of numerous works from the English and German into Polish.

SIDELIGHTS: Polish-born author and educator Elzbieta Ettinger's first-hand experience of the Nazi occupation of her native country during the Third Reich has informed much of her work. Her novel

Kindergarten is set during World War II, while *Rosa Luxemburg: A Life* and *Hannah Arendt/Martin Heidegger* examine prominent Jewish figures from Germany and Poland, exploring the political upheavals of the first half of the twentieth century from a personal perspective.

Ettinger's 1970 novel, *Kindergarten,* is a poignant portrayal of the Jewish experience in Nazi-occupied Poland, told from the point of view of Elli, a young woman who, along with her family, would successfully evade discovery by the Nazis through all the years of World War II. Miriam Halahmy, reviewing the work in the *Times Literary Supplement,* praises *Kindergarten* as "a highly self-conscious work, written with exceptional insight into the suffering of the individual in hiding."

Ettinger followed her novel with a work of nonfiction, *Rosa Luxemburg,* a life of the ardent revolutionary who transcended a childhood in a bourgeois family of declining fortune in Poland to become a leader of the German Social Democratic Party. Before her death in Berlin in January, 1919, at the hands of a German assassin, Rosa Luxemburg was hailed as one of the radical leaders of German Communism, both for her work in cofounding the Spartacus League and for her efforts at sustaining the fragmenting German Social Democratic Party several years later. Although her antimilitarist, internationalist, proletariat-based brand of communism has been the subject of a great deal of written scrutiny, Ettinger has adjusted the focus of Luxemburg's life story to reveal the details of Red Rosa's personal life. Surprisingly, considering Luxemburg's radical political views, the relationships she maintained with family members, friends, and lovers, were almost mundane by comparison. Using as a basis of her study the romantic letters Luxemburg wrote to lover and fellow politico Leo Jogiches, Ettinger found that her subject's "erotic nature gave her cause for anguish as well as elation but that she could always find strength for the cause of international Socialism," according to London *Observer* critic Faith Evans. While praised for her ability to bring to life the social and political backdrop of Luxemburg's early years, Ettinger was criticized by some reviewers for occasional lapses into instances of melodrama and psychobiography—for example, referring to Luxemburg's internal "hurt child"—which they considered to be ill-founded when judged according to the historical evidence available. However, her biography is lauded by James Joll in the *New York Times*

Review of Books: "Ettinger has provide us with many clues to help us understand Rosa's troubled, sensitive, and impetuous nature and her reactions to the tumult of her time."

The four-year love affair between assimilated German Jewish philosophy student Hannah Arendt and her married professor, soon-to-be Nazi Martin Heidegger, ended in 1928. However, Ettinger shows, in *Hannah Arendt/Martin Heidegger,* that their complex relationship extended far longer; Arendt, who vehemently condemned fascism in her 1950 work *The Origins of Totalitarianism,* would defend her ex-lover and his role as intellectual defender of Nazi racism until her death in 1974. Reconstructing the relationship of what she terms "starcrossed" lovers through the correspondence that they sustained from the time of their affair through their deaths in the mid-1970s, Ettinger's work has been credited by several critics with being the first historical account to document possible motivations for Arendt's formerly incomprehensible, emotionally based defense of the actions of her former lover during the war years. As such, it has caused a certain amount of controversy among Arendt scholars, as well as setting off several law suits due to its author's singular access to formerly-sealed letters. "The love affair of Martin Heidegger and Hannah Arendt . . . has been public knowledge for years," explains Richard Wolin in the *New Republic.* "But not in its details; and so there has been a great deal of speculation about the personal and intellectual consequences of the liaison. In her important and laconic book," Wolin concludes, "Elzbieta Ettinger puts all speculation to rest."

BIOGRAPHICAL/CRITICAL SOURCES:

PERIODICALS

London Review of Books, June 4, 1987, pp. 12-13.
Los Angeles Times Book Review, August 27, 1995, p. 6.
New Republic, October 9, 1995, pp. 27-37.
New York Review of Books, March 26, 1987.
New York Times Book Review, February 8, 1970; June 14, 1987, pp. 13-14; September 24, 1995, p. 41; October 1, 1995, p. 39.
Observer (London), July 5, 1987.
Times Literary Supplement, February 10, 1989, p. 148.

EVANS, Howard Ensign   1919-

PERSONAL: Born February 23, 1919, in East Hartford, CT; son of Archie J. and Adella (Ensign) Evans; married Mary Alice Dietrich, June 6, 1954; children: Barbara, Dorothy, Timothy. *Education:* University of Connecticut, B.A., 1940; Cornell University, M.S., 1941, Ph.D., 1949. *Avocational interests:* Photography, backpacking, fishing.

ADDRESSES: Home—79 McKenna Ct., Livermore, CO 80536. *Office*—Department of Entomology, Colorado State University, Fort Collins, CO 80523.

CAREER: Kansas State University (now Kansas State University of Agriculture and Applied Science), Manhattan, assistant professor, 1949-52; Cornell University, Ithaca, NY, assistant professor of entomology, 1954-59; Harvard University, Cambridge, MA, associate curator, Museum of Comparative Zoology, 1959-64, curator, 1964-70, Alexander Agassiz Professor of Zoology, 1970-73; Colorado State University, Fort Collins, professor of entomology, 1973-85, professor emeritus, 1986—. *Military service:* U.S. Army, 1942-45; became second lieutenant.

MEMBER: Animal Behavior Society, National Academy of Sciences.

AWARDS, HONORS: National Book Award nomination, 1964, for *Wasp Farm.*

WRITINGS:

The Song I Sing: Verses, Humphries, 1951.
(With Cheng Shan Lin) *Studies on the Larvae of Digger Wasps (Hymenoptera, Sphecidae)* [Philadelphia], 1956.
Studies on the Comparative Ethology of Digger Wasps of the Genus Bembix, Cornell University Press (Ithaca, NY), 1957.
Wasp Farm, Natural History Press (Garden City, NY), 1963.
A Synopsis of the American Bethylidae (Hymenoptera, Aculeata), Museum of Comparative Zoology, Harvard University (Cambridge, MA), 1964.
The Comparative Ethology and Evolution of the Sand Wasps, Harvard University Press (Cambridge, MA), 1966.
Life on a Little-Known Planet, Dutton (New York City), 1968.

(With Mary Jane West Eberhard) *The Wasps,* University of Michigan Press (Ann Arbor, MI), 1970.
(With wife, Mary Alice Evans) *William Morton Wheeler, Biologist,* Harvard University Press, 1970.
(With Robert W. Matthews) *Systematics and Nesting Behavior of Australian Bembix Sand Wasps (Hymenoptera, Sphecidae),* American Entomological Institute (Ann Arbor, MI), 1973.
The Bethylidae of America North of Mexico, American Entomological Institute, 1978.
(Editor with Michael D. Breed and Charles D. Michener) *The Biology of Social Insects: Proceedings of the Ninth Congress of the International Union for the Study of Social Insects,* Westview Press (Boulder, CO), 1982.
(With Evans) *Australia: A Natural History,* Smithsonian Institution Press (Washington, DC), 1983.
Insect Biology, Addison-Wesley (Reading, MA), 1984.
The Pleasures of Entomology, Smithsonian Institution Press, 1985.
(With Kevin M. O'Neill) *The Natural History and Behavior of North American Bee Wolves,* Cornell University Press, 1988.
(With Evans) *Cache la Poudre: The Natural History of a Rocky Mountain River,* University Press of Colorado, 1991.
Pioneer Naturalists: The Discovery and Naming of North American Plants and Animals, Henry Holt (New York City), 1993.

Contributor to scientific journals.

SIDELIGHTS: Howard Ensign Evans' *Life on a Little-Known Planet* describes the life histories and mating habits of several common insects. *New York Times Book Review* writer Robert W. Stock comments: "Evans, a skilled writer in the unlikely guise of a Harvard University entomologist, has the wit and charm to make us care about the life-styles of locusts and bedbugs." "The 'little-known planet' of the title is earth," he continues, "and Evans is pleading for a greater understanding of earth life—even unto the smallest bug. Seldom, if ever, has the case for the natural sciences—and for conservation—been presented with such reasoned, convincing eloquence."

BIOGRAPHICAL/CRITICAL SOURCES:

PERIODICALS

Audubon, March, 1994, p. 123.
Booklist, October 15, 1993, p. 401.

Library Journal, September 15, 1993, p. 100.
Natural History, October, 1979; December, 1981.
Nature, March 7, 1985.
New York Times Book Review, November 17, 1968.
Times Literary Supplement, April 8, 1965; May 28, 1970.

F

FAIRFIELD, John
   See **LIVINGSTONE, Harrison Edward**

*   *   *

FELDMAN, Gerald D(onald)   1937-

PERSONAL: Born April 24, 1937, in New York, NY; son of Isadore and Lillian (Cohen) Feldman; married Philippa Blume, June 22, 1958 (divorced, 1982); married Norma von Ragenfeld, November 30, 1983; children: (first marriage) Deborah Eve, Aaron. *Education:* Columbia University, B.A. (magna cum laude), 1958; Harvard University, M.A., 1959, Ph.D., 1964. *Politics:* Democrat. *Religion:* Jewish.

ADDRESSES: Home—Berkeley, CA. *Office*—Department of History, University of California, Berkeley, CA 94720.

CAREER: University of California, Berkeley, assistant professor, 1963-68, associate professor, 1968-70, professor of history, 1970—, Institute of International Studies, member of advisory and program committees, 1969-70, acting chair of committee on Advanced Industrial Societies and West European Studies, 1971-72, member of executive committee, 1975-76 and 1979-81, director, Center for German and European Studies, 1994—. Delegate to Council for European Studies, 1971-72; member of Curatorium for State and the Economy in the Weimer Republic conference, 1973; cochair of conference on twentieth-century capitalism, 1974; participant in consultation program, Historische Kommission zu

Berlin, summer, 1976; Stephen Allen Kaplan Memorial Lecturer, University of Pennsylvania, 1984.

MEMBER: American Historical Association (conference group for Central European History, vice-chair, 1989, chair, 1990), Historische Kommission zu Berlin (corresponding member), Friends of the German Historical Institute in Washington (member of executive committee, 1990—), Historical Society of the Deutsche Bank (member of board of directors, 1991—), European Association for Banking History (member of advisory board, 1991—), Historical de la Grande Guerre, Peronne (member of advisory board, centre de recherche), Phi Beta Kappa.

AWARDS, HONORS: Woodrow Wilson fellow, 1958-59, 1991-92; Harvard fellow, 1961-63; Social Science Research Council fellow, 1961-63; honorary Sheldon traveling fellow, 1961-62; American Council of Learned Societies (ACLS) fellow, 1966-67, 1970-71; Social Science Research Council grant, 1966-67; honorary mention for best article, Conference Group on Central European History, 1970; University of California Humanities research fellow, 1970-71, 1992; Guggenheim fellow, 1973-74; Newcomen Prize (with Ulrich Nocken) for best essay in *Business History Review,* 1975; National Endowment for the Humanities fellow, 1977-78; Volkswagen Foundation grant, 1979-82; Lehrman Institute fellow, 1981-82; German Marshall Fund fellow, 1981-82; stipendiat and Prize of the Historisches Kolleg, Munich, 1982-83; ACLS grants, 1986; appointment to the Wissenschaftskolleg, Berlin, 1987-88; Stinnes Foundation research grant, 1988-89; Book Prize, Conference Group for Central European History of the American Historical Association, 1995; Deutscher Akademischer Austauschdienst (DAAD) Book Prize, German Studies Association, 1995.

WRITINGS:

Army, Industry and Labor in Germany, 1914-1918, Princeton University Press, 1966, revised version published in German translation as *Armee, Industrie und Arbeiterschaft in Deutschland 1914 bis 1918,* J. H. Dietz (Berlin/Bonn), 1985.

Iron and Steel in the German Inflation, 1916-1923, Princeton University Press, 1977.

(With Heidrun Homburg) *Industrie und Inflation: Studien und Dokumente zur Politik der deutschen Unternehmer 1916 bis 1923,* Hoffman und Campe (Hamburg), 1977.

Vom Weltkrieg zur Weltwirtschaftskrise. Studien zur deutschen Wirtschafts-und Sozialgeschichte 1914-1932, Vandehoeck & Ruprecht (Goettingen), 1984.

(With Irmgard Steinisch) *Industrie und Gewerkschaften 1918-1924. Die ueberforderte Zentralarbeitgemeinschaft,* Oldebourg (Stuttgart), 1985.

The Great Disorder: Politics, Economics, and Society in the German Inflation, 1914-1924 Oxford University Press, 1993.

EDITOR

German Imperialism, 1914-1917: The Development of a Historical Debate, Wiley, 1972.

(With Thomas G. Barnes) *A Documentary History of Europe,* Volume 3: *Nationalism, Industrialization, and Democracy, 1814-1914,* Volume 4: *Breakdown and Rebirth, 1914 to the Present,* Little, Brown (Boston), 1972.

(With Otto Beusch, and contributor) *Historische Prozesse der deutschen Inflation 1914-1924. Ein Tangungsbericht,* Colloquium-Verlag (Berlin), 1978.

(With Carl-Ludwig Holtfrerich, Gerhard A. Ritter, and Peter-Christian Witt, and contributor) *The German Inflation: A Preliminary Balance,* De Gruyter, 1982, published as *The German Inflation Reconsidered: A Preliminary Balance,* 1984.

(With Holtfrerich, Ritter, and Witt) *The Experience of Inflation: International and Comparative Studies,* De Gruyter, 1984.

(With Elizabeth Mueller-Luckner, and contributor) *Die Nachwirkungen der Inflation auf die deutsche Geschichte 1924-1933,* Oldenbourg, 1985.

(With Holtfrerich, Ritter, and Witt, and contributor) *The Adaption to Inflation/Die Anpassung an die Inflation,* De Gruyter, 1986.

(With Holtfrerich, Ritter, and Witt) *Konsequenzen der Inflation/Consequences of Inflation* (introduction by Gerald D. Feldman), Einzelveroffentlichungen der Historischen Kommission zu Berlin (Berlin), 1989.

(With Klaus Tenfelde) *Arbeiter, Unternehmer und Staat im Bergbau, Industrielle Bexiehungen im internationalen Vergleich* [Munich], 1989, translated into English as *Workers, Owners and Politics in Coal Mining, An International Comparison of Industrial Relations,* Berg Publications, 1990.

(With Ulf Olssen, Michael D. Bordo, and Youssef Cassis) *The Evolution of Modern Financial Institutions in the Twentieth Century. Proceedings. Eleventh International Economic History Congress. Milan, September 1994,* [Milan], 1994.

(With Cassis and Olssen) *The Evolution of Financial Institutions and Markets in Twentieth-Century Europe,* Ashgate, 1995.

OTHER

Contributor to history books in the United States and Germany, including *Arbeiter und Buerger im 19. Jahrhundert,* edited by Juergen Kocka, Oldenbourg, 1986 and *The Changing Boundaries of the Political,* edited by Charles Meier, Cambridge University Press, 1987. Contributor to proceedings and historical journals in the United States and Germany. Member of editorial boards of *Journal of Social History,* 1970—, *Central European History,* 1973-75, *Journal of Modern History,* 1973-75, *Geschichte und Gesellschaft,* 1974—, and *German Yearbook on Business History,* 1982—, *Contemporary European History,* 1991-95, *German Studies Review,* 1991—.

WORK IN PROGRESS: A Merchant from Mulheim: Hugo Stinnes, 1870-1924, a biography.

* * *

FIELD, Hartry H(amlin)   1946-

PERSONAL: Born November 30, 1946, in Boston, MA; son of Donald T. (a lawyer) and Adelaide (an editor; maiden name, Anderson) Field; children: Elizabeth. *Education:* University of Wisconsin—Madison, B.A., 1967; Harvard University, M.A., 1968, Ph.D., 1972.

ADDRESSES: Office—Department of Philosophy, Graduate Center, City University of New York, 33 West 42nd St., New York, NY 10036.

CAREER: Princeton University, Princeton, NJ, assistant professor of philosophy, 1970-76; University of Southern California, Los Angeles, associate professor, 1976-81, professor of philosophy, 1981-91; City University of New York, Graduate Center, Distinguished Professor of Philosophy and Kornblith Chair, 1991—.

MEMBER: American Philosophical Association, Philosophy of Science Association.

AWARDS, HONORS: Grants from National Endowment for the Humanities, 1972-73, and National Science Foundation, 1979-80 and 1982; Guggenheim fellowship, 1979-80; Lakatos Award, 1986.

WRITINGS:

Science without Numbers: A Defence of Nominalism, Basil Blackwell (Cambridge, MA), 1980.
Realism, Mathematics and Modality, Basil Blackwell, 1989.

Contributor to philosophy journals.

WORK IN PROGRESS: Research on the philosophy of logic, the philosophy of space and time, and theories of truth and of the content of mental states.

SIDELIGHTS: Hartry H. Field told *CA:* "A general theme throughout my work is the development of a scientific metaphysics and an account of the place of thought, reasoning, and values within such a metaphysics."

Hartry's goal in *Science without Numbers: A Defence of Nominalism,* according to *Times Literary Supplement* critic Geoffrey Hunter, is to demolish the traditional argument that the existence of mathematical entities is necessary to an understanding of the physical world and to the science of physics. Field's view, Hunter wrote, is "that there is no need to postulate mathematical entities, or to regard mathematical claims about them as true, in order to pursue science." The author believes that, though mathematics provides convenient symbols for working with physical theories and concepts, the same scientific conclusions can be reached without the use of numbers. Even if numbers are used, he adds, it is not neces-

sary to assume that the mathematical theories are true. They work equally well when mathematical entities are treated as fictions.

BIOGRAPHICAL/CRITICAL SOURCES:

PERIODICALS

Times Literary Supplement, February 20, 1981.

* * *

FISHER, Robert (Tempest) 1943-

PERSONAL: Born August 2, 1943, in Perivale, England; son of John Tempest (a civil servant) and Doris (an antique dealer; maiden name, Hiscock) Fisher; married Celia Margaret Fulton (an editor), April 13, 1969; children: Jacob Alexander, Thomas Gabriel. *Education:* Goldsmiths College, London, B.A. (with honors), 1976. *Avocational interests:* Creating educational games for children and adults, reviewing books, lecturing on educational topics.

ADDRESSES: Home—7 Maze Rd., Kew, Surrey TW9 3DA, England.

CAREER: Teacher at primary schools in London, England, 1964-66 and 1969-72, and Addis Ababa, Ethiopia, 1966-69; Beacon Hill School (primary school), Hong Kong, deputy principal, 1972-74; St. Mary's Primary School, Twickenham, England, deputy headmaster, 1974-82; Archdeacon Cambridge School, Twickenham, head teacher, 1983-87; West London Institute of Higher Education, London, England, senior lecturer of higher education, 1988—, director of Centre for Thinking Skills.

MEMBER: National Association of Primary Education, Thinking Skills Network.

AWARDS, HONORS: Research grant from Schools Curriculum Development Council (U.K.), 1985-86, for setting up a program to teach thinking skills to three- to eleven-year-olds.

WRITINGS:

EDITOR; CHILDREN'S POETRY ANTHOLOGIES

Amazing Monsters: Verses to Chill and Thrill, Faber (London), 1982.

Ghosts Galore: Haunting Verse, Faber, 1983.
Funny Folk: Poems about People, Faber, 1986.
Witch Words: Poems of Magic and Mystery, Faber, 1987.
Pet Poems, Faber, 1989.
Minibeasts: Poems about Little Creatures, Faber, 1992.

OTHER

Together Today: Themes and Stories for Assembly (for teachers), Evans Brothers (London), 1981.
Together with Infants: Themes and Stories for Assembly (for teachers), Evans Brothers, 1982.
The Assembly Year (for teachers), Collins (London), 1985.
Religions (reference for children), Macdonald (London), 1987.
Problem Solving in Primary Schools, Basil Blackwell (London), 1987.
Investigating Mathematics, Basil Blackwell, 1988.
Teaching Juniors, Basil Blackwell, 1991.
Recording Achievement in Primary Schools, Basil Blackwell, 1991.

Also author of *Teaching Children to Think, Teaching Children to Learn, Investigating Maths,* and *Investigating Technology,* published by Basil Blackwell. Contributor to education journals. Consultant to *Pictorial Education,* 1980-81; editorial consultant to educational publishers, 1981—.

SIDELIGHTS: Robert Fisher is the editor of many poetry anthologies for children and author of books on fostering learning skills in young people. Fisher told *CA:* "I have taught in the United Kingdom, Ethiopia, and Hong Kong, at all age levels from preschool to adult. I write books for teachers to foster a creative and integrative approach to education. In my poetry books for children, my aim is to freshen and stimulate the imagination, whether the child is eight or eighty. The distinction between child and adult is often a false one. Poetry is one aspect of creative education which can reach both the mind of the child and the child within the adult. My recent research is into teaching children thinking and problem solving skills. I would welcome contacts with people working in this field, or in the field of children's poetry."

*   *   *

FISK, Nicholas
    See HIGGINBOTTOM, David

FORREST, Leon   1937-

PERSONAL: Born January 8, 1937 in Chicago, IL; married Marianne Duncan. *Education:* Attended Wilson Junior College, 1955-56, Roosevelt University, 1957-58, and University of Chicago, 1958-60, 1962-64.

ADDRESSES: Office—Department of African-American Studies, Northwestern University, 633 Clark, Evanston, IL 60201.

CAREER: Woodlawn Observer, managing editor, 1967-69; *Muhammed Speaks,* associate editor, 1969-71, managing editor, 1972-73; Northwestern University, Evanston, IL, professor of African-American Studies, 1973—, chair of African-American Studies department, 1985-94. Lecturer at Yale University, Rochester Institute of Technology, and Wesleyan University, 1974-79. *Military service:* United States Army, 1960-62.

MEMBER: Authors Guild, Authors League of America, Society of Midland Authors (president, 1981).

AWARDS, HONORS: Grant from Northwestern University, 1975; Chicago Public Library, Sandburg Medallion, 1978; Friends of the Chicago Public Library Carl Sandburg Award and Society of Midland Authors Award, both 1985, for *Two Wings to Veil My Face;* April 14, 1985 declared Leon Forrest Day by proclamation of Chicago Mayor Harold Washington; *Chicago Sun-Times,* Chicago Book of the Year Award, 1992, and *New York Times* Notable Book of the Year, 1993, both for *Divine Days.*

WRITINGS:

There Is a Tree More Ancient Than Eden, introduction by Ralph Ellison, Random House (New York City), 1973.
The Bloodworth Orphans, Random House, 1977.
Two Wings to Veil My Face, Random House, 1984.
Divine Days, Another Chicago Press (Chicago, IL), 1992.
Relocations of the Spirit (essays), Moyer Bell (Wakefield, RI), 1994.

Also author of an opera libretto commissioned by the Indiana University School of Music, 1980, and a play.

SIDELIGHTS: Leon Forrest's novels reveal his debts to the oral traditions of storytellers and songwriters and the literary traditions of writers such as James Joyce, William Faulkner, and Ralph Ellison. "Like Joyce, like Faulkner, like Ellison, Forrest focuses on a particular people in a particular time and place, and in telling their story, touches universal themes that speak to us all," writes Bernard Rodgers in the *Chicago Tribune Book World.* Like these authors, Forrest employs a stream of consciousness style, and his novels are often interrelated through reappearing characters as well as structural and stylistic similarities.

There Is a Tree More Ancient Than Eden concerns the complex relationships between the illegitimate children of an old family who once owned slaves. The book "represents an awe-inspiring fusion of American cultural myth, Black American history, Black fundamentalist religion, the doctrine and dogma of Catholicism (stations of the Cross and the Precious Blood Cathedral), and an autobiographical recall of days of anxiety and confusion in the city," writes Houston A. Baker, Jr., in *Black World.* Another *Black World* reviewer, Zack Gilbert, notes that "Forrest has woven an hypnotic fabric with words that are part jazz, part blues, part gospel," and likening the work to Ralph Ellison's *Invisible Man,* describes it as equally "moving and forceful in its poetic flow." Other critics, noting the novel's stream of consciousness style and impending sense of doom, compare the work to William Faulkner's writing. *Harvard Advocate* contributor Joel Motley calls the book "a powerful work of literature," and adds that while Forrest does use a Faulknerian style, he makes it into his own to express the "urban black experience." Baker concludes that *There Is a Tree More Ancient Than Eden* "contains insight, streaks of brilliance, and a finely-formed intelligence that promises further revelations." L. J. Davis of the *New York Times Book Review* was not so impressed with Forrest's style, arguing that stream-of-consciousness "is just fine, but only if we know from whom it is streaming and why it is streaming that way and not another. And a pervading sense of doom is certainly a nasty thing to have." Davis concludes that Forrest is "one of those black writers who appear to suffer from the unhappy delusion that they are really William Faulkner."

Forrest's 1977 novel *The Bloodworth Orphans* is the story of the many black and white orphaned children of the Bloodworths, a Southern, former slave-owning plantation family. A critic for *Booklist* calls comments that Forrest's writing is "an intense, breathless stream of prose" that develops the nonlinear plot. Arguing that the novel reveals "evidence of a large

talent," a *Publishers Weekly* reviewer finds the storyline "tiresomely complex" but admires many aspects of the novel including its "torrential eloquence, vivid characterization and occasional infectious humor." The reviewer concludes that there are great riches in the novel "if one wants to work hard to gather them."

In *Two Wings to Veil My Face,* Nathaniel Witherspoon, a character from Forrest's first novel, records the life story of Momma Sweetie Reed, a former slave. "As she tells her story, Nathaniel is forced to redefine his own identity, to translate as well as transcribe the meaning of her memories," writes Rodgers. "In the end, the secrets Great-Momma Sweetie reveals to Nathaniel . . . radically alter both their lives." *New York Times Book Review* contributor Benjamin DeMott observes that while the novel is at times overwritten and poorly structured, these "defects somehow fail to sink it." He explains: "The reason lies in the quality and complication of the feelings breathing in Sweetie Reed as she labors to teach young black generations the uses of the souls of black folk." Rodgers concludes: "It is a novel . . . that's not for everyone. Just for those who love the excitement of watching a truly unique writer practice his art; for those who can recognize the magic beneath the mundane, as Forrest does; for those who are willing to accept the challenge of a novel that really is extraordinary and unforgettable."

Forrest's 1,138 page 1992 novel *Divine Days* is the journal of Joubert Jones, an aspiring playwright living on Chicago's south side. Jones is searching for Sugar-Groove, a legend to the Chicago black people, who has apparently disappeared. Noting that *Divine Days* has been referred to as "the *Ulysses* of Chicago's South Side" by Forrest himself among others, Joseph Coates of Chicago *Tribune Books* argues that "the real model for *Divine Days* is *Finnegans Wake,* with its shifty cast of multi-masked selves, its intent to encapsulate the history of a people in the endless swirl of their personal and social identities and its playfully punful language, all organized around a death or deaths and at least one funeral." Coates, despite finding that Forrest's "natural prose voice too often flags when it should soar," concludes that *Divine Days* is "wonderfully entertaining . . . a late, brave attempt at Modernism." Critic Stanley Crouch of the *New York Times Book Review* calls *Divine Days* "an adventurous masterwork. . . . The work's exceptional strength arrives through the virtuoso fusion of idiomatic detail and allusions to the worlds of literature, religion and folklore."

In 1994, Forrest published a collection of essays entitled *Relocations of the Spirit.* Culled largely from his articles and reviews in periodicals, *Relocations* contains Forrest's thoughts on various prominent African-American figures, including Toni Morrison, Ralph Ellison, and Billie Holiday, as well as white writers, focusing substantially on William Faulkner. A *Kirkus Reviews* critic comments that *Relocations* is "lit-crit of a milder sort, not so dense that you can't more or less follow it," and concludes that some may find the collection "luminous, others windy." Donna Seaman in *Booklist* claims that the same "exhilarating and confounding atmosphere of talk" that was evident in *Divine Days* is also evident in *Relocations,* adding that Forrest moves "easily from memory to anecdote to musings on questions of faith, race, pride, prejudice, politics, justice, and art."

BIOGRAPHICAL/CRITICAL SOURCES:

BOOKS

Contemporary Authors Autobiography Series, Volume 7, Gale (Detroit, MI), 1988.
Contemporary Literary Criticism, Volume 4, Gale, 1975.
Dictionary of Literary Biography, Volume 33: *Afro-American Fiction Writers after 1955,* Gale, 1984.
Lee, A. Robert, *Black Fiction: New Studies in the Afro-American Novel since 1945,* Barnes & Noble (New York City), 1980.

PERIODICALS

Black World, January, 1974.
Booklist, May 15, 1977, p. 1399; July, 1992; February 15, 1994, p. 1052.
Chicago Tribune Book World, February 5, 1984.
College Language Association Journal, December, 1978.
Harvard Advocate, Volume CVII, number 4, 1974.
Kirkus Reviews, December 15, 1993, p. 1565.
Massachusetts Review, winter, 1977.
New Leader, July 9, 1973.
New York Times, June 8, 1973.
New York Times Book Review, October 21, 1973; May 1, 1977; February 26, 1984; July 25, 1993; December 5, 1993.
Publishers Weekly, March 21, 1977, pp. 79-80.
Review of Contemporary Fiction, spring, 1994.
Tribune Books (Chicago), August 2, 1992.

FRIEDMAN, Bruce Jay   1930-

PERSONAL: Born April 26, 1930, in New York, NY; son of Irving (a manufacturer) and Molly (Liebowitz) Friedman; married Ginger Howard (an actress and model), June 13, 1954 (divorced, 1978); married Patricia J. O'Donohue, July 3, 1983; children: (first marriage) Josh Alan, Drew Samuel, Kipp Adam; (second marriage) Molly. *Education:* University of Missouri, B.J., 1951.

ADDRESSES: Home—P.O. Box 746, Water Mill, NY 11976. *Agent*—Candida Donadio, 231 West 22nd St., New York, NY 10011.

CAREER: Writer. Magazine Management Co., New York, NY, editorial director, 1954-66. *Military service:* U.S. Air Force, 1951-53.

MEMBER: PEN, Phi Sigma Delta.

AWARDS, HONORS: With Lowell Ganz and Babaloo Mandel, nomination for best original screenplay, Academy of Motion Picture Arts and Sciences, 1985, for *Splash!*

WRITINGS:

Stern (novel; also see below), Simon & Schuster (New York City), 1962, reprinted, Atlantic Monthly Press (New York City), 1990.
Far from the City of Class, and Other Stories, Frommer-Pasmantier (New York City), 1963.
A Mother's Kisses (novel; also see below), Simon & Schuster, 1964.
(Editor and author of introduction) *Black Humor* (anthology), Bantam (New York City), 1965.
Stern [and] *A Mother's Kisses,* Simon & Schuster, 1966.
Black Angels (stories), Simon & Schuster, 1966.
(Contributor with Gregory Corso and others) *Pardon Me, Sir, But Is My Eye Hurting Your Elbow?,* Geis, 1968.
The Dick (novel), Knopf (New York City), 1970.
About Harry Towns (novel), Knopf, 1974, reprinted, Atlantic Monthly Press, 1990.
The Lonely Guy's Book of Life (essays), McGraw (New York City), 1978, published as *The Lonely Guy,* McGraw, 1984.
Let's Hear It for a Beautiful Guy, and Other Works of Short Fiction, Fine, 1984.
Tokyo Woes (novel), Fine, 1985.
The Current Climate (novel), Atlantic Monthly Press, 1989.

The Slightly Older Guy (nonfiction), Simon & Schuster, 1995.

The Collected Short Fiction of Bruce Jay Friedman, Fine, 1995.

A Father's Kisses, Fine, 1996.

PLAYS

23 Pat O'Brien Movies (one-act), produced Off-Broadway on a triple bill, with *The Floor,* by May Swenson, and *Miss Pete,* by Andrew Glaze, as *Double Opposites,* at American Place Theatre, May 11, 1966.

Scuba Duba: A Tense Comedy (first produced Off-Broadway at New Theatre, October 10, 1967), Simon & Schuster, 1968.

A Mother's Kisses (musical; based on Friedman's novel of the same name), first produced in New Haven, CT, September 21, 1968.

Steambath (first produced Off-Broadway at Truck and Warehouse Theatre, June, 1970), Knopf, 1971.

(With Jacques Levy, and co-director) *First Offenders,* produced in New York, 1973.

A Foot In the Door, produced at American Place Theatre, 1979.

Have You Spoken to Any Jews Lately?, produced in New York City at the American Jewish Theatre, 1995.

SCREENPLAYS

Stir Crazy, Columbia, 1980.

(With Carl Gottlieb and Robert Boris) *Doctor Detroit* (based on a story by Friedman), Universal, 1983.

(With Lowell Ganz and Babaloo Mandel) *Splash!* (based on a screen story by Friedman), Buena Vista, 1984.

ADAPTATIONS: The film *The Heartbreak Kid,* based on a story by Friedman, was produced by Palomar Pictures in 1972; *The Lonely Guy,* a film based on Friedman's essay collection *The Lonely Guy's Book of Life,* was produced by Universal in 1984; the film option for *Scuba Duba: A Tense Comedy* has been acquired by Filmways; screen rights for *Stern* and *The Dick* have been sold; *Steambath* was adapted for television and produced for the Public Broadcasting System.

WORK IN PROGRESS: A novel and a play.

SIDELIGHTS: Although Bruce Jay Friedman trained to be a journalist, he established himself as a popular novelist, short-story writer, and playwright in the mid-1960s. "Labeled a black humorist, an ambiguous term he himself coined, Friedman caricatures the lives of neurotic, partially assimilated Jewish-Americans," according to *Dictionary of Literary Biography* writer Evelyn Avery. With his first novel, *Stern,* in fact, Friedman prefigured the success of such other Jewish-American wits as Philip Roth and Woody Allen with his stories of "Jews alienated from Christian America and ignorant of their own roots," as Avery sees it. "Episodically structured and very colloquial, Friedman's fiction depicts an absurd and fragmented America. In such a world, the individual is weakened; the family is perverted; and the once taboo—adultery, alcoholism, drug abuse, and random violence—becomes common."

Stern is true to these themes. The novel's title character is a thirty-four-year-old suburbanite who, despite his best efforts, cannot assimilate into "mainstream" American life. Everything goes wrong for Stern—his homelife is a wreck, as is his house; the entire neighborhood seems anti-Semitic. But the protagonist is determined to prevail. "No matter that it takes him two hours to commute each way,. . . or that the shrubs outside develop a mysterious cancer so they're naked on one side (they look better in the winter)—life can be beautiful," as *Village Voice* critic Eliot Fremont-Smith remarks. "This is cruel, sadistic stuff, and helplessly funny," Fremont-Smith adds. "Stern has no airs; violent fantasies notwithstanding, he is a truly decent man—liberal, kind, eager to make the best of an extremely lousy lot. His urge to 'belong' isn't selfish; what he wants, really, is to enhance the spirit of community, do human good. It's the world that's grotesque, indecent, vengeful for no reason. And one laughs because Stern is so relentlessly naive and also because he is so *right,* which brings pain. *Stern* is—black humor is—the retelling of *Job.* Only this Job gets an ulcer instead of a benediction."

Friedman followed *Stern* with a short-story collection, *Far from the City of Class, and Other Stories,* and in 1964 produced his second novel, the well-received *A Mother's Kisses.* Joseph, the main character in this work, "is a younger version of Stern," as Karen Rood notes in another *Dictionary of Literary Biography* piece. Instead of a wife and children to harry him, though, Joseph finds himself a slave to his mother, Meg, a flamboyant, oversexed woman whose "favorite joke is to insist that people probably mistake her and [her son] for lovers," as Rood writes. "What is more, his mother's control extends to all aspects of his life. Joseph seems incapable of making the simplest choices. . . . But despite her image of herself as a person of influence who can make things happen her way, his mother is nearly as inept as Joseph."

Despite Joseph's obvious problems, *A Mother's Kisses* presents "an unusually happy description of the pains, fears and sexual experiments of adolescence: a sane and touching picture of an unusually close mother-son relationship; and an engaging account of Jewishness," says a *Times Literary Supplement* critic. And *Chicago Tribune Book World* writer Clarence Peterson hails the novel as a comic masterpiece and calls Joseph's "seductive, possessive, embarrassing mother" one of the "strongest characters in recent fiction."

By 1970 Friedman's reputation as a black humorist preceded most critical views of his work, and many reviewers agreed that the author's third novel, *The Dick,* was not well served by Friedman's sense of the absurd. The tale of Kenneth LePeters (ne Sussman), a deskbound homicide inspector who feels inadequate because his badge is only half the size of the badges of his colleagues who work the streets, *The Dick* examines LePeters's reactions to failure and depression, liberal anxiety, and racist underpinnings. "What was so interesting in Friedman's first two novels, *Stern* and *A Mother's Kisses*—a wildly imaginative gift for characters with unique personality quirks—seems a gimmick in this unsolid novel," writes Haskel Frankel in *Saturday Review.* "The characters come through, not as participants in a black comedy but as inventions, each with shtick attached. There is something outlandish about everyone; they are characters not in a novel, but in search of one."

"More a collection of short stories with the same central character than a unified novel, *About Harry Towns* [Friedman's 1974 book] returns to the theme of the inner life lurking beneath the public image," remarks Rood. Harry Towns, like his creator, is a successful writer in his mid-forties, separated from his wife and tasting the array of pleasures that Los Angeles has to offer. "Shortly after our introduction to him, Harry returns to Manhattan, where we see him ensconced in a deluxe high-rise apartment,. . . stalking and snaring as many young women as will have him," Jane Larkin Crain explains in a *Saturday Review* article. But Harry, awash in material delights, nonetheless is a sad, desperate man. Addicted to alcohol and cocaine, his life "grows tawdry as the

language with which Friedman describes it," notes *Washington Post Book World* critic Toby Thompson. Harry's solution is to abandon his wild lifestyle and to cultivate "a semi-contemplative life alone: Jogging, reading old classics, enjoying women as friends, eating simply, facing the prospect of 10 years hard work,. . . [and suddenly Towns] is back on his feet," Thompson relates. What the author has done with *About Harry Towns,* the critic concludes, is to have "created a character straight out of a fiction writer's dreams: unique, haunting and completely memorable. Short fiction is possibly the most demanding prose medium, in that one has so little space to sketch so much. Each of Friedman's Harry Towns stories stands on its own . . . and each complements the other brilliantly. The book is novel, it is short fiction, it is essay. It is a goddamn heartbreaking delight and you are a fool if you miss it."

Harry Towns's dramatic turnabout—from playboy to homebound bachelor—may have foretold the theme to Friedman's next publication, *The Lonely Guy's Book of Life.* In this collection of essays, the author provides descriptions of and advice to the legions of solitary men (and their female counterparts, the Lonely Gals) who, Friedman says, have missed out on the legendary swinging singlehood. Such chapters as "The Lonely Guy's Apartment" (chosen for its chumminess, humility, and nap potential), and "Eating Alone in Restaurants" (where Friedman suggests displaying a walkie-talkie, so that the lone diner will be taken for a daring undercover cop on a stakeout) are played for laughs. But "on another level, Friedman appears to be getting at soberer matters here," muses *New Republic* reviewer Peter LaSalle. "What makes this writing more than just the strutting of a stand-up comic is the pain whispering behind the gags. . . . Friedman is implying that the embarrassment of loneliness is worse than the loneliness itself."

While LaSalle mentions that the humor in *The Lonely Guy's Book of Life* can be hit-or-miss at times, he and *New York Times Book Review* critic Herbert Gold share the view that the tract has value as a comment on today's society. To Gold, "a combination of subtle chisel and naked need is what makes the lonely guy book work so well. This is not exactly laugh-clown-laugh time; it's time for the clowns to look at themselves."

Mike Halsey, the hero of Friedman's 1985 novel *Tokyo Woes,* follows in the author's tradition of lonely guys. Mike's impulsive decision to change his life results in a trip to Japan, where he meets an Asian version of himself, William ("Call Me Bill") Atenabe, who takes Mike into his offbeat family, "a lineup that could keep a sitcom in business for several seasons," as Richard Fuller points out in the *New York Times Book Review*. In fact, several critics likened *Tokyo Woes* to a situation comedy—effective as a gag manual, ineffective as a novel. "Merely being funny is never enough," in *Chicago Tribune Book World* writer L. J. Davis's opinion. "It is important to be funny about something and [in this book] Bruce Jay Friedman isn't." And while Michiko Kakutani cites a lack of "the anger and tenderness" that marked many of the author's earlier works, the *New York Times* critic finds that the novel's slapstick routines "make for tangy, if unfilling, reading."

In *The Current Climate,* Friedman offers a sequel to *About Harry Towns*. In this new novel, Harry lives in a small town outside New York City. He is remarried and has a young daughter. His career is on the upswing, having written a proposal for a television show starring a dog. He seems to have made a turnabout from his earlier days and nights of cocaine and womanizing. Yet, he still makes occasional trips to the city to relive the old days. It is in this overlapping of old and new that Harry struggles to maintain his self-respect. And, as Bill Franzen explains in the *New York Times Book Review,* "Maintaining some dignity, some little bit of self-respect, is pretty much what it comes down to, too, for the leading men in Mr. Friedman's brilliantly funny novels 'Stern,' 'A Mother's Kisses,' 'About Harry Towns,' and, most recently, 'The Current Climate.'"

In this sequel, Friedman is "funny and reliably irrelevant," comments a *Time* reviewer. *New York Times Book Review* contributor Craig Bloom admits that "the intended humor occasionally works," but he adds, "Mr. Friedman's look at the movie business and the rest of Harry's world lacks incisiveness. It remains inconsequential and flat." In the opinion of *New York* contributor John Taylor, the book works on a different level. "In Harry Towns [Friedman] has created a true Hemingwayesque character. Towns is a man in pursuit of existentially challenging Hemingwayesque experience." Even so, Taylor concludes, "While it's a funny book and a good book, *The Current Climate* isn't a big book." To this comment, Friedman has a response. As he told Taylor, "What's wrong with a bunch of little ones? All Voltaire's big ones are moldering in the library. What people read is *Candide,* the little one."

Though he has received a great deal of critical attention for his novels, Friedman enjoys an avid following for his shorter fiction. *The Collected Short Fiction of Bruce Jay Friedman* was published in 1995 for these readers and to bring the stories to a wider audience. In the words of *Newsweek* contributor David Gates, "The return to print of some of Friedman's best work is a bona fide literary event." The collection reveals Friedman turning his comic eye on a wide variety of people and issues. "Mr. Friedman's stories are about psychiatrists, Jewish mothers, Hollywood, death, the Air Force, cocaine, sex, getting cheated on, suicide, guilt and exquisitely bizarre situations," writes Christopher Buckley in the *New York Times Book Review*. These stories, according to Buckley, "tend to divide into two kinds: the first leave you whispering, 'Wow'; the second go whistling over your head like an artillery round and leave you muttering, 'Huh?'" Or as Gates characterizes the works, "Only half of these stories resemble the post-[Raymond] Carver realism now in vogue. Elsewhere Friedman exploits the conventions of pulp fiction . . . and his fantasy parables might now be deemed subliterary for their snap endings and over-the-top fun." Whatever their effect or affinity, "Shame, anxiety, self-delusion and miscommunication drive his stories," maintains Gates, "and like [Harold] Pinter or [David] Mamet—or Carver—he makes his characters' blurtings into out-of-kilter poetry." "Mr. Friedman has been likened to everyone from J. D. Salinger to Woody Allen," notes Buckley. "No further comparisons are necessary."

Friedman the playwright and screenwriter has seen a number of commercial and critical successes, including the acerbic 1967 stage comedy *Scuba Duba: A Tense Comedy*. This play "examines the racial attitudes of middle-class liberals, an issue which first appears in *Stern*," according to Rood in the *Dictionary of Literary Biography*. "When Harold Wonder discovers that his wife is having an affair with a black man, he immediately imagines the man to be a black skin diver who fits the typical oversexed, fast-talking stereotype. On the contrary, the man Wonder's wife has actually run off with wears Brooks Brothers suits and writes poetry for the *Partisan Review;* he is a middle-class liberal intellectual."

Friedman's play *Have You Spoken to Any Jews Lately?* is another of the author's dark comedies. "In the course of the two acts, played as very dark, but often wildly funny vaudeville entertainment," *New York Times* theater critic Vincent Canby explains, "Jack and Danny [the main characters] become convinced that a new Holocaust is at hand. They are assaulted by the past and present, by memories and fantasies, which are acted out, and by their own bizarre panic." Frank Scheck concedes in the *Christian Science Monitor* that "there are plenty of outrageous laughs" in the play, but the reviewer feels that Friedman's premise in the play fell short as an overall comedy. Canby finds more merit in the play. "There's a lot of anger, fear and compassion," he writes, "sometimes expressed in terms that are as horrific as they are funny." Canby also addresses criticism that the play is targeted too narrowly. "It would be a mistake to consider the play as narrowly ethnic as it sounds. Beneath its engagingly disreputable particulars, the play is another consideration of the same kind of moral aimlessness Sam Shepard examined in 'Simpatico.'"

Less lofty themes characterize Friedman's film scripts. *The Lonely Guy* and *Doctor Detroit,* both based on his earlier writings, did not fare as well with audiences as did *Stir Crazy* and *Splash!,* each a box-office hit. Perhaps not coincidentally, most of Friedman's screen heroes display the moods and motivations of the author's prototypical urban lonely guy.

BIOGRAPHICAL/CRITICAL SOURCES:

BOOKS

Contemporary Literary Criticism, Gale (Detroit), Volume 3, 1975, Volume 5, 1976, Volume 56, 1989.
Dictionary of Literary Biography, Gale, Volume 2: *American Novelists since World War II,* 1978, Volume 28: *Twentieth-Century American-Jewish Fiction Writers,* 1984.
Gilman, Richard, *Common and Uncommon Masks: Writings on Theatre 1961-1970,* Random House (New York City), 1971.
Hyman, Stanley Edgar, *Standards: A Chronicle of Books for Our Time,* Horizon, 1966.
Schulz, Max F., *Black Humor Fiction of the Sixties: Pluralist Definition of Man and His World,* Ohio University Press (Athens, OH), 1973.
Schulz, Max F., *Bruce Jay Friedman,* Twayne (Boston), 1974.

PERIODICALS

Atlantic Monthly, May, 1974.
Chicago Tribune, January 2, 1979.

Chicago Tribune Book World, September 16, 1984; July 7, 1985.
Christian Science Monitor, February 2, 1995, p. 11.
Commonweal, December 7, 1962, p. 294; November 20, 1964, p. 302.
Esquire, August, 1976.
Library Journal, August, 1989, p. 162; May 1, 1995, p. 96.
Los Angeles Times, September 24, 1984; May 16, 1985.
Nation, December 1, 1962, p. 380; September 21, 1964, p. 142; November 23, 1970, p. 536.
New Leader, March 26, 1979, p. 12.
New Republic, October 8, 1966; July 27, 1974; December 16, 1978, p. 29.
Newsweek, July 13, 1970, p. 101; November 6, 1995, p. 88.
New York, October 9, 1989, p. 46.
New Yorker, October 21, 1967, p. 82; July 11, 1970, p. 48; June 10, 1985.
New York Review of Books, November 5, 1970, p. 22.
New York Times, September 23, 1962; March 8, 1979; August 29, 1984, p. C21; April 27, 1985, p. 13; January 24, 1995, p. C13.
New York Times Book Review, August 16, 1964, p. 5; October 2, 1966, p. 4; August 16, 1970; September 27, 1970; June 23, 1974; February 11, 1979, p. 10; November 18, 1984, p. 32; May 19, 1985, p. 21; October 1, 1989, p. 26; June 18, 1995, p. 34; November 5, 1995, p. 9.
New York Times Magazine, January 14, 1968.
Notre Dame Review, March 1, 1974.
People, April 30, 1979.
Saturday Review, October 13, 1962, p. 38; September 19, 1970; June 1, 1974.
Studies in Short Fiction, fall, 1973.
Studies in the Twentieth Century, spring, 1972, p. 15.
Time, December 21, 1962; October 20, 1967, p. 82; July 13, 1970; September 7, 1970; April 22, 1985, p. 70; October 16, 1989, p. 90.
Times Literary Supplement, June 17, 1965; April 16, 1971; February 14, 1975.
Tribune Books, September 16, 1984; July 7, 1985; September 16, 1990, p. 23.
Variety, January 30, 1995. p. 57.
Village Voice, February 23, 1982; October 4, 1983.
Washington Post Book World, September 13, 1970, p. 4; June 16, 1974; November 26, 1989, p. 3.

G

GERAS, Adele (Daphne)   1944-

PERSONAL: Surname begins with a hard "G" and rhymes with "terrace"; first name accented over the first "e"; born March 15, 1944, in Jerusalem, Palestine (now Israel); daughter of Laurence David (a lawyer) and Leah (Hamburger) Weston; married Norman Geras (a lecturer and writer), August 7, 1967; children: Sophie, Jenny. *Education:* St. Hilda's College, Oxford, B.A., 1966. *Religion:* Jewish. *Avocational interests:* "I enjoy the movies more than anything and read an enormous amount of everything, but my great love is thrillers and detective stories. I am very lazy, and like sleeping in the afternoons."

ADDRESSES: Home—10 Danesmoor Rd., Manchester M20 3JS, England. *Agent*—Laura Cecil, 17 Alwyne Villas, London N1 2HG, England.

CAREER: Fairfield High School, Droylsden, Lancashire, England, French teacher, 1968-71; writer, 1976—. Actress in *Four Degrees Over* (play), London, 1966.

AWARDS, HONORS: Taylor Award, 1991, for *My Grandmother's Stories: A Collection of Jewish Folktales;* National Jewish Book Council Award, 1994, for *Golden Windows and Other Stories of Jerusalem.*

WRITINGS:

CHILDREN'S FICTION

Tea at Mrs. Manderby's, illustrated by Doreen Caldwell, Hamish Hamilton (London), 1976.

Apricots at Midnight and Other Stories from a Patchwork Quilt, illustrated by Caldwell, Hamish Hamilton, 1977, Atheneum (New York City), 1982.

Beyond the Cross-Stitch Mountains, illustrated by Mary Wilson, Hamish Hamilton, 1977.

The Painted Garden, illustrated by Caldwell, Hamish Hamilton, 1979.

A Thousand Yards of Sea, illustrated by Joanna Troughton, Hodder & Stoughton (London), 1980.

The Rug that Grew, illustrated by Priscilla Lamont, Hamish Hamilton, 1981.

The Christmas Cat, illustrated by Caldwell, Hamish Hamilton, 1983.

Little Elephant's Moon, Illustrated by Linda Birch, Hamish Hamilton, 1986.

Ritchie's Rabbit, illustrated by Vanessa Julian-Ottie, Hamish Hamilton, 1986, Random House (New York City), 1987.

Finding Annabel, illustrated by Alan Marks, Hamish Hamilton, 1987.

Fishpie for Flamingoes, illustrated by Birch, Hamish Hamilton, 1987.

The Fantora Family Files, illustrated by Tony Ross, Hamish Hamilton, 1988.

The Strange Bird, illustrated by Birch, Hamish Hamilton, 1988.

The Coronation Picnic, illustrated by Frances Wilson, Hamish Hamilton, 1989.

Bunk Bed Night, Dent (London), 1990.

My Grandmother's Stories: A Collection of Jewish Folktales, illustrated by Jael Jordan, Knopf (New York City), 1990, Heinemann (London), 1990.

Nina's Magic, Hamish Hamilton, 1990.

Pink Medicine, Dent, 1990.

A Magic Birthday, Simon & Schuster (London), 1992.

The Fantora Family Photographs, illustrated by Ross, Hamish Hamilton, 1993.

Golden Windows and Other Stories of Jerusalem, HarperCollins (New York City), 1993, Heinemann, 1995.

Baby's Bedclothes, illustrated by Prue Greener, Longman (Essex, England), 1994.

The Dolls' House, illustrated by Greener, Longman, 1994.

Keith's Croak, illustrated by Greener, Longman, 1994.

Mary's Meadow, illustrated by Greener, Longman, 1994.

Mimi; and, Apricot Max, illustrated by Teresa O'Brien, Longman, 1994.

Josephine, illustrated by O'Brien, Longman, 1994.

The Return of Archibald Gribbet, illustrated by Sumiko, Longman, 1994.

Toey, illustrated by Duncan Smith, Heinemann, 1994.

Gilly the Kid, illustrated by Sue Heap, Simon & Schuster, 1995.

Little Swan, illustrated by Johanna Westerman, Random House, 1995.

Stories for Bedtime (with cassette), illustrated by Amanda Benjamin, HarperCollins, 1995.

A Candle in the Dark (part of the "Flashbacks" historical fiction series), A. & C. Black (London), 1995.

Contributor to periodicals, including *Cricket.*

YOUNG ADULT FICTION

The Girls in the Velvet Frame, Hamish Hamilton, 1978, Atheneum, 1979.

The Green behind the Glass, Hamish Hamilton, 1982, published as *Snapshots of Paradise: Love Stories,* Atheneum, 1984.

Other Echoes, Atheneum, 1983.

Voyage, Atheneum, 1983.

Letters of Fire and Other Unsettling Stories, Hamish Hamilton, 1984.

Happy Endings, Hamish Hamilton, 1986, Harcourt (San Diego), 1991.

Daydreams on Video, Hodder & Stoughton, 1989.

The Tower Room, Hamish Hamilton, 1990, Harcourt, 1992.

Watching the Roses, Hamish Hamilton, 1991, Harcourt, 1992.

Pictures of the Night, Harcourt, 1993.

A Lane to the Land of the Dead, Hamish Hamilton, 1994.

OTHER

(With Pauline Stainer) *Up on the Roof* (adult poetry), Smith Doorstep (Huddersfield, England), 1987.

Yesterday (memoirs), Walker (London), 1992.

Voices from the Dolls' House (adult poetry), Rockingham Press (Ware, England), 1994.

Geras's work has been translated into several languages, including Dutch and German.

SIDELIGHTS: A childhood spent following her father on his wide-ranging assignments for the Colonial Service had a great influence on the work of novelist and short story writer Adele Geras. Using her experiences of historic Jerusalem, where she was born, exotic Africa, and Great Britain, where she attended boarding school and now lives, Geras weaves a strong sense of place and time into her fiction. "I write because I enjoy it," Geras once told *CA.* "I write about places and things that have been important to me in one way or another." Her portraits of vivid characters, also often drawn from recollections of the people she encountered during her childhood years, have been praised by reviewers and readers alike. Sea travel, Jewish culture, and a love of tradition also play strong roles in shaping her stories for children and teenage readers.

"I used to write a lot as a child," Geras explained to *CA,* "and then I found that what happened was, as you got more and more educated and had more and more academic work given to you, you had less and less time to do your own stuff. And of course the other thing is that, as you become an adolescent, you become very self-conscious, and you get the idea that if you can't be Tolstoy or Jane Austen, then you're not going to be anybody at all and you should stop. So I did stop when I was about fourteen, and I didn't start again until after my daughter was born. Then I rediscovered what fun it was—which is what every child knows."

Geras's first attempt at writing as an adult was spurred on by a competition in the London *Times.* "As soon as I saw the contest announced,. . . I wrote a story and sent it off," she recalled in an essay for *Something about the Author Autobiography Series* (*SAAS*), "and although it did not win, it did become the starting point for *Apricots at Midnight.* It's a ghost story called 'Rose' and the moment I'd finished it, I knew that this was what I wanted to do from now on."

"Rose" was be joined by several other short tales and published by Geras in 1977 as *Apricots at Midnight,* a collection of story "patches" narrated by Aunt Piney, a dressmaker, as she works on a quilt with her young niece. A *Publishers Weekly* reviewer finds the collection an "unusual and entrancing book," while *Horn Book* contributor Kate M. Flanagan praises the tales as "rich in detail and delightfully recounted." Geras's enthusiasm for her newfound craft also found an outlet in writing picture books for young children; the first, *Tea at Mrs. Manderby's,* is a story about a young girl who resigns herself to taking afternoon tea with an elderly neighbor at her parent's urging. Several more books for young readers would follow, including *A Thousand Yards of Sea,* about a fisherman who releases a mermaid from his net and is rewarded with beautiful sea-colored cloth that the women of his village make into skirts; and *Toey,* about two children who hope for a new pet and end up with a pair of playful kittens. Geras has also published many short stories in magazines such as *Cricket;* several of her tales have also been collected in 1995's *Stories for Bedtime.*

In addition to short stories and picture books for young children, Geras is the author of several collections of short fiction with older readers in mind. In 1983 she wrote *The Green behind the Glass,* a set of eight tales about young love that was released in the United States as *Snapshots of Paradise: Love Stories.* Called "an intriguing departure from the sunny sentimentality of so many romance collections for young adults" by *Booklist* reviewer Stephanie Zvirin, *The Green behind the Glass* includes "Don't Sing Love Songs," narrated by a young woman who is on her own with a friend in Paris until their shared attraction towards handsome Jim threatens their friendship; the title story, in which a woman's older sister knows herself to be the real object of the sister's now-dead fiance's true affections; and "Tea in the Wendy House," which tells of a young, pregnant woman's lament for her soon-to-be-lost youth as she faces a shotgun wedding and a future as wife and mother in a tiny house. *Horn Book* writer Mary M. Burns hails the variety of styles and settings of Geras's love stories, calling them "distinguished by perceptive insight into human nature, dexterity in plot construction, and a sense of style remarkable for its readability and its imagery and constraint."

In 1994's *A Lane to the Land of the Dead,* Geras uses suspense and elements of the supernatural to add spice and a touch of melancholy to the lives of her young protagonists. "Geras shows her usual lightness

of touch," Elspeth S. Scott observes in *School Librarian,* predicting the collection would have wide appeal. In contrast, the five tales in *Golden Windows and Other Stories of Jerusalem* show readers what life was like in early twentieth-century Jerusalem. In "Beyond the Cross-Stitch Mountains," one story from this collection, eleven-year-old Daskeh conspires with friend Danny to escape the care of her aunt Phina and visit his own aunt, despite the danger in leaving the bomb shelter where they routinely spend the nights during Israel's 1948 War for Independence. And "Dreams of Fire" shows the aftereffects of this experience on young Danny as memories of death and violence return to haunt him in the form of a memorial built to honor the War. Reviewer Ellen Mandel praises *Golden Windows* in *Booklist* as "well-written, laced with subtleties of history, and rich in personal emotion."

In addition to being included in *Golden Windows,* Geras's "Beyond the Cross-Stitch Mountains" is the title of another book for younger readers that draws on the author's Jewish heritage. Similarly, the 1978 novel *The Girls in the Velvet Frame* takes as its setting the city of Jerusalem in 1913. It tells the story of five girls whose only brother, Isaac, has left for the United States and from whom they have not heard for months. "The appeal of this charming book comes . . . from the accurate, penetrating and quite unsentimental portraits of the five children and of their elders," Marcus Crouch notes in the *Times Literary Supplement.* Cyrisse Jaffee similarly acclaims Geras's characters, and adds in *School Library Journal* that "marvelous descriptions of time and place add contours."

The 1983 novel *Voyage* also focuses on the history of the Jewish people, as it follows a group of characters who flee from the poverty of Eastern Europe by enduring a fifteen-day crossing of the Atlantic Ocean aboard a tightly packed ship. The sight of the Statue of Liberty in New York Harbor at journey's end is the beginning of a new life for the characters. The book's vignettes "cleverly [reveal] not only the happenings on board but the thoughts, hopes, fears, and memories of the little community," Ethel L. Heins writes in *Horn Book.*

Geras has also written several other novels for young adult readers. Among the most notable are three books that comprise her "Egerton Hall" series. Set in Egerton Hall boarding school in 1963, the stories revolve around three friends—Alice, Bella, and Megan. In 1990's *The Tower Room,* Megan becomes a modern-day Rapunzel as she is freed from a lack-luster tower room in the boarding school after falling in love with a handsome young laboratory assistant at Egerton Hall. In 1992's *Watching the Roses,* Geras draws from the Sleeping Beauty legend in telling Alice's story. On the night of her eighteenth birthday party, Alice is attacked and raped by the son of her family's gardener. Her story is told to her diary as she tries to recover from the shock of the event. Time seems to stop while Alice deals with her concerns over how the rape will affect her relationship with Jean-Luc, her own handsome prince. Florence H. Munat praises *Watching the Roses* in *Voice of Youth Advocates,* noting that Geras "has deftly added just the right modern twists and details to allure older readers back to the story that enchanted them as children." Geras's fairy-tale trilogy is completed with a modern re-telling of Snow White's story, casting eighteen-year-old Bella in the lead. *Pictures of the Night* features an evil stepmother, Marjorie, who becomes so jealous of her stepdaughter's budding singing career that she tries to kill the young woman. In a *Kirkus Reviews* assessment of the novel, one critic calls Geras "a writer distinguished for her imaginative power and fresh, vivid writing." "The fairy tale parallels become more apparent as the trilogy proceeds," notes Sheila Ray in *Twentieth-Century Young Adult Writers,* "gradually moving through the momentous year when the girls fall in love and face their emerging sexuality, creating a powerful tour de force, outstanding in young adult literature."

BIOGRAPHICAL/CRITICAL SOURCES:

BOOKS

Something about the Author Autobiography Series, Volume 21, Gale (Detroit), 1996.
Twentieth-Century Young Adult Writers, St. James Press (Detroit), 1994.

PERIODICALS

Booklist, August 1984, p. 1609; October 15, 1993.
Books for Your Children, autumn, 1992, p. 27.
Christian Science Monitor, May 13, 1983.
Horn Book, February, 1983, pp. 43-44; August, 1983, p. 452; September/October, 1984, p. 596; March/April, 1993, p. 211.
Junior Bookshelf, December, 1976, p. 326; June, 1994, p. 100; August, 1994, p. 134.
Kirkus Reviews, September 1, 1984, p. J8; March 15, 1993.
Publishers Weekly, October 15, 1982, p. 66.

School Librarian, June, 1983, pp. 162, 165; November, 1992, p. 157; May, 1994, p. 60; May, 1995, p. 77.
School Library Journal, September, 1979, p. 138.
Times Literary Supplement, September 29, 1978, p. 1083; March 27, 1981, p. 340; January 27, 1984; November 30, 1984; June 6, 1986.
Voice of Youth Advocates, December, 1992, p. 278.

*   *   *

GIBSON, William (Ford)   1948-

PERSONAL: Born March 17, 1948, in Conway, SC; son of William Ford (a contractor) and Otey (a homemaker; maiden name, Williams) Gibson; married Deborah Thompson (a language instructor), June, 1972; children: Graeme Ford Gibson, Claire Thompson Gibson. *Education:* University of British Columbia, B.A., 1977.

ADDRESSES: Agent—Martha Millard Literary Agency, 204 Park Ave., Madison, NJ 07940; (for film and television) Martin S. Shapiro, Shapiro-Lichtman Talent, 8827 Beverly Blvd., Los Angeles, CA 90048.

CAREER: Writer.

AWARDS, HONORS: Nebula Award nomination from Science Fiction Writers of America, c. 1983, for short story "Burning Chrome"; Hugo Award, World Science Fiction Society, 1984, Philip K. Dick Award, Philadelphia Science Fiction Society, 1984, Nebula Award, Science Fiction Writers of America, 1984, Porgie Award, *West Coast Review of Books,* 1984, and Ditmar Award from Australian National Science Fiction Convention, all for *Neuromancer.*

WRITINGS:

Neuromancer (novel; first in "Cyberspace" trilogy), Ace Books (New York City), 1984.
Count Zero (novel; second in "Cyberspace" trilogy), Arbor House, 1986.
(With John Shirley, Bruce Sterling, and Michael Swanwick) *Burning Chrome* (short stories; includes "Burning Chrome," "Johnny Mnemonic," "New Rose Hotel," and one story with each coauthor), introduction by Sterling, Arbor House, 1986.

Mona Lisa Overdrive (novel; third in "Cyberspace" trilogy), Bantam (New York City), 1988.

Dream Jumbo (text to accompany performance art by Robert Longo), produced in Los Angeles, California, at UCLA Center for the Performing Arts, 1989.

(With Sterling) *The Difference Engine* (novel), Gollancz, 1990, Bantam, 1991.

(With Dennis Ashbaugh and Kevin Begos, Jr.) *Agrippa: A Book of the Dead* (limited edition book and computer disk), Kevin Begos Publishing, 1992.

Virtual Light, Bantam, 1993.

Johnny Mnemonic (screenplay), Tristar, 1995.

Work represented in anthologies, including *Shadows 4,* Doubleday, 1981; *Nebula Award Stories 17,* Holt, 1983; and *Mirrorshades: The Cyberpunk Anthology,* edited with an introduction by Sterling, Arbor House, 1986. Contributor of short stories, articles, and book reviews to periodicals, including *Omni, Rolling Stone,* and *Science Fiction Review.*

ADAPTATIONS: Neuromancer, featuring the music of Stuart Argabright, William Barg, Black Rain and the group U2, was recorded for Time Warner Audio Books in 1994.

WORK IN PROGRESS: Screenplay adaptations of his short stories "Burning Chrome" and "New Rose Hotel."

SIDELIGHTS: Science-fiction author William Gibson had published only a handful of short stories when he stunned readers with his debut novel, *Neuromancer.* Published in 1984, *Neuromancer* became the first work ever to sweep the major honors of science fiction—the Hugo, Nebula, and Philip K. Dick awards. Combining the hip cynicism of the rock music underground and the dizzying powers of high technology, the novel was hailed as the prototype of a new style of writing, promptly dubbed "cyberpunk." Gibson, who was also earning praise as a skillful prose stylist, disliked the trendy label but admitted that he was challenging science fiction traditions. "I'm not even sure what cyberpunk means," he told the *Philadelphia Inquirer,* "but I suppose it's useful as a tip-off to people that what they're going to read is a little wilder."

The surface features of Gibson's allegedly cyberpunk style—tough characters facing a tough world, frantic pacing, bizarre high-tech slang—alienated some reviewers. "Like punk rock . . . Cyberpunk caters to

the wish-fulfillment requirements of male teenagers," complained science-fiction novelist Thomas M. Disch in the *New York Times Book Review,* "and there is currently no more accomplished caterer than William Gibson." In *Science Fiction Review,* Andrew Andrews blasted the "style and execution" of *Count Zero,* a novel typical of Gibson's work during the 1980s. "It is hodgepodge; spastic; incomprehensible in spots, somehow just *too much,*" the reviewer declared. "I prefer a novel that is concise, with fleshy, human characters."

Beneath the flash, however, admirers detected a serious purpose. Writers like Gibson, suggested J. R. Wytenbroeck in *Canadian Literature,* are really describing the world "in which we live today, with all its problems taken to their logical extreme." In particular, the advance of technology is shown to cause as many problems as it solves. "Technology has *already* changed us, and now we have to figure out a way to stay sane," Gibson observed in *Rolling Stone.* "If you were to put this in terms of mainstream fiction and present readers with a conventional book about modern postindustrial anxiety, many of them would just push it aside. But if you put it in the context of science fiction, maybe you can get them to sit still for what you have to say." Along with "adrenalin verve and random pyrotechnics," wrote Colin Greenland in the *Times Literary Supplement,* Gibson's work is "intellectually substantial." "His style," Greenland wrote, "is deadpan and precise, with the tone of the classic crime thriller: canny, cool and undeceived, yet ultimately the very opposite of the callousness it imitates, because motivated by a desire for justice."

Gibson grew up in a small town in southwest Virginia, on the edge of the Appalachian Mountains. "It was a boring, culturally deprived environment," he recalled in the *Sacramento Union.* "The library burned down in 1910, and nobody bothered to rebuild it." In such a place, he told *Interview,* "science-fiction books were the only source I had for subversive information." By his late teens Gibson had left behind the conventional authors who filled the genre with shining cities and benevolent scientists. Instead he began to prefer iconoclasts, such as J. G. Ballard and Philip K. Dick, who described a grim and frightening future. Some of his favorites might not qualify with purists as science-fiction writers at all: both William S. Burroughs and Thomas Pynchon were intricate stylists whose core following was among literary intellectuals. Such writers used the fantastic element of science fiction as a device to explore the ugly potentials of the human heart. Science fiction, Gibson realized, was a way to comment on the reality of the present day.

The 1960s youth culture also drew Gibson's attention. (A long-term rock fan, he counts the hard-edged music of Lou Reed as a major influence.) In 1967 he dropped out of high school and journeyed to Canada, ending up in Toronto, which had a thriving hippie scene. "We had our own version of the Summer of Love there," he said in the *Sacramento Union*. "If I'd gone to New York or San Francisco, I can't imagine what would have happened to me." Not wanting to be drafted into the Vietnam War, he remained in Canada and eventually married. The couple settled in Vancouver, where their lives soon centered around the University of British Columbia (UBC)—Gibson's wife was a teacher and he was a "permanent pseudo-grad student" who earned his bachelor's degree shortly before he turned thirty. After graduating, "I was clueless," he recalled in the *Chicago Tribune*. "A lot of my friends were becoming lawyers and librarians, things that filled me with horror." So he became a science-fiction writer, even though at the time "it seemed like such a goofy, unhip thing to do," as he told *Rolling Stone*. Gibson began his career almost in spite of himself, after he enrolled in a science-fiction course at UBC in hope of an easy credit. Unwilling to submit a term paper, he accepted the teacher's challenge to compose a short story—an ordeal that lasted three months. As Gibson settled into life as a househusband, however, he realized that writing more stories was the best way he could earn money while watching over his children.

Gibson's writing blossomed with amazing speed. By the early 1980s he was a favorite of fiction editor Ellen Datlow, who helped make *Omni* magazine a showcase of rising science-fiction talent. In *Omni* stories such as "Johnny Mnemonic" (1981) and "Burning Chrome" (1982) Gibson began to sketch his own grim version of the future, peopled with what *Rolling Stone* called "high-tech lowlifes." The title character of "Johnny Mnemonic," for instance, stashes stolen computer data on a microchip in his brain. He is marked for murder by the Yakuza, a Japanese syndicate that has moved into high-tech crime, but he is saved by Molly Millions, a bionic hitwoman with razors implanted under her fingernails. "I thought I was on this literary kamikaze mission," Gibson informed *Rolling Stone*. "I thought my work was so disturbing it would be dismissed and ignored by all but a few people." Instead, on the

basis of a few short stories, he began to gain a powerful reputation: "Burning Chrome" was nominated for a Nebula Award, and Ace Books editor Terry Carr encouraged him to expand his vision into a novel. Meanwhile, "cyberpunk" was becoming a trend throughout the science-fiction world. After writing a third of his novel, Gibson went to see the 1982 film *Blade Runner,* director Ridley Scott's stylish, punked-out interpretation of a book by Philip K. Dick. "It looked so much like the inside of my head," reported Gibson in *Saturday Night,* "that I fled the theatre after about thirty minutes and have never seen the rest of it."

Neuromancer, together with its sequels *Count Zero* and *Mona Lisa Overdrive,* fleshes out the future society of Gibson's short stories. Here technology is the main source of power over others, and the multinational corporations that develop and control technology are more important than governments. The world is a bewildering splatter of cultures and subcultures; Gibson skirts the issue of whether the United States or Canada are still viable countries, but his multinationals are generally based in Europe or Japan. While shadowy figures run the world for their own benefit, a large underclass—the focus of Gibson's interest—endures amid pollution, overcrowding, and pointlessness. People commonly drug themselves with chemicals or with "simstims," a form of electronic drug that allows users to experience vicariously the life of another, more glamorous, human being.

Though such a future seems hopeless, Gibson remains in some sense a romantic, observers note, for he chronicles the efforts of individuals to carve out a life for themselves in spite of hostile surroundings. His misfit heroes often exist on the crime-infested fringes of society, thus lending his works some of the atmosphere of a traditional crime thriller. Along with the expected cast of smugglers, prostitutes, murderers, and thieves, Gibson celebrates a distinctly modern freebooter, the computer hacker. Computers of the future, Gibson posits, will be linked worldwide through "cyberspace"—an electronically generated alternate reality in which all data, and the security programs that protect it, will appear as a palpable three-dimensional universe. Computer operators will access cyberspace by plugging into it with their brains, and hackers—known as "cowboys"—will sneak in to steal data, fill their bank accounts with electronic money, or suffer death when a security program uses feedback to destroy their minds.

"The Street," wrote Gibson in *Rolling Stone,* "finds its own uses for things—uses the manufacturers never imagined."

Gibson's wandering youth did not hinder—and may have helped—his ability to create such a world. "I didn't invent most of what's strange in the [books'] dialogue," Gibson told the *Mississippi Review,* as quoted in *Whole Earth Review.* "There are so many cultures and subcultures around today that if you're willing to listen, you start picking up different phrases, inflections, metaphors everywhere you go. A lot of stuff in *Neuromancer* and *Count Zero* that people think is so futuristic is probably just 1969 Toronto dope-dealers' slang, or bikers' slang." Gibson lacked an education in computers, but he knew about computer people. "They have this whole style of language . . . which attracted me simply for the intensity with which they talked about their machines," he said in *Rolling Stone.* "I immediately heard in that a real echo of the teenagers I grew up with talking about cars." Cyberspace came from watching a new generation of youth in video arcades. "I could see in . . . their postures how *rapt* these kids were," Gibson informed *Mississippi Review,* adding: "Everyone who works with computers seems to develop an intuitive faith that there's some kind of actual *space* behind the screen."

The plots of Gibson's works, some reviewers suggest, are less important than the way of life he describes: even admirers find the narratives rather complicated and difficult to summarize. As Gibson told *Interview,* he doesn't "really start with stories" but prefers to assemble images, "like making a ball out of rubber bands." *Neuromancer* centers on Henry Case, a skilled computer "cowboy" who has been punished for his exploits by being given a powerful nerve poison that leaves him unable to plug into cyberspace. As the book opens he is scrounging a living on the seamy side of Japan's Chiba City when a mysterious patron offers him restorative surgery in exchange for more computer hacking. Case assents, and in the company of Molly (one of Gibson's many recurring characters) he travels from one bizarre setting to the next in pursuit of a goal he cannot even understand. Finally Case arrives on a space station controlled by the wealthy Tessier-Ashpool clan, a family of genetic clones that owns two Artificial Intelligences—powerful computers which, like humans, have self-awareness and free will. Case realizes that one of the computers, named Wintermute, has hired him to help it take control of the other,

named Neuromancer; the combined Artificial Intelligence that would result could break free of its human masters.

"*Neuromancer* was a bit hypermanic—simply from my terror at losing the reader's attention," Gibson recalled in *Rolling Stone.* For the sequel, *Count Zero,* "I aimed for a more deliberate pace. I also tried to draw the characters in considerable detail. People have children and dead parents in *Count Zero,* and that makes for different emotional territory." Thus instead of taking one main character on a manic ride throughout human society, *Count Zero* tells the stories of three more fleshed-out individuals whose lives gradually intertwine. The "Count Zero" of the title is really Bobby Newmark, a poor teenage computer "cowboy" with dreams of greatness. On his first illicit run into cyberspace, he finds it much more colorful than Case did a few years earlier: the Artificial Intelligences of *Neuromancer* seem to have broken apart into many cyberspace entities, some of whom manifest themselves as voodoo gods. The "gods" have human worshippers who take custody of Bobby after he apparently has a religious experience while he is hacking. Meanwhile, art dealer Marly Krushkova tries to find an artist with mysterious powers, only to encounter an old "cowboy" who also believes that God lives in cyberspace. And Turner, a mercenary who rounds up scientists for multinationals, finds himself the protector of a strange young woman named Angie Mitchell. Angie has a unique gift: her scientist father placed microchips in her brain that give her direct access to cyberspace and sometimes make her the mouthpiece for its ghostly inhabitants. "The resolution [of the plot] is figuratively left in the hands of the Haitian Computer Gods," wrote Dorothy Allison of the *Village Voice.* "They are particularly marvelous, considering that the traditional science-fiction model of an intelligent computer has been an emotionless logician."

Gibson's third novel, *Mona Lisa Overdrive,* "brilliantly pyramids the successes of its predecessors," wrote Edward Bryant in *Bloomsbury Review.* The book is set several years after *Count Zero,* using a similar structure of plot-lines that slowly interconnect. When *Mona Lisa* opens, Bobby Newmark has grown up into an accomplished cowboy. Now he leaves his body in a coma so that he can explore the electronically generated universe inside a unique and costly microchip that he stole from the Tessier-Ashpool clan. Angie Mitchell, Bobby's sometime girlfriend, has become a simstim star, struggling against drug abuse and unsure of her future. In *Mona*

Lisa Overdrive, wrote Richard Mathews of the *St. Petersburg Times,* "Gibson employs the metaphor of addiction as the central fact of existence. Addictions to drugs, information, and sensuality permeate society and form the basis of all economic transactions." The drug-abusing Angie, for example, is herself a "mere fix . . . piped to millions of simstim addicts to enrich [her producers]." Bobby is also a junkie— "a metaphor for society, increasingly techno-dependent, and hopelessly addicted to the excitement of high-tech power trips and head games."

As *Mona Lisa* unfolds amid complex intrigues, the power of technology looms so large as to challenge the meaning of human identity itself. Characters seek friendship and advice from the personalities recorded on microchips; Angie comes face-to-face with "Mona Lisa," a confused teenage junkie who has been surgically altered to resemble Angie herself as part of a bizarre abduction plot. In the violent climax of the novel, during which Angie dies of a brain hemorrhage, the simstim producers stumble upon Mona and gladly recruit her as a new star. Then, in an astonishing burst of fantasy, Gibson shows Angie reunited with Bobby in his microchip universe—a computer-generated heaven. By then, Mathews observed, "Gibson has us re-evaluating our concepts of 'life,' 'death' and 'reality,' all of which have been redefined by the impact of the information matrix. What makes Gibson so exceptional a writer is that you haven't just seen or thought about this future; you've been there."

Increasingly Gibson was hailed as a master of observant, evocative, economical prose. "If the pace [of *Mona Lisa Overdrive*] is rather less frantic than in the earlier books," observed Paul Kincaid of the *Times Literary Supplement,* "it is because Gibson's writing has improved, and the space given to more vividly presenting mood, place and character slows the action." Even the skeptical Disch quoted a passage from *Mona Lisa* and, as other reviewers have done, observed how deftly Gibson could suggest a whole society with a handful of words. "Gibson is writing brilliant prose," declared Ellen Datlow in the *Philadelphia Inquirer,* "work that can be compared to anything being written inside or outside the science-fiction field."

Gibson seemed bemused by his new life as a best-selling novelist. At book signings he was greeted by disparate groups of hackers and punks whom he termed "M & M's" (for "modems and Mohawks"). As a soft-spoken, conservatively dressed father of two, Gibson realized that his wilder fans were sometimes disappointed to see him in person. "There was a classic case in San Francisco when two huge motorcyclists came screeching up," he continued in the *Chicago Tribune.* "One of them looked at me, picked up a book and shook his head and said, 'You can sign it anyway.'" To Gibson's surprise he quickly attracted the attention of the Hollywood film industry, and two years after *Neuromancer* was published he sold the rights for $100,000. Soon he was recruited as screenwriter for the projected third film in the highly profitable *Aliens* series. But after he wrote several drafts, the film studio had a management shuffle and he lost his job—a common fate in Hollywood. Paradoxically, the very fact that he was involved with such a high-profile effort made it easy for him to find more film work. Though Gibson stresses that *Mona Lisa Overdrive* is not autobiographical, he admits that the simstim subplot was inspired by his introduction to America's film capital. As he told the *Philadelphia Inquirer:* "Sitting in the Polo Lounge talking to 20-year-old movie producers with money coming out of their ears—*that's* science fiction, boy."

By the time *Mona Lisa Overdrive* was published in 1988, Gibson and many reviewers were glad to say farewell to the cyberpunk era. "It's becoming fashionable now to write 'cyberpunk is dead' articles," he noted in the *Bloomsbury Review.* The author teamed with fellow novelist Bruce Sterling to write *The Difference Engine,* a sort of retroactive science-fiction novel set in Victorian England. The book is named for one of several mechanical computers that were designed during the nineteenth century by mathematician Charles Babbage. Babbage failed to build his most sophisticated machines, for their manufacture was beyond his budget and he was unable to secure public funding. Gibson and Sterling, however, imagine the consequences if he had succeeded. With the help of mechanical computers, the Victorians develop airplanes, cybernauts, and a huge steam-powered television. *The Difference Engine,* Gibson warned, "sounds cuter than it is. It's really a very, very chilly semi-dystopia." In this novel, as in most of Gibson's work, technology proves corrupting, and society is painfully divided between the haves and have-nots. Gibson knows that a Victorian fantasy may baffle his old fans; at last, however, he might free himself of labels. "One of the reasons we cooked this up was so people wouldn't be able to say it was more cyberpunk writing," Gibson told the *Chicago Tribune.* "There won't be one guy with a silver Mohawk in the whole book."

Despite his rejection of the cyberpunk label, Gibson returned to technologically-based action and drama in *Virtual Light,* his 1993 novel. "Somewhere in the not-too-far-away in a quasi-anarcho-future, in the land of holograms, light-pens and tele-presence phones, in a world where many wear respirator-masks against the muck of dense viral air," explained *Los Angeles Times Book Review* contributor Frederic Tuten, "lives Rydell, former police officer turned, by force of circumstance, private cop for the 'residential armed response branch' of Inten-Secure, a private security organization in Los Angeles." Rydell is assigned to locate a pair of stolen sunglasses with a peculiar ability—through a technique called Virtual Light, they send stored information directly to the optic nerve of the person who is wearing them. The stored information in this pair of glasses contains industrial secrets that are very valuable to the Japanese corporation that plans to rebuild San Francisco. The glasses have been taken by a bicycle courier named Chevette Washington, from the community that has set itself on the remains of the Oakland Bay Bridge. Chevette has no idea of the value of what she has, and she and Rydell team up when he finally locates her. "Together they flee their pursuers," said *New York Times* contributor Christopher Lehmann-Haupt, "and then foil them by setting up what might be called a cyber-sting," recruiting helpers from a band of renegade computer hackers. "This is one of your basic crime-genre plots, of course," declared Bruce Cook in the *Chicago Tribune,* "and Gibson uses it well. Just as *Neuromancer* was essentially a caper story, the first half of *Virtual Light* is built around a criminal investigation, theft and murder."

Reviewers commented on Gibson's departure from the bitter, *noir* edge that characterized *Neuromancer, Count Zero,* and *Mona Lisa Overdrive.* Cyberspace itself does not figure in *Virtual Light.* "Is William Gibson mellowing?" asked *New York Times Book Review* contributor Gerald Jonas. "Compared to his earlier work, *Virtual Light* . . . offers more likable characters, a more subdued style, a less claustrophobic setting and a more upbeat ending." "There are action elements here," commented Charles Platt in the *Washington Post Book World,* "that wouldn't seem out of place in 'L. A. Law' or even 'Hawaii Five-O,' including a scene where an assassin wastes 15 minutes or more, holding his victims at gunpoint while he conveniently explains the plot." Still, according to Julian Loose in the *London Review of Books,* "although [Gibson's] thrillers increasingly make room for humour and reflection, essentially they remain like the machines he loves to describe: fast, showy and relentlessly slick."

In 1995, the motion picture *Johnny Mnemonic* was released. Gibson wrote the screenplay, based on a short story he published in 1986. It is an action-adventure story about an information courier (played in the movie by Keanu Reeves) who carries sensitive information electronically stored in his brain. Johnny has been surgically engineered to discharge the information according to a particular code, which he does not know and cannot access. Johnny's current assignment far exceeds his storage capacity, and he will die if he cannot get the information to its recipients within a single day. In addition, Johnny is being chased by a band of information hijackers intent on stealing his information. "It's a beautiful setup," exclaimed a reviewer for the *New Yorker,* "and Gibson embellishes the premise ingeniously." However, the critic opined that the film does not match the promise of Gibson's screenplay: "There's a terrific, wildly inventive science-fiction picture trapped in here somewhere, but the director can't find the images to give us access to it."

Working on the screenplay and the film was a great revelation for Gibson. He told the *New York Times'* Peter H. Lewis, "I thought that computer special effects in movies appear magically, because they have wonderful, powerful computers. It turns out to be 28 guys in a basement tapping in strings of code, changing pixels. It's very labor-intensive, and really slow." "I can see one of the flaws in the realism of my work is that in my fiction, technology almost always works," Gibson concluded. "I didn't have nearly enough things that break or that don't work and nobody knows why. It's all so cranky."

BIOGRAPHICAL/CRITICAL SOURCES:

BOOKS

Contemporary Literary Criticism, Gale (Detroit), Volume 39, 1986, Volume 63, 1991.

McCaffery, Larry, editor, *Across the Wounded Galaxies: Interviews with Contemporary American Science Fiction Writers,* University of Illinois Press (Champaign), 1990.

Olsen, Lance, *William Gibson,* Borgo Press (San Bernardino, CA), 1992.

Sterling, Bruce, editor, *Mirrorshades: The Cyberpunk Anthology,* Arbor House, 1986.

PERIODICALS

Analog, November, 1984; December, 1986; January, 1987; April, 1989; October, 1989.

Austin American-Statesman, November 27, 1988.

Best Sellers, July, 1986.

Bloomsbury Review, September, 1988.

Boston Globe, May 30, 1993, p. 65; October 10, 1993, p. 8.

Canadian Literature, summer, 1989.

Chicago Tribune, November 18, 1988; November 23, 1988; August 8, 1993, p. 1.

Christian Science Monitor, August 26, 1993, p. 11.

Entertainment Weekly, August 26, 1994, p. 106.

Esquire, May, 1992, p. 33.

Fantasy Review, July, 1984; April, 1986.

Film Comment, January, 1990.

Guardian Weekly (Manchester), October 3, 1993, p. 29.

Heavy Metal, May, 1985.

Impulse, winter, 1989.

Interview, January, 1989.

Isaac Asimov's Science Fiction Magazine, August, 1986.

Listener, October 11, 1990.

Locus, August, 1988; July, 1993, p. 19.

London Review of Books, November 4, 1993, pp. 40-42.

Los Angeles Times, September 12, 1993, p. 34; May 24, 1995, p. D1.

Los Angeles Times Book Review, January 29, 1989; May 12, 1991, p. 9; October 17, 1993, p. 13.

Maclean's, September 6, 1993, p. 52; June 5, 1995, p. 60.

Magazine of Fantasy and Science Fiction, August, 1985; August, 1986.

Mississippi Review, Volume 16, numbers 2 and 3, 1988.

Nation, May 8, 1989; November 15, 1993, pp. 580-88.

New Statesman, June 20, 1986; September 26, 1986.

New Yorker, August 16, 1993, p. 24; June 12, 1995, p. 111.

New York Times, October 3, 1993, p. 8; November 18, 1993, p. C22; May 22, 1995, p. D3.

New York Times Book Review, November 24, 1985; December 11, 1988; March 10, 1991, p. 5; August 29, 1993, p. 12; September 12, 1993, p. 36.

Oregonian (Portland), November 24, 1988.

PC Magazine, August, 1992, p. 34.

People, June 10, 1991, p. 103.

Philadelphia Inquirer, April 15, 1986; October 30, 1988.

Pittsburgh Press, October 19, 1986.

Publishers Weekly, September 6, 1993, pp. 70-71.

Punch, February 6, 1985.

Rolling Stone, December 4, 1986; June 15, 1989.

Sacramento Union, October 26, 1988.

St. Petersburg Times, December 18, 1988.

San Francisco Chronicle, January 1, 1987.

Saturday Night, March, 1989; December, 1994, p. 82.

Science Fiction Chronicle, April, 1994, p. 48.

Science Fiction Review, fall, 1985; summer, 1986; winter, 1986.

Science Fiction Studies, March, 1995, p. 63.

Seattle Times, October 24, 1988.

South Atlantic Quarterly, fall, 1993.

Spin, December, 1988.

Times Literary Supplement, December 7, 1984; June 20, 1986; August 12, 1988; October 1, 1993, p. 21.

Tribune Books (Chicago), August 8, 1993, pp. 1, 11; July 24, 1994, p. 2.

USA Today, January 3, 1992, p. 4; September 2, 1993, p. D1.

Utne Reader, July, 1989.

Village Voice, July 3, 1984; July 16, 1985; May 6, 1986; January 17, 1989.

Washington Post, October 18, 1993, p. D1.

Washington Post Book World, July 29, 1984; March 23, 1986; October 25, 1987; November 27, 1988; March 31, 1991, p. 9; August 22, 1993, p. 5.

West Coast Review of Books, September, 1985.

Whole Earth Review, summer, 1989.*

* * *

GINZBERG, Eli 1911-

PERSONAL: Born April 30, 1911, in New York, NY; son of Louis (a Talmudist) and Adele (Katzenstein) Ginzberg; married Ruth Szold, July 14, 1946 (deceased); children: Abigail, Jeremy, Rachel. *Education:* Attended University of Heidelberg and University of Grenoble, 1928-29; Columbia University, A.B., 1931, A.M., 1932, Ph.D., 1934.

ADDRESSES: Home—845 West End Ave., New York, NY. *Office*—Graduate School of Business, Columbia University, New York, NY 10027.

CAREER: Columbia University, Graduate School of Business, New York City, member of faculty, 1935—, A. Barton Hepburn Professor of Economics, 1967-79, professor emeritus, 1979—, director of Research Economics and Group Behavior, 1939-42 and 1948-49, Staff Studies of National Manpower

Council, 1941-61, Eisenhower Center for Human Resources, 1950—, and Revson Fellows Program on the Future of New York City, 1979—. Honorary member of faculty, Industrial College of the Armed Forces, 1971—. Adjunct professor of health and society, Barnard College, 1981-88; special lecturer at Graduate School of Business, 1979—, and School of Public Health, 1988—.

Chair or member of numerous professional boards on human resources/labor management/employment policy. Research director, United Jewish Appeal, 1941; member of Committee on Wartime Requirements for Scientific and Specialized Personnel, 1942; special assistant to chief statistician, U.S. Department of War, 1942-47; director of Resources Analysis Division, Surgeon General's Office, 1944-46; U.S. Representative, Five Power Conference on Reparations for Non-Repatriable Refugees, 1946; member of medical advisory board, Secretary of War, 1946-48; director of New York State Hospital Study, 1948-49; member of board of governors, Hebrew University of Jerusalem, 1953-59; member of National Advisory Mental Health Council, 1959-63, and National Advisory Allied Health Professions Council, 1969-72; chair of studies committee, White House Conference on Children and Youth, 1960; member of scientific advisory board, U.S. Air Force, 1970-74; member of personnel advisory committee, National Academy of Sciences Office of Science and Engineering; advisor, International Institute Management Science Center, Berlin.

Consultant to U.S. Department of the Army, 1946-70, Department of State, 1953, 1956, 1965-69, Department of Labor, 1954—, Department of Defense, 1964-71, Department of Commerce, 1965-66, General Accounting Office, 1973—, and Department of Health, Education, and Welfare; consultant to private business, including IBM, Citicorps, and Digital Equipment; consultant to Federation of Jewish Philanthropies of New York, Rockefeller Foundation, Robert Wood Johnson Foundation, Ford Foundation, and McKinsey Foundation for Management Research.

MEMBER: American Association for the Advancement of Science (fellow), American Economic Association, Academy of Political Science, American Academy of Arts and Sciences (fellow), American Association of University Professors, Society of Medical Consultants to the Armed Forces (associate member), Industrial Relations Research Association, Allen O. Whipple Surgical Society (honorary mem-

ber), National Academy of the Sciences, Institute of Medicine, Phi Beta Kappa, Beta Gamma Sigma.

AWARDS, HONORS: U.S. Department of War Medal, 1946, for exceptional civilian service; International University of Social Studies Medal (Rome), 1957, for research contributions to the study of human resources; McKinsey Management Journal Award, University of California, 1964; D.Litt., Jewish Theological Seminary of America, 1966; LL.D., Loyola University (Chicago), 1969; certificate of merit, U.S. Department of Labor, 1972; Litt.D., Columbia University, 1982; Special Service Award, Department of Labor, 1982; Distinguished Service Award, Teachers College, Columbia University, 1984; L.H.D., Rush University, 1985, and Kirkville Osteopathic College, 1994; LL.D, Philadelphia College of Osteopathic Medicine, 1994; D.H.L., State College of Optometry, New York, 1995.

WRITINGS:

Studies in the Economics of the Bible, Jewish Publication Society (Philadelphia, PA), 1932.

The House of Adam Smith, Columbia University Press (New York City), 1934, new edition published as *The House of Adam Smith Revisited,* Temple University Press (Philadelphia, PA), 1977.

The Illusion of Economic Stability, Harper (New York City), 1939.

Grass on the Slag Heaps: The Story of the Welsh Miners, Harper, 1942.

Report to American Jews on Overseas Relief, Palestine, and Refugees in the United States, Harper, 1942.

(With Ethel L. Ginsberg, Dorothy L. Lynn, and others) *The Unemployed,* Harper, 1943.

(With Joseph Carwell) *The Labor Leader,* Macmillan (New York City), 1948.

Program for the Nursing Profession, Macmillan, 1949.

A Pattern for Hospital Care, Columbia University Press, 1949.

Agenda for the American Jews, King's Crown Press, 1950.

(With others) *Occupational Choice,* Columbia University Press, 1951.

(With John L. Herma and Sol W. Ginsberg) *Psychiatry and Military Manpower Policy: A Reappraisal of the Experience in World War II,* King's Crown Press, 1953.

(With Douglas W. Bray) *The Uneducated,* Columbia University Press, 1953.

(With others) *What Makes an Executive?* (symposium), Columbia University Press, 1955.

(With Bray, James K. Anderson, and Robert W. Smuts) *The Negro Potential*, Columbia University Press, 1956.

(With Ewing W. Reilley, Bray, and Herma) *Effecting Change in Large Organizations*, Columbia University Press, 1957.

Human Resources: The Wealth of a Nation, Simon & Schuster (New York City), 1958.

(With Anderson) *Manpower for Government: A Decade's Forecast*, Public Personnel Association (Chicago), 1958.

(With Anderson and others) *The Ineffective Soldier: Lessons for Management and the Nation*, Volume 1: *The Lost Divisions*, Volume 2: *Breakdown and Recovery*, Volume 3: *Patterns of Performance*, Columbia University Press, 1959.

(With Peter Rogatz) *Planning for Better Hospital Care*, King's Crown Press, 1961.

(With Anderson and Herma) *The Optimistic Tradition and American Youth*, Columbia University Press, 1962.

(With Ivar E. Berg) *Democratic Values and the Rights of Management*, Columbia University Press, 1963.

(With Hyman Berman) *The American Worker in the Twentieth Century: A History through Autobiographies*, Free Press of Glencoe, 1964.

(With Alfred S. Eichner) *The Troublesome Presence: American Democracy and the Negro*, Free Press of Glencoe, 1964, enlarged and expanded edition, Transaction (New Brunswick, NJ), 1993.

(With Herma) *Talent and Performance*, Columbia University Press, 1964.

(With Dale L. Hiestand and Beatrice G. Reubens) *The Pluralistic Economy*, McGraw (New York City), 1965.

Louis Ginzberg: Keeper of the Law, Jewish Publication Society, 1966.

(With others) *Life Styles of Educated Women: Self-Portraits* (also see below), Columbia University Press, 1966.

(With Alice M. Yohalem) *Educated American Women: Self-Portraits* (also see below), Columbia University Press, 1966.

(With Herbert A. Smith) *Manpower Strategy for Ethiopia*, Central Press (Addis Ababa, Ethiopia), 1966, enlarged edition published as *Manpower Strategy for Developing Countries: Lessons from Ethiopia*, Columbia University Press, 1967.

The Development of Human Resources, McGraw, 1966.

(With others) *The Middle-Class Negro in a White Man's World*, Columbia University Press, 1967.

(With Carol A. Brown) *Manpower for Library Services*, Columbia University Press, 1967.

(With Hiestand) *Mobility in the Negro Community: Guidelines for Research on Social and Economic Progress*, U.S. Commission on Civil Rights, 1968.

Manpower Agenda for America, McGraw, 1968.

(With others) *Manpower Strategy for the Metropolis*, Columbia University Press, 1968.

People and Progress in East Asia, Columbia University Press, 1968.

One Fifth of the World: Manpower Reports on Iran and South Asia, Conservation of Human Resources Project, Columbia University Press, 1969.

(With Miriam Ostow) *Men, Money, and Medicine*, Columbia University Press, 1969.

Manpower for Development: Perspectives on Five Continents, Praeger (New York City), 1971.

Educated American Women: Life Styles and Self-Portraits (contains *Life Styles of Educated Women* and *Educated American Women: Self-Portraits*), Columbia University Press, 1971.

Career Guidance: Who Needs It, Who Provides It, Who Can Improve It, McGraw, 1971.

Perspectives on Indian Manpower, Employment, and Income, [New Delhi], 1971.

(With others) *Urban Health Services: The Case of New York*, Columbia University Press, 1971.

Manpower Advice for Government, U.S. Department of Labor (Washington, DC), 1972.

The Outlook for Educated Manpower, Engineering Manpower Commission (New York City), 1972.

Federal Manpower Policy in Transition, U.S. Department of Labor, 1974.

The Manpower Connection: Education and Work, Harvard University Press (Cambridge, MA), 1975.

The Human Economy, McGraw, 1976.

The Limits of Health Reform: The Search for Realism, Basic Books (New York City), 1977.

Health Manpower and Health Policy, Allanheld, Osmun (Totowa, NJ), 1978.

Good Jobs, Bad Jobs, No Jobs, Harvard University Press, 1979.

The School/Work Nexus, Phi Delta Kappa (Bloomington, IN), 1980.

(In Hebrew) *American Jews: The Building of Voluntary Community*, Schocken, 1980.

(With others) *Home Health Care: Its Role in the Changing Health Services Market*, Rowman & Allanheld (Totowa, NJ), 1984.

The Coming Physician Surplus: In Search of a Policy, Rowman & Allanheld, 1985.

American Medicine: The Power Shift, Rowman & Allanheld, 1985.

(With others) *Local Health Policy in Action: The Municipal Health Services Program*, Rowman & Allanheld, 1985.

(With George Vojta) *Beyond Human Scale: The Large Corporation at Risk*, Basic Books, 1985.

Understanding Human Resources: Perspectives, People and Policy, Abt Books (Cambridge, MA), 1985.

(With others) *From Health Dollars to Health Services: New York City 1965-85*, Rowman & Allanheld, 1986.

(With others) *Technology and Employment: Concepts and Clarifications*, Westview Press (Boulder, CO), 1986.

Medicine and Society, Westview Press, 1987.

The Skeptical Economist, Westview Press, 1987.

Tomorrow's Executives, Wiley (New York City), 1988.

Young People at Risk: Is Prevention Possible?, Westview Press, 1988.

Executive Talent: Developing Tomorrow's Leaders, Wiley, 1988.

The Financing of Biomedical Research, Johns Hopkins University Press (Baltimore, MD), 1989.

My Brother's Keeper, Transaction (New Brunswick, NJ), 1989.

Does Job Training Work?: The Clients Speak Out, Westview Press, 1989.

The Medical Triangle, Harvard University Press, 1990.

World without Work, Transaction, 1991.

(With Berliner and Ostow) *Changing U.S. Health Care: A Study of Four Metropolitan Areas*, Westview, 1993.

The Eye of Illusion, Transaction, 1993.

The Economics of Medical Education, Josiah Macy, Jr. Foundation (New York City), 1993.

The Road to Reform: The Future of Health Care in America, Free Press (New York City), 1994.

Critical Issues in U.S. Health Care Reform, Westview Press, 1994.

Medical Gridlock and Health Reform, Westview Press, 1994.

The Financing of Medical Schools in an Era of Health Care Reform, Josiah Macy, Jr. Foundation, 1995.

Tomorrow's Hospital: A Look to the 21st Century, Yale University Press (New Haven, CT), 1996.

EDITOR

The Nation's Children, Volume 1: *The Family and Social Change*, Volume 2: *Development and Education*, Volume 3: *Problems and Perspectives*, Columbia University Press, 1960.

Values and Ideals of American Youth, with foreword by John W. Gardner, Columbia University Press, 1961, new edition, Books for Libraries, 1972.

The Negro Challenge to the Business Community, McGraw, 1964.

Technology and Social Change, Columbia University Press, 1964.

Business Leadership and the Negro Crisis, McGraw, 1968.

(With Yohalem) *Corporate Lib: Women's Challenge to Management*, Johns Hopkins University Press, 1973.

New York Is Very Much Alive: A Manpower View, McGraw, 1973.

(With Robert M. Solow) *The Great Society: Lessons for the Future*, Basic Books, 1974.

(With Yohalem) *The University Medical Center and the Metropolis*, Josiah Macy, Jr. Foundation, 1974.

The Future of the Metropolis: People, Jobs, Income, Olympus, 1975.

Economic Impact of Large Public Programs: The NASA Story, Olympus, 1976.

Jobs for Americans, Prentice-Hall (Englewood Cliffs, NJ), 1976.

Regionalization and Health Policy, U.S. Department of Labor, 1977.

Employing the Unemployed, Basic Books, 1980.

The U.S. Health Care System: A Look to the 1990s, Rowman & Allanheld, 1985.

From Physician Shortage to Patient Shortage: The Uncertain Future of Medical Practice, Westview Press, 1986.

Medicine and Society: Clinical Decisions and Societal Values, Westview Press, 1987.

The AIDS Patient: An Action Agenda, Westview Press, 1988.

Public and Professional Attitudes toward AIDS Patients, Westview Press, 1989.

(With David Rogers) *Improving the Life Chances of Children at Risk*, Westview Press, 1990.

(And author of introduction) *Science and the Transformation of Academic Life*, Emanuel Piore, Transaction, 1990.

Health Services Research, Key to Health Policy, Harvard University Press, 1991.

OTHER

Also author of *The Skilled Work Force of the United States*, 1955, *The Negro and His Work*, 1961, and *Kavim le-heker haye ka-kalkalah shel Yehude hatefutsot*, 1972. Author of manpower studies for Israeli Ministry of Labor, 1961, 1964, and 1968, for Industrial College of the Armed Forces, 1964, and for National Commission on Productivity, 1971. Contributor to *The Public Interest.*

SIDELIGHTS: Eli Ginzberg and coauthor George Vojta discuss the problems of multinational corporations in *Beyond Human Scale: The Large Corporation at Risk.* Their thesis, an *Economist* reviewer relates, "is that huge firms are losing their competitive edge because they can no longer motivate workers enough." The problem is "bigness," writes Robert Krulwich. In the *New York Times Book Review* he summarizes, "As companies grow, they create internal monitoring systems to keep the boss aware of what is going on below—but after a while these systems take on a life of their own, and division chiefs and would-be division chiefs spend their days filling out reports and holding endless meetings instead of focusing on what counts in the business: the product, the customer, and the competition." According to Ginzberg and Vojta, today's managerial talent may prefer attachment to smaller companies where they don't spend as much time stalled in middle- management positions attending, for the most part, to corporate politics.

Smaller companies offer higher productivity incentives and advancement opportunity. Therefore, say the authors, large corporations are at risk unless they learn to reward talented managers with a greater voice in decision making to compensate for other missing motivators. To redirect energy from infighting back to the outside competitors, they prescribe a renewed emphasis on company-wide growth, and a decentralization of power. The multinational company may not be as endangered as Ginzberg and Vojta depict, states Krulwich, but he agrees that its survival will depend on its ability to attract and keep "the best recruits" in the manner that *Beyond Human Scale* suggests.

Ginzberg told *CA:* "The simplest answer as to why I write so much is that I am probably still competing with my father who was a great and prolific scholar. But there is more to the story. I like to write, among other reasons, because it helps me to clarify what I know and believe; and further it enables me to write *finis* to a subject which I have been exploring.

"Further, as an academic who is currently celebrating his sixtieth year of teaching at Columbia University, I have found that writing with an eye to publication has forced me—and encouraged me—to shift my research focus as the world changes. I have consistently challenged myself and others by picking up new theories and approaches starting with my early 'historical' efforts and carried down to date in dealing with womanforce, the blacks, etc.

"Finally, I would be less than honest if I did not admit that I get a great deal of satisfaction in being able to give form and direction to a broad assortment of ideas, and further, I get considerable satisfaction from seeing my efforts emerge in a published book. Clearly, without such satisfaction, I would not have kept on writing and published so much."

BIOGRAPHICAL/CRITICAL SOURCES:

BOOKS

Ginzberg, Eli, *The Eye of Illusion,* Transaction, 1993.

PERIODICALS

American Journal of Sociology, March, 1981.
Black Scholar, summer, 1993, p. 98.
Booklist, March 1, 1994, p. 1167.
Business Week, April 22, 1985.
Choice, November, 1993, p. 488.
Contemporary Sociology, January, 1994, p. 138.
Current History, July, 1985.
Economic Books: Current Selections, September, 1985; June, 1986; September, 1986.
Economist, May 10, 1986.
Industrial and Labor Relations Review, January, 1965; July, 1965; October, 1969; July, 1973; July, 1977.
International Labour Review, July, 1966; May, 1967; October, 1968; August, 1972.
Journal of Economic Literature, March, 1977; March, 1981; September, 1986.
Kirkus Reviews, February 1, 1994, p. 113.
Nation, January 23, 1967.
New Leader, December 9, 1974.
New Republic, December 8, 1979.
New York, May 7, 1973.
New York Review of Books, December 17, 1970; December 16, 1971.
New York Times, January 11, 1965; August 4, 1965.
New York Times Book Review, February 21, 1965; January 15, 1967; July 14, 1985; March 13, 1994, p. 18.
Personnel and Guidance Journal, June, 1965; April, 1972; December, 1982.
Personnel Psychology, winter, 1985.

Publishers Weekly, March 8, 1985.
Saturday Review, April 17, 1965; April 23, 1966; January 25, 1969; January 22, 1972.
SciTech Book News, February, 1986.
Times Literary Supplement, February, 25, 1965; October 21, 1965.
Virginia Quarterly Review, winter, 1994, p. 33.
Washington Post Book World, January 26, 1969.
West Coast Review of Books, March, 1978.
Wilson Quarterly, winter, 1980; spring, 1981; spring, 1982.

*   *   *

GIROUX, Robert   1914-

PERSONAL: Born April 8, 1914, in New Jersey; son of Arthur J. (a weaver and cabinetmaker) and Katharine (a teacher; maiden name, Lyons) Giroux; married Carmen de Arango, August 30, 1952 (divorced, 1969). *Education:* Columbia University, A.B. (with honors), 1936. *Politics:* Democrat. *Religion:* Roman Catholic. *Avocational interests:* "Going to movies, attending the opera, walking, sailing."

ADDRESSES: Office—Farrar, Straus & Giroux, Inc., 19 Union Sq. W., New York, NY 10003.

CAREER: Columbia Broadcasting System, Inc., New York City, editor of program book, 1936-39; Harcourt, Brace & Co., New York City, editor, 1940-47, editor-in-chief of trade books, 1948-55; Farrar, Straus & Giroux, Inc., New York City, vice president, editor-in-chief, and director, 1955-79, partner, 1963—, chairperson of board of editors, 1979-96. President of National Board of Review of Motion Pictures, Inc., 1975-82. *Military service:* U.S. Naval Reserve, active duty, 1942-45; became lieutenant commander.

MEMBER: Phi Beta Kappa, Century Club.

AWARDS, HONORS: Ivan Sandrof Award for "distinguished contribution to the enhancement of American literary and critical standards" from National Book Critics Circle, 1987; Alexander Hamilton Medal from Columbia University, 1987; Campion Award for service in the cause of Christian letters from *America,* 1988.

WRITINGS:

(Contributor) Allen Tate, editor, *T. S. Eliot: The Man and His Work,* Delacorte (New York City), 1966.
(Author of introduction) *The Complete Stories of Flannery O'Connor,* Farrar, Straus & Giroux (New York City), 1971.
(Author of preface) John Berryman, *The Freedom of the Poet,* Farrar, Straus & Giroux, 1976.
The Education of an Editor, Bowker (New York City), 1982.
The Book Known as Q: A Consideration of Shakespeare's Sonnets, Atheneum (New York City), 1982.
The Future of the Book, Grolier Club (Charlottesville, VA), 1984.
(Editor and author of introduction) Elizabeth Bishop, *The Collected Prose,* Farrar, Straus & Giroux, 1984.
(Editor and author of introduction) Robert Lowell, *Robert Lowell: Collected Prose,* Farrar, Straus & Giroux, 1987.
A Deed of Death: The Story behind the Unsolved Murder of Hollywood Director William Desmond Taylor, Knopf (New York City), 1990.
(Compiler, editor and author of introduction) Elizabeth Bishop, *One Art: Selected Letters,* Farrar, Straus & Giroux, 1994.

Also author of the radio drama "Delia Bacon: The Yankee Seeress and the Stratford Booby," for British Broadcasting Corporation (BBC-Radio), 1987. Contributor of articles to periodicals, including *Atlantic, New York Times Book Review* and *Yale Review.*

SIDELIGHTS: After four decades of working with such writers as Carl Sandburg, Flannery O'Connor, Bernard Malamud, Katherine Anne Porter, William Golding, T. S. Eliot, Jack Kerouac, Robert Lowell, Susan Sontag, and Walker Percy, Robert Giroux has become, in the words of Donald Hall for the *New York Times Book Review,* "the only living editor whose name is bracketed with Maxwell Perkins." Giroux began his publishing career at Harcourt Brace and one of his first books was Edmund Wilson's treatise on nineteenth-century socialist thinkers entitled *To the Finland Station.* Giroux observes in his 1981 Bowker Memorial Lecture, later published as *The Education of an Editor,* that Wilson's manuscript was almost flawless: "Thus at the start of my life as an editor I experienced the rarest and most ideal situation: a manuscript needing few or no changes. This is what every editor, and author, really wants."

Giroux has discovered many young authors, including Jean Stafford, whose first novel, *Boston Adventure,* came to Harcourt in 1943. Giroux took the manuscript with him on a train one afternoon and became so engrossed in the story that he missed his stop. Stafford, in turn, brought the work of her husband, the poet Robert Lowell, to the publisher's attention, and later Giroux edited Lowell's essays in *Robert Lowell: Collected Prose.* Giroux also discovered Bernard Malamud, accepting his first novel, *The Natural,* for Harcourt after it had been rejected by another publisher. After Giroux moved to the Farrar, Straus publishing company in 1955, Harcourt rejected Malamud's novel *The Assistant;* accepted by Giroux, it won a National Book Award. Giroux also worked on nineteen books by Isaac Bashevis Singer (who won the Nobel Prize for Literature in 1979) and brought the work of the Nobel Prize-winning poets Derek Walcott and Seamus Heaney to the Farrar, Straus & Giroux list.

Giroux's taste is renowned in the book trade. He was granted the Ivan Sandrof Award from the National Book Critics Circle in 1987 for his "distinguished contribution to the enhancement of American literary and critical standards." He is also a recipient of the Alexander Hamilton Medal from Columbia University and the Campion Award from *America.* Ted Morgan in the *Saturday Review* maintains that "[Giroux's] standards can be held up as an example in today's publishing industry, where the bottom line often takes precedent over the printed word. . . . As an editor who relies on his taste, the strongest statement he can make about a book is not its earn-out figure or its sub-rights potential, but simply 'I like it.'" Giroux, who deplores the many diet, self-help, financial, and beauty books that are prevalent in today's market, insists that if a publisher cannot find quality books to publish, he or she should not resort to publishing junk. Giroux quipped in his Bowker Memorial Lecture that "editors used to be known by their authors; now some of them are known by their restaurants." Furthermore, Giroux explained to Morgan: "To keep going, publishers must make money, and they like to make it as much as authors do. Commercial success is not only desirable, it's necessary. What I dislike is the great number of what I call *ooks,* publications that are almost but not quite books. You have trouble remembering them two weeks after they come out."

In *The Book Known as Q: A Consideration of Shakespeare's Sonnets,* Giroux examines the evidence for various theories about the date of composition and the autobiographical content of Shakespeare's sonnets, which were published in 1609. Scholars have long debated the identity of the young man who is the subject of many of the poems; Giroux identifies him as the third Earl of Southampton and offers his explanation of why the sonnets were not published until more than fifteen years after most of them were written and why they were virtually unknown until nearly a century after Shakespeare's death. Michael Dirda for the *Washington Post Book World* writes: "*The Book Known as Q* beguiles with the charm of a well-told historical detective story," whereas Christopher Lehmann-Haupt of the *New York Times* is somewhat more analytical; he identifies the thesis of the book as "highly inferential. Practically everything we know about Shakespeare is inferential. . . . Giroux goes out on a limb when he assumes that the sonnets must be autobiographical. . . . [He] . . . feels strongly on the subject and attacks what he calls 'the anti-biographical fallacy' at length. But however strong or weak his thesis, its value lies in this: It offers us a plausible and coherent explanation of what the sonnets, personal statements that they formally are, might actually be referring to. This, in turn, gives them an added dimension of dramatic life." Finally, according to Frances Taliaferro for the *New York Times Book Review, The Book Known as Q* "makes no flamboyant claims; it is a modest, fair-minded introduction to the history and scholarship of the sonnets and to that period when, in Colette's words, 'Shakespeare worked without knowing that he would become Shakespeare'. . . . [Giroux's] enthusiasm inspires the reader to intimacy with the sonnets themselves; as is fitting, the last section of this book is a facsimile of 'Q.'"

Giroux told *CA:* "During 1995 I enjoyed a Rockefeller Foundation fellowship at their Lake Como retreat, the Villa Serbelloni at Bellagio, where I began work on my memoirs. I recount fifteen years at Harcourt Brace, my wartime experiences on an aircraft carrier (the *Essex,* with Air Group Nine), notable and little known authors I have worked with, and the changes in the world of book publishing since I began in 1940. Fifty-five years—how have I survived! It will take at least another year or so before the book is finished."

BIOGRAPHICAL/CRITICAL SOURCES:

PERIODICALS

New York Times, May 31, 1982.
New York Times Book Review, January 6, 1980; August 29, 1982.

Saturday Review, September 1, 1979.
Washington Post Book World, June 13, 1982.

*   *   *

GOODMAN, Linda 1925-1995

PERSONAL: Born Mary Alice Kemery, on April 19, 1925, in Parkersburg, WV, died of complications from diabetes, October 21, 1995, in Colorado Springs, CO; daughter of Robert Stratton and Mazie (McBee) Kemery; married William Herbert Snyder (a writer), April 29, 1949 (divorced); married Sam O. Goodman (a disc jockey), September 28, 1955 (separated); children: (first marriage) Melissa Anne, James, John Anthony, Sarah Elizabeth, William Dana; (second marriage) Jill Kemery, Michael Aaron.

CAREER: Astrologer and author. WAMP-Radio, Pittsburgh, PA, writer and broadcaster for "Letters from Linda" show (from which she adopted the name "Linda"), 1958-61; writer for radio shows, 1962-64; WHN-Radio New York, NY, continuity chief, 1964-66; speech writer for National Urban League, 1966-67. Member of Universal Research Foundation, Sedona, AZ, and Association for Research and Enlightenment, Virginia Beach, VA.

MEMBER: Authors League of America, American Federation of Television and Radio Artists, Writers Guild of New York.

AWARDS, HONORS: Named Daughter of the Year by the West Virginia Society, Washington, DC, 1971.

WRITINGS:

Sun Signs (nonfiction), Taplinger (New York City), 1968, published as *Linda Goodman's Sun Signs,* Bantam (New York City), 1975.

Venus Trines at Midnight: Verses about Lions, Rams, Bulls, Twins, Archers, and Other Sun Signs and You (poetry), Taplinger, 1970.

Linda Goodman's Love Signs: A New Approach to the Human Heart, Harper (New York City), 1978.

Linda Goodman's Love Poems: Levels of Love Awareness, Harper, 1980.

Linda Goodman's Star Signs: The Secret Codes of the Universe, St. Martin's (New York City), 1987.

Goobers (prose), Hampton Roads (Norfolk, VA), 1989.

Contributor to popular magazines. Goodman's books have been translated into fifteen languages.

SIDELIGHTS: Due to the success of her first book, *Sun Signs,* published in 1968 at the height of the "Age of Aquarius," Linda Goodman has become one of America's most influential and famous astrologers. Although she claimed to be over four-hundred years old and been interested in astrology "since the time of Atlantis and before," according to her husband Sam and *People* magazine, it was only after Sam brought home a copy of *The Coffee Table Book of Astrology* that she "stayed in a nightgown studying astrology 20 hours a day for a year."

Sun Signs, credited for bringing astrology out of the occult section and into the mainstream, quickly sold several million copies and became the hip book to be seen with in the late 1960s; even Jane Fonda could be spotted reading it in the movie *Klute.* Many reviewers cited the playful nature of Goodman's writing as a reason for the book's success: "Don't move the food dish of a Virgo cat to a strange spot," was typical advice. Tapping into society's current interests, Goodman's follow up book, *Linda Goodman's Love Signs: A New Approach to the Human Heart,* broke the industry record when its paperback rights sold for $2.3 million. According to a *Newsweek* reviewer, "what seems to set [Goodman's books] apart from other stargazing guides is their knowledgeable approach and comprehensive reach." For example, *Love Signs* covers "every possible pairing of signs—all 166 combinations—for romantic possibilities." Other reviewers surmise that the author's penchant for dispensing pop psychology along with astrological forecasts is a large factor in her popularity. *Linda Goodman's Star Signs: The Secret Codes of the Universe,* Goodman's third book, discusses other popular New Age topics, including numerology, reincarnation, channeling, and crystal healing, and introduces the concept of the lexigram. *Linda Goodman's Love Poems: Levels of Love Awareness* was the author's second collection of published poetry, which reviewers likened to the pop sensibilities of Rod McKuen and other free-form advocates. Many of the poems draw on nature and astrology for their images, though reviewers were lukewarm in their praise: "colloquial and banal," stated one *Publishers Weekly* writer. However, many reviewers conceded that fans of Goodman's astrology books would find her poetry collections worthwhile.

In 1973, Goodman's daughter Sarah committed suicide, but the author, after consulting various astrological charts, refused to believe that she was dead or that the body identified by her husband was Sarah's. Thus ensued a search for her daughter's whereabouts that lasted for years, a quest that brought Goodman to the brink of financial ruin, even as she remained certain that her daughter would return.

Goodman once remarked, "I admit that to be an astrologer you live a great deal in the imagination." In addition to her career as an astrologer, Goodman also founded a religion, "Mannu," which combines the teachings of St. Francis of Assisi with American Indian beliefs.

BIOGRAPHICAL/CRITICAL SOURCES:

PERIODICALS

Booklist, February 15, 1979, p. 894; February 1, 1980, p. 752; January 1, 1988, p. 731.
Kirkus Reviews, July 15, 1968, p. 794.
Library Journal, January 1, 1969, p. 89; March 1, 1979, p. 636; February 1, 1980, p. 409; January, 1988, p. 90.
Newsweek, December 18, 1978.
New York Times, October 25, 1995, p. D21.
People, May 14, 1979.
Publishers Weekly, August 5, 1968, p. 49; November 13, 1978, p. 60; November 5, 1979.
Washington Post Book World, December 17, 1978.

OBITUARIES:

PERIODICALS

Chicago Tribune, October 29, 1995, sec 4, p. 4.
Washington Post, October 27, 1995, p. B7.*

H-I

HAMMOND, Ralph
See HAMMOND INNES, Ralph

* * *

HAMMOND INNES, Ralph   1913-
(Ralph Hammond, Hammond Innes)

PERSONAL: Indexed in some sources under Innes; born July 15, 1913, in Horsham, England; son of William and Dora Beatrice (Crisford) Hammond Innes; married Dorothy Mary Lang (an actress, playwright, and author; deceased, 1989), 1937. *Education:* Educated in England. *Avocational interests:* Traveling, forestry, ocean racing and cruising.

ADDRESSES: Home—Ayres End, Kersey, Suffolk, England. *Agent*—Curtis Brown, 28129 Haymarket, London SW1Y 4SP, England.

CAREER: Member of staff, *Financial News,* 1934-40; freelance writer, 1946—. *Military service:* British Army, Royal Artillery, 1940-46; served with Eighth Army in Sicily landings and as war correspondent, British Army Newspaper Unit invasion of S. France; became major.

MEMBER: Society of Authors, PEN, Royal Ocean Racing Club, Royal Cruising Club, Royal Yacht Squadron, English Speaking Union (vice president), World Ship Trust.

AWARDS, HONORS: Decorated Commander of the British Empire, 1978; Bouchercon Lifetime Achievement award; received honorary degree from Bristol University.

WRITINGS:

NOVELS; UNDER HAMMOND INNES

The Doppelganger, Jenkins (Lancaster, England), 1937.
Air Disaster, Jenkins, 1937.
Sabotage Broadcast, Jenkins, 1938.
All Roads Lead to Friday, Jenkins, 1939.
Trapped, Putnam (New York City), 1940, published in England as *Wreckers Must Breathe,* Collins (London), 1940.
The Trojan Horse, Collins, 1940, reprinted, 1974.
Attack Alarm, Collins, 1941, Macmillan (New York City), 1942, reprinted, Fontana (London), 1969.
Dead and Alive, Collins, 1946, reprinted, Fontana, 1970.
The Killer Mine, Harper (New York City), 1947, reprinted, Collins, 1973, published as *Run by Night,* Bantam (New York City), 1951.
Fire in the Snow, Harper, 1947, reprinted, 1985, published in England as *The Lonely Skier,* Collins, 1947.
Gale Warning, Harper, 1948, published in England as *Maddon's Rock,* Collins, 1948, reprinted, Fontana, 1970.
The Blue Ice, Harper, 1948, reprinted, 1985.
The White South (Book Society selection), Collins, 1949, published as *The Survivors,* Harper, 1950, reprinted, 1985.
The Angry Mountain, Collins, 1950, Harper, 1951, reprinted, Avon (New York City), 1980.
Air Bridge, Collins, 1951, Knopf (New York City), 1952.
Campbell's Kingdom (also see below; Book Society selection), Knopf, 1952, reprinted, Carroll & Graf (New York City), 1986.

The Naked Land, Knopf, 1954, reprinted, Carroll & Graf, 1986, published in England as *The Strange Land,* Collins, 1954.

The Wreck of the "Mary Deare" (Literary Guild selection), Knopf, 1956, reprinted, Carroll & Graf, 1985, also published as *The "Mary Deare"* (Book Society selection), Collins, 1956.

The Land God Gave to Cain, Knopf, 1958, reprinted, Carroll & Graf, 1985.

The Doomed Oasis (Literary Guild selection), Knopf, 1960, reprinted, Carroll & Graf, 1986.

Atlantic Fury, Knopf, 1962, reprinted, Carroll & Graf, 1985.

The Strode Venturer, Knopf, 1965.

Lekvas Man, Knopf, 1971.

Golden Soak, Knopf, 1973.

North Star, Collins, 1974, Knopf, 1975.

The Big Footprints, Knopf, 1977.

Solomon's Seal, Knopf, 1980.

The Black Tide, Collins, 1982, Doubleday (New York City), 1983.

High Stand, Collins, 1985, Atheneum (New York City), 1986.

Medusa, Atheneum, 1988.

Isvik, Chapmans (London), 1990, St. Martin's Press (New York City), 1991.

Target Antarctica, Chapmans, 1993.

The Delta Connection, Macmillan, 1996.

OTHER; UNDER HAMMOND INNES

(Editor) Richard Keverne, *Tales of Old Inns,* 2nd edition, Collins, 1947.

(With Robin Estridge) *Campbell's Kingdom* (screenplay; based on the novel of same title), Rank (Leicester), 1957.

Harvest of Journeys (travel), Collins, 1959, Knopf, 1960.

(With the editors of *Life*) *Scandanavia* (travel), Time-Life Books (London), 1963.

Sea and Islands (travel), Knopf, 1967.

The Conquistadors (history), Knopf, 1969, reprinted, Collins, 1986.

Hammond Innes Introduces Australia, edited by Clive Turnbull, McGraw (New York City), 1971.

The Last Voyage: Captain Cook's Lost Diary, Collins, 1978, Knopf, 1979.

Hammond Innes' East Anglia, Hodder & Stoughton (London), 1986.

Also author of television play, *The Story of Captain James Cook,* 1975. Contributor to *Saturday Evening Post* and *Holiday.*

JUVENILE; UNDER RALPH HAMMOND

Cocos Gold, Harper, 1950.

Isle of Strangers, Collins, 1951, published as *Island of Peril,* Westminster (Philadelphia), 1953.

Cruise of Danger, Westminster, 1952, published in England as *Saracen's Tower,* Collins, 1952.

Black Gold on the Double Diamond, Collins, 1953.

ADAPTATIONS: Fire in the Snow was filmed as *Snowbound,* RKO, 1948; *The White South* was filmed by Columbia, 1953; *Campbell's Kingdom* was filmed by Rank, 1957; *The Wreck of the "Mary Deare"* was filmed by Metro-Goldwyn-Mayer, 1959; *Golden Soak* and *Levkas Man* were adapted for television; *The Doomed Oasis* was adapted by the British Broadcast Corporation (BBC).

SIDELIGHTS: Ralph Hammond Innes draws upon his many years as a seafaring yachtsman and world traveler to write highly-acclaimed adventure novels set on the high seas or in exotic foreign locales. When she was alive, he would normally spend six months each year travelling with his wife and six months writing at his fourteenth-century home in the Suffolk countryside. His adventure novels have been set in East Africa, the Antarctic, the Canadian Northwest, Morocco, and the South Pacific—all places Hammond Innes himself has visited. "I seldom make notes on these trips," he tells Alan Bestic of the *Radio Times.* "I'm like a sponge, absorbing people, atmospheres." The resulting novels are as often praised for their vividly recreated settings as for their exciting plots. "It is the authenticity of [Hammond Innes's] background," Ernle Bradford writes in the *New York Times Book Review,* "which provides the frame of reality for his tales of adventure." Hammond Innes "has taken his readers," a *Newsday* reviewer writes, "from the Outer Hebrides to the Maldive Islands and from Labrador . . . to the Empty Quarter of Arabia. Any follower of [his] . . . winds up a world traveler by proxy if not in fact." Hammond Innes is one of the most popular adventure writers in the world; some forty million copies of his books have been sold in over fifty different languages.

Hammond Innes's success as a writer came after a grueling apprenticeship. His first four novels, published in the 1930s, earned him a total of 120 English pounds, and are now out of print. He was obliged to work on the staff of the *Financial News,* a daily newspaper for the banking industry, to support himself. But with *Attack Alarm,* published in 1941, Hammond Innes began to receive critical recognition for his work. Set in London during the early years of the Second World War, the novel was written while Hammond Innes was serving as a gunner during the Battle of Britain, a period when the Nazis made nightly bombing raids over England. His description of those harrowing nights has been critically praised. David Tilden of *Books,* for example, claims that *Attack Alarm* "contains pages of some of the most convincing and graphic descriptions of air raids, air fighting and bombing, especially of the work of anti-aircraft, yet to come out of the war, and all in human and story terms." "The description of daily life at the station," the reviewer for the *Times Literary Supplement* believes, "and the almost terrifyingly graphic picture of a dive-bombing attack on the aerodome bear the imprint of truth."

After his time in the British Army, Hammond Innes embarked on a freelance writing career in 1946. Since then, he has turned out an average of one book per year, "all of them bestsellers in the most extravagant sense of the term," as William Green maintains in the *Telegraph Sunday Magazine.* Although the novels do not follow a predictable formula, there are qualities they all share. Roger Baker of *Books and Bookmen* finds that all of Hammond Innes's work is characterized by "a narrative that possesses . . . pace, excitement, theatrical set-pieces and open-air drama." Green reports that "familiar elements recur in every story—the first person narrator and the lone girl he falls for; the half-legendary father-figure; the sense of quest. But they are only a kind of jumping-off point." Hammond Innes explains to Green: "If I wrote to a formula, I would have got bored long ago, and so would the reader."

Among Hammond Innes's most successful novels is *The Blue Ice,* an adventure story set in the rugged Norwegian mountains. It tells of the hunt for an escaped criminal who knows the location of a valuable mine. But "the plot," writes Anthony Boucher of the *New York Times,* "is merely a just-strong-enough thread to hold together a series of descriptions . . . as breathtaking as anything you'll find in contemporary adventure literature, fact or fiction." R. W. Henderson of *Library Journal* describes *The Blue Ice* as "a typical Innes thriller, packed with suspense, mystery, horror, murder and surprises."

Another critically-acclaimed novel, *The Doomed Oasis,* is set in Arabia where a young Englishman has gone to work in the oilfields. There he meets his long-lost father and gets entangled in the dangerous machinations of Arab chieftains and British oil ty-

coons. According to Rex Stout, in his appraisal for the *New York Times Book Review, The Doomed Oasis* "is the best tale of adventure I have read in many desert moons, and I thank Mr. Innes warmly, and salute him." Taliaferro Boatwright of the *New York Herald Tribune Book Review* calls the novel "bloody, exotic, colorful, and completely plausible. . . . [It] is an adult adventure story complex and involute, solidly anchored to today's headlines and yet adequately escapist, entertaining but nonetheless engaging to the mind. This is the way adventure stories ought to be written."

Perhaps Hammond Innes's most popular novel has been *The Wreck of the "Mary Deare,"* the story of a sea captain who struggles to save his ship when it runs aground on a treacherous reef in the English Channel. A bestseller in several countries and adapted as a successful film, *The Wreck of the "Mary Deare"* has also garnered critical acclaim as one of the finest sea adventures of recent times. "I have been reading sea stories for more than half a century," Gene Markey maintains in the *Chicago Sunday Tribune,* "and this is the most exciting one I've read." Although she has some reservations about the quality of the prose, Isabel Quigly of the *Spectator* calls *The Wreck of the "Mary Deare"* "first-rate and the climax one of the most thrilling, in the old danger-and-endurance tradition, that I remember meeting." Several critics especially praise the portrait of the ship's captain in his struggle with the sea. A *New Yorker* critic believes that "the characterization of Patch, master of the Mary Deare, is expertly done." G. H. Favre of the *Christian Science Monitor* believes that the novel is "dominated by the bold figures of a man and a ship, both equally scarred by the vicissitudes of a hard life and seafaring."

The novel was so popular that Hammond Innes named his own boat, a 42-foot ocean racer, the *Mary Deare.* For over ten years he and his wife used it to explore the European coastline from Scandinavia to Turkey. His travels have made him sensitive to the ecological damage that man has caused in all parts of the world. Several of his books focus on environmental issues: *The Big Footprints* concerns the dwindling herds of African elephants; *The Black Tide,* the damaging spills from huge oil tankers; and *High Stand,* the destruction of forestland.

Hammond Innes has been involved with reforesting projects for over twenty-five years. During that time he has, Bestic reports, "planted a million trees." He also owns four forest areas in England

and Wales, and has devoted so much of his time to forestry that he was obliged in the late 1970s to give up sailing the *Mary Deare*. Speaking of his reforesting projects to Bestic, Hammond Innes explains: "I'm replacing some of the timber used up by my books." In *High Stand,* "an old-fashioned tale of intrigue and treachery," as *Maclean's* describes it, Hammond Innes builds his plot around efforts to preserve a forest of red cedars from some unscrupulous loggers. But the plot is almost incidental to the novel. Hammond Innes is more concerned with the forest setting of the story than with its characters and their actions. There are "lovely descriptive passages" of the forest, Jack Sullivan writes in the *New York Times Book Review.* But ultimately, *High Stand* is "a book where the nonhuman world is depicted," Sullivan writes, "as more admirable and more alive, than the human."

Hammond Innes is usually described as a master storyteller whose novels are invariably exciting, entertaining, and believable. "There is no one in our time," D. B. Hughes writes in *Book Week,* "who can compare with him in creating the saga of man against the elements." William Hogan of the *San Francisco Chronicle* calls him "a born story-teller," while T. J. Binyon of the *Times Literary Supplement* finds that he "always spins a good solid yarn." Edwin Fadiman, Jr., believes that Hammond Innes is part of an important literary tradition. "Hammond Innes," Fadiman explains in the *Saturday Review,* "belongs to a group of British writers whose artistic heritage derives from such craftsmen as Somerset Maugham. To these men, novel writing represents an opportunity to serve the reader, to entertain, to amuse and, occasionally, to educate him—unobtrusively." Hammond Innes's own evaluation of his work is modest. "I write by the seat of my pants," he tells Green. "I don't know where the story comes from, and I never know quite how it will turn out. . . . I rely on what I know I can do well—tell a story." Speaking to Green of his life as a freelance writer, Innes remarks: "I am a novelist. I am one of the self-employed. I have to rely on myself."

BIOGRAPHICAL/CRITICAL SOURCES:

BOOKS

Innes, Hammond, *Harvest of Journeys,* Knopf, 1960.
Innes, *Sea and Islands,* Knopf, 1967.

PERIODICALS

Atlantic, June, 1971; April, 1979.
Best Sellers, November 15, 1967.
Books, April 12, 1942; May, 1994, p. 15.
Books and Bookmen, March, 1971.
Book Week, November 21, 1965.
Chicago Sunday Tribune, October 21, 1956.
Christian Science Monitor, November 8, 1956; April 22, 1968.
Globe and Mail (Toronto), November 15, 1985.
Harper's, May, 1971.
Library Journal, July, 1949; December, 1988, p. 132; March 15, 1989, p. 98; October 15, 1989, p. 118; May 15, 1990, p. 118.
Los Angeles Times Book Review, September 15, 1981; March 27, 1983.
Maclean's, October 21, 1985.
National Observer, December 15, 1969.
Newsday, May 22, 1971.
New Yorker, October 27, 1956.
New York Herald Tribune Book Review, October 21, 1956; November 25, 1956; November 13, 1960.
New York Times, March 8, 1942; August 14, 1949; October 21, 1956; May 26, 1977.
New York Times Book Review, November 25, 1956; November 13, 1960; December 24, 1967; December 7, 1969; April 14, 1974; February 8, 1981; June 21, 1985; December 21, 1986.
Observer, August 6, 1967.
Radio Times, August 18-24, 1984.
San Francisco Chronicle, October 21, 1956.
Saturday Review, July 3, 1971; April 28, 1979.
Spectator, July 13, 1956; February 19, 1977.
Telegraph Sunday Magazine, August 10, 1980.
Times (London), September 26, 1985.
Times Literary Supplement, October 25, 1941; May 28, 1970; March 4, 1977.
Village Voice, August 6, 1979.
Washington Post Book World, January 21, 1968; June 29, 1971; July 22, 1979; December 27, 1980; April 3, 1983; October 20, 1985.
Wilson Library Bulletin, September, 1954.
World Literature Today, winter, 1979.
Writer, March, 1970.

*   *   *

HARRIS, Fred (Roy) 1930-

PERSONAL: Born November 13, 1930, in Walters, OK; son of Fred B. (a farmer) and Alene (Person)

Harris; married LaDonna Crawford, April 8, 1949 (divorced, 1981); married Margaret S. Elliston, September 7, 1982; children: (first marriage) Kathryn Tijerina, Byron, Laura. *Education:* University of Oklahoma, B.A., 1952, J.D., 1954. *Politics:* Democrat.

ADDRESSES: Home—P. O. Box 1203, Corrales, NM 87048. *Office*—Department of Political Science, University of New Mexico, Albuquerque, NM 87131.

CAREER: Admitted to Oklahoma Bar, 1954; Harris, Newcomre, Redman & Doolin, Lawton, OK, founder and senior partner, 1954-64; member of Oklahoma State Senate, 1956-64; member of U.S. Senate from Oklahoma, 1964-73; Peoples Policy Center (public interest and research organization), Washington, DC, president, 1973-75; campaigned for Democratic Party presidential nomination, 1975-76; University of New Mexico, Albuquerque, professor of political science, 1976—. Adjunct professor of government, American University, 1973-75. Member of National Advisory Commission on Civil Disorders, 1967-68; chairperson of Democratic National Committee, 1969-70.

MEMBER: Phi Beta Kappa.

WRITINGS:

Alarms and Hopes, Harper (New York City), 1968.
Now Is the Time, McGraw (New York City), 1971.
The New Populism, Saturday Review Press (New York City), 1973.
Potomac Fever, Norton (New York City), 1977.
America's Democracy: The Ideal and the Reality, Scott, Foresman (Glenview, IL), 1980, 3rd edition, 1985.
(With Paul L. Hain) *America's Legislative Processes: Congress and the States,* Scott, Foresman, 1983.
(With David Cooper) *Estudios sobre Estados Unidos y su Relacion Bilateral con Mexico,* Universidad Nacional Autonoma de Mexico, 1986.
(With Randy Roberts and Margaret S. Elliston) *Understanding American Government,* Scott, Foresman, 1988.
(With Gary Wasserman) *America's Government,* Little, Brown (Boston), 1990.
Deadlock of Decision: The U.S. Senate and the Rise of National Politics, Oxford University Press (New York City), 1993.

In Defense of Congress, St. Martin's (New York City), 1994.

EDITOR

Social Science and Public Policy, Transaction Books (Brunswick, NJ), 2nd revised edition, 1973.
Readings on the Body Politic, Scott, Foresman, 1987.
(With Roger W. Wilkins) *Quiet Riots: Race and Poverty in the United States,* Pantheon, 1988.
Los Obstaculos para el Desarrollo, University of New Mexico, 1991.

SIDELIGHTS: Fred Harris, the "neo-populist" candidate for president in 1976, was the emotional, if not the practical, favorite of Democratic liberals, as several political commentators have noted. Philip Terzian in the *New Republic* describes Harris's neo-populism as "a spellbinding combination of affirmative action, Naderism, youthophilia, elitist-baiting, and good old fashioned legislative know-how." Although Harris began his career as a moderate Democratic senator from Oklahoma, during the late 1960s he drifted leftward politically and became known as a critic of the country's maldistribution of wealth.

Harris's presidential campaign was predicated, Jules Witcover relates in *Progressive,* "on a perception of an electorate that is tired of old trappings, that yearns for a new kind of open, straightforward candidate and politics, but that is justifiably suspicious of anyone who projects himself as different from the pack of old jacks." In a 1974 memo outlining his campaign plans, Harris wrote about himself as candidate: "The candidate must be plain-spoken, candid, open. He must demonstrate, from the very first and even in little things, that he will tell the people the truth. None of this 'people are asking me to run' business. No coy 'non-candidate' status. . . . The candidate must articulate in blunt language the real frustrations that people rightly feel because of elitism, privilege, bigness, and concentrated power. No twelve-point programs and new bureaucracies, but common sense steps to diffuse economic and political power more widely."

The style of Harris's campaign was in accordance with his political stance. He ran what Witcover termed a "guerilla-type campaign," crossing the country with his family in their camper, sponsoring $4.76 a plate fund-raising dinners, and generally conducting the campaign in a manner that made

"Jimmy Carter look like John Connally," as Jeff Greenfield states in the *New York Times Book Review.*

Many Democrats likened Harris to George McGovern, the Democrat Party's 1972 candidate, and avoided supporting him for that reason. They feared that if Harris became the nominee, he would be defeated in the national election as McGovern had because he was perceived by the electorate as a "radical." Harris explained the difference between himself and McGovern to *Time* magazine correspondent Stanley Cloud: "I never tell people that they ought to do something because it's morally right. I show how it's in their own self-interest. My dad used to listen to McGovern and then say, 'Well, it sounds fine, but when's he gonna start talking to me?' Dad was right, and that's what I try to do—talk a language that ordinary people can understand."

After bowing out of the race for the presidential nomination, Harris wrote his political memoirs. In the book *Potomac Fever,* he discusses his own case of "Potomac Fever": Harris felt that he concerned himself more with Washington and neglected his home state of Oklahoma. Colman McCarthy, writing in the *Washington Post Book World,* finds that Harris misdiagnosed his affliction—that instead Harris was suffering from "Potomac Blahs." Harris's problem, according to McCarthy, "was in believing that he, the mighty liberal and champion of the little guy, could bring on reforms quickly. He couldn't, and he got the Potomac Blahs. . . . The value of Harris's book is what it says about one person's failure to deal with the frustrations of reform."

In a *Progressive* review of the book, Les Whitten describes Harris's image during the campaign: "With his penultimate shirt button open, flesh showing through the gap, a suit too small, a 1930's hairstyle, he was a portrait in noble disorganization—caused by doing too much for others, his wife, LaDonna, and himself, in that order. Sometimes, he was a sudden dry handful of Dust Bowl wit in our surprised faces." On the other hand, complains Whitten, "*That* vivid Harris isn't enough in evidence in this book, and it is badly flawed thereby." Philip Terzian, writing in the *New Republic,* says he was drawn to the anecdotal humor of the book. He comments: "If Hollywood had any imagination, it would buy the rights for this book of Fred Harris's memoirs and film it as a political *Pilgrim's Progress* of the past two decades. Except, of course, it would require a

script writer with more humor than Bunyan to bring the tale off, because Fred Harris's career has not only been instructive, but funny."

Harris told *CA:* "In Moscow once, the Soviet Union's Americanologist chief, Georgi Arbatov, and I were talking, and I mentioned that I was at a disadvantage in commenting on the Soviet economic and political system, as compared to his ability to comment on ours, because the Soviet system was not open to outside researchers. 'That's no disadvantage for you,' he replied. 'We study your system, but we still cannot understand it.'

"The American system looks simple, but it is a labyrinth of complexity. I enjoy writing about it, to make it more understandable—not just *how* a bill goes through Congress, but also *why,* for example—to point the way for citizen participation and suggest ways to make participation opportunities better."

BIOGRAPHICAL/CRITICAL SOURCES:

BOOKS

MacPherson, Myra, *Power Lovers,* Putnam, 1975.

PERIODICALS

Best Sellers, June 15, 1968; July, 1977.
Nation, February 8, 1975.
New Republic, August 7, 1971; September 8, 1973; May 21, 1977.
Newsweek, November 3, 1975; December 22, 1975; January 12, 1976.
New Yorker, August 24, 1968; August 13, 1973.
New York Times Book Review, June 5, 1977.
Progressive, January, 1976; July, 1977.
Time, December 22, 1975.
U.S. News & World Report, December 1, 1975.
Washington Post Book World, May 15, 1977.

*   *   *

HAUSMAN, Patricia   1953-

PERSONAL: Born December 17, 1953, in Philadelphia, PA; daughter of Melvin Burton (a pharmacist) and Ruth Gilda (a pharmacist; maiden name, Weinstock) Hausman. *Education:* Kirkland College (now Hamilton College), B.A., 1975; University of Maryland, M.S., 1977. *Avocational interests:* Ballroom dancing, jazz music, animals, reading.

ADDRESSES: Office—NutriProse, P.O. Box 868, Gaithersburg, MD 20884-0884. *Agent*—Riverside Literary Agency, Keets Brook Rd., Leyden, MA 01337.

CAREER: Center for Science in the Public Interest, Washington, DC, research associate, 1974-76, editor of *Nutrition Action,* 1976-78, staff nutritionist, 1978-81; NutriProse, Gaithersburg, MD, owner, 1981—; writer and consultant in health, regulatory issues, and public policy. Scientific advisor to law firm of Emord & Associates, 1994-95. Lecturer.

MEMBER: Certification Board for Nutrition Specialists (board member and treasurer, 1992-94; national chair, legislative committee, 1993—), American Nutritionists Association (executive director, 1990-91), American Preventive Medical Association (member of Advisory Board, 1995—), American College of Nutrition, Maryland Nutritionists Association.

WRITINGS:

Jack Sprat's Legacy: The Science and Politics of Fat and Cholesterol, Richard Marek, 1981.
Foods That Fight Cancer, Rawson Associates, 1984.
At-a-Glance Nutrition Counter, Ballantine (New York City), 1985.
The Calcium Bible: How to Have Better Bones All Your Life, Rawson Associates, 1985.
The Right Dose: How to Take Vitamins and Minerals Safely, Rodale Press (Emmaus PA), 1987.
(With Judith Hurley) *The Surgeon General's Report on Nutrition and Health* (how-to sections), Warner, 1989.
(With Hurley) *The Healing Foods,* Rodale Press, 1989.
(With Hurley) *The Healthy Gourmet: A Cookbook of Culinary Discoveries for a Longer Life,* NAL, 1989.

Contributor to periodicals, including *FIT, Chicago Tribune, Washington Post, McCall's, Nutrition Action,* and *Runner's World.*

WORK IN PROGRESS: Various writings on health and public policy.

SIDELIGHTS: Patricia Hausman's *Jack Sprat's Legacy: The Science and Politics of Fat and Cholesterol* is deemed "readable and engaging" by a reviewer for the *Journal of the American Dietetic As-* *sociation.* In the book, Hausman, who has a master's degree in nutrition from the University of Maryland, asserts that traditionally accepted foods, such as eggs, milk, and meat, are promoting heart disease and cancer in Americans, a proven fact she believes the U.S. Government is suppressing. According to Hausman, the Wisconsin chapter of the American Heart Association publishes little information on the dangers of high fat diets, a condition Hausman says is due to submission to the Wisconsin dairy industry. She also charges the American Cancer Society with slighting the relation between fat and cancer. "The [American] Cancer Society just hasn't been progressive," she told the *Baltimore Evening Sun;* "it's stuck on smoking and [finding a cancer] cure and hardly does anything with diet." *Washington Post*'s Jean Carper writes: "Even though one may not agree absolutely with Hausman, she is an author to be trusted and listened to. Few who read her book can still think it is anything but lunacy to put a high premium on fat in a nation where fat-laden products pose a major health problem."

Hausman told *CA:* "In *Jack Sprat's Legacy,* I propose that the controversy about diet and heart disease is the predictable component of a scientific revolution now underway in the field of nutrition. Throughout its history, the science of nutrition has been concerned almost exclusively with essential nutrients and deficiency diseases; meat, milk fat, and egg yolk were long ago dubbed 'protective foods' in recognition of their protein, vitamin, and mineral value. This view, however, is challenged by the vast body of scientific research linking the saturated fat and cholesterol of such foods to coronary heart disease. I believe that the controversy surrounding this research results not from inconclusive or equivocal data but rather from the inability of some scientists to part with long-time notions that deemed high-fat, high-cholesterol foods to be the most nutritious. Thomas Kuhn's book *The Structure of Scientific Revolutions* strongly influenced the view that I present in *Jack Sprat's Legacy.*"

Foods That Fight Cancer is Hausman's book of practical advice regarding the much-publicized topic of diet and cancer. Hausman comes at her topic from two angles by pointing out nutrients and foods that promote cancer and those that may prevent it. In *Interview* magazine, Hausman tells Mark Matousek: "It's only a slight exaggeration to say that there are carcinogens in virtually every food—from mushrooms to steaks to oranges—some of them very weak, some of them very potent. It's impossible to avoid all of these chemicals because they're every-where. I've started telling people to stop trying to avoid all of these foods and to concentrate on eating other foods that provide the protective substances that counteract them. . . . People have been hearing for so long that food causes cancer. . . . If they'd open [my] book, they'd find out that they can stop worrying about how food is going to hurt them and learn how it can help." Although the link between fat and cancer has been much touted, Hausman points to four seemingly protective nutrients and foods: vita-min A, vitamin C, whole-grain fiber, and the "in-hibitors" known as indoles found in vegetables of the cabbage family. Hausman says medical research in-dicates that "better nutrition could reduce colon can-cer by 90 percent, breast cancer by 50 percent and lung cancer by 20 percent. Total reduction might reach 35 percent. That translates into about 150,000 lives a year, and that's a lot of people," records Peggy Brawley for *People*.

Hausman stepped onto controversial ground with two succeeding books which advocate the necessity of vitamin and mineral supplementation. While re-searching for *The Calcium Bible: How to Have Better Bones All Your Life*, Hausman came to the conclusion that calcium supplementation for women who were not getting sufficient calcium in their diets made better sense than pushing a greater intake of calcium-rich but high-fat dairy products. The message of Hausman's *The Right Dose: How to Take Vitamins and Minerals Safely* is at odds with national nutrition organizations, like the American Dietetic Association and the American Society for Clinical Nutrition.

Whereas these organizations urge people to get their nutrients from foods rather than from pills since, among other things, there is the potential for toxicity from pills, Chicago *Tribune Books* contributor Barbara Sullivan records Hausman's stance: "Supplements 'can help make up for short-comings in your diet. There is no doubt in my mind that an inadequate diet plus a safe supple-ment program is certainly better than an inad-equate diet alone.'" Hausman claims documenta-tion of the dangers of supplementation is just not prevalent in the medical research. In *The Right Dose*, Hausman recommends safe dosage levels and provides information on the general roles of vitamins and minerals, food sources in which they can be found, useful recipes, current scientific lit-erature and medical case studies regarding toxic-ity, and more. According to *Baltimore Evening*

Sun reviewer Linell Smith, Hausman professes: "Electricity can kill you, but you don't ban electricity. What most of my colleagues are saying is 'Don't take any Vitamin D because it can be toxic.' I think my job is to tell people how to take vitamins safely, not to tell them 'Don't touch them!'"

BIOGRAPHICAL/CRITICAL SOURCES:

BOOKS

Hausman, Patricia, *The Right Dose: How to Take Vitamins and Minerals Safely*, Rodale Press, 1987.

PERIODICALS

Baltimore Evening Sun, May 18, 1981; July 1, 1987.
Detroit News, April 9, 1987.
Glamour, February, 1986.
Interview, April, 1985.
Journal of Nutrition Education, December, 1981.
Journal of the American Dietetic Association, April, 1982.
Milwaukee Journal, August 12, 1981.
New England Journal of Medicine, September 10, 1981; December 10, 1981.
People, March 12, 1984.
Tribune Books (Chicago), May 7, 1987.
Washington Post, August 20, 1981.

*   *   *

HAWORTH-BOOTH, Mark 1944-

PERSONAL: Surname is pronounced "Hay-worth"; born August 20, 1944, in Westow, York-shire, England; son of Anthony Brough (a con-tractor and journalist) and Eva (a homemaker; maiden name, Holm) Haworth-Booth; married Rosemary Joanna Miles (a curator), July 19, 1979; children: Emily, Alice. *Education:* Cam-bridge University, English tripos, 1966; Univer-sity of Edinburgh, Post Graduate Diploma in Fine Art, 1969. *Religion:* Church of England.

ADDRESSES: Office—Department of Prints, Draw-ings, and Paintings, Victoria and Albert Museum, South Kensington, London SW7 2RL, England.

CAREER: City Art Gallery, Manchester, England, assistant keeper, 1969-70; Victoria and Albert Museum, London, assistant keeper of circulation, 1970-77, curator of photographs, 1977—.

WRITINGS:

E. McKnight Kauffer: A Designer and His Public, Gordon Fraser (London), 1979.

(With Brian Coe) *A Guide to Early Photographic Processes,* Victoria and Albert Museum (London), 1983.

(Editor) *The Golden Age of British Photography, 1839-1900,* Aperture (Millerton, NY), 1984.

(With David Mellor) *Bill Brandt: Behind the Camera,* Aperture, 1985.

Photography Now, Nishen Verlag and Victoria and Albert Museum, 1989.

Camille Silvy: River Scene, France, J. Paul Getty Museum (Malibu, CA), 1992.

Contributor of poems to periodicals, including *Spectator, New Statesman,* and *London.*

WORK IN PROGRESS: "A history of the photography collection at the Victoria and Albert Museum, which began in 1856."

SIDELIGHTS: Mark Haworth-Booth's *E. McKnight Kauffer: A Designer and His Public* is both a biography and a critique of the modernist advertising designer's social concerns. Celina Fox wrote in the *Times Literary Supplement:* "Mr. Haworth-Booth's book is imaginatively conceived and meticulously executed."

A Guide to Early Photographic Processes is a step-by-step guide for identifying the photographic processes used from 1840 to 1914. It should enable the reader to distinguish among five types of negative, three types of transparency, and twenty-seven types of print. Critic Colin Ford told readers of the *Times Literary Supplement* that Haworth-Booth's illustrations "are always revealing, excellently printed" to achieve "a better 'feel' of the processes than usual."

Haworth-Booth also edited *The Golden Age of British Photography, 1839-1900,* which studies the work of photographic pioneers of the Victorian era, including William Henry Fox Talbot, who invented calotype, Roger Fenton, who covered the Crimean War with his photographs, and Julia Margaret Cameron, who is famous for her portrait studies. In the *New Yorker,*

a reviewer declared that the "large and faithful-looking reproductions of these early calotypes and albumen, carbon, and platinum prints are stunning."

In 1992, Haworth-Booth produced *Camille Silvy: River Scene, France.* In this volume, the author closely examines the 1858 photograph, "River Scene, France," by French diplomat and photographer Silvy, pointing out its historical significance. Assessing the book, *Aperture*'s John Szarkowski called it an "excellent work."

Haworth-Booth told *CA:* "The Victoria and Albert Museum holds the national collection of the art of photography in the United Kingdom. As curator, I am responsible for looking after a collection of 300,000 photographs and for adding new acquisitions, mounting exhibitions, and editing and writing books bringing this collection to new audiences in Great Britain, the United States, and elsewhere.

"I am interested in photography of the 1850s because the medium was then in its pristine heyday and exploring roles which later became characteristic of the medium. Looking at the pioneering days is a good way to crystallize new ideas about the nature of photography—such as, for example, the interesting relationship between photography and detection (made explicit in the writings of Charles Dickens)."

BIOGRAPHICAL/CRITICAL SOURCES:

PERIODICALS

Aperture, winter, 1994.
New Yorker, November 26, 1984.
Times Literary Supplement, January 25, 1980; June 24, 1983.

*   *   *

HEBERT, Jacques 1923-

PERSONAL: Surname pronounced "Hay-bear"; born June 21, 1923, in Montreal, Quebec, Canada; son of Louis-Philippe (a doctor) and Denise (Saint-Onge) Hebert; married Therese DesJardins, October 20, 1951; children: Michel, Pascale, Isabelle, Bruno, Sophie. *Education:* Attended College Sainte-Marie, Montreal, and University St. Dunstan, Charlottetown; Ecole Des Hautes Etudes Commercials de Montreal, license en sciences commerciales.

ADDRESSES: Home—3480 Prud-homme, Montreal, Quebec, Canada H4A 3H4; 285 Laurier St., Apt. 505, Hull, Quebec, Canada J8X 3W9. *Office*—Senate Parliament Bldg., Ottawa, Ontario, Canada K1A 0A4; Canada World Youth, 2330 Notre-Dame St. West, 3rd floor, Montreal, Quebec, Canada H3J 1N4.

CAREER: Editions de l'Homme, Montreal, Quebec, founder, 1958, general manager, 1958-61; Editions du Jour, Montreal, founder, president, and director general, 1961-74; Canada World Youth, Montreal, founder and president, beginning 1971; member of senate, Canadian Parliament, Ottawa, Ontario, 1983—, chief government whip. President of the Association des Editeurs Canadiens, 1965-74. Founder and president, Katimavik, 1976—. Commissioner, Canadian Radio Television Commission, 1971-81. Cochair, Federal Cultural Review Committee, 1981-82. Order of Canada, officer, 1979.

MEMBER: International Association of French-Speaking Parliamentarians, Canada-US Inter-parliamentary Group, Canada-France Interparliamentary Association, Canada-Cuba Friendship Group (chair), Commonwealth Parliamentary Association, Canadian Parliamentarians for Global Action, Liberal National Caucus (vice chair), Canadian Human Rights Foundation (member of national council), Liberal Caucus of Quebec (vice chair), Civil Liberties Union, Quebec (founding member and past president).

AWARDS, HONORS: Rose Award, 1987; Lewis Perinbam Award in International Development, 1995.

WRITINGS:

IN FRENCH

Autour des trois Ameriques, Beauchemin (Montreal), 1948.
Autour de l'Afrique, Fides (Montreal), 1950.
Aicha l'Africaine (stories), Fides, 1950.
Aventure autour du Monde, Fides, 1952.
Nouvelle aventure en Afrique, Fides, 1953.
Coffin etait innocent, Editions de l'Homme (Montreal), 1958.
Scandale a Bordeaux, Editions de l'Homme, 1959.
(With Pierre Elliott Trudeau) *Deux innocents en Chine rouge,* Editions de l'Homme, 1960.

J'accuse les assassins de Coffin, Editions du Jour (Montreal), 1963.
Trois jours en prison, Club du Livre du Quebec (Montreal), 1965.
Les Ecoeurants (novel), Editions du Jour, 1966.
Ah! mes Aieux!, Editions du Jour, 1968.
Obscenite et Liberte, Editions du Jour, 1970.
Blablabla du bout de monde, Editions du Jour, 1971.
L'Affaire Coffin, Domino (Montreal), 1980.
La jeunesse des annees 80: etat d'urgencer, Editions Heritage (Montreal), 1982.
Voyager en pays tropical, Boreal Express (Montreal), 1984.
Trois semaines dans le hall du Senat, Editions de l'Homme, 1986.
Yemen-Invitation au voyage en Arabie heureuse, Editions Heritage, 1989.
Deux Innocents dans un igloo, Heritage Jeunesse (Montreal), 1990.
Deux Innocents au Mexique, Heritage Jeunesse, 1990.
Deux Innocents au Guatemala, Heritage Jeunesse, 1990.
Deux Innocents au Amerique centrale, Heritage Jeunesse, 1991.

IN ENGLISH

The Temple on the River, Harvest House (Montreal), 1967.
The World Is Round, McClelland & Stewart (Toronto), 1976.
Have Them Build a Tower Together, McClelland & Stewart, 1979.
(With Maurice F. Strong) *The Great Building-Bee,* General Publishing (Don Mills), 1980.

TRANSLATED FROM FRENCH INTO ENGLISH

(With Pierre Elliott Trudeau) *Two Innocents in Red China* (translated from *Deux innocents en Chine rouge*), Oxford University Press (Toronto), 1968.
I Accuse the Assassins of Coffin (translated from *J'accuse les assassins de Coffin*), Editions du Jour, 1964.
The Coffin Affair (translated from *L'Affaire Coffin*), General Publishing, 1982.
Travelling in Tropical Countries (translated from *Voyager en pays tropical*), Hurtig Publishers (Montreal), 1986.
Twenty-one Days: One Man's Fight for Canada's Youth (translated from *Trois semaines dans le*

hall du Senat), Optimum Publishing (Montreal), 1986.

Yemen-Invitation to a Voyage in Arabia Felix (translated from *Yemen-Invitation au voyage en Arabie heureuse*), Heritage Publishing (Montreal), 1989.

Two Innocents in an Igloo (translated from *Deux Innocents dans un igloo*), Heritage Jeunesse, 1990.

Two Innocents in Mexico (translated from *Deux Innocents au Mexique*), Heritage Jeunesse, 1990.

Two Innocents in Guatemala (translated from *Deux Innocents au Guatemala*), Heritage Jeunesse, 1990.

Two Innocents in Central America (translated from *Deux Innocents au Amerique centrale*), Heritage Jeunesse, 1991.

OTHER

Contributor to *Le Devoir,* 1951-53. Founder, 1954, and editor, 1954-59 of *VRAI.* Script writer and host of public affairs television programs for Canadian Broadcasting Company, 1962-70.

*   *   *

HEDRICK, Joan D(oran)   1944-

PERSONAL: Born May 1, 1944, in Baltimore, MD; daughter of Paul Thomas (a financier) and Jane (Connorton) Doran; married Travis K. Hedrick (a professor), August 26, 1967; children: Jessica, Rachel. *Education:* Vassar College, A.B., 1966; Brown University, Ph.D., 1974.

ADDRESSES: Office—Department of History, Trinity College, Hartford, CT 06106.

CAREER: Wesleyan University, Middletown, CT, instructor, 1972-74, assistant professor of English, 1974-80; Trinity College, Hartford, CT, visiting assistant professor, 1980-81, visiting associate professor of history and American studies, beginning 1981, currently associate professor of history and director of women's studies.

MEMBER: Modern Language Association of America, American Studies Association.

AWARDS, HONORS: Pulitzer Prize in history, 1995, for *Harriet Beecher Stowe: A Life.*

WRITINGS:

Solitary Comrade: Jack London and His Work, University of North Carolina Press (Chapel Hill, NC), 1982.

Harriet Beecher Stowe: A Life, Oxford University Press (New York City), 1994.

SIDELIGHTS: Joan D. Hedrick's Pulitzer Prize-winning *Harriet Beecher Stowe: A Life* examines the life and times of the most widely-read woman writer of nineteenth-century America. Stowe's controversial novel *Uncle Tom's Cabin* attracted an international audience and exposed the injustices of slavery on the plantations of the American South. Although the book lacks literary merit, *Uncle Tom's Cabin* enjoys a continuing place in American literary history as an important work of social protest.

The first biography of Stowe to be written in some fifty years, Hedrick's account draws on more recent feminist and racial approaches to literature and depicts Stowe as a woman crusader against the social evils of her time. James R. Mellow, writing for the *Washington Post Book World,* finds that Hedrick "does take a distinctly feminist approach" in her biography, "but her arguments are always well-taken and informative and not self-serving." While providing a biography of Stowe herself, Hedrick's study is also "an unforgettable view of the epic sweep of the era" in which Stowe lived, according to Martha Saxton in the *Nation.*

Not all commentators are as positive about Hedrick's biography. In a *Times Literary Supplement* review, Margaret Anne Doody argues that "one of the weaknesses of Hedrick's book seems to be a lack of understanding of, or interest in, the attitudes, thoughts and production of a pre-nineteenth-century past, which is sometimes very coarsely sketched." Peter Conrad, writing in the London *Observer,* contends that Hedrick apologizes for Stowe's lapse "into genteel racism" following the Civil War. Conrad states: "Hedrick's biography, evincing all the acrimonious separatism which envenoms intellectual debate in the United States, [sets] out to confer political correctness on the piously bigoted, unregenerately bourgeois Stowe." But Robert Dawidoff, writing in the *Los Angeles Times Book Review,* judges that "Hedrick's excellent biography gives the contemporary reader a fresh look at the life of a powerful writer . . . and an epochal figure in the modern history of women." Commenting on Hedrick's analysis of *Uncle Tom's Cabin,* E. L. Doctorow notes in the *New York Times Book Review* that Hedrick "makes no wild claims for *Uncle Tom's Cabin* on literary grounds. She concurs with critics who have pointed out Stowe's unacknowledged appropriation of published slave narratives . . . and she emphasizes the paternalistic racism of Stowe's stereotyping." However, Doctorow continues, Hedrick demonstrates that the novel's "internal flaws and moral self-contradictions" mirrored the conflicts then present in American society.

The task of writing a biography of Stowe took Hedrick ten years and involved working through what Lynn Karpen describes in the *New York Times Book Review* as an "extraordinary quantity and richness of . . . archival material." Hedrick told Karpen that the sheer amount of research material to be consulted, including Stowe's massive correspondence with her husband and scattered family members, "may just be what's kept other biographers away."

BIOGRAPHICAL/CRITICAL SOURCES:

PERIODICALS

America, March 19, 1994, p. 25.
American History, August, 1994, p. 20.
Belles Lettres, fall, 1994, p. 10.
Boston Globe, January 16, 1994, p. 63; May 3, 1995, p. 33.
Christian Science Monitor, April 8, 1994, p. 13.
Economist, February 5, 1994, p. 92.
Historian, autumn, 1994, p. 136.
Journal of American History, December, 1994, p. 1267.
Journal of American Studies, August, 1983, p. 311.
Los Angeles Times Book Review, August 21, 1994, p. 13.
Nation, May 16, 1994, pp. 676-78.
New Republic, April 18, 1994, p. 38.
New Yorker, March 7, 1994, p. 99.
New York Times, January 19, 1994, p. C22.
New York Times Book Review, February 13, 1994, pp. 3, 33.
Nineteenth-Century Literature, September, 1994, p. 264.
Observer (London), April 17, 1994, p. 20.
Times Literary Supplement, June 3, 1994, p. 13.
Wall Street Journal, March 22, 1994, p. 12.
Washington Post Book World, February 27, 1994, p. 3, 7.

Western American Literature, spring, 1983, p. 77.
Women's Review of Books, April, 1994, p. 13.*

* * *

HEILMAN, Robert Bechtold 1906-

PERSONAL: Born July 18, 1906, in Philadelphia, PA; son of Edgar James (a clergyperson) and Mary Alice (Bechtold) Heilman; married Elizabeth Wiltbank, 1927 (divorced, 1934); married Ruth Delavan Champlin, July 31, 1935; children: (first marriage) Robert W., (second marriage) Champlin. *Education:* Lafayette College, A.B., 1927; Tufts University, graduate study, 1927-28; Ohio State University, M.A., 1930; Harvard University, M.A., 1931, Ph.D., 1935. *Politics:* "Swing voter." *Religion:* Lutheran. *Avocational interests:* Watching football.

ADDRESSES: Home—900 University St. #7-0, Seattle, WA 98101-2729. *Office*—Department of English, Box 354330, University of Washington, Seattle, WA 98195.

CAREER: University of Maine, Orono, instructor in English, 1930-35; Louisiana State University, Baton Rouge, instructor, 1935-36, assistant professor, 1936-42, associate professor, 1942-46, professor of English, 1946-48; University of Washington, Seattle, professor of English, 1948-76, professor emeritus, 1976—, chair of department, 1948-71. Arnold Professor of English, Whitman College, 1977.

MEMBER: International Association of University Professors of English, International Shakespeare Association, Modern Language Association of America (member of national executive council, 1966-69), National Council of Teachers of English (distinguished lecturer, 1968), American Association of University Professors (member of national executive council, 1962-65), Shakespeare Association of America (trustee, 1977-80), Philological Association of Pacific Coast (president, 1958), Phi Beta Kappa (senator, 1967-85; member of executive committee, 1973-82; visiting scholar, 1983-84).

AWARDS, HONORS: Arizona Quarterly Essay Prize, 1956, for an essay on *Othello; Explicator* Award (for criticism), 1957, for *Magic in the*

Web: Action and Language in Othello; Huntington Library grant, 1959; Longview Award, 1960, for essay in *Texas Quarterly;* Guggenheim fellowship, 1964-65, and 1975-76; National Endowment for the Humanities senior fellow, 1971-72; Christian Gauss Prize of Phi Beta Kappa, 1979; recipient of honorary degrees, including D.Lit., Lafayette College, 1967; LL.D., Grinnell College, 1971; L.H.D., Kenyon College, 1973; HH.D., Whitman College, 1977; and Lit.D., University of the South, 1978.

WRITINGS:

America in English Fiction, 1760-1800, Louisiana State University Press (Baton Rouge), 1937.
This Great Stage: Image and Structure in King Lear, Louisiana State University Press, 1948.
Magic in the Web: Action and Language in Othello, University Press of Kentucky (Lexington), 1956.
Tragedy and Melodrama: Versions of Experience, University of Washington Press (Seattle), 1968.
The Iceman, the Arsonist, and the Troubled Agent: Tragedy and Melodrama on the Modern Stage, University of Washington Press, 1973.
The Ghost on the Ramparts and Other Essays in the Humanities, University of Georgia Press (Athens), 1973.

EDITOR AND AUTHOR OF CRITICAL INTRODUCTION

Jonathan Swift, *Gulliver's Travels,* Modern Library (New York City), 1950, revised edition, 1969.
Swift, *A Tale of a Tub* [and] *The Battle of the Books,* Modern Library, 1950.
An Anthology of English Drama before Shakespeare, Rinehart (Boulder, CO), 1952.
Joseph Conrad, *Lord Jim,* Rinehart, 1957.
Thomas Hardy, *The Mayor of Casterbridge,* Riverside (Riverside, CT), 1962.
George Eliot, *Silas Marner,* Riverside, 1962.
William Shakespeare, *Cymbeline,* Pelican (Gretna, LA), 1964.
Euripides, *Alcestis,* Chandler, 1965.
Hardy, *Jude the Obscure,* Harper (New York City), 1966.
Shakespeare, *The Taming of the Shrew,* Signet (New York City), 1966.
Hardy, *Tess of the D'Urbervilles,* Bantam (New York City), 1971.
Shakespeare; the Tragedies: Twentieth Century Views, New Perspectives, Prentice-Hall (Englewood Cliffs, NJ), 1984.

EDITOR

Aspects of Democracy, Louisiana State University Press, 1941.
Aspects of a World at War, Louisiana State University Press, 1943.
(With Cleanth Brooks) *Understanding Drama* (textbook), Holt (New York City), 1945, expanded edition, 1948.
Modern Short Stories: A Critical Anthology (textbook), Harcourt (New York City), 1950.

OTHER

Also author of *Charliad* (verse), 1973. Contributor to books, including *Studies for W. A. Read,* edited by T. A. Kirby and N. M. Caffee, Louisiana State University Press, 1941; *A Southern Vanguard,* edited by Allen Tate, Prentice-Hall, 1947; *Shakespeare 400,* edited by James G. McManaway, Holt, 1964; *Sense and Sensibility in Twentieth-Century Writings,* Southern Illinois University Press (Carbondale), 1970; *The Novels of Thomas Hardy,* edited by Anne Smith, Vision Press (London), 1979; *Walter Van Tilberg Clark: Critiques,* edited by Charlton Laird, University of Nevada Press (Reno), 1983; and *Concord in Discord: Essays on John Ford,* edited by Donald K. Anderson, Jr., AMS Press (New York City), 1986.

Also contributor to *English Institute Annual,* Columbia University Press (New York City), 1949; *The Range of English: NCTE Distinguished Lectures,* National Council of Teachers of English (Urbana, IL), 1968; and *Dictionary of American Biography,* 1981. Contributor of essays and reviews to journals. Member of editorial board, *Poetry Northwest,* 1962; *Studies in the Novel,* 1966—; *Shakespeare Studies,* 1966—; *Modern Language Quarterly,* 1973-77; *Sewanee Review,* 1974—; *Mississippi Studies in English,* 1981—; and *Interim,* 1987—. Regular reviewer for Phi Beta Kappa *Key Reporter,* 1959-91.

*   *   *

HELLER, David   1957-

PERSONAL: Born November 11, 1957, in Bridgeport, CT; son of Marcus and Blanche Heller. *Education:* Harvard University, B.A. (summa cum laude), 1979; University of Michigan, M.A., 1982, Ph.D., 1984. *Politics:* Independent. *Religion:* Jewish/Ecumenical.

ADDRESSES: Home—221 Massachusettes Ave. #1001, Boston, MA 02115.

CAREER: Writer.

MEMBER: American Psychological Association, PEN New England, Harvard Alumni Association, University of Michigan Alumni Association, Phi Beta Kappa.

AWARDS, HONORS: White House fellow finalist, 1985; Roothbert Humanities Fellowship, 1985; *Power in Psychotherapeutic Practice* was chosen as a Macmillan Behavioral Sciences Book Club Selection, 1985.

WRITINGS:

Power in Psychotherapeutic Practice, Macmillan (New York City), 1985.
(With Dan Goleman) *The Pleasures of Psychology,* New American Library (New York City), 1986.
The Children's God, University of Chicago Press, 1986.
Dear God: Children's Letters to God, Doubleday (New York City), 1987.
Talking to Your Child about God, Bantam (New York City), 1988.
Dear God, What Religion Were the Dinosaurs?, Doubleday, 1990.
The Soul of a Man, Ballantine (New York City), 1990.
Growing Up Isn't Hard to Do If You Start Out as a Kid, Villard, 1991.
Mr. President, Ballantine, 1991.
Love Is like a Crayon because It Comes in All Colors, Villard, 1993.
My Mother Is the Best Gift I Ever Got, Villard, 1993.
Fathers Are like Elephants because They're the Biggest Ones Around, Villard, 1993.
Grandparents Are Made for Hugging, Villard, 1993.
The Best Christmas Presents Are Wrapped in Heaven, Villard, 1993.
Just Build the Ark and the Animals Will Come, Villard, 1994.
Children on Happiness, Villard, 1994.
The Kids' Prayer Book about All Sorts of Things, St. Paul Books & Media (Boston), 1995.
Parenting, New Leaf (Harrison, AR), 1995.
Angels Must Get Their Wings by Helping Little Angels like Me, Kensington Books (San Diego, CA), 1995.

Contributor to magazines, including *Psychology Today* and *Working Mother,* and to newspapers, including *Boston Herald, Sun* (Baltimore), *Washington Times, Sun-Times* (Chicago), *Miami Herald,* and *Newsday.* Author of column on children and religion, syndicated by Religious News Service.

SIDELIGHTS: David Heller told *CA:* "I am interested in the cultivation of spiritual values in popular culture. I would like to contribute to that in some meaningful and influential way."

The Children's God, Heller's 1986 book, is derived from forty interviews of children, conducted by psychologist David Heller in Ann Arbor, Michigan. He interviewed boys and girls, aged four to twelve, of several religious faiths and concluded that sex, age, and religious orientation influence a child's perspective of God.

Heller added: "My own religious views are my motivation and source of guidance in all my writing. I believe in a great and uncategorizable God who is beyond religion and science, a God who is visible only with keen perception and personalized imagery—the tools of the human heart."

BIOGRAPHICAL/CRITICAL SOURCES:

PERIODICALS

Psychology Today, December, 1985.
Washington Post Book World, July 13, 1986.

*   *   *

HELLER, Michael (David)   1937-

PERSONAL: Born May 11, 1937, in New York, NY; son of Peter Frank (a publicist) and Martha (Rosenthal) Heller; married Doris C. Whytal, June 10, 1962 (divorced March 23, 1978); married Jane Augustine (writer), March 5, 1979; children: (first marriage) Nicholas Solomon. *Education:* Rensselaer Polytechnic Institute, B.S. Eng., 1959; New York University, M.A., 1986; graduate study at New School for Social Research.

ADDRESSES: Home—P.O. Box 1289, Stuyvesant Station, New York, NY 10009. *Office*—American Language Institute, New York University, New York, NY 10003.

CAREER: Norelco, New York City, chief technical writer, 1963-65; private teacher of English in Spain, 1965-66; freelance industrial and advertising writer, 1966-67; New York University, American Language Institute and Washington Square College, New York City, master teacher in English, 1967—, acting director, 1986-87, academic coordinator, 1987-92. Lecturer, New York City Community College, 1973. Curator, "Poetry—An Exhibition," City University of New York, 1977. Participant in Poetry-in-the-School programs in New York and Wyoming; member of advisory panel, New York Poetry-in-the-Schools, 1970—; Naropa Institute, summer faculty in MFA program. Has lectured on poetry for New York Sculpture Symposium and has given readings.

MEMBER: PEN (member of Freedom to Write committee), American Language Institute, Academy of American Poets, Poetry Society of America, Poets and Writers, Modern Language Association, National Book Critics Circle, New York State Poets in the Schools, Poets House (advisory board member).

AWARDS, HONORS: The Coffey Poetry Prize, New School for Social Research, 1964; Poetry fellowship from New York State Creative Artists Public Service, 1975; Poetry in Public Places Award, 1975; grants from National Endowment for the Humanities, 1979, 1986; Alice Fay di Castagnola Award from Poetry Society of America, 1980; Yaddo fellow, 1989; New York Foundation for the Arts fellow, 1989.

WRITINGS:

Conviction's Net of Branches: Essays on the Objectivist Poets and Poetry, Southern Illinois University Press (Carbondale, IL), 1984.
(Editor) *Carl Rakosi: Man and Poet,* National Poetry Foundation (Orono, ME), 1993.

POETRY

Two Poems, Perishable Press , 1970.
Accidental Center, Sumac Press (Fremont, MI), 1972.
Figures of Speaking, Perishable Press, 1977.
Knowledge, SUN (New York City), 1979.
Marginalia in a Desperate Hand, Staple Diet Pig Press, 1985.
In the Builded Place, Coffee House Press, 1989.

OTHER

Contributor of articles and poems to literary journals and national publications, including *Nation, Caterpillar, Sumac, Paris Review, Extensions, Ohio Review, Ironwood,* and *Parnassus.* Editor of *Origin: Fifth Series* and *American Language Institute Alumni Newsletter;* former contributing editor, *Montemora;* advisory editor, *Pequod;* contributing editor, *Sagetrieb.*

WORK IN PROGRESS: The Uncertainty of the Poet: Essays on Contemporary Poets and Poetry; Europe of the Last, a novel; *Living Root,* a memoir.

SIDELIGHTS: Michael Heller told *CA:* "My formal education has been in science and engineering, and recently, in philosophy, interests which continually play a great part in my thinking and writing. Science, thought—these later gods—deny the comforts of the old animisms; they too, however, are in need of demystification, not because they are wrong, but because they are not sufficient. I try to pose something as language which gives more force to a human argument of the world. Nevertheless, I would not want to call it a 'fine art.'"

BIOGRAPHICAL/CRITICAL SOURCES:

PERIODICALS

Contemporary Literature, fall, 1991.
Contemporary Poetry: A Journal of Criticism, spring, 1978.

*   *   *

HENDERSON, Michael (Douglas)   1932-

PERSONAL: Born March 15, 1932, in London, England; came to the United States, 1978; son of Arthur Douglas (a businessperson) and Erina (Tilly) Henderson; married Erica Mildred Hallowes, March 16, 1966; children: Juliet Rachel Erina. *Education:* Attended schools in England and the United States. *Religion:* Christian.

ADDRESSES: Home—10605 Southwest Terwilliger Pl., Portland, OR 97219.

CAREER: KOAP-TV, Portland, OR, moderator of "World Press in Review" program, 1979-81; KBOO-Radio, Portland, commentator, 1981—; Oregon Public Broadcasting Radio (KOAC/KOAP-FM), Portland, 1987-93. Columnist, *Lake Oswego Review,* Lake Oswego, OR, and *For a Change* magazine (UK). Voluntary religious worker with Moral Re-Armament, 1950—. Cable television host and freelance journalist; does voice-overs for film and video; video producer.

MEMBER: World Affairs Council of Oregon (president, 1983), English-speaking Union (president, 1982-83), Willamette Writers (president, 1983), Britain's Institute of Journalists, Society of Professional Journalists, Sigma Delta Chi.

AWARDS, HONORS: George Washington Honor Medal, Freedoms Foundation at Valley Forge, 1986, for *A Different Accent,* and 1989, for *On History's Coattails;* Academy of Religions Broadcasting Award of Excellence for radio commentary, 1987; Oregon Christian Writer of the Year, 1989-90; first place for radio commentary, Pacific Northeast Excellence in Journalism competition, Society of Professional Journalists, and Portland Baha'i Peace Award, both 1989.

WRITINGS:

From India with Hope, Grosvenor (London), 1972.
Experiment with Untruth: India under Emergency, Macmillan (India), 1977, South Asia Books (Columbia, MO), 1979.
A Different Accent (a collection of transcribed radio talks), Grosvenor, 1985.
On History's Coattails, Grosvenor, 1988.
Hope for a Change: Commentaries by an Optimistic Realist, Grosvenor, 1991.
All Her Paths Are Peace: Women Pioneers in Peacemaking, Kumarian Press (West Hartford, CT), 1994.

Coauthor of musical reviews, including *GB,* produced in London's West End. Also author of pamphlets. Contributor to numerous periodicals, including *Christian Science Monitor, Washington Times, Minneapolis Star Tribune, Asian Reporter,* and *Lake Oswego Review.*

All Her Paths Are Peace: Women Pioneers in Peacemaking has been translated into Chinese.

WORK IN PROGRESS: Making a World of Difference, a compilation of stories of conflict resolution.

SIDELIGHTS: Michael Henderson once told *CA:* "I was interviewed by a journalist . . . who asked me,

'What is your philosophy of writing?' I was a bit taken aback. I suppose I shouldn't have been. I had just never been asked it like that before, never really taken time to think out why I write what I write. I had taken my writing philosophy for granted; seen it simply as an extension of how I lived and what I lived for.

"That journalist's question to me has caused me to consider the why of my commentaries. Basically I write and speak to change the way people live and think. I write to share insights, lessons, attitudes, and hopes I have gleaned as the fruit of contact with very fine men and women all over the world, many of them associated with the program of Moral Re-Armament.

"One motive I have [for writing] is to enlarge horizons. In this dangerous age in which we live it is vital to be knowledgeable about other countries and what motivates their peoples. We are, whether we like it or not, interdependent. What is in the world interest is in our national interest, though we don't always realize it.

"There are so many ways in which society gets polarized, and I would like to work for a greater tolerance and understanding of those who differ from us. I would like in my writing to reduce the us and them syndrome. In the peace movement people who should be working together are at odds. . . . As Peter Howard, the English journalist to whom I owe most of what I know about writing, said about his own work: 'I write to encourage men to accept the growth in character that is essential if civilization is to survive.'"

BIOGRAPHICAL/CRITICAL SOURCES:

PERIODICALS

Christian Science Monitor, September 20, 1985.
Oregonian, February 6, 1983.

*　　*　　*

HERTZ, David Michael　1954-

PERSONAL: Born May 30, 1954, in Bay Shore, NY; son of Joseph H. (a teacher) and Sarah (a teacher) Hertz. *Education:* Indiana University—Bloomington, B.A. (with honors), 1976, B.S. (with distinction),

1977, M.A., 1979; New York University, M.Phil., 1982, Ph.D., 1983.

ADDRESSES: Home—Bloomington, IN. *Office*—Department of Comparative Literature, Ballantine Hall, Indiana University—Bloomington, Bloomington, IN 47401.

CAREER: New York University, New York City, lecturer in liberal studies and instructor in comparative literature, 1981-83, Mellon postdoctoral fellow, 1983-84, assistant professor of comparative literature, 1984-86; Indiana University—Bloomington, visiting assistant professor, 1987-89, associate professor, 1989-94, professor of comparative literature, 1994, director of graduate studies, 1994—. Director of Eastern Comparative Literature Conference, 1985-86; pianist and composer for orchestra and string quartet.

MEMBER: PEN, American Comparative Literature Association, Modern Language Association, International Comparative Literature Association, Lyrica: Society for Word-Music Relations, Association of Literary Scholars and Critics (member of steering committee).

WRITINGS:

The Tuning of the Word: The Musico-Literary Poetics of the Symbolist Movement, Southern Illinois University Press (Carbondale), 1987.
Angels of Reality: Emersonian Unfoldings in Wright, Stevens, Ives, Southern Illinois University Press, 1993.
Frank Lloyd Wright: In Word and Form, G. K. Hall (Boston), 1995.

Composer of *The Rose Garden Conspiracy,* 1988, and *China Songbook,* 1995. Contributor of articles and reviews to comparative literature journals.

WORK IN PROGRESS: Sublimation: Toward a Psychology of Creativity.

SIDELIGHTS: David Michael Hertz told *CA:* "My goal is to live the double life of artist and scholar. As a composer I always try to build on the great achievements of the past yet above all to be sensitive—in every sense of the word—to the sounds of *today.* From both a scholarly and artistic point of view, I believe that real originality must happen organically, from within, and must never be self-conscious.

"My first book is the logical result of my in-depth study of two art forms that have become unnecessarily distinct in the modern world—literature and music. *The Tuning of the Word* reflects, too, my continuing interest in musical poetry and poetic music. My title grew out of my gradual realization that the 'word,' as used by the poets, was literally 'tuned up' to approximate the condition of the musical note in the nineteenth century. I focused on the Symbolists because one can trace, in many important respects, the origins of modern styles in art to them.

"*Angels of Reality: Emersonian Unfoldings in Wright, Stevens, Ives,* is a search for my own roots as an American artist. The title comes from a poem by Stevens in which he argues that reality is the 'necessary angel.' The work is a study of how three major American artists found unique, fresh, and distinctly un-European voices in architecture, poetry, and music, respectively. These three Americans were influenced by dominant European intellectuals. In the case of Stevens, the major presence was [French symbolist poet Stephane] Mallarme. For Ives, it was [French composer Claude] Debussy. For Wright, [French architect Eugene Emmanuel] Viollet-le-duc. Yet all three were able to find their individuality through the contemplation of ordinary American reality. For them, the reality of everyday America was the 'necessary angel' that linked imaginative ideas of the possibilities of art to the surrounding world. The celebration of everyday reality is what distinguishes Wright, Stevens, and Ives from their European predecessors."

*   *   *

HEXHAM, Irving   1943-

PERSONAL: Born April 14, 1943, in Whitehaven, Cumbria, England; son of Thomas Johnson and Elsie (Bell) Hexham; married second wife, Karla Poewe (an anthropologist), 1988; children: (first marriage) Jeremy, Janet. *Education:* University of Lancaster, B.A. (with honors), 1970; University of Bristol, M.A. (with commendation), 1972, Ph.D., 1975. *Politics:* Liberal. *Religion:* Anglican.

ADDRESSES: Home—55 Hawksbrow Dr. N.W., Calgary, Alberta, Canada T3G 3H4. *Office*—Department of Religious Studies, University of Calgary, Calgary, Alberta, T2N 1N4, Canada.

CAREER: North-Western Gas Board, Stockport, England, apprentice gas fitter, 1958-64, manager in Ashton-under-Lyne, England, 1964-65; Stretford Technical College, Stretford, England, lecturer in gas technology, 1967; Bishop Lonsdale College, Derby, England, assistant professor of religious studies, 1974-77; Regent College, Vancouver, British Columbia, assistant professor of philosophy of religion, 1977-80; University of Manitoba, Winnipeg, assistant professor of religious studies, 1980-84; University of Calgary, Calgary, Alberta, assistant professor of religious studies, 1984-88; associate professor, 1988-92, full professor, 1992—. Religious broadcaster on Canadian Broadcasting Corp. weekly program "The Calgary Eyeopener."

MEMBER: Canadian Society for the Study of Religion, Evangelical Theological Society, Society for the Scientific Study of Religion, American Academy of Religion, Royal African Society, South African Institute of Race Relations, Berlin Society for Mission Studies, South African Missiological Society.

AWARDS, HONORS: Grants from Social Science and Humanities Research Council of Canada.

WRITINGS:

The Irony of Apartheid, Mellen, Edwin (Lewiston, NY), 1982.
(With wife, Karla Poewe) *Understanding Cults and New Religions,* Eerdmans (Grand Rapids, MI), 1986.
A Concise Dictionary of Religion, Inter-Varsity (Downers Grove, IL), 1993.
(With Poewe) *New Religions as Global Cultures,* Westview Press (Boulder, CO), in press.

EDITOR

(With Walter Block) *Religion, Economics, and Social Thought: Proceedings of an International Symposium,* Fraser Institute, 1987.
Texts on Zulu Religion: Traditional Zulu Ideas about God, Mellen, Edwin, 1988.
(With G. C. Oosthuizen) *Afro-Christian Religion and Healing in Southern Africa,* Mellen, Edwin, 1989.
(Consulting with Robert G. Clouse et. al.) *The Twentieth Century Encyclopedia of Religious Knowledge,* Baker (Grand Rapids, MI), 1991.
(With Oosthuizen) *Afro-Christianity at the Grassroots in Southern Africa,* Mellen, Edwin, 1991.

(With Oosthuizen) *Empirical Studies of African Independent/Indigenous Churches,* Mellen, Edwin, 1992.
Some Prayers and Writings of the Servant of Sorrows: Thumekile Isaiah Shembe (translated from the Zulu by Rt. Rev. Londaukosi iNsiKayakho Shembe), University of Calgary Press (Alberta, Canada), 1994.
(With Oosthuizen) *Studies on the Nazareth Baptist Church: the ibandla lamaNazaretha. Volume One: The Life and Work of Isaiah Shembe According to the Sacred History and Oral Traditions of the ibandla lamaNazaretha* (translated by Hans-Jurgen Becker), Mellen, Edwin, in press.

OTHER

Also author of several monographs, including *The New Paganism: Yoga and UFO's,* Potchefstroom University, 1973, and *The Bible, Justice, and the Culture of Poverty,* London Social Affairs Unit, 1985. General editor of several books on African religion, including *Heavens of Health in a Zulu City* by J. Kiernan, Edwin Mellen, 1990.

WORK IN PROGRESS: Charismatic Christianity: A Cross-Cultural Perspective, publication expected in 1997; *Atoms, Ancestors and the Nature of Religion,* revised version of F. B. Welbourn's *Atoms and Ancestors,* for Paragon House; *Christians, Germans and Holocaust Denial,* for Inter-Varsity Press; editing the works of F. B. Welbourn; editing several books on African religion, including *Notes and Index to the Oral Histories of the ibandla lamaNazaretha;* research on religion and racial reconciliation in South Africa.

SIDELIGHTS: Irving Hexham told *CA:* "I am an evangelical Christian working in the field of religious studies. My particular interests are new religious movements and religion and society in South Africa. Since 1969 I have been involved in the study of South African society and a member of the South African Institute of Race Relations, which led the struggle against apartheid. I am interested in the Afrikaners and the role of religion, especially Calvinism, in forming their social and political views.

"I became interested in South Africa as an undergraduate student because of the claim that it was the Calvinist religion of the Afrikaners which had originally created apartheid. If true, this created a major problem for my understanding of Christianity. My interest in new religious movements arose as a result of meeting 'hippies' in the late 1960s and early 1970s. Originally I intended to write my master's thesis on South Africa but Fred Welborn insisted that I had to 'get my hands dirty' by studying a religious group through participant observation and not simply from books. Therefore, he argued, I could only study the Afrikaners by going to South Africa, learning their language and living among them. As this was not feasible when I was studying for my master's degree, I had to find a local subject where I could immerse myself in the culture of the group I was studying. The result was that in my master's thesis I analysed the lifestyles and beliefs of the 'hippies' of Glastonbury, England. I then went to South Africa and spent two years in the Afrikaner Nationalist heartland where I did my archival work at the University of Potchefstroom. At the same time I made every effort to follow an anthropological approach to understanding the Afrikaners by simply living with them. Throughout my career I have believed that understanding precedes criticism and that informed criticism of any position, whether cults or Afrikaner Nationalism, can only be made after the critic has thoroughly immersed him or herself in the beliefs and lifestyle of people being studied."

Hexham later told *CA:* "Since 1986 I have worked on African religions, especially the lamaNazaretha and other Zulu groups, and new religions in Europe."

BIOGRAPHICAL/CRITICAL SOURCES:

PERIODICALS

Globe and Mail (Toronto), June 6, 1987.

*   *   *

HEYER, Marilee 1942-

PERSONAL: Born May 7, 1942, in Long Beach, CA; daughter of Arthur Henry (a machinist) and Esther May (Orth) Heyer. *Education:* Art Center College of Design, B.A. (with honors), 1965.

ADDRESSES: Home—1619 6th St., Los Osos, CA 93402. *Agent*—Toni Mendez, 141 56th St., New York, NY 10022.

CAREER: Scene designer for children's television cartoon shows, including "The Lone Ranger," "Journey to the Center of the Earth," "The Hardy Boys," and "The Archies," 1965-70; Liberty House Department Store, San Francisco, CA, fashion illustrator, 1970-77; Compendium Design Studio, San Francisco, illustrator, 1977-80; I. Magnin Department Store, San Francisco, fashion illustrator, 1980—. Assistant storyboard artist for *Return of the Jedi,* 1982.

MEMBER: San Francisco Society of Illustrators.

WRITINGS:

SELF-ILLUSTRATED JUVENILE

The Weaving of a Dream, Viking-Penguin (New York City), 1986.
The Forbidden Door, Viking-Penguin, 1988.
Iron Hans, Viking-Penguin, 1993.
The Girl, the Fish, and the Crown, Viking-Penguin, 1995.

SIDELIGHTS: Marilee Heyer told *CA:* "Although being listed in *CA* is a great honor for me, writing is the part of book publishing that I find most difficult, being first and foremost an illustrator. Almost all of my books have been written with the *great* help of an editor, with the exception of *The Forbidden Door,* which I wrote myself. The other stories are also folk tales or fairy tales which I and my editor have adapted.

"[The] first book I started on was *The Forbidden Door,* although it was not the first one published. In fact my book career started, not with the intent to do children's books for I was a fashion illustrator for I. Magnin at the time, but because I did a series of Science Fiction drawings to show Lucas Film, with the idea of getting some freelance work on the last "Star Wars" film (which also did come about). When friends saw these illustrations they thought they would make a great children's book. I found myself thinking then, of what story I could write to go along with the illustrations, and thus *The Forbidden Door* was born. *The Weaving of a Dream* then came about when some friends—Judy and Hap Kliban (the cartoonist), came upon a story called "The Chuang Brocade" in a book of Taoist tales and suggested I illustrate it in the style I had used for the Science

Fiction illustrations. Since then, one after the other, the books filled a place in my life.

"I'm always reading fairy tales looking for which one I want to do next. First I read them for the images that they bring to mind and then for the content of the story itself. Is it something (almost like a dream) that speaks to me—about something that is happening currently in my life? Then if they both meet the points I'm looking for I start doing the drawings. It takes me a year to complete the book so I have to really love the story to spend that much time with it.

"I have been greatly influenced by the turn of the century children's book illustrator Arthur Rackham and Edmond Dulac and also the Italian renaissance artists such as Leonardo da Vinci. I love the great care that they have shown in their desire to portray the human forms and the forms of nature with love and accuracy.

"My advice to aspiring writers and illustrators would be to do it because you love it and love doing it. Not in the hopes of selling it but because it is so much a part of your life that you can't not do it."

BIOGRAPHICAL/CRITICAL SOURCES:

PERIODICALS

School Library Journal, April, 1994, p. 43.

*   *   *

HICKMAN, Martha Whitmore   1925-

PERSONAL: Born December 9, 1925, in Holyoke, MA; daughter of George Deming (a lawyer) and Ruth Olive (Carr) Whitmore; married Hoyt Leon Hickman (a minister of United Methodist Church), December 16, 1950; children: Peter Carr, John Whitmore, Stephen Hoyt, Mary Esther. *Education:* Mount Holyoke College, B.A. (cum laude), 1947. *Politics:* Democrat. *Religion:* United Methodist. *Avocational interests:* Painting, drawing, swimming, travel.

ADDRESSES: Home—2034 Castleman Dr., Nashville, TN 37215.

CAREER: Writer. American Baptist Convention, Philadelphia, PA, assistant editor, 1947-50; nursery school teacher in New Haven, CT, 1951-52. Consultant, Information Services, Nashville, 1974-80.

MEMBER: Authors Guild, Authors League of America, Society of Children's Book Writers, Mount Holyoke College Alumnae Association, Nashville Writers Alliance, Phi Beta Kappa.

AWARDS, HONORS: Friends of American Writers award in Juvenile Division, 1976, for *I'm Moving;* Golden Kite nomination, 1987, for *Lost and Found;* Associated Church Press Fiction Award, 1991, for "The Last Hour."

WRITINGS:

(Contributor) *Days of Grass* (anthology), Channel Press, 1965.
How to Marry a Minister, Lippincott (Philadelphia), 1968.
Love Speaks Its Voice, Word, Inc. (Waco, TX), 1976, paperback edition published as *The Growing Season,* Upper Room (Nashville, TN), 1980.
(Contributor) *Images: Women in Transition,* Upper Room, 1976.
I Will Not Leave You Desolate: Some Thoughts for Grieving Parents, Upper Room, 1982.
Waiting and Loving: Thoughts Occasioned by the Illness and Death of a Parent, Upper Room, 1984.
Fullness of Time: Short Stories of Women and Aging, Upper Room, 1990.
And God Created Squash: How the World Began, Albert Whitman (Niles, IL), 1993.
Healing after Loss: Daily Meditations for Working through Grief, Avon (New York City), 1994.
Robert Lives with His Grandparents, Albert Whitman, 1995.
Such Good People (novel), Warner Books, 1996.

PUBLISHED BY ABINGDON (NASHVILLE, TN)

I'm Moving, 1975.
My Friend William Moved Away, 1979.
The Reason I'm Not Quite Finished Tying My Shoes, 1981.
When Can Daddy Come Home?, 1983, published as *When Andy's Father Went to Prison,* Albert Whitman, 1990.
Eeps Creeps, It's My Room, 1984.

Last Week My Brother Anthony Died, 1984.
With Crown: Good Manners for Girls and Boys, 1985.
When James Allen Whitaker's Grandfather Came to Stay, 1985.
When Our Church Building Burned Down, 1986.
Lost and Found, 1987.
Prayers and Devotions for Teachers, 1989.

OTHER

Contributor to books, including *365 Meditations for Women,* Abingdon, 1989, *365 More Meditations for Women,* Abingdon, 1992, and *The Storyteller's Companion to the Bible,* Abingdon, 1993. Also contributor to numerous periodicals, including *Good Housekeeping, Christian Science Monitor, Pastoral Psychology, Presbyterian Life, Christian Herald, Creative Years, Image,* and *Weavings.*

SIDELIGHTS: Martha Whitmore Hickman told *CA:* "I've been writing and publishing for a long time, but the advent of my first novel (April, 1996) is a gratifying development at this time in my life."

*   *   *

HIGGINBOTTOM, David   1923-
   (Nicholas Fisk)

PERSONAL: Born October 14, 1923, in London, England; married Dorothy Antoinette, 1949; children: Moyra and Nicola (twins), Steven, Christopher. *Education:* Ardingly College, Sussex, England.

ADDRESSES: *Home*—59 Elstree Rd., Bushey Heath, Hertfordshire, WD2 3QX, England. *Agent*—Laura Cecil, 17 Alwyne Villas, Canonbury, London, N1 2HG, England.

CAREER: Writer and illustrator. Head of creative groups, Lund Humphries Ltd. (printers/publishers), London, England. Former advertising creative director and consultant; has worked as an actor, publisher, editor, journalist, musician, and speaker to children and adults. *Military service:* Royal Air Force during World War II.

MEMBER: Saville Club.

WRITINGS:

SCIENCE FICTION FOR YOUNG ADULTS; UNDER PSEUDONYM NICHOLAS FISK

Space Hostages, Hamish Hamilton (London), 1967, Macmillan (New York City), 1969.
Trillions, Hamish Hamilton, 1971, Pantheon (New York City), 1973.
Grinny, Heinemann (London), 1973, Nelson (Nashville, TN), 1974.
High Way Home, Hamish Hamilton, 1973.
Little Green Spaceman, illustrated by Trevor Stubley, Heinemann, 1974.
Time Trap, Gollancz (London), 1976.
Wheelie in the Stars, Gollancz, 1976.
Antigrav, Viking Kestrel (London), 1978.
Escape from Splatterbang, Pelham (London), 1978, Macmillan, 1979, published as *Flamers,* Knight (London), 1979.
Monster Maker, Pelham, 1979, Macmillan, 1980.
A Rag, a Bone, and a Hank of Hair, Viking Kestrel, 1980, Crown (New York City), 1982.
Robot Revolt, Pelham, 1981.
Sweets from a Stranger and Other Science Fiction Stories, Viking Kestrel, 1982.
On the Flip Side, Viking Kestrel, 1983.
You Remember Me!, Viking Kestrel, 1984, Hall (Boston), 1987.
Bonkers Clocks, illustrated by Colin West, Viking Kestrel, 1985.
Dark Sun, Bright Sun, illustrated by Brigid Marlin, Blackie (Glasgow), 1986.
Living Fire (short stories), Corgi (London), 1987.
Mindbenders, Viking Kestrel, 1987.
Backlash, Walker (London), 1988.
The Talking Car, illustrated by Ann John, Macmillan, 1988.
The Telly Is Watching You, Macdonald (London), 1989.
The Model Village, illustrated by Alan Cracknell, Walker, 1990.
A Hole in the Head, Walker, 1991.
Extraterrestrial Tales, Puffin (New York City), 1991.
Broops! Down the Chimney, illustrated by Russell Ayto, Walker, 1991.
(Editor) *The Penguin Book of Science Fiction: Stories Chosen by Nicholas Fisk,* Viking (New York City), 1993, published as *The Puffin Book of Science Fiction: Stories Chosen by Nicholas Fisk,* Puffin, 1994.

Also contributor to *Twisted Circuits,* edited by Mick Gowar, Beaver Books (London), 1987; and *Electric*

Heroes, edited by Mick Gowar, Bodley Head (London), 1988.

"STARSTORMER SAGA"; SCIENCE FICTION FOR YOUNG ADULTS; UNDER PSEUDONYM NICHOLAS FISK

Starstormers, Knight, 1980.
Sunburst, Knight, 1980.
Catfang, Knight, 1981.
Evil Eye, Knight, 1982
Volcano, Knight, 1985.

FICTION; UNDER PSEUDONYM NICHOLAS FISK

(Illustrator) Beryl Cooke, *A Fishy Tale,* Angus & Robertson (London), 1957.
(Illustrator) Lettice Cooper, *The Bear Who Was Too Big,* Parrish, 1963.
(Illustrator) Geoffrey Morgan, *Tea with Mr. Timothy,* Parrish, 1964, Little, Brown (Boston), 1966.
(And illustrator) *The Bouncers,* Hamish Hamilton, 1964.
The Fast Green Car, illustrated by Bernard Wragg, Hamish Hamilton, 1965.
There's Something on the Roof, illustrated by Dugald Macdougall, Hamish Hamilton, 1966.
(Illustrator) William Mayne, *Skiffy,* Hamish Hamilton, 1973.
Emma Borrows a Cup of Sugar (for children), illustrated by Carol Baker, Heinemann, 1973.
Der Ballon, Junior Press (Germany), 1974.
The Witches of Wimmering, illustrated by Trevor Stubley, Pelham, 1976.
Leadfoot, Pelham, 1980, revised edition, Piper (London), 1992.
Snatched, Hodder & Stoughton, 1983.
The Worm Charmers, Walker, 1989.
The Back-Yard War, illustrated by Valeria Petrone, Macmillan, 1990.
Fantastico, illustrated by Mick Reid, Longman (New York City), 1994.

Also contributor to *Young Winter's Tales,* edited by D. J. Denney, Macmillan, 1978; *An Oxford Book of Christmas Stories,* edited by Dennis Pepper, Oxford University Press, 1986; and *I Like This Story,* Puffin, 1986.

NONFICTION; UNDER PSEUDONYM NICHOLAS FISK

(And illustrator) *Look at Cars* (for children), Hamish Hamilton, 1959, revised edition, Panther (London), 1969.

(Illustrator) Sir Philip Joubert de la Ferte, *Look at Aircraft,* Hamish Hamilton, 1960.
Look at Newspapers (for children), illustrated by Eric Thomas, Hamish Hamilton, 1962.
Cars, Parrish, 1963.
The Young Man's Guide to Advertising, Hamish Hamilton, 1963.
Making Music, illustrated by Donald Green, Joseph (London), 1966, Crescendo (Boston), 1969.
Lindbergh the Lone Flier (for children), illustrated by Raymond Briggs, Hamish Hamilton/Coward McCann (London and New York City), 1968.
Richthofen the Red Baron, Raymond Briggs, Hamish Hamilton/Coward McCann, 1968.
(Editor and contributor of photographs) Eric Fenby, *Menuhin's House of Music,* Icon Books, 1970.
Pig Ignorant (a teenage memoir), Walker, 1991.

Contributor to *The Thorny Paradise* (anthology for children), edited by Edward Blishen, Viking Kestrel, 1975.

OTHER

Also writer for television. Author of cassettes. General editor of "Hamish Hamilton Monographs," Hamish Hamilton, 1964. Contributor, "Take Part" series, Ward Lock, 1977. Contributor to *Pears Junior Encyclopaedia.* Contributor of articles and science fiction stories to magazines.

ADAPTATIONS: Grinny was adapted for "CBS Storybreak," 1985.

SIDELIGHTS: David Higginbottom, who writes under the pseudonym Nicholas Fisk, is an English writer best known for his young adult science fiction stories. "[While] my main interest lies in writing books for children," Higginbottom once commented: "I am also an illustrator and photographer and often an impresario of adult printed works." He is also a journalist, sometime musician, public speaker, and creative consultant. Although he writes both fiction and nonfiction, Higginbottom's name is primarily associated with his science fiction works. "I write science fiction because it is liberating," Higginbottom explained. "I greatly regret the label 'SF,' incidentally. SF were better named IF—stories centered on an If, a possibility, a leap." Often employing the traditional sci-fi plot device of the outside threat of an advanced technology, Higginbottom always returns to character development to carry the story. According to Gillian Cross, writing in the *Times Literary Supplement,* Higginbottom "has a gift for combining the fantastic with the down-to-earth. In books like *Grinny* and *Trillions,* the interest comes not merely from the central events, but also from the effect of those events on recognizable characters."

Higginbottom, after serving in the Royal Air Force during World War II, began writing and illustrating children's nonfiction, including *Look at Cars, Look at Aircraft, Look at Newspapers,* and *The Young Man's Guide to Advertising,* combining his knowledge of things mechanical with the world of the publicist. In 1967 he published the first of his science fiction novels, *Space Hostages,* and since that time has, with a few departures into children's picture books and mainstream juvenile novels, written almost solely in the science fiction field. Higginbottom related that he began writing science fiction because "the writer is free to invent his own games, rules, and players."

Trillions deals with an invasion from outer space in a completely novel form: trillions of glittering multifaceted baubles rain to earth, charming the children and alarming the militarists who declare martial law and prepare to nuke the mysterious jewel-like objects. Young Scott manages to communicate with the sentient trillions and warn them away in time to prevent their mass destruction. This theme, that of the innocent and unspoiled youths who are able to understand and see more clearly than befuddled adults, is common in Higginbottom's work. "Higginbottom has created an exciting story that should be enjoyed by all," noted Jean Mercier in a *Publishers Weekly* review of *Trillions.*

One of Higginbottom's best-known science fiction novels—which was also adapted for television—*Grinny,* tells another story of a disguised planetary visitor to earth, but with a new twist. In this case the visitor comes in the form of a sweet old lady who claims to be a long lost great-aunt to one family who has never met her, and whose words, "You remember me!," seem to have the power to make adults forgetful enough to accept her as kin. Not so, however, for young Tim and Beth, who soon realize Great-Aunt Emma is not the sweetheart she pretends to be but a sinister extraterrestrial, and they manage to foil her mission. "The nicely crafted story has suspense, action, and a frisson here and there," noted a reviewer for the *Bulletin of the Center for Children's Books.* A *Kirkus Reviews* critic commented that "the children have substantial, well-differentiated personalities not usually encountered in genre sci fi."

Higginbottom continued his science fiction explorations with the Cold War allegory *Antigrav,* in which a group of children vacationing with their parents on a tiny island off the coast of Scotland discover a red stone with the power to defy gravity. They set up clever experiments to prove the stone's power, but soon become the object of a chase by scientists trying to steal the antigravity rock. Finally the children throw the stone into the sea to keep its power out of the wrong hands.

Writing in *The Thorny Paradise,* an anthology on the art of children's fiction, Higginbottom noted his own development as a writer from his initial "childish little books for little children," to the point where his own children were demanding something quite different from him. "My child readers might, occasionally, be persuaded to share my nostalgias and fancies—even my childhood—but this was not to be relied upon. Better to devise stories that belonged either to a period the reader would recognize—the period of *now;* or to go so far back, or so far forward, that the reader must simply take my word for it."

Higginbottom returned to his own youth in England with one of his most well-received books, *A Rag, a Bone, and a Hank of Hair.* Venturing into the realm of DNA engineering, he created an altered world of the twenty-third century. As a result of a nuclear accident, very few humans can give birth, and so to avoid extinction the human race is now repopulated from the gene patterns found in fragments (the bits and pieces of the title) of those who died before the accident. These humans are known as Reborns, and young, brilliant Brin is given the job of observing three who have been resurrected from the twentieth century in an experiment to see how well such Reborns might adapt to the brave new world of Brin's time. These three, a boy, a girl, and a cleaning lady, inhabit a shabby kitchen in the London of the Blitz—something out of Higginbottom's own memories. Initially contemptuous of these primitive forms, Brin soon comes to sympathize with their free will, so at odds with the controlled, sterile society he lives in. Finally Brin allies himself with these Reborns against the Seniors who have engineered them, creating a "heart-stopping crisis in Higginbottom's unforgettable novel," according to one *Publishers Weekly* reviewer. Norman Culpan, writing in *School Librarian,* found the book to be "absorbing and thought-provoking," and *Horn Book* contributor Paul Heins called it an "unconventional science fiction novel that develops a moral theme."

This play of individual self-determination pitted against regulated human society helps to make *A Rag, a Bone, and a Hank of Hair* Higginbottom's "science fiction masterpiece," according to Dennis Hamley in the *Twentieth-Century Young Adult Writers.*

Higginbottom returned to his earlier protagonists Tim and Beth from *Grinny* with *You Remember Me!,* enlisting them once again in the fight against a disguised alien. This time the invasion comes in the form of beautiful television personality Lisa Treadgood who is able to charm an entire nation—even the clever writer N. Frisk who has a cameo appearance in his own book—but not cub reporter Tim or his sister Beth. Treadgood attracts a huge following to her proto-fascist political party that marches under a banner of "Decency, Discipline, and Dedication." Beth and Tim once again are able to defeat the evil machinations of this extraterrestrial. A *Junior Bookshelf* critic noted that the book had "enough tension and buoyancy to keep young readers eager to find out what happens next," while *Times Literary Supplement* contributor Stephanie Nettell thought it was "a lively sequel" to *Grinny.*

Higginbottom's obvious love for adventure stories gets full play in the "Starstormer Saga," a five-novel sequence in which four young protagonists—Vawn, Ispex, Tsu, and Makenzi—blast off from twenty-first-century Earth in a homemade rocket ship, partly in search of their space colonist parents, partly in search of adventure. They get plenty of the latter, including a fight against the power-drunk maniac, the Emperor of Tyrannopolis, who wants to rule the universe, and a test of survival on a hostile planet populated by talking lizards. "Mr. Fisk manipulates the cut and thrust of disturbing forces and sinister conflict with assured professionalism," commented a reviewer for *Junior Bookshelf* on the second in the series, *Sunburst.* Summing up the appeal of the series as a whole, another *Junior Bookshelf* critic concluded that it lay in "is futuristic thrills and spills and the enterprise of the children who face and solve what so often appear to be overwhelming challenges."

Higginbottom has also written thrillers and adventure novels for young readers without the science fiction angle. Books such as *Leadfoot,* about a young boy's dream of being a racing car driver and *Snatched,* about the kidnapping of an ambassador's two children, are more realistic in tone than his science fiction books. "Higginbottom's characters inhabit a world in which millions starve and individuals struggle, hit, love and hate," noted Mike Hayhoe in a review of *Snatched* for *School Librarian.* Higginbottom's realism was also noted by Margery Fisher in a *Growing Point* review of *Leadfoot:* "Terse and low-keyed even in moments of crisis, the book goes beyond the pace and excitement of action."

Writing in *The Thorny Paradise,* Higginbottom summarized why he writes for children and teenagers, whether it is science fiction or any other genre. "It is arguable," Higginbottom wrote, "that the highest expression of humankind takes the form of a child. It is very easy indeed to argue that the human mind is at its most agile, adventurous, generous and receptive stage during childhood. So the children's writer is mixing with and working for the Right People."

BIOGRAPHICAL/CRITICAL SOURCES:

BOOKS

Fisk, Nicholas, *The Thorny Paradise,* edited by Edward Blishen, Viking Kestrel, 1975.
Something about the Author, Volume 87, Gale (Detroit), 1996.
Twentieth-Century Young Adult Writers, edited by Laura Standley Berger, St. James Press (Detroit), 1994.

PERIODICALS

Bulletin of the Center for Children's Books, March, 1975, p. 112.
Growing Point, May, 1976, p. 2887; December, 1976, p. 3011; November, 1979, p. 3614; November, 1980, p. 3782; January, 1981, p. 3816; September, 1982, p. 3953; May, 1983, 4077; November, 1985, p. 4538; July, 1988, p. 5004; May, 1989, p. 5155.
Horn Book, June, 1982, pp. 286-87.
Junior Bookshelf, August, 1976, p. 198; February, 1977, p. 32; August, 1977, p. 234; October, 1978, p. 266; October, 1979, p. 277; August, 1980, p. 188; August, 1982, p. 151; June, 1983, p. 122; February, 1985, p. 38; April, 1985, p. 89; June, 1985, p. 139; December, 1986, p. 224; February, 1987, p. 27; August, 1987, p. 178; June, 1988, p. 137; April, 1990, p. 84; April, 1992, p. 61; June, 1993, p. 104.
Kirkus Reviews, August 1, 1974, p. 804.
Publishers Weekly, March 26, 1973; June 4, 1982, p. 67.

School Librarian, June, 1981, pp. 150-51; December, 1983, p. 376.

School Library Journal, March, 1979, p. 138; March, 1980, p. 139; April, 1982, p. 81.

Times Educational Supplement, November 23, 1984, p. 38; March 1, 1985, p. 29; April 5, 1985, p. 22; February 14, 1986, p. 28; June 17, 1988, p. B3; May 26, 1989, p. B15; July 10, 1992, p. 28; March 5, 1993, p. 12.

Times Literary Supplement, June 17, 1965, p. 500; May 19, 1966, p. 447; November 30, 1967, p. 1160; June 6, 1968, p. 582; April 6, 1973, p. 380; March 29, 1974, p. 331; December 10, 1976, p. 1553; July 7, 1978, p. 764; July 18, 1980, p. 812; November 20, 1981, p. 1361; July 23, 1982, p. 791; March 23, 1986, p. 574.

*   *   *

HILDEBRAND, Verna 1924-

PERSONAL: Born August 17, 1924, in Dodge City, KS; daughter of Carrell E. (a farmer) and Florence Butcher; married John R. Hildebrand (an economist), June 24, 1946; children: Carol, Steve. *Education:* Kansas State University, B.S., 1945, M.S., 1957; University of California, Berkeley, graduate study, 1946-48; Texas Woman's University, Ph.D., 1970.

ADDRESSES: Home—308 Michigan, No. 8, East Lansing, MI 48823. *Office*—Department of Family and Child Ecology, Michigan State University, East Lansing, MI 48824-1030.

CAREER: Kansas State University, Manhattan, instructor in family relations, 1953-54, instructor in student counseling center, 1958; Oklahoma State University, Stillwater, instructor in family relations and child development, 1955-56; Texas Technological College (now Texas Tech University), Lubbock, assistant professor of home and family life, 1962-67; Michigan State University, East Lansing, 1967—, currently professor of family and child ecology.

MEMBER: National Association for the Education of Young Children, American Home Economics Association (chair of family relations and child development section, 1975-77), World Association for Early Childhood Education, National Association of Early Childhood Teacher Educators (president, 1982-84).

AWARDS, HONORS: Award for meritorious leadership and professionalism, 1995.

WRITINGS:

Introduction to Early Childhood Education, with laboratory workbook, Macmillan (New York City), 1971, 5th edition, 1991.

Guiding Young Children, Macmillan, 1975, 5th edition, 1994.

Parenting and Teaching Young Children, McGraw-Hill (New York City), 1981, 3rd edition, 1990.

(With John R. Hildebrand) *China's Families: Experiment in Societal Change,* Burgess, 1981.

(Contributor) *Patterns of Supplementary Parenting,* Plenum, 1982.

Management of Child Development Centers, Macmillan, 1984, 4th edition, 1996.

Parenting: Rewards and Responsibilities, McGraw-Hill, 1994, second edition, 1997.

(With Lillian A. Phenice, Mary McPhail Gray, and Rebecca Pena Hines) *Knowing and Serving Diverse Families,* Prentice-Hall (Englewood Cliffs, NJ), 1996.

Contributor of articles to journals.

Some of Hildebrand's works have been translated into Spanish.

SIDELIGHTS: Verna Hildebrand told *CA:* "I am strongly committed to improving the quality of early childhood schools, child care centers, and kindergartens. Quality care and education for young children is an investment in our future."

*   *   *

HILL, John
   See KOONTZ, Dean R(ay)

*   *   *

HOLLANDER, John 1929-

PERSONAL: Born October 28, 1929, in New York, NY; son of Franklin (a physiologist) and Muriel (Kornfeld) Hollander; married Anne Loesser, June 15, 1953 (divorced, 1977); married Natalie Charkow, December 15, 1981; children: (first marriage) Martha, Elizabeth. *Education:* Columbia University, A.B., 1950, M.A., 1952; Indiana University, Ph.D., 1959.

ADDRESSES: Office—Department of English, Yale University, P.O. Box 208302, New Haven, CT 06520.

CAREER: Harvard University, Cambridge, MA, junior fellow, Society of Fellows, 1954-57; Connecticut College, New London, lecturer in English, 1957-59; Yale University, New Haven, CT, instructor, 1959-61, assistant professor, 1961-63, associate professor, 1964-66, professor of English, 1977—, A. Bartlett Giamatti Professor, 1987—; Hunter College of the City University of New York, New York City, professor of English, 1966-77. Visiting professor at the Linguistic Institute, Indiana University, 1964, and at the Salzburg Seminar in American Studies, 1965. Member of the poetry board, Wesleyan University Press, 1959-62.

MEMBER: Academy of American Poets, American Academy of Arts and Letters, American Academy of Arts and Sciences, Phi Beta Kappa.

AWARDS, HONORS: Yale Younger Poets Award, 1958, for *A Crackling of Thorns;* Poetry Chap-Book Award, 1962, for *The Untuning of the Sky: Ideas of Music in English Poetry, 1500-1700;* National Institute of Arts and Letters grant for creative work in literature, 1963; senior fellow, National Endowment for the Humanities, 1973-74; Levinson Prize, *Poetry* magazine, 1974; Guggenheim fellowship, 1979-80; Bollingen Prize, 1983; Mina P. Shaughnessy Award, 1983; Melville Cane Award, 1990; MacArthur Foundation fellow, 1990—; Ambassador Book Award, 1994.

WRITINGS:

POETRY

A Crackling of Thorns, Yale University Press (New Haven, CT), 1958.
Movie Going and Other Poems, Atheneum (New York City), 1962.
Various Owls, Norton (New York City), 1963.
Visions from the Ramble, Atheneum, 1965.
The Quest of the Gole, Atheneum, 1966.
Types of Shape, Atheneum, 1969, expanded edition, Yale University Press, 1991.
The Night Mirror, Atheneum, 1971.
Town and Country Matters, David R. Godine (Boston), 1972.

Selected Poems, Secker & Warburg (London), 1972.
The Head of the Bed, David R. Godine, 1974.
Tales Told of the Fathers, Atheneum, 1975.
Reflections on Espionage, Atheneum, 1976.
Spectral Emanations: New and Selected Poems, Atheneum, 1978.
In Place, Abattoir, 1978.
Blue Wine and Other Poems, Johns Hopkins Press (Baltimore, MD), 1979.
Looking Ahead, Nadja (New York City), 1982.
Powers of Thirteen: Poems, Atheneum, 1983.
In Time and Place, Johns Hopkins University Press, 1986.
Harp Lake: Poems, Knopf (New York City), 1988.
Selected Poetry, Knopf, 1993.
Tesserae and Other Poems, Knopf, 1993.
The Gazer's Spirit: Poems Speaking to Silent Works of Art, University of Chicago Press (Chicago), 1995.

EDITOR

(With Harold Bloom) *The Wind and the Rain,* Doubleday (New York City), 1961.
(With Bloom) *Selected Poems of Ben Johnson,* Dell (New York City), 1961.
(With Anthony Hecht) *Jiggery-Pokery: A Compendium of Double Dactyls,* illustrated by Milton Glaser, Atheneum, 1966.
Poems of Our Moment, Pegasus (Indianapolis, IN), 1968.
American Short Stories since 1945, Harper (New York City), 1968.
Modern Poetry: Modern Essays in Criticism, Oxford University Press, 1968.
(With Frank Kermode) *The Oxford Anthology of English Literature,* Oxford University Press, 1973.
(With Reuben Brower and Helen Vendler) *I. A. Richards: Essays in His Honor,* Oxford University Press, 1973.
American Poetry: The Nineteenth Century, Volume 1: *Philip Freneau to Walt Whitman,* Volume 2: *Herman Melville to Trumbull Stickney; American Indian Poetry; Folk Songs and Spirituals,* Library of America, 1994.

OTHER

The Untuning of the Sky: Ideas of Music in English Poetry, 1500-1700, Princeton University Press (Princeton, NJ), 1961, reprinted with a new preface, Archon Books (Hamden, CT), 1993.

Images of Voice, Chelsea House (New York City), 1969.

An Entertainment for Elizabeth, Being a Masque of the Seven Motions; or, Terpsichore Unchained (play), produced in New York, 1969.

The Immense Parade on Supererogation Day, Atheneum, 1972.

Vision and Resonance: Two Senses of Poetic Form, Oxford University Press, 1975, 2nd edition, Yale University Press, 1985.

The Figure of Echo: A Mode of Allusion in Milton and After, University of California Press (Berkeley, CA), 1981.

Rhyme's Reason: A Guide to English Verse, Yale University Press, 1981.

(Author of text) Saul Steinberg, *Dal Vero* (portraits), Library Fellows of the Whitney Museum of American Art (New York City), 1983.

Melodious Guile: Fictive Pattern in Poetic Language, Yale University Press, 1988.

(Author of introduction) Dante Gabriel Rossetti, *The Essential Rossetti,* Ecco Press (New York City), 1990.

Contributor of verse and prose to *New Yorker, Partisan Review, Kenyon Review, Paris Review, Esquire, Commentary,* and other popular and scholarly journals and magazines. Editorial associate for poetry, *Partisan Review,* 1959-64. Contributing editor, *Harper's,* 1970-71.

ADAPTATIONS: The poem "The Head of the Bed" was set to music by Milton Babbitt and recorded as part of "Concerto for Piano and Orchestra: The Head of the Bed," New World Records (New York City), 1987; "Blue Wine" was adapted into a song cycle by Hugo Weisgall and recorded as "Lyrical Interval: Song Cycle for Piano and Low Voice," Library of Congress, 1985.

SIDELIGHTS: John Hollander "has been a formidable presence in American literary life for a quarter century now," J. D. McClatchy asserts in a 1987 *New Republic* article. "His work as scholar, teacher, and editor is held in high esteem, and no critic of poetry is his superior. . . . But his true importance is as a poet, and [yet] to judge by the crudest measures—critical reckonings and anthology appearances—Hollander's poems are either merely respected or totally ignored." McClatchy attributes this in part to the "'difficulty' of his work." *Dictionary of Literary Biography* contributor Stephen A. Parris finds Hollander's poems "filled with a variety of lit-

erary, philosophical, and religious allusions; and his poetic technique, displaying an immense knowledge of prosody, is reminiscent of the neoclassical writers of the seventeenth century. Not surprisingly, it is precisely this difficulty that has prompted both the highest praise and severest criticism of his verse."

Hollander's first poetry collection, *A Crackling of Thorns,* caught the attention of W. H. Auden, who selected it for publication in the Yale Series of Younger Poets in 1958 and also contributed an introductory essay. *Southern Review* contributor James K. Robinson finds that Hollander's "early poetry resembles Auden's in its wit, its learned allusiveness, its prosodic mastery. . . . Yet, though the resonance of Hollander's poetry often reminds one of Auden, his vision is his own. He has paid his debt to the sassenach and is clearly an American poet."

From *A Crackling of Thorns* through *Spectral Emanations: New and Selected Poems,* Parris notes a heightening of Hollander's technical skill, leading to a body of work progressively more challenging to the reader. Parris describes *A Crackling of Thorns* as "a series of minor technical triumphs," finds *Visions from the Ramble* "a significant achievement . . . in its cumulativeness and broadness of scope," and recognizes the emergence of "a more direct poetic voice" in *The Night Mirror.* Later works such as *Tales Told of the Fathers* and *Spectral Emanations,* Parris adds, are "marked by a stunning yet troublesome technical brilliance that sets [them] apart from the bulk of modern poetry and indeed from Hollander's earlier work. . . . The demands of Hollander's poetry are great—greater perhaps than some readers are willing to accept. Hollander brings to a poem everything he possesses—his sense of form, his wit, his probing intellect—and he demands no less from those who choose to read his works. One should not expect an easy time from John Hollander; one will not, however, if he makes the effort, come away empty-handed."

Reviewing *Spectral Emanations* for the *New Republic,* Harold Bloom reflects on his impressions of Hollander's work in the twenty years since the appearance of his first collection: "I read [*A Crackling of Thorns*] . . . soon after I first met the poet, and was rather more impressed by the man than by the book. It has taken twenty years for the emotional complexity, spiritual anguish, and intellectual and moral power of the man to become the book. The enormous mastery of verse was there from the start, and is there still. . . . But there seemed almost always to be more knowledge and insight within Hollander than the verse could accommodate." He finds in *Spectral Emanations* "another poet as vital and accomplished as [A. R.] Ammons, [James] Merrill, [W. S.] Merwin, [John] Ashbery, James Wright, an immense augmentation to what is clearly a group of major poets."

In *Blue Wine and Other Poems* Hollander "reveals once more the qualities for which his poems have long been admired: wit, color, nuance, and charm," *World Literature Today* reviewer John Boening observes. While the critic notes that the poems "are scratched in spots by the gritty terminology of contemporary criticism," particularly Hollander's overuse of the word "text," Boening nonetheless cites poems such as "Monuments" and "Three of the Fates" as reasons to "forgive, readily forgive, and be glad to have such fine, clear, thoughtful music as Hollander, at his best, can give." *Poetry*'s William H. Pritchard finds a "passionate simplicity" in "The Dying Friend" which is "something new and welcome in Hollander's work." But, he adds, "there is also plenty of the old exuberance and brilliance of invention: in the title poem, in some of the poems about sculpture . . . and in what one might call transport poems—'The Train' and 'Just for the Ride.'"

A number of critics have identified *Blue Wine* as an important milestone in Hollander's life and career. Phoebe Pettingell, reviewing the work for the *New Leader,* remarks, "I would guess from the evidence of *Blue Wine* that John Hollander is now at the crossroads of his own midlife journey, picking out a new direction to follow." Pritchard notes, "That such a book can be published but a year after the retrospective *Spectral Emanations* . . . suggests that Hollander is writing at the top of his powers."

"Though it will be catalogued under poetry, *In Time and Place* is actually a hybrid of verse and prose, the extremes on either side of 'poetry,'" McClatchy remarks in *New Republic*. The work is divided into three sections—"In Time," "In Between," and "In Place"—of which "half the poems," according to *Poetry* contributor Linda Gregerson, "derive their subjectivity, and their daily labor, from a marriage lost. The other half revive a venerable tradition by contemplating the expulsion myth as a theory of language. In between, and called 'In Between,' is a . . . simultaneously self-effacing and self-asserting antimonument written in the form of a disappearing jour-

nal." Poet and *Times Literary Supplement* contributor Jay Parini believes "an elegiac tone dominates this book, which begins with a sequence of thirty four poems in the *In Memoriam* stanza. These interconnecting lyrics are exquisite and moving, superior to almost anything else Hollander has ever written." Of the lyrics in this section, the *New York Times Book Review*'s Robert von Hallberg notes that "some of the best, like 'Orpheus Alone' and 'A Defense of Rhyme,' would be memorable in any book, but here they are bright moments in a sustained meditation on a single subject: the loss of a lover, apparently a wife, and the loss of years, memory, abilities—in all, a former life." Remarking on the prose poems making up the second and third portions of *In Time and Place,* Parini describes them as "an intriguing if unrealized attempt to come to grips with what Hollander, in a footnote, calls 'life after verse.' Full of aphoristic lines . . . and bright images . . ., they seem oddly irrelevant after the astonishing performance that precedes them. . . . None the less, *In Time and Place* is a landmark in contemporary poetry." McClatchy holds *In Time and Place* as evidence that Hollander is "part conjurer and part philosopher, one of our language's true mythographers and one of its very best poets."

"The work collected in [*Tesserae and Other Poems* and *Selected Poetry*] makes clear that John Hollander is a considerable poet," *New Republic* reviewer Vernon Shetley remarks, "but it may leave readers wondering still, thirty-five years after his first book, . . . exactly what kind of poet Hollander is." The critic attributes this not only to the variety of Hollander's work, but also to his "strict avoidance of anything that might seem merely an expression of personality, as if the poet had taken to heart, much more fully than its author, Eliot's dictum that poetry should embody 'emotion which has its life in the poem and not in the history of the poet.'" Thomas M. Disch comments in *Poetry,* "Except for the fact that, on the evidence of *Tesserae,* Hollander is still working at full throttle, I think the poet would be better served by a *Complete Poems* than by a second *Selected,* generous as it is. But half a loaf of Hollander is still a surfeit of riches."

BIOGRAPHICAL/CRITICAL SOURCES:

BOOKS

Contemporary Literary Criticism, Gale (Detroit), Volume 2, 1974, Volume 5, 1976, Volume 8, 1978.

Dictionary of Literary Biography, Volume 5: *American Poets since World War II,* edited by Donald J. Greiner, Gale, 1980.

Hoffman, Daniel, editor, *Harvard's Guide to Contemporary American Writing,* Harvard University Press (Cambridge, MA), 1979.

Howard, Richard, *Alone with America: Essays on the Art of Poetry in the United States since 1970,* Atheneum, 1969.

PERIODICALS

America, June 17, 1989, p. 592; November 13, 1993, p. 18.

American Scholar, spring, 1994, p. 302.

American Spectator, September, 1994, p. 64.

Boston Globe, January 16, 1989, p. 17; May 16, 1993, p. B40.

Chicago Tribune, March 20, 1994, sec. 14, p. 6.

Christian Science Monitor, August 18, 1976, p. 27; June 2, 1989, p. 13.

Commentary, September, 1975, p. 94; March, 1994, p. 54.

Georgia Review, summer, 1977, p. 533; spring, 1994, pp. 162-72.

Harper's, November, 1975.

Library Journal, June 15, 1978.

London Review of Books, November 9, 1989, p. 24.

Nation, December 6, 1971, p. 86; November 11, 1978, p. 517; December 26, 1981, p. 714; October 3, 1994, p. 350.

New Leader, November 5, 1979, pp. 21-22.

New Republic, April 6, 1974, p. 33; November 29, 1975, p. 25; November 20, 1976, p. 23; September 9, p. 42; February 9, 1987, pp. 44-46; February 4, 1991, p. 34; September 6, 1993, pp. 36-40; November 22, 1993, p. 27.

Newsweek, January 23, 1984, p. 65.

New Yorker, December 6, 1993, p. 147.

New York Review of Books, October 2, 1975, p. 30; June 1, 1978, p. 27; December 16, 1993, p. 20.

New York Times, August 13, 1965, p. 27; September 26, 1969, p. 5; November 2, 1993, p. C20.

New York Times Book Review, November 21, 1965, p. 74; November 20, 1966, p. 58; October 17, 1971, p. 4; February 13, 1972, p. 3; November 5, 1972, p. 47; August 3, 1975, p. 17; June 16, 1974, p. 6; April 6, 1975, p. 5; May 28, 1978; February 15, 1987, p. 42; October 22, 1989, p. 16; July 18, 1993, p. 81.

Poetry, August, 1972, p. 296; January, 1975, p. 229; April, 1977, p. 41; August, 1980, pp. 299-302; December, 1984, p. 171; February, 1988, p. 433; February, 1994, pp. 285-95.

Southern Review, April, 1978, pp. 348-358.

Times Literary Supplement, May 11, 1973, p. 516; August 30, 1974, p. 932; January 18, 1980, p. 65; May 7, 1982, p. 499; March 28, 1986, p. 343; July 17, 1987, p. 767; August 11, 1989, p. 880; March 4, 1994, p. 4.

Washington Post Book World, December 17, 1978; February 1, 1987, p. 6; December 25, 1988, p. 6; December 26, 1993, p. 1.

World Literature Today, spring, 1980, p. 285; winter, 1990, p. 118.

Yale Review, autumn, 1972, p. 81; autumn, 1987, p. 115.*

* * *

HOLSTI, Ole R(udolf)   1933-

PERSONAL: Born August 7, 1933, in Geneva, Switzerland; became American citizen, 1954; son of Rudolf W. (a diplomat) and Liisa (Franssila) Holsti; married Ann Wood, September 20, 1953; children: Eric Lynn, Maija. *Education:* Stanford University, B.A., 1954, Ph.D., 1962; Wesleyan University, Middletown, CT, M.A.T., 1956.

ADDRESSES: Home—608 Croom Ct., Chapel Hill, NC 27514. *Office*—Department of Political Science, Duke University, Durham, NC 27708-0204.

CAREER: Stanford University, Stanford, CA, instructor, 1962-63, acting assistant professor, 1963-65, assistant professor of political science, 1965-67, research coordinator and associate director of Studies in International Conflict and Integration, 1962-67; University of British Columbia, Vancouver, associate professor, 1967-71, professor of political science, 1971-74; Duke University, Durham, NC, George V. Allen Professor of Political Science, 1974—, chairman of department, 1978-83; University of California, Davis, professor of political science, 1978-79. National Science Foundation, chairman of oversight committee, 1981-84. Member of advisory committee on historical diplomatic documentation, U.S. Department of State, 1983-86. Member of advisory board, University Press of America, 1976—. *Military service:* U.S. Army, 1956-58. U.S. Army Reserve, 1954-56, 1958-62; became staff sergeant.

MEMBER: International Institute of Strategic Studies (London), Peace Science Society (southern section president, 1975-77), International Studies Association (western secretary-treasurer, 1967-69; president, 1969-70 and 1979-80; southern president, 1975-76; member of communications committee, 1987-89), American Political Science Association (council member, 1982-85), Western Political Science Association (executive council member, 1971-74), Interuniversity Consortium for Political Research, Fleet Feet Running Club, Carolina Godiva Track Club, North Carolina Road Runners, Duke Master Runners, Phi Beta Kappa.

AWARDS, HONORS: Owen D. Young Fellowship, General Electric Foundation, 1960-61; research fellowship, Haynes Foundation, 1961-62; Canada Council, research grant, 1969, leave fellowship, 1970-71; fellowship, Center for Advanced Study in the Behavioral Sciences, 1972-73; faculty research fellowship, Ford Foundation, 1972-73; research grants, National Science Foundation, 1975-77, 1979-81, 1983-85, 1988-90, 1992-94, 1996-98; Best Published Paper award, *International Studies Quarterly,* 1979-81, for "The Three Headed Eagle"; Guggenheim fellowship, 1981-82; runner of the year award, Carolina Godiva Track Club, 1987, 1993; Nevitt Sanford Award, International Society for Political Psychology, 1988, for professional contributions to political psychology; Alumni Award, for distinguished undergraduate teaching, 1995.

WRITINGS:

(With Robert C. North, M. George Zaninovich, and Dina A. Zinnes) *Content Analysis: A Handbook with Application for the Study of International Crisis,* Northwestern University Press (Evanston, IL), 1963.

(With David J. Findlay and Richard R. Fagen) *Enemies in Politics,* Rand McNally (New York City), 1967.

Content Analysis for the Social Sciences and Humanities, Addison-Wesley (Reading, MA), 1969.

(With George Gerbner, Klaus Krippendorff, Philip J. Stone and William Paisley) *The Analysis of Communication Content: Developments in Scientific Theories and Computer Techniques,* Wiley (New York City), 1969.

Crisis, Escalation, War, McGill-Queens University Press (Buffalo, NY), 1972.

(With Terrence Hopmann and John D. Sullivan) *Unity and Disintegration in International Alliances,* Wiley, 1973.

The 'Operational Code' as an Approach to the Analysis of Belief Systems, report to the National Science Foundation, 1977.

(With James N. Rosenau) *Vietnam, Consensus, and the Belief Systems of American Leaders,* Institute for Transnational Studies, University of Southern California Press (Los Angeles, CA), 1977, Allen and Unwin (Winchester, MA), 1984.

(Editor with Alexander L. George and Randolph M. Siverson) *Change in the International System,* Westview (Boulder, CO), 1980.

The Three-Headed Eagle: Who Are the Cold War Internationalists, Post-Cold War Internationalists, and Isolationists?, Duke University (Durham, NC), 1981.

(With Rosenau) *Consensus and Change in Foreign Policy Opinions among American Leaders,* report to the National Science Foundation, 1982.

(With Rosenau) *American Leadership in World Affairs: The Breakdown of Consensus,* Allen & Unwin, 1984.

Public Opinion and American Foreign Policy, University of Michigan Press (Ann Arbor, MI), 1984.

The Lessons of Vietnam and the Breakdown of Consensuses on Foreign and Domestic Policy: A Study of American Leadership, report to the National Science Foundation, 1985.

The Domestic and Foreign Policy Beliefs of American Leaders: 1988, report to the National Science Foundation, 1990.

OTHER

Also author, with Rosenau, of *Does Where You Stand Depend on When You Were Born? The Impact of Generation on Post-Vietnam Foreign Policy Beliefs,* 1978. Contributor to "Peace Research Society Papers," 1964-65; contributor of articles and reviews to professional journals, including *Journal of Politics, Diplomatic History,* and *International Political Science Review;* contributor to numerous books including *Micropolitics,* edited by George Cole, John H. Kessel, and Robert G. Seddig, Holt, 1970, *Classics of International Relations,* edited by John A. Vasquez, Prentice-Hall, 1986, and *The Future of American Foreign Policy,* edited by Eugene R. Wittkopf, St. Martin's, 1994. Associate editor, *Journal of Conflict Resolution,* 1969-72, *International Studies Quarterly,* 1970-75, and *Western Political Quarterly,* 1970-79. Member of board of editors, *International Studies Quarterly,* 1967-70, 1975-80, and 1985—, *Computer Studies in the Humanities and Verbal Behavior,* 1968-76, *American Journal of Political Science,* 1975-80, and *International Interaction,* 1980—. Corresponding editor, *Running Journal,* 1985—; correspondent, *Racing South.*

WORK IN PROGRESS: Articles on crisis decision-making, and models of international relations and foreign policy; a book on the domestic and foreign policy attitudes of American leaders.

*   *   *

HUBBARD, L(afayette) Ron(ald) 1911-1986
(Winchester Remington Colt, Elron, Frederick
Engelhardt, Michael Keith, Rene Lafayette,
Ken Martin, B. A. Northrup, John Seabrook,
Kurt Von Rachen; Tom Esterbrook, a house
pseudonym)

PERSONAL: Born March 13, 1911, in Tilden, NE; died of a stroke, January 24, 1986, in Creston, CA; cremated, ashes scattered in the Pacific Ocean; son of Harry Ross (a naval officer) and Dora May (Waterbury de Wolfe) Hubbard; married Margaret Louise Grubb (divorced); married Sarah Northrup (divorced, May, 1951); married Mary Sue Whipp, October 30, 1952; children: Diana Meredith de Wolfe, Mary Suzette Rochelle, L. Ron Hubbard, Jr. (Ronald DeWolf), Arthur Ronald Conway. *Education:* Attended George Washington University, 1930-34, and Princeton University, 1945.

CAREER: Freelance writer, 1932-50; founder and director of the Dianetic Research Foundation, Hubbard Dianetic Foundation, Hubbard Association of Scientologists, Hubbard College Graduate School, and other organizations, during the 1950s; founder of Church of Scientology, 1954; conducted research into drug abuse, education, music, and photography, beginning 1966. Leader of Caribbean Motion Picture Expedition, 1931, West Indies Minerals Survey Expedition, 1932, Alaskan Radio Experimental Expedition, 1940, and Mission into Time Expedition, 1968. *Military service:* U.S. Navy, during World War II; became lieutenant.

AWARDS, HONORS: Explorers Club Flag for geological expeditions, 1940, 1961, and 1968; Highest Certificate of Merit from the Governor of Louisiana, 1974; Ingrams West Award, 1977, for *Dianetics: The Modern Science of Mental Health;* Tully Marketing Business Administration Award, 1977, for contributions of technology in the field of marketing; Saturn Science Fiction Award, 1982, for *Battlefield Earth: A Saga of the Year 3000;* Gutenberg Honorary Literary Award, 1986.

WRITINGS:

FICTION

Buckskin Brigades, Macaulay, 1937, reprinted, Bridge Publications (Los Angeles), 1987.

Death's Deputy (also see below), Fantasy Publishing (Alhambra, CA), 1948, reprinted, Leisure Books (Norwalk, CT), 1971.

Slaves of Sleep, Shasta (Cincinnati, OH), 1948, reprinted, Dell (New York City), 1979.

Final Blackout, Hadley, 1948, reprinted, Garland Publishing (New York City), 1975.

The Kingslayer (also see below), Fantasy Publishing, 1949.

Triton, and Battle of Wizards, Fantasy Publishing, 1949.

Typewriter in the Sky [and] *Fear* (also see below), Gnome Press, 1951, published as *Fear* [and] *Typewriter in the Sky,* Popular Library, 1977; *Fear* published separately, Galaxy Publishing (Miami Beach, FL), 1957, published in hardcover, Bridge Publications, 1991; *Typewriter in the Sky* published separately, Author Services (Hollywood, CA), 1994.

From Death to the Stars (includes *Death's Deputy* and *The Kingslayer* [also see below]), Fantasy Publishing, 1953.

Return to Tomorrow, Ace Books (New York City), 1954, published as *To the Stars,* Garland Publishing, 1975.

Ole Doc Methuselah (stories), DAW Books (New York City), 1970, reprinted, Bridge Publications, 1992.

Fear [and] *The Ultimate Adventure,* Berkley Publishing (New York City), 1970; *The Ultimate Adventure* published separately, Author Services, 1992.

Seven Steps to the Arbiter, Major Books, 1975.

Lives You Wished to Lead but Never Dared (stories), edited by V. S. Wilhite, Theta Books, 1978.

Battlefield Earth: A Saga of the Year 3000, St. Martin's (New York City), 1982.

Spy Killer, Author Services, 1990.

L. Ron Hubbard Classic Fiction: A Special Collection of Short Stories, Author Services, 1991.

Arctic Wings, Author Services, 1991.

Black Towers to Danger, Author Services, 1991.

Carnival of Death, Author Services, 1991.

Empty Saddles, Author Services, 1991.

The Ghoul, Author Services, 1991.

Six-Gun Caballero, Author Services, 1991.

Guns of Mark Jardine, Author Services, 1991.

Hell's Legionnaire, The Conroy Diary, Buckley Plays a Hunch: A Special Collection of Short Stories, Author Services, 1991.

The Case of the Friendly Corpse, Author Services, 1991.

The Kingslayer, Author Services, 1991.

The Red Dragon, Author Services, 1991.

Hot Lead Payoff, Author Services, 1992.

Inky Odds, Author Services, 1992.

The Kilkenny Cats Series, Author Services, 1992.

Wind-Gone-Mad [and] *Hurricane's Roar,* Author Services, 1992.

Sea Fangs, Author Services, 1992.

Forbidden Gold, Author Services, 1992.

The Chee-Chalker, Author Services, 1992.

Adventure Short Stories, Author Services, 1992.

Western Short Stories, Author Services, 1992.

The Tramp, Author Services, 1992.

The Indigestible Triton, Author Services, 1993.

Fantasy Short Stories, Author Services, 1993.

Brass Keys to Murder, Author Services, 1993.

Hurtling Wings, Author Services, 1993.

The Battling Pilot, Author Services, 1993.

Tinhorn's Daughter, Johnny, the Town Tamer [and] *Vengeance Is Mine,* Author Services, 1993.

The Sky-Crasher, Author Services, 1993.

The Invaders and the Beast, Author Services, 1993.

Science Fiction Short Stories, Author Services, 1993.

Mystery/Suspense Short Stories, Author Services, 1994.

Branded Outlaw, Author Services, 1994.

Trouble on His Wings, Author Services, 1994.

Sabotage in the Sky, Author Services, 1994.

Hostage to Death [and] *Killer Ape,* Author Services, 1994.

The Falcon Killer, Author Services, 1994.

"MISSION EARTH" SERIES

The Invaders Plan, Bridge Publications, 1985.

Black Genesis, Bridge Publications, 1986.

The Enemy Within, Bridge Publications, 1986.

An Alien Affair, Bridge Publications, 1986.

Fortune of Fear, Bridge Publications, 1986.

Death Quest, Bridge Publications, 1987.

Voyage of Vengeance, Bridge Publications, 1987.

Disaster, Bridge Publications, 1987.

Villainy Victorious, Bridge Publications, 1987.

The Doomed Planet, Bridge Publications, 1987.

Also contributor to *My Best Science Fiction Story,* Merlin Press (San Jose, CA), 1949, and *Men against the Stars,* Gnome Press, 1950.

NONFICTION

Dianetics: The Modern Science of Mental Health, Hermitage House, 1950, reprinted, Bridge Publications, 1984.

Dianetics: The Evolution of a Science, Hubbard, 1950, reprinted, Bridge Publications, 1983.

Science of Survival, Hubbard, 1951, reprinted, Bridge Publications, 1989.

Advanced Procedure and Axioms, Hubbard, 1951, 3rd edition, American St. Hill Organization, 1971.

Dianetics: The Original Thesis, Wichita Publishing, 1951.

Handbook for Preclears, Scientic Press (Palo Alto, CA), 1951, 2nd edition, Hubbard Scientology Organization, 1962.

Notes on the Lectures of L. Ron Hubbard, Hubbard, 1951, reprinted, Bridge Publications, 1989.

Introduction to Scientology Ethics, Hubbard, 1951, 4th edition, American St. Hill Organization, 1973.

Self-Analysis, International Library of Arts and Science, 1951, reprinted, Bridge Publications, 1968.

A Key to the Unconscious, Scientic Press, 1952.

Electropsychometric Auditing, Scientic Press, 1952.

Scientology: What to Audit, Scientic Press, 1952.

Scientology: A History of Man, Hubbard, 1952.

How to Live Though an Executive, Hubbard, 1953, 5th edition, Scientology Department of Publications World Wide, 1968.

The Creation of Human Ability: A Handbook for Scientologists, Hubbard, 1954.

Dianetics '55, Hubbard, 1954, 9th edition, American St. Hill Organization, 1973.

This Is Scientology: The Science of Certainty, Hubbard, 1955.

The Key to Tomorrow, Hubbard, 1955.

Scientology: The Fundamentals of Thought, Hubbard, 1956, reprinted, Bridge Publications, 1988.

The Problems of Work, Hubbard, 1957, reprinted, Bridge Publications, 1988.

Have You Lived before This Life? Hubbard, 1958, 3rd edition, Bridge Publications, 1978.

Self-Analysis in Scientology, Hubbard, 1959.

Scientology: Plan for World Peace, Scientology, 1964.

Scientology Abridged Dictionary, Hubbard, 1965.

A Student Comes to Saint Hill, Sidney Press, 1965.

Scientology: A New Slant on Life, Hubbard, 1965, revised edition published as *A New Slant on Life,* Bridge Publications, 1988.

The Phoenix Lectures, Scientology Department of Publications World Wide, 1968.

How to Save Your Marriage, Scientology Department of Publications World Wide, 1969.

When in Doubt, Communicate, Scientology Ann Arbor, 1969.

Mission into Time, Scientology Department of Publications World Wide, 1973.

The Management Series, 1970-74, American St. Hill Organization, 1974.

The Organization Executive Course, American St. Hill Organization, 1974.

Dianetics Today, Scientology Department of Publications World Wide, 1975.

Dianetics and Scientology Technical Dictionary, Scientology Department of Publications World Wide, 1975.

The Technical Bulletins of Dianetics and Scientology, ten volumes, Scientology Department of Publications World Wide, 1976.

The Volunteer Minister's Handbook, Scientology Department of Publications World Wide, 1976.

Hubbard Communications Office Policy Letter Subject Index under Likely Titles, Bridge Publications, 1976.

Modern Management Technology Defined, Bridge Publications, 1977.

Success through Communication, Bridge Publications, 1980.

The Effective Communication Course, Bridge Publications, 1980.

The Way to Happiness: A Non-Religious Moral Guide, Bridge Publications, 1986, republished as *The Way to Happiness: A Common Sense Guide to Better Living,* 1989.

Hubbard Advanced Auditor Course: Academy Level IV, Bridge Publications, 1987.

Hubbard Certified Auditor Course: Academy Level II, Bridge Publications, 1987.

Introducing the E-Meter, Bridge Publications, 1988.

Understanding the E-Meter: A Book on the Basics of How the E-Meter Works, Bridge Publications, 1988.

E-Meter Essentials: A Startling and Thorough Coverage of the E-Meter Incorporating All Modern Developments and Its Use in Assessments and Confessionals, Bridge Publications, 1988.

Individual Track Map, Bridge Publications, 1988.

Scientology 0-8: The Book of Basics, Bridge Publications, 1988.

Scientology, A History of Man: A List and Description of the Principal Incidents to be Found in a Human Being, Bridge Publications, 1988.

Scientology 8-80: The Discovery and Increase of Life Energy in the Genus Homo Sapiens, Bridge Publications, 1989.

Scientology 8-8008, Bridge Publications, 1989.

Introduction to Scientology Ethics, Bridge, 1989.

(With Gene Denk and Farley R. Spink) *All about Radiation,* Bridge Publications, 1989.

Child Dianetics, Bridge Publications, 1989.

Self Analysis: A Simple Self-help Volume of Tests and Techniques Based on the Discoveries Contained in Dianetics, Bridge Publications, 1989.

Advanced Procedure and Axioms, Bridge Publications, 1989.

Clay Table Processing Picture Book: The New Hubbard Professional TR Course, Bridge Publications, 1989.

Dianetics: The Evolution of a Science, Bridge Publications, 1989.

The Creation of Human Ability: A Handbook for Scientologists, Bridge Publications, 1989.

Hubbard False Purpose Rundown Auditor Course Lectures, Golden Era Productions (Los Angeles), 1989.

Dianetics 55!: A Guide to Effective Communications, Bridge Publications, 1989.

Dynamics of Life, Bridge Publications, 1989.

Clear Body, Clear Mind: The Effective Purification Program, Bridge Publications, 1990.

Staff Status II, Bridge Publications, 1990.

Dianetics: The Modern Science of Mental Health, Bridge Publications, 1990.

Purification: An Illustrated Answer to Drugs, Bridge Publications, 1990.

The New Grammar, Bridge Publications, 1990.

The Hubbard Life Orientation Course, Bridge Publications, 1990.

Hubbard Class V Graduate: Case Supervisor Course, Bridge Publications, 1990.

Understanding, the Universal Solvent: Quotations from the Works of L. Ron Hubbard, Bridge Publications, 1990.

How to Use a Dictionary Picture Book, Bridge Publications, 1990.

Hubbard Expanded Dianetics: Case Supervisor Course, Bridge Publications, 1991.

The Technical Bulletins of Dianetics and Scientology, Bridge Publications, 1991.

The Organization Executive Course and Management Series, Bridge Publications, 1991.

Knowingness: The Second Volume of Quotations from the Works of L. Ron Hubbard, Bridge Publications, 1991.

The Professional Registrations Course, Bridge Publications, 1991.

The Management Series, Bridge Publications, 1991.

The Book of Case Remedies, Bridge Publications, 1991.

Art, Bridge Publications, 1992.

Games and the Spirit of Play: Transcripts and Glossary, Golden Era Productions, 1992.

Introductory and Demonstration Processes Handbook, Bridge Publications, 1992.

Technical Specialist Source, Bridge Publications, 1992.

The Professional Product Debug Course, Bridge Publications, 1993.

The Automagic Horse, Bridge Publications, 1994.

Expanded Grades Reference, Bridge Publications, 1994.

Also author of other books, pamphlets, and courses on Scientology and Dianetics.

SOUND RECORDINGS

Differences between Scientology and Other Studies, Scientology Cassette (Los Angeles), 1989.

Operation Manual for the Mind, Scientology Cassette, 1989.

Miracles, Scientology Cassette, 1989.

Universes and the War between Theta and Mest, Bridge Publications, 1989.

Hubbard Senior Security Checker Course Lectures, Golden Era Productions, 1990.

Freedom Congress Lectures, Scientology Cassette, 1990.

Fear, Bridge Audio (Los Angeles), 1991.

The Ability Congress, Scientology Cassette, 1991.

Dianetics: Lectures and Demonstrations, Bridge Audio, 1992.

OTHER

The Hymn of Asia: An Eastern Poem, Scientology Department of Publications World Wide, 1974.

Also author of novel, *Excalibur,* and coauthor of screenplay, "The Secret of Treasure Island," Columbia. Also author of radio scripts. Contributor, sometimes under pseudonyms, to *Astounding Science Fiction, Unknown, Thrilling Wonder Stories, Startling Stories, Famous Western, Five Novels Monthly, Argosy, Thrilling Mystery, Western Story Magazine,* and other publications.

SIDELIGHTS: "The life of L. Ron Hubbard is the stuff of which myths are made," Charles Platt maintained in *Dream Makers,* Volume II: *The Uncommon Men and Women Who Write Science Fiction.* This mythological aspect to Hubbard's life lies in the many varied accomplishments and careers credited to him. He was an explorer in the 1930s, leading several expeditions to the Caribbean and Pacific on mapping or geological surveys. For a time he also worked as a stunt pilot. During the 1930s and 1940s, he was a prolific writer of pulp adventure fiction. He wrote music, travelled in the Orient as a teenager, was a sailor and photographer, and developed drug rehabilitation and educational techniques. But it is as the founder of the controversial Church of Scientology that Hubbard is primarily remembered. The church has branches in countries throughout the world and claims some six million members. In the booklet *L. Ron Hubbard: The Man and His Work,* published by Hubbard's followers upon his death in 1986, Hubbard was described as "a man whose tremendous contributions to virtually all walks of life have made him the greatest humanitarian in history . . . . Few men have achieved so much in so many different fields."

Hubbard first came to public attention as a writer for the pulp magazines of the 1930s. During the next two decades he turned out a host of westerns, mysteries, sea adventures, and science fiction stories under his own name and several pseudonyms. *Xignals* reported that at his peak he wrote "over 100,000 words a month." Hubbard's writing, Martin Gardner explained in his *In the Name of Science,* "is done at lightning speed. (For a while, he used a special electric IBM typewriter with extra keys for common words like 'and,' 'the,' and 'but.' The paper was on a roll to avoid the interruption of changing sheets.)" Hubbard published nearly six hundred books, stories, and articles during his life. His fiction volumes sold over 23 million copies, while his nonfiction books sold over 27 million copies.

Among science fiction enthusiasts, Hubbard is considered to be one of the great writers of the field's "Golden Age"—the 1940s. His name is often grouped with such other writers as Isaac Asimov, Robert Heinlein, Theodore Sturgeon, and A. E. Van Vogt, all of whom first came to prominence at that time. Under the tutelage of *Astounding Science Fiction* editor John W. Campbell, these writers created realistic characters for the science fiction stories they wrote, transforming the nature of the genre. Hubbard's science fiction works, ranging from outer space adventures to whimsical fantasies, proved popular with readers. Many of his works from the 1940s have remained in print ever since.

During the late 1940s, Hubbard began to synthesize concepts from Eastern religions and modern psychology into a new system for mental health. Called Dianetics, after the Greek word for thought, this system promised to cure all mental disorders and psycho-somatic physical ailments. "The hidden source of all psycho-somatic ills and human aberration has been discovered," Hubbard explained in *Dianetics: The Modern Science of Mental Health,* "and skills have been developed for their invariable cure." Dianetics sees the human mind as "blocked" by traumatic emotional memories called engrams. By talking over these emotional memories in a process similar to conventional psychoanalysis, a patient can remove the engrams and "clear" his mind. Hubbard believed that a treated patient—called a "clear"—was "to a current normal individual as the current normal is to the severely insane," and claimed that those treated by Dianetics had higher IQs, healed faster, had better eyesight, and never got colds. "The clear is, literally, a superman—an evolutionary step toward a new species," Gardner summarized. A writer for *Fantasy Review* saw a parallel between Dianetics and Hubbard's outer space adventures, claiming that "like the quasi-superman heroes of most of Hubbard's fiction, initiates were encouraged to believe their mental powers were unlimited."

In 1950, Hubbard published *Dianetics,* the first public explication of his discoveries. Bought at first only by the science fiction fans who were most familiar with Hubbard's work, *Dianetics* quickly became a national bestseller. Groups were formed to learn and practice Dianetics; the system was popular on college campuses and became a craze among the Hollywood set. Hubbard left freelance writing in 1950 to promote Dianetics, writing a score of books on the subject in the following decade, delivering some 4,000 lectures, and founding a string of research organizations to spread the word. The Church of Scientology, founded by Hubbard in 1954, became the largest and best known of these groups.

As the Church of Scientology grew, the ideas it presented to the public were altered by Hubbard's continuing research and later writings. Hubbard found, for example, that engrams can be formed not only in a patient's earlier life but in his previous lives as

well, reincarnation being a reality. These engrams could be located by a device Hubbard invented called an E-meter, a kind of lie detector. He wrote books explaining the use of the device and offered courses for those who wished to use it to clear others.

Such claims met with skepticism in some circles. Gardner, for one, maintained that the idea of engrams "is so completely unsupported by anything faintly resembling controlled research that not a single psychiatrist of standing has given it a second thought." It has even been claimed that Hubbard's motives in founding Scientology were purely monetary. One story, William A. Henry III recounted in *Time,* alleges that at a writers' convention in 1949, a year before publishing *Dianetics,* Hubbard remarked: "Writing for a penny a word is ridiculous. If a man really wants to make a million dollars, the best way would be to start his own religion." Writing in the *Detroit News,* Bud Foote listed several possible ways to evaluate Hubbard and his religious teachings. Hubbard, Foote wrote, "is (1) the greatest genius since Isaac Newton; (2) the greatest religious leader since St. Paul; (3) a wretched charlatan who tired of writing penny-a-word SF and decided his creative abilities would be better paid by pseudo-science; (4) a nut who really believes all of his own stuff; (5) any combination of the above."

Still, Hubbard's controversial ideas proved popular throughout the 1960s and 1970s. Scientology established over 600 churches, missions, and groups around the world and saw a peak membership of some six million people. Hubbard's *Dianetics,* the bible of the movement, has sold over eight million copies since it first appeared and reportedly still sells nearly 400,000 copies a year. Scientology revenues were estimated at about two million dollars a week by the 1970s.

Allegations concerning the misuse of church funds and charges that Scientology was a fraud and used illegal methods to stifle criticism, led to a series of lawsuits in the late 1970s and early 1980s. Gerald Armstrong, former archivist for Scientology, left the church after becoming disillusioned with its teachings. He claimed that documents he had seen in the Scientology archives, the *Los Angeles Times* reported, "proved that [Hubbard] had misrepresented his background and achievements." Armstrong sued Scientology for fifteen million dollars. Hubbard's wife and ten other church officials were convicted in 1979 of burglarizing and wire-tapping government agencies the church alleged had been harassing the organization. Several former Scientology officials claimed in a 1984 lawsuit that "Hubbard had directed them to secretly divert more than $100 million from church coffers into foreign bank accounts," the *New York Times* reported. And Jacqueline Adams of the *Washington Times* reported that "the church of Scientology also has filed and won a number of lawsuits challenging the FBI, Central Intelligence Agency, National Security Agency, and Internal Revenue Service." Many of the lawsuits against the church were finally settled out of court in 1986.

Because of Scientology's legal problems, Hubbard went into seclusion in the early 1980s, reportedly living on his yacht in international waters, in one of his homes in England, and on a ranch in rural California. But Hubbard seemed unable to avoid the legal battles of the time. Although Scientology officials explained that Hubbard simply wanted his privacy, some observers outside the organization found his seclusion to be suspicious. In 1982, Hubbard's son Ronald DeWolf contended in a California court that his father was either dead or mentally incompetent and asked the court to appoint a trustee for church funds. DeWolf further charged that Scientology officials had stolen millions of dollars from his father's estate and described his father as "one of the biggest con men of the century," according to Henry. The subsequent legal investigation ended when a judge declared that Hubbard was, based on handwritten documents submitted to the court, still alive, in voluntary seclusion, and capable of handling his business affairs.

Ironically, while Hubbard was entangled in these legal problems, he managed to write and publish several new works of best-selling science fiction after an absence from the field for some three decades. In 1982, to celebrate the fiftieth anniversary of his writing career, Hubbard published *Battlefield Earth: A Saga of the Year 3000,* a massive, 819-page novel that soon broke all sales records for science fiction. Published in thirty-six countries, the novel has sold over 1.5 million copies. Platt found the book to be "just as vigorous and dramatic as the writing of [Hubbard's] youth," while Foote called it "fine thud-and-blunder stuff."

In 1983, following the success of *Battlefield Earth,* Hubbard published the first volume in a ten-volume series entitled "Mission Earth." This 1.2 million-word epic, labeled a "dekalogy" by Hubbard, is a

satirical science fiction adventure set in the far future. The first volume, *The Invaders Plan,* is told "from the villain's point of view," Lisa See explained in *Publishers Weekly.* The book quickly shot to the top of the best-seller lists, as have the subsequent volumes in the series.

Hubbard's death from a stroke on January 24, 1986, was officially announced by church officials several days later, after Hubbard's body had been cremated and his ashes scattered in the Pacific Ocean. In accordance with Hubbard's will, "no autopsy was performed," according to the *Chicago Tribune,* and the bulk of his estate—"estimated in the tens of millions of dollars," according to Mark Brown of the *County Telegram-Tribune*—was bequeathed to the Church of Scientology.

Many eulogies for Hubbard praised his wide-ranging contributions. Ken Hoden, president of the Church of Scientology, commented to the *Chicago Tribune:* "I feel what he has accomplished in the brief span of one lifetime will have impact on every man, woman and child for the next 10,000 years." Adams noted that Hubbard had "changed the way millions of people thought of religion through his novel and controversial theories on the mind." A leaflet issued by the Friends of L. Ron Hubbard organization quoted the reactions of such well-known figures as Karen Black, Chick Corea, Sonny Bono, Jeff Pomerantz, and Julia Migenes-Johnson. Corea stated that "L. Ron Hubbard set a star-high goal for us. He documented it with pure science. He taught it with pure love. He's left nothing but pure inspiration." "My own philosophy," Hubbard once told *CA,* "is that one share what wisdom he has, one should help others to help themselves, and one should keep going despite heavy weather for there is always a calm ahead. . . . If things were a little better known and understood, we would all lead happier lives. And there is a way to know them and there is a way to freedom. The old must give way to the new, falsehood must become exposed by truth, and truth, though fought, always in the end prevails."

Years after its founder's death, the Church of Scientology continues to flourish, as do accusations against it. In the early 1990s, *Time* magazine conducted an in-depth investigation into Scientology that included more than 150 interviews and the examination of hundreds of internal Scientology documents and public court records. Summarizing the findings of the investigation in a *Time* feature story, Richard Behar announced: "In reality the church is a hugely profitable global racket that survives by intimidating members and critics in a Mafia-like manner." Behar described numerous businesses that, while hiding their ties to the Church of Scientology, exist to draw new members into Hubbard's organization. The front groups include publishing houses, consulting firms, health-care clinics, drug rehabilitation centers, and even remedial education programs. Behar quoted Cynthia Kisser, executive director of the Cult Awareness Network, as saying that "Scientology is quite likely the most ruthless, the most classically terroristic, the most litigious and the most lucrative cult the country has ever seen." At the time the article was published, the Church of Scientology and its satellite organizations were paying an estimated $20 million per year to a staff of more than 100 lawyers to deal with the many charges brought against it. "Yet the outrage and litigation have failed to squelch Scientology," noted Behar, who also stated that during the course of his research, "at least 10 attorneys and six private detectives were unleashed by Scientology and its followers in an effort to threaten, harass and discredit me." He concluded that "the group . . . threatens to become more insidious and pervasive than ever."

BIOGRAPHICAL/CRITICAL SOURCES:

BOOKS

Atack, John, *A Piece of Blue Sky: Scientology, Dianetics, and L. Ron Hubbard Exposed,* Carol, 1990.
Contemporary Literary Criticism, Volume 43, Gale (Detroit), 1987.
Corydon, Bent, *L. Ron Hubbard: Messiah or Madman?,* Barricade Books (Fort Lee, NJ), 1992.
Del Rey, Lester, *The World of Science Fiction, 1926-1976: The History of a Subculture,* Garland Publishing, 1980.
Evans, Christopher, *Cults of Unreason,* Farrar, Straus, 1973.
Gardner, Martin, *In the Name of Science,* Putnam, 1952, published as *Fads and Fallacies in the Name of Science,* Dover, 1957.
Hubbard, L. Ron, *Dianetics: The Modern Science of Mental Health,* Hermitage House, 1950, reprinted, Bridge Publications, 1984.
L. Ron Hubbard: The Man and His Work, North Star Publishing, 1986.
Lamont, Stuart, *Religion Inc.,* Harrap (London), 1986.

Littler, June D., *The Church of Scientology and L. Ron Hubbard,* Garland Publishing, 1992.
Miller, Russell, *Bare-Faced Messiah: The True Story of L. Ron Hubbard,* Holt, 1988.
Platt, Charles, *Dream Makers,* Volume II: *The Uncommon Men and Women Who Write Science Fiction,* Berkley Publishing, 1983.
Shepard, Leslie A., editor, *Encyclopedia of Occultism and Parapsychology,* Gale, 2nd edition, 1985.
Widder, William J., *The Fiction of L. Ron Hubbard: A Comprehensive Bibliography and Reference Guide to Published and Selected Unpublished Works,* Bridge Publications, 1994.

PERIODICALS

Analog, March, 1973; February, 1983; April, 1986.
Biography News, July/August, 1975.
Chicago Tribune, January 30, 1986; March 27, 1991, section 2C, p. 2.
County Telegram-Tribune, January 30, 1986.
Detroit News, November 14, 1982.
Economist, April 7, 1984.
Freedom!, May/June, 1975.
Locus, December 17, 1975.
Los Angeles Times, December 17, 1986; January 1, 1987; April 16, 1987, section II, p. 3; September 29, 1987, section II, p. 8; July 24, 1988, section II, p. 2; June 24, 1990, pp. A1, A38-A40; June 28, 1990, p. A1.
Los Angeles Times Book Review, November 21, 1982; February 9, 1986.
Luna Monthly, April, 1971; April-May, 1972.
Magazine of Fantasy and Science Fiction, August, 1988, p. 34; April, 1991, p. 28; July, 1992, p. 32.
Newsweek, September 23, 1974; June 14, 1993, p. 76.
New York Times, December 18, 1986; August 11, 1988, p. C24; May 27, 1990, section 1, p. 24.
New York Times Book Review, January 12, 1986; March 20, 1988, p. 27.
Psychology Today, January, 1983; June, 1988, p. 79.
Publishers Weekly, March 1, 1985.
Reader's Digest, May, 1980; October, 1991, p. 87.
Science Fiction & Fantasy Book Review, March, 1983.
Science Fiction Review, summer, 1986.
Time, April 5, 1976; January 31, 1983; May 6, 1991, pp. 50-57.
Wall Street Journal, January 31, 1990, p. B7; February 21, 1990, p. A5; May 25, 1990, p. B5;

April 19, 1991, p. A1; March 22, 1995, p. A1;
April 10, 1995, p. A21.
Washington Post, December 25, 1994, p. C1.
Washington Post Book World, February 23, 1986.
Xignals, April/May, 1986.

OBITUARIES:

PERIODICALS

Chicago Tribune, January 29, 1986.
Detroit News, January 28, 1986.
Fantasy Review, February, 1986.
Los Angeles Times, January 28, 1986.
Newsweek, February 10, 1986.
New York Times, January 29, 1986.
Publishers Weekly, February 14, 1986.
Time, February 10, 1986; May 6, 1991, pp. 50-57.
Washington Post, January 29, 1986.
Washington Times, January 29, 1986.*

* * *

HUNTER, Bernice Thurman   1922-

PERSONAL: Born November 3, 1922, in Toronto,
Ontario, Canada; daughter of William Henry (a laborer) and Francelina (a homemaker; maiden name,
Coe) Thurman; married Lloyd George Hunter (a telephone company employee), November 16, 1942;
children: Anita, Heather. *Education:*Runnymede Collegiate Institute, commercial diploma, 1939.

ADDRESSES: Home—3333 Finch Ave. E., Apt. 703,
Scarborough, Ontario, Canada M1W 2R9.

CAREER: Writer. Eaton Co. Ltd., Toronto, Ontario,
bookkeeper and machine operator, 1942-70, general
office clerk, 1970-75. Guest speaker at schools and
libraries; volunteer worker for Canadian Cancer Society.

MEMBER: Writers' Union of Canada, Canadian Society of Children's Authors, Illustrators and Performers.

AWARDS, HONORS: Imperial Order of Daughters of
the Empire Book Award (Toronto Chapter), 1981,
and City of Toronto Book Award Contest finalist,
1982, both for *That Scatterbrain Booky;* Ruth

Schwartz Award finalist, 1983, for *With Love from
Booky;* Vicky Metcalf Award, Canadian Authors
Association, 1990, for body of work.

WRITINGS:

CHILDREN'S FICTION

That Scatterbrain Booky, Scholastic/Tab (New York
City), 1981.
With Love from Booky, Scholastic/Tab, 1983.
A Place for Margaret, Scholastic/Tab, 1984.
As Ever, Booky, Scholastic/Tab, 1985.
Margaret in the Middle, Scholastic/Tab, 1986.
Lamplighter, Scholastic/Tab, 1987.
Margaret on Her Way, Scholastic/Tab, 1988.
That Scatterbrain Booky, With Love from Booky,
[and] *As Ever, Booky* (boxed set), Scholastic/
Tab, 1989.
The Railroader, Scholastic/Tab, 1990.
The Firefighter, Scholastic/Tab, 1991.
Hawk and Stretch, Scholastic/Tab, 1993.

OTHER

Also contributor to books, readers, magazines, and
newspapers, including the *Toronto Star, Crackers,*
and *JAM.*

SIDELIGHTS: One of Canada's leading writers for
children, Bernice Thurman Hunter is praised for the
authenticity of the historical settings she recreates in
her fictional tales. This accuracy often stems from
Hunter's own experiences. Her "Booky" trilogy is
autobiographical, while many of the elements in the
"Margaret" trilogy come from these same childhood
memories. "Hunter attracts middle school audiences
through her consistent ability to create likeable, but
ordinary, central juvenile characters whom she
places in loving, supporting environments and sur-
rounds with interesting, historically accurate details," asserts David H. Jenkinson in *Twentieth-Century Children's Writers.*

Hunter was born and educated in Toronto, but her
great-grandparents were pioneers, settling in the
wilds of Muskoka and the village of Swansea, which
is now a part of Toronto. "These pioneer roots have
furnished me with lots of ideas to incorporate into
my books and stories," Hunter once told *CA.* Hunter
first began writing in early childhood and read her
stories to friends. "My cousin used to hate it when
I was asked to read my composition in class and she

was next," Hunter recalls in an interview for *Children's Book Centre*. "I'd have pages and pages—and hers would be quite short."

Inspired by L. M. Montgomery's *Anne of Green Gables,* Hunter was fortunate enough to meet the author. But this meeting, during the course of which Montgomery stressed the importance of higher education, made Hunter's writing ambitions seem unreachable. "No one in my family had gone to university," she explains in her *Children's Book Centre* interview. "So it put a damper on my ambitions. . . . When I quit school, I went to work for Eaton's and I thought I could never be a writer."

Despite this belief, Hunter did continue to write, and it was Alexander Ross of the *Toronto Star* who finally gave her the encouragement she needed to be published. After reading and publishing Hunter's column on becoming a grandmother, Ross sent a letter urging the author to keep writing. So Hunter did, and her first book, *That Scatterbrain Booky,* was accepted by Scholastic and published in 1981.

Based on Hunter's own childhood during the Depression in Toronto, *That Scatterbrain Booky* led to two sequels that follow Booky as she grows up: *With Love from Booky* and *As Ever, Booky.* The trilogy begins when Booky is ten, and her tale concludes seven years later at the beginning of World War II. The trials of Booky's financially poor but emotionally rich family are episodically related by Booky herself, and each chapter stands alone as a separate story. Adding to the historical detail are actual pages reproduced from the Eaton's Catalog, as well as photos of Hunter's family and passages from newspapers of the time period. "The three volumes that comprise the Booky series have the special strength of novels that were lived and researched," maintains Nancy Colpitts in *Canadian Children's Literature,* adding: "Bits and pieces of family life form an unpretentious, seemingly unconscious lesson in history without relying on galloping story lines or great events whirling in the background."

Set in a similar historical time period, Hunter's "Margaret" series—*A Place for Margaret, Margaret in the Middle,* and *Margaret on Her Way*—begins in 1925 when eleven-year old Margaret contracts tuberculosis. Sent to stay at her Aunt Marg and Uncle Herb's farm during her illness, Margaret forms a bond with these relatives, who ask her to remain permanently. Coming from a family of ten children,

Margaret decides to stay, forming a special friendship with the farm's Clydesdale horse, which eventually leads to her decision to become a veterinarian.

Lynn Wytenbroek, writing in *Canadian Literature,* praises the characters Hunter creates in the "Margaret" trilogy and pointed out that Margaret's adventures are "so captivating" that the "novels come alive and hold a fascination rare in any genre. There is no doubt that Hunter is one of Canada's best writers for young people." Callie Israel observes in *Books for Young People* that "young readers will recognize and empathize with Margaret's growing-up problems, laughing with her as she learns to drive and when the roof falls in on her." Israel concludes: "Margaret's fans will be sorry to see the story end, but hopefully Hunter has a new heroine or hero waiting in the wings."

Hunter once told *CA:* "My greatest satisfaction comes from today's children who tell me that they wish they had lived in 'the old days' so they could be my characters' friends. Many times I have been asked where Starr, the horse in *A Place for Margaret,* lives now so that they can go and visit him. They do not consider for a minute that a horse that was adult in 1925 could not possibly be grazing in some green meadow."

BIOGRAPHICAL/CRITICAL SOURCES:

BOOKS

Twentieth-Century Children's Writers, 4th edition, St. James Press (Detroit), 1995.

PERIODICALS

Books for Young People, December, 1988, p. 10.
Books in Canada, December, 1981, p. 6; December, 1983, p. 16.
Canadian Children's Literature, number 44, 1986, pp. 73-75; number 62, 1991, pp. 62-63; number 65, 1992, pp. 102-104.
Canadian Literature, winter, 1992, pp. 191-192; summer, 1992, p. 191.
Children's Book Centre, December, 1983.
Emergency Librarian, autumn, 1985.
Quill and Quire, January, 1982, p. 35; November, 1983, p. 24; October, 1985, pp. 21-22; December, 1986, p. 13.
Toronto Star, October 15, 1981.

OTHER

Meet the Author: Bernice Thurman Hunter (filmstrip
   with cassette or videocassette), Mead, 1987.*

* * *

HUNTER, Dawe
   See DOWNIE, Mary Alice (Dawe)

* * *

INNES, Hammond
   See HAMMOND INNES, Ralph

J

JACKSON, Shirley 1919-1965

PERSONAL: Born December 14, 1919, in San Francisco, CA; died of heart failure, August 8, 1965, in North Bennington, VT; daughter of Leslie Hardie (president of Stecher-Traung Lithograph, Inc.) and Geraldine (Bugbee) Jackson; married Stanley Edgar Hyman (an author and critic), 1940 (died, 1970); children: Laurence Jackson, Joanne Leslie, Sarah Geraldine, Barry Edgar. *Education:* Attended University of Rochester, 1934-36; Syracuse University, B.A., 1940.

CAREER: Novelist and freelance writer.

AWARDS, HONORS: Edgar Allan Poe Award, 1961, for story, "Louisa, Please"; Arents Pioneer Medal for Outstanding Achievement, Syracuse University, 1965.

WRITINGS:

The Road through the Wall (novel), Farrar, Straus (New York City), 1948, 2nd edition, Manor, 1973, published as *The Other Side of the Street,* Pyramid (New York City), 1956, reprinted under original title, Popular Library (New York City), 1976.

The Lottery; or, The Adventures of James Harris (short stories), Farrar, Straus, 1949.

Hangasman (novel), Farrar, Straus, 1949.

Life among the Savages (semiautobiographical essays), Farrar, Straus, 1953.

The Bird's Nest (novel), Farrar, Straus, 1954, published as *Lizzie,* Signet, 1957, reprinted under original title, Popular Library, 1976.

The Witchcraft of Salem Village (juvenile nonfiction), Random House (New York City), 1956.

Raising Demons, Farrar, Straus, 1957.

The Sundial (novel), Farrar, Straus, 1958.

The Haunting of Hill House (novel), Viking (New York City), 1959.

The Bad Children (play), Dramatic Publishing, 1959.

(Contributor) *Special Delivery,* Little, Brown (Boston), 1960, published as *And Baby Makes Three,* Grosset (New York City), 1966.

We Have Always Lived in the Castle (novel), Viking, 1962.

9 Magic Wishes (juvenile), Crowell-Collier (New York City), 1963.

The Magic of Shirley Jackson (eleven stories and three novels), edited by husband, Stanley Edgar Hyman, Farrar, Straus, 1966.

Famous Sally (juvenile), Quist, 1966.

Come along with Me (part of a novel, sixteen stories, and three lectures), edited by S. E. Hyman, Viking, 1968.

The Lottery (single story), Creative Education (Mankato, MN), 1983.

One Ordinary Day (single story), Creative Education, 1990.

Charles (single story), Creative Education, 1991.

The Lottery and Other Stories, Noonday Press (New York City), 1991.

Also author of radio and television scripts. Contributor of numerous stories to *New Yorker, Good Housekeeping, Hudson Review, Woman's Day, Yale Review* and other publications.

Jackson's papers are housed in the manuscript division of the Library of Congress.

ADAPTATIONS: The novel *The Bird's Nest* was filmed as *Lizzie* by Metro-Goldwyn-Mayer (MGM), 1957; the novel *The Haunting of Hill House* was filmed as *The Haunting,* starring Julie Harris and Claire Bloom, by MGM in 1963, and adapted for the stage by F. Andrew Leslie; the novel *We Have Always Lived in the Castle* was adapted for the stage by Hugh Wheeler and first produced on Broadway in 1966; the story "The Lottery" was filmed by the University of Southern California's Division of Cinema and Television, 1981, and adapted for the stage by Brainerd Duffield; the story "The Renegade" was filmed by Phoenix/BFA Films & Video, 1984. Three recordings have been made of Shirley Jackson's work: "The Demon Lover" and "The Lottery," read by the author for Folkway Records, 1963; *The Lottery and Other Stories,* read by Maureen Stapleton for Caedmon, 1976; and "The Summer People" and "The Little House," also read by Stapleton for Caedmon, 1976.

SIDELIGHTS: A master of modern gothic fiction, Shirley Jackson wrote of the essentially evil nature of human beings. Her most famous story, "The Lottery," tells of a ritual in a typical New England town in which local residents choose one among their number to be sacrificed. Other Jackson stories turn on ironic twists and black humor. Her novels include *The Sundial,* in which a group of people who believe the end of the world is near takes refuge in a large estate; *The Haunting of Hill House,* the story of a research project at a supposedly haunted manor house; and *We Have Always Lived in the Castle,* the tale of two sisters ostracized by their community for allegedly murdering the rest of their family. Jackson's dark fiction, wrote Martha Ragland in the *Dictionary of Literary Biography,* "earned her a reputation as a 'literary sorceress,' a writer with a peculiar talent for the bizarre, a creator of psychological thrillers, an adroit master of effect and suspense."

"The Lottery," Jackson's most famous short story, was first published in the *New Yorker* on June 26, 1948. Reader reaction was intense, and the publishers announced that the story had prompted more mail than anything published in the magazine up to that time: 450 letters from twenty-five states, two territories, and six foreign countries, most expressing outrage at the allegory of man's darker nature. In this story Jackson stated a theme which, according to Ragland, carries through much of the author's fiction: "Humankind is more evil than good. The mass of men is profoundly misguided, seemingly incapable

of enlightenment. Lacking either the capacity to reason or the strength to act upon moral convictions, their lives are dictated by habit and convention. They often behave with callous disregard of those around them."

Speaking of the reaction provoked by "The Lottery," Jackson wrote in *The Story and Its Writer: An Introduction to Short Fiction:* "One of the most terrifying aspects of publishing stories and books is the realization that they are going to be read, and read by strangers. I had never fully realized this before. . . . It had simply never occurred to me that these millions and millions of people . . . would sit down and write me letters I was downright scared to open. . . . Even my mother scolded me."

"The Lottery" firmly established Jackson as a master of the gothic horror tale. But according to her husband, Stanley Edgar Hyman, the story also led many critics to misunderstand both the author and her work. He wrote: "Her fierce visions of dissociations and madness, of alienation and withdrawal, of cruelty and terror, have been taken to be personal, even neurotic fantasies. Quite the reverse: They are a sensitive and faithful anatomy of our times, fitting symbols for our distressing world of the concentration camp and The Bomb. She was always proud that the Union of South Africa banned 'The Lottery,' and she felt that they, at least, understood the story."

Jackson's novel *The Sundial* concerns a group of people who, believing that the end of the world is near, hide out in a remote estate. Various supernatural events, which the group takes to be omens, have convinced them of this looming apocalypse. "Showing her ability to find pity and terror in the ludicrous and the ludicrous in terror," wrote John G. Parks in *Twentieth Century Literature,* "Jackson created [in *The Sundial*] a fantasy of the end of the world which parodies the apocalyptic imagination, while at the same time portraying it." Mary Kittredge, writing in *Discovering Modern Horror Fiction,* noted that "the book was written in a comic style and many of its episodes are quite funny."

Jackson used a similar setting in *The Haunting of Hill House,* this time taking the gothic situation more seriously than she had in the earlier novel. As Parks noted, "while a setting for what begins as a mad masquerade party in *The Sundial,* the gothic house in a real sense is the chief character of *The Haunting of Hill House.*" In this novel, a group of researchers gathers at an old estate house as part of a psychic investigation to see if the building is haunted. One of the women invited to participate on the project because of her sensitivity to the supernatural becomes obsessed with or possessed by the house. Carol Cleveland explained in *And Then There Were Nine . . . More Women of Mystery* that with this novel Jackson had given the traditional gothic story a twist. "The classic gothic formula," Cleveland wrote, "brings a vulnerable young girl to an isolated mansion with a reputation for ghosts, exposes her to a few weird happenings to heighten the suspense, then explains the 'supernatural' away by a perfectly human, if evil, plot and leaves the heroine in the strong arms of the hero. In *House,* the heroine is exceedingly vulnerable, the weird happenings quite real, the house really haunted." In *The Haunting of Hill House,* Kittredge wrote, "Jackson for the first time gives the devil his due. She puts her damsel into mortal distress and leaves her there, completely unrescued. The potential for disaster is fully explored; the evil force is developed into a completely independent and alien entity, and is shown to be a power that can triumph."

In *We Have Always Lived in the Castle* Jackson tells the story of two sisters who have become outcasts in their town. Merricat and Constance Blackwood have survived the arsenic poisoning which has killed four members of their family. Although Constance has been acquitted by a jury of murdering the family, the townspeople still view the two sisters with suspicion and hostility. Their isolation is violated when cousin Charles arrives and, hoping to get his hands on the family fortune, woos Merricat. She rejects his advances. In the resulting fracas, a fire breaks out in the house and the townspeople who arrive to help are soon tempted instead to wreck the house further. "The novel closes," wrote Parks, "with the image of a ruin nearly completely covered with vines with two sisters huddled in fragile happiness within it." According to Lynette Carpenter in *Frontiers: A Journal of Women Studies, We Have Always Lived in the Castle* is Jackson's "most radical statement on the causes and consequences of female victimization and alienation, a theme that runs throughout her work."

Despite her talent for macabre fiction, Jackson also published humorous books about family life. In *Life among the Savages* and *Raising Demons,* two collections of short sketches originally published in women's magazines, Jackson wrote a "domestic saga spanning from the time of her family's first house in Vermont until the year her youngest child [enrolled]

in school," Ragland explained. Speaking of the book *Life among the Savages,* Orville Prescott said he read "until I laughed so much the tears came to my eyes and I had to stop." Ragland claimed that these two books on domestic life "reveal Jackson as a comic writer who at her best belongs in the ranks of the great American humorists." Referring to the two distinct styles in Jackson's published work, a writer for the *New York Times* explained: "Shirley Jackson wrote in two styles. She could describe the delights and turmoils of ordinary domestic life with detached hilarity; and she could, with cryptic symbolism, write a tenebrous horror story in the Gothic mold in which abnormal behavior seemed perilously ordinary."

Although William Kennedy agreed that Jackson was a master of the Gothic narrative, he called her work "dated excellence. She was modern in the sense that mysticism is modern; she represented the twilight zone as genre. But she treated her subject matter as an old-time storyteller. She was a *good* storyteller, fully conscious of the demands of the short-story form—but today they are old-fashioned demands." In contrast to Kennedy, Guy Davenport, writing in the *New York Times Book Review,* found that Jackson "recognized the strange discontinuousness of things. . . . That the familiar can become alien, that the level flow of existence can warp in the batting of an eye, was the theme to which she most often returned." Granville Hicks, in an article for *Saturday Review,* stated: "Jackson was certainly not the first writer to assert that there is evil in everybody, but what might be merely a platitude becomes a great truth because of the depth and consistency of her own feeling about life and because she was so extraordinarily successful in making her readers feel what she felt."

BIOGRAPHICAL/CRITICAL SOURCES:

BOOKS

Bakerman, Jane S., editor, *And Then There Were Nine . . . More Women of Mystery,* Bowling Green State University Popular Press (Bowling Green, OH), 1985, pp. 199-219.

Brooks, Cleanth, and Robert Penn Warren, editors, *Understanding Fiction,* Appleton-Century-Crofts, 1959, pp. 72-76.

Charters, Ann, editor, *The Story and Its Writer: An Introduction to Short Fiction,* St. Martin's (New York City), 1983, pp. 1192-195.

Contemporary Literary Criticism, Gale (Detroit), Volume 11, 1979, Volume 60, 1990, Volume 87, 1995.

Dictionary of Literary Biography, Volume 6: *American Novelists since World War II,* second series, Gale, 1980.

Eisenger, Chester E., *Fiction of the Forties,* University of Chicago Press (Chicago), 1963.

Friedman, Lenemaja, *Shirley Jackson,* Twayne (New York City), 1975.

Hall, Joan Wylie, *Shirley Jackson: A Study of the Short Fiction,* Twayne, 1993.

Hyman, Stanley Edgar, *The Promised End,* World (New York City), 1963.

Kessler-Harris, Alice, and William McBrien, editors, *Faith of a (Woman) Writer,* Greenwood Press (Westport, CT), 1988, pp. 143-48.

Oppenheimer, Judy, *Private Demons: The Life of Shirley Jackson,* Putnam (New York City), 1988.

Schweitzer, Darrell, editor, *Discovering Modern Horror Fiction,* Starmont House (Mercer, WA), 1985, pp. 3-12.

Short Story Criticism, Volume 9, Gale, 1992.

PERIODICALS

America, November 26, 1966, p. 709.
American Literature, March, 1974, pp. 100-07.
Atlantic, October, 1968, p. 150.
Bibliographical Society of America Papers, January, 1962, pp. 110-13; April, 1966, pp. 203-13.
Christian Science Monitor, September 29, 1966, p. 15; February 6, 1969, p. 7.
English Journal, December, 1971, pp. 1204-208.
Essays in Literature, fall, 1988, pp. 259-65.
Explicator, March, 1954.
Frontiers: A Journal of Women's Studies, Volume VIII, number 1, 1984, pp. 32-38.
Harper's, October, 1968.
Listener, November 27, 1969, p. 750.
National Observer, October 14, 1968.
New Leader, September 9, 1968, pp. 18-19.
New Orleans Review, spring, 1985, pp. 27-32.
Newsweek, August 23, 1965.
New Yorker, October 24, 1959.
New York Herald Tribune Book Review, May 1, 1949, p. 4; October 25, 1959.
New York Review of Books, December 15, 1967.
New York Times, August 10, 1965; September 21, 1966.
New York Times Book Review, April 17, 1949, p. 4; June 26, 1949, p. 15; October 18, 1959; September 23, 1962; October 9, 1966, p. 58; September 15, 1968, p. 4; July 3, 1988, p. 1.

Observer, August 10, 1969, p. 24.
Papers of the Bibliographical Society of America, first quarter, 1962, 1966.
Publishers Weekly, August 23, 1965.
Saturday Evening Post, December 18, 1965, p. 63.
Saturday Review, September 17, 1966, pp. 31-32; September 14, 1968.
Southwest Review, September, 1967, pp. 152-62.
Spectator, August 26, 1960.
Studies in American Humor, spring-summer, 1985, pp. 62-73.
Studies in Short Fiction, summer, 1978, pp. 320-23; spring, 1982, pp. 133-39.
Studies in Weird Fiction, fall, 1989, pp. 15-24.
Time, September 21, 1962; August 20, 1965.
Times Literary Supplement, September 16, 1960; May 29, 1969.
Twentieth Century Literature, spring, 1984, pp. 15-29.
Vogue, July, 1988, p. 70.
Washington Post Book World, November 16, 1969, p. 21.
Writer, January, 1969.

OBITUARIES:

PERIODICALS

Antiquarian Bookman, September 6-13, 1965.
Books Abroad, spring, 1966.
Newsweek, August 23, 1965.
New York Times, August 10, 1965.
Publishers Weekly, August 23, 1965.
Time, August 20, 1965.*

*   *   *

JANOWITZ, Tama   1957-

PERSONAL: Born April 12, 1957, in San Francisco, CA; daughter of Julian Frederick (a psychiatrist) and Phyllis (a poet and professor; maiden name, Winer) Janowitz; married Tim Hunt, 1992. *Education:* Barnard College, B.A., 1977; Hollins College, M.A., 1979; postgraduate studies at Yale University School of Drama, 1980-81; Columbia University, M.F.A., 1985.

ADDRESSES: Agent—c/o Crown Publishers, 201 East 50th Street, New York, NY 10022.

CAREER: Model with Vidal Sassoon (international hair salon) in London, England, and New York City, 1975-77; Kenyon & Eckhardt, Boston, MA, assistant art director, 1977-78; Fine Arts Work Center, Provincetown, MA, writer in residence, 1981-82; freelance journalist, 1985—. Member of Barnard College Arts and Literature Committee (member of board of directors, 1974-75). Appeared in film *Slaves of New York,* 1989.

MEMBER: Poets and Writers, Writers' Community (fellow, 1976), Associated Writing Program.

AWARDS, HONORS: Breadloaf Writers' Conference, 1975; Elizabeth Janeway Fiction Prize, 1976 and 1977; Amy Loveman Prize for poetry, 1977; Hollins College fellowship, 1978; National Endowment for the Arts grants, 1982 and 1986; CCLM/General Electric Foundation award, 1984; Ludwig Vogelstein Foundation award, 1985; Alfred Hodder Fellow in the Humanities, Princeton University, 1986-87.

WRITINGS:

NOVELS

American Dad, Putnam (New York City), 1981.
A Cannibal in Manhattan, Crown (New York City), 1987.
The Male Cross-Dresser Support Group, Crown, 1992.

SHORT STORIES

Slaves of New York, Crown, 1986.

Contributor of short stories to magazines and periodicals, including *Paris Review, Mississippi Review,* and *Pawn Review.*

OTHER

Author of *Slaves of New York* (screenplay; based on her novel of the same name; directed by Ismail Merchant and James Ivory), 1989. Contributor of articles to magazines, including *Rolling Stone* and *Mademoiselle.*

SIDELIGHTS: Since the publication of her first novel, *American Dad,* at age twenty-three, author Tama Janowitz has captured media headlines, as much for her flamboyant and engaging personality and notoriety as friend to the late Andy Warhol as for her postmodernist fiction. A witty and sensitive observer of New York City's inner life, she has sometimes been taken to task—along with fellow novelists Bret Easton Ellis and Jay McInerney—for, as Terrence Rafferty comments in the *New Yorker,* "believing that the goal of their [literary] elders' activity was their celebrity . . . rather than their vision." Thomas De Pietro describes the Janowitz "vision" as follows in the *Hudson Review:* "Her rock-and-roll sensibility is new-wave and, although her characters prefer groups like Teenage Jesus and The Circle Jerks, she herself comes off like a literary Cyndi Lauper, a connoisseur of kitsch capable of being assimilated into the mainstream."

Earl Przepasniak, the protagonist and narrator of Janowitz's debut novel, *American Dad,* is eleven years old when his parents divorce. Earl's father, a psychiatrist, is an amiable, self-absorbed, pot-smoking philanderer whose unrepressed behavior upsets and embarrasses the family. His mother, a poet, is killed halfway through the novel during a fight with her ex-husband over alimony payments. Earl's father is convicted of involuntary manslaughter—Earl testifies against him at the trial—and sentenced to ten to fifteen years in prison. With his mother dead and his father in jail, Earl decides to travel abroad and goes to London, where he pursues women and indulges in various other misadventures. Upon his return from Europe, Earl is, as several reviewers of *American Dad* observe, predictably wiser, and his enhanced sense of self leads to improved relations with his father.

Although Arnold Klein of the *Soho News* finds *American Dad* "episodic and trivial," he notes that it has the "considerable virtue of being funny." Klein is also delighted with Janowitz's depiction of Earl's psychiatrist father, which he calls "an uncannily acute portrayal of a distinct social type." Garrett Epps concurs in the *New Republic,* saying, "There is not a false note in the presentation of this engaging villain." David Quammen, writing for the *New York Times Book Review,* laments the untimely death of Earl's mother, whom he believes to be the novel's most well-drawn and endearing character. Echoing the reaction of several other reviewers, Quammen praises the novelist for her "fine comedic inventiveness, especially as applied in light dabs to character." According to Epps, Janowitz also has "a sharp eye for the things of this world . . . and her sensuous writing enlivens the book." Reviewers generally agree that the first half of *American Dad* is the stronger half, and the novel flounders, according to some, after Earl embarks on what one reviewer terms a

European rite-of-passage trip. "Earl's adventures are mostly filler," writes Epps, "[and they mar] what is otherwise one of the most impressive first novels I've read in a long time."

Slaves of New York, Janowitz's follow-up to *American Dad,* is a collection of twenty-two interconnected short stories—many of which originally appeared in the *New Yorker.* The stories center on Eleanor, a shy young jeweller who is financially bound to her boyfriend Stash—a self-proclaimed artist—because he has enough money to pay the rent. *Slaves* takes readers into the behind-the-scenes lives of Manhattan's bohemian elite: painters who adopt blood and ground-up bones as an artistic medium, pimps who contemplate the categorical imperative of philosopher Immanuel Kant, and a host of "couples" whose relationships are dictated by the lack of affordable housing in the Big Apple. "Janowitz writes about people who are not terribly nice," notes Victoria Radin in *New Statesman,* "with an underlying hopefulness that they'll get nicer; and she shows how little control they have over themselves or their lives without pitying or inflating them." While agreeing that *Slaves* is "resoundingly successful as a comedic look" at city dwellers, a reviewer for the *Los Angeles Times Book Review* also finds that "pleasantly distracted by Janowitz' solid sense of humor, we don't notice that her characters' spiritual quest is largely for show." Indeed, the main criticism of *Slaves of New York* is that Janowitz's characters possess no depth: *Village Voice* reviewer Carol Ashnew terms them "permanent transients in a dress-up and play-act milieu full of style without the slightest pretense of substance." Despite the mixed critical response, Janowitz was asked to write the screenplay for a film version of *Slaves of New York,* which starred Bernadette Peters and was released in 1989.

After the popular success of *Slaves of New York,* its publisher, Crown, released a work of Janowitz juvenilia in an attempt to continue her momentum on the best-seller lists. Heavily indebted to the literature of the past, *A Cannibal in Manhattan* "begins as a travesty of *Robinson Crusoe,*" according to *Newsweek*'s David Lehman, and "borrows liberally from Evelyn Waugh's *Black Mischief,* [and] broadly imitates the satire of *Candide.*" Unlike its predecessors, *A Cannibal in Manhattan* fared poorly with critics, who, as Rafferty notes in the *New Yorker,* had been fast becoming inured to the "death of the novel. . . . In more idealistic times,. . . the publication of . . . *A Cannibal in Manhattan* . . . might have been the occasion of panic in the streets of

Morningside Heights, or for hastily convened symposia in *Partisan Review.*" Taking place in the heart of the Big Apple, Janowitz's romp finds noble cannibal savage Mgungu Yabba Mgungu plucked from his South Sea island home—where he lived with three wives and assorted children and pigs—and transplanted to New York City by a society heiress playing part-time Peace Corps volunteer. Believing himself to have been selected to become her spouse, Mgungu attempts to fit in with his fiance's high-society friends, where, according to *Times Literary Supplement* reviewer Peter Reading, his activities serve "to accentuate the real absurdity, viciousness and debasement of the sophisticated civilization into which he is deposited." At the close of a dinner party after the couple's wedding, some so-called friends finally reveal to Mgungu that all his new bride really wanted was the recipe for a native hallucinogen and that it doesn't really matter now because his new wife has been freshly offed by underworld pals and served up as the main course at dinner. Some critics consider the cynical humor that redeemed *Slaves* to be unsuccessful in Janowitz's second novel. "Given the book's grisly central metaphor, the tone is shockingly light," observes Rafferty. "If we're really living in a country—or, at least, a city—of cannibals, shouldn't we be a little disturbed?"

Janowitz's same comic voice "is instantly recognizable," Robert Plunket notes in a review of her next novel, *The Male Cross-Dresser Support Group* for the *New York Times Book Review.* Janowitz is, he states, "precise, fearless, with the intuitive rhythm of someone who was born funny. . . . Most of all, it's great fun to see a first-rate comic mind tackle the important issues of the day—sexual identity, family values, the shocking behavior of rich WASP's with enormous trust funds." In Janowitz's 1992 effort, readers are introduced to Pamela Trowel, a woman who lives a meaningless existence in a Manhattan apartment and supports herself with a mindless job selling advertising space for a low-budget hunting magazine until she encounters meaning in the form of a nine-year-old boy called Abdhul. She and the homeless waif become attached to each other and, after Pamela gets fired from her job, they decide to escape from New York rather than be separated by a city bureaucracy seemingly intent upon destroying supportive relationships between children and caring adults. The problem of sexual identity implied by the novel's title comes into play after Abdhul becomes lost; Pamela must adopt the identity of the popular "Paul" in order to discover his whereabouts. "In this post-feminist era, when women still suffer from a lack of status and a lot of disillusionment,. . . Pamela is a kind of comic urban Everywoman," explains Susan Heeger in the *Los Angeles Times Book Review*. "But she's loyal and courageous," Heeger adds, "and it's heartening to watch her find her way in the wilderness, despite all those who want to trample her." The author commented on the plight of her protagonist in the *Boston Globe*, telling interviewer Matthew Gilbert: "God knows the men don't come off well in this book, but the women are even worse. I mean women are so rotten to each other, particularly in New York. They're so competitive and back-stabbing and desperate."

Like her protagonist Earl in *American Dad*, Janowitz is the product of a broken marriage between a psychiatrist and a poet; critics note that she interjects in the fictional lives of the characters she creates the ability to seek unusual ways of dealing with permissive parents or unstructured lifestyles. Several critics also note parallels between Janowitz and Eleanor, the heroine of *Slaves of New York*. "Her story isn't as much mine as eighty of my girlfriends," Janowitz responded to Gini Sikes in an interview for *Mademoiselle*. "Just because I write that stuff doesn't mean it has anything to do with me." However, she also admitted to *CA* that an autobiographical element does run through her work. "I write about myself by pretending to be others," Janowitz explained. "In my first novel I am a young boy trying to win his father's approval; in my second I am an elderly 'primitive' cannibal visiting 'civilized' New York City for the first time; and in [*Slaves of New York*] I am a young painter who is burdened with the weight of all of history, and is preoccupied with death and immortality."

In commenting on the "writing life," Janowitz once described the act of rising from bed as a daily struggle. "But generally the need to go to the bathroom and the desire for Wheat Chex forces me to get up," she quipped to *CA*. "Then there is the floor to be swept, and the thought that perchance on this day some mail will come. . . . This is not to say that I despise life. On the contrary, life is an overwhelming experience for me, so much so that getting out of bed becomes an Everest of Olympian proportions for me to climb. The glory of eating Wheat Chex is quite beyond belief. And then if I can actually drag myself to the typewriter and get some words down on paper, what joy I experience!

"For me, writing is overwhelmingly difficult, yet not so difficult, it seems, as actually having to go out and get a job. . . . Some people, sadly, are not meant to work, but I have learned this about myself at an early age. Certain people (though whom I cannot say) might feel that as a writer I should be working in order to collect experience; but it was Flannery O'Connor who said that each person has had enough experiences by the age of twenty to write for the rest of his or her life. Or something to that effect."

BIOGRAPHICAL/CRITICAL SOURCES:

BOOKS

Contemporary Literature Criticism, Gale (Detroit), Volume 43, 1987.

PERIODICALS

Baltimore News-American, May 24, 1981.
Baltimore Sun, June 7, 1981.
Boston Globe, September 9, 1992, p. 69.
Boston Phoenix, May 12, 1981.
Hudson Review, autumn, 1986, p. 489.
Horizon, June, 1981.
Houston Chronicle, April 4, 1981.
Interview, August, 1981.
Listener, February 19, 1987, p. 36.
London Review of Books, February 5, 1987, pp. 12-13.
Los Angeles Times Book Review, April 26, 1987, p. 14; October 18, 1987, p. 10; September 13, 1992, p. 1.
Mademoiselle, April, 1989, pp. 102, 104, 276.
New Republic, June 6, 1981; February 1, 1988, pp. 29-34.
New York Daily News, May 21, 1981.
Newsweek, September 7, 1987, p. 72.
New York Times Book Review, May 17, 1981; October 4, 1987, p. 12; August 20, 1992, p. 3.
New Yorker, October 26, 1987, pp. 142-46.
New Statesman, February 27, 1987; March 4, 1988, p. 26.
Newark Star-Ledger, April 26, 1981.
Pittsburgh Press, July 20, 1981.
Soho News, April 15, 1981.
Time, October 19, 1987, pp. 77-79.
Times Literary Supplement, March 4-10, 1988, p. 245.
Springfield Republican, August 30, 1981.
Village Voice, August 5, 1986.
Washington Post Book World, August 30, 1992, p. 2.
West Coast Review of Books, July, 1981.

JASEN, David A(lan) 1937-

PERSONAL: Born December 16, 1937, in New York, NY; son of Barnet (a dentist) and Gertrude (Cohen) Jasen; married Susan Pomerantz (a registered nurse), December 30, 1963; children: Raymond Douglas. *Education:* American University, B. A., 1959; Long Island University, M. S., 1972.

ADDRESSES: Home—225 East Penn St., Long Beach, NY 11561. *Office*—C. W. Post Center, Long Island University, Greenvale, NY 11548.

CAREER: Columbia Broadcasting System, New York City, supervisor of news videotape, 1959-66; American Educational Theatre Association, Washington, DC, administrative assistant, 1967; Florists' Transworld Delivery Association, Detroit, MI, field service representative, 1968-69; Reading Development Center, Inc., New York City, assistant to president, 1969-70; Long Island University, C. W. Post Center, Greenvale, NY, assistant professor, 1971-77, associate professor in School of Art, 1977—, professor of communication arts, 1982—, director of communication arts, 1975—, chairman of communication arts department, 1979—, director of Popular Music Archive, 1983—. Ragtime composer and pianist; record producer; public speaker.

MEMBER: American Library Association, Ragtime Society, Maple Leaf Club, Pi Delta Epsilon, Alpha Psi Omega.

AWARDS, HONORS: Scott Joplin Award, 1995, for contributions to the field of ragtime music.

WRITINGS:

Bibliography and Reader's Guide to the First Editions of P. G. Wodehouse, Archon (Hamden, CT), 1970, revised edition, Greenhill, 1986.
Recorded Ragtime, 1897-1958 (discography), Archon, 1973.
P. G. Wodehouse: A Portrait of a Master, Mason & Lipscomb, 1974, revised edition, Continuum (New York City), 1981.
(Editor) *The Uncollected Wodehouse,* Seabury (New York City), 1976.
(With Trebor Jay Tichenor) *Rags and Ragtime: A Musical History,* Seabury, 1978, revised edition, Dover (New York City), 1989.
(Editor) *Ragtime: 100 Authentic Rags* (music), Big 3 Music, 1979.

(Editor) P. G. Wodehouse, *The Swoop! and Other Stories,* Seabury, 1979.
The Theatre of P. G. Wodehouse, Batsford, 1979.
(Editor) Wodehouse, *The Eighteen-Carat Kid, and Other Stories,* Continuum, 1980.
(Editor) Wodehouse, *Not George Washington: An Autobiographical Novel,* Continuum, 1980.
(Editor) George Barr McCutcheon, *Brewster's Millions,* Continuum, 1980.
(Editor) Jerome K. Jerome, *Three Men in a Boat,* Continuum, 1980.
(Editor) *P. G. Wodehouse: Four Plays,* Methuen (New York City), 1983.
(Editor) *Alexander's Ragtime Band and Other Favorite Song Hits, 1901-1911,* Dover, 1987.
(Editor) *Scott Joplin: Complete Piano Rags,* Dover, 1988.
Tin Pan Alley, Fine, 1988.
(Editor) *For Me and My Gal and Other Favorite Song Hits, 1915-1917,* Dover, 1994.
(Editor) *A Pretty Girl Is Like a Melody and Other Favorite Song Hits, 1918-1919,* Dover, 1996.

RECORDINGS

Creative Ragtime, Euphonic Sound.
Fingerbustin' Ragtime, Blue Goose Records.
Rompin' Stompin' Ragtime, Blue Goose Records.
Rip-Roarin' Ragtime, Folkways.
Dave Jasen's Ragtime, Archive.
26 Happy Honky Tonk Memories, Special Music.
(Producer) *They All Played the Maple Leaf Rag,* Archive.
(Producer) *Zez Confrey Plays Zez Confrey,* Archive.

Also author of several ragtime pieces, included in his sound recordings. Contributor to *Ragtimer.*

SIDELIGHTS: In editing the collection *The Swoop! and Other Stories,* "David A. Jasen has performed a valuable service in combing through turn-of-the-century popular British periodicals . . . in search of pieces from the earliest years of [P. G.] Wodehouse's long career," remarks *New York Times Book Review* contributor Robert Kiely. "The result is a collection of fresh and delightful entertainments, many of which had been thought lost and none of which has been published in book form in this country," continues the critic. Jasen has edited several volumes of Wodehouse's work, and was the first to publish a biography of the great British humorist.

In addition to his work as an editor of Wodehouse fiction, Jasen is also a composer, performer, and producer of ragtime music. He has written and recorded several albums of ragtime, and has helped propogate the popularity of rags through concerts, radio shows, university classes, and books. His discography, *Recorded Ragtime, 1897-1958,* "is a landmark of ragtime scholarship," notes *Washington Post* writer Joseph McLellan. His historical work, *Rags and Ragtime,* written with fellow composer-performer Trebor Jay Tichenor, is "commendably lucid, accurate, detailed, and well-arranged, with interesting illustrations," comments McLellan. The critic adds that the work helps "fill widespread needs which have begun to be felt only in the last generation and have reached their peak in the present decade."

BIOGRAPHICAL/CRITICAL SOURCES:

PERIODICALS

Los Angeles Times, June 1, 1980.
Melody Maker, September 1, 1973.
Mississippi Rag, June, 1979.
Newsday, October 22, 1972; January 15, 1992.
New York Times, November 14, 1971; February 10, 1985.
New York Times Book Review, July 1, 1979.
Time, May 4, 1981.
Washington Post, July 24, 1978.

*   *   *

JONES, Geraldine
    See McCAUGHREAN, Geraldine

*   *   *

JONG, Erica   1942-

PERSONAL: Born March 26, 1942, in New York, NY; daughter of Seymour (an importer) and Eda (a painter and designer; maiden name, Mirsky) Mann; married Michael Werthman (divorced), married Allan Jong (a child psychiatrist), 1966 (divorced, September 16, 1975); married Jonathan Fast (a writer), 1977 (divorced, 1983); married Ken Burrows (a lawyer), 1989; children: (third marriage) Molly Miranda. *Education:* Barnard College, B.A., 1963; Columbia University, M.A., 1965; post-graduate study at Columbia School of Fine Arts, 1969-70.

Politics: "Left-leaning feminist." *Religion:* "Devout pagan."

ADDRESSES: Office—Erica Jong Productions, 205 E. 68th St., Suite T3G, New York, NY 10021. *Agent*—Ed Victor, 6 Bayley St., Bedford Sq., London WC1, England.

CAREER: Writer and lecturer. Member of English faculty, City College of the City University of New York, 1964-65 and 1969-70; member of faculty, University of Maryland, Overseas Division, Heidelberg, West Germany (now Germany), 1966-69; instructor in English, Manhattan Community College, 1969-70; instructor in poetry, YM/YWCA Poetry Center, New York City, 1971-73; instructor, Bread Loaf Writers Conference, 1981, and Salzburg Seminar, 1993. Judge in fiction, National Book Award, 1995. Member, New York State Council on the Arts, 1972-74.

MEMBER: PEN, Authors League of America, Authors Guild (president, 1991-93), Dramatists Guild of America, Writers Guild of America, Poetry Society of America, National Writers Union (member of advisory board), Poets and Writers, Phi Beta Kappa.

AWARDS, HONORS: American Academy of Poets Award, 1963; New York State Council on the Arts grant, 1971; Borestone Mountain Award in poetry, 1971; Bess Hokin prize, *Poetry* magazine, 1971; Madeline Sadin Award, *New York Quarterly,* 1972; Alice Faye di Castagnolia Award, Poetry Society of America, 1972; Creative Artists Public Service (CAPS) award, 1973, for *Half-Lives;* National Endowment for the Arts fellowship, 1973-74; Premio International Sigmund Freud, 1979.

WRITINGS:

NOVELS

Fear of Flying, Holt (New York City), 1973.
How to Save Your Own Life, Holt, 1977.
Fanny, Being the True History of the Adventures of Fanny Hackabout-Jones, New American Library (New York City), 1980.
Parachutes and Kisses, New American Library, 1984.
Serenissima: A Novel of Venice, Houghton (Boston), 1987, published as *Shylock's Daughter,* HarperCollins (New York City), 1995.
Any Woman's Blues, Harper (New York City), 1990.

POETRY

Fruits and Vegetables, Holt, 1971.
Half-Lives, Holt, 1973.
Loveroot, Holt, 1975.
Here Comes, and Other Poems, New American Library, 1975.
The Poetry of Erica Jong (three volumes), Holt, 1976.
Selected Poetry, Granada (London), 1977.
The Poetry Suit, Konglomerati Press, 1978.
At the Edge of the Body, Holt, 1979.
Ordinary Miracles: New Poems, New American Library, 1983.
Becoming Light: New and Selected Poems, Harper-Collins (New York City), 1991.

OTHER

Fear of Flying (sound recording; includes selections from poetry and from the novel of the same title; read by the author), Spoken Arts, 1976, Harper Audio, 1990.
(Contributor) *Four Visions of America,* Capra Press (Santa Barbara, CA), 1977.
Witches (miscellany), illustrated by Joseph A. Smith, Abrams (New York City), 1981.
Megan's Book of Divorce: A Kid's Book for Adults, illustrated by Freya Tanz, New American Library, 1984.
Serenissima (sound recording of the novel of the same title; read by the author), Brilliance Corp./ Houghton, 1987.
Becoming Light (sound recording of the book of the same title), Dove Audio (Beverly Hills, CA.), 1992.
The Devil at Large: Erica Jong on Henry Miller, Turtle Bay (New York City), 1993.
Fear of Fifty: A Midlife Memoir, HarperCollins, 1994.

Also author of introduction to the Book-of-the-Month Club Facsimile first edition of Vladimir Nabokov's *Lolita,* 1988, and author, with Jonathan Fast, of screenplay *Love al Dente.* Contributor of poems and articles to newspapers and periodicals, including *Esquire, Ladies Home Journal, Los Angeles Times, Ms., Nation, New Republic, New York, New Yorker, New York Times Book Review, Poetry,* and *Vogue.*

WORK IN PROGRESS: "Currently developing *Fanny* as a Broadway musical."

SIDELIGHTS: Best known as the author of the 1973 best-selling novel *Fear of Flying,* Erica Jong has received critical attention for her frank and unabashed portrayal of female sexuality. Despite Jong's literary output in the areas of poetry and social criticism, *Interview* contributor Karen Burke notes that "her fame from the enormous success of *Fear of Flying* has overshadowed these accomplishments." Recounting one woman's escapades during her search for sexual realization, *Fear of Flying* won its author "a special place in woman's literary history" in the opinion of *Ms.* reviewer Karen Fitzgerald. "Jong was the first woman to write in such a daring and humorous way about sex," Fitzgerald declares. "She popularized the idea of a woman's ultimate sexual fantasy . . . sex for the sake of sex."

Dictionary of Literary Biography contributor Benjamin Franklin V also acknowledges the fact that the success of Jong's novels "tended to obscure the fact that she is a popular and good poet." Jong's first collection of poetry, *Fruits and Vegetables,* appeared two years before her first novel, and her early verse was generally well-received by critics. "Welcome Erica Jong," announced *Saturday Review* contributor James Whitehead in his review of *Fruits and Vegetables,* "and welcome the sensuality she has so carefully worked over in this wonderful book. . . . Clearly she has worked hard to gain this splendid and various and serious comic vision." "Too frequently commercial success comes to poets of little ability," adds Franklin. "Such is not the case with Jong. In deft verse she addresses life's difficulties with ever-increasing maturity. As a poet of substance, she speaks to the human condition."

Jong's poetry is written in the confessional mode, the "crazed exposure of the American ego," according to Douglas Dunn in *Encounter.* Dunn notes the similarity of Jong's verse to the work of confessional poets such as Sylvia Plath and Anne Sexton, who wrote extensively on existential despair and the relations between men and women—and who each ultimately committed suicide. Unlike such literary predecessors, Jong chooses to affirm life; according to Franklin, her work is "generally positive and optimistic about the human condition." John Ditsky, writing for the *Ontario Review,* explains that Jong is "a Sexton determined to survive"; he sees the influence of sensualist poet Walt Whitman in her verse. Above all, says Franklin, "her own work illustrates women's victory and that, instead of flaunting their success and subduing men, women and men should work together and bolster each other."

Fear of Flying protagonist Isadora Zelda White Stollerman Wing—a poet and writer like her creator—is a woman "unblushingly preoccupied with her own libido," according to Elizabeth Peer of *Newsweek. Fear of Flying* recounts Isadora's adventures in search of the ideal sexual experience. While accompanying her Chinese-American Freudian analyst husband to a congress of psychoanalysts in Vienna, she meets Adrian Goodlove, an English analyst and self-proclaimed free spirit. Goodlove coaxes Wing to leave her husband and run off with him on an existential holiday across Europe where they can gratify their sexual appetites without guilt and remorse. In the course of this sensual odyssey, Isadora realizes that Adrian, who had epitomized sex-for-the-sake-of-sex, is in fact impotent, and that the freedom she sought in the encounter is false. As Carol Johnson writes in the *Dictionary of Literary Biography*, Isadora finds Adrian's "promised 'liberation' to be simply a new style of confinement." After two weeks he deserts Isadora to keep a planned rendezvous with his own family and she returns to her husband unrepentant, if unfulfilled.

While sex plays a major role in *Fear of Flying*, it is only one of the novel's main focuses. Johnson remarks that the story "revolves around themes of feminism and guilt, creativity and sex," and indeed, Jong told *Interview*'s Burke that *Fear of Flying* is "not an endorsement of promiscuity at all. It [is] about a young woman growing up and finding her own independence and finding the right to think her own thoughts, to fantasize." Emily Toth points out in the *Dictionary of Literary Biography* that "*Fear of Flying* is essentially a literary novel, a Bildungsroman with strong parallels to the *Odyssey*, Dante's *Inferno*, and the myths of Daedalus and Icarus." Parts of the book may be regarded as satirical: Johnson states that Jong's most erotic scenes "are parodies of contemporary pornography, her liberated woman [is] openly thwarted and unfulfilled." Other aspects of the novel, according to an *Atlantic* contributor, include a "diatribe against marriage—against the dread dullness of habitual, connubial sex, against the paucity of means of reconciling the desire for freedom and the need for closeness, against childbearing," and a search for personal creativity.

Fear of Flying was a smashing popular success, translated into several languages and selling more than twelve million copies. Whether read for its graphic eroticism, for its wry humor, or for its portrayal of women as people with a right to sexual expression, it revolutionized readers'perceptions of

female sexuality with its depiction of Isadora's passions. Jong's work proclaimed to a generation of women that they need not be ashamed of their own sensuality. In an interview with Cynthia Wolfson in the *Chicago Tribune Magazine*, Jong declared, "My spirit and the world's spirit happened to be in the same place at the same time, and I was the mouth." As Isa Kapp puts it in the *Washington Post Book World*, the women of America "had been endowed with freedoms even the women's liberation movement was afraid to ask for and did not know it wanted: to bathe in steamy fantasies of seduction by strangers, and to turn the tables on men and treat them as sex objects."

Critical reaction to *Fear of Flying* has varied. John Updike notes in the *New Yorker* that Jong's work possesses "class and sass, brightness and bite." He compares the author to Chaucer and her protagonist to the Wife of Bath in the *Canterbury Tales*, and finds parallels between *Fear of Flying* and both J. D. Salinger's *Catcher in the Rye* and Philip Roth's *Portnoy's Complaint*. Christopher Lehmann-Haupt of the *New York Times* praises Jong's characterization of Isadora, saying, "I can't remember ever before feeling quite so free to identify my own feelings with those of a female protagonist." He concludes that "Isadora Wing, with her unfettered yearnings for sexual satisfaction and her touching struggle for identity and self-confidence, is really more of a person than a woman (which isn't to deny in the least Mrs. Jong's underlying point that it's harder to become a person if you're a woman than it is if you're a man)." In a *New York Times* appraisal, novelist Henry Miller compares *Fear of Flying* to his own *Tropic of Cancer*—only "not as bitter and much funnier"—and predicts that "this book will make literary history, that because of it women are going to find their own voice and give us great sagas of sex, life, joy, and adventure."

Other reviewers have not been so enthusiastic. *New Statesman* contributor Paul Theroux accuses the novel of "misusing vulgarity to the point where it becomes purely foolish, picturing woman as a hapless organ animated by the simplest ridicule, and devaluing imagination in every line," and concludes that it "represents everything that is to be loathed in American fiction today." Jonathan Raban in *Encounter*, while comparing a reading of the book to "being locked in a lift with a woman who tells you her life story twice over, rapes you, and stops you reaching for the Emergency button," does admit that Isadora "has a crude genius for reality. . . . She persuades one of her existence by brute force, and she will not be budged." However, he asserts, Jong's heroine is "botheringly close to the insatiably willing dream-girl of male fantasies and male fiction." Although Michael Wood of the *New York Review of Books* feels that the novel "has far too much maudlin or portentous self-examination which it seems we are to take seriously," and comments that "the wit often seems to be working harder than it ought to be," he concludes: "Nevertheless, or even partly because of all this, the book has a helplessness, a vulnerability that makes it very likable, and in some backhanded way successful."

Isadora's story is continued in *How to Save Your Own Life*. Now a successful author of the very daring and explicit novel *Candida Confesses*, she strikes out on her own after her husband confesses to an affair with another woman early in their marriage. "Despite herb tea and sympathy" from various female friends, says Kapp, "her frame of mind is gloomy." Her sexual experiments continue, Kapp adds, and include "a Lesbian episode justified as research, and an orgy itemized like the instructions for stuffing a holiday turkey." Isadora leaves her husband and travels to California to visit a movie producer interested in filming her book. There she meets and falls in love with Josh Ace, an aspiring screenwriter some years younger than herself. Convinced that she has found her ideal man, she prepares to settle down. *New York Review of Books* contributor Diane Johnson praises *How to Save Your Own Life* as "a plain, wholesome American story, containing as it does that peculiarly American and purely literary substance Fulfillment, [the] modern equivalent of fairy gold." However, in the *New York Times Book Review*, John Leonard finds the novel lacking in the "energy and irreverence of 'Fear of Flying'. . . . Whereas the author of 'Fear of Flying' was looking inside her own head, shuffling her fantasies, and with a manic gusto playing out her hand, the author of 'How to Save Your Own Life' is looking over her shoulder, afraid that the critics might be gaining on her."

Some seven years later Isadora's latest romance sours; now almost forty and the mother of a three-year-old girl, she is deserted by Josh. Jong's 1984 novel *Parachutes and Kisses* tells of Isadora's attempt to cope with the pressures and problems of being a single mother, of approaching middle age, and of supporting a household on a writer's income. "It is about having it all in the 1980s," Jong explained to Gil Pyrah of the London *Times*. "Isadora exemplified the 1970s woman and now, in the 1980s, we are trying to be single parents, breadwinners and feminine at the same time." In the course of her journey toward self-realization, Jong's heroine tours Russia, characteristically encountering a number of sexual adventures on the way. She eventually finds contentment of sorts with a young actor named Bean in the novel, which *Washington Post Book World* reviewer Grace Lichtenstein notes "is funny and searching enough to suggest that *How to Save Your Own Life* was Jong's sophomoric jinx."

Any Woman's Blues, which Jong published in 1990, is linked to the author's previous three novels in that it is presented in an introduction by a fictitious literary scholar as a manuscript left behind by Isadora Wing after she boards an airplane headed for the South Pacific and mysteriously disappears. "I knew I wanted to write a fable of a woman living in the Reagan era of excess and greed and avarice," Jong explained to Lynn Van Matre of the *Chicago Tribune* in describing the novel, "an artist at the height of her powers who is hopelessly addicted to a younger man and goes through all the different states of change to get free." Protagonist Leila Sand is a wealthy and successful artist who is obsessed by her unfaithful and manipulative young lover. Focusing on Sand's codependence upon male attention, *Any Woman's Blues* follows Sand's downward spiral into alcoholism, sexual depravity, and drug abuse, coming up for air as she gains a spiritual strength that enables her to take control of her life. By the end of the story, Sand emerges as has Isadora before her: a more self-assured, emotionally integrated, focused person. "Co-dependency is just a trendy term for being a well-socialized woman," Jong explained to Josh Getlin in the *Los Angeles Times*. "We're all trained to put other people's needs before our own. We're trained to be validated by what our husbands, children and lovers think of us. It's not uniquely feminine, but it's considered normal in women, whereas in men it's considered a disease."

Critics and readers have consistently confused fictional characters Isadora Wing and Leila Sand with their creator; Jong and her protagonists come from similar backgrounds and have led similar lives. Both Jong and Wing are New York born, were educated at Barnard and Columbia, have Jewish origins, and have published poetry. Jong herself has added somewhat to the confusion by being ambivalent about her sources. As Peer says, "There are days when Erica

Jong flies into a fit at the suggestion that 'Fear of Flying' is autobiographical. 'It's not true,' she protests. 'I resent that question.' There are other days when Jong, with a buoyant giggle, admits, 'I cannibalized real life.'" In fact, Jong has capitalized on her readers' confusion in the novels subsequent to *Fear of Flying.* Lehmann-Haupt points out in a *New York Times* article that the main character of Isadora's novel *Candida Confesses,* in *How to Save Your Own Life,* is a promiscuous woman whom her readers insist on confusing with Isadora, "much to her distress, because everyone ought to know the difference between fiction and autobiography." The distinction is very clear in Jong's mind; in a *Publishers Weekly* interview with Barbara A. Bannon, she maintains that "the sophisticated reader who has read Colette, Proust, Henry Miller knows that what I am writing is a mock memoir, allowing for a complete range of interpretations in between fact and fancy." "I always write as if what I'm writing will never be published," she would later tell Rick Kogan in an interview for the *Chicago Tribune.* "I write for that intimate space where the reader is lying in bed at night. The reader is reading. The writer is naked on the page."

In 1994 Jong published *Fear of Fifty: A Midlife Memoir,* described by Lynn Freed in the *Washington Post Book World* as "a funny, pungent, and highly entertaining memoir of her growing up, her men, her marriages, her motherhood, her writing, her successes and her failures on all fronts. And she has done so . . . with all her customary candor." The autobiography draws from the drama of the artist's own life, which has caused some critics to comment on the newsworthy Jong's obvious inability to either totally empathize with or reflect a global midlife female consciousness. Several critics have also noted the author's continued defense and reiteration of the sexually liberated attitudes embodied over twenty years earlier in *Fear of Flying.* "Two decades is a long time to go on playing the naughty girl who can sling dirty words and sleep around just like the guys," states reviewer Nancy Mairs in the *New York Times Book Review.* "What might have been outre at age 30 seems passe at age 50." However, *Fear of Fifty* has been praised for its engaging style: what Roberta Rubenstein lauds in the *Chicago Tribune* as a "funny, wise, candid, poignant, brash, painful, soul-baring, occasionally moralistic, but never dull memoir."

In addition to her series of novels revolving around the very modern, forward-thinking Isadora Wing,

Jong has also explored the fictional terrain of past literary periods. *Fanny, Being the True History of the Adventures of Fanny Hackabout-Jones* is "a picaresque of intelligence, buoyant invention and wonderful Rabelaisian energy" in the opinion of *New York Times Book Review* contributor Michael Malone. According to Judy Klemesrud in the *New York Times,* it is also "a radical departure from the so-called confessional style of her first two novels." A longtime student of the eighteenth-century English novels of Lawrence Sterne, Henry Fielding, and John Cleland, Jong designed *Fanny* as "a cross between *Tom Jones* and *Moll Flanders,* with a wink at *Fanny Hill,*" according to Julia M. Klein in the *New Republic.* But *Fanny* resembles its predecessors in more than plot: Jong adopts archaic language, spelling and diction. As *Washington Post Book World* contributor Judith Martin illustrates, "She also hath this funny Way with Words that can drive the faithful Reader nuts in the extreme, but 'tis a pleasant Prose when once the Reader hath accustom'd herself to't."

In other ways, however, *Fanny* is firmly grounded in the twentieth century; notes Toth, "Jong uses the eighteenth-century novel form to satirize both Fanny's century and her own." "At heart," comments *Chicago Tribune* contributor James Goldman, "this novel is a vehicle for Jong's ideas about Woman and Womanhood." Still, Fanny remains a woman of her times; as Alan Friedman in the *New York Times Book Review* says, Fanny is "a contemporary heroine chained to a romantic sage with neoclassical links."

Jong explores another period of history in *Serenissima: A Novel of Venice,* the story of Jessica Pruitt, a much-married and much-divorced actress who comes to Venice to judge a film festival and come to terms with the death of her mother, her own middle age, and the lack of direction in her life. Jessica falls ill and, either in the delirium of her fever or through a magic ring given her by a witchlike silent film star, finds herself in the sixteenth century. There she meets William Shakespeare, on tour with his patron and lover, the Earl of Southampton, and becomes the inspiration for the Dark Lady of his sonnets and for Jessica, daughter of Shylock in *The Merchant of Venice.*

Critics have praised *Serenissima* for its evocation of the atmosphere of Venice; Joan Aiken, writing for the *Washington Post Book World,* lauds the author's descriptive prowess: "the Adriatic, the shimmer of

Venice—Jong's control of narrative is beautiful, floating, hypnotic." At the same time, however, other reviewers find her use of sixteenth-century literature overdone and disappointing. For instance, Shakespeare talks in quotes from his as yet unwritten work, "Southampton reels off sonnets, [and] Shylock wails in passages from 'Lear,'" notes Malone. Susan Jacoby agrees in *Tribune Books:* "This would have been a good joke if it were used sparingly, but repetition makes it truly tedious."

Throughout Jong's literary career, critics have drawn comparisons between her work and that of Henry Miller, whose novels, including 1934's *Tropic of Cancer*—not published in the United States until the repeal of obscenity laws in 1964—shocked readers due to its graphic portrayal of sexuality and liberal use of four-letter words. A friendship grew between the two authors following a letter Miller wrote to Jong in 1974 in praise of *Fear of Flying;* the two met face to face a year later when Jong spent two years in an area of California near Miller's home in Pacific Palisades. Although after Jong's return to New York in 1976 the two would end their contact—Miller would die four years later, at the age of eighty-eight—she worked on a book about the late author over the next decade. Finally published in 1993, *The Devil at Large: Erica Jong on Henry Miller* attempts to place Miller's work among the most valuable and creative American literature of the twentieth century. The book includes a brief discussion of the parallels between Jong's life and career as a writer and those of her subject, a biography of Miller, several essays discussing the importance of his work, an "imaginary dialogue" between Miller and herself, and transcripts of twenty-six letters that the two exchanged prior to Miller's death.

Several critics have disagreed with the literary stature that Jong strives to accord Miller, as well as with the similarities she attempts to draw between their two lives. "Perhaps Ms. Jong resents being, like Miller, critically dismissed, not taught in most universities," posits Walter Kendrick in the *New York Times Book Review.* "But is the reader . . . supposed to conclude that the perfection of humanity hinges on reading Erica Jong? No doubt that would be pushing the analogy too far." However, Gerald Nicosia finds Jong's focus effective, noting in the *Washington Post Book World* that she "champions one of the most controversial of literary causes—the writing of Henry Miller—and in doing so builds a case not only for Miller's importance in 20th-century literature but for her own as well." "Jong has given back a lot in [*The Devil at Large*]," Nicosia continues, "not only in the essence of a writer lost to us through a series of unfortunate misapprehensions, but also the very possibility of literature as a medium for healing." Brooke Horvath also lauds the work in *Review of Contemporary Fiction,* citing the "freedom from the pretentious tedium of so much academic [literary] criticism" and Jong's ability to write "a study aimed at the general reader" as two of the work's strengths. "For Jong, Miller's work enacts an against-the-grain search for life-enhancing truths and stands as the repository of those found," Horvath comments. "The same can be said of *The Devil at Large.*"

Within each of Jong's fictional works are "women who are in an ambiguous position, philosophically confused, emotionally overwrought," according to Burke, who maintains that the author uses these women to create "a realistic collage of the woman's situation today." Jong agrees, describing the void she attempted to fill in literature about women to Burke in *Interview:* "Nobody was writing honestly about women and the variousness of their experience." What was missing from the American literary scene, she concluded, was "a thinking woman who also had a sexual life," a woman who could be as heroic as any man. As Peer has observed, Jong's protagonists make it clear "that women and men are less different than literature has led us to believe. With a courage that ranges from deeply serious to devil-may-care, Jong . . . [has] stripped off the pretty masks that women traditionally wear, exposing them as vulgar, lecherous and greedy, frightened and flawed—in short, as bewilderingly human. Sort of like men." For the author, writing such works has been a process of personal self-exposure as well. "It's a very profound self-analysis. It's like meditation," Jong confided to Dana Micucci of the *Chicago Tribune.* "I try to tell a certain truth about the interior of my life and other women's lives. If you're writing the kinds of books I write, you come out a changed person."

BIOGRAPHICAL/CRITICAL SOURCES:

BOOKS

Authors in the News, Volume 1, Gale (Detroit), 1976.

Contemporary Literary Criticism, Gale, Volume 4, 1975, Volume 6, 1976, Volume 8, 1978, Volume 18, 1981, Volume 85, 1994.

Dictionary of Literary Biography, Gale, Volume 2: *American Novelists since World War II,* 1978,

Volume 5: *American Poets since World War II,* 1980, Volume 28: *Twentieth-Century Jewish-American Fiction Writers,* 1984.

Jong, Erica, *Ordinary Miracles: New Poems,* New American Library, 1983.

Templin, Charlotte, *Feminism and the Politics of Literary Reputation: The Example of Erica Jong,* University of Kansas Press (Lawrence), 1995.

PERIODICALS

Atlantic, December, 1973; April, 1977; November, 1981.

Books of the Times, November, 1980.

Chicago Tribune, April 25, 1990, sec. 7, pp. 11-13; April 25, 1993, sec. 6, p. 3; July 31, 1994, sec. 14, p. 3; August 18, 1994, sec. 5, pp. 1-2.

Chicago Tribune Magazine, December 12, 1982.

Courier-Journal and Times (Louisville, KY), October 13, 1974.

Detroit Free Press, May 17, 1987.

Encounter, July, 1974; December, 1974.

Globe and Mail (Toronto), November 24, 1984; November 21, 1987.

Harpers Bazaar, August, 1984.

Hudson Review, summer, 1974.

Interview, July, 1987.

Listener, May 2, 1974.

Los Angeles Times, November 4, 1981; May 16, 1987; May 18, 1987; January 22, 1990, pp. E1-2.

Los Angeles Times Book Review, August 17, 1980; June 24, 1984; November 11, 1984; August 21, 1994, pp. 2, 10.

Moons and Lion Tailes, Volume II, number 1, 1976.

Ms., November, 1980; July, 1981; July, 1986; June, 1987.

Nation, January 12, 1974.

National Review, May 24, 1974; April 29, 1977.

New Republic, February 2, 1974; September 20, 1980.

New Review, May, 1974.

New Statesman, April 19, 1974.

Newsweek, November 12, 1973; May 5, 1975; March 28, 1977; November 5, 1984.

New Yorker, December 17, 1973; April 4, 1977; October 13, 1980; November 19, 1984.

New York Review of Books, March 21, 1974; April 28, 1977; November 6, 1980.

New York Times, August 25, 1973; November 6, 1973; September 7, 1974, June 11, 1975; March 11, 1977; August 4, 1980; August 28, 1980; March 8, 1984; October 10, 1984.

New York Times Book Review, August 12, 1973; November 11, 1973; September 7, 1975; March 20, 1977; March 5, 1978; September 2, 1979; August 17, 1980; April 12, 1981; October 31, 1982; July 1, 1984; October 21, 1984; April 19, 1987; June 5, 1988; February 14, 1993, p. 10; July 24, 1994, p. 6.

North American Review, summer, 1975.

Ontario Review, fall/winter, 1975-76.

Parnassus: Poetry in Review, spring/summer, 1974.

People, May 25, 1987.

Poetry, March, 1974.

Publishers Weekly, February 14, 1977; January 4, 1985; February 22, 1985.

Review of Contemporary Fiction, fall, 1993, pp. 242-43.

Saturday Review, December 18, 1971; April 30, 1977; August, 1980; November, 1981; December, 1981.

Spectator, September 3, 1994, p. 37.

Time, March 14, 1977; June 22, 1987.

Times (London), November 2, 1984.

Times Literary Supplement, April 27, 1973; July 26, 1974; May 6, 1977; October 24, 1980; September 18-24, 1987; June 23, 1993, pp. 4-5; October 7, 1994, p. 44.

Tribune Books (Chicago), June 10, 1979; August 10, 1980; April 5, 1981; October 14, 1984; April 5, 1987; April 25, 1990, pp. 11-13; July 31, 1994, p. 3.

Virginia Quarterly Review, summer, 1979.

Washington Post, July 27, 1994, pp. 1, 12.

Washington Post Book World, December 19, 1971; July 6, 1975; March 20, 1977; August 17, 1980; October 21, 1984; April 19, 1987; June 6, 1993, pp. 4-5; July 31, 1994, p. 5.

Washington Star-News, January 2, 1974.

Women's Review of Books, November, 1994, pp. 15-16.

*   *   *

JUGENHEIMER, Donald W(ayne)   **1943-**

PERSONAL: Surname is pronounced "*You*-gen-high-mer"; born September 22, 1943, in Manhattan, KS; son of Robert William (a professor) and Mabel Clara (Hobert) Jugenheimer; married Bonnie Jeanne Scamehorn, August 30, 1970 (died, 1983); married Kaleen Brown (a marketing executive), July 25, 1987; children: (first marriage) Beth Carrie. *Education:* University of Illinois at Urbana-Champaign, B.S., 1965, M.S., 1968, Ph.D., 1972. *Religion:* Presbyterian.

ADDRESSES: Office—School of Journalism, Southern Illinois University, Carbondale, IL 62901-6601.

CAREER: Fillman and Associates, Champaign, IL, advertising copywriter, 1963-64; Leo Burnett Co., Chicago, IL, media buyer, 1965-66; Fillman and Associates, advertising copywriter, 1966; University of Kansas, Lawrence, assistant professor, 1971-75, associate professor, 1975-80, professor of journalism, 1980-85, chair of advertising, 1974-78; Louisiana State University, Baton Rouge, Manship Professor of Journalism, 1985-87; Fairleigh Dickinson University, Teaneck, NJ, professor of journalism and chair of department of communications, 1987-95; Southern Illinois University, Carbondale, director of school of journalism, 1996—. President of Lawrence School-Community Relations Council, 1974-75. Consultant to U.S. Army and Louisiana Dairy Promotion Board. *Military service:* U.S. Air Force, 1961-67; became captain.

MEMBER: American Academy of Advertising (president, 1985-87), Association for Education in Journalism (head of Advertising Division, 1977-78), American Association of University Professors, Kappa Tau Alpha, Alpha Delta Sigma.

AWARDS, HONORS: Kellogg national fellow of W. K. Kellogg Foundation, 1984-87.

WRITINGS:

(With Arnold Barban and Peter B. Turk) *Advertising Media Sourcebook and Workbook,* NTC Business Books (Lincolnwood, IL), 1975, 4th edition, 1996.

(With Ronald D. Michman) *Strategic Advertising Decisions,* Grid Publishing (Columbus, OH), 1976.

(With Gordon E. White) *Basic Advertising,* Southwestern Publishing, 1979, 2nd edition, 1988.

(With Turk) *Advertising Media,* Wiley (New York City), 1980.

(With Alan D. Fletcher) *Problems and Practices in Advertising Research; Readings and Workbook,* Wiley, 1982.

(Editor) *Proceedings of the Convention of the American Academy of Advertising,* American Academy of Advertising (Provo, UT), 1983.

(With Barban and Turk) *Advertising Media: Strategy and Tactics,* Brown & Benchmark, 1992.

Contributor to scholarly journals. *Journal of Advertising,* subscription manager, 1971-74, business manager, 1974-79, member of board of editors, 1985—.

WORK IN PROGRESS: Intimidation: How to Use It and How to Escape It; How to Succeed in College.

SIDELIGHTS: Donald W. Jugenheimer told *CA:* "Because the teaching of advertising has grown drastically in the past decade, the number of available textbooks has not kept pace. There are many texts for the introductory level, but few for the specific and advanced courses. I have tried to fill in some of these gaps with specialized materials. Because of this shortage of texts, some of our books have been adopted for teaching courses for which they were not originally intended: research courses using advertising media texts and campaign courses using basic anthologies.

"As the discipline grows and matures, I hope that the quality of books will improve in content and that the advertising industry will cooperate in this effort."

K

KALLIR, Jane K(atherine) 1954-

PERSONAL: Born July 30, 1954, in New York, NY; daughter of John Otto (an advertising executive) and Joyce (a school principal; maiden name, Ruben) Kallir. *Education:* Brown University, B.A., 1976.

ADDRESSES: Office—Galerie St. Etienne, 24 West 57th St., New York, NY 10019.

CAREER: Galerie St. Etienne, New York, NY, co-director, 1979—.

MEMBER: Art Dealers Association of America (member of board of directors, 1994—).

AWARDS, HONORS: Award from Art Library Society of New York, 1982, for *The Folk Art Tradition;* Elie Faure Award and Prix des Lesteurs des *Beaux-Arts Magazine.*

WRITINGS:

Gustav Klimt/Egon Schiele, Crown (New York City), 1980.
Austria's Expressionism, Rizzoli (New York City), 1981.
The Folk Art Tradition, Viking (New York City), 1981.
Grandma Moses, C. N. Potter (New York City), 1982.
Arnold Schoenberg's Vienna, Rizzoli, 1984.
Viennese Design & the Wiener Werkstaette, Braziller (New York City), 1986.

Gustav Klimt: 25 Masterworks, Abrams (New York City), 1989.
Egon Schiele: The Complete Works, Including a Biography and a Catalogue Raisonne, Abrams, 1990.
Egon Schiele, Abrams, 1994.

WORK IN PROGRESS: Women and Expressionism.

SIDELIGHTS: Jane K. Kallir told *CA:* "My writing career began as an adjunct to my work in gallery management—books complemented exhibitions as a way of making art accessible to the public. Inevitably, however, certain themes began to recur in my writing. In particular, I am interested in the discrepancies that exist between artists' perceptions of art, public taste, and the critical judgments of the art historians. Folk art—literally the art of the people—has always held a special appeal for me because it has generally existed beyond the confines of the European academic tradition. Grandma Moses, especially, personifies the conflict between folk and 'high' culture, between popular and elitist taste. Austrian Expressionism, my second area of expertise, on the other hand, poses an entirely different sort of challenge. My Schiele catalogue raissone involved documenting a massive output—some 3,000 works—as well as compiling a comprehensive new biography from first-hand sources."

*   *   *

KEITH, Michael
See HUBBARD, L(afayette) Ron(ald)

KELLEY, Mary 1943-

PERSONAL: Born June 12, 1943, in Missoula, MT; daughter of George and June Bremer. *Education:* Mount Holyoke College, B.A., 1965; New York University, M.A., 1970; University of Iowa, Ph.D., 1974.

ADDRESSES: Office—Department of History, Dartmouth College, Hanover, NH 03755.

CAREER: Time, New York City, researcher and reporter, 1965-70; Herbert H. Lehman College of the City University of New York, New York City, assistant professor of American history, 1974-76; University of North Carolina, Charlotte, assistant professor of history, 1976-77; Dartmouth College, Hanover, NH, assistant professor, 1977-83, associate professor, 1983-89, professor of history, 1989—.

MEMBER: American Historical Association, Organization of American Historians, American Studies Association.

WRITINGS:

(Editor and contributor) *Women, Identity, and Vocation in American History,* G. K. Hall (Boston), 1979.
Private Woman, Public Stage: Literary Domesticity in Nineteenth-Century America, Oxford University Press (New York City), 1984.
(Editor and author of introduction) Catharine Maria Sedgwick, *Hope Leslie; or, Early Times in the Massachusetts,* Rutgers University Press (New Brunswick, NJ), 1987.
(Coauthor) *The Limits of Sisterhood: The Beecher Sisters on Women's Rights and Woman's Sphere,* University of North Carolina Press (Chapel Hill), 1988.
(Editor and author of introduction) *The Portable Margaret Fuller,* Viking (New York City), 1994.

*　　*　　*

KING, Stephen (Edwin) 1947-
(Steve King; pseudonyms: Richard Bachman, John Swithen)

PERSONAL: Born September 21, 1947, in Portland, ME; son of Donald (a merchant sailor) and Nellie Ruth (Pillsbury) King; married Tabitha Jane Spruce (a novelist), January 2, 1971; children: Naomi Rachel, Joseph Hill, Owen Phillip. *Education:* University of Maine at Orono, B.Sc., 1970. *Politics:* Democrat. *Avocational interests:* Reading (mostly fiction), jigsaw puzzles, playing the guitar ("I'm terrible and so try to bore no one but myself"), movies, bowling.

ADDRESSES: Home—Bangor and Center Lovell, ME. *Office*—P.O. Box 1186, Bangor, ME 04001; also c/o Penguin USA, 375 Hudson St., New York, NY 10014; *Agent*—Arthur Greene, 101 Park Ave., New York, NY 10178.

CAREER: Writer. Has worked as a janitor, a laborer in an industrial laundry, and in a knitting mill. Hampden Academy (high school), Hampden, ME, English teacher, 1971-73; University of Maine, Orono, writer in residence, 1978-79. Owner, Philtrum Press, a publishing house, and WZON-AM, a rock 'n' roll radio station, both in Bangor, ME. Has made cameo appearances in films, including *Knightriders* (under name Steven King), 1981, *Creepshow,* 1982, *Maximum Overdrive,* 1986, and *Pet Sematary,* 1989; has also appeared in American Express credit card television commercial. Served as judge for 1977 World Fantasy Awards, 1978. Participated in radio honor panel with George A. Romero, Peter Straub, and Ira Levin, moderated by Dick Cavett on WNET in New York, October 30-31, 1980.

MEMBER: Authors Guild, Authors League of America.

AWARDS, HONORS: Carrie named to *School Library Journal's* Book List, 1975; World Fantasy Award nominations, 1976, for *'Salem's Lot,* 1979, for *The Stand* and *Night Shift,* 1980, for *The Dead Zone,* 1981, for "The Mist," and 1983, for *The Breathing Method: A Winter's Tale,* in *Different Seasons;* Hugo Award nomination from World Science Fiction Society and Nebula Award nomination from Science Fiction Writers of America, both 1978, both for *The Shining;* Balrog Awards, second place in best novel category for *The Stand* and second place in best collection category for *Night Shift,* both 1979; named to the American Library Association's list of best books for young adults, 1979, for *The Long Walk,* and 1981, for *Firestarter;* World Fantasy Award, 1980, for contributions to the field, and 1982, for story "Do the Dead Sing?"; Career Alumni Award, University of Maine at Orono, 1981; Nebula Award nomination from Science Fiction Writers of America,

1981, for story "The Way Station"; special British Fantasy Award for outstanding contribution to the genre, British Fantasy Society, 1982, for *Cujo;* Hugo Award, World Science Fiction Convention, 1982, for *Stephen King's Danse Macabre;* named Best Fiction Writer of the Year, *Us* Magazine, 1982; Locus Award for best collection, Locus Publications, 1986, for *Stephen King's Skeleton Crew.*

WRITINGS:

NOVELS

Carrie: A Novel of a Girl with a Frightening Power (also see below), Doubleday (New York City), 1974, movie edition published as *Carrie,* New American Library/Times Mirror (New York City), 1975 (also published in a limited edition with introduction by Tabitha King, Plume [New York City], 1991).
'Salem's Lot (Literary Guild alternate selection; also see below), Doubleday, 1975, television edition, New American Library (New York City), 1979 (also published in a limited edition with introduction by Clive Barker, Plume, 1991).
The Shining (Literary Guild main selection; also see below), Doubleday, 1977, movie edition, New American Library, 1980 (also published in a limited edition with introduction by Ken Follett, Plume, 1991).
The Stand (also see below), Doubleday, 1978, enlarged and expanded edition published as *The Stand: The Complete and Uncut Edition,* Doubleday, 1990.
The Dead Zone (Literary Guild dual main selection; also see below), Viking (New York City), 1979, movie edition published as *The Dead Zone: Movie Tie-In,* New American Library, 1980.
Firestarter (Literary Guild main selection; also see below), Viking, 1980, reprinted with afterword by King, 1981 (also published in a limited, aluminum-coated, asbestos-cloth edition, Phantasia Press [Huntington Woods, MI], 1980).
Cujo (also see below), Viking, 1981 (also published in limited edition, Mysterious Press, 1981, and Plume, 1994).
Pet Sematary (Literary Guild dual main selection; also see below), Doubleday, 1983.
Christine (Literary Guild dual main selection; also see below), Viking, 1983 (also published in a limited edition illustrated by Stephen Gervais, Donald M. Grant [Hampton Falls, NH], 1983).
(With Peter Straub) *The Talisman,* Viking Press/Putnam (New York City), 1984 (also published in a limited two-volume edition, Donald M. Grant, 1984).
The Eyes of the Dragon (young adult; Book-of-the-Month Club alternate selection), limited edition illustrated by Kenneth R. Linkhauser, Philtrum Press, 1984, new edition illustrated by David Palladini, Viking, 1987.
It (Book-of-the-Month Club main selection; also see below), Viking, 1986 (first published in limited German edition as *Es,* Heyne [Munich, West Germany], 1986).
Misery (Book-of-the-Month Club main selection; also see below), Viking, 1987.
The Tommyknockers (Book-of-the-Month Club main selection; also see below), Putnam (New York City), 1987.
The Dark Half (Book-of-the-Month Club main selection; also see below), Viking, 1989.
Needful Things (also see below), Viking, 1991.
Gerald's Game, Viking, 1992.
Dolores Claiborne (also see below), Viking, 1993.
Insomnia, Viking, 1994.
Rose Madder, Viking, 1995.
The Green Mile (serialized novel), Signet, Chapter 1, "The Two Dead Girls," Chapter 2, "The Mouse on the Mile," Chapter 3, "Coffey's Hands," Chapter 4, "The Bad Death of Eduard Delacroix," Chapter 5, "Night Journey," Chapter 6, "Coffey on the Mile," March-August, 1996.
Desperation, Viking, 1996.

Also author of early unpublished novels "Sword in the Darkness" (also referred to as "Babylon Here"), "The Cannibals," and "Blaze," a reworking of John Steinbeck's *Of Mice and Men.*

"THE DARK TOWER" SERIES

The Dark Tower: The Gunslinger (also see below), Amereon Ltd., 1976, published as *The Gunslinger,* New American Library, 1988 (also published in limited edition illustrated by Michael Whelan, Donald M. Grant, 1982, 2nd limited edition, 1984).
The Dark Tower II: The Drawing of the Three (also see below), illustrated by Phil Hale, New American Library, 1989.
The Dark Tower III: The Waste Lands (also see below), illustrated by Ned Dameron, Donald M. Grant, 1991.
The Dark Tower Trilogy: The Gunslinger; The Drawing of the Three; The Waste Lands (box set), New American Library, 1993.

NOVELS; UNDER PSEUDONYM RICHARD BACHMAN

Rage (also see below), New American Library/Signet (New York City), 1977.

The Long Walk (also see below), New American Library/Signet, 1979.

Roadwork: A Novel of the First Energy Crisis (also see below) New American Library/Signet, 1981.

The Running Man (also see below), New American Library/Signet, 1982.

Thinner, New American Library, 1984.

The Regulators, Dutton, 1996.

SHORT FICTION

(Under name Steve King) *The Star Invaders* (privately published), Triad, Inc., and Gaslight Books (Durham, ME), 1964.

Night Shift (story collection; also see below), introduction by John D. MacDonald, Doubleday, 1978, published as *Night Shift: Excursions into Horror,* New American Library/Signet, 1979.

Different Seasons (novellas; Book-of-the-Month Club main selection; contains *Rita Hayworth and Shawshank Redemption: Hope Springs Eternal* [also see below; published in a large-type edition as *Rita Hayworth and Shawshank Redemption: A Story from "Different Seasons,"* Thorndike Press, 1983]; *Apt Pupil: Summer of Corruption; The Body: Fall from Innocence;* and *The Breathing Method: A Winter's Tale* [published in a large-type edition as *The Breathing Method,* Chivers Press, 1984]), Viking, 1982.

Cycle of the Werewolf (novella; also see below), illustrated by Berni Wrightson, limited portfolio edition published with "Berni Wrightson: An Appreciation," Land of Enchantment (Westland, MI), 1983, enlarged edition including King's screenplay adaptation published as *Stephen King's Silver Bullet,* New American Library/Signet, 1985.

Stephen King's Skeleton Crew (story collection), illustrated by J. K. Potter, Viking, 1985 (also published in a limited edition, Scream Press, 1985).

My Pretty Pony, illustrated by Barbara Kruger, Knopf (New York City), 1989 (also published in a limited edition, Library Fellows of New York's Whitney Museum of American Art, 1989).

Four Past Midnight (contains "The Langoliers," "Secret Window, Secret Garden," "The Library Policeman," and "The Sun Dog"; also see below), Viking, 1990.

Nightmares & Dreamscapes, Viking, 1993.

Also author of short story "Slade" (a western), and (under pseudonym John Swithen) "The Fifth Quarter." Contributor of short story "Squad D" to Harlan Ellison's *The Last Dangerous Visions.* Also contributor to anthologies and collections, including *The Year's Finest Fantasy,* edited by Terry Carr, Putnam, 1978; *Shadows,* edited by Charles L. Grant, Doubleday, Volume 1, 1978, Volume 4, 1981; *New Terrors,* edited by Ramsey Campbell, Pocket Books (New York City), 1982; *World Fantasy Convention 1983,* edited by Robert Weinberg, Weird Tales Ltd., 1983; *The Writer's Handbook,* edited by Sylvia K. Burack, Writer, Inc. (Boston), 1984; *The Dark Descent,* edited by David G. Hartwell, Doherty Associates, 1987; *Prime Evil: New Stories by the Masters of Modern Horror,* by Douglas E. Winter, New American Library, 1988; and *Dark Visions,* Gollancz (London), 1989.

SCREENPLAYS

Stephen King's Creep Show: A George A. Romero Film (based on King's stories "Father's Day," "The Lonesome Death of Jordy Verrill" [previously published as "Weeds"], "The Crate," and "They're Creeping Up on You"; released by Warner Brothers as *Creepshow,* 1982), illustrated by Berni Wrightson and Michele Wrightson, New American Library, 1982.

Cat's Eye (based on King's stories "Quitters, Inc.," "The Ledge," and "The General"), Metro Goldwyn-Mayer/United Artists, 1984.

Stephen King's Silver Bullet (based on and published with King's novella *Cycle of the Werewolf;* released by Paramount Pictures/Dino de Laurentiis's North Carolina Film Corp., 1985), illustrated by Berni Wrightson, New American Library/Signet, 1985.

(And director) *Maximum Overdrive* (based on King's stories "The Mangler," "Trucks," and "The Lawnmower Man"; released by Dino de Laurentiis's North Carolina Film Corp., 1986), New American Library, 1986.

Pet Sematary (based on King's novel of the same title), Laurel Production, 1989.

Stephen King's Sleepwalkers, Columbia, 1992.

Author of unproduced screenplays, including *Children of the Corn, Cujo, The Dead Zone, The Shotgunners, The Shining, Something Wicked This Way Comes,* and *Daylight Dead* (based on three stories from *Night Shift*—"Strawberry Spring," "I Know What You Need," and "Battleground").

TELEPLAYS

Stephen King's Golden Years, CBS-TV, 1991.
(And executive producer) *Stephen King's The Stand* (based on King's novel *The Stand*), ABC-TV, 1994.

Also author of *Battleground* (based on short story of same title; optioned by Martin Poll Productions for NBC-TV), and "Sorry, Right Number," for television series *Tales from the Dark Side,* 1987.

RECORDINGS

The Dark Tower: The Gunslinger, New American Library, 1988.
The Dark Tower II: The Drawing of the Three, New American Library, 1989.
The Dark Tower III: The Waste Lands, Penguin-HighBridge Audio (St. Paul, MN), 1991.
Needful Things, Penguin-HighBridge Audio, 1991.

OMNIBUS EDITIONS

Stephen King (contains *The Shining, 'Salem's Lot, Night Shift,* and *Carrie*), W. S. Heinemann/Octopus Books (London), 1981.
The Bachman Books: Four Early Novels (contains *Rage, The Long Walk, Roadwork,* and *The Running Man*), with introduction "Why I Was Richard Bachman," New American Library, 1985.

OTHER

Another Quarter Mile: Poetry, Dorrance, 1979.
Stephen King's Danse Macabre (nonfiction), Everest House, 1981 (also published in limited edition).
The Plant (privately published episodes of a comic horror novel in progress), Philtrum Press (Bangor, ME), Part I, 1982, Part II, 1983, Part III, 1985.
Black Magic and Music: A Novelist's Perspective on Bangor (pamphlet), Bangor Historical Society, 1983.
Stephen King's Year of Fear 1986 Calendar (color illustrations from novels and drawings from King's short stories published in horror magazines with accompanying text), New American Library, 1985.
Nightmares in the Sky: Gargoyles and Grotesques, photographs by f.Stop FitzGerald, Viking, 1988.
Dolan's Cadillac, Lord John Press (Northridge, CA), 1989.

Also author of weekly column "King's Garbage Truck" for *Maine Campus,* February 20, 1969 through May 21, 1970, and of monthly book review column for *Adelina,* June through November, 1980. Contributor of short fiction and poetry to numerous magazines, including *Art, Castle Rock: The Stephen King Newsletter, Cavalier, Comics Review, Cosmopolitan, Ellery Queen's Mystery Magazine, Fantasy and Science Fiction, Gallery, Great Stories from Twilight Zone Magazine, Heavy Metal, Ladies' Home Journal, Magazine of Fantasy and Science Fiction, Maine, Maine Review, Marshroots, Marvel Comics, Moth, Omni, Onan, Playboy, Redbook, Reflections, Rolling Stone, Science Fiction Digest, Startling Mystery Stories, Terrors, Twilight Zone Magazine, Ubris, Whisper,* and *Yankee.*

Most of King's papers are housed in the special collection of the Folger Library at the University of Maine at Orono.

ADAPTATIONS: Several of King's novels have been adapted for the screen. *Carrie* was produced as a motion picture in 1976 by Paul Monash for United Artists, screenplay by Lawrence D. Cohen, directed by Brian De Palma, featuring Sissy Spacek and Piper Laurie, and was also produced as a Broadway musical in 1988 by Cohen and Michael Gore, developed in England by the Royal Shakespeare Company, featuring Betty Buckley; *'Salem's Lot* was produced as a television miniseries in 1979 by Warner Brothers, teleplay by Monash, featuring David Soul and James Mason; *The Shining* was filmed in 1980 by Warner Brothers/Hawks Films, screenplay by director Stanley Kubrick and Diane Johnson, starring Jack Nicholson and Shelley Duvall; *Cujo* was filmed in 1983 by Warner Communications/Taft Entertainment, screenplay by Don Carlos Dunaway and Lauren Currier, featuring Dee Wallace and Danny Pintauro; *The Dead Zone* was filmed in 1983 by Paramount Pictures, screenplay by Jeffrey Boam, starring Christopher Walken; *Christine* was filmed in 1983 by Columbia Pictures, screenplay by Bill Phillips; *Firestarter* was produced in 1984 by Frank Capra, Jr., for Universal Pictures in association with Dino de Laurentiis, screenplay by Stanley Mann, featuring David Keith and Drew Barrymore; *Stand by Me* (based on King's novella *The Body*) was filmed in 1986 by Columbia Pictures, screenplay by Raynold Gideon and Bruce A. Evans, directed by Rob Reiner; *The Running Man* was filmed in 1987 by Taft Entertainment/Barish Productions, screenplay by Steven E. de Souza, starring Arnold Schwarzenegger; *Misery* was filmed in 1990 by Columbia, directed by

Reiner, screenplay by William Goldman, starring James Caan and Kathy Bates; *Graveyard Shift* was filmed in 1990 by Paramount, directed by Ralph S. Singleton, adapted by John Esposito; *Stephen King's It* (based on King's novel *It*) was filmed as a television mini-series by ABC-TV in 1990; *The Dark Half* was filmed in 1993 by Orion, written and directed by George A. Romero, featuring Timothy Hutton and Amy Madigan; *Needful Things* was filmed in 1993 by Columbia/Castle Rock, adapted by W. D. Richter and Lawrence Cohen, directed by Fraser C. Heston, starring Max Von Sydow, Ed Harris, Bonnie Bedelia, and Amanda Plummer; *The Tommyknockers* was filmed as a television mini-series by ABC-TV in 1993; *The Shawshank Redemption*, based on King's novella *Rita Hayworth and Shawshank Redemption: Hope Springs Eternal*, was filmed in 1994 by Columbia, written and directed by Frank Darabont, featuring Tim Robbins and Morgan Freeman; *Dolores Claiborne* was filmed in 1995 by Columbia.

Several of King's short stories have also been adapted for the screen, including *The Boogeyman,* filmed by Tantalus in 1982 and 1984 in association with the New York University School of Undergraduate Film, screenplay by producer-director Jeffrey C. Schiro; *The Woman in the Room,* filmed in 1983 by Darkwoods, screenplay by director Frank Darabont, broadcast on public television in Los Angeles, 1985 (released with *The Boogeyman* on videocassette as *Two Mini-Features from Stephen King's Nightshift Collection* by Granite Entertainment Group, 1985); *Children of the Corn,* produced in 1984 by Donald P. Borchers and Terrence Kirby for New World Pictures, screenplay by George Goldsmith; *The Word Processor* (based on King's "The Word Processor of the Gods"), produced by Romero and Richard Rubenstein for Laurel Productions, 1984, teleplay by Michael Dowell, broadcast November 19, 1985 on *Tales from the Darkside* series and released on videocassette by Laurel Entertainment, Inc., 1985; *Gramma,* filmed by CBS-TV in 1985, teleplay by Harlan Ellison, broadcast February 14, 1986, on *The Twilight Zone* series; *Creepshow 2* (based on "The Raft" and two unpublished stories by King, "Old Chief Wood'nhead" and "The Hitchhiker"), was filmed in 1987 by New World Pictures, screenplay by Romero; *Sometimes They Come Back,* filmed by CBS-TV in 1987; "The Cat from Hell" is included in a three-segment anthology film entitled *Tales from the Darkside—The Movie,* produced by Laurel Productions, 1990; *The Lawnmower Man,* written by director Brett Leonard and Gimel Everett for New Line Cinema, 1992; *The Mangler,* filmed by

New Line Cinema, 1995; and *The Langoliers,* filmed as a television mini-series by ABC-TV in 1995.

Unabridged readings of the novellas from *Different Seasons,* entitled *Rita Hayworth and Shawshank Redemption: Different Seasons I, The Body: Different Seasons II, Apt Pupil: Different Seasons III,* and *The Breathing Method: Different Seasons IV,* were recorded on audiocassettes in 1984 by Recorded Books; readings by Frank Muller of stories from *Skeleton Crew* ("The Ballad of the Flexible Bullet," "Gramma," and "The Mist") were recorded for Recorded Books in 1985; a set of six audiocassettes of *Night Shift,* read by Colin Fox, David Purdham, and Deidre Westervelt, have also been recorded; an abridged version by Sue Dawson of *Thinner* was recorded on two audiocassettes by Paul Sorvino for Listen for Pleasure in 1986; readings by David Purdham and Gale Garnett of "The Monkey," "Mrs. Todd's Shortcut," "The Reaper's Image," and "Gramma" were recorded by Warner Audio in 1986; readings of "Strawberry Spring," "The Boogeyman," "Graveyard Shift," "The Man Who Loved Flowers," "One for the Road," "The Last Rung on the Ladder," "I Know What You Need," "Jerusalem's Lot," and "I Am the Doorway" were recorded for Walden; "The Langoliers" was recorded as *One Past Midnight: The Langoliers,* read by Willem Dafoe, Penguin/HighBridge Audio, 1990; "Secret Window, Secret Garden" was recorded as *Two Past Midnight: Secret Window, Secret Garden,* read by James Woods, Penguin/HighBridge Audio, 1991; "The Library Policeman" was recorded as *Three Past Midnight: The Library Policeman,* read by Ken Howard, Penguin/HighBridge Audio, 1991; and "The Sun Dog" was recorded as *Four Past Midnight: The Sun Dog,* Penguin/HighBridge, 1991. A dramatization of "The Mist" was performed on public radio in Boston; a 90-minute adaptation written by Dennis Etchinson was recorded on audiocassette by Simon & Schuster Audioworks, 1986; it has also served as the basis of an "interactive fiction" software for a computer game of the same title, Mindscape, Inc.

WORK IN PROGRESS: The Cannibals: Livre Noir, a detective story in French; a sequel to *'Salem's Lot;* original story for television to be broadcast in more than fourteen episodes; *The Dark Tower IV: Wizard and Glass,* due in 1997.

SIDELIGHTS: "With Stephen King," muses Chelsea Quinn Yarbro in *Fear Itself: The Horror Fiction of Stephen King,* "you never have to ask 'Who's afraid

of the big bad wolf?'—You are. And he knows it."
Throughout a prolific array of novels, short stories,
and screen work in which elements of horror, fantasy, science fiction, and humor meld, King deftly
arouses fear from dormancy. The breadth and dura-
bility of his popularity alone evince his mastery as a
compelling storyteller. "Nothing is as unstoppable as
one of King's furies, except perhaps King's word
processor," remarks Gil Schwartz in *People* magazine, which selected King as one of twenty individuals who have defined the decade of the eighties. And
although the critical reception of his work has not
necessarily matched its sweeping success with readers, colleagues and several critics alike discern
within it a substantial and enduring literary legiti-
macy. In *American Film,* for instance, Darrell Ewing
and Dennis Meyers call him "the chronicler of contemporary America's dreams, desires, and fears."
And fantasy writer Orson Scott Card, citing King's
"brilliant" exploration of current American myths
and legends, proclaims in a *Contemporary Authors*
interview with Jean W. Ross: "If someone in the
future wants to see what American life was like,
what Americans cared about, what our stories were
in the seventies and eighties, they'll read Stephen
King." Moreover, says Card, in fifty years, King
will be "regarded as the dominant literary figure of
the time. A lot of us feel that way."

Credited with revivifying the macabre in both fiction
and film, "this maker of nightmares," says Andrew
Klavan in the *Village Voice,* has finally become syn-
onymous with the genre itself. A publishing marvel
with nearly one hundred million copies of his work
in print worldwide, not only is he the first writer to
have had three, four, and finally five titles appear
simultaneously on the *New York Times*' bestseller
lists, he remained on those lists continuously for
more than a decade—frequently at the top for months
at a stretch. Moreover, his 1989 novel *The Dark Half*
commanded a record-shattering first printing for
hardcover fiction of one and a half million copies.
As David Streitfeld assesses in the *Washington Post,*
"King has passed beyond bestsellerdom into a special
sort of nirvana reserved for him alone." Widely
translated, King's work has also been regularly
adapted for the screen and recorded on audio and
video, prompting Curt Suplee, in the *Washington
Post Book World,* to call him "a one-man entertainment industry." While pointing out that King has not
"single-handedly and overnight" transformed horror
into the marketing sensation that it is, literary critic
Leslie Fiedler concedes in *Kingdom of Fear: The
World of Stephen King* that "no other writer in the

genre [has] ever before produced so long a series of
smash successes . . . so that he has indeed finally
become—in his own words—a 'brand name.'" But as
Paul Weingarten makes clear in the *Chicago Tribune
Magazine,* "Stephen King, like any good brand
name, delivers."

The genre of horror fiction, which boasts an avid and
loyal readership, dates almost to the origins of the
novel itself. Fiedler explains, for instance, that just
as the portrayal of mundanity in Samuel Richardson's
work represents a disavowal of the fantastic elements
of Medieval and Renaissance Romance, "a kind of
neo-fantastic fiction which abandoned the recognizable present in favor of an exotic past" emerged near
the end of the eighteenth century as a partial reaction
against the popular, sentimental, domestic novel.
Consequently, in the aftermath of the French Revolution, continues Fiedler, "the fantastic was reborn in
sinister form, as terrifying nightmare rather than
idyllic dream," and was manifested in 1818 by the
first and perhaps the best known of horror stories—
Mary Wollstonecraft Shelley's *Frankenstein, or, The
New Prometheus.* The novel was not critically well
regarded during its time, though, and a similar reception awaited its successors—Robert Louis Stevenson's *Dr. Jekyll and Mr. Hyde* and Bram Stoker's
Dracula. Although the modern horror tale is founded
in these three works, King notes in *Stephen King's
Danse Macabre,* his study of the Gothic arts, especially literature, film, and television, "all three live
a kind of half-life outside the bright circle of English
literature's acknowledged classics."

While striking a deep and responsive chord within its
readers, the genre of horror is frequently trivialized
by critics who tend to regard it, when at all, less
seriously than mainstream fiction. In an interview
with Charles Platt in *Dream Makers: The Uncommon
Men & Women Who Write Science Fiction,* King
suspects that "most of the critics who review popular
fiction have no understanding of it as a whole."
Regarding the "propensity of a small but influential
element of the literary establishment to ghettoize
horror and fantasy and instantly relegate them beyond the pale of so-called serious literature," King
tells Eric Norden in a *Playboy* interview, "I'm sure
those critics' nineteenth-century precursors would
have contemptuously dismissed [Edgar Allan] Poe as
the great American hack." But as King contends in
"The Horror Writer and the Ten Bears," his foreword to *Kingdom of Fear:* "Horror isn't a hack
market now, and never was. The genre is one of the
most delicate known to man, and it must be handled

with great care and more than a little love." Furthermore, in a panel discussion at the 1984 World Fantasy Convention in Ottawa, reprinted in *Bare Bones: Conversations on Terror with Stephen King,* he predicts that horror writers "might actually have a serious place in American literature in a hundred years or so."

The genre survived on the fringe of respectability through movies and comic books, observes Fiedler, adding that during the repressive 1950s, "the far-from-innocent kids . . . fought back; surreptitiously indulging in the literature of horror, even as they listened to the rock music disapproved of by their fathers and mothers." Profoundly an offspring of the 1950s, King imparts the influence of its music and movies to the content and style of his fiction. In *Esquire,* Barney Cohen describes King's writing style as "American yahoo—big, brassy, and bodacious"; and according to Gary Williams Crawford in *Discovering Stephen King,* it derives not only from the American literary tradition of Realism, but from the horror and science fiction film and the horror comic book as well. King grew up with rock 'n' roll, played rhythm guitar in a rock band, and still enjoys playing—even though the family feline invariably leaves the room, he told the audience in a talk presented at a public library in Billerica, Massachusetts, reprinted in *Bare Bones.* As owner of a local rock radio station, he often works to the blare of its music and laces much of his fiction with its lyrics. And as a lifelong fan of film, he conveys a cinematic immediacy to his books: "I see them almost as movies in my head," he explains to Michael Kilgore in a *Tampa Tribune* interview.

The first motion picture King remembers seeing is *The Creature from the Black Lagoon,* but another film proved more portentous. He relates to Norden that he still has difficulty expressing how "terribly frightened and alone and depressed" he felt when, in 1957, a theatre manager interrupted *Earth vs. the Flying Saucers* to announce to the audience that the Soviet Union had launched the satellite "Sputnik": "At that moment, the fears of my fictional horror vividly intersected with the reality of potential nuclear holocaust; a transition from fantasy to a real world suddenly became far more ominous and threatening." King believes that his entire generation is beset with terrifying itself because it is the first to mature under the threat of nuclear war. In a *Penthouse* magazine interview with Bob Spitz, King adds that consequently, his generation has been "forced to

live almost entirely without romance and forced to find some kind of supernatural outlet for the romantic impulses that are in all of us." King suggests in *Danse Macabre* that "we make up horrors to help us cope with the real ones"; and, as he relates to Keith Bellows in a *Sourcebook* interview, "The more frightened people become about the real world, the easier they are to scare." Douglas E. Winter comments in the *Washington Post Book World* that "in a time of violence and confusion, it is little wonder then that so many readers have embraced the imaginative talents of Stephen King."

King's ability to comprehend "the attraction of fantastic horror to the denizen of the late 20th century" according to Deborah L. Notkin in *Fear Itself: The Horror Fiction of Stephen King,* partially accounts for his unrivaled popularity in the genre. But what distinguishes him is the way in which he transforms the ordinary into the horrific. Pointing out in the *Atlantic* that horror frequently represents "the symbolic depiction of our common experience," Lloyd Rose observes that "King takes ordinary emotional situations—marital stress, infidelity, peer-group-acceptance worries—and translates them into violent tales of vampires and ghosts. He writes supernatural soap operas." But to Crawford, King is "a uniquely sensitive author" within the Gothic literary tradition, which he describes as "essentially a literature of nightmare, a conflict between waking life and the darkness within the human mind." Perpetuating the legacy of Edgar Allan Poe, Nathaniel Hawthorne, Herman Melville, Henry James, and H. P. Lovecraft, "King is heir to the American Gothic tradition in that he has placed his horrors in contemporary settings and has depicted the struggle of an American culture to face the horrors within it," explains Crawford, and because "he has shown the nightmare of our idealistic civilization."

Some critics, though, attribute King's extraordinary accomplishments simply to a deep and genuine enjoyment of, as well as respect for, the genre itself. According to Don Herron in *Discovering Stephen King,* for instance, "The fact that King *is* a horror fan is of more importance to his fiction than his past as a teacher, his aims as an artist, or even his ability as a craftsman." Herron suggests that although King's work may very well represent "a psychological mirror of our times," he doubts whether "the majority of fans or even his most intelligent critics read him for Deep Meaning." In Herron's estimation, most readers begin "a new Stephen King book with thrills of expectation, waiting for this guy who's *really* a horror *fan,* see, to jump out of the old closet and yell 'Boo!!!'"

"We value his unique ability to scare the living daylights out of us," says William F. Nolan in *Kingdom of Fear,* because "King, more than any other modern master of Dark Fantasy, knows how to activate our primal fears." Referring to himself as a "sort of Everyman" where fear is concerned, King admits to Kilgore that perhaps his books succeed because his own fears, some of which are the natural residue of childhood, are simply "very ordinary fears." Only through exercising his imagination, he adds, has he honed his "perceptions of them." Although he indicates to Norden that he never experienced anything paranormal as a child, he does recall being "terrified and fascinated by death—death in general and my own in particular—probably as a result of listening to all those radio shows as a kid and watching some pretty violent TV shows." Religion, too, provided its share of trepidations. "It scared me to death as a kid," he confesses to Spitz. "I was raised Methodist, and I was scared that I was going to hell. The horror stories that I grew up on were biblical stories . . . the best horror stories ever written." As an adult, though, he shares a widespread anxiety over society's propensity toward self-destruction, frets about his family's security, is resolutely superstitious, and is prey to such pedestrian terrors as bugs, airplanes, and getting stuck in crowded elevators. He also retains a vigorous fear of the dark. "The dark is a big one," he admits in the talk presented at the Billerica library. "I don't like the dark." Or as he elaborates to Norden: "There's a lot of mystery in the world, a lot of dark, shadowy corners we haven't explored yet. We shouldn't be too smug about dismissing out of hand everything we can't understand. The dark can have *teeth,* man!"

"The desire to be scared is a childish impulse, belonging to innocence rather than to experience," writes Barbara Tritel in the *New York Times Book Review.* "Frightening escapist literature lets us escape not to a realm of existential terror . . . but to the realm of childhood, when, within some cozy setting, we were able to titillate ourselves with fear." And in Tritel's opinion, "King has understood and answered a profound and popular need." While most of his fiction is aimed at an adult audience, young people are especially drawn to it, and children are vital to it. Unlike his portrayals of women, which he acknowledges are at times weak, some of his strongest characters are children; and his realistic depictions of them have earned much critical praise. Lauding King's "energetic and febrile imagination," Richard R. Lingeman adds in the *New York Times* that he has "a radar fix on young people."

Observing that children suspend their disbelief easily, King argues in *Danse Macabre* that, ironically, they are actually "better able to deal with fantasy and terror *on its own terms* than their elders are." In an interview for *High Times,* for instance, he marvels at the resilience of a child's mind and the inexplicable, yet seemingly harmless, attraction of children to nightmare-inducing stories: "We start kids off on things like 'Hansel and Gretel,' which features child abandonment, kidnapping, attempted murder, forcible detention, cannibalism, and finally murder by cremation. And the kids love it." Adults are capable of distinguishing between fantasy and reality, but in the process of growing up, laments King in *Danse Macabre,* they develop "a good case of mental tunnel vision and a gradual ossification of the imaginative faculty"; thus, he perceives the task of the fantasy or horror writer as enabling one to become "for a little while, a child again." In *Time,* King discusses the prolonged obsession with childhood that his generation has had. "We went on playing for a long time, almost feverishly," he recalls. "I write for that buried child in us, but I'm writing for the grown-up too. I want grown-ups to look at the child long enough to be able to give him up."

Of his own childhood, King recounts to Norden that he was only two when his father (whose surname was originally Spansky, but was also known as Pollack before he legally changed his name to King) caroused his way out of the family one night, never to be heard from again. Several years thereafter, King discovered that his father had also had an affection for science fiction and horror stories, and had even submitted, albeit unsuccessfully, stories of his own to several men's magazines. With few resources after the departure of King's father, the family moved to the Midwest then back East to Connecticut before returning to Maine when King was about eleven to live with and help care for his ailing grandparents. Despite his mother's valiant efforts to provide for herself and two sons, King tells Norden that theirs was a "pretty shirttail existence." Remembering being "prey to a lot of conflicting emotions as a child," King explains, "I had friends and all that, but I often felt unhappy and different, estranged from other kids my age."

The empowerment of estranged young people is a theme that recurs throughout King's fiction. "If Stephen King's kids have one thing in common," declares young-adult novelist Robert Cormier in the *Washington Post Book World,* "it's the fact that they all are losers. In a way, all children are losers, of course—how can they be winners with that terrifying adult world stacked against them?" His first novel, *Carrie,* is about a persecuted teenaged girl. "The novel examines female power," states *Dictionary of Literary Biography* contributor Carol Senf, "for Carrie gains her telekinetic abilities with her first menstruation." "It is," Senf concludes, "a compelling character study of a persecuted teenager who finally uses her powers to turn the table on her persecutors. The result is a violent explosion that destroys the mother who had taught her self-hatred and the high-school peers who had made her a scapegoat." An alienated teenaged boy is the main character in King's *Christine,* and *Rage* features Charlie Decker, a young man who tells the story of his descent into madness and murder. In *The Shining* and *Firestarter,* Danny Torrance and Charlie McGee are alienated not from their families—they have loving, if sometimes weak, parents—but through the powers they possess and by those who want to manipulate them: evil supernatural forces in *The Shining,* the U.S. Government in *Firestarter.* Children also figure prominently, although not always as victims, in *'Salem's Lot, The Tommyknockers, Pet Sematary, The Eyes of the Dragon,* and *The Talisman.*

King's most explicit examination of alienation in childhood, however, comes in the novel *It.* The eponymous IT is a creature that feeds on children—on their bodies and on their emotions, especially fear. IT lives in the sewers of Derry, Maine, having arrived there ages ago from outer space, and emerges about every twenty-seven years in search of victims. "*It* begins, demonically enough, in 1957," explains *New York Review of Books* contributor Thomas R. Edwards, "when a six-year-old boy has his arm torn off by what appears to be a circus clown lurking down a storm drain. . . . King organizes the tale as two parallel stories, one tracing the activities of seven unprepossessing fifth-graders ('The Losers' Club') who discovered and fought the horror in 1958, the other describing their return to Derry in 1985 when the cycle resumes." The surviving members of the Losers' Club return to Derry to confront IT and defeat IT once and for all. The only things that appears to hurt IT are faith, humor, and child-like courage. "Only brave and imaginative children, or adults who learn to remember and honor their childish selves," Edwards concludes, "can hope to foil It, as the Losers finally do in 1985."

"*It* involves the guilts and innocences of childhood and the difficulty for adults of recapturing them," Christopher Lehmann-Haupt states in the *New York Times.* "*It* questions the difference between necessity and free will. *It* also concerns the evil that has haunted America from time to time in the forms of crime, racial and religious bigotry, economic hardship, labor strife and industrial pollution." The evil takes shape among Derry's adults and older children, especially the bullies who terrorize the members of the Losers' Club. "The bullies, who have names like Belch Huggens and Boogers Taliendo, are loutish, dumb, racist, sexist, cowardly, working class and unbelievable," opines *Nation* contributor George Stade. However, in King's world even the oppressors can be victims. "Henry Bowers, who is committed to Juniper Hill, an institution for the criminally insane," Senf explains, "is a bully long before IT uses him to persecute the members of the Losers Club and long before he kills his father. King examines the cycle of abuse in the dysfunctional Bowers family, for Butch Bowers is responsible for making his son a bully. Butch is also a victim, however for his experiences during World War II have left him an emotional cripple and unfit father."

Not surprisingly, throughout most of King's adolescence, the written word afforded a powerful diversion. "Writing has always been it for me," King indicates in a panel discussion at the 1984 World Fantasy Convention in Ottawa, reprinted in *Bare Bones.* Science fiction and adventure stories comprised his first literary efforts. Having written his first story at the age of seven, King began submitting short fiction to magazines at twelve, and published his first story at eighteen. In high school, he authored a small, satiric newspaper entitled "The Village Vomit"; and in college, he penned a popular and eclectic series of columns called "King's Garbage Truck." He also started writing the novels he eventually published under the short-lived pseudonymous ruse of Richard Bachman—novels that focus more on elements of human alienation and brutality than supernatural horror. After graduation, King supplemented his teaching salary through various odd jobs and by submitting stories to men's magazines. Searching for a form of his own, and responding to a friend's challenge to break out of the machismo mold of his short fiction, King wrote what he describes to Peck as "a parable of women's consciousness." Retrieving the discarded manuscript from the trash, though, King's wife Tabitha, a writer herself, suggested that he ought to expand it. And because King completed the first draft of *Carrie* at the time William Peter Blatty's *The Exorcist* and Thomas Tryon's *The Other* were being published, the novel was marketed as horror fiction, and the genre had found its juggernaut. Or, as Herron puts it in *Fear Itself,* "Like a mountain, King is there."

"Stephen King has made a dent in the national consciousness in a way no other horror writer has, at least during his own lifetime," states Alan Warren in *Discovering Stephen King.* "He is a genuine phenomenon." A newsletter—"Castle Rock"—has been published since 1985 to keep his ever-increasing number of fans well-informed; and Book-of-the-Month Club is reissuing all of his bestsellers as the Stephen King Library collection. In his preface to *Fear Itself,* "On Becoming a Brand Name," King describes the process as a fissional one in that a "writer produces a series of books which ricochet back and forth between hardcover and softcover at an ever increasing speed." Resorting to a pseudonym to get even more work into print accelerated the process for King; but according to Stephen P. Brown in *Kingdom of Fear,* although the ploy was not entirely "a vehicle for King to move his earliest work out of the trunk," it certainly triggered myriad speculations about, as well as hunts for, other possible pseudonyms he may also have used. In his essay "Why I Was Bachman" in *The Bachman Books: Four Early Novels by Stephen King,* King recalls that he simply considered it a good idea at the time, especially since he wanted to try to publish something without the attendant commotion that a Stephen King title would have unavoidably generated. Also, his publisher believed that he had already saturated the market. King's prodigious literary output and multi-million-dollar contracts, though, have generated critical challenges to the inherent worth of his fiction. Deducing that he has been somehow compromised by commercial success, some critics imply that he writes simply to fulfill contractual obligations. But as King tells Norden, "Money really has nothing to do with it one way or the other. I love writing the things I write, and I wouldn't and *couldn't* do anything else."

King writes daily, exempting only Christmas, the Fourth of July, and his birthday. He likes to work on two things simultaneously, beginning his day early with a two- or three-mile walk: "What I'm working on in the morning is what I'm *working* on," he says in a panel discussion at the 1980 World Fantasy Convention in Baltimore, reprinted in *Bare Bones.*

He devotes his afternoon hours to rewriting. And according to his *Playboy* interview, while he is not particular about working conditions, he is about his output. Despite chronic headaches, occasional insomnia, and even a fear of writer's block, he produces six pages daily; "And that's like engraved in stone," he tells Moore.

Likening the physical act of writing to "auto-hypnosis, a series of mental passes you go through before you start," King explains to Peck that "if you've been doing it long enough, you immediately fall into a trance. I just write about what I feel I want to write about. I'm like a kid. . . . I like to make believe." King explains to Moore that although he begins with ideas and a sense of direction, he does not outline: "I'm never sure where the story's going or what's going to happen with it. It's a discovery." Neither does he prepare for his novels in any particularly conscious way: "Some of the books have germinated for a long time," he tells Christopher Evans in a *Minneapolis Star* interview. "That is to say, they are ideas that won't sink." Also, research follows the writing so as not to impede it: "Afterward," he comments to Moore, "I develop the soul of a true debater . . . and find out the things that support my side." Besieged by questions about where his ideas originate, King tells Norden, "Like most writers, I dredge my memory for material, but I'm seldom really explicitly autobiographical." And, while he indicates to Randi Henderson in a *Baltimore Sun* interview that his ideas often begin in a dreamlike fashion in which "disconnected elements . . . will kind of click together," he adds in his foreword to *Kingdom of Fear* that they can also come from his nightmares: "Not the nighttime variety, as a rule, but the ones that hide just beyond the doorway that separates the conscious from the unconscious."

King describes himself in *Waldenbooks Book Notes* as one of the eternal "Halloween people," replete with a "vampire bat and a rattlesnake on my desk— both mercifully stuffed"; but a customary response when people first encounter him is that he does not seem weird enough. Noting that "they're usually disappointed," he tells Joyce Lynch Dewes Moore in *Mystery:* "They say, 'You're not a monster!'" And when he is asked, endlessly, "Why do you write that stuff?," he replies that aside from being "warped, of course," writing horror fiction serves as "a kind of psychological protection. It's like drawing a magic circle around myself and my family," he explains to the audience at the Billerica library. But King also approximates the role of horror writer to that of an "old Welsh sin eater" called upon to consume the sins of the dying so their souls might hurry unblemished into heaven. "I and my fellow horror writers are absorbing and defusing all your fears and anxieties and insecurities and taking them upon ourselves," King tells Norden. "We're sitting in the darkness beyond the flickering warmth of your fire, cackling into our caldrons and spinning out our spider webs of words, all the time sucking the sickness from your minds and spinning it out into the night."

Aware that "people want to be scared," as he relates to Abe Peck in a *Rolling Stone College Papers* interview, and truly delighted to be able to accommodate them, King rejects the criticism that he preys on the fears of others. As he explains to Jack Matthews in a *Detroit Free Press* interview, some people simply avoid his books just as those who are afraid of speed and heights, especially in tandem, shun roller coasters. And that, he declares to Paul Janeczko in *English Journal,* is precisely what he believes he owes his readers—"a good ride on the roller coaster." Regarding what he finds to be an essential reassurance that underlies and impels the genre itself, King remarks in *Danse Macabre* that "beneath its fangs and fright wig," horror fiction is really quite conservative. The scare we experience from reading it is safe, he tells Henderson, because "there's a real element of, thank God it isn't me, in the situation." Comparing horror fiction with the morality plays of the late middle ages, for instance, he believes that its primary function is "to reaffirm the virtues of the norm by showing us what awful things happen to people who venture into taboo lands." Also, there is the solace in knowing "when the lights go down in the theatre or when we open the book that the evildoers will almost certainly be punished, and measure will be returned for measure." But King admits to Norden that despite all the discussion by writers generally about "horror's providing a socially and psychologically useful catharsis for people's fears and aggressions, the brutal fact of the matter is that we're still in the business of public executions."

"Death is a significant element in nearly all horror fiction," writes Michael A. Morrison in *Fantasy Review,* "and it permeates King's novels and short stories." Noting in *Danse Macabre* that a universal fear with which each of us must personally struggle is "the fear of dying," King explains to Spitz that "everybody goes out to horror movies, reads horror novels—and it's almost as though we're trying to preview the end." But he submits that "if the horror story is our rehearsal for death, then its strict morali-

ties make it also a reaffirmation of life and good will and simple imagination—just one more pipeline to the infinite." While he believes that horror is "one of the ways we walk our imagination," as he tells Matthews, he does worry about the prospect of a mentally unstable reader patterning behavior after some fictional brutality. Remarking that "evil is basically stupid and unimaginative and doesn't need creative inspiration from me or anybody else," King tells Norden, for instance, that "despite knowing all that rationally, I have to admit that it is unsettling to feel that I could be linked in any way, however tenuous, to somebody else's murder."

King, who was absorbed as an adolescent by the capacity of evil to appear deceptively benign, separates the evil with which horror fiction is concerned into two types: that which resides within the human mind or heart and represents "an act of free and conscious will" and that which threatens from without and is "predestinate . . . like a stroke of lightning," he says in *Danse Macabre.* "He is obviously an intelligent, sensitive and voluptuously terrified man who writes horror stories as a way of worrying about life and death," observes Annie Gottlieb in the *New York Times Book Review.* "He knows that we have been set down in a frightening universe, full of real demons like death and disease, and perhaps the most frightening thing in it is the human mind." King recognizes, as he says in *Time,* that "there is a part of us that needs to vicariously exorcise the darker side of our feelings," and much of his fiction probes mental perturbation. Relating to Norden that one of his darkest childhood fears was of going suddenly and completely insane, King explains that writing is a way of exorcising his own nightmares and destructiveness: "Writing is necessary for my sanity. I can externalize my fears and insecurities and night terrors on paper, which is what people pay shrinks a small fortune to do." While the process is therapeutic for the writer, it seems to extend its benefits to the reader, as well. Summarizing what he finds as one of King's most important qualities as a writer, Clive Barker states in *Kingdom of Fear:* "He shows us . . . that on the journey which he has so eloquently charted, where no terror shows its face but on a street that we have ourselves trodden, it is not, finally, the stale formulae and the trite metaphysics we're taught from birth that will get us to the end of the ride alive; it is our intimacy with our dark and dreaming selves."

Although King has frequently referred to his own work as "the literary equivalent of a Big Mac and a large fries from McDonalds," Winter cites the general hallmarks of King's fiction as "effortless, colloquial prose and an unerring instinct for the visceral." Yet, because King likes to work within traditional themes, myths, and forms, some critics find his work derivative and contend that he ought to be concentrating his considerable creative energy and talent in areas traditionally deemed more literary or serious. King indicates to Norden that while he has never considered himself "a blazingly original writer in the sense of conceiving totally new and fresh plot ideas," what he tries to do is "to pour new wine from old bottles." Acknowledging that he has always viewed his own work as "more humdrum or more mundane than the sort of thing the really great writers do," King tells Moore that "you take what talent you have, and you just try to do what you can with it. That's all you can do."

An example of King's ability to "pour new wine from old bottles" is his experimentation with narrative structure. In *It, Carrie,* and *The Stand,* declares Tony Magistrale in the study *Landscape of Fear: Stephen King's American Gothic,* King explores story forms—"stream of consciousness, interior monologues, multiple narrators, and a juggling of time sequences—in order to draw the reader into a direct and thorough involvement with the characters and events of the tale." Both *The Dark Half* and *Misery,* according to George Stade in the *New York Times Book Review,* are "parable[s] in chiller form of the popular writer's relation to his audience." *Gerald's Game*'s Jessie Burlingame has lost her husband to heart failure. He "has died after handcuffing her to the bed at their summer home," Senf explains, "and Jessie must face her life, including the memory that her father had sexually abused her, and her fears alone." *Dolores Claiborne* is the story of a woman suspected of murdering her employer, a crusty old miser named Vera Donovan. Dolores maintains her innocence, but she freely confesses that she murdered her husband thirty years previously when she caught him molesting their daughter.

"There are a series of dovetailing, but unobtrusive, connections," states *Locus* contributor Edward Bryant, "linking the two novels and both Jessie and Dolores." Like *It,* both *Gerald's Game* and *Dolores Claiborne* are set in the town of Derry, Maine. They are also both psychological portraits of older women who have been subjected to sexual abuse. *Dolores Claiborne* differs from *Gerald's Game,* however, because it uses fewer of the traditional trappings of horror fiction, and it is related entirely from the

viewpoint of the title character. *Dolores Claiborne* "is, essentially, a dramatic monologue," states Kit Reed in the *Washington Post Book World,* "in which the speaker addresses other people in the room, answers questions and completes a narrative in actual time." "All but the last page is one long quote from Dolores Claiborne," asserts a *Rapport* reviewer. "King has taken horror literature out of the closet and has injected new life into familiar genres," Senf concludes. "He is not afraid to mix those genres in fresh ways to produce novels that examine contemporary American culture."

Insomnia, King's 1994 novel, continues the example set by *Gerald's Game* and *Dolores Claiborne.* It is also set in Derry, and its protagonist is an elderly man named Ralph Roberts, a retired salesman, newly widowed and suffering severely from insomnia. Ralph begins to see people in a new way: their auras become visible to him. "Ralph finds himself a man in a classic situation, a mortal in conflict with the fates—literally," declares *Locus* reviewer Bryant. "How much self-determination does he really possess? And how much is he acted upon?" Ralph also finds himself in conflict with his neighbor Ed Deepeneau, a conservative Christian and an anti-abortion activist who beats his wife and has taken up a crusade against a visiting feminist speaker. "There are some truly haunting scenes in the book about wife abuse and fanaticism, as well as touching observations about growing old, but they're quickly consumed by more predictable sensationalism," explains Chris Bohjalian in the *New York Times Book Review.* "In a world teeming with timeless, omnipotent entities," declares novelist Kinky Friedman in the *Washington Post Book World,* "King has provided Ralph Roberts, that ancient vulnerable, white-haired widower, with the ultimate weapon, the power of the human spirit."

Over the years, King has been careful to keep his own fame in perspective. King tells Mel Allen in *Yankee* magazine, "I'm very leery of thinking that I'm somebody. Because nobody really is. Everybody is able to do something well, but in this country there's a premium put on stardom." Describing what he calls the "occupational hazard of the successful writer in America," King tells Kilgore that "once you begin to be successful, then you have to avoid being gobbled up. America has developed this sort of cannibalistic cult of celebrity, where first you set the guy up, and then you eat him." Pertaining to such disparaging critiques as a *Time* condemnation of him as a master of "postliterate prose" and an uncomplimentary *Village Voice* profile, King tells Norden: "People like me really do irritate people like them, you know. In effect, they're saying, 'What right do you have to entertain people. This is a serious world with a lot of serious problems. Let's sit around and pick scabs; *that's* art.'" But as Cohen points out, "People consume horror in order to be scared, not *arted*." King, however, suggests in *Danse Macabre* that horror actually "achieves the level of art simply because it is looking for something beyond art, something that predates art: it is looking for what I would call phobic pressure points. The good horror tale will dance its way to the center of your life and find the secret door to the room you believed no one but you knew of."

Although he does not necessarily feel that he has been treated unfairly by the critics, King expresses what it is like to witness the written word turned into filmed images that are less than generously received by critics. "Whenever I publish a book, I feel like a trapper caught by the Iroquois," he tells Peck. "They're all lined up with tomahawks, and the idea is to run through with your head down, and everybody gets to take a swing. . . . Finally, you get out the other side and you're bleeding and bruised, and *then* it gets turned into a movie, and you're there in front of the same line and everybody's got their tomahawks out again." Nevertheless, in his essay "Why I Was Bachman," he readily admits that he really has little to complain about: "I'm still married to the same woman, my kids are healthy and bright, and I'm being well paid for doing something I love." And despite the financial security and recognition, or perhaps because of its intrinsic responsibility, King strives to improve at his craft. "It's getting later and I want to get better, because you only get so many chances to do good work," he states in a panel discussion at the 1984 World Fantasy Convention in Ottawa. "There's no justification not to at least try to do good work when you make the money."

According to Warren in *Discovering Stephen King*, there is absolutely nothing to suggest that success has been detrimental to King: "As a novelist, King has been remarkably consistent." Noting, for instance, that "for generations it was given that brevity was the soul of horror, that the ideal format for the tale of terror was the short story," Warren points out that "King was among the first to challenge that concept, writing not just successful novels of horror, but long novels." Moreover, says Warren, "his novels have gotten longer." King quips in the *Chicago Tribune*

Magazine that his "philosophy has always been take a good thing and beat it 'til it don't move no more." Although some critics fault him for overwriting, Warren suggests that "the sheer scope and ambitious nature of his storytelling demands a broad canvas." Referring to this as "the very pushiness of his technique," the *New York Times'* Lehmann-Haupt similarly contends that "the more he exasperates us by overpreparing, the more effectively his preparations eventually pay off."

"I just want to scare people," King remarks to Kilgore. "I'm very humble about that." And in Yarbro's estimation, "King knows how to evoke those special images that hook into all the archetypal forms of horror that we have thrived on since earliest youth." Recognized for the varied and vivid descriptions he consistently renders of the emotion he so skillfully summons, King claims no other technique for inducing fear than lulling a reader into complacency and then "turn[ing] the monsters loose," as he relates in a *Shayol* interview. To create a comfortably familiar world for the reader so that the horrors experienced within it will seem more real, he imbues his fiction with touchstones of reality—recognizable brand names, products, people, and events. King does, however, delineate a certain hierarchy of fear that he tries to attain, telling Norden: "There's terror on top, the finest emotion any writer can induce; then horror; and, on the very lowest level of all, the gag instinct of revulsion. Naturally, I'll try to terrify you first, and if that doesn't work, I'll try to horrify you, and if I can't make it there, I'll try to gross you out. I'm not proud. . . . I suppose the ultimate triumph would be to have somebody drop dead of a heart attack, literally scared to death. I'd say, 'Gee, that's a shame,' and I'd mean it, but part of me would be thinking, Jesus, that really *worked!*"

Influenced by the naturalistic novels of writers such as Theodore Dreiser and Frank Norris, King confesses to Janeczko that his personal outlook for the world's future is somewhat bleak. On the other hand, one of the things he finds most comforting in his own work is an element of optimism. "In almost all cases, I've begun with a premise that was really black," he says in a panel discussion at the 1980 World Fantasy Convention in Baltimore, reprinted in *Bare Bones*. "And a more pleasant resolution has forced itself upon that structure." But as Andrew M. Greeley maintains in *Kingdom of Fear:* "Unlike some other horror writers who lack his talents and sensitivity, Stephen King never ends his stories with any cheap or easy hope. People are badly hurt, they suffer and some of them die, but others survive the struggle and manage to grow. The powers of evil have not yet done them in." According to Notkin, though, the reassurance King brings to his own readers derives from a basic esteem for humanity itself, "For whether he is writing about vampires, about the death of 99 percent of the population, or about innocent little girls with the power to break the earth in half, King never stops emphasizing his essential liking for people."

"You have got to love the people in the story, because there is no horror without love and without feeling," King explains to Platt. "Horror is the contrasting emotion to our understanding of all the things that are good and normal." While stressing the importance of characterization, he regards the story itself as the most integral part of crafting fiction. "If you can tell a story, everything else becomes possible," he explains to Mat Schaffer in the *Boston Sunday Review,* reprinted in *Bare Bones.* "But without story, nothing is possible, because nobody wants to hear about your sensitive characters if there's nothing happening in your story. And the same is true with mood. Story is the only thing that's important." Harris speaks for several critics when he observes that King is at his best when he "is simply himself, and when he loses consciousness of himself as a writer—the way the old tale-teller around the campfire occasionally will—he can be outstanding." Praising King's "page-flipping narrative drive, yanking the reader along with eye-straining velocity," Brown describes his prose as "invisible" and points to those moments of pure transport in which "the reader is caught in the rush of events and forgets that words are being read. It is a quality as rare as it is critically underappreciated."

"There's unmistakable genius in Stephen King," admits Walter Kendrick in the *Village Voice,* adding that he writes "with such fierce conviction, such blind and brutal power, that no matter how hard you fight—and needless to say, I fought—he's irresistible." The less reserved critical affirmations of King's work extend from expressions of pragmatism to those of metaphor. Lehmann-Haupt, for example, a self-professed King addict, offers his evaluation of King's potential versus his accomplishments as a writer of horror fiction: "Once again, as I edged myself nervously toward the climax of one of his thrillers, I found myself considering what Stephen King could accomplish if he would only put his storytelling talents to serious use. And then I had to

ask myself: if Mr. King's aim in writing . . . was not entirely serious by some standard that I was vaguely invoking, then why, somebody please tell me, was I holding on to his book so hard that my knuckles had begun to turn white?" Winter assesses King's contribution to the genre in his study *Stephen King: The Art of Darkness* this way: "Death, destruction, and destiny await us all at the end of the journey—in life as in horror fiction. And the writer of horror stories serves as the boatman who ferries people across that Reach known as the River Styx. . . . In the horror fiction of Stephen King, we can embark upon the night journey, make the descent down the dark hole, cross that narrowing Reach, and return again in safety to the surface—to the near shore of the river of death. For our boatman has a master's hand."

BIOGRAPHICAL/CRITICAL SOURCES:

BOOKS

Authors and Artists for Young Adults, Volume 1, Gale (Detroit), 1989.

Beahm, George W., *The Stephen King Story,* Andrews & McMeel (Kansas City, MO), 1991, revised and updated edition, 1992.

Beahm, editor, *The Stephen King Companion,* Andrews & McMeel, 1989.

Blue, Tyson, *The Unseen King,* Starmont House (Mercer Island, WA), 1989.

Blue, *Observations from the Terminator: Thoughts on Stephen King and Other Modern Masters of Horror Fiction,* Borgo Press (San Bernardino, CA), 1995.

Collings, Michael R., *Stephen King as Richard Bachman,* Starmont House, 1985.

Collings, *The Many Facets of Stephen King,* Starmont House, 1985.

Collings and David Engebretson, *The Shorter Works of Stephen King,* Starmont House, 1985.

Collings, *The Annotated Guide to Stephen King: A Primary and Secondary Bibliography of the Works of America's Premier Horror Writer,* Starmont House, 1986.

Collings, *The Films of Stephen King,* Starmont House, 1986.

Collings, *The Stephen King Phenomenon,* Starmont House, 1987.

Collings, *The Works of Stephen King: An Annotated Bibliography and Guide,* edited by Boden Clarke, Borgo Press, 1993.

Collings, *Scaring Us to Death: The Impact of Stephen King on Popular Culture,* 2nd edition, Borgo Press, 1995.

Contemporary Literary Criticism, Gale, Volume 12, 1980, Volume 26, 1983, Volume 37, 1985, Volume 61, 1990.

Davis, Jonathan P., *Stephen King's America,* Bowling Green State University Popular Press (Bowling Green, OH), 1994.

Dictionary of Literary Biography, Volume 143: *American Novelists since World War II, Third Series,* Gale, 1994.

Dictionary of Literary Biography Yearbook: 1980, Gale, 1981.

Docherty, Brian, editor, *American Horror Fiction: From Brockden Brown to Stephen King,* St. Martin's (New York City), 1990.

Heron, Don, editor, *Reign of Fear: Fiction and Film of Stephen King,* Underwood-Miller (Lancaster, PA), 1988.

Hoppenstand, Gary, and Ray B. Browne, editors, *The Gothic World of Stephen King: Landscape of Nightmares,* Bowling Green State University Popular Press, 1987.

Horsting, Jessie, *Stephen King: At the Movies,* Signet/Starlog, 1986.

Keyishian, Amy, and Marjorie Keyishian, *Stephen King,* Chelsea House (New York City), 1995.

Kimberling, C. Ronald, *Kenneth Burke's Dramatism and Popular Arts,* Bowling Green State University Popular Press, 1982.

King, Stephen, *Stephen King's Danse Macabre,* Everest House, 1981.

Lloyd, Ann, *The Films of Stephen King,* St. Martin's, 1993.

Magistrale, Tony, *Landscape of Fear: Stephen King's American Gothic,* Bowling Green State University Popular Press, 1988.

Magistrale, *The Moral Voyages of Stephen King,* Starmont House, 1989.

Magistrale, *The Shining Reader,* Starmont House, 1991.

Magistrale, editor, *The Dark Descent: Essays Defining Stephen King's Horrorscape,* Greenwood Press (New York City), 1992.

Magistrale, editor, *A Casebook on "The Stand,"* Starmont House, 1992.

Magistrale, *Stephen King: The Second Decade— "Danse Macabre" to "The Dark Half,"* Twayne (New York City), 1992.

Platt, Charles, *Dream Makers: The Uncommon Men & Women Who Write Science Fiction,* Berkley Books (New York City), 1983.

Reino, Joseph, *Stephen King: The First Decade— "Carrie" to "Pet Sematary,"* Twayne, 1988.

Saidman, Anne, *Stephen King, Master of Horror,* Lerner Publications (Minneapolis), 1992.

Schweitzer, Darrell, editor, *Discovering Stephen King,* Starmont House, 1985.

Short Story Criticism, Volume 17, Gale, 1995.

Spignesi, Stephen, *The Shape under the Sheet: The Complete Stephen King Encyclopedia,* Popular Culture (Ann Arbor, MI), 1991.

Underwood, Tim, and Chuck Miller, editors, *Fear Itself: The Horror Fiction of Stephen King,* Underwood-Miller, 1982.

Underwood and Miller, editors, *Kingdom of Fear: The World of Stephen King,* Underwood-Miller, 1986.

Underwood and Miller, editors, *Bare Bones: Conversations on Terror with Stephen King,* McGraw-Hill (New York City), 1988.

Underwood and Miller, editors, *Feast of Fear: Conversations with Stephen King,* Carroll & Graf (New York City), 1992.

Underwood and Miller, editors, *Fear Itself: The Early Works of Stephen King,* foreword by King, introduction by Peter Straub, afterword by George A. Romero, Underwood-Miller, 1993.

Winter, Douglas E., editor, *Shadowings: The Reader's Guide to Horror Fiction, 1981-1982,* Starmont House, 1983.

Winter, *Stephen King: The Art of Darkness,* New American Library, 1984.

Zagorski, Edward J., *Teacher's Manual: Novels of Stephen King,* New American Library, 1981.

PERIODICALS

American Film, June, 1986.

Atlantic Monthly, September, 1986.

Boston, October, 1980.

Boston Globe, October 10, 1980; April 15, 1990, p. A1; May 16, 1990, p. 73; July 15, 1990, p. 71; September 11, 1990, p. 61; October 31, 1990, p. 25; November 17, 1990, p. 12; December 5, 1990, p. 73; July 16, 1991, p. 56; September 28, 1991, p. 9; November 22, 1991, p. 1; August 21, 1992, p. 21; August 30, 1992, p. 14; May 8, 1993, p. 21; May 24, 1993, p. 43; October 16, 1994, p. 14; May 13, 1995, p. 21.

Boston Sunday Review, October 31, 1983.

Castle Rock: The Stephen King Newsletter, July, 1986.

Chernobog, Volume 18, 1980 (King issue).

Chicago Daily News, July 7, 1977.

Chicago Tribune, August 26, 1990, p. 3; October 29, 1990, p. 5; November 16, 1990, p. 1; November 30, 1990, p. C29; June 29, 1992, p. 3; November 18, 1992, p. 3; November 7, 1993, p. 9; October 26, 1994, p. 1; May 14, 1995, p. 5.

Chicago Tribune Book World, June 8, 1980.

Chicago Tribune Magazine, October 27, 1985.

Christian Science Monitor, January 22, 1990, p. 13.

Cinefantastique, spring, 1981; Volume 12, numbers 2 and 3, 1982; Volume 15, number 2, 1985.

Detroit Free Press, November 12, 1982.

Detroit News, September 26, 1979.

English Journal, January, 1979; February, 1980; January, 1983; December, 1983; December, 1984.

Entertainment Weekly, October 14, 1994, pp. 52-53; June 16, 1995, p. 54.

Esquire, November, 1984.

Fangoria, December, 1979; June, 1980.

Fantasy Review, January, 1984.

Film Comment, May/June, 1981; May/June, 1986.

Film Journal, April 12, 1982.

High Times, January, 1981; June, 1981.

Horizon, February, 1978.

Locus, September, 1992, pp. 21-22, 67; November, 1992, pp. 19, 21; February, 1994, p. 39; October, 1994, pp. 27, 29.

Los Angeles Times, April 23, 1978; December 10, 1978; August 26, 1979; September 28, 1980; May 10, 1981; September 6, 1981; May 8, 1983; November 20, 1983; November 18, 1984; August 25, 1985; March 9, 1990, p. F16; October 29, 1990, p. F9; November 18, 1990, p. F6; November 30, 1990, p. F1; July 16, 1991, p. F1; May 28, 1992, p. E7; April 16, 1995, p. 28.

Los Angeles Times Book Review, August 29, 1982; July 15, 1990, p. 12; June 9, 1991, p. 6; April 23, 1995, p. 14.

Maclean's, August 11, 1986.

Miami Herald, March 24, 1984.

Minneapolis Star, September 8, 1979.

Mystery, March, 1981.

New Statesman, September 15, 1995, p. 33.

Newsweek, August 31, 1981; May 2, 1983.

New Yorker, January 15, 1979.

New York Review of Books, October 19, 1995, p. 54.

New York Times, March 1, 1977; August 14, 1981; August 11, 1982; April 12, 1983; October 21, 1983; November 8, 1984; June 11, 1985; April 4, 1987; January 25, 1988; June 17, 1990, p. 13; October 27, 1990, p. A12; November 16, 1990, p. C38; December 2, 1990, p. 19; June 3, 1991, p. C14; July 14, 1991, p. 25; October 2, 1991, p. C23; June 29, 1992, p. C13; November 16, 1992, p. C15; March 15, 1993, p. D6; June 27, 1993, p. 23; September 17, 1993, p. B8; May 12, 1995, p. D18.

New York Times Book Review, May 26, 1974; October 24, 1976; February 20, 1977; March 26, 1978; February 4, 1979; September 23, 1979; May 11, 1980; May 10, 1981; September 27, 1981; August 29, 1982; April 3, 1983; November 6, 1983; November 4, 1984; June 9, 1985; February 22, 1987; December 6, 1987; May 13, 1990, p. 3; September 2, 1990, p. 21; September 29, 1991, pp. 13-14; August 16, 1992, p. 3; December 27, 1992, p. 15; October 24, 1993, p. 22; October 30, 1994, p. 24.

New York Times Magazine, May 11, 1980.

Observer (London), October 1, 1995, p. 15.

Parent's Magazine, January, 1982.

Penthouse, April, 1982.

People, March 7, 1977; December 29, 1980-January 5, 1981; May 18, 1981; January 28, 1985; fall, 1989.

Playboy, June, 1983.

Prevue, May, 1982.

Psychology Today, September, 1975.

Publishers Weekly, January 17, 1977; May 11, 1984.

Rapport, Volume 17, number 3, p. 20.

Rolling Stone, April, 1982.

Rolling Stone College Papers, winter, 1980; winter, 1983.

San Francisco Chronicle, August 15, 1982; August, 1995, p. 48.

Saturday Review, September, 1981; November, 1984.

Self, September, 1981.

Shayol, summer, 1979; winter, 1982.

Sourcebook, 1982.

Tampa Tribune, August 31, 1980.

Time, August 30, 1982; July 1, 1985; October 6, 1986; December 7, 1992, p. 81.

Tomb of Dracula, April, 1980; June, 1980.

TV Guide, June 13-19, 1981; December 5-11, 1981.

Twilight Zone Magazine, April, 1981; June, 1981; May, 1982.

USA Today, October 14, 1982; May 10, 1985; April 13, 1990, p. D1; November 16, 1990, pp. D1, D3; July 16, 1991, p. D1; August 8, 1991, p. D3; October 31, 1991, p. D8; April 13, 1992, p. D6; July 23, 1992, p. D4; February 18, 1993, p. D3.

Village Voice, April 29, 1981; October 23, 1984; March 3, 1987.

Voice Literary Supplement, September, 1982; November, 1985.

Waldenbooks Book Notes, August, 1983.

Wall Street Journal, July 7, 1992, p. B2; October 5, 1992, p. B3.

Washington Post, August 26, 1979; April 9, 1985; May 8, 1987; October 29, 1990, p. B8; July 16, 1991, p. B1; April 13, 1992, p. C7; May 21,

1993, p. 16; May 27, 1993, p. D9; May 14, 1995, p. G1.

Washington Post Book World, May 26, 1974; October 1, 1978; August 26, 1980; April 12, 1981; August 22, 1982; March 23, 1983; October 2, 1983; November 13, 1983; June 16, 1985; August 26, 1990, p. 9; September 29, 1991, p. 9; October 31, 1991, p. C7; July 19, 1992, p. 7; December 13, 1992, p. 5; October 10, 1993, p. 4; October 9, 1994, p. 4; March 6, 1995, p. D6.

Writer, July, 1986; July, 1988.

Writer's Digest, November, 1973; June, 1977; October, 1978.

Yankee, March, 1979.*

*   *   *

KING, Steve
See KING, Stephen (Edwin)

*   *   *

KINNEY, Harrison   1921-

PERSONAL: Born August 16, 1921, in Mars Hill, ME; son of Charles S. and Blanche (Clark) Kinney; married Doris Getsinger, 1952; children: Susan Edith, Barbara Lee, Joanne Leslie, John Harrison. *Education:* Washington & Lee University, A.B., 1947; Columbia University, M.A., 1949. *Politics:* Democrat. *Religion:* Unitarian Universalist.

CAREER: New Yorker, New York City, reporter, 1949-54; *McCall's,* New York City, senior editor, 1955-58; International Business Machines Corp. (IBM), Armonk, NY, writer, 1960—. *Military service:* U.S. Army, 1943-46; became captain.

MEMBER: Phi Beta Kappa.

WRITINGS:

The Lonesome Bear (juvenile), Whittlesey House (New York City), 1949.

DaVinci's Last Supper, Coward (New York City), 1953.

Has Anybody Seen My Father?, Simon & Schuster (New York City), 1960.

The Kangaroo in the Attic (juvenile), Whittlesey House, 1960.

James Thurber: His Life and Times, Holt (New York City), 1995.

Also coauthor of *Bronco Charlie of the Pony Express.* Contributor to *Saturday Evening Post* and other publications.

SIDELIGHTS: In 1949 Harrison Kinney interviewed James Thurber, the humorist and "writer of light pieces" for the *New Yorker* magazine, as part of his master's thesis. He subsequently began to interview friends, family members and associates of Thurber in order to write a biography of the famous author. In the following decades Kinney wrote books for children and adults, and worked as a journalist (including a stint at the *New Yorker*) and as a speechwriter for business executives. In 1995, his 1,200-page study of Thurber's career—*James Thurber: His Life and Times*—finally saw print. "Had its subject been more conventional," writes John McAleer in the *Chicago Tribune,* "this biography's long period of gestation might have been hazardous. But Thurber's deceptively simple surface concealed complexities that only painstaking effort could bring to full disclosure."

Kinney's biography of Thurber uncovers many hitherto unknown facts. "Over the course of his two score and seven years of labor," notes Ben Yagoda in the *New York Times Book Review,* "[Kinney] unearthed what appears to be every relevant written source and spoke to everyone worth speaking to about Thurber." Yagoda asserts that Kinney's biography is noteworthy not only for its size, but also for the insights it offers into Thurber's life-long misogyny. "Kinney demonstrates that a strong strain of misogyny coursed through [Thurber's] conversation and correspondence," Yagoda notes. McAleer asks: "Was Thurber a misogynist? Consider the facts." He then details Thurber's fear of sex, his inability to sustain intimate relationships, and his many portrayals of women as domineering.

Although it reveals some negative facts about Thurber's personality, Kinney's biography also clarifies some periods in the author's life which have until now not been fully understood. Among these periods are Thurber's first years at the *New Yorker* and his life in the 1950s, when he suffered from continuing ill health. McAleer notes that Kinney's biography shows that when Thurber began his career at the *New Yorker,* he "actually maximized himself at [editor] Harold Ross' expense." Rivalry among the magazine's staff was intense, as Kinney reveals with an early Thurber cartoon depicting his co-workers glowering angrily at him. Heywood Hale Broun, writing in the *Washington Post Book World,* finds that "Thurber's love-hate relationship with the *New Yorker* makes up the most compelling portion of this book." Thurber's later years, when he suffered from blindness and periods of depression, are also presented in a more complete manner than previous accounts have given.

A critic for *Publishers Weekly* finds that *James Thurber: His Life and Times* is a "marvelous biography. . . . liberally sprinkled with excerpts from Thurber's letters, conversations, essays and poems, and charmingly illustrated throughout with his cartoons." Broun praises the insight Kinney offers into Thurber's creative processes and McAleer concludes by praising Kinney's "deft handling of friendships, romantic attachments, working relationships, conflicts of personality and personal crises" to provide "access to a mind that learned, by hard necessity, to supplant outer vision with inner vision."

BIOGRAPHICAL/CRITICAL SOURCES:

PERIODICALS

Chicago Tribune, December 17, 1995, pp. 1, 9.
New York Times Book Review, December 10, 1995, p. 7.
Publishers Weekly, October 9, 1995, p. 70.
Washington Post Book World, December 31, 1995, p. 5.*

*   *   *

KNEALE, Matthew (Nicholas Kerr)   **1960-**

PERSONAL: Born November 24, 1960, in London, England; son of Nigel (a playwright) and Judith (a writer; maiden name, Kerr) Kneale. *Education:* Magdalen College, Oxford, B.A., 1982. *Avocational interests:* Travel, long-distance hill and mountain walking, cycling.

ADDRESSES: Home—Oxford, England. *Agent*—Deborah Rogers, Rogers, Coleridge & White, 20 Powys Mews, London W11 1JN, England.

CAREER: Teacher of English as a foreign language in Tokyo, 1982-83, and in Rome; tutor of English and history. Freelance photographer.

MEMBER: Society of Authors.

AWARDS, HONORS: Winner of Somerset Maugham Award, 1988, for *Whore Banquets;* winner of John Llewellyn Rhys Award, 1993, for *Sweet Thames;* speaker at Adelaide Festival, 1994, and at Singapore Festival, 1995.

WRITINGS:

Whore Banquets, Gollancz (London), 1987.
Inside Rose's Kingdom, Gollancz, 1989.
Sweet Thames, Sinclair-Stevenson (London), 1992, Black Swan Books (Redding Ridge, CT), 1994.

SIDELIGHTS: Matthew Kneale told *CA:* "I contracted a severe case of the travel bug sometime early on in life and till now have visited some seventy countries and all seven continents. I have also spent a year living in both Tokyo and, later, Rome. The areas I feel I have got to know best are Italy, Latin America, Australia, and Asia. My strangest journey was probably in Indonesian New Guinea, where I walked and stayed with the Dani people, who are only recently emerged from the stone age. My saddest journey was in China in June, 1989, where I found myself a witness to the quiet bravery of the student demonstrators. All this journeying about, together with a study of history, has left me with a fascination with how cultures work, and their seemingly limitless ability to believe that they alone have found the right and normal way of going about things. My first novel, *Whore Banquets,* was based on my year in Tokyo, and is a study of cultural miscomprehensions. My latest, *Sweet Thames,* is set in London in 1849, and is a wry look at Victorian English thinking, from the starting point of an obsessively ambitious drainage engineer whose wife vanishes in the middle of a cholera epidemic."

Kneale also noted that he resides in "a Victorian castle on an island in the center of Oxford, England."

BIOGRAPHICAL/CRITICAL SOURCES:

PERIODICALS

Canberra Times, February 7, 1989.
Cosmopolitan, January 5, 1987; June, 1989.
Daily Telegraph, February 6, 1987; May 6, 1989; September 12, 1992.
Evening Standard, July 23, 1992.
Financial Times, January 31, 1987.

Guardian, January 30, 1987; April 17, 1989.
Independent, February 10, 1987.
Independent on Sunday, August 2, 1992.
Literary Review, April, 1987; March, 1989.
Mail on Sunday, July 19, 1992.
New Statesman, March 27, 1987.
Observer (London), February 1, 1987; August 16, 1992.
Spectator, August 8, 1992.
Sunday Telegraph, February 2, 1987.
Sunday Times, April 4, 1989; July 19, 1992.
Time Out, January 1, 1987; April 5, 1989; August 5, 1992.
Times Literary Supplement, January 30, 1987; April 4, 1987; March 30, 1989; August 8, 1992.
Weekend Australian, December 31, 1988.

*   *   *

KOONTZ, Dean R(ay)   1945-
(David Axton, Brian Coffey, Deanna Dwyer, K. R. Dwyer, John Hill, Leigh Nichols, Anthony North, Richard Paige, Owen West)

PERSONAL: Born July 9, 1945, in Everett, PA; son of Ray and Florence Koontz; married Gerda Ann Cerra, October 15, 1966.

ADDRESSES: Home—Newport Beach, CA. *Office*—P.O. Box 9529, Newport Beach, CA 92658-9529. *Agent*—Robert Gottlieb, William Morris Agency, 1325 Avenue of the Americas, New York, NY 10019.

CAREER: Teacher-counselor with Appalachian Poverty Program, 1966-67; high school English teacher, 1967-69; writer, 1969—.

AWARDS, HONORS: Atlantic Monthly college creative writing award, 1966, for story "The Kittens"; Hugo Award nomination, World Science Fiction Convention, 1971, for novella *Beastchild;* Litt.D., Shippensburg State College, 1989.

WRITINGS:

NOVELS

Star Quest, Ace Books (New York City), 1968.
The Fall of the Dream Machine, Ace Books, 1969.
Fear That Man, Ace Books, 1969.

Anti-Man, Paperback Library (New York City), 1970.
Beastchild, Lancer Books (New York City), 1970 (published in limited illustrated edition by Charnel House [Lynbrook, NY], 1992).
Dark of the Woods, Ace Books, 1970.
The Dark Symphony, Lancer Books, 1970.
Hell's Gate, Lancer Books, 1970.
The Crimson Witch, Curtis Books (New York City), 1971.
A Darkness in My Soul, DAW Books (New York City), 1972.
The Flesh in the Furnace, Bantam (New York City), 1972.
Starblood, Lancer Books, 1972.
Time Thieves, Ace Books, 1972.
Warlock, Lancer Books, 1972.
A Werewolf among Us, Ballantine (New York City), 1973.
Hanging On, M. Evans (New York City), 1973.
The Haunted Earth, Lancer Books, 1973.
Demon Seed, Bantam, 1973.
(Under pseudonym Anthony North) *Strike Deep,* Dial (New York City), 1974.
After the Last Race, Atheneum (New York City), 1974.
Nightmare Journey, Putnam (New York City), 1975.
(Under pseudonym John Hill) *The Long Sleep,* Popular Library (New York City), 1975.
Night Chills, Atheneum, 1976.
(Under pseudonym David Axton) *Prison of Ice,* Lippincott (Philadelphia), 1976, revised edition under name Dean R. Koontz published as *Icebound* (also see below), Ballantine, 1995 .
The Vision (also see below), Putnam, 1977.
Whispers (also see below), Putnam, 1980.
Phantoms (also see below), Putnam, 1983.
Darkfall (also see below), Berkley (New York City), 1984, published in England as *Darkness Comes,* W. H. Allen (London), 1984.
Twilight Eyes, Land of Enchantment (Westland, MI), 1985.
(Under pseudonym Richard Paige) *The Door to December,* New American Library (New York City), 1985.
Strangers (Literary Guild main selection; also see below), Putnam, 1986.
Watchers (Literary Guild main selection; also see below), Putnam, 1987.
Lightning (Literary Guild main selection; also see below), Putnam, 1988.
Midnight, Putnam, 1989.
The Bad Place (Literary Guild main selection; also see below), Putnam, 1990.

Cold Fire (Literary Guild main selection; also see below), Putnam, 1991.

Three Complete Novels: Dean R. Koontz: The Servants of Twilight; Darkfall; Phantoms, Wings Books (New York City), 1991.

Hideaway (Literary Guild main selection; also see below), Putnam, 1992.

Dragon Tears (Literary Guild main selection; also see below), Berkley, 1992 (also published in a limited edition, Putnam, 1993).

Dean R. Koontz: A New Collection (contains *Watchers, Whispers,* and *Shattered* [originally published under pseudonym K. R. Dwyer; also see below]), Wings Books, 1992.

Mr. Murder (Literary Guild main selection; also see below), Putnam, 1993.

Winter Moon, Ballantine, 1993.

Three Complete Novels: Dean Koontz: Lightning; The Face of Fear; The Vision (*The Face of Fear* originally published under pseudonym Brian Coffey), Putnam, 1993.

Three Complete Novels: Dean Koontz: Strangers; The Voice of the Night; The Mask (*The Voice of the Night* originally published under pseudonym Brian Coffey; *The Mask* originally published under pseudonym Owen West), Putnam, 1994.

Dark Rivers of the Heart (also see below), Knopf (New York City), 1994.

Strange Highways (Literary Guild main selection; also see below), Warner Books (New York City), 1995.

Intensity (Literary Guild main selection; also see below), Knopf, 1995.

Tick-Tock, Ballantine, 1996.

UNDER PSEUDONYM BRIAN COFFEY

Blood Risk, Bobbs-Merrill (Indianapolis, IN), 1973.

Surrounded, Bobbs-Merrill, 1974.

The Wall of Masks, Bobbs-Merrill, 1975.

The Face of Fear, Bobbs-Merrill, 1977.

The Voice of the Night, Doubleday (New York City), 1981.

Also author of script for *CHiPs* television series, 1978.

UNDER PSEUDONYM DEANNA DWYER

The Demon Child, Lancer Books, 1971.

Legacy of Terror, Lancer Books, 1971.

Children of the Storm, Lancer Books, 1972.

The Dark of Summer, Lancer Books, 1972.

Dance with the Devil, Lancer Books, 1973.

UNDER PSEUDONYM K. R. DWYER

Chase (also see below), Random House, 1972.

Shattered (also see below), Random House, 1973.

Dragonfly, Random House, 1975.

UNDER PSEUDONYM LEIGH NICHOLS

The Key to Midnight, Pocket Books (New York City), 1979.

The Eyes of Darkness, Pocket Books, 1981.

The House of Thunder, Pocket Books, 1982.

Twilight, Pocket Books, 1984, revised edition under name Dean R. Koontz published as *The Servants of Twilight,* Berkley, 1990.

Shadowfires, Avon (New York City), 1987.

UNDER PSEUDONYM OWEN WEST

The Funhouse (novelization of screenplay), Jove (New York City), 1980.

The Mask, Jove, 1981.

OTHER

(With wife, Gerda Koontz) *The Pig Society* (nonfiction), Aware Press (Granada Hills, CA), 1970.

(With G. Koontz) *The Underground Lifestyles Handbook,* Aware Press, 1970.

Soft Come the Dragons (story collection), Ace Books, 1970.

Writing Popular Fiction, Writer's Digest (Cincinnati), 1973.

How to Write Best-Selling Fiction, Writer's Digest, 1981.

Contributor to books, including *Infinity 3,* edited by Robert Haskins, Lancer Books, 1972; *Again, Dangerous Visions,* edited by Harlan Ellison, Doubleday, 1972; *Final Stage,* edited by Edward L. Ferman and Barry N. Malzberg, Charterhouse, 1974; *Night Visions IV,* Dark Harvest, 1987; *Stalkers: All New Tales of Terror and Suspense,* edited by Ed Gorman and Martin H. Greenberg, illustrated by Paul Sonju, Dark Harvest, 1989; and *Night Visions VI: The Bone Yard,* Berkley, 1991.

ADAPTATIONS: *Demon Seed* was filmed by Metro-Goldwyn-Mayer/Warner Bros., 1977; *Shattered* was filmed by Warner Bros., 1977; *Watchers* was filmed by Universal, 1988; *Hideaway* was filmed by Tri-Star, starring Jeff Goldbloom, 1994. Many of Koontz's works were recorded unabridged on audiocassette, including *Cold Fire, Hideaway,* and *The*

Bad Place, Reader's Chair (Hollister, CA), 1991; *Mr. Murder,* and *Dragon Tears,* Simon and Schuster Audio; *Dark Rivers of the Heart, Icebound,* and *Intensity,* Random House Audio; and *Strange Highways,* and *Chase,* Warner Audio.

SIDELIGHTS: Dean R. Koontz is one of popular fiction's most successful novelists. Originally a science fiction writer, Koontz branched out from the genre in 1972, focusing mainly on suspense fiction. His novels, many of which have been bestsellers, are known for tightly constructed plots and rich characters—often combining elements of horror, science fiction, suspense and romance.

Koontz explained to *CA:* "I began writing when I was a child, for both reading and writing provided much needed escape from the poverty in which we lived and from my father's frequent fits of alcohol-induced violence. I started selling my work while I was still in college, and by the time I was twenty-five I had sold a dozen novels. This prolific production was both a boon and a curse. Even the low advances from my early science fiction novels were welcome, for my wife and I began married life with much less than five hundred dollars to our name. The curse lies in the fact that much of the early work is of lower quality than what came after, both because I was so young and unself-critical and because the low earnings of each book forced me to write a lot of them in order to keep financially afloat. Of all my science fiction . . . I am only well pleased with *The Flesh in the Furnace, Beastchild,* and to a lesser extent, *Demon Seed.*

"I mark the beginning of my *real* career as a writer with the publication of *Chase* (a suspense novel that dealt with the effects of Vietnam on a veteran, which must have been one of the first novels to do so), in 1972, and *Hanging On* (a comic novel) in 1973, when I moved out of science fiction into the mainstream and suspense fields. Since then, I have attempted, book by book, to speak to the reader's intellect and emotions as well as to his desire for a 'good read.' I believe the best fiction does three things well: tells an involving story, makes the reader think, and makes the reader feel."

With regard to sales and mainstream popular success, Koontz's breakthrough was his 1980 novel *Whispers.* According to Michael A. Morrison in *Sudden Fear: The Horror and Dark Suspense Fiction of Dean R. Koontz, Whispers* seems at first to be "a simple genre novel of the psychopathic-madman-assaults-woman variety." The novel revolves around Bruno Frye and his obsession with Hilary Thomas, a Hollywood screenwriter. But, Morrison argues, the parallels between the two characters become evident: "Both are victims of parental abuse, and both carry deep-seated neuroses as a consequence. Indeed, all the main figures of Koontz's novel reflect the constricting influence of childhood on adult life—the sins of the fathers and mothers." Elizabeth Massie, also a contributor to *Sudden Fear,* points out that Hilary emerges as a much stronger character than she initially appears after surviving the second attack and apparently killing Frye. For Massie, this "allow[s] the story to take off flying. It allows the tale to spend the majority of its energy with . . . Frye, which it is well advised to do. Having seen Hilary in action against Frye, the reader can know that, regardless of peril, Hilary will put up the good fight." Morrison concludes that Frye ranks "as one of the most original psychological aberrations in horror fiction."

Critical reaction to *Whispers* was mixed. A *Publishers Weekly* reviewer argues that readers will need "strong stomachs to tolerate the overheated scenes of rape and mayhem." The reviewer praises Koontz's portrait of Frye but finds the mystery too easy to solve because the author gives too many clues. *Library Journal* contributor Rex E. Klett sees Koontz edging "dangerously close to a ruinous occultism" with *Whispers,* but also finds the novel a smooth read. Denis Pitts, reviewing the novel in *Punch,* calls *Whispers* a "superior crime read." Pitts advises: "*Whispers* is not a book to be read by women of a nervous disposition living alone in a country house. Or men, come to think of it."

Strangers, published in 1986, is the story of a group of people connected only by a weekend each spent at a motel in Nevada two years prior—a weekend none of them remember. The characters begin to experience nightmares, unusual, intense fears, and even supernormal powers, driving each toward uncovering the mystery and conspiracy that joins them all. Deborah Kirk in the *New York Times Book Review* finds some of the characters unconvincing but concludes that *Strangers* is "an engaging, often chilling, book." *Library Journal's* Eric W. Johnson calls the novel an "almost unbearably suspenseful page-turner." A *Booklist* reviewer deems Koontz a "true master," and finds *Strangers* "a rich brew of gothic horror and science fiction, filled with delectable turns of the imagination."

Koontz considers *Whispers* and *Strangers* among his best work. He told *CA*: "*Strangers* . . . and *Whispers* are the exemplars to which I will refer while working on future novels. Both of these books rely heavily on character and background for their impact. Without doubt, both novels have strong, suspenseful plots, as well, and I intend that all of my future novels will be what are called 'page turners'; however, the older I get the more I find that well-drawn characters and vivid backgrounds are just as important as plot to the success of a book."

Koontz's *Dark Rivers of the Heart,* published in 1994, is a suspense thriller and political parable revolving around Spencer Grant, an ex-policeman who "confronts a maniacally fascistic secret government agency, an underground web of computer espionage and his own hideous past," summarizes Curt Suplee in the *Washington Post Book World.* As Edward Bryant notes in *Locus,* Spencer has ample paramilitary and cyberspace navigational skills himself, which "is lucky, since the bad guys are *so* bad and so well-equipped with high-tech surveillance gadgets and weaponry." Spencer becomes involved with Valerie Keene, a waitress and computer hacker, and finds that federal agents are soon pursuing them both. Suplee comments that this familiar ground, in which "boy can't get girl until the nefarious father/ superego figures are adequately purged," is offset by Koontz's narrative, which is replete with "so much novelty and so many odd asides, new characters and screwball subthemes that there's a fresh surprise on virtually every page." Suplee argues that readers may be put off by Koontz's implausible character motivations and "uneconomical" prose style, but concludes that, with regard to "narrative pace and incessant invention, Koontz delivers." Bryant sees *Dark Rivers* as reflecting Koontz's trust in his readers, finding that the narrative "flows better than many of Koontz's other recent novels because the characters spend less time explaining important issues to each other at length," and calls the novel "enormously entertaining."

The prolific Koontz published two works in 1995, *Strange Highways* and *Intensity. Strange Highways* is a collection of short stories, novellas, and two novel-length pieces. A *Publishers Weekly* reviewer argues that a few of the stories in *Strange Highways* are "slight, but none is a failure," and concludes that Koontz's collection is "well crafted and imaginative." Brad Hooper in *Booklist* concurs, commenting that Koontz's "legion of fans won't be let down."

Koontz's bestselling novel *Intensity* is the story of Chyna Shepherd, a psychology student who must combat Edgler Vess, a killer obsessed with intensity of sensation, be it pleasure or pain. Colin Harrison in a *New York Times Book Review* piece on *Intensity* laments that despite Koontz's "gift for gruesome storytelling," the novel's killer is cliche due to overexposure in popular culture. A *Publishers Weekly* reviewer, however, finds *Intensity* "masterful, if ultimately predictable," and lauds Koontz's racing narrative, calling it a contender for the most "viscerally exciting thriller of the year."

Koontz's fictional characters are often pitted against unspeakable evil and amazing odds but nonetheless emerge victorious. Concerning this optimism Koontz told *CA*: "For all its faults, I find the human species—and Western culture—to be primarily noble, honorable, and admirable. In an age when doomsayers are to be heard in every corner of the land, I find great hope in our species and in the future we will surely make for ourselves. I have no patience whatsoever for misanthropic fiction, of which there is too much these days. In fact, that is one reason why I do not wish to have the 'horror novel' label applied to my books even when it is sometimes accurate; too many current horror novels are misanthropic, senselessly bleak, and I do not wish to be lumped with them. I am no pollyanna, by any means, but I think we live in a time of marvels, not a time of disaster, and I believe we can solve every problem that confronts us if we keep our perspective and our freedom. Very little if any great and long-lasting fiction has been misanthropic. I strongly believe that, in addition to entertaining, it is the function of fiction to explore the way we live, reinforce our noble traits, and suggest ways to improve the world where we can."

BIOGRAPHICAL/CRITICAL SOURCES:

BOOKS

Contemporary Literary Criticism, Volume 78, Gale (Detroit), 1994.

Greenberg, Martin H., and others, editors, *Dean Koontz Companion,* Berkley, 1994.

Munster, Bill, editor, *Dean R. Koontz's Cold Terror,* Underwood-Miller (San Francisco), 1990.

Munster, editor, *Sudden Fear: The Horror and Dark Suspense Fiction of Dean R. Koontz,* second edition, Borgo (San Bernardino, CA), 1995.

Twentieth-Century Science-Fiction Writers, St. James Press (Detroit), 1996.

PERIODICALS

Analog, January, 1984.
Armchair Detective, summer, 1995, p. 329.
Booklist, March 1, 1986, p. 914; April 15, 1995, p. 1452.
Chicago Tribune Book World, April 12, 1981.
Library Journal, May 15, 1980, p. 1187; April 15, 1986, p. 95.
Locus, February, 1989, p. 21; March, 1992, p. 62; September, 1994, p. 29; October, 1994, p. 21; December, 1994, p. 58; January, 1995, p. 49; February, 1995, p. 39.
Los Angeles Times, March 12, 1986.
Los Angeles Times Book Review, January 31, 1988; January 21, 1990; November 13, 1994, p. 14; May 21, 1995, p. 10.
New York Times Book Review, January 12, 1975; February 29, 1976; May 22, 1977; September 11, 1977; June 15, 1986, p. 20; November 13, 1994, p. 58; February 25, 1996, p. 9.
Observer (London), February 12, 1995, p. 22.
People, April 13, 1987; April 24, 1989.
Publishers Weekly, April 4, 1980, p. 61; March 7, 1986, p. 82; December 18, 1987; December 19, 1994, p. 52; April 24, 1995, p. 60; November 6, 1995, p. 81.
Punch, July 15, 1981, p. 109.
Rapport, April, 1994, p. 27.
Science Fiction and Fantasy Book Review, October, 1983, pp. 25-26.
Science Fiction Chronicle, March, 1995, p. 39.
Times Literary Supplement, September 11, 1981.
Washington Post Book World, December 11, 1994, p. 8.

* * *

KUNDERA, Milan 1929-

PERSONAL: Born April 1, 1929, in Brno, Czechoslovakia; immigrated to France, 1975, naturalized French citizen, 1981; son of Ludvik (a pianist and musicologist) and Milada (Janosikova) Kundera; married Vera Hrabankova, September 30, 1967. *Education:* Studied music under Paul Haas and Vaclav Kapral; attended Charles University, Prague, and Film Faculty, Academy of Music and Dramatic Arts, Prague, 1956.

CAREER: Writer. Worked as a laborer and jazz pianist in provincial Czechoslovakia; Film Faculty, Academy of Music and Dramatic Arts, Prague, Czechoslovakia, assistant professor, 1958-69; Universite de Rennes II, Rennes, France, invited professor of comparative literature, 1975-79; Ecole des hautes etudes en sciences sociales, Paris, France, professor, 1980—.

MEMBER: Czechoslovak Writers Union (member of central committee, 1963-69), American Academy of Arts and Letters.

AWARDS, HONORS: Klement Lukes Prize, 1963, for *Majitele klicu;* Czechoslovak Writers Union prize, 1968, for *Zert;* Czechoslovak Writers' Publishing House prize, 1969, for *Smesne lasky;* Prix Medicis, 1973, for *La Vie est ailleurs;* Premio Letterario Mondello, 1978, for *The Farewell Party;* Common Wealth Award for distinguished service in literature, 1981, for the body of his novelistic work; Prix Europa for literature, 1982, for the body of his novelistic work; honorary doctorate, University of Michigan, 1983; *Los Angeles Times* Book Prize for fiction, 1984, for *The Unbearable Lightness of Being;* Jerusalem Prize for Literature on the Freedom of Man in Society, 1985; finalist for Ritz Paris Hemingway Award, 1985; Academie Francaise critics prize, 1987; *Independent* Award for foreign fiction, 1991.

WRITINGS:

NOVELS

Zert (also see below), Ceskoslovensky Spisovatel (Czechoslovak Writers Union; Prague), 1967, translation by David Hamblyn and Oliver Stallybrass published as *The Joke,* Coward, 1969, new complete translation by Michael Henry Heim with author's preface, Harper (New York City), 1982, fully revised edition by Kundera, HarperCollilns (New York City), 1992.
Zivot je jinde, Sixty-Eight Publishers (Toronto), 1979, translation from the original Czech manuscript by Francois Kerel first published as *La Vie est ailleurs,* Gallimard (Paris), 1973, translation from the original Czech manuscript by Peter Kussi published as *Life Is Elsewhere,* Knopf (New York City), 1974.
Valcik na rozloucenou, Sixty-Eight Publishers, 1979, translation from the original Czech manuscript by Kussi published as *The Farewell Party,* Knopf, 1976.

Kniha smichu a zapomneni, Sixty-Eight Publishers, 1981, translation from the original Czech manuscript by Kerel first published as *Le Livre du rire et de l'oubli,* Gallimard, 1979, translation from the original Czech manuscript by Heim published as *The Book of Laughter and Forgetting,* Knopf, 1980, published with an interview with the author by Philip Roth, Penguin Books (New York City), 1981.

Nesnesitelna lehkost byti, Sixty-Eight Publishers, 1984, translation from the original Czech manuscript by Heim published as *The Unbearable Lightness of Being,* Harper, 1984.

Nesmrtelnost, 1990, translation from the original Czech manuscript by Kussi published as *Immortality,* Grove Weidenfeld (New York City), 1990, Faber (London), 1991.

Lenteur, 1996, translation from the French by Linda Asher published as *Slowness,* HarperCollins, 1996.

OTHER

Clovek zahrada sira (poetry; title means "Man: A Broad Garden"), Ceskoslovensky Spisovatel, 1953.

Posledni maj (poetry; title means "The Last May"), Ceskoslovensky Spisovatel, 1955, revised edition, 1963.

Monology (poetry; title means "Monologues"), Ceskoslovensky Spisovatel, 1957, revised edition, 1964.

Umeni romanu: cesta Vladislava Vancury za velkou epikou (study of writer Vladislav Vancura; title means "The Art of the Novel"), Ceskoslovensky Spisovatel, 1961.

Majitele klicu (play; title means "The Owners of the Keys"; first produced in Prague at National Theatre, April, 1962), Orbis, 1962.

Smesne lasky: Tri melancholicke anekdoty (short stories; title means "Laughable Loves: Three Melancholy Anecdotes"; also see below), Ceskoslovensky Spisovatel, 1963.

Druhy sesit smesnych lasek (short stories; title means "The Second Book of Laughable Loves"; also see below), Ceskoslovensky Spisovatel, 1965.

Dve usi dve svatby (play), Dilia (Prague), 1968.

Treti sesit smesnych lasek (short stories; title means "The Third Book of Laughable Loves"; also see below), Ceskoslovensky Spisovatel, 1968.

(With Jaromil Jires) *The Joke* (screenplay; based on Kundera's novel *Zert*), directed by Jires, Smida-Fikar—Studio de Cinema de Barrandov, 1968.

Ptakovina (two-act play), first produced in Liberec, Czechoslovakia at Divadlo F. X. Saldy, January, 1968.

Smesne lasky (selection of seven of the short stories previously published in *Smesne lasky: Tri melancholicke anekdoty, Druhy sesit smesnych lasek,* and *Treti sesit smesnych lasek*), Ceskoslovensky Spisovatel, 1970, translation by Suzanne Rappaport with introduction by Roth published as *Laughable Loves,* Knopf, 1974.

Jacques et son maitre: Hommage a Denis Diderot (three-act play; first produced in Paris at Theatre des Maturins, 1981), published with an introduction by the author, Gallimard, 1981, translation by Heim published as *Jacques and His Master* (produced in Cambridge, MA, at American Repertory Theatre, January, 1985), Harper, 1985, translation by Simon Callow produced as *Jacques and His Master* in Toronto at Free Theatre, May 14, 1987.

L'art du roman, 1986, translation from the original French by Linda Asher published as *The Art of the Novel,* Perennial Library (New York City), 1988.

Testaments Betrayed: An Essay in Nine Parts, HarperCollins, 1995.

Kundera's works have also been translated into German, Dutch, Danish, Norwegian, Swedish, Finnish, Portuguese, Spanish, Italian, Serbian, Slovene, Greek, Turkish, Hebrew, and Japanese.

Contributor of essays to *New York Times Book Review.* Member of editorial board of *Literarni noviny,* 1963-67 and 1968, and of *Literarni listy,* 1968-69.

ADAPTATIONS: The Unbearable Lightness of Being was adapted for film by Jean-Claude Carriere and produced by Ingram International Films, 1988.

SIDELIGHTS: Milan Kundera, a Czech novelist now living in France, "is one of the finest and most consistently interesting novelists in Europe and America," writes Richard Locke in the *Washington Post Book World.* Writing from experience, Kundera "has brought Eastern Europe to the attention of the Western reading public, and he has done so with insights that are universal in their appeal," notes Olga Carlisle in the *New York Times Magazine.* His novels, according to David Lodge in the *Times Literary Supplement,* "[investigate], with a bold combination of abstraction, sensuality and wit, the problematic interrelationship of sex, love, death and the ultimate mystery of being itself." "Playfully mixing history with philosophy and fantasy," adds Michiko Kakutani in the *New York Times,* "Mr. Kundera creates a world in which routine expectations are undercut, ideals and reason mocked." Kundera's blending of fact and fiction has earned him international recognition and major awards from France, Italy, Israel, and the United States.

In June 1967, Kundera appeared before the Fourth Czechoslovak Writers Congress to introduce the policy statement of the Writers Union, a document prepared in advance, cleared by the Czechoslovak Communist Party Central Committee, and traditionally approved without significant discussion by the writers. It was a critical time for the Czechoslovak nation. A campaign by some of the writers to speed reform and liberalization of cultural policy together with their criticism of Czechoslovakia's role in the Arab-Israeli conflict had prompted the Party to increase censorship and other repressive tactics. The Union and the Party were heading for a confrontation, and the Congress provided an occasion. Rejecting convention, Kundera opened discussion of the draft statement with "a defence of open criticism and an attack on the repression of it," notes A. French in *Czech Writers and Politics, 1945-1969.* Many who followed spoke freely; immediately following the Congress, the government stepped up repressive measures against the outspoken writers.

By January 1968, however, the reform movement, which had spread into the political arena, emerged into the open. Alexander Dubcek replaced the dictatorial Antonin Novotny as First Secretary of the Party and steps were taken to humanize Czechoslovakia's socialism. Many credited the writers—especially visible were Ludvik Vaculik, Ivan Klima, Kundera, and the Slovak Ladislav Mnacko—with initiating this progress, and as French points out, "political realists at the center of power recognised their influence and the moral authority they had acquired in the eyes of the public."

Kundera had begun writing his first novel, *Zert (The Joke),* in 1962 and had submitted it to a Prague publisher in December 1965. "Though they promised to do their best to bring it out," he writes in the preface to the 1982 edition of *The Joke,* "they never really believed they would succeed. The spirit of the work was diametrically opposed to the official ideology." But Kundera had held firm against the demands of government censors; finally in 1967, the novel was published, unchanged. "Three editions of *The Joke* appeared in quick succession and incredibly

large printings, and each sold out in a matter of days," the author explains. During the enlightened Prague Spring of 1968, a time when Czechoslovakia was rediscovering its cultural freedom and writers were held in high esteem, Milan Kundera was one of the major literary figures of the day.

Within four months, however, Czechoslovakia was invaded by troops from the U.S.S.R., Poland, East Germany, Hungary, and Bulgaria, and the occupation brought the reform movement to an end. During the next few years, Kundera's books were removed from libraries and bookstores, his plays were banned; he lost his job and his right to work and publish in Czechoslovakia. At first, he was also forbidden to travel in the West, but finally in 1975 he was permitted to accept a teaching position in Rennes, France. Four years later, after the publication of *Le Livre du rire et de l'oubli (The Book of Laughter and Forgetting),* the Czechoslovak government revoked his citizenship.

Silenced in Czechoslovakia immediately after the invasion, Kundera became a writer without an audience. He did write two novels that were published in translation abroad, but not until he had settled in France did he feel at home with this new audience. As an artist, Kundera had experimented with music, painting, cinema, and theater, but he found his home in the novel. Today, although he has become one of the West's most respected novelists, in essays and interviews he directs discussion away from himself toward literature; he is an outspoken proponent of the novel. "I often hear it said that the novel has exhausted all its possibilities," he writes in a 1985 essay in the *New York Times Book Review.* "I have the opposite impression: during its 400-year history, the novel has missed many of its possibilities; it has left many great opportunities unexplored, many paths forgotten, calls unheard."

To take advantage of the possibilities offered by the novel, Kundera combines autobiography and fiction, history and fantasy, satire and philosophical discourse. From his reading of Laurence Sterne, Denis Diderot, Franz Kafka, Hermann Broch, and others, the author has formulated his own aesthetic of the novel, an outline of the characteristics that define his work. He offers this outline in a 1982 essay in the *New York Times Book Review:* "The novel [is] an investigation into human existence. . . . A novel makes sense only when it reveals an unknown side to human existence. . . . The novel proclaims no truth, no morality. . . . The novel represents a great intellectual synthesis. . . . The novel is the only form of art capable of moving in time with complete ease."

Structure is another important element in the Kundera novel which is often of interest to reviewers. Some believe that because of their structure, his novels should be placed in other categories—*The Book of Laughter and Forgetting* as a collection of short stories, for instance. Kundera has little regard for labels, but in interviews and essays he rejects any attempts to exclude his work from the roll of novels. "There is enormous freedom latent within the novelistic form," he tells Philip Roth in the *New York Times Book Review.* "It is a mistake to regard a certain stereotyped structure as the inviolable essence of the novel." He adds that in his view of the novel "the unity of a book need not stem from the plot, but can be provided by the theme."

For a number of practitioners of the novel, plot suggests causality, but for Kundera, as he explains in his aesthetic, "the novel is composed like a piece of music, . . . on the principle of a theme and variations, the elaboration of a theme. The unity of a novel comes from several basic words, which gradually take on the force of philosophical categories." In order to elaborate a theme, the author must "master the technique of ellipsis, the art of condensation. Otherwise, [he falls] into the trap of endless length," he explains to Christian Salmon in the *Paris Review.* In this way, following the example of modern composers, juxtaposing variations and emphasizing only the essential, Kundera hopes to renew the novel. He suggests in his interview with Salmon that too often the novel "is encumbered by 'technique,' by rules that do the author's work for him: present a character, describe a milieu, bring the action into its historical setting, fill up the lifetime of the characters with useless episodes. Every change of scene requires new expositions, descriptions, explanations. My purpose is . . . to rid the novel of the automatism of novelistic technique, of novelistic word-spinning."

An additional element of the novel in Kundera's aesthetic is its form. This varies from author to author, he believes, but each individual author has characteristic forms that recur in his writing. "The architectural blueprint of a work, [form] is something the writer bears within him as an obsession," Kundera writes in the *New York Times Book Review;* "it is an archetype, the irreducible pattern of his personality." Kundera's novels are dominated by a form based on the number seven. Except for *Valcik na rozloucenou* (*The Farewell Party*), each was writ-

ten with seven sections. Even *Smesne lasky* (*Laughable Loves*), originally ten short stories published in Czechoslovakia in three books, became a single book of seven stories. The author tells Salmon that in writing *The Unbearable Lightness of Being* he consciously tried to vary the pattern, but it still emerged in the end. "I am not indulging in some superstitious affectation about magic numbers, nor making a rational calculation. Rather, I am driven by a deep, unconscious, incomprehensible need, a formal archetype from which I cannot escape."

While growing up in Czechoslovakia, Kundera witnessed the dismemberment of a young republic by Nazis in search of *Lebensraum,* or living space. He also witnessed the postwar political purges. Then, in the rise of Communism, he had found the promise of better times; but the promise was broken after the Communist coup of 1948. "I was 19," he writes in the *New York Times Book Review.* "I learned about fanaticism, dogmatism and political trials through bitter experience; I learned what it meant to be intoxicated by power, be repudiated by power, feel guilty in the face of power and revolt against it." Twenty years later, he saw another promise crushed, this time by invading Soviet tanks.

As a writer, Kundera is fascinated by the individual's struggle against power, and this conflict emerges as a central theme of his novels. Power—sterile, serious, focused on the future—dominates his public world and strives to rob the individual of authority, understanding, and history, absorbing him into "the people." Kundera believes that the small world of intimate life is the only refuge available. As he tells Philip Roth in the *Village Voice,* "Intimate life [is] understood as one's personal secret, as something valuable, inviolable, the basis of one's originality." Here, to a small degree, the individual can attempt to exercise his freedom and react against the state. Through eroticism, humor, and memory, Kundera's characters make their stand in the face of power. By setting in opposition eroticism and sterility, humor and seriousness, memory and forgetting, Kundera "discovers" the variations of his central theme.

"Sex, in Kundera, is a means of rebelling against authority," writes J. Hoberman in the *Voice Literary Supplement.* "Often, it's the only means." As Roth points out in *Reading Myself and Others,* "Erotic play and power are the subjects frequently at the center of the stories that Kundera calls, collectively, *Laughable Loves.*" In these stories, some characters use sexual encounters to exercise their personal power; others see them as a measure of self-worth. In "Symposium," for example, "Doctor Havel . . . refuses to go to bed with an importunate nurse because to refuse is an assertion of freedom," relates Gabriele Annan in the *Times Literary Supplement*. In another story, the same character explains to a young admirer of his exploits: "In life, my friend, it is not a question of winning the greatest number of women, because that is too external a success. Rather, it is a question of cultivating one's own demanding taste, because in it is mirrored the extent of one's personal worth."

In a review in the *Nation,* Elizabeth Pochoda discusses the role of sexuality in *Laughable Loves:* "For many of the young men in Kundera's stories love comes primarily in the form of sexual conquest, and promises adventures outside of the life plan, a rare chance to experience the unexpected and to acquire a sense of power." She adds that "the would-be seducers attempt to circumvent the habitual oppression of their daily lives through love because love is voluntary, or so they think." In the end, according to Pochoda, "the characters who push hardest for certainty in love are the most laughable and the most disappointed. They take a holiday from one form of tyranny and unwittingly uncover another, their own."

"Sexuality as a weapon (in this case, the weapon of he who is otherwise wholly assailable) is to the point of *The Joke* as well," explains Roth. "To revenge himself upon the political friend who had turned upon him back in his remote student days, Ludvik Jahn . . . coldly conceives a plan to seduce the man's wife." In *The Farewell Party,* a young girl tries to seduce her guardian "simply so that she can feel, for once, the triumph of her will over circumstance," Elizabeth Pochoda observes in the *Nation.*

Tamina of *The Book of Laughter and Forgetting* submits to Hugo, hoping that in return he will retrieve her precious diaries from Czechoslovakia. And, as Thomas DePietro relates in *Commonweal,* "Like so many of Kundera's Don Juans, Tomas [of *The Unbearable Lightness of Being*] finds in his private, erotic life the freedom and power he so lacks in the public sphere." In the end, however, Kundera's characters fail to achieve their aims. Their stories reveal Kundera's belief that as an escape, a weapon, or a tool, sex creates its own hazards. "Something must always go wrong when sex and love are made to bear the whole burden of personal freedom," suggests Pochoda, the reason being that

"as individuals, [Kundera's characters] operate on too small a scale. Everyone has his plot, but there is always another and larger plot which gathers up and transforms the designs of individuals."

"Few contemporary writers have succeeded as Kundera has in combining a cool, elegant, formal objectivity with warm, intimate (almost embarrassingly intimate) pictures of the imperfect realities of adult love," maintains Edmund White in the *Nation.* But as an artist, Kundera finds in the sexual exchange more than examples of flawed love and failed rebellion. "I have the feeling that a scene of physical love generates an extremely sharp light which suddenly reveals the essence of characters and sums up their life situation," he explains to Roth in the *New York Times Book Review.* He continues, "The erotic scene is the focus where all the themes of the story converge and where its deepest secrets are located."

For Kundera, the seriousness of a world dominated by power fosters self-deception, evident in misunderstanding and extremism among individuals. In such a world, humor becomes an important characteristic. "I learned the value of humor during the time of Stalinist terror," Kundera tells Roth. "I could always recognize a person who was not a Stalinist, a person whom I needn't fear, by the way he smiled. A sense of humor was a trustworthy sign of recognition. Ever since, I have been terrified by a world that is losing its sense of humor." In his fiction, Kundera explores the nature of humor under totalitarian pressure, often focusing on the roles of the joke and laughter.

The dangers of a world lacking a sense of humor are evident in *The Joke.* Having missed an opportunity to cultivate his desire for Marketa because of her choice to attend a Party training session, Ludvik responds to her enthusiastic letters with a spiteful joke, written on a postcard: "Optimism is the opium of the people! A healthy atmosphere stinks of stupidity! Long live Trotsky!" But members of the power structure have no appreciation of jokes. His comrades learn of the card and expel him from the Party and the university. He is banished to work the provincial coal mines. Years later, his revenge, an "erotic power play, is thwarted, and turns into yet another joke at his expense," writes Roth in *Reading Myself and Others.*

The jokes that turn against Ludvik and other Kundera characters often seem cruel. Yet as Josephine Woll points out in the *New Republic,* the backfired joke serves to illuminate the character's self-deception:

"With no illusions left to cover his nakedness, Ludvik comes to an acceptance—of himself, his past, those who wronged him and those whom he wronged. He accepts the possibility of innocence in the midst of devastation, and the need not only to hate that devastation, but to commiserate with the things thus devastated." Antonin J. Liehm adds in *The Politics of Culture:* "We are too grave about our lives; we moan and wring our hands and curse and explain and beg for understanding, and yet most likely what we need, above all, is the courage to laugh at our existence and through laughter to clear the way for understanding. And in this way, we earn the right to laugh at cowards, at those who refuse to understand."

In *The Book of Laughter and Forgetting,* Kundera constructs an inquiry into the meaning of laughter. "People nowadays do not even realize that one and the same external phenomenon embraces two completely contradictory internal attitudes," he writes in this novel. "There are two kinds of laughter, and we lack the words to distinguish them." Kundera explains that the first, the laughter of the devil, is not associated with evil, but rather with the belief that God's world is meaningless; the second, the laughter of angels, is not associated with good, but the belief that in God's world, everything has meaning. "Both kinds of laughter belong among life's pleasures, but when it is carried to extremes it also denotes a dual apocalypse," he observes in the *New York Times Book Review* interview. In the extreme, the devil's laughter is absolute skepticism; the angel's laughter is fanaticism.

Kundera's writings illustrate how in a totalitarian state both fanaticism and skepticism can promote self-deception. "In fact," writes Peter Kussi in *World Literature Today,* "self-deception is such a striking element in Kundera's stories and novels that his protagonists could really be divided into two moral types: those who are satisfied to remain self-deluded and those struggling for a measure of self-awareness." The author believes that the happily self-deluded, who he associates with the laughter of angels, and with immaturity and lyricism, have been the dominant group in recent Czech history and culture. In his second novel, *Zivot je jinde* (*Life Is Elsewhere*), Kundera focuses on this. "The novel is a sly and merciless lampoon of revolutionary romanticism," observes a *Time* reviewer, "and it deals with lyric poetry as a species of adolescent neurosis." The author tells Liehm that the lyrical age "is the period of youth when a person is a mystery to himself and

therefore exhausts himself in endless self-contemplation. Other people are merely mirrors in which he searches for his own significance and worth." Jaromil, the young poet of *Life Is Elsewhere,* is of this age. Notes the *Time* reviewer: "He tries to spy on the maid as she takes her bath, and fails, but produces a vivid poem about his 'aquatic love.' The genius of lyric poetry, Kundera observes, 'is the genius of inexperience.'" Eventually, as Neal Ascherson points out in the *New York Review of Books,* Jaromil dies an "absurd death (from a chill caught deliberately on a balcony, after he has been insulted at a party)."

In *The Book of Laughter and Forgetting,* Kundera presents the image of poet Paul Eluard dancing in a circle lifted aloft by a girl laughing the laughter of angels. In 1950, Eluard was called upon by Dada-founding poet Andre Breton to help save their mutual friend Zavis Kalandra from hanging. (Kalandra, a Prague surrealist, had been accused by the Stalinists of betraying the people.) "But Eluard was too busy dancing in the gigantic ring encircling Paris, Moscow, Warsaw, Prague, Sofia, and Athens, encircling all the socialist countries and all the Communist parties of the world; too busy reciting his beautiful poems about joy and brotherhood," Kundera writes in his novel. As a poet himself during this period, Kundera tells Liehm, "I got a close look at poets who adorned things that weren't worth it, and am still able to remember vividly this state of passionate lyrical enthusiasm which, getting drunk on its frenzy, is unable to see the real world through its own grandiose haze." In Czechoslovakia, where poetry is the preferred literary form, he adds, "on the other side of the wall behind which people were jailed and tormented, Gullibility, Ignorance, Childishness, and Enthusiasm blithely promenaded in the sun." "Milan Kundera," notes Ascherson, "who made his own transition from poetry to novel-writing, is one of the deadliest exponents of the argument that [there] have been too many poets, too few novelists: too much romantic narcissism and too little sober illustration of what is within the capacity of the human animal and what is not."

"The struggle of man against power is the struggle of memory against forgetting." Kundera declares through Mirek, one of his characters in *The Book of Laughter and Forgetting.* In the *New York Times Book Review* interview, he elaborates: "[Forgetting] is the great private problem of man: death as the loss of the self. . . . [The self] is the sum of everything we remember. Thus, what terrifies us about death is not the loss of the future but the loss of the past. Forgetting is a form of death ever present within life." The loss of the past can make learning impossible and present actions meaningless. After completing the act that he hoped would bring him revenge, Ludvik of *The Joke* relates: "I contemplated how I too (at this very moment) was caught up in that vast and inevitable forgetting. . . . A wave of depression came over me, not so much because the day had been futile as because not even its futility would remain; it would be forgotten. . . . And the society itself would be forgotten and all the errors and injustices that obsessed me, consumed me, that I'd vainly attempted to fix, right, rectify."

For Kundera, memory is a means of self-preservation, but one with its own burdens. "Mirek . . . ultimately does himself in by trying to destroy memories that are embarrassing to his present self-esteem," observes Charles Michener in *Newsweek*. Those not buoyed up by blissful forgetting often drown in tragedy. "Ludvik's boyhood friend Jaroslav [is] a simple man who is capable of remembering and who suffers in his inability to forget," notes Hana Demetz in the *Washington Post Book World*. Tamina, the central character of *The Book of Laughter and Forgetting*, hopes that recovering the diaries she left in Czechoslovakia will enable her to revive the fading memory of her dead husband and the love they shared. Hers is a "personal struggle . . . to remember details that give life emotional continuity," John Updike indicates in the *New York Times Book Review*. Unable to give in to forgetting, Tamina is destroyed by the offspring of totalitarian power, Kundera's "nation of children." In *The Unbearable Lightness of Being*, "this sense of the past, of continuity—heaviness—is seen as a positive foil to the fleeting sensations and frivolity—lightness—which form contemporary existence," observes Christopher Hawtree in the *Spectator*. Even so, like Tamina, Tereza in *The Unbearable Lightness of Being* is burdened by her sense of the past and is often victimized by the lightness of others.

Charles Michener calls *The Book of Laughter and Forgetting* "an impassioned plea for the struggle of memory against the obliterating forces of modern life [and] an eloquent act of personal memory by a Czech writer living abroad who is forbidden to publish in his own country." In each of his novels, Kundera, aware of the terrible loss associated with forgetting, attempts to retain the past, especially his own. "He writes variations on that past," observes Joseph McLellan in the *Washington Post*, "but his purpose is not to alter or destroy it; rather, through these variations, he seeks to understand it, to penetrate its reality to the microscopic level, and to share with the rest of us what he has found."

Kundera's experience within the world of publishing, both in the East and West, has on occasion resembled the jokes turned against his characters. *The Joke* itself emerged from the Czechoslovak state censor unchanged. It rapidly became a bestseller until it was banned after the Soviet invasion. Louis Aragon hailed the French edition among the twentieth century's greatest novels. The publishers of the first English edition then issued the work in a greatly altered form. "Individual chapters have been shortened, rewritten, simplified, some of them omitted," Kundera protested in a letter to the *Times Literary Supplement*. Comparing these changes to those made to one of his plays before it was staged in the Soviet Union, he added, "the mentality of a London bookseller and that of a Moscow official responsible for art seem to have a mysterious kinship. The depth of their contempt for art is equally unfathomable."

In his preface to the novel's 1982 edition, Kundera proposes that "the ideologues in Prague took *The Joke* for a pamphlet against socialism and banned it; the foreign publisher took it for a political fantasy that became reality for a few weeks and rewrote it accordingly." Both turned *The Joke* into a joke at Kundera's expense. The "ideological dictatorship" of the East combined with the "journalistic oversimplification" of the West "to prevent a work of art from telling its own truth in its own words," he contends.

A critical debate to determine Kundera's significance has accompanied each of his books published in the West. Some reviewers emphasize the political nature of his work; others focus on the universal quality of his art. Viewed together, these critical variations suggest the complexity of Kundera's work. *National Review* contributor D. Keith Mano observes in his discussion of *The Joke*: "Eastern European novels are often exploited for their convenient psywar impact. And, of course, Czech or Russian art can never be wholly neutral or without accent. To some degree it *must* sound dissident." But he adds that Kundera's novel "sets out to transcend this inherent dissidence. For that reason it is a brilliant, an exquisite, and a very problematical book."

Woll praises the author's insight into the interplay between the individual and the difficult social situation in which he finds himself. "Kundera's brilliance resides in his ability to strip away the lies and disguises which Ludvik and the others need to survive, and which their society has institutionalized and sanctified," she writes. But Vivian Gornick, writing in the *Village Voice,* is critical of Kundera's technique. She maintains that "with all his great gifts for imaginative writing [the author] has essentially forsworn the novelist's obligation to make people out of his characters. He is content to let his characters serve as cartoon figures in a landscape of indictment that lacks sufficient dimension to declare itself a portrait of the human condition." In the judgment of *Saturday Review* contributor Vasa D. Mihailovich, however, what Kundera does is probe "his characters' minds by constantly shifting the focus and by letting them tell of their own thoughts and feelings in a confessional style."

In Mihailovich's view, Kundera employs his novelistic skills to illuminate a political issue. "The author's fine instinct for the right detail, his knack for wry humor, biting satire, and even grotesque, and his subtle philosophizing underscore the tragedy of the Czech people." And as Michael Berman suggests, this tragedy has implications beyond its immediate context. He concludes in his *New York Times Book Review* article that *The Joke* does reveal "a great deal about the background to liberalization in Czechoslovakia, and—more important—it offers a genuinely humane look at inhumanity. [It] is a work of sharp psychological perception and great literary finesse."

With the publication of *The Book of Laughter and Forgetting* five years after Kundera's flight to France, some critics began to view his work in the context of exile literature. In Elaine Kendall's estimation, "*The Book of Laughter and Forgetting* is a model of the exile's novel: bittersweet and sardonic but somehow neither corrosive nor sentimental." She adds in her *Los Angeles Times* review that "Kundera deals in the gradual erosions of totalitarianism: the petty indignities, the constant discomforts and the everyday disillusions."

The book "calls itself a novel," writes John Leonard in the *New York Times,* "although it is part fairy tale, part literary criticism, part political tract, part musicology and part autobiography. It can call itself whatever it wants to, because the whole is genius." Norman Podhoretz relates his response to the book in an open letter to Kundera printed in *Commentary:* "What compelled me most when I first opened [it]

was not its form or its aesthetic character but its *intellectual* force, the astonishing intelligence controlling and suffusing every line." *New York Review of Books* contributor Robert M. Adams spotlights Kundera's control when he notes, "Again and again, in this artfully artless book an act or gesture turns imperceptibly into its exact opposite—a circle of unity into a circle of exclusion, playful children into cruel monsters, a funeral into a farce, freedom into lockstep, nudity into a disguise, laughter into sadism, poetry into political machinery, artificial innocence into cynical exploitation. These subtle transformations and unemphasized points of distant correspondence are the special privileges of a meticulously crafted fiction." Concludes Adams, "That a book which combines so delicately dry wit and a deep sense of humanity should cause the author to be deprived of his citizenship is one more of the acute ironies of our time."

The Unbearable Lightness of Being focuses on the connected lives of two couples—Tomas and Tereza, and Franz and Sabina. Set in Czechoslovakia around the time of the Russian invasion, this work is often considered an examination of the hardships and limitations that can result from commitment and the meaninglessness of life without such responsibility.

In his review of *The Unbearable Lightness of Being* in the *Times Literary Supplement,* David Lodge describes the relationship between the intimate concerns of the individual and the larger concerns of politics in Kundera's world: "Although the characters' lives are shaped by political events, they are not determined by them. Tereza and Tomas return to Czechoslovakia for emotional, not ideological reasons. He refuses to retract his article not as a courageous act of political defiance, but more out of bloody-mindedness and complicated feelings about his son, who is involved in the dissident movement." As Richard Eder observes in the *Los Angeles Times,* "For the most part, *The Unbearable Lightness* succeeds remarkably in joining a series of provocative and troubling speculations about human existence to characters that charm and move us." He adds, "Kundera leads us captivatingly into the bleakness of our days." Thomas DePietro offers a similar view: "For all its burning compassion, extraordinary intelligence, and dazzling artistry, [this novel] leaves us with many questions, questions about love and death, about love and transcendence. These are our burdens, the existential questions that never change but need to be asked anew." "Often witty, sometimes terrifying and always profound, Kundera brings genuine wisdom to his novels at a time when many of his fellow practitioners of the craft aspire only to cleverness," concludes Ian Pearson in *Maclean's*.

Published in English in 1988, *The Art of the Novel* contains three essays, two interviews, Kundera's acceptance speech for the Jerusalem prize, and the definitions of sixty-three words Kundera believes are frequently mistranslated. In the essays Kundera traces the development of the European novel. Although most critics praise Kundera's belief that the novel is a "sequence of discoveries," they also accuse him of being arrogant and ethnocentric for his failure to consider any works by non-European or women writers. Terrence Rafferty, in *The New Yorker*, notes that "Kundera's polemical fervor in *The Art of the Novel* annoys us, as American readers, because we feel defensive, excluded from the transcendent 'idea of the novel' that for him seems simply to have been there for the taking." Kundera states in the work, "Need I stress that I intend no theoretical statement at all, and that the entire book is simply a *practitioner's confession*? Every novelist's work contains an implicit vision of the history of the novel, an idea of what the novel is: I have tried to express here the idea of the novel that is inherent in my own novels." Kundera continues his exploration of the novel in his *Testaments Betrayed: An Essay in Nine Parts,* which traces the evolution of the novel from Francois Rabelais to Franz Kafka and relates literature to music.

Kundera's novel *Immortality* is his first to be set in France. In this work, Kundera examines how media manipulation, popular culture, and capitalist technocracy have developed into instruments of propaganda that distort mankind's perception of reality. In addition to discussing the love triangles between Agnes, her husband Paul, and Anges's sister, Laura, *Immortality* contains episodes from the lives of such literary figures as Johann Wolfgang von Goethe and Ernest Hemingway. While Kundera has consistently won praise for juxtaposing fictitious and biographical elements and simultaneously exploring recurring themes, some critics faulted *Immortality* for its disjointed plot and episodic characterizations. Jonathan Yardley, writing in the *Washington Post Book World,* notes that while "*Immortality* is ingenious, witty, provocative, and formidably intelligent," it, unlike the best of Kundera's earlier novels, "is all talk and no story." D. M. Thomas, however, writes in *The New York Times Book Review*, "*Immortality* is certainly a daunting novel: almost devoid of the good-natured or ill-tempered bustle of ordinary humanity . . . and yet the novel fascinates."

Kundera's 1996 novel, *Slowness,* ostensibly concerns "the failure of our speed-obsessed age to appreciate the delights of slowness (in lovemaking, in travel, in the rituals of daily life)," comments Kakutani in the *New York Times*. But, she continues, *Slowness* "is really concerned with the storytelling process itself, with the means by which the facts of real life are turned into fiction, the means by which people sell one version of themselves to the world, to friends, to lovers and to political rivals." Like other Kundera novels, *Slowness* does not employ a traditional narrative structure, juxtaposing different stories and characters connected by a central theme. Fredric Koeppel in the *Detroit News* comments: " . . . Kundera carries his tangled tales off with wisdom, sweetness and wit that permeate each word and sentence." Kakutani claims that, in Kundera's earlier works, humor and sex were "wonderfully anarchic," but in *Slowness,* his "humor has turned sour: it's no longer a gesture of liberation; it's become a symptom of weariness and cynicism." Koeppel disagrees, arguing that "Kundera handles his material with a lightness which, far from being unbearable, sparkles with the deftness of a magician shuffling cards for our delectation and mystification."

Since losing his Czech home, audience, and citizenship, Kundera has found each in France. He tells Roth in the *Village Voice* that "the years in France have been the best years of my life." Moreover, as Edmund White comments in the *Nation,* "Kundera—despite his irony, his abiding suspicion of any cant, any uniformity of opinion and especially of kitsch—is currently the favored spokesman for the uneasy conscience of the French intellectual." But Kundera understands the laughable nature of fame. He says in the *Village Voice* interview: "When I was a little boy in short pants I dreamed about a miraculous ointment that would make me invisible. Then I became an adult, began to write, and wanted to be successful. Now I'm successful and would like to have the ointment that would make me invisible."

BIOGRAPHICAL/CRITICAL SOURCES:

BOOKS

Aji, Aron, editor, *Milan Kundera and the Art of Fiction: Critical Essays,* Garland Publishing (New York City), 1992.

Banerjee, Maria Nemcove, *Terminal Paradox: The Novels of Milan Kundera,* Grove, 1990.

Contemporary Literary Criticism, Gale (Detroit), Volume 4, 1975, Volume 9, 1978, Volume 19, 1981, Volume 32, 1985, Volume 68, 1991.

Dolezel, Lubomir, *Narrative Modes in Czech Literature,* University of Toronto Press, 1973.

French, A., *Czech Writers and Politics, 1945-1969,* East European Monographs, 1982.

Goetz-Stankiewicz, Marketa, *The Silenced Theatre: Czech Playwrights without a Stage,* University of Toronto Press, 1979.

Kundera, Milan, *Laughable Loves,* translation by Suzanne Rappaport with introduction by Philip Roth, Knopf, 1974.

Kundera, *The Book of Laughter and Forgetting,* translation by Michael Henry Heim published with an interview with the author by Philip Roth, Penguin Books, 1981.

Kundera, *The Joke,* translation by Heim with author's preface, Harper, 1982.

Liehm, Antonin J., *The Politics of Culture,* translation from the Czech by Peter Kussi, Grove, 1972.

Misurella, Fred, *Understanding Milan Kundera: Public Events, Private Affairs,* University of South Carolina Press (Columbia), 1993.

O'Brien, John, *Milan Kundera and Feminism: Dangerous Intersections,* St. Martin's (New York City), 1995.

Porter, Robert, *Milan Kundera: A Voice from Central Europe,* Arkona (Denmark), 1981.

Roth, Philip, *Reading Myself and Others,* Farrar, Straus (New York City), 1975.

Trensky, Paul I., *Czech Drama since World War II,* M. E. Sharpe, 1978.

Zeman, Z. A. B., *Prague Spring,* Hill & Wang (New York City), 1969.

PERIODICALS

Commentary, December, 1980; October, 1984.

Commonweal, May 18, 1984; June 2, 1989, pp. 339-41.

Contemporary Literature, fall, 1990, pp. 281-99.

Critical Quarterly, spring/summer, 1984.

Detroit News, July 20, 1996, p. D30.

Dissent, winter, 1983.

Globe and Mail (Toronto), April 28, 1984.

Hudson Review, winter, 1995, p. 616.

London Review of Books, December 4, 1986, pp. 10, 12; June 13, 1991, pp. 13-14.

Los Angeles Times, January 5, 1981; May 2, 1984.

Maclean's, May 14, 1984.

Nation, August 28, 1967; November 6, 1967; August 26, 1968; September 18, 1976; October 2, 1976; May 12, 1984; June 10, 1991, pp. 770-75.

National Review, March 20, 1981; January 21, 1983.

New Criterion, January, 1986, pp. 5-13.

New Republic, May 18, 1968; September 6, 1975; February 14, 1983; July 29, 1991, pp. 36-9.

Newsweek, July 29, 1974; November 24, 1980; November 8, 1982; April 30, 1984; February 4, 1985.

New York Review of Books, May 21, 1970; August 8, 1974; September 16, 1976, February 5, 1981; May 10, 1984.

New York Times, November 6, 1980; January 18, 1982; April 2, 1984; December 17, 1992, p. C18; September 21, 1995; May 14, 1996, p. B2.

New York Times Book Review, January 11, 1970; July 28, 1974; September 5, 1976; November 30, 1980; October 24, 1982; April 29, 1984; January 6, 1985; April 28, 1991, p. 7.

New York Times Magazine, May 19, 1985.

New Yorker, May 16, 1988, pp. 110, 113-18.

Paris Review, summer, 1984.

Partisan Review, Volume LI, 1985; Volume LII, 1985.

Publishers Weekly, July 24, 1995, p. 54.

Review of Contemporary Fiction, summer, 1989, pp. 7-11.

San Francisco Review, spring, 1991, pp. 6, 12.

Saturday Review, December 20, 1969.

Spectator, June 10, 1978; February 13, 1982; June 23, 1984; November 22, 1986, pp. 38-9.

Time, August 5, 1974.

Times (London), February 17, 1983; May 24, 1984.

Times Literary Supplement, October 30, 1969; March 3, 1978; July 21, 1978; February 5, 1982; May 25, 1984; January 16, 1987, p. 55; May 17, 1991, p. 17.

Village Voice, December 24, 1980; November 23, 1982; June 26, 1984; March 29, 1988, p. 70.

Voice Literary Supplement, November, 1983.

Washington Post, November 22, 1980.

Washington Post Book World, December 19, 1982; April 22, 1984; May 5, 1991, p. 3.

World Literature Today, spring, 1983.*

L

LaCAPRA, Dominick 1939-

PERSONAL: Born July 13, 1939, in New York, NY; son of Joseph and Mildred (Sciascia) LaCapra; married Anne-Marie Hlasny, 1965 (divorced, 1970); children: Veronique. *Education:* Cornell University, B.A., 1961; Harvard University, Ph.D., 1970.

ADDRESSES: Home—119 Terrace Place, Ithaca, NY 14850. *Office*—Department of History, Cornell University, Ithaca, NY 14853.

CAREER: Cornell University, Ithaca, NY, assistant professor, 1969-74, associate professor, 1974-79, professor of history, 1979—, Goldwin Smith Professor of European Intellectual History, 1985-92, Bryce and Edith M. Bowmar Professor of Humanistic Studies, 1992—.

MEMBER: International Association of Philosophy and Literature, American Historical Association, Modern Language Association.

AWARDS, HONORS: Fulbright fellow, 1961; Woodrow Wilson fellow, 1962; Harvard University fellow, 1963, 1964; Foreign Area Studies fellow, 1965, 1966; National Endowment for the Humanities senior fellow, 1976; Cornell Society for the Humanities senior fellow, 1979.

WRITINGS:

Emile Durkheim: Sociologist and Philosopher, Cornell University Press (Ithaca, NY), 1972.
A Preface to Sartre, Cornell University Press, 1978.

(Editor with Steven L. Kaplan) *Modern European Intellectual History: Reappraisals and New Perspectives,* Cornell University Press, 1982.
"Madame Bovary" on Trial, Cornell University Press, 1982.
Rethinking Intellectual History: Texts, Contexts, Language, Cornell University Press, 1983.
History and Criticism, Cornell University Press, 1985.
History, Politics, and the Novel, Cornell University Press, 1987.
Soundings in Critical Theory, Cornell University Press, 1989.
(Editor) *The Bounds of Race,* Cornell University Press, 1991.
Representing the Holocaust: History, Theory, Trauma, Cornell University Press, 1994.

Contributor to journals, including *American Historical Review, Journal of Modern History, Diacritics, Philosophical Review,* and *Modern Language Notes.*

WORK IN PROGRESS: "Studies of the relationships among history, reading, memory, and psychoanalysis. I am also working on the Southwest as the site of ethnographic encounter between Euro-Americans and Native Americans."

SIDELIGHTS: Dominick LaCapra's *Emile Durkheim: Sociologist and Philosopher* is a "serious, intelligent, and important study" concerning one of sociology's foremost pioneers, comments Philip Rosenberg in the *New York Times Book Review.* Durkheim, whose works *Suicide* and *The Elementary Forms of the Religious Life* helped define and explain the behavior of nineteenth-century humanity, is represented in LaCapra's work as both an innovator within the budding field of sociology, and as a perceptive analyst of his own society. Rosenberg asserts that "Durkheim, as LaCapra interprets him, emerges as a social critic who recognized that it is not merely the case that our social system is subject to pathological distortions; rather, the system itself is, for its members, pathogenic." LaCapra traces Durkheim's contention that the disorder within society has reached crisis proportions, but faults the sociologist for his refusal to acknowledge Karl Marx's observations on social conflict; nevertheless, the author contends that Durkheim's work has provided the foundation for modern-day sociology.

"For almost a decade, Dominick LaCapra has been urging intellectual historians to pay closer attention to developments in literary criticism and philosophy in order to 'acquire the conceptual means to come to terms with problems in their own field,'" summarizes John E. Toews in the *American Historical Review.* LaCapra believes that fields such as intellectual and social history need to become less technical and more concerned with the relation between the present and the past; he is "among the few historians currently prepared to rethink the assumptions underlying the craft," states Peter Burke in the *Times Literary Supplement.* In his review of *History and Criticism, Times Literary Supplement* contributor Hayden White observes that LaCapra "openly defines his purpose as an attempt to 'revive a Renaissance ideal of historiography'" which utilizes interpretative techniques from disciplines such as literary criticism and philosophy. The author wants to depart from "the ideal of the historian as writer of 'realistic' narrative prose whose sole concern is to tell the true story of what really happened in the past," states White. Instead, LaCapra "implies that, if there is a literary dimension to historical discourse, it might well be expressed in the writing of historical narratives in the manner of modernist or even post-modernist novels, as well as in that of the nineteenth century 'realists.'" Toews similarly notes that "LaCapra perceives the intellectual historian's vocation of historical scholar to be a crucial element in the more general vocation as cultural critic." As the author once described his work to *CA,* "My primary objective has been to reconceptualize the way intellectual history is written, in part by employing approaches developed in recent literary criticism and philosophy. My focus has been upon complex texts and the various contexts that inform them."

Recently LaCapra has turned to the relationship between psychoanalysis and history, especially in its bearing on such problems as fascism and Nazism. Of his *Representing the Holocaust: History, Theory, Trauma,* Toews writes in the *American Historical Review* that "LaCapra has succeeded in organizing his criticism around a specific historiographical issue that has wide-ranging ethical, philosophical, political, and cultural resonance" and that this book "establishes his position as the most sensitive, trenchant professional gadfly and historiographical critic of his generation."

BIOGRAPHICAL/CRITICAL SOURCES:

PERIODICALS

American Historical Review, February, 1983; October, 1987; June, 1995.
Contemporary Review, June, 1979.
iichiko intercultural, June, 1994, pp. 109-26.
Los Angeles Times Book Review, February 18, 1979.
New York Times Book Review, July 15, 1973.
Times Literary Supplement, July 28, 1972; December 14, 1979; July 8, 1983; January 31, 1986; November 6, 1987; February 12; 1988.

* * *

LAFAYETTE, Rene
    See HUBBARD, L(afayette) Ron(ald)

* * *

LAMIS, Alexander P.   1946-

PERSONAL: Born May 10, 1946, in Charleston, SC; son of Pano A. (a hat cleaner) and Olympia Lynn (a secretary; maiden name, Moses) Lamis; married Karen Aldridge (a librarian), December 28, 1968. *Education:* College of Charleston, B.A., 1968; Vanderbilt University, M.A., 1975, Ph.D., 1982; University of Maryland, Baltimore, J.D., 1984. *Politics:* Democrat. *Religion:* Greek Orthodox. *Avocational interests:* Travel (Europe, West Africa, Mexico, Central America).

ADDRESSES: Office—Department of Political Science, Case Western Reserve University, Cleveland, OH 44106.

CAREER: WCSC-TV, Charleston, SC, evening news reporter, 1966-67; *Arizona Daily Star,* Tucson, reporter, 1971-72; *Columbia Record,* Columbia, SC, reporter, 1972; *Tennessean,* Nashville, TN, part-time copy editor, 1974-75; *Bergen Record,* Hackensack, NJ, assistant news editor, 1976; *Baltimore Sun,* Baltimore, MD, copy editor, 1976-81; Towson State University, Baltimore, instructor in political science, 1978-80; Brookings Institution, Washington, DC, research assistant, 1981; University of Mississippi, Oxford, assistant professor of political science, 1981-85; University of North Florida, Jacksonville, associate professor of political science, 1985-88; Case Western Reserve University, Cleveland, OH, associate professor of political science, 1988—. *Military service:* U.S. Navy, supply officer, 1968-71; served in Iceland; became lieutenant junior grade.

MEMBER: American Political Science Association, Southern Political Science Association.

AWARDS, HONORS: Co-recipient of V. O. Key Book Award from Southern Political Science Association, 1985, for *The Two-Party South.*

WRITINGS:

The Two-Party South, Oxford University Press (New York City), 1984, new edition, 1990.
(Editor with Mary Anne Sharkey) *Ohio Politics,* Kent State University Press (Kent, OH), 1994.

Contributor to *Encyclopedia of Southern Culture.* Contributor to political science and history journals.

WORK IN PROGRESS: Research on U.S. electoral change since 1964; editing a book, *Southern Politics in the 1990s.*

SIDELIGHTS: Alexander P. Lamis told *CA:* "My interest in southern politics began in the 1960s, when as a television news reporter in Charleston, South Carolina, I observed in action many of the South's leading political figures of the day. Some of these leaders who left vivid impressions on me were George Wallace, Martin Luther King, Jr., and Strom Thurmond. After entering graduate school at Vanderbilt University, I encountered the analytical tools and instruction I needed to make sense of what I had been witnessing in the politics of my native region."

Samuel C. Patterson in *Perspective* describes *The Two-Party South* as a "gracefully written and co-

gently argued book" and "a readable and timely account of the southern politics of the present day." The book begins with a history of southern politics, emphasizing the movement away from a traditionally solid, Democratic South. Lamis then offers an analysis of the politics of each southern state, focusing on the period that followed the waning of the civil rights movement of the 1960s. These analyses reveal the author's view that the Republican party has established itself in each southern state, providing, as Patterson explains, "an opportunity for fully seated partisan realignment in the South, but only if the Republican party capitalizes on its opportunity." David D. Lee explains in the *American Historical Review* that Lamis writes "in an engaging manner that blends colorful quotations and quantitative analysis," adding, what is "particularly appealing is his final chapter that draws on survey research to provide some generalizations about the current status of southern politics."

BIOGRAPHICAL/CRITICAL SOURCES:

PERIODICALS

American Historical Review, October, 1985.
Choice, May, 1995.
Journal of Politics, volume 48, 1986.
Journal of Southern History, November, 1985.
Perspective, November-December, 1984.
Times Literary Supplement, August 30, 1985.

*   *   *

LEE, William
See BURROUGHS, William S(eward)

*   *   *

LEE, Willy
See BURROUGHS, William S(eward)

*   *   *

Le GUIN, Ursula K(roeber) 1929-

PERSONAL: Surname pronounced "luh-gwin"; born October 21, 1929, in Berkeley, CA; daughter of

Alfred L. (an anthropologist) and Theodora Covel Brown (a writer; maiden name, Kracaw) Kroeber; married Charles Alfred Le Guin (a historian), December 22, 1953; children: Elisabeth, Caroline, Theodore. *Education:* Radcliffe College, A.B., 1951; Columbia University, A.M., 1952.

ADDRESSES: Home—Portland, OR. *Agent*—Virginia Kidd, 538 East Harford St., Milford, PA 18337; and Ilse Lahn, Paul Kohner Inc., 9169 Sunset Blvd., Los Angeles, CA 90069.

CAREER: Writer. Part-time instructor in French at Mercer University, 1954-55, and University of Idaho, 1956; Emory University, department secretary, 1955; visiting lecturer and writer in residence at various locations, including Pacific University, Portland State University, University of California, San Diego, University of Reading, Kenyon College, Tulane University, and First Australian Workshop in Speculative Fiction; guest of honor at science fiction conventions, including World Science Fiction Convention, 1975. Creative consultant for Public Broadcasting Service for television production of *The Lathe of Heaven,* 1979.

MEMBER: Authors League of America, Writers Guild, PEN, Science Fiction Research Association, Science Fiction and Fantasy Writers of America, Science Fiction Poetry Association, Writers Guild West, Amnesty International of the USA, National Abortion Rights Action League, National Organization for Women, Nature Conservancy, Planned Parenthood Federation of America, Women's International League for Peace and Freedom, Phi Beta Kappa.

AWARDS, HONORS: Fulbright fellowship, 1953; *Boston Globe-Horn Book* Award, 1968, Lewis Carroll Shelf Award, 1979, *Horn Book* honor list citation, and American Library Association Notable Book citation, all for *A Wizard of Earthsea;* Nebula Award nomination for best novelette, Science Fiction Writers of America (now Science Fiction and Fantasy Writers of America), 1969, for "Nine Lives"; Nebula Award and Hugo Award, International Science Fiction Association, both for best novel, 1970, for *The Left Hand of Darkness;* Nebula Award nomination, 1971, and Hugo Award nomination and *Locus* Award, both 1973, all for best novel, for *The Lathe of Heaven;* Newbery Silver Medal Award and finalist for National Book Award for Children's Literature, both 1972, and American Library Association Notable Book citation, all for *The Tombs of*

Atuan; Child Study Association of America's Children's Books of the Year citation, 1972, and National Book Award for Children's Books, 1973, both for *The Farthest Shore;* Nebula Award nomination, 1972, and Hugo Award, 1973, both for best novella, for *The Word for World Is Forest;* Hugo Award for best short story, 1974, for "The Ones Who Walk Away from Omelas"; American Library Association's Best Young Adult Books citation, 1974, Hugo Award, Nebula Award, and Jupiter Award, all for best novel, 1975, and Jules Verne Award, 1975, all for *The Dispossessed: An Ambiguous Utopia;* Nebula Award and Jupiter Award, both for best short story, 1975, for "The Day before the Revolution"; Nebula Award nomination for best novelette, 1975, for "The New Atlantis"; Nebula Award nomination for best novelette and Jupiter Award, both 1976, for "The Diary of the Rose"; National Book Award finalist, American Library Association's Best Young Adult Books citation, Child Study Association of America's Children's Books of the Year citation, and *Horn Book* honor list citation, all 1976, and Prix Lectures-Jeunesse, 1987, all for *Very Far Away from Anywhere Else;* Gandalf Award (Grand Master of Fantasy) nomination, 1978; D.Litt., Bucknell University, 1978, and Lawrence University, 1979; Gandalf Award, 1979; Balrog Award nomination for best poet, 1979; Nebula Award nomination for best novelette, 1979, for "The Pathways of Desire"; D.H.L., Lewis and Clark College, 1983, and Occidental College, 1985; *Locus* Award, 1984, for *The Compass Rose;* American Book Award nomination, 1985, and Janet Heidinger Kafka Prize for Fiction, University of Rochester English Department and Writer's Workshop, 1986, both for *Always Coming Home;* Nebula Award nominations for best novelette, 1987, for *Buffalo Gals, Won't You Come Out Tonight,* and 1990, for "The Shobies' Story"; Nebula Award for best novel, 1991, for *Tehanu: The Last Book of Earthsea;* Nebula Award nomination for best novelette, 1994, for "The Matter of Seggri"; Nebula Award nomination for best novella, 1994, and Sturgeon Award, both for "Forgiveness Day."

WRITINGS:

NOVELS

Rocannon's World (bound with *The Kar-Chee Reign* by Avram Davidson; also see below), Ace Books (New York City), 1966.
Planet of Exile (bound with *Mankind under the Lease* by Thomas M. Disch; also see below), Ace Books, 1966.

City of Illusions (also see below), Ace Books, 1967.

Three Hainish Novels (contains *Rocannon's World, Planet of Exile,* and *City of Illusions*), Doubleday (New York City), 1967.

A Wizard of Earthsea (also see below), illustrated by Ruth Robbins, Parnassus Press (Berkeley, CA), 1968.

The Left Hand of Darkness, Walker (New York City), 1969, with new afterword and appendixes by author, 1994.

The Tombs of Atuan (sequel to *A Wizard of Earthsea;* also see below), illustrated by Gail Garraty, Atheneum (New York City), 1971.

The Lathe of Heaven, Scribner (New York City), 1971.

The Farthest Shore (sequel to *The Tombs of Atuan;* Junior Literary Guild selection; also see below), illustrated by Garraty, Atheneum, 1972.

The Dispossessed: An Ambiguous Utopia, Harper (New York City), 1974.

Very Far Away from Anywhere Else, Atheneum, 1976, published in England as *A Very Long Way from Anywhere Else,* Gollancz (London), 1976.

Earthsea (contains *A Wizard of Earthsea, The Tombs of Atuan,* and *The Farthest Shore*), Gollancz, 1977, published as *The Earthsea Trilogy,* Penguin (London), 1979.

Malafrena, Putnam (New York City), 1979.

The Beginning Place, Harper, 1980, published in England as *Threshold,* Gollancz, 1980.

The Eye of the Heron, and Other Stories (includes a novella originally published in collection *Millennial Women;* also see below), Panther, 1980, Harper, 1983.

The Visionary: The Life Story of Flicker of the Serpentine (bound with *Wonders Hidden: Audubon's Early Years,* by Scott Russell Sanders), Capra (Santa Barbara, CA), 1984.

Always Coming Home (includes audiocassette of "Music and Poetry of the Kesh," with music by Todd Barton; also see below), illustrated by Margaret Chodos, diagrams by George Hersh, Harper, 1985, published without audiocassette, Bantam (New York City), 1987.

Tehanu: The Last Book of Earthsea (sequel to *The Farthest Shore*), Atheneum, 1990.

FOR CHILDREN

Solomon Leviathan's Nine Hundred Thirty-First Trip around the World (originally published in collection *Puffin's Pleasures*), illustrated by Alicia Austin, Puffin, 1976, Cheap Street (New Castle, VA), 1983.

Leese Webster, illustrated by James Brunsman, Atheneum, 1979.

The Adventures of Cobbler's Rune, illustrated by Austin, Cheap Street, 1982.

Adventures in Kroy, Cheap Street, 1982.

A Visit from Dr. Katz (picture book), illustrated by Ann Barrow, Atheneum, 1988, published as *Dr. Katz,* Collins (London), 1988.

Catwings, illustrated by S. D. Schindler, Orchard Books (New York City), 1988.

Catwings Return, illustrated by Schindler, Orchard Books, 1989.

Fire and Stone, Atheneum, 1989.

Fish Soup, illustrated by Patrick Wynne, Atheneum, 1992.

A Ride on the Red Mare's Back, illustrated with paintings by Julie Downing, Orchard Books, 1992.

Buffalo Gals, Won't You Come Out Tonight, illustrated by Susan Seddon Boulet, Pomegranate Artbooks (San Francisco, CA), 1994.

Wonderful Alexander and the Catwings, illustrated by Schindler, Orchard Books, 1994.

POEMS

Wild Angels (collection of early works), Capra, 1975.

(With mother, Theodora K. Quinn) *Tillai and Tylissos,* Red Bull, 1979.

Torrey Pines Reserve (broadsheet), Lord John (Northridge, CA), 1980.

Hard Words, and Other Poems, Harper, 1981.

Gwilan's Harp, Lord John, 1981.

(With artist Henk Pander) *In the Red Zone,* Lord John, 1983.

Wild Oats and Fireweed, Harper, 1988.

Going Out with Peacocks and Other Poems, Harper-Perennial (New York City), 1994.

OTHER

The Word for World Is Forest (novella; originally published in collection *Again, Dangerous Visions;* also see below), Berkley (New York City), 1972.

From Elfland to Poughkeepsie (lecture), introduction by Vonda N. McIntyre, Pendragon Press (Portland, OR), 1973.

The Wind's Twelve Quarters: Short Stories, Harper, 1975.

Dreams Must Explain Themselves (critical essays), Algol Press (New York City), 1975.

(With Gene Wolfe and James Tiptree, Jr.) *The New Atlantis and Other Novellas of Science Fiction,* edited by Robert Silverberg, Hawthorn Books (New York City), 1975.

Orsinian Tales (short stories), Harper, 1976.

The Water Is Wide (short story), Pendragon Press, 1976.

(With others) *The Altered I: An Encounter with Science Fiction* (includes Le Guin's play *No Use to Talk to Me*), edited by Lee Harding, Norstrilia Press (Melbourne, Australia), 1976.

(Editor) *Nebula Award Stories 11,* Gollancz, 1976, Harper, 1977.

The Language of the Night: Essays on Fantasy and Science Fiction (critical essays), edited by Susan Wood, Putnam, 1979, revised edition, edited by Le Guin, Women's Press, 1989.

(Editor with Virginia Kidd) *Interfaces: An Anthology of Speculative Fiction,* Ace Books, 1980.

(Editor with Kidd) *Edges: Thirteen New Tales from the Borderlands of the Imagination,* Pocket Books (New York City), 1980.

The Compass Rose (short stories), Harper, 1982.

King Dog: A Screenplay (bound with *Dostoevsky: The Screenplay,* by Raymond Carver and Tess Gallagher), Capra, 1985.

(With Barton) *Music and Poetry of the Kesh* (audiocassette), Valley Productions, 1985.

(With David Bedford) *Rigel Nine: An Audio Opera* (recording), Charisma, 1985.

(With composer Elinor Armer) *Uses of Music in Uttermost Parts* (music and text), first performed in part in San Francisco, CA, and Seattle, WA, 1986, 1987, and 1988.

Buffalo Gals and Other Animal Presences (short stories and poems), Capra, 1987, published as *Buffalo Gals,* Gollancz, 1990.

Dancing at the Edge of the World: Thoughts on Words, Women, Places (essays), Grove (New York City), 1989.

The Way the Water's Going: Images of the Northern California Coastal Range, photographs by Ernest Waugh and Alan Nicolson, Harper, 1989.

Searoad: Chronicles of Klatsand (short stories), HarperCollins (New York City), 1991.

Myth and Archetype in Science Fiction, Pulphouse, 1991.

Talk about Writing, Pulphouse, 1991.

Blue Moon over Thurman Street, photographs by Roger Dorband, NewSage Press (Portland, OR), 1993.

Earthsea Revisioned (lecture), Children's Literature New England (Cambridge, MA), 1993.

The Ones Who Walk Away from Omelas (short story), Creative Education (Mankato, MN), 1993.

(Editor with Brian Attebery) *The Norton Book of Science Fiction: North American Science Fiction, 1960-1990,* Norton (New York City), 1993.

A Fisherman of the Inland Sea: Science Fiction Stories, HarperPrism (New York City), 1994.

Four Ways to Forgiveness (contains "Betrayals," "Forgiveness Day," "A Man of the People," and "A Woman's Liberation"), HarperPrism, 1995.

Unlocking the Air: And Other Stories (includes "Standing Ground," "Poacher," "Half Past Four," and "Limberlost"), HarperCollins, 1996.

Author of postcard short story, *Post Card Partnership,* 1975, and *Sword & Sorcery Annual,* 1975. Contributor to anthologies, including *Orbit 5,* 1969, *World's Best Science Fiction,* 1970, *The Best Science Fiction of the Year #5,* 1976, and *The Norton Anthology of Short Fiction,* 1978. Contributor of short stories, novellas, essays, and reviews to numerous science fiction, scholarly, and popular periodicals, including *Amazing Science Fiction, Science-Fiction Studies, New Yorker, Antaeus, Parabola, New Republic, Redbook, Playgirl, Playboy, New Yorker, Western Humanities Review, Yale Review,* and *Omni.*

ADAPTATIONS: The Lathe of Heaven was televised by the Public Broadcasting Service in 1979; *The Tombs of Atuan* was adapted as a filmstrip with record or audiocassette by Newbery Award Records, 1980; "The Ones Who Walk Away from Omelas" was performed as a drama with dance and music at the Portland Civic Theatre in 1981. Le Guin has made recordings of several of her works, including "The Ones Who Walk Away from Omelas" (includes excerpt from *The Left Hand of Darkness*), Alternate World, 1976, *Gwilan's Harp and Intracom,* Caedmon, 1977, and *The Left Hand of Darkness* (abridged recording), Warner Audio, 1985; an abridged version of *The Earthsea Trilogy* was made into a sound recording by Colophone, 1981; *The Word for World Is Forest* was made into a sound recording by Book of the Road, 1986.

SIDELIGHTS: Critics have often found it difficult to classify Ursula K. Le Guin: while some consider her writing science fiction or fantasy, Le Guin herself discounts any narrow genre categorizations. She told *CA* that "some of my fiction is 'science fiction,' some of it is 'fantasy,' some of it is 'realist,' and some of it is 'magical realism.'" Le Guin has also written several volumes of poetry and essays. "A significant amount of science fiction has been profoundly thoughtful about the situation of contemporary humanity in the light of its possible futures and its imaginable alternatives," writes Derek de Solla Price in the *New Republic*. "In recent years, no [writer] inside the field of science fiction or outside of it [has] done more to create a modern conscience than . . . Ursula K. Le Guin." Le Guin, however, "is not competing with [George] Orwell or [Ernest] Hemingway," according to George Edgar Slusser in his book *The Farthest Shores of Ursula Le Guin*. "Her social analysis is acute, but its purpose is not indignation or reform. She has no social program, offers no panaceas." And a *Cambridge Review: Fantasy in Literature* contributor finds Le Guin "an elegant, but not a light writer: not to be trifled with. Superficially, her work charms because it has all the glitter of high intelligence and efficiency."

In his essay on Le Guin for the *Dictionary of Literary Biography* volume on science fiction writers, Brian Attebery writes that the author "has brought to science fiction a new sensitivity to language, a powerful set of symbols and images, and a number of striking and sympathetic characters." He judges her work "extraordinarily risky: it is full of hypotheses about morality, love, society, and ways of enriching life expressed in the symbolic language found in myth, dream, or poetry. However, the greater the risk, the greater the reward, and for the reader . . . the reward is a glimpse of something glowing, something very much like truth." Similarly, Joseph D. Olander and Martin Harry Greenberg say in the introduction to their edited volume *Ursula K. Le Guin* that while "Le Guin's fiction may be filled with wizards, aliens, and clones, . . . the vision contained in her stories and novels is, above all, concerned with what is most permanent about the human condition." *Modern Fiction Studies* contributor Keith N. Hull notes: "Certainly one of the most important lessons in Le Guin's novels is that humanity is a broader, deeper entity than we ordinarily think and that the definition of humanity requires constant expansion as our experience broadens. Because of this theme, Le Guin's work risks being polemical and sentimental, but her best work exploits it beautifully."

Le Guin was born in Berkeley, California, to the prominent anthropologist Alfred Kroeber and the writer Theodora Kroeber. She studied Renaissance history as a graduate student at Columbia University and after obtaining her master's degree married a history professor, Charles Le Guin. In addition to exposing her to history and anthropology, Le Guin's formative environment gave her a perspective on religion different from that of many Americans. She

told Jean W. Ross in an interview for *Contemporary Authors,* "My father was a cultural relativist. He had been brought up in the Ethical Culture movement in New York in the late nineteenth century, which was a nonreligious but, as the title implies, highly moral system of thought. I was brought up in an un-religious household; there was no religious practice of any kind. There was also no feeling that any religion was better than another, or worse; they just weren't part of our life."

Le Guin began her writing career with short fiction. Her first short story, "An die Musik," appeared in the *Western Humanities Review* in 1961. A later story, "The Dowry of Angyar," appeared originally in *Amazing Science Fiction* in 1964 and provided the impetus for Le Guin's first novel, *Rocannon's World.* "I always wanted to write, and I always knew it would be hard to make a living at it," she explained to *Boston Globe* contributor Maureen Dezell. "I was very arrogant and wanted to be free to write what I wanted to write and see if I could get it published on my own terms. I did, eventually. But it took a long time." Le Guin has been rewarded for her persistence and her vision on numerous occasions, winning the prestigious Nebula and Hugo awards for her short works, including *The Word for World Is Forest* and "The Ones Who Walk Away from Omelas."

These two shorter works introduce and explore themes that recur throughout Le Guin's fiction. *The Word for World Is Forest* looks at the use of force levied against an alien people and has been said to reflect in many ways the American intervention in Vietnam during the 1960s and early 1970s. "At the same time," cautions Ian Watson in *Science-Fiction Studies,* "the obvious Vietnam analogy should not blind one to other relevant contemporary analogies—the genocide of the Guyaki Indians of Paraguay, or the genocide and deforestation along the Trans-Amazon Highway in Brazil, or even the general destruction of rain-forest habitats from Indonesia to Costa Rica. Le Guin's story is multi-applicable—and multifaceted." "The Ones Who Walk Away from Omelas." explains the necessity of individual morality. The society of Omelas is one of utopian happiness based on the unhappiness of a single scapegoat, who suffers for the entire community. "In *Omelas,*" writes Shoshana Knapp in the *Journal of Narrative Technique,* "the world created is unfit for human habitation. The bargain on which it rests violates not only decency but logic. . . . To choose between torturing a child and destroying one's society (which includes other children) is a diabolical choice, not a human one."

Le Guin first began to receive extensive critical and popular attention with her Earthsea novels, the first being *A Wizard of Earthsea.* The Earthsea trilogy, considered by Le Guin to be among her best work, displays a holistic conception of the universe. As Robert Scholes suggests in a *Hollins Critic* article, "What Earthsea represents, through its world of islands and waterways, is the universe as a dynamic, balanced system . . . which include[s] a role for magic and for powers other than human, but only as aspects of the great Balance or Equilibrium, which is the order of this cosmos. Where C. S. Lewis worked out of a specifically Christian set of values, Ursula Le Guin works not with a theology but with an ecology, a cosmology, a reverence for the universe as a self-regulating structure." The theme of equilibrium between opposing forces works on several levels within the trilogy. On the most immediate and recognizable level is the integration of man with himself. In *A Wizard of Earthsea* it is the young mage, or wizard, Ged who undertakes the journey to maturity and self-knowledge; in *The Tombs of Atuan,* it is the girl-priestess, Tenar; and in *The Farthest Shore,* it is the young prince Arran, accompanying Ged on a search for the source of an evil spreading through Earthsea. Writing in Olander and Greenberg's *Ursula K. Le Guin,* Margaret P. Esmonde suggests that "all of these journeys symbolize the journey every human being must make, one through pain and fear, aided only by trust in the goodness of man, hand holding hand, to the acceptance of mortality." A *Times Literary Supplement* contributor praises the trilogy's depth and concludes: "After Earthsea-lore, with its weight and substance, most other modern fantasies must ring thin."

"Two Le Guin novels of unquestionably high standing, even among readers who generally do not care for science fiction, are *The Left Hand of Darkness* and *The Dispossessed,*" writes Hull. "In these novels Le Guin . . . describes herself as writing science fiction based on 'social science, psychology, anthropology [and] history,'. . . [The result] is an emphasis on culture." *The Left Hand of Darkness* explores the themes of sexual identity, incest, xenophobia, fidelity, and betrayal in a tale of an Earth ambassador, Genly Ai, who is sent to the planet of Gethen, whose inhabitants are androgynous. Through his relationship with a native, Estraven, Ai gains understanding both of the consequences of his fixed sexual orienta-

tion and of Gethenian life. As in many of her works, Le Guin incorporates a social message in her science fiction tale. Scholes feels that "the great power of the book comes from the way it interweaves all its levels and combines all its voices and values into an ordered, balanced, whole." In *The Dispossessed: An Ambiguous Utopia,* another character is an alien in a strange culture; the physicist Shevek, however, is also at odds with his home planet's values. He is devoted to the spread of knowledge, but the development of his theories will inevitably bring his isolated colonial planet and its mother-planet into contact, although the two cultures bitterly oppose one another. Attebery describes the novel's form as "slow, sober, down-to-earth. The writing verges on pure naturalistic reporting, except that the places being written about do not exist on Earth." He adds that *The Dispossessed* "is fuller than any other of [Le Guin's] stories in character and in social and political interplay."

Le Guin has invented many beings to inhabit the alien worlds of her fiction and has endowed them with a variety of physical and mental characteristics. The Athsheans of *The Word for World Is Forest,* for instance, are an intelligent hominid species covered with green fur and capable of perceiving reality through daydreams. Several different species live on the planet called Rocannon's World, including a large winged creature much like an angelic robot; the Liuar, a feudal society of very tall, lordly people with yellow hair and dark skin; the Clayfolk, short, pale, intelligent troglodytes; and the Fiia, simple-minded, elfish humanoids. And while Le Guin's societies are sometimes utopian in concept, the inhabitants are capable of very human and imperfect actions. According to the *Cambridge Review* critic, "The satisfaction of [Le Guin's] stories is that her heroes and heroines are constantly on the brink of doing the wrong thing, and sometimes do: a reader holds his breath at every turn."

Le Guin's characters and settings vary widely, and her books take place on many different planets and in varying time spans. Some, like the books of the Earthsea trilogy, take place wholly outside the known universe, much as does J. R. R. Tolkien's *Lord of the Rings.* Some of Le Guin's other novels adhere to somewhat more familiar spatial and temporal structures, or are at least set within the parameters of human history. The works which form Le Guin's Hainish Cycle, for example (including *Ro-cannon's World, Planet of Exile, City of Illusions, The Left Hand of Darkness, The Dispossessed,* and many of her short stories), are bound by a common historical context—their characters and cultures originated with a race called the Hain, whose history encompasses Earth.

Always Coming Home concerns a people known as the Kesh, who reside in northern California after a nuclear war. The format moves between poetry and prose and includes stories, legends, and "autobiography"; the book was originally published with an audiocassette of Kesh music. Brian D. Johnson in *Maclean's* describes *Always Coming Home* as "an 'archaeological dig' into the distant future—a search for 'shards of the broken pot at the end of the rainbow.'" Science fiction author Samuel R. Delany in the *New York Times Book Review* praises the work: "With high invention and deep intelligence, *Always Coming Home* presents, in alternating narratives, poems and expositions, Ursula K. Le Guin's most consistently lyric and luminous book in a career adorned with some of the most precise and passionate prose in the service of a major imaginative vision." H. J. Kirchhoff in the Toronto *Globe and Mail* expresses the belief that Le Guin "has created an entire culture, not just a cast of characters—an impressive achievement from an impressive writer." And Delany concludes: "This is her most satisfying text among a set of texts that have provided much imaginative pleasure."

Le Guin's excursions into the world of children's fiction have included *Solomon Leviathan's 931st Trip around the World, Catwings,* and *Catwings Return.* In *Catwings,* four flying cats—Harriet, James, Thelma and Roger—escape city dangers to live in the country, where they are adopted by two children. *New York Times Book Review* contributor Crescent Dragonwagon finds that Le Guin's "dialogue, humor, skill as a storyteller and emotional veracity combine near-flawlessly in a story that is both contemporary and timeless. One of the book's weaknesses is that, other than for their wings, the kittens are not so remarkable, at least as individuals. . . . Still, their collective winged adventures, their looking after one another, and the understated charm of Ms. Le Guin's writing keeps us captivated." "I don't know the artist—we'd never met," Le Guin explained to Ross, "but I asked the editor please to tell him that the cats' wings should be furry, tabby, like the cats, though of course they have to have a feather structure. I thought he did that splendidly. I've had a lovely letter from a little boy, my first fan letter for *Catwings,* and he said, 'I keep looking at my cats and telling them, "Fly! Fly!"'" Dragonwagon continues: "[When Susan] whispers to her brother, 'Oh, Hank . . . their wings are furry,' as kitten Harriet

whispers to her brother, 'Oh, James . . . their hands are kind'—well, who could fail to recognize the enduring, healing power of love?"

A Ride on the Red Mare's Back, a book for younger children, looks at the issue of avoidance of responsibility. In it, a young girl learns that her little brother has been taken by trolls, and she goes out alone to rescue him, taking only a toy red horse, a warm scarf, knitting needles and yarn, and a bit of bread. Once she locates the boy in the trolls' castle, she finds that he has changed: he now wants to become a troll. "The boy's desire is an old one," Michael Dirda explains in the *Washington Post Book World:* "Is it better to be a happy pig or an unhappy Socrates? Most of us don't get the chance to be quite either." Dirda concludes that the volume "is indisputably suspenseful, thought-provoking, and beautifully illustrated."

Dancing at the Edge of the World: Thoughts on Words, Women, Places is a collection of essays, addresses and reviews. *Los Angeles Times Book Review* critic Nancy Mairs finds the collection "unpredictable and uneven but, for those very reasons, a trove of delights: insightful, impassioned, sometimes lyrical, often funny. . . . Those who appreciate Le Guin's novels will find the pieces in [*Dancing at the Edge of the World*] no substitute for their intricacies of vision and language. But this volume makes a fine companion, and on occasion a guide, to her fiction, offering insight into the writer at work." And Elizabeth Hand in the *Washington Post Book World* thinks the grouping shows "Ursula Le Guin at her best: insightful, funny, sharp, occasionally tendentious and nearly always provocative."

Eighteen years after the publication of *The Farthest Shore,* Le Guin produced another volume in the chronicles of Earthsea: *Tehanu: The Last Book of Earthsea.* The story concerns both Ged and Tenar, who are now old. Ged abandoned his power at the end of *The Farthest Shore;* Tenar has lived a "normal" life and is a farmer's widow. Their lives become enmeshed with that of a little girl, Therru, who has been raped and burned but survives. "The astonishing clearsightedness of *Tehanu,*" explains novelist Robin McKinley in the *New York Times Book Review,* "is in its recognition of the necessary and lifegiving contributions of female magic—sometimes disguised as domesticity." Although Dirda sees the novel as "meditative, somber, even talky," he acknowledges that it "builds to a climax of almost pornographic horror, nearly too shocking for its supposedly young adult pages." "The first three books lay out the answer to the problem of evil with some confidence (lack of balance)," relates Meredith Tax in the *Village Voice;* "this one asks, like Gertrude Stein on her deathbed, 'What is the question?'" Dirda adds that while *Tehanu* may be "less sheerly exciting" than the Earthsea trilogy, it "may be the most moving of them all."

Searoad: Chronicles of Klatsand is a collection of short fiction that breaks away from the science fiction with which Le Guin is most often identified. Set in the Oregon town of Klatsand, *Searoad* follows the outwardly unremarkable lives of its inhabitants. "In understated stories that ask the reader not to pity their marginal characters but to respect their courage," explains Yvonne Fraticelli in the *Women's Review of Books,* "Le Guin summons up a host of visionaries, dreamers and solitaries." Reviewing the work for *Belles Lettres,* Juli Duncan asserts that "the stories are uneven in tone and style" but that "each is perfectly tailored to its characters, who are so lovingly drawn that they will live on in the reader's mind for a long time." The collection represents a notable achievement for Le Guin, in the opinion of Patricia Dubrava Keuning in the *Bloomsbury Review,* who notes that it is "Le Guin's first purely mainstream book of fiction, and with it, she has accomplished squarely what few writers succeed in doing: She has liberated herself from the genre pigeonhole."

BIOGRAPHICAL/CRITICAL SOURCES:

BOOKS

Authors and Artists for Young Adults, Volume 9, Gale (Detroit), 1992.

Authors in the News, Volume 1, Gale, 1976.

Bittner, James, *Approaches to the Fiction of Ursula K. Le Guin,* UMI Research Press (Ann Arbor, MI), 1984.

Bucknall, Barbara J., *Ursula K. Le Guin,* Ungar (New York City), 1981.

Children's Literature Review, Gale, Volume 3, 1978, Volume 28, 1992.

Cogell, Elizabeth Cummins, *Ursula K. Le Guin: A Primary and Secondary Bibliography,* G. K. Hall (Boston), 1983.

Cogell, *Understanding Ursula K. Le Guin,* University of South Carolina Press (Columbia), 1990.

Concise Dictionary of American Literary Biography: Broadening Views, 1968-1988, Gale, 1989.

Contemporary Literary Criticism, Gale, Volume 8, 1978, Volume 13, 1980, Volume 22, 1982, Volume 45, 1987, Volume 71, 1992.

Contemporary Novelists, sixth edition, St. James Press (Detroit), 1996.

De Bolt, Joseph W., editor, *Ursula K. Le Guin: Voyage to Inner Lands and to Outer Space,* Kennikat (Port Washington, NY), 1979.

Dictionary of Literary Biography, Gale, Volume 8: *Twentieth-Century American Science Fiction Writers,* 1981, Volume 52: *American Writers for Children since 1960: Fiction,* 1986.

Gay and Lesbian Literature, St. James Press, 1994.

Keulen, Margarete, *Radical Imagination: Feminist Conceptions of the Future in Ursula Le Guin, Marge Piercy, and Sally Miller Gearhart,* Peter Lang (New York City), 1991.

Olander, Joseph D., and Martin Harry Greenberg, editors, *Ursula K. Le Guin,* Taplinger (New York City), 1979.

Reference Guide to Short Fiction, St. James Press, 1993.

Scholes, Robert, *Structural Fabulation: An Essay on Fiction of the Future,* University of Notre Dame Press (Notre Dame, IN), 1975.

Short Story Criticism, Volume 12, Gale, 1993.

Slusser, George Edgar, *The Farthest Shores of Ursula Le Guin,* Borgo (San Bernardino, CA), 1976.

Slusser, *Between Two Worlds: The Literary Dilemma of Ursula K. Le Guin,* second edition, Borgo, 1995.

Slusser and Robert Reginald, editors, *Zephyr and Boreas: Winds of Change in the Fiction of Ursula K. Le Guin; A Festschrift in Memory of Pilgrim Award Winner Marjorie Hope Nicolson (1894-1981),* Borgo, 1995.

Spivack, Charlotte, *Ursula K. Le Guin,* Twayne (Boston), 1984.

St. James Guide to Science Fiction Writers, St. James Press, 1996.

Twentieth-Century Children's Writers, third edition, St. James Press, 1989.

Twentieth-Century Young Adult Writers, St. James Press, 1994.

Wayne, Kathryn Ross, *Redefining Moral Education: Life, Le Guin, and Language,* Austin & Winfield, 1994.

PERIODICALS

Analog Science Fiction/Science Fact, February, 1985, pp. 183-84.

Belles Lettres, spring, 1992, pp. 53-54; spring, 1994, pp. 27-28.

Bloomsbury Review, June, 1992, pp. 9, 22.

Book Report, March/April, 1989.

Boston Globe, July 13, 1994, p. 65.

California Quarterly, spring-summer, 1978, pp. 38-55.

Cambridge Review: Fantasy in Literature, November 23, 1973.

Extrapolation, December, 1976, pp. 28-41; May, 1977, pp. 131-41; fall, 1980, pp. 197-208.

Globe and Mail (Toronto), December 7, 1985.

Hollins Critic, April, 1974.

Journal of Narrative Technique, winter, 1985, pp. 75-81.

Locus, October, 1994, pp. 17, 19.

Los Angeles Times, September 5, 1982.

Los Angeles Times Book Review, September 5, 1982; March 5, 1989.

Maclean's, November 4, 1985.

Modern Fiction Studies, spring, 1986, pp. 65-74.

New Republic, February 7, 1976; October 30, 1976.

New York Review of Books, October 2, 1975, pp. 3-7.

New York Times Book Review, September 29, 1985; November 13, 1988; May 20, 1990, p. 38; March 3, 1996, p. 10.

Science Fiction Review, spring, 1983, p. 41.

Science-Fiction Studies, spring, 1974, pp. 164-73; March, 1975, pp. 67-75; November, 1975, pp. 231-37; March, 1976; November, 1978, pp. 215-42; March, 1987, pp. 34-43; July, 1994, pp. 164-72.

Times Literary Supplement, April 6, 1973; June 3-9, 1988; March 11, 1994, p. 24.

Village Voice, February 25, 1986.

Voice of Youth Advocates, April, 1991, pp. 14-16, 18.

Washington Post, October 31, 1993, p. 8.

Washington Post Book World, October 6, 1985; January 29, 1989; February 25, 1990; August 9, 1992, p. 11.

Women's Review of Books, July, 1992, pp. 29-30.

OTHER

DISCovering Authors: British Edition (CD-ROM product), Gale, 1995.

DISCovering Authors Modules (CD-ROM product), Gale, 1996.

Junior DISCovering Authors (CD-ROM product), Gale, 1995.

*   *   *

LENZ, Frederick   1950-
(Rama)

PERSONAL: Born February 9, 1950, in San Diego, CA. *Education:* University of Connecticut, received B.A.; State University of New York at Stony Brook, M.A., 1974; Ph.D., 1978. *Avocational interests:* Atlantis.

ADDRESSES: Home—8528 Cliffridge Ave., La Jolla, CA 92037. *Office*—Relaxation Studies, Inc., P.O. Box 589, LaJolla, CA 92036. *Agent*—James Seligmann Agency, 280 Madison Ave., New York, NY 10016.

CAREER: President of Relaxation Studies, Inc., La Jolla, CA; member of staff of New School for Social Research, New York City. Guest on television and radio programs in the United States and Canada; lecturer at universities in the United States and abroad, including Oxford University, Harvard University, State University of New York, and University of Heidelberg; also conducts seminars.

MEMBER: Phi Beta Kappa.

WRITINGS:

Lifetimes: True Accounts of Reincarnation, Bobbs-Merrill (Indianapolis, IN), 1979.

Total Relaxation: The Complete Program for Overcoming Stress, Tension, Worry, and Fatigue, Bobbs-Merrill, 1980.

The Wheel of Dharma, Lakshmi (Malibu, CA), 1982.

Meditation: The Bridge is Flowing but the River Is Not, Lakshmi, 1983.

The Last Incarnation: Experiences with Rama in California, Lakshmi, 1983.

SIDELIGHTS: Frederick Lenz teaches meditation, relaxation, and eastern philosophy, but as an expert on psychic phenomena and reincarnation, his lectures and television-radio discussions include such topics as parapsychology, UFOs, the Bermuda Triangle, and the spirit world. He has created an advanced method of overcoming stress and tension, which he calls Total Relaxation, which he teaches at two-day seminars. Kate Stone Lombardi in the *New York Times* summarizes: "To his followers, he is Rama, a gifted teacher and spiritual leader with special powers who offers a path to enlightenment, happiness and career success. To his detractors, he is everything from a sophisticated con man to a dangerous cult leader."

Lenz writes: "As an author my primary interest is presenting health and psychic information that will be of use to the public. My interests are sharply divided between classical literary studies and contemporary issues."

BIOGRAPHICAL/CRITICAL SOURCES:

PERIODICALS

Newsweek, February 1, 1988, p. 58.
New York Times, June 20, 1993, section WC, p. 8.*

*   *   *

LESCHAK, Peter M. 1951-

PERSONAL: Born May 11, 1951, in Chisholm, MN; son of Peter (a miner) and Agnes (in retail sales; maiden name, Pavelich) Leschak; married Pamela Cope (a writer), May, 1974. *Education:* Attended College of St. Thomas, St. Paul, MN, 1969-70; Ambassador College, B.A., 1974.

ADDRESSES: Home—Box 51, Side Lake, MN 55781.

CAREER: Lumberjack in Roseburg, OR, 1973; printer in Baton Rouge, LA, 1974; water plant operator in Chisolm, MN, 1975-79; City of Hibbing, Hibbing, MN, operator of waste water plant, 1979-84; writer, 1984—. Fire chief of French, MN, volunteer fire department.

MEMBER: Authors Guild, Minnesota Fire Chiefs Association.
WRITINGS:

Letters from Side Lake: A Chronicle of Life in the North Woods, Harper (New York City), 1987.
The Bear Guardian, North Star Press (St. Cloud, MN), 1990.
Bumming with the Furies, North Star Press, 1993.
Seeing the Raven, University of Minnesota Press (Minneapolis), 1994.
Hellroaring, North Star Press, 1994.
The Snow Lotus, University of Minnesota Press, 1996.

Author of regular column in *TWA Ambassador,* 1985-86. Contributor to magazines. Contributing editor of *Twin Cities,* 1984-86, and *Minnesota Monthly,* 1984-89.

WORK IN PROGRESS: The Witness Post.

SIDELIGHTS: Peter M. Leschak grew up in a small mining town in northern Minnesota. In 1969 he left the Mesabi Iron Range to attend college in the city of St. Paul. The author never felt comfortable with city life, however, so, after earning his college degree, Leschak returned to rural Minnesota. He and his wife settled near Side Lake, where they built a log home and began to explore the wilderness around them. Their experiences form the core of *Letters from Side Lake.*

"Mr. Leschak is an acute observer with genuine affection for his material," writes John Tallmadge in the *New York Times Book Review.* His book is a collection of "dozens of stories told in a breezy, journalistic style." *Washington Post Book World* critic Vic Sussman agrees that Leschak is "a fine writer with an eye both for natural wonder and for irony . . . [and with a] great sense of humor that carries this lively book along." He adds: "Leschak's engaging essays are happily free of bile, evangelism, and Thoreauvian moralizing on the evils of modern life." Sussman sees *Letters from Side Lake* as a celebration of "the beauty and adventure of the north woods . . . and the simplicity of small-town life."

Leschak told *CA:* "I agree with novelist Philip Roth that 'We writers are lucky: nothing truly bad can happen to us. It's all material.' One of the goals of a writer is to weave his own life into the tapestry of the culture. We're entertainers as well as reporters and teachers, and if we wish to reach others, we must be willing to offer a piece of ourselves. If you can tell a story (and all writing boils down to that) in such a way that the reader feels he knows you, then you are successful. In the terms of our ancient forebears, we are closer to the shaman than the scribe. It's just too bad it doesn't pay better."

BIOGRAPHICAL/CRITICAL SOURCES:

PERIODICALS

New York Times Book Review, June 28, 1987; February 12, 1995.
St. Paul Pioneer Press-Dispatch, July 7, 1993.
Washington Post Book World, July 12, 1987.

*   *   *

LESTER, Alison 1952-

PERSONAL: Born November 17, 1952, in Foster, Australia; daughter of Donald Robert (a grazier) and

Jean Rosalind (a nurse; maiden name, Billings) Lester; married Edwin Hume (a solicitor), January 22, 1977; children: Will, Clair, Lachlan. *Education:* Melbourne State College, Higher Diploma of Teaching, 1975. *Avocational interests:* Horses, basketball, the beach, gardening, music, skiing, cooking, travel, photography, shopping for clothes.

ADDRESSES: Home—Dore Rd., Nar Nar Goon North, Victoria, Australia.

CAREER: Victorian Education Department, high school art teacher in Alexandra, Australia, 1976-77, high school art teacher at correspondence school in Melbourne, Australia, 1977-78; writer and illustrator, 1978—.

AWARDS, HONORS: Received medal for best children's picture book of the year from Australian Children's Book Council, 1983, for illustrating *Thing;* Australian Children's Book Council, commendation, 1986, for *Clive Eats Alligators,* and honour, 1990, for *The Journey Home;* Australian Book Publishers Association design award, 1989, for *Rosie Sips Spiders,* and 1990, for *Imagine.*

WRITINGS:

Clive Eats Alligators (juvenile), self-illustrated, Oxford University Press (Oxford), 1985.
Ruby (juvenile), self-illustrated, Oxford University Press, 1987.
Rosie Sips Spiders, Oxford University Press, 1988.
"Australian Baby Books" series (contains *Bibs and Boots, Happy and Sad, Crashing and Splashing,* and *Bumping and Bouncing*), Penguin (West Drayton, England), 1989.
Imagine, Allen and Unwin (London), 1989.
The Journey Home, Oxford University Press, 1989.
Magic Beach, Allen and Unwin, 1990.
Tessa Snaps Snakes, Oxford University Press, 1990.
Isabella's Bed, Oxford University Press, 1991.
My Farm, Allen and Unwin, 1992.
I'm Green and I'm Grumpy, Penguin, 1993.
Monsters Are Knocking, Penguin, 1993.
Yikes!, Allen and Unwin, 1993.
When Frank Was Four, Hodder and Stoughton (London), 1994.
The Quicksand Pony, Allen and Unwin, 1996.
Alice and Aldo, Allen and Unwin, 1996.
Celeste Sets Sail, Hodder Headline, 1996.

ILLUSTRATOR

June Epstein, "Big Dipper" (series), Oxford University Press, 1980-84.
Robin Klein, *Thing,* Oxford University Press, 1982.
R. Klein, *Thingnapped,* Oxford University Press, 1984.
R. Klein, *Ratbags and Rascals,* Dent (London), 1984.
Morris Lune, *Night-Night,* Oxford University Press, 1986.
June Factor, *Summer,* Penguin, 1987.
R. Klein, *Birk the Berserker,* Omnibus Press (London), 1987.

WORK IN PROGRESS: Running with the Horses, for Penguin, 1997.

SIDELIGHTS: "After a happy childhood on my parents' farm," Alison Lester told *CA,* "I finished my secondary education and, like many of my contemporaries, had no ambition other than to have a good time. Years of traveling, hiking, riding, and partying ensued. After I married Edwin, we traveled in South America for a year. I've also traveled in Australia and Southeast Asia.

"The birth of our first child woke me up with a start, and I began illustrating then. Anything was preferable to being stuck at home with the housework! As I get more confident about my own writing, though, I find it difficult to illustrate for other people.

"As my imagination increases, I can't think of any work I would rather be doing, unless it is droving cattle. Still, I'm not sure that I'll keep writing children's books forever. I'm full of ideas about fabric design, toys, gardens, et cetera, and I may choose to follow one of these follies. It is hard to find time to work on all these creative things.

"My own children and my childhood memories are my greatest sources of inspiration. I'm a country girl and still live in the bush, so the horses, dogs, cats, and garden also inspire me. I love to see the funny side of things. Kids are very funny and sharp, but it is difficult to communicate humor to them without being patronizing. I also love the exotic and strange.

"I have been doing more and more writing, progressing on to a junior novel to be published next year. Increasingly my time is taken up travelling around Australia and overseas talking about my work and running writing and illustrating workshops."

LEVANT, Victor 1947-

PERSONAL: Born November 26, 1947, in Winnipeg, Manitoba, Canada; son of Edgar (a fur cutter) and Sarah (Blackerman) Levant. *Ethnicity:* "Jewish." *Education:* Attended Sorbonne, University of Paris, 1968-69; McGill University, B.A. (with distinction), 1968, M.A. (with distinction), 1973, Ph.D., 1981.

ADDRESSES: Home—2243 Oxford, Montreal, Quebec, Canada HYA 2X7. *Office*—Department of Humanities, John Abbott College, Box 2000, de Bellevue, Quebec, Canada H9X 3L9.

CAREER: Dawson College, lecturer in sociology, 1971-72; Concordia University, lecturer in political science, 1972-74; John Abbott College, de Bellevue, Quebec, professor of humanities, 1972-93. Lecturer at University of Quebec, summers, 1976 and 1977; lecturer at international conferences; interviewed on Canadian television and radio programs; political commentator for Radio-Canada. Director of research for Via le Monde Film Productions, 1982-84; film and television consultant; consultant to National Film Board of Canada, 1984-86.

MEMBER: Gestalt Association of Quebec, Provincial Association of Art Teachers, l'Association des arts therapeutes du Quebec, Canadian Guidance and Counselling Association, Societe quebecoise des psychotherapeutes professionnel-le-s.

AWARDS, HONORS: Guy Drummond Fellowship, 1968-69, 1969-70; McConnell Fellowship, 1970-71, 1971-72, 1972-73; Conseil des Arts: Doctoral Fellowship, 1976-77.

WRITINGS:

(Coauthor) *How to Make a Killing: Canadian Military Involvement in the Indo-China War,* Presse Solidaire, 1972.
(Coeditor) *How to Buy a Country: Research Monograph on Pentagon Contracts,* Presse Solidaire, 1973.
Capital and Labour: Partners?, Steel Rail Press (Toronto), 1977, published in French as *Capital et travail,* Les editions de l'etincelle (Montreal), 1978.
Quiet Complicity: Canada and the Vietnam War, foreword by Gwynne Dyer, Between the Lines (Toronto), 1987, published in French as *Secrete*

Alliance: Le Canada dans la guerre du Vietnam, foreword by Pierre Nadeau, Hurtubise (Montreal), 1990.
The Neighbourhood Gourmet, Hurtubise, 1989.

Contributor to newspapers and periodicals.

WORK IN PROGRESS: Sacrifice, a screenplay; *Grandpa's Gone, My House,* and *Lost,* children's books.

BIOGRAPHICAL/CRITICAL SOURCES:

PERIODICALS

Globe and Mail (Toronto), February 21, 1987.

*   *   *

LEVENKRON, Steven 1941-

PERSONAL: Born March 25, 1941, in New York, NY; son of Joseph A. (a paperhanger) and Florence (a salesperson; maiden name, Shader) Levenkron; married Abby Rosen (a therapist), May 25, 1963; children: Rachel, Gabrielle. *Education:* Queens College of the City of New York, B.A., 1963; Brooklyn College of the City of New York, M.S., 1969.
ADDRESSES: Office—16 East 79th Street, New York, NY 10021. *Agent*—George Wieser, Wieser and Wieser, Inc., 79 Valley View, Chappaqua, NY 10514.

CAREER: Social studies teacher at secondary schools, New York City, 1963-68; guidance counselor at secondary schools, New York City, 1968-74; part-time private practice of psychotherapy, 1972-74; Montefiore Hospital and Medical Center, Bronx, NY, visiting psychotherapist, 1975—; Center for the Study of Anorexia, New York City, clinical consultant, 1981—.

MEMBER: National Association of Anorexia Nervosa and Associated Disorders (member of advisory board), American Personnel and Guidance Association, American Orthopsychiatric Association.

AWARDS, HONORS: The Best Little Girl in the World was named best book for young adults by the American Library Association, 1978-79; annual award from the National Association of Anorexia Nervosa and Associated Disorders, 1981, for bringing anorexia nervosa to public attention.

WRITINGS:

YOUNG ADULT NOVELS

The Best Little Girl in the World, Contemporary Books (Chicago), 1978.
Kessa, Popular Library (New York City), 1986.

ADULT NONFICTION

Treating and Overcoming Anorexia Nervosa, Scribner (New York City), 1982.

ADAPTATIONS: The Best Little Girl in the World was adapted as a film for television.

SIDELIGHTS: One of the world's foremost authorities on anorexia nervosa, Steven Levenkron is a psychotherapist whose specialty is treating people suffering from this disease in which a person starves himor herself in an attempt to be thinner. As defined by an article in *Los Angeles Times,* anorexia nervosa is a "hysterical aversion to food, leading to severe weight loss and malnutrition." While the remedy for anorexia nervosa is simple—just eat—that is the last thing persons suffering from this disease can bring themselves to do. Instead, they will resort to every kind of deceit to keep from eating.

Statistics show that the mortality rate for those suffering from anorexia nervosa is the highest of any psychiatric disorder. Once rare, this eating disorder is now thought to afflict more than 100,000 people in the United States, almost all of them white, middle-class women under the age of twenty-five. Anorexia nervosa can lead to such complications as infection, heart failure, irreversible hypoglycemia, and death. Levenkron's young adult novel, *The Best Little Girl in the World,* was the first to bring this disease and its dangers to the public's awareness.

Levenkron based *The Best Little Girl in the World* on his work with anorexics, most of whom are teenage girls. In it, he describes the experiences of Francesca, a fictional anorexic teen, who began dieting in an attempt to qualify for a very prestigious ballet camp. As her health deteriorates from not eating, Francesca's thinking becomes muddled because of malnutrition. Her family is distraught. Finally Francesca's physicians hospitalize her in an attempt to keep her alive. Writing in *Publishers Weekly,* Barbara A. Bannon refers to Levenkron as "an impassioned and skillful author" who uses a method "more powerful than dry facts" to raise public awareness.

In 1986 Levenkron published *Kessa,* the sequel to *The Best Little Girl,* continuing the story of Francesca. Although it is a sequel, Linda Polomski suggests in *School Library Journal* that Kessa "can be read independently." Called a "thoughtful sequel" by *Voice of Youth Advocates* reviewer Evie Wilson, *Kessa* follows Francesca through her ongoing battle to save herself and her attempts to keep a friend from falling prey to the same disease. *Kessa* "may help some [young adults] to understand the pressures and insecurities of their own lives while also providing a good read," Wilson writes in *Voice of Youth Advocates.* However, a critic in *Publishers Weekly* finds less to prause about *Kessa,* noting that "the story is difficult to follow [and] the transitions are not smooth."

Levenkron explains the symptoms of anorexia nervosa and how he treats his patients in *Treating and Overcoming Anorexia Nervosa. Voice of Youth Advocates* reviewer Susan Levine states that Levenkron writes with "clarity and compassion." Although Priscilla Johnson concludes in *School Library Journal* that *Treating and Overcoming* was "a clear, concise guide" she then states that "the lack of a bibliography and/or more footnotes limits the use of this book as a source for further study."

Levenkron once told *CA:* "I am interested in shaping psychotherapy for adolescents who have anorexia nervosa by integrating contemporary psychotherapy with feminism. This calls for a rethinking of the kinds of interpretations and meanings attributed to patients' statements in psychotherapy. Such interpretations would take into consideration the effects of role modeling within the family and existential dilemmas of mothers—and women in general—in today's society. This implies less emphasis on traditional Freudian-analytical concepts that were not formulated with an empathic approach to women."

BIOGRAPHICAL/CRITICAL SOURCES:

PERIODICALS

Discover, May, 1982.
Kirkus Reviews, July 15, 1978, p. 767.

Life, February, 1982.

Los Angeles Times, August 24, 1979.

Publishers Weekly, July 17, 1978, p. 163; December 6, 1985, p. 73.

School Library Journal, March, 1979, p. 152; December, 1982, pp. 89-90; March, 1986, p. 177.

Voice of Youth Advocates, October, 1983, p. 234; August/October, 1986, p. 146.

* * *

LEVINE, Peter D. 1944-

PERSONAL: Born June 23, 1944, in Brooklyn, NY; son of Sam (a teacher) and Pearl (a teacher) Levine; married Gale Auerbach (an artist), June 19, 1965; children: Ruth. *Education:* Columbia University, B.A., 1965, M.A., 1966; Rutgers University, Ph.D., 1971. *Religion:* Jewish.

ADDRESSES: Home—1895 Melrose, East Lansing, MI 48823. *Office*—Department of History, 336 Morrill Hall, Michigan State University, East Lansing, MI 48824.

CAREER: Michigan State University, East Lansing, instructor, 1969-70, assistant professor, 1970-71, associate professor, 1971-82, professor of American history and associate chair of department of history, 1982—, director of American studies program, 1994—.

WRITINGS:

State Legislative Parties in the Jacksonian Era: New Jersey, 1829-1844, Fairleigh Dickinson University Press (East Brunswick, NJ), 1977.

A. G. Spalding and the Rise of Baseball, Oxford University Press (New York City), 1985.

American Sport: A Documentary History, Prentice-Hall (Englewood Cliffs, NJ), 1989.

Ellis Island to Ebbets Field: Sports and the American Jewish Experience, Oxford University Press, 1992.

(With Robert Lipsyte) *Idols of the Game: A Sporting History of the American Century,* Turner, 1995.

Editor of series on sport and history for Oxford University Press. Contributor to history journals. Editor of *Journal of Baseball History.*

WORK IN PROGRESS: The Rabbi of Swat, a novel.

LEVINE, Philip 1928-

PERSONAL: Born January 10, 1928, in Detroit, MI; son of A. Harry (a businessman) and Esther Gertrude (a bookseller; maiden name, Priscoll) Levine; married Frances Artley (an actress and costumer), July 4, 1954; children: Mark, John, Theodore Henri. *Education:* Wayne University (now Wayne State University), A.B., 1950, A.M., 1954; University of Iowa, M.F.A., 1957. *Politics:* "Anarchist." *Religion:* "Anarchist."

ADDRESSES: Home—4549 North Van Ness Ave., Fresno, CA 93704. *Office*—Department of English, California State University, Fresno, CA 93710; (autumn) Program on Creative Writing, New York University, 19 University Place, Room 200, New York, NY 10003.

CAREER: Poet. Worked at "a succession of industrial jobs" in Detroit, MI, during the early 1950s, for companies including Chevy Gear and Axle, Detroit Transmission, and Wyandotte Chemical. University of Iowa, Iowa City, member of faculty, 1955-57; California State University, Fresno, professor of English, 1958-92; Tufts University, Medford, MA, professor of English, 1981-88; Elliston Professor of Poetry, University of Cincinnati, 1976; poet in residence, National University of Australia, Canberra, summer, 1978; visiting professor of poetry, Columbia University, 1978, 1981, 1984, New York University, 1984 and 1991, and Brown University, 1985; teacher at Squaw Valley Writers Community, Bread Loaf, and Midnight Sun. Has read his poetry at the Library of Congress, Poetry Center of San Francisco, Pasadena Art Gallery, Guggenheim Museum, Princeton University, Massachusetts Institute of Technology, University of Michigan, University of California, Stanford University, Wayne State University, University of Iowa, San Francisco State University, Harvard University, Yale University, Brown University, and other schools. Chair of literature board, National Endowment for the Arts, 1984-85.

AWARDS, HONORS: Stanford University poetry fellowship, 1957; Joseph Henry Jackson Award, San Francisco Foundation, 1961, for manuscript "Berenda Slough and Other Poems" (later published as *On the Edge,* 1963); Chaplebrook Foundation grant, 1969; National Endowment for the Arts grant, 1969, 1970 (refused), 1976, 1981, 1987; named outstanding lecturer, California State University, Fresno, 1971; named outstanding professor, California State University System, 1972; Frank O'Hara Prize, *Poetry,* 1973; National Institute of Arts and Letters grant, 1973; award of merit, American Academy of Arts and Letters, 1974; Frank O'Hara Prize and Levinson Prize, *Poetry,* 1974; Guggenheim fellowship, 1974, 1981; Harriet Monroe Memorial Prize for Poetry, University of Chicago, 1976; Lenore Marshall Award for Best American Book of Poems, 1976, for *The Names of the Lost;* National Book Award for Poetry, 1979, for *Ashes: Poems New and Old;* National Book Critics Circle Prize, 1979, for *Ashes: Poems New and Old* and *7 Years from Somewhere;* notable book award, American Library Association, 1979, for *7 Years from Somewhere; Selected Poems* nominated for *Los Angeles Times* Book Prize, 1984; Golden Rose Award, New England Poetry Society, 1985; Ruth Lilly Award, Modern Poetry Association and American Council for the Arts, 1987, "in recognition of outstanding achievement"; Elmer Holmes Bobst Award, New York University, 1990, for "a life in poetry"; *Los Angeles Times* Book Prize, and National Book Award for Poetry, both 1991, both for *What Work Is;* Pulitzer Prize in Poetry, 1995, for *The Simple Truth: Poems.*

WRITINGS:

POETRY

On the Edge (limited edition), Stone Wall Press (Iowa City, IA), 1961, second edition, 1963.

Silent in America: Vivas for Those Who Failed (limited edition), Shaw Avenue Press (Iowa City, IA), 1965.

Not This Pig, Wesleyan University Press (Middletown, CT), 1968.

5 Detroits, Unicorn Press (Greensboro, NC), 1970.

Thistles: A Poem Sequence (limited edition), Turret Books (London), 1970.

Pili's Wall, Unicorn Press, 1971, second edition, 1980.

Red Dust, illustrated with prints by Marcia Mann, Kayak (Santa Cruz, CA), 1971.

They Feed They Lion, Atheneum (New York City), 1972.

1933, Atheneum, 1974.

New Season (pamphlet), Graywolf Press (Port Townsend, WA), 1975.

On the Edge and Over: Poems Old, Lost, and New, Cloud Marauder, 1976.

The Names of the Lost (limited edition), Windhover Press (Iowa City), 1976, 2nd edition, Atheneum, 1976.

7 Years from Somewhere, Atheneum, 1979.

Ashes: Poems New and Old, Atheneum, 1979.

One for the Rose, Atheneum, 1981.

Selected Poems, Atheneum, 1984.

Sweet Will, Atheneum, 1985.

A Walk with Tom Jefferson, Knopf (New York City), 1988.

New Selected Poems, Knopf, 1991.

What Work Is, Knopf, 1991.

The Simple Truth: Poems, Knopf, 1994.

EDITOR

(With Henri Coulette) *Character and Crisis: A Contemporary Reader,* McGraw (New York City), 1966.

(And translator with Ernesto Trejo) Jaime Sabines, *Tarumba: The Selected Poems of Jaime Sabines,* Twin Peaks Press, 1979.

(With Ada Long, and translator) Gloria Fuertes, *Off the Map: Selected Poems,* Wesleyan University Press, 1984.

(With D. Wojahn and B. Henderson) *The Pushcart Prize XI,* Pushcart (Wainscott, NY), 1986.

OTHER

Don't Ask (collection of interviews with Levine), University of Michigan Press (Ann Arbor), 1979.

(Selector and author of introduction) *The Essential Keats,* Ecco Press (New York City), 1987.

The Bread of Time: Toward an Autobiography (essays), Knopf, 1994.

Also author of introduction, Dennis Sampson, *Forgiveness,* Milkweed Editions, 1990. Contributor of poems to numerous anthologies, including *Midland,* Random House, 1961; *New Poets of England and America,* Meridian, 1962; *Poet's Choice,* Dial, 1962; *American Poems,* Southern Illinois University Press, 1964; and *Naked Poetry,* Bobbs-Merrill, 1969. Contributor of poems to periodicals, including *New Yorker, Poetry, New York Review of Books, Hudson Review, Paris Review,* and *Harper's.* Also narrator of sound recordings, *The Poetry and Voice of Philip Levine,* Caedmon, 1976, and *Hear Me,* Watershed Tapes.

SIDELIGHTS: Poet Philip Levine "is a large, ironic Whitman of the industrial heartland," who, according to Edward Hirsch in *New York Times Book Review,* should be considered "one of our quintessentially urban poets." The son of Russian-Jewish immigrants, Levine was born and raised in industrial

Detroit and acquired a left-wing political awareness early. As a young boy in the midst of the Great Depression, he listened to his elders discuss the political "isms" and was fascinated by the events of the Spanish Civil War. His heroes were not only those individuals who struggled against fascism and the state but ordinary folks who worked at hopeless jobs simply to stave off poverty. Joan Taylor writes in the *Dictionary of Literary Biography:* "Levine met his enemy in the gray arenas of industrialism, . . . of factory hum and stink, vacant lots, junkyards, and railroad tracks. . . . Levine's hero is the lonely individual who tries and often fails within this big industrial machine."

While working in the auto plants of Detroit during the 1950s, Levine resolved "to find a voice for the voiceless," he told *CA.* "I saw that the people that I was working with . . . were voiceless in a way," he explains in *Detroit Magazine.* "In terms of the literature of the United States they weren't being heard. Nobody was speaking for them. And as young people will, you know, I took this foolish vow that I would speak for them and that's what my life would be. And sure enough I've gone and done it. Or I've tried anyway. . . . I just hope I have the strength to carry it all the way through." For more than three decades, Levine has spoken for the working men and women of America's industrial cities.

In the *Hudson Review,* Vernon Young finds that Levine "has never acknowledged the claim of any society save that of the bluecollar dispossessed, the marginal and crunched for whom he has elected to be the evangelist and spokesman." Herbert Leibowitz, in a *New York Times Book Review* article on Levine's award-winning collection *Ashes: Poems New and Old,* comments: "Levine has returned again and again in his poems to the lives of factory workers trapped by poverty and the drudgery of the assembly line, which breaks the body and scars the spirit." However, the speaker in Levine's poems "is never a blue-collar caricature," argues Richard Tillinghast in his *New York Times Book Review,* "but someone with brains, feelings and a free-wheeling imagination that constantly fights to free him from his prosaic environment."

In addition to concentrating on the working class in his work, Levine has paid tribute to the Spanish anarchist movement of the 1930s, especially in *The Names of the Lost.* According to Leibowitz, "Though he was too young to fight in that war, it embodies for him the historical exemplum: a people's uprising that succeeded, quixotically, for a few rare days in hinting at what a genuine egalitarian society might be." Charles Molesworth explains in *The Fierce Embrace* that Levine connected the Spanish revolutionaries with Detroit's laboring class during a brooding stay in Barcelona: "Both cities are built on the backs of sullen, exploited workers, and the faded revolution in one smolders like the blunting, racist fear in the other." As Leibowitz sums up, "The poet's 'Spanish self,' as he calls it, is kin to his Detroit self. Both bear witness to the visionary ideal destroyed."

Levine's concentration on the negative aspects of working class life has led many critics to describe his work as dark, brooding, and without solace. However, in *Cry of the Human,* Ralph J. Mills Jr. notes that a certain resigned acceptance of the harshness of industrial life leads Levine to "an acceptance of pain and the admission that failure, defeat, and imperfection—but not surrender!—are unavoidable." Levine is extremely sensitive to people who feel trapped in their jobs or their lives, and his portraits can't help but convey this feeling of doom. *Time*'s Paul Gray, for instance, calls Levine's speakers "guerrillas, trapped in an endless battle long after the war is lost." This sense of defeat is particularly strong when the poet recalls scenes from his Detroit childhood, where unemployment and violence colored his life.

Despite its painful quality, Levine's verse displays a certain joyfulness, a sense of victory-in-defeat, suggests Marie Borroff. Writing in the *Yale Review,* she describes the title poem of *They Feed They Lion* as "a litany celebrating, in rhythms and images of unflagging, piston-like force, the majestic strength of the oppressed, rising equally out of the substances of the poisoned industrial landscape and the intangibles of humiliation." Hirsch finds that while anger and indignation lie at the core of Levine's poetry, his later poems "have developed a softer edge while maintaining their brooding intensity." Mazzocco asserts that Levine is "affectionate in his hate, hard in his compassion," and fully aware of "the twilit other world where the negative and the positive seem to be twins of the same coin, where the poet is both victor and victim, and at times blessed because he is both." And Richard Hugo comments in the *American Poetry Review:* "Levine's poems are important because in them we hear and we care." Though Levine's poems tell of despair, pain, and inadequacy, Hugo feels that they still hold out the hope that people can triumph over sadness through language and song. Because Levine has kept alive in himself "the impulse to sing," Hugo concludes that Levine "is destined to become one of the most celebrated poets of the time."

W. S. Di Piero asserts in *Commonweal* that Levine's consistent desire to trumpet the cause of the common man sometimes "risks a kind of melodrama," which tends to weaken the impact of his verse. In the *New York Times Book Review,* Robert Pinsky says that "it must be admitted that Levine's work is uneven and that its failing is the maudlin, . . . the locking of tone into a flaw or groove, running there without the capacity for modulation of emotion: a single, sustained whine, piercing but not penetrating." Di Piero, however, believes "that in Levine's case this is a flaw of a high order, commensurate with his high ambition." Pinsky qualifies his criticism as well, stating that "Levine has earned and undertaken the hardness of high standards."

Levine's poetry for and about the common man is distinguished by simple diction and a rhythmic narrative style—by what Pinsky calls "the strength of a living syntax." In an *American Poetry Review* appraisal of *Ashes* and *7 Years from Somewhere,* Dave Smith notes that in Levine's poems "the language, the figures of speech, the narrative progressions are never so obscure, so truncated as to forbid less sophisticated readers. Though he takes on the largest subjects of death, love, courage, manhood, loyalty, etc., he brings the mysteries of existence down into the ordinarily inarticulate events and objects of daily life." "Levine's poetic world values reality above all else," Robert D. Spector remarks in the *Saturday Review,* "a reality that is reinforced by his earthy language, colloquial syntax, and natural rhythms." Molesworth believes that Levine's work reflects the mistrust of language that characterizes the laboring people of whom he writes. Therefore, rather than compressing multiple meanings into individual words and phrases, and balancing their tonal and semantic qualities, as in traditionally conceived poetry, Levine's simple narratives work to reflect the concrete and matter-of-fact speech patterns of working people. Taylor describes this aspect of Levine's work as a concern with what is "*out there*" rather than the more typical "postmodernist concern with words as the process by which one perceives what is out there." Levine himself, in an interview with Calvin Bedient in *Parnassus,* defines his "ideal poem" as one in which "no words are noticed. You look through them into a vision of . . . the people, the place."

Several critics have faulted Levine for the very reliance on narrative descriptions of realistic situations that are his hallmark. Finding Levine to be too realistic, Clayton Eshleman claims in a *Los Angeles Times* review of *Selected Poems* that "the literal perspective admits only a single actor in a single life scene." Because Levine's poetic stance "boils down to: This is what happened to me and this is what I am," Eshleman concludes that more imaginative poetic devices such as association, word play, and ambiguity would be alien in his verse. Helen Vendler thinks that this lack of traditional poetic devices makes Levine "simply a memoir-writer in prose who chops up his reminiscent paragraphs into short lines," and asks in her *New York Review of Books* appraisal of *One for the Rose,* "Is there any compelling reason why it should be called poetry?" This objection to Levine's verse originates in "the primarily narrative nature" of his poems, says Taylor, who concludes that "Levine may now be approaching the solution more closely than ever in his growing concern with his language and his lines as they reflect his poetic vision." Thomas Hackett, in his *Village Voice Literary Supplement* review of *A Walk with Tom Jefferson,* argues that, rather than being a weakness, Levine's "strength is the declarative, practically journalistic sentence. He is most visual and precise when he roots his voice in hard, earthy nouns."

Levine has also been criticized, as Leibowitz puts it, for "digging for gold in a nearly exhausted vein." "Some have said he has written the same poem for years, that he lacks variety and vision," Smith comments. "True, his vision is such a relentless denunciation of injustice that he has occasionally engaged in reductive oversimplifications." Smith believes that despite this objection and others, Levine's poetry is "nearly a national treasure." According to Jack Anderson in *Prairie Schooner,* "Levine achieves a calm resolution, . . . one devoid of easy sentimentality and consonant with his flinty perceptions."

Levine's ability to craft deeply affecting poems has long been his hallmark, and he is among the few contemporary poets who write convincingly about working people without being condescending. "His poems are personal, love poems, poems of horror, poems about the experiencing of America," Stephen Spender writes in the *New York Review of Books.* Joyce Carol Oates says in the *American Poetry Review,* "He is one of those poets whose work is so emotionally intense, and yet so controlled, so concentrated, that the accumulative effect of reading a number of his related poems can be shattering. . . . I really think he is extraordinary," Oates calls Levine "a visionary of our dense, troubled mysterious time." David Baker, writing about *What Work Is* in *Kenyon Review,* says Levine has "one of our most resonant voices of social conviction and witness, and he speaks with a powerful clarity. . . . *What Work Is* may be one of the most important books of poetry of our time. Poem after poem confronts the terribly damaged conditions of American labor, whose circumstance has perhaps never been more wrecked."

Some reviewers find Levine's Pulitzer Prize-winning poetry collection, *The Simple Truth,* published in 1994, somewhat more subdued than his previous work. While Levine covers his usual subjects in the book, he does so with a different tone—one of wistful remembrance, several critics report. A writer for *Virginia Quarterly Review* asserts the volume's poems lack "the hard edge and passion" found in *What Work Is,* but they still are "deeply felt, leavened with personal experience and family memories." At the same time, Levine carefully avoids becoming maudlin, says a reviewer for *Publishers Weekly:* "Wryness intervenes to temper mourning."

Levine explores the forces that have shaped his life and poetry in *The Bread of Time: Toward an Autobiography,* a collection of nine essays. Levine deals with his experiences as a factory worker, his family and friends, the writers who served as his mentors, and his fascination with the Spanish Civil War and Spanish poets. One notable aspect of the book, several critics point out, is that Levine portrays his mentors John Berryman and Yvor Winters much more sympathetically than have other observers. Richard Eder, writing in the *Los Angeles Times Book Review,* considers the essays on Berryman, Winters, and the Spanish poet Antonio Machado to be the strongest in the book. Through it all, adds Tod Marshall in the *Georgia Review,* "the book's main focus—much to the benefit and delight of anyone interested in the formative years of one of our best contemporary poets—is Levine's relationship with poetry." Mary Kaiser, reviewing for *World Literature Today,* describes that relationship in this way: "In this novel approach to the memoir, Philip Levine comes across as a man dedicated to poetry with a romantic faith in its power to reflect and affect the real world." Levine's "novel approach" does not please all, however; Dana Gioia asserts in the *New York Times Book Review* that Levine's "inspired subjectivity aggravates the problems inherent in the book's episodic structure. For all its energy, *The*

Bread of Time never develops much narrative momentum." Gioia also criticizes Levine's "self-dramatization" and "his obsession with settling old scores." A different view comes from Phoebe Pettingell, in the *New Leader.* She writes that "Levine hardly plays the hero" and shows a sense of humor about himself. "All of the chapters in this memoir," she adds, "engage us as much as short stories do." Marshall further finds the collection an excellent companion to Levine's poems: "If one knows his poetry, I'd recommend keeping it handy while reading this book; if a reader is unfamiliar with Levine's work, then *The Bread of Time* should serve as an effective stimulus to seek it out."

BIOGRAPHICAL/CRITICAL SOURCES:

BOOKS

Buckley, Christopher, *Stranger to Nothing: On the Poetry of Philip Levine,* University of Michigan Press, 1991.

Contemporary Literary Criticism, Gale (Detroit), Volume 2, 1974, Volume 4, 1975, Volume 5, 1976, Volume 9, 1978, Volume 14, 1980, Volume 33, 1984.

Dictionary of Literary Biography, Volume 5: *American Poets since World War II,* Gale, 1980.

Levine, Philip, *Don't Ask,* University of Michigan Press, 1979.

Levine, *The Bread of Time: Toward an Autobiography,* Knopf, 1994.

Mills, Ralph J., Jr., *Cry of the Human,* University of Illinois Press (Champaign), 1975.

Molesworth, Charles, *The Fierce Embrace: A Study of Contemporary American Poetry,* University of Missouri Press (Columbia), 1979.

PERIODICALS

American Poetry Review, November, 1972; May, 1973; March, 1974; May, 1974; May, 1977; November, 1979.

Antioch Review, spring/summer, 1977.

Boston Globe, February 2, 1994, p. 63.

Carleton Miscellany, fall, 1968.

Chicago Tribune, March 2, 1994, section 5, p. 3.

Chicago Tribune Book World, August 5, 1984.

Commonweal, October 12, 1979.

Detroit Magazine, February 26, 1978.

Georgia Review, spring, 1980; winter, 1994, pp. 821-24.

Harper's, January, 1980.

Hudson Review, winter, 1979-80.

Kenyon Review, fall, 1989; summer, 1992, pp. 166-73.

Los Angeles Times, September 10, 1984; May 16, 1995, p. A1.

Los Angeles Times Book Review, October 21, 1984; September 8, 1991, p. 11; August 30, 1992, p. 6; January 16, 1994, p. 3.

Nation, February 2, 1980; December 30, 1991, p. 864.

New Leader, January 17, 1977; August 13, 1979; December 27, 1993, pp. 12-13.

New York Review of Books, April 25, 1968; September 20, 1973; April 3, 1975; December 17, 1981.

New York Times, May 29, 1985.

New York Times Book Review, July 16, 1972; February 20, 1977; October 7, 1979; September 12, 1982; August 5, 1984; December 8, 1991, p. 7; May 31, 1992, p. 28; February 20, 1994, p. 14.

New York Times Magazine, February 3, 1980.

Parnassus, fall/winter, 1972; fall/winter, 1974; fall/winter, 1977; spring/summer, 1978.

Poetry, July, 1972; March, 1975; August, 1977; December, 1980; December, 1989; May, 1992, p. 94.

Prairie Schooner, winter, 1974.

Publishers Weekly, September 26, 1994, p. 58; November 7, 1994, p. 41.

Saturday Review, June 1, 1968; March 11, 1972; September 7, 1977.

Sewanee Review, spring, 1976.

Shenandoah, summer, 1972.

Southern Review, spring, 1992.

Time, June 25, 1979.

Times Literary Supplement, September 11, 1981; July 2, 1982.

Village Voice Literary Supplement, May, 1982; July 19, 1988.

Virginia Quarterly Review, autumn, 1972; spring, 1995, pp. 64-65.

Wall Street Journal, March 15, 1994, p. A18.

Washington Post, February 14, 1994, p. D2.

Western Humanities Review, autumn, 1972.

World Literature Today, spring, 1995, pp. 371-72.

Yale Review, autumn, 1972; autumn, 1980.

* * *

LINDBERG, Richard 1953-

PERSONAL: Born June 14, 1953, in Chicago, IL; son of Oscar Waldemar (a contractor) and Helen (a clerk; maiden name, Stone) Lindberg; married Denise Janda (a claims supervisor), July 1, 1978. *Education:* Northeastern Illinois University, B.A., 1974, M.A., 1987. *Politics:* "Moderate Republican." *Religion:* Methodist.

ADDRESSES: Home—5915 N. Navarre Ave., Chicago, IL 60631. *Office*—Combined Counties Police Association, 55 S. Northwest Hwy., Palatine, IL 60067. *Agent*—Connie Goddard, Goddard Book Group, 203 N. Wabash Ave., Chicago, IL 60601.

CAREER: Sears, Roebuck & Co., Inc., Chicago, IL, beginning 1971, department manager, 1982-84; The Signature Group, Schaumburg, IL, senior scriptwriter, 1984-88; Chicago White Sox, Chicago, IL, team historian, 1985—; Americall Corp., Downers Grove, IL, account executive, 1988; Crime Books, Inc., Wilmette, IL, senior editor, 1989-92; *The Illinois Police & Sheriff's News,* Palatine, IL, managing editor, 1992—. Reporter for Lerner Newspaper Chain, 1977-81.

MEMBER: Society for the Study of American Baseball Research, Merry Gangsters Literary Society (co-founder), Society of Midland Authors, Chicago Crime Commission, Chicago Press Veterans Association, Phi Alpha Theta (Pi Gamma chapter president, 1988-89).

AWARDS, HONORS: Robert Zegger Memorial Award, Phi Alpha Theta, Pi Gamma chapter, 1987, for graduate thesis "The Impact of Politics, Gambling, and Vice on the Chicago Police Department, 1855-1920."

WRITINGS:

Stuck on the Sox, Sassafrass Press (Evanston, IL), 1978.

(With Cindy Cooney, Ron Pazola, Fritz Plous, and Linda Warner) *A Kid's Guide to Chicago,* G. T. Nelson Publishing (Chicago, IL), 1980.

Who's on Third?: The Chicago White Sox Story, Icarus (South Bend, IN), 1983.

The Macmillan White Sox Encyclopedia, Macmillan (New York City), 1984.

To Serve and Collect: Chicago Politics and Police Corruption from the Lager Beer Riot to the Summerdale Scandal, 1855-1960, Praeger Press (New York City), 1991.

Passport's Guide to Ethnic Chicago, Passport Books (Chicago, IL), 1992.

Stealing First in a Two Team Town, Sagamore Publishing (Champagne, IL), 1994.

Chicago Ragtime: Another Look at Chicago, 1880-1920, Icarus, 1995, paperback edition published as *Chicago by Gaslight,* Academy Chicago Publishers (Chicago, IL), 1995..

OTHER

Contributor to *The Baseball Biographical Encyclopedia,* Morrow, 1990; contributor to periodicals, including *Chicago History, Inside Chicago* and *U. S. A. Today Magazine;* contributor to newspapers, including *Chicago Sun Times, Chicago Tribune,* and *Lifetimes.*

WORK IN PROGRESS: The White Sox Encyclopedia, for Temple University Press; *Quotable Chicagoans,* for Wild Onion Books; *The Whiskey Breakfast,* a memoir of my father and growing up.

SIDELIGHTS: Richard Lindberg told *CA:* "As a boy I was an insecure loner, bullied by my school classmates and not finding much joy in childhood. Coming from a broken home I turned inward and expressed my private thoughts in a diary I have maintained for the past 30 years. This practical experience provided the foundation for my future writing endeavors.

"After seven books exploring various Chicago themes, I hope to write a more personal memoir about my childhood on the Southwest Side of Chicago, and the struggle to come to terms with my immigrant father—a distant and aloof figure who emigrated from Sweden in 1924 because of his political convictions. Only after he died in 1986 did I learn the full truth about my father who had left his native land illegally in order to escape from the Swedish draft and an illegitimate child he had sired.

"I hope to juxtapose these incidents from his life with a broader story about the Northwest Side of Chicago. For I have discovered over the years that there exists two Chicagos. The creative spirit—or what there is of it in Chicago—exists in a narrow corridor hugging the Chicago lakefront. The writers, poets, musicians, and 'glitterati' of the lakefront Gold Coast know so very little about the neighborhoods west of Ashland Avenue and fanning out across Cook County, north, west, and south. The *real* Chicago of bungalows, two-flats, manicured lawns, and average work-a-day people have very little interaction with the city dwellers. There are really two Chicagos, and one could build a wall down this Ashland avenue dividing line and no-one from either side would notice the difference.

"As a product of this bungalow belt culture, and presently 'exiled' in the suburbs, I am somewhat of an anomaly among my peers in the writing field. Yet we all have a story to tell, and if I am to be remembered at all, I hope it will be as the voice of the Northwest Side, even if I am a *solitary* voice."

*   *   *

LIVINGSTONE, Harrison Edward   1937-
    (John Fairfield)

PERSONAL: Born May 23, 1937, in Urbana, IL. *Education:* Eastern College (now merged with University of Baltimore), LL.B., 1965; Harvard University, B.A., 1970. *Politics:* "Neutral." *Religion:* "Episcopal—not a formal member." *Avocational interests:* Back-packing, sailing.

ADDRESSES: Home—1609 Park Grove Ave., Baltimore, MD 21228.

CAREER: Writer. Teacher at seminars in creative writing at Harvard University, 1969-70. *Military service:* U.S. Air Force.

WRITINGS:

Poems, privately printed, 1967.
(Under pseudonym John Fairfield) *David Johnson Passed through Here,* Little, Brown (Boston), 1971.
Harvard, John: A Story of the Sixties (novel), Conservatory Press (Baltimore), 1987.
(With Robert J. Groden) *High Treason: The Assassination of President John F. Kennedy: What Really Happened,* Conservatory Press, 1989.
High Treason 2: The Great Cover-up: The Assassination of President John F. Kennedy, Carroll & Graf (New York City), 1992.
Killing the Truth: Deceit and Deception in the JFK Case, Carroll & Graf, 1993.
Killing Kennedy and the Hoax of the Century, Carroll & Graf, 1995.

Also author of an unpublished novel, *The Wild Rose.*

SIDELIGHTS: Harrison Edward Livingstone has written several books dealing with the assassination of President John Kennedy and an alleged conspiracy behind his death. Speaking of *Killing the Truth: Deceit and Deception in the JFK Case,* the reviewer for *Library Journal* notes that "sloppy scholarship and argumentative writing destroy whatever merit exists in Livingstone's case." But a critic for *Kirkus Reviews* finds that in *High Treason 2: The Great Cover-up: The Assassination of President John F. Kennedy,* "the author has much new evidence to offer, and is good at exploding evidence put forth by others."

BIOGRAPHICAL/CRITICAL SOURCES:

PERIODICALS

Baltimore Sun, November 28, 1971.
Booklist, April 15, 1992, p. 1489.
Kirkus Reviews, April 1, 1992, pp. 446-447; October 15, 1993, p. 1313.
Library Journal, November 15, 1993, pp. 87-88.
New York Times Book Review, November 21, 1993, p. 15.

* * *

LOMPERIS, Timothy J.   1947-

PERSONAL: Born March 6, 1947, in Guntur, India; U.S. citizen; son of Clarence G. (an American missionary) and Marjorie (an American missionary; maiden name, Larsen) Lomperis; married Ana Maria Turner (a university professor), May 15, 1976; children: Kristina Maria, John Scott Anders. *Ethnicity:* "Caucasian." *Education:* Augustana College, Rock Island, IL, A.B. (magna cum laude), 1969; Johns Hopkins School of Advanced International Studies, M.A., 1975; Duke University, M.A., 1978, Ph.D., 1981. *Religion:* Lutheran.

ADDRESSES: Home—5 Peterson Road, Monroe, NY 10950. *Office*—Department of Social Sciences, U.S. Military Academy, West Point, NY 10996-1798. *E-mail*—jt5435@westpoint-emh2.army.mil.

CAREER: U.S. Embassy Defense Attache Office, Saigon, South Vietnam, Intelligence Liaison Officer, 1973; Lutheran Immigration and Refugee Service,

New York, NY, special assistant to the director and head of Lao program, 1975-76; Louisiana State University, Baton Rouge, assistant professor of political science, 1980-83; Duke University, Durham, NC, visiting assistant professor of political science, 1983-84; assistant professor of political science, 1984-94; U.S. Military Academy, West Point, NY, associate professor of political science, 1994—. WTVD News, on-air Persian Gulf consultant, 1990-91. *Military service:* U.S. Army, 1969-73; served in Vietnam; became first lieutenant; received Bronze Star and Vietnam Army Staff Medal first class.

MEMBER: International Studies Association, American Political Science Association, American Studies Association.

AWARDS, HONORS: Helen Dwight Reid Award, American Political Science Association, 1982, for dissertation in international relations, "A Conceptual Framework for Deriving the Lessons of History: The U.S. Involvement in Vietnam as a Case Study"; Olin fellow at Harvard University's Center for International Affairs, 1985-86; fellow at Woodrow Wilson International Center for Scholars, Smithsonian Institution, Washington, DC, 1988.

WRITINGS:

Hindu Influence on Greek Philosophy: The Odyssey of the Soul from the Upanishads to Plato, Minerva Associates, 1984.
The War Everyone Lost—and Won: America's Intervention in Vietnam's Twin Struggles, Louisiana State University Press (Baton Rouge), 1984, revised edition, CQ Press, 1993.
"Reading the Wind": The Literature of the Vietnam War, Duke University Press (Durham, NC), 1987.
From People's War to People's Rule: Insurgency, Intervention, and the Lessons of Vietnam, University of North Carolina Press (Chapel Hill), 1996.

Contributor to periodicals.

SIDELIGHTS: Timothy J. Lomperis told *CA:* "My interest in Vietnam was sparked by the two tours of duty I served there, during which time a fear gnawed at me: we Americans didn't seem to know what we were doing in Indochina. Since I had invested too much of myself in this war, I was determined, for myself at least, to plumb the depths of this experience. This 'plumbing' is continuing, but one of the first things to strike me was that after 1968 the communists had lost their direction as well. It is from this perspective on mutual ignorance that I developed the thesis for *The War Everyone Lost—and Won: America's Intervention in Vietnam's Twin Struggles,* that victory and defeat were shared by both sides. Obviously, then, when the subject turns to lessons, I have come to strongly believe that the Vietnam War is too complicated for easy historical lessons.

"In my next book, *From People's War to People's Rule: Insurgency, Intervention, and the Lessons of Vietnam,* I explore the quest for lessons from the vantage point that whatever lessons there are will have to be teased out from the political setting of each historical case. There is an enormous amount of literature on Vietnam, both nonfiction and fiction. It was the weighing of the relative contributions of each against an overall understanding of the war that I sought to analyze in my recent *'Reading the Wind': The Literature of the Vietnam War.*

"*From People's War to People's Rule* was eleven years in the making. Inevitably, the book became the centerpiece of my struggle for tenure at Duke. Intended as the definitive work on the lessons of Vietnam, its complexity and politically incorrect message led my detractors to insist that no major press would publish the work, and my bid for tenure was denied. Its enthusiastic subsequent publication by the University of North Carolina Press makes this, more than a book, the vindication of my career."

*   *   *

LOURIE, Helen
    See STORR, Catherine (Cole)

*   *   *

LUCAS, Henry C(ameron), Jr.   1944-

PERSONAL: Born September 4, 1944, in Omaha, NE; son of Henry Cameron (an advertising executive) and Lois (a teacher; maiden name, Himes) Lucas; married Ellen Kuhbach, June 8, 1968; children: Scott Cameron, Jonathan Gerdes. *Education:* Yale University, B.S. (magna cum laude), 1966; Massachusetts Institute of Technology, M.S., 1968, Ph.D., 1970. *Avocational interests:* Jogging, cycling, sailing, travel.

ADDRESSES: Home—18 Portland Rd., Summit, NJ 07901. *Office*—Information Systems Area, School of Business, New York University, New York, NY 10003.

CAREER: Arthur D. Little, Inc., Cambridge, MA, consultant on information systems, 1966-70; Stanford University, Graduate School of Business, Stanford, CA, assistant professor of computer and information system, 1970-74; New York University, New York City, associate professor of computer applications and information systems, 1974-78, professor of computer applications and information systems and chair of department, Schools of Business, both 1978-84, professor of information systems, Graduate School of Business Administration, 1984-88, Research Professor of Information Systems, Leonard N. Stern School of Business, 1988—. Visiting professor at INSEAD, Fontainebleau, France, 1985; visiting researcher, Bell Communications Research, Morristown, NJ, 1991. Vice president of publications, Association for Information Systems, 1995.

MEMBER: Association for Computing Machinery, Institute of Management Sciences, Insitute of Electrical and Electronics Engineers, Association of Information Systems, Phi Beta Kappa, Tau Beta Pi.

AWARDS, HONORS: Award for Excellence in teaching, Schools of Business, 1982; Westside Alumni Hall of Fame Award, 1991.

WRITINGS:

Computer-Based Information Systems in Organizations, Science Research Associates (Palo Alto, CA), 1973.
Toward Creative Systems Design (monograph), Columbia University Press (New York City), 1974.
Why Information Systems Fail (monograph), Columbia University Press, 1975.
The Implementation of Computer-Based Models (monograph), National Association of Accountants (New York City), 1976.
The Analysis, Design, and Implementation of Information Systems, McGraw (New York City), 1976, 4th edition, 1992.

(With C. F. Gibson) *Casebook for Management Information Systems,* McGraw, 1976, 3rd edition, 1985.

Information Systems Concepts for Management, McGraw, 1978, 6th edition, 1996.

(Editor with F. Land, T. J. Lincoln, and K. Supper) *The Information Systems Environment,* North-Holland (New York City), 1980.

Implementation: The Key to Successful Information Systems (monograph), Columbia University Press, 1981.

Coping with Computers: A Manager's Guide to Controlling Information Processing, Free Press (New York City), 1982.

Introduction to Computers and Information Systems, Macmillan (New York City), 1987.

Managing Information Services, Macmillan, 1989.

(Senior Editor with R. Schwartz) *The Challenge of Information Technology for Securities Markets: Liquidity, Volatility and Global Trading,* Dow Jones-Irwin (Homewood, IL), 1989.

The T-Form Organization: Using Technology to Design Organizations for the 21st Century, Jossey-Bass (San Francisco), 1996.

CONTRIBUTOR

F. Gruenberger, editor, *Efficient versus Effective Computing,* Prentice-Hall (Englewood Cliffs, NJ), 1973.

R. Schultz and D. Slevin, editors, *Implementing Operations Research/Management Science: Research Findings and Implications,* Elsevier Science (New York City), 1975.

R. Goldberg and H. Lorin, editors, *The Economics of Information Processing,* Volume 2, Wiley (New York City), 1982.

G. Salvendi, editor, *The Handbook of Industrial Engineering,* Wiley, 1982.

H. Ansoff, A. Bosman, and P. Storms, editors, *Understanding and Managing Strategies Change,* North-Holland, 1982.

OTHER

Contributor to information systems and management journals. Editor in chief of *Systems, Objectives, Solutions;* associate editor of *MIS Quarterly,* 1978-83, *Management Science,* 1985-87, *ACM Transactions on Office Information Systems,* 1985-87, and *Information and Management;* editor of *Industrial Management* (now *Sloan Management Review*), 1967-68, and *Performance Evaluation Review,* 1972-73; member of editorial board of *Sloan Management Review,* 1980-91.

WORK IN PROGRESS: Research on information technology and organization design and the management of information technology.

SIDELIGHTS: Henry C. Lucas, Jr., told *CA:* "The powerful combination of computers and networks make it possible to design radically new organizations, a topic I explore in *The T-Form Organization: Using Technology to Design Organizations for the 21st Century.*"

* * *

LUTTRELL, Ida (Alleene) 1934-

PERSONAL: Surname is accented on first syllable; born April 18, 1934, in Laredo, TX; daughter of Pelton Bruce (a rancher) and Helen (a teacher and rancher; maiden name, Sewell) Harbison; married William S. Luttrell (in real estate and insurance), January 20, 1959; children: Robert, Anne, Billy, Richard. *Education:* University of Texas, B. A., 1955; also attended University of Houston, 1960, and Houston Baptist University, 1969, 1970, 1971. *Religion:* Protestant. *Avocational interests:* "One of my favorite activities is helping in the school library and reading to the primary grades. I also enjoy gardening, plays, family get-togethers, and sharing my husband's interest in old and contemporary art glass. I also like to do needlework occasionally, including designing and stitching quilts."

ADDRESSES: Home—12211 Beauregard, Houston, TX 77024.

CAREER: Writer. University of Texas, Main University (now University of Texas at Austin), laboratory technician at Biochemical Institute, 1954-55; Texas Children's Hospital, Houston, bacteriologist, 1955-63; Luttrell Insurance Agency, Houston, TX, part-time secretary, 1963—.

MEMBER: Authors Unlimited of Houston.

WRITINGS:

JUVENILES

Not Like That, Armadillo, illustrated by Janet Stevens, Harcourt (San Diego, CA), 1982.
One Day at School, illustrated by Jared D. Lee, Harcourt, 1984.

Lonesome Lester, illustrated by Megan Lloyd, Harper (New York City), 1984.

Tillie and Mert, illustrated by Doug Cushman, Harper, 1985.

Mattie and the Chicken Thief, illustrated by Thacher Hurd, Dodd (New York City), 1988.

Ottie Slockett, illustrated by Ute Krause, Dial (New York City), 1990.

Three Good Blankets, illustrated by Michael McDermott, Atheneum (New York City), 1990.

Be Nice to Marilyn, illustrated by Lonnie Sue Johnson, Atheneum, 1992.

Milo's Toothache, illustrated by Enzo Giannini, Dial, 1992.

Mattie's Little Possum Pet, illustrated by Betsy Lewin, Atheneum, 1993.

The Star Counters, illustrated by Korinna Pretro, Tambourine Books, 1994.

Contributor to books, including *Collectible Glass,* edited by A. Christian Revi, Everybody's Press, 1980, and *Three Ingredient Cookbook,* edited by Phyllis Prokop, 1981.

Contributor to *Antique Trader, Collectible Glass,* and *Spinning Wheel.*

SIDELIGHTS: Ida Luttrell commented to *CA:* "I grew up on a small ranch in south Texas, in a family where children were plentiful and money was scarce. We could not buy books, but I can still remember the thrill of checking out my first book from the county library—*Angus and the Ducks* by Marjorie Flack, the even greater thrill when I could finally read it, and the longing to have A. A. Milne's *Winnie the Pooh* for my very own. Because ranch life was so isolated, books were a great diversion for us, as well as taming baby rabbits, mice, quail, owls, or ground squirrels for pets, and the joy we found in the profusion of wild flowers that bloomed in the fields and pastures.

"Both parents stressed the importance of an education, and there was never any doubt that we would all go to college. So I went to the University of Texas and became a bacteriologist. During the time I worked at Texas Children's Hospital I met my husband, and we now have four children. Through my children I once again became interested in children's books. I have very happy memories of reading to my children when they were small, and the closeness that sharing pleasures brings.

"Because books and reading have been so important to me, it distresses me to hear of the cutbacks in funding for public libraries. Citizens whose only source of reading material is the public library are being robbed of the enrichment books provide. With test scores declining, we need more exposure to books, and I feel the cutbacks could be made in other areas."

BIOGRAPHICAL/CRITICAL SOURCES:

BOOKS

Goettsche, Jacque, and Phyllis Prokop, *A Kind of Splendor,* Broadman (Nashville, TN), 1980.

*   *   *

LYON, Bryce Dale   1920-

PERSONAL: Born April 22, 1920, in Bellevue, OH; son of E. Paul and Florence (Gundrum) Lyon; married Mary Elizabeth Lewis, June 3, 1944; children: Geoffrey P., Jacqueline M. *Education:* Baldwin-Wallace College, A.B., 1942; Cornell University, Ph.D., 1949.

ADDRESSES: Home—6 Stratford Park, Balbrae, Bloomfield, CT 06002. *Office*—Department of History, Brown University, Brown Station, Providence, RI 02912.

CAREER: University of Colorado, Boulder, assistant professor of history, 1949-51; Harvard University, Cambridge, MA, assistant professor of history, 1951-56; University of Illinois at Urbana-Champaign, associate professor of history, 1956-59; University of California, Berkeley, professor of history, 1959-65; Brown University, Providence, RI, Barnaby and Mary Critchfield Keeney Professor of History, 1965-86, professor emeritus, 1986—, chair of department, 1968-75. *Military service:* U.S. Army Air Forces, 1942-46.

MEMBER: American Academy of Arts and Sciences (fellow), Medieval Academy of America (fellow), American Historical Association, Economic History Association, Conference on British Studies, Royal Historical Society (fellow), Belgian Royal Academy (fellow).

AWARDS, HONORS: Fellow of Belgian American Educational Foundation, 1951-52, 1959, American Council of Learned Societies, 1962-63, and National

Endowment for the Humanities, 1973-74; Guggenheim fellow, 1954-55 and 1972-73; Doctor of Pedagogy from Baldwin-Wallace College, 1972; honorary degree in letters and philosophy from University of Ghent, 1988.

WRITINGS:

(Editor) Carl Stephenson, *Medieval Institutions: Selected Essays,* Cornell University Press (Ithaca, NY), 1954.

From Fief to Indenture: The Transition from Feudal to Non-Feudal Contract in Western Europe, Harvard University Press (Cambridge, MA), 1957.

A Constitutional and Legal History of Medieval England, Harper (New York City), 1960, 2nd edition, Norton (New York City), 1980.

(With others) *A History of the World,* Rand McNally (Chicago), 1960.

(With Stephenson) *Medieval History,* 4th edition, Harper, 1962.

The High Middle Ages, 1000-1013, Free Press of Glencoe, 1964.

(With A. E. Verhulst) *Medieval Finance: A Comparison of Financial Institutions in Northwestern Europe,* Brown University Press (Providence, RI), 1967.

(Translator with wife, Mary Lyon) Francois L. Ganshof, *Frankish Institutions Under Charlemagne,* University Press of New England (Hanover, NH), 1968.

(With Herbert H. Rowen and Theodore S. Hamerow) *A History of the Western World,* Rand McNally, 1969, 2nd edition, 1974.

The Origins of the Middle Ages: Pirenne's Challenge to Gibbon, Norton, 1972.

Henri Pirenne: A Biographical and Intellectual Study, E. Story-Scientia, 1974.

(Editor with M. Lyon) *The Journal de Guerre of Henri Pirenne,* North-Holland Publishing (New York City), 1976.

Studies of West European and Medieval Institutions, Variorum Reprints, 1978.

Magna Carta, the Common Law, and Parliament in Medieval England, Forum Press (Arlington Heights, IL), 1980.

(With Henry S. Lucas and M. Lyon) *The Wardrobe Book of William de Norwell: 12 July 1338 to 27 May 1340,* Palais de Academies (Brussels), 1983.

The Birth of Annales History: The Letters of Lucien Febvre and Marc Bloch to Henri Pirenne (1921-1935), Palais des Academies, 1994.

Reflexions d'un solitaire by Henri Pirenne, Palais des Academies, 1994.

Contributor to history journals. Contributor to *Encyclopedia Americana* and *World Book Encyclopedia.*

SIDELIGHTS: Bryce Dale Lyon told *CA:* "My primary motivation for writing is to investigate unexplored areas in medieval history. I have written a number of textbooks to make knowledge of the Middle Ages available to college students. My articles have been for the general reader. I was much influenced by Professor Carl Stephenson of Cornell University with whom I did my doctorate degree in medieval history. He had studied with the celebrated medievalist Henri Pirenne in Belgium. This led me to Belgium for further study in medieval history, and gave me an interest in the history of medieval England, France, Germany, and the Low Countries. Becoming very familiar with the writing of Henri Pirenne, I determined to write his biography. For this purpose his son Jacques made available from his library all the pertinent sources. I also was assisted by conversations with many of Pirenne's students."

BIOGRAPHICAL/CRITICAL SOURCES:

PERIODICALS

American Historical Review, June, 1968, October, 1975.
Times Literary Supplement, October 3, 1975.

M

MACY, Joanna Rogers   1929-

PERSONAL: Born May 2, 1929, in Los Angeles, CA; daughter of Hartley (a stockbroker) and Margaret (a homemaker and office manager; maiden name, Kinsey) Rogers; married Francis Underhill Macy (an educator), May 30, 1953; children: Christopher, John, Margaret. *Education:* Wellesley College, B.A., 1950; graduate study at the University of Bordeaux; Syracuse University, Ph.D., 1978.

ADDRESSES: Home—2812 Cherry St., Berkeley, CA 94705.

CAREER: Syracuse University, Syracuse, NY, lecturer in religion, 1976-77; American University, Washington, DC, lecturer in religion, 1978-79; writer and researcher, 1980-86; California Institute of Integral Studies, San Francisco, professor, 1987—.

MEMBER: Society for Values in Higher Education, Society for General Systems Research, American Academy of Religion, Buddhist Peace Fellowship.

AWARDS, HONORS: Fulbright scholarship; Ford Foundation grant, 1979-80.

WRITINGS:

Dharma and Development, Kumarian (West Hartford, CT), 1982, revised edition, 1985.
Despair and Personal Power in the Nuclear Age, New Society (Philadelphia, PA), 1983.
(With John Seed, A. Naess, and P. Fleming) *Thinking Like a Mountain,* New Society, 1988.
World as Lover, World as Self, Parallax Press, 1991.
Mutual Causality in Buddhist Teachings and General Systems Theory, Syracuse University Press (Syracuse, NY), 1991.
(With A. Barrows) *Rilke's Book of Hours,* Putnam Riverhead, 1996.

Contributor of articles on Buddhist metaphysics and ethics to philosophy journals.

WORK IN PROGRESS: Research on Buddhism as a resource for social action; research on the theory and practice of "deep ecology."

SIDELIGHTS: Joanna Rogers Macy told *CA:* "I am active as a speaker, trainer, and workshop leader within the context of citizen action for justice, peace, and ecological survival. My teaching at the California Institute of Integral Studies and Graduate Theologian Union focuses on general systems theory, Buddhism, and ecology."

*   *   *

MAITAL, Shlomo   1942-

PERSONAL: Born November 10, 1942, in Regina, Saskatchewan, Canada; son of Morris Malt and Sally (Fages) Maital; married Sharone Levow (a school psychologist), June 25, 1967; children: Temira, Ronen, Yochai, Noam Shai. *Education:* Queen's University, B.A., M.A., 1964; University of Manchester, M.A., 1965; Princeton University, Ph.D., 1967. *Avocational interests:* Writing fiction.

ADDRESSES: Home—18 Freud St., Haifa 34753, Israel. *Office*—Faculty of Industrial Engineering and

Management, Technion-Israel Institute of Technology, Technion City, Haifa 32000, Israel; National and Economic Planning Authority, Building C, Kiryat Ben Gurion, Jerusalem, Israel.

CAREER: Technion-Israel Institute of Technology, Haifa, Israel, chairman of department of economics, 1980—. Director, National and Economic Planning Authority, Ministry of Economics and Planning, Government of Israel. *Military service:* Israel Defense Forces, 1968—; in artillery and naval reserve.

MEMBER: American Economics Association, Econometric Society.

AWARDS, HONORS: General Motors scholarship, 1960; Commonwealth fellowship, 1964.

WRITINGS:

Minds, Markets, and Money: Psychological Foundations of Economic Behavior, Basic Books (New York City), 1982.
(With wife, Sharone L. Maital) *Economic Games People Play,* Basic Books, 1984.
Executive Economics: Ten Essential Tools for Managers, The Free Press (New York City), 1994.

EDITOR

(With Noah M. Meltz) *Lagging Productivity Growth: Causes and Remedies,* Ballinger (Cambridge, MA), 1980.
(With Irwin Lipnowski) *Macroeconomic Conflict and Social Institutions,* Ballinger, 1985.
Applied Behavioral Economics, Wheatsheaf Books/ New York University Press (New York City), 1988.
(With S. L. Maital) *Economics and Psychology,* E. Elgar (Aldershot, Britain), 1993.

SIDELIGHTS: In *Minds, Markets, and Money: Psychological Foundations of Economic Behavior,* Shlomo Maital suggests a closer study of psychological motivations and implications in the supply-and-demand structure of economic systems. A reviewer in *Business Week* finds the book "persuasive, especially for people more interested in understanding the economy than in preaching about it," while Peter Passell comments in the *New York Times Book Review* that "*Minds, Markets and Money* is a delight, the rare important book about economics that charms as it informs."

In *Economic Games People Play,* Maital and his wife, Sharone L. Maital, "provide an insightful analysis of how we have arrived at some of our current economic dilemmas," writes R. Duncan Luce in the *New York Times Book Review.* Luce also notes that in a discussion of the type of economic analysis referred to as "game theory," the Maitals make clear that "some of the most difficult and unstable dilemmas involve three or more players who may form coalitions. The example they treat in detail is the interdependence of labor leaders, businessmen and government officials and the way in which their decisions have produced such undesirable outcomes as inflation." As an important potential solution for some economic dilemmas, Luce indicates that the Maitals "urge a nationwide rethinking of our social contract," or the government's role.

In *Executive Economics: Ten Essential Tools for Managers,* says reviewer B. Joseph Pine II in *Sloan Management Review,* "Shlomo Maital has made microeconomics not only intelligible to even the most 'economically challenged' managers but also applicable to everyday problems and situations. He synthesizes tried-and-true economic concepts with fascinating stories and latest research to create an effective guide to managerial decision making." He continues: "Each chapter of *Executive Economics* is a guide to a particular tool of the economic trade, made real by application to specific company situations." Chapters include information on such subjects as: the three components of profit—cost, value, and price; hidden costs; the economic swing from products to services; mass customization; the transition to variety from volume; and markets and demand.

Maital once told *CA:* "As an economist, my objective is to persuade my colleagues to pay attention to the people who buy and sell in markets, and not just the objects bought and sold and the prices at which they trade."

BIOGRAPHICAL/CRITICAL SOURCES:

PERIODICALS

Business Week, June 21, 1982.
New York Times Book Review, August 15, 1982; August 26, 1984.
Savvy, June, 1982.
Sloan Management Review, spring, 1995, p. 97.
Wall Street Journal, August 11, 1982.

MAMALAKIS, Markos J(ohn) 1932-

PERSONAL: Born October 30, 1932, in Salonica, Greece; son of Ioannis P. (a historian) and Renate (Rocha) Mamalakis; married Angelica Athanasiou, January 31, 1960; children: Anna, Katja, Marina, John, Andreas, Philip, Irene, Peter, Joanna, Alexandra, Emmanuel, Thomas. *Education:* University of Salonica, B.A. (summa cum laude), 1955; attended University of Munich, 1955-57; University of California, Berkeley, M.A., 1959, Ph.D., 1962. *Religion:* Greek Orthodox.

ADDRESSES: Home—2977 North Shepard Ave., Milwaukee, WI 53211. *Office*—Bolton 804, University of Wisconsin, Milwaukee, WI 53201.

CAREER: University of Western Ontario, London, instructor, 1961-62, assistant professor of economics, 1962-63; Yale University, New Haven, CT, assistant professor of economics, 1963-67; University of Wisconsin—Milwaukee, associate professor, 1967-69, professor of economics, 1969—, director of Center for Latin American Studies, 1967-72. Visiting professor, Universidad de Chile, 1964-66; Ford Foundation visiting professor, summer, 1966; visiting professor, University of Goettingen, 1975-76. Guest scholar, Woodrow Wilson International Center for Scholars, Smithsonian Institution, summers, 1990, 1991. Has also lectured at University of London, University of Chicago, University of Kansas, Getulio Vargas Foundation, Oxford University, University of Sussex, and numerous other universities; has appeared on radio and television programs. Member of Institute for Economic Research, Queen's University, Kingston, Ontario, summer, 1962-63.

MEMBER: International Association for Income and Wealth, American Economic Association, Latin American Studies Association.

AWARDS, HONORS: Prize for Outstanding Scholastic Performance, University of Salonica, 1952-54; German Academic Exchange Program Scholarship to University of Munich, 1955-57; Fulbright Smith-Mundt exchange program scholarship, University of California, Berkeley, 1957-58, 1958-61; Social Science Research Council grant to analyze the service sector in Latin America, 1950-65, 1969; Canada Council research grants, 1962, 1963; Ford Foundation fellow, 1963; Yale A.I.D. Grants to work on employment and unemployment in Chile, 1970-73; Fulbright-Hays faculty research grant to examine

role of services in the economic development of the Iberian Peninsula, 1971; German Research Foundation grant to analyze role of minerals in economic development, 1975-76; Tinker Foundation grants to write four volumes of *Historical Statistics of Chile,* 1977, 1979; National Endowment for the Humanities grants, 1981, 1984; Fulbright lecture grants, 1987, 1988.

WRITINGS:

(With Clark Reynolds) *Essays on the Chilean Economy,* Irwin (Homewood, IL), 1965.

La Teoria de los Choques entre Sectores (title means "The Theory of Sectoral Clashes"), Instituto de Economia, Universidad de Chile (Santiago), 1966.

The Role of the Government in the Resource Transfer and Resource Allocation Process: The Chilean Nitrate Sector, 1880-1930, University of Wisconsin—Milwaukee, Center for Latin America (Milwaukee), 1968.

(Contributor) Raymond Mikesell and others, editors, *Foreign Investment in Minerals and Petroleum,* Johns Hopkins Press for Resources for the Future (Baltimore, MD), 1971.

(Contributor) Gustav Ranis, editor, *Government and Economic Development,* Yale University Press (New Haven, CT), 1971.

The Growth and Structure of the Chilean Economy: From Independence to Allende, Yale University Press, 1976.

(Compiler) *Historical Statistics of Chile,* Greenwood Press (Westport, CT), Volume I: *National Accounts,* 1978, Volume II: *Demography and Labor Force,* 1980, Volume III: *Forestry and Related Activities,* 1982, Volume IV: *Money, Prices, and Credit Services,* 1983, Volume V: *Banking and Financial Services,* 1985, Volume VI: *Government Services and Public Sector and a Theory of Services.*

Contributor of articles and reviews to professional journals, including *Eastern Economic Journal, Handbook of Latin American Studies, Latin American Research Review, Journal of Development Studies, Journal of Interamerican Studies,* and *Economia.*

WORK IN PROGRESS: "Working on topics of economic development in an effort to assist in the formulation of policies alleviating poverty in all areas and forms."

BIOGRAPHICAL/CRITICAL SOURCES:

PERIODICALS

American Reference Books Annual, Volume 11, 1980, Volume 12, 1981, Volume 17, 1986.
Hispanic American Historical Review, February, 1980, August, 1981, August, 1983, August, 1984.
Journal of Economic History, June, 1979, December, 1985.

* * *

MANN, David Douglas   1934-

PERSONAL: Born September 13, 1934, in Oklahoma City, OK; son of Loftin Harry and Jeannette (Kneer) Mann; married Jane McKenzie, August 12, 1962 (divorced); married Cathy Hoyser, June 18, 1972 (divorced); married Susan Garland, August 15, 1983. *Education:* Oklahoma State University, B.S., 1956, M.A., 1963; Indiana University, Ph.D., 1969.

ADDRESSES: Home—379 South "D" St., Hamilton, OH 45056. *Office*—Department of English, Miami University, Oxford, OH 45056.

CAREER: Wabash College, Crawfordsville, IN, instructor in English, 1965-67; Miami University, Oxford, OH, instructor, 1968-69, assistant professor, 1969-73, associate professor, 1973-79, professor of English, 1979—. Scholar in residence, University of Luxembourg, 1978-80 and 1985-87. *Military service:* U.S. Navy, 1956-59; became lieutenant commander.

MEMBER: Modern Language Association of America, American Society for Eighteenth-Century Studies, Samuel Johnson Society Midwest.

AWARDS, HONORS: Folger Shakespeare Library fellowship, 1970; National Endowment for the Humanities grant, 1976; Bibliographic Society of America fellowship, 1988; Beinecke Library fellowship, 1989; Ball Brothers grant to the Lilly Library, 1990.

WRITINGS:

(Editor) *A Concordance to the Plays of William Congreve,* Cornell University Press (Ithaca, NY), 1973.

(Editor and author of introduction) *The Plays of Theophilus and Susannah Cibber,* Garland Press (New York City), 1981.
Sir George Etherege: A Reference Guide, G. K. Hall (Boston), 1981.
(Editor) *A Concordance to the Plays and Poems of Sir George Etherege,* Greenwood Press (Westport, CT), 1985.
(With Susan Garland Mann) *British Women Playwrights, 1660-1823,* Indiana University Press (Bloomington), 1996.

Contributor to *An Encyclopedia of British Women Writers,* 2nd edition, and *Beecham's Guide to Literature and Biography for Young Adults.* Also contributor to journals, including *Analytical & Enumerative Bibliography, Essays in Literature, PMLA, Computers and the Humanities, Mississippi Valley Review, Studies in Scottish Literature, Georgia Review, Review of English Studies, Papers of the Bibliographical Society of America, The Scriblerian, Wabash Review, Old Northwest, Journal of Narrative Technique,* and *Eighteenth-Century Studies.* Assistant editor, *Old Northwest,* 1975-78.

WORK IN PROGRESS: A critical edition of *The Wonder: A Woman Keeps a Secret,* by Susanna Centlivre (1714).

* * *

MARCUS, George E.   1946-

PERSONAL: Born October 17, 1946, in Pittsburgh, PA; son of Samuel C. and Rose (Shriber) Marcus; married Patricia Seed (a historian), June 21, 1984; children: Rachel Abigail, Avery Garth, Eliot. *Education:* Yale University, B.A. (magna cum laude), 1968; graduate study at Cambridge University, 1968-69; Harvard University, Ph.D., 1976.

ADDRESSES: Home—8211 Lorrie Dr., Houston, TX 77025. *Office*—Department of Anthropology, Rice University, Box 1892, Houston, TX 77251.

CAREER: Rice University, Houston, TX, assistant professor, 1975-80, associate professor, 1980-85, professor of anthropology, 1985—, chair of department, 1980—. Senior fellow in communications at East-West Institute, 1981; visiting member of School of Social Science, Institute for Advanced Study, Princeton, NJ, 1982-83; visiting scholar, Getty Center for the History of Art and the Humanities, Santa Monica, CA, 1988-89. *Military service:* U.S. Army, 1969-71.

MEMBER: Phi Beta Kappa.

WRITINGS:

The Nobility and the Chiefly Tradition in the Modern Kingdom of Tonga, University Press of Hawaii (Honolulu, HI), 1980.

(With Michael Fischer) *Anthropology as Cultural Critique: An Experimental Moment in the Human Sciences,* University of Chicago Press (Chicago, IL), 1986.

(With Peter Dobkin Hall) *Lives in Trust: The Fortunes of Dynastic Families in Late Twentieth Century America,* Westview Press (Boulder, CO), 1992.

EDITOR

Elites: Ethnographic Issues, University of New Mexico Press (Albuquerque, NM), 1983.

(With James Clifford, and contributor) *Writing Culture: The Politics and Poetics of Ethnography,* University of California Press (Santa Cruz, CA), 1986.

Rereading Cultural Anthropology, Duke University Press (Durham, NC), 1992.

Cultural Studies for the End of the Century, University of Chicago Press, Late Editions 1: *Perilous States: Conversations on Culture, Politics, and Nation,* 1993; Late Editions 2: *Technoscientific Imperatives: Profiles, Memoirs, and Conversations,* 1995; Late Editions 3: *Connected: Engagements with Media at the End of the Century,* in press.

(With Fred Myers) *The Traffic in Culture: Refiguring Art and Anthropology,* University of California Press, 1995.

Critical Anthropology in Fin-de-Siecle America: New Locations, Non-Standard Fieldwork, School of American Research Press (Santa Fe, NM), in press.

OTHER

Coeditor of series "New Directions in Anthropological Writing," University of Wisconsin Press. Editor of *Cultural Anthropology,* 1986-91.

WORK IN PROGRESS: Additional volumes for the *Cultural Studies for the End of the Century* series,

". . . a decade-long project of Late Editions, annuals which deal with the fin-de-siecle. I edit one volume each year until the year 2000." These are scheduled to be published by University of Chicago Press.

SIDELIGHTS: George E. Marcus told *CA:* "My initial project in anthropology was a field study of contemporary nobles and chiefs of the Kingdom of Tonga, and I have continued this sort of interest with more current field work and research on the legacies and strategies of perpetuation among established elites of wealth, talent, and power in various American and European settings. Specifically, in the United States, I am concerned with elite self-images of superiority, first in an ideologically pervasive liberal era, and now in a widely perceived era of national decline.

"During my earlier research project, the process of turning notes, memories, and data into a series of academic writings preoccupied me for several years. My temperamental resistance to writing conventional ethnography and my introduction to recent techniques of literary criticism led me to a critique of anthropology from the perspective of its rhetoric and writing strategies. Out of this, in turn, came my effort to rethink the purposes of anthropological writing itself as a form of cultural criticism. Trying to revive certain long-standing but underdeveloped critical tendencies in anthropology by connecting them to a modernist tradition of critical thought in the West, I have tried to think of innovative, if not experimental, strategies for writing ethnography. Most of these strategies involve working back and forth between contexts of intellectual and academic debates and analogous contexts in the 'real life' of those who become subjects in ethnographic research, where versions of these same debates in very different idioms and for different purposes are also conducted.

"Rather than being privileged above or outside the world of one's subjects, academic discourse and concerns become comparable and equivalent to those of subjects. The demotion of the scientific gaze in relation to its distanced object, without establishing a total context of subjectivity, makes possible the exposure of the processes by which knowledge is produced in the human sciences at the same time that it is being presented as knowledge. In short, I am interested in the various ways of realizing the practice of a cultural hermeneutics in the framework of a now thoroughly critiqued tradition of ethnographic writing in anthropology. My recent theoretical work has been devoted to both this practice and this critique, and my hope is that this work has been registered in the way that I am writing about elites in decline."

BIOGRAPHICAL/CRITICAL SOURCES:

PERIODICALS

Times Literary Supplement, February 27, 1987.
Washington Post Book World, May 4, 1986.

* * *

MARMOR, T(heodore) R(ichard) 1939-

PERSONAL: Born February 24, 1939, in New York, NY; son of James and Mira (Karpf) Marmor; married Jan Schmidt, October 20, 1961; children: Laura Carleton, Sarah Rogers. *Education:* Harvard University, B.A., 1960, Ph.D., 1966; attended Wadham College, Oxford, 1961-62. *Politics:* Democrat.

ADDRESSES: Home—139 Armory St., Hamden, CT 06511. *Office*—School of Management, Yale University, Box 17A Yale Station, New Haven, CT 06520.

CAREER: Harvard University, Cambridge, MA, instructor, 1965-66; research fellow at University of Essex, Colchester, England, and Nuffield College, Oxford University, Oxford, England, 1966-67; University of Wisconsin—Madison, 1967-70, began as assistant professor, became associate professor of political science; fellow at Adlai Stevenson Institute, Chicago, IL, 1969, and John F. Kennedy Institute, Cambridge, 1970; University of Minnesota, Minneapolis, associate professor of political science, 1970-73; University of Chicago, Chicago, professor, School of Social Service Administration, 1973-79, research fellow, Center for Health Administration, 1974-79, associate professor, Committee on Public Policy Studies, 1976-79; Yale University, New Haven, CT, professor of public health and political science and chair of Center for Health Studies, 1979-83, professor of public policy and management and political science, 1983—.

Visiting fellow, Russell Sage Foundation, 1987-88; fellow, Canadian Institute for Advanced Research, 1987—. Member of board of directors, Center for the Study of Drug Development and National Academy of Social Insurance, both 1986—. Senior advisor on health and social security, Mondale/Ferraro cam-

paign, 1983-84. Consultant to the U.S. Department of Health, Education, and Welfare, Senator Ribacoff (Connecticut), the state of Illinois governor's office, the Medicare, Congressional Committee on Ways and Means, 1984, 1986, 1991-93, the state of Texas Health Policy Task Force, 1992, and the states of Kentucky, Vermont, and Delaware on Health Care Reform, 1993.

MEMBER: Association of Public Policy and Management (institutional representative, 1984—), American Political Science Association (member of executive committee), Center for National Policy (member of advisory board, 1986-92), Connecticut Academy of Arts and Sciences.

AWARDS, HONORS: Woodrow Wilson Fellowship, 1961-62; Rotary International Fellowship, 1961-62; Harvard Graduate School Fellowship, 1962-65; Kennedy School of Government Fellowship, 1966-67; Flinn Foundation Distinguished Scholar in Health Care Management and Policy, Arizona State University, and University of Arizona, 1986; fellow, National Academy of Social Insurance, 1993; grants from Ford Foundation, Donner Foundation, Robert Wood Johnson Foundation, and other foundations.

WRITINGS:

(With wife, Jan S. Marmor) *The Politics of Medicare,* Routledge & Kegan Paul (London), 1970, Aldine-Atherton (Chicago), 1973.
(Editor and contributor) *Poverty Policy: A Compendium of Cash Transfer Proposals,* Aldine-Atherton, 1971.
(Editor with Judith Feder and John Holahan) *National Health Insurance: Conflicting Goals and Policy Choices,* Urban Institute (Washington, DC), 1980.
(With Stephen M. Davidson) *The Cost of Living Longer,* Lexington Books (Lexington, MA), 1980.
(With Jon B. Christianson) *Health Care Policy: A Political Economy Approach,* Sage Publications (Beverly Hills, CA), 1982.
Political Analysis and American Medical Care: Essays, Cambridge University Press (New York City), 1983.
(Contributor) J. Doig and E. Hargrove, editors, *Leadership and Innovation: A Biographical Perspective on Entrepreneurs in Government,* Johns Hopkins University Press (Baltimore, MD), 1987.

(Editor with Jerry L. Mashaw) *Social Security: Beyond the Rhetoric of Crisis,* Princeton University Press (Princeton, NJ), 1988.

The Career of John C. Calhoun, Garland Publishing (New York City), 1988.

(Editor with Mashaw) *Social Security: Beyond the Rhetoric of Crisis,* Princeton University Press, 1988.

(With Mashaw and Philip L. Harvey) *America's Misunderstood Welfare State: Persistent Myths, Enduring Realities,* Basic Books, 1990.

Why Some People Are Healthy and Others Not: The Determinants of Health of Populations, Aldine de Gruyter (New York City), 1994.

Economic Security and Intergenerational Justice, Urban Institute, 1994.

Understanding Health Care Reform, Yale University Press (New Haven, CT), 1994.

Contributor to periodicals, including *American Political Science Review, American Prospect, Washington Monthly,* and *Political Quarterly.* Editor, *Public Policy Studies,* 1972, *International Journal of Health Services,* 1974-1980, and *Journal of Health Politics, Policy and Law,* 1980-84.

WORK IN PROGRESS: "A book on what happened to health care reform to be published by Westview."

SIDELIGHTS: T. R. Marmor told *CA:* "I write for much the same reasons I became a professor of politics and public policy. It is to work on subjects that interest me, that involves the controversial issues of the day, and for which research and thought are necessary ingredients. I once assumed that good writing on my subjects would have beneficial effects, that one could slay the dragons of distortion with op-eds in the *Los Angeles Times,* sharp articles in *The Washington Monthly,* or, turning to scripts, the illuminating interview on National Public Radio. I believe that no longer, but continue to write for a broader public for the same reasons mountain climbers continue: the mountains are there, just as the spring creeks of nonsense are there in our public life."

BIOGRAPHICAL/CRITICAL SOURCES:

PERIODICALS

American Political Science Review, September, 1986.

American Prospect, spring, 1995.

Annals of the American Academy of Political Social Sciences, May, 1984.

Economist, September 12, 1970.

Ethics, January, 1987.

Journal of Political Economy, August, 1983.

Journal of Politics, February, 1986.

Washington Monthly, August, 1995.

*   *   *

MARNEY, Dean   1952-

PERSONAL: Born December 30, 1952, in Waterville, WA; son of Keith S. (a postmaster) and Alice (a piano teacher; maiden name, Osborne) Marney; married Susan Carr (a psychiatric nurse practitioner), July 12, 1975; children: Blythe, Dylan, Luke. *Education:* University of Washington, Seattle, B.A., 1975; University of Oregon, M.L.S., 1977.

ADDRESSES: Home—2996 Riviera Blvd., Malaga, WA 98828. *Office*—North Central Regional Library, 238 Olds Station Rd., Wenatchee, WA 98801.

CAREER: North Central Regional Library, Wenatchee, WA, assistant director, 1985-90, director, 1990—.

WRITINGS:

YOUNG ADULT NOVELS

Just Good Friends, Addison-Wesley (Reading, MA), 1982.

The Computer That Ate My Brother, Houghton (Boston), 1985.

The Trouble with Jake's Double, Scholastic Inc. (New York City), 1988.

You, Me, and Gracie Makes Three, Scholastic Inc., 1989.

The Christmas Tree That Ate My Mother, Scholastic Inc., 1992.

Dirty Socks Don't Win Games, Scholastic Inc., 1992.

The Jack O'Lantern That Ate My Brother, Scholastic Inc., 1994.

The Turkey That Ate My Father, Scholastic Inc., 1995.

The Easter Bunny That Ate My Sister, Scholastic Inc., 1996.

The Valentine That Ate My Teacher, Scholastic Inc., 1997.

SIDELIGHTS: Dean Marney told *CA:* "I'm amazed at where writing for children has taken me. Certainly on an inward journey to all those weird dark places in my own childhood that demand to be written about, but also on an outward journey that has put me in contact with kids all over the world. I love the letters I get. I'm always slightly surprised by how up front kids are. If they like what I did in a book, they tell me, and if they don't like what I did, they tell me too. I've also been extremely fortunate to meet and work with terrific editors. If editors didn't exist, I'd invent them.

"People always ask me where I get my ideas. I think they are politely wondering if I'm as weird as the subjects I write about. I tell them I have a very rich and full dream life that tends to spill out every now and then. They also ask me why I got into writing books about things eating my family. I tell them they've obviously never met my family.

"Writing a series has allowed me to get even closer to some of my characters. To see these characters that are parts of me grow and falter, taking one step forward and two steps back is both invigorating and humbling. A day does not go by that I'm not in awe of the workings of the unconscious. I feel guilty that writing books should be as fun as it has been. The process of writing, although at times frustrating, always has the potential to make me laugh out loud at myself and the world.

"I grew up in a very small rural town and as a boy dreamed of the possibilities that lay beyond the horizon. I now live, write, and still dream about those possibilities as a man. Isn't life strange and wonderful?"

BIOGRAPHICAL/CRITICAL SOURCES:

PERIODICALS

School Library Journal, November, 1982.
Seattle Times, June 6, 1982.

*   *   *

MARSH, Mary Val 1925-

PERSONAL: Born April 28, 1925, in Uniontown, PA; daughter of Roy William (an osteopathic physician) and Mary (a teacher; maiden name, Hickman) Marsh; married Dwight Ellsworth Twist (a school superintendent), August 4, 1962; step-children: Barbara, Charles Russell. *Education:* University of California, Los Angeles, B.A., 1946; Claremont Graduate School, M.A., 1953. *Politics:* Republican. *Religion:* Presbyterian.

ADDRESSES: Home—879 Rosecrans St., San Diego, CA 92106.

CAREER: Elementary school teacher in Redlands, CA, 1946-48; San Bernadino County Department of Education, San Bernadino, CA, curriculum consultant, 1948-52, music coordinator, 1952-59; music supervisor for public schools in Beverly Hills, CA, 1959-62; San Diego State University, San Diego, CA, part-time lecturer in music education, 1963-73; freelance writer, music arranger, and consultant in music education, 1973—. Faculty member at University of Redlands, Claremont Graduate School and University Center, and Idyllwild School of Music and the Arts; director of music education workshops in the United States and Canada. Member of Music Educators National Conference-Ford Foundation "Contemporary Music Project" Committee, San Diego, 1963-65; supervisor of local "Opera Participation Project for Youth," 1971-75; member of board of directors of Civic Youth Orchestra, 1976-91.

MEMBER: International Society for Music Education, Music Educators National Conference (life member), California Music Educators Association (life member), Sigma Alpha Iota, Delta Kappa Gamma, Pi Lambda Theta, P.E.O. Sisterhood.

WRITINGS:

Choruses and Carols (for unchanged voices), Summy-Birchard (Princeton, NJ), 1964.
Here a Song, There a Song (for elementary and junior high school choruses), Shawnee Press (Delaware Water Gap, PA), 1969.
Explore and Discover Music: Creative Approaches to Music Education in Elementary, Middle, and Junior High Schools, Macmillan (New York City), 1970.
(With Carroll Rinehart and Edith Savage) *The Spectrum of Music* (textbook series for elementary and junior high school), Macmillan, 1974-75, 1978, 1980, 1983.
(With Rinehart) *Wish I Had a Song: Music for Today's Children* (with record or cassette), Alfred Publishing, 1987.

(With Rinehart) *Zingers and Swingers for Young Singers: New Music for a New Generation* (with compact disc or cassette), Belwin Mills (now Warner Publications), 1994.

CHORAL COMPOSITIONS AND ARRANGEMENTS

Aardvarks on the Ark (unison/2 pt.), Alfred Publishing, 1978.
Singin' a Song (unison/2 pt.), Alfred Publishing, 1980.
Watah Come a Me Eye (unison/2 pt.), Alfred Publishing, 1982.
I'd Rather Be Sailing (unison/2 pt.), Alfred Publishing, 1982.
Linstead Market (unison/2 pt.), Alfred Publishing, 1983.
Sing for America (unison/2 pt.), Alfred Publishing, 1984.
The Yellow Sun (unison/2 pt.), Alfred Publishing, 1985.
Christmas Time (unison/2 pt.), Alfred Publishing, 1988.
I Have Music (unison/2 pt.), Alfred Publishing, 1988.
Hold On (2-pt., SAB), Alfred Publishing, 1988.
Time to Sing-a Noel (2-pt., SAB, SATB), Alfred Publishing, 1989.
Baby's Born in Bethlehem (2-pt., 3-pt. mixed), Alfred Publishing, 1991.
Deliver Me (3-pt. mixed), Plymouth Music, 1993.
Sing Hey, Sing Ho! (3-pt. mixed), Plymouth Music, 1993.
Hallelujah to the Newborn King (2-pt., 3-pt. mixed), Alfred Publishing, 1993.
Psalm of Praise (SATB), Plymouth Music, 1994.

OTHER

Contributor to *Music Educators Journal.* Editor, *CMEA News,* 1978-82, and *Soundings,* 1982-86.

WORK IN PROGRESS: Choral arranging and composing; additional music textbook materials.

SIDELIGHTS: Mary Val Marsh told *CA:* "I am committed to the belief that arts education is essential to improving the quality of life for all, and that without a commitment to the arts, a culture will gradually deteriorate. Only as children and youth encounter the arts in meaningful situations will they develop aesthetic sensitivity. As a specialist in music education, I believe that *creating music* is one of the most effective means of learning about music and of

developing a continuing interest in it. This belief led me a number of years ago to organize an experimental creative music class, which subsequently led to my writing of *Explore and Discover Music.*"

*   *   *

MARTER, Joan M.   1946-

PERSONAL: Born August 13, 1946, in Philadelphia, PA; daughter of Anthony and Rita (DiMascio) Mastrangelo; married Walter Marter (a broadcasting company director), November, 1967; children: Julia. *Education:* Temple University, B.A. (magna cum laude), 1968; University of Delaware, M.A., 1970, Ph.D., 1974.

ADDRESSES: Office—Department of Art History, Voorhees Hall, Rutgers University, New Brunswick, NJ 08903.

CAREER: Sweet Briar College, Sweet Briar, VA, assistant professor of art history, 1974-77; Rutgers University, New Brunswick, NJ, associate professor, 1977-90, professor of art history, 1990—. Guest curator, Pennsylvania Academy of the Fine Arts, 1976, Detroit Institute of Arts and Metropolitan Museum of Art, 1982-83, and at List Visual Arts Center, Cambridge, MA, 1986—.

MEMBER: International Association of Art Critics (member, executive board of American section, 1987-89), College Art Association of America, Women's Caucus for Art.

AWARDS, HONORS: Chester Dale fellow at National Gallery of Art, 1973-74; Charles Montgomery Prize from Decorative Arts Society of Society of Architectural Historians, 1983, for *Design in America: The Cranbrook Vision;* George Wittenborn Award, Art Libraries Society of North America, 1985; Diamond Achievement Award in the Humanities, Temple University, 1993.

WRITINGS:

(With R. Boyle and F. Goodyear) *In This Academy,* Pennsylvania Academy of the Fine Arts (Philadelphia), 1976.
(With Roberta K. Tarbell and Jeffrey Wechsler) *Vanguard American Sculpture 1913-1939,* Rutgers University (New Brunswick, NJ), 1979.

Jose de Rivera Constructions, introduction by Dore Ashton, Taller Ediciones JB (Madrid, Spain), 1980.

Alexander Calder, Cambridge University Press (New York City), 1991.

(With R. J. Clark and David DeLong) *Design in America: The Cranbrook Vision,* Abrams (New York City), 1983.

Theodore Roszak, The Drawings, University of Washington Press (Seattle, WA), 1992.

OTHER

Contributor to books, including *In This Academy, The Pennsylvania Academy of the Fine Arts,* edited by Doreen Bolger, Richard Boyle, Frank Goodyear, and others, Museum Press (Washington, DC), 1976; *Abstract Painting and Sculpture in America: 1927-44,* edited by John R. Lane and Susan Larsen, Abrams, 1983; *A Gallery of Modern Art at Washington University in St. Louis,* Washington University Gallery (St. Louis, MO), 1994; and *American National Biography,* Oxford University Press (New York City), in press. Contributor to museum publications, including *Alexander Calder: Artist as Engineer,* List Visual Arts Center, Massachusetts Institute of Technology (Cambridge, MA), 1986; *Dorothy Dehner, Journeys, Dreams, and Realities,* Baruch College Gallery (New York City), 1991; and *Dorothy Dehner, Sixty Years of Art,* University of Washington Press, 1993. Contributor to art journals, including *American Art Journal, American Art Review, Drawing, Kresge Art Museum Bulletin, Sculpture, Women's Art Journal, Women's Studies Quarterly.*

WORK IN PROGRESS: (With others) *American Sculpture, The Collection of The Metropolitan Museum of Art, New York,* to be published in 1996; a book on American sculpture since 1930.

*   *   *

MARTIN, Don W.   1934-

PERSONAL: Born April 22, 1934, in Grants Pass, OR; son of George E. (a dairyman) and Irma Ann (Dallas) Martin; married Kathleen Elizabeth Murphy, 1969 (divorced, 1981); married Betty Woo (a pharmacist, realtor, and writer), March 18, 1985; children: Kimberly Ann, Daniel Clayton. *Education:*

Attended high school in Wilder, Idaho. *Politics:* Liberal Republican. *Religion:* Protestant ("not active").

ADDRESSES: Home and office—P.O. Box 1494, 11362 Yankee Hill Rd., Columbia, CA 95310.

CAREER: Blade-Tribune, Oceanside, CA, member of editorial staff, 1960-64; *Press-Courier,* Oxnard, CA, entertainment and feature editor, 1964-69; *Argus-Courier,* Petaluma, CA, managing editor, 1969-70; *Motorland* (travel magazine), San Francisco, CA, associate editor, 1970-88; freelance writer and photographer, 1988—. Established Pine Cone Press, with wife Betty Woo Martin, in 1988. *Military service:* U.S. Marine Corps, correspondent, 1952-58; became staff sergeant.

WRITINGS:

WITH WIFE, BETTY WOO MARTIN; GUIDEBOOKS

The Best of San Francisco, Chronicle Books (San Francisco), 1986, third edition, 1994.

The Best of the Gold Country, Pine Cone Press (Columbia, CA), 1987, revised edition, 1992.

San Francisco's Ultimate Dining Guide, Pine Cone Press, 1988.

The Best of the Wine Country, Pine Cone Press, 1989, revised edition, 1995.

Coming to Arizona, Pine Cone Press, 1991.

Inside San Francisco, Pine Cone Press, 1991.

Northern California Discovery Guide, Pine Cone Press, 1991.

Oregon Discovery Guide, Pine Cone Press, 1993.

The Ultimate Wine Book, Pine Cone Press, 1993.

Washington Discovery Guide, Pine Cone Press, 1994.

Utah Discovery Guide, Pine Cone Press, 1995.

Arizona Discovery Guide, Pine Cone Press, 1996.

Adventure Cruising, Pine Cone Press, 1996.

Nevada Discovery Guide, Pine Cone Press, 1996.

Contributor of articles to periodicals.

WORK IN PROGRESS: A fourth edition of *The Best of San Francisco,* for publication in spring, 1997.

SIDELIGHTS: Don W. Martin told *CA:* "I was moved to begin writing guidebooks because I felt that most of the ones on the market were dry and bland. The guidebooks I write with my wife are highly opinionated, yet written in a light and humorous style. They are intended to entertain the armchair traveler, as well as the functioning tourist. The books reflect our personal tastes, but then, our tastes are closer to middle-of-the-road than to lunatic fringe. Hopefully, our writings chart for the traveler a useful course through the good, the bad, and the awful."

* * *

MARTIN, Herbert Woodward   1933-

PERSONAL: Born October 4, 1933, in Birmingham, AL; son of David Nathaniel and Willie Mae (Woodward) Martin. *Education:* University of Toledo, B.A., 1964; State University of New York at Buffalo, M.A., 1967; Middlebury College, M.Litt., 1972; Carnegie-Mellon University, D.A., 1979. *Religion:* Lutheran.

ADDRESSES: Home—320 West Hudson Ave., Dayton, OH 45406-4830. *Office*—Department of English, 300 College Park, Dayton, OH 45469-0001.

CAREER: State University of New York at Buffalo, instructor, summer, 1966; Aquinas College, Grand Rapids, MI, 1967-70, began as instructor, became assistant professor and poet in residence; University of Dayton, Dayton, Ohio, 1970—, began as assistant professor, became professor of English and poet in residence. Visiting distinguished professor of poetry at Central Michigan University, fall, 1973. Associated with Writer Workshop at Antioch Writer's Conference, 1993—, and Ohio Arts Council Writer's Workshop, 1995—. Consultant for contemporary black writers collection at University of Toledo, 1974—; consultant in poetry for *World Order*.

WRITINGS:

Dialogue (one-act play), produced in New York City at Hardware Poets Playhouse, 1963.
Three Garbage Cans, first produced in Grand Rapids, Michigan, fall, 1968.
New York: The Nine Million and Other Poems, Abracadabra Press, 1969.
The Shit-Storm Poems, Pilot Press, 1972.
The Persistence of the Flesh (poems), Lotus Press, 1976.
Paul Laurence Dunbar: A Singer of Songs (booklet), State Library of Ohio, 1979.
The Forms of Silence, Lotus Press, 1980.

Also author of libretti, including, with Adolphus Hailstork, *Paul Laurence Dunbar: Common Ground* (one-act opera), 1995; with Philip Carl Magnuson, *Seven Songs on Seven Poems of Herbert Woodward Martin;* and with Magnuson, *It Pays to Advertize* (one-act opera), 1995. Author of *Letters from the World.* Work represented in anthologies, including *The Poetry of Black America, Introduction to Black Literature, Urban Reader, 10 Michigan Poets,* and *Face the Whirlwind.* Contributor of poetry to journals, including *Poetry, Massachussett Review, Aura Literary Arts Review, Grand Street, George Washington Review, Spindrift,* and *Synaesthetic: A Journal of Prose and Poetry.* Editor, *Great Lakes Review,* 1978—; guest editor, *University of Dayton Review,* 1988.

WORK IN PROGRESS: The Last Days of William Short, poems on AIDS; *Final W.,* poems on dying of cancer; *The Edge of Being; Private Poems: Public Portraits, Public Wars.*

SIDELIGHTS: Herbert Woodward Martin told *CA:* "You want to try and say something sensible in public, and especially if it is to appear in print. We forget what we hear or we reproduce it inaccurately. It is hard to deny print when it is contradictory. The best I can say is that I try to make the best poems possible, to allow them a life of their own and to try and instill in them a music that is accessible and natural.

"I write and act and sing when I can because those are the disciplines which I understand or seem to understand the most. I try to put elements of each discipline in my poems. I am not always sure that I achieve the effect.

"A thumbnail sketch of my life might be that I was born in Birmingham, Alabama, grew into adolescence in Toledo, Ohio, matured in New York City (doesn't everyone?), began teaching in Michigan, and got married and started a family in Dayton, Ohio, where I have lived for the past twenty-five years. Of course, when I see this in print, I will wish that I had sat this one out as well."

* * *

MARTIN, Ken
See HUBBARD, L(afayette) Ron(ald)

MARTIN, Tony 1942-

PERSONAL: Born February 21, 1942, in Port-of-Spain, Trinidad and Tobago; son of Claude G. and Vida (Scope) Martin. *Education:* Honourable Society of Gray's Inn, Barrister-at-Law, 1965; University of Hull, B.Sc. (with honors), 1968; Michigan State University, M.A., 1970, Ph.D., 1973.

ADDRESSES: Office—Department of Africana Studies, Wellesley College, Wellesley, MA 02181.

CAREER: Called to English Bar, 1966, and to Trinidad Bar, 1969; accounts clerk in water department, Trinidad Public Service, 1961; accounts clerk, Office of the Prime Minister, Federal Government of the West Indies, Trinidad and Tobago, 1961-62; Master of Latin, French, Spanish, English, history, and geography, St. Mary's College, Trinidad and Tobago, 1962-63; lecturer in economics and politics, Cipriani Labour College, Trinidad and Tobago, 1968-69; Michigan State University, East Lansing, instructor in history, 1970-71; University of Michigan—Flint, assistant professor of history and coordinator of African-American studies program, 1971-73; Wellesley College, Wellesley, MA, associate professor, 1973-79, professor of Africana studies, 1979—, chair of department, 1976-78, 1981-84, and 1985-90. Visiting professor at Brandeis University, fall, 1974 and 1981, and at University of Minnesota, fall, 1975; visiting professor at Colorado College, 1985 and 1986; visiting professor, Brown University, 1992.

MEMBER: African Heritage Studies Association (member of executive board, 1982), Association of Caribbean Historians (member of executive board, 1985-86, 1986-87), Association for the Study of Afro-American Life and History, Association for the Study of Classical African Civilizations, National Council for Black Studies (vice president of New England region, 1984-86), Organization of American Historians.

WRITINGS:

Race First: The Ideological and Organizational Struggles of Marcus Garvey and the Universal Negro Improvement Association, Greenwood Press (Westport, CT), 1976.
(Coauthor) *Rare Afro-Americana: A Reconstruction of the Adger Library,* G. K. Hall (Boston), 1981.

Literary Garveyism: Garvey, Black Arts, and the Harlem Renaissance, Majority Press (Dover, MA), 1983.
Marcus Garvey, Hero, Majority Press, 1983.
The Pan-African Connection: From Slavery to Garvey and Beyond, Majority Press, 1984.
The Jewish Onslaught: Despatches from the Wellesley Battlefront, Majority Press, 1993.
Amy Ashwood Garvey: Pan-Africanist, Feminist, and Wife Number One, Majority Press, 1996.

EDITOR

The Poetical Works of Marcus Garvey, Majority Press, 1983.
In Nobody's Backyard: The Grenada Revolution in Its Own Words, Majority Press, Volume 1: *The Revolution at Home,* 1984, Volume 2: *Facing the World,* 1985.
Marcus Garvey, *Message to the People: The Course of African Philosophy,* Majority Press, 1986.
African Fundamentalism: A Literary Anthology of the Garvey Movement, Majority Press, 1989.

OTHER

Also author of pamphlets. Contributor of numerous articles and reviews to professional journals, including *African Studies Review, American Historical Review, Journal of Modern African Studies, Journal of Human Relations, Journal of Negro History, Mazungumzo, Negro History Bulletin,* and *Race.* Guest editor, *Pan-African Journal,* 1974.

WORK IN PROGRESS: Audrey Jeffers, a biography; *Auntie Kay,* a biography.

*   *   *

MARZOLF, Marion Tuttle 1930-

PERSONAL: Born July 6, 1930, in Greenville, MI; daughter of Stuart K. and Signe M.(Johnson) Tuttle; married Kingsbury Marzolf, May 7, 1953. *Education:* Michigan State University, B.A., 1952; University of Michigan, M.A., 1963, Ph.D., 1972.

ADDRESSES: Home—1420 Granger St., Ann Arbor, MI 48104. *Office*—Department of Communication, University of Michigan, Ann Arbor, MI 48109.

CAREER: Wallace-Lindeman, Grand Rapids, MI, advertising copywriter, 1952-53; *Biloxi Bulletin,* Biloxi, MS, reporter, 1953-54; *Washington Post,* Washington, DC, reporter and assistant, 1955-57; *National Geographic,* Washington, DC, editorial layout assistant, 1957-63; Eastern Michigan University, Ypsilanti, lecturer in journalism, 1964-68; University of Michigan, Ann Arbor, lecturer, 1967-73, assistant professor, 1973-78, associate professor of journalism, 1978-95, associate chair of department of communication, 1987—, professor emerita, 1995. Copy editor on city desk of *Ann Arbor News,* 1973.

MEMBER: Association for Education in Journalism and Mass Communications, Society for the Advancement of Scandinavian Studies, Danish-American Historical Society, Detroit Women Writers.

AWARDS, HONORS: Outstanding achievement award for leadership from Status of Women Committee of Association for Education in Journalism and Mass Communications, 1982.

WRITINGS:

Up from the Footnote: A History of Women Journalists, Hastings House (New York City), 1977.
The Danish-Language Press in America, Arno, 1979.
Civilizing Voices: American Press Criticism, 1880-1950, Longman (New York City), 1991.

WORK IN PROGRESS: Women Who Wrote the News.

SIDELIGHTS: Marion Tuttle Marzolf told *CA:* "My research has been motivated by an interest in the unsung and unnoticed in American journalism history. First I wrote about the immigrant press in a dissertation that became a book. Then I studied the women who were so overlooked by mainstream history that I found them mentioned mostly in footnotes. This led to an interest in journalistic values and press criticism and critics who have been noticed, but not studied. Currently, I am exploring the life and work of 20th-century women journalists, using oral histories and my own interviews."

*   *   *

MATHES, W(illiam) Michael   1936-

PERSONAL: Born April 15, 1936, in Los Angeles, CA; son of William C. (a U.S. district judge) and Rilla (Moore) Mathes. *Education:* Loyola University, Los Angeles, CA, B.S., 1957; University of Southern California, M.A., 1962; University of New Mexico, Ph.D., 1966. *Religion:* Roman Catholic.

ADDRESSES: Home—P.O. Box 1090, Plainview, TX 79073. *Office*—Director, Biblioteca, El Colegio de Jalisco, 5 De Mayo 321, 45100 Zapopan, Jalisco, Mexico.

CAREER: University of New Mexico, Albuquerque, special collections librarian in Coronado Room, 1963-65; University of San Francisco, San Francisco, CA, assistant professor, 1966-71, associate professor, 1971-75, professor of history, 1975-93, professor emeritus, 1993—. Taught course at Universidad Autonoma de Guadalajara, 1978; visiting professor at "First History Week" observance at Universidade Federal do Acre (Brazil), 1978, and at Colegio de Michoacan (Mexico), 1981. Academico supernumerario, Academia de la Historia de Occidente Guadalajara, and academico, Academia Sudcaliforniana de la Historia, La Paz, both 1982—; academico, El Colegio de Historia, Guadalajara, 1984—.

Agente de canje, National Archives of Mexico, 1960-74; "Pablo L. Martinez" Historical Archives, La Paz, technical director, 1974-77, director of microfilming project, 1975-76; Commission of the Californias, archivist-historian, 1975-92, and chair of history committee, 1982-92; Patronato para la Preservacion del Patrimonio Historico-Cultural de Baja California Sur, assessor, 1975-77, secretary, 1977-78; cultural representative, Camara nacional de Comercio, Ensenada, Baja California, 1977; special researcher, Centro de Investigaciones Historicas of Universidad Nacional Autonoma de Mexico and Universidad Autonoma de Baja California, 1977-93; special representative to Archivo General de Indias for Bancroft Library of University of California, 1981; honorary curator of Mexican collection of California State Library—Sutro Branch, 1981—; technical director, microfilm project in the Archivo Historico de Zacatecas, Bancroft Library, 1986-91.

California Historical Society, associate editor, 1967-69, review editor, 1981-87, member of publications committee, 1982-87; San Diego Historical Society, advisory editor, 1970-74, member of board of editors, 1981—; member of board of editors, Universidad de Baja California Sur, 1977-87. Member of Serra bicentennial commission, 1984; corresponding member, Academia Mexicana de la

Historia, 1985—. Consultant, Oakland Museum, 1967-69; advisor-consultant, Automobile Club of Southern California, 1975-76; consultant, Depot Museum, Sonoma Valley Historical Society, Consejo Consultivo del Archivo del Poder Ejecutivo, Estado de Baja California Sur, and Museo del Hombre, Naturaleza y Cultura, all 1982—, and National Geographic Society, California State Library, and Mundus Novus Foundation, 1984—.

MEMBER: American Catholic Historical Association, American Historical Association, Western History Association, Westerners International (member of executive board, 1978-85), Asociacion Cultural de las Californias (representative, 1983—), California Historical Society, Texas State Historical Association, San Diego Historical Society, Sigma Delta Pi (honorary member), Phi Alpha Theta.

AWARDS, HONORS: Fulbright grant to Spain, 1962-63; Del Amo fellow in Spain, 1965-66; California Historical Society, award of merit, 1977, for contributions to California history, and Henry R. Wagner Memorial Award, 1979; Diploma de Merito, Universidade Federal do Acre (Brazil), 1978; certificate of award, Sonoma Valley Historical Society, and Medalla de Plata, Asociacion Espanola de Amigos de los Castillos, Madrid, both 1984; Condecoracion del Orden del Aguila Azteca, Secretaria de Relaciones Exteriores, Mexico, 1985; miembro academico, Seminario de Historia de Baja California.

WRITINGS:

Vizcaino and Spanish Expansion in the Pacific Ocean, 1580-1630, California Historical Society (San Diego), 1968.

Reparo a errores de la navegacion espanola (title means "*Correction of Errors in Spanish Navigation*"), Ediciones Jose Porrua Turanzas (Madrid, Spain), 1970.

To Save a City: The Desague, Americas, 1970.

The Conquistador in California: The Voyage of Fernando Cortes to Baja California in Chronicles and Documents, 1535, Dawson's Book Shop (Los Angeles, CA), 1973.

A Brief History of the Land of Calafia: The Californias, 1533-1795, Gobierno del Territorio de Baja California Sur (La Paz, Mexico), 1974, 2nd edition, Patronato del estudiante sudcaliforniano, 1977.

*Geographic and Hydrographic Descriptions of Many Northern and Southern Lands and Seas in the Indies: Specifically of the Discovery of the King-*dom of California (1632), Dawson's Book Shop, 1974.

Spanish Approaches to the Island of California, 1628-1632, Book Club of California, 1975.

Piratas en la costa de Nueva Galicia en el siglo XVII (title means "*Pirates on the Coast of New Galicia during the Seventeenth Century*"), Libreria Font (Guadalajara, Mexico), 1976.

Las misiones de Baja California—The Missions of Baja California: Una resena historica-fotografica—An Historical-Photographic Survey, Gobierno del Estado de Baja California Sur, 1977.

Cattle Brands of Baja California Sur, 1809-1885: Los registros de marcas de Baja California Sur, Dawson's Book Shop-Archivo Historico de Baja California Sur "*Pablo L. Martinez,*" 1978.

Cortes en California, 1535, Universidad Autonoma de Baja California (Mexicali, Mexico), 1978.

Clemente Guillen: Explorer of the South, Dawson's Book Shop, 1979.

Baja California cartografica: Catalogo de mapas, planos y disenos del siglo XIX que se encuentran en el Archivo Historico de Baja California Sur "Pablo L. Martinez" (title means "*Cartographic Baja California: A Catalog of Maps, Plans, and Designs from the Nineteenth Century Found in the 'Pablo L. Martinez' Historical Archives of Baja California Sur*"), Gobierno del Estado de Baja California Sur, 1979.

Missions, with photographs by Stanley Truman, California Historical Society, 1980.

Obras californianas del Padre Miguel Venegas, S.J., Universidad Autonoma de Baja California Sur, five volumes, 1980.

(With John H. R. Polt) *Vignettes of Early California: Childhood Reminiscences of Juan Bautista Alvarado,* Book Club of California, 1982.

(With J. Andres Cota Sandoval) *Importancia de Cabo San Lucas,* FONAPAS, 1982.

Santa Crus de Tlatelolco: La primera biblioteca academica de las Americas, Secretaria de relaciones exteriores, 1982, English translation published as *The America's First Academic Library: Santa Cruz de Tlatelolco,* California State Library Foundation (Sacramento), 1985.

Las defensas de Mexico en 1824 (monograph), Universidad Autonoma de Nuevo Leon, 1983.

Mexico on Stone: Lithography in Mexico, 1826-1900, Book Club of California, 1984.

La geografia mitologica de California: Origenes, desarrollo, concrecion y desaparicion (monograph), Academia Mexicana de la Historia, 1984.

Pensil Americano, edited by Ignacio Carrillo Perez, Edmundo Avina Levy (Guadalajara, Mexico), 1985.

Un centro cultural novogalaico: La biblioteca del convento de San Francisco de Guadalajara en 1610, Instituto Cultural Cabanas (Guadalajara, Mexico), 1986.

The America's First Academic Library, Santa Cruz de Tlatelolco, California State Library Foundation, 1985.

Un Centro Cultural Novogalaico: La Biblioteca del Convento de San Francisco de Guadalajara en 1610, Insituto Cultural Cabanas, 1986.

America Socorrido, edited by Bruno Francisco Larranaga, Edmundo Avina Levy 1987.

Californiana IV: Aportacion a la Historiografia de California en el Siglo XVIII, 2 volumes, Ediciones Jose Porrua Turanzas, 1987.

Baja California Textos de Su Historia, 2 volumes, Instituto de Investigaciones Dr. Jose Maria Luis Mora SEP/Programa Cultura de las Fronteras/ Gobierno del Estado de Baja California (Mexico), 1988.

Breviary of the Instituto Cultural Cabanas, Instituto Cultural Cabanas, 1988.

Noticias de la Peninsula Americana de California, edited by Juan Jacobo Baegert, Gobierno del Estado de Baja California Sur (Guadalajara, Mexico), 1989.

Mexico en piedra: La Litografia en Mexico (1826-1900), Gobierno del Estado de Jalisco, Imprejal S. A. (Guadalajara, Mexico), 1990.

La Frontera Ruso-Mexicana 1808-1842, Secretaria de Relaciones Exteriores (Mexico), 1991.

Memoria, D. Miguel Ramos Arizpe, Ayuntamiento de Guadalajara (Guadalajara, Mexico), 1991.

Ethnology of the Baja California Indians, Garland Publishing (New York City), 1992.

TRANSLATOR

(And transcriber and author of annotations) Juan Cavallero Carranco, *The Pearl Hunters in the Gulf of California, 1668,* Dawson's Book Shop, 1966.

(And transcriber and author of annotations) *The Capture of "Santa Ana," Cabo San Lucas, November, 1587: The Accounts of Francis Pretty, Antonio de Sierra, and Tomas de Alzola,* Dawson's Book Shop, 1969.

Muria, *A Thumbnail History of Guadalajara,* Editorial Colomos, 1983.

CONTRIBUTOR

Some California Catholic Reminiscences for the United States Bicentennial, Knights of Columbus (Los Angeles), 1976.

Cabrillo and His Compatriots: The Explorers and Their Expeditions, Cabrillo Historical Association, 1979.

Pioneer Trails West, Caxton Printers (Caldwell, CA), 1985.

El Impacto del Encuentro de dos Mundos, Memorias, Universidad de Tel Aviv, 1988.

Vision Historica de la Frontera Norte de Mexico, Universidad Autonoma de Baja California, 1988.

Columbian Consequences, Archaeological and Historical Perspectives on the Spanish Borderlands West, Smithsonian Institution Press (Washington, DC), 1989.

Los Vascos y America, ideas, hechos, hombres, Espasa-Calpe (Madrid, Spain), 1990.

Presencia Jesuita en el Noroeste, Difocur (Culiacan, Mexico), 1992.

San Blas de Nayarit, El Colegio de Jalisco (Zapopan, Mexico), 1993.

Nacion de Imagenes: La Litografia Mexicana del Siglo XIX, Consejo Nacional para la Cultura y las Artes (Mexico), 1994.

Doscientos Anos de la Imprenta En Guadalajara, Camara Nacional de la Industria de Artes Graficas (Guadalajara, Mexico), 1994.

AUTHOR OF PROLOGUE

Coronado, *Kino y Salvatierra en la Conquista de las Californias,* FONAPAS, 1981.

Lopez, *Documentalia Novogalaica en los archivos de Espana,* Editorial Rocinante, 1982.

Coronado, *Descripcion e inventarios de las misiones de Baja California, 1773,* Institut D'Estudis Balearics (Palma de Mallorca, Spain), 1988.

Santa Rosalia Baja California Sur: Tres Enfoques Historicos, Ayuntamiento de Mulege (Santa Rosalia), 1992.

EDITOR

Californiana (in Spanish), nine volumes, Ediciones Jose Porrua Turanzas, 1965-87.

Documentos para la historia de la demarcacion comercial de California, 1583-1632 (title means "Documents for the History of the Commercial Charting of California"), Ediciones Jose Porrua Turanzas, 1965.

Documentos para la historia de la explotacion comercial de California, 1611-1679 (title means "Documents for the History of Commercial Exploitation of California"), Ediciones Jose Porrua Turzanas, 1968.

Eusebio Francisco Kino, *First from the Gulf to the Pacific,* Dawson's Book Shop, 1969.

(With others) Miguel del Barco, *The Natural History of Baja California,* Dawson's Book Shop, 1980.

(With Joseph Ignacio Bartolache) *Manifesto Satisfactorio,* Edmundo Avina Levy, 1988.

Juan de Urtassum, *La Gracia Triunfante en la Vida de Catharina Tegakovita India Iroquesa,* Ediciones Jose Porrua Turanzas, 1994.

OTHER

Contributor to *Diccionario enciclopedico de Baja California,* Enciclopedia de Mexico, Gobierno de Baja California (Mexico), 1989; *Encyclopedia of Library History,* edited by Wayne A. Wiegand and Donald Davis, Jr., Garland Publishing, 1994; *Encyclopedia of Latin American History,* Scribner (New York City), 1994. Also contributor to books, including article "Posible Origen del Nombre Tijuana" (title means "Possible Origen of the Name Tijuana"), *Historia de Tijuana—Semblanza General,* Centro de Investigaciones Historica UNAM-UABC (Tijuana, Mexico), 1985, reprinted in *Historia de Tijuana 1889-1989,* Edicion Conmemorativa del Centenario de su Fundacion (Tijuana, Mexico), 1989; *De la Historia Homenaje a Jorge Gurria Lacroix,* UNAM (Mexico), 1986; *American National Biography,* Oxford University Press (New York City), 1994.

Contributor to periodicals, including *Americas, Calafia, California History, Californians, Colonial Latin American Historical Review, Cronicas, Estudios Jaliscienses, Hispanic American Historical Review, Journal of San Diego History, Lector, Meyibo, Quinto Centenario, St. Anthony Messenger,* and *Western Historical Quarterly.*

Member of board of editors, *Calafia,* 1977—, *Meyibo,* 1977—, and *California History,* 1982-87; member of editorial committee, *The Californians,* 1982—. Editorial consultant, *The Journal of San Diego History,* 1975-80.

WORK IN PROGRESS: Research on the history of California in the seventeenth century, on the history of printing in colonial Mexico.

*   *   *

MAXWELL, Patricia   1942-
(Patricia Ponder; pseudonyms: Jennifer Blake, Maxine Patrick; Elizabeth Treahearne, a joint pseudonym)

PERSONAL: Born March 9, 1942, in Winn Parish, LA (one source lists Goldonna, LA); daughter of John H. (an electrician) and Daisy (Durbin) Ponder; married J. R. Maxwell (a retail automobile dealer), August 1, 1957; children: Ronnie, Ricky, Delinda, Kathy.

ADDRESSES: Home—P.O. Box 9218, Quitman, LA 71268.

CAREER: Writer.

MEMBER: National League of American Pen Women, Romance Writers of America.

AWARDS, HONORS: "Best Historical Romance Novelist of the Year" citation, *Romantic Times,* 1985; "Best Historical Romance with a Southern Background" citation, Georgia Romance Writers in association with Waldenbooks, 1985, for *Midnight Waltz,* and 1987, for *Southern Rapture;* Golden Treasure Award, Romance Writers of America, 1987, for lifetime achievement in the romance genre; Reviewer's Choice, *Romantic Times,* 1994, for *Arrow to the Heart,* and 1995, for *Shameless;* Best Contemporary Romance, Affaire de Coeur, 1995, for *Shameless;* Romance Hall of Fame, Affaire de Coeur, 1995.

WRITINGS:

The Secret of Mirror House, Fawcett (New York City), 1970.
Stranger at Plantation Inn, Fawcett, 1971.
(With Carol Albritton, under joint pseudonym Elizabeth Treahearne) *Storm at Midnight,* Ace Books (New York City), 1973.
Dark Masquerade, Fawcett, 1974.
The Bewitching Grace, Popular Library, 1974.
The Court of the Thorn Tree, Popular Library, 1974.
Bride of a Stranger, Fawcett, 1974.
The Notorious Angel, Fawcett, 1977, reprinted under pseudonym Jennifer Blake, 1983.
(Under name Patricia Ponder) *Haven of Fear,* Manor Books (New York City), 1977.
(Under name Patricia Ponder) *Murder for Charity,* Manor Books, 1977.
Sweet Piracy, Fawcett, 1978.
Night of the Candles, Fawcett, 1978.

*UNDER PSEUDONYM JENNIFER BLAKE; HISTORICAL RO-
    MANCES*

Love's Wild Desire, Popular Library, 1977.
Tender Betrayal, Popular Library, 1979.
The Storm and the Splendor, Fawcett, 1979.
Golden Fancy, Fawcett, 1980.
Embrace and Conquer, Fawcett Columbine (New
    York City), 1981.
Royal Seduction, Fawcett Columbine, 1983.
Surrender in Moonlight, Fawcett Columbine, 1984.
Midnight Waltz, Fawcett Columbine, 1985.
Fierce Eden, Fawcett Columbine, 1985.
Royal Passion, Fawcett Columbine, 1986.
Prisoner of Desire, Fawcett Columbine, 1986.
Southern Rapture, Fawcett Columbine, 1987.
Louisiana Dawn, Fawcett Columbine, 1987.
Perfume of Paradise, Fawcett Columbine, 1988.
Spanish Serenade, Fawcett Columbine, 1990.
Arrow to the Heart, Fawcett Columbine, 1993.
Silver-Tongued Devil, Fawcett Columbine, 1996.

*UNDER PSEUDONYM JENNIFER BLAKE; CONTEMPORARY
    ROMANCES*

Love and Smoke, Fawcett Columbine, 1989.
Joy and Anger, Fawcett Columbine, 1991.
Wildest Dreams, Fawcett Columbine, 1992.
Shameless, Fawcett Columbine, 1994.
Tigress, Fawcett Columbine, 1996.

UNDER PSEUDONYM MAXINE PATRICK

The Abducted Heart, Signet (New York City), 1978.
Bayou Bride, Signet, 1979.
Snowbound Heart, Signet, 1979.
Love at Sea, Signet, 1980.
Captive Kisses, Signet, 1980.
April of Enchantment, Signet, 1981.

OTHER

Contributor to anthologies, under pseudonym Jennifer Blake, including *A Dream Come True,* Topaz,
1994; *Secrets of the Heart,* Topaz, 1994; *Stardust,*
Avon (New York City), 1994; *Honeymoon Suite,* St.
Martin's Press (New York City), 1995; and *A
Purrfect Romance,* Harper Monogram, 1995. Also
contributor to *Vignettes of Louisiana History* and
Louisiana Leaders; contributor of poetry, short stories, and articles to newspapers.

WORK IN PROGRESS: Under pseudonym Jennifer
Blake, *Forbidden Delights,* for MIRA Books, publi-

cation expected in 1997; contributions to anthologies,
Christmas Wishes, for Zebra Press, and *Masked Ball,*
for MIRA.

SIDELIGHTS: Patricia Maxwell once told *CA:* "I
write for the classic reason, to entertain, but also for
the joy of the mental exercise and for that rare
moment of euphoria that comes when the writer's
subconscious takes over and pours out the story with
little interference from the conscious mind. The [Jen-
nifer] Blake historical romances give me particular
pleasure because of a love affair with history that is
long standing. I like to recreate the past as closely as
possible. If I can take readers with me back in time,
if I can make them see what I see, feel what I feel,
even if only for a brief moment, then I am satisfied."

BIOGRAPHICAL/CRITICAL SOURCES:

BOOKS

Falk, Kathryn, editor, *Love's Leading Ladies,* Pin-
    nacle Books (New York City), 1982.

PERIODICALS

Booklist, June 1, 1994, p. 1724.
Kirkus Reviews, April 1, 1994, p. 411.
Library Journal, May 1, 1994, p. 135; May 15,
    1994, p. 64.
Publishers Weekly, April 18, 1994, p. 43.

*   *   *

**McCAUGHREAN, Geraldine   1951-
    (Geraldine Jones)**

PERSONAL: Surname is pronounced "Mc-*cork*-ran";
born June 6, 1951, in Enfield, London, England;
daughter of Leslie Arthur (a fireman) and Ethel (a
teacher; maiden name, Thomas) Jones; married John
McCaughrean. *Education:* Attended Southgate Technical College, Middlesex, 1969-70; Christ Church
College, Oxford, B.A. (honors), 1977. *Religion:*
"Almost Catholic." *Avocational interests:* Playing
the concertina; "I have a dilapidated cabin cruiser on
the local canal."

ADDRESSES: Home—3 Melton Dr., Didcot,
Oxfordshire OX11 7JP, England. *Agent*—Giles Gor-
don, Anthony Sheil Associates Ltd., 43 Doughty St.,
London WC1N 2LF, England.

CAREER: Thames Television, London, England, secretary, 1970-73; Marshall Cavendish Ltd., London, assistant editor, 1977-80, staff writer, beginning 1982, subeditor, 1978-79, 1983-88; Carreras-Rothman Ltd., Aylesbury, England, editorial assistant, 1980-81; freelance writer, 1981—.

MEMBER: National Union of Journalists, Journalists Against Nuclear Extermination.

AWARDS, HONORS: Winner in short story category, All-London Literary Competition, Wandsworth Borough Council, 1979, for "The Pike"; Whitbread Award, 1987, for *A Little Lower Than the Angels;* Carnegie Medal, British Library Association, and *Guardian* Award, both 1989, for *A Pack of Lies.*

WRITINGS:

CHILDREN'S BOOKS

One Thousand and One Arabian Nights, illustrated by Stephen Lavis, Oxford University Press (New York City), 1982.

The Canterbury Tales, illustrated by Victor Ambrus, Oxford University Press, 1984, Rand McNally (Chicago), 1985.

Seaside Adventure, illustrated by Chrissie Wells, Hamlyn (London), 1986.

(With Wells) *Tell the Time,* illustrated by Wells, Hamlyn, 1986.

The Story of Noah and the Ark, illustrated by Helen Ward, Templar, 1987.

The Story of Christmas, illustrated by Ward, Templar, 1988.

Saint George and the Dragon, illustrated by Nicki Palin, Doubleday (New York City), 1989.

El Cid, Oxford University Press, 1989.

My First Space Pop-Up Book, illustrated by Mike Peterkin, Simon & Schuster (New York City), 1989.

My First Earth Pop-Up Book, illustrated by Peterkin, Simon & Schuster, 1990.

The Orchard Book of Greek Myths, Orchard Books (London), 1992.

Greek Myths, illustrated by Emma Chichester Clark, Margaret K. McElderry Books, 1993.

The Odyssey, illustrated by Ambrus, Oxford University Press, 1993.

Blue Moon Mountain, illustrated by Palin, Golden Press (New York City), 1994.

Blue Moo, illustrated by Colin Smithson, Longman (London), 1994.

Stories from Shakespeare, illustrated by Antony Maitland, Orion Children's, 1994.

The Orchard Book of Stories from the Ballet, illustrated by Angela Barrett, Orchard Books, 1994, published as *The Random House Book of Stories from the Ballet,* Random House (New York City), 1995.

How the Reindeer Got Their Antlers, illustrated by Debi Gliori, Orchard Books, 1995.

On The Day the World Began, illustrated by Norman Bancroft-Hunt, Longman, 1995.

The Quest of Isis, illustrated by David Sim, Longman, 1995.

Wizziwig and the Crazy Cooker, Orchard Books, 1995.

Wizziwig and the Singing Chair, Orchard Books, 1995.

Wizziwig and the Sweet Machine, Orchard Books, 1995.

Wizziwig and the Wacky Weather Machine, Orchard Books, 1995.

YOUNG ADULT FICTION

A Little Lower Than the Angels, Oxford University Press, 1987.

A Pack of Lies, Oxford University Press, 1988.

Gold Dust, Oxford University Press, 1993.

TRANSLATOR

Michel Tilde, *Who's That Knocking on My Door?,* Oxford University Press, 1986.

The Snow Country Prince, Knopf (New York City), 1991.

Daisaku Ikeda, *The Princess and the Moon,* Knopf, 1991.

Ikeda, *The Cherry Tree,* illustrated by Brian Wildsmith, Knopf, 1992.

Ikeda, *Over the Deep Blue Sea,* illustrated by Wildsmith, Knopf, 1993.

UNDER NAME GERALDINE JONES

Adventure in New York (textbook), illustrated by Cynthia Back, Oxford University Press, 1979.

Raise the Titanic (textbook) Oxford University Press, 1980.

Modesty Blaise (textbook), Oxford University Press, 1981.

OTHER

Fires' Astonishment, Minerva, 1991.

Vainglory (adult novel), J. Cape, 1991.

Also author of *The Maypole* (adult novel), 1989, and *Heart's Blood* (adult novel), 1994. Editor, *Banbury Focus,* 1981-82; subeditor and writer of stories for *Storyteller* and *Great Composers.*

SIDELIGHTS: Geraldine McCaughrean has written novels for young adults and stories for young children; she has translated and adapted tales, myths, and legends from various cultures; and she has written adult fiction and textbooks. Whatever her subject, however, the author brings a flair for intricate prose and exciting storytelling to her writing. "Reading McCaughrean," Eileen Dunlop asserted in *Twentieth-Century Children's Writers,* "reinforces the belief that a good book is for everyone capable of reading it, regardless of its intended primary audience."

A former editor and writer for various British publishers, McCaughrean started writing for young people by retelling the stories of *One Thousand and One Arabian Nights,* the series of tales told by the legendary Shahrazad. McCaughrean was immediately praised for her inspired storytelling, and her ability to make the familiar stories of Sinbad, Aladdin, and Ali Baba seem exciting and original. M. Crouch commented in *Junior Bookshelf* that with *One Thousand and One Arabian Nights* McCaughrean had achieved a "brilliant tour de force in what is not so much a translation as a thorough reworking of the tales" and that she had "used the original as the starting point of a piece of individual creative enterprise." Several reviewers also praised the way McCaughrean interpreted Shahrazad's own story; Anne Wilson, for instance, noted in *Signal* that "the personal story of Shahrazad, which links her tales much as the sources do, can never have been told with so much warmth, suspense and appreciation of the ridiculousness of her situation." The result, added the critic, is "spellbinding. The language in which the stories are told is a constant excitement throughout the book. . . . Feelings and scenes are powerfully evoked, and Geraldine McCaughrean's arts show limitless versatility in the undertaking of a variety of narrative."

In *The Canterbury Tales,* McCaughrean takes Geoffrey Chaucer's classic series of stories from the fourteenth century and focuses on the pilgrimage to Canterbury itself. The author tones down the content of some of the more ribald tales, and then, "in colorful style and language", creatively adding

conversatation and detail, as Ruth M. McConnell described it in the *School Library Journal.* While he felt that some of the tales lose something in the retelling, *Times Educational Supplement* contributor Terry Jones noted that "McCaughrean's real achievement is the way she has succeeded in turning the whole pilgrimage itself into a story, and has brought that far-off medieval expedition to life in a quite remarkable way." Calling *The Canterbury Tales* "one of the best buys of 1984" in another *Junior Bookshelf* review, Crouch concluded that McCaughrean "captures most beautifully the mood of the pilgrimage."

McCaughrean's first novel, *A Little Lower Than the Angels,* was published to great acclaim, winning the Whitbread Award in 1987. A complex, multi-level drama of medieval England during the time when travelling players performed their Mystery and Morality plays in towns and villages across the countryside, the story centers around Gabriel, a stonemason's apprentice who runs away from his cruel master to join a troupe of players. The playmaster Garvey, seizing a chance to increase the troupe's wealth and popularity, convinces Gabriel to play an off-stage role as a "miracle healer." Gabriel almost believes in his own power until he is confronted by townspeople, dying of the plague and desperate for a miracle. McCaughrean "has triumphed in her first novel in presenting the lives of ordinary people of the past, in direct, present-day language, with just a few archaisms to set the scene, and relevant historical information," Jessica Yates wrote in *British Book News Children's Books.* As Crouch similarly concluded in *Junior Bookshelf:* "This is a very good novel, rich in uncluttered historical detail, written with sensitive fluency, and with a gallery of memorable characters."

McCaughrean's versatility was highlighted by her next book, *A Pack of Lies.* This 1989 winner of the *Guardian* Award and the Carnegie Medal tells of Ailsa Povery and her mother, who eke out a living selling antiques. One day, Ailsa meets a mysterious young man named MCC Berkshire, who offers to help in the shop in exchange for room and board. He is spectacularly successful, as he weaves elaborate stories about each item available, enthralling customers into making purchases. Every tale displays his (and McCaughrean's) brilliance as a storyteller, as each one is written in a different literary style. "Each is an utterly convincing example of its kind, enthralling the reader in a web of make-believe," Valerie Caless observed in *School Librarian.* A reviewer in *Publishers Weekly* similarly hailed the author's "leaps from genre to genre, in the writing equivalent of sleight of hand," and added that she "pulls off each meta-fictional complexity with finesse and humor."

A Pack of Lies is more than just a collection of stories, however, as the ending reveals. MCC does not stay around the shop for long. After his departure, the disconsolate Ailsa picks up a book and finds herself a character in a story about MCC, their meeting, and his time in the shop. Caless asked, "Who, then, is the fiction and who the liar telling it? Is Ailsa a figment of MCC's imagination or he of hers?" As Stephanie Nettell concluded in introducing this award-winner in *Books for Keeps:* "More than anything, *A Pack of Lies* is an exuberant celebration of fiction's spell, a smiling surrender to the grip of the unruly imagination, a playful introduction to the riches of style that lie waiting in books."

McCaughrean again showed the depth of her imagination with her third novel, 1993's *Gold Dust,* which is set in a poor mining town in Brazil. The effects of uncontrolled greed caused by the discovery of gold are seen through the eyes of Inez de Souza and her brother Maro, who watch as their town is slowly destroyed and its inhabitants corrupted by a gold rush. "Sharp observations on a kaleidoscope of topics enliven every page, often underlined by ironic humour, whether understated . . . or sharper," Brian Slough wrote in *Times Educational Supplement.* "All we can be confident about each book [by McCaughrean] is that it will be admirable—but in which way?" Crouch asked in his *Junior Bookshelf* review. With its "sparkling" language and "wonderfully inventive, consistent and hideously convincing" plot, the critic concluded, *Gold Dust* is "an engrossing, funny, tragic blockbuster of a story."

In addition to writing fiction, McCaughrean continued her retelling and translating activities, in 1989 producing her version of *Saint George and the Dragon,* the story of England's patron saint. Traveling across the countryside, George of Lydda comes across Sabra, the king's daughter, who has been tied to the stake as a sacrifice to the dragon—a slimy, lizard-like creature called Wickedness, whose father is Evil and whose mother is Darkness. In *El Cid,* McCaughrean retells the story of one of Spain's most famous heroes, Rodrigo Diaz, who was exiled from Castile only to become a brilliant warrior who recaptured territory from the invading Moors. "McCaughrean shows herself a grand storyteller," a *Kirkus Reviews* critic remarked; "she presents this prototypical chivalric knight in a lively narrative

sparked with humor, drama, and her hero's daring trickery."

In her retellings of both *The Odyssey* and *Greek Myths,* McCaughrean uses humor to create interest and excitement for younger readers. Janet Tayler, reviewing for *School Librarian,* noted that the adventures of Odysseus had been retold in a "lively, rather tongue-in-cheek manner," while Hazel Rochman, writing for *Booklist,* called the stories in *Greek Myths* "direct, robust, and gleeful." Pauline Long noted that *Greek Myths* would not serve as a reference tool, but she added in *School Librarian* that "its real purpose is to delight and entertain—and this it does in flamboyant style." As Rochman commented, the stories have the "dramatic immediacy" of familiar legends: "'Long ago, when fortune-tellers told the truth, there lived a very frightened man.' How can you not read on?"

McCaughrean has been widely praised for her translations as well as her adaptations. She has translated several books by Japanese author Daisaku Ikeda, including *The Cherry Tree* and *Over the Deep Blue Sea.* The first is the story of a sister and brother in a village that has been devastated by war. The children's father is now dead, and their mother goes off to work every day. They find hope and the possibility of rebirth when they work to help an old man protect a badly damaged cherry tree against the winter months, and watch as it blooms again in the spring. A *Kirkus Reviews* critic commented that McCaughrean's translation had "poetic vigor and grace." *Over the Deep Blue Sea* is a story of hatred dissipated through friendship. When a Japanese family goes to live on a South Sea island, the children make friends with a native boy named Pablo. But Pablo cuts off the friendship when he learns that the Japanese had bombed the island during the war. In the end, the children reunite and are told that they may have all come from the "same place" in "tiny boats" from around the world. Although some reviewers found the ending trite, a *Kirkus Reviews* writer praised the "vividly phrased text."

McCaughrean once commented: "Having struggled with several unsuccessful and unpublished novels, I have now found that my true talent lies in writing for children. In doing so, I have cleaned up a previously elaborate and overwritten style into one that is both more valid and of more use to publishers. This pure luck of being in the right place at the right time has led to the remarkable good fortune of making a living from the thing I like doing best."

BIOGRAPHICAL/CRITICAL SOURCES:

BOOKS

Children's Literature Review, Volume 38, Gale (Detroit), 1996.
Twentieth-Century Children's Writers, St. James Press (Detroit), 1995.

PERIODICALS

Booklist, March 15, 1986, p. 1079; October 15, 1989, p. 461; December 15, 1989, p. 834; February 1, 1993, p. 982.
Books for Keeps, May, 1989, p. 25.
British Book News Children's Books, June, 1987, p. 30.
Bulletin of the Center for Children's Books, April, 1988, pp. 161-62.
Growing Point, July, 1987, pp. 4824-26.
Horn Book, June, 1983, p. 342-43.
Junior Bookshelf, February, 1983, p. 44; February, 1985, p. 41-42; June, 1987, p. 135; August, 1989, pp. 159-60; February, 1990, p. 47; February, 1994, pp. 34-35; February, 1995, pp. 38-39.
Kirkus Reviews, November 1, 1987, p. 1577; September 15, 1989, p. 1406; October 15, 1989, p. 1532; April 1, 1992, p. 466; May 15, 1993.
Publishers Weekly, April 28, 1989, p. 82.
School Librarian, December, 1982, pp. 339-40; September, 1985, p. 239; February, 1989, p. 31; February, 1993, p. 22; May, 1994, pp. 62, 72, 74.
School Library Journal, February, 1986, p. 82; April, 1988, p. 102; March, 1990, p. 209; April, 1993, pp. 136-37.
Signal, January, 1983, pp. 26-29.
Times Educational Supplemental, January 14, 1983, p. 33; February 1, 1985, p. 27; March 10, 1989, p. B13; June 9, 1989, p. B12; November 10, 1989, p. 58; October 30, 1992, sec. 2, p. 7; November 12, 1993, p. 3.
Times Literary Supplement, November 25-December 1, 1988, p. 1322.*

* * *

McDONALD, Ian A(rchie)   1933-

PERSONAL: Born April 18, 1933, in Trinidad, West Indies; son of John Archie (in business) and Thelma (Seheult) McDonald; married Myrna Camille Foster, December 5, 1959 (divorced); married Mary Angela Callender, 1983; children: (first marriage) Keith Ian; (second marriage) Jamie, Darren. *Education:* Attended Queens Royal College, Trinidad, 1941-51; Cambridge University, B.A.(honors), 1955, M.A., 1959. *Avocational interests:* Tennis (captained the Cambridge University team, the Guyana team, and the West Indian Davis Cup team and has played at Wimbledon, 1952-59).

ADDRESSES: Home—16 Bel Air Gardens, East Coast, Demerara, Guyana, South America. *Office*—c/o Guyana Sugar Corp., 22 Church St., Georgetown, Guyana, South America.

CAREER: Bookers Group Committee, Georgetown, Guyana, secretary, 1955-59; Bookers Sugar Estates Ltd., Georgetown, company secretary, 1959-64, administrative secretary, 1964-70; currently director of Marketing and Administration, Guyana Sugar Corp., Georgetown.

MEMBER: Fellow of the Royal Society of Literature (London).

AWARDS, HONORS: Winifred Holtby Memorial Prize of Royal Society of Literature, 1969, for best regional novel, *The Humming-Bird Tree;* Golden Arrow of Achievement; Guyana Prize for Literature, 1992, for poetry.

WRITINGS:

The Humming-Bird Tree (novel), Heinemann (London), 1969.
Poetry Introduction 3, Faber (London), 1975.
Selected Poems, Labour Advocate (Georgetown), 1983.
(Editor) *A. J. S. at 70: A Celebration on his 70th Birthday of the Life, Work, and Art of A. J. Seymour,* Autoprint (Georgetown), 1984.
Mercy Ward, Peterloo Poets (Cornwall, England), 1988.
Essequibo, Peterloo Poets, 1992.
Jaffo the Calypsonian, Peepal Tree Press (Leeds, England), 1994.

Kyk-Over-Al (literary magazine), joint editor, 1984-89, editor, 1989—. Editorial consultant for West Indian Commission, 1990-92. Contributor of short stories and poems to *Penthouse, Bim, Outposts, Chicago Tribune,* and *Greenfield Review.*

WORK IN PROGRESS: Two volumes of poems; a novel; short stories. Editing *The Collected Poems of A. J. Seymour.*

BIOGRAPHICAL/CRITICAL SOURCES:

PERIODICALS

Books and Bookmen, June, 1969.
Times Literary Supplement, March 6, 1969.

*   *   *

McWHINNEY, Edward Watson 1926-

PERSONAL: Born May 19, 1926, in Sydney, New South Wales, Australia; son of Matthew Andrew and Evelyn Annie (Watson) McWhinney; married Emily Ingalore (an economist and stockbroker), June 27, 1951. *Education:* University of Sydney, LL.B., 1949; Yale University, LL.M.,1951, Sc.Jur.D., 1953; Academy of International Law, Diploma in International Law, 1951. *Avocational interests:* Golf, tennis, swimming, walking.

ADDRESSES: Home—1949 Beach Ave. Ste. 402, Vancouver, British Columbia, Canada V6G 1Z2. *Office*—House of Commons, 555-D Centre Block, Parliament, Ottawa, Ontario, Canada K1A OA6.

CAREER: Yale University, New Haven, CT, lecturer in law, 1951-53, assistant professor of political science and fellow of Silliman College, 1953-55; University of Toronto, Toronto, Ontario, professor of international and comparative law and member of Centre for Russian Studies, 1955-66; McGill University, Montreal, Quebec, professor of law and director of Institute of Air and Space Law, 1966-71; Indiana University—Bloomington, professor of law and director of international and comparative legal studies, 1971-74; Simon Fraser University, Burnaby, Vancouver, British Columbia, professor of international law and relations and chair of department of politics, 1974-92; member of parliament, 1993—.

Visiting professor at Ecole Libre des Hautes Etudes, 1952, University of Heidelberg and Max-Planck Institut, 1960-61 and 1990, National University of Mexico, 1965, University of Paris and University of Madrid, 1968, University d'Aix-Marseille, 1969, Institut Universitaire, Luxembourg, 1972, 1974, 1976, Academy of International Law, The Hague,

1973 and 1990, Aristotelian University of Thessaloniki, 1975, 1978, 1982, University of Nice, 1976-77, Jagellonian University of Cracow, 1976, University of Paris, 1982, 1985, College of France, Paris, 1983, Meiji University, 1987, and Institute of Contemporary International Relations, Beiging, China, 1987. Queen's counsel, Canada, 1967—; royal commissioner, Quebec, 1968-72; royal commissioner, British Columbia, 1974-75. Legal consultant to United Nations, 1953-54, U.S. Naval War College, 1961-68, government of Ontario, 1969-71, government of Quebec, 1969-70, 1974-75, and government of Canada, 1979. Special advisor, Canadian delegation to the United Nations, 1981-83. *Military service:* Australian Air Force, 1943-45; became flying officer (first lieutenant).

MEMBER: Institut de Droit International (membre titulaire), Academie International de Droit Compare, Canadian Society of International Law (chair of executive committee, 1972-75), American Society of International Law (member of executive council, 1965-68), American Foreign Law Association, Institut Grand-Ducal (Luxembourg), Instituto Interamericano de Estudios Juridicos Internacionales, Deutsche Gesellschaft fur Volkerrecht, Knights of Mark Twain (United States; honorary member).

AWARDS, HONORS: Rockefeller Foundation fellowship, 1960-61, 1966-68; Canada Council fellowship, 1960-61.

WRITINGS:

NONFICTION

Judicial Review in the English-Speaking World, University of Toronto Press, 1956, 4th edition, 1969.
Foederalismus und Bundesverfassungsrecht, Quelle & Meyer, 1961.
Constitutionalism in Germany, Sijthoff, 1962.
Comparative Federalism, University of Toronto Press, 1962, 2nd edition, 1965.
Peaceful Coexistence and Soviet-Western International Law, Sijthoff, 1964.
Federal Constitution-Making for a Multi-National World, Sijthoff, 1966.
International Law and World Revolution, Sijthoff, 1967.
Conflit ideologique et ordre public mondial, A. Pedone (Paris), 1969.
The Illegal Diversion of Aircraft and International Law, Sijthoff, 1975.

The International Law of Detente, Sijthoff, 1978.

The World Court and the Contemporary International Law-Making Process, Sijthoff, 1979.

Quebec and the Constitution, 1960-1978, University of Toronto Press, 1979.

Constitution-Making: Principles, Process, Practices, University of Toronto Press, 1981.

Conflict and Compromise: International Law and World Order in a Revolutionary Age, Holmes & Meier, 1981.

Supreme Courts and Judicial Law-Making, Holmes & Meier, 1986.

Les Nations—Unies et la formation du droit, Pedone/ UNESCO (Paris), 1986.

Aerial Piracy and International Terrorism, Martinus Nijhoff, 1987.

The International Court of Justice and the Western Tradition of International Law, Martinus Nijhoff, 1987.

(With Nagendra Singh) *Nuclear Weapons and Contemporary International Law,* Martinue Nijhoff, 1988.

Judicial Settlement of International Disputes, Martinus Nijhoff, 1991.

Judge Shigeru Oda and the Progressive Development of International Law, Martinus Nijhoff, 1993.

Judge Manfred Lochs and Judicial Law-Making, Martinus Nijhoff, 1995.

Also author of *Canada and the Constitution,* 1982, and *United Nations Law-Making,* 1983.

EDITOR AND CONTRIBUTOR

Canadian Jurisprudence: The Civil Law and Common Law in Canada, University of Toronto Press, 1958.

Law, Foreign Policy, and the East-West Detente, University of Toronto Press, 1964.

The International Law of Communications, Oceana, 1971.

Aerial Piracy and International Law, Oceana, 1971.

(With P. Pescatore) *Federalism and Supreme Courts and the Integration of Legal Systems,* Editions UGA (Brussels), 1973.

(With G. T. Tunkin) *From Coexistence to Cooperation: International Law and Organization in the Post-Cold War Era,* Martinus Nijhoff, 1991.

Federalism-in-the-Making, Martinus Nijhoff, 1992.

OTHER

(Editor with Martin A. Bradley) *The Freedom of the Air,* Oceana, 1968.

(Editor with Bradley) *New Frontiers in Space Law,* Oceana, 1969.

Contributor to *International Encyclopaedia of the Social Sciences* and *Encyclopaedia Britannica.* Also contributor of articles and essays to *Harvard Law Review, Revue Generale de Droit/International Public,* and other journals in the United Kingdom, United States, France, Germany, Spain, and India. Member of international editorial advisory board, *Encyclopaedia Britannica.*

SIDELIGHTS: Edward Watson McWhinney is fluent in French and German and competent in Russian, Italian, and Spanish.

* * *

MELONE, Albert P(hilip) 1942-

PERSONAL: Born April 25, 1942, in Chicago, IL; son of Dominic A. (an electronics technician) and Catherine (Bongeorno) Melone; married Peggy Harles, August 26, 1971; children: Dominic, Ann, Peter. *Education:* Mount San Antonio College, A.A., 1962; California State University, Los Angeles, B.A., 1964, M.A., 1967; attended Loyola Marymount University, 1964-65; University of Iowa, Ph.D., 1972.

ADDRESSES: Home—109 North Rod Lane, Carbondale, IL 62901. *Office*—Department of Political Science, Southern Illinois University at Carbondale, Carbondale, IL 62901.

CAREER: Idaho State University, Pocatello, lecturer, 1966, instructor in government, 1967; California State University, Los Angeles, instructor in political science, 1968; North Dakota State University, Fargo, assistant professor, 1970-75, associate professor of political science, 1975-80, chairperson of department, 1973-76; Southern Illinois University, Carbondale, visiting associate professor, 1979-80, associate professor, 1980-85, professor of political science, 1985—. Manuscript referee for Southern Illinois University Press, Brooks/Cole Publishing Co., North Dakota Institute for Regional Studies, and Minnesota Academy of Science. Consultant to various universities, North Dakota Supreme Court, and Professional Market Research Audits and Surveys, New York.

MEMBER: American Political Science Association, Law and Society Association, American Judicature Society, Midwest Political Science Association, Western Political Science Association, Pi Sigma Alpha.

WRITINGS:

Lawyers, Public Policy, and Interest Group Politics, University Press of America (Lanham, MD), 1977.

(With Carl Kalvelage) *Primer on Constitutional Law,* Palisades (Palisades, CA), 1982.

(Contributor) Stuart S. Nagel, Erika Fairchild, and Anthony Champagne, editors, *The Political Science of Criminal Justice,* C. C. Thomas (Springfield, IL), 1982.

Administrative Law Primer, Palisades, 1983.

(Contributor) Bruce Leone, editor, *Criminal Justice: Opposing Viewpoints,* Greenhaven Press (St. Paul, MN), 1983.

(With H. B. Jacobini and Kalvelage) *Research Essentials of Administrative Law,* Palisades, 1983.

Bridges to Knowledge in Political Science: A Handbook for Research, Palisades, 1984.

(Contributor) Ericka Fairchild and Vincent Webb, editors, *The Politics of Crime and Criminal Justice,* Sage Publications (Beverly Hills, CA), 1985.

(Contributor) Walter F. Murphy and C. Herman Pritchett, editors, *Courts, Judges, and Politics,* 4th edition, Random House (New York City), 1986.

Judicial Review and American Democracy, Iowa State University Press (Ames), 1988.

Researching Constitutional Law, Scott, Foresman (Glenview, IL), 1990.

The Legal System and American Constitutional Democracy, St. Kliment Ohridski University Press (Sofia, Bulgaria), 1993.

Also contributor to books, including *Encyclopedia of the American Judicial System,* Volume II, edited by Robert J. Janosik, Scribner, 1987, and *Point-Counterpoint: Readings in American Government,* 5th edition, edited by Herbert M. Levine, St. Martin's Press, 1995. Contributor of articles and reviews to law and political science journals, including *Policy Studies Journal, Journal of Politics, Judicature, Western Political Quarterly, International Political Science Review,* and *Political Science and Politics.* Manuscript referee for *Journal of Politics, American Politics Quarterly, Western Politics Quarterly* and *American Political Science Review.*

SIDELIGHTS: Albert P. Melone told *CA:* "In the last several years, much of my writing attention has shifted from an exclusive preoccupation with American government to comparative politics. Specifically, the transition to democracy around the world is the most dramatic and interesting question in political science today. Because of a combination of world events and being in the right place at the right moment, I became interested in studying the transition to democracy in Bulgaria. I have written several articles on the topic and currently I am preparing a book length manuscript on the subject. An author gives up much when shifting attention from one field of study to another. It requires retooling and in a sense it is necessary to start all over. But the task is an interesting intellectual challenge that serves to expand one's knowledge. Unlike some others who have shifted fields, I will try to keep at least one leg in the old camp. It may prove to be quite a stretch."

*   *   *

MILLER, Lillian B(eresnack)   1923-

PERSONAL: Born February 15, 1923, in Boston, MA; daughter of Samuel M. and Ida Frances (Curland) Beresnack; married Nathan Miller (a professor of history), November 3, 1948; children: Hennah E. Lieberman, Joel A., Rebecca S. *Education:* Radcliffe College, A.B. (magna cum laude), 1943; Columbia University, A.M., 1948, Ph.D., 1962.

ADDRESSES: Office—National Portrait Gallery, Smithsonian Institution, Washington, DC 20560.

CAREER: Bard College, Annandale-on-Hudson, NY, instructor in literature, 1946-49; University of Wisconsin—Milwaukee, instructor, 1961-62, lecturer, 1962-67, associate professor of history, 1967-71; Smithsonian Institution, National Portrait Gallery, Washington, DC, historian, 1971-74, historian of American culture, 1974—. Professorial lecturer in American Studies, George Washington University, 1972—; Caroline Werner Gannett Professor of the Humanities, Rochester Institute of Technology, 1981-82; special member of American Studies graduate faculty, University of Maryland, 1986—. Creator of historical paintings exhibitions held in National Portrait Gallery, 1972, 1974, 1975, 1982-83, 1987, and 1992, Amon Carter Museum and Metropolitan Museum, 1982-83, and Philadelphia Museum of Art,

1996. Commissioner, Commission on Artistic Properties for the State of Maryland, 1973-76; panel member and evaluator, National Endowment for the Humanities, 1977—. Presenter of over 100 slide-illustrated lectures relating to art history and American cultural history to public and academic audiences all over the United States and in Canada, France, and Yugoslavia. Consultant in American cultural history and art history to a variety of organizations throughout the United States.

MEMBER: American Historical Association, Organization of American Historians, American Studies Association (member, program committee, 1979, council and executive board, 1983-86; chair, publications committee, 1984-86; delegate, American Council of Learned Societies, 1986-90), American Society for Eighteenth-Century Studies, Institute of Early American History and Culture (member of council, 1983-86), Commonwealth Center (member of council, 1990-93), Association for Documentary Editing, Society of Federal Historians, Phi Beta Kappa.

AWARDS, HONORS: American Council of Learned Societies fellowship, 1949-51; university essay contest prize, New York Historical Association, 1950; research grant, University of Wisconsin, 1969-71; research grants, Smithsonian Institution, 1978, 1981, 1986, and 1991.

WRITINGS:

Patrons and Patriotism: The Encouragement of the Fine Arts in the United States, 1790-1860, University of Chicago Press (Chicago, IL), 1966.

"If Elected . . .": Unsuccessful Candidates for the Presidency, 1796-1968, Smithsonian Institution Press (Washington, DC), 1972.

The Lazzaroni: Science and Scientists in Mid-19th Century America, Smithsonian Institution Press, 1972.

In the Minds and Hearts of the People: Prologue to the American Revolution, 1760-1774, New York Graphic Society (Boston, MA), 1974.

The Dye Is Now Cast: The Road to American Independence, 1774-1776, Smithsonian Institution Press, 1975.

(Editor and author of foreword) *Charles Fenderich, Lithographer,* University of Chicago Press, 1978.

(Editor) *The Collected Papers of Charles Willson Peale and His Family,* three volumes, Kraus Microform, 1980.

(With Edgar P. Richardson and Brooke Hindle) *Charles Willson Peale and His World,* Abrams (New York City), 1982.

(Editor with Sidney Hart and David C. Ward) *The Selected Papers of Charles Willson Peale and His Family,* Yale University Press (New Haven, CT), Volume I, *Charles Willson Peale: Artist in Revolutionary America, 1735-1791,* 1983, Volume II, *Charles Willson Peale: The Artist as Museum Keeper, 1791-1810,* 1987, Volume III, *The Belfield Farm Years, 1810-1820,* 1991, Volume IV, *Charles Willson Peale: His Last Years, 1820-1827,* 1996.

(With Nancy A. Johnson) *Portraits from the American Academy and Institute of Arts and Letters,* National Portrait Gallery, Smithsonian Institution, 1987.

(Editor with Ward) *New Perspectives on Charles Willson Peale: A 250th Anniversary Celebration,* University of Pittsburgh Press (Pittsburgh, PA), 1991.

In Pursuit of Fame: Rembrandt Peale, 1778-1860, University of Washington Press (Seattle), 1992.

The Peale Family: Creation of a Legacy, 1770-1870, Abbeville Press (New York City), 1996.

CONTRIBUTOR

Indiana Historical Society Lectures for 1972-1973, Indiana Historical Society, 1974.

John Browning and Richard Morton, editors, *1776,* Samuel Stevens & Co., 1976.

John C. Milley, editor, *Papers on American Art,* Edinburgh Press, 1976.

The Best of the Smithsonian, Smithsonian Institution Press, 1982.

(Author of introduction) Wendy C. Wick, *George Washington, an American Icon: The Eighteenth Century Graphic Portraits,* University Press of Virginia (Charlottesville), 1982.

David D. Hall and David Grayson Allen, editors, *Seventeenth-Century New England,* Colonial Society of Massachusetts (Charlottesville, VA), 1985.

Rembrandt Peale, 1778-1860: A Life in the Arts, Historical Society of Pennsylvania (Philadelphia), 1985.

1888. Frederick Layton and His World, Milwaukee Art Museum, 1988.

Irma Jaffe, editor, *The Italian Preserve in American Art, 1760-1860,* Fordham University Press (Bronx, NY), 1989.

Jaffe, editor, *The Italian Presence in American Art, 1860-1920,* Fordham University Press, 1992.

OTHER

The Legacy of James Bowdoin III, Bowdoin College Museum of Art (Brunswick, ME), 1994.

Also contributor to *Meaning in American Art,* 1976. Editor of the Charles Wilson Peale papers for the National Portrait Gallery. Member of board of managing editors, *American Quarterly,* 1989-92. Member of editorial advisory board, *Winterthur Journal of Material Culture,* 1978-82, and *William and Mary Quarterly,* 1983-86; member of editorial board, *American Studies,* 1986-90. Contributor to periodicals, including *American Magazine of Art, American Art Journal, Smithsonian, American Historical Review, Modern Language Journal, Journal of American History, Journal of the Early Republic,* and *Virginia Historical Magazine.*

WORK IN PROGRESS: The Hereditary Tradition: Patronage of the Fine Arts in the United States, 1865-1915; Selected Papers of Charles Willson Peale and His Family series, vols. 5-7, for Yale University Press; *The Great American Collectors.*

SIDELIGHTS: Lillian B. Miller told *CA:* "I left the academic world in 1971 to join the Smithsonian Institution's National Portrait Gallery as Historian, in order to bring new historical ideas and methodologies to the attention of the general public through publications, exhibitions, and research. Since the time I joined the Smithsonian, museums have assumed great importance in the country's intellectual life, and I am pleased to have been part of this effort. Continuing to teach in nearby universities and at the National Portrait Gallery (by advising interns and fellows) through research and writing, I continue to try to make available to the non-scholarly audience that visit museums new approaches to the study of American art and cultural history. The Peale Family Papers project is one means of doing so; by elucidating the significance of materials in their letters, publications, and painted works, we are able to clarify and deepen understanding of the times in which they lived (1735-1885) and the artistic and cultural ideas that underlay their achievement. To convey these ideas visually through exhibitions is another challenge that has its own satisfactions.

"My longstanding interest in patronage of the arts continues but slowly and in small pieces, which I hope to pull together some day into a more comprehensive study."

BIOGRAPHICAL/CRITICAL SOURCES:

PERIODICALS

Art Bulletin, June, 1988, pp. 188-207.
Los Angeles Times Book Review, April 4, 1984.
Washington Post, April 2, 1984.

*   *   *

MISHLER, William (Thomas Earle II)   1947-

PERSONAL: Born October 14, 1947, in Miami, FL; son of William Thomas Earle (in business) and Marie (a homemaker; maiden name, Schmitz) Mishler; married Catherine Tanner (a librarian), August 5, 1972. *Education:* Stetson University, B.A. (magna cum laude), 1969; Duke University, M.A., 1971, Ph.D., 1973.

ADDRESSES: Home—165 Arwen Ln., Columbia, SC 29212. *Office*—Department of Government and International Studies, University of South Carolina at Columbia, Columbia, SC 29208.

CAREER: Duke University, Durham, NC, assistant professor of political science, 1972-78; State University of New York at Buffalo, associate professor, 1978-83, professor of political science and chair of department 1983-86; University of South Carolina at Columbia, professor of government and chair of department of government and international studies, 1986-89, professor of government, 1989-95, James F. and Maude B. Byrnes Professor of government, 1995—. Visiting professor at University of Strathclyde, 1976-77; director of National Science Foundation's Political Science Program, 1982-84, 1990-91. *Military service:* U.S. Army Reserve, 1969-77; became captain.

MEMBER: International Political Science Association, International Studies Association, American Political Science Association, Southern Political Science Association, Midwestern Political Science Association, Association of Canadian Studies in the United States, Phi Beta Kappa, Omicron Delta Kappa.

AWARDS, HONORS: Woodrow Wilson fellowship, 1969-70.

WRITINGS:

(With Allan Kornberg) *Influence in Parliament: Canada,* Duke University Press (Durham, NC), 1976.

Political Participation in Canada, Macmillan of Canada, 1979.

(With Kornberg and Harold Clarke) *Representative Democracy in the Canadian Provinces,* Prentice-Hall of Canada, 1982.

(Editor with Kornberg and Barry Cooper) *The Resurgence of Conservatism in Anglo-American Democracies,* Duke University Press, 1987.

(With Clarke and others) *Controversies in Political Economy,* Westview (Boulder, CO), 1992.

WORK IN PROGRESS: With Richard Rose, *Bringing Democracy In: Public Support for Democratization in Post-Communist Europe,* and with Reginald Sheehan and Donald Songen, *The Supreme Court and American Democracy.*

* * *

MOFFAT, Gwen 1924-

PERSONAL: Born July 3, 1924, in Brighton, Sussex, England; married Gordon Moffat, 1948 (divorced); married John Lees (a mountain guide), 1956; children: (first marriage) Sheena. *Education:* Attended English schools. *Avocational interests:* Mountaineering, exploring the American West, music, cooking.

ADDRESSES: Home—The English Lake District. *Agent*—Laurence Pollinger Ltd, 18 Maddox St, Mayfair, London W1R 0EU, England.

CAREER: Mountain guide; first woman to be granted guides' certificates of British Mountaineering Council, 1953, and Association of Scottish Climbing Clubs, 1957; specialized in English Lake District and North Wales, and in winter, Glencoe and Ben Nevis Areas. Radio and television broadcaster. *Military service:* Auxiliary Territorial Service, 1943-47.

MEMBER: Society of Authors, Crime Writers' Association, Sierra Club, Alpine Club, Pinnacle Club, Mystery Writers of America.

AWARDS, HONORS: Welsh Arts Council grant, 1973.

WRITINGS:

Space below My Feet (autobiographical), Houghton (Wirral, England), 1961.

Two Star Red: A Book about R.A.F. Mountain Rescue, Hodder & Stoughton (London), 1964.

On My Home Ground, Hodder & Stoughton, 1968.

Survival Count (nonfiction), Gollancz (London), 1972.

Hard Option (novel), Gollancz, 1975.

Hard Road West: Alone on the California Trail (nonfiction), Viking (London), 1981.

The Buckskin Girl, David & Charles (Newton Abbot, England), 1982.

Also author of *The Storm Seekers,* Secker & Warburg (London).

CRIME NOVELS

Lady with a Cool Eye, Gollancz, 1973.

Deviant Death, Gollancz, 1974.

The Corpse Road, Gollancz, 1974.

Miss Pink at the Edge of the World, Scribner (New York City), 1975.

Over the Sea to Death, Scribner, 1976.

A Short Time to Live, Gollancz, 1976.

Persons Unknown, Gollancz, 1978.

Die Like A Dog, David & Charles, 1982.

Last Chance Country, Gollancz, 1983.

Grizzly Trail, Gollancz, 1984.

Snare, Macmillan (London), 1987.

The Stone Hawk, Macmillan, 1989.

Rage, Macmillan, 1990.

The Raptor Zone, Macmillan, 1990.

Pit Bull, Macmillan, 1991.

Veronica's Sisters, Macmillan, 1992.

The Outside Edge, Macmillan, 1993.

Cue the Battered Wife, Macmillan, 1994.

OTHER

Contributor to *Daily Express, Sunday Express, Glasgow Herald, Guardian, She,* and *Woman.* Also contributor to anthologies.

WORK IN PROGRESS: A Melinda Pink crime novel, and "a crime novel set in the Scottish Highlands and the American West."

SIDELIGHTS: Gwen Moffat told *CA:* "My advice to youngsters who want to become authors is to read voraciously and to indulge their natural curiosity. And to persist. I first appeared in print when I was

10 years old, winning an essay competition, but I didn't earn any money—from the articles that began my career—until 14 years later. Four books followed, at long intervals: nonfiction books on climbing, mountain rescue, and the environment. Meanwhile I worked as a mountain guide until Livia Gollancz, of Victor Gollancz Ltd, persuaded me to try crime fictions. Subsequently, she encouraged me to travel (I had never been beyond the Alps), and the first commission was to follow the nineteenth-century California Trail for *Hard Road West: Alone on the California Trail.* The next book was a novel on the Trail: *The Buckskin Girl.*"

I write because this is what I do best, and in order to make the money to indulge my love of wilderness: in the West or the Scottish Highlands. Whether I'm traveling, climbing, or working on a book, I aim to write 1,000 words a day. I write best when I'm deeply committed: to the red rock country of Utah, as in *The Stone Hawk,* with old-growth forests in *The Raptor Zone,* with its sub-plot of the threat to spotted owls in Oregon. But although the natural environment is my background, it is the peculiar horror of people driven beyond endurance in a wild and lovely setting that is the main feature of all my work.

"I move around, renting homes in the backwoods for months while writing a book about the last place I investigated. So I have lived in a log cabin in the Rockies, in a house in the Mojave Desert, on the bank of the Colorado River, in an adobe above the Rio Grande in New Mexico. I worked on a Montana ranch where Yellowstone's grizzly bears holed up in winter, and where I was taught to ride by a great cutting horse called Sergeant.

"The joy of old age is like America: everything is more extreme. One falls in love at the drop of a feather: with a horse, a desert, with evening shadows on tomorrow's mountain. That's the good part. The bad news is the frightened child, the battered wife, the drowned dog in a sack floating down Green River. The good citizen reports the crime and retreats—to be racked by rage. Authors channel the rage. Art is passion disciplined."

BIOGRAPHICAL/CRITICAL SOURCES:

PERIODICALS

Christian Science Monitor, December 6, 1961.
New York Times Book Review, January 1, 1984.

MONKMAN, Leslie
   See MONKMAN, Leslie G.

*   *   *

MONKMAN, Leslie G.   1946-
   (Leslie Monkman)

PERSONAL: Born August 13, 1946, in Owen Sound, Ontario, Canada; son of Gordon Emerson and Islay Annie (Sinclair) Monkman; married Marni Isobel Lockington, December 19, 1975 (separated, 1993); children: Lindsay Alexandra, Fraser Douglas. *Education:* University of Western Ontario, B.A., 1968; University of Toronto, M.A., 1969; York University, Ph.D., 1975.

ADDRESSES: Office—Department of English, Queen's University, Kingston, Ontario, Canada K7L 3N6.

CAREER: University of Guelph, Guelph, Ontario, lecturer, 1969-71, 1973-76, assistant professor, 1976-80, associate professor of English, 1980-84; Queen's University, Kingston, Ontario, associate professor, 1984-88, professor of English, 1988—, associate dean, Faculty of Arts and Science, 1990-95, associate vice-principal (academic), 1995—.

MEMBER: Association for Commonwealth Language and Literature Studies (vice-chair, 1980-83), Association of Canadian University Teachers of English, Association of Canadian Studies, Modern Language Association.

WRITINGS:

(Editor with Douglas M. Daymond) *Towards a Canadian Literature: Essays, Editorials, and Manifestos,* Tecumseh Press, Volume I: *1752-1940,* Volume II: *1940-1983,* 1984-85.
(Editor with Daymond) *On Middle Ground* (novellas), Methuen, 1987.

UNDER NAME LESLIE MONKMAN

(Editor with Daymond) *Literature in Canada,* Volumes I-II, Gage Publishing, 1978.
(Editor with Daymond) *Stories of Quebec,* Oberon Press, 1980.
(Editor with Daymond) *Canadian Novelists and the Novel,* Borealis Press, 1981.

A Native Heritage: Images of the Indian in English-Canadian Literature, University of Toronto Press, 1981.

(Editor with Daymond) John Richardson, *Tecumseh,* Canadian Poetry Press, 1992.

Contributor to *The Commonwealth Novel since 1960,* edited by Bruce King, and *The Native in Literature,* edited by Tom King, et al. Contributor of essays to *Canadian Literature, Journal of Canadian Fiction, Etudes Canadiennes, African Literature Today, Essays on Canadian Writing,* and *Profiles in Canadian Literature.* Associate editor of *World Literature Written in English,* 1982-89.

WORK IN PROGRESS: Research on Canadian, New Zealand, and Australian fiction, and on "genre theory in relation to postcolonial literatures."

SIDELIGHTS: In his 1981 book, *A Native Heritage: Images of the Indian in English-Canadian Literature,* Leslie G. Monkman dispels "conclusively a prevalent idea that the Indian has always been . . . a minor figure" in the literature of Canada, wrote Alfred G. Bailey in *Canadian Poetry.* Exploring how these native Americans are variously depicted in some 250 English-language works, the author discusses an array of genres and writers. The study covers an "impressive range of material," wrote Carole Gerson in *Canadian Literature.* "Especially interesting are Monkman's ventures into some of the narrower byways of [Canada's] cultural history."

Commending the topical rather than historical arrangement of Monkman's investigation, Bailey noted that the author provides "coherent accounts of diverse themes and with a degree of illumination not . . . obtainable" in volumes that adhere to a strictly historical framework. Also noteworthy is Monkman's "lengthy examination" of the Indian mythology and legend revealed in the numerous writings. According to Bailey, questions "of authenticity" are raised concerning physical and anthropological attributes, which many of the authors employed as literary devices to describe the native Americans.

"From Monkman's study emerges the irony that . . . writers have presented simultaneously conflicting stereotypes of Canada's native peoples," observed Gerson. Native Americans have been presented as both vicious savages and children of nature, "a group without a history" that has "supplied identity-hungry white writers with indigenous historical heroes." Asserting that Monkman makes "consistently just

interpretations of the intent of many authors," Bailey determined that *A Native Heritage* stands as "a major contribution to the growing body of critical studies" addressing Canadian literature.

BIOGRAPHICAL/CRITICAL SOURCES:

PERIODICALS

Books in Canada, December, 1985.
Canadian Literature, autumn, 1982.
Canadian Poetry, spring/summer, 1982.
Globe and Mail (Toronto), September 7, 1985.

*   *   *

MOORE, Susanna   1948-

PERSONAL: Born December 9, 1948, in Bryn Mawr, PA; daughter of Richard Dixon (a physician) and Anne (Shields) Moore; married Richard Sylbert (a film production designer), 1972 (divorced); children: Lulu Linnane Sylbert. *Education:* Attended a private preparatory school in Honolulu, Hawaii.

ADDRESSES: Agent—Wallace & Sheil Agency, Inc., 177 East 70th St., New York, NY 10021.

CAREER: Home script reader for actors and motion picture studios, 1967-80; motion picture art director, 1980-82. Writer.

AWARDS, HONORS: American Book Award nomination for best first novel of 1982 and Sue Kaufman Prize for first fiction from American Academy-Institute of Arts and Letters, both 1983, both for *My Old Sweetheart;* Literary Lion Award from New York Public Library, 1993.

WRITINGS:

NOVELS

My Old Sweetheart, Houghton (Boston), 1982.
The Whiteness of Bones, Doubleday (New York City), 1989.
Sleeping Beauties, Knopf (New York City), 1993.
In the Cut, Knopf, 1995.

Contributor of essay to photography book, *Fighting Fish, Fighting Birds,* photos by Hiro, Abrams (New York City), 1990.

SIDELIGHTS: Susanna Moore's novels frequently deal with young women who come from unhappy families and who suffer emotional and sexual difficulties. Moore grew up in Hawaii during the 1950s, where her novel *My Old Sweetheart,* which recounts Lily Shields's journey to maturity, takes place. "*My Old Sweetheart* is one of those rare books that really does show us how people grow and change," Bruce Allen comments in the *Chicago Tribune Book World.* "Moore's prose is modestly lyrical," he continues, "yet it succeeds admirably in casting her troubled characters in vivid relief: They loom larger than life, seem, somehow, emblems of the age that weighs so heavily on them."

Moore's second novel, *The Whiteness of Bones,* also is a female coming-of-age story. The primary character, Mamie Clarke, is the elder daughter of well-off sugar cane farmers on the Hawaiian island of Kauai. At the age of twelve, Mamie is molested by a long-time family servant. In the aftermath of the incident, Mamie grows deeply uncomfortable with her body and sexuality. Several years later, she and her younger sister, Claire, move to New York City, where their Aunt Alysse, a retired model, introduces them to her circle of socialite friends. Claire is swept up in a world of drug use and abusive sex, while Mamie suffers a sexual assault before finding a man who helps her deal with the problems that have plagued her since childhood.

Chicago *Tribune Books* reviewer Hilma Woltzer considers *The Whiteness of Bones* less tightly constructed than Moore's first novel but admires much in it, including its humor. "Moore deftly juxtaposes frankly brutal and hilariously funny events," according to Woltzer. Jonathan Yardley, writing in the *Washington Post Book World,* praises Moore's powers of observation and her "large and understanding heart"; he finds many passages that have "the ring of absolute truth." To the *Voice Literary Supplement*'s Carol Anshaw, however, much in the book rings false. She criticizes Moore's view of 1980s New York as anachronistic: "No crime or grime or homelessness here. . . . Moore's Manhattan is a stage set of the Upper East Side, a My Sister Eileenish froth of gossip and bitchiness." Anshaw finds the characters to be caricatures and the portrayal of Mamie's sexual difficulties and eventual awakening to be sexist. "If sex were politics," states Anshaw, "Susanna Moore might be the new Ayn Rand." Other critics, though, deem Moore's voice a feminist one. "The shaping of Mamie's feminine self-esteem is wisely and poignantly drawn," asserts Wolitzer.

In *Sleeping Beauties,* Moore again deals with a Hawaiian woman who escapes to a new environment. After her mother leaves the family and her father proves to be indifferent to the needs of his children, Clio—Mamie Clarke's cousin—runs away at age thirteen to her Aunt Emma's Hawaiian estate. She and Clio have mixed native Hawaiian and white European ancestry; Emma considers herself the custodian of native culture, seeking to maintain traditions against the onslaught of outsiders, and she schools Clio in her beliefs. Clio becomes a mythology researcher and marries a self-centered movie star, Tommy Haywood, and moves with him to California. The "West Coast [is a] version of the frivolous world of New York socialites . . . in *The Whiteness of Bones,*" observes Michiko Kakutani in the *New York Times.* Tommy becomes physically abusive, and when Clio extricates herself from him she returns to Hawaii, where a return to her roots and a new relationship offer her a second chance at happiness.

Several critics praise Moore's writing style in *Sleeping Beauties* but express reservations about her handling of plot and character. Chicago *Tribune Books* reviewer Joyce Johnson calls the book "a weak novel by an elegant writer." Moore's description of the island environment, Johnson writes, is marked by "spare lyricism," but her characters and their motivations are unrealistic; Johnson also finds the book's ending maudlin. Particularly puzzling, Johnson and some other reviewers observe, is what attracted Clio to Tommy in the first place. Kakutani opines that *Sleeping Beauties* would be a superior novel if Tommy and his world were portrayed in less cartoonish terms. A different view comes from a *Belles Lettres* critic, who asserts that Moore's characters are "distinct and quirky," when they could have been walking cliches. Certain reviewers find the book a worthy effort; "Flawed as it is, *Sleeping Beauties* expands a body of work that is eloquent and disturbing," writes Abby Frucht in the *New York Times Book Review.* The *Washington Post Book World*'s Francine Prose comments that the book "leaves us with images . . . that stay with us long after we've finished the novel," although readers must make it through "much steamy tropical excess" to find them. Kakutani concludes that *Sleeping Beauties,* despite its problems, "ratifies Ms. Moore's earlier achievements and attests to her lucid, poetic gifts as a writer."

With *In the Cut,* Moore leaves her Hawaiian milieu in favor of a New York-based murder mystery that features explicit sex and violence. Written in first-person, the book's narrator is a teacher, linguist and writer who becomes involved in the police investigation of an especially brutal murder and falls for one of the investigators. "Though the novel's themes of rebellion and erotic violence are hardly new to the author, the book is a major departure from Ms. Moore's earlier work," writes Kakutani in the *New York Times.* However, Kakutani states that in trying to create a heroine different from those of her other novels, Moore has created "a disembodied creature subject only to perverse desires and whims." Kakutani and some other reviewers consider the book's descriptions of sex and violence to be overheated yet ordinary. Larissa MacFarquhar comments in the *Los Angeles Times Book Review* that Moore's sex scenes are "selected from the catalogue of Basic Hetero Porn Plots." Molly Haskell, writing in the *New York Times Book Review,* deems Moore's "refusal to express horror or outrage" when describing violent incidents "refreshing" yet troubling: "her Zenlike, unflappable sensibility doesn't quite work with material so loaded with the toxic ill will of our ever more divided culture." Conversely, Haskell praises many of the book's details as evidence of Moore's perceptiveness, as does Kakutani, who expresses a wish that Moore would have used this ability to create a more credible heroine instead of writing scenes designed to shock. If she had done so, Kakutani says, "she might have written a novel more commensurate with her rich talent."

BIOGRAPHICAL/CRITICAL SOURCES:

PERIODICALS

Belles Lettres, winter, 1993-94, pp. 50-51.
Boston Globe, April 2, 1989, p. B15; September 12, 1993, p. B46.
Chicago Tribune Book World, February 13, 1983.
Journal and Constitution (Atlanta), April 23, 1989, p. N11.
Los Angeles Times, March 23, 1989, p. V10.
Los Angeles Times Book Review, November 14, 1993, pp. 3, 8; November 5, 1995, pp. 3, 7.
New York Review of Books, April 27, 1989, pp. 50-51.
New York Times, March 10, 1989, p. C31; September 14, 1993, p. C15; October 31, 1995, p. B3.
New York Times Book Review, March 26, 1989, pp. 5-6; September 5, 1993, p. 2; November 12, 1995, p. 9.
Publishers Weekly, August 28, 1995, p. 100; November 6, 1995, pp. 72-73.

Tribune Books (Chicago), March 12, 1989, p. 6; November 7, 1993, pp. 3, 13.
USA Today, October 1, 1993, p. D5.
Voice Literary Supplement, July, 1989, p. 29.
Washington Post Book World, February 26, 1989, p. 3; September 12, 1993, p. 9.
Women's Review of Books, July, 1989, pp. 31-32.

—*Sketch by Trudy Ring*

* * *

MORRESSY, John   1930-

PERSONAL: Born December 8, 1930, in Brooklyn, NY; son of John Emmett and Jeanette (Geraghty) Morressy; married Barbara Turner, August 11, 1956. *Education:* St. John's University, Jamaica, NY, B.A., 1953; New York University, M.A., 1961.

ADDRESSES: Home—East Sullivan, NH. *Agent*—William Morris Agency, Inc., 1350 Avenue of the Americas, New York, NY 10019.

CAREER: Teacher, intermittently, 1956-63; St. John's University, Jamaica, NY, instructor in English, 1963-66; Monmouth College, West Long Branch, NJ, assistant professor of English, 1966-67; Franklin Pierce College, Rindge, NH, 1968-95, began as associate professor, retired as professor of English and writer in residence. *Military service:* U.S. Army, 1953-55.

MEMBER: Science Fiction Writers of America, Authors League of America, Authors Guild.

AWARDS, HONORS: Bread Loaf Writers' Conference fellowship, 1968; University of Colorado Writers' Conference fellowship, 1970; Balrog Award for best short fantasy, 1984.

WRITINGS:

NOVELS

The Blackboard Cavalier, Doubleday (New York City), 1966.
The Addison Tradition, Doubleday, 1968.
Starbrat, Walker & Co. (New York City), 1972.
Nail Down the Stars, Walker & Co., 1973.
A Long Communion, Walker & Co., 1974.
Under a Calculating Star, Doubleday, 1975.

A Law for the Stars, Laser Books, 1976.
The Extraterritorial, Laser Books, 1977.
Frostworld and Dreamfire, Doubleday, 1977.
Ironbrand, Playboy Press (Chicago), 1980.
Graymantle, Playboy Press, 1981.
Kingsbane, Playboy Press, 1982.
The Mansions of Space, Berkley Publishing (New York City), 1982.
The Time of the Annihilator, Ace Books (New York City), 1985.
A Voice for Princess, Ace Books, 1986.
The Questing of Kedrigern, Ace Books, 1987.
Kedrigern in Wanderland, Ace Books, 1988.
Kedrigern and the Charming Couple, Ace Books, 1990.
A Remembrance for Kedrigern, Ace Books, 1990.
Kedrigern a Drak Comme Il Faut (title means "Kedrigern and the Dragon Comme Il Faut"), Polaris (Czech Republic), 1994.
The Juggler, Holt (New York City), 1996.

OTHER

The Humans of Ziax II (juvenile), Walker & Co., 1974.
The Windows of Forever (juvenile), Walker & Co., 1975.
Drought on Ziax II (juvenile), Walker & Co., 1978.
Other Stories, Northern New England Review Press, 1983.
Kedrigern Doma a Na Cestach (title means "Kedrigern at Home and On the Road"), Polaris, 1994.

Contributor to *Magazine of Fantasy and Science Fiction, Harper's, Esquire, Omni, Playboy,* and other magazines.

WORK IN PROGRESS: An historical novel; a story collection.

SIDELIGHTS: John Morressy told *CA:* "I began writing seriously while I was in college, and sold my first story to a magazine during my junior year. My career after that was meteoric: i.e., it vanished underground and was not seen again for a long time. And that was a good and necessary thing, because I had a lot to learn, and early success would have convinced me that I already knew it all. In writing, as in life, no one knows it all, or even very much of it. No one is perfect, no work is without a flaw, and that is the best part of this profession, because it makes us keep on working, always hoping that the next one will be better.

"Perhaps because of this, perhaps because I've spent so much of my life in and around classrooms, learning plays an important part in all my work. I write about what one must know, and how it is to be learned, and how taught. My characters all learn something, though what they learn is not always what they hope, or expect, or want, to learn. Life is like that too.

"Much of my writing has been in fantasy and science fiction. Others may choose to chronicle contemporary life—usually at its worst—and write of people crushed by neuroses, failure, anxiety, loneliness, despair, anomie, frustration, loss of identity, and lack of purpose. That is not for me. A writer spends a lot of time in intimate association with his characters, and I prefer to be with those who try, not those who wring their hands. The seekers and strivers may fare no better than the whiners in the end, but they're much better company along the way."

BIOGRAPHICAL/CRITICAL SOURCES:

PERIODICALS

Best Sellers, August 15, 1968.
Booklist, December 1, 1989, p. 726.
Christian Science Monitor, August 29, 1968.
Fantasy Newsletter, September, 1980.
Locus, January, 1990, p. 27; February, 1990, p. 53; November, 1990, pp. 29, 59.
Newsday, October 30, 1977.
New York Times Book Review, July 28, 1968.
Times Literary Supplement, February 2, 1967.
Virginia Quarterly Review, winter, 1969.

* * *

MOSSE, George L(achmann)   1918-

PERSONAL: Born September 20, 1918, in Berlin, Germany; naturalized U.S. citizen; son of Hans (a publisher) and Felicia Lachmann-Mosse. *Education:* Attended Cambridge University, 1936-39; Haverford College, B.S., 1941; Harvard University, Ph.D., 1946.

ADDRESSES: Home—36 Glenway, Madison, WI 53705.

CAREER: University of Iowa, Iowa City, 1945-55, began as instructor, became associate professor;

University of Wisconsin—Madison, 1955-65, began as associate professor, became professor of history, John C. Bascom Professor of History, 1965-82, Weinstein-Bascom Professor, Jewish Studies, 1982-88, Emeritus, 1988—; Hebrew University, Jerusalem, Koebner Professor of History, 1978-85, Emeritus, 1985—, A. D. White Professor at Large, 1993—. Visiting professor and fellow at universities in the United States, Europe, Africa, and Australia, including Stanford University, 1963-64, Hebrew University, 1969-78, University of Munich, 1982-83, Cornell University, 1989, 1992, and Pembroke College, Cambridge University, 1990, 1991, 1994. Member of board of directors, Wiener Library, 1973-93, and Leo Baeck Institute, 1978—; member of board of overseers, Tauber Center for Jewish Studies, Brandeis University, 1980—; Conseil Scientifique, Centre de Recherche de L'Historial de la Grande Guerre, Peronne, 1990—. Consultant, U.S. High Commission in Germany (U.S. Information Service), 1951, 1955.

MEMBER: American Society for Reformation Research (president, 1961-62), American Historical Association, American Society for Church History, American Association of University Professors (president, Iowa Conference, 1953-54), American Academy of Arts and Sciences (fellow), Phi Beta Kappa, Phi Eta Sigma.

AWARDS, HONORS: Huntington Library grant, 1953; Social Science Research Council grant, 1961; E. Harris Harbison Prize, Danforth Foundation, 1970; D.Litt., Carthage College, 1973; Aqui Storia Prize, 1975; Premio Prezzolini (Florence), 1985; L.H.D., Hebrew Union College, 1987; Goethe-Medallie, Goethe Institut, 1988; Hilldale Award, University of Wisconsin, 1989; DR.L.C., Universita Degli Studi di Camerino, 1995.

WRITINGS:

The Struggle for Sovereignty in England: From the Reign of Queen Elizabeth to the Petition of Right, Michigan State College Press (East Lansing, MI), 1950, reprinted, Octagon (New York City), 1968.

The Reformation, Holt (New York City), 1953, 3rd revised edition, 1963.

The Holy Pretence: A Study of Christianity and Reason of State from William Perkins to John Winthrop, Basil Blackwell (Oxford, England), 1957, Fertig (New York City), 1968.

(Editor with Hill, Cameron, and Petrovich) *Europe in Review: Readings and Sources since 1500,* Rand McNally (Chicago), 1957, revised edition, 1964.

The Culture of Western Europe: The Nineteenth and Twentieth Centuries, Rand McNally, 1961, 3rd edition, Westview (Boulder, CO), 1988.

The Crisis of German Ideology: The Intellectual Origins of the Third Reich, Grosset (New York City), 1964, reprinted, Schocken (New York City), 1981.

(Compiler with Walter Ze'ev Laqueur) *1914: The Coming of the First World War,* Harper (New York City), 1966.

(With Laqueur) *The Left-Wing Intellectuals between the Wars: 1919-1939,* Gannon (Santa Fe, NM), 1966.

(Editor) *Nazi Culture: Intellectual, Cultural, and Social Life in the Third Reich,* Grosset, 1966, reprinted, Schocken, 1981.

(Editor and contributor) *International Fascism, 1920-1945,* Harper, 1966.

(Editor with Laqueur) *Literature and Politics in the Twentieth Century,* Harper, 1967.

(Editor with Laqueur) *The New History: Trends in Historical Research and Writing since World War Two,* Harper, 1967.

(Editor) *Education and Social Structure in the Twentieth Century,* Harper, 1967.

(With Helmut Georg Koenigsberger) *Europe in the Sixteenth Century,* Holt, 1968.

(Author of introduction) Max Nordau, *Degeneration,* Fertig, 1968.

Germans and Jews: The Right, the Left, and the Search for a "Third Force" in Pre-Nazi Germany, Fertig, 1970, reprinted, Wayne State University Press (Detroit), 1987.

(Editor with Bela Vago) *Jews and Non-Jews in Eastern Europe: 1918-1945,* Wiley (New York City), 1974.

(Editor with Laqueur) *Historians in Politics,* Sage Publications (New York City), 1974.

(Editor) *Police Forces in History,* Sage Publications, 1974.

The Nationalization of the Masses: Political Symbolism and Mass Movements in Germany from the Napoleonic Wars through the Third Reich, Fertig, 1977.

Toward the Final Solution: A History of European Racism, Fertig, 1977.

Interviste Sul Nazismo, Laterza (Bari, Italy), 1977, translation published as *Nazism: A Historical and Comparative Analysis of National Socialism,* Transaction Books (New Brunswick, NJ), 1978.

(Editor) *International Fascism: New Thoughts and New Approaches,* Sage Publications, 1979.

Masses and Man: Nationalist and Fascist Perceptions of Reality, Fertig, 1980.

Nationalism and Sexuality: Middle Class Morality and Sexual Norms in Modern Europe, Fertig, 1985.

German Jews beyond Judaism, Indiana University Press (Bloomington, IN), 1985.

Fallen Soldiers: Shaping the Memory of the World Wars, Oxford University Press (New York City), 1990.

Ebrei in Germania fra Assimilazione e Antisemitismo, Editrice La Giuntina (Florence, Italy), 1991.

(Editor with Jehuda Reinharz) *The Impact of Western Nationalisms,* Sage Publications, 1992.

Confronting the Nation: Jewish and Western Nationalism, University Press of New England (Hanover, NH), 1993.

Image of Man: The Creation of Modern Masculinity, Oxford University Press, 1996.

Contributor to numerous scholarly books on European history, culture, and politics; contributor to encyclopedias and yearbooks; contributor to numerous academic journals. Coeditor, *Journal of Contemporary History,* 1966—.

Mosse's works have been translated into Polish, Italian, Spanish, and French.

SIDELIGHTS: In his study *Nationalism and Sexuality: Middle Class Morality and Sexual Norms in Modern Europe,* historian George L. Mosse examines the contrasting views of European countries on homosexual and gender questions. While the study focuses on sexual roles, Robert Dawidoff in the *Los Angeles Times Book Review* argues that "Nazism is Mosse's real subject." Mosse, the critic explains "broadens the definition of the victims of the Third Reich and the kinds of attitudes that energized their victimization." Dawidoff concludes that *Nationalism and Sexuality* "tries to guide our thinking about the human cost of the Third Reich in suggestive and significant ways."

BIOGRAPHICAL/CRITICAL SOURCES:

BOOKS

Drescher, Seymour and others, editors, *Political Symbolism in Modern Europe: Essays in Honor of George L. Mosse,* Transaction Books (New Brunswick, NJ), 1982.

Runge, Irene and Uwe Stelbrink, *George L. Mosse: Ich bleibe Emigrant,* Dietz (Berlin), 1991.

PERIODICALS

Commentary, October, 1970.

Los Angeles Times Book Review, May 19, 1985.

New German Critique, winter, 1986.

New York Times Book Review, July 12, 1970; February 8, 1981.

Times Literary Supplement, July 23, 1971; September 26, 1975; December 23, 1977.

*   *   *

MOST, Bernard   1937-

PERSONAL: Born September 2, 1937, in New York, NY; son of Max (a painter) and Bertha (Moskowitz) Most; married Amy Beth Pollack, February 12, 1967; children: Glenn Evan, Eric David. *Education:* Pratt Institute, B.F.A. (with honors), 1959. *Politics:* Independent.

ADDRESSES: Home—Scarsdale, NY.

CAREER: McCann-Erickson, Inc. (advertising agency), New York City, art director, 1959-65; Benton & Bowles, Inc. (advertising agency), New York City, associate creative director, 1965-78; MCA Advertising, Inc., New York City, senior vice-president and creative director, 1978-86; Bernie & Walter, Inc. (creative consulting company), partner, 1986-89.

MEMBER: Authors Guild, Authors League of America.

AWARDS, HONORS: Awards from Art Directors Club, Type Directors Club, and American Institute of Graphic Arts; Clio Award; Andy Award; *If the Dinosaurs Came Back, My Very Own Octopus, Boo!,* and *There's an Ant in Anthony* were each selected as a Children's Choice Book by the International Reading Association and Children's Book Council; *There's an Ant in Anthony* was chosen as an American Library Association Notable Book.

WRITINGS:

SELF-ILLUSTRATED CHILDREN'S BOOKS

If the Dinosaurs Came Back (Book-of-the-Month Club selection), Harcourt (New York City), 1978.

There's an Ant in Anthony, Morrow (New York City), 1980.

Turn Over, Prentice-Hall (Englewood Cliffs, NJ), 1980.

My Very Own Octopus, Harcourt, 1980.

Boo!, Prentice-Hall, 1980.

There's an Ape behind the Drape, Morrow, 1981.

Whatever Happened to the Dinosaurs? (Book-of-the-Month Club selection), Harcourt, 1984.

Dinosaur Cousins? (Book-of-the-Month Club selection), Harcourt, 1987.

The Littlest Dinosaurs, Harcourt, 1989.

Four & Twenty Dinosaurs, HarperCollins (New York City), 1990.

The Cow That Went Oink, Harcourt, 1990.

A Dinosaur Named after Me, Harcourt, 1991.

Pets in Trumpets, Harcourt, 1991.

Happy Holidaysaurus, Harcourt, 1992.

Zoodles, Harcourt, 1992.

Where to Look for a Dinosaur, Harcourt, 1993.

Can You Find It?, Harcourt, 1993.

How Big Were the Dinosaurs?, Harcourt, 1994.

Hippopotamus Hunt, Harcourt, 1994.

Catbirds & Dogfish, Harcourt, 1995.

Dinosaur Questions, Harcourt, 1995.

Cock-a-Doodle-Moo!, Harcourt, 1996.

OTHER

Contributor of illustrations to national magazines.

If the Dinosaurs Came Back has been translated into Chinese, Japanese, French, and Spanish; *The Cow That Went Oink* has been translated into Spanish.

SIDELIGHTS: Bernard Most commented: "My books are 'concept books' in that they get children to participate in the ideas of the books beyond the actual reading of them."

*   *   *

MOYERS, Bill   1934-

PERSONAL: Given name legally changed from Billy Don; born June 5, 1934, in Hugo, OK; son of John Henry (a laborer) and Ruby (Johnson) Moyers; married Judith Suzanne Davidson, December 18, 1954; children: William Cope, Alice Suzanne, John Davidson. *Education:* Attended North Texas State University, 1952-54; University of Texas, Austin, B.J. (with honors), 1956; attended University of Edinburgh, 1956-57; Southwestern Baptist Theological Seminary, B.D., 1959.

ADDRESSES: Office—356 West 58th St., New York, NY 10019.

CAREER: News Messenger, Marshall, TX, reporter and sports editor, 1949-54; KTBC Radio and Television, Austin, TX, assistant news editor, 1954-56; assistant pastor of churches in Texas and Oklahoma, 1956-59; special assistant to Senator Lyndon B. Johnson, 1959-60; executive assistant for vice presidential campaign, 1960-61; Peace Corps, Washington, DC, director of public affairs, 1961, deputy director, 1962-63; special assistant to President Lyndon B. Johnson, 1963-65, White House press secretary, 1965-67; *Newsday,* Garden City, NY, publisher, 1967-70; television executive and series host, 1970—; host of "This Week," National Educational Television, 1970, and of "Bill Moyers' Journal," Educational Broadcasting Corp., 1971-76, 1978-81; editor and chief correspondent, "CBS Reports," Columbia Broadcasting System (CBS), 1976-80, senior news analyst and commentator, "CBS News," 1981-86; executive editor, Public Affairs TV, Inc., 1987—; commentator on "NBC Nightly News," National Broadcasting Company (NBC), 1995—. President, Florence and John Schumann Foundation and Schumann Fund of New Jersey.

AWARDS, HONORS: Emmy Awards from National Academy of Television Arts and Sciences for outstanding broadcaster, 1974, 1978, 1980, 1982-87; Silver Gavel Award from American Bar Association (ABA), 1974, for distinguished service to the American law system; Certificate of Merit, ABA, 1975; Ralph Lowell Medal for contributions to public television, 1975; George Peabody Awards, 1976, 1980, 1985, and 1986-89; Monte Carlo Television Festival Grand Prize, Jurors Prize, and Nymph Award, all 1977, all for "The Fire Next Door"; Robert F. Kennedy Journalism Grand Prize, 1978, 1988; Christopher Award, 1978; Sidney Hillman Prize for Distinguished Service, 1978, 1981, 1987; Distinguished Urban Journalism Award, National Urban Coalition, 1978; George Polk awards, 1981, 1986, and 1987; Alfred I. du Pont-Columbia University Award, 1981, 1987, 1988, 1991, 1992; Medal of Excellence from

University of the State of New York, 1984; Overseas Press Award, 1986; Gold Baton for the body of his work and Silver Baton for documentaries, both 1992, from Alfred I. du Pont-Columbia University.

WRITINGS:

Listening to America: A Traveler Rediscovers His Country, Harper Magazine Press, 1971.

TELEVISION SERIES

Creativity, first broadcast by the Public Broadcasting System (PBS), January, 1982.

A Walk through the Twentieth Century, first broadcast by PBS, January, 1984.

In Search of the Constitution, first broadcast by PBS, April, 1987.

Joseph Campbell and the Power of Myth, first broadcast by PBS, 1987.

The Secret Government: The Constitution in Crisis (first broadcast by PBS, 1987), Seven Locks Press (Washington, DC), 1988.

Facing Evil, first broadcast by PBS, March, 1988.

Moyers: The Power of the Word, first broadcast by PBS, September, 1989.

A World of Ideas, Volume 1: *Conversations with Thoughtful Men and Women about American Life Today and the Ideas Shaping Our Future* (first broadcast by PBS, 1988), Doubleday (New York City), 1989, Volume 2: *Public Opinions from Private Citizens,* Doubleday, 1990.

Global Dumping Ground: The International Traffic in Hazardous Waste (first broadcast by PBS, 1990), Seven Locks Press, 1990.

Healing and the Mind (first broadcast by PBS, February, 1993), Doubleday, 1993.

The Language of Life: A Festival of Poets (first broadcast by PBS, 1995), Doubleday, 1995.

Also creator of "The Fire Next Door," and "The Vanishing Family." Host or creator of the following public television series: *The Arab World,* Public Affairs Television, April, 1991; *Listening to America with Bill Moyers,* April, 1992. Also host or creator of the following public television specials: "All Our Children," 1991; "Moyers: Project Censored," 1991; "The Home Front," 1991; "Sports for Sale," 1991; "Moyers: Beyond Hate," Public Affairs Television, May, 1991; "Special Report: After the War with Bill Moyers," Public Affairs Television, June, 1991; "Moyers: Hate on Trial," 1992; "Minimum Wages: The New Economy," 1992; "What Can We Do about Violence? A Bill Moyers Special," 1995.

Contributing editor, *Newsweek.*

SIDELIGHTS: Broadcast journalist Bill Moyers is well-known for providing American television audiences with "news of the mind." His erudite political commentaries, historical essays, and series on such subjects as myth and evil challenge the limits of television programming and offer educational alternatives to standard prime-time fare. "The conventional wisdom is that ideas and intelligent conversation make bad TV," writes Geoffrey C. Ward in *American Heritage* magazine. "Within the industry, human beings with something to say are dismissed as 'talking heads.' Moyers knows better and has proved it time and again. His is an earnest presence . . . but it is also intelligent, humane, and intensely curious. He seems genuinely affected by what he sees and hears, and more important, he possesses the mysterious power to pass along his amusement or astonishment or horror intact to the viewer." Most of Moyers's work, including his series *Creativity, A Walk through the Twentieth Century,* and *Facing Evil,* have appeared on public television, a forum well-suited to his intellectual style and scope. He has also served as a commentator and investigative reporter for CBS Television, both on the nightly news and in specials. According to a *Saturday Review* correspondent, Moyers "asks the questions we ourselves would like to [ask] and, unlike most of us, never interrupts the answer. His passing comment seems designed not to draw attention to himself, . . . but to bring out something in the interviewee that a direct question might not evoke. . . . He's an intellectual. . . . He's a man of political acuity. . . . He's moral but not a preacher, political but not a politician."

Moyers was born in 1934 and christened Billy Don. The younger of two sons, he grew up in Marshall, Texas, where his father held a variety of blue collar jobs. In *People* magazine, Moyers reminisced about his youth. Marshall, he said, "was a wonderful place to be poor if you had to be poor. It was a genteel poverty in which people knew who you were and kind of looked after you. Status was important in Marshall, but more important was being part of the community." As a child during the Second World War, Moyers was particularly drawn to the overseas broadcasts of journalist Edward R. Murrow. "This stout voice coming across the ocean night after night, describing the horrors of war," he told *People.* "He brought history alive for me." A good student who also found time to work and engage in extracurricular activities, Moyers began his own journalism career at the Marshall *News Messenger* in 1949. He changed his name to Bill because he thought the name more appropriate for a budding sports writer. After graduating from high school he enrolled at North Texas State University, where he met his future wife, Judith Suzanne Davidson.

In the spring of his sophomore year of college, Moyers wrote to Senator Lyndon B. Johnson, offering to help with Johnson's reelection campaign. Johnson hired Moyers for a summer internship, then, impressed with the young man's work habits, persuaded Moyers to transfer to the University of Texas at Austin. There Moyers studied journalism and theology, worked as assistant news director at KTBC-TV, and preached at two small Baptist churches two Sundays per month. He received his Bachelor's degree in journalism in 1956 and spent the following year at the University of Edinburgh in Scotland as a Rotary International fellow. In 1957 he entered the Southwestern Baptist Theological Seminary to train for the ministry, and he earned another Bachelor's degree with honors in 1959. Moyers never served as a fulltime minister, however. He told *People:* "I knew I couldn't be a preacher. I thought that my talents lay elsewhere." Apparently Lyndon Johnson agreed with that assessment, offering Moyers a position as special assistant in Washington, D.C. Soon after Johnson was elected vice president, Moyers was appointed associate director of public affairs of the newly-created Peace Corps. He was made deputy director in 1962—one of the youngest presidential appointees ever approved by Congress.

Moyers returned to the White House in 1963, when John F. Kennedy's assassination elevated Johnson to the presidency. Moyers first served as one of Johnson's advisors on domestic affairs, overseeing the far-reaching Great Society legislation. Then, in 1964, he became White House chief of staff, and in 1965 he assumed the position of press secretary. As the *Saturday Review* reporter notes, the Washington press corps "was fascinated by the young man who seemed to have Lyndon Johnson's full confidence. Part of the appeal was his background—son of an East Texas dirt farmer, former divinity student, and ordained Baptist teacher. Part was his age—30. Part was his already impressive political credentials. . . . And part was his character—he was bright, and he was calm and efficient. This inner fortitude took its toll. Moyers suffered from a chronic ulcer when he worked for Johnson, and the strain is obvious even in photographs, which show a tense, skinny young man with heavy, black-rimmed glasses." Indeed,

Moyers became increasingly disillusioned as Johnson intensified America's military involvement in Southeast Asia while placing less stress on domestic improvements. In 1967 he left public service, over Johnson's strenuous objections, to become publisher of *Newsday,* one of the nation's largest suburban daily newspapers.

Under Moyers's tenure at *Newsday,* the paper garnered thirty-three major journalism awards, including two Pulitzer Prizes. Still Moyers quit *Newsday* in the summer of 1970 for a more leisurely adventure. He boarded a bus with a notebook and tape recorder and embarked on a 13,000-mile trip across the United States. Claiming that he had been out of touch with Americans for too long, he interviewed numerous ordinary folk from all walks of life and described his subjects in *Listening to America: A Traveler Rediscovers His Country,* published in 1971. The book became a best-seller as well as a critical success.

Moyers also began his long association with public television in 1970. He recognized the then-fledgling medium as the perfect forum for a free and unhurried discussion of important issues. "You know that your [public television] viewer has a tolerance for ideas, a willingness to be patient, a mind that wants to be stretched," Moyers commented in *Saturday Review.* "Commercial television paces itself so rapidly that it's hard to absorb. It's racing—it wants to keep the action flowing like the Indianapolis speedway. . . . My work on public broadcasting wants to almost infiltrate—to insinuate itself into the consciousness of the viewer." In 1971 Moyers became host of *Bill Moyers' Journal,* a weekly show that addressed the political and social issues of the time. To quote the *Saturday Review* reporter, the program "epitomized public-affairs broadcasting at its best"; it won its host a total of five Emmy Awards. After a decade in commercial television at CBS, he returned to public television because, as he put it in the *Chicago Tribune,* "I've always thought there's no limit to what you can do in this world if you don't want to get rich or gain credit. . . . I've done 500 hours of television or more by staying loose, by going to where I could create the opportunity."

Since returning to public television, Moyers has worked through PBS and Public Affairs TV, a production company, to create programs that focus on ideas and issues. These programs often involve an interview format, in which Moyers engages, questions, provokes, and listens to thinkers, experts, policy-makers, and others. As James Gardner observes in *Commentary,* "The popular success of . . . projects with which Bill Moyers has been associated over the years, evidently results from the distinctive chemistry generated among the three parts in the equation—Moyers, his subjects, and his audience." Programs which use this interview format include series such as *Joseph Campbell and the Power of Myth, A World of Ideas with Bill Moyers, The Arab World, Listening to America with Bill Moyers,* and *The Language of Life: A Festival of Poets.* Moyers has also been the host or driving force for numerous documentaries and special reports aired on PBS on subjects such as government excess, toxic pollution, violence, and hate crimes.

Several of Moyers's television projects have a more permanent impact and reach a wider audience through books published as companions to the television series. Among these, *Joseph Campbell and the Power of Myth,* the two volumes of *A World of Ideas, Healing and the Mind,* and *The Language of Life: A Festival of Poets* have received significant attention in the world of readers.

A World of Ideas is just the kind of project that Bill Moyers is known for creating. The first volume, subtitled *Conversations with Thoughtful Men and Women about American Life Today and the Ideas Shaping Our Future,* contains over forty interviews with authors, poets, scientists, social scientists, policy-makers, and other thinkers and doers from a variety of social groups, countries, and walks of life. (The second volume, subtitled *Public Opinions from Private Citizens,* adds almost thirty similar interviews.) "Although Mr. Moyers imposes few constraints, he does have an overall agenda, albeit a broad one," notes Alison Friesinger Hill in the *New York Times Book Review.* "He is inquiring into contemporary values and concerns, within the United States and in global society." Characteristically, in exploring these issues "Moyers doesn't lower the level of the dialogue for TV. On the contrary," Alex Raksin observes in the *Los Angeles Times Book Review,* "he consistently focuses these conversations through thoughtful comments and enlivens them by playing provocateur."

Publishing the transcripts of these interviews in a book form not only makes them permanent, but also gives the reader a chance to savor some of the comments and Moyers a chance to further highlight some of the issues. "This new format is generally more satisfying than the original broadcasts because it permits us to study more closely those arguments that possess real substance, and to skip over much cant and attitudinizing," Gardner points out. "Thus, while the broadcasts were generally duller than polite people were willing to concede at the time, these transcripts do provide some moments of genuine intelligence and illumination."

In *Healing and the Mind,* Moyers explores Chinese medicine, psychoneuroimmunology, meditation and other unconventional approaches to healing, as well as old-fashioned, personal and humane medicine in traditional settings. Moyers's investigation of the growing interest in alternative approaches to healing "frequently reinforces Western medicine's domination and underscores how little is really known about the mind's effect on the body," admits M. S. Mason in the *Christian Science Monitor.* "He is scrupulously careful not to undermine the biomedical model. Yet implicit in all the information provided is an important challenge to the medical establishment's mechanistic approach to curing: A human being is more than a 'ghost in a machine.'" Mason concludes that "the most important insights 'Healing and the Mind' has to offer concern the importance of community, the importance of respect for the whole person, and the direct effect of thought on the body."

The Language of Life: A Festival of Poets is Moyers's celebration of poetry and its place in American life. The book brings together Moyers's public television series of the same name with two television specials, one on Rita Dove and another on Donald Hall and Jane Kenyon. Here again Moyers employs his characteristic interviewing style to probe the issues, public and personal, on the minds and in the poetry of twenty-nine poets. He also includes short speeches given by five other poets at the Doge Poetry Festival, a regular gathering in Stanhope, New Jersey. Author Helen Vendler finds fault with the companion book in a *New York Times Book Review* piece. "Mr. Moyers's earnestly proclaimed love for poetry turns out to be a love of its human narratives, its therapeutic power and its unifying messages," she observes. "The poets themselves try to return Mr. Moyers to what he is missing: to imagination, to language, to rhythms, to structure," she adds. "But these are not grist for television, with its abhorrence of analytic talk. So each interview is relentlessly diverted from the discussion of poetry itself to human-interest topics, which usually produce statements of thoughtless banality." Vendler also finds that "the poems quoted are strikingly uneven in worth," but she admits "everyone will find something to like."

Critical acclaim and viewer support from a surprising cross-section of the population has assured Moyers a lasting berth on public television. As Jane Hall notes in *People,* Moyers "has been honored as perhaps the most insightful broadcast journalist of our day, an astute interviewer to whom philosophers, novelists and inarticulate workers have revealed their deepest dreams." *Newsweek* contributor Harry F. Waters writes that Bill Moyers "looks at America and sees freeways of the mind connecting great and complex issues, a landscape of ethical cloverleafs that affords a natural habitat for the journalist as moralist. . . . Along with his gifts of insight and eloquence, this Texas populist and former Baptist preacher possesses a special knack for bringing big issues down to human dimension." Waters concludes: "Besides choosing fertile thematic terrain, Moyers always brings a point of view to his craft that . . . at least dares to challenge and provoke. Agree with him or not, he never leaves your mind in neutral."

BIOGRAPHICAL/CRITICAL SOURCES:

BOOKS

Authors in the News, Volume 1, Gale (Detroit), 1976.

PERIODICALS

American Film, June, 1990, pp. 17-20, 44.
American Heritage, December, 1983.
Booklist, November 15, 1988, p. 536.
Boston Globe, April 4, 1993, M8.
Chicago Tribune, March 28, 1988.
Christian Science Monitor, February 19, 1993, p. 13.
Commentary, October, 1989, p. 70.
Esquire, October, 1989, p. 139.
Harper's, October, 1965.
Los Angeles Times, April 20, 1987.
Los Angeles Times Book Review, April 16, 1989, p. 6; March 7, 1993, p. 6.
Los Angeles Times Magazine, March 27, 1994, p. 26.
National Review, March 10, 1989, pp. 22-25.
New Republic, August 19, 1991, p. 22; October 7, 1991, p. 14.
Newsday, June 4, 1974.
Newsweek, March 1, 1965; April 15, 1974; October 21, 1974; July 4, 1983.
New York Times Book Review, March 14, 1971, pp. 2, 37; June 4, 1989, p. 23; November 25, 1990, p. 14; May 23, 1993, p. 29; June 18, 1995, p. 14.

New York Times Magazine, April 3, 1966.
People, February 22, 1982; August 1, 1983.
San Francisco Review of Books, winter, 1990-91, p. 54.
Saturday Review, February, 1982, p. 16-18, 20.
Time, July 15, 1974; June 13, 1977.
Times Literary Supplement, November 8, 1991, p. 32.
Washington Magazine, July/August, 1974.
Washington Post, July 14, 1991, p. WSP18.*

*   *   *

MULDOON, Paul   1951-

PERSONAL: Born June 20, 1951, in Armagh, Northern Ireland; son of Patrick (a laborer and gardener) and Brigid (a schoolteacher; maiden name, Regan) Muldoon; married Jean Hannff Kovelitz, 1987. *Education:* Received B.A. from Queen's University, Belfast, Northern Ireland.

ADDRESSES: Office—c/o Faber & Faber, 3 Queen Sq., London WC1N 3AU, England.

CAREER: Poet. British Broadcasting Corporation (BBC Radio), Belfast, Northern Ireland, radio producer, 1973-86; Princeton University, Princeton, NJ, lecturer in writing, 1987—; professor, 1995—.

MEMBER: Royal Society of Literature (fellow).

AWARDS, HONORS: Eric Gregory Award from the Society of Authors, 1972; Geoffrey Faber Memorial Prize for *Why Brownlee Left,* 1982; T. S. Eliot Prize, 1994.

WRITINGS:

POETRY

Knowing My Place, Ulsterman, 1971.
New Weather, Faber & Faber (London), 1973.
Spirit of Dawn, Ulsterman, 1975.
Mules (also see below), Faber & Faber, 1977.
Names and Addresses, Ulsterman, 1978.
Why Brownlee Left (includes "Immram"), Faber & Faber, 1980, Wake Forest University Press (Winston-Salem, NC), 1981.
Immram, illustrations by Robert Ballagh, Gallery Press (Dublin), 1980.

Out of Siberia, illustrations by Timothy Engelland, Deerfield Press (Deerfield, MA), 1982.

Quoof, University of North Carolina Press (Chapel Hill), 1983.

The Wishbone, Gallery, 1984.

Mules, and Early Poems, Wake Forest University Press, 1985.

Selected Poems: 1968-86, Faber & Faber, 1986, Ecco Press (New York City), 1987.

Meeting the British, Faber & Faber, 1987.

Madoc: A Mystery, Farrar (New York City), 1991.

The Annals of Chile, Farrar, 1995.

EDITOR

The Scrake of Dawn: Poems by Young People from Northern Ireland, Blackstaff (Belfast), 1979.

The Faber Book of Contemporary Irish Poetry, Faber & Faber, 1986.

The Essential Byron, Ecco Press, 1988.

OTHER

Czeslaw Milosz and Paul Muldoon Reading Their Poems (sound recording), Archive of Recorded Poetry and Literature, 1991.

(Translator) Nuala Ni Dhomhnaill, *The Astrakhan Cloak,* Gallery Press, 1992, Wake Forest University Press, 1993.

SIDELIGHTS: Paul Muldoon is one of Ireland's leading contemporary poets. His short lyrics, modified sonnets and ballads, and dramatic monologues touch on themes of love, maturation, and self-discovery, as well as Irish culture and history. Terse and highly original, Muldoon's poetry is noted for its multiplicity of meaning. In a *Stand* review, Rodney Pybus asserted that the poet's works reveal a "quirky, offbeat talent for sudden revelatory flights from mundane consequences. . . . He found very early a distinctively wry and deceptively simple-sophisticated lyric voice."

Muldoon is the youngest member of a group of Northern Irish poets—including Seamus Heaney, Michael Longley, and Derek Mahon—which gained prominence in the 1960s and 1970s. As a student at Queen's University, Muldoon studied under Heaney, and refined his own analytical and critical skills in weekly discussions with other poets. In 1971, at the age of nineteen, Muldoon had completed his first short collection, *Knowing My Place.* Two years later, he published *New Weather,* his first widely reviewed volume of poetry. The book secured Muldoon's

place among Ireland's finest writers and helped establish his reputation as an innovative new voice in English-language poetry.

The poems in *New Weather* generally illuminate the complexities of seemingly ordinary things or events. Several critics have noted that the collection's multilayered, heavily imagistic, and metaphoric verse explores psychological development with apparent simplicity and eloquence while offering keen insights into the subjective nature of perception. Calling the collection "the result of continuous age and aging," Roger Conover suggested in a review for *Eire-Ireland,* "Muldoon's is a poetry which sees *into* things, and speaks of the world in terms of its own internal designs and patterns." A *Times Literary Supplement* reviewer, however, felt that the poems in Muldoon's "highly promising collection are flawed by a vagueness of focus that dissipates the strength of original ideas."

Muldoon followed *New Weather* with the 1977 collection *Mules,* which opens with a poem reflecting Northern Ireland's civil strife. Recurring themes of political and social relevance inform the other pastorals and ballads in *Mules.* "The Narrow Road to the North," for instance, depicts the debilitating effects of war on a Japanese soldier who emerges from hiding, unaware that World War II has ended. The poem subtly parallels the soldier's deadened emotional state with the toll that the struggle in Ireland has taken on its citizens. As Peter Scupham noted in his *Times Literary Supplement* review, "Muldoon's taste for anecdote, invention, and parable shows strongly [in *Mules*]," and claimed that the collection is "a handsome promise of good poems to come." In *Preoccupations: Selected Prose, 1968-1978,* Heaney deemed *Mules* "a strange, rich second collection" and judged the poet "one of the very best."

By the time Muldoon's next volume of poetry, *Why Brownlee Left,* was published in 1980, the poet had attracted considerable attention for his technical acumen, dry verbal wit, and provocative use of language. Some critics considered *Why Brownlee Left* a more mature effort than Muldoon's earlier collections. According to Alan Hollinghurst in *Encounter,* "the key to the book" lies in a seemingly straightforward and elemental poem titled "October 1950." Chronicling the poet's own conception, the poem reflects Muldoon's preoccupation with the search for self and acknowledges, noted Hollinghurst, that life "refut[es] any philosophical attempts to organise or direct it." Feeling that Muldoon's poetry in *Why*

Brownlee Left was composed mainly of "blueprints, sketches, [and] fragments," and that Muldoon is not "a truly satisfying poet," *Anglo-Welsh Review*'s David Annwn nonetheless praised Muldoon for his "unnerving knack of capturing most elusive atmospheres, manipulating the inflexions of Anglo-Irish . . . and conveying a whole spectrum of humour."

Muldoon's 1983 collection, *Quoof,* takes its title from his family's name for a hot-water bottle. The imaginative poems in the volume offer varying perceptions of the world. "Gathering Mushrooms" opens the book with the narrator's drug-induced reminiscences of his childhood, his father, and the turmoil in Ireland. "The More a Man Has the More a Man Wants," the final poem and the volume's longest, is a narrative that follows the exploits of the mercenary-like figure Gallogly as he voyages through Northern Ireland. Writing in the *London Review of Books,* John Kerrigan asserted that the poetry in *Quoof* is "a bewildering display of narrative invention . . . written with that combination of visual clarity and verbal panache which has become the hallmark of Paul Muldoon." Muldoon, in an interview with Michael Donaghy in *Chicago Review,* commented on the violence in *Quoof:* "I don't think it's a very likeable or attractive book in its themes."

Meeting the British, Muldoon's 1987 collection, contains several poems of recollection as well as more unusual selections such as "7, Middagh Street," which, according to Terry Eagleton in the *Observer,* blends fantasy and history with "dramatic energy and calculated irony . . . to produce a major poem." A series of imaginary monologues by such prominent artistic and literary figures as W. H. Auden, Salvador Dali, Gypsy Rose Lee, Carson McCullers, and Louis MacNeice, "7, Middagh Street" contains provocative commentary on the importance of politics in Irish art. Comparing *Meeting the British* with *Quoof,* Mark Ford in the *London Review of Books* found that whereas "*Quoof* tended to push its metaphors, trance-like, to the point of no return, its mushroom hallucinations not deviation from but a visionary heightening of reality: the poems in *Meeting the British* seem more self-aware. . . . *Meeting the British* adds some wonderful new tricks to Muldoon's repertoire." Deeming *Meeting the British* Muldoon's "most ambitious collection," Mick Imlah, writing in the *Times Literary Supplement,* noted that the volume proves an innovative addition "to a difficult and delightful body of poetry." Responding to several critics' attempts to compare the poet's style to that of his contemporaries, Conover proclaimed that

Muldoon's "poems are too individual to characterize very effectively in terms of anyone else's work. . . . [His] conception of the poem is unique."

Muldoon's next collection was the ambitious *Madoc: A Mystery,* summarized by Geoffrey Stokes in the *Village Voice* as "quite funny, very difficult, highly ambitious, more than a little unsettling, and . . . subtitled 'A Mystery.' Which it surely is." Named after the title of a Robert Southey poem concerning a Welsh prince who discovers America in the 12th century, the narrative flow of *Madoc* revolves around "what might have happened if the Romantic poets Robert Southey and Samuel Taylor Coleridge had indeed come (as they planned in 1794) to America and created a 'pantisocracy' ('equal rule for all') on the banks of the Susquehanna River in Pennsylvania," commented Lucy McDiarmid in her *New York Times Book Review* piece on *Madoc.* Coleridge becomes entranced by peyote and Native American culture while Southey becomes vengeful and tyrannical after a loss of idealism. The question, in the words of Thomas M. Disch in *Poetry,* is whether or not *Madoc*'s "helter-skelter narrative pattern, with its excursions into such parallel lives as those of Thomas Moore, Lord Byron, Lewis and Clark, Aaron Burr, Thomas Jefferson, and George Catlin, add up either to a memorable drama or to a coherent vision of history?" Despite finding *Madoc* "readable for its entire length," Disch's answer remained: "I don't think so." Michael Hoffman in the *London Review of Books* concluded, however, that each "reading—and still more, every new bit of information—makes *Madoc* a cleverer and more imposing piece of work." Stokes countered Disch, and commented: "The question is whether it's worth stepping into *Madoc* even once; the answer is an unqualified yes."

"*The Annals of Chile* is easier of access and more emotionally direct than *Madoc,* while more allusive and arcane than [Muldoon's] earlier work," argued Richard Tillinghast in the *New York Times Book Review.* "Incantata," one of two central poems in *The Annals of Chile,* remembers Muldoon's lover Mary Farl Powers in a "beautiful and heartfelt elegy" in the words of *Times Literary Supplement* reviewer Lawrence Norfolk. "It is Muldoon's most transparent poem for some time, and also his most musical." "Yarrow," the second, "jazzily juxtaposes swashbuckling daydreams . . . with real life's painful memories of a druggy girlfriend's breakdown and the death of [Muldoon's] mother," commented Michael Dirda in a *Washington Post Book World* review. Mark Ford, in a review of *Annals* in the *London*

Review of Books, found the themes of "less scope for the kinds of all-synthesising wit characteristic of Muldoon." William Pratt concluded in *World Literature Today* that for those readers "who enjoy having a leg pulled, Muldoon is your man; to those who expect something more substantial from poetry, Muldoon rhymes with buffoon." *Los Angeles Times Book Review*'s Katherine McNamara, however, found that in *Annals,* "every word, every reference, every allusion, carries meaning. Muldoon never flinches in his brilliant verbal workings."

Muldoon told *CA:* "I started [writing poetry] when I was fifteen or sixteen. I'd written a few poems before then, as I suppose most people do. It seems to me that children of eight or nine—though I don't remember writing anything myself when I was that age—are in a way some of the best poets I've come across. Poems by children of that age are quite fresh, untrammeled by any ideas of what a poem might be or what a poem should look like. While I think it's perhaps a little romantic to suggest it, I believe it's something of that quality that people a little older are trying to get back to, something of that rinsed quality of the eye.

"I wrote lots of poems as a teenager, many of them heavily under the influence of T. S. Eliot, who seemed to me to be quite a marvelous person. I devoured Eliot and learned everything I could about him. He's a bad person, though, for anyone trying to write to learn from, since his voice is so much his own; I ended up doing parodies of Eliot. I read a lot of poetry, modern poetry as well as poetry by writers all the way through in English and indeed in Irish. And gradually I began to learn, particularly from writers who were round about, like Seamus Heaney, Michael Longley, Derek Mahon, and other Irish writers who were writing about things I knew about. I think it's quite important to have people round about who remind one that writing poetry is not an entirely weird occupation, that one isn't the only one trying to do it.

"As to choosing poetry rather than some other form of writing, in a way I chose poetry over the weekly essay. We had a teacher who used to assign an essay every week, and rather than an essay, I wrote a poem one week because it seemed to me a much easier, certainly a shorter, thing to do. In a way it was out of laziness that I felt I might try to write poems, and I continued to do it. I'd love to be able to write prose, and I've written the occasional little autobiographical piece for radio or whatever, but I find it takes me so long to write a sentence, or to write anything. I don't have a natural fluency in writing. The poems I do try to write are aimed to sound very off-the-cuff, very simple and natural, as if they were spoken, or as if they were composed in about the same time as it takes to speak them. But I spend a lot of time getting that effect; it doesn't come naturally.

"There is a school of thought that holds that the writer is dead, and really anyone can read whatever they like into this text, as they insist on calling it nowadays. I think one of the jobs of a writer is to contain and restrict the range of possible meanings and readings and connotations that a series of words on a page can have. There's an element of the manipulative about the process of writing. The writer is very truly a medium if things are ideal. The writer should be open to the language and allowing the language to do the work. I don't want to sound like somebody who's heavily into Zen, but I really do believe in all of that; I believe in inspiration in some way.

"On the other hand, there is this other part involved in the writing, the part that is marshaling and is looking on as an acute, intense reader. When I am writing, I'm in control of this uncontrollable thing. It's a combination of out of control and in control. What I'm interested in doing, usually, is writing poems with very clear, translucent surfaces, but if you look at them again, there are other things happening under the surface. And I am interested in poems that go against their own grain, that are involved in irony, that seem to be saying one thing but in fact couldn't possibly be saying that. I am interested in what's happening in those areas, and I do try to control that and hope that I have controlled it. But sometimes when I reread a poem much later (which I don't usually do), I wonder, What on earth was I thinking of there?"

BIOGRAPHICAL/CRITICAL SOURCES:

BOOKS

Birkerts, Sven, *The Electric Life: Essays on Modern Poetry,* Morrow (New York City), 1989.

Contemporary Literary Criticism, Volume 32, Gale (Detroit), 1985.

Dictionary of Literary Biography, Volume 40: *Poets of Great Britain and Ireland since 1960,* Gale, 1985.

Haffenden, John, *Viewpoints: Poets in Conversation,* Faber & Faber, 1980.

Heaney, Seamus, *Preoccupations: Selected Prose, 1968-1978,* Farrar, 1980.

Longley, Edna, *Poetry in the Wars,* Bloodaxe Books (Newcastle upon Tyne, England), 1986.

PERIODICALS

Anglo-Welsh Review, 1981, p. 74.

Chicago Review, autumn, 1985, p. 76.

Concerning Poetry, Volume 14, number 2, 1981, p. 125.

Eire-Ireland, summer, 1975, p. 127; Volume 13, number 2, 1978; spring, 1984, p. 123; spring, 1989, p. 79.

Encounter, February-March, 1981; March, 1984.

Kenyon Review, summer, 1988, p. 127.

Listener, October 13, 1977.

London Magazine, October, 1977.

London Review of Books, February 16, 1984; December 10, 1987, p. 20; December 20, 1990, p. 18; August 19, 1993, p. 22; January 12, 1995, p. 19.

Los Angeles Times Book Review, November 11, 1994, p. 13.

New England Review and Bread Loaf Quarterly, winter, 1989, p. 179.

New Statesman, September 26, 1980.

New York Review of Books, May 30, 1991, p. 37.

New York Times Book Review, July 28, 1991, p. 14; December 11, 1994, p. 25.

Observer (London), May 3, 1987, p. 25.

Poetry, May, 1992, p. 94; November, 1994, p. 101.

Shenandoah, summer, 1974.

Stand, Volume 22, number 3, 1981.

Times Literary Supplement, April 20, 1973, p. 442; July 1, 1977, p. 801; March 28, 1980; November 14, 1980, p. 1287; May 30, 1986; September 4, 1987; October 12, 1990, p. 1105; October 7, 1994, p. 32.

Village Voice, July 30, 1991, p. 68.

Voice Literary Supplement, March, 1984.

Washington Post Book World, January 31, 1988; January 1, 1995, p. 8.

World Literature Today, spring, 1995, p. 365.

*   *   *

MULLER, (Lester) Robin 1953-

PERSONAL: Born October 30, 1953, in Toronto, Ontario, Canada; son of Frederick Walter and Sara Ada (Thomas) Muller. *Education:* Algonquin College, 1979; attended George Brown College, 1982.

ADDRESSES: Home—26 Wardell St., Toronto, Ontario, Canada.

CAREER: Fine artist, editorial illustrator, and set designer. University of Toronto, Fine Art Department, Toronto, Ontario, studio coordinator, 1977-83; Graph Em, Toronto, art director, 1984.

MEMBER: Canadian Writers Union, Canadian Society of Children's Authors, Illustrators, and Performers (CANSCAIP).

AWARDS, HONORS: Toronto Art Directors Award, 1982, and Silver Birch Award, Ontario Library Association, 1995, both for *Mollie Whuppie and the Giant;* New York Art Directors Award, 1984, for "Carrion Comfort"; Best Children's Book of the Year Award, I.O.D.E. (International Order of the Daughters of the Empire), 1985, and Alcuin Award for excellence in book design, 1986, both for *The Sorcerer's Apprentice;* Ezra Jack Keats Memorial Silver Medal, 1986, for various works; Governor General's Award for illustration, 1989, for *The Magic Paintbrush;* Studio Magazine Award, 1991, and Canadian Library Association Notable Book citation, 1992, both for *The Nightwood.*

WRITINGS:

Mollie Whuppie and the Giant, Scholastic (New York City), 1982.

Tatterhood, Scholastic, 1984.

The Sorcerer's Apprentice, Kids Can Press, 1985.

The Lucky Old Woman, Kids Can Press, 1987.

Little Kay, Scholastic, 1988.

The Magic Paintbrush, Doubleday (Canada), 1989, Viking (New York City), 1992.

The Nightwood, Doubleday, 1991.

Hickory Dickory Dock, illustrated by Suzanne Dureanceau, Scholastic, 1992.

SELF-ILLUSTRATED

Row, Row, Row Your Boat, North Winds/Scholastic, 1993.

Little Wonder, North Winds/Scholastic, 1994.

SIDELIGHTS: "Like all good adaptors of traditional narratives," Jon C. Stott comments in *Twentieth-Century Children's Writers,* "Robin Muller discovers the contemporary relevance of old motifs and tale types, and in the timeless essences of the stories, themes that speak to young readers of the late twentieth century." Muller's first work is about Mollie Whuppie, the youngest of three sisters abandoned in the woods, whose story is told in *Mollie Whuppie and the Giant*. In text that Anne Gilmore describes in *Quill & Quire* as "elegant" with "simple yet evocative similes," Muller tells how Mollie succeeds at three demanding tests of courage before she can destroy the giant. Gilmore also praises the black and white illustrations as being "rich in detail" and "startlingly effective," and Mary Ainslie Smith finds in *Books in Canada* that Muller's artwork has "all the details just right."

The heroine in Muller's *Tatterhood* is less immediately likable. She is wild and mischievous, rides a goat and wears outrageous clothing, and suffers in comparison to her beautiful, lovable sister Belinda. But when a witch removes Belinda's head and replaces it with that of a calf, Tatterhood comes to the rescue. When the two girls flee they meet two young princes, one of whom is immediately smitten with Belinda. When the other prince, Galen, admires Tatterhood's courage, she is transformed into a lovely maiden. In *Canadian Children's Literature,* Murray J. Evans admires Muller's skill at portraying expressive faces, especially "Galen's astonished visage at Tatterhood's transformation, with her back as yet to the reader, until the page turns to reveal the beautiful face which we saw Galen seeing."

The Sorcerer's Apprentice is the story of Robin, a hungry, homeless young boy apprenticed to a wicked magician. Robin is determined to learn good spells to countermand his master's evil schemes. He is helped by a white dove, who turns out in the end to be an enchanted princess. Ellen Mandel, writing for *Booklist,* notes the "masterfully phrased text in this magical retelling of a fanciful classic," and Ronald A. Van De Voorde, in his *School Library Journal* review, praises the "realistically drawn" illustrations in blues, browns, and yellows as "dramatic, detailed, and effective." Muller explained the technique he used for the effective illustrations in *The Sorcerer's Apprentice:* "I splattered the paper with a dusting of black ink flicked off of a toothbrush and modeled it into a background, foreground, and middle ground with the use of an exacto knife. I then used pencil crayons for color, rubbing the color in with tissue paper."

The only one of Muller's books to have an elderly heroine, *The Lucky Old Woman* is described as a "refreshing change" from the typical fairy tale by Andy Butcher in a *Books for Your Children* review, explaining that in this tale "mild manners, rather than muscle and might, earn the best." An old woman who makes her living running errands for wealthier people one day runs into Grumpleteaser, a malevolent gnome. Although he teases and tricks the old woman continuously, he is finally worn down by her simplicity and goodness. Smith praises the "lively" story in *Books in Canada,* and calls Muller's elderly protagonist "a sympathetic creation."

In *Little Kay,* Muller returns to creating stories revolving around younger heroines. Susan Perren, writing in *Books for Young People,* describes Muller's language as "simple, forceful, and funny," and hails the "simply wonderful" illustrations. *Books in Canada* contributor Linda Granfield similarly finds the illustrations "glorious, filled with textures and swirls of colour, moving from silhouette to patterned borders and back," and concludes that this artwork, when added to the action-filled and humorous text, creates "a refreshing and amusing look" at equality.

The essence of art and artists is the theme of Muller's *The Magic Paintbrush*. Based on an old Chinese tale, it is the story of Nib, a talented young artist who rescues an old wizard, and, as a reward, is given a paintbrush that will make his paintings real. When the king hears of Nib's talent, he wants the boy to make him even more powerful than he already is. Nib outsmarts the king with his clever use of the paintbrush (he sends the king and his newly painted navy out to sea in a storm), then throws away the brush because he realizes the best pictures are "the ones you make with your heart." While she finds the text "too complicated," *School Library Journal* contributor Shirley Wilton observes that the "richly detailed and sophisticated" artwork, full of details and references to classic artists, will appeal to both adults and children.

The Nightwood is a retelling of Tamlynne, one of the oldest Scottish folktales. One evening, Elaine, the daughter of the Earl of March, journeys into the forbidden Nightwood. There she plucks a single red rose that summons the young knight Tamlynne, who is doomed to be sacrificed unless the love of a mortal can save him. Elaine stands fast during the fight for his soul, and because of her love, Tamlynne becomes mortal. In a review for *Canadian Children's Literature,* Terri L. Lyons comments that "the story literally pulsates with suspense and foreboding, but, as with every good folktale, all is right with the world in the end." She adds that Muller's unique illustrations of the faery dance, filled with evil creatures who look out of the page right at the reader, are "eerie and deliciously disconcerting."

Muller has also retold two of the most familiar of all children's rhymes: *Row, Row, Row Your Boat* and *Hickory, Dickory, Dock.* Muller, who drew the illustrations on bond paper with colored pencils, has dressed all his characters in Edwardian garb and, according to Granfield in *Quill & Quire,* "taken a monotonous childhood tune and given it new life."

"I draw my inspirations from folk and fairy tales," Muller once told *CA.* "These stories are often the first introduction a child has to the world at large, to his or her own heritage, and the importance of history. . . .

"Being an author/illustrator is a full-time endeavor; the majority of that time is spent on the illustrations, for which I set high standards. The reader is rewarded with a high quality picture that pulls them into the story and leaves them lingering on the page. . . .

"I believe there should be a richness to children's illustration," Muller concluded, "something that will embroider the imaginations of young readers."

BIOGRAPHICAL/CRITICAL SOURCES:

BOOKS

Muller, Robin, *The Magic Paintbrush,* Doubleday, 1989.
Twentieth-Century Children's Writers, 4th edition, St. James Press (Detroit), 1995, p. 687.

PERIODICALS

Booklist, January 17, 1987, p. 787; May 1, 1994, p. 1609.
Books for Young People, February, 1989, p. 9.
Books for Your Children, spring, 1988, p. 7.
Books in Canada, December, 1982, p. 9; December, 1987, p. 14; April, 1989, p. 37; April, 1992, pp. 44-45.
Canadian Children's Literature, number 39/40, 1985, pp. 145-48; number 57/58, 1990, pp. 116-117; number 63, 1991, pp. 83-87; number 73, 1994, p. 88-89.
Junior Bookshelf, February, 1987, p. 22.

Quill and Quire, February, 1983, pp. 35-36; February, 1985, pp. 10, 12, 14; September, 1993, p. 68; September, 1994, p. 69.
School Library Journal, February, 1987, p. 72; July, 1990, p. 78; May, 1994, p. 109.

*   *   *

MURRAY, Albert L.   1916-

PERSONAL: Born June 12, 1916, in Nokomis, AL; son of John Lee and Sudie (Graham) Young; married Mozelle Menefee, May 31, 1941; children: Michele. *Education:* Tuskegee Institute, B.S., 1939; New York University, M.A., 1948; postgraduate work at University of Michigan, 1940, Northwestern University, 1941, and University of Paris, 1950. *Avocational interests:* Recordings, photography, cookbooks, and gourmet cooking.

ADDRESSES: Home and office—45 West 132nd St., New York, NY 10037.

CAREER: U.S. Air Force, 1943-62, retired as major. Instructor, Tuskegee Institute, 1940-43, 1946-51, director of College Little Theatre; lecturer, Graduate School of Journalism, Columbia University, 1968; Colgate University, O'Connor Professor of Literature, 1970, O'Connor Lecturer, 1973, professor of humanities, 1982; visiting professor of literature, University of Massachusetts, Boston, 1971; Paul Anthony Brick lecturer, University of Missouri, 1972; writer in residence, Emory University, 1978; adjunct associate professor of creative writing, Barnard College, 1981-83; lecturer and participant in symposia.

MEMBER: PEN International, Authors League of America, Authors Guild, Alpha Phi Alpha.

AWARDS, HONORS: Lillian Smith Award for fiction, 1974, for *Train Whistle Guitar;* Litt.D., Colgate University, 1975; Deems Taylor Award, ASCAP, for music criticism, 1976, for *Stomping the Blues;* Lincoln Center Directors Emeriti Award, 1991.

WRITINGS:

The Omni-Americans: New Perspectives on Black Experience and American Culture (essays),

Outerbridge & Dientsfrey, 1970, published as *The Omni-Americans: Some Alternatives to the Folklore of White Supremacy,* Vintage Book (St. Paul, MN), 1983.

South to a Very Old Place, McGraw (New York City), 1972.

The Hero and the Blues, University of Missouri Press (Columbia), 1973.

Train Whistle Guitar (novel), McGraw, 1974.

Stomping the Blues, McGraw, 1976.

(With Count Basie) *Good Morning Blues: The Autobiography of Count Basie,* Random House (New York City), 1985.

The Spyglass Tree, Pantheon (New York City), 1991.

The Seven League Books, Pantheon, 1996.

The Blue Devils of Nada, Pantheon, 1996.

SIDELIGHTS: "As a writer, [Albert L. Murray] implicitly perceives himself as proceeding in the same fashion as he maintains legendary heroes, early Americans, and black Americans have always proceeded: by conceptualizing their lives out of chaos and against hostile forces," states *Dictionary of Literary Biography* contributor Elizabeth Schultz. Schultz declares that the "abiding concern of [Murray's] writing is the triumph, of Afro-American people, who, despite and, indeed, in Murray's view, because of centuries of difficulties, created a courageous, complex, life-sustaining, and life-enhancing culture—apparent in their language, religion, sports, fashions, food, dance, and above all in their music." Murray articulates these views in his collection of essays *The Omni-Americans: New Perspectives on Black Experience and American Culture,* in which he argues that black Americans have a distinctive identity of their own, developing a unique culture "which allows them to see themselves 'not as the substandard, abnormal *non-white* people of American social science surveys and the news media, but rather as if they were, so to speak, fundamental *extensions* of contemporary possibilities,'" says Schultz. "Like jam session musicians and blues singers," she continues, "they have learned the skills of improvisation, not only translating white models of excellence into their own terms, but also transforming degrading conditions into culture."

Murray expresses an interest in jazz in other works, especially in *The Hero and the Blues* and *Stomping the Blues,* an attempt to redefine "the music and its connotations for American culture," according to Jason Berry of the *Nation.* S. M. Fry, writing in the *Library Journal,* points out that Murray "views the music not as a primitive musical expression of black suffering but as an antidote to the bad times." Murray, the reviewer says, also emphasizes the importance of the performance, "the performing style and the music itself over the lyrics and social or political connotations." These books have made Murray "one of the foremost literary interpreters of blues, jazz and improvisation," states Brent Staples in the *New York Times Book Review.*

BIOGRAPHICAL/CRITICAL SOURCES:

BOOKS

Dictionary of Literary Biography, Volume 38: *Afro-American Writers since 1955: Dramatists and Prose Writers,* Gale (Detroit), 1985.

PERIODICALS

Chicago Tribune Book World, January 19, 1986.
Library Journal, February 1, 1977.
Los Angeles Times Book Review, March 26, 1986.
Nation, January 15, 1977.
Newsweek, March 23, 1970; January 31, 1972; December 20, 1976.
New Yorker, October 17, 1970; January 8, 1972; July 22, 1974.
New York Review of Books, February 24, 1972; June 18, 1974; January 16, 1986.
New York Times, April 4, 1972; December 11, 1976.
New York Times Book Review, May 3, 1970; January 2, 1972; June 4, 1972; December 3, 1972; May 12, 1974; December 1, 1974; December 26, 1976; December 26, 1982; February 2, 1986.
Rolling Stone, January 13, 1977.
Saturday Review, January 22, 1972.
Time, January 10, 1972; March 10, 1986.
Times Literary Supplement, July 28, 1978; July 11, 1986.
Voice Literary Supplement, February, 1982.
Washington Post Book World, March 22, 1970; December 26, 1971; December 8, 1974; January 8, 1986.

*   *   *

MYRSIADES, Kostas J.   1940-

PERSONAL: Born May 21, 1940, in Vourliotes, Samos, Greece; came to the United States in 1948, naturalized citizen, 1957; son of John (a vintner) and Mary (Laghos) Myrsiades; married Linda Suny (an associate professor of English), 1965; children: Yani, Leni. *Education:* University of Iowa, B.A., 1963; Indiana University, M.A., 1965, Ph.D., 1972; University of Athens, Certificate in Classical and Modern Greek, 1966.

ADDRESSES: Home—370 North Malin Rd., Newtown Square, PA 19073. *Office*—Department of English, West Chester University, Philips 210, West Chester, PA, 19380.

CAREER: Homer English Institute, Athens, Greece, instructor in English, 1965-66, 1969; West Chester University, West Chester, PA, assistant professor of English, 1969-73; Deree College, Athens, assistant professor of modern Greek literature and director of Center for Hellenic Studies, 1973-74; West Chester University, associate professor, 1974-77, professor of English, 1977—, assistant dean of College of Arts and Sciences, 1982-83, director of comparative literature studies, 1983—, director of graduate English studies, 1983-85, chair of English department, 1985-90.

MEMBER: Modern Language Association of America, Modern Greek Studies Association, American Literary Translators Association, American Comparative Literature Association, Association for the Departments of English, Association of Pennsylvania State Colleges and University Faculty, English Association of Pennsylvania State Universities, Teachers for a Democratic Culture, Temple University Center for Hellenic Studies (fellow, 1995).

AWARDS, HONORS: Lily fellow at University of Pennsylvania, 1981; West Chester University grants, 1980, 1982, 1986, 1987, 1989, 1994, 1995; Philadelphia Council of the Humanities grant, 1983; Delaware Valley Faculty Exchange grant, 1984; Faculty Merit Awards for Scholarship and Service, 1984, 1987; University Scholars grant, 1988; College of Arts and Sciences Development grant, 1988, 1990, 1991; Phoenix Award for significant editorial achievement, Council of Editors of Learned Journals, 1991; Outstanding Academic Book of the Year, American Library Association, 1991, for *Yannis Ritsos: Selected Poems, 1938-1988;* grant from American Philosophical Society, 1992; research grant from Pennsylvania State System of Higher Education, 1993; College of Arts and Sciences grant incentive award, 1993.

WRITINGS:

Takis Papatsonia, G. K. Hall (Boston), 1974.

(Contributor) Kostas E. Tsiropoulos, editor, *Timi ston T. K. Papatsoni* (title means "In Honor of Takis K. Papatsonis"), Tetradhia Eythinis (Athens, Greece), 1976.

(Contributor) G. Valetas, editor, *Afieroma ston Yanni Ritso* (title means "Festschrift for Yannis Ritsos"), Aiolika Ghramata, 1976.

(Editor and translator, with Kimon Friar) Yannis Ritsos, *Scripture of the Blind,* Ohio State University Press (Columbus), 1979.

(Contributor) Athina Kallaianesi, editor, *Afieroma ston Yanni Ritso* (title means "Festschrift for Yannis Ritsos"), Kedhros (Athens), 1981.

(Editor and author of introduction) *Approaches to Teaching Homer's Illiad and Odyssey,* Modern Language Association of America (New York City), 1987.

(Editor and translator, with Friar) Yannis Ritsos, *Monovasia and The Women of Monemvasia,* Nostos Press (Minneapolis, MN), 1987.

(Author and translator, with Linda S. Myrsiades) *The Karagiozis Heroic Performance in Greek Shadow Theater,* University Press of New England (Hanover, NH), 1988.

(With Friar) *Takis Papatsonis, Ursa Minor and Other Poems,* Nostos Press, 1988.

(With Friar) *Yannis Ritsos: Selected Poems, 1938-1988,* Boa Editions (New York City), 1989.

(With L. S. Myrsiades) *Karagiozis: Culture and Comedy in Greek Puppet Theater,* Kentucky University Press (Lexington), 1992.

Let Others Dance for the Lord Dionysus Now, Pella Publishing (New York City), 1993.

(Editor with L. S. Myrsiades) *Margins in the Classroom: Teaching Literature,* University of Minnesota Press (Minneapolis), 1994.

(Editor with Jerry Mcguire) *Order and Partialities: Theory, Pedagogy, and the "Postcolonial",* Syracuse University Press (Syracuse, NY), 1995.

Contributor to *Encyclopedia of World Literature in the Twentieth Century, Dictionary of Literary Biography, The World Book Encyclopedia,* and *European Writers.* Contributor of articles, poems, translations, and reviews to language and literature journals in the United States and Greece. Guest editor of *Falcon,* 1978, *Grove: Contemporary Poetry and Translation,* 1979, and *Durak: An International Magazine of Poetry,* 1980. *College Literature,* guest editor, 1976, 1978, 1988, editor, 1990—; editor, *The Journal of the Hellenic Diaspora,* 1991—.

WORK IN PROGRESS: With L. S. Myrsiades, *Writing the Resistance: Guerrilla Theater in World War II Greece; Conversations with an Oral Performer: The Art of Greek Shadow Puppet Theater,* taped interviews with Karagiozis performer Yiorgos Haridimos (1965-1992) and the oral art of Greek shadow puppet theater; *Drinking from the Pit of Blood: (Re)Writing a Created Past,* stories and poems on ancient and modern Greece; *The Poetry of Yannis Ritsos,* study of the poet's oeuvre; *Greek Guerrilla Texts,* translations and interviews from Greek resistance texts; *Custom as Law in Homer's* Iliad *and* Odyssey.

SIDELIGHTS: Kostas J. Myrsiades told *CA:* "My interests in the field of literature are twofold: first the poetry of the Western world's longest continuous literary traditions from Homer to the poetry of twentieth-century Greece, and secondly, the way all literatures should be taught in our nation's colleges and universities. In Greek poetry, I am especially interested in modern Greek poets who, like Kazantzakis, Constantine Cavafy, Seferis Elytis, and Ritsos, use the Greek past of Homer to speak of man and the human condition in new and contemporary ways.

Translating from the modern Greek provides me with an opportunity to explode both the richness and Greekness (*romiosini*) of these poets into an equally rich language—English. Moreover, dealing with separate languages (classical, Byzantine, and modern Greek) permits me to emphasize the Hellenic (that which is universally Greek without regard to specific locality) rather than the Greek (purely local).

In translating from the modern Greek folk culture tradition (Karagiozis shadow theater and resistance literature of WWII), I am interested in experimenting with new translation theories in new ways of applying these to the Greek texts. My second interest, that of pedagogy, stems from a desire to explore new ways of reading, understanding, expanding, and defining that which we call 'literature.' The great variety of literary theories that have surfaced since the 60s, and which continue to multiply have enriched the field of literature and all the different type of 'texts'incorporated under that term. Finding new ways of approaching and teaching these new texts and rereading old texts in new ways presents a true challenge for the contemporary teacher of literatures."

N-O

NAMIOKA, Lensey 1929-

PERSONAL: Born June 14, 1929, in Beijing, China; daughter of Yuen Ren (a linguist) and Buwei (a physician and writer; maiden name, Yang) Chao; married Isaac Namioka (a mathematician), September 9, 1957; children: Aki, Michi (daughters). *Education:* Attended Radcliffe College, 1947-49; University of California, Berkeley, B.A., 1951, M.A., 1952. *Avocational interests:* Music, gardening.

ADDRESSES: Home—2047 23rd Ave. E., Seattle, WA 98112. *Agent*—Ruth Cohen Inc. Literary Agency, Box 7626, Menlo Park, CA 94025.

CAREER: Wells College, Aurora, NY, instructor in mathematics, 1957-58; Cornell University, Ithaca, NY, instructor in mathematics, 1958-61; Japan Broadcasting Corp., broadcasting monitor, 1969. Translator for American Mathematical Society, 1958-66.

MEMBER: Authors Guild, Society of Children's Book Writers, Mystery Writers of America, PEN Center USA West, Seattle Free Lances.

AWARDS, HONORS: Reading Magic Award, *Parenting* magazine, for *Yang the Youngest and His Terrible Ear;* Washington State Governor's Award, for *April and the Dragon Lady;* Gold Award, *Parents' Choice,* for *Yang the Third and Her Impossible Family.*

WRITINGS:

(Translator) Buwei Y. Chao, *How to Order and Eat in Chinese,* Vintage, 1974.

The Samurai and the Long-Nosed Devils (juvenile), McKay (New York City), 1976.
White Serpent Castle (juvenile), McKay, 1976.
Japan: A Traveler's Companion, Vanguard, 1979.
Valley of Broken Cherry Trees (juvenile), Delacorte (New York City), 1981.
Who's Hu? (juvenile), Vanguard, 1981.
China: A Traveler's Companion, Vanguard, 1985.
Phantom of Tiger Mountain (juvenile), Vanguard, 1986.
Island of Ogres, Harper (New York City), 1989.
Coming of the Bear, HarperCollins (New York City), 1992.
Yang the Youngest and His Terrible Ear, Little, Brown (Boston), 1992.
April and the Dragon Lady, Harcourt (San Diego), 1994.
Yang the Third and Her Impossible Family, Little, Brown, 1995.
The Loyal Cat, Harcourt, 1995.

Also contributor of short stories and a one-act play to anthologies and of articles to textbooks. Contributor of travel and humor articles to magazines and newspapers.

WORK IN PROGRESS: Den of the White Fox; Yang the Second and the Bashful Athletes.

SIDELIGHTS: Lensey Namioka once told *CA:* "For my writings, I draw heavily on my Chinese cultural heritage and on my husband's Japanese cultural heritage. My involvement with Japan started before my marriage, since my mother spent many years in Japan. My long years of training in mathematics had little influence on my writing, except for an urge to economy."

BIOGRAPHICAL/CRITICAL SOURCES:

PERIODICALS

Chicago Tribune Book World, July 5, 1981.

* * *

NAVONE, John J(oseph)   1930-

PERSONAL: Surname is pronounced Na-*vo*-nay; born October 19, 1930, in Seattle, WA; son of James and Juliet (Micheli) Navone. *Education:* Gonzaga University, M.Phil., 1956; St. Mary's University, Halifax, Nova Scotia, Canada, S.T.M., 1963; Gregorian University, Th.D., 1965. *Avocational interests:* Drama, literature, music, art, European history, sociology, international relations, geopolitics, communications, Italian culture.

ADDRESSES: Home and office—Gregorian University, Piazza della Pilotta 4, Rome 00187, Italy.

CAREER: Entered Society of Jesus in 1949, ordained Roman Catholic priest, 1962. Seattle Preparatory School, Seattle, WA, teacher, 1956-59; Gregorian University, Rome, Italy, 1967—, began as assistant professor, currently professor of theology. Annually teaches summer school, Seattle University.

WRITINGS:

History and Faith in the Thought of Alan Richardson, SCM Press, 1966.
Personal Witness: A Biblical Spirituality, Sheed, 1967.
Themes of St. Luke, Gregorian University Press, 1970.
Everyman's Odyssey: Seven Plays Seen as Modern Myths about Man's Quest for Personal Integrity, Seattle University Press, 1974.
A Theology of Failure, Paulist Press (Ramsey, NJ), 1974.
Communicating Christ, St. Paul Publications (Australia), 1976.
Towards a Theology of Story, St. Paul Publications, 1977.
The Jesus Story: Our Life as Story in Christ, Liturgical Press (Collegeville, MN), 1979.
(With Thomas Cooper) *Tellers of the Word,* Le Jacq Publishers, 1981.

Gospel Love: A Narrative Theology, Michael Glazier (Wilmington, DE), 1984.
Triumph through Failure, St. Paul Publications, 1984.
Freedom and Transformation in Christ, Gregorian University Press, 1985.
The Story of the Passion, Gregorian University Press, 1985.
The Dynamic of the Question in Narrative Theology, Gregorian University Press, 1986.
Self-Giving and Sharing: The Trinity and Human Fulfillment, Liturgical Press, 1990.
Seeking God in Story, Liturgical Press, 1990.
Towards a Theology of Beauty, Liturgical Press, 1996.
The Land and the Spirit of Italy: The Texture of Italian Religious Culture, Legas, 1996.

Contributor to *Foundations of Theology,* Macmillan (New York City), 1972. Contributor to several periodicals in the United States and in Europe, including *La Civilta Cattolica,* a semi-official publication of the Vatican. Member of the board of editors for *Italian Journal: A Quarterly Digest of Italian Affairs.*

SIDELIGHTS: John J. Navone once told *CA* that "an important motivating factor for writing is the need to prepare and improve or update lectures at the graduate level. Writing for the lecture and revising afterwards makes for both better lectures and better writing. Secondly, the discipline of writing is an excellent aid to clarifying and organizing and critically reflecting upon our thinking."

Navone is competent in Italian, French, German, Spanish, Latin, Portuguese, and Greek. Some of his works have been translated into Italian, French, Spanish, and Portuguese.

BIOGRAPHICAL/CRITICAL SOURCES:

PERIODICALS

Weekly (Seattle), August 10, 1983.

* * *

NETANYAHU, B(enzion)   1910-

PERSONAL: Born March 25, 1910; son of Nathan (a rabbi) and Sarah (Lurie) Mileikowsky; married Cela Segal, September 7, 1944; children: Jonathan, Benjamin, Iddo. *Education:* Hebrew Teachers Seminary, Jerusalem, Israel, teacher's diploma, 1929; Hebrew University of Jerusalem, M.A., 1933; Dropsie College, Ph.D., 1947.

ADDRESSES: Home—30 Uptown Village, Ithaca, NY 14850. *Office*—Department of Semitic Languages and Literatures, Cornell University, 166 Rockefeller Hall, Ithaca, NY 14853.

CAREER: Coeditor of *Betar* (Hebrew monthly), 1933-34; *Hayarden* (daily newspaper), Jerusalem, Israel, editor, 1934-35; Zionist Political Library, Jerusalem and Tel-Aviv, Israel, editor, 1935-40; New Zionist Organization of America, New York, NY, executive director, 1940-48; *Encyclopedia Hebraica,* Jerusalem, editor-in-chief, 1948-62; Dropsie College, Philadelphia, PA, professor of Hebrew language and literature, and chairman of department, 1957-66, professor of medieval Jewish history and Hebrew literature, 1966-68; University of Denver, Denver, CO, professor of Hebraic studies, 1968-71; Cornell University, Ithaca, NY, professor of Judaic studies, beginning 1971, currently professor emeritus, chairman of department of Semitic languages and literatures, 1971-75; Hebrew University, Jerusalem, professor emeritus in history. Member of American Zionist Emergency Council, 1945-48.

MEMBER: American Academy for Jewish Research (fellow; executive member, 1967—), Institute for Advanced Religious Studies (member of advisory council, 1967—).

WRITINGS:

(Contributor) Max Nordau, editor, *Political Writings* (in Hebrew), two volumes, Hozaah Medinit (Tel-Aviv), 1936-37, 2nd edition, 1946.

(Editor and contributor) Theodore Herzl, *Letters, 1896-1904* (in Hebrew), Hozaah Medinit, 1937, 2nd edition, 1949.

(Editor) Israel Zangwill, *Road to Independence: Collected Works on the Jewish Question* (in Hebrew), Hozaah Medinit, 1938.

(Contributor) Zangwill, editor, *Collection of Essays,* Hozaah Medinit, 1939.

(Editor and contributor) *Max Nordau to His People,* Scopus Publishing, 1941.

(Editor and contributor) Leo Pinsker, *Road to Freedom,* Scopus Publishing, 1944.

Don Isaac Abravanel: Statesman and Philosopher, Jewish Publication Society, 1953, 3rd edition, 1972.

(Editor and contributor) Nordau, *Collected Works* (in Hebrew), four volumes, World Zionist Organization Publications, 1954-62.

The Marranos of Spain, American Academy for Jewish Research, 1966, 2nd edition, 1973.

The Origins of the Inquisition in 15th-Century Spain, Random House (New York City), 1995.

General editor of *The World History of the Jewish People,* Volume 1, Rutgers University Press, 1964. Contributor to *Proceedings* of American Academy for Jewish Research, and to *Encyclopedia Hebraica.* Coeditor of *Jewish Quarterly Review,* 1959-60; editor of *Zionews* (of New Zionist Organization of America), 1942-44.

SIDELIGHTS: A 1,300-page historical study, B. Netanyahu's *The Origins of the Inquisition in 15th-Century Spain* examines the origins of a period in Spanish history when the Catholic Church persecuted those it considered to be heretics. "The power of Mr. Netanyahu's intellect, the grandeur of his themes and his moral passion give *The Origins of the Inquisition* great narrative power," writes Richard Bernstein in the *New York Times.*

Among scholars in the field there has been a long-standing debate over why the Spanish Inquisition focused its attention on Jews who had converted to Catholicism. The Church's explanation at the time was that many of these converted Jews were actually not Christians at all but were secretly practicing their old religion. Accepting this version of events, some historians see the Spanish Jews who died during the Inquisition as martyrs who heroically gave their lives for their Judaic religion.

But Netanyahu disputes that argument. When the Muslims were forced out of the Iberian Peninsula, the triumphant Christian forces did force some Jews to convert to Christianity. But many others, Netanyahu shows, converted voluntarily from a sincere religious conviction. Netanyahu believes that intolerance of the converts stemmed from the "Spanish habit of defining the Jews not religiously, but racially," as Bernstein explains. This racial classification gave the converts no safety based on their religious beliefs or behavior. Such classification was also a forerunner to the genocidal policies of such 20th-century regimes as Soviet Russia and Nazi Germany. Bernstein concludes that *The Origins of the Inquisition* is a "scholarly monument against which future works will be measured."

BIOGRAPHICAL/CRITICAL SOURCES:

PERIODICALS

New York Times, August 23, 1995, p. C16.
New York Times Book Review, August 27, 1995, p.
    15.

* * *

NICHOLS, Leigh
    See KOONTZ, Dean R(ay)

* * *

NIMMO, Jenny   1942-

PERSONAL: Born January 15, 1942 (some sources
say 1944), in Windsor, Berkshire, England; married
David Wynn Millward (an artist and illustrator),
1974; children: two daughters, one son. *Education:*
Private boarding schools, 1950-60.

ADDRESSES: Home—Henllan Mill, Llangynyw,
Welshpool, Powys SY21 9EN, Wales. *Agent*—
Murray Pollinger, 4 Garrick St., London WC2E
9BH, England.

CAREER: Theatre Southeast, Sussex and Kent, England, actress and assistant stage manager, 1960-63;
governess in Amalfi, Italy, 1963; British Broadcasting Corp. (BBC-TV), London, England, photographic researcher, 1964-66, assistant floor manager,
1966-68, 1971-74, director and writer of children's
programs for "Jackanory," 1970; full-time writer,
1975—.

AWARDS, HONORS: Smarties Prize in ages 7-11
category, Rowntree Mackintosh Co., 1986, and Tir
Na n'Og Award, Welsh Arts Council, 1987, both for
The Snow Spider.

WRITINGS:

CHILDREN'S FICTION

The Bronze Trumpeter, illustrated by Caroline
    Scrace, Angus & Robertson (London), 1975.
Tatty Apple, illustrated by Priscilla Lamont, Methuen
    (London), 1984.

The Snow Spider (first book in the "Snow Spider"
    trilogy), illustrated by Joanna Carey, Methuen,
    1986, Dutton (New York City), 1987.
Emlyn's Moon (second book in the "Snow Spider"
    trilogy), illustrated by Carey, Methuen, 1987,
    published as *Orchard of the Crescent Moon,*
    Dutton, 1989.
The Red Secret, illustrated by Maureen Bradley,
    Hamish Hamilton (London), 1989.
The Chestnut Soldier (third book in the "Snow Spi-
    der" trilogy), Methuen, 1989.
The Bears Will Get You!, Methuen, 1990.
Jupiter Boots, Heinemann, 1990.
Ultramarine, Methuen, 1990.
Delilah and the Dogspell, Methuen, 1991.
Rainbow and Mr. Zed (sequel to *Ultramarine*),
    Methuen, 1992, Dutton, 1994.
(Reteller) *The Witches and the Singing Mice,* illus-
    trated by Angela Barrett, Dial (New York City),
    1993.
The Stone Mouse, illustrated by Helen Craig, Walker
    (London), 1993.
(Reteller) *The Starlight Cloak,* illustrated by Justin
    Todd, Dial, 1993.
Griffin's Castle, Methuen, 1994.
Wilfred's Wolf, illustrated by husband, David Wynn
    Millward, Bodley Head (London), 1994.
Granny Grimm's Gruesome Glasses, illustrated by
    Millward, A. & C. Black (London), 1995.
Ronnie and the Millipede, Walker, 1995.

ADAPTATIONS: The "Snow Spider" trilogy, comprised of *The Snow Spider, Emlyn's Moon,* and *The
Chestnut Soldier,* has been adapted as children's programs for British television. Several of Nimmo's
works have been recorded.

SIDELIGHTS: Jenny Nimmo began to receive much
notice as a children's author in the 1980s. Her first
book, *The Bronze Trumpeter,* was published in 1975,
and led *Times Literary Supplement* contributor Ann
Thwaite to call her "a new writer of considerable
imagination and skill." The responsibility of raising
her three children kept her from publishing another
book until 1984, and Nimmo related in the *Twentieth-Century Children's Writers:* "I live and work in
a rural community in Wales where my three bilingual
children are growing into an old but vigorous culture. Here place names hark back to legend and it
seems to me that the past is still part of the rhythm
of everyday life. My books are concerned with the
very real problem of growing children, and most of
them are set in a landscape which is undeniably
magical; they are described as fantasies." As a result,

"Wales has a powerful hold on [the] imagination" of this "relative newcomer to children's fantasy," as Donna White revealed in the *School Librarian*.

Nimmo has received accolades for her Welsh-inspired books. To win the Tir Na n'Og Award, as she did for *The Snow Spider,* one must present a Welsh language book, or, for an English language book, depict an authentic Welsh setting while raising the standard of writing for children and young people. The protagonist of *The Snow Spider* concerns the story of ten-year-old Gwyn Griffiths, whose family is torn apart by his sister's death. In order to help heal his relationship with his parents, Gwyn is given five strange birthday gifts from his mystic grandmother which are to be used to rediscover the magical powers that have long resided in his bloodline. Gwyn is taken aback when he sees his dead sister's ghostly image appear in a spider's sorcerous web. His newfound magic creates a dichotomy, for now he must choose between returning home or joining his sister in a different world. According to *Horn Book* critic Mary M. Burns, "Gwyn is a very real ten-year-old . . . conscious that he is different from his classmates, touchingly anxious to belong and to be loved." Zena Sutherland, writing for the *Bulletin of the Center for Children's Books,* found *The Snow Spider* a "cohesive and compelling" story that has "depth and nuance."

The mysterious alternate world of Gwyn's Welsh home returns in *Orchard of the Crescent Moon* (published in England as *Emlyn's Moon*); this time Gwyn's neighbor Nia is the person seeking a special talent, which she must then use to rescue her friend Emlyn. Like its predecessor, *Orchard of the Crescent Moon* demonstrates "the 'realness' of the child characters, despite their close access to ancient magical powers," David Bennett noted in *Books for Keeps*. A *Publishers Weekly* critic similarly observed that while the story has fantasy elements, it is "rooted in the miseries of family misunderstandings and sorrows." "*Emlyn's Moon* confirms all our hopes" about Nimmo's "unusual talents," Marcus Crouch asserted in *Junior Bookshelf*. "This is a rich, moving and amusing story, one which demands and receives the reader's total capitulation."

The trilogy concludes with *The Chestnut Soldier,* in which Gwyn is approaching his fourteenth birthday and still exercising his magical powers. Irresponsibility causes him to lose control of one of his powers, and his carelessness endangers a weak-spirited, wounded soldier resting at a home in the village.

Since the power can thwart Gwyn, he must call on his grandmother and Uncle Gwydion to exorcise the evil force from the soldier's abducted spirit. *The Chestnut Soldier* contains the most parallels to the ancient Welsh legends known as the Mabinogion, but was favored least by critic Beth E. Andersen. In *Voice of Youth Advocates,* the reviewer faulted the "relentlessly oppressive moodiness" of the characters and the "disappointingly anti-climactic finish." *School Library Journal* contributor Virginia Golodetz, however, applauded the book and stated that "Nimmo has skillfully woven the ancient story into the modern one, making it accessible to those who do not know the legend." White also praised the concluding volume, calling it "Nimmo's best book to date," showing that the author has been "stirred to new depths."

"As her major work grows in scale and complexity, Nimmo has turned to the creation of small, simpler worlds," Crouch observed in *Twentieth-Century Children's Writers. The Red Secret,* for instance, is a simple tale of Tom, a city boy whose family moves to the country, and how he rescues a wounded fox cub and makes friends in the process. Similarly told with "quiet assurance and [Nimmo's] instinct for the right turn of phrase," according to Crouch in *Junior Bookshelf,* is *Jupiter Boots,* the story of young Timothy's encounter with fancy footwear.

Nimmo returned to a supernatural setting for *Ultramarine,* which "again combines fantasy elements with the psychological growth of her protagonists to weave solid entertainment," according to a *Publishers Weekly* critic. Ned and Nell learn the truth about their parents while staying with their aunt and grandmother, a discovery with leads them to aid a mysterious stranger in rescuing sea creatures, creating a "tantalizing blend" of elements where the children's "realities are every bit as fascinating as their fantasies," Jody McCoy remarked in *Voice of Youth Advocates. Rainbow and Mr. Zed* continues the story of Nell, who is adjusting to life without Ned, on the estate of the mysterious Mr. Zed, whom she discovers is her late mother's evil brother. "In a chilling and eerie story that weaves back and forth between fantasy and reality," as *Booklist* writer Kay Weisman described it, "Nell comes to terms with her uniqueness" and thwarts her uncle's sinister plans. *Rainbow and Mr. Zed* "is exciting, moving, and deeply committed to the preservation of the world," Crouch asserted in *Junior Bookshelf*.

In an assessment of the author's career in *Twentieth-Century Children's Writers,* Crouch further lauded

Nimmo, stating that she "is a living example of the basic formula for success in an author: write what you know. She works in big ideas on a small canvas, which she fills with the figures of her own rural community. Magic or no magic, hers is a real world, viewed with a keen and understanding eye and with rich appreciation of its fun and its folly."

BIOGRAPHICAL/CRITICAL SOURCES:

BOOKS

Twentieth-Century Children's Writers, 4th edition, St. James Press (Detroit), 1995.

PERIODICIALS

Booklist, May 1, 1993, p. 1605; August, 1994, p. 2064; February 15, 1995.
Books for Keeps, September, 1986, p. 25; March, 1989, p. 19.
Bulletin of the Center for Children's Books, July-August, 1987, p. 216; July-August, 1992, p. 301.
Growing Point, May, 1989, p. 5172; November, 1991, p. 5602.
Horn Book, September-October, 1987, p. 613; September, 1993, p. 611.
Junior Bookshelf, February, 1985, p. 28; February, 1988, p. 51; April, 1989, pp. 65-66; February, 1991; August, 1992, pp. 158-59; December, 1993, p. 235; December, 1995, pp. 214-15.
Publishers Weekly, June 9, 1989, p. 68; March 9, 1992, p. 58; August 2, 1993, p. 81.
School Librarian, February, 1988, p. 21; November, 1991, pp. 130-31; February, 1992, p. 21; November, 1993, p. 157; May, 1994, p. 62.
School Library Journal, July, 1991, p. 74; November, 1992, p. 74; February, 1995.
Times Literary Supplement, April 4, 1975, p. 362.
Voice of Youth Advocates, October, 1991, p. 248; June, 1992, p. 113.*

* * *

NOLIN, Bertil   1926-

PERSONAL: Born December 6, 1926, in Tingsryd, Sweden; son of C. O. (a member of the Riksdag) and Hulda (Carlsson) Nolin; married Elly Hjertonsson, 1955; children: Bo, Jan. *Education:* University of Uppsala, M.A., 1954; University of Stockholm, Ph.D., 1966.

ADDRESSES: Home—Hoejdenvagen 127, 443 35 Lerum, Sweden. *Office*—Department of Literature, University of Gothenburg, Lundgrensgatan, Goeteborg, Sweden.

CAREER: University of Gothenburg, Goeteborg, Sweden, assistant professor of literature, 1965-68, associate professor of drama, 1972-82, head of literature department, 1982-87; University of Chicago, Chicago, IL, visiting professor of literature, 1968-70; University of Washington, Seattle, visiting professor, 1987, 1988.

MEMBER: Royal Society for Arts and Sciences of Gothenburg.

WRITINGS:

Den gode europen, Svenska Bokfoerlaget (Stockholm), 1965.
Georg Brandes, Twayne (Boston), 1976.
(Editor) *The Modern Breakthrough in Scandinavian Literature 1871-1905,* Goeteborg, 1988.
(Editor) *Lorensbergsteatern 1916-1934,* Goeteborg, 1988.
(Editor) *Kulturradikalismen. Det moderna genombrottets andra fas,* (Stockholm), 1993.

* * *

NORMAN, Lilith   1927-

PERSONAL: Surname is pronounced "*lie*-lith"; born November 27, 1927, in Sydney, New South Wales, Australia. *Education:* Studied with Library Association of Australia. *Politics:* "Small 'l' liberal, left of center." *Avocational interests:* Animals, films, opera, conservation, reading, food, and "what makes people tick."

ADDRESSES: Home—21 Rhodes Ave., Naremburn, New South Wales 2065, Australia. *Agent*—Margaret Connelly & Associates, 37 Ormond St., Paddington, New South Wales 2021, Australia.

CAREER: Newtown Municipal Library, Sydney, Australia, library assistant, 1947-49; Bonnington Hotel, London, England, telephonist, 1950-51; Angus & Robertson Books, Sydney, book shop assistant, 1951-53; Balmain District Hospital, Sydney, nursing trainee, 1953-56; City of Sydney Public Library, Sydney, library assistant, 1956-58, research officer, 1958-66, children's librarian, 1966-70; New South Wales Department of Education, *School Magazine,* Sydney, assistant editor, 1970-76, editor, 1976-78; full-time writer, 1978—.

MEMBER: Library Association of Australia (branch councillor, 1969-70; president of Children's Libraries Section, New South Wales Division, 1969-71), Australian Society of Authors, Children's Book Council of New South Wales (treasurer, 1968-70).

AWARDS, HONORS: Commendation from Children's Book Council Australian Book Awards, 1971, for *Climb a Lonely Hill;* Queen's Silver Jubilee Medal, 1977; IBBY Honour Book, Australia, 1980, for *A Dream of Seas.*

WRITINGS:

FOR CHILDREN

Climb a Lonely Hill, Collins (London), 1970, Walck, 1972.
The Shape of Three, Collins, 1971, Walck, 1972.
The Flame Takers, Collins, 1973.
Mocking-Bird Man (reader), illustrated by Astra Lacis, Hodder & Stoughton (London), 1977.
A Dream of Seas, illustrated by Edwina Bell, Collins, 1978.
My Simple Little Brother, illustrated by David Rae, Collins, 1979.
The Hex, Nelson Educational, 1989.
The Laurel & Hardy Kids, Random House (New York City), 1989.
The Paddock: A Story in Praise of the Earth (picture book), illustrated by Robert Roennfeldt, Random House, 1992.
Aphanasy (picture book), illustrated by Maxim Svetlanov, Random House, 1994.
The Beetle (picture book; retelling of a Hans Christian Andersen tale), illustrated by Maxim Svetlanov, Random House, 1995.

FOR ADULTS

The Brown and Yellow: Sydney Girls' High School 1883-1983, Oxford University Press (New York City), 1983.

NONFICTION

The City of Sydney: Official Guide, Sydney City Council, 1959.
Facts about Sydney, Sydney City Council, 1959.

Asia: A Select Reading List, Sydney City Council, 1959.
Some Notes on the Early Land Grants at Potts Point, Sydney City Council, 1959.
A History of the City of Sydney Public Library, Sydney City Council, 1960.
Notes on the Glebe, Sydney City Council, 1960.
Historical Notes on Paddington, Sydney City Council, 1961.
Historical Notes on Newtown, Sydney City Council, 1962.

OTHER

Also author of episode for television series, *Catch Kandy,* 1973. Contributor to periodicals, including *Reading Time* and *School Magazine.* Editor of *Felis,* a journal of the Siamese Cat Society of New South Wales, 1965-69.

SIDELIGHTS: Lilith Norman creates works for children that are consistent in their loving portrayal of the author's native Australian landscape and their realistic young protagonists. A librarian by profession, Norman did not begin writing for children until she was in her forties. "I managed to avoid becoming a writer for quite a long time, mainly, I think, because it seemed like very hard work for a very speculative result," she said in *Twentieth-Century Children's Writers.* "It wasn't until I started working as a children's librarian that I realized *these* were the books I wanted to write. . . . I like to write about ordinary children trying to cope, for I believe that most of us can cope with whatever is thrown at us, *if we really have to*—otherwise we'd all be living in caves still."

Norman's first two novels, *Climb a Lonely Hill* and *The Shape of Three,* depict just these types of children. The former work is an adventure tale set in the Australian outback. Young Jack and Sue Clarke are stranded when the truck they are riding in with their uncle crashes and the uncle dies. With little food and water to help them survive until they can be rescued, they have to risk a trek into the distant hills to find a waterhole. What follows is a realistic depiction of their grueling journey under the unrelenting desert sun and eventual rescue. Though critics didn't find the premise of the story particularly original, and one *Booklist* critic called the conclusion "contrived," reviewers admired the novel for its skillful characterization and faithful rendering of the Australian outback. As one *Times Literary Supplement* contributor commented, Norman is able to draw the reader into the story because "the children are real children, frail and recognizable; one cares about their fate." The critic concluded, "The book will be a sad experience for soft-hearted readers and yet a worthwhile one, for it is an honest book."

With her second novel, *The Shape of Three,* Norman examines a different type of challenge in an inhospitable environment. In this case, a newborn twin is accidentally switched with the boy of another mother while they're at the hospital. Bruce is sent home to become the only child of the wealthy Protestant Cunningham family, while Shane is taken home with Bruce's twin brother, Greg, to the large Catholic Herbert family. Greg and Shane are raised together as fraternal twins, and all seems well until Greg and Bruce meet and discover their remarkable similarity in appearance. When their mothers learn of this—and blood tests prove who the real twins are—they insist that Bruce and Shane be switched back again, which results in both boys being miserable, since they are not used to the new families that have been forced upon them. Only after much emotional suffering is it finally decided that the boys should be returned again to the families they have known since birth. Critical reaction to *The Shape of Three* was mixed. A reviewer in *Bulletin of the Center for Children's Books* felt that the "characterization and dialogue are adroit," and that Norman's comparisons of Catholic and Protestant households is well done, but added that the "book's weakness is that it smacks of the documentary approach to a case history."

After her first two books, Norman began to venture into the genre of fantasy. *The Flame Takers* is an unusual blend of reality and fantasy about the talented Malory family—the parents are actors and their son is a musician—who are subjected to the wicked machinations of a sadistic schoolmaster and the mysterious "flame takers" who destroy people's talent, and then helped by a rotund German chess aficionado. The schoolmaster and the flame takers seek to extinguish the family's flame of talent and turn them into uninspired, materialistic, card-carrying members of the bourgeoisie, but are thwarted by the German and by the boy's sister who, having no particular talent, are able to stand up to the flame takers. "Put like this," one critic in *Times Literary Supplement* remarked, "it sounds ridiculous but it is in fact a powerful and exciting allegory."

Norman once again blends fantasy and reality in *A Dream of Seas*. Taking a much more lyrical approach to the genre than in her previous novel, Norman writes about a young Australian boy nicknamed "Seasie," whose father has recently drowned. His mother takes him to live near Bondi Beach, where Seasie becomes obsessed with the sea (thus his nickname). The story of his growing interest in the sea is paralleled by the tale of a young seal's maturation from pup to young adult. As the novel progresses, Seasie's existence among humans becomes more like a dream, while the life of the sea becomes increasingly real. Boy and seal's lives draw closer together, and when Seasie's mother remarries and becomes pregnant his final ties to human civilization are broken—he embraces the ocean and becomes one with the seal. The story shows "how a boy achieves independence and a separate identity," Margery Fisher pointed out in *Growing Point*. As Seasie matures, so does the seal, so that the ending "seems an inevitable if fantastic climax to a perfectly rational story."

Norman's love for the Australian landscape, seen throughout her work, is especially poignant in her picture book *The Paddock: A Story in Praise of the Earth*. Focusing on a particular plot of land in Australia, the author follows its history from original formation, through the age of dinosaurs, to the first human settlements, and finally to its death from industrial usage. The ending, however, implies that the land will be reborn again after mankind leaves. Calling this picture book a "hymn to the resilience and dominance of the land," a *Publishers Weekly* critic felt that Norman's "dense imagery will likely be beyond the book's intended audience." On the other hand, a *Junior Bookshelf* reviewer praised the "beautifully composed text" adding that "today's children will understand what it is saying."

As Betty Gilderdale observed in *Twentieth-Century Children's Writers,* Norman's books tend to be interested in "the effect of environment on character." Whether she is writing about the influences and challenges of the natural environment on her young protagonists, or the effects of family and other social pressures, her themes have often been related in at least some way to this subject. The author, however, does not like to analyze her books, believing instead that they should be self-explanatory. As she once commented, "It seems to me that a book should speak directly to the reader. If I have anything worth saying it is there, in my books, in a far more entertaining and accessible (I hope) way than a pretentious self-analysis would provide."

BIOGRAPHICAL/CRITICAL SOURCES:

BOOKS

Saxby, H. M., *A History of Australian Children's Literature, 1941-1970*, Wentworth Books, 1971.
Twentieth-Century Children's Writers, fourth edition, St. James Press (Detroit), 1995.

PERIODICALS

Booklist, September 15, 1972, p. 101; January 1, 1973, p. 450.
Bulletin of the Center for Children's Books, February, 1973, p. 96.
Growing Point, July, 1979, pp. 3539-42.
Horn Book, fall, 1993, p. 270.
Junior Bookshelf, June, 1979, p. 171; April, 1993, p. 61.
Kirkus Reviews, March 1, 1993, p. 303.
Library Journal, September 15, 1972, p. 2965; March 15, 1973, p. 1015.
Publishers Weekly, January 1, 1973, p. 57; March 29, 1993, p. 55.
School Librarian, August, 1993, p. 104.
Times Literary Supplement, October 30, 1970, p. 1266-67; December 3, 1971, p. 1516; July 5, 1974, p. 717.

*   *   *

NORTH, Anthony
   See KOONTZ, Dean R(ay)

*   *   *

NORTHRUP, B. A.
   See HUBBARD, L(afayette) Ron(ald)

*   *   *

OLIN, John C(harles)   1915-

PERSONAL: Born October 7, 1915, in Buffalo, NY; son of Newell and Dorothy (Britt) Olin; married Marian Gouse, January 10, 1943; children: Marybeth Olin Deambrosis, Margaret Olin Santos, John Charles, Jr., Thomas. *Education:* Canisius College, B.A.,

1937; Fordham University, M.A., 1941; Columbia University, Ph.D., 1960. *Religion:* Roman Catholic.

ADDRESSES: Home—133 Van Houten Fields, West Nyack, NY 10994.

CAREER: Fordham University, Bronx, NY, instructor, 1946-52, assistant professor, 1952-62, professor of history, 1962-86, professor emeritus, 1986—. *Military service:* U.S. Navy, 1942-46; became lieutenant senior grade.

MEMBER: Renaissance Society of America, American Catholic Historical Association, Erasmus of Rotterdam Society, Amici Thomae Mori.

AWARDS, HONORS: A Festschrift entitled *Religious Orders of the Catholic Reformation*, edited by Richard L. DeMolan was published by Fordham University Press in 1994 in honor of Olin's 75th birthday.

WRITINGS:

Christian Humanism and the Reformation, Harper (New York City), 1965, revised, Fordham University Press (Bronx, NY), 1987.
(Editor) *A Reformation Debate*, Harper, 1966.
The Catholic Reformation: Savonarola to Ignatius Loyola, Harper, 1969.
(Editor) *The Autobiography of St. Ignatius Loyola*, Harper, 1974.
Six Essays on Erasmus, Fordham University Press, 1979.
(Editor) *Interpreting Thomas More's Utopia*, Fordham University Press, 1989.
Catholic Reform from Cardinal Ximenes to the Council of Trent, Fordham University Press, 1990.
(Editor with James F. Brady) *The Edition of St. Jerome* (collected works of Erasmus), University of Toronto Press (Toronto, ON), 1992.

SIDELIGHTS: John C. Olin once told *CA:* "My field of study and teaching as a historian has been the Renaissance and the Reformation, and I have worked extensively on Erasmus. I have also been interested in Catholic reform (as contrasted with Protestant reform) in the sixteenth century. My interest in Erasmus has been both because of his views and his pivotal role in his own times and because of the relevance of his ideas in ours. My concern with Catholic reform has been personal, but it is also part and parcel of an attempt to broaden out the story of the Reformation and to see and evaluate it in a much fuller context."

OOSTHUIZEN, G(erhardus) C(ornelis)   1922-

PERSONAL: Born June 18, 1922, in Alexandria District, South Africa; son of Carel Adam (a farmer) and Anna Johanna (Potgieter) Oosthuizen; married Anna Cornelia Opperman (a medical practitioner); children: Carel, Rudolf, Gerhardus. Education: University of Stellenbosch, B.A., 1941, M.Th., 1953; University of South Africa, M.A., 1946, Ph.D., 1955; Union Theological Seminary, New York, STM, 1958; Free University, Amsterdam, Netherlands, Th.D., 1958.

ADDRESSES: Home—2 Jamieson Dr., Westville, Durban, South Africa.

CAREER: Ordained minister of Dutch Reformed Church, 1944; pastor of church in Bulawayo, Rhodesia, 1950-56, and Queenstown, South Africa, 1956-59; University of Fort Hare, Alice, Cape Province, South Africa, professor of missiology, 1959-68; University of Durban-Westville, South Africa, professor of religious studies, 1969-1984. Visiting professor in West Berlin, 1966-67, and the Netherlands, 1970-71. New Religions and Independent Indigenous Churches in South Africa, director of research unit, 1984-94, honorary director, 1995—. Former mayor of Alice, Cape Province. Military service: South African Air Force, chaplain, 1944-46.

MEMBER: International Association for Missiological Studies, International Association for the History of Religions, International Association for the Study of Prehistoric Religions and Ethnology, South African Academy for Arts and Science, Missiological-Anthropological Research Association.

AWARDS, HONORS: Honorary doctorates from University of Natal, 1992, University of Zululand, 1995, and University of Durban-Westville, 1995.

WRITINGS:

Theological Discussions and Confessional Developments in the Churches of Asia and Africa, Wever (Netherlands), 1958.
(Contributor) Delayed Action, Gollancz (London), 1961.
Die kerk in gistende Asie en Afrika, Lovedale Press (South Africa), 1962.
The Theology of a South African Messiah, E. J. Brill (Long Island City, NY), 1967.
Post-Christianity in Africa: A Theological and Anthropological Study, Eerdmans (Grand Rapids, MI), 1968.

Shepherd of Lovedale: A Life for Southern Africa, Keartlands, 1970.
(Contributor) World Mission Handbook, Lutterworth (Cambridge, England), 1970.
Theological Battleground in Asia and Africa: The Issues Facing the Churches and the Efforts to Overcome Western Division, Humanities, 1972.
(Editor) The Ethics of Tissue Transplantation, Howard Timmons (Cape Town), 1972.
(Coeditor) The Great Debate: Abortion in the South African Context, Howard Timmins, 1974.
Pentecostal Penetration into the Indian Community in Metropolitan Durban, Human Sciences Research Council (Pretoria), 1975.
Moving to the Waters: Fifty Years of Pentecostal Revival in Bethesda, 1925-1975, Bethesda (Bethesda, MD), 1975.
(Editor with H. A. Shapiro and S. A. Strauss) Euthanasia, Oxford University Press (Oxford, England), 1977.
Iconography of Afro-Christian Religions, E. J. Brill, 1979.
(With J. H. Hofmeyr) Socio-religious Survey of Chatsworth, Institute for Economic and Social Research, University of Durban-Westville (South Africa), 1979.
(Editor with Shapiro and Strauss) Genetics and Society, Oxford University Press, 1980.
(Editor with A. A. Clifford-Vaughan, A. L. Behr, and G. A. Rauche) Challenge to a South African University, Oxford University Press, 1981.
Succession Conflict within the Church of the Nazarites, Institute for Social and Economic Research, University of Durban-Westville, 1981.
(With Hofmeyr) Religion in a South African Community, Institute for Social and Economic Research, University of Durban-Westville, 1981.
(Editor with Shapiro and Strauss) Professional Secrecy in South Africa, Oxford University Press, 1983.
(Editor with Shapiro and Strauss) Clinical Experimentation in South Africa, Hodder & Stoughton (London), 1985.
(Editor) Religion Alive: The New Movements and Indigenous Churches in South Africa, Hodder & Stoughton, 1986.
(With others) Religion, Social Change, and Intergroup Relations in South Africa, Greenwood Press (Westport, CT), 1986.
The Birth of Christian Zionism in South Africa, University of Zululand Publication Series, 1987.

(Editor with S. D. Edwards, W. H. Wessels, and I. Hexham) *Afro-Christian Religion and Healing in Southern Africa, Lewiston,* Edwin Mellen (Lewiston, NY), 1988.

(Editor with Hexham) *Afro-Christian Religion at the Grassroots in Southern Africa, Lewiston,* Edwin Mellen, 1991.

(Editor with Hexham) *Empirical Studies of African Independent/Indigenous Churches,* Edwin Mellen, 1992.

The Healing Prophet in the African Independent Churches, E. J. Brill, 1992.

(Editor with M. C. Kitshoff and S. W. D. Dube) *Afro-Christianity at the Grassroots,* E. J. Brill, 1994.

Contributor of articles to journals in the Netherlands, Germany, Switzerland, South Africa, South East Asia, and the United States.

SIDELIGHTS: G. C. Oosthuizen told *CA:* "I grew up on a farm called Arizona in the Alexandria district, Eastern Province, South Africa. I attended a farm school (three years), then Alexandria Secondary School (two years), and Kirkwood High School (two years). At sixteen years of age, I went to the University of Stellenbosch. Thereafter, I went to a Missionary Theological Seminary for three years, was ordained as a missionary of the Dutch Reformed Church in 1944, joined the South African forces during December 1944, and was ordained and sent to the war zone in Italy, January 1945.

"When the Germans surrendered, I signed on for the Far East; while on our way through the Suez Canal (from Northern Italy) to Burma, the Japanese surrendered. I returned to South Africa. I was demobilised in March 1946 and studied at the University of Cape Town. I went to the Theological School at Stellenbosch, 1947-49, and then worked as a minister in Southern Rhodesia (the present Zimbabwe), 1950-56. I returned to Queenstown in South Africa as a minister of the Dutch Reformed Church, 1956-59. Although, I received a scholarship sponsored by Rockefeller, I studied at Union Theological Seminary (UTS), New York, where I stayed in a compartment building with twenty-four others selected from seventeen different countries to study and deliberate together. This was perhaps the most meaningful period in the formation of my future.

"I worked simultaneously on an STM and a Th.D. (I had already received an M.A. and doctorate in phi-

losophy and an Mth.) UTS had a fantastic missionary research library. The STM and Th.D. theses were completed in seven months and after receiving, in 1958, both the STM at UTS and the Th.D. at the Vrije (Free) University of Amsterdam, Holland, I proceeded with my ministerial duties at Queenstown in October 1958.

"I left Queenstown in July 1959 for the University College of Fort Hare, where I accepted a post in the Department of Theology. I went to the University of Durban-Westville (UDW) in 1969, where I accepted the headship in the department of theology, but soon afterwards, in 1971, started a Department of Science of Religion. This was the first department of its kind in South Africa. An Association for the Study of Religion was formed in 1973.

"In 1975 I became a member of the International Association for the History of Religions. I did work on medical ethics and organised conferences. I accepted upon retirement from UDW in 1984, a directorship of the Research Unit from the Study of New Religions and Indigenous Churches at the University of Zululand; I retired from here on December 31, 1994. I still continue as honorary director and assist researches from abroad and in South Africa. I regularly attend international conferences in my field of study and research. In 1992 I received a special medal from the Human Sciences Research Council of South Africa, a prestigious body, concerning the research done through more than three decades.

"I was a hockey and rugby player and an athlete receiving 'full blues' (colours) for performance from the Universities of Stellenbosch and Cape Town. I took part in standard marathons and in ultra distance running for which I received medals. My wife is a medical practitioner. I have three sons who are all well qualified at various universities and are well placed with their families in Pretoria, Johannesburg, and Cape Town respectively. None of them supported the apartheid policy; I always had a critical stance towards this ideology.

"I am still associated with various universities and colleagues here and abroad. I have served on a university council since 1972, except for the last four years. I serve on committees, regularly assist visiting research students from abroad, and remain thus active. I still run on average of fifty kilometres per week. My wife and myself refuse to accept the retirement label. There is too much to do in the new South Africa."

P-Q

PAIGE, Richard
See KOONTZ, Dean R(ay)

*   *   *

PARKER, Robert B(rown) 1932-

PERSONAL: Born September 17, 1932, in Springfield, MA; son of Carroll Snow (a telephone company executive) and Mary Pauline (Murphy) Parker; married Joan Hall (an education specialist), August 26, 1956; children: David F., Daniel T. Education: Colby College, B.A., 1954; Boston University, M.A., 1957, Ph.D., 1970.

ADDRESSES: Agent—Helen Brann Agency, 94 Curtis Rd., Bridgewater, CT 06752.

CAREER: Curtiss-Wright Co., Woodridge, NJ, management trainee, 1957; Raytheon, Co., Andover, MA, technical writer, 1957-59; Prudential Insurance Co., Boston, MA, advertising writer, 1959-62; Parker-Farman Co. (advertising agency), Boston, partner, 1960-62; Boston University, Boston, lecturer in English, 1962-64; Massachusetts State College at Lowell (now University of Lowell), instructor in English, 1964-66; Massachusetts State College at Bridgewater, instructor in English, 1966-68; Northeastern University, Boston, assistant professor, 1968-74, associate professor, 1974-76, professor of English, 1976-79; novelist, 1979—. Lecturer, Suffolk University, 1965-66. Film consultant to Arthur D. Little, 1962-64. Military service: U.S. Army, 1954-56.

AWARDS, HONORS: Edgar Allan Poe Award, Mystery Writers of America, 1976, for Promised Land.

WRITINGS:

(With others) The Personal Response to Literature, Houghton (Boston), 1970.
(With Peter L. Sandberg) Order and Diversity: The Craft of Prose, Wiley (New York City), 1973.
(With John R. Marsh) Sports Illustrated Weight Training: The Athlete's Free-Weight Guide, Lippincott (Philadelphia), 1974.
(With Joan Parker) Three Weeks in Spring (nonfiction), Houghton, 1978.
Wilderness (novel), Delacorte (New York City), 1979.
Love and Glory (novel), Delacorte, 1983.
The Private Eye in Hammett and Chandler, Lord John (Northridge, CA), 1984.
Parker on Writing, Lord John, 1985.
(With Raymond Chandler) Poodle Springs, Putnam (New York City), 1989.
(With Joan Parker; photographs by William Strode) A Year at the Races, Viking (New York City), 1990.
Perchance to Dream: Robert B. Parker's Sequel to Raymond Chandler's "The Big Sleep" (novel), Putnam, 1991.
All Our Yesterdays (novel), Delacorte, 1994.
(With photographs by Kasho Kumagai) Spenser's Boston, Otto Penzler (New York City), 1994.

"SPENSER" DETECTIVE SERIES

The Godwulf Manuscript, Houghton, 1974.
God Save the Child, Houghton, 1974.
Mortal Stakes, Houghton, 1975.

Promised Land, Houghton, 1976.
The Judas Goat, Houghton, 1978.
Looking for Rachel Wallace, Delacorte, 1980.
Early Autumn, Delacorte, 1981.
A Savage Place, Delacorte, 1981.
Surrogate: A Spenser Short Story, Lord John, 1982.
Ceremony, Delacorte, 1982.
The Widening Gyre, Delacorte, 1983.
Valediction, Delacorte, 1984.
A Catskill Eagle, Delacorte, 1985.
Taming a Sea-Horse, Delacorte, 1986.
Pale Kings and Princes, Delacorte, 1987.
Crimson Joy, Delacorte, 1988.
Playmates, Putnam, 1989.
The Early Spenser: Three Complete Novels (contains *The Godwulf Manuscript, God Save the Child,* and *Mortal Stakes*), Delacorte, 1989.
Stardust, Putnam, 1990.
Pastime, Putnam, 1991.
Double Deuce, Putnam, 1992.
Paper Doll, Putnam, 1993.
Walking Shadow, Putnam, 1994.
Thin Air, Putnam, 1995.
Chance, Putnam, 1996.

OTHER

Also author with wife, Joan Parker, of several television scripts for series "Spenser: For Hire," two "B.L. Stryker" television movies for Burt Reynolds, and four television movies based on Spenser television series. Contributor to *Lock Haven Review* and *Revue des langues vivantes.* Contributor of restaurant reviews to *Boston Magazine,* 1976.

ADAPTATIONS: The "Spenser: For Hire" television series, American Broadcasting Corp. (ABC), 1985-88, was based, in part, on Parker's works; film rights have been sold to many of the Spenser novels.

SIDELIGHTS: Robert B. Parker's "Spenser" series represents "the best American hardboiled detective fiction since Ross Macdonald and Raymond Chandler," according to *Armchair Detective* writer Anne Ponder. Parker's career as a novelist began only after he spent years producing ad copy and technical writing for various companies. At his wife's urging, he completed his Ph.D. and entered the teaching profession to gain more time for his own writing projects. "Being a professor and working are not the same thing," Parker explained to Wayne Warga in the *Los Angeles Times.* In a Toronto *Globe and Mail* interview with Ian Brown, Parker expressed his feelings about the university environment even more

frankly: "The academic community is composed largely of nitwits. If I may generalize. People who don't know very much about what matters very much, who view life through literature rather than the other way around. . . . In my 14 or 16 years in the profession, I've met more people that I did not admire than at any other point in my life. Including two years in the infantry, where I was the only guy who could read."

It took two and a half years of writing in his spare time for Parker to complete his first fiction manuscript, but only three weeks for it to be accepted for publication. Parker's doctoral thesis had treated the classic detective fiction of Raymond Chandler and Dashiell Hammett, and his first novel, *The Godwulf Manuscript,* presented a detective in the tradition of Philip Marlowe and Sam Spade. A Boston policeman turned private eye after being fired for insubordination, Spenser is "a man's man, all six feet plus of him, a former professional fighter, a man who can take on any opposition," relates Newgate Callendar in the *New York Times Book Review.*

The character's traditional toughness is balanced by his "honesty and his sensitivity," continues Callendar. "Spenser may be something of a smart aleck but only when he is faced with pomposity and pretension. Then he reacts, sometimes violently. He is educated and well read, though he never parades his knowledge. His girlfriend is the perfect woman, as smart as he is, and so he never has to chase around. Pushed as he is by his social conscience, he is sometimes dogged enough to seem quixotic."

Parker followed *The Godwulf Manuscript* with *God Save the Child, Mortal Stakes, Promised Land* and other Spenser novels. Their growing success soon enabled him to quit his teaching post and devote himself to writing full-time. The author now estimates that it takes him three to five months to write a Spenser adventure. Many critics point to Parker's plotting as his weakness, but he is widely praised for his evocative descriptions, for his sharp, witty dialogue, and for introducing a more human, emotional tone to the hard-boiled detective genre. H. R. F. Keating comments in the London *Times* that in the Spenser books "there is a concern with human beings that rises at times to compassion and perhaps falls at other times to that commonish complaint among American novelists 'psychology showing through.' But the seriousness that this indicates is always well-compensated for by Parker's dialogue. Spenser is a wisecracking guy in the firm tradition of the Chandler shamus, and above and beyond this all the conversations in the books are splendidly swift and sharp." In her review of *Pale Kings and Princes,* *Washington Post Book World* writer Jean M. White concurs that "Parker . . . writes some of the snappiest and sauciest dialogue in the business," and calls the book "lean and taut and crisply told with moments of genuine humor and genuine poignancy."

One of Parker's most notable departures from the detective novelists before him is Spenser's monogamous commitment to his psychologist lover, Susan Silverman. "By all the unwritten rules of private-eye fiction, that [relationship] should have handicapped Spenser's future literary prospects disastrously," declares Derrick Murdoch in the Toronto *Globe and Mail.* "Instead it has allowed him to develop into the most fully rounded characterization of an intelligent human being in the literature—a mixture of idealism, passion, strength, frailty and unselfish tenacity." In his book *Sons of Sam Spade, The Private-Eye Novel in the 70s: Robert B. Parker, Roger L. Simon, Andrew Bergman,* David Geherin also states his belief that the Spenser character has "grown significantly, especially in the area of self-knowledge, thanks in part to the frequent confrontations between his ever-deepening relationship with Susan. Even when she is absent . . . her presence is felt . . . Parker's handling of Spenser's relationship with Susan effectively disproves Chandler's assertion that the love story and the detective story cannot exist in the same book. Not only do they coexist in Parker's novels, the love story adds an element of tension by serving as a poignant reminder of the vast distance that separates the mean streets from the quiet ones." A *Time* reviewer emphasizes, however, that for all the intellectual and romantic dialogue, Parker's novels never lack "slambang action."

"Robert B. Parker's influence on the [detective] genre is unquestioned," summarizes Margaret Cannon in the Toronto *Globe and Mail.* "Spenser liberated the PI from California, gave him a whole new line of inquiry, and taught him to love." Furthermore, "with each novel Parker has exhibited growing independence from his predecessors, confidently developing his own themes, characters, and stylistic idiom," concludes Geherin. "However, despite his innovative efforts, he has remained faithful to the conventions of the genre, so effectively laid down by his predecessors. He has thus earned for himself the right to be designated *the* legitimate heir to the Hammett-Chandler-Macdonald tradition, which,

thanks to the efforts of writers like Parker, shows no signs of diminishing."

Parker is so clearly the heir of Raymond Chandler in particular that in 1988 the Chandler estate asked him to complete the 30-page manuscript that Chandler was working on when he died. The result is *Poodle Springs,* but Parker proceeded to write a sequel to Chandler's classic *The Big Sleep* as well, calling it *Perchance to Dream: Robert B. Parker's Sequel to Raymond Chandler's "The Big Sleep."* Not liking either novel, John Williams of *New Statesman and Society* says "*Poodle Springs* is the better of the two," finding less fault with Parker's work than with Chandler's. In the *New York Times Book Review,* Martin Amis also criticizes Chandler, citing the master's stylistic lapses and his homophobia among other flaws, but Amis is even less charitable to Parker. *Perchance to Dream,* he says, "is a chaos of tawdry shortcuts" and the "character of Marlowe collapses" into an "affable goon." Parker's fellow mystery writer Ed McBain has high praise for the Chandler recreations, however, lamenting the inadequacy of the original *Poodle Springs* manuscript but lauding Parker's work with it "as a tribute to his enormous skill."

Another departure for Parker—or a harking back to his two mainstream novels, *Wilderness* and *Love and Glory*—is *All Our Yesterdays,* which Walter Walker of the *New York Times Book Review* feels Parker wrote from a self-conscious desire to be taken seriously by the mainstream literary world. "*All Our Yesterdays,*" writes Walker, "embraces two countries, two families, three generations, love, war, guilt, corruption, and angst." Despite some misgivings, however, Walker feels the novel to be "a most satisfying reading experience" in the same sense as the Spenser novels—that is, as "entertainment." Wendy Smith of the *Washington Post* has similar misgivings, finding the novel to be "thoughtful, though structurally flawed." Karl Miller of *Times Literary Supplement,* however, concludes that "the novel is expertly plotted and tersely written" and that "Spenser fans, and a fair number of professors of English, may be unable to put it down."

Yet with all his departures, the Spenser novels remain Parker's bread-and-butter. Some critics, such as David Papineau in the *Times Literary Supplement,* feel that the series has lost its early energy. Writing of *Stardust,* Papineau declares that it's "about as close to Chandler as Barbara Cartland is to Emily Bronte." Similarly, Maureen Corrigan laments in the

Washington Post Book World that the "Spenser series has grown weaker" and that reading its later entries is "like attending a seance to commune with the departed." But Parker can still "create characters who live and dialogue that talks," says Marilyn Stasio in her review of *Thin Air* in the *New York Times*. Writing in the *Chicago Tribune*, Dick Allen calls *Walking Shadow* "a really good story" that "offers several surprises and only a few annoyances." In fact, warns Adler, "the message here is clear. Never underestimate Spenser or his creator, Robert B. Parker."

BIOGRAPHICAL/CRITICAL SOURCES:

BOOKS

Carr, John C., *Craft of Crime,* Houghton, 1983.
Contemporary Literary Criticism, Volume 27, Gale (Detroit), 1984.
Geherin, David, *Sons of Sam Spade, The Private-Eye Novel in the 70s: Robert B. Parker, Roger L. Simon, Andrew Bergman,* Ungar (New York City), 1980.
Parker, Robert B., *Three Weeks in Spring,* Houghton, 1978.

PERIODICALS

Armchair Detective, fall, 1984; winter, 1991, p. 113; summer, 1992, p. 343; winter, 1993, p. 112.
Boston Globe, May 20, 1994.
Chicago Tribune, September 20, 1985; May 29, 1994.
Chicago Tribune Book World, June 28, 1987.
Christian Science Monitor, September 3, 1991, p. 13.
Clues: A Journal of Detection, fall/winter, 1980; spring/summer, 1984. *Critique,* fall, 1984.
Globe and Mail (Toronto), May 12, 1984; June 6, 1984; June 15, 1985; June 21, 1986.
Library Journal, April 1, 1992; October 1, 1994.
Los Angeles Times, January 26, 1981; March 20, 1981; June 21, 1982; January 17, 1984; February 16, 1986; July 3, 1994, p. 10; October 9, 1994, p. 15.
Los Angeles Times Book Review, July 6, 1986; May 10, 1987.
New Republic, March 19, 1977; November 4, 1978.
New Statesman and Society, April 19, 1991, p. 37.
Newsweek, June 7, 1982; June 17, 1985; July 7, 1986.
New Yorker, July 13, 1987.
New York Times, January 21, 1981; September 20, 1985; July 2, 1987; June 4, 1992; May 11, 1995.

New York Times Book Review, January 13, 1974; December 15, 1974; November 11, 1979; August 2, 1981; May 1, 1983; May 20, 1984; June 30, 1985; June 22, 1986; May 31, 1987; April 23, 1989; October 15, 1989; January 27, 1991; May 12, 1991, p. 34; July 28, 1991, p. 10; May 31, 1992, p. 34; February 12, 1995, p. 32; May 21, 1995.
Observer (London), March 31, 1991, p. 54; May 19, 1991, p. 59; January 12, 1992, p. 7.
People, May 7, 1984.
Publishers Weekly, May 4, 1990; November 23, 1990; April 4, 1994; March 20, 1995.
Southwest Review, autumn, 1974.
Time, July 1, 1985; July 7, 1986; July 27, 1987.
Times (London), November 4, 1978; May 4, 1987.
Times Literary Supplement, November 30, 1990, p. 1287; November 25, 1994, p. 21.
USA Today, March 20, 1987.
Washington Post, May 17, 1983; March 7, 1984; June 19, 1992; December 20, 1994.
Washington Post Book World, April 15, 1984; June 15, 1986; June 21, 1987; May 24, 1992, p. 6.

*   *   *

PATRICK, Maxine
See MAXWELL, Patricia

*   *   *

PEACOCK, Molly   1947-

PERSONAL: Born June 30, 1947, in Buffalo, NY; daughter of Edward Frank and Pauline (Wright) Peacock. *Education:* State University of New York at Binghamton, B.A. (magna cum laude), 1969; Johns Hopkins University, M.A. (with honors), 1977.

ADDRESSES: Home—505 E. 14th St., #3G, New York, NY 10009; 229 Emery St. East, London, Ontario, N6C 2E3, Canada.

CAREER: State University of New York at Binghamton, director of academic advising, 1970-73, coordinator of innovational projects in office of the dean, 1973-76; Johns Hopkins University, Baltimore, MD, honorary fellow, 1977-78; Delaware State Arts Council, Wilmington, poet in residence, 1978-81; Friends Seminary, New York City, learning specialist, 1981-92; Bucknell University, Lewisburg, PA, poet in residence, 1993—. Visiting lecturer at Columbia University, Barnard College, Sarah Lawrence College, New York University, 1989; writer in residence, University of Western Ontario, 1995-96.

MEMBER: Poetry Society of America (president, 1989-94)

AWARDS, HONORS: Resident at MacDowell Colony, 1975-76, 1979, 1982, 1985, 1989, and Yaddo Colony, 1980, 1982; awards from Creative Artists Public Service, 1977; award from Ingram Merrill Foundation, 1981; National Endowment for the Arts Fellowship, 1990; Lila Wallace Fellowship, 1994; Woodrow Wilson Fellowship, 1995.

WRITINGS:

POETRY

And Live Apart, University of Missouri Press (Columbia), 1980.
Raw Heaven, Random House (New York City), 1984.
Take Heart, Random House, 1989.
Original Love, W. W. Norton (New York City), 1995.

Contributing editor, House and Garden magazine, 1996. Also contributor to journals, including *Shenandoah, Mississippi Review, New Letters, Southern Review, Massachusetts Review, Ohio Review, Paris Review, New Yorker, Nation,* and *New Republic.*

SIDELIGHTS: American poet Molly Peacock uses strong rhyme schemes, skillful alliteration, and biting humor to explore such themes as fate, family, sexuality, pain, and the many facets of love. Writing in the *Washington Post Book World,* David Lehman observed that "Peacock has a luxuriantly sensual imagination—and an equally sensual feel for the language. In mood her poems range from high-spirited whimsy . . . to bemused reflection. . . . Whatever the subject, rich music follows the tap of her baton." Annette Allen, in *Dictionary of Literary Biography,* commented on Peacock's poetic structures, stating that "Peacock's skillful wielding of form ensures a continual dialectic between the inner world of memory and feeling and the external world. She accomplishes this dynamic, the balance between inner and outer worlds, by employing sound patterns that keep the poem close to unconscious rhythms and

by using images or metaphors from the civilized and the natural worlds."

Peacock's first collection, *And Live Apart,* introduces her preoccupation with the past. Instead of employing a bitter or hostile approach, Peacock views her personal history from the enlightened perspective of one who has reconciled herself to its shortcomings. Robert Phillips noted in the *Hudson Review* that Peacock's "concerns are big ones: the separations we make between one another, the reversals of love, the inescapability of fate, inevitabilities of inheritance, a concern for the language of emotion in conversation." He went on to say that *And Live Apart* "is notable for plumbing the past without sentimentality, and for finding new solutions to old dilemmas."

Raw Heaven, which received wider critical attention, stresses the manipulative aspects of desire and the ineffable quality of sex and sensuality. In the poem "Desire," for example, Peacock compares sexual yearning to a pet's constant demands for affection. Several critics expressed admiration for her vivid, illuminating imagery, elegant rhymes, and bold consideration of such taboo topics as menstruation, childbirth, and masturbation. *Boston Review* critic Matthew Gilbert observed, "What makes this book a 'drive for what is real,' even more than her forceful longings, is Peacock's devotion to the strength of vision. She reveres the power of uninhibited perception, imagining herself as one daring to witness the world." Some reviewers, however, criticized what they considered Peacock's overabundant use of wordplay, rhyme, and the sonnet form. J. D. McClatchy noted in the *New York Times Book Review* that Peacock's "wordplay, so high-spirited, is often aimless," while Christopher Benfey observed in *Parnassus* that "her rhymes—and these sonnets are relentlessly rhyming—are rarely part of the sense of the poem, nor are they particularly adept."

In *Take Heart* Peacock continues to address inviolable topics, including the horrors and repercussions of physical and mental child abuse. Many of the volume's opening poems deal with the death of Peacock's father and her childhood memories of his alcoholism. Several critics praised her ability to illuminate universal concerns through intimate memories. In "Say You Love Me," for instance, her drunken father's aggressive demand for her unconditional love evolves into a study of humanity's need for acceptance and reassurance. Similarly, "Buffalo"—in which Peacock harshly recollects waiting in bars while her father drank—becomes a condolence for the bartenders who "shrink / from any conversation to endure / the serving, serving, serving of disease." *Los Angeles Times Book Review* critic Ian Gregson noted, "Peacock is conspicuously courageous in the subjects she is willing to tackle. The [reason] she's mostly successful in doing so in *Take Heart* . . . is because she's discovered a technique that meticulously follows the labyrinthine twists and turns of these emotional tangles."

Peacock begins to move away from more formally structured verse in *Original Love*. In this work, as Frank Allen stated in *Library Journal,* she addresses "the boundaries between men and women, mother and daughter, and one's mind, body, and senses." A reviewer in *Publishers Weekly* also noted that Peacock uses "explicit eroticism" to explore "three loves—for lover, mother, self." Like her other works, *Original Love* directly and unrelentlessly examines such subjects as sexuality, desire, death, and human fallibility. Regarding Peacock's work as a whole, Allen observed, "the intelligence and music of her work, the belief in exploring consciousness with honesty, the sheer beauty of the language—all contribute to the 'pleasure of the text.' Because all the pain and joy of living are in [Peacock's] poetry, people will continue to turn to her poems."

BIOGRAPHICAL/CRITICAL SOURCES:

BOOKS

Contemporary Literary Criticism, Volume 60, Gale (Detroit), 1990.
Dictionary of Literary Biography, Volume 120: *American Poets since World War II,* Third Series, Gale, 1992.

PERIODICALS

Booklist, November 1, 1984, p. 30; March 15, 1995, p. 1302.
Boston Review, December, 1984, pp. 30-1.
Georgia Review, fall, 1984, p. 628; fall, 1989, p. 589.
Hudson Review, autumn, 1981, p. 427.
Library Journal, February 15, 1995, p. 159.
Los Angeles Times Book Review, August 20, 1989, p. 3; October 22, 1989, p. 16.
New Republic, July 17, 1989, pp. 31-4.
New York Times Book Review, December 2, 1984, pp. 54-5; October 22, 1989, p. 16.
Parnassus, spring, 1985, pp. 500-12.
Poetry, April, 1990, p. 38.

Publishers Weekly, July 13, 1984, p. 42; February 27, 1995, p. 98.
Virginia Quarterly Review, spring, 1985, p. 54.
Washington Post Book World, September 2, 1984, p. 6.

*   *   *

PICANO, Felice   1944-

PERSONAL: Born February 22, 1944, in New York, NY; son of Phillip (a grocer) and Ann (Del Santo) Picano. *Education:* Queens College of the City University of New York, B.A. (cum laude), 1964.

ADDRESSES: Home—95 Horatio St., #423, New York, NY 10014. *Agent*—Jane Berkey, Jane Rotrosen Agency, 226 East 32nd St., New York, NY 10016.

CAREER: New York City Department of Welfare, New York City, social worker, 1964-66; *Art Direction,* New York City, assistant editor, 1966-68; Doubleday Bookstore, New York City, assistant manager, 1969-70; freelance writer, 1970-72; Rizzoli's Bookstore, New York City, assistant manager and buyer, 1972-74; freelance writer, 1974—; founder and publisher of the Sea Horse Press Ltd., 1977—; cofounder and copublisher of the Gay Presses of New York, 1980—. Instructor of fiction writing classes, YMCA West Side Y Writers Voice Workshop, 1982—.

MEMBER: PEN, Writers Guild of America, Authors Guild, Triangle.

AWARDS, HONORS: Ernest Hemingway Award nomination; PEN Syndicated Short Fiction Award; Poetry Society of America Chapbook Award.

WRITINGS:

NOVELS

Smart as the Devil, Arbor House (New York City), 1975.
Eyes, Arbor House, 1976.
The Mesmerist, Delacorte (New York City), 1977.
The Lure, Delacorte, 1979.
Late in the Season, Delacorte, 1981.
House of Cards, Delacorte, 1984.

Ambidextrous: The Secret Lives of Children (memoir), Volume 1, Gay Presses of New York, 1985, published as *Ambidextrous: The Secret Lives of Children, A Memoir in the Form of a Novel,* New American Library (New York City), 1989.

Men Who Loved Me: A Memoir in the Form of a Novel, New American Library, 1989.

To the Seventh Power, Morrow (New York City), 1989.

Dryland's End, Masquerade Books (New York City), 1995.

Like People in History: A Gay American Epic, Viking (New York City), 1995.

OTHER

The Deformity Lover and Other Poems, Sea Horse Press (New York City), 1978.

(Editor) *A True Likeness: An Anthology of Lesbian and Gay Writing Today,* Sea Horse Press, 1980.

An Asian Minor: The True Story of Ganymede (novella), Sea Horse Press, 1981.

Slashed to Ribbons in Defense of Love and Other Stories, Gay Presses of New York (New York City), 1983.

Window Elegies (poetry), Close Grip Press, 1986.

Immortal (play with music; based on Picano's novella *An Asian Minor: The True Story of Ganymede*), produced Off-Off Broadway, 1986.

One o'Clock (one-act play), produced Off-Off Broadway, 1986.

(With Charles Silverstein) *The New Joy of Gay Sex,* HarperCollins (New York City), 1992.

Also author of the screenplay *Eyes* (based on his novel), 1986. Contributor to numerous anthologies. Contributor of articles, poems, stories, and reviews to periodicals, including *OUT, Mouth of the Dragon, Islander, Cumberland Review, Connecticut Poetry Review, Cream City Review,* and *Soho Weekly News.* Book editor, *New York Native,* 1980-83.

Several of Picano's works have been translated into French, Japanese, Spanish, and Portuguese.

SIDELIGHTS: Described as "a leader of the modern gay literary movement" by Howard E. Miller in *Library Journal,* Felice Picano has written a number of books of fiction and nonfiction about gay life in America. His *Like People in History: A Gay American Epic,* a panoramic novel spanning some forty years, is his most ambitious work.

Like People in History traces the lives of two gay cousins, Roger Sansarc and Alistair Dodge, from the 1960s to the 1990s. While following the two characters' respective careers in the arts and publishing in New York City, the novel presents a gay social history of the time. Such events as the Woodstock music festival of the 1960s, the Fire Island scene of the 1970s and the AIDS epidemic of 1980s Manhattan form the backdrop to the careers of the two successful cousins.

Although Miller calls *Like People in History* a "compelling novel" that "may well be the breakthrough gay-themed best seller of the decade," Kevin Allman in the *Washington Post Book World* describes the novel as "what old Hollywood used to term a 'weepie' and what modern readers will likely call overwrought, overwritten and overripe." Writing in *Booklist,* Charles Harmon admits that "the book doesn't work all that well as a serious chronicle of gay America," but finds nonetheless that "it succeeds as a story that doesn't take itself too seriously." Suzanne Berne in the *New York Times Book Review* writes that "the main appeal of the novel . . . is its irreverence, extending even to the horror of AIDS itself."

Picano describes his writing to *CA:* "In fiction I write about the possible rather than the actual, and so, I suppose, 'Romances' in Hawthorne's sense of the word, even with 'realistic' settings, characters, and actions. My novels, novellas, and short stories deal with ordinary individuals who are suddenly thrust into extraordinary situations and relationships which test their very existence. Unusual perceptions and abilities, extrasensory powers, and psychological aberrations become tools and weapons in conflicts of mental and emotional control. Previous behavioral patterns are inadequate for such situations and must be changed to enable evolved awareness and survival, or they destroy their possessor. Thus, perspective is of the utmost importance in my fiction, both for structure and meaning. I am dedicated to experimenting with new and old points of view, which seem to have progressed very little since the pioneering work of Henry James and James Joyce."

BIOGRAPHICAL/CRITICAL SOURCES:

BOOKS

Nelson, Emmanuel S., editor, *Contemporary Gay American Novelists: A Bio-bibliographical Critical Sourcebook,* Greenwood Press (Westport, CT), 1993.

PERIODICALS

Booklist, July, 1995, pp. 1860-1861.
Lambda Book Report, January, 1991, p. 40.
Library Journal, February 15, 1989, p. 178; November 1, 1989, p. 112; June 15, 1995, p. 96.
New York Times Book Review, December 2, 1979; July 16, 1995, p. 21.
Publishers Weekly, December 9, 1988, p. 46; September 22, 1989, p. 40.
Tribune Books (Chicago), March 5, 1989, p. 6; June 3, 1990, p. 5.
Village Voice, December 24, 1979.
Washington Post Book World, June 18, 1995, p. 6.*

* * *

PILEGGI, Nicholas   1933-

PERSONAL: Born February 22, 1933, in New York, NY; son of Nick (a shoestore owner) and Susan (Defaslo) Pileggi. *Education:* Attended Long Island University.

ADDRESSES: Agent—Sterling Lord, 660 Madison Ave., New York, NY 10021.

CAREER: Associated Press, New York City, reporter, 1956-68; *New York* (magazine), New York City, contributing editor, 1968—.

MEMBER: PEN, Players.

AWARDS, HONORS: Awards from New York State Bar Association and Detective Association; Golden Globe nomination for best screenplay and Academy Award nomination for best adapted screenplay, both 1995, for *Goodfellas.*

WRITINGS:

Blye, Private Eye (nonfiction), Playboy Press, 1976.
Wiseguy: Life in a Mafia Family (nonfiction), Simon & Schuster (New York City), 1985.
(With Martin Scorcese) *Goodfellas* (screenplay based on novel *Wiseguy: Life in a Mafia Family*), Faber (London), 1990.
Casino: Love and Honor in Las Vegas, Simon & Schuster, 1995.
(With Scorsese) *Casino* (screenplay based on novel *Casino: Love and Honor in Las Vegas*), 1995.

Contributor to periodicals, including *Esquire, Saturday Evening Post, New York Times,* and *Life.*

ADAPTATIONS: Wiseguy: Life in a Mafia Family was recorded by Simon & Schuster Audioworks, 1990; *Goodfellas,* was filmed in 1990, directed by Martin Scorsese, starring Robert De Niro, Ray Liotta, Joe Pesci, Paul Sorvino, and Lorraine Bracco; *Casino: Love and Honor in Las Vegas* was recorded by Simon & Schuster Audioworks, 1995; *Casino* was filmed in 1995, directed by Scorsese, starring De Niro, Pesci, and Sharon Stone.

SIDELIGHTS: A long-time crime reporter in New York City, Nicholas Pileggi has written several books about criminal life based on real people he has met. In *Blye, Private Eye,* Pileggi presents the story of a real-life private detective; *Wiseguy: Life in a Mafia Family* is the biography of a minor organized-crime figure who betrayed his associates; and *Casino: Love and Honor in Las Vegas* is a behind-the-scenes account of the mobsters and their role in Nevada's world of legalized gambling. Pileggi is, according to Joseph Barbato in *Publishers Weekly,* "an old-fashioned street reporter who still retains the enthusiasm that he first brought to his trade."

In his first book, *Blye, Private Eye,* Pileggi focuses on the work of real-life private detective Irwin Blye. Pileggi's aim is to debunk the aura of glamour surrounding Blye's profession created by the fictional exploits of such private-eye characters as Sam Spade and Philip Marlowe. Andrew C. J. Bergman points out in the *New York Times Book Review* that "slinky temptresses do not drop by [Blye's] office . . . and his life is not packed with, or even occasionally punctuated by adventure and carnage, libidinous or otherwise." Instead Pileggi relates that Blye is a family man who has far more frequent need of various legal forms than of guns. With the right papers, Blye can gather information about anyone who pays taxes, owns a car, or receives a telephone bill. His cases concern everything from compiling evidence to clear accused criminals to assembling facts for clients contemplating divorce, and he is often involved in taking depositions for attorneys. Though Pileggi convinced reviewers that detective work is not as exciting as it is often portrayed in fiction, many of them find *Blye, Private Eye* interesting. Bergman reports that "Pileggi is an alert observer and a deft writer, capable of creating large effects with small strokes," and concludes that the book is "a virtual primer on detection."

Pileggi's next book, *Wiseguy: Life in a Mafia Family,* explores the life of organized crime figure Henry Hill. In a series of phone conversations and meetings, Hill, a member of the U.S. government's Witness Protection Program who now lives under a newly fabricated identity, told Pileggi of his escapades under various crime bosses. In the words of Vincent Patrick, reviewing *Wiseguy* in the *New York Times Book Review,* "Pileggi molds Mr. Hill's life story into an absolutely engrossing book that rings with authenticity." Hill began working at the age of eleven for Paul Vario, allegedly a member of the Lucchese crime family, and became involved in illegal gambling, arson, and counterfeiting. He later became acquainted with James (Jimmy the Gent) Burke, and claims to have given Burke the tip that helped him plan the 1978 six-million-dollar robbery of the Lufthansa airline. Hill ended up testifying against Burke, who contracted ten murders that followed the theft because he did not want to share the takings. For protection, Hill was given a new identity by the government and allowed to start a new life, but according to Pileggi, Hill misses his life as a criminal. As Walter Clemons concludes in *Newsweek,* "One believes the book because Henry Hill is unrepentant. Pileggi has done a terrific job of reporting, without moralizing."

In *Casino: Love and Honor in Las Vegas,* Pileggi tells the story of several criminal figures in Las Vegas, who, because of their own greed and rivalry, allowed control of the gambling casinos to slip away from the mob. Central to the story are Frank (Lefty) Rosenthal and Tony Spilotro, two Chicago gangsters sent to Las Vegas in the 1960s to oversee the mob's casinos, skim money and distribute it among mob leaders, and run the daily operations. All went well until Spilotro began an affair with Rosenthal's young wife; the resulting betrayals led to government investigations, a series of arrests, and the end of mob domination in Las Vegas casinos. Dave Hickey writes in the *Los Angeles Times Book Review* that "in getting Las Vegas right, Pileggi's *Casino* ends up feeling a bit like a casino itself—a good, scary ride and a generous spectacle." "Pileggi," writes Robert Lacey in the *New York Times Book Review,* "captured the spirit of the outlaw that is the bedrock of the criminal netherworld—the romance, the greed, the deceit, the grandiosity, the delight in inflicting pain and death on your fellow human beings—in his 1986 book *Wiseguy,* and he has done it again in *Casino.*"

BIOGRAPHICAL/CRITICAL SOURCES:

PERIODICALS

Armchair Detective, spring, 1991, p. 245.
Atlantic, June, 1986, p. 84.
Los Angeles Times, March 22, 1991, pp. F10, F12.
Los Angeles Times Book Review, April 6, 1986, p. 4; October 22, 1995, pp. 4, 10.
National Review, August 15, 1986, p. 53.
New Republic, October 12, 1987, p. 33.
Newsweek, February 10, 1986, p. 72.
New Yorker, February 17, 1986, p. 104.
New York Review of Books, May 8, 1986, p. 43.
New York Times, January 16, 1986, p. 17; September 19, 1990, p. C11.
New York Times Book Review, February 27, 1977; January 26, 1986, p. 7; June 21, 1987, p. 34; October 8, 1995, p. 28.
Publishers Weekly, February 7, 1986, pp. 56-57; August 28, 1995, p. 94.
Quill and Quire, April, 1986, p. 41.
Time, March 28, 1977; March 3, 1986, p. 75.
Tribune Books (Chicago), March 1, 1987, p. 8.
USA Today, February 14, 1986, p. D5; July 26, 1994, p. D3.
Wall Street Journal, February 10, 1986, p. 18.
Washington Post Book World, January 19, 1986.*

*   *   *

PINION, F(rancis) B(ertram)   1908-

PERSONAL: Born December 4, 1908, in Glinton, Peterborough, England; married Marjorie Fidler, August, 1935; children: Andrew, Catherine. *Education:* Cambridge University, B.A., 1930, M.A., 1936; Oxford University, diploma in education, 1944.

ADDRESSES: Home—65 Ranmoor Crescent, Sheffield S10 3GW, England.

CAREER: Headmaster of a grammar school in England, 1950-61; University of Sheffield, Sheffield, England, lecturer, 1961-68, senior lecturer, 1968-73, reader in English studies, 1973-74, sub-dean of Faculty of Arts, 1965-74. Visiting lecturer in English, University of Michigan, 1964-65. Lecturer at universities in the United States, Canada, and Norway. Active in promoting work of the American Field Service in Yorkshire and East Midlands region, and former chair of the committee for the selection of British students placed in America.

MEMBER: Victorian Studies Association of Western Canada, Thomas Hardy Society (honorary vice president), George Eliot Fellowship (honorary vice president).

AWARDS, HONORS: Litt.D. from Cambridge University, 1981; Mid-American State Universities Distinguished Foreign Scholar, 1981-82.

WRITINGS:

Educational Values in the Age of Technology, Pergamon (Elmsford, NY), 1964.
(Author of critical commentary) Thomas Hardy, *The Mayor of Casterbridge,* Macmillan (New York City), 1966.
A Hardy Companion, Macmillan, 1968.
A Jane Austen Companion, Macmillan, 1973.
A Bronte Companion, Macmillan, 1975.
A Commentary on the Poems of Thomas Hardy, Macmillan, 1976.
Thomas Hardy: Art and Thought, Macmillan, 1977.
A D. H. Lawrence Companion, Macmillan, 1978.
A George Eliot Companion, Macmillan, 1981.
A Wordsworth Companion, Macmillan, 1983.
A Tennyson Companion, Macmillan, 1984.
A T. S. Eliot Companion, Macmillan, 1986.
A Wordsworth Chronology, Macmillan, 1988.
A Thomas Hardy Dictionary, Macmillan, 1989.
A Tennyson Chronology, Macmillan, 1990.
Thomas Hardy: His Life and Friends, Macmillan, 1992.
A Keats Chronology, Macmillan, 1992.

Contributor to *Thomas Hardy Annual,* 1986, and to professional journals.

EDITOR

Robert Browning, *The Ring and the Book* (abridged edition), Macmillan, 1957.
A Selection of Shelley's Poetry, Macmillan, 1958.
Thomas Hardy, *Tess of the d'Urbervilles,* Macmillan, 1959.
A Wordsworth Selection, Macmillan, 1963.
Browning, *Men and Women,* Macmillan, 1963.
A Lamb Selection, Macmillan, 1965.
Browning, *Dramatis Personae,* Collins, 1969.
(With Evelyn Hardy) *One Rare Fair Woman,* Macmillan, 1972.

(And contributor) *Thomas Hardy and the Modern World,* Thomas Hardy Society, 1974.
Hardy, *The Mayor of Casterbridge,* Macmillan, 1975.
Hardy, *The Woodlanders,* Macmillan, 1975.
Hardy, *Two on a Tower,* Macmillan, 1975.
(And contributor) *Budmouth Essays on Thomas Hardy,* Thomas Hardy Society, 1976.
A George Eliot Miscellany, Macmillan, 1982.
(With wife, Marjorie Pinion) *The Collected Sonnets of Charles (Tennyson) Turner,* Macmillan, 1988.

Also editor of additional selections of poetry for school use, published between 1941-64. Editor, *Thomas Hardy Society Review,* 1975-84.

*   *   *

PONDER, Patricia
    See MAXWELL, Patricia

*   *   *

PRADO, C(arlos) G(onzalez)   **1937-**

PERSONAL: Born June 19, 1937, in Guatemala City, Guatemala; son of Carlos Gonzalez (an attorney) and Concha Prado; married Catherine Buchanan, August 26, 1962. *Education:* University of California, Berkeley, B.A. (with honors), 1961, M.A., 1965; Queen's University, Kingston, Ontario, Ph.D., 1970.

ADDRESSES: Home—P.O. Box 105, Kingston, Ontario, Canada K7L 4V6. *Office*—Department of Philosophy, Queen's University, Kingston, Ontario, Canada   K7L   3N6.   *E-mail*—pradocg@post. queensu.ca.

CAREER: Chaminade University, Honolulu, HI, instructor in philosophy, 1965-66; Queen's University, Kingston, Ontario, lecturer, 1968-70, assistant professor, 1970-75, associate professor, 1975-83, professor of philosophy, 1983—. Visiting fellow at Princeton University, 1981-82, 1988-89; lecturer at colleges and universities.

WRITINGS:

Illusions of Faith: A Critique of Noncredal Religion, Kendall/Hunt (Dubuque, IA), 1980.

Making Believe: Philosophical Reflections on Fiction, Greenwood Press (Westport, CT), 1984.

Rethinking How We Age, Greenwood Press, 1986.

The Limits of Pragmatism, Humanities (Atlantic Highlands, NJ), 1987.

The Last Choice: Preemptive Suicide in Advanced Age, Greenwood Press, 1990.

Descartes and Foucault, University of Ottawa Press, 1992.

Starting with Foucault: An Introduction to Genealogy, Westview (Boulder, CO), 1995.

OTHER

Also contributor to *The Challenge of Religion Today,* edited by John King-Farlow, Neale Watson (New York City), 1976. Contributor of about thirty-five articles and reviews to philosophy journals. Member of board of referees of *Dialogue,* 1983.

WORK IN PROGRESS: An introduction to philosophy.

*   *   *

PRINCE, Alison (Mary)   1931-

PERSONAL: Born March 26, 1931, in Beckenham, Kent, England; daughter of Charles (a bank official) and Louise (David) Prince; married Goronwy Siriol Parry (a teacher), December 26, 1957 (separated); children: Samantha, Andrew, Benjamin. *Education:* Slade School of Fine Art, London, diploma in fine art, 1952; Goldsmiths' College, London, art teachers' certificate 1954. *Politics:* Green. *Religion:* Agnostic. *Avocational interests:* Films, music, art, children, schools, animals.

ADDRESSES: Home—Burnfoot House, Whiting Bay, Isle of Arran KA27 8QL, Scotland.

CAREER: Author and illustrator. Elliott Comprehensive School, London, England, head of art department, 1954-58; adult education art teacher in Bromley, Kent, England, beginning 1960; Jordanhill College of Education, Glasgow, Scotland, fellow in creative writing, 1988.

MEMBER: International PEN, Society of Authors, Royal Society of Painter-Etchers and Engravers.

AWARDS, HONORS: Best books for young adults citation, American Library Association, 1980, for *The Turkey's Nest.*

WRITINGS:

SELF-ILLUSTRATED CHILDREN'S BOOKS

The House on the Common, Methuen (London), 1969, Farrar, Straus (New York City), 1970.

The Red Alfa, Methuen, 1971, published as *The Red Jaguar,* Atheneum (New York City), 1972.

(With Jane Hickson) *Whosaurus? Dinosaurus!* (nonfiction), Studio Vista (London), 1975.

Who Wants Pets?, Methuen, 1980.

The Type One Super Robot, Deutsch (London), 1986, Four Winds Press (New York City), 1988.

How's Business, Deutsch, 1987, Four Winds Press, 1988.

The Blue Moon Day, Deutsch, 1988.

CHILDREN'S FICTION

Joe and the Horse, and Other Short Stories about Joe from "Watch with Mother," British Broadcasting Corp. (London), 1969.

(With Joan Hickson) *Joe and the Nursery School,* British Broadcasting Corp., 1972.

(With Hickson) *Joe Moves House,* British Broadcasting Corp., 1972.

(With Chris Connor) *Ben's Fish,* illustrated by Connor, Benn (London), 1972.

The Doubting Kind, Methuen, 1975, Morrow (New York City), 1977, published in two volumes as *A Friend in Need* and *All Who Love Us,* Macmillan (New York City), 1977.

The Night I Sold My Boots (young adult), Heinemann (London), 1979.

The Turkey's Nest, Methuen, 1979, Morrow, 1980, published as *Willow Farm,* Ace Books (New York City), 1980.

Haunted Children (stories), illustrated by Michael Bragg, Methuen, 1982.

The Sinister Airfield, illustrated by Edward Mortelmans, Methuen, 1982, Morrow, 1983.

Goodbye Summer, Methuen, 1983.

Night Landings, illustrated by Mortelmans, Methuen, 1983, Morrow, 1984.

The Ghost Within (stories), Methuen, 1984.

The Others, Methuen, 1984.

Scramble!, illustrated by Anne Knight, Methuen, 1984.

A Job for Merv, illustrated by David Higham, Deutsch, 1986.

Nick's October, Methuen, 1986.
A Haunting Refrain (stories), Methuen, 1988.
A Dog Called You, Macmillan, 1993.
Merv on the Road, Young Piper, 1993.
The Sherwood Hero, Macmillan, 1995.

"MILL GREEN" SERIES

Mill Green on Fire, Armada (New York City), 1982.
Mill Green on Stage, Armada, 1982.
A Spy at Mill Green, Armada, 1983.
Hands Off, Mill Green!, Armada, 1984.
Rock On, Mill Green, Armada, 1985.

ILLUSTRATOR

(With Samantha Parry) Audrey Coppard, *Don't Panic!,* Heinemann, 1975.
Audrey Coppard, *Keeping Time,* Heinemann, 1976.
Coppard, *Get Well Soon,* Heinemann, 1978.
Jane Allen and Mary Danby, *Hello to Ponies,* Heinemann, 1979.
Allen and Danby, *Hello to Riding,* Heinemann, 1980.

Also illustrator of *Let's Explore Mathematics* and *Jessica on Her Own.*

OTHER

The Joe Annual, Polystyle Publications, 1968-71.
The Good Pets Guide, Armada, 1981.
(Self-illustrated) *The Necessary Goat* (essays), Taranis, 1992.
(Editor with Cicely Gill) *A Book of Arran Poetry,* illustrated by Saji Gill, Arran Theatre and Arts Trust, 1993.
On Arran, Argyll Publications, 1994.
Kenneth Grahame: An Innocent in the Wild Wood, Allison & Busby (London), 1994.
Having Been in the City (poems), Taranis, 1994.
The Witching Tree (adult novel), Allison & Busby, 1996.

Also author of television plays for children, including *Joe* series, 1968-71; *War Stories,* 1970 (part of *Jackanory* series); *Trumpton,* 1970; and scripts for *Watch with Mother* series. Author of adult radio play, *Ellie Bagg's Account,* 1984. Author of column "On the Green," *Arran Banner;* contributor to *Times Educational Supplement.*

WORK IN PROGRESS: A biography of Hans Christian Andersen; a second adult novel.

SIDELIGHTS: In over thirty children's books that range from picture stories to young adult novels, Alison Prince has demonstrated that she is "a writer of great versatility," according to *Twentieth-Century Children's Writers* contributor Valerie Bierman. Since the 1969 publication of her first book, the first of a series of stories also produced on television, Prince has written mysteries, science fiction, ghost stories, historical fiction, school stories, and contemporary "problem" novels; she has even illustrated several of her works. Also the author of adult works, including a newspaper column and a biography of *The Wind in the Willows* creator Kenneth Grahame, Prince once explained: "Writing for me is something which happens all the time."

In one of her earliest works, *The House on the Common,* Prince recreates the wartime England of her childhood. The year is 1943, and young Jane and Derek are convinced that their new neighbors, an elderly couple who speak German, are potential enemy spies who need to be watched. The two learn a lesson about jumping to conclusions when they embarrass themselves during a nighttime "patrol" and discover the Liepmanns are Jewish refugees. A *Kirkus Reviews* critic praises the depth of Prince's portrayal of the time, noting that within "the facade of a conventional mystery . . . [and] family story is the long and the short of people in wartime."

The author returned to the World War II era for a literary experiment in which she collaborated with twenty-one schoolchildren in developing the plot and characters for a novel. *How's Business* takes place in the Lincolnshire countryside, where young Howard Grainger—who goes by the name How—has left his friends and successful trading business in London to live with an aunt and uncle during the war. An outsider because he is an evacuee, How's only friend is Anna, who is also an outcast because of her German background. When his mother stops sending him letters, How returns to London, where he discovers his home has been destroyed by bombs and his mother has been hospitalized. *Bulletin of the Center for Children's Books* critic Zena Sutherland finds the "all-problems-solved" ending too unrealistic, but notes that "the period details, wartime atmosphere, and writing style are effective" and How's return to London is "exciting and credible." Louise L. Sherman likewise observes in *School Library Journal* that "Prince excels in recreating the historical period," and adds that the characters, even the minor ones, "are convincing and well-drawn."

While Prince often includes some type of puzzle in her books—such as the background of the Liepmanns in *The House on the Common* or the identity of a button thief in *The Red Jaguar*—she has also written pure mystery stories filled with suspense. In *The Sinister Airfield,* for instance, Harrie, her brother Ian, and their new friend Neil are exploring the woods near a reputedly "haunted" airport when they discover a dead body that disappears before they can return with the police. The children's persistence in investigating the airfield leads them to a gang of rustlers, and during an adventurous night chase the criminals are caught. While "less ambitious" than Prince's other novels, a *Kirkus Reviews* writer remarks that *The Sinister Airfield* is "a straightforward mystery with adeptly tuned suspense and more than the usual texture." *School Library Journal* writer Drew Stevenson similarly hails the story as "a good solid mystery with a touch of the macabre for spice and a wild climax."

The three friends return in *Night Landings* and "have lost none of their grit" in this story of smugglers and kidnapping, Stevenson observes. This time mysterious nighttime activity at the airstrip alerts Harrie, and when she discovers a boy hiding in a nearby barn the young sleuths have another riddle to solve. "This has just as much action as the first book, but is better structured," Sutherland notes in the *Bulletin of the Center for Children's Books,* adding praise for the book's "firmly drawn" characters and "brisk" pace. As Stevenson concludes, the ending "is as wild as anyone could want," and *Night Landings* provides readers with "good fun all the way around."

Suspense of a higher order is found in several of Prince's collections of ghost stories—"a genre in which Prince has had considerable success," according to Bierman. In the nine stories of *Haunted Children,* for example, ghosts ranging from the friendly to the sinister confront ordinary children; by using a "rather low-keyed style," Margery Fisher remarks in *Growing Point,* Prince "throws into relief the sensational, supernatural moments rising from everyday circumstances." The eight stories of *The Ghost Within* all feature a lonely child whose supernatural encounter triggers, or is triggered by, an internal conflict; the stories again demonstrate the author's "knack of being able to juxtapose convincingly the banal and the bizarre," according to *School Librarian* contributor Robert Dunbar. The tales in *A Haunting Refrain* deal with voyages through time and the mixture of past and present. While Prince's use of detail and narrative skill create a believable present,

D. A. Young writes in *Junior Bookshelf,* "she manipulates the transition into the past so smoothly that it seems the most natural thing in the world." Whatever the degree of horror she uses, the hallmark of Prince's ghost stories is their believability. As A. Thatcher concludes in a *Junior Bookshelf* review of *Haunted Children,* "Alison Prince is a master of suspense writing, able to create out of simple everyday occurrences a menacing atmosphere in which anything can happen."

Less menacing but just as thoughtful is Prince's science fiction novel *The Others,* which is set in a post-nuclear society where people's bodies are genetically engineered to fit their occupations, and their minds are given implants to prevent unsocial behavior. Ergo, whose thumb and forefinger have been given sharp edges for gardening, discovers and joins an underground movement that teaches him about forbidden things like books and feelings. As Ergo assumes the dangerous life of a dissenter, he learns more about his restrictive society; nevertheless, "human strengths and weaknesses play the major part in keeping the story moving," Young notes in *Junior Bookshelf.* The critic praises the author for "fleshing out" her fictional society, as well as for creating characters that are "drawn in depth." A completely different approach to science fiction distinguishes *The Type One Super Robot,* a humorous story about a housekeeping robot that has its hands full babysitting a young boy. As young Humbert tests Manders's skills with unusual activities such as kite-building, the pair's "comic antics should keep readers chuckling," a *Kirkus Reviews* critic declares, adding that "Manders has unusual charm, even for a robot."

Not all of Prince's books contain elements of adventure or the supernatural, however. Her "Mill Green" series follows the amusing incidents and everyday happenings at a traditional British school. Like the very popular "Grange Hill" books, another British series about school life, Prince's cycle is "authentic in its hierarchies and power struggles, and . . . alive and alert in style," Fisher notes in a *Growing Point* review of *Mill Green on Fire.* Some of the author's picture books also deal with commonplace experiences. *Merv on the Road,* for instance, shows a handyman and his employer both learning to drive a car, with hilarious complications. Jean Needham remarks in *School Librarian* that Prince's pictures "ably demonstrate the eccentricities of the main characters" in this "funny" book.

It is Prince's young adult novels, however, that "are perhaps the most accurately observed," Bierman claims, with "language, sexuality, and unconventional lifestyles [that] are accurately and perceptively described." In addition, the critic relates, Prince's "dialogue is honest, fresh, and often humorous, and controversial subjects such as pregnancy are handled in a sympathetic and straightforward manner." *The Doubting Kind,* for instance, follows two fifteen-year-olds through a particularly difficult week in their lives. Fanny has a crush on the leader of her theater group, but he has feelings for one of her teachers instead; Fanny's friend Bobbie has just lost her father in a car accident and has run off to a religious cult to avoid dealing with her alcoholic mother. While Sutherland, writing in the *Bulletin of the Center for Children's Books,* faults the book for a "lack of a strong story line," she nevertheless observes that readers will appreciate the true-to-life characters and writing that is "casual and brisk, sophisticated in its candor." In taking her characters through the turmoil of adolescence, Prince shows "a good deal of understanding" of teenage life, Graham Hammond says in *Children's Literature in Education,* and examines her themes "with wit, pace, insight, and responsibility." Best of all, the critic concludes, "Prince pays her readers the compliment of showing rather than preaching, of looking at a question all round and not rushing into judgments."

In 1979 Prince published both *The Night I Sold My Boots,* a romance told from the boy's point of view, and *The Turkey's Nest,* a story of a teen's unexpected pregnancy. In the former, Ken's story of how he moves from London to the country and learns to adjust with the help of a free-spirited older girl is "right on the wavelength of mid-teenage readers," Thatcher states in *Junior Bookshelf.* In *The Turkey's Nest,* Kate also makes a journey to the country; there she plans to have her baby, although her boyfriend, who has reconciled with his dying wife, wants Kate to have an abortion. While the resolution to Kate's problems is "a bit pat," Sutherland remarks in recommending the book, Prince's writing "is smooth, the characters sturdy if a bit stock, and the pace even." *Horn Book* critic Ethel L. Heins likewise finds the novel's ending "somewhat too neat," but praises the "nicely individualized" characters and the "cool objectivity that matches the unusual, dispassionate tone of the book."

Prince wrote two novels that explore the turbulent relationship of a pair of working-class teens, one from each individual's point of view. In *Goodbye*

Summer, Sasha is working at her first job—a dead-end position as a clerk in a shoe shop—when she meets Nick, a mechanic who is a bit of a bad boy. As her attachment to Nick develops, she also gains insight into her parents' lives and improves her relationship with them as well. While *Times Literary Supplement* writer Nicholas Tucker calls Prince "a good writer . . . [whose] sentences have an authority that normally makes it easy for readers to sit back and let the story take over," he asserts that Nick's powerful attraction for someone "so clearly his superior" weakens the believability of the story line. *Junior Bookshelf* critic R. Baines, on the other hand, notes that for the most part *Goodbye Summer* "is a realistic and interesting novel." Nick's side of the story is explored in *Nick's October:* his strained relationship with his parents; his search for a meaningful job; and his fear of being caught in a routine. Nick's tale of his feelings of rebellion is "distinguished from others . . . by its affectionate and humorous realism," Caroline Heaton comments in *British Book News.* Taken together, the books reveal "the uncertainty and insecurity of young people and explore their fears with friends and parents," Bierman concludes. "They also portray the pressures of parental manipulation—all refreshingly realistic."

Prince once explained how she develops her books: "Sitting down at a typewriter is just the last stage of a process which has usually been going on for weeks, or often months. The tantalizing beginnings of stories are everywhere; in a turn of phrase, a funny anecdote, a casual incident. Yet none of these things are in themselves a story, any more than flour and eggs and milk are pancakes. They need rearranging and altering before they start to form an interesting plot, and even after that there is a lot of careful development to do before the characters and the things which happen to them are really convincing.

"A story won't always 'come' through aggressive hard work. When the raw materials are all there, it needs to be shut away in the mysterious subconscious workings of the mind, rather as an egg starts to live in the dark warmth under a hen. Periodically one can, so to speak, 'take it out' and see how it is getting on. When it is ready to enter the 'finished writing' stage then the job seems fascinating and not difficult. If it is mind-bafflingly hard, then it's not ready.

"Running a small farm fits in well with writing. The routine work of caring for animals gives me exercise and fresh air as well as constant interest and, most importantly, it does not interfere with the mental process of writing. In fact, many of the knottiest plot problems seem to solve themselves while I am peacefully milking my Jersey cow!"

BIOGRAPHICAL/CRITICAL SOURCES:

BOOKS

Micklethwait, Lucy, and Brigid Peppin, *Book Illustrators of the Twentieth Century,* Arco (New York City), 1984.
Twentieth-Century Children's Writers, 4th edition, St. James Press (Detroit), 1995.

PERIODICALS

Books for Keeps, May, 1986, p. 22.
British Book News, March, 1987, p. 33.
Bulletin of the Center for Children's Books, April, 1978, p. 133; June, 1980, p. 199; May, 1983, p. 175; May, 1984, pp. 172-73; June, 1988, p. 215; October, 1988, pp. 50-51.
Children's Literature in Education, summer, 1982, pp. 61-62.
Growing Point, September, 1982, p. 3946; November, 1982, p. 3986.
Horn Book, June, 1980, p. 308.
Junior Bookshelf, June, 1980, p. 146; February, 1983, p. 47; June, 1984, p. 149; February, 1985, p. 45; October, 1986, p. 193; April, 1987, pp. 98-99; December, 1988, pp. 309-10.
Kirkus Reviews, May 1, 1970, p. 508; October 15, 1972, p. 1191; February 15, 1983, p. 185; March 15, 1988, p. 457.
Library Journal, November 15, 1972, p. 3808.
School Librarian, March, 1984, p. 74; June, 1985, p. 163; August, 1993, p. 111.
School Library Journal, December, 1977, p. 55; May, 1983, p. 93; May, 1984, p. 102; September, 1988, p. 185.
Times Literary Supplement, December 3, 1971, p. 1517; November 25, 1983.
Voice of Youth Advocates, December, 1988, p. 241.

*   *   *

PROCHNAU, William W.   1937-

PERSONAL: Surname is pronounced *Prock*-now; born August 9, 1937, in Everett, WA; son of Emil W. (in business) and Florence (Foley) Prochnau; married Lani Gruger (a nurse), January 7, 1961 (divorced, 1978); children: Monica, Anna, Jennifer. *Education:* Attended Everett Junior College and Seattle University.

ADDRESSES: Home—2525 Minor E., Seattle, WA 98102. *Office*—*Post-Intelligencer,* Sixth and Wall Sts., Seattle, WA 98111.

CAREER: Everett Daily Herald, Everett, WA, reporter, 1955-56; *Anchorage Daily News,* Anchorage, AK, sports editor, 1957; *Seattle Times,* Seattle, WA, sports writer, 1958-62, Washington correspondent, 1963-73; manager of reelection campaign of Senator Warren G. Magnuson, 1974; freelance writer, 1975; *Bellevue Daily Journal-American,* Bellevue, WA, editor, 1975-76; *Post-Intelligencer,* Seattle, special projects reporter, beginning 1977; *Washington Post,* Washington, DC, former national affairs reporter.

MEMBER: National Press Club.

AWARDS, HONORS: National Headliners Award for best domestic reporting of the first landing on the moon, 1969.

WRITINGS:

(With Richard W. Larsen) *A Certain Democrat: Senator Henry M. Jackson,* Prentice-Hall (Englewood Cliffs, NJ), 1972.
Trinity's Child, Putnam (New York City), 1983.
Once Upon a Distant War: Young War Correspondents and the Early Vietnam Battles, Times Books (New York City), 1995.

Author of several documentary films. Contributor to magazines.

SIDELIGHTS: An experienced journalist who has covered national and foreign news for over thirty years, William W. Prochnau has written of war in two very different books. In *Trinity's Child* he tells of a fictional nuclear war of the near future, while in *Once Upon a Distant War: Young War Correspondents and the Early Vietnam Battles,* he analyzes the early coverage of the Vietnam War and the conflict that developed between some of the nation's top journalists and the military establishment over how the war was being conducted.

In the novel *Trinity's Child,* Prochnau "describes the first fifteen hours of World War III," as Martin Morse Wooster explains in *Fantasy Review.* Concerned not with the science-fictional aftermath of such a war, as are many writers who speculate about future world conflict, Prochnau examines instead the events just after the war begins, when both sides are trying desperately to end the destruction while there is still time. Although finding fault with Prochnau's fictional talent, Gregg Easterbrook in the *New Republic* finds that "the book contains a thorough and well-written explanation of how the strategic nuclear system works" and is "strong on analysis of important factual matters."

Prochnau turns his attention from imaginary to actual war in *Once Upon a Distant War*, a study of how the early stages of the Vietnam War were covered by the nation's leading war correspondents. Specifically, Prochnau outlines how an antagonism developed between the reporters covering the war and the military officials conducting operations. This antagonism developed during a two-year period in the early 1960s when several reporters for the *New York Times*, United Press and Associated Press began to reveal that American military involvement in Vietnam was more than was being officially reported by the Kennedy Administration. Prochnau's story of this conflict is narrated, according to Richard Eder in the *Los Angeles Times Book Review*, "with vivid and exciting detail," while his portrayal of the journalists themselves is the work of a "sensitive reporter and thoughtful analyst." According to a critic for *Publishers Weekly*, Prochnau's vivid account explains "how a handful of young reporters became the vanguard of the antiwar movement."

BIOGRAPHICAL/CRITICAL SOURCES:

PERIODICALS

Best Sellers, January, 1984, p. 362.
Booklist, September 1, 1983, p. 32.
Fantasy Review, August, 1984, p. 21.
Kirkus Reviews, August 15, 1983, p. 906.
Library Journal, September 15, 1983, p. 1809.
Los Angeles Times Book Review, November 12, 1995, pp. 3, 6.
New Pages, fall, 1984, p. 11.
New Republic, August 6, 1984, pp. 40-42.
New York Times Book Review, November 19, 1995, p. 11.
Publishers Weekly, August 26, 1983, p. 369; October 9, 1995, pp. 69-70.*

QUIRK, Lawrence J.   1923-

PERSONAL: Born September 9, 1923, in Lynn, MA; son of Andrew Lawrence and Margaret Louise (Connery) Quirk. *Education:* Suffolk University, B.A. (cum laude), 1949; graduate study at Boston University, 1949-50.

ADDRESSES: Home—74 Charles St., New York, NY 10014.

CAREER: Writer for film magazines, and former editor of *Screen Life, Screen Parade, Screen Stars, Movie World,* and *Hollywood Stars;* editor and publisher, *Quirk's Reviews,* 1972—. Has also worked for *Lynn Item,* Lynn, MA, *Boston Record-American,* Boston, MA, *New York World-Telegram and Sun,* and as film critic for *Motion Picture Herald, Motion Picture Daily,* and other periodicals. *Military service:* U.S. Army, 1950-53; public relations assignments, 1951-53; became sergeant.

AWARDS, HONORS: Walt Whitman Award, 1979, for *Some Lovely Image.*

WRITINGS:

Robert Francis Kennedy, Holloway (Los Angeles), 1968.
The Films of Joan Crawford, Citadel (Secaucus, NJ), 1968.
The Films and Career of Ingrid Bergman, Citadel, 1970, revised edition published as *The Complete Films of Ingrid Bergman*, 1989.
The Films of Paul Newman, Citadel, 1971, revised edition, 1981.
The Films of Fredric March, Citadel, 1971.
The Films of William Holden, Citadel, 1973.
The Great Romantic Films, Citadel, 1974.
The Films of Robert Taylor, Citadel, 1975.
Some Lovely Image (novel), Quirk Publishing, 1976.
The Films of Ronald Colman, Citadel, 1977.
The Films of Warren Beatty, Citadel, 1979.
The Films of Myrna Loy, Citadel, 1980.
The Films of Gloria Swanson, Citadel, 1984.
Claudette Colbert: An Illustrated Biography, Crown (New York City), 1985.
Bette Davis: Her Films and Career, revised edition, Citadel, 1985.
Lauren Bacall: Her Films and Career, Citadel, 1986.
The Complete Films of William Powell, Citadel, 1986.
Jane Wyman: The Actress and the Woman, Norton (New York City), 1986.

Margaret Sullavan: Child of Fate, St. Martin's (New York City), 1987.

Norma: The Story of Norma Shearer, St. Martin's, 1988.

Fasten Your Seat Belts: The Passionate Life of Bette Davis, William Morrow, 1990.

Totally Uninhibited: The Life and Wild Times of Cher, William Morrow, 1991.

The Great War Films, Citadel, 1994.

Also author of introduction, *Anthology of Photoplay Magazine, 1928-1940,* Dover, 1971. Contributor to *Variety, Photoplay, Modern Screen, New York Times, Cosmopolitan, Films in Review,* and *Theatre.*

WORK IN PROGRESS: The Kennedys in Hollywood; a definitive biography of James Stewart; a biography of James R. Quirk.

SIDELIGHTS: One of the country's leading film authorities, Lawrence J. Quirk is the nephew of James R. Quirk, founder of *Photoplay* and editor and publisher of the magazine during its glory days of the 1920s. Lawrence J. Quirk established the James R. Quirk Awards in 1973, for meritorious achievements in film-related fields. The award has been given to over twenty-two people, including Lillian Gish, Joan Crawford, and Blanche Sweet.

BIOGRAPHICAL/CRITICAL SOURCES:

PERIODICALS

Booklist, January 1, 1990, p. 868.
Choice, September, 1990, p. 127.
Films in Review, June, 1990, p. 380.
Film Quarterly, summer, 1990, p. 25.
Kirkus Reviews, December 1, 1989, p. 1733.
Los Angeles Times, August 1, 1988.
New York Times Book Review, March 11, 1990, p. 19.

R

RAMA
See LENZ, Frederick

* * *

RATCLIFFE, F(rederick) W(illiam)   1927-

PERSONAL: Born May 28, 1927; son of Sydney and Dora (Smith) Ratcliffe; married Joyce Brierley (a college lecturer), August 20, 1952; children: Richard George, Helen Laura Ratcliffe Wareham, Robert John. *Education:* Victoria University of Manchester, B.A. (with honors), 1951, M.A., 1952; Ph.D., 1954; Cambridge University, M.A., 1980. *Religion:* Church of England.

*ADDRESSES: Home—*Ridge House, Rickinghall Superior, Diss, Norfolk, IP22 1DY, England. *Office—* The Parker Library, Corpus Christi College, Cambridge, CB2 1RH, England.

CAREER: Victoria University of Manchester, Manchester, England, began as assistant cataloger at university library, became cataloger, 1954-62; University of Glasgow, Glasgow, Scotland, sub-librarian, 1962-63; University of Newcastle upon Tyne, Newcastle upon Tyne, England, deputy librarian, 1963-65; Victoria University of Manchester, university librarian, 1965-80, director of John Rylands University Library, 1972-80, honorary lecturer in historical bibliography, 1970-80; Cambridge University, Cambridge, England, university librarian and fellow of Corpus Christi College, 1980-94, university librarian emeritus and life fellow of Corpus Christi College, 1994—, Parker Librarian of Corpus Christi College, 1995—. Visiting professor at Loughborough University of Technology, 1981-86. Chair of advisory committee of National Preservation Office, British Library, 1984-94, and Library Committee, Wellcome Institute for the History of Medicine, 1989-94; trustee, St. Deiniol's Library, Hawarden, England, 1975—, Woodard Corporation, 1982—, and Cambridge Foundation, 1989-94. Justice of the peace of Stockport, 1972-80, and Cambridge, 1981. *Military service:* British Army, North Staffordshire Regiment, 1945-48.

MEMBER: Bibliographical Society, Royal Society for the Encouragement of the Arts, Magistrates' Association, Library Association, Cambridge Society.

AWARDS, HONORS: Encomienda de la Order del Merto Civil (Spain), 1988; decorated Commander of the British Empire, 1994.

WRITINGS:

The Psalm Translation of Heinrich von Muegeln, John Rylands University Library, Victoria University of Manchester (Manchester, England), 1961.
(With D. Patterson) *Preservation Policies and Conservation in British Libraries: Report of the Cambridge University Library Conservation Project,* British Library (London), 1984.

Contributor to library, German, and literary journals.

Some of Ratcliffe's works have been translated into German.

WORK IN PROGRESS: Research on English academic librarianship since 1851.

BIOGRAPHICAL/CRITICAL SOURCES:

PERIODICALS

Times Literary Supplement, October 5, 1984.

* * *

RAYNER, Mary   1933-

PERSONAL: Born December 30, 1933, in Mandalay, Burma; daughter of A. H. and Yoma Grigson; married E. H. Rayner, 1960 (divorced, 1982); married Adrian Hawksley, 1985; children: Sarah, William, Benjamin. *Education:* University of St. Andrews, M.A. (second class honors), 1956.

ADDRESSES: Home—Wiltshire, England. *Office*—c/o Macmillan Children's Books, Cavaye Place, London SW10 9PG, England. *Agent*—Laura Cecil, 17 Alwyne Villas, London N1 2HG, England.

CAREER: Freelance writer and book illustrator. Former production assistant at Hammond, Hammond Ltd. (publisher), London, England; Longmans, Green & Co. Ltd. (publisher), London, copywriter, 1959-62.

MEMBER: Society of Authors, Association of Illustrators.

AWARDS, HONORS: Horn Book Honor List citation, 1977, for *Mr. and Mrs. Pig's Evening Out,* 1978, for *Garth Pig and the Ice Cream Lady,* and 1986, for *Babe: The Gallant Pig;* Parents' Choice Award, 1987, for *Mrs. Pig Gets Cross and Other Stories.*

WRITINGS:

SELF-ILLUSTRATED JUVENILES

The Witch-Finder, Morrow (New York City), 1976.
Mr. and Mrs. Pig's Evening Out, Atheneum (New York City), 1976.
Garth Pig and the Ice Cream Lady, Atheneum, 1977.
The Rain Cloud, Atheneum, 1980.
Mrs. Pig's Bulk Buy, Atheneum, 1981.
Crocodarling, Collins (London), 1985, Bradbury Press, 1986.

Mrs. Pig Gets Cross and Other Stories, Collins, 1986, Dutton (New York City), 1987.
Reilly, Gollancz (London), 1987.
Oh Paul!, Heinemann (London), 1988, Barron, 1989.
Bathtime for Garth Pig, Picture Lions, 1989.
Marathon and Steve, Dutton, 1989.
Rug, Forest House, 1989.
Garth Pig Steals the Show, Dutton, 1993.
One by One: Garth Pig's Rain Song, Dutton, 1994.
Ten Pink Piglets: Garth Pig's Wall Song, Dutton, 1994.

JUVENILES

Open Wide, illustrated by Kate Simpson, Longman (London), 1990.
The Echoing Green, illustrated by Michael Foreman, Viking (New York City), 1992.

ILLUSTRATOR

Daphne Ghose, *Harry,* Lutterworth, 1973.
Stella Nowell, *The White Rabbit,* Lutterworth, 1975.
Griselda Gifford, *Because of Blunder,* Gollancz, 1977.
Gifford, *Cass the Brave,* Gollancz, 1978.
Partap Sharma, *Dog Detective Ranjha,* Macmillan, 1978.
Dick King-Smith, *Pigs Might Fly,* Viking, 1982.

Also illustrator of *Silver's Day,* 1980, and *Revenge of the Wildcat,* both by Gifford; *The Boggart,* by Emma Tennant, 1980; *Daggie Dogfoot,* 1980, *Magnus Powermouse,* 1982, and *The Sheep-Pig,* 1983 (published in the United States as *Babe: The Gallant Pig,* 1993), all by King-Smith; *The Dead Letter Box,* by Jan Mark, 1982; *Mr. Weller's Long March,* by Anthea Colbert, 1983; *Lost and Found,* by Jill Paton Walsh, 1984; and *Thank You for the Tadpole,* by Pat Thomson, 1987.

OTHER

Contributor to anthologies, including *Allsorts Six,* edited by Ann Thwaite, Methuen, 1974; *Allsorts Seven,* edited by Thwaite, Methuen, 1975; *Young Winters' Tales Seven,* edited by M. R. Hodgkin, Macmillan, 1976; and *Hidden Turnings.* Contributor of stories to *Cricket.*

SIDELIGHTS: Mr. and Mrs. Pig and their ten lively little piglets are the focus in several picture books by author and illustrator Mary Rayner. Often finding themselves in life-threatening situations involving a wolf, the ten youngsters manage to wriggle their way out of trouble in such stories as *Mr. and Mrs. Pig's Evening Out, Garth Pig and the Ice Cream Lady,* and *Garth Pig Steals the Show.* "There are numerous outstanding children's books featuring pigs," maintains Karen Jameyson in *Horn Book,* "but when it comes to stories about families of them, Mary Rayner has practically cornered the market."

"The pig stories," Rayner once explained, "began as stories invented for my children and, although they have now grown beyond picture books, their comments and criticisms are a great help to me still." The first Pig family book, *Mr. and Mrs. Pig's Evening Out,* begins with Mother and Father Pig going out for the evening and a baby sitter coming to watch the ten piglets. When this baby sitter arrives, Mr. and Mrs. Pig fail to realize that it is really a wolf in disguise. As the evening wears on, the wolf gets hungry and attempts to eat Garth Pig for a snack, but his nine brothers and sisters quickly formulate a plan and come to his rescue. "How lucky children are now!," exclaims Liz Waterland in her *Books for Keeps* review of *Mr. and Mrs. Pig's Evening Out.* "Who could fail to want to read when there are books like this about?" A *Bulletin of the Center for Children's Books* reviewer also praises Rayner's story, pointing out that it "has a felicitous blend of familiar situation, drastic crisis, and resourceful solution by a team of children."

A wolf figures into *Garth Pig and the Ice Cream Lady,* the second of Rayner's books about the Pig family. In this adventure, young Garth is sent by his brothers and sisters to get treats from the ice cream truck, which turns out to be driven by a wolf who kidnaps him. When Garth's return seems to be taking too long, his siblings once again come to his rescue just in the nick of time. Writing in *Books for Keeps,* Moira Small concludes that *Garth Pig and the Ice Cream Lady* "is a lovely romp with plenty of pace and adventure."

Seven different stories about the Pig family can be found in Rayner's *Mrs. Pig Gets Cross and Other Stories.* During the course of these tales, the piglets manage to lock themselves in the bathroom, fight over the chores they are assigned, leave a messy trail throughout the house, disrupt their parents' sleep, and cause more damage than good while "helping" with household projects. "These are very much family read-aloud stories, true to the humorous experiences of everyday life and embellished with imagina-

tive flourishes of phrase and watercolor illustration," comments a *Bulletin of the Center for Children's Books* reviewer. *New York Times Book Review* contributor Merri Rosenberg similarly finds that "once again Mrs. Rayner amusingly, and honestly, deals with the ordinary experiences of family life in a manner that is entertaining to the small fry—and blessedly comforting to the parent." Rosenberg goes on to add: "*Mrs. Pig Gets Cross* is one of those rare finds that are as much fun for a parent to read as they are for a child to hear."

In addition to her popular Pig books, Rayner has written and illustrated several other stories, including *The Rain Cloud, Reilly,* and *Marathon and Steve. The Rain Cloud* follows the cloud of the title as it moves across the sky on a nice summer day, holding in its rain so it does not ruin anyone's day. The rain is finally released where it is needed and wanted—over a farmer's crops. During its travels, the cloud passes over the beach, a picnic in the country, and villagers doing their wash, all of which are depicted in Rayner's watercolors. Paul Heins, writing in *Horn Book,* finds that *The Rain Cloud* is "a quiet picture book extolling a fanciful interplay between man and nature."

A precocious cat who has already lost eight of his nine lives is the title character of *Reilly.* Almost drowning as a kitten, Reilly is now leading the life of a stray cat, until he manages to find a home with Betty and Joyce Braithwaite and win over the affection of most of their neighbors, much to the dismay of the other cats on the street. "This hilarious and touching story shows an intimate and unsentimental knowledge of cats and their humans," observes Julie Blaisdale in *British Book News.* Richard Brown, writing in the *School Librarian,* also praises Rayner's insights into cats, concluding: "This book deserves to be loved not just by cat-lovers, but by any child who enjoys a good read."

More animal and human interaction is presented in *Marathon and Steve,* the tale of Steve the jogger and his dog Marathon, who does not like to exert himself. In fact, Marathon dreads being forced to run alongside his master in the cold wind on the hard cement. It is a relief for Marathon when Steve strains a tendon and changes his sport of choice to swimming, leaving Marathon at home with the television. "Gentle fun is poked at the trendy human tendency to exhaust one's self exercising while the sensible dog knows how to combine enjoyable activity with leisure," notes *School Library Journal* reviewer

Patricia Pearl. "With her delightful, fresh humor," writes Jameyson in *Horn Book*, "Rayner is sure to collect herself a new crowd of fans."

BIOGRAPHICAL/CRITICAL SOURCES:

BOOKS

Twentieth-Century Children's Writers, 4th edition, St. James Press (Detroit), 1995.

PERIODICALS

Books for Keeps, September, 1988, p. 9; January, 1989, p. 18.
British Book News, June, 1987, p. 30.
Bulletin of the Center for Children's Books, January, 1977; May, 1981, p. 179; June, 1986; April, 1987; March, 1989, p. 179.
Growing Point, May, 1989, p. 5172.
Horn Book, February, 1978; October, 1980, pp. 514-15; February, 1982; May/June, 1987, pp. 338-39; October, 1987, pp. 240-41; March/April, 1989, p. 203.
Junior Bookshelf, October, 1991, p. 217; February, 1993, p. 34.
Kirkus Reviews, August 15, 1976, p. 906; May 15, 1993.
New York Times Book Review, May 17, 1987.
Publishers Weekly, November 6, 1981, p. 79.
School Librarian, August, 1987, pp. 234, 237; November, 1988, p. 135; May, 1993, p. 63.
School Library Journal, December, 1976, p. 68; November, 1980, p. 66; September, 1981, p. 114; March, 1985, p. 137; May, 1986, p. 84; April, 1989, p. 90; May, 1993; August, 1994, p. 144.

*   *   *

RENDELL, Ruth (Barbara)   1930-
(Barbara Vine)

PERSONAL: Born February 17, 1930, in London, England; daughter of Arthur Grasemann (a teacher) and Ebba (a teacher) Kruse; married Donald Rendell, 1950 (divorced, 1975; remarried, 1977); children: Simon. *Education:* Educated in Essex, England. *Avocational interests:* Reading, walking, opera.

ADDRESSES: Home—Nussteads, Polstead, Colchester, Suffolk CO6 5DN, England; 26 Cornwall Terrace Mews, NW1 5LL. *Agent*—Sterling Lord Agency, 660 Madison Ave., New York, NY 10021.

CAREER: Writer. Express and Independent Newspapers, West Essex, England, reporter and subeditor for the Chigwell *Times*, 1948-52.

AWARDS, HONORS: Edgar Allan Poe Award, Mystery Writers of America, 1974, for story "The Fallen Curtain," 1976, for collection *The Fallen Curtain and Other Stories*, 1984, for story "The New Girlfriend," and 1986, for novel *A Dark-Adapted Eye*; Gold Dagger Award, Crime Writers Association, 1977, for *A Demon in My View*, 1986, for *Live Flesh*, and 1987, for *A Fatal Inversion*; British Arts Council bursary, 1981; British National Book Award, 1981, for *The Lake of Darkness*; Popular Culture Association Award, 1983; Silver Dagger Award, Crime Writers Association, 1984, for *The Tree of Hands*.

WRITINGS:

MYSTERY NOVELS

From Doon with Death (also see below), John Long (London), 1964, Doubleday (Garden City, NY), 1965.
To Fear a Painted Devil, Doubleday, 1965.
Vanity Dies Hard, John Long, 1966, published as *In Sickness and in Health*, Doubleday, 1966.
A New Lease of Death (also see below), Doubleday, 1967, published as *Sins of the Fathers*, Ballantine (New York City), 1970.
Wolf to the Slaughter, John Long, 1967, Doubleday, 1968.
The Secret House of Death, John Long, 1968, Doubleday, 1969.
The Best Man to Die (also see below), John Long, 1969, Doubleday, 1970.
A Guilty Thing Surprised, Doubleday, 1970.
No More Dying Then, Hutchinson (London), 1971, Doubleday, 1972.
One Across, Two Down, Doubleday, 1971.
Murder Being Once Done, Doubleday, 1972.
Some Lie and Some Die, Doubleday, 1973.
The Face of Trespass, Doubleday, 1974.
Shake Hands Forever, Doubleday, 1975.
A Demon in My View, Hutchinson, 1976, Doubleday, 1977.
A Judgment in Stone, Hutchinson, 1977, Doubleday, 1978.
A Sleeping Life, Doubleday, 1978.
Make Death Love Me, Doubleday, 1979.

The Lake of Darkness, Doubleday, 1980.
Put on by Cunning, Hutchinson, 1981, published as
   Death Notes, Pantheon (New York City), 1981.
Master of the Moor, Pantheon, 1982.
The Speaker of Mandarin, Pantheon, 1983.
The Killing Doll, Pantheon, 1984.
The Tree of Hands, Pantheon, 1984.
An Unkindness of Ravens, Pantheon, 1985.
Live Flesh, Pantheon, 1986.
Heartstones, Harper, 1987.
Talking to Strangers, Hutchinson, 1987, published as
   Talking to Strange Men, Pantheon, 1987.
The Veiled One, Pantheon, 1988.
The Bridesmaid, Mysterious Press (New York City),
   1989.
Going Wrong, Mysterious Press, 1990.
Kissing the Gunner's Daughter, Mysterious Press,
   1992.
The Crocodile Bird, Crown (New York City), 1993.
Simisola, Random House (New York City), 1995.

STORY COLLECTIONS

The Fallen Curtain and Other Stories, Hutchinson,
   1976, published as *The Fallen Curtain: Eleven
   Mystery Stories by an Edgar Award-Winning
   Writer,* Doubleday, 1976.
Means of Evil and Other Stories, Hutchinson, 1979,
   published as *Five Mystery Stories by an Edgar
   Award-Winning Writer,* Doubleday, 1980.
The Fever Tree and Other Stories, Hutchinson, 1982,
   Pantheon, 1983, published as *The Fever Tree
   and Other Stories of Suspense,* Ballantine, 1984.
The New Girlfriend and Other Stories, Hutchinson,
   1985, Pantheon, 1986.
Collected Short Stories, Hutchinson, 1987, published
   as *Collected Stories,* Pantheon, 1988.
The Copper Peacock and Other Stories, Mysterious,
   1991.

OTHER

(Editor) *A Warning to the Curious: The Ghost Stories
   of M. R. James,* Hutchinson, 1986.
Wexford: An Omnibus (contains *From Doon with
   Death, A New Lease of Death,* and *The Best Man
   to Die*), Hutchinson, 1988.
(With Colin Ward) *Undermining the Central Line,*
   Chatto & Windus (London), 1989.
The Fifth Wexford Omnibus (contains *Means of Evil,
   An Unkindness of Ravens,* and *The Veiled One*),
   Hutchinson, 1991.
(With photographs by Paul Bowden) *Ruth Rendell's
   Suffolk,* Hutchinson, 1992.

Contributor of short stories to *Ellery Queen's Mystery Magazine.*

UNDER PSEUDONYM BARBARA VINE

A Dark-Adapted Eye, Viking (London), 1985, G.K.
   Hall (Boston), 1986.
A Fatal Inversion, Viking, 1987.
(With others) *Yes, Prime Minister: The Diaries of the
   Right Honorable James Hacker,* Salem House
   Publishers, 1988.
The House of Stairs, Harmony Books, 1989.
Gallowglass, Harmony Books, 1990.
King Solomon's Carpet, Harmony Books, 1992.
Anna's Book, Harmony Books, 1993.
No Night Is Too Long, Harmony Books, 1994.
The Brimstone Wedding, Harmony Books, 1996.

ADAPTATIONS: A Judgment in Stone was filmed as
The Housekeeper, Rawfilm/Schulz Productions,
1987; several of Rendell's Wexford mysteries have
been adapted for British television and subsequently
aired on the Arts and Entertainment network's "Masters of Mystery" series.

SIDELIGHTS: "It's infuriating to see Ruth Rendell
consistently referred to as the new Agatha Christie,"
writes Cryptus in the *Detroit News.* "The fact is that
Rendell . . . is incomparably better, attempting more
and achieving more." Indeed, since issuing her first
novel, *From Doon with Death,* in which she introduced her popular sleuth Chief Inspector Reginald
Wexford of murder-plagued Kingsmarkham, Sussex,
England, Rendell has been applauded by critics for
her deftness of characterization, ingenious plots, and
surprising conclusions. Francis Wyndham of the
Times Literary Supplement praises Rendell's "masterly grasp of plot construction [and] highly developed faculty for social observation." David Lehman
of *Newsweek* reports that "few detective writers are
as good at pulling such last-second rabbits out of
their top hats—the last page making us see everything before it in a strange, new glare."

Rendell writes two different kinds of mystery novels.
In her Wexford books, she creates traditional "police
procedural" stories, while her non-series books are
psychological thrillers, "energized by the startling,
disturbing, seductive notion that all psychology is
abnormal psychology and that the criminal mind isn't
all that different from our own," as Lehman notes.
Wyndham remarks on Rendell's agility in both areas
of mystery fiction: "Ruth Rendell's remarkable talent
has been able to accommodate the rigid rules of the

reassuring mystery story (where a superficial logic conceals a basic fantasy) as well as the wider range of the disturbing psychological thriller (where an appearance of nightmare overlays a scrupulous realism)."

Rendell's popular character Chief Inspector Wexford is middle-aged, married, and the father of two grown daughters. His extensive reading allows him to quote from a wide range of literature during his murder investigations. "Wexford is quite witty, I think," Rendell tells Marilyn Stasio of the *New York Times*. "He is also a big, solid type, very cool and calm. He also likes women very much and always has time for them. What more could you want in a man?" Along with his assistant, Michael Burden, Wexford solves mysterious murders in the town of Kingsmarkham in rural Sussex, a gritty and rather glum setting. "I don't want people to see [Kingsmarkham] as a pretty village," Rendell explains to Stasio.

Rendell's adroitness at building suspense in all her mystery books is admired by reviewers. In a *New York Times Book Review* critique of *A Demon in My View*, Newgate Callender writes: "Nothing much seems to happen, but a bit here, a bit there, a telling thrust, and suddenly we are in a sustained mood of horror. Rendell is awfully good at this kind of psycho-suspense." Writing in the *Los Angeles Times Book Review* about *The Lake of Darkness*, Charles Champlin calls the book "a cleverly plotted story whose several strands, seemingly only tentatively connected at the start, move toward a last, violent knotting (the sort of construction Alfred Hitchcock, who preferred suspense to the classic timetable mystery, might well have enjoyed)." Commenting on *Master of the Moor*, T. J. Binyon of the *Times Literary Supplement* finds it "immaculately written and constructed, . . . another of Ruth Rendell's skillful studies in abnormal psychology; a powerful, intriguing, if ultimately depressing novel." Speaking of *The Bridesmaid*, Carol Kleiman of the *Chicago Tribune* remarks that "it is a fine, psychological novel that holds its own as good literature." Similarly, John Gross of the *New York Times* claims that "Rendell's work . . . is equally notable for subtle psychological tension and sharp social observation."

Chicago Tribune critic Joyce Slater notes that Rendell's ability to make "irrational behavior seem perfectly plausible" accounts for the success of what many feel to be her best book, *The Crocodile Bird*. The novel is a chilling, atmospheric tale of Eve, a murderess who raises her daughter Liza in an iso-lated country mansion. Eve is violent toward the outside world but loving and protective—even normal—with her daughter. "More evident than ever," writes Charles Champlin in the *Los Angeles Times Book Review*, "is Rendell's ability to evoke, with poetic exactness, the life and look of the English countryside," not to mention "the brutal lives of the poor and the cruel indifferences of the rich."

Lynn Simross reports in the *Los Angeles Times* that Rendell, with the publication of *Kissing the Gunner's Daughter*, begins to show a certain impatience with Wexford. "If I get an idea and it's very good, I'll do another [Wexford book] . . . but yet, I am bored with him," Rendell said. Nonetheless, *Kissing the Gunner's Daughter* was well received. Simross states that *Kissing the Gunner's Daughter* "is a first-rate novel with an inventive plot and subplots, skillful portraits of its characters and succinct social comments about greed," while Catherine Foster observes in the *Christian Science Monitor* that "Rendell provides a mystery that is rich in physical and sociological detail."

The opportunity to comment on contemporary life was apparently good reason to bring Wexford back yet another time in *Simisola*. As Guy Walters notes in the London *Times*, "Wexford's Kingsmarkham patch is a subtly different place in *Simisola*. The town has a more recessionary feel; the unemployed and the halt are more in evidence, and it has lost its comfortable atmosphere of sated bourgeois life. Wexford himself is a gloomier figure; irritated by his family, and emotionally drained by the nature of his work. The subject matter of *Simisola* is more gritty too—racial prejudice." Rendell herself observes in the *New York Times*: "I thought I would really try to examine unemployment and racism in [England]."

In addition to her Wexford mysteries, Rendell has also published novels written under the pseudonym Barbara Vine. The Vine novels include the Edgar Award-winning *A Dark-Adapted Eye* and the Gold Dagger Award-winning *A Fatal Inversion*. Rendell explained to *CA* that she began writing under the pseudonym Barbara Vine when a planned novel she was working on relied heavily on historical research. The story of a narrator trying to locate a missing mother, *A Dark-Adapted Eye* was quite different from Rendell's usual books. "I understood," Rendell told *CA*, "that what I was going to do would be a semi-historical novel with a great deal of research in that period, and that my readers would find this quite straight. They might find it acceptable, but I thought they would want to know what was going on. So I chose a pseudonym, but at the same time deciding not to keep my own identity a secret.... I'm not trying to deceive anybody. I constantly get letters from my readers saying that they understand why I do this."

BIOGRAPHICAL/CRITICAL SOURCES:

BOOKS

Bestsellers 90, Issue 4, Gale (Detroit), 1991.
Contemporary Literary Criticism, Gale, Volume 28, 1984, Volume 48, 1988, Volume 50, 1988.
Dictionary of Literary Biography, Volume 87: *British Mystery and Thriller Writers since 1940,* Gale, 1989.

PERIODICALS

Belles Lettres, summer, 1993, p. 50; spring, 1994, p. 13.
Chicago Tribune, August 29, 1989; October 31, 1993.
Chicago Tribune Book World, December 19, 1982.
Christian Science Monitor, July 6, 1992, p. 13.
Detroit News, August 12, 1979.
Globe and Mail (Toronto), May 31, 1986; September 16, 1989.
Library Journal, October 1, 1991, p. 144; October 15, 1995.
Los Angeles Times, June 3, 1992, p. E1.
Los Angeles Times Book Review, August 3, 1980; May 8, 1983; November 21, 1993, p. 12.
Maclean's, May 19, 1986; April 10, 1995, p. 58.
Newsweek, September 21, 1987.
New York Times, September 9, 1988; February 4, 1990; June 12, 1992, p. C12; April 10, 1995, p. C9.
New York Times Book Review, June 25, 1967; June 23, 1968; August 24, 1969; February 26, 1974; June 2, 1974; December 1, 1974; April 27, 1975; November 23, 1975; February 27, 1977; January 23, 1979; October 14, 1979; February 24, 1980.
Publishers Weekly, August 16, 1991, p. 49; October 23, 1995.
Saturday Review, January 30, 1971.
Spectator, November 19, 1994, p. 47.
Times (London), December 11, 1987; October 5, 1995.
Times Literary Supplement, February 23, 1967; December 21, 1967; April 23, 1970; October 1, 1976; June 5, 1981; July 23, 1982, October 7, 1994, p. 30.

Washington Post, May 19, 1992, p. B2.
Washington Post Book World, September 20, 1981; October 31, 1993.

*   *   *

RICHTER, William L.   1942-

PERSONAL: Surname is pronounced *"Rick*-ter"; born January 20, 1942, in Fort Madison, IA; son of Gerard R. (a professor of international trade) and Lillian (maiden name, Werner) Richter; married Lynne Chalmers (a medical technologist), August 26, 1967. *Education:* Arizona State University, B.A., 1964, M.A., 1965; Louisiana State University, Ph.D., 1970; postdoctoral study at Kentucky State College (now University), 1971; University of Arizona, M.L.S., 1980.

ADDRESSES: Home—2917 East Elm St., Tucson, AZ 85716.

CAREER: U.S. National Park Service, Grand Canyon, AZ, laborer, 1961-67; Louisiana State University, Baton Rouge, visiting instructor in history, 1970; Cameron University, Lawton, OK, assistant professor of history, 1970-75; Bill's Farrier Service, Tucson, AZ, owner and operator, 1975—.

MEMBER: American Historical Association, Organization of American Historians, American Farriers Association, Southern Historical Association, Texas State Historical Association, Missouri State Historical Association, Association of Oklahoma College History Professors.

WRITINGS:

The Army in Texas During Reconstruction, 1865-1870, Texas A & M University Press (College Station), 1987.
Overreached on All Sides: The Freedmen's Bureau Administrators in Texas, 1865-1868, Texas A & M University Press, 1991.
(With Ronald D. Smith) *Fascinating People and Astounding Events from American History,* ABC-CLIO (Santa Barbara, CA), 1993.
The ABC-CLIO Companion to Transportation in America, ABC-CLIO, 1995.
The ABC-CLIO Companion to Reconstruction, ABC-CLIO, 1996.

Contributor to *Plantation, Town, and Country: Essays on the Local History of American Slave Society,* edited by Elinor Miller and Eugene D. Genovese, University of Illinois Press (Champaign), 1974; *Great Events in American History: American Series,* three volumes, edited by Frank N. Magill and John L. Loos, Salem Press (Englewood Cliffs, NJ), 1975. Also contributor of more than twenty articles and reviews to history journals.

*   *   *

ROSEN, Michael (Wayne)   1946-

PERSONAL: Born May 7, 1946, Harrow, Middlesex, England; son of Harold (a professor) and Connie Ruby (a college lecturer; maiden name, Isakovsky) Rosen. *Education:* Attended Middlesex Hospital Medical School, 1964-65; attended Wadham College, Oxford, 1965-69; attended National Film School, 1973-76. *Politics:* Socialist. *Religion:* Atheist.

ADDRESSES: Agent—Charles Walker, Peters, Fraser and Dunlop, 503/4 The Chambers, Chelsea Harbour, London SW10 0XF, England.

CAREER: Writer, poet, playwright, and broadcaster. Has appeared regularly on British Broadcasting Company (BBC) television and radio shows, including *Meridian Books, Treasure Islands,* and *Best Worlds.*

MEMBER: National Union of Journalists.

AWARDS, HONORS: Best original full-length play award, *Sunday Times* National Union of Students Drama Festival, 1968, for *Backbone;* poetry award, *Signal,* 1982, for *You Can't Catch Me!;* other award, *Children's Book Bulletin,* 1983, for *Everybody Here;* Smarties' best children's book of the year award and *Boston Globe-Horn Book* award, both 1990, and Japanese picture book award, 1991, all for *We're Going On a Bear Hunt;* Cuffies Award for best anthology, *Publishers Weekly,* 1992, and best book award, National Association of Parenting Publications, 1993, for *Poems for the Very Young.*

WRITINGS:

Once There Was a King Who Promised He Would Never Chop Anyone's Head Off, illustrated by Kathy Henderson, Deutsch (London), 1976.

The Bakerloo Flea, illustrated by Quentin Blake, Longman (London), 1979.

(Reteller) *A Cat and Mouse Story,* illustrated by William Rushton, Deutsch, 1982.

Nasty!, illustrated by Amanda Macphail, Longman, 1982, revised edition, Puffin (London), 1984.

You're Thinking about Doughnuts, illustrated by Tony Pinchuck, Deutsch, 1987.

Beep Beep!: Here Come—The Horribles!, illustrated by John Watson, Walker (New York City), 1988.

Norma and the Washing Machine, illustrated by David Hingham, Deutsch, 1988.

The Class Two Monster, illustrated by Maggie King, Heinemann (London), 1989.

We're Going on a Bear Hunt, illustrated by Helen Oxenbury, Walker, 1989.

(Reteller) *The Wicked Tricks of Till Owlyglass,* illustrated by Fritz Wegner, Walker, 1989.

The Golem of Old Prague, illustrated by Val Biro, Deutsch, 1990.

(Reteller) *Little Rabbit Foo Foo,* illustrated by Arthur Robins, Simon & Schuster (New York City), 1990.

The Royal Huddle [and] *The Royal Muddle,* illustrated by Colin West, Macmillan (New York City), 1990.

Clever Cakes, Walker, 1991.

The Deadman Tapes, Lion Tracks, 1991.

(Reteller) *How the Animals Got Their Colours: Animal Myths from Around the World,* illustrated by John Clementson, Harcourt (San Diego), 1991.

Burping Bertha, Andersen, 1993.

(Reteller) *How Giraffe Got Such a Long Neck . . . and Why Rhino Is So Grumpy,* illustrated by Clementson, Dial (New York City), 1993.

Moving, illustrated by Sophy Williams, Viking (New York City), 1993.

Songbird Story, illustrated by Jill Dow, F. Lincoln, 1993.

The Arabian Frights and Other Gories, illustrated by Chris Fisher, Scholastic Inc. (New York City), 1994.

(Reteller) *Crow and Hawk: A Traditional Pueblo Indian Story,* illustrated by Clementson, Harcourt, 1995.

Even Stevens, F.C., Collins (London), 1995.

POETRY, VERSE, AND JOKE COLLECTIONS

Mind Your Own Business, illustrated by Blake, Deutsch, 1974.

(With Roger McGough) *You Tell Me,* illustrated by Sara Midda, Kestrel, 1979.

Wouldn't You Like to Know, illustrated by Blake, Penguin, 1981.

You Can't Catch Me!, illustrated by Blake, Deutsch, 1981.

Quick, Let's Get Out of Here, illustrated by Blake, Deutsch, 1983.

Bloody L.I.A.R.S., illustrated by Alan Gilbey, privately printed, 1984.

How to Get Out of the Bath and Other Problems, illustrated by Graham Round, Scholastic Inc., 1984.

Don't Put Mustard in the Custard, illustrated by Blake, Deutsch, 1985.

Hairy Tales and Nursery Crimes, illustrated by Alan Baker, Deutsch, 1985.

Under the Bed, illustrated by Blake, Walker, 1986.

When Did You Last Wash Your Feet?, illustrated by Pinchuck, Deutsch, 1986.

The Hypnotiser, illustrated by Andrew Tiffen, Deutsch, 1988.

Silly Stories (jokes), illustrated by Mik Brown, Kingfisher, 1988.

Freckly Feet and Itchy Knees, illustrated by Sami Sweeten, Collins, Doubleday, 1990.

Never Mind!, BBC, 1990.

Who Drew on the Baby's Head, Deutsch, 1991.

Mind the Gap, Scholastic Inc., 1992.

Nuts about Nuts, Collins, 1993.

Off the Wall: A Very Silly Story Book, illustrated by Brown, Larousse Kingfisher Chambers, 1994.

"SCRAPBOOK" SERIES

Smelly Jelly Smelly Fish, illustrated by Blake, Prentice-Hall (Englewood Cliffs, NJ), 1986.

Under the Bed, illustrated by Blake, Prentice-Hall, 1986.

Hard-Boiled Legs, illustrated by Blake, Prentice-Hall, 1987.

Spollyollydiddilytiddlyitis, illustrated by Blake, Walker, 1987, published as *Down at the Doctors,* Simon & Schuster, 1987.

EDITOR

Everybody Here (miscellany), Bodley Head (London), 1982.

(With Susanna Steele), *Inky Pinky Ponky: Children's Playground Rhymes,* illustrated by Dan Jones, Granada (London), 1982.

(With David Jackson) *Speaking to You,* Macmillan, 1984.

(With Joan Griffiths) *That'd Be Telling,* Cambridge University Press (New York City), 1985.

The Kingfisher Book of Children's Poetry, Kingfisher, 1985.

A Spider Bought a Bicycle, and Other Poems for Young Children, illustrated by Inga Moore, Kingfisher, 1986.

The Kingfisher Book of Funny Stories, illustrated by Tony Blundell, Kingfisher, 1988.

Experiences (contains *The Attic: Fear, The Oar: Friendship, The Tree: Imagination, The Formula: Intelligence, Isabel: Shyness,* and *The Nose: Lying*), Firefly, 1989.

Tell Tales (contains *Peter Pan, Aladdin, Alice in Wonderland, Cinderella, Goldilocks and the Three Bears, Hansel and Gretel, Little Red Riding Hood, The Little Tin Soldier, The Princess and the Pea, Sinbad the Sailor,* and *Snow White*), Firefly, 1989-90.

Culture Shock, Viking, 1990.

Goodies and Daddies: An A-Z Guide to Fatherhood, Murray, 1991.

Give Me Shelter, Bodley Head, 1991.

A World of Poetry, Kingfisher, 1991.

(With David Widgery), *The Chatto Book of Dissent,* Chatto & Windus (London), 1991.

Mini Beasties, illustrated by Baker, Firefly, 1991, published as *Itsy-Bitsy Beasties: Poems from around the World,* Carolrhoda Books (Minneapolis, MN), 1992.

Rude Rhymes, Signet (New York City), 1992.

Sonsense Nongs, illustrated by Shoo Rayner, A & C Black (London), 1992.

(With Jill Burridge) *Treasure Islands II: An Adult Guide to Children's Writers,* BBC Books (London), 1992.

South and North, East and West: The Oxfam Book of Children's Stories, Walker/Candlewick, 1992.

Action Replay, illustrated by Andrzej Krauze, Viking, 1993.

The Kingfisher Book of Children's Poetry, illustrated by Alice Englander, Kingfisher, 1993.

Poems for the Very Young, illustrated by Bob Graham, Kingfisher, 1993.

Rude Rhymes II, Signet, 1994.

Penguin Book of Childhood, Penguin, 1994.

Pilly Soems, illustrated by Rayner, A & C Black, 1994.

OTHER

Backbone (play; first produced at Oxford University, 1967; produced on the West End at Royal Court Theatre, London, February, 1968), Faber (London), 1968.

Stewed Figs (play), first produced in Edinburgh at the University of Durham, 1968.

Regis Debray (radio play), first produced on BBC-Radio 4, 1971.

I See a Voice (on poetry), Thames Television-Hutchinson, 1981.

Did I Hear You Write?, illustrated by Pinchuck, Deutsch, 1989.

Rap with Rosen, Longmans, 1995.

The Best of Michael Rosen, RDR Books, 1995.

Also author of a retelling of von Chamisso's version of a Faust tale, *The Man with No Shadow*. Writer of television series, including *The Juice Job*, Thames TV, 1981, 1984; *You Tell Me*, Thames TV, 1982; *Everybody Here*, Channel 4, 1982; *Black and White and Read All Over*, Channel 4, 1984; and *Talk Write Read*, Central TV, 1986. Contributor of drama features for radio and articles to *New Statesman*.

WORK IN PROGRESS: This Is Our House, illustrated by Bob Graham, for Walker.

SIDELIGHTS: As *School Librarian* critic Margaret Meek states, anyone "who has seen Michael Rosen on TV, at work with children in school," or reading to children "testifies to his Pied Piper magic with words." Rosen's love of words, his talent for combining them in fresh and exciting ways, and his ability to speak the words of a child in the way a child would speak them has made him one of England's most popular children's poets.

Rosen's love of words is reflected in his enthusiasm for writing, collecting, and sometimes piecing together anecdotes, jokes, songs, folktales, fairytales, vignettes, and nonsense verse, which he has published in informal poetry collections. Rosen's habit of collecting stories—or parts of them—is apparent in such novels as *You're Thinking about Doughnuts* and *The Deadman Tapes*, which contain several stories within a larger plot. Rosen once explained that some "people are worried about whether what I write is 'poetry.' If they are worried, let them call it something else, for example, 'stuff.'"

Rosen first realized the importance of pursuing his own style after reading James Joyce's novel, *Portrait of the Artist as a Young Man*, when he was young. He tells an interviewer for *Language Matters*: "That book really came home to me. . . . For the first time I realized that you could actually play around with different ways of saying something. So, for example, you could do a stream of consciousness or you could

write about things that happened to you when you were six, and you could do it in the voice of a child of six. So I became absolutely fascinated by this idea and I started to write a few things of that sort."

In college, Rosen developed an interest in theater and wrote a play that was performed at the Royal Court in London. Later, when he noticed the poems his mother selected for a British Broadcasting Corporation show she helped produce, Rosen decided to write poems for radio and television programs. Although Rosen's poems made the air waves, it took a little longer for them to find a home on the printed page. As Rosen explains in *Language Matters*, publishers rejected his submissions, "saying that 'Children don't like poems written from the child's point of view.'" Then, according to Rosen, "Pam Royds, from [publisher] Andre Deutsch, saw them and they said 'What lovely fun!,' 'Tremendous!' and so they married me to [illustrator] Blake, and that's how *Mind Your Own Business* came about."

Since the publication of that first poetry collection in 1974, Rosen's reputation for writing nonsense verse and humorous dialogue has grown. He is especially known for the childlike voice of his poetry, which, as he points out in *Language Matters*, is uncommon. While "plenty of people have written about their childhood, they haven't written about it in the kind of speaking voice that is totally accessible to a child, so that they can read it out loud."

According to *Times Educational Supplement* critic Edward Blishen, reviewing *You Can't Catch Me!* and *Wouldn't You Like to Know*, two of Rosen's early collections, the poet's talent lies in his ability to show "how far from being ordinary are the most ordinary of events." These ordinary events include in *You Can't Catch Me!*, for example, a father and child teasing one another, the joy of sailing, and the fear of the dark. Noting the compatibility of Quentin Blake's illustrations with Rosen's verse, a reviewer for *Junior Bookshelf* concludes that *You Can't Catch Me!* is a "gorgeous book." Speaking of *Wouldn't You Like to Know*, John Fuller in the *Times Literary Supplement* finds that "Rosen satisfies most of the demands that children make of poems, playing for family sentiment, inventing silly phrases, insulting authority." Similarly, the free-verse poems in *Quick, Let's Get Out of Here* recall the events, episodes, and special moments of childhood, and describe fights, birthday parties, tricks, and schemes. As Helen Gregory relates in *School Library Journal*, Rosen evokes emotions ranging from the "hysteria of silly joking" to "the agony of breaking a friend's toy." *Horn Book* contributor Ann A. Flowers remarks that, with its "irrepressible" and "outrageous" poems, *Quick, Let's Get Out of Here* is a "far cry from Christopher Robin."

Rosen's talent for humor is found in his collections of silly verses, songs, fairytales, and folktales as well as in his poetry. *Freckly Feet and Itchy Knees* presents a list of body parts, describes their owners, and explains their functions in rhythmic verse. Rosen contemplates the nose: "I'm talking about noses / wet noses / warty noses / sleepy noses / when someone dozes." Before the end of the book, children are encouraged to wiggle and jiggle their own body parts. In the words of Diane Roback and Richard Donahue in *Publishers Weekly, Freckly Feet and Itchy Knees* is "always lighthearted" and "ideal for reading aloud." *Nuts about Nuts* is another list of things described in verse. This time, the focus is on food: sweets like ice cream, cake, and honey as well as staples like bread, eggs, nuts, and rice are, as a *Junior Bookshelf* critic notes, "celebrated and examined."

The works in *Sonsense Nongs*—eight ballads, parodies, and silly songs written by Rosen with contributions from children—are meant to be sung out loud. According to a *Junior Bookshelf* reviewer, *Sonsense Nongs* may help children gain a "deeper understanding of language as well as much fun and laughter." Children may also sing the words to *Little Rabbit Foo Foo*, which is based on the old children's fingerplay song in which Little Rabbit Foo Foo bops his helpless victims on the head. Judith Sharman claims in *Books for Keeps* that her son found *Little Rabbit Foo Foo* so charming that she had to "sneak" the book away from him while he slept to write her review of it.

The fables in *Hairy Tales and Nursery Crimes* are written in verse which lampoons traditional fairy tales. For example, Rosen's version of Hansel and Gretel begins, "Once a plum time, in the middle of a forest, there lived a poor wood- / nutter and his woof. They lived in a little wooden sausage with their two / children, Handsel and Gristle." In the opinion of George Szirtes, in his *Times Literary Supplement* review, the jokes in these fables "are improved in the telling aloud. Hansel's pocketful of stones . . . become a rocket full of phones." According to *School Librarian* reviewer Colin Walter, however, the book is "not for hearing, and therein lies its secret and appeal."

Rosen's treatment of folktales is tempered by his respect for their origins. His version of an African *porquoi* tale, *How Giraffe Got Such a Long Neck . . . and Why Rhino Is So Grumpy,* according to *School Library Journal* contributor Lee Bock, is "lively" and "bright." *The Golem of Old Prague* is a collection of stories concerning the legendary Rabbi Loeb of Prague. The stories tell how Rabbi Loeb creates a Golem—a huge, strong, but mindless creature—from clay and gives him life. With the help of the powerful and loyal Golem, Rabbi Loeb ensures the Jewish community's survival as they are persecuted by the monk Thaddeus. Writing in *Books for Your Children,* S. Williams concludes that *The Golem of Old Prague* "gives insight to Jewish thinking, customs, and way of life" in sixteenth-century Prague.

Rosen's work for older children and teenagers frequently addresses serious issues. His poetry collection, *When Did You Last Wash Your Feet?,* for example, deals with topics from racism to terminal illness. *Mind the Gap,* a collection Sue Rogers describes in *School Librarian* as "brilliant," features "comic, sad," and "controversial" poems, including one that recalls the past as the narrator's mother is dying. *Books for Keeps* critic Adrian Jackson advises librarians to buy many copies: "Teenagers will love it."

In his fiction, Rosen raises questions often found in his poetry as well. The novel *You're Thinking about Doughnuts,* for example, tells the story of Frank, a little boy who must wait in the dark halls of the museum where his mother works every Friday night. One night, the exhibits, including a skeleton, a space suit, a few Greek statues, and a stuffed tiger, come alive. As these exhibits tell Frank about their lives before they were taken to the quiet museum, asserts Tom Lewis in *School Librarian,* Rosen thoughtfully questions the "honesty and integrity of an institutional building like a museum." Rosen's novel, *The Deadman Tapes,* also presents a series of stories within a larger plot. When Paul Deadman plays some tapes he has found in the attic of his new house, he is introduced to the voices and stories of eight teens. With occasional interruptions from Paul, these stories make up the text of *The Deadman Tapes.* Like some of Rosen's more serious poetry, they deal with various social problems that many teenagers face.

Rosen also enjoys sharing the techniques that have made him a successful children's writer. He has published books on writing, including *Did I Hear You Write?,* and visits schools and libraries. Rosen even reveals one of the secret's of his unique style to *Language Matters:* "What I try to do in my mind is to go back and write about my feelings when I was ten. . . . I write about my experience using the voice of a ten year old. I write in that voice, using what I know as a performer will work, knowing, that is, what children can take off a page."

"Children's literature," Rosen once told *CA,* "is as neglected as children. Writers of children's books are frequently regarded as less important than adult writers, except when we're dead. Society's attitude to children is that they are innocents, nuisances, or victims. As innocents we can imprint training and conditioning on them, as nuisances we can tame and control them, as victims we can abuse them (actively or vicariously). Children's writers try to approach children with ideas, fantasies, intrigues, hopes, failings—which, because they are in book form, can be put down, picked up, enjoyed or thrown away at will. Because we tend to be both democratic and serious with children, we are regarded with patronizing amusement by society except at moments of outrage when we are deemed to have overstepped bounds of decency, order and control."

BIOGRAPHICAL/CRITICAL SOURCES:

BOOKS

Language Matters, Centre for Language in Primary Education, 1983.

Nettell, Stephanie, editor, *Meet the Authors,* Scholastic Inc., 1994.

Powling, Chris, *What It's Like to be Michael Rosen,* Ginn (Aylesbury, England), 1990.

Styles, M., and H. Cook, editors, *There's a Poet behind You,* ArcBlack, 1988.

PERIODICALS

Books for Keeps, May, 1981; July, 1988; May, 1992, p. 11; September, 1992, p. 13.

Books for Your Children, spring, 1991, p. 24; autumn/winter, 1991, p. 24.

Bulletin of the Center for Children's Books, December, 1992, pp. 121-22.

Christian Science Monitor, February 21, 1968.

Horn Book, June, 1984, p. 345; December, 1989, p. 765.

Junior Bookshelf, February, 1982, p. 22; October, 1992, p. 201; June, 1993, pp. 93, 100; June, 1995, pp. 93-94.

Prompt, Number 12, 1968.

Publishers Weekly, June 8, 1990, p. 54; October 25, 1993, p. 62.

Punch, May 15, 1968.

School Librarian, August, 1988, p. 100; November, 1990, p. 148; August, 1991, p. 112; May, 1993, p. 71.

School Library Journal, October, 1984, p. 161; March, 1985, p. 40; May, 1988, p. 59; August, 1989, p. 128; November, 1992, p. 156; December, 1992, p. 127; October, 1993, pp. 121-22; January, 1994, p. 110; June, 1995, p. 104.

Times Educational Supplement, November 20, 1981, p. 34; January 1, 1982; April 28, 1995.

Times Literary Supplement, March 29, 1974; October 28, 1977; November 25, 1983; March 8, 1985, p. 270.

*   *   *

ROSENSTONE, Robert A(llan) 1936-

PERSONAL: Born May 12, 1936, in Montreal, Quebec, Canada; son of Louis (a businessman) and Anne (Kramer) Rosenstone. *Education:* University of California, Los Angeles, B.A., 1957, Ph.D., 1965.

ADDRESSES: Office—California Institute of Technology, Pasadena, CA 91125.

CAREER: Los Angeles Examiner, Los Angeles, CA, reporter and copy editor, 1960; *Los Angeles Times,* Los Angeles, public relations work, 1961-62; University of Oregon, Eugene, assistant professor of history, 1965-66; California Institute of Technology, Pasadena, professor of history, 1975—, executive officer of humanities, 1982-85. Summer professor, University of California, Los Angeles, 1966; visiting professor of American studies, Kyushu University and Seinan Gakuin University, Fukuoka, Japan, 1974-75. Member, board of trustees, Beyond Baroque Literary/Arts Foundation, 1988-92. *Military service:* California National Guard, 1961-67; active duty in U.S. Army, 1962.

MEMBER: PEN, American Historical Association, Organization of American Historians, Phi Beta Kappa.

AWARDS, HONORS: Old Dominion Fund grant, 1969-70; American Philosophical Society travel grant, 1970; Fulbright-Hays senior lecturer at Seinan Gakuin University, Fukuoka, Japan, 1974-75, and at

University of Barcelona, Spain, 1994; Silver Medal, Commonwealth Club of California, 1975, for *Romantic Revolutionary: A Biography of John Reed;* National Endowment for the Humanities, summer grant, 1977, senior fellowship, 1981-82, 1989-90; East-West Center fellow in Honolulu, 1982.

WRITINGS:

(Editor) *Protest from the Right,* Glencoe Press, 1968.

Crusade of the Left: The Lincoln Battalion and the Spanish Civil War, Pegasus, 1970.

(Coeditor) *Seasons of Rebellion: Protest and Radicalism in Recent America,* Holt (New York City), 1972.

(Coauthor) *Los cantos de la conmocion: Veinte anos de rock,* Tuquets (Barcelona), 1974.

Romantic Revolutionary: A Biography of John Reed, Knopf (New York City), 1975.

Mirror in the Shrine: American Encounters with Meiji Japan, Harvard University Press (Cambridge, MA), 1988.

Visions of the Past: The Challenge of Film to Our Idea of History, Harvard University Press, 1995.

(Editor) *Revisioning History,* Princeton University Press (Princeton, NJ), 1995.

Also author of narration for feature-length documentary film, *The Good Fight: The Lincoln Brigade and the Spanish Civil War,* 1983. Contributor to books, including *Affairs of the Mind: The Salon in Europe and America from the Eighteenth to the Twentieth Century,* New Republic, 1980; and *Reform and Reformers in the PROGRESSIVE Era,* Greenwood Press (Westport, CT), 1983. Contributor to periodicals, including *Michigan Quarterly Review, Partisan Review, Ploughshares, New Republic,* and *Progressive.* Coeditor, "Protest in the Sixties" issue of *Annals* of the American Academy of Political and Social Science, March, 1969; contributing editor for film, *American Historical Review,* 1989-95.

Romantic Revolutionary: A Biography of John Reed has been translated into Italian, Spanish, French, and Hungarian; *Mirror in the Shrine: American Encounters with Meiji Japan* has been translated into Japanese.

WORK IN PROGRESS: Romania, Romania, Romania: A Family Memoir.

BIOGRAPHICAL/CRITICAL SOURCES:

PERIODICALS

Los Angeles Times Book Review, October 16, 1988.
Nation, April 6, 1970.
New Republic, September 20, 1975; January 1, 1995.
New York Times Book Review, November 2, 1975; February 21, 1982.
Reviews in American History, June, 1976.
Times Literary Supplement, June 9, 1995.

*   *   *

RUSSELL, Jeffrey Burton   1934-

PERSONAL: Born August 1, 1934, in Fresno, CA; son of Lewis Henry (a publishers representative) and Ieda (Ogborn) Russell; married Diana Mansfield (a teacher of English), June 30, 1956; children: Jennifer, Mark, William, Penelope. *Education:* University of California, Berkeley, A.B., 1955, A.M., 1957; University of Liege, Belgium, graduate study, 1959-60; Emory University, Ph.D., 1960. *Politics:* Democrat. *Religion:* Catholic. *Avocational interests:* Conservation and preservation of wilderness, numismatics, Baroque music, British mystery stories.

ADDRESSES: Office—Department of History, University of California, Santa Barbara, CA 93106. *Agent*—Gerard McCauley Agency, Inc., P.O. Box 844, Katonah, NY 10536.

CAREER: University of New Mexico, Albuquerque, assistant professor of history, 1960-61; Harvard University, Cambridge, MA, junior fellow, Society of Fellows, 1961-62; University of California, Riverside, assistant professor, 1962-65, associate professor, 1965-69, professor of medieval and religious history, 1969-75; University of Notre Dame, Notre Dame, IN, Michael P. Grace Professor of Medieval Studies and director of Medieval Institute, 1975-79; University of California, Santa Barbara, professor of medieval and church history, 1979—.

MEMBER: Mediaeval Academy of America, American Society of Church History, Catholic Historical Association, Medieval Association of the Pacific, Sierra Club, Phi Beta Kappa.

AWARDS, HONORS: Fulbright fellowship, 1959; Guggenheim fellowship, 1968; National Endowment for the Humanities senior fellowship, 1972; grants in aid from American Council of Learned Societies and Social Science Research Council.

WRITINGS:

Dissent and Reform in the Early Middle Ages, University of California Press (Berkeley), 1965.
Medieval Civilization, Wiley (New York City), 1968.
A History of Medieval Christianity: Prophecy and Order, Crowell (New York City), 1968.
(Editor) *Religious Dissent in the Middle Ages,* Wiley, 1971.
Witchcraft in the Middle Ages, Cornell University Press (Ithaca, NY), 1972.
The Devil: Perceptions of Evil from Antiquity to Primitive Christianity, Cornell University Press, 1977.
A History of Witchcraft: Sorcerers, Heretics and Pagans, Thames & Hudson (New York City), 1980.
(With Carl T. Berkhout) *Medieval Heresies: A Bibliography 1960-1979,* Pontifical Institute of Mediaeval Studies, 1981.
Satan: The Early Christian Tradition, Cornell University Press, 1981.
Lucifer: The Devil in the Middle Ages, Cornell University Press, 1984.
Mephistopheles: The Devil in the Modern World, Cornell University Press, 1986.
The Prince of Darkness: Radical Evil and the Power of Good in History, Cornell University Press, 1988.
(Translator into Latin) Madeleine L'Engle, *Ruga in aevis* (title of original text: *A Wrinkle in Time*), Quidst Press, 1990.
Inventing the Flat Earth: Columbus and Modern Historians, Praeger (New York City), 1991.
Dissent and Order in the Middle Ages: The Search for Legitimate Authority, Twayne (Boston), 1992.

Also contributor to *The Transformation of the Roman World,* edited by Lynn White, University of California Press, 1966. Contributor to periodicals, including *Revue d'Histoire ecclesiastique, Medieval Studies, Church History, Speculum, American Historical Review,* and *Catholic Historical Review.*

SIDELIGHTS: Jeffrey Burton Russell once told *CA* that "using the history of evil as an example," he has explored "the ways in which concepts may be most fully understood and accurately defined in terms of their history and sociology." One of the results of Russell's efforts "to develop an historical method uniting philosophy and content analysis with traditional historical approaches," as he describes it, is his tetralogy which traces the history of the idea of the Devil in philosophy, literature, and theology from ancient to modern times. The series includes *The Devil: Perceptions of Evil from Antiquity to Primitive Christianity, Satan: The Early Christian Tradition, Lucifer: The Devil in the Middle Ages,* and *Mephistopheles: The Devil in the Modern World.*

In a review of *Mephistopheles, New York Times Book Review* contributor Robert Coles calls the tetralogy "impressive." He writes that "the author is not only a conscientious historian, . . . [he] is also an introspective essayist who acknowledges his own continuing struggle to understand the nature and source of evil." Russell, says D. J. Enright in the *Times Literary Supplement,* avoids the problem of choosing "between what might be deplored as insufficient documentation and the risk, or certainty, of boring, or maddening, the modern reader" by branching "out into a number of interesting and entertaining cognate topics."

While holding his readers interest, the author pursues his main goal of exploring, as *New York Times Book Review* contributor D. J. R. Bruckner phrases it, "the devil in the mind." In other words, Russell explains how the idea of what the Devil is (and, by association, what God is) has evolved over time. Collectively, these books explain to "us a lot about the attention and passion we have given to that idea," concludes Coles. Russell's "books tell us much about what we were and what we are today—people who all along have been trying to make sense of the world and to stay around in it as a species, our devilish capacity for hate and slaughter notwithstanding."

BIOGRAPHICAL/CRITICAL SOURCES:

PERIODICALS

New York Times Book Review, April 28, 1985; March 8, 1987.
Times Literary Supplement, March 22, 1985.
Washington Post Book World, January 8, 1989.

RYDELL, Robert W(illiam) 1952-

PERSONAL: Born May 23, 1952, in Evanston, IL; son of Robert and Cristol Rydell; married Kiki Leigh. *Education:* University of California, Berkeley, A.B., 1974; University of California, Los Angeles, M.A., 1975, C.Phil., 1977, Ph.D., 1980.

ADDRESSES: Office—Department of History and Philosophy, Montana State University, Bozeman, MT 59717.

CAREER: Montana State University, Bozeman, assistant professor, 1980-84, associate professor, 1984-89, professor of history, 1989—. Visiting assistant professor at University of California, Los Angeles, summer, 1981; John Adams Professor at University of Amsterdam, 1985-86; visiting associate professor at University of Michigan, 1987. Fellow at Smithsonian Institution, 1982-83.

MEMBER: American Historical Association, American Studies Association, Organization of American Historians.

AWARDS, HONORS: Alan Nevins Prize from Society of American Historians, 1981, for Ph. D. dissertation "All the World's a Fair: American International Expositions, 1876-1916"; Netherlands Institute for Advanced Study fellowship, 1991-92.

WRITINGS:

All the World's a Fair: Visions of Empire at American International Expositions, 1876-1916, University of Chicago Press (Chicago), 1985.
Books of the Fairs, American Library Association (Chicago), 1992.
World of Fairs: The Century of Progress Expositions, University of Chicago Press, 1993.
(Coauthor) *In the People's Interest: A Centennial History of Montana State University,* Montana State University Foundation, 1993.

Contributor to history journals.

WORK IN PROGRESS: Fair America and *A History of American Mass Culture,* both expected in 2000.

SIDELIGHTS: Robert W. Rydell told *CA:* "I became interested in world's fairs as vehicles for transmitting scientific ideas about race when I learned of the presence of 'living ethnological villages' at the fairs. I then tried to determine the function of the exhibits within the fairs and within American society as a whole. My current work seeks to expand these interests to include twentieth-century American expositions and expositions held around the world."

*   *   *

RYKEN, Leland 1942-

PERSONAL: Born May 17, 1942, in New Sharon, IA; son of Frank (in farming) and Eva (Bos) Ryken; married Mary Graham, August 22, 1964; children: Philip Graham, Margaret Lynn, Nancy Elizabeth. *Education:* Central College (now Central University of Iowa), B.A., 1964; University of Oregon, Ph.D., 1968. *Politics:* Republican. *Religion:* Presbyterian.

ADDRESSES: Home—1118 North Howard, Wheaton, IL 60187. *Office*—Department of English, Wheaton College, Wheaton, IL 60187.

CAREER: Wheaton College, Wheaton, IL, professor of English, 1968—.

WRITINGS:

The Apocalyptic Vision in "Paradise Lost," Cornell University Press (Ithaca, NY), 1970.
The Literature of the Bible, Zondervan (Grand Rapids, MI), 1974.
Triumphs of the Imagination: Literature in Christian Perspective, Inter-Varsity Press (Downers Grove, IL), 1979.
The Christian Imagination: Essays on Literature and the Arts, Baker Book (Grand Rapids, MI), 1981.
(Coeditor and contributor) *Milton and Scriptural Tradition: The Bible into Poetry,* University of Missouri Press (Columbia), 1984.
(Editor) *The New Testament in Literary Criticism,* Ungar (New York City), 1984.
How to Read the Bible as Literature, Zondervan, 1984.
Windows to the World: Literature in Christian Perspective, Zondervan, 1985.
Culture in Christian Perspective: A Door to Understanding and Enjoying the Arts, Multnomah (Portland, OR), 1986.
Worldly Saints: The Puritans as They Really Were, Zondervan, 1986.
Words of Delight: A Literary Introduction to the Bible, Baker Book, 1987.

Words of Life: A Literary Introduction to the New Testament, Baker Book, 1987.

Work and Leisure in Christian Perspective, Multnomah, 1987.

(Coauthor) *Effective Bible Teaching,* Baker Book, 1988.

The Liberated Imagination: Thinking Christianly about the Arts, Harold Shaw (Wheaton, IL), 1989.

Realms of Gold: The Classics in Christian Perspective, Harold Shaw, 1991.

(Coeditor) *Contemporary Literary Theory: A Christian Appraisal,* Eerdmans (Grand Rapids, MI), 1992.

(Coeditor) *A Complete Literary Guide to the Bible,* Zondervan, 1993.

(Coeditor) *The Discerning Reader: Christian Perspectives on Literature and Theory,* Baker Book, 1995.

Redeeming the Time: A Christian Approach to Work and Leisure, Baker Book, 1995.

Contributor to books, including *Literary Interpretations of Biblical Narratives,* edited by Kenneth Gros Louis, Abingdon (Nashville, TN), 1974. Contributor to scholarly journals.

WORK IN PROGRESS: A dictionary of biblical imagery.

S

SANDBERG, (Karin) Inger   1930-

PERSONAL: Born August 2, 1930, in Karlstad, Sweden; daughter of Johan and Hanna (a teacher; maiden name, Carlstedt) Erikson; married Lasse Sandberg (an artist), April 27, 1950; children: Lena, Niklas, Mathias. *Education:* Swedish Training College for Teachers, teacher's certificate, 1954.

ADDRESSES: Home—Praestaengsv. 7, 65230 Karlstad, Sweden; and Alvsbacka, Sweden (summer).

CAREER: Author of books and television and radio productions for children, 1953—. Teacher in Karlstad, Sweden public schools, 1957-63.

MEMBER: Swedish Union of Writers, Swedish PEN Club, Zonta International.

AWARDS, HONORS: Swedish Author's Fund award, 1963; Swedish Author's Society Awards, 1963, 1965-66, 1970-74; Swedish Literature Promotion Scholarship, 1964, 1969; Karlstad culture prize, 1965; Hans Christian Andersen honorable mention and International Board on Books for Young People (IBBY) honorable mention, both 1966, and Leipzig International Book Exhibit award, 1971, all for *Niklas roeda dag;* The Society of Building Worker culture award, 1969; Heffaklump award from *Expressen* newspaper (Sweden), 1969, for *Pappa, kom ut!;* Child Study Association Book of the Year, 1971; Nils Holgersson Medal, 1973; Astrid Lindgren Prize, 1974; Froeding Award, County Council of Vaermland, 1976; Garanterad foerfattarpenning, 1980-94; Wettergrens Bokollon, 1987, for *Sand-berg's ABCD;* Swedish Honour Award of the Year, Swedish Council of the International Reading Association, 1994.

WRITINGS:

Mina glada trojor (title means "Happy Knitting!"), Raben & Sjoegren, 1987, 2nd edition, 1988.

ILLUSTRATED BY HUSBAND, LASSE SANDBERG

Faaret Ullrik Faar medalj (title means "Woolrik the Sheep Gets a Medal"), Eklund, 1953.
Jag maalar en . . . (title means "I Paint a . . ."), Eklund, 1955.
Jonas bilen och aeventyret (title means "Jonas the Car and the Adventure"), Geber, 1959.
Godnattsagor paa rullgardinen (title means "Bedtime Stories on the Blind"), Geber, 1960.
Filuren paa aeventyr (title means "The Adventure of the Little Filur"), Geber, 1961.
Hemma hos mej (title means "At My Place"), Geber, 1962.
Lena beraettar, Geber, 1963, 3rd edition, 1971, translation by Patricia Crampton published as *Here's Lena,* Methuen (New York City), 1970.
Trollen i Lill-Skogen (title means "The Trolls in the Little Wood"), Karlstad Town, 1963.
Niklas roeda dag, Geber, 1964, 3rd edition, 1985, translation of second edition published as *Nicholas' Red Day,* Delacorte (New York City), 1967.
Barnens bildordlista (title means "Children's Word-book"), Skrivrit, 1965.
Den musikaliska myran (title means "The Musical Ant"), Geber, 1965, 2nd edition, 1970.
En morgon i varuhuset (title means "One Morning in the Department Store"), [Stockholm], 1965.

Johan, Raben & Sjoegren, 1965, 3rd edition, 1970, translation by Crampton published as *Johan's Year*, Methuen, 1971.

Pojken med de Hundra bilarna, Raben & Sjoegren, 1966, 2nd edition, 1980, translation of first edition published as *The Boy with 100 Cars*, Delacorte, 1967.

Tomtens stadsresa (title means "The Tomten Goes to Town"), General Post Office (Sweden), 1966.

En konstig foersta maj, Raben & Sjoegren, 1967.

Niklas oenskedjur, Raben & Sjoegren, 1967, translation by R. Sadler published as *Nicholas' Ideal Pet*, Sadler & Brown, 1968, published as *Nicholas' Favorite Pet*, Delacorte, 1969.

Pojken med de maanga husen, Raben & Sjoegren, 1968, translation published as *The Boy with Many Houses*, Delacorte, 1969.

Vi passar oss sjaelva (title means "We Look after Ourselves"), Geber, 1968.

Pappa, kom ut!, Raben & Sjoegren, 1969, 2nd edition, 1986, translation of first edition published as *Daddy Come Out!*, Sadler & Brown, 1970, published as *Come On Out, Daddy*, Delacorte, 1971.

Johan i2:an, Raben & Sjoegren, 1969, 2nd edition, 1970, translation by Crampton published as *Johan at School*, Methuen, 1972.

Filurstjaernan (title means "The Filurstar"), Geber, 1969.

Buffalo Bengt och indianerna, Raben & Sjoegren, 1970, translation published as *Buffalo Bengt and the Indians*, Sadler & Brown, 1971.

Lena staar i koe (title means "Lena Lines Up"), Geber, 1970.

Stora Tokboken (title means "The Big Crazybook"), Geber, 1970.

Vad aer det som ryker?, Raben & Sjoegren, 1971, translation by Merloyd Lawrence published as *Where Does All That Smoke Come From?*, Delacorte, 1972.

Fred Strid krymper (title means "Mr. Fred Strid Shrinks"), Raben & Sjoegren, 1972.

Vi leker oeken, Froeken, Raben & Sjoegren, 1973, translation published as *Let's Play Desert*, Delacorte, 1974, published in England as *The Desert Game*, Methuen (London), 1974.

Hej, vaelkommen till mej!, Raben & Sjoegren, 1974, translation published as *Let's Be Friends*, Methuen, 1975.

Perry och osynlige Wrolf (title means "Perry and the Invisible Wolf"), Raben & Sjoegren, 1975.

Tummens resa, Raben & Sjoegren, 1978.

Tummen tittar pa natten, Raben & Sjoegren, 1980.

Tummen far en vaen, Raben & Sjoegren, 1980.

Tummens mamma slutar roeka, Raben & Sjoegren, 1980.

En fin dag foer Johan, Raben & Sjoegren, 1981.

Tummen och Tossingarna, Raben & Sjoegren, 1982.

Tummesagor, Raben & Sjoegren, 1984.

Mera macka, sa Pulvret, Raben & Sjoegren, 1985.

Lilla Nollan och dom andra, Carlsen Lit., 1985.

Vit och Svart och alla dom andra, Raben & Sjoegren, 1986.

Sandberg's ABCD, Raben & Sjoegren, 1987.

Pojken, prinsessan och gront, Raben & Sjoegren, 1988.

Rundhunden, Raben & Sjoegren, 1989.

De hemliga i skogen, Raben & Sjoegren, 1991.

Tre paa Mallorca, Raben & Sjoegren, 1991.

Nej, sa lilla P, Raben & Sjoegren, 1992.

Fraan A till Oe, Erikson & Lindgren, 1993.

Beraetta mera, Matilda (diabetesbok), Sv. Diabetesfoerb, 1994.

Den modiga hunden BROOK, Natur & Kultur, 1995.

"LITTLE ANNA" SERIES; ILLUSTRATED BY L. SANDBERG

Vad Anna fick se, Raben & Sjoegren, 1964, 8th edition, 1987, translation published as *What Anna Saw*, Lothrop (New York City), 1964.

Lilla Anna och trollerihatten, Raben & Sjoegren, 1965, 8th edition, 1987, translation published as *Little Anna and the Magic Hat*, Lothrop, 1965, published in England as *Anna and the Magic Hat*, Sadler & Brown, 1965.

Vad lilla Anna sparade paa, Raben & Sjoegren, 1965, 8th edition, 1987, translation published as *What Little Anna Saved*, Lothrop, 1965, published in England as *What Anna Saved*, Sadler & Brown, 1965.

Lilla Annas mamma fyller aar, Raben & Sjoegren, 1966, 8th edition, 1987, translation published as *Little Anna's Mama Has a Birthday*, Sadler & Brown, 1965, Lothrop, 1966.

Naer lilla Anna var foerkyld, Raben & Sjoegren, 1966, 8th edition, 1987, translation published as *When Little Anna Had a Cold*, Lothrop, 1966, published in England as *When Anna Had a Cold*, Sadler & Brown, 1966.

Lilla Anna och Laanga Farbrorn paa havet, Raben & Sjoegren, 1971, translation published as *Little Anna and the Tall Uncle*, Methuen, 1973.

Var aer lilla Annas hund?, Raben & Sjoegren, 1972, translation published as *Where Is Little Anna's Dog?*, Methuen, 1974.

Lilla Annas julklapp, Raben & Sjoegren, 1972, 5th edition, 1987, translation published as *Kate's Christmas Present*, A. & C. Black, 1974.

Lilla Anna flyttar saker, Raben & Sjoegren, 1972, 5th edition, 1987, translation published as *Kate's Upside Down Day,* A. & C. Black, 1974.

Lilla Anna kom och hjaelp!, Raben & Sjoegren, 1972, 5th edition, 1987, translation published as *Kate, Kate Come and Help!,* A. & C. Black, 1974.

Lilla Anna leker med bollar, Raben & Sjoegren, 1973, 5th edition, 1987, translation published as *Kate's Bouncy Ball,* A. & C. Black, 1974.

Lilla Anna i glada skolan (title means "Little Anna in the Happy School"), Raben & Sjoegren, 1975.

Var aer Laanga Farbrorns hatt? (title means "Where's Tall Uncle's Hat?"), Raben & Sjoegren, 1976.

Lilla Anna och de mystiska froena, Raben & Sjoegren, 1979.

Lilla Anna reser till Landet Mittemot, Raben & Sjoegren, 1982.

"LITTLE SPOOK" SERIES; ILLUSTRATED BY L. SANDBERG

Lilla spoeket Laban, Geber, 1965, 3rd edition, 1976, translation by Nancy S. Leupold published as *Little Ghost Godfrey,* Delacorte, 1968, translation by Kertsi French published as *Little Spook,* Methuen, 1969.

Lilla spoeket Laban far en lillasyster, Raben & Sjoegren, 1977, translation published as *Little Spook's Baby Sister,* Methuen, 1978.

Labolinas Lina, Raben & Sjoegren, 1977, translation published as *Tiny Spook's Tugging Game,* Methuen, 1978.

Labolinas snubbeldag, Raben & Sjoegren, 1977, translation published as *Tiny Spook's Tumbles,* Methuen, 1978.

Gissa vem jag aer idag? sa Labolina, Raben & Sjoegren, 1977, translation published as *Tiny Spook's Guessing Game,* Methuen, 1978.

Kommer snart, sa Laban och Labolina, Raben & Sjoegren, 1977, translation published as *Little Spook's Grubby Day,* Methuen, 1978.

Pappa aer sjuk, sa lilla spoeket Laban, Raben & Sjoegren, 1977, translation published as *Little Spook Haunts Again,* Methuen, 1978.

Var aer Labolinas Millimina?, Raben & Sjoegren, 1979, translation published as *Little Spook and the Lost Doll,* Methuen, 1980.

Laban och Labolinas jul, Raben & Sjoegren, 1991.

Sov gott, sa Lilla Spoeket Laban, Raben & Sjoegren, 1992.

Rufus paa hundutstaellning, Raben & Sjoegren, 1992.

Haexkalaset, Raben & Sjoegren, 1993.

Spoekpappan i simskolan, Raben & Sjoegren, 1993.

Rufus och benet, Raben & Sjoegren, 1994.

Rufus och haexam, Raben & Sjoegren, 1994.

"MATHIAS" SERIES

Mathias bakar kakor, Raben & Sjoegren, 1968, 3rd edition, 1974, translation published as *Daniel and the Coconut Cakes,* A. & C. Black, 1973.

Mathias och trollet, Raben & Sjoegren, 1968, translation published as *Daniel's Mysterious Monster,* A. & C. Black, 1973.

Mathias maalar en . . ., Raben & Sjoegren, 1969, translation published as *Daniel Paints a Picture,* A. & C. Black, 1973.

Mathias hjaelper till, Raben & Sjoegren, 1969, 2nd edition, 1974, translation published as *Daniel's Helping Hand,* A. & C. Black, 1973.

"DUSTY" SERIES; ILLUSTRATED BY L. SANDBERG

Titta daer, sa Pulvret, Raben & Sjoegren, 1983.

Hjaelpa till, sa Pulvret, Raben & Sjoegren, 1983, translation by Judy Abbott Maurer published as *Dusty Wants to Help,* ROS Books/Farrar, Straus (New York City), 1987.

Lana den, sa Pulvret, Raben & Sjoegren, 1984, translation by Maurer published as *Dusty Wants to Borrow Everything,* ROS Books/Farrar, Straus, 1988.

Radd for, sa Pulvret, Raben & Sjoegren, 1984.

Hitta den, sa Pulvret, Raben & Sjoegren, 1986.

Laga mej, sa Pulvret, Raben & Sjoegren, 1990.

Fixa fisk, sa Pulvret, Raben & Sjoegren, 1991.

Ja det faar du, sa Pulvret, Raben & Sjoegren, 1993.

Var aer roesten, sa Pulvret, Raben & Sjoegren, 1994.

Staeda mindre, sa Pulvret, Raben & Sjoegren, 1995.

"BIG AND SMALL" BOOKS

Rimboken, Natur & Kultur, 1995.

Morris och Nifs, Natur & Kultur, 1995.

Vem bor haer?, Natur & Kultur, 1995.

Vem aer Skalle?, Natur & Kultur, 1995.

OTHER

Also author, with husband L. Sandberg, of children's books, and children's television and radio programs. Contributor to Swedish periodicals.

Sandberg's works have been translated into thirty-two languages. Also visiting author in Singapore,

Taiwan, South Korea, New Zealand, the United States, England, and the Nordic countries.

WORK IN PROGRESS: "The books of the future are secret."

SIDELIGHTS: "The big challenge," Inger Sandberg told *CA,* "is to write books which make tiny little ones, from one year of age, happy and make them laugh and also expand their emotions and artistic and linguistic ability. Give the children resources. Give them tools. Give them artistic books with fantasy, happiness and meaningful messages. A writer of children's books must *know* a lot about children, and above all, she must know what she wants and where her loyalties are.

"The environment, the life of the modern city, means a lot to our work, both in the fifties when we lived in a tall block of flats, and now when we in the winter live in town and in the summer in our country home. What we see and experience, we use, just like other writers use their own special environment. Ours is an environment where the big and the small play together and work together; an environment in which the little ones are rightful citizens with rights and responsibilities. We want to be on the side of the children in what we are doing, in our books and for people living in the world today.

"I don't think that any book for children can explain our complex, mad world to a child—hopefully the *good* book can explain a bit of what's going on—and make the world—the everyday life—more understandable."

*   *   *

SCHIFFER, Michael B(rian)   1947-

PERSONAL: Born October 4, 1947, in Winnipeg, Manitoba, Canada; came to the United States in 1953, naturalized in 1962; son of Louie (a salesperson) and Frances-Fera (Ludmer) Schiffer; married Annette Leve, December 22, 1968; children: Adam Joseph, Jeremy Alan. *Education:* University of California, Los Angeles, B.A. (summa cum laude), 1969; University of Arizona, M.A., 1972, Ph.D., 1973.

ADDRESSES: Office—Department of Anthropology, University of Arizona, Tucson, AZ 85721.

CAREER: University of Arkansas, Fayetteville, assistant professor of anthropology, 1973-75; University of Arizona, Tucson, assistant professor, 1975-79, associate professor, 1979-82, professor of anthropology, 1982—, assistant director of Archaeological Field School in Grasshopper, AZ, summer, 1973, director of Laboratory of Traditional Technology, 1984—. Visiting distinguished archaeologist at University of South Carolina, summer, 1977; visiting associate professor at University of Washington, summer, 1979; distinguished visiting professor at Arizona State University, autumn, 1982. Member of staff of Southwest Expedition of Field Museum of Natural History, summer, 1969, research assistant, summer, 1970, research associate, summer, 1971, co-director of excavations, 1970-71; director of Cache River Archaeological Project in northeastern Arkansas, 1973-74, Big Running Water Ditch Project and Village Creek Project, both spring, 1974, and Arkansas Eastman Archaeological Project, 1974-75; methodologist with Corduroy Creek Archaeological Project in east central Arizona, 1978-79, and with Tudor Aldea Project in Chile, summer, 1985; archaeologist with Phoenix District of U.S. Bureau of Land Management, summers, 1980-81; microstratigrapher for Kourion Project in Cyprus, summer, 1985.

MEMBER: American Anthropological Association (fellow), Society for American Archaeology, American Association for the Advancement of Science (fellow), Society for Historical Archaeology, Phi Beta Kappa, Phi Eta Sigma, Pi Gamma Mu.

AWARDS, HONORS: Woodrow Wilson fellowship, 1969-70; Cugnot Award of Distinction, Society of Automotive Historians, 1995, for *Taking Charge: The Electric Automobile in America.*

WRITINGS:

Behavioral Archaeology, Academic Press (San Diego), 1976.
(With William J. Rathje) *Archaeology,* Harcourt (San Diego and New York City), 1982.
Formation Processes of the Archaeological Record, University of New Mexico Press (Albuquerque), 1987.
The Portable Radio in American Life, University of Arizona Press (Tucson), 1991.
Technological Perspectives on Behavioral Change, University of Arizona Press, 1992.

(With Tamara C. Butts and Kimberly K. Grimm) *Taking Charge: The Electric Automobile in America,* Smithsonian Institution Press (Washington, DC), 1994.

Behavioral Archaeology: First Principles, University of Utah Press (Salt Lake City), 1995.

EDITOR

(With George J. Gumerman, and contributor) *Conservation Archaeology: A Guide for Cultural Resource Management Studies,* Academic Press, 1977.

Advances in Archaeological Method and Theory, Volumes 1-11, Academic Press, 1978-87.

(With Richard A Gould, and contributor) *Modern Material Culture: The Archaeology of Us,* Academic Press, 1981.

(With Randall H. McGuire, and contributor) *Hohokam and Patayan: Prehistory of Southwestern Arizona,* Academic Press, 1982.

Archaeological Method and Theory, Volumes 1-5, University of Arizona Press, 1989-93.

Contributor to more than a dozen books on anthropology, including *Sampling in Archaeology,* University of Arizona Press, 1975; *Transformations: Mathematical Approaches to Culture Change,* Academic Press, 1979; *Quandaries and Quests: Visions of Archaeology's Future,* Southern Illinois University Press, 1991; and *Expanding Archaeology* University of Utah Press, 1995. Also contributor of more than forty articles and reviews to anthropology and archaeology journals, including *American Antiquity, Kiva, Current Anthropology, American Anthropologist, Journal of Archaeological Science,* and *Science and Archaeology.* Assistant editor of *Kiva,* 1970. Editor of *Journal of Archaeological Method and Theory,* 1994—.

WORK IN PROGRESS: Research on archaeological epistemology, theory and methodology, experimental archaeology, ceramic technology, and modern material culture.

SIDELIGHTS: Michael B. Schiffer told *CA:* "One theme of my work has been the need to relate the past and present through artifacts. That's why I have used archaeological methods to study modern artifacts, and why I am using modern analytical approaches to unlock the secrets of ancient technologies. I hope in the years ahead to find new ways to apply archaeology to the benefit of modern society."

SCHLAFLY, Phyllis   1924-

PERSONAL: Born August 15, 1924, in St. Louis, MO; daughter of John Bruce (an engineer) and Odille (Dodge) Stewart; married John Fred Schlafly (a lawyer), October 20, 1949; children: John F., Bruce S., Roger S., P. Liza Forshaw, Andrew L., Anne V. *Education:* Attended Maryville College of the Sacred Heart for one year; Washington University, A.B., 1944, J.D., 1978; Radcliffe College, M.A., 1945.

ADDRESSES: Home—32 Briarcliff, St. Louis, MO 63124. *Office*—7800 Bonhomme Ave., St. Louis, MO 63105.

CAREER: Lawyer, 1979—. First National Bank and St. Louis Union Trust Company, St. Louis, librarian and researcher, 1946-49; homemaker, 1949—. Delegate to Republican national conventions, 1956, 1960, 1964, 1968, 1980, 1984, 1988, 1992; candidate for Congress, 1952, 1970; president, Illinois Federation of Republican Women, 1960-64; first vice president, National Federation of Republican Women, 1964-67; national chairperson, Stop ERA, 1972—; member, Illinois Commission on the Status of Women, 1975-85; founder and president, Eagle Forum, 1975—. Member, Administrative Conference of the United States, 1983-86, and Commission on the Bicentennial of the United States Constitution, 1985-91. Commentator on "Matters of Opinion," WBBM Radio, Chicago, 1973-75, on "Spectrum," CBS Radio Network, 1973-78, and on CNN Cable Television Network, 1980-83.

MEMBER: Authors Guild, Daughters of the American Revolution (national chairperson of American history committee, 1965-68; chairperson of bicentennial committee, 1967-70; chairperson of national defense committee, 1977-80, 1983-95), Junior League of St. Louis, Phi Beta Kappa, Pi Sigma Alpha.

AWARDS, HONORS: Named woman of achievement in public affairs by *St. Louis Globe-Democrat,* 1963; named Woman of the Year by Illinois Federation of Republican Women, 1969; awarded ten George Washington Honor Medals by Freedoms Foundation; Brotherhood Award, National Conference of Christians and Jews, 1975; LL.D., Niagara University, 1976; named one of the ten "most admired women in the world" by *Good Housekeeping* magazine, 1977-90; Illinois Mother of the Year, 1992.

WRITINGS:

A Choice Not an Echo, Pere Marquette (Alton, IL), 1964.
(With Chester C. Ward) *The Gravediggers,* Pere Marquette, 1964.
(With Ward) *Strike from Space,* Pere Marquette, 1965.
Safe—Not Sorry, Pere Marquette, 1967.
(With Ward) *The Betrayers,* Pere Marquette, 1968.
Mindszenty the Man, Cardinal Mindszenty Foundation, 1972.
(With Ward) *Kissinger on the Couch,* Arlington House (New York City), 1975.
(With Ward) *Ambush at Vladivostok,* Pere Marquette, 1976.
The Power of the Positive Woman, Arlington House, 1977.
The Power of the Christian Woman, Standard Publishing (Cincinnati, OH), 1981.
(Editor) *Equal Pay for UNequal Work,* Eagle Forum Education and Legal Defense Fund, 1984.
Child Abuse in the Classroom, Pere Marquette, 1984.
Pornography's Victims, Pere Marquette, 1987.
First Reader, Pere Marquette, 1994.

Also author of *The Phyllis Schlafly Report* (monthly national newsletter), 1967—. Contributor of syndicated column to newspapers through Copley News Service, 1976—. Editor of *Education Reporter,* 1986—.

SIDELIGHTS: Phyllis Schlafly, a homemaker turned political activist, is a leading spokeswoman for the conservative viewpoint on issues such as women's rights, national defense, education, the law, and politics. Schlafly's organizational techniques and outspoken personal leadership are often cited as primary reasons for the defeat of the Equal Rights Amendment (ERA) in 1982. A tireless worker known for her unflappable demeanor, Schlafly is "one of the best loved and the most loathed women in the country," according to *New York Review of Books* contributor Frances FitzGerald. Opinion is indeed sharply divided on Schlafly and her goals. In the *Washington Post,* Sally Quinn notes that on the podium Schlafly "comes on like a female George Wallace. She is tough and aggressive, totally unlike the role she espouses for most women." Conversely, a *National Review* correspondent calls her "one of the most remarkable women in American history," a dynamo who "has triumphed over the major media, the bureaucrats (and bureaucrettes), and the

'women's movement,' almost singlehandedly." Supporters and detractors alike concede, however, that Schlafly is enormously successful at galvanizing support and influencing public policy. In the *New York Times Magazine,* Joseph Lelyveld observes that she "has become one of the most relentless and accomplished platform debaters of any gender to be found on any side of any issue."

Schlafly published her first book, *A Choice Not an Echo,* in 1964. The paperback, published by a company she and her husband created, championed Senator Barry M. Goldwater for the Republican presidential nomination. Over 3 million copies of *A Choice Not an Echo* were sold; political analysts contend that the work helped Goldwater to secure his party's nomination. Thereafter Schlafly teamed with a retired military man, Admiral Chester Ward, to coauthor more titles on the subjects of national defense policy and nuclear strategy. In works such as *The Gravediggers, Strike from Space, The Betrayers,* and *Kissinger on the Couch,* Schlafly and Ward find fault with a series of presidential advisors who, in their view, weakened the United States' defenses and paved the way for Soviet nuclear superiority. FitzGerald explains: "The central thesis of these books was that certain powerful government officials were plotting the unilateral disarmament of the United States."

Schlafly's first blast against the Equal Rights Amendment was printed in the February, 1972 issue of *The Phyllis Schlafly Report.* Schlafly told *Newsweek* that she "didn't set out to confront the whole women's lib movement. These tasks were thrust upon me." Convinced that the ERA would undermine family life, take away the legal rights of wives, and thrust women into military combat, Schlafly turned her full attention to a crusade to defeat the amendment. She founded Stop ERA in 1972 and the Eagle Forum in 1975, both of which became sophisticated grass-roots lobby organizations with the goal of defeating ERA. Schlafly also testified against the amendment in thirty state legislatures. *New Republic* contributor Morton Kondracke observes that when state-by-state ratification of the amendment began to slow down, "it was caught up to and walloped by anti-feminist firebrand Phyllis Schlafly, one of the most gifted practitioners of political diatribe in the country today. Most of Schlafly's major arguments against ERA [were] outrageous fabrications, but they [were] so artful and so brazenly repeated that Schlafly . . . put ERA proponents on the defensive in state after state." Although polls showed that a majority of Americans favored

ERA, Schlafly and her corps of trained volunteers "made the ERA so controversial that legislators preferred to avoid it—thus turning the weight of inertia against the amendment," according to FitzGerald. Schlafly's pro-family movement pooled forces with the burgeoning American Conservative Union, the Moral Majority, and the Catholic, Baptist, Orthodox Jewish, and Mormon churches to reach state legislators individually. She made speeches against ERA repeatedly, often driving hostile audiences to hysteria with her calmly-expressed and unshakable convictions.

The Power of the Positive Woman outlines Schlafly's views on the status of American women. The Positive Woman, she writes, "rejoices in the creative capability within her body and the power potential of her mind and spirit. She understands that men and women are different, and that those very differences provide the key to her success as a person and fulfillment as a woman." The Women's Liberation Movement, she contends, is peopled by "a bunch of bitter women seeking a constitutional cure for their personal problems" and "Typhoid Marys carrying a germ called lost identity."

BIOGRAPHICAL/CRITICAL SOURCES:

BOOKS

Authors in the News, Volume 1, Gale (Detroit), 1976.
Contemporary Issues Criticism, Volume 1, Gale, 1982.
Felsenthal, Carol, *The Sweetheart of the Silent Majority: The Biography of Phyllis Schlafly,* Doubleday (New York City), 1981.
Gilder, George, *Men and Marriage,* Pelican (New York City), 1987.
Schlafly, Phyllis, *The Power of the Positive Woman,* Arlington House, 1977.

PERIODICALS

Christian Century, April 24, 1985.
Modern Age, winter, 1977.
Ms., March, 1974; May, 1981; January, 1982; September, 1982.
National NOW Times, December, 1977.
National Review, June 6, 1975; February 3, 1978; May 15, 1981; August 6, 1982.
New Republic, April 30, 1977.
Newsweek, July 25, 1977; February 28, 1983; December 23, 1985.
New York Daily News, November 22, 1977.
New York Review of Books, November 19, 1981.
New York Times, December 15, 1975; October 14, 1977; January 24, 1980.
New York Times Book Review, October 30, 1977.
New York Times Magazine, April 17, 1977.
People, March 30, 1981.
Rolling Stone, November 26, 1981.
Time, July 3, 1978; May 4, 1981; July 12, 1982.
Washington Post, July 11, 1974.

*   *   *

SCHLEIN, Miriam   1926-
  (Susan Dorritt)

PERSONAL: Born in 1926; children: Elizabeth, John. *Education:* Brooklyn College (now of the City University of New York), received degree.

ADDRESSES: Home—19 East 95th St., New York, NY 10128.

CAREER: Writer.

MEMBER: Authors Guild, Authors League of America, PEN American Center, National Writers Union.

AWARDS, HONORS: Junior Book Award Medal, Boys' Clubs of America, 1953, for *Fast Is Not a Ladybug: A Book about Fast and Slow Things;* Herald Tribune Honor Book, 1954, for *Elephant Herd;* Children's Spring Book Festival Honor Book, 1955, for *Little Red Nose;* Kirkus Reviews 100 Best citation, 1974, and Westchester Library Best books citation, 1974-75, both for *What's Wrong with Being a Skunk?;* Outstanding Science Trade Book for Children citation, National Science Teachers Association/Children's Book Council, 1976, and Showcase Title selection, Children's Book Council, 1977, for *Giraffe: The Silent Giant;* Outstanding Science Trade Book for Children citations, 1979, for *Snake Fights, Rabbit Fights, and More: A Book about Animal Fighting,* 1980, for *Lucky Porcupine!,* 1982, for *Billions of Bats,* 1986, for *The Dangerous Life of the Sea Horse,* and 1991, for *Discovering Dinosaur Babies;* Honor Book citation, New York Academy of Sciences, 1984, for *Project Panda Watch;* Children's Books of the Year citation, Child Study Association, 1989, for *Pigeons;* Outstanding Science Trade Book for Children citation, 1990, and Sunshine State Young Readers Award list and Nebraska Golden

Sower Award nominee, both 1992-93, all for *The Year of the Panda;* "Pick of the Lists" citation, American Booksellers Association, 1991, for *I Sailed with Columbus.* Several of Schlein's books have been selections of the Junior Library Guild and other book clubs.

WRITINGS:

PICTURE BOOKS

A Day at the Playground, illustrated by Eloise Wilkin, Golden Press (New York City), 1951.

Tony's Pony, illustrated by Van Kaufman, Simon & Schuster, 1952.

Go with the Sun, illustrated by Symeon Shimin, W. R. Scott, 1952.

The Four Little Foxes, illustrated by Luis Quintanilla, W. R. Scott, 1953.

When Will the World Be Mine?, illustrated by Jean Charlot, W. R. Scott, 1953, published as *The Rabbit's World,* illustrated by Peter Parnall, Four Winds Press (New York City), 1973.

Elephant Herd, illustrated by Shimin, W. R. Scott, 1954.

The Sun Looks Down, illustrated by Abner Graboff, Abelard Schuman (New York City), 1954.

How Do You Travel?, illustrated by Paul Galdone, Abingdon (Nashville), 1954.

Little Red Nose, illustrated by Roger Duvoisin, Abelard Schuman, 1955.

Puppy's House, illustrated by Katherine Evans, Albert Whitman (Niles, IL), 1955.

Big Talk, illustrated by Harvey Weiss, W. R. Scott, 1955, illustrated by Joan Auclair, Bradbury (Scarsdale, NY), 1990.

Lazy Day, illustrated by Weiss, W. R. Scott, 1955.

City Boy, Country Boy, illustrated by Katherine Evans, Children's Press (Chicago), 1955.

Henry's Ride, illustrated by Vana Earle, Abingdon, 1956.

Deer in the Snow, illustrated by Leonard Kessler, Abelard Schuman, 1956.

A Bunny, a Bird, a Funny Cat, illustrated by Graboff, 1957.

Little Rabbit, the High Jumper, illustrated by Theresa Sherman, W. R. Scott, 1957, published as *Just Like Me,* illustrated by Marilyn Janovitz, Hyperion (New York City), 1993.

Amazing Mr. Pelgrew, illustrated by Weiss, Abelard Schuman, 1957.

Here Comes Night, illustrated by Weiss, Albert Whitman, 1957.

The Bumblebee's Secret, illustrated by Weiss, Abelard Schuman, 1958.

Home, The Tale of a Mouse, illustrated by E. Harper Johnson, Abelard Schuman, 1958.

Herman McGregor's World, illustrated by Weiss, Albert Whitman, 1958.

Kittens, Cubs, and Babies, illustrated by Charlot, W. R. Scott, 1959, published as *Big Lion, Little Lion,* illustrated by Joe Lasker, Albert Whitman, 1964.

The Fisherman's Day, illustrated by Weiss, Albert Whitman, 1959.

The Sun, the Wind, the Sea, and the Rain, illustrated by Lasker, Abelard Schuman, 1960.

(Under pseudonym Susan Dorritt) *Laurie's New Brother,* illustrated by Elizabeth Donald, Abelard Schuman, 1961.

The Pile of Junk, illustrated by Weiss, Abelard Schuman, 1962.

Snow Time, illustrated by Lasker, Albert Whitman, 1962.

The Way Mothers Are, illustrated by Lasker, Albert Whitman, 1963, revised edition, 1993.

Who?, illustrated by Weiss, Walck, 1963.

The Big Green Thing, illustrated by Elizabeth Dauber, Grosset & Dunlap, 1963.

Billy, The Littlest One, illustrated by Lucy Hawkinson, Albert Whitman, 1966.

The Best Place, illustrated by Erica Merkling, Albert Whitman, 1968.

My House, illustrated by Lasker, Albert Whitman, 1971.

The Girl Who Would Rather Climb Trees, illustrated by Judith Gwyn Brown, Harcourt (San Diego), 1975.

I Hate It, illustrated by Brown, Albert Whitman, 1978.

That's Not Goldie!, illustrated by Susan Gough Magurn, Simon & Schuster, 1990.

More Than One, illustrated by Donald Crew, Greenwillow (New York City), 1996.

CHILDREN'S FICTION

Oomi, the New Hunter, illustrated by George Mason, Abelard Schuman, 1955.

Something for Now, Something for Later, illustrated by Leonard Weisgard, Harper (New York City), 1956.

The Big Cheese, illustrated by Joseph Low, W. R. Scott, 1958.

The Raggle Taggle Fellow, illustrated by Weiss, Abelard Schuman, 1959.

Little Dog Little, illustrated by Hertha Depper, Abelard Schuman, 1959.

Amuny, Boy of Old Egypt, illustrated by Thea Dupays, Abelard Schuman, 1961.

The Snake in the Carpool, illustrated by N. M. Bodecker, Abelard Schuman, 1963.

Bobo the Troublemaker, illustrated by Ray Cruz, Four Winds Press, 1976.

I, Tut: The Boy Who Became Pharaoh (historical), illustrated by Erik Hilgerdt, Four Winds Press, 1979.

The Year of the Panda, illustrated by Kim Mak, Crowell (New York City), 1990.

I Sailed with Columbus (historical), illustrated by Tom Newsom, Harper, 1991.

Secret Land of the Past, illustrated by Kees de Kiefte, Scholastic (New York City), 1992.

CONCEPT BOOKS

Shapes, illustrated by Sam Berman, W. R. Scott, 1952.

Fast Is Not a Ladybug: A Book about Fast and Slow Things, illustrated by Kessler, W. R. Scott, 1953 (published in England as *Fast Is Not a Ladybird,* World's Work, 1961).

Heavy Is a Hippopotamus, illustrated by Kessler, W. R. Scott, 1954.

It's about Time, illustrated by Kessler, W. R. Scott, 1955.

My Family, illustrated by Weiss, Abelard Schuman, 1960.

CHILDREN'S SCIENCE BOOKS

What's Wrong with Being a Skunk?, illustrated by Cruz, Four Winds Press, 1974.

Giraffe: The Silent Giant, illustrated by Betty Fraser, Four Winds Press, 1976.

On the Track of the Mystery Animal: The Story of the Discovery of the Okapi, illustrated by Ruth Sanderson, Four Winds Press, 1978.

Snake Fights, Rabbit Fights, and More: A Book about Animal Fighting, illustrated by Sue Thompson, Crown, 1979.

Antarctica: The Great White Continent, Hastings House (New York City), 1980.

Lucky Porcupine!, illustrated by Martha Weston, Four Winds Press, 1980.

Billions of Bats, illustrated by Walter Kessell, Lippincott (New York City), 1982.

Project Panda Watch, illustrated by Robert Shetterly, Atheneum (New York City), 1984.

What the Elephant Was: Strange Prehistoric Elephants, Atheneum, 1985.

The Dangerous Life of the Sea Horse, illustrated by Gwen Cole, Atheneum, 1986.

Pigeons, photographs by Margaret Miller, Crowell, 1989.

Discovering Dinosaur Babies, illustrated by Margaret Colbert, Four Winds, 1991.

Let's Go Dinosaur Tracking!, illustrated by Kate Duke, Harper, 1991.

Squirrel Watching, photographs by Marjorie Pillar, Harper, 1992.

The Dino Quiz Book, illustrated by Nate Evans, Scholastic, 1995.

Before the Dinosaurs, illustrated by Michael Rothman, Scholastic, 1996.

The Puzzle of the Dinosaur-Bird: The Story of Archaeopteryx, illustrated by Mark Hallett, Dial (New York City), 1996.

"JANE GOODALL'S ANIMAL WORLD" SERIES

Hippos, Atheneum, 1989.

Pandas, Atheneum, 1989.

Elephants, Atheneum, 1990.

Gorillas, Atheneum, 1990.

CHILDREN'S NONFICTION

Metric: The Modern Way to Measure, illustrated by Jan Pyk, Harcourt, 1975.

Rosh Hashanah and Yom Kippur, illustrated by Erika Weihs, Behrman (New York City), 1983.

Hanukkah, illustrated by Katherine Kahn, Behrman, 1983.

Shavuot, illustrated by Weihs, Behrman, 1983.

Shabbat, illustrated by Amy Blake, Behrman, 1983.

Prayers and Blessings, illustrated by Amye Rosenberg, Behrman, 1983.

Passover, illustrated by Kahn, Behrman, 1983.

Sukkot and Simhat Torah, illustrated by Rosenberg, Behrman, 1983.

Purim, illustrated by Ruth Heller, Behrman, 1983.

OTHER

Moon-Months and Sun-Days (folktales), illustrated by Shelly Sacks, W. R. Scott, 1972.

Juju-Sheep and the Python's Moonstone, and Other Moon Stories from Different Times and Different Places (folktales), illustrated by Lasker, Albert Whitman, 1973.

Also author of additional books under pseudonym Susan Dorritt, including *Wait Till Sunday,* illustrated by Duvoisin, *Jason's Lucky Day,* illustrated by John Strickland Goodall, and *Jellybean, the Puppy Who Was Born in the Time of the Snow,* illustrated by Pat Marriott, all for Abelard-Schuman.

Several of Schlein's books have been translated into Danish, Dutch, French, German, Italian, Norwegian, Russian, and Swedish, or are available in Braille editions.

ADAPTATIONS: Fast Is Not a Ladybug and *Shapes* were made into short films; other books have been included in school readers and on phonograph records for children.

WORK IN PROGRESS: Sleep Safe, Little Whale, illustrated by Peter Sis, a picture book for Greenwillow.

SIDELIGHTS: Miriam Schlein is best known for her many books which acquaint young readers with animals and their behaviors, dispelling myths about creatures such as bats, skunks, and porcupines. In addition to her inviting writing style, Schlein often approaches her subject from a fresh angle so that her readers are entertained as well as educated. As Joan McGrath remarks in *Twentieth-Century Children's Writers,* "Schlein is an extremely important and influential writer for the beginner, for she has made the difficult explication of concepts for the beginning reader her province."

Schlein's early concept books, particularly those illustrated by Leonard Kessler, were pioneers in the field, according to Barbara Bader in *American Picturebooks from Noah's Ark to the Beast Within.* "Her rackety-packety manner of writing for kids . . . , the bounce, the sunshine the two together brought to a book, their blithe young way with ideas, ordinary ideas—these were picked up in turn by many others." *Heavy Is a Hippopotamus,* for instance, has "a quirky kind of humor that fixes a point indelibly in the mind," *New York Times Book Review* writer Ellen Lewis Buell remarks; the critic observes that *Shapes* similarly uses "a deceptively light touch" to explain ideas of round and square, making for "a brilliant little book which will help to train a youngster's eye."

Many of Schlein's fictional picture books also contain more complex concepts—such as family relation-

ships and ownership—along with a pleasant story. The 1953 title *When Will the World Be Mine?,* for instance, tells of a young snowshoe hare whose mother teaches him how to enjoy the things of the forest which "belong" to him—the stream, the snow, the trees. Schlein's "experimental, imaginative" work is reminiscent of that of Margaret Wise Brown's "at its best," Buell asserts in the *New York Times Book Review,* "yet it has its own individuality." The story is "gentle in tone [and] unobtrusively informative," a *Bulletin of the Center for Children's Books* reviewer notes of the book's 1974 reissue as *The Rabbit's World;* the critic also praises the "warm" portrayal of the mother-child relationship. *The Four Little Foxes* likewise focuses on an animal family with which children can identify. Lois Palmer comments in *New York Times Book Review* that "the just-like-us quality of the story helps children to sense the parallel to their own progress from small to big," among other family interactions.

In her first natural science book, 1974's *What's Wrong with Being a Skunk?,* Schlein uses an informal, conversational approach to provide readers with "a wealth of information" that refutes the animal's negative reputation, according to a *Publishers Weekly* critic. While the "simply worded text" is "conversational in style and makes use of analogies to human behavior," Mary M. Burns observes in *Horn Book,* the skunk is never portrayed as anything other than an animal. Similarly, in *Lucky Porcupine!* "Schlein has created an anecdotal narrative of another misunderstood animal," Rebecca Keese remarks in *School Library Journal.* The myth that porcupines can "shoot" their quills is dismissed, and the creatures' behaviors "are depicted in an informative, thoughtful, and personalized manner," *Booklist's* Barbara Elleman states.

Another misunderstood animal is featured in 1982's *Billions of Bats,* which Timothy C. Williams calls "a very impressive book" in *Science Books and Films.* Looking at the anatomy, behavior, and feeding habits of bats—which do not include sucking people's blood or flying into their hair—Schlein shows how these flying mammals are an important part of environments all over the world. Williams also praises the author for conveying "mature zoological concepts without watering down the information." A less well-known creature is the focus of *The Dangerous Life of the Sea Horse,* a 1986 study that demonstrates Schlein's "usual care and thorough attention to facts," Elleman notes in *Booklist.* Beginning with the birth of baby sea horses—who are carried by their father, not their mother—the author traces the life cycle of these unusual fish, providing "extensive information about this small creature's struggle for survival, its means of propelling itself, and different types of sea horses," Peggy Ellen Leahy explains in *School Library Journal*. Not only is Schlein's text "easy to read," Susan D. Chapnick writes in *Appraisal*, but her style "flows well and keeps the interest of the reader even when introducing difficult biological facts" and terms.

While Schlein often writes about animals that are unfamiliar or misunderstood, she has also provided readers with information on creatures they can see every day. 1989's *Pigeons* is "a much-needed look at our cities' most common bird," Elizabeth S. Watson claims in *Horn Book*. Although the "interesting, factual text . . . is pared down to essentials," Watson continues, it also includes Schlein's own journal of the time she spent observing two new pigeon chicks. Containing "lots of facts," according to Betsy Hearne of the *Bulletin of the Center for Children's Books, Pigeons* is "a must for urban nature study." *Squirrel Watching* similarly "introduces the joy of wildlife observation to children," Susan Oliver comments in *School Library Journal,* with Schlein's style making the book "engaging and personable." *Bulletin of the Center for Children's Books* reviewer Roger Sutton also hails the writing, terming it "conversational, with short sentences that are easy to read and occasionally funny," and concludes that the book's emphasis "encourages readers to participate in the investigation."

Schlein has also communicated historical information to her readers through fiction. In *I, Tut: The Boy Who Became Pharaoh,* Schlein uses Tutankhamen himself to narrate the story of how he came to rule his ancient Egyptian kingdom at the age of nine. "By selecting such an inviting narrator," Jacqueline van Zanten explains in the *New York Times Book Review,* Schlein "manages to pack her text with glimpses of what life was like in Egypt 3,000 years ago without making her reader feel overwhelmed." Tut describes his role as head of ancient Egypt's government and religion, and after his early death at eighteen, his friend Hekenefer relates how the king was mourned and buried, leaving behind the treasure trove we know today as "King Tut's Tomb." "Simple and dignified, the story should appeal to the many children who know of [Tut's] tomb," Zena Sutherland observes in the *Bulletin of the Center for Children's Books,* also praising Schlein's "carefully factual" writing.

Similarly, in *I Sailed with Columbus* the author's portrayal of Christopher Columbus's journey to the New World "is notable for its bits of navigational information eagerly revealed by its likable protagonist," Sylvia V. Meisner writes in *School Library Journal*. This time a fictional character, the ship's boy Julio, writes down in his journal all of the notable events he sees during Columbus's pioneering voyage to America. Schlein used details she found in Columbus's own diaries, and the facts that Julio "reports with refreshing simplicity and candor" make for a story that is "compelling as well as accurate," a *Publishers Weekly* critic states.

While she may be better known for her nonfiction works, Schlein has written distinctive stories as well, some of which have remained in print more than thirty years after they first appeared. *Big Talk,* for instance, is the story of a boastful baby kangaroo. As baby Joey brags about his bravery and his ability to run fast and jump high, his mother calmly accepts his inventions and then tells him he will be able to do all these things when he grows up. *Big Talk*'s "exotic" Australian background and gentle story make it "a natural for toddler storytimes," Jeanette Larson remarks in *School Library Journal,* while a *Publishers Weekly* critic praises Schlein's "straightforward, 'less is more' approach" in presenting "an appealingly offbeat look at mother-child relationships."

Two more of Schlein's classic stories of motherly love are *The Way Mothers Are* and *Just Like Me*. In *The Way Mothers Are* a mother cat reassures her offspring she will love it no matter what it does, good or bad. While the 1993 version contains a few changes from the original 1963 text, "the story still captures the interaction between" mother and child, Ilene Cooper states in *Booklist. Just Like Me* similarly shows a parent's love as a mother rabbit relates the legend of a great jumper while her child adds a "just like me" to all the related adventures; the storyteller echoes these words when she relates the joy of the jumper's mother at its return. *School Library Journal* contributor Beth Tegart finds *Just Like Me* "a delightful reissue," adding that "this lovely story belongs on the shelf" with classics by Margaret Wise Brown and Ann Tompert.

Whether in gentle stories of the mother-child bond, fictionalized histories, or straight nonfiction, "Schlein's especial talent lies in her ability to explain while entertaining," McGrath declares. In a book such as *Antarctica: The Great White Continent,* for example, "the writing is easy enough" for beginning readers, "yet has a verve and humor that older children will appreciate," Ellen D. Warwick observes in *School Library Journal*. In addition, Schlein rarely talks down to her readers; in books like *Giraffe: The Silent Giant* the author has "stuck to the facts and let the unusualness of [her] subject come through clearly without resort[ing] to a gee-whiz factor," an *Appraisal* critic remarks. As McGrath concludes, Schlein's books "are works of charm and simplicity that have stood the tests of time."

BIOGRAPHICAL/CRITICAL SOURCES:

BOOKS

Bader, Barbara, *American Picturebooks from Noah's Ark to the Beast Within,* Macmillan (New York City), 1976, pp. 394-97.
Twentieth-Century Children's Writers, 4th edition, St. James Press (Detroit), 1995.

PERIODICALS

Appraisal, winter, 1977, p. 36; spring, 1980, p. 72; summer, 1987, pp. 79-80; summer, 1992, pp. 50-51.
Booklist, December 15, 1978, p. 689; May 1, 1980, p. 1299; September 1, 1986, p. 67; December 1, 1990, p. 752; April 1, 1993, p. 1442.
Bulletin of the Center for Children's Books, February, 1967, pp. 97-98; May, 1974, pp. 148-149; September, 1974, p. 16; March, 1977, p. 113; March, 1979, p. 126; September, 1980, p. 21; February, 1985, p. 116; September, 1989, pp. 18-19; November, 1990, p. 69; October, 1991, pp. 28-29; March, 1992, p. 193.
Horn Book, August, 1974, p. 392; March/April, 1985, p. 199; November/December, 1989, p. 793; November/December, 1990, p. 745.
Kirkus Reviews, November 15, 1976, p. 1219; October 15, 1978, p. 1141; April 1, 1980, p. 442.
New York Times Book Review, November 16, 1952, p. 41; August 9, 1953, p. 14; January 17, 1954, p. 18; October 31, 1954, p. 36; May 6, 1979, p. 20.
Publishers Weekly, October 2, 1972, p. 54; May 20, 1974, p. 64; August 31, 1990, p. 62; October 25, 1991, p. 69.
School Library Journal, September, 1975, p. 111; March, 1976, p. 97; November, 1976, p. 63; November, 1978, p. 79; January, 1980, p. 60; August, 1980, pp. 56, 70; March, 1985, p. 171; January, 1987, pp. 78-79; December, 1989, p. 116; October, 1990, p. 119; November, 1990,

p. 98; January, 1991, p. 80; July, 1991, p. 86; October, 1991, p. 128; January, 1992, p. 106; March, 1992, p. 252; July, 1993, p. 71.
Science Books and Films, November/December, 1982, p. 93.

*   *   *

SCHOM, Alan (Morris) 1937-

PERSONAL: Born May 9, 1937, in Sterling, IL; married Juliana Leslie Hill, September 6, 1963 (divorced April 19, 1984); children: Sarah Elizabeth Rose, Emma Sofia Anne. *Education:* University of California, Berkeley, A.B.; School of Oriental Studies, University of Durham, Ph.D.

ADDRESSES: Agent—c/o HarperCollins, 10 E. 53rd St., New York, NY 10022.

CAREER: University of California, Riverside, associate of history department, 1968-69; Southern Connecticut State University, New Haven, assistant professor of modern French and European history, 1969-76; writer, 1976—.

MEMBER: Authors Guild; French Colonial Historical Society (founder; president, 1974-76).

AWARDS, HONORS: Grants from American Philosophical Society, 1970 and 1984, and Research Foundation of the City University of New York, 1985; fellow of Hoover Institution on War, Revolution, and Peace, 1982; Pulitzer Prize and National Book Award nominations for *One Hundred Days: Napoleon's Road to Waterloo*.

WRITINGS:

Lyautey in Morocco: Protectorate Administration, 1912-1925, University of California Press (Berkeley), 1970.
Emile Zola: A Bourgeois Rebel, Queen Anne Press, 1987, published in the United States as *Emile Zola: A Biography,* Holt (New York City), 1988.
Trafalgar: Countdown to Battle, 1803-1805, Atheneum (New York City), 1989.
One Hundred Days: Napoleon's Road to Waterloo, Atheneum, 1992.

Contributor of articles and reviews to history journals.

WORK IN PROGRESS: Napoleon: A Biography, to be published by HarperCollins in 1996.

SIDELIGHTS: Alan Schom's *Emile Zola: A Biography* concentrates on the nineteenth-century French novelist's personal and political life, his marriage, his love affair, and his role in the Dreyfus trial, rather than on a detailed analysis of Zola's creative work or its impact on literature. Writing in the London *Observer,* Anita Brookner praises Schom's eloquence in telling Zola's story: "For new visitors to this almost mythical island of integrity [Zola] in an ocean of duplicity Professor Schom's book will provide a good, sane introduction." A *Kirkus Reviews* reviewer finds the biography "penetrating" and "continuously absorbing," lauding Schom's meticulous research. Barbara Fisher Williamson, in the *New York Times Book Review,* credits Schom with providing the facts of Zola's life, but finds a critical appraisal of those facts lacking. According to Williamson, Schom "presents no evaluation of the novelist's work, never describes the artist's progression and attempts no discussion of the relation between this most socially conscious writer and his times." J. A. Cimon in *Choice* finds *Zola* "extremely well-documented," noting the appendixes, annotated bibliography, indexes, and notes, and recommends the book for both graduate and undergraduate students.

In *Trafalgar: Countdown to Battle, 1803-1805,* Schom draws on original French and British sources to depict the political and military events leading up to what is generally considered Britain's greatest naval victory, the battle of Trafalgar in October, 1805. Byron Farwell in the *Los Angeles Times Book Review* calls *Trafalgar* "a thoroughly researched and splendidly written book," and asserts that Schom has not only placed the Battle of Trafalgar "in its proper historical perspective," but that his battle descriptions are "superb." Farwell feels that Schom "has the rare ability to describe naval affairs and battles in words readily understood by landlubbers." Jay Freeman, writing in *Booklist,* calls *Trafalgar* "historical writing at its best: superbly researched and wrought with style and clarity."

One Hundred Days: Napoleon's Road to Waterloo, nominated both for a Pulitzer Prize and a National Book Award, covers the period from Napoleon's escape from Elba in March, 1815, to his second abdication in June of that same year. Schom again draws upon original French and British sources, emphasizing both the military and political aspects of the period. Richard Holmes in the *Times Literary*

Supplement states that "*One Hundred Days* draws its strength from this melding of the military and the political," and goes on to say that "Schom's mastery of English and French sources has enabled him to avoid that literary nationalism which still obscures our understanding of the period." He believes that Schom "has produced what is undoubtedly the best account of this episode in English."

BIOGRAPHICAL/CRITICAL SOURCES:

PERIODICALS

Booklist, November 15, 1990, p. 598.
Choice, September, 1988, p. 133; February 1991, p. 986.
Financial Times, September 5, 1987.
Glasgow Herald, February 4, 1993.
Kirkus Reviews, March 1, 1988, p. 351; October 15, 1990, p. 1444.
Los Angeles Times Book Review, December 16, 1990, p. 2.
New York Times, June 21, 1988.
New York Times Book Review, July 17, 1988, p. 21.
Observer (London), September 13, 1987, p. 26.
Punch, August 19, 1987.
Sunday Times (London), November 29, 1987.
Telegraph (London), January 24, 1993.
Times (London), October 14, 1990.
Times Educational Supplement, November 27, 1987.
Times Literary Supplement, September 9, 1988; March 19, 1993. p. 27.
Washington Post Book World, June 5, 1988, p. 6.

*   *   *

SCHREINER, Samuel A(gnew), Jr.   1921-

PERSONAL: Born June 6, 1921, in Mt. Lebanon, PA; son of Samuel Agnew (a lawyer) and Mary (Cort) Schreiner; married Doris Moon (an artist and antique dealer and appraiser), September 22, 1945; children: Beverly Ann (Mrs. Jonathan S. Carroll), Carolyn Cort (Mrs. Scott Calder). *Education:* Princeton University, A.B., 1942. *Politics:* Democrat. *Religion:* Presbyterian.

ADDRESSES: Home and office—111 Old Kings Highway S., Darien, CT 06820. *Agent*—Harold Ober Associates, Inc., 425 Madison Ave., New York, NY 10017.

CAREER: McKeesport Daily News, McKeesport, PA, reporter, 1946; *Pittsburgh Sun-Telegraph,* Pittsburgh, PA, reporter, 1946-51; *Parade,* New York, NY, writer and assistant managing editor, 1951-55; *Reader's Digest,* Pleasantville, NY, associate editor, 1955-68, senior editor, 1968-74; full-time writer, 1974—. President of Schreiner Associates. Elder, Noroton Presbyterian Church; secretary, Darien Library Association; former chair, Darien Youth Advisory Committee and Centre Store. *Military service:* U.S. Army, Office of Strategic Services, cryptographer, 1942-45; served in China-Burma-India theater; became first lieutenant; received Bronze Star and Presidential unit citation.

MEMBER: Princeton Club of New York, Noroton Yacht Club.

WRITINGS:

Urban Planning and Public Opinion, Bureau of Urban Research, Princeton University (Princeton, NJ), 1942.
Thine Is the Glory (novel), Arbor House (New York City), 1975.
Pleasant Places (novel), Arbor House, 1976.
The Condensed World of the Reader's Digest, Stein Publishing (Chicago), 1977.
Angelica (novel), Arbor House, 1977.
The Possessors and the Possessed (novel), Arbor House, 1980.
The Van Alens (novel), Arbor House, 1981.
A Place Called Princeton, Arbor House, 1984.
The Trials of Mrs. Lincoln (nonfiction), Donald I. Fine, 1987.
May Day! May Day! (nonfiction), Donald I. Fine, 1990.
(With Everett Alvarez) *Code of Conduct* (nonfiction), Donald I. Fine, 1991.
Henry Clay Frick (biography), St. Martin's (New York City), 1995.

Contributor of articles and stories to popular magazines, including *McCall's, Saturday Evening Post, Collier's, Redbook, Reader's Digest,* and *National Geographic.*

SIDELIGHTS: Samuel A. Schreiner, Jr., told *CA:* "Still going strong on the far side of seventy-three, I would recommend a freelance writing career as the answer to the 'problem' of retirement; you can't afford to retire. Seriously, if you can do without the act of writing as an essential part of daily life, you shouldn't be writing for a living in the first place.

The true rewards of writing come from the process not the profits, and there are very few human endeavors of which this can be said."

BIOGRAPHICAL/CRITICAL SOURCES:

PERIODICALS

Los Angeles Times, August 7, 1987.
Tribune Books (Chicago), August 9, 1987.

* * *

SCHUYLER, David   1950-

PERSONAL: Born April 9, 1950, in Albany, NY; son of Ruth C. Schuyler Cote; married Marsha Sener, September 6, 1985; children: Nancy. *Education:* University of North Carolina, M.A., 1976; University of Delaware, M.A., 1976; Columbia University, Ph.D., 1979.

ADDRESSES: Home—1221 Country Club Dr., Lancaster, PA 17601. *Office*—Department of American Studies, Franklin and Marshall College, Box 3003, Lancaster, PA 17604. *E-mail*—d_schuyler-@acad.fandm.edu.

CAREER: Franklin and Marshall College, Lancaster, PA, assistant professor, 1979-86, associate professor, 1986-92, professor of American Studies, 1992—, chair of department of American Studies, 1988—.

MEMBER: Organization of American Historians, American Studies Association, Society of Architectural Historians, Society of Winterthur Fellows, Athenaeum of Philadelphia.

AWARDS, HONORS: Richard B. Morris Dissertation Prize, Columbia University, 1981; Best Edited Book, Museum of the History of the Confederacy and the Southern Memorial Literary Society, 1982, for *The Papers of Frederick Law Olmsted,* Volume 2: *Slavery and the South, 1852-1857;* Preservation Planning award, Preservation League of New York State, 1991; Honor Award, Connecticut Chapter ASLA and Connecticut Society of Architects/AIA, 1993; Merit Award, Connecticut Trust for Historic Preservation, 1993; Christian R. and Mary F. Lindback Award for Distinguished Teaching, Franklin & Marshall College, 1994.

WRITINGS:

(Editor with Charles E. Beveridge and Charles C. McLaughlin) *The Papers of Frederick Law Olmsted,* Volume 2: *Slavery and the South, 1852-1857,* Johns Hopkins University Press (Baltimore), 1981.

(Editor with Beveridge) *The Papers of Frederick Law Olmsted,* Volume 3: *Creating Central Park, 1857-1861,* Johns Hopkins University Press, 1983.

The New Urban Landscape: The Redefinition of City Form in Nineteenth-Century America, Johns Hopkins University Press, 1986.

(Contributor) *The Best Planned City: The Olmsted Legacy in Buffalo,* edited by Francis R. Kowsky, Burchfield Art Center (Buffalo, NY), 1991.

(Editor with Jane Turner Censer) *The Papers of Frederick Law Olmsted,* Volume 6: *The Years of Olmsted, Vaux & Company, 1865-1874,* Johns Hopkins University Press, 1992.

(Contributor) *Landscape in America,* edited by George F. Thompson, University of Texas Press (Austin), 1995.

Apostle of Taste: Andrew Jackson Downing, 1815-1852, Johns Hopkins University Press, 1996.

"The Frederick Law Olmsted Papers Publication Project," associate editor, 1982-92, member of editorial board, 1993—. "Creating the North American Landscape Series," Johns Hopkins University Press, advisory editor. Contributor to periodicals, including *Journal of Urban History, Pennsylvania History, Planning History Present 7,* and *Landscape.*

WORK IN PROGRESS: A study of race, poverty, and urban renewal in Lancaster, Pennsylvania.

SIDELIGHTS: David Schuyler told *CA:* "As a boy I played in a park in Newburgh, New York, designed by Frederick Law Olmsted and Calvert Vaux in honor of Andrew Jackson Downing. Perhaps as a result of what Olmsted termed 'unconscious influence,' I became interested in studying how and why nineteenth-century Americans created openly-built recreational and domestic areas. After more than a decade of research I still find Olmsted a fascinating subject and the Olmsted papers the single best resource for understanding the development of American culture in the nineteenth century. I should probably spend less time studying and writing, though, and more time relaxing with my family in parks."

SCOTT, Bill
   See SCOTT, William N(eville)

*   *   *

SCOTT, W. N.
   See SCOTT, William N(eville)

*   *   *

SCOTT, William N(eville)   1923-
   (Bill Scott, W. N. Scott)

PERSONAL: Born October 4, 1923, in Bundaberg, Queensland, Australia; son of William (a railway worker) and Elizabeth Florence (a homemaker; maiden name, Christie) Scott; married Mavis Richards (a writer), 1949; child: Harry Alan. *Avocational interests:* Woodcarving, prospecting for gold and precious stones, playing the tin whistle, telling tall stories.

ADDRESSES: Home—157 Pratten St., Warwick, Queensland, 4370, Australia.

CAREER: Worked as a bookseller, publisher, and editor during the 1950s and 1960s; full-time writer, 1974—. *Military service:* Royal Australian Navy, 1942-46; served in Pacific theater.

MEMBER: Queensland Folk Federation, Australian Folklore Society, ISCLR Australian Folklore Association, Order of Australia Association.

AWARDS, HONORS: Mary Gilmore National Award, 1964, for the story, "One Is Enough"; Australian Council fellowship, 1977, 1980, 1981; runner-up for Book of the Year Award, Children's Book Council of Australia, 1979 and 1982; Medal of the Order of Australia, 1992.

WRITINGS:

FOR CHILDREN

(Under name Bill Scott) *Boori,* illustrated by A. M. Hicks, Oxford University Press, 1978.

(Under name Bill Scott) *Darkness under the Hills,* illustrated by Hicks, Oxford University Press, 1980.

Shadows among the Leaves, illustrated by Bill Farr, Heinemann (London), 1984.

Many Kinds of Magic: Tales of Mystery, Myth and Enchantment, illustrated by Lisa Herriman, Penguin (London), 1988.

Following the Gold (poetry), Omnibus (London), 1989.

Hey Rain (recording), Restless Music, 1992.

Songbird in Your Pocket (recordings), Restless Music, 1994.

The Currency Lad, illustrated by Annmarie Scott, Walter McVitty, 1994.

FOR ADULTS

Focus on Judith Wright, University of Queensland Press, 1967.

Some People (stories), Jacaranda Press (Brisbane, Australia), 1968.

(Under name W. N. Scott) *Brother and Brother* (poems), Jacaranda Press, 1972.

(Under name Bill Scott) *Portrait of Brisbane,* illustrated by Cedric Emanuel, Rigby, 1976.

My Uncle Arch and Other People (stories), Rigby, 1977.

(Under name Bill Scott) *Tough in the Old Days* (autobiography), Rigby, 1979.

Australian Bushrangers (originally published as *The Child and Henry Book of Bushrangers*), Child & Henry, 1983.

The Long and the Short and the Tall: Australian Yarns, Western Plains Publishing, 1985.

Brisbane Sketchbook, Herron, 1988.

EDITOR

The Continual Singing: An Anthology of World Poetry, Jacaranda Press, 1973.

(Under name Bill Scott) *The Complete Book of Australian Folklore,* Ure Smith, 1976.

(Under name Bill Scott; with Pro Hart) *Bushranger Ballads,* Ure Smith, 1976.

The Second Penguin Australian Songbook, Penguin Australia, 1980.

(Under name Bill Scott; with John Meredith) *Ned Kelly after a Century of Acrimony,* Lansdowne Press, 1980.

Impressions on a Continent (stories), Heinemann, 1983.

The Penguin Book of Australian Humorous Verse, Penguin Australia, 1984.

OTHER

Work represented in anthologies, including *More Australian Poetry for Fun,* Hamlyn, 1975. Author of narration for documentary film *Explorer Safari,* 1984. Editor of series "Australian Content Readers," 1981—. Contributor to folktale journals, including *Stringybark and Greenhide, Folklore Round Table,* and *Folklines.*

SIDELIGHTS: William N. Scott is an Australian writer and poet who has written extensively (and often sings) about the myths and customs of his native Australia. His writing style has been described as heroic, especially in reference to his writings on the Aborigine natives, which frequently concern their ties to their homeland, spiritualism, and their strict code of interpersonal and intertribal relationships.

Scott's path to becoming a writer was not evident in his early years. "I was brought up in a small country town during the bitter days of the Depression," he once stated. "I left school at age fourteen and worked at various jobs, mainly as a storeman [stock boy or salesperson], until I was old enough to enlist in the navy during World War II. I served on a minelayer and later in the small wooden ships of the Coastal Forces as a seaman and antiaircraft gunner. From 1946 to 1948, I traveled around eastern Australia, working as a gold prospector, miner, sugar cane cutter, and locomotive driver; this part of my life is recorded in the book *Tough in the Old Days.* After my marriage in 1949, I worked as a seaman on the ship which supplied the lighthouses along the Great Barrier Reef, and as a steam engine driver in various industries. Following an industrial accident in 1954, I began work as a bookseller, and later I became one of the people who founded the publishing house of what is now Jacaranda/Wiley Press in Brisbane, Australia. I resigned my position as trade manager in 1974 to write full time.

"I began writing poetry in the late 1940s," Scott continued, "and some of it was published in newspapers and magazines. In the mid-1950s I began writing short stories with some success and became involved in the investigation and collection of Australian folklore. I wrote, and sometimes presented, scripts for radio. As a folklorist, my interest is in the field of 'contemporary urban legends,'" Scott explained, "and I carry on a vigorous correspondence with fellow enthusiasts in England and the United States."

Two of Scott's most popular children's books, *Boori* and its sequel, *Darkness under the Hills,* are about an Aboriginal man of magical powers, not born as a human, but created out of clay by one of his tribe's most powerful elders. Since the elders cannot teach Boori all the skills and magic a person must have, Boori has to learn himself by serving his community, the Aboriginal law, and the spirits that govern both. Though alone on his quest, Boori does not have to endure all these trials and tests alone, for he is provided with a quick-witted spirit friend, Jaree, who lives in a leather pouch hanging from his neck. Together these two battle the forces of evil. According to the complex Australian Aboriginal law (the code of belief and honor that governs every facet of Aboriginal life), all people are responsible for their actions in nature, the spiritual world, and their human community. According to these beliefs, anyone—Aboriginal or not—who breaks this law must try to restore the delicate balance that has been upended. Woven into these stories are portions of songs, legends, dances, and dramas that form the basis of the native Australian culture.

Writing in *Booklist,* reviewer Betsy Hearne stated that those who study mythology might be interested in comparing *Boori* with "the more familiar exploits of Greco-Roman hero figures." A reviewer in *Kirkus Reviews* cautioned about the initial slow pace of *Boori,* stating that "stories drawn from the Australian aboriginal past have a fatal tendency to seem at once dense and aimless, and for some way into the book, [*Boori*] is no exception."

Patricia A. Morgans said in *Best Sellers* that *Darkness under the Hills* is "a beautifully, sometimes poetically, written book that will appeal to fantasy lovers in junior high school." Morgans's concern over the book's wordiness, however, was echoed by George Shannon of the *School Library Journal* who stated that "Dialogue falls into speech-making, and so many facts are deposited that narrative flow is impeded."

Scott's *Shadows among the Leaves,* classified by some critics as an ecological thriller, tells of the Shadows—formless, animated spirit forces which tear through the Australian rain forest destroying those who would harm the jungle habitat. Young Jo Brady must contend with these forces weekly as she travels from her father's farm to the home of an elderly, part-aboriginal neighbor woman. A *Junior Bookshelf* reviewer commented that "here are the makings of a strong story. It is enriched, and made more credible,

by the space devoted to the ordinary life of a country settlement."

BIOGRAPHICAL/CRITICAL SOURCES:

BOOKS

Scott, Bill, *Tough in the Old Days,* Rigby, 1979.

PERIODICALS

Best Sellers, April, 1981, p. 39.
Booklist, May 1, 1979, p. 1366.
Growing Point, September, 1979, p. 3563.
Junior Bookshelf, February, 1986, p. 40.
Kirkus Reviews, March 1, 1979, p. 267-68.
School Library Journal, April, 1981, p. 131; September, 1987, p. 133.
Voice of Youth Advocates, June, 1981, p. 55.

*   *   *

SEABROOK, John
   See HUBBARD, L(afayette) Ron(ald)

*   *   *

SEGAL, David R(obert) 1941-

PERSONAL: Born June 22, 1941, in New York, NY; son of Harry (a civil servant) and Daisy Rose (an educator; maiden name, Gold) Segal; married Mady Wechsler (a professor), December 25, 1966; children: Eden Heather. *Education:* Harpur College of the State University of New York (now Binghamton University), B.A. (cum laude), 1962; University of Chicago, M.A., 1963, Ph.D., 1967.

ADDRESSES: Home—9007 Gettysburg Ln., College Park Woods, MD 20740. *Office*—Department of Sociology, University of Maryland, College Park, MD 20742.

CAREER: University of Michigan, Ann Arbor, assistant professor, 1966-71, associate professor of sociology, 1971-75, acting director of Center for Research on Social Organization; University of Maryland, College Park, professor of sociology, government, and politics, 1975—, director of Center for Research on Military Organizations, 1995—. Special assistant to the Chief of Staff of the U.S. Army, 1993-95. Visiting member of faculty at U.S. Army War College, 1973-75; visiting professor at U.S. Military Academy at West Point, 1988-89; holder of S. L. A. Marshall Chair at U.S. Army Research Institute for the Behavioral and Social Sciences, 1992; guest lecturer at colleges and universities in the United States and Canada. Fellow at Center for Social Organization Studies, 1965-66; guest scholar at Brookings Institution, 1981-83; guest scientist at Walter Reed Army Institute of Research, 1982-90. Civilian chief of social processes technical area at U.S. Army Research Institute for the Behavioral and Social Sciences, 1973-75. Member of manpower, personnel, and training panel of Naval Research Advisory Committee, 1979-81; member of editorial board of National Defense University Press, 1981-83. Project director for Twentieth Century Fund, 1982-88; member of advisory panel of Advanced Technology, Inc., 1982. Consultant to Booz-Allen & Hamilton, Andrulis Research Corp., and General Research Corp.; staff consultant to the National Security and International Affairs Division, U.S. General Accounting Office, 1988-90.

MEMBER: International Sociological Association (member of executive council of research committee on armed forces and conflict resolution, 1982-86; vice-president, 1986-94; president, 1994—), International Studies Association, American Sociological Association (section on peace and war, member of council, 1988-90, chairperson, 1991-92), American Association for Public Opinion Research, American Society for Public Administration, Military Operations Research Society (chairperson of working group of human resource management, 1976), Inter-University Seminar on the Armed Forces and Society (member of executive council, 1974-82; associate chairperson, 1982-88; member of board of directors, 1987-95; president, 1995—).

AWARDS, HONORS: Horace H. Rackham fellow at University of Michigan, 1968; Ruth M. Sinclair Memorial Honors Program Award, 1970; James K. Pollock visiting research scholar at DATUM and University of Bonn, 1971; U.S. Department of the Army, commendation, 1975, certificate of achievement, 1976, medal for outstanding civilian service, 1989; Mid-Career Award, American Society for Public Administration, 1984; D.H.L., Towson State University, 1991; President's Award, District of Columbia Sociological Society, 1994.

WRITINGS:

Society and Politics, Scott, Foresman (Glenview, IL), 1974.

(With Jerald G. Bachman and John D. Blair) *The All-Volunteer Force: A Study of Ideology in the Military,* University of Michigan Press (Ann Arbor), 1977.

Recruiting for Uncle Sam, University Press of Kansas (Lawrence), 1989.

(With wife, Mady W. Segal) *Peacekeepers and Their Wives,* Greenwood Press (Westport, CT), 1993.

EDITOR AND CONTRIBUTOR

(With Nancy Goldman) *The Social Psychology of Military Service,* Sage Publications (Beverly Hills, CA), 1976.

(With H. Wallace Sinaiko) *Life in the Rank and File,* Pergamon (Elmsford, NY), 1986.

(With Louis Kriesberg) *The Transformation of European Communist Societies,* JAI Press (Greenwich, CT), 1992.

OTHER

Contributor to over thirty-eight books. Associate editor of "Sage Research Progress on War, Revolution, and Peacekeeping" series, Sage Publications, 1979-82. Contributor to over thirty-eight books. Also contributor of over 100 articles and reviews to political science and sociology journals. *Armed Forces and Society,* associate editor, 1980-82, editor, 1982-88; associate editor, *American Sociologist,* 1973-75, *Sociological Focus,* 1973-79, *Journal of Political and Military Sociology,* 1974-77, 1981-83, *Western Sociological Review,* 1977-81, and *Social Science Quarterly,* 1989-95; guest editor, *Youth and Society,* 1978.

WORK IN PROGRESS: A book on reserve military personnel.

SIDELIGHTS: David R. Segal once told *CA:* "My major field of interest in graduate school was political sociology, and this interest led to the publication of my first book. One could not study politics in the 1960s, however, without recognizing the central importance of the military as an instrument of policy. Social scientists at the time were avoiding studies of the military, afraid, I suspect, of being tainted by coming too close to the unclean. I felt the military was too important to go unstudied, and it was unlikely to go away, so I spent some time looking at it.

When the era of the all-volunteer force dawned, it was clear to me that it was one of the largest scale social experiments ever attempted, and it too was worthy of study. The military has transformed the basic relationship between the citizen and the state in America in ways that we are only beginning to understand."

*   *   *

SEULING, Barbara   1937-
(Carrie Austin)

PERSONAL: Surname pronounced "Soo-ling"; born July 22, 1937, in Brooklyn, NY; daughter of Kaspar Joseph (a postman) and Helen Veronica (Gadie) Seuling. *Education:* Attended Hunter College (now Hunter College of the City University of New York), 1955-57, Columbia University, 1957-59, and School of Visual Arts. *Avocational interests:* Movies (silent to modern).

ADDRESSES: Home—Manhattan, NY; Landgrove, VT. *Agent*—Miriam Attshuler Literary Agency, RR #1, Box 5, 5 Old Post Road, Red Hook, NY 12571.

CAREER: Freelance writer and illustrator, 1968—. Has worked for an investment firm, a university, and at the General Electric Co. exhibit at the New York World's Fair. Dell Publishing Co., New York City, children's book editor, 1965-71; J. B. Lippincott Co., New York City, children's book editor, 1971-73. Director, The Manuscript Workshop, 1982—. Lecturer, teacher, and consultant on children's books and writing for children.

MEMBER: Society of Children's Book Writers and Illustrators (board of directors).

AWARDS, HONORS: Award from American Institute of Graphic Arts, 1979, for *The Teeny Tiny Woman: An Old English Ghost Story;* Christopher Award, 1979, for *The New York Kids' Book;* first place, Harold Marshall Solstad Prize, Cameron University Children's Short Story Competition, 1982.

WRITINGS:

JUVENILE

The Last Legal Spitball and Other Little Known Facts about Sports, Doubleday (New York City), 1975.

Abracadabra!: Creating Your Own Magic Show from Beginning to End, Messner (New York City), 1975.

You Can't Eat Peanuts in Church and Other Little Known Laws, Doubleday, 1975.

The Teeny Tiny Woman: An Old English Ghost Story, Viking (New York City), 1976.

The Loudest Screen Kiss and Other Little Known Facts about the Movies, Doubleday, 1976.

The Great Big Elephant and the Very Small Elephant, Crown (New York City), 1977.

The Last Cow on the White House Lawn and Other Little Known Facts about the Presidency, Doubleday, 1978.

You Can't Count a Billion Dollars and Other Little Known Facts about Money, Doubleday, 1979.

The New York Kids' Book, Doubleday, 1979.

The Triplets, Clarion (Boston), 1980.

Just Me, Harcourt (New York City), 1982.

You Can't Show Kids in Underwear and Other Little Known Facts about T.V., Doubleday, 1982.

Elephants Can't Jump and Other Freaky Facts about Animals, Lodestar (New York City), 1984.

Stay Safe, Play Safe: A Book about Safety Rules, Western Publishing (New York City), 1985.

What Kind of Family Is This?, Western Publishing, 1985.

I'm Not So Different: A Book about Handicaps, Western Publishing, 1986.

Who's the Boss Here?: A Book about Parental Authority, Western Publishing, 1986.

You Can't Sneeze with Your Eyes Open and Other Freaky Facts about the Human Body, Lodestar, 1986.

It Is Illegal to Quack Like a Duck and Other Little Known Laws, Field/Weekly Reader, 1987, Lodestar, 1988.

(Under pseudonym Carrie Austin) *Julie's Boy Problem* (Party Line series), Berkeley (New York City), 1990.

(Under pseudonym Carrie Austin) *Allie's Wild Surprise* (Party Line series), Berkeley, 1990.

The Man in the Moon Is Upside Down in Argentina, Ivy Books/Ballantine (New York City), 1991.

Too Cold to Hatch a Dinosaur, Ivy Books/Ballantine, 1993.

Natural Disasters, Kidsbooks, 1994.

The Bug That Goes Blam!, Willowisp, 1995.

ILLUSTRATOR

Wilma Thompson, *That Barbara!,* Delacorte (New York City), 1969.

Nan Hayden Agle, *Tarr of Belway Smith,* Seabury Press (New York City), 1969.

Stella Pevsner, *Break a Leg!,* Crown, 1969.

Antonia Barber, *The Affair of the Rockerbye Baby,* Delacorte, 1970.

Pevsner, *Footsteps on the Stairs,* Crown, 1970.

Moses Howard, *The Ostrich Chase,* Holt (New York City), 1974.

Melinda Green, *Bembelman's Bakery,* Parents' Magazine Press (New York City), 1978.

OTHER

How to Write a Children's Book and Get It Published, Scribner (New York City), 1984, revised and expanded edition, 1991.

Contributor to books for and about children. Also contributor to journals for and about children, including *Cricket.*

WORK IN PROGRESS: A book showing kids how to become creative writers; a book about "sticking with it" for children's book writers; a biography.

SIDELIGHTS: "I love both writing and illustrating, but I find that writing takes much more discipline and a different sort of mental energy," Barbara Seuling told *CA.* "After an hour or two of steady writing, I am truly tired. With drawing, I can go on all day and tune in to my favorite radio station at the same time. Someone can interrupt me, talk to me, and I am still involved in my drawing without losing ground. A distraction when I'm writing, however, is serious, and often I cannot go back to work once this happens. I know a lot of it has to do with concentration, but I also wonder if a large part of it isn't the security I feel with drawing, which came naturally and was recognized early, and writing, which I discovered later, and with which I feel less on solid ground.

"My purpose is different for each book I create—to share an emotional experience, show some aspect of the world a little better, or more clearly; make it easier to get through a tough or stressful situation—and yet all this must be kept carefully hidden so that it doesn't frighten children away. So, on the surface, I want to make children laugh, to entertain them, tell them a good story, excite their interest.

"I feel fortunate to work at what I love so much—writing and illustrating children's books. Although it has never been easy, the rewards still outweigh the difficulties. Young people want to know more and more about the life around them, about people and relationships and feelings, and if we're truthful, we can support them in this quest for knowledge. Inevitably, it turns around, and we learn something from the kids.

"My advice to new writers is: be persistent. The saddest part of writing is the defeatism that is felt so early by writers. One's first work rarely gets published, but that is when our hopes and ideals are so high that they are easily dashed by rejection. It is a rough process, and if one can weather the first years, and keep writing in spite of the obstacles, the chances of success keep growing. A writer is a growing thing; we grow with each page we write, and therefore the more we write the more we learn and the better we become."

* * *

SHAARA, Michael (Joseph, Jr.) 1929-1988

PERSONAL: Born June 23, 1929, in Jersey City, NJ; died of a heart attack, May 5, 1988, in Tallahassee, FL; son of Michael Joseph, Sr. (a union organizer) and Alleene (Maxwell) Shaara; married Helen Krumweide, September 16, 1950 (marriage ended, June, 1980); children: Jeffrey, Lila Elise. *Education:* Rutgers University, B.A., 1951; graduate study at Columbia University, 1952-53, and University of Vermont, 1953-54. *Politics:* None. *Religion:* None.

ADDRESSES: Home and office—2074 Robinhood Dr., Melbourne, FL 32935.

CAREER: Writer. Worked as merchant seaman, 1948-49; St. Petersburg Police Department, St. Petersburg, FL, police officer, 1954-55; short story writer, 1955-61; Florida State University, Tallahassee, associate professor of English, 1961-73. Guest lecturer at universities. *Military service:* U.S. Army, 1946-49, paratrooper in 82nd Airborne Division; became sergeant. U.S. Army Reserve, 1949-53.

MEMBER: International Platform Association, Authors Guild, Omicron Delta Kappa, Gold Key.

AWARDS, HONORS: Award from the American Medical Association, 1966, for article, "In the Midst of Life"; Pulitzer Prize for fiction, 1975, for *The Killer Angels;* short story awards include Dikty's best science fiction of the year awards and citations from Judith Merrill.

WRITINGS:

The Broken Place (novel), New American Library (New York City), 1968.
The Killer Angels (novel), McKay (New York City), 1974.
The Herald (novel), McGraw, 1981.
Soldier Boy (short stories), Pocket Books (New York City), 1982.
For Love of the Game, Carroll & Graf (New York City), 1991.

Author of screenplay *Billy Boy,* 1980. Contributor of stories to magazines, including *Saturday Evening Post, Playboy, Galaxy, Redbook,* and *Cosmopolitan,* as well as to various newspapers.

ADAPTATIONS: The Killer Angels was adapted by Turner Pictures and aired as the television miniseries *Gettysburg,* 1993; *The Killer Angels* was also recorded in an unabridged audio version by Books on Tape, 1985.

SIDELIGHTS: Michael Shaara published his first story while still an undergraduate at Rutgers University, even though his creative writing teacher had been less than impressed with his manuscript and urged him instead to write "literature." His professor's criticism notwithstanding, Shaara continued to publish many more stories and four novels, one of which, *The Killer Angels,* won the Pulitzer Prize for fiction in 1975.

Shaara's work in science fiction and fantasy first became known in the 1950s, when a number of his stories were published in journals and literary magazines. These early works have been collected in the volume *Soldier Boy,* which a *Publishers Weekly* reviewer declared showed Shaara to be "a master of a particularly humanistic brand of SF." Shaara's humanistic bent is also evident in his novels, the first of which, *The Broken Place,* owes a debt to Ernest Hemingway. Like much of Hemingway's work, it follows a man emotionally scarred by war, whose psychological return to society is attained by grueling physical trials—boxing in the case of Shaara's Tom McClain. McClain searches for meaning in a world that seems devoid of it: "In all this world there are no signs and no miracles and nobody watching over and nobody caring," he tells a friend. "But I believe anyway." Shaara's novel was received favorably by

critics; John C. Pine of the *Library Journal* praised it for "a natural rhythm that is unmistakable."

The Killer Angels, Shaara's second novel, not only won the Pulitzer Prize, but it also became the 1993 television miniseries *Gettysburg.* The novel recounts the events of the July, 1863, battle in which nearly 50,000 men lost their lives; the four-day battle became the high-water mark of the Confederacy. Shaara's goal in writing the novel, Thomas Lask quotes the author explaining in the *New York Times,* was to know "what is was like to *be* there, what the weather was like, what men's faces looked like." To do this, he deployed multiple points of view, from Generals Lee and Longstreet of the Confederacy, to General John Buford and Colonel Joshua Chamberlain for the Union. He also blended two fictional elements, according to Lask: "a careful expository description of strategy and tactics,. . . and a graphic evocation of the clashes themselves." *Best Sellers* reviewer L. C. Smith praised the former, making note of Shaara's "particularly good description of the military problems caused by the terrain at Gettysburg." Lask praised the latter, observing that "The pages in which Win Hancock, the Union general, canters slowly along in the very hell of battle looking after his men, is not a passage a reader will soon forget."

Shaara's next novel, *The Herald,* was a departure from *The Killer Angels* in terms of subject matter. The story's hero, Nick Tesla, lands his plane in a town decimated by a scientist whose goal is to kill most of the world's inhabitants in his efforts to create a master race. Some dismissed the book's ideas as simplistic, including a *Science Fiction Review* contributor who wondered "how Michael Shaara could have won a Pulitzer prize." But others lauded the novel's philosophical import; Algis Budrys in the *Magazine of Fantasy and Science Fiction* called it "a must-read book that raises a profound question."

Shaara's last novel, *For Love of the Game,* was published posthumously after his children uncovered the manuscript while settling his estate. *For Love of the Game* is the tale of an aging baseball pitcher who, even as his life is falling apart, pitches a perfect game. As in Shaara's first novel, the story's central character plays out his emotional crises in the crucible of an all-out athletic challenge. Also as with Shaara's first novel, *For Love of the Game* garnered praise for its intense psychological exploration of an athlete pushed to his limits. Though criticized by some as falling short of Shaara's greatest work—a reviewer for *Publishers Weekly* noted that "one feels he might have liked to give it a rewrite"—Bill Brashler wrote for the *Chicago Tribune* that "Shaara obviously had a love of the game, of its tradition and natural grace, and he left it this lovely token."

Shaara once told *CA:* "I have written almost every known type of writing, from science fiction through history, through medical journalism and *Playboy* stories, always because I wrote only what came to mind, with no goal and little income, always for the joy of it, and it has been a great joy. The only trouble comes from the 'market mind' of the editor when the work is done. I have traveled over most of the world, lived three years in South Africa, two years in Italy, speak some foreign languages, and love airplanes, almost as much as women. I enjoyed teaching, because it taught me a lot."

BIOGRAPHICAL/CRITICAL SOURCES:

BOOKS

Authors in the News, Volume 1, Gale (Detroit), 1976.
Dictionary of Literary Biography Yearbook 1983, Gale, 1984.
Shaara, Michael, *The Broken Place,* New American Library, 1968.

PERIODICALS

American Heritage, October, 1992, p. 103; April, 1994, p. 116.
American Spectator, December, 1988, p. 17; December, 1989, p. 28; December, 1993, p. 25.
Analog, August, 1982, p. 125.
Atlantic Monthly, October, 1974, p. 118; April, 1975, p. 98; August, 1981, p. 86.
Best Sellers, September 15, 1974, p. 281.
Booklist, June 1, 1968, p. 1129; May 15, 1981, p. 1214; May 1, 1982, p. 1148; May 15, 1991, p. 1781.
Chicago Tribune, April 7, 1991, section 14, p. 5.
Fantasy Review, August, 1984, p. 26.
Forbes, October 19, 1992, p. 28; March 15, 1993, p. 172.
Inc., January, 1987, p. 64.
Kirkus Reviews, January 15, 1968, p. 72; July 1, 1974, p. 702; April 1, 1981, p. 457; March 15, 1991, p. 358.
Kliatt, fall, 1984, p. 19; September, 1992, p. 16; November, 1994, p. 65.

Library Journal, February 15, 1968, p. 772; September 1, 1974, p. 2091; June 1, 1981, p. 1246; March 15, 1982, p. 653; April 1, 1991, p. 156; February 1, 1992, p. 144; February 1, 1993, p. 132; October 1, 1994, p. 130.
Los Angeles Times Book Review, April 7, 1991, p. 6.
Magazine of Fantasy and Science Fiction, May, 1982, p. 33; September, 1984, p. 52.
New Republic, November 8, 1993, p. 32.
New Yorker, June 26, 1995, p. 57.
New York Times, May 10, 1975, p. 27.
New York Times Book Review, April 7, 1968, p, 36; October 20, 1974, p. 38; June 12, 1994, p. 20.
Observer (London), August 14, 1977, p. 23.
Publishers Weekly, January 15, 1968, p. 84; July 8, 1974, p. 69; June 2, 1975, p. 57; May 15, 1981, p. 49; January 29, 1982, p. 64; April 12, 1991, p. 44.
San Francisco Chronicle, May, 1986, p. 38.
School Library Journal, April, 1995, p. 91.
Science Fiction and Fantasy Book Review, June, 1982, p. 32.
Science Fiction Review, November, 1981, p. 54.
Tallahassee Democrat, September 15, 1974, pp. 410-411.
USA Today, July 10, 1991, p. D-5.
Washington Post, September 29, 1982, section B, p. 15.

OBITUARIES:

PERIODICALS

Atlanta Journal and Atlanta Constitution, May 7, 1988, p. E-7.
Los Angeles Times, May 7, 1988, p. I-22.
New York Times, May 9, 1988, p. D-11.*

* * *

SHANKS, Hershel 1930-

PERSONAL: Born March 8, 1930, in Sharon, PA; son of A. Martin and Mildred (Freedman) Shanks; married Judith Alexander Weil, February 20, 1966; children: Elizabeth Jean, Julia Emily. *Education:* Haverford College, B.A., 1952; Columbia University, M.A., 1953; Harvard University, LL.B., 1956.

ADDRESSES: Home—5208 38th St. NW, Washington, DC 20015. *Office*—4710 41st St. NW, Washington, DC 20016.

CAREER: U.S. Department of Justice, Washington, DC, trial attorney in Civil Division, 1956-59; private law practice in Washington, DC, 1959-64; Glassie, Pewett, Dudley, Beebe & Shanks, Washington, DC, partner, 1964-88. President of Jewish Educational Ventures, Inc., 1987—.

MEMBER: American Bar Association, National Press Club, Biblical Archaeology Society (president, 1975—), American Schools of Oriental Research, District of Columbia Bar Association, Lawyers Committee on Civil Rights, Phi Beta Kappa.

WRITINGS:

(Editor and author of introduction) *The Art and Craft of Judging: The Decisions of Judge Learned Hand,* Macmillan (New York City), 1968.

The City of David: A Guide to Biblical Jerusalem, Biblical Archaeology Society, 1973.

Judaism in Stone: The Archaeology of Ancient Synagogues, Harper (New York City), 1979.

(Editor with Benjamin Mazar) *Recent Archaeology in the Land of Israel,* Biblical Archaeology Society, 1984.

(Editor) *Ancient Israel: A Short History From Abraham to the Roman Destruction of the Temple,* Prentice-Hall (Englewood Cliffs, NJ), 1988.

(Editor) *Christianity and Rabbinic Judaism,* Biblical Archaeology Society, 1992.

(Editor) *Understanding the Dead Sea Scrolls,* Random House (New York City), 1992.

Jerusalem: An Archeological Biography, Random House, 1995.

Contributor to law books. Also contributor of articles and reviews to periodicals. Editor of *Biblical Archaeology Review,* 1975—, *Bible Review,* 1985—, and *Moment* magazine, 1988—.

SIDELIGHTS: Hershel Shanks told *CA:* "We should think more and write less. Mea culpa."

*   *   *

SHIVERS, Jay S(anford)   1930-

PERSONAL: Born July 7, 1930, in New York, NY; son of Ted M. and Mabel (Sinkoff) Shivers; married

Rhoda Goldstein (a teacher), February 14, 1951; children: Jed Mark. *Education:* Indiana University, B.S., 1952; New York University, M.A., 1953, additional study, 1953-55; University of Wisconsin, Ph.D., 1958. *Politics:* Independent.

ADDRESSES: Home—South Eagleville Rd., Storrs, CT 06268. *Office*—U-110, University of Connecticut, Storrs, CT 06268.

CAREER: Hillside Psychiatric Hospital, Glen Oaks, NY, recreational leader, 1952-53; Goldwater Memorial Hospital, Welfare Island, NY, director of recreational rehabilitation, 1953; University of Wisconsin—Madison, instructor in education, 1955-57; U.S. Veterans Administration Hospital, Madison, recreational supervisor, 1957-58; Mississippi Southern College (now University of Southern Mississippi), Hattiesburg, professor of recreational service education and chair of department, 1958-62; University of Connecticut, Storrs, assistant professor, 1962-66, associate professor, 1967-69, professor of recreational service education, 1970—. Visiting summer professor at Eastern Washington State College (now Eastern Washington University), 1963, and California State College at Hayward (now California State University, Hayward), 1967. Chair of Mansfield (CT) Park Planning Committee, 1962—. Mansfield Recreational Services, 1965—, and Connecticut Older Worker Employee Network, 1982—. Member of scientific committee, Van Cle Foundation, 1976. *Military service:* U.S. Army, 1953-55, Counter-Intelligence Corps, special agent.

MEMBER: World Leisure and Recreation Association, International Playground Association, International Rehabilitation Association, International Federation of Physical Education, National Recreation and Park Association, Society of Professional Recreation Educators, National Therapeutic Recreational Society, American Academy of Leisure Science (founding fellow, 1980), American Association of University Professors, Connecticut Recreation and Park Association, Phi Delta Kappa, Sigma Delta Psi.

AWARDS, HONORS: Certificate of Achievement from Hospital Section, American Recreation Society, 1965; honor award from Connecticut Recreation Society, 1968; National Literary Award of National Recreation and Park Association, 1979; distinguished service award of National Therapeutic Recreational Society, 1983; Hollis Fait Scholarly Contribution Award, National Consortium of Physical Education and Recreation for Disabled Persons, 1990.

WRITINGS:

Horizons Unlimited: The Organization of Recreational Services in the State of Mississippi, Mississippi Recreation Association, 1959.
(With George Hjelte) *Public Administration of Park and Recreational Services,* Macmillan (New York City), 1962.
Leadership in Recreational Service, Macmillan, 1963.
Principles and Practices of Recreational Service, Macmillan, 1967.
Camping: Management, Counseling Program, Appleton, 1971.
Planning Recreational Places, Barnes, A.S. (San Diego, CA), 1971.
(With Hjelte) *Public Administration of Recreational Services,* Lea & Febiger (Philadelphia, PA), 1972, 2nd edition, 1978.
(With C. R. Calder) *Recreational Crafts for School and Community,* McGraw (New York City), 1974.
(With Hollis F. Fait) *Therapeutic Recreational Service,* Lea & Febiger, 1975.
Essentials of Recreational Service, Lea & Febiger, 1978.
Perceptions of Recreation and Leisure, Holbrook, 1978.
(With H. Ibrahim) *Leisure: Emergence and Expansion,* Hwong Publishing (Los Alamitos, CA), 1979.
Recreational Leadership: Group Dynamics and Interpersonal Relations, Princeton Publishing, 1980, 2nd edition, 1985.
(With Fait) *Recreational Service for the Aging,* Lea & Febiger, 1980.
(With Joseph W. Halper) *The Crisis in Urban Recreational Service,* Fairleigh Dickinson University Press (East Brunswick, NJ), 1981.
Special Recreational Service: Therapeutic and Adapted, Lea & Febiger, 1984.
(With Charles Bucher) *Recreation for Today's Society,* 2nd edition (Shivers was not associated with previous edition), Prentice-Hall (Englewood Cliffs, NJ), 1984.
Recreational Safety: The Standard of Care, Associated University Presses, 1985.
Introduction to Recreational Service Administration, Lea & Febiger, 1987.
Camping: Organization and Operation, Prentice-Hall, 1988.
Advanced Management for Recreational Service, Prentice-Hall, 1988.
Introduction to Recreational Service, C.C. Thomas (Springfield, IL), 1993.

The Story of Leisure, Human Kinetics (Champaign, IL), 1995.

Also author of master plans for recreational service in various towns. Contributor of more than fifty articles to recreation and rehabilitation journals. *Recreation in Treatment Centers,* member of editorial board, 1962-69, editor, 1964-66.

WORK IN PROGRESS: Programming Recreational Services, for Human Kinetics.

* * *

SIMIC, Charles   1938-

PERSONAL: Born May 9, 1938, in Belgrade, Yugoslavia; came to United States in 1954; son of George (an engineer) and Helen (Matijevic) Simic; married Helene Dubin (a designer), October 25, 1965; children: Anna, Philip. *Education:* New York University, B.A., 1967. *Religion:* Eastern Orthodox.

ADDRESSES: Home—P.O. Box 192, Strafford, NH 03884. *Office*—Department of English, University of New Hampshire, Durham, NH 03824.

CAREER: Aperture (photography magazine), New York City, editorial assistant, 1966-69; University of New Hampshire, Durham, associate professor of English, 1974—. Visiting assistant professor of English, State University of California, Hayward, 1970-73, Boston University, 1975, and Columbia University, 1979. *Military service:* U.S. Army, 1961-63.

AWARDS, HONORS: PEN International Award for translation, 1970; Guggenheim fellowship, 1972-73; National Endowment for the Arts fellowships, 1974-75 and 1979-80; Edgar Allan Poe Award, American Academy of Poets, 1975; National Institute of Arts and Letters and American Academy of Arts and Letters awards, 1976; National Book Award nomination, 1978, for *Charon's Cosmology;* Harriet Monroe Poetry Award, University of Chicago, Di Castignola Award, Poetry Society of America, and PEN Translation award, all 1980; Fulbright travelling fellowship, 1982; Ingram Merrill fellowship, 1983-84; MacArthur Foundation fellowship, 1984-89; Pulitzer Prize nominations, 1986 and 1987; Pulitzer Prize, 1990, for *The World Doesn't End.*

WRITINGS:

POETRY

What the Grass Says, Kayak (Santa Cruz, CA), 1967.

Somewhere among Us a Stone Is Taking Notes, Kayak, 1969.

Dismantling the Silence, Braziller (New York City), 1971.

White, New Rivers Press (St. Paul, MN), 1972, revised edition, LogbridgeRhodes (Durango, CO), 1980.

Return to a Place Lit by a Glass of Milk, Braziller, 1974.

Biography and a Lament, Bartholemew's Cobble (Hartford, CT), 1976.

Charon's Cosmology, Braziller, 1977.

Brooms: Selected Poems, Edge Press (Point Reyes, CA), 1978.

School for Dark Thoughts, Banyan Press (Chicago, IL), 1978, sound recording of same title published by Watershed Tapes (Washington, DC), 1978.

Classic Ballroom Dances, Braziller, 1980.

Austerities, Braziller, 1982.

Shaving at Night, Meadow (San Francisco, CA), 1982.

The Chicken without a Head, Trace (Portland, OR), 1983.

Weather Forecast for Utopia and Vicinity, Station Hill Press (Barrytown, NY), 1983.

Selected Poems: 1963-1983, Braziller, 1985.

Unending Blues, Harcourt (San Diego, CA), 1986.

Nine Poems, Exact Change, 1989.

The World Doesn't End, Harcourt, 1989.

The Book of Gods and Devils, Harcourt, 1990.

Hotel Insomnia, Harcourt, 1992.

A Wedding in Hell: Poems, Harcourt, 1994.

Frightening Toys, Faber (London), 1995.

ESSAYS AND INTERVIEWS

The Uncertain Certainty: Interviews, Essays, and Notes on Poetry, University of Michigan Press (Ann Arbor, MI), 1985.

Wonderful Words, Silent Truth, University of Michigan Press, 1990.

Dime-Store Alchemy: The Art of Joseph Cornell, Ecco Press (Hopewell, NJ), 1992.

The Unemployed Fortune-Teller: Essays and Memoirs, University of Michigan Press, 1994.

TRANSLATOR

Ivan V. Lalic, *Fire Gardens,* New Rivers Press, 1970.

Vasko Popa, *The Little Box: Poems,* Charioteer Press (Washington, DC), 1970.

Four Modern Yugoslav Poets: Ivan V. Lalic, Branko Miljkovic, Milorad Pavic, Ljubomir Simovic, Lillabulero (Ithaca, NY), 1970.

(And editor with Mark Strand) *Another Republic: 17 European and South American Writers,* Viking (New York City), 1976.

Key To Dream, According to Djordje, Elpenor, 1978.

Vasko Popa, *Homage to the Lame Wolf: Selected Poems,* Field (Oberlin, OH), 1979.

(With Peter Kastmiler) Slavko Mihalic, *Atlantis,* Greenfield Review Press (Greenfield Center, NY), 1983.

(With others) Henri Michaux, *Translations: Experiments in Reading,* O.ARS (Cambridge, MA), 1983.

Tomaz Salamun, *Selected Poems of Tomaz Salamun,* Viking, 1987.

Ivan Lalic, *Roll Call of Mirrors,* Wesleyan University Press (Middletown, CT), 1987.

Aleksandar Ristovic, *Some Other Wine or Light,* Charioteer Press, 1989.

Slavko Janevski, *The Bandit Wind: Poems,* Dryad Press (Takoma Park, MD), 1991.

(And editor) *The Horse Has Six Legs: An Anthology of Serbian Poetry,* Graywolf Press (St. Paul, MN), 1992.

Novica Tadic, *Night Mail: Selected Poems,* Oberlin College Press (Oberlin, OH), 1993.

OTHER

(Author of introduction) Vernon Newton, *Homage to a Cat: As It Were: Logscapes of the Lost Ages,* Northern Lights, 1991.

(Author of introduction) *Prisoners of Freedom: Contemporary Slovenian Poetry,* edited by Ales Debeljak, Pedernal, 1992.

Contributor to books, including *The Young American Poets,* Follett (New York City), 1968; *Shake the Kaleidoscope: A New Anthology of Modern Poetry,* Pocket Books (New York City), 1973; *Contemporary American Poetry, 1950-1980,* Longman (New York City), 1983; *Harvard Book of American Poetry,* Harvard University Press (Cambridge, MA) 1985;

and *The Harper American Literature,* Volume 2, Harper (New York City), 1987. Also contributor of poetry to more than 100 magazines, including *American Poetry Review, Antaeus, Atlantic, Chicago Review, Esquire, Field, Georgia Review, Gettysburg Review, Grand Street, Harvard Magazine, Kayak, Nation, New Republic, New Yorker, Ontario Review, Paris Review, Ploughshares, Poetry, Poetry Miscellany, Southwest Review, Sulfur, Western Humanities Review,* and *Witness.*

SIDELIGHTS: Charles Simic, a native of Yugoslavia who emigrated to America in his teens, has been hailed as one of the finest of America's postmodern poets. Simic's work has won numerous prestigious awards for poetry and translation, among them the coveted MacArthur Foundation "genius grant" (1982), the Edgar Allan Poe Award, the PEN Translation Award, a Guggenheim Foundation Scholarship, an American Academy of Arts and Letters Prize, a Poetry Society of America Prize, and, in 1990, a Pulitzer Prize for his book of prose poems, *The World Doesn't End.* Although he writes in English, Simic draws heavily upon Eastern European tradition—and his own experiences of war-torn Belgrade—to compose poems about the physical and spiritual poverty of modern life. *Hudson Review* contributor Liam Rector notes that the author's work "has about it a purity, an originality unmatched by many of his contemporaries." In the *Chicago Review,* Victor Contoski characterizes Simic's work as "some of the most strikingly original poetry of our time, a poetry shockingly stark in its concepts, imagery, and language." *Georgia Review* correspondent Peter Stitt writes: "The fact that [Simic] spent his first eleven years surviving World War II as a resident of Eastern Europe makes him a going-away-from-home writer in an especially profound way. . . . He is one of the wisest poets of his generation, and one of the best."

Simic spent his formative years in Belgrade. His early childhood coincided with the Second World War, and several times his family members evacuated their home on foot to escape indiscriminate bombing. The atmosphere of violence and desperation continued after the war as well. Simic's father left the country for work in America, and his mother tried several times to follow, only to be turned back at the border by Yugoslavian authorities. In the meantime, young Simic was growing up in Belgrade, where he was considered a below-average student and a minor troublemaker.

When Simic was fifteen his mother finally arranged for the family to travel to Paris. After a year spent studying English in night school and attending French public schools during the day, Simic sailed for America to reunite with his father. He entered the United States at New York City and then moved with his family to Chicago, where he enrolled in high school. In that environment—a suburban school with caring teachers and motivated students—Simic began to take new interest in his courses, especially literature. After graduation he managed to attend college at night while holding a full-time job as an office boy with the *Chicago Sun Times.* Simic earned his bachelor's degree from New York University in 1967.

Simic's first poems were published in 1959, when he was twenty-one. Between that year and 1961, when he entered the service, he wrote a number of poems, many of which he has since destroyed. His first full-length collection of poems, *What the Grass Says,* was published in 1967. In a very short time, Simic's work—original poetry in English and translations of important Yugoslavian poets—began to attract critical attention. In *The American Moment: American Poetry in the Mid-Century,* Geoffrey Thurley notes that the substance of Simic's earliest verse—its material referents—"are European and rural rather than American and urban. . . . The world his poetry creates—or rather with its brilliant semantic evacuation decreates—is that of central Europe—woods, ponds, peasant furniture." *Voice Literary Supplement* reviewer Matthew Flamm also contends that Simic was writing "about bewilderment, about being part of history's comedy act, in which he grew up half-abandoned in Belgrade and then became, with his Slavic accent, an American poet."

Simic's work defies easy categorization. Some poems reflect a surreal, metaphysical bent and others offer grimly realistic portraits of violence and despair. *Hudson Review* contributor Vernon Young maintains that memory—a taproot deep into European folklore—is the common source of all of Simic's poetry. "Simic, a graduate of NYU, married and a father in pragmatic America, turns, when he composes poems, to his unconscious and to earlier pools of memory," the critic writes. "Within microcosmic verses which may be impish, sardonic, quasi-realistic or utterly outrageous, he succinctly implies an historical montage." Young elaborates: "His Yugoslavia is a peninsula of the mind. . . . He speaks by the fable; his method is to transpose historical actuality into a surreal key. . . . [Simic] feels the European yesterday on his pulses."

Some of Simic's best-known works challenge the dividing line between the ordinary and extraordinary. He gives substance and even life to inanimate objects, discerning the strangeness in household items as ordinary as a knife or a spoon. Shaw writes in the *New Republic* that the most striking perception of the author's early poems was that "inanimate objects pursue a life of their own and present, at times, a dark parody of human existence." *Chicago Review* contributor Victor Contoski concludes: "Simic's efforts to interpret the relationship between the animate and inanimate have led to some of the most strikingly original poetry of our time, a poetry shockingly stark in its concepts, imagery, and language." As Anthony Libby puts it in the *New York Times Book Review,* Simic "takes us to his mysterious target, the other world concealed in this one."

Childhood experiences of war, poverty, and hunger lie behind a number of Simic's poems. *Georgia Review* correspondent Peter Stitt claims that the poet's most persistent concern "is with the effect of cruel political structures upon ordinary human life. . . . The world of Simic's poems is frightening, mysterious, hostile, dangerous." Thurley too declares that Simic "creates a world of silence, waiting for the unspeakable to happen, or subsisting in the limbo left afterwards. . . . The dimension of menace in Simic becomes metaphysics in itself." Simic tempers this perception of horror with gallows humor and an ironic self-awareness. Stitt claims: "Even the most somber poems . . . exhibit a liveliness of style and imagination that seems to re-create, before our eyes, the possibility of light upon the earth. Perhaps a better way of expressing this would be to say that Simic counters the darkness of political structures with the sanctifying light of art."

Critics find Simic's style particularly accessible, a substantial achievement for an author for whom English is a second language. According to Shaw, the "exile's consciousness still colors [Simic's] language as well as his view of existence. Having mastered a second language, Simic is especially aware of the power of words, and of the limits which words grope to overcome. His diction is resolutely plain: as with the everyday objects he writes about, he uncovers unexpected depth in apparently commonplace language." In the *New Letters Review of Books,* Michael Milburn writes: "Charles Simic is a poet of original

vision. . . . He seems to challenge himself to write as plainly as possible, while still producing works of freshness and originality. But a brilliant method lies behind Simic's plainness. . . . Casual, unobtrusive language expresses the most fantastic images." Milburn concludes that the poet "mines ingredients of language and experience that readers may take for granted, and fuses them in a singular music."

Such praise by contemporary critics and poets prepared audiences for *Unending Blues* (1986). Although previous works by Simic drew, as Stephen Dobyns in the *New York Times Book Review* indicates, from "a sense of the world and a sense of history," and from the archetypal and surreal poems which had previously characterized his work, this collection represents a period of writing in which Simic began to draw from the autobiographical as well. Matthew Flamm in the *Voice Literary Supplement* sees this book as a movement "toward a more personally accessible poem," a book containing poems in which "the lines are longer, the language more discursive, the settings more specific. They're also rural instead of urban." In some senses, this book may be one of Simic's most "American" books, and in fact, a distinctly "New England" book, for, as Flamm points out, it "includes landscapes . . . and a long meditation addressed to Emily Dickinson."

After collecting nominations for several previous books, Simic's *The World Doesn't End,* won the 1990 Pulitzer Prize. Called "a flawless performance by a poet at the height of his powers" by John Ash in the *Washington Post,* Simic's collection of sixty-seven prose poems is "a beautifully designed box of verbal fireworks,. . . a seamless fusion of wild jazz and delicate, moonstruck, European chamber music." The book is divided into three sections of prose poems dealing with quasi-narratives, surrealist stagings, and meditations on, as David Starkey points out in the *Southern Humanities Review,* "everything from art and philosophy to the tenor of the century." The critic goes on to point out that the prose poems in this collection are "typically based on a surrealist premise which is described in precise, domestic detail" and range "in length from nearly a full page to a single whimsical sentence" and "in tone from extremely playful . . . to very dark." Simic has been quoted by Molly McQuade in *Publishers Weekly* as having selected the prose poem form for this collection since "nothing ever happens in a lyric poem. It's a great acknowledgment of the present moment. In a prose sentence, however, things *do* happen. You write in sentences, and tell a story, but the piece is like a poem because it circles back on itself." Despite the fact that there was considerable controversy over awarding the Pulitzer Prize to *The World Doesn't End,* "at least in part because most of the poems are in prose," as David Dooley points out in the *Hudson Review,* Starkey argues that "it is in the prose poem that Simic appears to have found the most fluid vehicle for his poetry," and that it is a prose "which is so lovely, so non-*prosaic* that it will surprise anyone who has dismissed the prose poem as 'anti-poetry.'"

Simic's 1990 collection, *The Book of Gods and Devils,* is a semi-autobiographical work that derives from memories of his early years in New York City. These are poems which return to an urban setting, showing the scenes set on 14th Street, in Hell's Kitchen, at old booksellers, in late-night coffee shops reading poetry, and in libraries. In an interview with Molly McQuade in *Publishers Weekly,* Simic states that although his work is often characterized as surrealist and grotesque, this work is "based upon the most factual stuff imaginable." "You could smell a certain high lunacy in New York," he says. "I used to spend evenings on long walks, looking at store windows, watching people. . . . Cities are places of sphinxes, enigmas." Simic explains further how he was "aware in writing *The Book of Gods and Devils,* of an almost pagan impulse. Pagans would invent gods or demons for any place where people had had intense experiences. A big city is a home of multiple gods, not just the obvious religions." In this work Simic moves from the enigma of form, like the prose poems in *The World Doesn't End,* to the enigma of the experiences, like those which one encounters in the big cities, and in doing so, Simic returns to his previous style. David Kirby in the *New York Times Book Review* calls this kind of style a "typical" Charles Simic poem: it "starts with a sentence fragment, an ungainly image crash-landing at the feet of the speaker who was expecting some thing else entirely," and has characters who "are often like the protagonists in fairy tales. . . . [They] begin as rather ordinary types and end up as heroes, their bemusement turning to amusement as they regain control over their interrupted lives." Helen Vendler in *Parnassus* characterizes "the Simic style" further by analyzing the poem "War" from this collection as "an apparently speakerless scene; an indefinite article establishing the vagueness of place and time—'a woman' somewhere, anywhere, in a wintry evening; then a menacing definite article focusing our gaze, in this instance on 'the' list; then a late entrance of the personal pronoun engaging the speaker's life and ours."

Hotel Insomnia, published in 1992, opens with the two-line poem "Evening Chess" ("The Black Queen raised high / In my father's angry hand"), which James Krusoe in the *Los Angeles Times Book Review* suggests "hangs above the reader throughout the entire volume." Children and childhood experiences illuminate many of these poems. As Krusoe goes on to discuss, images of "lost children . . . or a dead child . . . or a nose bleed," occur frequently, for even the language "is the language of a child's reader, forcing us to assume a child's vulnerable role." By way of contrast, Vendler cites how "Simic's world has aged. About one poem in three has something old in it—an old dog, a blind old woman, old snow, shoes grown old, a crippled old man, an old cemetery. In Simic's insomniac nights, the world shrivels, wrinkles, dwindles, both physically and metaphysically." Stylistically, Vendler views the fifty-two poems in the book as "more of an evolving sequence than a collection of separate poems." Most are written in verse, but some are presented in the prose poem style that Simic used exclusively in *The World Doesn't End.*

In 1994's *A Wedding in Hell: Poems,* Simic returned to a blend of the lyric poem and the prose poem to write what Christopher Merrill in the *Los Angeles Times Book Review* called "records of marvelous journeys. He addresses mystics, [the main character from Fedor Dostoevsky's novel *Crime and Punishment*] Raskolnikov and a certain Mr. Zoo Keeper." The poems, like previous works by Simic, are compact, economic, deceptively simple, and quickly swing from nostalgia and surreal settings to irony and tragedy. Images of urban landscapes, or street scenes set in generically European villages, often with the threat of war lurking just off the page, make this book seem as though, according to Lisa Sack in the *Voice Literary Supplement,* "Simic must be living through an unending flashback." This work includes, however, seven love poems, rather uncharacteristic for Simic, and offering some new directions in content and tone. Still, Sack points out how "flashes of the wily old skeptic do appear" in the half-dozen prose poems in this collection, where Simic "sounds like the great Shakespearean fools in these pieces—his motley ravings make us laugh even as they chill us with the accuracy of their observation."

In addition to collections of poems, Simic continues to publish a variety of other types of books. *Dime*

Store Alchemy: The Art of Joseph Cornell, 1992, is a tribute to the New York artist who constructed collages of objects inside small boxes. Simic's identification with Cornell is logical, for, as Craig Crist-Evans comments in the *Bloomsbury Review,* Simic's poetry "often resembles a Cornell box: found images and objects, fragments, inscriptions, dolls, birds, balls, bubble pipes—the wispy strains of a tarnished nostalgia, wire cages brought together to make a lyric poem-assemblage." *The Unemployed Fortune-Teller: Essays and Memoirs,* 1994, displays Simic's range of interests and experiences as he discusses topics as diverse as his time served in the U.S. Army, an affair he had as a young man, food, the blues, the poet's social role, or the creation of poetry. Simic's *The Horse Has Six Legs: An Anthology of Serbian Poetry,* 1992, generated controversy more for its publication during the breaking stories of the atrocities of the war in the former Yugoslavia than for the poems it included. Vasa Mihailovich in *World Literature Today* cautions readers that this is "not a conventional anthology" but rather a selection of Simic's translations of Serbian verse that "contains only those poets and poems he liked and felt he had translated adequately." The book has been praised by Edward Ifkovic in *Multicultural Review* as being "generous and eclectic, ranging from the early, oral verse and women's songs to the internationally known writing of poets like Vasko Popa."

A wide-ranging writer and translator, Simic remains a challenging and enigmatic poet for readers. As Mark Ford points out in the *Times Literary Supplement,* "Poetry is never figured by Simic as a solution to difficulties, but a paradigmatic means of charting them." Perhaps it is because Simic's work is, according to Ford, consistent in its "fidelity to the random and partial," and in its "embodiment of contradictions and unlikely connections," that readers continue to be attracted to Simic's poems.

BIOGRAPHICAL/CRITICAL SOURCES:

BOOKS

Contemporary Authors Autobiography Series, Volume 4, Gale (Detroit), 1986.
Contemporary Literary Criticism, Gale, Volume 6, 1976; Volume 9, 1978; Volume 22, 1982; Volume 49, 1988; Volume 68, 1991.
Dictionary of Literary Biography, Volume 105: *American Poets Since World War II, Second Series,* Gale, 1991.

Thurley, Geoffrey, *The American Moment: American Poetry in the Mid-Century,* St. Martin's (New York City), 1978.

PERIODICALS

Antioch Review, spring, 1977.
Bloomsbury Review, November/December, 1993, p. 12; January/February, 1995, p. 17.
Booklist, March 1, 1989, p. 1087; October 1, 1992, p. 230; October 15, 1994, p. 396.
Boston Globe, December 23, 1992, p. 39.
Boston Review, March/April, 1981; April, 1986, p. 28.
Chicago Review, spring, 1977, pp. 145-57.
Chicago Tribune, January 21, 1993.
Chicago Tribune Book World, June 12, 1983.
Choice, March, 1975.
Christian Science Monitor, July 14, 1992.
Contemporary Literature, winter, 1980, pp. 136-45; fall, 1982, pp. 528-549.
Crazy Horse, summer, 1972.
Gargoyle, number 22/23, 1983.
Georgia Review, winter, 1976; summer, 1986, p. 557; spring, 1987, p. 192; spring, 1992, pp. 157-59.
Hudson Review, spring, 1981; autumn, 1986, p. 511-12; spring 1991, pp. 157-59.
Interlochen Review, Volume 1, number 2, 1980.
Library Journal, September 15, 1985, p. 84; December, 1986, p. 116; March 15, 1989, p. 74; September 1, 1990, p. 224; August, 1992, p. 106; November 1, 1994, p. 80; November 15, 1994, p. 66.
Los Angeles Times Book Review, March 16, 1986, p. 9; December 7, 1986, p. 8; August 30, 1992, p.6; December 27, 1992, p. 1; September 5, 1993, p. 6; March 19, 1995, p. 8.
Manassas Review, winter, 1978.
Mid-America Review, Volume 8, number 1, pp. 89-96.
Missouri Review, Volume 7, number 3, 1984.
Multicultural Review, October, 1992, p 70.
New Boston Review, March/April, 1981.
New England Review, fall, 1993, p.192.
New Letters Review of Books, spring, 1987.
New Literary History, autumn, 1989, pp. 199-214, 215-21.
New Republic, January 24, 1976; March 1, 1993, pp. 28-32.
Newsweek, December 28, 1992, p. 60.
New Yorker, December 21, 1992, pp. 130-35.
New York Times, May 28, 1990.

New York Times Book Review, March 5, 1978; October 12, 1980; May 1, 1983; January 12, 1986, p. 17; October 18, 1987, p. 46; December 23, 1990, p. 16; March 21, 1993, p. 14.

Ohio Review, winter, 1973.

Parnassus, February, 1992, p. 86.

Ploughshares, Volume 2, number 3, 1975; Volume 7, number 1, 1981.

Poet and Critic, Volume 9, number 1, 1975.

Poetry, December, 1968; September, 1971; March, 1972; February, 1975, November, 1978; July, 1981; October, 1983; July, 1987, pp. 228-31; January, 1992, pp. 226-34.

Poetry Miscellany, number 8, 1978.

Poetry Review, June, 1983.

Publishers Weekly, July 26, 1985, p. 160; February 3, 1989, p. 101; November 2, 1990; September 1, 1992, p. 78; November 9, 1992, p. 44, p. 68; October 10, 1994, p. 68; October 31, 1994, p. 53.

Sewanee Review, April, 1992, pp. 311-23.

Southern Humanities Review, winter, 1991, pp. 101-2.

Stand, summer, 1984; summer, 1988, pp. 72-75; autumn, 1988, p. 61, p. 69.

Sulfur, spring, 1991, p. 220.

Times Literary Supplement, July 7, 1995, p. 15.

Village Voice, April 4, 1974; February 28, 1984.

Virginia Quarterly Review, spring, 1975; spring, 1993, p. 64; summer, 1993, p. 99.

Voice Literary Supplement, December, 1986, p. 18; February, 1994, p. 22; November, 1994, p. 35.

Washington Post, April 13, 1990.

Washington Post Book World, November 2, 1980; April 13, 1986; May 7, 1989.

World Literature Today, autumn, 1984, p. 609; spring, 1993, p. 409.

—*Sketch by Robert Miltner*

*   *   *

SIRE, James W(alter) 1933-

PERSONAL: Born October 17, 1933, in Inman, NE; son of Walter Guy and Elsie (Mulford) Sire; married Marjorie Ruth Wanner (a laboratory technician), June 14, 1955; children: Carol, Eugene, Richard, Ann. *Education:* University of Nebraska, B.A., 1955; Washington State University, M.A., 1958; University of Missouri—Columbia, Ph.D., 1964. *Religion:* Christian.

ADDRESSES: Office—InterVarsity Press, 430 East Plaza, Downers Grove, IL 60559.

CAREER: University of Missouri—Columbia, instructor in English, 1958-64; Nebraska Wesleyan University, Lincoln, assistant professor, 1964-66, associate professor of English, 1966-68; Inter-Varsity Press (now InterVarsity Press), Downers Grove, IL, editor, 1968-84, senior editor and campus lecturer for InterVarsity Christian Fellowship, 1984—. Part-time associate professor at Northern Illinois University, 1969-70, and Trinity College, Deerfield, IL, 1971-75; visiting summer professor at University of Nebraska, 1966, University of Missouri, 1967, Regent College, 1977, and New College, Berkeley, 1983-84. *Military service:* U.S. Army, Ordnance, 1955-57; became first lieutenant.

MEMBER: Conference on Christianity and Literature, American Scientific Affiliation.

WRITINGS:

(With Robert Beum) *Papers on Literature: Models and Methods,* Holt (New York City), 1970.

Program for a New Man, InterVarsity Press (Downers Grove, IL), 1973.

Jeremiah, Meet the Twentieth Century, InterVarsity Press, 1975.

The Universe Next Door, InterVarsity Press, 1976, 2nd edition, 1988.

How to Read Slowly, Harold Shaw, 1978.

Scripture Twisting, InterVarsity Press, 1980.

Beginning with God, InterVarsity Press, 1981.

Meeting Jesus, Harold Shaw (Wheaton, IL), 1988.

Shirley MacLaine and the New Age Movement, InterVarsity Press, 1988.

Discipleship of the Mind, InterVarsity Press, 1990.

Chris Chrisman Goes to College, InterVarsity Press, 1993.

Why Should Anyone Believe Anything at All?, InterVarsity Press, 1994.

The Universe Next Door has been translated into ten languages.

SIDELIGHTS: James W. Sire once told *CA:* "Though I have written since 1976 a number of books, articles, and reviews, *The Universe Next Door* remains my own favorite and, apparently, a favorite among readers. While the book concentrates on outlining seven basic worldviews, including Christian theism, naturalism, pantheism, and the new consciousness, it does so from a uniquely Christian perspective. I have been pleased to see that over two hundred colleges and universities, both state and private, have used this book as a text in a wide variety of courses from philosophy and religion, on the one hand, to English and history on the other. I left the university teaching world over twenty years ago, but am pleased to see that my books have continued to keep me on campus. I have also been pleased that the Christian perspective in these books has been getting a hearing even on secular campuses."

He adds, "I now travel widely in the U.S., Canada, and Europe, lecturing on the Christian faith, primarily on university campuses."

*　　*　　*

SKINNER, Jeffrey　1949-

PERSONAL: Born December 8, 1949, in Buffalo, NY; son of Thomas F. (in business) and Doris Ann (Donhauser) Skinner; married Sarah Gorham (a poet), May 8, 1982; children: Laura Katherine, Bonnie Anne. *Education:*Rollins College, B.A., 1971; graduate study at University of Bridgeport, 1973-74; Columbia University, M.F.A., 1978.

ADDRESSES: Home—1637 Rosewood Ave., Louisville, KY 40204. *Office*—Department of English, University of Louisville, Louisville, KY 40292.

CAREER: University of Bridgeport, Bridgeport, CT, lecturer in English, 1978-86; Salisbury State College, Salisbury, MD, assistant professor of English, 1986-88; University of Louisville, Louisville, KY, assistant professor of English and creative writing, 1988-95, professor of English, 1995—. Vice president and general manager of Gleason Plant Security, Inc., 1978-86. Lecturer at Norwalk Community College, 1982; creative writing teacher at Liberation House, 1982-83, and Center for Creative Youth, Wesleyan University, Middletown, CT, 1986-88. Adviser to World Prison Poetry Center, 1984-86; editorial consultant for Sarabande Books, Louisville, KY; gives poetry readings at colleges and other institutions.

AWARDS, HONORS: Fellow at Indiana University Writers Conference, 1973, Colorado Writers Conference, 1975, and Provincetown Fine Arts Center, 1981-82; guest of MacDowell Colony and Yaddo, 1981; grants from Connecticut Commission on the Arts, 1983, Ingram Merrill Foundation, 1985, and Delaware State Arts Council; fellow of National Endowment for the Arts, 1987; Book Award from National Poetry Series, 1987, for *A Guide to Forgetting;* Howard Foundation fellowship, 1991-92; A. L. Smith Award, Kentucky Council on the Arts, 1992.

WRITINGS:

Late Stars (poems), Wesleyan University Press (Middleton, CT), 1985.
A Guide to Forgetting (poems), Graywolf Press (Port Townsend, WA), 1988.
(With Stephen Policott) *Real Toads in Imaginary Gardens* (creative writing text), Chicago Review Press (Chicago), 1991.
(With Sarah Gorham) *The Night Lifted Us* (poems) Larkspur (Bowmansville, NY), 1992.
The Company of Heaven (poems), University of Pittsburgh Press (Pittsburgh, PA), 1992.

Also author of two-act play *The Last Time I Saw Richard.* Work represented in anthologies, including *Anthology of Magazine Verse and Yearbook of American Poetry,* 1981 and 1984, and *Anthology of New England Poetry.* Contributor of more than fifty poems and reviews to magazines, including *Atlantic Monthly, Commonweal, Iowa Review, Nation, New Yorker, Paris Review,* and *Poetry.* Literary editor of *Small Press Book Review.*

WORK IN PROGRESS: A book of poems; editing *Last Call: Poems of Alcoholism, Drug Addiction, and Deliverance,* to be published by Sarabande Books in 1997.

SIDELIGHTS: Jeffrey Skinner once told *CA:* "I was a businessman for ten years, and I like to include that experience in my writing when possible; it's a way of life lived by many millions of people, but rarely addressed in our literature. I also write 'form' poetry—sonnets, sestinas, villanelles, etc.—and I find the effort to simultaneously satisfy the demands of form while still speaking in a twentieth-century voice challenging and, oddly, liberating.

"I want, at bottom, to address directly and without sentimentality the issues that have always been most important to us as humans—love, death, family, and the dimensions of our spiritual selves, an area sadly ignored or treated by our culture as yet another commodity to be acquired and flaunted."

SNOW, Donald M(erritt)   1943-

PERSONAL: Born June 22, 1943, in Fort Wayne, IN; son of C. A. and Dorothea (a writer; maiden name, Johnston) Snow; married Donna Bock (an administrator), May 30, 1969; children: Eric DeVries. *Education:* University of Colorado, B.A., 1965, M.A., 1967; Indiana University, Ph.D., 1969. *Avocational interests:* Racquetball, squash, coaching, running.

ADDRESSES: Home—2935 Juniper Lane, Tuscaloosa, AL 35405. *Office*—Department of Political Science, University of Alabama, Box 870213, Tuscaloosa, AL 35487-0213.

CAREER: University of Alabama, Tuscaloosa, assistant professor, 1969-77, associate professor, 1977-82, professor of political science, 1982—, director of international studies, 1972—. Professor at Air Command and Staff College, 1980; visiting professor, U.S. Army War College, 1989-91; guest lecturer at Air War College, Army War College, Naval War College, and U.S. Military Academy. Secretary of the Navy Senior Research Fellow, Naval War College, 1985-86.

MEMBER: International Studies Association (chair of section on military studies, 1983-85), Academy of Political Science, Air Force Association, Inter-University Seminar on the Armed Forces and Society.

WRITINGS:

Introduction to Game Theory, Consortium for International Studies Education, 1978.
Nuclear Strategy in a Dynamic World: American Policy in the Nineteen Eighties, University of Alabama Press (University, AL), 1981.
(Editor) *Introduction to World Politics: A Conceptual and Developmental Perspective,* University Press of America (Lanham, MD), 1981.
(With Dennis M. Drew) *Introduction to Strategy,* Air Command and Staff College, 1981.
The Nuclear Future: Toward a Strategy of Uncertainty, University of Alabama Press, 1983.
(With Gary L. Guertner) *The Last Frontier: An Analysis of the Strategic Defense Initiative,* Lexington Books (Lexington, MA), 1986.
National Security: Enduring Problems of U.S. Defense Policy, St. Martin's (New York City), 1986, 2nd edition published as *National Security: Enduring Problems in a Changing Defense Environment,* 1991, 3rd edition published as *National*

Security: Defense Policy for a New International Order, 1995.
The Necessary Peace: Nuclear Weapons and Superpower Relations, Lexington Books, 1987.
(With Drew) *Making Strategy,* Air University Press, 1987.
(Editor) *Fencers: U.S.-Soviet Relations Face the 1990s,* Lexington Books, 1988.
(With Drew) *The Eagle's Talons: War, Politics, and the American Experience,* Air University Press, 1988.
The Shape of the Future: The Post-Cold War World, Sharpe, M.E. (Armonk, NY), 1991, 2nd edition, 1995.
Distant Thunder: Third World Conflict and the New International Order, St. Martin's Press, 1993.
(With Drew) *From Lexington to Desert Storm: War and Politics in the American Experience,* Sharpe, M.E., 1993.
(With Eugene Brown) *Puzzle Palaces and Foggy Bottom: Foreign and Defense Policy-Making in the 1990s,* St. Martin's Press, 1994.
(With Brown) *The Contours of Power: A Contemporary Introduction to International Relations,* St. Martin's Press, 1996.

Contributor to political science and military journals.

WORK IN PROGRESS: Beyond the Water's Edge, a coauthored American foreign policy textbook; *Rampage: The "New" Problem of Internal War,* a manuscript dealing with changes in the pattern of violence since the end of the Cold War.

SIDELIGHTS: Donald M. Snow told *CA:* "The operation of the international system has changed markedly since the demise of communism and the end of the Cold War. One of the most dramatic changes has been in the pattern of violence in the system and especially how the United States and other major countries should deal with that violence. Policy and academic understandings of these matters are principal concerns for me as an author and analyst."

*   *   *

SOBOSAN, Jeffrey G.   1946-

PERSONAL: Born March 30, 1946, in Chicago, IL; son of John (an executive) and Louise (a homemaker; maiden name, Maurier) Sobosan. *Education:* University of Notre Dame, A.B., 1969, M.Th., 1972; Graduate Theological Union, Th.D., 1977.

ADDRESSES: Office—Department of Theology, University of Portland, 5000 North Willamette Blvd., Portland, OR 97203.

CAREER: Entered Congregatio a Sancta Cruce (Fathers and Brothers of the Holy Cross; C.S.C.), 1962, ordained Roman Catholic priest, 1973. University of Portland, Portland, OR, assistant professor, 1978-84, associate professor of theology, 1984—.

WRITINGS:

The Tapestry of Faith, Alba House, 1976.
Act of Contrition, Ave Maria Press (Notre Dame, IN), 1979.
The Ascent to God: Faith as Art, Risk, and Humor, Thomas More Press (Chicago), 1981.
Guilt and the Christian: A New Perspective, Thomas More Press, 1982.
Christian Commitment and Prophetic Living, Twenty-Third (Mystic, CT), 1986.
Bless the Beasts: A Spirituality of Animal Care, Crossroad, 1991.
The Turn of the Millennium: An Agenda for Christian Religion in an Age of Science, Pilgrim Press (New York City), 1996.

Contributor to journals and magazines.

*   *   *

SPIRES, Elizabeth   1952-

PERSONAL: Born May 28, 1952, in Lancaster, OH; daughter of Richard C. (in grounds maintenance) and Sue (a real estate broker; maiden name, Wagner) Spires; married Madison Smartt Bell (a novelist), June 15, 1985; children: Celia Dovell. *Education:* Vassar College, B.A. (with honors in English), 1974; Johns Hopkins University, M.A., 1979.

ADDRESSES: Office—Department of English, Goucher College, Towson, MD 21204.

CAREER: Charles E. Merrill Publishing Co., Columbus, OH, assistant editor, 1976-77; freelance writer, 1977-81; Washington College, Chestertown, MD,

visiting assistant professor of English, 1981; Loyola College, Baltimore, MD, poet in residence, 1981-82; Johns Hopkins University, visiting professor in Writing Seminars, 1984-85, 1988-96; Goucher College, Towson, MD, writer in residence, 1985-86, 1988-96.

AWARDS, HONORS: Academy of American Poets' Prize, 1974; *Mademoiselle* Magazine College Poetry Prize, 1974; W. K. Rose fellowship, Vassar College, 1976; Individual Artist's Grant, Ohio Arts Council, 1978; National Endowment for the Arts fellowship, 1981, 1992; Pushcart Prize, Pushcart Press, 1981, 1995; Ingram Merrill Foundation award, 1981; Artist's Fellowship, Maryland State Arts Council, 1982, 1989; Amy Lowell Travelling Poetry scholarship, Harvard University, 1986-87; Sara Teasdale Poetry Award, Wellesley College, 1990; Towson State University Prize for Literature, 1992; Guggenheim Fellowship in Poetry, 1992.

WRITINGS:

Boardwalk (poems), Bits Press (Cleveland, OH), 1980.
Globe (poems), Wesleyan University Press (Middletown, CT), 1981.
The Falling Star (juvenile), C. E. Merrill (Columbus, OH), 1981.
Count with Me (juvenile), C. E. Merrill, 1981.
The Wheels Go Round (juvenile), C. E. Merrill, 1981.
Swan's Island (poems), Holt (New York City), 1985.
Annonciade (poems), Viking (New York City), 1989.
Worldling (poems), Norton (New York City), 1995.
With One White Wing (juvenile; "Margaret K. McElderry Books"), Simon & Schuster (New York City), 1995.

Contributor of poems to anthologies, including five volumes of *Best American Poems,* and to periodicals, including *Antaeus, New Yorker, New Republic, Mademoiselle, Poetry, American Poetry Review, Yale Review, Partisan Review, New Criterion,* and *Paris Review.*

WORK IN PROGRESS: "A fifth collection of poetry (for adults) and several picture books for children."

SIDELIGHTS: Elizabeth Spires told *CA:* "I think by the time I was twelve, I knew I would be a writer, though at the time I thought I would write short stories, not poetry (I was under the influence of Flannery O'Connor at the time).

"My most recent book of poems, *Worldling* deals, in part, with motherhood and mortality. The first section of the book chronicles the birth of my daughter, Celia, who is now five years old. I think for many people the experience of having a child is a transformative experience, one in which you feel your mortality quite strongly; the poems in *Worldling* try to chronicle, directly or obliquely, how I have been changed by the ongoing experience of motherhood, how it has pushed me deeper into my life. Underlying these poems is the constant tension between the insistent movement of each person towards individuation and the equally strong claims of relatedness, the push/pull of the mother/daughter bond. Some of my new poems, written since *Worldling,* continue these explorations, although I envision that my next book will reach beyond mother/child concerns, and have a wider (though not deeper) scope. In particular, I feel preoccupied with my sense not only of rapid change in my own life, but in the world around me. This feeling that the world is shaping itself into something new and different as it approaches the year 2000 will certainly enter into some of the poems I am hoping to write. In fact, it already has.

"My poetry has been influenced by my close reading, and love, of the poetry of John Donne, George Herbert, Robert Frost, John Berryman, Robert Lowell, Elizabeth Bishop, Josephine Jacobsen, and A. R. Ammons. That's not an exhaustive list, just some of the high points. These are poets who, for me, are always fresh and alive on the page, and towards whom I feel a debt of gratitude."

BIOGRAPHICAL/CRITICAL SOURCES:

BOOKS

Dictionary of Literary Biography, Volume 120: *American Poets since World War II, Third Series,* Gale (Detroit), 1992.

PERIODICALS

Baltimore Evening Sun, October 9, 1981.
Boston Review, April, 1989.
New Criterion, November, 1995.
New York Times Book Review, March 14, 1982; June 1, 1986.
Philadelphia Inquirer, January 14, 1996.
Southwest Review, winter, 1995.

SPURLING, Hilary　1940-

PERSONAL: Born December 25, 1940, in Stockport, England; daughter of G. A. (a judge) and E. M. (a teacher; maiden name, Armstrong) Forrest; married John Spurling (a playwright), April 4, 1961; children: Amy Maria, Nathaniel Stobart, Gilbert Alexander. *Education:* Somerville College, Oxford, B.A., 1962.

ADDRESSES: Home—London, England. *Agent*—David Higham Associates Ltd., 5-8 Lower John St., Golden Square, London W1R 4HA, England.

CAREER: Spectator, London, arts editor and theatre critic, 1964-70, literary editor, 1967-70; freelance writer, 1970—.

AWARDS, HONORS: Rose Mary Crawshay Prize from British Academy, 1976, for *Ivy When Young: The Early Life of I. Compton-Burnett, 1884-1919;* traveling scholarship from Society of Authors, 1984; Duff Cooper Memorial Prize, 1984, and Heinemann Award from Royal Society of Literature, 1985, both for *Secrets of a Woman's Heart: The Later Life of I. Compton-Burnett, 1920-1969.*

WRITINGS:

Ivy When Young: The Early Life of I. Compton-Burnett, 1884-1919 (also see below), Gollancz (London), 1974.
(Editor) *Mervyn Peake: Drawings,* Davis Poynter, 1974.
Handbook to Anthony Powell's Music of Time, Heinemann (London), 1977.
Secrets of a Woman's Heart: The Later Life of I. Compton-Burnett, 1920-1969 (also see below), Hodder & Stoughton (London), 1984.
Ivy: The Life of I. Compton-Burnett (contains *Ivy When Young: The Early Life of I. Compton-Burnett, 1884-1919* and *Secrets of a Woman's Heart: The Later Life of I. Compton-Burnett, 1920-1969*), Knopf (New York City), 1984.
Elinor Fettiplace's Recipe Book: Elizabethan Country House Cooking, Viking (New York City), 1986.
Paul Scott: A Life, Norton (New York City), 1990.
Paper Spirits, Chatto & Windus (London), 1992.

WORK IN PROGRESS: Biography of Henri Matisse, for Knopf, 1997.

SIDELIGHTS: Hilary Spurling published her biography of novelist Ivy Compton-Burnett in two separate volumes, *Ivy When Young: The Early Life of I. Compton-Burnett, 1884-1919* and *Secrets of a Woman's Heart: The Later Life of I. Compton-Burnett, 1920-1969.* According to Peter Kemp in the *Listener,* Spurling's reasoning for this division rests on the fact that Compton-Burnett's life was essentially split in two, "with 1918 acting as watershed. . . . The first book, *Ivy When Young,* which appeared [in 1974], was packed to bursting-point with the domestic Grand-Guignol, frock-coated imperiousness and corsetted aggression that became the stock-in-trade of Ivy's subsequent fiction." Several catastrophes marred the early years of Compton-Burnett's life, including the sudden death of her father, the oppressiveness arising from her mother's subsequent grief, and the loss of her favorite brother in World War I. Kemp continues: "When Spurling's biography broke off at 1918, in fact, it looked as though Ivy's life was virtually finished. Her family had fallen apart—and so had she, prostrated by panic and grief. What the second volume, *Secrets of a Woman's Heart,* . . . fascinatingly relates is the way she rehabilitated herself until she was able to exorcise in her fiction the traumas of her past." Reviewers note that after the tragedies of Compton-Burnett's early decades, her remaining years were essentially nondescript. With this in mind, such critics as A. N. Wilson in the *Times Literary Supplement* commend Spurling for having the "panache" to flesh out an interesting biography. Writes Wilson: "[Spurling] has made one of the most fascinating of modern biographies out of what must have been one of the most boring of all modern lives. . . . [She] has guaranteed that [Compton-Burnett] will live on as a tragicomic figure in her own right."

Praise for Spurling's biography is plenteous in another regard, also. As the critics note, Compton-Burnett was an enigma. She was the inscrutable woman known to her public in the 1950s as the "English Secret." "Ivy Compton-Burnett kept few personal papers and declined to write her memoirs," writes Nigel Cross in the *New Statesman.* "Consequently . . . Spurling, who did not know her subject, has had to rely on the memories and papers of friends and relatives and on her reading of the novels. It seems the perfect combination." In a similar vein, J. I. M. Stewart remarks in the *London Review of Books* that "Spurling must surely have been at work from the dawn of life, determined to know as much as God himself about Ivy's ancestors, parents, siblings, enemies, rivals, friends, acquaintances, servants, mentors and (above all) sources and channels of inspiration. . . . Endlessly curious as she ought to

be, she brings sound judgment and taste to bear upon almost everything she finds, and her conclusions are embodied in an admirable expository prose." Though *Newsweek* critic Walter Clemons argues that Spurling draws too heavily on Compton-Burnett's novels as a means of explaining Compton-Burnett's early life, he admits that "Spurling has done as much as anyone can to penetrate [Compton-Burnett's] inscrutability." Minor complaints of other reviewers aside, in the opinion of Cross, "*Secrets of a Woman's Heart* completes a two-volume life of Ivy Compton-Burnett that ranks as one of the more important literary biographies of the century. It is not only an engrossing account of a curiously static life, it is a critical reassessment that enhances an already formidable, if narrow, literary reputation. . . . Few biographies written so soon after their subject's death are definitive. This one must be."

BIOGRAPHICAL/CRITICAL SOURCES:

BOOKS

Contemporary Literary Criticism, Volume 34, Gale (Detroit), 1985.

PERIODICALS

Books and Bookmen, July, 1984.
Listener, June 7, 1984.
London Review of Books, July 19-August 1, 1984.
Los Angeles Times Book Review, December 30, 1984.
New Statesman, June 15, 1984.
Newsweek, December 24, 1984.
New Yorker, November 4, 1985.
New York Review of Books, December 20, 1984.
New York Times, November 9, 1984.
New York Times Book Review, December 9, 1984.
Spectator, March 16, 1974.
Times (London), June 7, 1984; December 18, 1986.
Times Educational Supplement, June 8, 1984.
Times Literary Supplement, June 8, 1984.
Washington Post Book World, December 9, 1984.
World Literature Today, summer, 1985.

*   *   *

STAINES, David   1946-

PERSONAL: Born August 8, 1946, in Toronto, Ontario, Canada; son of Ralph McKenzie (a florist) and Mary Rita (a secretary and accountant; maiden name, Hayes) Staines. *Education:* University of Toronto, B.A., 1967; Harvard University, A.M., 1968, Ph.D., 1973. *Politics:* Liberal. *Religion:* Roman Catholic.

ADDRESSES: Home—12 Galt St., Ottawa, Ontario, Canada K1S 4R4. *Office*—Department of English, University of Ottawa, Ottawa, Ontario, Canada K1N 6N5.

CAREER: Harvard University, Cambridge, MA, assistant professor of English, 1973-78; University of Ottawa, Ottawa, Ontario, associate professor, 1978-85, professor of English, 1985—, chair, department of English, 1990-93, vice-dean, faculty of arts, 1994-95, acting dean, faculty of arts, 1995-96.

MEMBER: International Arthurian Society, Mediaeval Academy of America (vice-chair, 1975-81; chair of standing committee on centers and regional associations, 1981-87), Modern Language Association of America.

AWARDS, HONORS: Fellow of National Endowment for the Humanities, 1977-78; honorary research fellow at University College, London, 1977-78; fellow of Social Sciences and Humanities Research Council of Canada, 1986-87.

WRITINGS:

CRITICISM

Tennyson's Camelot: The Idylls of the King and Its Medieval Sources, Wilfrid Laurier University Press, 1982.
Beyond the Provinces: Literary Canada at the Century's End, University of Toronto Press (Toronto), 1995.

EDITOR

The Canadian Imagination: Dimensions of a Literary Culture, Harvard University Press (Cambridge, MA), 1977.
Responses and Evaluations: Essays on Canada by E. K. Brown, McClelland & Stewart (Toronto), 1977.
The Callaghan Symposium: A Reappraisal, University of Ottawa Press (Ottawa), 1981.
(With Andrew Garrod) *Illuminations: The Days of Our Youth,* Gage Publishing (Scarborough, Canada), 1984.

The Forty-ninth and Other Parallels: Contemporary Canadian Perspectives, University of Massachusetts Press (Amherst, MA), 1986.
Stephen Leacock: A Reappraisal, University of Ottawa Press, 1986.
(With Robert Scholes, Nancy R. Comley, and Carl H. Klaus) *Elements of Literature: Fiction, Poetry, Drama,* Oxford University Press (New York City), 1987, revised edition, 1990.
(With Neil Besner) *The Short Story in English,* Oxford University Press, 1991.
Stephen Leacock: My financial Career and Other Follies, McClelland & Stewart, 1993.

OTHER

(Translator) *The Complete Romances of Chretien de Troyes,* Indiana University Press (Bloomington, IN), 1990.

Editor of *Journal of Canadian Poetry.*

WORK IN PROGRESS: An edition of the letters of Stephen Leacock, a reader of Leacock's writings, and a biography of Leacock.

SIDELIGHTS: David Staines told *CA:* "I began my academic career as a medievalist, focusing on medieval Arthurian literature. My publications include studies of Arthuriana, both medieval and modern. My interest has now turned to the literature of twelfth-century France and fourteenth-century England. In addition, I have become a frequent lecturer and essayist on Canadian literature and culture. As a critic, editor, and scholar I have been a careful observer of the Canadian cultural scene. In my writings there is a consistent vision of Canada as a mature, challenging, and exciting world of the arts. The Canadian preference for a mosaic structure in which all the ethnic and social regions retain their distinctness is central to an understanding of the nation. As a country Canada is not only a mosaic of ethnic cultures but also a mosaic of regions, each with its own sense of identity; the nation, therefore, exists in a dialectic of regional and ethnic tensions."

*   *   *

STEPHENS, W(illiam) P(eter)   1934-

PERSONAL: Born May 16, 1934, in Penzance, Cornwall, England; son of Alfred Cyril William Joseph and Jennie Eudora (Trewavas) Stephens. *Education:* Clare College, Cambridge University, B.A., 1955, M.A., 1959, B.D., 1971; University of Strasbourg, Docteur es sciences religieuses, 1967; attended University of Lund, 1957-58, and University of Muenster, 1965-67. *Avocational interests:* "Theatre, opera, hill walking, gardening, and sport. I play squash and tennis regularly, and swim and surf on holiday."

ADDRESSES: Office—Faculty of Divinity, Kings College, Old Aberdeen AB9 2UB, Scotland.

CAREER: Hartley Victoria College, Manchester, England, assistant tutor in New Testament, 1958-61, Ranmoor Chair of Church History, 1971-73; University of Nottingham, Nottingham, England, Methodist chaplain, 1961-65; minister of Methodist church in Shirley, Croydon, England, 1967-71; Wesley College, Bristol, England, Randles Chair of Historical and Systematic Theology, 1973-80; The Queens College, Birmingham, England, research fellow, 1980-81, lecturer in church history, 1981-86; University of Aberdeen, Aberdeen, Scotland, professor of church history, 1986—, dean of faculty of divinity, 1987-89; provost of faculty of divinity, 1989-90. Fernley Hartley Lecturer, 1972; James A. Gray Lecturer at Duke University, 1976. Chair of Shirley Group of Churches, 1969-70, Croydon Anti-Apartheid Group, 1970-72, Withington World Development Movement, 1972-73, and British Council of Churches Advisory Committees on Western Europe, 1974-85, and East-West Relations, 1975-86. Member of British Roman Catholic-Methodist Commission, 1972-80, Bristol City Council, 1976-83, World Methodist Council and Lutheran World Federation International Commission, 1981-84.

MEMBER: Society for Study of Theology (secretary, 1963-76), Conference of European Churches (member of advisory committee, 1974-92), Society for Reformation Studies (president, 1995—).

WRITINGS:

(Co-translator) Martin Luther, *Luther's Works,* Volume 41, Fortress (Philadelphia, PA), 1966.
The Holy Spirit in the Theology of Martin Buber, Cambridge University Press (Cambridge), 1970.
Faith and Love (sermons), Epworth (London), 1971.
Christians Conferring, Epworth, 1978.
Our Churches, Catholic Truth Society (London), 1978.
Methodism in Europe, [Cincinnati], 1982.

The Theology of Huldrych Zwingli, Oxford University Press (Clarendon), 1986.
Zwingli: An Introduction to His Thought, Oxford University Press, 1992.
(Editor and contributor) *The Bible, the Reformation and the Church,* Sheffield Academic Press (Sheffield, England), 1995.

Contributor to books, including *The Holy Spirit,* edited by Dow Kirkpatrick, Tidings, 1974; *Prophet, Pastor, Protestant,* edited by E. J. Furcha and H. W. Pipkin, Pickwick, 1984; *John Wesley: Contemporary Perspectives,* edited by John Stacey, Epworth, 1988; and *Martin Bucer,* edited by D. F. Wright, Cambridge University Press, 1994. Also contributor of articles on theological and pastoral issues and on churches in Eastern and Western Europe to periodicals, including *Epworth Review* and *Scottish Journal of Theology.*

WORK IN PROGRESS: The Theology of Heinrich Bullinger.

SIDELIGHTS: W. P. Stephens told *CA:* "My writing on the reformation is primarily for scholars and students. My other works are intended for a wider audience, frequently interpreting . . . a theology or a tradition which [is not the readers] own."

Stephens is competent in French, German, Swedish, Latin, and Greek.

* * *

STERN, Richard (Gustave) 1928-

PERSONAL: Born February 25, 1928, in New York, NY; son of Henry George (a dentist) and Marion (Veit) Stern; married Gay Clark, March 14, 1950 (divorced, February 1972); married Alane Rollings, August 9, 1985; children: Christopher, Kate, Andrew, Nicholas. *Education:* University of North Carolina, B.A., 1947; Harvard University, M.A., 1949; University of Iowa, Ph.D., 1954.

ADDRESSES: Office—Department of English, University of Chicago, 1050 East 59th St., Chicago, IL 60637.

CAREER: Jules Ferry College, Versailles, France, lecturer, 1949-50; University of Heidelberg, Heidelberg, Germany, lektor, 1950-51; educational advisor, U.S. Army, 1951-52; Connecticut College, New London, instructor, 1954-55; University of Chicago, Chicago, IL, assistant professor, 1956-61, associate professor, 1962-64, professor of English, 1965—, Helen Regenstein professor of English, 1990—. Visiting lecturer, University of Venice, 1962-63, University of California, Santa Barbara, 1964 and 1968, State University of New York at Buffalo, 1966, Harvard University, 1969, University of Nice, 1970, University of Urbino, 1977.

MEMBER: American Academy of Arts and Sciences, Philological Society (University of Chicago), Phi Beta Kappa.

AWARDS, HONORS: Longwood Award, 1960; Friends of Literature Award; Rockefeller grant, 1965; *Stitch* was selected as one of the American Library Association's books of the year, 1965; National Institute of Arts and Letters grant, 1968; Guggenheim fellowship, 1973-74; Carl Sandburg Award, Friends of the Chicago Public Library, 1979, for *Natural Shocks;* Award of Merit for the Novel, American Academy and Institute of Arts and Letters, 1986; Chicago *Sun-Times* book of the year award for *Noble Rot: Stories 1949-1988,* 1989; Hearland Award, best work of non-fiction, 1995.

WRITINGS:

Golk (novel), Criterion (Torrance, CA), 1960.
Europe; or, Up and Down with Schreiber and Baggish (novel), McGraw (New York City), 1961, published in England as *Europe; or, Up and Down with Baggish and Schreiber,* MacGibbon & Kee, 1962.
In Any Case (novel), McGraw, 1963, published as *The Chaleur Network,* Second Chance (Sag Harbor, NY), 1981.
Teeth, Dying, and Other Matters [and] *The Gamesman's Island: A Play,* Harper (New York City), 1964.
Stitch (novel), Harper, 1965.
(Editor) *Honey and Wax: Pleasures and Powers of Narrative,* University of Chicago Press (Chicago), 1966.
1968: A Short Novel, an Urban Idyll, Five Stories, and Two Trade Notes, Holt (New York City), 1970.
The Books in Fred Hampton's Apartment (essays), Dutton (New York City), 1973.
Other Men's Daughters (novel), Dutton, 1973.
Natural Shocks (novel), Coward, 1978.
Packages (short story collection), Coward, 1980.

The Invention of the Real (collected essays and poems), University of Georgia Press (Athens), 1982.
A Father's Words (novel), Arbor House (New York City), 1986.
The Position of the Body, Northwestern University Press, 1986.
Noble Rot: Stories 1949-1988, Grove Press (New York City), 1988.
Shares and Other Fictions, Delphinium (Harrison, NY), 1992.
One Person and Another: On Writers and Writing, Baskerville (Dallas), 1993.
A Sistermony, Donald I. Fine, 1995.

Contributor to numerous periodicals, including *Partisan Review* and the *New York Times.*

SIDELIGHTS: "Richard Stern is American letters' unsung comic writer about serious matters," writes Doris Grumbach in the *Chicago Tribune.* "He is, further, that oddity among novelists, a writers' writer, a critics' writer, whose name is not part of household vocabulary." Unlike Saul Bellow, with whom he shares artistic and thematic concerns, Stern has not gained wide recognition in popular circles and among the mainstream of academe. As Julian Barnes observes in the *New Statesman,* "An obstinate and selfish attachment to lucidity debars his work from the attention of problem-solving academics; while his tense intelligence discourages holiday skimmers." Yet, the long-time University of Chicago professor has in over fifty years of writing poetry, fiction, and nonfiction earned a significant amount of respect in the world of literature, as is evidenced by the Award of Merit for the Novel given him in 1986 by the American Academy and Institute of Arts and Letters.

Stern's approach to his writing has often been at the heart of critical evaluation of his work. "A novelist who began by writing poetry," Peter Straub notes in the *New Statesman,* "[he] was always concerned with, and fiercely delighted by, the possibilities within language and narrative technique, and shares with the best American prose its self-awareness and daring." Typically, in his writing less means more. "Stern's short stories are short," explains *New Republic* contributor Mark Harris. "His novels and reportage have always been concise, compressed. Economy of language is his rule." As the reviewer points out, this characteristic, while viewed by Stern's proponents as an important strength, may be one of the reasons the author's works have not enjoyed more popular readership. "This is regrettable," concludes Harris, "since, if the task of reading him requires a greater concentration than we are accustomed to apply to mere jewels of literary art, the reward of reading him is proportionately greater as well."

Stern emerged on the literary scene in 1960, publishing his first novel in that year and two others by 1963. "What struck one from the first was Stern's command of the novelist's resources: an ample and supple language, a lively, vigorous narrative style, a sense of character and scene, of place, person and significant action," asserts Saul Maloff in *Commonweal*. "The generosity and sophistication of his mind, those characteristics which emerge first in depth of style, evident in his first novel, *Golk,* were fully present a year later in his second, *Europe; or, Up and Down with Baggish and Schreiber,*" comments Straub, "giving deep tones to that book's comedy— the bank he's been drawing on ever since." Of Stern's third novel, *In Any Case,* a story of espionage and treason during World War II, Straub adds: "Every chapter is packed with know-how and knowingness, a hundred different kinds of sentence, stunning usages, metaphorically apt information, brilliant speculation and question."

In his 1973 novel, *Other Men's Daughters,* Stern addresses the theme of a middle-aged, married man's love for a young college student. Robert Merriwether, a doctor who teaches at Harvard University, is caught in an unhappy marriage to Sara when he meets Cynthia, half his age, "beautiful, witty, intelligent, understanding, well-educated and wholly in love with him," explains *New York Times* critic Anatole Broyard. "He is decent, kindly and modest, she is eager, intelligent and sad, and without his wife or her father their relationship would have no problems," a *Times Literary Supplement* reviewer observes, "unless one perversely concludes that without these problems there would be no relationship, a view Merriwether himself seems to have some time for."

Other Men's Daughters "is a consideration, at once witty and painful, of marital malaise, extra-marital rejuvenation and the hard emotional burdens attendant to both," writes Jonathan Yardley in the *Washington Post Book World*. While the reviewer does point out that the novel's subject is nothing new—it is, in fact, common to the time in which it was written—he admits, "I cannot recall its being treated elsewhere in recent fiction with more fidelity to and

understanding of the truths of separation, divorce and readjustment."

Here as before, Stern's technique and style draw significant critical attention. James R. Frakes comments in the *New York Times Book Review* that "though not really experimental in structure, *Other Men's Daughters* makes use of some unusual time-patterns, with convolutions and overlays, flashbacks and flash-forwards." In the reviewer's opinion, "The end result is not obscurantism but enrichment."

New York Review of Books contributor Michael Wood focuses on the style conveyed in the novel. "Style," he maintains, "is what saves buried lives from extinction, style is the mark of an exceptional and delicate attention." Moreover, according to Wood, "Stern has a style in a perfectly old-fashioned sense, and *Other Men's Daughters* is an old-fashioned novel, an impressive plea for the private life as a continuing subject for serious fiction."

Natural Shocks examines another, yet more complicated, older man/younger woman relationship. Frederick Wursup, a worldly, caustic journalist, accepts an assignment for an article on death. His subject becomes Cicia, a young woman losing her battle with cancer. As he becomes more involved with Cicia's case, Wursup's private feelings begin to intrude on his professional decisions, and he begins to realize, as *Newsweek*'s Peter S. Prescott observes, "how fully his life had become mired in the trivialities of his profession, how stunted his education in feeling."

Prescott finds the author of *Natural Shocks* "a remarkably deft and witty writer" and characterizes the novel as "wound so tight as to have a springy texture; aphorisms abound." Looking beyond the author's style, *National Review* contributor Paul Lukacs expresses his reservations about Stern's emphasis of idea over character. He describes *Natural Shocks*'s supporting characters as "formless; they are specimens of life . . . but they are not characters in a work of fiction." He also argues that the novel is not so much the story of Wursup's growing self-awareness; "in truth it is about Stern's one dominant *idea*—namely, a man's relationship with death and with his self."

New York Times book reviewer Christopher Lehmann-Haupt draws different conclusions. He writes that the novel "has a superstructure that is as solid and timeless as a folktale,. . . fairly teems with vividly realized men and women,. . . and prose—energetic, muscular, intelligent, playful prose, bristling with epigrams and allusions, yet never distracting from the onward rush of the story it unfolds." Furthermore, Lehmann-Haupt remarks that "the book is about death, yes, but more than that, it is about the deaths of fathers and children and lovers and mentors. And it is about journalism—public events viewed by public men for the consumption of the public. And about the relationship between the public and the private."

In his 1986 novel *A Father's Words,* Stern offers the story of Cy Riemer, editor of a Chicago science newsletter, and his four grown children. Divorced from his children's mother, Cy is setting up a new relationship with a young girlfriend and trying to set in order his relationships with his sons and daughters. "Family is the novel's subject," writes Geoffrey Wolff in the *Los Angeles Times Book Review,* "and particularly the idiom of a particular family, particularly American."

Central to this examination of the family is Cy's troubles with his son Jack. "The discord between father and son is one of the oldest stories and traditionally told from the son's point of view," comments Prescott in another *Newsweek* article. But as the reviewer points out, "What Stern has done here is to explore it from the father's perspective." This break from tradition can also be seen in the role given Cy in this novel. In an interview with Garry Abrams published in the *Los Angeles Times,* the author discussed his novel and the changing nature of fatherhood in our day and age. Fathers are "having relationships with their children that they didn't have in the past," he said. "The father is a competitor, a brother, a friend in a way that didn't exist for most of human history. . . . The old paternal-filial decorum is under a lot of pressure."

In *A Father's Words,* comments John Bowers in the *New York Times Book Review,* "Stern gives us a glimmer of fatherhood and how it goes to the marrow of one's bones." The author creates his portrait of the present-day father "by forgoing straight narrative and employing intelligent bits of business, little snippets of comment, disregarding sequence of time," adds Bowers. This effort earns Stern praise from *New York Times* contributor John Gross. The reviewer writes: "he is an unusually crisp and intelligent writer, with a sharp edge to his wit; and in *A Father's Words* he runs true to form. Many of the book's pleasures are incidental: jokes, intellectual

cadenzas, agile turns of phrase." Concludes Bowers, "Richard Stern may be compared to a jeweler. He worries and frets and tinkers to get the smallest matters just right—the jewellike *Father's Words* is an example."

A collection of Stern's short works of fiction are found in *Noble Rot, Stories 1949-1988,* published by Grove Press. The title alludes to the putrid soil that is necessary to produce fine wines. Among the characters in the book's thirty-two stories are what Sven Birkerts of the *New Republic* calls "grumbling husbands and wives, depressed grad students, small-time operators, lovelorn spinsters, struggling retirees. . . . All have been rendered with a fascination for circumstance and setting . . . and with an eye for their psychological particularity." David R. Slavitt observes in *American Book Review* that "the stories are lively, well-crafted pieces, with a tough-guy Chicago voice that allows the narrator a certain freedom."

Stern stays with the shorter form in his next book, *Shares and Other Fictions,* which contains two novellas and several short stories. The theme of the collection is the uncertain emotional ground between fathers and sons. "This ancient theme becomes original in Stern's hands," writes Joseph Coates for the *Chicago Tribune Book World,* "because it is handled so consistently from the father's viewpoint." In *One Person and Another,* a collection of essays also culled from a period of forty years, Stern examines the literary world with his usual forthright style. "Stern's observations are resolutely intelligent and interesting," notes August Kleinzahler of *Small Press,* who adds that the author is "opinionated and proud of it." Mark Shechner of the *Chicago Tribune* writes, "This flurry of auto-compilation is good news for the reader who has acquired a taste for that mixture of piquant detail and sharp irony that is Stern's signature." Among the subjects for Stern's analysis are twentieth-century authors Lillian Hellman, Ezra Pound, Samuel Beckett, Joyce Carol Oates, and Norman Mailer. The collection also includes a satirical play that speculates on how Dante and Shakespeare would fare in a modern litigious society.

In the memoir titled *Sistermony,* Stern chronicles his sister's battle with uterine cancer and his own insights into their ambivalent relationship. The effect, according to Scott Donaldson of the *Chicago Tribune,* is far from a romantic tribute. While Stern honestly presents what he considers his sister's shortcomings, the author is even harder on himself. But, as Donaldson notes, "as Ruth's illness runs its course, Richard begins to emerge from such obsessive self-repugnance into what his sister meant to him." This new insight also extends to other areas of the writer's life. A review in the *Los Angeles Book Review* chides Stern for the book's solipsism, but for Aaron Cohen of *Booklist,* the book's wide-ranging scope is a sign of craft. "Stern can conjure up a complex characterization in a few paragraphs," Cohen comments.

Stern's writing stands apart from much of the fiction created by his contemporaries in that, as Charles Monaghan suggests in *Commonweal,* it concentrates on "personal moral questions." David Kubal elaborates on the author's place in contemporary fiction in an essay in the *Hudson Review:* "Mr. Stern's lucidity, together with his capacity for affection and the comic, are very rare qualities, shortages in contemporary literature. The informed reading public, at least, wants its fictive realities uncontaminated by an author's suggestion that human character is greater than its circumstances, or that the condition itself has its goodness, or that anyone should be forgiven or tolerated." Yet, as Kubal concludes, "That Mr. Stern continues to offer these consolations in a body of work . . . tells us of his artistic integrity."

BIOGRAPHICAL/CRITICAL SOURCES:

BOOKS

Contemporary Literary Criticism, Gale (Detroit), Volume 4, 1975, Volume 39, 1986.
James Schiffer, *Richard Stern,* Twayne (New York City), 1993.

PERIODICALS

American Book Review, October-November, 1994.
Booklist, June 15, 1992; October 15, 1993; February 15, 1995, p. 1054.
Chicago Tribune, April 6, 1986; December 11, 1986; January 22, 1989; October 31, 1993, p. 6; March 19, 1995, p. 3.
Chicago Tribune Book World, April 6, 1986; September 6, 1992, pp. 4-5.
Commonweal, May 13, 1960; December 14, 1962.
Current Biography, June, 1994.
Encounter, July, 1974.
Hudson Review, autumn, 1987.
Los Angeles Times, June 15, 1986; February 17, 1989; October 11, 1992; April 2, 1995.

Los Angeles Times Book Review, May 4, 1986; April 2, 1995, p.6.
National Review, May 26, 1978.
New Republic, November 15, 1980; February 20, 1989.
New Statesman, May 10, 1974; September 22, 1978, pp. 46-48.
Newsweek, January 2, 1978; November 3, 1980; March 24, 1986.
New York Review of Books, August 13, 1970; December 13, 1973; February 23, 1978.
New York Times, October 16, 1973; January 9, 1978; April 11, 1986.
New York Times Book Review, May 1, 1960; October 14, 1962; December 19, 1965; March 25, 1973; November 18, 1973; January 1, 1978; January 9, 1978; September 7, 1980; June 15, 1986; September 27, 1992.
Partisan Review, spring, 1965.
Publishers Weekly, January 20, 1989; June 22, 1992; January 2, 1995, pp. 64-65.
Saturday Review, December 11, 1965; January 21, 1978.
Small Press, spring, 1994, p. 79.
Times Literary Supplement, May 10, 1974; October 27, 1978; November 21, 1980.
Virginia Quarterly Review, winter, 1983.
Washington Post, May 9, 1986.
Washington Post Book World, October 28, 1978; October 19, 1980; February 1, 1987.

*   *   *

STITT, Peter   1940-

PERSONAL: Born October 9, 1940, in Minneapolis, MN; son of Allison Bacon (a forester) and Josephine (a homemaker; maiden name, Eichhammer) Stitt; married Judith Hatling, August 12, 1961 (divorced April 16, 1981); married Jean Straub (a management consultant), July 6, 1985; children: Peter II, Jon, Justin Redd (stepson). *Education:* University of Minnesota, B.A., 1962, M.A., 1964; University of North Carolina at Chapel Hill, Ph.D., 1970.

ADDRESSES: Home—435 Carlisle St., Gettysburg, PA 17325. *Office*—*Gettysburg Review,* Gettysburg College, Gettysburg, PA 17325.

CAREER: University of North Carolina at Chapel Hill, editor of *Carolina Quarterly,* 1967-68; Middlebury College, Middlebury, VT, assistant professor of American literature, 1969-76; University of Houston, Houston, TX, associate professor of English, 1976-86; Gettysburg College, Gettysburg, PA, professor of English and editor of *Gettysburg Review,* 1986—. Member of literature panel of National Endowment for the Arts, 1985-86, 1993-94 and American literature panel of National Endowment for the Humanities, 1994.

MEMBER: Modern Language Association of America, Associated Writing Programs, Academy of American Poets, Association of Literary Scholars and Critics.

AWARDS, HONORS: Choice named *The World's Hieroglyphic Beauty: Five American Poets* one of the year's outstanding academic books in 1986; fellow of National Endowment for the Humanities, 1986-87, 1994-96; inaugural recipient of the Nora Magid Award for excellence in editing, PEN, 1993.

WRITINGS:

The World's Hieroglyphic Beauty: Five American Poets, University of Georgia Press (Athens), 1985.
(Editor with Frank Graziano) *James Wright: The Heart of the Light,* University of Michigan Press (Ann Arbor), 1990.

Contributor of articles and reviews to literature journals. Associate editor of *Minnesota Review,* 1963-64; contributing editor of *Georgia Review,* 1982-87.

WORK IN PROGRESS: The Oxford Book of American Humor, coedited with Veronica Geng and Garrison Keillor; *The Authorized Biography of James Wright; The Art of Contemporary Poetry: Essays on Nine Writers.*

SIDELIGHTS: Peter Stitt told *CA:* "I began my career as the poetry editor of the *Ivory Tower,* the literary magazine of the University of Minnesota. The commitment at first was to poetry, then it broadened to include various types of prose, such as fiction, essays, and reviews. With fellow staffer Garrison Keillor, I used to write much of the magazine under pseudonyms. I don't write much poetry anymore, and I publish none, but the love remains—that is the key word for me."

Stitt believes that creative literature, particularly poetry, is alive and well in America today. He com-

mented in an interview in the *Gettysburg Times* that one role of the critic is to popularize such work, to "make the reading act an easier one for the reader," and "to open poetry up to people, to get them to read it." He added that his work as a critic is a labor of love and that he does not believe literary criticism can be valid without this dimension. In an interview with *Pride* magazine's Fran Dressman, Stitt noted that he generally confines his criticism to works he admires, reasoning, "It doesn't make sense to write about things you don't like."

Stitt's *The World's Hieroglyphic Beauty: Five American Poets,* examines the work of Richard Wilbur, William Stafford, Louis Simpson, James Wright, and Robert Penn Warren. It includes the author's critical views as well as illuminating interviews with the poets themselves. The theme that binds their work, according to Andy Brumer of the *New York Times Book Review,* is one of a struggle to reconcile the human spirit with the daily events of the real world. Brumer observed: "It is unusual to find such a unifying thesis in a single study of so many writers. . . . This cooperative rather than combative atmosphere adds a personal touch too often missing from more standard academic works."

BIOGRAPHICAL/CRITICAL SOURCES:

PERIODICALS

Gettysburg Times, February 28-March 1, 1987.
New York Times Book Review, August 17, 1986.
Pride, summer, 1986.

*   *   *

STORR, Catherine (Cole)   1913-
   (Irene Adler, Helen Lourie)

PERSONAL: Born July 21, 1913, in London, England; daughter of Arthur Frederick (a lawyer) and Margaret (Gaselee) Cole; married Anthony Storr (a psychiatrist and writer), February 6, 1942 (marriage ended); married Lord Balogh (an economist), 1970; children: (first marriage) Sophia, Cecilia, Emma. *Education:* Newnham College, Cambridge, 1932-36 and 1939-41, B.A. (honors) in English, 1935; West London Hospital, 1941-44, qualified medical practitioner, 1944; Licensee, Royal College of Physicians. *Religion:* Agnostic.

ADDRESSES: Home—12 Frognal Gardens, No. 5, London NW3 6UX, England. *Agent*—Peters, Fraser, and Dunlop, 5th Floor, The Chambers, Chelsea Harbour, Lots Road, London SW10 0XF, England.

CAREER: West London Hospital, London, assistant psychiatrist, 1948-50; Middlesex Hospital, London, assistant psychiatrist, 1950-62; assistant editor, Penguin Books Ltd., London, 1966-70. Writer, 1952—.

MEMBER: Society of Authors, Royal College of Surgeons.

WRITINGS:

CHILDREN'S FICTION

Ingeborg and Ruthy, Harrap (London), 1940.
Clever Polly and Other Stories, illustrated by Dorothy Craigie, Faber (London), 1952.
Stories for Jane, illustrated by Peggy Jeremy, Faber, 1952.
Clever Polly and the Stupid Wolf, illustrated by Marjorie-Ann Watts, Faber, 1955.
Polly, the Giant's Bride, illustrated by Marjorie-Ann Watts, Faber, 1956.
The Adventures of Polly and the Wolf, illustrated by Marjorie-Ann Watts, Faber, 1957, Macrae Smith, 1970.
Marianne Dreams, illustrated by Marjorie-Ann Watts, Faber, 1958, revised edition, Penguin (London), 1964, published as *The Magic Drawing Pencil,* A. S. Barnes (Kent, England), 1960.
Marianne and Mark, illustrated by Marjorie-Ann Watts, Faber, 1960.
Lucy, illustrated by Dick Hart, Bodley Head (London), 1961, Prentice Hall, 1968.
Lucy Runs Away, illustrated by Dick Hart, Bodley Head, 1962, Prentice Hall, 1969.
Robin, illustrated by Peggy Fortnum, Faber, 1962, published as *The Freedom of the Seas,* Duell, 1965.
The Catchpole Story, Faber, 1965.
Rufus, illustrated by Peggy Fortnum, Faber, 1969, Gambit (Ipswich, MA), 1969.
Puss and Cat, illustrated by Carolyn Dinan, Faber, 1969.
Thursday, Faber, 1971, Harper (New York City), 1972.
Kate and the Island, illustrated by Gareth Floyd, Faber, 1972.
The Painter and the Fish, illustrated by Alan Howard, Faber, 1975.

The Chinese Egg, Faber, 1975, McGraw Hill (New York City), 1975.
The Story of the Terrible Scar, illustrated by Gerald Rose, Faber, 1976.
Who's Bill?, Macmillan (New York City), 1976.
Hugo and His Grandma, illustrated by Nita Sowter, Dinosaur (Amherst, MA), 1977.
Hugo and His Grandma's Washing Day, illustrated by Nita Sowter, Dinosaur, 1978.
Winter's End, Macmillan, 1978, Harper, 1979.
Tales of Polly and the Hungry Wolf, illustrated by Jill Bennett, Faber, 1980.
Vicky, Faber, 1981.
The Bugbear, illustrated by Elaine McGregor Turney, Hamish Hamilton (London), 1981.
It Couldn't Happen to Me, Dinosaur, 1982.
February Yowler, illustrated by Gareth Floyd, Faber, 1982.
The Castle Boy, Faber, 1983.
Two's Company, Hardy, 1984.
It Shouldn't Happen to a Frog, Macmillan, 1984.
Wagga Storybooks (Enter Wagga, Lost and Found Wagga, Wagga's Magic Ears, Watchdog Wagga), illustrated by Colin Caket, 4 vols., Hamlyn (London), 1984.
Cold Marble and Other Ghost Stories, Faber, 1985.
The Underground Conspiracy, Faber, 1987.
The Boy and the Swan, illustrated by Laszlo Acs, Deutsch (London), 1987.
Not Too Young and Other Stories, with Griselda Gifford and Jill Kent, Macmillan, 1987.
Mrs. Circumference, Deutsch, 1989.
Daljit and the Unqualified Wizard, Heinemann (London), 1989.
The Spy before Yesterday, Hamish Hamilton, 1990.
We Didn't Think of Ostriches, Longman (Essex, England), 1990.
Last Stories of Polly and the Wolf, illustrated by Jill Bennett, Puffin (New York City), 1992.
Babybug, illustrated by Fiona Dunbar, Simon & Schuster (New York City), 1992.
Finn's Animal, illustrated by Paul Howard, Heinemann, 1992.
The Mirror Image Ghost, Faber, 1994.
Watcher at the Window, illustrated by Judith Lawton, Longman, 1995.

CHILDREN'S NONFICTION AND RETELLINGS

Pebble (reader), Macmillan, 1979.
Pen Friends (reader), illustrated by Charles Front, Macmillan, 1980.
Feasts and Festivals, illustrated by Jenny Rhodes, Hardy, 1983.

Easy Piano Picture Books (includes *Swan Lake, The Nutcracker, The Sleeping Beauty, Hansel and Gretel, Peter & the Wolf*), first volume with Dianne Jackson, 5 vols., Faber, 1987-92.

Let's Read Together series (*A Fast Move, Find the Specs, Grandpa's Birthday, Gran Builds a House*) illustrated by Toni Goffe, 4 vols., Macdonald & Co. (London), 1987, 3 vols., Silver Burdett (Morristown, NJ), 1987, *Gran Builds a House* was published as *Building a House*, Silver Burdett, 1987.

Competitions and Ponies, Macmillan, 1987.

"PEOPLE OF THE BIBLE" SERIES

Noah and His Ark, Joseph and His Brothers, The Birth of Jesus, Jesus Begins His Work, Adam and Eve, Jonah and the Whale, The Prodigal Son, Miracles by the Sea, Moses of the Bulrushes, Joseph the Dreamteller, The First Easter, The Good Samaritan, Abraham and Isaac, Moses and the Plagues of Egypt, David and Goliath, St. Peter and St. Paul, Jesus and John the Baptist, Joseph the Long Lost Brother, Moses Leads His People, The Trials of Daniel, King David, Sampson and Delilah, Ruth's Story, Jesus the Healer, 24 vols., Watts (London), 1982-86, Raintree (Milwaukee, WI), 1982-86.

"GREAT TALES FROM LONG AGO" SERIES

Robin Hood, Hiawatha, The Pied Piper of Hamelin, Rip Van Winkle, Joan of Arc, King Midas and His Gold, King Arthur's Sword, Odysseus and the Enchanters, Theseus and the Minotaur, Dick Whittington, Androcles and the Lion, The Wooden Horse, Richard the Lionheart, 13 vols., Methuen (London), 1984-87, 12 vols., Raintree, 1984-89; *The Wooden Horse* was published as *The Trojan Horse*, Raintree, 1985.

FICTION FOR ADULTS

(Under pseudonym Helen Lourie) *A Question of Abortion*, Bodley Head, 1962.

(Under pseudonym Irene Adler) *Freud for the Jung; Or, Three Hundred and Sixty-Six Hours on the Couch*, Cresset Press (Philadelphia, PA), 1963.

The Merciful Jew, Barrie and Rockliff, 1968.

Black God, White God, Barrie and Jenkins (Covent Gardens, England), 1972.

Unnatural Fathers, Quartet (London), 1976.

Tales from the Psychiatrist's Couch, Quartet, 1977.

NONFICTION FOR ADULTS

Cook's Quick Reference: Essential Information on Cards, Penguin, 1971.

(Editor) Isabelle Jan, *On Children's Literature*, Allen Lane (London), 1973, Schocken (New York City), 1974.

Growing Up: A Practical Guide to Adolescence for Parents and Children, Arrow (London), 1975.

OTHER

Author of *Flax into Gold: The Story of Rumpelstiltskin*, a children's libretto with music by Hugo Cole, Chappell (Essex), 1964, of the children's television plays in the *Starting Out* series, 1973-78, and the adult radio play, *Bevil*, 1984. Also contributor of reviews to *Times Literary Supplement* and of articles to *Nova* and *Cosmopolitan*.

Some of Storr's manuscripts are housed in the Kerlan Collection, University of Minnesota—Minneapolis.

SIDELIGHTS: Trained as a psychiatrist, the English writer Catherine Storr has found her most effective form of personal therapy in writing. "I started writing when I was ten years old," she once stated, "and it has become an addiction. . . . I think in story form and my dreams often take the form of stories, though hardly ever useful as plots. . . . I don't write with a child readership in mind, I write for the childish side of myself, and find it often acts as psychotherapy."

Psychotherapy, compulsion, or pure enjoyment, Storr's writings have spanned four decades, several genres, and include some 100 picture books, retellings, and novels for both children and adults. Exploring such themes as the power of dreams and adolescent sexuality, Storr's books often employ elements of myth and folktale, blending realism with fantasy. On the whole, her work has been better received in her own country than in the United States where some reviewers have tended to take her empowering stories for children a bit too literally: Her encouragement to readers to understand their dreams has been criticized as promoting avoidance of real-life problems. Perhaps best known for her children's books, Storr has also produced an impressive array of young adult novels, including *Rufus, Thursday,* and *Marianne Dreams*, which Fred Inglis, writing in *Twentieth-Century Children's Writers*, called Storr's "best book."

Though she had been interested in writing since she was a child and graduated from college with a degree in English, Storr chose medicine as a career partly, as she wrote in *The Thorny Paradise,* because "I thought that as a doctor I would get that experience of life which was wanted in my writing." But just before embarking on her medical studies, she sold her first children's book, *Ingeborg and Ruthy,* a fantasy about a doll she'd had as a child.

Some of Storr's earliest children's books, the Polly stories, were also among her most popular. *Clever Polly and the Stupid Wolf* and *The Adventures of Polly and the Wolf* appeared in the mid-1950s and found an eager readership. Employing the big bad wolf motif, Storr inverts the standard myth by making the young girl intelligent and indifferent to the clumsy and gullible wolf who tries to capture her. Survival and empowerment are also themes explored in the Lucy books, in which the young tomboy tries to gain acceptance, as in *Lucy,* or embarks on faraway adventures, as in *Lucy Runs Away.* While a *Kirkus Reviews* writer thought the latter book was "bouncy and brash enough" to appeal to young girls, Marguerite M. Murray of the *Library Journal* called it "A pedestrian adventure that should not be allowed to circulate," and felt that it might incite children to run away from home.

With *Marianne Dreams* and *Marianne and Mark,* Storr moved into the realm of juvenile and young adult fiction. In *Marianne Dreams* the title character is afforded the chance to explore her interior world during a long convalescence. The book can be seen as a discourse on the power of dreams as well as a suspense novel. Fred Inglis in *Twentieth-Century Children's Writers* calls the book "a metaphor for nursing. . . . [It] has gravity and power . . . unquestionably a classic." *Marianne and Mark* finds Marianne on a holiday at the seashore where a fortuneteller's prophecy interrupts her relationship with Mark.

Sometimes criticized for her use of the dream world and the unconscious in her stories, Storr nevertheless has admitted to employing such forces in her creative process. "As a writer I rely enormously on the unconscious," she commented in *The Thorny Paradise,* though she conceded that "however rich the material and great the impetus given by the dynamic unconscious, there must always be the more objective attitude, the power to judge, evaluate and shape into coherence, provided by the conscious intelligence."

Storr deals with adolescent and teenage sexuality in two novels, *Winter's End* and *Two's Company.* In the former she blends elements of Gothic romance with realism and fantasy: Two young undergraduate couples take a study holiday at a country house one of them has inherited. "Catherine Storr has the ability to capture the stark misty atmosphere of the countryside," noted Drew Stevenson in *School Library Journal,* and a *Bulletin of the Center for Children's Literature* reviewer concluded that while the element of fantasy gave the story color and force, "it is the realistic problems and relationships that give it substance . . . [and which are] presented with depth and perception." In *Two's Company,* two sisters embark on a holiday in France which leads them into the realm of homosexuality and bisexuality when they meet two boys. Nicholas Tucker in *Times Literary Supplement* found *Two's Company* to be "a moving story, its heart in the right place," while Margaret Meek in the *School Librarian* commented that the book avoided prurient traps and told a universal story: "A more grown-up book than many books for grown-ups," Meek concluded.

A magpie of genre forms, Storr has also ventured into ghost stories with *Cold Marble and Other Stories* and *The Mirror Image Ghost,* as well as suspense novels with *The Castle Boy* and *The Underground Conspiracy.* Additionally, she has written retellings of Biblical stories and favorite tales such as *Robin Hood* and *Rip Van Winkle.* "I've continued to write for the young," Storr wrote in *The Thorny Paradise,* "not only long after I should have ceased to be childish, but also after my own children were grown up, because of my lasting need for the story form."

BIOGRAPHICAL/CRITICAL SOURCES:

BOOKS

Blishen, Edward, editor, *The Thorny Paradise,* Kestrel Books (London), 1975, pp. 25-33.
Twentieth-Century Children's Writers, 4th edition, St. James Press (Detroit), 1995, pp. 909-12.

PERIODICALS

Booklist, January 1, 1969, p. 500; November 15, 1972, p. 303; December 15, 1975, pp. 574, 581; December 15, 1976, p. 615; August 1, 1982, p. 1529; February 1, 1985, p. 791; February 15, 1996, p. 861.
Books for Keeps, November, 1988, pp. 29-30.

Bulletin of the Center for Children's Books, January, 1969, p. 85; May, 1970, p. 152; March, 1976, p. 119; May, 1979, p. 164; July-August, 1979, p. 202; April, 1983, p. 143; April, 1985, p. 150.

Horn Book, April, 1973, p. 148; February, 1976, p. 58.

Junior Bookshelf, April, 1977, p. 101; February, 1979, p. 61; April, 1981, p. 73; April, 1982, p. 76; June, 1982, p. 101; April, 1983, p. 79; August, 1983, p. 174; December, 1983, p. 250; February, 1985, p. 31; June, 1985, p. 135; April, 1986, p. 61, 72; April, 1987, p. 95; December, 1987, p. 289; October, 1990, p. 213; December, 1990, p. 284; December, 1991, p. 255; June, 1994, p. 111.

Library Journal, April 15, 1970, p. 1630; September 15, 1970, p. 3054; October 15, 1972, p. 3465.

Kirkus Reviews, October 1, 1969, pp. 1065-66; December 15, 1969, p. 1317. July 1, 1972, p. 730.

New York Times Book Review, November 9, 1969, p. 38.

Publishers Weekly, August 14, 1972, p. 46.

School Librarian, March, 1985, p. 62-63; February, 1991, p. 25.

School Library Journal, January, 1976, p. 56-7; May, 1979, p. 83; January, 1980, p. 62; March, 1980; April, 1981, p. 117; October, 1981, p. 136; November, 1982, p. 91; April, 1985, p. 89; March, 1986, p. 179.

Times Educational Supplement, November 15, 1985, p. 49; November 6, 1987, p. 46; March 18, 1988, p. 32; October 6, 1989, p. 32; April 1, 1994, p. 22.

Times Literary Supplement, November 30, 1967, p. 1137; August 8, 1968, p. 841; April 3, 1969, p. 355; December 4, 1969, p. 1384; December 8, 1972, p. 1491; October 1, 1976, p. 1248; December 1, 1978, p. 1394; November 20, 1981, p. 1355; March 26, 1982, p. 344; July 23, 1982, p. 797; July 13, 1984, p. 794; May 29, 1987, p. 589; January 1, 1988, p. 21.*

*   *   *

STREET, Pamela   1921-

PERSONAL: Born March 3, 1921, in Wilton, Wiltshire, England; daughter of Arthur George (an author, broadcaster, and farmer) and Vera Florence (Foyle) Street; married David Francis Hamilton McCormick, July 3, 1945 (divorced, 1971); children: Miranda. *Education:* Godolphin School, England. *Politics:* Socialist. *Religion:* Church of England.

ADDRESSES: Home—47 South St., Flat 5, London W1Y 5PD, England.

CAREER: Writer. Secretary and researcher for Sir Arthur Bryant (a historian), beginning 1971. *Wartime service:* British Auxiliary Territorial Service, 1942-45; became second lieutenant.

WRITINGS:

My Father, A. G. Street, Hale (London), 1969, 2nd edition, 1984.

Portrait of Wiltshire, International Publications Service, 1971, 3rd revised edition published as *Illustrated Portrait of Wiltshire,* Hale, 1986.

Arthur Bryant: Portrait of a Historian, Collins (London), 1979.

NOVELS

Light of Evening, Hale, 1981.
Morning Glory, Hale, 1982.
The Stepsisters, Hale, 1982.
The Mill-Race (also see below), Hale, 1983.
The Way of the River (also see below), Hale, 1984.
Many Waters (also see below), Hale, 1985.
Unto the Fourth Generation (also see below), Hale, 1985.
Portrait of Rose, Hale, 1986.
Personal Relations, Hale, 1987.
The Mill-Race Quartet (contains *The Mill-Race, The Way of the River, Many Waters,* and *Unto the Fourth Generation*), Pan Books (London), 1988.
The Timeless Moment, Hale, 1988.
The Beneficiaries, Hale, 1989.
Doubtful Company, Hale, 1990.
Guilty Parties, Hale, 1990.
Late Harvest, Hale, 1991.
The Colonel's Son, Hale, 1992.
Hindsight, Hale, 1993.
Keeping It Dark, Hale, 1994.
King's Folly, Hale, 1995.

OTHER

Also author of the radio short story "Mr. Brown and Prudence" for British Broadcasting Corp. (BBC-Radio), 1988.

SIDELIGHTS: Pamela Street told _CA:_ "I have always wanted to write since childhood, probably inspired by my late father, A. G. Street, who broke into print with the best-seller, _Farmer's Glory,_ in 1932 and about whom I wrote my first book, _My Father, A. G. Street,_ in 1969."

BIOGRAPHICAL/CRITICAL SOURCES:

PERIODICALS

Times Literary Supplement, January 18, 1980.

*   *   *

SWINBURNE, Richard   1934-

PERSONAL: Born December 26, 1934, in Smethwick, England; son of William Henry (a college professor) and Gladys (Parker) Swinburne; married Monica Holmstrom, August 4, 1960 (separated, 1985); children: Juliet Caroline, Nicola Margaret. _Education:_ Exeter College, Oxford, B.A., 1957; St. Johns College, Oxford, B.Phil., 1959, M.A., 1961. _Religion:_ Greek Orthodox.

ADDRESSES: Office—Oriel College, University of Oxford, OX1 4EW, England.

CAREER: University of Leeds, Leeds, England, Leverhulme research fellow in history and philosophy of science, 1961-63; University of Hull, Hull, England, lecturer, 1963-69, senior lecturer in philosophy, 1969-72; University of Keele, Keele, England, professor of philosophy, 1972-84; University of Oxford, Oxford, England, Nolloth Professor of the Philosophy of the Christian Religion, 1985—. Visiting associate professor of philosophy, University of Maryland, 1969-70; Wilde Lecturer in Natural and Comparative Religion, University of Oxford, 1975-78; Gifford Lecturer, University of Aberdeen, 1983-84.

MEMBER: British Academy (fellow).

WRITINGS:

Space and Time, St. Martin's (New York City), 1968, 2nd edition, 1981.
The Concept of Miracle, St. Martin's, 1970.
An Introduction to Confirmation Theory, Methuen (London), 1973.
(Editor) _The Justification of Induction,_ Oxford University Press (Oxford, England), 1974.
The Coherence of Theism, Oxford University Press, 1977, revised edition, 1993.
The Existence of God, Oxford University Press, 1979.
Faith and Reason, Oxford University Press, 1981.
(Editor) _Space, Time, and Causality,_ D. Reidel (Dordrecht, The Netherlands), 1983.
(With Sydney Shoemaker) _Personal Identity,_ Basil Blackwell (Oxford, England), 1984.
The Evolution of the Soul, Oxford University Press, 1986.
Responsibility and Atonement, Oxford University Press, 1989.
(Editor) _Miracles,_ Macmillan (London), 1989.
Revelation, Oxford University Press, 1991.
The Christian God, Oxford University Press, 1994.
Is There a God?, Oxford University Press, 1996.

Contributor to professional journals.

WORK IN PROGRESS: Providence, the final book in his tetralogy on Christian doctrine.

SIDELIGHTS: In connection with his dual interest in the philosophy of science and religion, Richard Swinburne writes: "I believe that detailed philosophical examination of large claims of science or theology can elucidate the meaning of those claims and the ways in which they are to be established or refuted. _Space and Time_ puts modern theories of physics under the philosophical microscope. _An Introduction to Confirmation Theory_ analyzes what in science and elsewhere is evidence for what. _The Coherence of Theism, The Existence of God,_ and _Faith and Reason_ form a trilogy on the philosophy of theism. _The Coherence of Theism_ examines the meaning of the claim that there is a God; _The Existence of God_ examines the evidence for and against that claim and concludes that probably there is a God; _Faith and Reason_ examines the relation of reasoned arguments to religious faith. _The Evolution of the Soul,_ of which my contribution to _Personal Identity_ was a first installment, examines the differences between humans and the primeval matter out of which they have evolved, and claims that these differences are to be explained by humans having souls."

Swinburne adds: "I am now completing a tetralogy on the philosophical issues involved in Christian doctrines. Each of the four books contains a first part discussing straight philosophical issues and a second part in which the results of the first part are applied to Christian doctrines. The first book, *Responsibility and Atonement,* examines the meaning and applicability of such notions as guilt, merit, atonement, forgiveness, reward, and punishment. It then applies these results to relevant Christian doctrines—sin, original sin, the Atonement, heaven, and hell. The second book, *Revelation,* examines how truth can be conveyed by genres of poetry and parable, by analogy and metaphor, within false presuppositions about history and science. It then considers whether the practice of religion requires revealed truth and goes on to consider what would show that the Christian creeds and Bible reveal truth. The third book, *The Christian God,* examines the basic metaphysical categories of substance, cause, time, and necessity. It then goes on to examine the Christian doctrine of the divine nature and the resultant doctrines of the Trinity and the Incarnation. The final volume of the tetralogy, to be called *Providence,* will consider the various good and bad states which can happen to humans and show how many great goods for humans would logically require some bad states on the way. It then seeks to show how God who is concerned to give humans very great good may allow evil to occur on the way to that good.

"In my trilogy on theism, my book on the soul, and the tetralogy on Christian doctrine, I believe that I shall have developed a well-integrated account of the meaning and justification of central Christian doctrines, in the light of twentieth-century philosophy and science. Conscious of the need to make these results more generally accessible, I have just written a short book *Is There a God?,* which is a popular version of *The Existence of God,* the book which is perhaps the central volume of all these writings."

BIOGRAPHICAL/CRITICAL SOURCES:

BOOKS

Padgett, Alan G., editor, *Reason and the Christian Religion: Essays in Honour of Richard Swinburne,* Clarendon Press (Oxford, England), 1994.

PERIODICALS

Times Literary Supplement, August 14, 1969; April 2, 1971; October 19, 1973; January 25, 1980; May 28, 1982; February 15, 1985; December 11, 1987.

SWITHEN, John
See KING, Stephen (Edwin)

*   *   *

SYMONDS, Craig L.   1946-

PERSONAL: Born December 31, 1946, in Long Beach, CA; son of Lee and Virginia (Garrison) Symonds; married Marylou Hayden, January 17, 1969; children: Jeffrey K. *Education:* University of California, Los Angeles, B.A., 1967; University of Florida, M.A., 1969, Ph.D., 1976.

ADDRESSES: Office—Department of History, U.S. Naval Academy, Annapolis, MD 21402.

CAREER: U.S. Naval War College, Washington, DC, assistant professor of strategy, 1973-74; U.S. Naval Academy, Annapolis, MD, assistant professor, 1976-80, associate professor, 1980-85; professor of history, 1985—, chair of department, 1988-92. Visiting lecturer, Britannia Royal Naval College, Dartmouth, England, 1994-95. *Military service:* U.S. Navy, 1971-74; became lieutenant.

MEMBER: American Military Institute, Southern Historical Association.

WRITINGS:

Navalists and Antinavalists: The Naval Policy Debate in the United States, 1785-1827, University of Delaware Press (East Brunswick, NJ), 1980.
A Battlefield Atlas of the Civil War (Book-of-the-Month Club selection), Nautical and Aviation (Annapolis, MD), 1983.
A Battlefield Atlas of the American Revolution (Book-of-the-Month Club selection), Nautical and Aviation, 1986.
Joseph E. Johnston: A Civil War Biography, Norton (New York City), 1992.
Gettysburg: A Battlefield Atlas, Nautical and Aviation, 1992.
The Naval Institute Historical Atlas of the U. S. Navy, Naval Institute Press (Annapolis, MD), 1995.

Contributor to books, including *The Chiefs of Naval Operations,* edited by Robert W. Love, Jr., Naval Institute Press, 1980; *Command under Sail,* edited by James Bradford, Naval Institute Press, 1985; and

Against All Enemies: Interpretations of American Military History from Colonial Times to the Present, edited by Kenneth J. Hagan and William R. Roberts, Greenwood Press (Westport, CT), 1986.

EDITOR

John B. Marchand, *Charleston Blockade: The Journals of John B. Marchand, USN,* Naval War College Press, 1976.

New Aspects of Naval History, Naval Institute Press, 1981.

William H. Parker, *Recollections of a Naval Officer, 1941-1965,* Naval Institute Press, 1985.

Alvah F. Hunter, *A Year on a Monitor,* University of South Carolina Press (Columbia), 1987.

WORK IN PROGRESS: A biography of Confederate general Patrick R. Cleburne, to be published by University Press of Kansas in March, 1997.

T-U

TABRAH, Ruth Milander 1921-

PERSONAL: Born February 28, 1921, in Buffalo, NY; daughter of Henry and Ruth H. (Flock) Milander; married Frank L. Tabrah (a physician), May 8, 1943 (divorced August, 1971); children: Joseph Garner, Thomas. *Education:* University of Buffalo, B.A., 1941; University of Washington, Seattle, graduate study, 1944-45. *Politics:* Democrat. *Religion:* Buddhist. *Avocational interests:* Painting, skin diving.

ADDRESSES: Home—876 Curtis St., Apt. 3905, Honolulu, HI 96813-5134.

CAREER: Writer, editor, and freelance photojournalist; editor, Buddhist Study Center Press, 1980—; ordained Shin Buddhist priest in Kyoto, Japan, 1983. Hawaii School Advisory Council, elected member, 1962-66, chairperson, 1964-66; Hawaii State Board of Education, Honolulu, elected member, 1966-68; National Association of State Boards of Education, vice-president of Western Division, 1968-72, director-at-large, 1971. Co-host of weekly series on Hawaii public television, *Hawaii Now.* Consultant to U.S. Office of Education, 1969-72, and Consulting Organization, 1972—.

MEMBER: International Association of Shin Buddhist Studies, Authors League of America, Hawaii Association of International Buddhists, Honpa Hongwanji Hawaii Betsuin (president, 1994-96), Hawaii Watercolor Society, Phi Beta Kappa.

AWARDS, HONORS: Distinguished Woman in Education Award, American Association of University Women, 1970.

WRITINGS:

Pulaski Place, Harper (New York City), 1950.
The Voices of Others, Putnam (New York City), 1959, published as *Town for Scandal,* Pocket Books (New York City), 1960.
Hawaiian Heart, Follett, 1964.
Hawaii Nei, Follett, 1967.
The Red Shark, Follett, 1970.
Buddhism: A Modern Way of Life and Thought, Jodo (Honolulu), 1970.
The Old Man and the Astronauts: A Melanesian Tale, Island Heritage (Honolulu), 1975.
Lanai, Island Heritage, 1975.
Living Shin Buddhism, Press Pacifica (Waipahu, HI), 1979.
Hawaii: A Bicentennial History, Norton (New York City), 1980.
Maui: The Romantic Island, K.C. Publications (Portland, OR), 1985.
Emily's Hawaii, Press Pacifica, 1986, 3rd edition, 1994.
(Translator) *Shoshinge,* Buddhist Study Center Press (Kailua, HI), 1986.
Hawaii's Incredible Anna, Press Pacifica, 1987.
The Golden Children of Hawaii, Island Heritage, 1987.
Kauai: The Unconquerable Island, K.C. Publications, 1988.
Ajata Satru: The Story That Tells Us Who We Are, Buddhist Study Center Press, 1988.
Shin Sutras to Live By, Buddhist Study Center Press, 1992.
The Natural Way of Shin Buddhism, Buddhist Study Center Press, 1994.
The Monk Who Dared (novel), Press Pacifica, 1995.

Also author of *Niihau: The Last Hawaiian Island,* 1987.

George Suyeoka, *Momotaro,* 1972.
Guy Buffet and Pam Buffet, *Adventures of Kama Puaa,* 1972.
G. Buffet and P. Buffet, *Pua Pua Lena Lena and the Magic Kiha-Pu: An Adaptation from the Hawaiian Legends,* 1972.
G. Buffet and P. Buffet, *Kahala: Where the Rainbow Ends,* 1973.
Shan Mui, *The Seven Magic Orders,* 1973.
Robert B. Goodman and Robert A. Spicer, *Urashima Taro,* 1973.
Goodman and Spicer, *The Magic Brush,* 1974.
Issunboshi, 1974.
Philipo Springer, *Makaha: The Legend of the Broken Promise,* 1974.

OTHER

Contributor to periodicals.

WORK IN PROGRESS: Writing My Life, an autobiography.

SIDELIGHTS: Ruth Milander Tabrah once told *CA* that she is "a writer who was born wanting to do exactly what I've spent my life doing—putting into words what it means to be fully human, exciting readers by opening new windows in their minds, telling what I see and feel and think with honesty and without shame."

Tabrah speaks French and German as well as some Japanese and Spanish. She has traveled extensively while researching her books.

*   *   *

TANSELLE, G(eorge) Thomas   1934-

PERSONAL: Surname is pronounced "*Tan*-sell"; born January 29, 1934, in Lebanon, IN; son of K. Edwin and Madge R. (Miller) Tanselle. *Education:* Yale University, B.A. (magna cum laude), 1955; Northwestern University, M.A., 1956, Ph.D., 1959.

ADDRESSES: Office—John Simon Guggenheim Memorial Foundation, 90 Park Ave., New York, NY 10016.

CAREER: Chicago City Junior College, Chicago, IL, instructor in English, 1958-60; University of Wisconsin—Madison, instructor, 1960-61, assistant professor, 1961-63, associate professor, 1963-68, professor of English, 1968-78; John Simon Guggenheim Memorial Foundation, New York City, vice president, 1978—. Adjunct professor of English and comparative literature, Columbia University, 1980—; member of faculty, Summer Rare Book School, Columbia University School of Library Service, 1984-87. Board of directors, Literary Classics of the United States, Inc., 1979—, and 18th-century short title catalog, North America, Inc., 1988—, chair, 1994—. Member of Planning Institute of Commission on English, Ann Arbor, MI, summer, 1961; executive committee, Center for Editions of American Authors, 1970-73; Soviet-American symposium on editing, Indiana University, 1976; executive committee, Center for Scholarly Editions, 1976-81. Member of advisory committees and advisory boards of various organizations, including Center for the Book Library of Congress, 1978—. Speaker before many literary organizations and at numerous conferences.

MEMBER: Modern Language Association of America, Modern Humanities Research Association, Society for Textual Scholarship (president, 1981-83), Renaissance Society of America, American Society for Eighteenth-Century Studies, American Printing History Association (member of board of trustees, New York Chapter, 1979-85), Printing Historical Society, Private Libraries Association, Manuscript Society (member of board of directors, 1974-79), Melville Society (president, 1982—), Typophiles, Guild Book Workers, American Antiquarian Society (council member, 1974-92), Bibliographical Society of America (member of council, 1970-94; president, 1984-88), Fellows Morgan Library, Bibliographical Society (London), Edinburgh Bibliographical Society, Oxford Bibliographical Society, Cambridge Bibliographical Society, Bibliographical Society of the University of Virginia (president, 1992—), Wisconsin Academy of Sciences, Arts, and Letters, Society for the History of Authorship, Reading, and Publishing (board of directors, 1993—), The Johnsonians (chair, 1993), Book Club of California, Yale Club,

Century Club, Grolier Club (secretary, 1982-86, president, 1986-90), Caxton Club, Phi Beta Kappa.

AWARDS, HONORS: Kiekhofer Teaching Award, University of Wisconsin, 1963; Guggenheim fellowship, 1969-70; Jenkins Prize for Bibliography, Union College, 1973; American Council of Learned Societies fellowship, 1973-74; National Endowment for the Humanities fellowship, 1977-78; English-Speaking Union "Books-Across-the-Sea Ambassador of Honor" book awards for *Herman Melville: Typee, Omoo, Mardi,* 1983, and *Herman Melville: Redburn, White-Jacket, Moby-Dick,* 1984; Laureate Award, American Printing History Association, 1987, "for distinguished contribution to the study of the history of publishing and printing."

WRITINGS:

NONFICTION

T. Royall Tyler, Harvard University Press (Cambridge, MA), 1967.
A Guide to the Study of the United States Imprints, Belknap, 1971.
A Checklist of Editions of Moby-Dick, Northwestern University Press and Newberry Library, 1976.
Selected Studies in Bibliography, University Press of Virginia (Charlottesville), 1979.
Textual Criticism since Greg: A Chronicle, 1950-1985, University Press of Virginia, 1988.
A Rationale of Textual Criticism, University of Pennsylvania Press (Philadelphia), 1989.
Hawthorne and Melville ("Parkman Dexter Howe Library" series, part 6), University of Florida Press (Gainsville), 1989.
Textual Criticism and Scholarly Editing, University Press of Virginia, 1990.
The Life and Work of Fredson Bowers, Bibliographic Society of the University of Virginia, 1993.

EDITOR

(Coeditor) *The Writings of Herman Melville,* Northwestern University Press and Newberry Library (Evanston, IL), 1968.
Herman Melville: Typee, Ommo, Mardi, Library of America (New York City), 1982.
Herman Melville: Redburn, White-Jacket, Moby-Dick, Library of America, 1983.
Gordon N. Ray, *Book on a Way of Life,* Grolier Club and Morgan Library (Charlottesville, VA), 1988.

OTHER

Contributor to books and scholarly journals, including *Studies in Bibliography,* 1964—, *Book Collector, Library, Shakespeare Quarterly, Gutenberg Jahrbuch, Papers of the Bibliographical Society of America, Modern Language Review, American Literature,* and *PMLA.* Member of editorial board, *Contemporary Literature,* 1962-91, *Abstracts of English Studies,* 1964-78, *Papers of the Bibliographical Society of America,* 1968-80, *Resources for American Literary Study,* 1971—, *Analytical and Enumerative Bibliography,* 1977—, *Review,* 1978—, *American Literature,* 1979-82, *Literary Research,* 1986-90, and *Common Knowledge,* 1991—. Member of advisory board of *Burtons Anatomy of Melancholy,* 1978—, *James Fenimore Cooper Editions,* 1990—, and *Mark Twain Editions,* 1991—.

*   *   *

TARR, Judith   1955-

PERSONAL: Born January 30, 1955, in Augusta, ME; daughter of Earle A., Jr. (a waterworks manager and real estate salesman) and Regina (a teacher; maiden name, Gallagher) Tarr. *Education:* Mount Holyoke College, A.B., 1976; Newnham College, Cambridge, B.A., 1978, M.A., 1983; Yale University, M.A., 1979, M.Phil., 1983, Ph.D., 1988.

ADDRESSES: Home—94 Foster St. #23, New Haven, CT 06511. *Agent*—Jane Butler, Box 278, 212 3rd St., Milford, PA 18337.

CAREER: Edward Little High School, Auburn, ME, Latin teacher, 1979-81; writer, 1985—. Wesleyan University, Middletown, CT, visiting lecturer in liberal studies and visiting writer, 1989—, visiting assistant professor of classics, 1990—.

MEMBER: Modern Language Association of America, Medieval Academy of America, Science Fiction Writers of America.

AWARDS, HONORS: Crawford Memorial Award, 1987; Mary Lyon Award, Mt. Holyoke College, 1989.

WRITINGS:

A Wind in Cairo, Bantam (New York City), 1989.
Ars Magica, Bantam, 1989.
Alamut, Doubleday (New York City), 1989.
The Dagger and the Cross: A Novel of the Crusades, Doubleday, 1991.
His Majesty's Elephant (juvenile), Jane Yolen Books (San Diego, CA), 1993.
Lord of the Two Lands, Tor Books (New York City), 1993.
Throne of Isis, Forge (New York City), 1994.
The Eagle's Daughter, Forge, 1995.
Pillar of Fire, Forge, 1995.

"THE HOUND AND THE FALCON" SERIES; FANTASY NOVELS

The Isle of Glass, Bluejay Books (New York City), 1985.
The Golden Horn, Bluejay Books, 1985.
The Hounds of God, Bluejay Books, 1986.

"AVARYAN RISING" SERIES; FANTASY NOVELS

The Hall of the Mountain King, Bluejay Books, 1986.
The Lady of Han-Gilen, Bluejay Books, 1986.
A Fall of Princes, Bluejay Books, 1987.
Avaryan Rising (includes *The Hall of the Mountain King, The Lady of Han-Gilen,* and *A Fall of Princes*), Doubleday, 1988.
Arrows of the Sun, Tor Books, 1993.
Spear of Heaven, Tor Books, 1994.

OTHER

Work represented in anthologies, including *Moonsinger's Friends,* edited by Susan Schwartz, Bluejay Books, 1985. Contributor to *Isaac Asimov's Science Fiction Magazine.*

SIDELIGHTS: "Judith Tarr," writes a reviewer for the *Washington Post Book World,* "has plumbed the well of ancient lore for her novels." A trained historian, Tarr uses her academic background to add depth and realism to her works. All her novels to date use historical characters, settings, or prototypes: the three volumes of her "Hound and the Falcon" series, for instance, take place in the late twelfth and early thirteenth centuries in Europe and the Middle East; *Lord of the Two Lands* is set in Egypt during the conquests of Alexander the Great in the fourth century B.C.; and *Pillar of Fire* tells an alternative version of the fate of the ancient pharaoh Akhenaten,

credited with developing monotheism before the ancient Hebrews. Although her work is at heart fantastic rather than historical, explains Faren Miller in *Locus* magazine, "Tarr grounds it as firmly in research as the soundest historical novel."

Tarr's "Hound of the Falcon" fantasy series, consisting of *The Isle of Glass, The Golden Horn,* and *The Hounds of God,* traces the adventures of Alfred, a half-human, half-elf hybrid. Alfred was abandoned at birth, as many unwanted children were in ancient and medieval times, and was raised in a monastery as an oblate. Because of his ancestry, Alfred suffers from a conflict between "his spiritual needs as a monk, his magical ability, and his physical reality as a non-human," explains Phyllis J. Day in *Fantasy Review.* In *The Isle of Glass* Alfred is sent on an important mission to the Crusader king, Richard I of England. *The Golden Horn* finds him and his elf lover Thea in the city of Constantinople, which is besieged by Crusaders, while *The Hounds of God* places Alfred as chancellor of the kingdom of Rhiyana, where the few surviving elves are under attack by the Inquisition. Many critics react positively to Tarr's mix of history, romance, and fantasy: "Tarr provides loving detail to each characterization, subplot, image and interaction—her craft is exceptional," Day concludes. Other reviewers, however, faulted these works. "*The Golden Horn,*" notes Colin Greenwood in *New Statesman,* "is a bit like *The Sound of Music* set in Byzantium, 1204, though with rather more carnage."

In the "Avaryan Rising" series, Tarr's historical erudition is less explicit. According to a *Publishers Weekly* reviewer, *The Lady of Han-Gilen,* the second volume in the series, is "less original than Tarr's 'The Hound and the Falcon' trilogy, but it's also livelier and more engaging." Elian, the title character in this work, recalls the ancient Greek legend of Atalanta: she is beautiful, intelligent, and determined not to marry until she finds someone she cannot best. Her chosen mate turns out to be a childhood friend named Mirain, who is a demigod. "Proving herself an able warrior as well as a royal hellion with prophetic gifts," Anne Raymer writes in *Voice of Youth Advocates,* "Elian wins more than the admiration of her child love." Later volumes in the series tell about the future of the kingdom Mirain and Elian establish. *Spear of Heaven,* about one of their descendants, "owes more to adventure novels such as *Kim* and—in particular—*Lost Horizons,*" states Faren Miller in *Locus,* and it reads like "an exotic hybrid of *Lost Horizons* and *The Taming of the Shrew.*" "With elegant prose," declares a *Publishers Weekly* reviewer, "Tarr beautifully conveys splendid regal settings, realistic politics, convincing cultural details—and cultural clashes."

In her other novels, Tarr takes historical characters and places them in fantastic contexts. The title character of *His Majesty's Elephant,* for instance, is Abul Abbas, an elephant given by the Caliph of Baghdad, Haroun al-Rashid, to the Frankish emperor Charlemagne in the early ninth century. Tarr adds a subplot about a magical talisman that arrives with Abul Abbas. A sorcerer wishes to use it to cast a spell that will kill the king. Charlemagne's youngest daughter Rowan and a British slave named Kerrac confront the sorcerer. "Tarr has written a marvelous fantasy tale," asserts Renee Troselius in *Book Report.* "Rowan is a strong-willed character that readers will care about." Three of Tarr's works—*Lord of the Two Lands, Throne of Isis,* and *Pillar of Fire*—are set in ancient Egypt, and tell, respectively, of the country's conquest by Alexander the Great, of the reign of Cleopatra and her romance with the Roman soldier Marc Anthony, and of the career of the pharaoh Akhenaten and the prophet Moses. "If she hasn't yet proven herself a successor to the likes of Mary Renault and Bryher and Rosemary Sutcliff," *Washington Post Book World* reviewer concludes, "Judith Tarr . . . [takes] a step in the right direction."

Judith Tarr told *CA:* "As a writer of fantasy, I have found my academic training to be truly invaluable. Fantasy is more than an illogical escape, or a conglomeration of elements from Tolkien, C. S. Lewis, and the *Dungeons and Dragons Monster Manual.* Good fantasy requires a knowledge of history, a feeling for language—one's own and, preferably, a number of others (I have classical and medieval Latin, classical Greek, Old and Middle English, medieval and modern French, some German, and some Provencal)—and an affinity for plain old hard work. The training and techniques required to earn a Ph.D. adapt themselves very well indeed to the exigencies of creating and populating a world. If nothing else, I have learned where to look for what I need, what to look for, and what to do with it when I have it—not to mention the ability to produce work of consistent and, I can hope, high quality, on command and against a deadline.

"I write what I write, and not (by choice) scholarly monographs or historical novels, or, for that matter, contemporary fiction, because I *like* writing fantasy. The challenge of historical fantasy is to adhere as closely as possible to actual historical events, while incorporating elements of fantasy: magical beings and powers, imaginary kingdoms, and straight-forward alternate history. In high fantasy, the challenge becomes at once simpler and more complex. The need for scrupulous historical research is less, but in its place comes the task of creating lands, people, languages, histories, cultures, and all the manifold aspects of a living world. Not only must I create them, I must create them as a whole, connected logically and plausibly, with characters drawn to the best of my ability. It is not easy. There are few shortcuts. The result is never as close to perfection as it might be, but the sheer, exhilarating fun of it is well worth the effort."

BIOGRAPHICAL/CRITICAL SOURCES:

PERIODICALS

Booklist, June 1 & 15, 1995, p. 1732.
Book Report, May/June, 1994, pp. 46-7.
Fantasy Review, January, 1986, p. 26.
Kirkus Reviews, February 15, 1994, p. 173.
Library Journal, November 15, 1994, p. 89; June 15, 1995, p. 96.
Locus, August, 1993, p. 49; November, 1993, p. 54; February, 1994, p. 76; April, 1994, p. 53; October, 1994, p. 57.
New Statesman, July 24, 1987, p. 23.
Publishers Weekly, April 10, 1987, p. 85; August 30, 1993, p. 80; March 20, 1995, p. 44.
Science Fiction Chronicle, April, 1986, p. 42; December, 1992, p. 57; August, 1993, p. 39.
Voice of Youth Advocates, October, 1987, p. 181; August, 1993, p. 171; February, 1994, p. 387; August, 1994, p. 150.
Washington Post, May 30, 1993, p. 9.
Washington Post Book World, May 20, 1993, p. 9; October 17, 1994, p. 68; May 22, 1995, p. 50.

*   *   *

TATCHELL, Peter   1952-

PERSONAL: Born January 25, 1952, in Melbourne, Australia; son of Gordon (a lathe operator) and Mardi (a factory packer; maiden name, Rhodes) Tatchell. *Education:* West London College, Certificate in Applied Sociology, 1974; Polytechnic of North London, B.Sc. in sociology (with honors), 1977. *Politics:* "Leftwing socialist." *Religion:* None.

ADDRESSES: Home and office—45 Arrol House, Rockingham St., London SE1 6QL, England.

CAREER: Freelance journalist and researcher in Malawi, Papua New Guinea, and New Hebrides, 1977-79; housing adviser and campaigner for the rights of the homeless, 1979-82; freelance writer and political campaigner, 1982-83; freelance journalist and writer, 1983—. Labour candidate for Parliament, 1983; member of Campaign for Nuclear Disarmament, Labour Movement Campaign for Palestine, Labour Campaign for Lesbian and Gay Rights, and Socialist Environment and Resources Association, 1981-90; member of executive committee of Vietnam Moratorium Campaign, 1971; activist, London Gay Liberation Front, 1971-74; member of Malawi Support Committee, 1979-82; coordinator, UK AIDS Vigil Organization, 1987-89; cofounder, London ACT UP (AIDS Coalition To Unleash Power), 1989-90; cofounder and organizer, Outrage, 1990—.

WRITINGS:

The Battle for Bermondsey, Heretic (New York City), 1983.
Democratic Defence: A Non-Nuclear Alternative, GMP, 1985.
AIDS: A Guide to Survival, GMP, 1986, 3rd edition, 1990.
Out in Europe—A Guide to Lesbian and Gay Equality in 30 European Countries, Channel Four Television, 1990.
Europe in the Pink—Lesbian and Gay Equality in the New Europe, GMP, 1992.
Safer Sex—The Guide to Gay Sex Safely, Cassell (London), 1994.
We Don't Want to March Straight—Masculinity, Queers, and the Military, Cassell, 1995.

Contributor of articles and reviews to magazines and newspapers, including *Gay Times, The Guardian, The Independent, New Statesman and Society,* and *The Observer.* Contributor to books, including *Nuclear-Free Defence,* edited by Louis Mackay and David Fernbach, Heretic Books, 1983; *The Betrayal of Youth,* edited by Warren Middleton, CL Publications, 1986; *Into the Twenty-First Century—An Agenda for Political Realignment,* edited by Felix Dodds, Green Print, 1988; *Getting There—Steps to a Green Society,* edited by Derek Wall, Green Print, 1990; and *How Can You Write a Poem When You're Dying of AIDS?,* edited by John Harold, Cassell, 1993.

WORK IN PROGRESS: Fighting Back Against HIV—Self-Help for the Newly Diagnosed, for Cassell, 1996.

SIDELIGHTS: Peter Tatchell told *CA:* "Most of my writings, both fiction and nonfiction, blend a mixture of personal commitment, involvement, and experience with a broader and more general progressive political insight, message, and vision. For me, writing is an instrument for human understanding and liberation.

"*The Battle for Bermondsey* is a personal account of my campaign for election as a Labour member of Parliament in the southeast London constituency of Bermondsey in 1983. The subject of a violent hate campaign by the far Right and of vicious press smears which vilified me as an extremist, foreigner, draft-dodger, homosexual, traitor, and 'nigger-lover,' I told in *The Battle for Bermondsey* the inside story of the dirtiest election in Britain in this century.

"*Democratic Defence: A Non-Nuclear Alternative* proposes an alternative to nuclear weapons that is non-provocative, self-reliant, and democratic. This includes a switch to strictly self-defensive weapon systems; withdrawal from NATO and the remnants of Empire to a nonthreatening home-based defense posture; the reorientation of the armed forces around a Swedish-style guerrilla strategy and citizen's army; the incorporation of nonviolent civilian resistance as a component of defense policy; and a radical democratization of the armed forces.

"*AIDS: A Guide to Survival* brings a message of hope to the many people already exposed to the AIDS virus. No one need face this disease as a passive victim. By fighting back mentally and physically, people with the virus can reduce their chances of developing AIDS, and those who already have AIDS can increase their likelihood of survival. Drawing on studies of immune-deficient cancer patients, my book sets out a comprehensive practical program for strengthening the body's natural defenses by means of diet, exercise, sleep, and relaxation. It explains how to fight AIDS psychologically, using the techniques of meditation and mental imagery, and gives useful advice on how to sustain self-valuation and the will to live.

"*Out in Europe—A Guide to Lesbian and Gay Equality in 30 European Countries* documents what has been achieved, and what remains to be done, in securing the civil rights of lesbians and gay men in each of the countries of Europe, including the brave efforts of the movements for gay emancipation in the former Soviet block states. It cites the positive initiatives for homosexual equality from the European Parliament and the European Court of Human Rights, and summarizes the lobbying successes of the International Lesbian and Gay Association.

"*Europe in the Pink—Lesbian and Gay Equality in the New Europe* argues that with moves towards a more united Europe, the European Community (EC) is becoming an increasingly important forum for the advancement of lesbian and gay equality. As the EC acquires growing powers and introduces pan-European legislation binding in all the members states, the homosexual rights movement cannot afford to ignore European institutions. The book proposes ways the movement can use the European Parliament and Commission to overturn homophobic discrimination, urging a Europe-wide campaign for queer civil rights and setting out a radical European agenda for homosexual equality.

"*Safer Sex—The Guide to Gay Sex Safely* is a raunchy, sizzling guide to gay sexuality, relationships and HIV prevention. The most explicit gay sex book ever published, its no-holds-barred language and photographs give frank, in-your-face information about how to have exciting and satisfying sex, safely. Erotic, entertaining, educative and empowering, it looks at new ways of understanding and enjoying sex, presenting irreverent and provocative arguments in praise of sexual deviance and perversion. This book celebrates queer desire and encourages gay self-esteem. With practical hints on how to enliven sex and enhance relationships, it offers a sex-positive and homo-affirmative guide to all aspects of gay love and lust without risk.

"*We Don't Want to March Straight—Masculinity, Queers, and the Military* takes a dissenting view from the cosy gay consensus in favor of queers in the military. Why should we homosexuals enlist in the armed forces to help defend a society that treats us as second-class citizens? Since we know the pain of injustice, it doesn't make sense for gay people to collude with an oppressive institution like the armed forces, which symbolizes the worst aspects of straight male machismo: violence, domination, conformity and authoritarianism. Moreover, it cannot be right for us queers to demand freedom for ourselves, yet participate in a military system that has fre-

quently trampled on the freedom of others, as in Vietnam and Ireland. The campaign for lesbians and gays in the military is based on the mistaken premise that all the rights heteros have are desirable and that homos should have them too. I argue that it's important for lesbians and gay men to maintain a skeptical attitude towards heterosexual institutions. Our claim for equal rights should always be discerning. There are some aspects of straight culture, such as the armed forces, that are not worthy of queer emulation."

BIOGRAPHICAL/CRITICAL SOURCES:

PERIODICALS

London Review of Books, December 22, 1983.
New Statesman, November 4, 1983; April 19, 1985.
Sunday Times Magazine, April 23, 1995.
Times Literary Supplement, May 17, 1985.

*   *   *

**TAYLOR, Andrew (John Robert) 1951-
   (John Robert Taylor)**

PERSONAL: Born October 14, 1951, in Stevenage, England; son of Arthur John (a teacher and minister) and Hilda (a physiotherapist; maiden name, Haines) Taylor; married Caroline Silverwood (a librarian), September 8, 1979; children: Sarah Jessica, William John Alexander. *Education:* Emmanuel College, Cambridge, B.A. (with honors), 1973, M.A., 1976; University of London, M.A. (library and information studies), 1979. *Politics:* None.

ADDRESSES: Home and office—The Carriage House, 13 Lords Hill, Coleford, Gloucestershire GL16 8BG, England. *Agent*—Vivien Green, Richard Scott Simon Ltd., 43 Doughty St., London WC1N 2LF.

CAREER: Borough of Brent, London, England, librarian, 1976-78, 1979-81; freelance writer and subeditor for London area publishers, 1981—.

AWARDS, HONORS: John Creasey Memorial Award, Crime Writers Association, 1982, and Edgar nomination, Mystery Writers of America, both for *Caroline Minuscule;* Gold Dagger nomination, Crime Writers Association, 1985, for *Our Fathers' Lies.*

WRITINGS:

"DOUGAL" SERIES

Caroline Minuscule, Gollancz (London), 1982, Dodd (New York City), 1983.
Waiting for the End of the World, Dodd, 1984.
Our Fathers' Lies, Dodd, 1985.
An Old School Tie (Book-of-the-Month Club alternate selection), Dodd, 1986.
Freelance Death, Gollancz, 1987, Dodd, 1988.
Blood Relation, Gollancz, 1990, Doubleday (New York City), 1991.
The Sleeping Policeman, Gollancz, 1992.
Odd Man Out, Gollancz, 1993.

"THE BLAINES TRILOGY"

The Second Midnight, Dodd, 1987.
Blacklist, Collins (New York City), 1988.
Toyshop, Collins, 1990.

"LYDMOUTH" SERIES

An Air That Kills, Hodder and Stoughton (London), 1994, St. Martin's (New York City), 1995.
The Mortal Sickness, Hodder and Stoughton, 1995, St. Martin's, 1996.

CRIME NOVELS AND THRILLERS

(Under name John Robert Taylor) *Hairline Cracks* (young adult), Dutton/Lodestar (New York City), 1988.
(Under name John Robert Taylor) *The Private Nose* (juvenile), Walker, 1989, Candlewick, 1993.
Snapshot (young adult), Collins, 1989.
Double Exposure (young adult), Collins, 1990.
The Raven on the Water, HarperCollins, 1991.
Negative Image (young adult), HarperCollins, 1992.
The Barred Window, Sinclair Stevenson, 1993.
The Invader (young adult), HarperCollins, 1994.

WORK IN PROGRESS: "I am at present (January 1996) writing *The Four Last Things,* the first of a trilogy commissioned by HarperCollins; these will be psychological thrillers which look at the vulnerability of children and at some of the links between crime and religion. Next I plan to write *The Lover of the Grave,* the third volume of my Lydmouth series (Hodder and St. Martin's), which is set on the Anglo-Welsh borders in c. 1950. This series uses crime novels as medium for a portrait of a provincial society in the grip of the sea-change that followed World War II."

SIDELIGHTS: Andrew Taylor told *CA:* "The urge to write fiction is mysterious, but you ignore it at your peril. For most of my 20s I was one of those writers who managed to avoid actually writing anything. One lunchtime on a grey February in 1980, I realized that a lifetime of undemanding and unsatisfying jobs stretched before me: if I didn't start writing now, I never would. Then and there, I pushed aside the sandwich crumbs and scribbled the first few pages of what eventually became *Caroline Minuscule.* Long before I'd finished the first draft, I knew I was hooked. Before the book had been accepted by a publisher, I left my safe, sensible job and became precariously self-employed.

"I chose to write a crime novel because I knew and liked the genre. Although my work has broadened out—I have written adventure thrillers, psychological novels and espionage, as well as mysteries—crime remains a constant ingredient. Patricia Highsmith remarked in her *Plotting and Writing Suspense Fiction* that a wise author knows what makes his or her creative juices flow. For me, crime in fiction offers a way of revealing and examining both character and society: under stress we show ourselves as we really are. I am fascinated, too, by the long shadows cast by events in the past, and by the way in which family life acts on personality as an emotional hothouse, forcing strange growths.

"Since 1981 I have been fortunate enough to make my living as a writer. In that time I have written over twenty books, including some for children. I see myself primarily as a storyteller whose medium happens to be the written word. My novels sell in English and in translation. Writing fiction is hard work and still financially precarious; it's both a business and a vocation; and I would not happily do anything else.

"In writing fiction there are no rules, only precedents you may or may not follow. When I talk to writers' classes, I can give only one piece of advice with absolute confidence. And that is: write."

BIOGRAPHICAL/CRITICAL SOURCES:

PERIODICALS

New York Times Book Review, October 23, 1983; January 26, 1986.

Scorpion, November, 1994.
Times (London), August 5, 1982.
Times Literary Supplement, January 29, 1993.

*   *   *

TAYLOR, John Robert
   See TAYLOR, Andrew (John Robert)

*   *   *

TOMALIN, Claire   1933-

PERSONAL: Born June 20, 1933, in London, England; daughter of Emile (a scholar) and Muriel (a songwriter; maiden name, Herbert) Delavenay; married Nicholas Tomalin, September 17, 1955 (died October, 1973); married Michael Frayn, June 5, 1993; children: (first marriage) Josephine, Susanna, Emily, Thomas. *Education:* Newnham College, Cambridge, M.A., 1954. *Religion:* None.

ADDRESSES: Home—57 Gloucester Cres., London NW1 7EG, England. *Agent*—Deborah Rogers, 5-11 Mortimer St., London W.1, England. *Office*—57 Gloucester Cres., London NW1 7EG, England.

CAREER: Reader and editor for publishing firms in London, England, 1955-67; *Evening Standard,* London, staff member, 1967-68; *New Statesman,* London, assistant literary editor, 1968-74, literary editor, 1974-77; *Sunday Times,* London, reviewer, 1977-79, literary editor, 1979-86.

MEMBER: National Portrait Gallery (trustee), Royal Literature Fund (registrar), Royal Society of Literature (fellow; council member, 1994—).

AWARDS, HONORS: Whitbread Prize, 1974, for *The Life and Death of Mary Wollstonecraft;* NCR Book Award, Hawthornden Prize, and the James Tait Black Memorial Prize, all for *The Invisible Woman: The Story of Nelly Ternan and Charles Dickens.*

WRITINGS:

The Life and Death of Mary Wollstonecraft, Weidenfeld & Nicolson (London), 1974, Harcourt (New York City), 1975.

Shelley and His World, Thames & Hudson (London), 1979.
Katherine Mansfield: A Secret Life, Knopf (New York City), 1987.
The Invisible Woman: The Story of Nelly Ternan and Charles Dickens, Knopf, 1990.
The Winter Wife (play; produced in Sheffield at the Nuffield Theatre, 1991), Nick Hern Books (London), 1991.
Mrs. Jordan's Profession: The Story of a Great Actress and a Future King, Viking (New York City), 1994, published as *Mrs. Jordan's Profession: The Actress and the Prince,* Knopf, 1995.

Contributor to *Punch* and other English periodicals.

SIDELIGHTS: Claire Tomalin is best known for writing biographies of prominent literary women. Loraine Fletcher, writing in the *New Statesman and Nation,* comments that Tomalin's biographies often concern those who have been "obscured by prudent contemporaries or written out of the record by academics." Writing in the *Dictionary of Literary Biography,* James King explains that "central to [Tomalin's] books is a concern with how the experience of females is fundamentally different from that of men."

Tomalin began her career as a biographer in the early 1970s, when she was approached by publishers to do a full-length biography on Mary Wollstonecraft, after Tomalin published an essay on the 18th-century feminist in the *New Statesman.* Noted for her 1792 book *Vindication of the Rights of Women,* Wollstonecraft was a controversial feminist in her time, arguing that women should be afforded equal education and should be as self-supporting and independent as they wished. Her daughter, Mary Shelley, went on to write the classic novel *Frankenstein.* Ellen Moers in the *New York Review of Books* criticizes *The Life and Death of Mary Wollstonecraft* as a "slanted, carping, and unreliable" account of the feminist's life. But Arthur M. Wilson, writing in the *New York Times Book Review,* finds that although "not very fond of Mary, Claire Tomalin is tolerant and just. In her hands we are able . . . to know much more about Mary Wollstonecraft than any one person did in her lifetime and indeed more than she knew about herself."

In *Katherine Mansfield: A Secret Life,* Tomalin focuses on the secretive side of British short story writer Mansfield, "a theatrical and mercurial creature who was addicted to disguise and impersonation, mendacity and deception," as Pearl K. Bell notes in the *New York Times Book Review.* Tomalin begins her account of the author's short and stormy life with a description of "Mansfield's masks and performances, her lies, her sexual ambiguities, her 'dizzying' changes of face and heart," according to Hermione Lee in the London *Observer.* Lee finds that Tomalin's biography "departs from and surpasses its rivals" in its coverage of the friendship between Mansfield and D. H. Lawrence. "This is so powerful," Lee writes, "I almost wished it had been the book's only subject." Bell concludes that *Katherine Mansfield: A Secret Life* is a "vivid and crisply authoritative book," while John Gross in the *New York Times* believes that "perhaps Mrs. Tomalin's greatest achievement is that the parts cohere, that we are left with a portrait as consistent as Mansfield's own inconsistencies allow."

Tomalin explores the mystery of whether or not the actress Nelly Ternan was the mistress of British novelist Charles Dickens in *The Invisible Woman: The Story of Nelly Ternan and Charles Dickens.* Gathering material and proof for this story was difficult because Dickens took great pains to keep his public image untarnished. The children of both Ternan and Dickens destroyed all correspondence and any other evidence that might have been considered incriminating; Dickens himself burned all his personal letters and dairies.

Dickens met Ternan in 1857 when the author hired the 18-year-old for the stage production of *The Frozen Deep.* At that time, Dickens was 45 years old, married for 22 years and the father of ten children. In 1858, Dickens separated from his wife. At about the same time, Ternan gave up her stage career and began to live in luxury. Tomalin surmises that Ternan's sudden wealth came from Dickens. When Dickens died in 1879, his will left Ternan one thousand pounds. There is also speculation that Ternan bore a child by Dickens. Michiko Kakutani in the *New York Times* calls Tomalin "a careful and judicious writer, using her gifts of sympathy and insight to flesh out the bare bones of her detective work." "Tomalin, in her brilliant, compassionate and sometimes indignant biography, has brought off something very difficult," Penelope Fitzgerald writes in the London *Observer.* "She gives us, for the first time, Nelly Ternan's own point of view."

Dora Jordan, the eighteenth-century actress profiled in Tomalin's *Mrs. Jordan's Profession: The Story of a Great Actress and a Future King,* is considered one of the greatest theatrical comediennes of all time. She was also for some twenty years the lover of Prince William, the Duke of Clarence, later to become King William IV. Although she bore him children, the Prince left Jordan suddenly when court pressure to find a suitable woman to be his queen became unbearable. David Cannadine in the *London Review of Books* finds that Jordan was "a remarkable female personality . . . whose life was more dramatic than any of the parts she played . . . and which still possesses the power to captivate, to move, to shock and to anger." Writing in the *Spectator,* Helen Osborne calls *Mrs. Jordan's Profession* an "altogether enthralling biography" and "a wonderful book about a remarkable actress." Pat Rogers, writing in the *Times Literary Supplement,* notes that "it is hard to find a fault in [Tomalin's] performance. It is one her subject would have esteemed, for its technique, brio, and human warmth."

BIOGRAPHICAL/CRITICAL SOURCES:

BOOKS

Dictionary of Literary Biography, Volume 155: *Twentieth-Century British Literary Biographers,* Gale (Detroit), 1995.

PERIODICALS

London Review of Books, November 26, 1987, pp. 24-26; November 8, 1990, p. 18; October 20, 1994, p. 35.
New Statesman & Society, October 21, 1994, pp. 38-39.
New York Review of Books, February 19, 1976, p. 38.
New York Times, March 22, 1988; March 26, 1991.
New York Times Book Review, January 5, 1975, p. 5; May 15, 1988, pp. 15-18; April 21, 1991, p. 12; May 14, 1995, p. 9.
Observer (London), November 1, 1987, p. 27; October 28, 1990; October 16, 1994.
Spectator, October 29, 1994, pp. 31-32.
Times Literary Supplement, September 6, 1974, pp. 941-944; October 21, 1994, pp. 4-5.
Washington Post Book World, March 24, 1991; April 16, 1995.

*   *   *

TREAHEARNE, Elizabeth
See MAXWELL, Patricia

**UTTLEY, Alice Jane (Taylor)   1884-1976
(Alison Uttley)**

PERSONAL: Born December 17, 1884, in Cromford, Derbyshire, England; died May 7, 1976, in High Wycombe, England; daughter of Henry (a farmer) and Hannah (Dickens) Taylor; married James A. Uttley, August 10, 1911 (died, 1930); children: John. *Education:* Manchester University, B.Sc. (honours), 1906; Cambridge University, graduate study, 1907. *Politics:* Conservative. *Religion:* Church of England. *Avocational interests:* Music, gardening, birds, art (specifically seventeenth-century Dutch painting).

CAREER: Writer. Fulham Secondary School for Girls, London, science mistress, 1908-11.

AWARDS, HONORS: D.Litt., Manchester University, 1970.

WRITINGS:

CHILDREN'S FICTION; UNDER NAME ALISON UTTLEY

The Squirrel, the Hare and the Little Grey Rabbit, illustrated by Margaret Tempest, Heinemann, 1929, new edition illustrated by Jennie Corbett, 1968.

How Little Grey Rabbit Got Back Her Tail, illustrated by Tempest, Heinemann, 1930, new edition illustrated by Corbett, 1968.

The Great Adventure of Hare, illustrated by Tempest, Heinemann, 1931, new illustrated edition, 1968.

Moonshine and Magic, illustrated by Will Townsend, Faber, 1932.

The Story of Fuzzypeg the Hedgehog, illustrated by Tempest, Heinemann, 1932.

Squirrel Goes Skating, illustrated by Tempest, Collins, 1934.

Wise Owl's Story, illustrated by Tempest, Collins, 1935.

The Adventures of Peter and Judy in Bunnyland, illustrated by L. Young, Collins, 1935.

Candlelight Tales, illustrated by Elinor Bellingham-Smith, Faber, 1936.

Little Grey Rabbit's Party, illustrated by Tempest, Collins, 1936, abridged edition, 1978.

The Adventures of No Ordinary Rabbit, illustrated by Alec Buckels, Faber, 1937.

The Knot Squirrel Tied, illustrated by Tempest, Collins, 1937.

Fuzzypeg Goes to School, illustrated by Tempest, Collins, 1938.

Mustard, Pepper and Salt, illustrated by Gwen Raverat, Faber, 1938.

A Traveller in Time, Faber, 1939, Putnam, 1940, new edition illustrated by Phyllis Bray, Viking, 1964, new edition illustrated by Faith Jaques, Puffin, 1977.

Tales of the Four Pigs and Brock the Badger, illustrated by Buckels, Faber, 1939.

Little Grey Rabbit's Christmas, illustrated by Tempest, Collins, 1939, abridged edition, 1978.

Moldy Warp, The Mole, illustrated by Tempest, Collins, 1940.

The Adventures of Sam Pig, illustrated by Francis Gower, Faber, 1940.

Six Tales of the Four Pigs, illustrated by Buckels, Faber, 1941.

Sam Pig Goes to Market, illustrated by A. E. Kennedy, Faber, 1941.

Ten Tales of Tim Rabbit, illustrated by Buckels and Gower, Faber, 1941.

Six Tales of Brock the Badger, illustrated by Buckels and Gower, Faber, 1941.

Six Tales of Sam Pig, illustrated by Buckels and Gower, Faber, 1941.

Nine Starlight Tales, illustrated by Irene Hawkins, Faber, 1942.

Little Grey Rabbit's Washing-Day, illustrated by Tempest, Collins, 1942, abridged edition, 1980.

Sam Pig and Sally, illustrated by Kennedy, Faber, 1942.

Hare Joins the Home Guard, illustrated by Tempest, Collins, 1942.

Water-Rat's Picnic, illustrated by Tempest, Collins, 1943, abridged edition, 1980.

Cuckoo Cherry-Tree, illustrated by Hawkins, Faber, 1943.

Sam Pig at the Circus, illustrated by Kennedy, Faber, 1943.

The Spice Woman's Basket and Other Tales, illustrated by Hawkins, Faber, 1944.

Little Grey Rabbit's Birthday, illustrated by Tempest, Collins, 1944, abridged edition, 1978.

Mrs. Nimble and Mr. Bumble, illustrated by Horace Knowles, James, 1944.

The Weather Cock and Other Stories, illustrated by Nancy Innes, Faber, 1945.

The Speckledy Hen, illustrated by Tempest, Faber, 1945.

Some Moonshine Tales, illustrated by Sarah Nechamkin, Faber, 1945.

The Adventures of Tim Rabbit, illustrated by Kennedy, Faber, 1945.

Little Grey Rabbit and the Weasels, illustrated by Tempest, Collins, 1947.

Grey Rabbit and the Wandering Hedgehog, illustrated by Tempest, Collins, 1948, abridged edition, 1978.

Sam Pig in Trouble, illustrated by Kennedy, Faber, 1948.

John Barleycorn: Twelve Tales of Fairy and Magic, illustrated by Philip Hepworth, Faber, 1948.

Macduff, illustrated by Kennedy, Faber, 1950.

Little Grey Rabbit Makes Lace, illustrated by Tempest, Collins, 1950.

The Cobbler's Shop and Other Tales, illustrated by Hawkins, Faber, 1950.

Yours Ever, Sam Pig, illustrated by Kennedy, Faber, 1951.

Hare and the Easter Eggs, illustrated by Tempest, Collins, 1952.

Little Red Fox and the Wicked Uncle, illustrated by Katherine Wigglesworth, Heinemann, 1954, Bobbs-Merrill, 1962.

Little Grey Rabbit Goes to the Sea, illustrated by Tempest, Collins, 1954.

Sam Pig and the Singing Gate, illustrated by Kennedy, Faber, 1955.

Hare and Guy Fawkes, illustrated by Tempest, Collins, 1956.

Little Red Fox and Cinderella, illustrated by Wigglesworth, Heinemann, 1956.

Magic in My Pocket: A Selection of Tales, illustrated by Judith Brook, Penguin, 1957.

Little Red Fox and the Magic Moon, illustrated by Wigglesworth, Heinemann, 1958.

Little Grey Rabbit's Paint-Box, illustrated by Tempest, Collins, 1958.

Snug and Serena Count Twelve, illustrated by Wigglesworth, Heinemann, 1959, Bobbs-Merrill, 1962.

Tim Rabbit and Company, illustrated by Kennedy, Faber, 1959.

Grey Rabbit Finds a Shoe, illustrated by Tempest, Collins, 1960.

John at the Old Farm, illustrated by Jennifer Miles, Heinemann, 1960.

Sam Pig Goes to the Seaside: Sixteen Stories, illustrated by Kennedy, Faber, 1960.

Grey Rabbit and the Circus, illustrated by Tempest, Collins, 1961.

Snug and Serena Go to Town, illustrated by Wigglesworth, Heinemann, 1961, Bobbs-Merrill, 1963.

The Little Knife Who Did All the Work: Twelve Tales of Magic, illustrated by Pauline Baynes, Faber, 1962.

Little Red Fox and the Unicorn, illustrated by Wigglesworth, Heinemann, 1962.

Grey Rabbit's May Day, illustrated by Tempest, Collins, 1963.

Tim Rabbit's Dozen, illustrated by Shirley Hughes, Faber, 1964.

Hare Goes Shopping, illustrated by Tempest, Collins, 1965.

The Sam Pig Storybook, illustrated by Cecil Leslie, Faber, 1965.

The Mouse, the Rabbit and the Little White Hen, illustrated by Corbett, Heinemann, 1966.

Enchantment, illustrated by Corbett, Heinemann, 1966.

Little Grey Rabbit's Pancake Day, illustrated by Tempest, Collins, 1967.

Little Red Fox, illustrated by Wigglesworth, Penguin, 1967.

The Little Red Fox and the Big Big Tree, illustrated by Corbett, Heinemann, 1968.

Little Grey Rabbit's Valentine, illustrated by Tempest, Collins, 1969.

Lavender Shoes: Eight Tales of Enchantment, illustrated by Janina Ede, Faber, 1970.

Little Grey Rabbit Goes to the North Pole, illustrated by Wigglesworth, Collins, 1970.

The Sam Pig Storybook, illustrated by Leslie, Faber, 1971.

The Brown Mouse Book: Magical Tales of Two Little Mice, illustrated by Wigglesworth, Heinemann, 1971.

Fuzzypeg's Brother, illustrated by Wigglesworth, Heinemann, 1971.

Little Grey Rabbit's Spring Cleaning Party, illustrated by Wigglesworth, Collins, 1972.

The Little Red Fox Book, illustrated by Wigglesworth, Heinemann, 1972.

Little Grey Rabbit and the Snow-Baby, illustrated by Wigglesworth, Collins, 1973.

Fairy Tales, edited by Kathleen Lines, illustrated by Ann Strugnell, Faber, 1975.

Hare and the Rainbow, illustrated by Wigglesworth, Collins, 1975.

More Little Red Fox Stories, illustrated by Wigglesworth, Penguin, 1975.

Stories for Christmas, edited by Lines, illustrated by Gavin Rowe, Faber, 1977.

Little Grey Rabbit's Storybook, illustrated by Tempest, Collins, 1977.

From Spring to Spring: Stories of the Four Seasons, edited by Lines, illustrated by Hughes, Faber, 1978.

Tales of Little Grey Rabbit, illustrated by Jaques, Heinemann, 1980.

Little Grey Rabbit's Second Storybook, illustrated by Tempest, Collins, 1981.

Foxglove Tales, edited by Lucy Meredith, illustrated by Shirley Felts, Faber, 1984.

"LITTLE BROWN MOUSE" BOOKS; UNDER NAME ALISON UTTLEY; ILLUSTRATED BY KATHERINE WIGGLES-WORTH

Snug and Serena Pick Cowslips, Heinemann, 1950.
Snug and Serena Meet a Queen, Heinemann, 1950.
Going to the Fair, Heinemann, 1951.
Toad's Castle, Heinemann, 1951.
Mrs. Mouse Spring-Cleans, Heinemann, 1952.
Christmas at the Rose and Crown, Heinemann, 1952.
The Gypsy Hedgehogs, Heinemann, 1953.
Snug and the Chimney-Sweeper, Heinemann, 1953.
The Flower Show, Heinemann, 1955.
The Mouse Telegrams, Heinemann, 1955.
Mr. Stoat Walks In, Heinemann, 1957.
Snug and the Silver Spoon, Heinemann, 1957.

CHILDREN'S PLAYS; UNDER NAME ALISON UTTLEY

Little Grey Rabbit to the Rescue, illustrated by Tempest, Collins, 1946.
The Washerwoman's Child: A Play on the Life and Stories of Hans Christian Andersen, illustrated by Hawkins, Faber, 1946.
Three Little Grey Rabbit Plays (includes *Grey Rabbit's Hospital, The Robber,* and *A Christmas Story*), Heinemann, 1961.

NOVELS; UNDER NAME ALISON UTTLEY

High Meadows, Faber, 1938, new edition, 1966.
When All Is Done, Faber, 1945.

NONFICTION; UNDER NAME ALISON UTTLEY; ILLUSTRATED BY C. F. TUNNICLIFFE

The Country Child, Macmillan, 1931, new edition, Faber, 1945.
Ambush of Young Days (autobiographical reminiscences), Faber, 1937, new edition, 1952.
Country Hoard, Faber, 1943.
Carts and Candlesticks, Faber, 1948.
Plowmen's Clocks, Faber, 1952.
Here's a New Day, Faber, 1956.
A Year in the Country, Faber, 1957.
The Swans Fly Over, Faber, 1959.
Something for Nothing, Faber, 1960.
Wild Honey, Faber, 1962.
Cuckoo in June, Faber, 1964.
A Peck of Gold, Faber, 1966.
The Button Box and Other Essays, Faber, 1968.

Secret Places and Other Essays, Faber, 1972.
Country World: Memories of Childhood, edited by Lucy Meredith, Faber, 1984.
Our Village: Alison Uttley's Cromford, edited by Jacqueline Mitchell, Scarthin, 1984.

OTHER; UNDER NAME ALISON UTTLEY

The Farm on the Hill, Faber, 1941, new edition, 1949.
Ten Candlelight Tales, Faber, 1942.
Country Things, Faber, 1946.
(Editor) *In Praise of Country Life* (anthology), Muller, 1949.
Buckinghamshire, Faber, 1950.
The Stuff of Dreams, Faber, 1953.
Recipes from an Old Farmhouse, illustrated by Baynes, Faber, 1966, Merrimack Book Service, 1973.
A Ten O'Clock Scholar and Other Essays, Faber, 1970.

Uttley's manuscript collection is housed in the Kerlan Collection, University of Minnesota, Minneapolis.

SIDELIGHTS: The English countryside of Alice Jane Uttley's childhood forms the basis for most of her gentle, sensitive, and tradition-filled children's stories. The majority of these stories are filled with various animal characters who possess very distinct personalities. Among her most famous characters is Little Grey Rabbit, whose calm and giving nature keeps peace in her country neighborhood that includes several other animal residents, as well as in her own cottage, which she shares with Hare and Squirrel. "There is a lot of Uttley herself in the character of Grey Rabbit: the resourceful country-woman, the lover of traditional customs and festivals, the sensitive observer who enjoyed all the signs and sounds and smells of the countryside," as Peter du Sautoy related in *Twentieth-Century Children's Writers.*

Uttley was born and raised in the countryside of Derbyshire, England, where she lived on a farm that offered continuous views of hills and valleys. "My family had lived there for over 200 years," she once stated, "but the house itself had been rebuilt on the old foundations of rock only a hundred years before, when the family lived for some months in a barn during the work. I was devoted to my home, and most of my books have taken this house for the scene of the action."

This countryside was Uttley's playground as a child, and she spent much of her time exploring the woods, the meadows, and the many animals who inhabited these areas. "I made up stories ever since I can remember," she once recalled, "but I did not write any down, for I never thought of such a thing. I could always tell stories, so why write them?" It was not until Uttley was married, in fact, and her son John started going away to school that the author put her first story on paper. This story, *The Squirrel, the Hare and the Little Grey Rabbit,* was quickly picked up by a publisher, presenting Uttley's most famous characters to children for the first time.

These characters and their many adventures can be found in such books as *Little Grey Rabbit's Party, Squirrel Goes Skating, Little Grey Rabbit and the Weasels, Hare Goes Shopping,* and several others. In all, though, the characters stay true to their natures. Little Grey Rabbit is like a mother to all the other animals, always there in times of need, ready to offer a word of advice or comfort. Hare is much more mischievous and is often at the center of all the action and excitement in the woods. Squirrel, on the other hand, is too caught up in her appearance and fine tail to cause much of a commotion. And although Wise Owl often eats everything in sight, he too can be called on to help out when danger befalls his friends. "The lives of the little animals run in secret parallel with human existence for the most part," Margery Fisher explained in *Growing Point,* "with their own version of the [human] scenes they watch from far off."

"Alison Uttley's characters are robust," maintained *Times Literary Supplement* reviewer William Feaver. "She knew her species. Grey Rabbit is more complex than she at first appears, not a stuffed bunny but Teacher, Mother and Big Sister rolled into one; a great comforter. Living together in their dell, Hare, Squirrel and Little Grey Rabbit are an endearing menage a trois." Since their first publication, many of the individual stories featuring Uttley's animal characters have been combined into classic collections. Writing of the collection *Tales of Little Grey Rabbit,* Mary Cadogan pointed out in *Books and Bookmen* that although the books first appeared nearly fifty years ago, "they have since become nursery classics. . . . The tales will delight child readers, and possibly become a collector's item for many adults." As Fisher likewise noted, "as each generation of children is introduced to the stories, their historical basis gains more resonance." Marcus Crouch concluded in *Junior Bookshelf,* the newly

collected stories of *Tales of Little Grey Rabbit* demonstrate "how masterly they are in technique, exquisite in their language and scrupulous in the consistency of their characterisation."

The countryside that forms the basis for Uttley's casts of animals is also the foundation on which the author built her other fairy tales and stories, many of which were collected in *Fairy Tales, From Spring to Spring: Stories of the Four Seasons,* and *Stories for Christmas.* The selections found in *Fairy Tales* portray the magic and wonder that can be found in the country and in the lives of village people. In *From Spring to Spring* the cycle of one year is spanned, focusing on both animal and magical tales that take place in every season. Mary F. Birkett wrote in *School Library Journal* that in this collection contains "a sweet fairy-tale quality," adding that Uttley's "descriptions reveal a singular understanding and love of nature." And the collection *Stories for Christmas,* which focuses on English traditions and other holiday customs, "rings with an old-fashioned charm of Christmases past," asserted *Booklist* contributor Barbara Elleman, which is filled with "nostalgia and magic."

During the course of her career, Uttley stayed true to what she saw as the basis for children's books. "A story for children, however fanciful, should have truth in the background," she once explained. "There should be a solid foundation for the thistledown tale. This weaving of truth and countrylore into a tale is fascinating to the writer, and I bring natural effects into the wildly imaginative situations. Flowers that Grey Rabbit or Sam Pig gather are the flowers which would be in bloom at that season. They pick herbs, tansy, eyebright, houseleek, and the uses to which they put them are the uses of countrymen for hundreds of years. I want them to be remembered. . . . In each story I hide something, a legend, a proverb, scraps of wisdom which I heard when I was a child."

Writing of this same blending of fact and fantasy, du Sautoy asserted: "It is characteristic of Uttley that magic and fantasy play a part in all her writing. This element was a fundamental part of her mind and her imagination." Du Sautoy went on to add that "Uttley herself is quoted as saying: 'So each and every tale holds everyday magic, and each is connected with awareness of everyday life, where reality is made visible, and one sees what goes on with new eyes.' Here is the essence of much of Uttley's writing for children."

BIOGRAPHICAL/CRITICAL SOURCES:

BOOKS

du Sautoy, Peter, "Alison Uttley," *Twentieth-Century Children's Writers,* 4th edition, St. James Press (Detroit), 1995, pp. 977-80.

Judd, Denis, *The Country Child: A Biography of Alison Uttley,* Joseph, 1986.

Saintsbury, Elizabeth, *The World of Alison Uttley,* Baker, 1980.

PERIODICALS

Booklist, February 15, 1965, p. 581; November 15, 1977, p. 558.

Books and Bookmen, June, 1980, pp. 45-46.

Bulletin of the Center for Children's Books, January, 1971, p. 82; February, 1978, p. 103; January, 1979, p. 91.

Growing Point, January, 1976, p. 2807; May, 1982, pp. 3897-98.

Junior Bookshelf, February, 1978, pp. 51-52; August, 1978, p. 196; October, 1980, pp. 242-43; October, 1981, p. 203.

School Library Journal, September, 1981, p. 116; October, 1981, p. 154.

Times Literary Supplement, August 14, 1970, p. 909; October 22, 1971, p. 3618; April 2, 1976, p. 396; March 26, 1982, p. 346.*

* * *

UTTLEY, Alison
   See UTTLEY, Alice Jane (Taylor)

V

van KAAM, Adrian (L.) 1920-

PERSONAL: Born April 19, 1920, in The Hague, Netherlands; son of Charles L. van Kaam. *Education:* Spiritan Seminary, Gemert, Netherlands, B.A., 1939; Hoogveld Institute, Nijmegen, Netherlands and Dutch Study Center, Gulemborg, M.O., 1954; Western Reserve University (now Case Western Reserve University), Cleveland, OH, Ph.D., 1958.

ADDRESSES: Office—Institute of Formative Spirituality, Duquesne University, Pittsburgh, PA 15282.

CAREER: Roman Catholic priest, member of Congregation of the Spiritans. Psychological consultant to life schools for young adults in Netherlands, 1949-52; counselor in psychological observation center for juvenile delinquents, Veenendaal, Netherlands, 1952-54; Duquesne University, Pittsburgh, PA, instructor, 1957, assistant professor, 1959-60, associate professor, 1961-65, professor of psychology, 1965—, founder and director of Institute of Man (now Institute of Formative Spirituality), 1963-80, director emeritus and professor of foundational formation, 1980—. Visiting professor, University of Heidelberg, summer, 1966, and Brandeis University, Waltham, MA, 1958-59. Lecturer at Universities of Heidelberg and Oslo, 1963; lecturer throughout United States with Institute of Man workshop, and on radio and television. *Military service:* Honorary chaplain, U.S. Navy, 1987—; Developed training course for U.S. Navy chaplains, 1987—.

MEMBER: American Psychological Association, Epiphany Association (founding member, 1979, corporation board, board of directors), St. John's Seminary (board of directors), St. Paul's Seminary (board of directors).

AWARDS, HONORS: President's Award for excellence in scholarship, Duquesne University, 1978; William C. Bier Award, American Psychological Association, 1982; Dallas University established a yearly Adrian van Kaam Honor Award for outstanding psychology student in 1993; Honorary Doctor of Christian Letters, Franciscan University, Steubenville, OH, 1994.

WRITINGS:

A Light to the Gentiles (translation of *De Jood Van Saverne,* a biography of Frances Libermann), Duquesne University Press (Pittsburgh, PA), 1959, revised edition, Bruce Publishing (Milwaukee, WI), and Dimension Books (Denville, NJ), 1962.
The Third Force in European Psychology, Psychosynthesis Research Foundation (Greenville, DE), 1960.
The Vocational Director and Counseling, St. Paul Publications (Derby, NY), 1962.
Religion and Personality, Prentice-Hall (Englewood Cliffs, NJ), 1964.
Personality Fulfillment in the Spiritual Life, Dimension Books, 1966.
Existential Foundations of Psychology, Duquesne University Press, 1966.
The Art of Existential Counseling, Dimension Books, 1966.
Personality Fulfillment in Religious Life, Volume 1: *Religious Life in a Time of Transition,* Dimension Books, 1967.

(With Kathleen Healy) *The Demon and the Dove,* Duquesne University Press, 1967.

The Vowed Life, Dimension Books, 1968.

(With Bert van Crooenburg and Susan Annette Muto) *The Emergent Self,* four volumes, Dimension Books, 1968.

(With van Crooenburg and Muto) *The Participant Self,* two volumes, Dimension Books, 1969.

On Being Involved, Dimension Books, 1970.

On Being Yourself, Dimension Books, 1972.

Envy and Originality, Doubleday, 1972.

Spirituality and the Gentle Life, Dimension Books, 1974.

In Search of Spiritual Identity, Dimension Books, 1975.

The Dynamics of Spiritual Self Direction, Dimension Books, 1976.

The Woman at the Well, Dimension Books, 1976.

(Coauthor) *Tell Me Who I Am,* Dimension Books, 1977.

Looking for Jesus, Dimension Books, 1978.

Living Creatively, Dimension Books, 1978.

(With Muto) *Am I Living a Spiritual Life?,* Dimension Books, 1978.

The Transcendent Self: Formative Spirituality of the Middle, Early, and Late Years of Life, Dimension Books, 1979.

(Coauthor) *Practicing the Prayer of Presence,* Dimension Books, 1980.

The Mystery of Transforming Love, Dimension Books, 1982.

(Coeditor) *Creative Formation of Life and World,* University Press of America (Washington, DC), 1982.

Foundations for Personality Study: An Adrian van Kaam Reader, Dimension Books, 1983.

The Science of Formative Spirituality, Crossroad/Continuum (New York City), Volume 1: *Fundamental Formation,* 1983, Volume 2: *Human Formation,* 1985, Volume 3: *Formation of the Human Heart,* 1986, Volume 4: *Scientific Formation,* 1987, Volume 5: *Traditional Formation,* 1992, Volume 6: *Transcendent Formation,* 1995, Volume 7: *Transcendent Therapy,* 1995.

Roots of Christian Joy, Dimension Books, 1985.

(Coauthor) *Songs for Every Season,* St. Bede's Publications (Petersham, MA), 1989.

(Coauthor) *Commitment: Key to Christian Maturity,* Paulist Press, 1989.

Music of Eternity, Ave Maria Press (Notre Dame, IN), 1990.

Commitment: Key to Christian Maturity, A Workbook and Guide, Paulist Press, 1991.

(Coauthor) *Formation Guide for Becoming Spiritually Mature,* Epiphany Books (Pittsburgh, PA), 1991.

(Coauthor) *Aging Gracefully,* St. Paul Books & Media (Boston), 1992.

(Coauthor) *The Power of Appreciation: A New Approach to Personal and Relational Healing,* Crossroad/Continuum, 1993.

(Coauthor) *Stress and the Search for Happiness: A New Challenge for Christian Spirituality,* Resurrection Press (Williston Park, NY), 1993.

(Coauthor) *Harnessing Stress: A Spiritual Quest,* Resurrection Press, 1993.

(Coauthor) *Healthy and Holy Under Stress: A Royal Road to Wise Living,* Resurrection Press, 1993.

(Coauthor) *Practicing the Prayer of Presence,* Resurrection Press, 1993.

(Coauthor) *Divine Guidance: Seeking to Find and Follow the Will of God,* Servant Publications (Ann Arbor, MI), 1994.

Author of audio and video cassettes on Christian spirituality. Contributor to books on religion and psychology, including *The Christian Intellectual,* edited by Samuel Hazo, Duquesne University Press, 1963; *Explorations in Human Potentialities,* edited by Herbert C. Otto, C. C Thomas, 1966; and *Handbook of Innovative Psychotherapies,* edited by Raymond J. Corsini, Wiley, 1981. Also contributor to *Jahrbuch fuer Psychologie und Medizinische Anthropologie,* 1966; *Wiley Encyclopedia of Psychology,* 1984; *Dictionary of Pastoral Care and Counseling,* 1986; *New Catholic Encyclopedia;* and *International Encyclopedia of Psychiatry, Psychoanalysis, and Psychology.* Contributor of more than thirty articles to scientific periodicals in the Netherlands, 1952-54; also contributor to *Journal of Individual Psychology, American Journal of Nursing, Review of Existential Psychology and Psychiatry, Current Psychiatric Therapies,* and *Journal of Humanistic Psychology.* Consulting editor, *Journal of Individual Psychology,* 1958—, and *Journal of Humanistic Psychology,* 1963—; editor of *Studies in Formative Spirituality* (formerly *Humanitas*) and of *Envoy* (publications of the Institute of Formative Spirituality), 1965—; former editor of *Review of Existential Psychology and Psychiatry.*

*   *   *

Van LEEUWEN, Jean   1937-

PERSONAL: Surname is pronounced "Van *Loo-*en"; born December 26, 1937, in Glen Ridge, NJ; daughter of Cornelius (a member of the clergy) and Dorothy (Charlton) Van Leeuwen; married Bruce David Gavril (a digital computer systems designer), July 7, 1968; children: David Andrew, Elizabeth Eva. *Education:* Syracuse University, B.A., 1959. *Avocational interests:* Reading, gardening, music, antiques.

ADDRESSES: Home—7 Colony Row, Chappaqua, NY 10514.

CAREER: Writer. Began career working for *TV Guide;* Random House, Inc., New York City, 1963-68, began as assistant editor, became associate editor of juvenile books; Viking Press, Inc., New York City, associate editor of juvenile books, 1968-70; Dial Press, New York City, senior editor of juvenile books, 1971-73.

AWARDS, HONORS: William Allen White Award, 1978, and South Carolina Children's Book Award, 1978-79, both for *The Great Christmas Kidnapping Caper; Seems like This Road Goes on Forever* was named one of the best books of 1979 by the American Library Association (ALA), Young Adult Services Division; Massachusetts Honor Book Award, 1981, for *The Great Cheese Conspiracy; More Tales of Oliver Pig, Amanda Pig and Her Big Brother Oliver,* and *Tales of Amanda Pig* have all received ALA Notable Book citations.

WRITINGS:

FOR CHILDREN

(Editor) *A Time of Growing,* Random House (New York City), 1967.
Timothy's Flower, illustrated by Moneta Barnett, Random House, 1967.
One Day in Summer, illustrated by Richard Fish, Random House, 1969.
The Great Cheese Conspiracy, Random House, 1969.
(Adaptor) Hans Christian Andersen, *The Emperor's New Clothes,* illustrated by Jack Delano and Irene Delano, Random House, 1971.
I Was a Ninety-Eight Pound Duckling, Dial (New York City), 1972, reprinted, Bantam (New York City), 1987.
Too Hot for Ice Cream, illustrated by Martha Alexander, Dial, 1974.
The Great Christmas Kidnapping Caper, illustrated by Steven Kellog, Dial, 1975.
Seems like This Road Goes on Forever (young adult novel), Dial, 1979.

Tales of Oliver Pig, illustrated by Arnold Lobel, Dial, 1979.
More Tales of Oliver Pig, illustrated by Lobel, Dial, 1981.
The Great Rescue Operation, illustrated by Margot Apple, Dial, 1982.
Amanda Pig and Her Big Brother Oliver, illustrated by Ann Schweninger, Dial, 1982.
Benjy and the Power of Zingies, illustrated by Apple, Dial, 1982.
Tales of Amanda Pig, illustrated by Schweninger, Dial, 1983.
Benjy in Business, illustrated by Apple, Dial, 1983.
More Tales of Amanda Pig, illustrated by Schweninger, Dial, 1985.
Benjy the Football Hero, illustrated by Gail Owens, Dial, 1985.
Oliver, Amanda, and Grandmother Pig, illustrated by Schweninger, Dial, 1987.
Oliver and Amanda's Christmas, illustrated by Schweninger, Dial, 1989.
Dear Mom: You're Ruining My Life (young adult novel), Dial, 1989.
Oliver Pig at School, illustrated by Schweninger, Dial, 1990.
Amanda Pig on Her Own, illustrated by Schweninger, Dial, 1991.
Going West, illustrated by Thomas B. Allen, Dial, 1991.
The Great Summer Camp Catastrophe, illustrated by Diane de Groat, Dial, 1992.
Oliver and Amanda's Halloween, illustrated by Schweninger, Dial, 1992.
Emma Bean, Juan Wijngaard, Dial, 1993.
Two Girls in Sister Dresses, illustrated by Linda Benson, Dial, 1994.
Bound for Oregon, Dial, 1994.
Oliver and Amanda and the Big Snow, illustrated by Schweninger, Dial, 1995.
Across the Wide Dark Sea, illustrated by Allen, Dial, 1995.
Blue Sky, Butterfly, Dial, 1996.

SIDELIGHTS: About Jean Van Leeuwen's "Easy-to-Read" series involving sister and brother Amanda and Oliver Pig, *New York Times Book Review* contributor Mary Gordon writes: "One of the great values of these books is their ability to dramatize the ridiculous and trivial and sickeningly frequent fights that siblings endure every day of their lives, and yet suggest the siblings essential fondness for one another, their dependency, their mutual good will." The critic concludes by remarking that "at their best, and there are no real failures, the Oliver and Amanda stories can provide the early reader . . . with pleasant, solid, buoying experiences of the commodity all too rare in real life: the happy family."

Reviewers have consistently praised the warm yet realistic celebrations of family life in Van Leeuwen's books, emphasizing her gentle humor and insightful portrayal of common childhood experiences. In a review of *Oliver, Amanda, and Grandmother Pig,* a *Horn Book* writer states: "With perceptiveness and gentle humor Jean Van Leeuwen shapes even the most mundane subjects into pleasing, warm tales."

Van Leeuwen once told *CA:* "I write because of a need to capture time and force it to stand still, to record that cozy moment of a mother and child baking cookies so it won't vanish for me. I write to rework childhood experiences and try to find the meaning in them that once escaped me. And perhaps most of all, I write in the hope of touching the life of another person."

BIOGRAPHICAL/CRITICAL SOURCES:

BOOKS

Something about the Author Autobiography Series, Volume 8, Gale (Detroit), 1989, pp. 317-30.

PERIODICALS

Bulletin for the Center for Children's Books, November, 1975; July-August, 1982; March, 1983; October, 1989, p. 47; March, 1991, pp. 180-81.
Horn Book, April, 1983, pp. 168-69; March-April, 1986, pp. 199-200; September, 1987, pp. 606-7; September-October, 1990, p. 599.
New York Times Book Review, November 5, 1967; November 11, 1979; April 25, 1982; November 10, 1985; January 19, 1986; January 10, 1988.
School Library Journal, August, 1982, p. 123; December, 1982, p. 75; December, 1983, p. 70; May, 1985, p. 111; December, 1985, p. 110; April, 1992, p. 126.

*   *   *

VIERTEL, Peter   1920-

PERSONAL: Born November 16, 1920, in Dresden, Germany; naturalized U.S. citizen; son of Berthold (a poet, novelist and director) and Salka (a screenwriter; maiden name Steuerman) Viertel; married Deborah Kerr (an actress), July, 1960; children: Christine. *Education:* Attended Dartmouth College and University of California, Los Angeles. *Politics:* Democrat.

ADDRESSES: Home—Wyhergut, Klosters, Switzerland 7250. *Agent*—I. P. Lazar, 211 South Beverly Dr., Beverly Hills, CA 90212.

CAREER: Freelance writer. *Military service:* U.S. Marine Corps, 1942-45; served in Pacific and European theaters; received Bronze Star and three battle stars.

MEMBER: Authors League, Screen Writers Guild.

AWARDS, HONORS: Christopher Award for screenplay, *The Old Man and the Sea.*

WRITINGS:

NOVELS

The Canyon, Harcourt (New York City), 1940.
Line of Departure, Harcourt, 1947.
White Hunter, Black Heart (see also below), Doubleday (New York City), 1953.
Love Lies Bleeding, Doubleday, 1964.
Bicycle on the Beach, Delacorte (New York City), 1971.
American Skin, Houghton (Boston, MA), 1984.
Loser Deals, Donald Fine (New York City), 1995.

OTHER

(With James Bridges and Burt Kennedy) *White Hunter, Black Heart* (screenplay based on novel of same title), Warner Bros., 1990.
Dangerous Friends: At Large with Hemingway and Huston in the Fifties (memoir), Doubleday/Talese (New York City), 1992, published in England as *Dangerous Friends: Hemingway, Huston and Others,* Viking (London), 1992.

Also author, with Irwin Shaw, of play, *The Survivors,* 1948. Writer of screenplays, including *Decision Before Dawn.* Adaptor for the screen of *The Old Man and the Sea* and *The Sun Also Rises,* based on the novels by Ernest Hemingway, and, with John Huston, of *The African Queen,* based on the novel by C. S. Forester.

SIDELIGHTS: German-born Peter Viertel is an acclaimed novelist, screenwriter and memoirist. Viertel's work is often compared to the work of his childhood hero, Ernest Hemingway, whom he met and befriended in the late 1940s. Viertel adapted two Hemingway novels for the screen as well as co-adapting *The African Queen,* based on the novel by C. S. Forester. Working on *The African Queen* with director John Huston became the focus of Viertel's *White Hunter, Black Heart,* and Huston and Hemingway both are a large part of Viertel's *Dangerous Friends: At Large with Hemingway and Huston in the Fifties.*

Viertel's 1964 novel, *Love Lies Bleeding,* is the story of the rise and fall of Spanish toreador Juan Ramon Vasquez. As *America* reviewer Richard C. Crowley notes, pushed on by the crowd's "lust for blood, and his own arrogance," Vasquez "grows increasingly weary, disdainful of the crowd's fickleness and afraid of physical disaster." Crowley compares *Love Lies Bleeding* to Ernest Hemingway's *Death in the Afternoon* and though he finds Viertel a "fine writer, but not a master," he admires Viertel's capturing of the "spirit of a filled Sunday arena in Spain right down to the last ole." *Saturday Review's* Maia W. Rodman finds Viertel's narrator Richard Belden "a bore," and sees an excess of detail making for an "extremely sluggish start." Rodman, like Crowley, admires the fiction once it "enters the ring," where Viertel "becomes as good a writer as Ramon is a bullfighter."

Caroline Seebohm in the *New York Times Book Review* sees Viertel's *American Skin* as "one of those wonderful old-fashioned novels in which men are men and women are girls and everyone knows a cute Spanish saying to indicate depth of character." *American Skin* is the story of David Brandt, an American in the Costa del Sol to ostensibly recover from losing his wife to another man. Brandt becomes entangled in a sea of murderous intrigue and infidelity with Max, a British financier and Hope, his American wife (who later turn out not to be married). Seebohm also compares Viertel to Hemingway, arguing that Viertel's use of Spanish phrases reflects Hemingway's own, and concludes that *American Skin* is a "rattling good yarn." Although a *Kirkus Reviews* critic finds *American Skin* no more than "competent, old-fashioned fiction in an imitation-Hemingway mode," a *Publishers Weekly* reviewer argues that in *American Skin,* Viertel "skillfully conveys his characters' cynical, pleasure-seeking lives."

In 1990 Viertel adapted *White Hunter, Black Heart,* his 1953 semi-fictional account of working with John Huston on *The African Queen,* for the screen. In a *New York Times* review, Janet Maslin argues that the John Huston portrayed in the film, "selfish, regal, grandly playful at the expense of others and always supremely self-assured—is the same one captured by Peter Viertel in *White Hunter, Black Heart.*" The film, directed by and starring Clint Eastwood, received mixed reviews. Maslin finds that Eastwood "dispenses choice Hustonisms in a singsong, mellifluous growl," but concludes that the film is "as brave as it is improbable." Caryn James in the *New York Times Book Review* notes that Viertel's version of Huston is the portrait of a "charming bully who spends his time in Africa hunting elephants instead of making his movie." Huston claimed to be unaffected by Viertel's portrait.

In 1992 Viertel published a semi-autobiography and memoir of the post-World War II literary scene, *Dangerous Friends: At Large with Hemingway and Huston in the Fifties.* The book recounts Viertel's meeting both Hemingway, whom he met in Ketchum, Idaho, and Huston, who was the director of the first film that Viertel worked on in Hollywood. Bruce Cook in the *Chicago Tribune Books* finds that of the two, "Huston comes off far better than Hemingway," arguing that Viertel focuses on Hemingway's decline—a "social bully with a swollen ego," as opposed to Huston's "authentic and spontaneous charm." Other "dangerous friends" in Viertel's memoir include Luis Miguel Dominguin, a Spanish matador and Franco supporter, Orson Welles, Ava Gardner and Viertel's wife Jigee. Philip French, writing in the *Times Literary Supplement,* sees *Dangerous Friends* as "inclined to present [Viertel's] peripatetic crowd of writers and socialites as a new 'lost generation.'" A *New Leader* reviewer calls *Dangerous Friends* "bracingly direct [and] well-fashioned," and finds that Viertel presents "nicely rounded portraits" rather than "denigrating the recent and not-so-recent dead." Noting that there is little in the way of "the sort of summing-up we might expect from a man in his 70s looking back at his younger self," Cook nonetheless concludes: "with such a star-studded cast and such a narrative, perhaps it is greedy to expect more from this spectacular production."

In 1995 Viertel returned to fiction with *Loser Deals,* the story of expatriate Robert Masters, an ex-B-movie actor whose adventures in Spain and memories of his spotted past provide the material of the narrative. When Masters joins his son-in-law's detective agency, he becomes embroiled in the divorce of the Collinses, a British nobleman and his attractive wife who suspects her husband of extra-marital proclivities. Elaine Kendall of the *Los Angeles Times* calls *Loser Deals* "exactly the sort of delight you would expect from [Viertel]," and recommends the author as a "witty and sophisticated storyteller." A *Rapport* reviewer agrees, commenting that "Viertel is a master at this sort of writing, able to conjure ambience and marvelous characterization with a minimum of words." The *Chicago Tribune*'s Penelope Mesic also gives *Loser Deals* a positive reading, arguing that "even the [book's] surroundings conspire to create a sense of happy self-sufficiency."

BIOGRAPHICAL/CRITICAL SOURCES:

PERIODICALS

America, January 23, 1965, p. 132.
Booklist, January 1, 1972; February 15, 1995, p. 1061.
Chicago Tribune, May 11, 1995, section 5, p. 3.
Chicago Tribune Books, October 4, 1992, p. 4.
Kirkus Reviews, August 1, 1971, p. 834; November 1, 1983, p. 1145.
Los Angeles Times, February 28, 1995, p. E5.
New Leader, October 5, 1992, p. 18.
New York Times, September 14, 1990, p. 1.
New York Times Book Review, March 18, 1984, p. 10; August 9, 1992, p. 3; May 14, 1995, p. 16.
Observer (London), December 6, 1992, p. 59.
Publishers Weekly, October 28, 1983, p. 60; July 6, 1992, p. 43; January 2, 1995, p. 59.
Rapport, Volume 18, number 6.
Saturday Review, January 9, 1965, p. 55.
Times Literary Supplement, January 22, 1993, p. 16.
Washington Post Book World, July 26, 1992, p. 5.*

* * *

VINE, Barbara
  See RENDELL, Ruth (Barbara)

* * *

VON RACHEN, Kurt
  See HUBBARD, L(afayette) Ron(ald)

W

WALKER, C(larence) Eugene 1939-

PERSONAL: Born January 8, 1939, in Monongahela, PA; son of Lewis G. (an auditor) and Olga Thresa (Brioli) Walker; married Lois E. Strom (a chemist), February 28, 1964 (divorced, 1980); children: Chad Eugene, Kyle Lewis, Cass Emanuel. *Education:* Geneva College, B.S. (summa cum laude), 1960; Purdue University, M.S., 1963, Ph.D., 1965. *Politics:* Democrat. *Religion:* Methodist.

ADDRESSES: Home—1133 North Bank Side Circle, Edmond, OK 73003. *Office*—Department of Psychiatry and Behavioral Sciences, University of Oklahoma Health Science Center, P.O. Box 26901, Oklahoma City, OK 73190.

CAREER: Licensed psychologist in state of Oklahoma. Veterans Administration Neuropsychiatric Hospital, Marion, IN, psychology trainee, 1961-62; Veterans Administration Regional Office, Mental Hygiene Clinic, Indianapolis, IN, psychology trainee, 1962-63; West Tenth Street Veterans Administration Hospital, Indianapolis, psychology trainee, 1963, intern in clinical psychology, 1963-64; Riley Childrens Hospital, Indianapolis, intern in clinical psychology, 1963-64; Westmont College, Santa Barbara, CA, assistant professor of psychology, 1964-68, chair of Division of Education and Psychology, 1966-68; private practice of clinical psychology in Santa Barbara, 1965-68; Camarillo State Hospital, Camarillo, CA, consulting psychologist, 1965-68; Baylor University, Waco, TX, assistant professor, 1968-70, associate professor of psychology, 1970-74; private practice of clinical psychology in Waco, 1970-74; Oklahoma Childrens Memorial Hospital, Oklahoma City, OK, director of Outpatient Pediatric Psychol-

ogy Clinic, 1974-79, associate chief of Mental Health Services, 1980—; University of Oklahoma, College of Medicine, Oklahoma City, associate professor, 1974-79, professor of psychology, 1980—, chief of Pediatric Psychology Service, 1974-80, director of Pediatric Psychology Training, 1977—. Has presented numerous scientific papers and reports at psychological symposiums and conventions. Member of student appeals board, College of Medicine, University of Oklahoma, 1979-80. Member of several governance committees at Oklahoma Childrens Memorial Hospital, 1977—. Consultant to several hospitals, educational programs, and institutions in California, Texas, and Oklahoma.

MEMBER: American Psychological Association (fellow; chair of Newsletter Editors Committee), Association for the Advancement of Psychology, American Association for the Advancement of Science, Society of Pediatric Psychology (former president), American Society of Clinical Hypnosis, American Scientific Affiliation (fellow), Corresponding Committee of Fifty (former chair), Southwestern Psychological Association (former secretary-treasurer and former president), Oklahoma Psychological Association (former president), Central Texas Psychological Association (former president), Sigma Xi.

WRITINGS:

Learn to Relax, Prentice-Hall (Englewood Cliffs, NJ), 1975.
(With Allen G. Hedberg) *An Introduction to Behavior Therapy,* Behavioral Advances, 1975.
(With Hedberg, Paul Clement, and Logan Wright) *Clinical Procedures for Behavior Therapy,* Prentice-Hall, 1981.

(With B. L. Bonner and K. Kaufman) *The Physically and Sexually Abused Child: Evaluation and Treatment,* Pergamon (Elmsford, NY), 1988.

EDITOR

(And contributor) *Research Symposium #2,* California Department of Mental Hygiene, 1968.

(With Hedberg, Wright, and Donald K. Freedheim) *A Newsletter Editors Handbook,* Division of State Psychological Association Affairs, American Psychological Association (Washington, DC), 1974.

(With Hedberg and Larry E. Beutler) *Careers in Clinical Psychology: Is There a Place for Me?* (booklet), Section II, Division of Clinical Psychology, American Psychological Association, 1977.

Clinical Practice of Psychology, Pergamon, 1981.

(With M. C. Roberts) *Handbook of Clinical Child Psychology,* Wiley (New York City), 1983, 2nd edition, 1992.

Handbook of Clinical Psychology, Dow Jones-Irwin (Homewood, IL), 1983.

(With A. Zeiner and D. Bendell) *Health Psychology: Treatment and Research Issues,* Plenum (New York City), 1985.

(With Roberts) *Casebook of Child and Pediatric Psychology,* Guilford (New York City), 1989. *Clinical Psychology: Historical and Research Foundations,* Plenum, 1990.

History of Clinical Psychology in Autobiography, Brooks/Cole (Pacific Grove, CA), Volume 1, 1991, Volume 2, 1993.

CONTRIBUTOR

O. H. Herron, editor, *New Dimensions in Student Personnel Administration,* International Textbook Co., 1970.

G. R. Collins, editor, *Our Society in Turmoil,* Creation House (Wheaton, IL), 1970.

Paul J. Woods, editor, *Source Book on the Teaching of Psychology,* Scholars Press (Chico, CA), 1973.

Phyllis McGrab, editor, *Psychological Management of Pediatric Problems,* University Park Press (Baltimore), 1978.

Wright, editor, *Encyclopedia of Pediatric Psychology,* University Park Press, 1979.

John McNamara, editor, *Behavioral Approaches to Medicine: Application and Analysis,* Plenum, 1980.

D. M. Doleys, R. L. Meredith, and A. R. Ciminero, editors, *Behavioral Psychology in Medicine: Assessment and Treatment Strategies,* Plenum, 1981.

J. H. Humphrey, editor, *Stress in Childhood,* AMS Press (New York City), 1984.

D. J. Keyser and R. C. Sweetland, editors, *Test Critiques,* Test Corp. (Kansas City, MO), Volume 1, 1985, Volume 5, 1986.

P. Keller and L. Ritt, editors, *Innovations in Clinical Practice,* Professional Resource Exchange (Sarasota, FL), Volume 4, 1985, Volume 7, 1988, Volume 9, 1990.

P. Karoly, editor, *Handbook of Child Health Assessment: Biopsychosocial Perspectives,* Wiley, 1988.

T. Ollendick and M. Hersen, editors, *Handbook of Child Psychopathology,* Plenum, 1989.

D. J. Willis, E. Wayne Holden, and M. Rosenburg, editors, *Prevention of Physical Abuse of Children through Parent Training,* Wiley, 1992.

R. A. Olson, L. L. Mullins, J. M. Chaney, and J. B. Gillman, editors, *Sourcebook of Pediatric Psychology,* Allyn & Bacon (Newton, MA), 1994.

Roberts, editor, *Handbook of Pediatric Psychology,* Guilford, 1995.

OTHER

Also author of "The Sex Form," a test for assessing sexual functioning and adjustment. Author of audio tapes produced by Self Control Systems, *Creative Parenting: Helping Children Learn to Be Happy Adults,* 1980, and *Stress Management* and *Effective Communications between Parents and Teenagers,* both 1981. Contributor of articles to psychology journals, including *Journal of Consulting and Clinical Psychology, Archives of Sexual Behavior, Journal of Child and Adolescent Psychotherapy, Behavior Therapist, Clinical Psychologist,* and *Psychological Reports.* Contributing editor of *Journal of the American Scientific Affiliation,* 1966-68, and *Professional Psychology,* 1969-76; book review editor of *Clinical Psychologist,* 1968-69, *Journal of Clinical Child Psychology,* 1975—, *Journal of Pediatric Psychology,* 1975—, and *American Psychologist,* 1980—.

WORK IN PROGRESS: With S. D. Netherton and D. Holmes, *Comprehensive Textbook of Child and Adolescent Disorders,* for Oxford University Press; with J. R. Matthews, *Professional Issues in Clinical Psychology,* for Allyn & Bacon. Also, books for parents on creative parenting and a college-level textbook on health and personal adjustments.

WALSH, P(atrick) G(erard) 1923-

PERSONAL: Born August 16, 1923, in Accrington, Lancashire, England; son of Peter and Joanna (Fitzpatrick) Walsh; married Eileen Quin, July 18, 1953; children: Anthony, Patricia, Stephen, John, David. *Education:* Attended Preston Catholic College, 1934-42; University of Liverpool, B.A., 1949, M.A., 1951; University College, Dublin, Ph.D., 1957. *Religion:* Roman Catholic.

ADDRESSES: Home—17 Broom Rd., Glasgow G43 2TP, Scotland. *Office*—Department of Classics, University of Glasgow, Glasgow G12 8QQ, Scotland.

CAREER: University College, Dublin, Ireland, lecturer in classics, 1952-59; University of Edinburgh, Edinburgh, Scotland, lecturer, 1959-66, reader in humanity, 1967-71, professor of Medieval Latin, 1971-72; University of Glasgow, Glasgow, Scotland, professor of humanity, 1972-93. Visiting professor, University of Toronto, 1966-67, Yale University, 1970-71, University of North Carolina at Chapel Hill, 1978, Georgetown University, 1990, and Pamona College, 1992. *Military service:* British Army, Intelligence Corps, 1943-46.

AWARDS, HONORS: Fellow of the Royal Society of Edinburgh, 1982; Knight Commander of St. Gregory (Britain), 1993; Hon. D.Litt (Edinburgh), 1993.

WRITINGS:

Livy: His Historical Aims and Methods, Cambridge University Press (Cambridge, England), 1961.
(Translator) Paulinus of Nola, *Letters,* two volumes, Paulist/Newman, 1966-67.
(Translator with Anthony Ross) St. Thomas Aquinas, *Courage,* Eyre & Spottiswoode (Andover, England), 1966.
The Roman Novel, Cambridge University Press, 1970.
Courtly Love in the Carmina Burana, Edinburgh University Press (Scotland), 1972.
Livy, Oxford University Press, 1974.
(Editor) Livy, *Book XXI,* University Tutorial Press (London), 1974.
(Translator) O. Quasten, editor, *Poems of Paulinus of Nola,* Paulist/Newman, 1975.
(Editor) *Thirty Poems from the Carmina Burana,* University of Reading (Reading, England), 1976.
(Editor and translator) *Andreas Capellanus on Love,* Duckworth (London), 1982.

(Editor) Livy, *Ab urbe condita libri XXVI-XXVII,* Teubner, 1982, *Ab urbe condita libri XXVIII-XXX,* 1986.
(Editor with P. Sharratt) *George Buchanan Tragedies,* Scottish Academic Press (Edinburgh, Scotland), 1984.
(Editor and translator) Livy, *Book XXXVI,* Aris & Phillips (Warminster, England), 1990, *Book XXXVII,* 1992, *Book XXXVIII,* 1993, *Book XXXIX,* 1994, *Book XL,* 1996.
(Translator) Cassiodorus, *Commentary on the Psalms,* 3 Volumes, Paulist/Newman, 1990-93.
(Editor and translator) *More Lyrics from the Carmina Burana,* University of North Carolina Press (Chapel Hill), 1993.
(Translator) Apuleius, *The Golden Ass,* Oxford University Press, 1994.
(Translator) Petronius, *The Satyricon,* Oxford University Press, 1996.

Contributor to classical journals.

WORK IN PROGRESS: Translations of Cicero, *The Nature of the Gods,* and of the Oxford classical text of Livy.

BIOGRAPHICAL/CRITICAL SOURCES:

PERIODICALS

Classical Review, February, 1993, p. 429.
Library Journal, February 1, 1991, p. 82.
Times Literary Supplement, March 18, 1983.

*   *   *

WARREN, Mary Bondurant 1930-

PERSONAL: Born February 5, 1930, in Athens, GA; daughter of John Parnell (a lumber dealer) and Mary Claire (a personnel director; maiden name, Brannon) Bondurant; married James Randolph Warren (a farm equipment dealer), November 27, 1953 (divorced); children: Eve Bondurant (Mrs. James Corbin Weeks), Mark Standard, Amy Moss Sanders, Stuart Heard, Lisa Brannon David. *Education:* University of Georgia, B.S., 1951; Oak Ridge Institute of Nuclear Studies, D.R.I.P., 1952.

ADDRESSES: Home—170 Windsor Ct., Athens, GA 30606-2956. *Office*—P.O. Box 7776, Athens, GA 30604-7776.

CAREER: Union Carbide, Oak Ridge, TN, staff member, 1950-51; Oak Ridge Institute of Nuclear Studies, Medical Division, Oak Ridge, conducted radio biophysics research, 1951-52; Emory University, School of Medicine, Atlanta, GA, conducted radioisotope research, 1952-53; Georgia Institute of Technology, Atlanta, technical editor for engineering experiment station, 1954; Veterans Administration Hospital, Atlanta, radioassay consultant, 1956-57; Heritage Papers, Athens, GA, owner, 1964—. Chair of Clarke County (GA) Civil War Centennial Commission, 1961-65.

MEMBER: South Caroliniana Society (life member), Georgia Genealogical Society, Athens Historical Society (charter member; member of board of directors; president, 1962-63).

WRITINGS:

(Contributor) John Stegeman, *These Men She Gave,* University of Georgia Press (Athens), 1964.

Family Puzzlers, twenty-two volumes, Heritage Papers, 1964-95.

Jackson Street Cemetery, Athens, GA, Heritage Papers (Athens), 1966.

Mars Hill Baptist Church, Oconee County, GA, Heritage Papers, 1966.

Marriage Book "A", Clarke County, GA, Heritage Papers, 1966.

Georgia Genealogical Bibliography, 1963-67, Heritage Papers, 1968.

Marriages and Deaths, 1763 to 1820: Abstracted from Extant Georgia Newspapers, Heritage Papers, 1968.

(Editor and author of revisions) L. M. Hill, *Hills of Wilkes County, Ga., and Allied Families,* Heritage Papers, 1972, 2nd edition, 1987.

Marriages and Deaths, 1820 to 1830: Abstracted from Extant Georgia Newspapers, Heritage Papers, 1972.

South Carolina Jury Lists: 1718 through 1783, Heritage Papers, 1977.

Citizens and Immigrants: South Carolina, 1768, Heritage Papers, 1978.

(Editor) Bowen, *Chronicles of Wilke's County, Georgia,* Heritage Papers, 1978.

(Editor) A. L. Hull, *Annals of Athens, Georgia* (Warren was not associated with the previous edition), Heritage Papers, 1978.

South Carolina Wills, Heritage Papers, 1981.

(Editor) A. B. Stroud, *The Strouds,* 2nd edition (Warren was not associated with previous edition), Heritage Papers, 1983.

(Compiler) *Georgia Marriages, 1811-1820,* Heritage Papers, 1984.

(Annotator and indexer) Reverend Morgan Edwards, *Materials toward a Baptist History, 1770-1772,* Heritage Papers, Volume I: *Pennsylvania, Rhode Island, New Jersey, Delaware,* 1984, Volume II: *Maryland, Virginia, North Carolina, South Carolina, Georgia,* 1984.

(Coauthor) *Whites among the Cherokee, Georgia, 1828-1838,* Heritage Papers, 1987.

(Compiler) *Georgia Land Owners' Memorials, 1758-1776,* Heritage Papers, 1988.

(Coauthor) *South Carolina Newspapers, 1760: The South Carolina Gazette,* Heritage Papers, 1988.

South Carolina Immigrants, 1760-70, Heritage Papers, 1988.

South Carolina Newspapers, 1760, Heritage Papers, 1988.

Gilmer's Georgians, Heritage Papers, 1989.

Georgia Governor and Council Journals, 1753-1760, Heritage Papers, 1991.

The Macon Telegraph, 1826-1832, Heritage Papers, 1991.

Halifax Co., VA, Tithables and Voters, 1755-1780, Heritage Papers, 1991.

Virginia's District Courts, Prince Edward District, 1789-1809, Heritage Papers, 1991.

Georgia Governor and Council Journals, 1761-1767, Heritage Papers, 1992.

Georgia Revolutionary Bounty Land Records, 1783-1785, Heritage Papers, 1992.

Washington County, GA, Land Warrants, 1785-1787, Heritage Papers, 1992.

Buckingham Co., VA, Church and Marriage Records, 1764-1822, Heritage Papers, 1993.

The Macon Telegraph, 1833-1839, Heritage Papers, 1993.

Revolutionary Memoirs and Musters, Heritage Papers, 1994.

Also author of "Athens Lives and Legends," a column published in *Athens Daily News,* and "Family Puzzlers," a column published in *Athens Banner Herald, Oglethorpe Echo,* and *Athens Daily News,* 1964-67. Editor of *Family Puzzlers,* 1964—, *Carolina Genealogist,* 1970-85, and *Georgia Genealogist,* 1970-85.

WORK IN PROGRESS: Georgia Governor and Council Journals 1768-1783, and *Jean-Pierre Bondurant, Cevenole.*

SIDELIGHTS: Mary Bondurant Warren told *CA:* "My interest is research—discovering, codifying, and publishing records of historical and genealogical value in a useful form. With computers and micro-films to assist, we now explore obscure documents and voluminous collections avoided in the past!"

Warren goes on to write, "*Family Puzzlers,* our weekly genealogical magazine, strives to enhance the research skills of its readers by bringing to light just such sources.

"My current research and writing project is the Eu-ropean family history of our immigrant ancestor Jean-Pierre Bondurant, of the Cevennes Mountains, France. He was a descendant of Huguenots and left France for Switzerland, and then London, arriving in Virginia in September 1700. This has taken me to France and Switzerland where records of the Hugue-not exodus still can be found. It has been a fascinat-ing effort."

*   *   *

WEISSMANN, Gerald   1930-

PERSONAL: Born August 7, 1930, in Vienna, Aus-tria; immigrated to the United States, 1938, natural-ized citizen, 1943; son of Adolf (a medical doctor) and Greta (Lustbader) Weissmann; married Ann Raphael, 1953; children: Andrew, Lisa Beth. *Ethnicity:* "Austrian." *Education:* Columbia Univer-sity, B.A., 1950; New York University, M.D., 1954.

ADDRESSES: Office—Department of Medicine, School of Medicine, New York University, 550 First Ave., New York, NY 10016. *E-mail*—gerald.weissmann@ mcccm.med.nyu.edu.

CAREER: Licensed to practice medicine in New York. Mt. Sinai Hospital, New York City, intern, 1954-55; Bellevue Hospital, New York City, resident and chief resident, 1955-58; Arthritis and Rheuma-tism Foundation, New York City, research fellow in biochemistry, 1958-59; New York University, New York City, instructor, 1959-61, assistant professor, 1961-65, associate professor, 1965-70, professor of medicine, 1970—, director of Division of Rheumatology, 1974—. Diplomate of American Board of Internal Medicine, 1963; U.S. Public Health Service special research fellow at Strangeways Research Laboratory, Cambridge University, 1960-61; senior investigator

of Arthritis and Rheumatism Foundation, 1961-65; career investigator of Health Research Council of New York, 1966-70; investigator and instructor at Woods Hole Marine Biological Laboratory, 1970—; consultant to U.S. Food and Drug Administration and National Heart and Lung Institute; Rockefeller Foundation resident at the Villa Serbelloni, Bellagio, Italy, 1987; centennial lecturer at the Marine Bio-logical Laboratory, 1988, and at Johns Hopkins Medical School, 1989. Ethicon Company, scientific advisory board, 1973-76; BioResponse, scientific advisory board, 1982-86; Pfizer, Searle, Riker, Upjohn, consultant, 1972—; The Liposome Com-pany, director, cofounder, and chair of scientific advisory board, 1982—. *Military service:* U. S. Medical Corps, 1955-57, became captain.

MEMBER: American Society of Cell Biology, American Society of Biological Chemistry and Mo-lecular Biology, American Society of Experimental Pathology, American Society for Clinical Investiga-tion, Harvey Society (president, 1981-82), American Rheumatism Association, American College of Rheumatology (president, 1982-83), American Asso-ciation for the Advancement of Science (fellow, 1982), Society for Experimental Biology and Medi-cine, New York Academy of Medicine (fellow, 1993), PEN American Center, Phi Beta Kappa, Al-pha Omega Alpha, Interurban Club.

AWARDS, HONORS: Alessandro Robecchi Prize for Rheumatology, International League Against Rheu-matism, 1972, for research on mechanisms of inflam-mation; Guggenheim fellow at Center of Immunol-ogy and Physiology, Paris, France, 1973-74; Marine Biology Laboratory Prize in cell biology, 1974 and 1979, for work in cell biology of inflammation; Lila Gruber Cancer Research Award (coholder with Emil Frei, Jr.), 1979; Solomon A. Berson Medical Alumni Achievement Award in Clinical Sciences, New York University, 1980; National Institutes of Health MERIT Award, 1987; Marine Biological Laboratory Centennial Award for Leadership in Biomedical Sci-ences, 1988; Hiram Maxim Award for Scientific Communication, 1990; American College of Rheumatology Distinguished Investigator Award, 1992; Charles Plotz Award, Arthritis Foundation (NY), 1993.

WRITINGS:

(Editor) *Mediators of Inflammation,* Plenum Press (New York City), 1974.

(Editor) *Cell Membranes, Biochemistry, Cell Biology & Pathology,* Hospital Practice Press (New York City), 1975.

(Editor) *The Biological Revolution: Applications of Cell Biology to Public Welfare,* Plenum Press, 1979.

The Woods Hole Cantata: Essays on Science and Society, Dodd (New York City), 1985.

They All Laughed at Christopher Columbus: Tales of Medicine and the Art of Discovery (essays), Times Books (New York City), 1987.

The Doctor with Two Heads: And Other Essays, Knopf (New York City), 1990.

The Doctor Dilemma, Whittle Books (New York City), 1992.

(Editor with Robert Barlow and John Dowling) *The Biological Century: Friday Evening Talks at the Marine Biological Laboratory,* Harvard University Press (Cambridge, MA), 1994.

Democracy and DNA: American Dreams and Medical Progress (essays), Hill & Wang (New York City), 1996.

Contributor of articles, book reviews, and essays to books, periodicals, and scholarly journals.

SIDELIGHTS: Gerald Weissmann, a professor of medicine at New York University Medical Center, is the author of four volumes of essays on the art and science of medicine. The essays in his first collection, *The Woods Hole Cantata: Essays on Science and Society,* relate the science of medicine to its social context. One piece concerns a medical researcher who is a prisoner in a concentration camp. Another describes the fate of a severe schizophrenic whose physical illness is treated with new wonder drugs; the patient is then released to the community with little apparent regard for the psychological and social aspects of her illness. The author discusses a wide range of medical and social issues that reflect his own routine as a scientific researcher. Anna Fels, a reviewer for the *New York Times Book Review,* found Gerald Weissmann's insights "original and provocative." She wrote: "It is not only Dr. Weissmann's observations that enliven these essays, but also the palpable delight he derives from the occasions that gave rise to them."

Weissmann's second volume of essays, *They All Laughed at Christopher Columbus: Tales of Medicine and the Art of Discovery,* was published in 1987. In an article for the *New York Times Book Review,* Martha Weinman Lear called the book a "graceful, feisty collection" that conveys "the promise of ad-venture, of voyages of discovery, near-palpable each morning . . . when the laboratory doors are opened." Weissmann uses examples from his own practice to inform the general reader about the world of scientific discovery and to air his views on some of the medico-social issues of our time. An essay on one of his asthma patients allows the physician to discuss the fluctuations in the history of asthma treatment over the years and the debate between those who consider it a physical ailment and others who treat asthma as a psychosomatic disorder. A female AIDS victim prompts Weissmann to consider the fear of science that permeates our age. Lear recommended *They All Laughed at Christopher Columbus* as "a book filled with graceful and generous themes, written in a spirit of caring that defines medicine in the fullest sense."

In his third collection, *The Doctor with Two Heads: And Other Essays,* Weissmann comments on the relationship between art and medicine. Gloria Hochman, writing in the *New York Times Book Review,* stated that the "reader comes away with a tasty repertory of cultural hors d'oeuvres."

In 1996, Weissmann published his fourth book of essays, *Democracy and DNA: American Dreams and Medical Progress,* in which he presents his arguments against the use of nontraditional therapies, pointing out the ineffectiveness of unconventional medicine on pandemics and the positive effects of American meliorists. *New York Times Book Review* contributor Lance Morrow described the book as "surprising and elegantly indignant."

Weissmann told *CA:* "I have been writing all my life and am always pleased when someone actually reads my work, not in the course of duty, but in the pursuit of pleasure."

BIOGRAPHICAL/CRITICAL SOURCES:

PERIODICALS

New York Times Book Review, September 29, 1985; April 5, 1987; July 15, 1990; March 3, 1996, pp. 11-12.

*   *   *

WELLS, John Jay
See COULSON, Juanita (Ruth)

WEST, Owen
  See KOONTZ, Dean R(ay)

*   *   *

WILSON, Robert Anton   1932-

PERSONAL: Born January 18, 1932, in Brooklyn, NY; son of John Joseph (a longshoreman) and Elizabeth (Milli) Wilson; married Arlen Riley (a freelance writer), December 14, 1958; children: Karuna, Djoti, Graham, Luna (deceased). *Education:* Attended Brooklyn Polytechnical College, 1952-57, and New York University, 1957-58; Paidea University, Cotati, CA, Ph.D. in psychology, 1979. *Politics:* "Internet." *Religion:* "LSD."

ADDRESSES: Agent—Al Zuckerman, Writers House, 21 West 26th St., New York, NY 10010.

CAREER: Author and lecturer. Ebasco Services, New York, NY, engineering aide, 1952-58; Antioch Bookplate, Yellow Springs, OH, assistant sales manager, 1962-65; *Playboy,* Chicago, IL, associate editor, 1966-71. Educational director of School of Living, Brookville, OH, 1962; director of Institute for the Study of the Human Future, Berkeley, CA, 1979-82.

MEMBER: World Esoteric Order (founding member, 1974—), Bavarian Illuminati, John Dillinger Died for You Society (treasurer, 1966—), Prometheus Society (director), L5 Society, Ordo Templi Celatus, New Reformed Orthodox Order of the Golden Dawn, Sociedad Magico de Chango.

WRITINGS:

NONFICTION

Playboy's Book of Forbidden Words, Playboy Press (Chicago, IL), 1973.
Sex and Drugs: A Journey beyond Limits, Playboy Press, 1973, 2nd edition, New Falcon (Tempe, AZ), 1991.
The Book of the Breast, Playboy Press, 1974, reprinted as *Ishtar Rising: Why the Goddess Went to Hell and What to Expect Now that She's Returning,* New Falcon, 1989.
Cosmic Trigger, And/Or Press (Berkeley, CA), Volume 1: *The Final Secret of the Illuminati,* fore-

word by Timothy Leary, 1977, revised edition, New Falcon, 1991, Volume 2: *Down to Earth,* New Falcon, 1991, Volume 3: *My Life after Death,* New Falcon, 1995.
The Illuminati Papers, And/Or Press, 1977, 2nd edition, Ronin (Berkeley, CA), 1991.
(With Timothy Leary and George Koopman) *Neuropolitics: The Sociobiology of Human Metamorphosis,* Peace Press, 1977.
Right Where You Are Sitting Now: Further Tales of the Illuminati, And/Or Press, 1977, 2nd edition, Ronin, 1992.
Prometheus Rising: Brain Power in Evolution, Falcon Press (Phoenix, AZ), 1983, revised edition, New Falcon, 1991.
The New Inquisition: Irrational Rationalism and the Citadel of Science, Falcon Press, 1986, revised edition, New Falcon, 1991.
Natural Law, or Don't Put a Rubber on Your Willy, Loompanics (Port Townsend, WA), 1987.
Coincidance: A Head Test, Falcon Press, 1989, revised edition, New Falcon, 1991.
Quantum Psychology, Falcon Press, 1990, revised edition, New Falcon, 1993.
Chaos & Beyond: The Best of Trajectories, Permanent Press (San Jose, CA), 1994.

FICTION

The Sex Magicians, Jaundice Press (Los Angeles, CA), 1974, revised and expanded edition published as *Schroedinger's Cat* (trilogy), Pocket Books (New York City), Volume 1: *The Universe Next Door,* 1979, Volume 2: *The Trick Top Hat,* 1981, Volume 3: *The Homing Pigeons,* 1981.
(With Robert Shea) *Illuminatus!* (trilogy), Dell (New York City), Volume 1: *The Eye in the Pyramid,* 1975, Volume 2: *The Golden Apple,* 1975, Volume 3: *Leviathan,* 1975.
Masks of the Illuminati, Pocket Books, 1981.
The Earth Will Shake (Historical Illuminatus Chronicles series), J. P. Tarcher (Los Angeles, CA), 1982.
The Widow's Son (Historical Illuminatus Chronicles series), Bluejay Books (New York City), 1985.
Nature's God (Historical Illuminatus Chronicles series), Roc (New York City), 1991.

OTHER

Wilhelm Reich in Hell (play), first produced in Dublin, 1985, Falcon Press, 1987.

(With Rudy Rucker and Robert Lamborn Wilson) *Semiotext(e)* (anthology), Autonomedia (New York City), 1990.

Reality Is What You Can Get Away With: A Screenplay, Dell, 1992.

Contributor of over 2,000 articles, sometimes under pseudonyms, to periodicals. Editor of *Verbal Level,* 1957-59; *Fact,* associate editor, 1965, contributing editor, 1965-66; coeditor, with wife Arlen Wilson and D. Scott Apel, of *Trajectories: The Journal of Futurism and Heresy,* 1988—.

ADAPTATIONS: Illuminatus! was adapted as a play, first produced in Liverpool, 1976, and by the National Theatre of Great Britain, 1977.

SIDELIGHTS: "Robert Anton Wilson . . . has spent much of his life writing and lecturing on the challenges and opportunities of man's future," notes Jeffrey M. Elliot in *Literary Voices #1.* Elliot calls Wilson "an important thinker and doer, a renowned mystic and revolutionary whose books and articles are read and debated with gusto and fervor." Wilson's published works, most often characterized as science fiction, transcend that genre in Elliot's view, synthesizing "new trends in physics and parapsychology, combining elements of science fiction and political satire, and revolving around such contemporary interests as UFOs, holistic health, cosmology, quantum mechanics, and human consciousness." Novelist Tom Robbins praises Wilson as a "dazzling barker, hawking tickets to the most thrilling tilt-a-whirls and daring loop-o-planes on the midway of higher consciousness."

Wilson has conducted both psychic experimentation upon himself and extensive research into secret societies, referred to in his books as the Illuminati. This work informs his fiction and nonfiction alike—within his novels, and in his essay collections, such as the autobiographical *Cosmic Trigger* series. While some critics claim that Wilson satirizes the concept of secret societies and conspiracies to rule the world, others feel that his work is not only serious, but also profound and revolutionary. Wilson told Elliot: "There has always been an element of self-mockery in my writing, because I feel uncomfortable being on a pedestal, and so I try to encourage the reader not to take me too seriously. . . . My novels are written so as to force the reader to see things through different reality grids rather than through a single grid. It's important to abolish the unconscious dogmatism

that makes people think their way of looking at reality is the only sane way of viewing the world. My goal is to try to get people into a state of generalized agnosticism, not agnosticism about God alone, but agnosticism about everything."

In a *Science Fiction Review* interview, Wilson further explains his "Transcendental Agnosticism." "There are realities and intelligences greater than conditioned normal consciousness recognizes, but it is premature to dogmatize about them at this primitive stage of our evolution. We've hardly begun to crawl off the surface of the cradle-planet," he states. "The most advanced shamanic techniques—such as Tibetan Tantra or [Aleister] Crowley's system in the West—work by alternating faith and skepticism until you get beyond the ordinary limits of both. With such systems, one learns how arbitrary are the reality-maps that can be coded into laryngeal grunts by hominids or visualized by a mammalian nervous system. . . . Most people are trapped in one static reality-map imprinted on their neurons when they were naive children."

Wilson expounds his views in his fiction, especially in the *Illuminatus!* books, co-written with Robert Shea. The seeds of the ideas behind the *Illuminatus!* books were planted in the late 1960s. "It's 1968," Charles Platt writes in an introduction to his interview with Wilson in *Dream Makers II: The Uncommon Men and Women Who Write Science Fiction,* "and Robert Anton Wilson, self-described skeptic, is playing games with what he calls 'absurdly ridiculous conspiracy theories.' He links up with like-minded prankster-radicals and they plant all kinds of bogus scare stories in the American underground press, claiming that everyone from Richard Nixon to Lee Harvey Oswald belonged to the Bavarian Illuminati, an extinct secret society that Wilson and his friends 'prove' is plotting to rule the world. Only the Discordians (another cult, invented by Wilson *et al.*) can save us."

Wilson and Shea took this idea and worked it into the original *Illuminatus!* trilogy of books. "By and large the basic plot was Shea's," Wilson tells Platt, "and I did the digressions. But I also started adding things to the main line of the plot, as we went along." Their presentation of a world dominated by a great secret conspiracy won much public attention, but not as much as Wilson had hoped for. "To be absolutely honest," he says to Platt, "I expected it to be more successful than it was. And I still do. I still think

Illuminatus! hasn't reached its full potential yet. I feel that it could reach as big an audience as *Catch-22* did. It's that kind of book. It's a satirical comedy. I think promoting it as science fiction limited the audience; I never thought of it as science fiction until Dell promoted it that way."

In fact, Wilson regards all his novels as less science fiction than mystery or detective fiction. His work also has many similarities with twentieth-century experimental writers, such as James Joyce and Jorge Luis Borges. Michael Orgill, writing in the *Washington Post Book World,* explains that the three volumes of Wilson's *Schroedinger's Cat* trilogy make "a bid to rectify alternate history's lack of explicitly philosophical foundations." Throughout the trilogy, Orgill continues, "Wilson continues to touch on everything from metaphysics and social history to love and man's destiny." "What is not provided," the reviewer concludes, "is a denouement that convincingly ties the disparate elements of the trilogy together. Instead, the work flies apart like galaxies speeding away from earth at light speed." "What I'm *always* doing is trying to break down the one-model view of reality," Wilson tells Platt. "Whatever the reader takes for granted is going to be knocked out fifty pages later, and, if they think they know what one book is saying, if they go on with the series they'll find it wasn't that simple after all."

Both *Illuminatus!* and *Schroedinger's Cat* were acclaimed by critics for their humorous content. "*Illuminatus!,*" writes Platt, "had been one big belly-laugh." *Analog Science Fiction/Science Fact* reviewer Tom Easton refers to the "zany" antics of both trilogies. Science fiction novelist Orson Scott Card writes in the *Washington Post Book World* that *Schroedinger's Cat* "survives being a fundamentally silly book because the language is so much fun. The attitude and rhythm of the book are even more like Vonnegut than Vonnegut's most recent imitations of himself; the cynical send-ups of practically everything in the world are often painfully accurate, always amusing." Card finds a lack of foundation in *Schroedinger's Cat* and views it as a weakness. "There is no one in the book to care about, nothing in the book to believe in," he states. "Satire especially requires a moral platform, and because Wilson's book lacks one, *Schroedinger's Cat* left me feeling entertained but empty."

Despite Wilson's depiction of conspiracies in his works (both fiction and nonfiction), much of his work remains optimistic in tone, looking forward to a time when humankind will be free to realize its own full potential. His historical fiction—such as *The Earth Will Shake,* set in eighteenth-century England and Italy, and *Masks of the Illuminati,* set in the early twentieth century—demonstrates his belief that increased freedom leads to increased enlightenment. "The ultimate message of *Masks of the Illuminati,*" declare Alexei and Cory Panshin in the *Washington Post Book World,* "is the suggestion that the disorder and misery of the 20th century has been for a higher purpose—the alchemical production of the new and more flexible-minded humanity." The protagonist of *The Earth Will Shake,* according to Melody Hardy of *Best Sellers,* is led "to doubt and revise his fundamental assumptions about religion, justice, his family and himself." "I think anything that interferes with human freedom prevents the maximum success that we're capable of," Wilson tells Platt. "We're capable of a world in which everybody is not only affluent but super-affluent." In a *Locus* review of *Nature's God,* Tom Whitmore argues that it is "good to know that there are popularizers of philosophy that can turn out as good a read as some of the popularizers of science, and Wilson is certainly high among them."

Wilson once told *CA:* "I regard all my books, fiction and nonfiction, as one long experiment in guerilla ontology. My way of looking at the world is derived from sources as varied as the spy novels of Ambler, Le Carre and Deighton (in which you can't believe anything any of the characters say), the skeptical philosophers such as Hume and Nietzsche (who have shown that reality is not known but only guessed), and such revolutionary artists and movements as Joyce, surrealism, 'Pataphysics,' and Borges, who were all challenging everything we take for granted. I live in the world beyond dogma and certitude, and I use both humor and horror, both story and ideas, to shock the reader into a similarly relativistic and perplexed mentality.

"If my books, or any of them, do what I intend, they should leave the reader feeling that the universe is capable of doing something totally shocking and unexpected in the next five minutes. The Existentialists, of course, share this sense of uncertainty, but they sound rather desperate about it; I am trying to show that life without certainty can be exhilarating, liberating, a great adventure. I want to create a real sense of awe, which is all the religion we need, and all we can honestly hold in this day and age."

BIOGRAPHICAL/CRITICAL SOURCES:

BOOKS

Elliot, Jeffrey M., *Literary Voices #1,* Borgo, 1980.
Platt, Charles, *Dream Makers Volume II: The Uncommon Men and Women Who Write Science Fiction,* Berkley Publishing, 1983.
Wilson, Robert Anton, *Cosmic Trigger,* And/Or Press, Volume 1: *The Final Secret of the Illuminati,* foreword by Timothy Leary, 1977, revised edition, New Falcon, 1991, Volume 2: *Down to Earth,* New Falcon, 1991, Volume 3: *My Life after Death,* New Falcon, 1995.

PERIODICALS

Analog Science Fact/Science Fiction, December 7, 1981, pp. 93-94.
Best Sellers, April, 1983, p. 11.
Booklist, June 15, 1978, p. 1604.
Locus, July, 1990, p. 56; March, 1991, p. 60; May, 1991, p. 50; July, 1991, p. 27, 49.
Los Angeles Times Book Review, March 27, 1983.
New York Times Book Review, November 26, 1972.
Science Fiction Review, May, 1976; fall, 1987, pp. 44-45.
Village Voice Literary Supplement, December, 1993, p. 28.
Washington Post Book World, December 23, 1979; April 26, 1981; June 28, 1981.

*   *   *

WOOD, David   1944-

PERSONAL: Born February 21, 1944, in Sutton, Surrey, England; son of Richard Edwin and Audrey Adele (Fincham) Wood; married Sheila Ruskin, 1966 (marriage dissolved, 1970); married Jacqueline Stanbury (an actress), January 17, 1975; children: Katherine, Rebecca. *Education:* Worcester College, Oxford, B.A. (with honors), 1966. *Avocational interests:* Writing, conjuring, collecting old books.

ADDRESSES: Agent—(for plays) Cavarotto Ramsay Ltd., National House, 60-66 Wardour St., London W1V 3HP, England; (for children's books) Eunice McMullen, 38 Clewer Hill Rd., Windsor, Berkshire SL4 4BW, England.

CAREER: Actor, composer, producer, director, and playwright. W.S.G. Productions Ltd., director, 1966—; Whirligig Theatre (touring children's theatre company), cofounder and director, 1979—; Verronmead Limited (television production company), founder and director, 1983—; Westwood Theatre Productions, founder and director, 1986—. Member of drama advisory panel of Arts Council of Great Britain, 1978—.

MEMBER: British Actors Equity Association, Society of Authors, Green Room Club.

AWARDS, HONORS: Nottinghamshire Children's Book of the Year Award, 1990, for *Sidney the Monster.*

WRITINGS:

CHILDREN'S PLAYS

The Tinder Box (two-act; adaptation of a story by Hans Christian Andersen), produced in Worcester, England, at Swan Theatre, 1967.
Cinderella (book by Sid Collin, music by John Gould), produced in Glasgow, Scotland, 1968.
(With Sheila Ruskin) *The Owl and the Pussycat Went to See. . .* (two-act musical; adaptation of works by Edward Lear; produced in Worcester at Swan Theatre, 1968, and in London at Jeannetta Cochrane Theatre, 1969), Samuel French (London), 1970.
(With Ruskin) *Larry the Lamb in Toytown* (two-act musical; adaptation of stories by S. G. Hulme Beaman; produced in Worcester at Swan Theatre, 1969, and in London at Shaw Theatre, 1973), Samuel French, 1977.
The Plotters of Cabbage Patch Corner (two-act musical; produced in Worcester at Swan Theatre, 1970, and in London at Shaw Theatre, 1971), Samuel French, 1972.
Flibberty and the Penguin (two-act musical; produced in Worcester at Swan Theatre, 1971, and in London, 1977), Samuel French, 1974.
Tickle (produced on tour in England, 1972, and in London at Arts Theatre, 1977), Samuel French, 1978.
The Papertown Paperchase (two-act musical; produced in Worcester at Swan Theatre, 1972, and in London at Greenwich Theatre, 1973), Samuel French, 1976.
Hijack over Hygenia (two-act musical; produced in Worcester at Swan Theatre, 1973), Samuel French, 1974.

Old Mother Hubbard (two-act musical; produced in Hornchurch, Essex, England, at Queen's Theatre, 1975), Samuel French, 1976.

Old Father Time (two-act musical; produced in Hornchurch, Essex, at Queen's Theatre, 1976), Samuel French, 1977.

The Gingerbread Man (two-act musical; produced in Basildon, Essex, England, at Towngate Theatre, 1976, and in London at Old Vic, 1977), Samuel French, 1977.

Mother Goose's Golden Christmas (two-act; produced in Hornchurch, Essex, at Queen's Theatre, 1977), Samuel French, 1978.

Nutcracker Sweet (two-act; produced in Farnham, Surrey, England, at Redgrave Theatre, 1977, and in London, 1980), Samuel French, 1981.

Babes in the Magic Wood (two-act; produced in Hornchurch, Essex, at Queen's Theatre, 1978), Samuel French, 1979.

There Was an Old Woman . . . (two-act; produced in Leicester, England, at Haymarket Theatre, 1979), Samuel French, 1980.

Cinderella (produced in Hornchurch, Essex, at Queen's Theatre, 1979), Samuel French, 1980.

The Ideal Gnome Expedition (produced as *Chish and Fips,* Liverpool, England, 1980; produced as *The Ideal Gnome Expedition,* on tour and in London, 1981), Samuel French, 1982.

Aladdin (produced in Hornchurch, Essex, 1980), Samuel French, 1981.

(With Dave and Toni Arthur) *Robin Hood* (produced in Nottingham, England, 1981, and in London, 1982), Samuel French, 1985.

Meg and Mog Show (adaptation of stories by Helen Nicoll and Jan Pienkowski; produced in London, 1981), published as *Meg and Mog: Four Plays for Children,* Puffin (New York City), 1994.

Dick Whittington and Wondercat (produced in Hornchurch, Essex, 1981), Samuel French, 1982.

Jack and the Giant (produced in Hornchurch, Essex, 1982), Samuel French, 1987.

Magic and Music Show, produced in London, 1983.

The Selfish Shellfish (produced in Farnham, Surrey, England, and London, 1983), Amber Lane Press (Summertown, Oxford), 1983.

(With Dave and Toni Arthur) *Jack the Lad,* produced in Manchester, England, 1984.

The Old Man of Lochnagar (adaptation of the story by Prince Charles; produced in Aberdeen and London, 1986), Amber Lane Press, 1986.

Dinosaurs and All That Rubbish (music by Peter Pontzen; adaptation of the story by Michael Foreman; produced in Denbigh, Wales, 1986, and in London, 1988), Amber Lane Press, 1986.

The See-Saw Tree (produced in Farnham, Surrey, 1986, and in London, 1987), Amber Lane Press, 1987.

Play Theatre (includes *The Nativity Play* and *Jack and the Beanstalk*), two volumes, illustrated by Richard Fowler, Holt (New York City), 1987.

(Adaptor) *The BFG (Big Friendly Giant)* (adapted for the stage from the book by Roald Dahl), Samuel French, 1991.

(With Dave and Toni Arthur) *The Pied Piper* (based on the tale by Robert Browning), Samuel French, 1991.

The BFG: Plays for Children, illustrated by Jane Walmsley, Puffin, 1993.

(Adaptor) *The Witches* (adapted for the stage from the book by Dahl), Samuel French, 1994.

Also author of the plays *Rupert and the Green Dragon,* 1993, and *Save the Human!* Contributor of plays to books, including *Robin Hood and Friar Tuck* and *Marian and the Witches' Charm,* in *Playstages,* edited by John Alcock, Methuen, 1987.

CHILDREN'S FICTION

The Operats of Rodent Garden, illustrated by Geoffrey Beitz, Methuen (New York City), 1984.

The Gingerbread Man (from Wood's own play), illustrated by Sally Anne Lambert, Salem House, 1985.

The Discorats, illustrated by Beitz, Methuen, 1985.

(With Don Seed) *Chish 'n' Fips,* Boxtree, 1987.

Sidney the Monster, illustrated by Clive Scruton, Walker, 1988.

Happy Birthday, Mouse!: A First Counting Book, illustrated by Fowler, Grosset, 1990.

Save the Human! (from Wood's own play), illustrated by Tony Husband, Hamish Hamilton (London), 1991.

Bedtime Story: A Slip-in-the-Slot Book, Ingram, 1994.

Kingfisher Pop-up Theatre: Cinderella, illustrated by Fowler, Kingfisher (London), 1994.

Also author of *Baby Bear's Buggy Ride,* illustrated by Fowler, 1993.

PLAYS

(With David Wright) *Hang Down Your Head and Die* (two-act), produced in Oxford, England, at Oxford Playhouse, in London at Comedy Theatre, and in New York City at Mayfair Theatre, 1964.

(With John Gould) *Four Degrees Over* (two-act), produced in Edinburgh, Scotland, and in London at Mermaid Theatre, 1966.

(With Mick Sadler and Gould) *And Was Jerusalem,* produced in Oxford, 1966; produced as *A Present from the Corporation* in Worcester, England, at Swan Theatre, and in London, 1967.

(With David Wright) *A Life in Bedrooms* (two-act), produced in Edinburgh at Traverse Theatre, 1967; produced as *The Stiffkey Scandals of 1932* in London at Queen's Theatre, 1968.

(With Gould) *Three to One On* (two-act), produced in Edinburgh at Edinburgh Festival, 1968.

(With Gould) *Postscripts* (two-act), produced in London at Hampstead Theatre Club, 1969.

(With Gould) *Down Upper Street* (two-act), produced in London at King's Head Theatre Club, 1971.

(With Gould) *Just the Ticket* (two-act), produced in Leatherhead, Surrey, England, at Thorndike Theatre, 1973.

Rock Nativity (two-act musical; music by Tony Hatch and Jackie Trent; produced in Newcastle-upon-Tyne, England, at University Theatre, 1974; produced as *A New Tomorrow* in Wimbledon, England, at Wimbledon Theatre, 1976), Weinberger, 1977.

(With Iwan Williams) *Maudie* (two-act), produced in Leatherhead, Surrey, at Thorndike Theatre, 1974.

(With Bernard Price and Julian Sluggett) *Chi-Chestnuts* (two-act), produced in Chichester, England, at Assembly Rooms, 1975.

(With Gould) *Think of a Number* (two-act), produced in Peterborough, England, at Key Theatre, 1975.

(Coauthor) *More Chi-Chestnuts* (two-act), produced in Chichester at Assembly Rooms, 1976.

(With Gould) *Bars of Gould* (two-act revue), produced in Exeter, England, at Northcott Theatre, 1977.

(With Gould) *The Luck of the Bodkins* (two-act; adaptation of a work by P.G. Wodehouse), produced in Windsor at Theatre Royal, 1978.

Abbacadabra (music by Bjoern Ulvaeus and Benny Andersson, lyrics by Don Black, Mike Batt, and Ulvaeus), produced in London, 1983.

OTHER

Also writer for television, including the series *Playaway,* 1973-77, *Emu's Christmas Adventure,* 1977, *Chish 'n' Fips,* 1984, *Chips' Comic,* 1984, *Seeing and Doing,* 1986, and *Back Home* (adaptation of the story by Michelle Magorian), 1989. Author of the screenplay *Swallows and Amazons,* released by Anglo EMI Ltd., 1974, and *Tide Race,* 1989. Contributor of articles to *Drama* and *London Drama.*

ADAPTATIONS: Wood's stage adaptation of Enid Blyton's books was adapted into the video production *Noddy,* BBC Video, 1994.

SIDELIGHTS: An actor, director, and writer, David Wood is the cofounder of the Whirligig Theatre, a touring company devoted entirely to bringing his plays, as well as the works of others, to children throughout England. Among these plays are those that give a new spin to old tales, including *The Gingerbread Man* and *The Owl and the Pussycat Went to See. . . ,* and those that bring original, new stories to audiences, such as *Flibberty and the Penguin* and *The See-Saw Tree.* Wood's "musical plays appeal to children's love of action, movement, colour, and spectacle," asserts Colin Mills in *Twentieth-Century Children's Writers.* And a *Plays and Players* contributor adds: "It might be said, now that he has cornered the market, that Wood is our first, and only children's dramatist."

Wood first began to write seriously while a student at Oxford University; his first play, *Hang Down Your Head and Die,* was produced at the Comedy Theatre in 1964 while he was still a student. From that point on, he has written, directed, and acted in several plays, both for children and adults. In addition, Wood writes for television, films, and radio, and has also broken into the children's book market. It is his children's plays, however, for which he is best known. Mills writes that among the reasons for the success of these plays is that "they all have an actor's instinct for their impact, as well as a gifted storyteller's feel for character, plot, and theme."

The plays that are based on well-known stories, such as *Robin Hood* and *Old Mother Hubbard,* are familiar to children, offering a level of comfort. At the same time, though, they "have imaginative and convoluted fun with their sources—and celebrate minor characters," points out Mills. Wood's original plays utilize traditional stock characters like those found in his adaptations—friendly dragons, well-intentioned but bumbling characters, and evil villains—and place them in action-filled adventures that incorporate audience participation. "The original plays are vital and unflagging," maintains Mills, adding that Wood "is a superb creator of names that capitalise upon children's love of word play: Blotch and Carbon,

Kernal Walnut, Herr Von Cuckoo. In his dialogue and songs, he exploits the fun to be had from the topsy-turvy and the illogical."

Wood's imaginative children's plays and his work with Whirligig make theater much more accessible to his young patrons. "The dream was to form a company to tour the shows, one that was not four actors and a hamper, that would sit upon the set that happened to be there," he explains in his *Plays and Players* interview. "We give a fully staged show, with 60 or 70 lighting cues. My belief is that we've short-changed children over the years—we've only given them theatre where it has been convenient. The mere phrase 'children's theatre', in this country, has always had a second division tag on it. But these are tomorrow's theatregoers: they deserve more."

BOOKS

Mills, Colin, "David Wood," *Twentieth-Century Children's Writers*, 4th edition, St. James Press (Detroit), 1995, pp. 1038-40.

PERIODICALS

Books for Keeps, March, 1988, p. 17.
British Book News, December, 1987, p. 27.
Junior Bookshelf, February, 1986, p. 30.
Plays and Players, December, 1987, pp. 8-9.
School Librarian, February, 1992, p. 22; May, 1994, p. 69.

*　　*　　*

WRIGHT, Austin (McGiffert) 1922-

PERSONAL: Born September 6, 1922, in Nepperhan, NY; son of John Kirtland (a geographer) and Katharine (McGiffert) Wright; married Sara Kathleen Hull, 1950; children: Katharine Edith, Joanna Louise, Margaret Hull. *Education:* Harvard University, A.B., 1943; University of Chicago, M.A., 1948, Ph.D., 1959.

ADDRESSES: Home—3454 Lyleburn Pl., Cincinnati, OH 45220.

CAREER: Augustana College, Rock Island, IL, instructor in English, 1948-50; Wright Junior College, Chicago, teacher of English, 1955-60; University of Chicago, Chicago, assistant professor of English, 1960-62; University of Cincinnati, Cincinnati, OH, assistant professor, 1962-66, associate professor, 1966-69, professor of English, 1969-93, professor emeritus, 1993—, acting chairperson of department, 1976-77, director of Graduate Studies, 1973-76. Teacher of college-credit courses on educational television, Chicago, 1959, 1961. *Military service:* U.S. Army, 1943-46; became first lieutenant.

MEMBER: Modern Language Association of America, American Association of University Professors, Authors Guild, Steamship Historical Society of America.

WRITINGS:

The American Short Story in the Twenties, University of Chicago Press (Chicago), 1961.
(Editor with J. Leeds Barroll) *The Art of the Short Story: An Introductory Anthology*, Allyn & Bacon (Newton, MA), 1969.
The Formal Principle in the Novel, Cornell University Press (Ithaca, NY), 1982.
Recalcitrance, Faulkner, and the Professors: A Critical Fiction, University of Iowa Press (Iowa City), 1990.

NOVELS

Camden's Eyes, Doubleday (New York City), 1969.
First Persons, Harper (New York City), 1973.
The Morley Mythology, Harper, 1977.
Tony and Susan, Baskerville Publishers (Dallas), 1993.
After Gregory, Baskerville Publishers, 1994.
Telling Time, Baskerville Publishers, 1995.

SIDELIGHTS: In his novels, Austin Wright experiments "with the mechanics of narration and the interactions between mind and reality," as Christopher Lehmann-Haupt explains in the *New York Times*. "As a novelist I have been most interested," Wright once told *CA,* "in making things as vivid and bright and clear as I can . . . through experiments with shifting points of view and explorations into people's divided minds. The question of how people identify themselves to themselves is a fascinating one. Also how they compose the world around them."

In the novel *Camden's Eyes,* Wright explores the divided mind of William Camden as he confronts the fact of his wife's adultery. As Lehmann-Haupt describes it, "Reader and narrator are forced to peer out at the world through Camden's eyes—prisms fracturing experience into separate, varying, contradictory fragments, tellingly arranged like the planes of a cubist painting." This presentation of a character's inner experiences can be disorienting for the reader. One of the characters in *First Persons,* for example, complains, "'I just been reading this goddam French novel . . . and you can't tell what is real and what is imaginary or in fact you can't tell whether there is any difference between the real and the imaginary in the novel at all.'"

In *The Morley Mythology,* a professor finds that his private memories of childhood are known intimately by a strange telephone caller. The odd revelation causes Morley to break down into a number of distinct personalities, only to be reunited when the private mythology of his life is restored. A reviewer for *Choice* calls *The Morley Mythology* "a psychological comedy" that is "well but fussily crafted, intelligent, and insightful," while Dennis Pendleton in *Library Journal* describes it as a "cautiously experimental novel . . . successfully realized." John Yohalem in the *New York Times Book Review* finds *The Morley Mythology* to be "a fiction of many contradictory textures," although he finds that Morley's world of childhood memories "has depth and substance and the crazy rationales of childhood imagination."

In *Tony and Susan,* Wright creates a novel within a novel. The story begins when Susan Morrow receives a manuscript for a novel written and sent by her ex-husband with a request for her to read it. As she reads the manuscript—a thriller about Tony Hastings, who loses his wife and daughter in a double murder—Susan sees disturbing parallels between the fictional story and her own life. The Tony Hastings novel, Brendan Bernhard writes in the *New York Times Book Review,* "is exciting and persuasive enough to stand on its own," while Lehmann-Haupt calls it "a harrowing exploration of the border between civilization and barbarity, between justice and revenge." According to Joseph Coates in his *Chicago Tribune* review of *Tony and Susan,* "this brilliantly original novel, and the one nestled inside it, are both thrillers, each in a different way and each way different from and infinitely superior to most thrillers, because they play for keeps."

Wright creates another examination of personal psychology in *After Gregory,* in which a despondent Peter Gregory throws himself into the Ohio River only to reemerge a different man, shedding the problems of his life to begin anew. The novel is, Lehmann-Haupt explains, "a mesmerizing parable of the way Americans search for themselves by throwing away their used-up pasts." Writing in Chicago *Tribune Books,* Geoffrey Johnson finds *After Gregory* to be "at heart an old-fashioned mystery story" but also "a novel that ultimately challenges (and involves) readers more than any lurid potboiler, it's the kind of book that asks big, philosophical questions—like 'What is a person anyway?'" While Wendy Smith in the *New York Times Book Review* believes that *After Gregory* "lacks any real passion either for the characters or for the existential questions their plights embody," she also finds the novel to be "cleverly constructed and thematically provocative." Lehmann-Haupt concludes that *After Gregory* is "a satisfying philosophical thriller."

Wright's novel *Telling Time* begins with a situation from a thriller as a man takes his wife and children hostage and holds off the local police with gunfire. Attempting to intervene, an elderly neighbor, Thomas Westerly, suffers a stroke when the gunman fires at him. On his deathbed, Westerly tells his eldest son to go through his papers and destroy whatever might be embarrassing to the family. His son uncovers personal secrets that surprisingly tie Westerly to the man who has taken his family hostage. The story, writes a critic for *Publishers Weekly,* "unfolds kaleidoscopically through dialogues, letters, diary entries and interior monologues." Lehmann-Haupt describes *Telling Time* as "an epistolary novel in an up-to-date sense, using faxes, answering-machine messages and imaginary letters to God, among other devices," and concludes that the work is "an oddly dissonant novel that touches the mind and stretches the heart as only Mr. Wright can do with his tragicomic take on the human predicament."

BIOGRAPHICAL/CRITICAL SOURCES:

BOOKS

Wright, Austin, *First Persons,* Harper, 1973.

PERIODICALS

American Literature, September, 1991.
Boston Globe, March 7, 1993, p. B45; October 9, 1994, p. B18.
Chicago Tribune, March 4, 1993, p. 3.
Choice, September, 1977, p. 868.
Christian Science Monitor, August 18, 1977, p. 21.
Commonweal, December 19, 1969.
Library Journal, April 15, 1977, p. 951.
Mississippi Quarterly, summer, 1991.

New York Review of Books, January 29, 1970, p.45;
    August 4, 1977, p. 37.
New York Times, July 2, 1969; November 28, 1973;
    June 3, 1977; March 22, 1993, p. C15; September 29, 1994, p. C18; October 12, 1995.
New York Times Book Review, November 18, 1973;
    June 19, 1977, p. 40; August 4, 1977; May 23,
    1993, p. 29; November 13, 1994, p. 63.
Observer, September 18, 1994, p. 19.
Publishers Weekly, August 21, 1995, p. 47.
Small Press, summer, 1993, p. 72.
Tribune Books (Chicago), November 6, 1994, p. 6.
Western Humanities Review, autumn, 1983, p. 274.
World Literature Today, summer, 1983, p. 521.

Y

YEAZELL, Ruth Bernard 1947-

PERSONAL: Born April 4, 1947, in New York, NY; daughter of Walter and Annabelle (Reich) Bernard; married Stephen C. Yeazell, August 14, 1969 (marriage ended, 1980). *Education:* Swarthmore College, B.A. (with high honors), 1967; Yale University, M.Phil., 1970, Ph.D., 1971.

ADDRESSES: Office—Department of English, Yale University, P.O. Box 8302, New Haven, CT 06520-8302.

CAREER: Boston University, Boston, MA, assistant professor of English, 1971-75; University of California, Los Angeles, assistant professor, 1975-77, associate professor, 1977-80, professor of English, 1980-91; Yale University, New Haven, CT, professor, 1991—, Clace Family professor, 1995—.

MEMBER: Modern Language Association of America (member of executive council, 1985-88), Phi Beta Kappa.

AWARDS, HONORS: Woodrow Wilson fellow, 1967-68; Guggenheim fellow, 1979-80; National Endowment for the Humanities fellow, 1988-89; President's Research fellow, University of California, 1988-89; Harvey L. Eby Award for the art of teaching, University of California, Los Angeles, 1990.

WRITINGS:

Language and Knowledge in the Late Novels of Henry James, University of Chicago Press (Chicago), 1976.

(Editor) *The Death and Letters of Alice James: Selected Correspondence,* University of California Press (Berkeley), 1981.

(Editor) *Sex, Politics, and Science in the Nineteenth Century Novel,* John Hopkins University Press (Baltimore, MD), 1986.

Fictions of Modesty: Women and Courtship in the English Novel, University of Chicago Press, 1991.

(Editor) *Henry James: New Century Views,* Prentice-Hall (Englewood Cliffs, NJ), 1994.

Associate editor, *Nineteenth-Century Fiction,* 1977-80; member of advisory board, *Publications of the Modern Language Association,* 1980-84.

WORK IN PROGRESS: A book on representations of the harem in England and France, tentatively entitled *Harems of the Mind: Some Passages in Western Art and Literature.*

SIDELIGHTS: In *The Death and Letters of Alice James,* editor Ruth Bernard Yeazell has collected some of the writings from the last years of the brilliant but repressed younger sister of noted writer Henry James and famed psychologist William James. "Yeazell's discriminating selection of Alice James's often witty and sad letters was chosen for their 'inherent appeal and for the representativeness, to help the reader sense the range of [Alice James's] concerns and the shape of her mortal career," notes Diane Johnson in the *New York Times Book Review.* While the James children were all encouraged to develop their intellectual talents, Alice, perhaps because of her gender, felt herself held back in many ways; from an early age she experienced numerous "nervous" conditions that kept her an invalid until her death from cancer. Nevertheless, observes Johnson, "Yeazell in her introduction to Alice James's letters . . . avoids the temptation to make of the talented and wasted Alice either a heroine or a victim" "Working with one thread, the theme of death," continues the critic, the editor "illumines in detail a preoccupation with death that seems, from a perspective more strictly psychological, to have controlled Alice's life."

Despite Alice James's physical and emotional problems, her writings demonstrate her considerable literary gifts. *Yale Review* contributor Patricia Meyer Spacks writes that Yeazell "calls attention to the fictionalizing process in Alice James's correspondence, exemplified in several letters where she imaginatively converts herself to a corpse and triumphs over her mortality by using the fantasized cadaver as an argumentative counter." "Ably edited by Yeazell," claims R. J. Kelly in *Library Journal,* these letters "offer a fascinating glimpse of a remarkable woman and of one of Americas most distinguished families." Katherine Winton Evans concurs, calling *The Death and Letters of Alice James* a "well-edited and intelligently annotated collection." Evans comments in the *Washington Post Book World* that the book will "shed light on the curious Victorian phenomenon of nervous prostration and give a vivid picture of a self-imprisoned 19th-century woman."

BIOGRAPHICAL/CRITICAL SOURCES:

PERIODICALS

Library Journal, November 1, 1980.
Los Angeles Times Book Review, January 4, 1981.
New Republic, December 20, 1980.
New York Times Book Review, December 14, 1980.
Review of English Studies, May, 1994, p. 284.
Signs: Journal of Women in Culture and Society, autumn, 1993, p. 241.
Times Literary Supplement, May 20, 1977.
Washington Post Book World, November 30, 1980.
Yale Review, summer, 1981.

*   *   *

YERBY, Frank G(arvin)   1916-1991

PERSONAL: Born September 5, 1916, in Augusta, GA; died of heart failure, November 29, 1991, in Madrid, Spain; buried in Almudena Cemetery,

Madrid, Spain; son of Rufus Garvin (a postal clerk) and Wilhelmina (Smythe) Yerby; married Flora Helen Claire Williams, March 1, 1941 (divorced); married Blanca Calle-Perez (Yerby's secretary, translator, researcher, and "general manager"), July 27, 1956; children: (first marriage) Jacques Loring, Nikki Ethlyn, Faune Ellena, Jan Keith. *Education:* Paine College, A.B., 1937; Fisk University, M.A., 1938; graduate study, University of Chicago, 1939. *Politics:* Independent. *Religion:* Agnostic.

CAREER: Novelist. Florida Agricultural and Mechanical College (now University), Tallahassee, instructor in English, 1939-40; Southern University and Agricultural and Mechanical College, Baton Rouge, LA, instructor in English, 1940-41; Ford Motor Co., Dearborn, MI, laboratory technician, 1941-44; Ranger (Fairchild) Aircraft, Jamaica, NY, chief inspector, Magnaflux, 1944-45; resident of Madrid, Spain, beginning 1955; also lived in France for an extended period in the 1950s.

MEMBER: Authors Guild, Authors League of America, Real Sociedad Hipica Espanola (Madrid), Madrid Country Club.

AWARDS, HONORS: O. Henry Memorial Award, 1944, for best first short story, "Health Card"; Doctor of Letters, Fisk University, 1976, and Doctor of Humane Letters, Paine College, 1977; named honorary citizen of State of Tennessee by Governor's Proclamation, 1977.

WRITINGS:

NOVELS; ORIGINALLY PUBLISHED BY DIAL (NEW YORK CITY)

The Foxes of Harrow, 1946, reprinted, Buccaneer Books (Cutchogue, NY), 1976.
The Vixens, 1947, reprinted, Dell (New York City), 1976.
The Golden Hawk, 1948.
Pride's Castle, 1949.
Floodtide, 1950.
A Woman Called Fancy, 1951.
The Saracen Blade, 1952.
The Devil's Laughter, 1953.
Benton's Row, 1954.
The Treasure of Pleasant Valley, 1955.
Captain Rebel, 1956.
Fairoaks, 1957.
The Serpent and the Staff, 1958.
Jarrett's Jade, 1959.

Gillian, 1960.
The Garfield Honor, 1961.
Griffin's Way, 1962.
The Old Gods Laugh: A Modern Romance, 1964.
An Odor of Sanctity: A Novel of Medieval Moorish Spain, 1965.
Goat Song: A Novel of Ancient Greece, 1968.
Judas My Brother: The Story of the Thirteenth Disciple, 1968.
Speak Now: A Modern Novel, 1969.
The Dahomean: An Historical Novel, 1971 (published in England as *The Man from Dahomey*, Heinemann (London), 1972).
The Girl from Storyville: A Victorian Novel, 1972.
The Voyage Unplanned, 1974.
Tobias and the Angel, 1975.
A Rose for Ana Maria, 1976.
Hail the Conquering Hero, 1977.
A Darkness at Ingraham's Crest: A Tale of the Slaveholding South, 1979.
Western: A Saga of the Great Plains, 1982.

NOVELS; PUBLISHED BY DOUBLEDAY (NEW YORK CITY)

Bride of Liberty, 1954.
Devilseed, 1984.
McKenzie's Hundred, 1985.

OTHER

Work represented in numerous anthologies, including *The Best Short Stories by Negro Writers: An Anthology from 1899 to the Present*, edited by Langston Hughes, Little, Brown (Boston), 1967; *The Poetry of the Negro, 1746-1970*, edited by Hughes and Arna Bontemps, Doubleday, 1970; and *Blacklash*, edited by Stewart H. Benedict, Popular Library, 1970. Contributor to *Harper's, Liberty, Colliers, France Soir, Le Meuse, La Laterne, Berlin Zeitung*, and numerous other periodicals.

ADAPTATIONS: The Foxes of Harrow was filmed by Twentieth Century-Fox in 1951; *The Golden Hawk* and *The Saracen Blade* were filmed by Columbia in 1952 and 1954, respectively; *Pride's Castle* was filmed for television.

SIDELIGHTS: A prolific novelist who published thirty-three tales of adventure, Frank G. Yerby sold over fifty-five million hardback and paperback books during the course of his lifetime. While many of these novels were best-sellers, their popularity had little effect on Yerby's critical stature. Since the appearance of his first novel, *The Foxes of Harrow*, in 1946, the author was routinely—and some say unfairly—slighted by critics. Early in his career, for instance, when Yerby was producing mainstream fiction, black reviewers attacked him for abandoning his race. Those who knew his work, but not his color, accused him of squandering his writing talent on cardboard characters and hackneyed plots. Still others objected to his "over-blown" prose and the way he sensationalized his material. Writing in *The Negro Novel in America*, Robert A. Bone dubbed him "the prince of the pulpsters."

In the face of such criticism, Yerby steadfastly maintained his integrity: "The only excuse for writing is that you love it beyond measure and beyond reason," he once told *CA*, adding that "to make any compromise whatsoever for the sake of sales or popularity is to join the world's oldest profession. I believe that a writer should have the guts to starve; and that if he doesn't come close to it most of the time, he'd better take a long, hard look at what he's doing. . . . I write only because I have to. What I get out of it financially doesn't come under consideration at all. I write exactly what I feel and think . . ., but within that framework I try to give pleasure to the reading public."

Yerby's novels are characterized by colorful language, complex plot lines, and a multiplicity of characters. Hugh M. Gloster called Yerby's formula "the recipe of Southern historical romance," listing the following ingredients in *Crisis* magazine: "a bold, handsome, rakish, but withal somewhat honorable hero; a frigid, respectable wife; a torrid unrespectable mistress; and usually a crafty, fiendish villain." According to the *Washington Post Book World*, "a typical Yerby plot seems to involve a strong man who has to choose between two women and . . . more-than-generous helpings of revenge, madness, suffering and violence." *Time* summed up his writing as "a crude, shrewd combination of sex, violence, sadism, costuming and cliche."

A common criticism of Yerby's fiction is that he habitually solved apparently insoluble problems through a *deus ex machina*, or stroke of fate. "Despite his skillful tangling and untangling of exciting narratives which mesmerize even many sophisticated readers, Yerby too often depends on contrived endings," wrote Darwin T. Turner in *The Black Novelist*. Nick Aaron Ford echoed this sentiment in *Phylon*, writing that in all Yerby's books "there are scenes of great literary power, followed by episodes of incredible adventure, with too little preparation for the miraculous results. . . . This is not to say that Yerby is an inferior writer. He has rich imagination, a talent for vivid expression, ability to create pity and terror, and an understanding of the suffering of the poor and the oppressed. In short, he possesses the qualifications that could make of him a great novelist. But it appears that Yerby is satisfied with popularity without greatness. He says emphatically, 'I think the novelist has a professional obligation to please his reading public.'"

A more sensitive arena is Yerby's treatment of racial issues. The second of four children of a racially mixed couple, Yerby encountered his share of discrimination as a boy. "When I was young," he told *People* magazine, "a bunch of us black kids would get in a fight with white kids and then I'd have to fight with a black kid who got on me for being so light." Though he was an excellent student, and, after graduation, secured teaching positions at a number of black universities, Yerby became dissatisfied with what he regarded as the "stifling" atmosphere of these "Uncle Tom factories" and abandoned academia for a wartime factory job in Detroit. His first published fiction, which earned him an O. Henry Memorial Award in 1944, was a bitter story of racial injustice called "Health Card." He published five other short stories during the early 1940s, each of them concerned with blacks and their living conditions.

He discovered, however, that most American readers were uninterested in reading about bigotry and race problems. *Dictionary of Literary Biography* contributor Jeffrey D. Parker quoted Yerby as saying in a *Harper's* magazine article: "The idea dawned on me that to continue to follow the route I had mapped out for myself was roughly analogous to shouting one's head off in Mammoth Cave." Accordingly, he abandoned the direct treatment of black themes in his fiction for almost thirty years. Instead, he set out to write a historical novel that would have broad appeal. Employed during the day at a defense plant, he worked on his book at night. Yerby described his philosophy at that time in a 1982 interview with the *New York Times Book Review,* quoted by Parker: "Nobody ever went broke underestimating the taste of the American public, so I set out to write the worst possible novel it was humanly possible to write and still get published." He admitted, however, that despite his cynical approach, the book "sort of got hold of me, and about half way through, I started revising and improving it." The result was *The Foxes of Harrow,* a lush southern romance which traces the fortunes of the dashing young Stephen Fox in his rise from poverty to great wealth.

It is "a good, old-fashioned obese historical novel of the Old South that seems, more than once, to be haunted by the affluent ghost of Scarlett O'Hara," according to the *New York Times*. While acknowledging Yerby's ability to hold the reader captive with his fast-paced plotting and vivid prose, many critics dismissed the book as socially insignificant melodrama. *New Yorker* contributor, Edmund Wilson, for instance, noted that Yerby "has packed everything in—passion, politics, creole society, sex, the clash of races, and war—but he never captures the faintest flutter of the breath of life." In N. L. Rothman's view, "the book rings throughout with colorful passions and the words to match. It is not a historical novel—for that must have some reality in it—," he continued in the *Saturday Review of Literature,* "but it is a good example of the technicolored fantasies that have been passing as such of late." In later years, Yerby himself belittled the work, telling *People* magazine that *The Foxes of Harrow* comprised "every romantic cliche in history."

The novel's literary shortcomings had no effect on its enormous popularity, however. With sales of over two million copies, *The Foxes of Harrow* became one of the hottest titles of the decade. It was translated into at least twelve languages, reprinted in several national magazines, and made into a lucrative movie starring Rex Harrison and Maureen O'Hara. Though Yerby despised the film adaptation, he was pleased with his novel's popular acceptance. He went on to publish a string of historical novels with Anglo-Saxon protagonists, leading Hugh M. Gloster to surmise that Yerby "gained his laurels by focusing upon white rather than Negro characters. Performance—and not pigmentation—has been the basis of his success."

Yerby staunchly defended his focus, explaining to *CA* that "the novelist hasn't any right to inflict on the public his private ideas on politics, religion or race. If he wants to preach he should go on the pulpit." Later he stated: "My mother was Scotch-Irish, a grandparent was an Indian; I've far more Irish blood than Negro. I simply insist on remaining a member of the human race. I don't think a writer's output should be dictated by a biological accident. It happens there are many things I know far better than the race problem." Yerby's personal solution to problems of discrimination was to leave the country. He moved from the United States to Spain in 1955 and remained there until his death in 1991.

Despite his contempt for didactic fiction, Yerby did address racial issues indirectly in several novels, some critics have said. "In his earliest novels, the racial problems are employed peripherally, almost perfunctorily, and occupy little space or overt interest in the novel," wrote Jack B. Moore in the *Journal of Popular Culture.* "None the less Yerby's racial attitudes pervade these early novels of the South, sometimes in obvious and sometimes in disguised fashion." Darwin T. Turner saw Yerby's position manifested in "the theme of the outcast who, as in existentialist literature, pits his will against a hostile universe. By intelligence and courage, he proves himself superior to a society which rejects him because of his alien, inferior, or illegitimate birth."

His second novel, *The Vixens,* utilized research material on the south he hadn't been able to incorporate into his first book. He followed *The Vixens* with a string of other southern romances, set for the most part in the nineteenth century. Commenting on Yerby's southern tales, Parker noted that although *A Darkness at Ingraham's Crest* is an unmistakable "indictment against the South and slavery," in other books the author had "done much to perpetuate the myths surrounding the 'Old South.'" With *The Golden Hawk,* in 1948, Yerby turned to picaresque adventure in other lands and earlier centuries. And his research, which had been admittedly careless in his first novels, became meticulous. One of his most ambitious projects was *Judas, My Brother: The Story of the Thirteenth Disciple,* published in 1969. Based on thirty years of research, it was the author's attempt to present a demythologized account of the origin of Christianity. Parker quoted Yerby as saying that this book examines the question of "whether any man truly has the right to impose, by almost imperial fiat, belief in things that simply are not so. To me, irrationality is dangerous; perhaps the most dangerous force stalking through the world today. This novel. . .is one man's plea for an ecumenicism broad enough to include reasonable men; and his effort to defend his modest intellect from intolerable insult." Still, Parker concludes that "for all the polemics, *Judas, My Brother* [is a] costume novel," best read as entertainment.

But while Yerby's novels of the 1950s and 1960s qualified as popular fiction, some critics were willing to admit that they also reflected serious concerns. In addition to escapism, they "exhibit another dimension, disregarded by the readers who lament Yerby's failure to write an historical novel and by the others who condemn his refusal to write an overtly polemical treatise on the plight of the American Negro," according to Darwin T. Turner in *The Black Novelist.* "Ideas—bitter ironies, caustic debunkings, painful gropings for meaning—writhe behind the soap-opera facade of his fiction." And, in 1971, after protesting his indifference to racial issues for many, many years, Yerby addressed the matter directly in *The Dahomean: An Historical Novel,* his novel of Black Africa.

Set in the nineteenth century, *The Dahomean* traces the life of Nyasanu/Hwesu as he advances in position from a chief's son to governor of an entire province, only to be sold into American slavery by two jealous relatives. "At the same time, his rise and fall illustrates the customs and folkways of his country: the rites of manhood and marriage; the feudal system; war," according to the *New York Times Book Review.* "Virtues of the book," said Turner, writing in *Black World,* "are the presentation of an exciting and illuminating history of Black people and a determined focus of the story on a single Black hero. But there is more. In *The Dahomean,* Yerby's strength reveals itself to best advantage and even his former weaknesses become strengths. . . . Yerby is at his best when he envelops his plot with a history he has unearthed painstakingly and with a serious or satirical but always devastating debunking of historical legends and myths. That achievement is superior in *The Dahomean,* not so much in the presentation of historical facts as in the presentation of a people and a culture."

In a prefatory note to the novel, Yerby explained that part of his reason for writing the book was "to correct, so far as possible, the Anglo-Saxon reader's historical perspective" on black history. By portraying the Dahomean culture in all its rich complexity, Yerby dispelled the myth of a totally primitive Africa, even hinting at times that the tribal cultures "sometimes surpassed in their subtlety, their complexity, their dignity the ones to which the slaves were brought," in the *Best Sellers* critic's words. But in depicting the cruelties that certain tribesmen perpetrated on their black brothers, including selling them into slavery, Yerby also shattered the illusion that blacks are inherently superior morally. What Yerby seemed to be suggesting, Turner maintained, is that "the differences between people do not stem from a difference of blood, but a difference of opportunity and power."

Hailed by several reviewers as Yerby's masterpiece, *The Dahomean* also settled an old score for the author, as he explained in a letter to *CA:* "I am much more relaxed about racial matters, that increased tranquility being due in part to the fact that *The Dahomean* received (with one lone exception) rave notices from the critics. Thereafter, reviewers seemed to have waked up to what I was actually writing as distinct from and opposed to 1) what I used to write; and 2) what they thought I was writing. In short, I seem to have succeeded in changing many critics' minds. Pleasantly surprising was the high praise bestowed upon this novel by the critics of the South African papers. Needless to say, black critics immediately removed me from the list of 'non-conductors' and welcomed me back into the fold like a sinner redeemed by faith."

Later, in that same letter, Yerby postulated that critical reaction to his books reflected the reviewers' biases: "Those who confuse literature with sexual morality damn them; those wise enough, emotionally mature enough to realize that the two things have practically nothing to do with each other, generally like them very much indeed." Since the publication of *The Dahomean,* Yerby admitted, "two things have been of considerable comfort to me. First is the fact that I am no longer accused of colorful, purplish over writing. And the second is the dawning realization that fifty-five million readers in eighty-two countries and twenty-three languages (who have bought and paid for my novels) are not necessarily all idiots. Strangely enough (or perhaps not so strangely after all) the degree of appreciation for a novel of mine is directly increased by the degree of knowledge the reader has of the subject. In other words, people who know the themes I've written about either by reason of having lived through them, or deeply and professionally studied them, find no fault with my novels. I am praised by experts, attacked by—well, let's be kind and call them amateurs."

Ultimately, however, critical reaction is incidental. Yerby, who in his later years turned increasingly to subjects he found personally—rather than commercially—appealing, worked from compulsion. As he told *People* magazine, "I won't stop writing as long as there's a breath in me."

Some of Yerby's manuscripts are held at the Mugar Memorial Library, Boston University.

BIOGRAPHICAL/CRITICAL SOURCES:

BOOKS

Bone, Robert A., *The Negro Novel in America,* Yale University Press (New Haven, CT), revised edition, 1965.
Breit, Harvey, *The Writer Observed,* World Publishing, 1956.
Contemporary Literary Criticism, Gale (Detroit), Volume 1, 1973, Volume 7, 1977, Volume 12, 1982.
Black Literature Criticism, Gale, Volume 3, 1992.
Dictionary of Literary Biography, Volume 76: *Afro-American Writers, 1940-1955,* Gale, 1988.
Hemenway, Robert, *The Black Novelist,* C. E. Merrill (Columbus, OH), 1970.
Yerby, Frank G., *The Dahomean: An Historical Novel,* Dial, 1971.

PERIODICALS

Best Sellers, February 15, 1968; January 1, 1969; September 1, 1971; November, 1982.
Black World, February, 1972.
Book Week, February 10, 1946; April 27, 1947.
Crisis, January, 1948.
Journal of Popular Culture, spring, 1975.
Los Angeles Times Book Review, November 7, 1982.
Negro Digest, July, 1968; April, 1969.
Newsweek, November 30, 1959.
New Yorker, February 9, 1946; April 24, 1948.
New York Herald Tribune Book Review, May 4, 1947; June 12, 1949; October 22, 1950; July 15, 1951; September 21, 1952; October 4, 1953; November 14, 1954; December 19, 1954; October 14, 1956; September 22, 1957.
New York Times, February 10, 1946; May 2, 1948; May 15, 1949; September 10, 1950; May 6, 1951; April 6, 1952; November 15, 1953; December 5, 1954; September 23, 1956; September 8, 1957; October 12, 1958.
New York Times Book Review, November 10, 1968; October 17, 1971; September 17, 1972.
People, March 30, 1981.
Phylon: The Atlanta University Review of Race and Culture, Volume XXV, number 1, 1954.
Publishers Weekly, May 10, 1971; June 4, 1982.
Saturday Review, May 10, 1952; October 27, 1956; August 24, 1957.

Saturday Review of Literature, February 23, 1946; May 8, 1948; June 18, 1949; September 30, 1950; June 23, 1951.
Time, May 5, 1947; September 4, 1950; April 7, 1952; November 23, 1953; November 29, 1954.
Times Literary Supplement, March 27, 1959.
Washington Post Book World, August 15, 1982.

OBITUARIES:

PERIODICALS

Chicago Tribune, January 12, 1992, p. 7.
Los Angeles Times, January 1, 1992, p. A22.
New York Times, January 8, 1992, p. D19.

*   *   *

YOUNG, Ian (George)   1945-

PERSONAL: Born January 5, 1945, in London, England; son of George Roland and Joan (Morris) Young. *Education:* Attended Malvern Collegiate Institute, 1957-63, and University of Toronto, 1964-67. *Politics:* Libertarian.

ADDRESSES: *Home and office*—2483 Gerrard St. East, Scarborough, Ontario, Canada M1N 1W7.

CAREER: Writer, editor, and publisher. Director of Catalyst Press, 1969-81; director of TMW Communications, 1990—.

MEMBER: Hermetic Order of the Silver Sword, Mackay Society.

AWARDS, HONORS: Various Canada Council and Ontario Arts Council awards.

WRITINGS:

(Translator) Count Jacques d'Adelsward Fersen, *Curieux d'Amour,* Timothy d'Arch Smith, 1970.
The Male Homosexual in Literature: A Bibliography, Scarecrow (Metuchen, NJ), 1975, 2nd edition, 1982.
Gay Resistance: Homosexuals in the Anti-Nazi Underground (essays), Stubblejumper Press, 1985.

The AIDS Dissidents: An Annotated Bibliography, Scarecrow, 1993.
The Stonewall Experiment: A Gay Psychohistory, Cassell, 1995.

POEMS

White Garland: 9 Poems for Richard, Cyclops, 1969.
Year of the Quiet Sun, Anansi, 1969.
Double Exposure, New Books, 1970, new edition, Crossing Press (Trumansburg, NY), 1974.
(With Richard Phelan) *Cool Fire: 10 Poems by Ian Young and Richard Phelan,* Catalyst (New York City), 1970.
(With Phelan) *Lions in the Stream,* Catalyst, 1971.
Some Green Moths, Catalyst, 1972.
Autumn Angels, Village Bookstore, 1973.
Yuletide Story, Catalyst, 1973.
Don, Catalyst, 1973.
Invisible Words, Missing Link (Phoenix, AZ), 1974.
Common-or-Garden Gods, Catalyst, 1976.
Alamo, Dreadnaught Co-Operative, 1976.
Whatever Turns You On in the New Year, Catalyst, 1976.
Schwule Poesie, Achenbach-Verlag, 1978.
Sex Magick, Stubblejumper Press, 1986.

EDITOR

(And contributor) *The Male Muse: A Gay Anthology,* Crossing Press, 1973.
On the Line: New Gay Fiction, Crossing Press, 1981.
Overlooked and Underrated: Essays on Some Twentieth-Century Writers, Little Caesar Press, 1982.
Son of the Male Muse, Crossing Press, 1983.

OTHER

Also author of introduction or editor of other books. Contributor to numerous anthologies, including *T. O. Now: The Young Toronto Poets,* Anansi, 1968; *The Speaking Earth,* edited by John Metcalf, Van Nostrand (New York City), 1973; *Fire,* edited by Peter Carver, Peter Martin, 1978; *The Penguin Book of Homosexual Verse,* edited by Stephen Coote, Penguin Books (New York City), 1983; *Brushes with Greatness,* Coach House Press, 1989; *Bizarre Dreams,* Badboy Books, 1994; and *Boys of the Night,* STARbooks, 1996. Book reviewer, *Torso* magazine (New York City), 1991—. Contributor to numerous periodicals, including *Advocate,*

Antigonish Review, Body Politic, Books in Canada, Canadian Forum, Descant, Gay News, Jewish Dialog, Poetry Canada Review, Quarry, and *Tamarack Review.*

WORK IN PROGRESS: Editing, with Gavin Dillard, *Return of the Male Muse,* a poetry anthology; a third edition of *The Male Homosexual in Literature;* Volume 2 of *The AIDS Dissidents;* an anthology on gay life in the 1970s; contributions to an anthology on the origins of AIDS.

SIDELIGHTS: Ian Young told *CA:* "Much of my writing, editing, and publishing activity has reflected my involvement in the gay liberation and anarchist movements. For some years I have been a member of the Hermetic Order of the Silver Sword, a nondenominational group practicing ceremonial magick in the service of understanding, healing, and enlightenment. I am the director of TMW Communications, a consultancy company for writers and artists."

BIOGRAPHICAL/CRITICAL SOURCES:

BOOKS

Ian Young: A Bibliography, 1962-1980, Canadian Gay Archives, 1981.

PERIODICALS

Advocate, April 25, 1973.
Arc (Ottawa), spring, 1994.
Books in Canada, May, 1976.
Carleton, February 6, 1970.
Christopher Street, Volume 1, number 6, 1976.
Gay Books Bulletin, fall/winter, 1982.
Gay News, September 3-16, 1982.
Gay Sunshine, January/February, 1973.
Heat (New York City), December, 1989.
Margins, March, 1976.
Quill and Quire, July, 1976.
Saturday Night, February, 1970.
Vancouver Province, February 7, 1969.
Varsity, February 6, 1970.